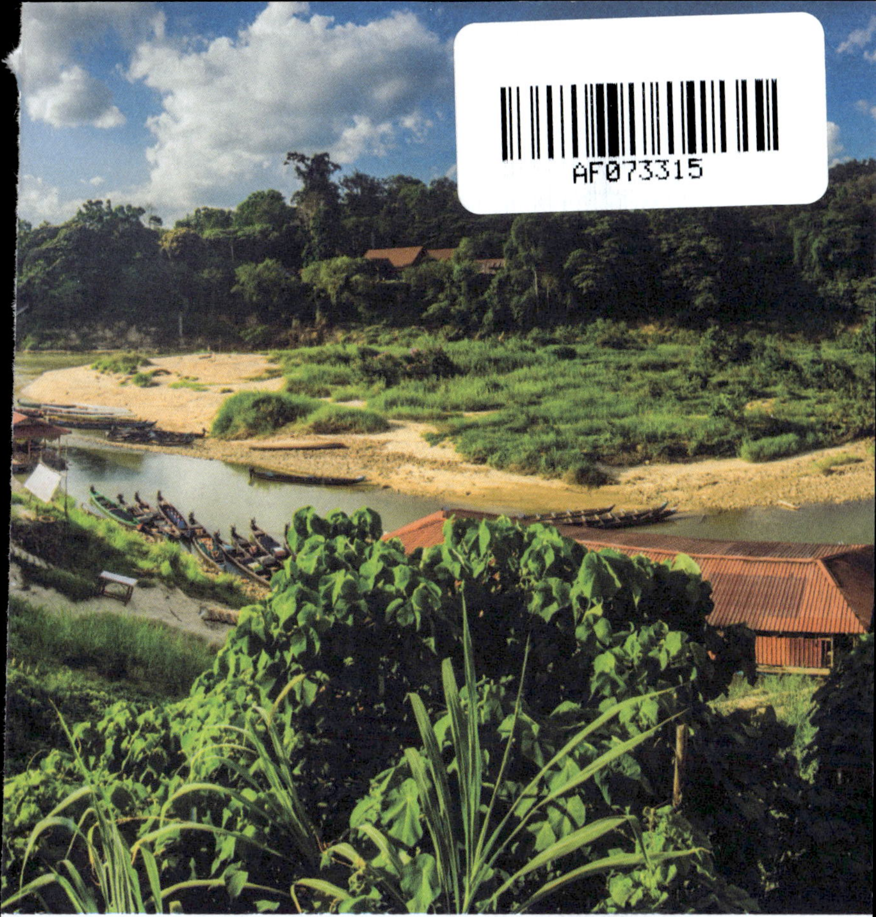

MALAYSIA, SINGAPORE AND BRUNEI

This eleventh edition updated by
Martin Zatko

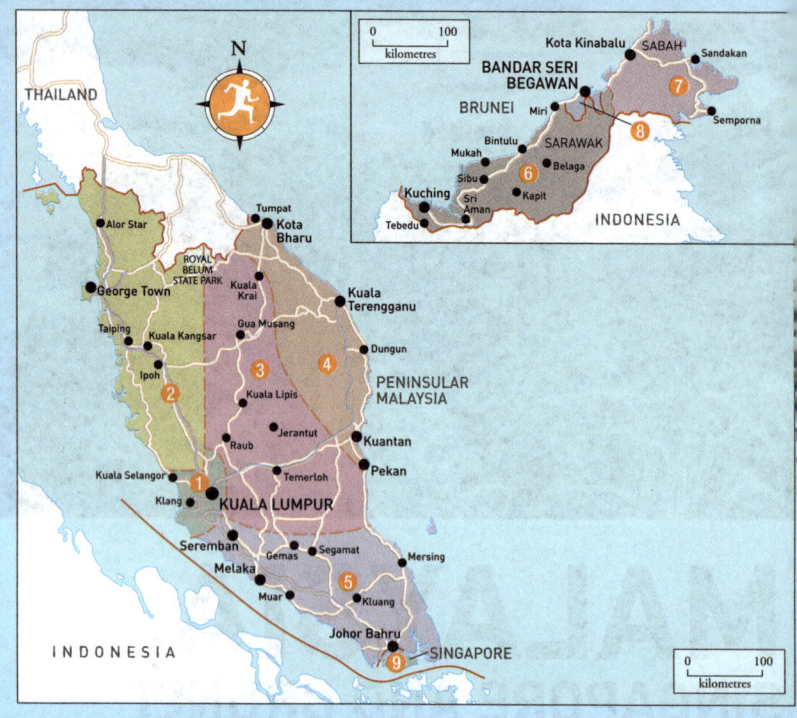

Contents

INTRODUCTION   4

Where to go	5	Things not to miss	14
When to go	11	Itineraries	24
Author picks	13		

BASICS   26

Getting there	27	The media	45
Visas and entry requirements	29	Festivals	47
Getting around	31	Sports and outdoor activities	48
Accommodation	36	Culture and etiquette	49
Food and drink	38	Shopping	51
Health	43	Travel essentials	52

THE GUIDE   58

1 Kuala Lumpur and around	59	6 Sarawak	295
2 The west coast	109	7 Sabah	365
3 The interior	177	8 Brunei	425
4 The east coast	205	9 Singapore	447
5 The south	251		

CONTEXTS   524

History	525	Wildlife	555
Religion	542	Books	559
Peoples	546	Language	563
Development and the environment	551	Glossary	573

SMALL PRINT AND INDEX   575

We've flagged up our favourite places – a perfectly sited hotel, an atmospheric café, a special restaurant – throughout the Guide with the ★ symbol

Introduction to
Malaysia, Singapore and Brunei

Populated by a blend of Malays, Chinese, Indians and Indigenous groups, Malaysia, Singapore and Brunei boast a rich cultural heritage, from a huge variety of annual festivals and wonderful cuisines, to traditional architecture and rural crafts. There's astonishing natural beauty to take in too, including gorgeous beaches and some of the world's oldest tropical rainforest, much of which is surprisingly accessible. Malaysia's national parks are superb for trekking and wildlife-watching, and sometimes for cave exploration and river rafting.

As part of the Malay archipelago, which stretches from Indonesia to the Philippines, Malaysia, Singapore and Brunei share not only similarities in their ethnic make-up but also part of their **history**. Each became an important port of call on the trade route between India and China, the two great markets of the early world, and later became important entrepôts for the Portuguese, Dutch and British empires. Malaysia has only existed in its present form since 1963, when the federation of the eleven Peninsula states was joined by Singapore and the two Bornean territories of Sarawak and Sabah. Singapore didn't last even two years inside Malaysia, becoming an independent city-state in 1965; Brunei chose to stay outside the federation and only became independent of the British in 1984.

Since then, Malaysia, Singapore and Brunei – particularly, of course, the latter two – have been united in their **economic predominance** among Southeast Asian nations. While Brunei is locked into a paternalistic regime, using its considerable oil wealth to guarantee its citizens a respectable standard of living, Singapore has become a giant in commerce, having transformed itself from a strategic port. Malaysia, always

SENTOSA ISLAND, SINGAPORE

competitive with its southern neighbour, is pursuing a similarly ambitious goal, to which end the country is investing heavily in new infrastructure, from highways to ports and factories.

Today, the dominant cultural force in the region is undoubtedly **Islam**, adopted by the Malays in the fourteenth century, though in Chinese-dominated Singapore, **Buddhism** and **Taoism** together hold sway among half the population. But it's the religious plurality – there are also sizeable Christian and Hindu minorities – that is so attractive, often providing surprising juxtapositions of mosques, temples and churches. Add the colour and verve of Chinese temples and street fairs, Indian festival days and everyday life in Malay kampungs (villages), as well as the Indigenous traditions of Borneo, and it's easy to see why visitors are drawn into this celebration of ethnic diversity; indeed, despite some issues, both Malaysia and Singapore have something to teach the rest of the world when it comes to building successful multicultural societies.

Where to go

Malaysia's capital, **Kuala Lumpur** (usually referred to as KL), is the social and economic driving force of a nation eager to better itself, a fact reflected in the relentless proliferation of air-conditioned shopping malls, designer bars and restaurants in the

FACT FILE
- **Malaysia** is a federation of nine **sultanates**, plus the states of Penang, Melaka and, on the island of Borneo, Sabah and Sarawak.
- **Peninsular Malaysia**, where the federal capital Kuala Lumpur is located, and **East Malaysia**, the northern section of Borneo, are separated by more than 600km of the South China Sea.
- In terms of **population**, Malays make up just over two-thirds of Malaysia's 34 million people, ethnic Chinese around 22 percent, Indigenous Orang Asli and Borneo groups together 12 percent, and ethnic Indians 7 percent.
- Tiny **Singapore**, just 700 square kilometres in size, is a wealthy city-state cramming in 6 million inhabitants, including a sizeable minority of expats.
- Made up of two enclaves in eastern Sarawak, **Brunei** is nearly ten times the size of Singapore, but holds less than one tenth of the population.
- Both Malaysia and Singapore are British-style **parliamentary democracies**, the former with a ceremonial head of state known as the Yang di-Pertuan Agung (the post rotates among the sultans of the federation). Brunei is ruled by its **sultan**.
- The world's largest flower, the **Rafflesia**, is a Malaysian rainforest plant measuring a metre across and smelling of rotten meat. It's named after the naturalist and founder of Singapore, Sir Stamford Raffles.
- Malaysia's **economy**, historically dominated by agriculture and mining, now features a healthy manufacturing sector, as does Singapore, where shipping and financial services are also key industries. Brunei profits handsomely from its reserves of oil and gas.

city, and in the continuing sprawl of suburbia and industry around it. But KL is also firmly rooted in tradition, where the same Malay executives who wear suits to work dress in traditional clothes at festival times, and markets and food stalls are crowded in among high-rise hotels and bank towers, especially in older areas such as Chinatown and Little India.

Just a couple of hours' drive south of the capital lies the birthplace of Malay civilization, **Melaka**, its historical architecture and mellow atmosphere making it a must on anybody's itinerary. Much further up the **west coast**, the island of **Penang** was the site of the first British settlement in Malaysia. Its capital, **George Town**, still features beautifully restored colonial buildings and a vibrant Chinatown district, and is, together with Melaka, recognized for its cultural and architectural diversity as a UNESCO World Heritage Site. The former hill station **Cameron Highlands** has lost most of its colonial atmosphere, but its cooler temperatures and lush countryside provide ample opportunities for walks, birdwatching, rounds of golf and cream teas. North of Penang, Malay, rather than Chinese, traditions hold sway at **Alor Setar**, the last major town before the Thai border. This far north, the premier tourist destination is **Langkawi**, an island with international-style resorts and picture-postcard beaches.

Crossing the Peninsula's mountainous **interior** by road or rail allows you to venture into the majestic tropical rainforests of **Taman Negara**. The national park's four thousand square kilometres hold enough to keep you occupied for days: trails, salt-lick hides for animal-watching, aerial forest-canopy walkways, limestone caves and waterfalls. Here you may well also come across the **Orang Asli**, the Peninsula's Indigenous peoples, a few of whom cling to a semi-nomadic lifestyle within the park.

WILDLIFE

Peninsular Malaysia, Borneo and Singapore are a paradise for wildlife-spotters, harbouring over 600 types of birds and 200 mammal species – including Asian elephants, sun bears, tigers, tapirs, barking deer, gibbons, hornbills and pythons. Borneo's speciality is the **proboscis monkey**, so-called because of its bulbous, drooping nose. The island is also one of only two natural habitats (with Sumatra) for **orangutans** – indeed, the name is Malay for "man of the forest". **Marine life** is equally diverse: divers can swim with white-tip sharks, clownfish and barracuda, not to mention green and hawksbill **turtles**, which drag themselves ashore in season to lay their eggs by night. Even cosmopolitan Singapore maintains a pocket of primary rainforest that's home to long-tailed macaques.

The Peninsula's **east coast** is much more rural and relaxing than the west, peppered with rustic villages and stunning islands such as **the Perhentians** and **Tioman**, busy with backpackers and package tourists alike. The state capitals of **Kota Bharu**, near the northeastern Thai border, and **Kuala Terengganu**, further south, still showcase something of the Malay traditions, craft production and performing arts.

Across the sea from the Peninsula lie the east Malaysian states of Sarawak and Sabah. For most travellers, their first taste of **Sarawak** comes at **Kuching**, the old colonial capital, and then the Iban **longhouses** of the Batang Ai river system. **Sibu**, much further north on the Rajang River, is the starting point for trips to less touristed Iban, Kayan and Kenyah longhouses. In the north, **Gunung Mulu National Park** is the principal destination; many come here to climb up to view its extraordinary razor-sharp limestone pinnacles, though spectacular caves also burrow into the park's mountains. More remote still are the **Kelabit Highlands**, further east, where the mountain air is refreshingly cool and there are ample opportunities for extended treks.

More so than any other part of Malaysia, **Sabah** draws visitors with its wildlife. The state's surviving forests are well enough protected to host elephants, orangutans, proboscis monkeys, hornbills and rare creatures such as the clouded leopard, while its southeastern islands, notably **Sipadan**, are home to some of the world's most cherished dive sites, which teem with stunning marine life. Perhaps the best-known attraction, though, is the 4095m granite peak of **Mount Kinabalu**, which needs no special gear or skills to hike up – though it's a pricey experience. The mountain is easily reached from the modern, lively capital Kota Kinabalu.

For those who venture into the tiny kingdom of **Brunei**, enveloped by Sarawak's two most northerly divisions, the capital **Bandar Seri Begawan** holds the entrancing Kampung Ayer, a sprawling stilt village built out over the Brunei River, plus a handful of interesting museums and mosques. In the sparsely populated Temburong district, you can visit unspoiled rainforest at the **Ulu Temburong National Park**, where abundant wildlife roams.

An easy entry-point for first-time visitors to Southeast Asia, **Singapore** is exceptionally safe, organized and accessible, thanks to its small size, excellent modern infrastructure and Western standards of hygiene – though prices are likewise at Western levels. The island has fascinating Chinese and Indian quarters, excellent historical museums and a smattering of colonial architecture as well as great shopping, all of which will keep you occupied for several days. Singapore also rightly holds a reputation as one of Asia's **gastronomic capitals**, where you can just as readily savour fantastic snacks at simple hawker stalls or an exquisite Chinese banquet in a swanky restaurant.

When to go

Temperatures vary little in Malaysia, Singapore and Brunei, hovering constantly at or just above 30°C by day, while humidity is high year-round. Showers occur year-round too, often in the mid-afternoon, though these short, sheeting downpours clear up as quickly as they arrive.

The major distinction in the seasons is marked by the arrival of the northeast monsoon (ushering in what is locally called the **rainy season**). This particularly

SHOPHOUSES

A standard feature of local townscapes is rows of **shophouses** – two- or three-storey buildings traditionally containing a shop at street level, with residential quarters behind and above. For visitors, their most striking feature is that at ground level the front wall is usually set back from the street. This creates a so-called "**five-foot way**" overhung by the upper part of the house, which shelters pedestrians from the sun and pelting rain.

Shophouses were fusion architecture: facades have **Western** features such as shuttered windows and gables, while inside there might be an area open to the sky, in the manner of **Chinese** courtyard houses. Some, especially from the early part of the last century, are bedecked with columns, floral plaster motifs and beautiful tilework, while later properties feature simpler Art Deco touches. Sadly, shophouses went out of favour in the 1980s, and recent ones tend to be bland, functional affairs; older buildings, however, have won a new lease of life as swanky restaurants and boutique hotels.

AVERAGE DAILY TEMPERATURES AND RAINFALL

	Jan	Feb	Mar	April	May	June	July	Aug	Sept	Oct	Nov	Dec
KOTA BHARU												
Max/min °C	29/22	30/23	31/23	32/24	33/24	32/24	32/23	32/23	32/23	31/23	29/23	29/23
Rain (mm)	163	60	99	81	114	132	157	168	195	286	651	603
KOTA KINABALU												
Max/min °C	30/23	30/23	31/23	32/24	32/24	31/24	31/24	31/24	31/23	31/23	31/23	31/23
Rain (mm)	153	63	71	124	218	311	277	256	314	334	296	241
KUALA LUMPUR												
Max/min °C	32/22	33/22	33/23	33/23	33/23	32/23	32/23	32/23	32/23	32/23	31/23	31/23
Rain (mm)	159	154	223	276	182	119	120	133	173	258	263	223
KUCHING												
Max/min °C	30/23	30/23	31/23	32/23	33/23	33/23	32/23	33/23	32/23	32/23	31/23	31/23
Rain (mm)	683	522	339	286	253	199	199	211	271	326	343	465
SINGAPORE												
Max/min °C	32/23	32/23	32/24	32/24	31/24	31/24	31/23	31/23	31/23	31/23	31/23	31/23
Rain (mm)	70	93	141	214	240	170	208	235	341	380	246	107

affects the east coast of Peninsular Malaysia and the western end of Sarawak, with late November to mid-February seeing the heaviest rainfall. On the Peninsula's west coast and in Sabah, September and October are the wettest months. Monsoonal downpours can be heavy and prolonged, sometimes lasting two or three hours and prohibiting almost all activity for the duration; boats to most islands in affected areas won't attempt the sea swell at the height of the rainy season. In mountainous areas like Cameron Highlands, the Kelabit Highlands and in the hill stations and upland national parks, you may experience more frequent rain as the high peaks gather clouds more or less permanently.

The **ideal time** to visit most of the region is between March and early October, when you will avoid the worst of the rains and there's less humidity, though both ends of this period can be characterized by a stifling lack of breezes. Despite the rains, the months of January and February are rewarding, and see a number of significant **festivals**, notably Chinese New Year and the Hindu celebration of Thaipusam. Visiting just after the rainy season can afford the best of both worlds, with verdant countryside and bountiful waterfalls, though there's still a clammy quality to the air. In late May and early June, a **rice harvest** festival takes place in both Sabah (where it's called Kaamatan) and Sarawak (Gawai). It's an excuse for extended merry-making, with much quaffing of rice wine, music and dancing – all best witnessed in longhouses, although Kota Kinabalu hosts more formal celebrations.

Author picks

Our author has traversed every corner of Malaysia, Singapore and Brunei, from KL's shopping malls and Sarawak's longhouses to the jungles of Taman Negara and the summit of Mount Kinabalu. Here are some of their favourite experiences.

Wildlife-spotting Hornbills and long-tailed macaques are widespread, and you can see elephants at the Kinabatangan River (see page 408), proboscis monkeys at Bako (see page 319) and orangutans at Sepilok (see page 405) and Semenggoh (see page 322).

Tastiest laksa Compare famous variations of the region's signature seafood soup in Penang (see page 152), Singapore (see page 516) and Kuching (see page 303).

Shadow puppets Experience the magical Malay tradition of *wayang kulit* at Kota Bharu's Cultural Centre (see page 212).

Amazing caves Sarawak has major cave systems which are both spectacular – especially at Gunung Mulu National Park (see page 350) – and of archeological significance, as in the case of Niah (see page 346).

Eccentric desserts Satisfy your sweet tooth with ABC – shaved ice drenched in condensed milk and luridly coloured fruit syrups (see page 41).

Turtle beaches Stay up late to catch marine turtles laying their eggs at Sabah's Turtle Islands Park (see page 407).

Glittering cityscapes Admire the night lights from atop Menara KL Tower (see page 76) or *Marina Bay Sands* in Singapore (see page 479).

Rowdiest festival You can't beat the crowds and slightly gory celebrations surrounding the Hindu festival of Thaipusam at KL's Batu Caves (see page 101).

Bizarre blooms Discover the weird *Rafflesia* flower, whose scent mimics rotting meat, at the Royal Belum State Park (see page 129), Gunung Gading (see page 323) or Tambunan (see page 420).

> Our author recommendations don't end here. We've flagged up our favourite places – a perfectly sited hotel, an atmospheric café, a special restaurant – throughout the Guide, highlighted with the ★ symbol.

TRADITIONAL LAKSA SOUP
MALAYSIAN SHADOW PUPPETS, KOTA BHARU

25
things not to miss

It's not possible to see everything that Malaysia, Singapore and Brunei have to offer in one trip – and we don't suggest you try. What follows is a selective taste, in no particular order, of their highlights: natural wonders, stunning buildings and colourful heritages. Each entry has a page reference to take you straight into the Guide, where you can find out more. Coloured numbers refer to chapters in the Guide section.

1 NIAH NATIONAL PARK
See page 346
This compact park is the site of a cave system holding important archeological remains, and also offers the chance to see edible swiftlet nests being harvested at certain times of year.

2 GEORGE TOWN
See page 141
A bustling, Chinese-dominated town with historic temples, colonial-era mansions and a blossoming cultural scene.

3 LANGKAWI
See page 166
Luxurious resorts and backpacker digs on sublime beaches: that pretty much sums up this west-coast island, close to the Thai border.

4 KAMPONG AYER
See page 433
Take a boat ride around this wooden village in the middle of the Brunei River.

5 TAMAN NEGARA
See page 178
Peninsular Malaysia's premier national park, Taman Negara is one of the world's oldest rainforests, with hides for wildlife-spotting, treetop walkways and many trekking options.

6 ADVENTURE TOURISM
See page 29
Whitewater rafting, caving and jungle trekking are among the activities widely available in Malaysia.

7 SINGAPORE'S ARTS SCENE
See page 519
As befits the largest city in the region, Singapore offers a dynamic range of artistic activities – catch anything from Chinese street opera to indie rock gigs.

8 KELABIT HIGHLANDS
See page 356
These remote uplands offer excellent walks and hikes, plus encounters with friendly communities along the way.

9 LITTLE INDIA, SINGAPORE
See page 464
On Serangoon Road you can almost believe you're in downtown Chennai – the area has all the sights, sounds and smells of the Indian subcontinent.

10 THE PERHENTIAN ISLANDS
See page 219
A popular pair of islands off the east coast, with beautiful beaches, great snorkelling and accommodation for all budgets.

11 GUNUNG MULU NATIONAL PARK
See page 350
A view of razor-sharp limestone pinnacles reward the challenging haul up Mount Api, and the park also boasts underground caves that teem with wildlife.

12 MELAKA
See page 258
The city's complex historical heritage is evident in its Portuguese, Dutch and British buildings, and Peranakan ancestral homes.

13 THE PETRONAS TOWERS
See page 72
KL's iconic towers not only hold your gaze from all angles, but also house one of the country's best shopping malls.

14 THE KINABATANGAN RIVER
See page 408
Boat trips here are brilliant for spotting proboscis monkeys, hornbills and, if you're lucky, elephants and orangutans.

15 MALIAU BASIN
See page 422
Billed as Sabah's "Lost World", this forest conservation area has excellent multi-day treks to remote waterfalls, plus decent wildlife-spotting opportunities.

16 TRADITIONAL CRAFTS
See page 51
Malaysia boasts a wide range of crafts, from batik and *songket* (brocade) to rattan baskets and *labu*, gourd-shaped ceramic jugs.

17 HAWKER CENTRE FOOD
See page 38
Simple stalls in markets and malls and on the street serve up mouthwatering noodles, snacks and desserts.

18 LONGHOUSES IN SARAWAK
See page 324
Large communal dwellings, home to members of Indigenous groups, are found along rivers and in remote mountain locations.

19 PROBOSCIS MONKEYS, BAKO
See page 319
These odd-looking creatures roam *kerangas* forest and mangrove swamps in the national park, not far from Kuching.

20 RAINFOREST MUSIC FESTIVAL
See page 318
Held annually near Kuching, this world music festival is an opportunity to see Indigenous performers alongside musicians from across the globe.

21 MOUNT KINABALU
See page 393
Watch dawn over Borneo from the summit of one of Southeast Asia's highest peaks.

22 DIVING AT SIPADAN
See page 415
Off southeast Sabah, Sipadan and neighbouring islands are world-renowned for their dive sites and astonishing marine life.

23 GARDENS BY THE BAY AT NIGHT
See page 481
Expansive park featuring assorted "supertrees" illuminated by night, with *Marina Bay Sands* – a modern architectural masterpiece – acting as a photogenic backdrop.

24 CAMERON HIGHLANDS
See page 130
Boasting pleasantly cool weather, by South East Asian standards, these highlands have many hiking routes, as well as scones, mock-Tudor buildings and more, all inherited from the British.

25 KL'S SPEAKEASY BARS
See page 96
Hidden speakeasy-style bars have burgeoned in popularity in KL, with a pleasing, always slightly secretive, variety to proceedings.

Itineraries

Malaysia, Singapore and Brunei cover such a spread-out area that it would be impossible to see everything in one trip, but each of the following routes makes a great way to spend two or three weeks in the region. While the Peninsula Circuit is the most varied, you can head east to Borneo if you prefer an outdoor-focused option. Singapore is more of a long-weekend destination, but a stay here could easily be tacked onto a wider trip north up into Peninsular Malaysia.

PENINSULA CIRCUIT

For a straightforward taster of everything the region has to offer, try this three-week circuit.

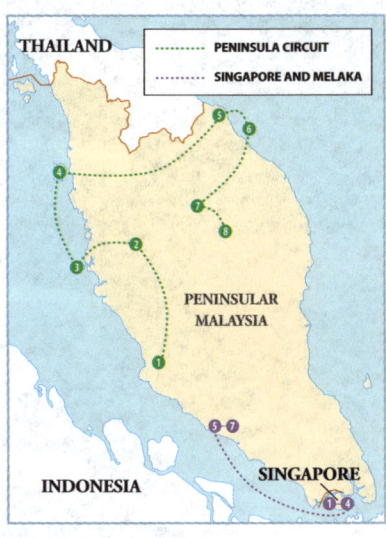

❶ **Kuala Lumpur** Malaysia's capital offers shiny malls, showcase architecture and a mix of Muslim, Chinese and Hindu districts, with some of the best street food in the country. See page 60

❷ **Cameron Highlands** This former retreat for colonial administrators is now a rural idyll of tea plantations and forest walks. See page 130

❸ **Pangkor Island** Kick back at this low-key resort island that's a favourite with Malaysian families. See page 119

❹ **Penang** Packed with historic guildhalls and streets, eccentric temples, surprisingly wild gardens and its own national park. See page 139

❺ **Kota Bharu** One of the few places where you can see shadow-puppet performances of the Hindu epics. See page 209

Create your own itinerary with Rough Guides. Whether you're after adventure or a family-friendly holiday, we have a trip for you, with all the activities you enjoy doing and the sights you want to see. All our trips are devised by local experts who get the most out of the destination. Visit **www.roughguides.com/trips** to chat with one of our travel agents.

❻ **Perhentian islands** Superb tropical hangouts with gorgeous beaches and splendid snorkelling and scuba diving. See page 219

❼ **Jungle Railway** This slow-moving commuter train chugs past languid towns, tiny kampungs and market gardens along the way. See page 193

❽ **Taman Negara** One of the world's oldest rainforests features superlative wildlife-spotting and jungle treks lasting up to a week or more. See page 178

SINGAPORE AND MELAKA

You can pack this round-up of the region's great food and centuries-old history into a week.

❶ **Little India, Singapore** Charismatic area of temples and shops selling gold and saris with the liveliest market in Singapore. See page 464

❷ **Chinatown, Singapore** Amid the modern shophouses, restaurants and markets, don't miss the Buddha Tooth Relic Temple, full of dynamic statuary and the tooth itself. See page 469

❸ **Night Safari, Singapore** The highlight of Singapore Zoo's superbly displayed collection of native wildlife, the Night Safari section lets you see creatures such as tigers, leopards, elephants and rhinos. See page 488

❹ **Bukit Timah, Singapore** The last patch of real rainforest left in Singapore offers an easy, leech-free introduction to jungle trails and colourful birdlife. See page 487

❺ **Istana Kesultanan, Melaka** Replica of an exquisite Malay palace, founded during the fifteenth century. See page 261

❻ **Baba-Nyonya Heritage Museum, Melaka** An elegant row of traditional houses decorated with the tiles, lanterns and woodcarvings of the Chinese-Malay Peranakan culture, now – aside from its cuisine – virtually extinct. See page 263

❼ **Bukit China, Melaka** Hilltop covered in many crescent-shaped Chinese graves, some dating to the seventeenth century. See page 265

SARAWAK AND MT KINABALU

Allow at least three weeks for this adventurous trip into Malaysia's least-developed corners.

❶ **Kuching** Find your bearings in Sarawak's small, likeable capital: the museum's is worth a browse, and the Semenggoh orangutan sanctuary makes a rewarding day-trip. See page 303

❷ **Bako** Sarawak's oldest national park, this patch of coastal forest is home to proboscis monkeys and pitcher plants. See page 318

❸ **Batang Ai** Take a boat through spectacular riverine forest in this often overlooked national park. See page 326

❹ **Gunung Mulu National Park** A three-day trek reveals a clutch of limestone towers and a network of rugged caverns. See page 350

❺ **Miri** A stepping stone to the more remote corners of Sarawak and to Sabah. Don't miss the caves at Niah National Park. See page 340

❻ **Bario** Set out on a multiday trek via Kelabit longhouses or up Mount Murud. See page 358

❼ **Kinabalu Park** This small reserve surrounds wind-seared Mount Kinabaulu, which hosts one of the toughest hikes in all of Malaysia. See page 392

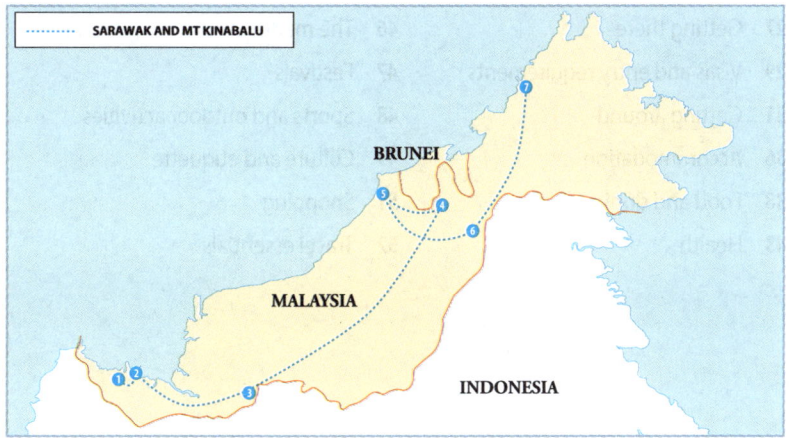

FLOATING MOSQUE, PANGKOR ISLAND

Basics

- **27** Getting there
- **29** Visas and entry requirements
- **31** Getting around
- **36** Accommodation
- **38** Food and drink
- **43** Health
- **46** The media
- **47** Festivals
- **48** Sports and outdoor activities
- **49** Culture and etiquette
- **51** Shopping
- **52** Travel essentials

Getting there

Located at the heart of Southeast Asia, on the busy aviation corridor between Europe and Australasia, Malaysia and Singapore enjoy excellent international air links – the former mainly through its main hub, Kuala Lumpur (KL). Of Malaysia's regional airports, those in Kota Kinabalu, Kuching and Penang have the most useful international connections, albeit chiefly with other East Asian cities. If you're heading to Brunei, you'll most likely have to stop over elsewhere in the region or in the Middle East, though there are plenty of direct flights there too.

During the **peak seasons** for travel to Southeast Asia – the Christmas/New Year period, typically from mid-December until early January, and July and August – prices can be fifty percent higher than at other times of year, though you can often avoid the steepest fares if you **book well in advance**. Fares also rise considerably at weekends and around major local festivals, such as Islamic holidays and the Chinese New Year. Sample fares given here are for **round-trip** journeys and include taxes and current fuel surcharges. If you're thinking of visiting on a **package trip**, note that it's generally cheaper to book one after you've arrived than with a tour operator in your home country.

From the UK and Ireland

London Heathrow has daily **nonstop** flights to KL with Malaysia Airlines (http://malaysiaairlines.com), and to Singapore with British Airways (http://britishairways.com) and Singapore Airlines (http://singaporeair.com). On these routes, reckon on the journey time being twelve to thirteen hours. Flying with any other airline or from any other airport in the UK and Ireland involves a change of plane in Europe, the Middle East or elsewhere in Asia, with nonstop flights always commanding a premium. You may be able to save money by booking two legs of the journey separately; at the time of writing, budget airline Scoot (http://flyscoot.com), Singapore Airlines' low-cost-arm, were flying to Singapore from Athens and Vienna, and the amount saved (particularly for one-way flights, which can be horrendous rip-offs with some of the big airlines) could buy you a couple of free days in one of those cities.

From the US and Canada

In most cases the trip from North America, including a stopover, will take at least twenty hours if you fly the **transatlantic** route from the eastern seaboard, or nineteen hours minimum if you cross the **Pacific** from the west coast. It is, however, possible to fly nonstop from San Francisco to Singapore on Singapore Airlines (http://singaporeair.com), and from Los Angeles to Singapore on United (http://united.com), with trips lasting around seventeen hours. From Honolulu, there's occasionally also the option of flying with Scoot (http://flyscoot.com), to Singapore, but these were not running at the time of writing.

The quickest route isn't always the cheapest: it can sometimes cost less to fly westwards from the east coast, stopping off in Northeast Asia en route.

Plenty of airlines operate to East Asia from major North American cities. If your target is Borneo, it's worth investigating connecting with one of the East Asian airlines – Kota Kinabalu, for example, has flights from Hong Kong, Shanghai and Seoul.

From Australia and New Zealand

Geographical proximity means there's a good range of flights from Australia and New Zealand into Malaysia, Singapore and Brunei, including a useful link between Melbourne and Borneo with Royal Brunei Airlines (http://flyroyalbrunei.com). **Budget flights** include services from Australia to KL with AirAsia (http://airasia.com) and Batik Air (http://batikair.com), and to Singapore with Scoot (http://flyscoot.com); there are, of course, more flights with the main flag carriers. From New Zealand, there's a direct service from Auckland to KL with Malaysia Airlines (http://malaysiaairlines.com).

A BETTER KIND OF TRAVEL

At Rough Guides we are passionately committed to travel. We believe it helps us understand the world we live in and the people we share it with – and of course tourism is vital to many developing economies. But the scale of modern tourism has also damaged some places irreparably, and climate change is accelerated by most forms of transport, especially flying. We encourage all our authors to consider the carbon footprint of the journeys they make in the course of researching our guides.

From South Africa

The quickest way to reach Malaysia or Singapore from South Africa is to fly with **Singapore Airlines** (http://singaporeair.com), which offers flights to Singapore from Cape Town via Johannesburg; reckon on ten hours' flying time from the latter. That said, it's often cheaper to book a ticket that involves changing planes en route, usually in the Middle East.

From elsewhere in Southeast Asia

Budget airlines make it easy to explore Malaysia, Singapore and Brunei as part of a wider trip through Southeast Asia. The most useful no-frills carriers for the three countries covered in this book are Malaysia's AirAsia (http://airasia.com), Firefly (http://fireflyz.com.my) and Batik Air (http://batikair.com), and Singapore's Scoot (http://flyscoot.com). Though fuel surcharges and taxes do take some of the shine off the fares, prices can still be good, especially if you book well in advance.

You can, of course, reach Malaysia or Singapore from their immediate neighbours by means other than flying. There are **road** connections from Thailand and from Kalimantan (Indonesian Borneo); **ferries** from Indonesia and from the southern Philippines, and **trains** from Thailand. Below is a round-up of the most popular routes.

From Thailand

A Special Express **train** service leaves Bangkok each afternoon on the 1000km journey south to the Malaysian border town of Padang Besar, where travellers can change for Malaysian ETS trains on the west-coast line (see page 32). The train calls at (among others) Hua Hin, Surat Thani and Hat Yai before reaching Padang Besar; you then have half an hour to board the train south to Butterworth, and another 40min (or a whole extra night, if you want to see Penang) to wait there for the train to KL. Also useful is the Thai rail service from Hat Yai across to Sungai Golok on the east coast of the Kra isthmus, close to the Malaysian border crossing at Rantau Panjang, from where buses run to Kota Bharu.

As regards **flights**, plenty of services connect Bangkok, Chiang Mai and Thai resorts with Malaysian airports and Singapore. Some are run by the low-cost airlines, while others are provided by the main carriers.

A few scheduled **ferry** services sail from the most southwesterly Thai town of Satun to the Malaysian west-coast town of Kuala Perlis (30min) and to the island of Langkawi (1hr 30min). If you're departing from Thailand by sea for Malaysia, ensure your passport is stamped at the immigration office at the pier to avoid problems with the Malaysian immigration officials when you arrive. Another option is the ferry from the southern Thai town of Ban Taba to the Malaysian town of Pengkalan Kubor, where frequent buses run to Kota Bharu, 20km away. Buses connect Ban Taba with the provincial capital, Narathiwat (1hr 30min).

The easiest **road** access from Thailand is via Hat Yai, from where buses, minivans and a few shared taxis run to Butterworth (4hr) and nearby George Town on Penang Island, with some buses continuing right to KL or Singapore. From the interior Thai town of Betong, there's a road across the border to the Malaysian town of Pengkalan Hulu, from where Route 67 leads west to Sungai Petani; share taxis serve the route. You can also get a taxi from Ban Taba for the few kilometres south to Kota Bharu.

From Indonesia

Plenty of **flights**, including many operated by the low-cost airlines, connect major airports in Java and Sumatra, plus Bali and Lombok, with Malaysia and Singapore. There's also a service between Manado in Sulawesi and Singapore with Scoot (http://flyscoot.com). As for Kalimantan, Malaysia Airlines (http://malaysiaairlines.com) and AirAsia (http://airasia.com) operate between Balikpapan and KL.

THE EASTERN & ORIENTAL EXPRESS

Unlike some luxury trains in other parts of the world, the **Eastern & Oriental Express** (http://belmond.com) isn't a re-creation of a classic colonial-era rail journey, but a sort of fantasy realization of how such a service might have looked had it existed in Southeast Asia. Employing 1970s Japanese rolling stock, given an elegant old-world cladding with wooden inlay work and featuring Thai and Malay motifs, the train travels between Bangkok and Singapore, with the option of starting or ending the trip in KL, at least monthly. En route there are extended stops at Kanchanaburi for a visit to the infamous bridge over the **River Kwai**, and at **Kuala Kangsar**. An observation deck at the rear of the train makes the most of the passing scenery. The trip doesn't come cheap, of course, and rates in swish, en-suite Pullman accommodation include meals, though alcohol costs extra.

It's possible to reach Sarawak from Kalimantan on just one **road route**, through the western border town of Entikong and onwards to Kuching. The bus trip from the western city of Pontianak to Entikong takes seven hours, crossing to the Sarawak border town of Tebedu; stay on the same bus for another three hours to reach Kuching.

As for **ferries**, Dumai, on the east coast of Sumatra, has a daily service to Melaka (2hr). There are also a few services from Bintan and Batam islands in the Riau archipelago (accessible by plane or boat from Sumatra or Jakarta) to Johor Bahru (1hr 30min–3hr) or Singapore (30min), and there's a minor ferry crossing from Tanjung Balai to Kukup (1hr), just southwest of Johor Bahru. Over in Borneo, ferries connect Tawau in Sabah with Nunakan (1hr) and Tarakan (3hr).

From the Philippines

A weekly ferry service operates between Zamboanga in the southern Philippines and Sandakan in Sabah, though Zamboanga and its whole surrounding area are no-go zones according to most Western governments, and travelling there may thus invalidate your travel insurance. Low-cost **flights** include from Clark to KL and Kota Kinabalu (both AirAsia; http://airasia.com), from Clark and Manila to Singapore (JetStar Asia; http://jetstar.com), and from Boracay and Cebu to Singapore (Scoot; http://flyscoot.com). Major airlines provide additional links, including Manila to Bandar Seri Begawan (Royal Brunei Airlines; http://flyroyalbrunei.com).

TRAVEL AGENTS AND TOUR OPERATORS

Absolute Asia Tours US http://absoluteasiatours.com. Luxury Malaysia tours, lasting ten days or more, taking in various parts of the country, and sometimes Singapore too.
Adventure Alternative UK http://adventurealternative.com. A superb range of off-the-beaten track Borneo tours.
Adventure World Australia http://adventureworld.com.au; New Zealand http://adventureworld.co.nz. Short Malaysia tours, covering cities and some wildlife areas.
Allways Dive Expeditions Australia http://allwaysdive.com.au. Dive holidays to the prime dive sites of Sabah.
Audley Travel US & Canada, UK, Ireland http://audleytravel.com. Luxury tours concentrating on East Malaysia.
Bestway Tours US & Canada http://bestway.com. A handful of cultural and wildlife tours featuring East Malaysia and Brunei, plus the peninsula and Singapore.
Borneo Eco Tours http://borneoecotours.com. Small-group, customizable tours of all of Borneo, covering wildlife, trekking and indigenous culture.
Dive Adventures Australia http://diveadventures.com.au. Sabah and Labuan dive packages.
Eastravel UK http://eastravel.co.uk. Bespoke Malaysia trips.

> ### ADDRESSES AND PLACE NAMES
> Place names in Malaysia present something of a linguistic dilemma. **Road signage** is often in Malay only, and some colonial-era names have been deliberately changed to Malay ones, but since **English** is widely used in much of the country, local people are just as likely to say "Kinta River" as "Sungai Kinta", or talk of "Northam Road" in George Town rather than "Jalan Sultan Ahmad Shah", and so on. The Guide mostly uses English-language names, for simplicity. The Glossary includes Malay terms for geographical features like beaches, mountains and so forth (see page 573).

Exodus Travels US, UK http://exodustravels.com. Several packages, mainly focused on East Malaysia, plus tailor-made trips.
Explore UK http://explore.co.uk. A handful of Malaysia tours.
Explorient US http://explorient.com. Malaysia and Singapore packages, including both city and jungle breaks.
InsideAsia UK http://insideasiatours.com. Excellent off-the-peg tours, and custom ones too, to Malaysia, Singapore, wider Borneo, or a combination of destinations.
Intrepid Travel US, Canada, UK, Australia, New Zealand http://intrepidtravel.com. Several Malaysia offerings, mainly focused on Borneo, or taking in Thailand and Singapore as well.
Jade Tours Canada http://en.jadetours.com. Borneo and Peninsular Malaysia trips.
Pentravel South Africa http://pentravel.co.za. Flight deals plus city breaks that combine Singapore with Bangkok or Hong Kong.
Premier Holidays UK http://premierholidays.co.uk. Tours of East Malaysia, plus holidays in Peninsular Malaysia and Singapore.
Reef & Rainforest US http://reefrainforest.com. Sabah dive packages based in resorts or a liveaboard.
Sayang Holidays US http://sayangholidays.com. City- or resort-based Peninsular Malaysia and Singapore tours, plus Borneo.
Symbiosis UK http://symbiosis-travel.com. Diving, trekking and longhouse stays in various Malaysian locations.
Trailfinders UK http://trailfinders.com; Ireland http://trailfinders.ie. Flights and a few tours, including major Malaysian cities, Borneo and Singapore.
USIT Ireland http://usit.ie. Student and youth travel.

Visas and entry requirements

Nationals of the UK, Ireland, US, Canada, Australia, New Zealand and South Africa do not need visas in advance to stay in

Malaysia, Singapore or Brunei, and it's easy to extend your permission to stay.

That said, check with the relevant embassy or consulate, as the rules on **visas** are complex and subject to change. Ensure that your passport is valid for at least six months from the date of your trip, and has several blank pages for entry stamps.

Malaysia

Upon arrival in **Malaysia**, citizens of the UK, Ireland, US, Canada, Australia, New Zealand and South Africa receive a passport stamp entitling them to a ninety-day stay.

It's straightforward to **extend** your permit through the Immigration Department, who have offices (listed in the Guide) in Kuala Lumpur and major towns. Visitors from the aforementioned countries can also cross into Singapore or Thailand and back to be granted a fresh Malaysia entry stamp.

Tourists travelling from the Peninsula to **East Malaysia** (Sarawak and Sabah) must be cleared again by immigration. Visitors to Sabah can remain as long as their original entry stamp is valid, but each state maintains its own border controls – which means you are always stamped in, even when arriving from other parts of Malaysia. For a full list of Malaysia's embassies and consulates, see http://kln.gov.my.

MALAYSIA EMBASSIES AND CONSULATES

Australia 7 Perth Ave, Yarralumla, Canberra 02 6120 0300.
Brunei 61, Junction 336, Jalan Duta, Bandar Seri Begawan 02 381096.
Canada 60 Boteler St, Ottawa 613 241 5182.
Indonesia Jalan H.R. Rasuna Said, Kav. X/6, No. 1–3 Kuningan, Jakarta South 021 522 4947.
Ireland Shelbourne House, Level 3A–5A, Shelbourne Rd, Ballsbridge, Dublin 01 667 7280.
New Zealand 10 Washington Ave, Brooklyn, Wellington 04 385 2439.
Singapore 301 Jervois Rd 6235 0111.
South Africa 1007 Francis Baard St, Arcadia, Pretoria 012 342 5990.
Thailand 46 North Sathon Rd, Bangkok 02 340 5720.
UK 45 Belgrave Sq, London 020 7242 4308.
US 3516 International Court, NW Washington DC 202 572 9700.

Singapore

Singapore reserves the term "visa" for permits that must be obtained in advance. Travellers from many countries, however, are granted a **visit pass** on arrival. Although the duration of the pass can vary at the discretion of immigration officials, citizens of the UK, Ireland, US, Canada, Australia, New Zealand and South Africa are usually given at least thirty days. There is a formal procedure for extending it, but it's usually much easier to simply do a day-trip by a bus to Johor Bahru just inside Malaysia and be given a fresh pass on returning to Singapore. Within three days prior to your arrival in Singapore, you'll have to complete an **arrival card** online (http://eservices.ica.gov.sg/sgarrivalcard).

For details of nationalities that require visas, along with how to apply and how to extend a visit pass, see http://ica.gov.sg. Full details of Singapore's embassies abroad are at http://mfa.gov.sg.

SINGAPORE EMBASSIES AND CONSULATES

Australia 17 Forster Crescent, Yarralumla, Canberra 02 6271 2000.
Brunei 8 Junction 74, Jalan Subok, Bandar Seri Begawan 02 262741.
Indonesia Block X/4 Kav No. 2, Jalan H.R. Rasuna Said, Kuningan, Jakarta South 021 5091 5400.
Ireland 2 Ely Place Upper, Dublin 01 669 1700.
Malaysia 209 Jalan Tun Razak, Kuala Lumpur 03 2161 6277.
New Zealand 17 Kabul St, Khandallah, Wellington 04 470 0850.
South Africa 980–982 Francis Baard St, Pretoria 012 430 6035.
Thailand 129 South Sathorn Rd, Bangkok 02 348 6700.
UK 9 Wilton Crescent, Belgravia, London 020 7235 8315.
US 3501 International Place NW, Washington DC 202 537 3100.

Brunei

UK and US nationals are allowed to stay in **Brunei** for up to ninety days on arrival; Australian and New Zealand passport holders are granted thirty days; and Canadians get fourteen days. South African citizens need to apply for a visa in advance. Once in Brunei, extending your permission to stay is usually a formality; apply at the Immigration Department in Bandar Seri Begawan. For full details of Brunei's embassies, see http://mfa.gov.bn.

BRUNEI EMBASSIES AND CONSULATES

Australia 16 Bulwarra Cl, O'Malley, Canberra 02 6285 4500.
Canada 395 Laurier Ave East, Ottawa 613 864 5656.
Indonesia 18 Jalan Cirebon, Jakarta 021 2911 0242.
Malaysia 2 Jalan Diplomatik 2/5, Putrajaya 03 8888 7777.
Singapore 325 Tanglin Rd 6733 9055.
South Africa c/o the embassy in Singapore.
Thailand 12 Soi Ekamai 2, 63 Sukhumvit Rd, Bangkok 02 714 7395.
UK 19–20 Belgrave Square, London 020 7581 0521.
US 3520 International Court NW, Washington DC 202 237 1838.

Customs allowances

Malaysia's duty-free allowances are 200 cigarettes (or 225g of tobacco) and one litre of wine, spirits or liquor. Entering **Singapore** from anywhere other than

Malaysia (when there are no duty-free allowances), you can bring in up to three litres of alcohol duty-free (including no more than a litre of spirits); duty is payable on all tobacco (and that which isn't packaged in line with Singapore's own restrictions will not be allowed into the country).

Visitors to **Brunei** may bring in 200 cigarettes, 50 cigars or 250g of tobacco, and 60ml of perfume; non-Muslims over seventeen can also import two litres of liquor and twelve cans of beer for personal consumption (any alcohol brought into the country must be declared upon arrival, and consumed in private), and 60ml of perfume or 250ml of eau de toilette.

> **DRUGS: A WARNING**
>
> In Malaysia, Singapore and Brunei, the possession of **illegal drugs** – hard or soft – carries a hefty prison sentence or even the death penalty. If you are arrested for drugs offences you can expect **no mercy** from the authorities and little help from your consular representatives. The simple advice, therefore, is not to have anything whatsoever to do with drugs in any of these countries. Never agree to carry anything through customs for a third party.

Getting around

Public transport in Malaysia, Singapore and Brunei is reliable and inexpensive. Much of your travelling, particularly in Malaysia, will be by bus, minivan or, occasionally, long-distance shared taxi. Budget flights are a good option for hopping around the region, especially given that no ferries connect Peninsular and East Malaysia. The Peninsula's rail system is now partly upgraded, slashing journey times.

Sabah and **Sarawak** have their own travel peculiarities – in parts of Sarawak, for instance, you're reliant on boats or light aircraft. The chapters on Sarawak, Sabah, Brunei and Singapore contain specific information on their transport systems; the focus in this section is largely on Peninsular Malaysia.

The transport system is subject to heavy pressure during any nationwide **public holiday** (see page 56) – particularly Muslim festivals, the Chinese New Year, Deepavali (Diwali), Christmas and New Year. A day or two before each festival, whole communities embark upon **balik kampung**, which literally means a return to the village (or hometown) to be with family. It's worth buying tickets at least one week in advance to travel at these times; if you're driving, steel yourself for more than the usual number of jams.

And finally, bear in mind that **chartering** transport – longboats, or cars with drivers – to reach some off-the-beaten-track national park or island is always pricey for what it is.

By bus

Malaysia's **bus network** is fairly comprehensive, at least in terms of serving major cities and towns. However, buses rarely stray off main roads to reach rural sites of the kind that tourists might want to get to – nature reserves, caves, hill resorts and so forth. In such instances, the best you can do is to ask the driver if you can get off at the start of the turning for your destination, after which you're left to your own devices.

> **LOCAL TICKET BOOKING ENGINES**
>
> Gone are the days when travellers had to rock up at a bus or train station, hoping there were still tickets available, or pay a cut to local travel agents for ticket purchase. This is still quite possible, of course, though booking online eliminates some linguistic problems or misunderstandings, plus the potential of being stuck at a bus terminal for hours. In addition, having more control over your schedule (even just a day in advance) enables you to book accommodation ahead, often at a significantly cheaper price.
>
> **Easybook** http://easybook.com. Slightly fiddly site offering ticket purchase for buses, trains and ferries across the region; though it doesn't always work splendidly, it includes more operators than rival site Redbus.
>
> **KTMB** http://www.ktmb.com.my. Official site of Malayan Railways (known to all and sundry in Malaysia as KTMB), with a pleasingly efficient ticket-purchase system.
>
> **Redbus** http://redbus.my. Excellent, easy-to-use site on which you can purchase bus tickets for destinations all over Malaysia, including connections to Singapore and Brunei.

BUS COMPANIES

A handful of well-established bus companies give reliable service in Peninsular Malaysia. The largest is **Transnasional** (http://transnasional.com.my) and its slightly pricier subsidiary **Plusliner** (same website), whose services have the entire Peninsula pretty well covered. Among many competitors are **Sri Maju** (http://srimaju.com), which is strong on the west coast. These are just a few companies, though, and there are absolutely loads of acceptable ones – book online through one of the main umbrella sites (see page 31) and you'll be able to see average review ratings (if not necessarily understand the reviews themselves).

Long-distance (express) buses

The **long-distance bus network** borders on the anarchic: a largish town can be served by a dozen or more express bus companies. **Timetabling** is a mess, too: every bus station has signs above a zillion ticket booths displaying a zillion routes and departure times, but these may be out of date, as may the websites of even the biggest bus companies. Given this, the route details in this Guide are a general indication of what you can expect; for specifics, you will need to call the bus company's local office (stations do not have central enquiry numbers), ask in person, or – of course – book online (see page 31), which is the recommended course of action.

At least the plethora of companies means you can often find **tickets** at the station for a bus heading to your destination within the next two hours. However, it can be worth booking a day in advance for specific departures or on routes where services are limited (in between, rather than along, the west and east coasts for example).

Most intercity buses are comfortable, with **air conditioning** and curtains to screen out the blazing sun, though seats can be tightly packed. There are rarely toilets on board, but longer journeys feature a rest stop every couple of hours, with a short meal stopover if needed. On a few plum routes, notably KL–Singapore and KL–Penang, additional **luxury** or "executive" coaches charge up to twice the regular fares and offer plush seats with greater legroom, plus on-board movies (not always a positive, especially when drivers have no idea how loud the speakers are through the bus).

Local buses

In addition to express buses, the Peninsula has a network of simple, somewhat sporadic **local buses** serving small towns on routes that can stretch up to 100km end to end. Local buses are organized at the **state level**, and this means that many services do not cross into adjacent states even when the same firm is active on both sides of the border. **Tickets**, usually bought on board from the driver or conductor, rarely cost very much at all. Note that services typically run only during **daylight hours**, winding down by 8pm if not earlier.

By train

For years, Malaysian **trains** were a laughing stock – antiquated and generally much slower than buses. The useful service to Singapore was also choked off in 2011, after Singapore station – previously owned by Malaysia – was taken over by the Singaporean government, and promptly closed down. Now, after belated investment, the trains are once again a competitive option in parts of Malaysia, and even bigger changes are in the pipeline, with a new, metro-like shuttle service between Johor Bahru and Singapore scheduled to open before 2027; unfortunately, plans for a long-envisioned high-speed rail link between Singapore and KL were scrapped in 2021.

The Peninsula's rail service is operated by **KTM** (short for Keretapi Tanah Melayu, literally "Trains of the Malay Land"; http:// ktmb.com.my). Its network is shaped roughly like a Y, with the southern end anchored at Johor Bahru and the intersection, for historical reasons, at the small town of Gemas. The northwest branch links up with Thai track at the border town of Padang Besar via KL, Ipoh and Alor Setar; the northeast branch cuts up through the interior to terminate at Tumpat, beyond Kota Bharu on the east coast. KTM also runs a useful **Komuter** rail service in the Kuala Lumpur area (see page 85) and the northwest (see page 110).

Trains are at their best on the west-coast line, which is electrified and double-tracked right from Gemas up to Padang Besar, enabling the modern, fast (and thus much in demand) **Electric Train Service (ETS)** to run. The fly in the ointment is that although there were at least a dozen services north of KL daily at the time of research, services between KL and Gemas were still sparse.

Intercity (*Antarabandar*) services make up the rest of the network, between Johor Bahru and the east via the interior. These remain backward and single-tracked, meaning a handful of slow, often basic, trains run in one direction each day – journeys can be mind-numbing and are often delayed. Even so, trains can still be the quickest way to reach some settlements here, and the **Jungle Railway** stretch is also entertaining in parts (see page 193). Unfortunately, there were no direct services between KL and the east coast at the time of research, although these may return in the future; in the meantime, passengers from KL and the west coast need to change at Gemas for the east-coast line.

Seats and fares

ETS trains have no **seat classes**, but fares still vary depending on whether you travel on a "platinum" service (faster, with fewer stops) or "gold". On intercity trains, seats theoretically divide into premier (first), superior (second) and economy (third) class, although not all trains feature all three; **sleeper services** are limited to the overnight trains between Johor Bahru and Tumpat, and are also split into three theoretical classes.

Tickets and timetables

You can buy **tickets** at stations via KTM's website or their KTMB Mobile app; for ETS trains, it's best to book at least a couple of days in advance.

Note that as KTM is continually upgrading and maintaining its lines, it has made frequent, often radical changes to its **timetables** and routes over the past few years – it's a good idea to check the latest details on the company's website before you travel.

By long-distance taxi

Long-distance taxis are fading away somewhat, but still run between some cities and towns, and are especially useful in Sabah. They can be a lot quicker than buses, but the snag is that they operate on a **shared** basis, so you have to wait for enough people to show up to fill the vehicle. In practice, you're unlikely to make much use of them unless you're travelling in a group or you want to travel to a destination that's off the beaten track. **Fares** usually work out at double the corresponding bus fare; official prices are usually chalked up on a board at the taxi rank or listed on a laminated tariff card (*senarai tambang*), which you can ask to see.

Some taxi operators assume any tourist who shows up will want to charter a taxi; if you want to use the taxi on a shared basis, say "*nak kongsi dengan orang lain*".

By ferry or boat

Regular **ferries** serve all the major islands, from Penang to Labuan off the coast of Sabah. Within

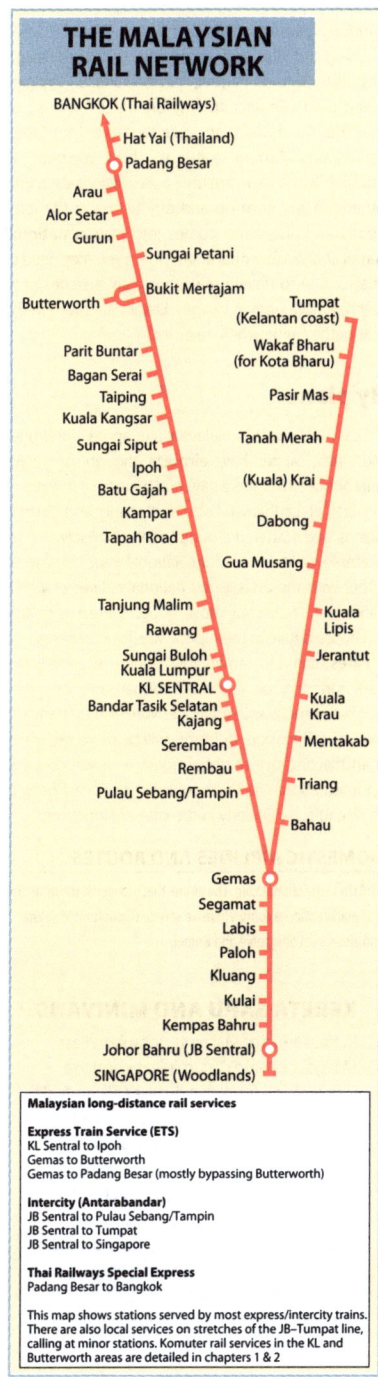

THE MALAYSIAN RAIL NETWORK

Malaysian long-distance rail services

Express Train Service (ETS)
KL Sentral to Ipoh
Gemas to Butterworth
Gemas to Padang Besar (mostly bypassing Butterworth)

Intercity (Antarabandar)
JB Sentral to Pulau Sebang/Tampin
JB Sentral to Tumpat
JB Sentral to Singapore

Thai Railways Special Express
Padang Besar to Bangkok

This map shows stations served by most express/intercity trains. There are also local services on stretches of the JB–Tumpat line, calling at minor stations. Komuter rail services in the KL and Butterworth areas are detailed in chapters 1 & 2

Sarawak, there are scheduled boat services between Kuching and Sibu, and up the Rejang River to Belaga. Vessels tend to be narrow, cramped affairs – imagine being inside an aircraft, only on water – and some may be no more than speedboats or motorized *penambang* (fishing craft). It's best to book in advance when there are only a few sailings each day; otherwise, just turn up and buy tickets at the jetty. Boat travel also often comes into play in **national parks** and in a few rural areas, where you may need to charter one to travel between coastal beaches or to reach remote upriver villages. Details are given in the text of the Guide where relevant.

By plane

It's easy to fly within Malaysia, Singapore and Brunei. Most state capitals have **airports** (though some have only one or two flights a day), and there are also regional airports at Langkawi, Labuan, Redang and Tioman islands, and scattered around Sabah and Sarawak – for example, at Mulu for Mulu National Park. You can fly either with the established national airlines or with a variety of low-cost operators, though there may be little to choose between them pricewise if you book late.

Fares can be remarkably cheap, especially for early-morning or late-night departures, or when booked some way in advance. Note also that any trip involving Singapore or Brunei will be more expensive than the distance might suggest, as it will count as an international flight, though fares can still be very reasonable, particularly in the case of Singapore.

DOMESTIC AIRLINES AND ROUTES

AirAsia http://airasia.com. The airline that pioneered the local low-cost market offers a comprehensive service throughout Malaysia and also serves Singapore and Brunei.

KERETA SAPU AND MINIVANS

In rural areas of Malaysia, notably in East Malaysia, private cars, minivans and (on rough roads) four-wheel-drives fill in handily for the lack of buses along certain routes. Sometimes called **kereta sapu** in Malay, or "taxis" as a shorthand, they may not be as ad hoc as they sound, even running at fixed times each day in some places.

Minivans also operate on a more formal level: travel agencies run them to take backpackers to destinations such as the Perhentians and Taman Negara, or just across the border to Hat Yai in Thailand.

Batik Air http://batikair.com. Previously known as Malindo Air, this has a good range of flights throughout Peninsular Malaysia and also serves Singapore.

Firefly http://fireflyz.com.my. Malaysia Airlines' discount subsidiary has some useful flights out of KL's Subang airport, Penang and Ipoh, serving other Peninsula cities and Singapore.

MASwings http://maswings.com.my. Once another subsidiary of Malaysia Airlines, though now owned by the government of Sarawak, MASwings operates on many routes, largely rural, within Borneo, often using nineteen-seater propeller-driven Twin Otter planes that are a lifeline for isolated communities.

Malaysia Airlines (MAS) http://malaysiaairlines.com. Flies between KL and many state capitals, plus Langkawi, Labuan, Singapore and Brunei.

Scoot http://flyscoot.com. Singapore's Airlines' low-cost wing serves major Peninsular destinations, plus Kuching, from Singapore.

By car

The roads in **Peninsular Malaysia** are good, making driving a viable prospect for tourists – though the cavalier local attitude to road rules takes some getting used to. It's mostly the same story in **East Malaysia** and **Brunei**, though here major towns tend to be linked by ordinary roads rather than wide highways. **Singapore** is in another league altogether, boasting modern highways and a built-in road-use charging system that talks to a black-box gizmo fitted in every car. All three countries **drive on the left**, and wearing seat belts is compulsory in the front of the vehicle (and in the back too, in Singapore). To **rent a vehicle**, you must be 23 or over and will need to show a clean driving licence.

The rest of this section concentrates on **Malaysia**. For more on driving in Singapore and Brunei, see the respective chapters in the Guide.

Malaysian roads

Malaysian highways – called **expressways** and usually referred to by a number prefixed "E" – are a pleasure to drive; they're wide and well maintained, and feature convenient **rest stops** with toilets, shops and small food courts. In contrast, the streets of major cities can be a pain, regularly traffic-snarled, with patchy signposting and confusing one-way systems. Most cities and towns boast plenty of **car parks**, and even where you can't find one, there's usually no problem with parking in a lane or side street.

Speed limits are 110km/h on expressways, 90km/h on the narrower trunk and state roads, and 50km/h in built-up areas. Whatever road you're on, keep to the speed limit; speed traps are not uncommon and fines hefty. If you are pulled up for a traffic offence, note that it's not unknown for Malaysian police to ask for a

MALAY VOCABULARY FOR DRIVERS

The following list should help decipher road signage in Peninsular Malaysia and parts of Brunei, much of which is in Malay.

Utara North
Selatan South
Barat West
Timur East
Di belakang Behind
Di hadapan Ahead
Awas Caution
Berhenti Stop
Beri laluan Give way
Dilarang meletak kereta No parking
Dilarang memotong No overtaking
Had laju/jam Speed limit/per hour
Ikut kiri/kanan Keep left/right
Jalan sehala One-way street
Kawasan rehat Highway rest stop
Kurangkan laju Reduce speed
Lebuhraya Expressway/highway
Lencongan Detour
Pembinaan di hadapan Road works ahead
Pusat bandar Town/city
bandaraya centre
Simpang ke Junction/turning for
Zon had laju Zone where speed limit applies

---

bribe, which will set you back less than the fine. Never offer to bribe a police officer and think carefully before you give in to an invitation to do so.

All expressways are built and run by private concessions and as such attract **tolls**, though on some roads a flat fee is levied. At some toll points (signed "Tol Plaza") you can pay in cash (cashiers can dispense change), but this is being phased out – some will only let you through with a stored-value **Touch 'n Go** card (http://touchngo.com.my), which you wave in front of a sensor (see page 85). Get in the appropriate lane as you approach the toll points: some lanes are for certain types of vehicle only.

Once out on the roads, you'll rapidly become aware of the behaviour of quite a few Malaysian motorists, which their compatriots might term *gila* (Malay for "insane"). Swerving from lane to lane in the thick of the traffic, overtaking close to blind corners and careering downhill are not uncommon, as are tragic press accounts of pile-ups and road fatalities. Not for nothing does the exhortation *"pandu cermat"* (drive safely) appear on numerous highway signboards, though the message still isn't getting through.

If you're new to driving in Malaysia, the best approach is to take all of this with equanimity and drive conservatively; concede the right of way if you're not sure of the intentions of others. One local habit that may confuse those more used to Western road customs is that drivers generally flash their headlights to claim the **right of way**, rather than concede it – you have been warned.

Car and bike rental

Car rental rates with the main multi-national chains are reasonable by international standards, although you may find better deals with local firms. The rates usually include unlimited mileage and collision damage waiver insurance; the excess can be hefty, but can be reduced by paying a surcharge of up to ten percent on the daily rental rate.

Motorbike rental tends to be informal, usually offered by Malaysian guesthouses and shops in more touristy areas. Officially, you must be over 21 and have an appropriate driving licence, though it's unlikely you'll have to show the latter; you'll probably need to leave your passport as a deposit. Wearing helmets is compulsory.

Transport in cities and towns

The companies that run local buses in each state also run city and town buses, serving urban centres and suburbs. Fares seldom amount to much, though schedules can be unfathomable to visitors (and even locals). KL also has an MRT and LRT metro system, plus local rail and monorail systems, which are badly connected to each other in a logistical sense, but as a whole get the job done quite well.

Outside the largest cities, **taxis** do not ply the streets looking for custom, so using one means heading to a taxi rank, typically outside big hotels and malls. Malaysian taxis are notorious for being **unmetered** except in a few big cities, notably KL, so it's worth asking locals what a fair price to your destination would be and haggling with the driver before you set off. At a few taxi ranks, notably at airports and train stations, you buy a voucher for your destination at a sensible price. In a few areas it can be worthwhile **chartering** a taxi for several hours, for example to reach a remote nature park and perhaps collect you when you're done; prices will depend on the area and your bargaining skills.

The good news for taxi users is that in an ever-increasing swathe of the area, including more or less all large cities in Malaysia, as well as Singapore, you can now book a ride using the homegrown Uber-style **Grab app** (http://grab.com/my); fares are distance-based and can work out a third cheaper than using an unmetered taxi, and drivers will pick you up from wherever you are. Dart (http://dartbrunei.com) is the only such option in Brunei.

Trishaws (bicycle rickshaws), seating two people, are seen less these days, but they're still part of the tourist scene in places like Melaka, Penang and Singapore. You're paying for an experience here, not transport as such; details are given in the relevant sections of the Guide.

> **CHALETS**
>
> Banish all thoughts of Alpine loveliness when it comes to Malaysian **chalets**: these are guesthouse and resort rooms in the form of little self-contained wooden or concrete cabins. They're mostly to be found in rural areas, especially at nature reserves and beaches. Chalets range from cramped, stuffy A-frames – sheds named for their steeply sloping roofs, sometimes with a tiny bathroom at the back – to luxury en-suite affairs with a veranda, sitting area, minibar and the like; prices vary accordingly.

Accommodation

Accommodation in Malaysia is good value: mid-range en-suite rooms can cost the same as you'd pay for a dorm bed in Europe or North America. Details of accommodation in Brunei and Singapore are given in the relevant chapters of the Guide.

The cheapest form of accommodation is offered by hostels, guesthouses and lodges, which usually have dorms and simple private rooms, sharing bathrooms. These places exist only in well-touristed areas, whether urban or rural. Elsewhere, you'll need to rely on hotels, which range from world-class luxury affairs to austere concrete blocks with basic rooms.

Advance reservations are essential to be sure of securing a budget or mid-range room during major festivals or school breaks (see page 56). The East Asian accommodation specialist http://agoda.com (founded and headquartered in Singapore) has a wide selection of hotels in all three countries, though so do most of the main international accommodation engines. In addition to "conventional" accommodation, it's also possible to find apartments in cities using the likes of Airbnb (http://airbnb.com).

Air conditioning is standard in all but the cheapest hotels, and is fairly common in guesthouses too. **Wi-fi** is practically standard. Baby cots are usually available only in more expensive places.

Guesthouses, hostels and lodges

The mainstay of the travellers' scene in Malaysia are **hostels** and **guesthouses** (also called backpackers or lodges – all these terms are somewhat interchangeable). These can range from basic affairs to smartly refurbished shophouses with satellite TVs and games consoles. Almost all offer **dorm beds**, though prices and standards vary widely. Basic double rooms, at the cheapest level, often have mere plywood partitions separating them from adjacent rooms, but at more modern establishments they're comparable to a simple hotel room – and occasionally far more attractive. **Breakfast** is usually available; this is often a simple self-service affair of coffee or tea and toast with jam and butter, but at some guesthouses they put in much more effort with their offerings.

Hotels

Malaysia's **cheapest hotels** tend to cater for a local clientele and seldom need to be booked in advance. Showers and toilets may be shared and can be pretty basic, although most places have some en-suite rooms. Another consideration at cheap and even some mid-range hotels is the **noise** level, as doors and windows offer poor sound insulation. Note that some cheap hotels also function as brothels, especially those that allow rooms to be paid for by the hour.

Mid-range hotels can be better value; you can expect air conditioning, en-suite facilities and relatively decent furnishings, sometimes also a refrigerator, in-room safe and access to a restaurant.

High-end hotels are as comfortable as you might expect, and many have state-of-the-art facilities, including a swimming pool, spa and gym. Some may add a touch of class by incorporating grand extrapolations of kampung-style architecture, such as saddle-shaped roofs with woodcarving. Rates can be surprisingly affordable, if you book in advance.

In the major cities, look out for **boutique hotels**, usually set in refurbished shophouses or colonial-era office buildings. They are the most characterful places to stay, offering either retro-style decor or über-hip contemporary features – although never at budget prices.

Hotel **breakfasts**, where available, are either Asian/Western buffets with trays of noodles next to beans and eggs, or simpler affairs where you order off a menu. They're usually included in the rate except at four- and five-star places, where the spread is so elaborate that there are two room rates – with and without breakfast. In the Guide listings, we have indicated when breakfast is included in the price.

Camping

There are few official opportunities for **camping** in Malaysia, perhaps because guesthouses are so reasonably priced, and because the heat and humidity, not to mention the copious insect population, make camping something only strange foreigners would willingly do. Where there are **campsites**, typically in nature parks, they are either free to use or entail a nominal fee; facilities are basic and may not be well maintained. A few lodges and camps have tents and other equipment for rent, but you generally need to bring your own gear (see box, page 49).

If you go trekking in very remote regions, for example in the depths of Taman Negara and the Kelabit Highlands in Sarawak, camping is just about your only option. Specialist tour operators or local guides can often provide gear.

Longhouses

A stay in a **longhouse**, *de rigueur* for many travellers visiting Sarawak (and also possible in Sabah), offers the chance to experience Indigenous community life, do a little trekking and try activities such as weaving and using a blowpipe. It used to be that visitors could simply turn up and ask the *tuai rumah* (headman) for a place to stay, paying only for meals and offering some gifts as an additional token of thanks. While some tourists still try to work things like this, these

ACCOMMODATION PRICING AND TAXES

Many mid-range hotels in Malaysia have a published tariff or rack rate and a so-called **promotional rate**, generally around a third less. What's important to realize is that the promotional rate is the de facto price, applying all year except, perhaps, during peak periods such as important festivals. To be sure of getting the promotional rate, either book online or call in advance of your arrival.

Top-tier and some mid-range hotels, plus some hostels, have a different strategy: their online booking engines constantly adjust prices according to demand. This means the best rates usually go to those who book early, although some last-minute discounts may also pop up.

Note that mid-range and pricey hotels levy a **service charge** (usually ten percent) and that most hotels levy **GST** (six percent; see page 52). Unless otherwise stated, the accommodation prices **quoted in the reviews** in this Guide include such surcharges and are based on promotional rates or, at luxury hotels, typical rates.

Finally, there's the matter of the **tourism tax**. It essentially requires foreigners to pay a set additional fee per room per night. Naturally, this hits people staying in cheap hotels or in private rooms in hostels especially hard, though dorm occupants may find the tax is divided by the number of beds or even absorbed by the hostel owner. When booking online, if the tax isn't added you will probably have to pay it upon checking in (often in cash), though at the time of writing the fee was being waived, and may disappear entirely.

ACCOMMODATION PRICE CODES

All accommodation reviewed in this Guide is accompanied by a price category, based on the cost of a basic **room for two (or two dorm beds, in the case of hostels) in high season**. Price ranges don't include breakfast, unless stated otherwise. For camping, prices are given per pitch.

The codes for Singapore (see page 505) and Brunei (see page 438) appear elsewhere in the Guide, and those for **Malaysia** chapters are as follows:

$ = under RM120
$$ = RM120–200
$$$ = RM200–450
$$$$ = over RM450

days most longhouse visits are invariably arranged through a **tour operator** and can therefore be a little pricey. *Gawai* (see page 47) is the most exciting time of year to stay.

More expensive packages put visitors up in their own section of the longhouse, equipped with proper beds and modern washing facilities; meals will be prepared separately rather than shared with the rest of the community. More basic trips generally have you sleeping on mats or in hammocks rather than beds, either in a large communal room or on the veranda, and the main washing facilities may well be the nearest river. For meals, the party will be divided up into smaller groups, and each will dine with a different family.

Homestays

In many rural areas especially, **homestay programmes** offer the chance to stay with a Malaysian family, paying for your bed and board. The arrangement is an appealing one on paper, giving you a chance to sample home cooking and local culture. In practice, however, hosts may not be able to speak much English, a situation that effectively cuts foreign guests off from them and the community. As a result, homestays often end up being used by Malaysian travellers rather than foreigners. Tourist offices can usually furnish a list of local homestays on request, but be sure to raise the above issues if pursuing the idea.

Food and drink

One of the best reasons to come to Malaysia and Singapore (even Brunei, to a lesser extent) is the food, comprising two of the world's most venerated cuisines, Chinese and Indian, and one of the most underrated – Malay. Even if you think you know two out of the three pretty well, be prepared to be surprised: Chinese food here boasts a lot of the provincial diversity that you don't find in the West's Cantonese-dominated Chinese restaurants, while Indian food is predominantly southern Indian, lighter and spicier than the cuisine of the north.

Furthermore, each of the three cuisines has acquired more than a few tricks from the other two – the Chinese here cook curries, for example – giving rise to some distinctive fusion food. Add to this cross-fertilization a host of regional variations and specialities, plus excellent seafood and unusual tropical produce, and the result can be a dazzling gastronomic experience.

None of this need be expensive. From the ubiquitous food stalls and cheap street diners called **kedai kopis**, the standard of cooking is high and food everywhere is remarkably good value. Basic noodle- or rice-based one-plate meals at a stall or *kedai kopis* rarely cost more than a few ringgit or Singapore dollars. Even a full meal with drinks in a fancy restaurant can be quite affordable in Malaysia, though expect to pay Western prices at quite a few places in Singapore. The most renowned culinary centres are Singapore, George Town, KL, Melaka and Kota Bharu, although other towns have their own distinctive dishes too.

Food stalls and food courts

Some of the cheapest and most delicious food available in Malaysia and Singapore comes from **stalls**, traditionally wooden pushcarts on the roadside, surrounded by a few wobbly tables with stools. Most serve one or a few standard **noodle** and **rice dishes** or specialize in certain delicacies, from oyster omelettes to squid curry. One myth to bust immediately is the notion that you will get food poisoning eating at stalls or cheap diners. Standards of hygiene are usually good, and as most food is cooked to order (or, in the case of rice-with-toppings spreads, only on display for a few hours), it's generally pretty **safe**.

Many stalls are assembled into user-friendly **medan selera** (literally "appetite square") or **food courts**, also known as **hawker centres** in Singapore. Usually taking up a floor of an office building or shopping mall, or housed in open-sided market buildings, food courts feature stall lots with menus displayed and fixed tables, plus toilets. You generally don't have to sit close to the stall you're patronizing: find a free table, and the vendor will track you down when your food is ready (at some Singapore food centres you quote the table number when ordering). Play it by ear as to whether you pay when ordering, or when the food is delivered.

Stalls open at various times from morning to evening, with most closing well before midnight except in the big cities. During the Muslim fasting month of **Ramadan**, however, Muslim-run stalls don't open until mid-afternoon, though this is also when you can take advantage of the **pasar Ramadan**, afternoon food markets at which stalls sell masses of savouries and sweet treats to take away; tourist offices can tell you where one is taking place. Ramadan is also the time to stuff yourself at the massive fast-breaking buffets laid on by most major hotels.

EATING PRICE CODES

Throughout the Guide, every dining option reviewed is accompanied by a price category, based on the cost of a basic **two-course meal for one** (or similar, at cafés and hawker centres), without drinks.

The codes for Brunei (see page 439) and Singapore (see page 511) appear elsewhere in the Guide, and those for **Malaysia** chapters are as follows:

$ = under RM20
$$ = RM20–40
$$$ = RM40–80
$$$$ = over RM80

Kedai kopis

Few downtown streets lack a **kedai kopis**, sometimes known as a *kopitiam* in Hokkien Chinese. Although both terms literally mean "coffee shop", a *kedai kopi* is actually an inexpensive diner rather than a café. Most serve noodle and rice dishes all day, often with a *campur*-style spread (see page 39) at lunchtime, sometimes in the evening too. Some *kedai kopis* function as miniature food markets, housing a handful of vendors – perhaps one offering curries and griddle breads, another doing a particular Chinese noodle dish, and so on.

Most *kedai kopis* open at 8am to serve breakfast, and don't shut until the early evening; a few stay open as late as 10pm. Culinary standards are seldom spectacular but are satisfying all the same, and you're unlikely to spend more than small change for a filling one-plate meal. In some Malaysian towns, particularly on the east coast, the Chinese-run *kedai kopis* are often the only places where you'll be able to get **alcohol**.

Restaurants, cafés and bakeries

Sophisticated **restaurants** only exist in the big cities. Don't expect a stiffly formal ambience, however – while some places can be sedate, the Chinese, especially, prefer restaurants to be noisy, sociable affairs. Where the pricier restaurants come into their own is for **international food** – anything from Vietnamese to Tex-Mex. The chief letdown is that the service can be amateurish, reflecting how novel this sort of dining experience is for many of the staff.

Most large Malaysian towns feature a few attempts at Western **cafés**, serving passable fries, sandwiches, burgers, shakes and so forth. It's also easy to find **bakeries**, which can offer a welcome change from the local rice-based diet – though don't be surprised to find chilli sardine buns and other Asian Western hybrids, or cakes with decidedly artificial fillings and colourings. For anything really decent in the café or bakery line, you'll need to be in a big city.

Cuisines

A convenient, cheap way to get acquainted with local dishes is to sample the spreads available at many *kedai kopis*, particularly at lunchtime. The concept is pretty much summed up by the Malay term **nasi campur** ("mixed rice"), though Chinese and Indian *kedai kopis*, too, offer these arrays of stir-fries, curries and other savouries in trays. As in a cafeteria, you tell the person behind the counter which items you want, and a helping of each will be piled atop a mound of rice. If you don't like plain rice, ask for it to be doused with gravy (*kuah* in Malay) from any stew on display.

Nasi campur is not haute cuisine – and that's precisely its attraction. Whether you have, say, *ikan kembong* (mackerel) deep-fried and served whole, or chicken pieces braised in soy sauce, or bean sprouts stir-fried with salted fish or shrimp, a *campur* spread is much closer to **home cooking** than anything served in formal restaurants.

Nasi campur and noodle dishes are meals in themselves, but otherwise eating is generally a **shared** experience – stir-fries and other dishes arrive in quick succession, and everyone helps themselves to several servings of each, eaten with rice, as the meal progresses.

Breakfast can present a conundrum in small towns, where rice, *roti canai* and noodles may be all that's easily available. If you can't get used to the likes of rice porridge at dawn, you'll find that many a *kedai kopis* offers *roti bakar*, toast served with butter and **kaya**. The latter is a scrumptious sweet coconut curd jam,

EATING ETIQUETTE

Malays and Indians often eat with the **right hand**, using the palm as a scoop and the thumb to help push food into the mouth. **Chopsticks** are, of course, used for Chinese food, though note that a spoon is always used to help with rice, gravies and slippery food such as mushrooms or tofu, and that you don't pick up rice with chopsticks (unless you've a rice bowl, in which case you lift the bowl to your mouth and use the chopsticks as a sort of shovel). **Cutlery** is universally available; for local food, it's best to eat mainly with a spoon, using a fork to get food on to it.

either orange or green, not unlike English lemon curd in that egg is a major ingredient.

Malay food

In its influences, **Malay cuisine** looks to the north and east, most obviously to China in the use of noodles and soy sauce, but also to neighbouring Thailand, with which it shares an affinity for such ingredients as lemongrass, the ginger-like galangal and fermented fish sauce (the Malay version, *budu*, is made from anchovies). But Malay food also draws on Indian and Middle East cooking in the use of spices, and in dishes such as *biriyani* rice. The resulting cuisine is both spicy and a little sweet. Naturally there's an emphasis on **local ingredients**: *santan* (coconut milk) lends a sweet, creamy undertone to many stews and curries, while *belacan*, a pungent fermented prawn paste (something of an acquired taste), is found in chilli condiments and sauces. **Herbs**, including curry and kaffir lime leaves, also play a prominent role.

The cuisine of the southern part of the Peninsula tends to be more *lemak* (rich) than further north, where the Thai influence is stronger and *tom yam* stews, spicy and sour (the latter by dint of lemongrass), are popular. The most famous Malay dish is arguably **satay** (see page 41), though it can be hard to find outside big cities. Also quintessentially Malay, **rendang** is a dryish curry made by slow-cooking meat (usually beef) in coconut milk flavoured with galangal and a variety of herbs and spices.

For many visitors, one of the most striking things about Malay food is the bewildering array of **kuih-muih** (or just *kuih*), or sweets, on display at markets and street stalls. Often featuring coconut and sometimes *gula melaka* (palm-sugar molasses), *kuih* come in all shapes, sizes and colours (often artificial nowadays) – rainbow-hued layer cakes of rice flour are about the most extreme example.

Chinese food

The range of **Chinese cooking** available in Malaysia and Singapore represents a mouthwatering sweep through China's southeastern seaboard, reflecting the historical pattern of emigration from **Fujian**, **Guangzhou** and **Hainan Island** provinces. This diversity is evident in dishes served at hawker centres and *kopitiams*. Cantonese *char siew* (roast pork, given a reddish honey-based marinade) is frequently served over plain rice as a meal in itself, or as a garnish in noodle dishes such as *wonton mee* (*wonton* being Cantonese pork dumplings); also very common is Hainanese chicken rice, comprising steamed chicken accompanied by savoury rice cooked in chicken stock. Fujian province contributes dishes such as *hae mee*, yellow noodles in a rich prawn broth; *yong tau foo*, from the Hakka ethnic group on the border with Guangzhou, and comprising bean curd, fishballs and assorted vegetables, poached and served with broth and sweet dipping sauces; and *mee pok*, a Teochew (Chaozhou) dish featuring ribbon-like noodles with fishballs and a spicy dressing.

Restaurant dining tends to be dominated by **Cantonese** food. Menus can be formulaic, but the quality of cooking is usually high. Many Cantonese places also offer great **dim sum**, at which small servings of numerous savouries such as *siu mai* dumplings (of pork and prawn), crispy yam puffs and *chee cheong fun* (rice-flour rolls stuffed with pork and drenched in sweet sauce) are consumed. Traditionally, these would be served in bamboo steamers and ordered from waitress-wheeled trolleys, but these days you might well have to order from a menu.

Where available, take the opportunity to try **specialities** such as **steamboat**, a sort of fondue that involves dunking raw vegetables, meat and seafood into boiling broth to cook, or **chilli crab**, with a spicy tomato sauce. A humdrum but very commonplace stomach-filler is **pow**, steamed buns containing a savoury filling of *char siew* or chicken, or sometimes a sweet red bean paste.

Nyonya food

Named after the word used to describe womenfolk of the Peranakan communities (see page 528), **Nyonya food** is a product of the melding of Penang, Melaka and Singapore cultures. A blend of Chinese and Malay cuisines, it can seem more Malay than Chinese thanks to its use of spices – except that pork is widely used.

Nyonya **popiah** (spring rolls) are very common: rather than being fried, the rolls are assembled by coating a steamed wrap with a sweet sauce made of palm sugar, then stuffed mainly with stir-fried *bangkwang*, a crunchy turnip-like vegetable. Another classic is **laksa**, noodles in a spicy soup with the distinctive *daun kesom* – a herb fittingly referred to in English as *laksa* leaf. Other well-known Nyonya dishes include **asam fish**, a spicy, sour fish stew featuring tamarind (the *asam* of the name), and **otak-otak**, fish mashed with coconut milk and chilli paste then put in a narrow banana-leaf envelope and steamed or barbecued.

Indian food

The classic southern Indian dish is the *dosai* (aka dosa or *thosai*), a thin rice-flour pancake. It's usually served accompanied by *sambar*, a thin vegetable and lentil curry; *rasam*, a tamarind broth; and perhaps small helpings of other curries. Also very common are *roti* griddle breads, plus the more substantial **murtabak**, thicker than a *roti* and stuffed with egg, onion and

SIX OF THE BEST

The dishes listed below are mostly easy to find, and many of these cut across ethnic boundaries as well, with each group modifying the recipe slightly to suit its cooking style.

Nasi lemak Rice fragrantly cooked in coconut milk and served with fried peanuts, tiny fried anchovies, cucumber, boiled egg and spicy *sambal*.

Roti canai Basically Indian paratha (indeed it's called *roti prata* in Singapore), a delicious griddle bread served with a curry sauce. It's ubiquitous, served up by Malay and Indian *kedai kopis* and stalls.

Nasi goreng Literally, fried rice, though not as in Chinese restaurants; Malay and Indian versions feature a little spice and chilli, along with the usual mix of vegetables plus shrimp, chicken and/or egg bits.

Char kuay teow A Hokkien Chinese dish of fried tagliatelle-style rice noodles, often darkly coated in soy sauce and garnished with egg, pork and prawns. The Singapore version is decidedly sweet. Malay *kuay teow goreng* is also available and tends to be spicier.

Satay A dish of chicken, mutton or beef kebabs on bamboo sticks, marinated and barbecued. The meat is accompanied by cucumber, raw onion and *ketupat*, cubes of sticky rice steamed in a wrap of woven leaves. All are meant to be dipped in a spicy peanut sauce. Though most Westerners think of satay as Malay, it actually (shhhh) originated on the Indonesian island of Java. Chinese pork satay also exists.

Laksa A spicy seafood noodle soup, Nyonya in origin. Singapore *laksa*, served with fishcake dumplings and beansprouts, is rich and a little sweet thanks to copious use of coconut milk, while Penang's *asam laksa* features flaked fish and a tamarind tang.

---

minced meat, with sweet banana versions sometimes available. At lunchtime many South Indian cafés turn to serving *daun pisang* (literally, banana leaf) meals comprising rice heaped on a banana-leaf "platter" and small, replenishable heaps of various curries placed alongside. In some restaurants you'll find more substantial dishes such as the popular fish-head curry (don't be put off by the idea – the "cheeks" between the mouth and gills are packed with tasty flesh).

A notable aspect of the eating scene in Malaysia is the "**mamak**" *kedai kopis*, run by Muslims of South Indian descent (and easily distinguished from Hindu Tamil places by the framed Arabic inscriptions on the walls). *Mamak* establishments have become de facto meeting places for all creeds, being halal and open late, often round the clock. Foodwise, they're similar to other South Indian places, though with more emphasis on meat.

The food served in **North Indian** restaurants (found only in big cities), is richer, less fiery and more reliant on mutton and chicken. You'll commonly come across **tandoori** dishes – named after the clay oven in which the food is cooked – and in particular tandoori chicken, marinated in yoghurt and spices and then baked. Breads such as *naan* also tend to feature rather than rice.

Borneo cuisine

The diet of the Indigenous groups living in settled communities in **East Malaysia** can be not dissimilar to Malay and Chinese cooking. In remoter regions, however, or at festival times, you may have an opportunity to sample Indigenous cuisine. Villagers in **Sabah**'s Klias Peninsula and in **Brunei** still produce *ambuyat*, a gluey, sago-starch porridge; then there's the Lun Bawang speciality of *jaruk* – raw wild boar, fermented in a bamboo tube and definitely an acquired taste. Sabah's most famous dishes include *hinava*, raw fish pickled in lime juice. In **Sarawak**, Iban and Kelabit communities sometimes serve wild boar cooked on a spit or stewed, and served with rice (perhaps *lemang* – glutinous rice cooked in bamboo) and jungle ferns. River fish is a longhouse basic; the most easily available, tilapia, is usually grilled with pepper and herbs, or steamed in bamboo cylinders.

Desserts

Given the steamy climate, stalls offer a range of desserts that often revolve around **ice** milled down to something resembling slush. More jarringly, desserts often include ingredients such as **pulses**, **sticky rice** or even **yam** and **sweet potato**, all of which can be turned into a sweet stew or porridge.

At their best, local desserts are certainly a lot more interesting than most ice-cream sundaes ever get. Easy to find and worth trying is **eis kacang** (also known as *air batu campur* – "mixed ice" – or ABC), comprising a small helping of aduki beans, sweetcorn and bits of jelly, covered with a snowy mound doused in colourful syrups. Even better, though high in cholesterol, is **cendol**, luscious coconut milk sweetened with *gula melaka* and mixed with green threads of mung-bean-flour jelly. You'll even find delicious red-bean ice cream on sale, its flavour dominated by coconut milk rather than the beans.

Drinks

While **tap water** is generally safe to drink, **bottled water** is widely and cheaply available. Among freshly squeezed **juices**, watermelon, orange and carrot are pretty common, as is the faintly sappy but invigorating sugar cane, extracted by pressing the canes through mangles. Lychee and *longan* drinks can also be good, made with diluted tinned juices and served with some of the fruit at the bottom. Sweetened soya milk in cartons or – much tastier – freshly made at stalls is another popular local choice, as is the refreshing, sweet *chin chow*, which looks like cola but is in fact made from a seaweed and comes with strands of seaweed jelly.

Tea (*teh*) and **coffee** (*kopi*) are as much national drinks as they are in the West, and locals adore them served **tarik**, literally "pulled" – which means frothing the drink by repeatedly pouring it between mugs in each hand. If ordered with milk, they'll come with a generous dollop of the sweetened condensed variety or sometimes evaporated milk (only large hotels and smarter Western-style cafés have regular milk). If you don't have a sweet tooth, either ask for your drink *kurang manis* ("lacking in sweetness"), in which case less condensed milk will be added, or have it black. Note that there can be even more intricacies involved when ordering drinks (see page 571).

Alcohol

Alcohol is not generally hard to find in **Malaysia**. Most big cities have a bar scene, though in Malaysian towns drinking is limited to non-Muslim eating places, food courts (drink stalls usually have beer and perhaps stout) and Chinese-run bars – sometimes little more than tarted-up *kedai kopis*, the walls plastered with posters of Hong Kong showbiz poppets. However,

---

SPECIAL DIETS

Malay food is, unfortunately, a tough nut to crack for **vegetarians**, as meat and seafood are well blended into the cuisine. Among the standard savoury dishes, vegetarians can only really handle *sayur lodeh* (a rich mixed-veg curry made with coconut milk), *tauhu goreng* (deep-fried tofu with a peanut dressing similar to satay sauce) and *acar* (pickles). Chinese and Indian eating places are the best bets, thanks to the dietary influence of Buddhism and Hinduism. Chinese restaurants can always whip up veg stir-fries to order, and many places now feature **Chinese vegetarian** cuisine (usually also good for **vegans**), using textured veg protein and gluten mock meats – often uncannily like the real thing, and delicious when done right.

Strict vegetarians will want to avoid **seafood derivatives** commonly used in cooking. This means eschewing dishes like *rojak* (containing fermented prawn paste) and the chilli dip called *sambal belacan* (containing *belacan*, the Malay answer to prawn paste). Oyster sauce, often used in Chinese stir-fries, can easily be substituted with soy sauce or just salt. Note also that the gravy served with **roti canai** often comes from a meat curry, though some places offer a lentil version, too.

If you need to **explain in Malay** that you're vegetarian, try saying "*saya hanya makan sayuran*" ("I only eat vegetables"). Even if the person taking your order speaks English, it can be useful to list the things you don't eat; in Malay you'd say, for example, "*saya tak mahu ayam dan ikan dan udang*" for "I don't want chicken or fish or prawn". Expect a few misunderstandings; the cook may leave out one thing on your proscribed list, only to put in another.

HALAL FOOD

Halal food doesn't just feature at Malay and *mamak* eating places. The catering at mid-range and top-tier Malaysian hotels is almost always halal (or at least "**pork-free**"), to the extent that you get turkey or beef "bacon" at breakfast. Of course, the pork-free billing doesn't equate to being halal, but many local Muslims are prepared to overlook this grey area.

In areas where the population is largely Muslim, such as **Kelantan** and **Terengganu**, halal or pork-free food is the norm, even at Chinese and Indian restaurants. In largely Chinese **Singapore**, most hawker centres have a row or two of Muslim stalls.

TROPICAL FRUIT

Markets throughout the region feature a delightful range of locally grown **fruit**, though modern agricultural practices are leading to a decline in some varieties. Below are some of the more unusual fruits to watch out for.

Bananas (pisang) Look out for the delicious *pisang mas*, small, straight, thin-skinned and aromatically sweet; *pisang rastali*, slightly bigger, with dark blotches on the skin and not quite so sweet, and green- and even red-skinned varieties.

Cempedak This smaller version of the *nangka* (see jackfruit, below) is normally deep-fried, enabling the seed, not unlike a new potato, to be eaten too.

Ciku Looks like an apple; varies from yellow to pinkish brown when ripe, with a soft, pulpy flesh.

Durian One of Southeast Asia's most popular fruits, durians are also, for many visitors, the most repugnant thanks to their smell. In season (May–Aug & Nov–Feb), they're the size of footballs and have a thick green skin covered with sharp spikes. Inside, rows of large seeds are coated with squidgy yellow-white flesh, whose flavour has been likened by some to vomit-flavoured custard.

Jackfruit Like a giant grenade, the jackfruit (*nangka*) grows up to 40cm long and has a coarse greenish-yellow exterior, enclosing large seeds whose sweet flesh has a powerful odour like overripe pineapple. The unripe fruit, stir-fried, is a bit like bamboo shoots.

Langsat Together with its sister fruit, the *duku*, this looks like a small, round potato, with juicy, segmented white flesh containing small, bitter seeds.

Longan Not unlike the lychee, this stone fruit has sweet, juicy translucent flesh inside a thin brown skin.

Mangosteen Mangosteens have a segmented white flesh with a sweet, slightly tart flavour. Be warned: the thick purple rind can stain clothes indelibly.

Pomelo Much grown in Perak, this pale green citrus fruit is slightly smaller than a soccer ball and, at its best, is juicier and sweeter than grapefruit. Slice away the rind with a knife, then separate and peel the giant segments with your hands.

Rambutan The shape and size of chicken eggs, rambutans have a soft, spiny exterior that gives them their name – *rambut* means "hair" in Malay. To get at the sweet translucent flesh coating the stone inside, simply make a small tear in the peel with your nails and twist open.

Salak Teardrop-shaped, the *salak* has a skin rather like a snake's and a bitter taste.

Soursop Inside the bumpy, muddy-green skin is smooth white flesh that Margaret Brooke, wife of Sarawak's second rajah, Charles, described as "tasting like cotton wool dipped in vinegar and sugar".

Starfruit Also called carambola, this yellow-green fruit, star-shaped in cross section, is said to be good for high blood pressure – though it can be insipid to taste.

---

in strongly Muslim areas, particularly Kelantan and Terengganu, only a handful of establishments, usually Chinese, sell alcohol. **Brunei** is officially dry (see page 431), and different rules again apply for details of **Singapore** drinking (see page 516).

Anchor and Tiger **beer** (lager) are locally produced and easily available, and you can get Western and Thai beers as well as the Chinese Tsingtao and various **stouts**, including Guinness. More upmarket restaurants and bars serve beer on draught, cocktails and (generally pricey) imported **wine**. In the longhouses of East Malaysia, you will probably be invited to sample *tuak* (Sarawak) or *tapai* (Sabah), a rice wine that can be potent or weak and as sickly as sweet sherry.

At a food court or *kopitiam*, beer may be on sale at prices only slightly above what the same thing sells for at a supermarket or convenience store. Proper bars may charge up to fifty percent more, except during **happy hour** (which could last from opening time until 8pm), when prices are sharply lower. While some bars open from lunchtime, most tend to open from early evening until the small hours.

Health

No inoculations are required for visiting Malaysia, Singapore or Brunei, although the immigration authorities may require

a yellow-fever vaccination certificate if you have transited an endemic area, normally Africa or South America, within the preceding six days. Though levels of hygiene and medical care in Malaysia, Singapore and Brunei are higher than in much of Southeast Asia – with any luck, the most serious thing you'll go down with is an upset stomach – it's a wise precaution to visit your doctor no less than two months before you leave to check that you are up to date with your polio, typhoid, tetanus and hepatitis inoculations.

Heat problems

Travellers unused to tropical climates may suffer from sunburn and **dehydration**. The easiest way to avoid this is to restrict your exposure to the midday sun, use high-factor sunscreens, wear sunglasses and a hat. You should also drink plenty of water and, if you do become dehydrated, keep up a regular intake of fluids. **Heat stroke** is more serious and can require hospitalization: its onset is indicated by a high temperature, dry red skin and a fast pulse.

Stomach problems

The most common complaint is a stomach problem, which can range from a mild dose of diarrhoea to full-blown dysentery. The majority of stomach bugs may be unpleasant, but are unthreatening; however, if you notice blood or mucus in your stools, then you may have amoebic or bacillary dysentery, in which case you should seek medical help.

Stomach bugs are usually transmitted by contaminated food and water, so steer clear of raw vegetables and shellfish, always wash unpeeled fruit, and stick to freshly cooked foods, avoiding anything reheated. However careful you are, food that's spicy or just different can sometimes upset your system, in which case, try to stick to relatively bland dishes and avoid fried food.

Tap water is drinkable in Singapore and in parts of Malaysia and Brunei, although in rural areas it's best to buy bottled water, which is widely available.

Air quality

In general, **air quality** is not a major health issue. However, the region is occasionally blanketed by what's locally called "the haze", regularly caused by forest fires in Indonesia. On such occasions, schools sometimes find themselves closed and major outdoor events cancelled, while local people venture out wearing surgical-style masks. If a major haze returns (keep a close eye on the weather forecasts), people with respiratory problems should seek medical advice and try to avoid the worst-hit areas – or even postpone the trip.

Cuts, bites and stings

Wearing protective clothing when swimming, snorkelling or diving can help avoid sunburn and protect against any sea stings. **Sea lice**, minute creatures that cause painful though harmless bites are the most common hazard; more dangerous are **jellyfish**, whose stings must be doused with vinegar to deactivate the poison before you seek medical help.

Coral can also cause nasty cuts and grazes; any wounds should be cleaned and kept as dry as possible until properly healed. The only way to avoid well-camouflaged sea urchins and stone fish is by not stepping on the seabed: even thick-soled shoes don't provide total protection against their sharp spines, which can be removed by softening the skin by holding it over a steaming pan of water.

As for **mosquitoes**, you can best avoid being bitten by covering up as much as is practical, and applying repellent to exposed flesh. Note that most repellents sold locally are based on **citronella**; if you want one containing **DEET**, which some say is more effective, buy it at home as it's not sold locally. Rural or beachside accommodation often features **mosquito nets**, and some places also provide slow-burning **mosquito coils** that generate a little smoke that can deter the insects.

For many people, the ubiquitous **leech** – whose bite is not actually harmful – is the most irritating aspect to jungle trekking (see page 45). Venomous **snakes** are not that common, and any that you might encounter will usually slink away. If you are unlucky enough to be bitten then remain still and call for an ambulance, or get someone else to summon help. If one of your limbs has been bitten, ideally a pressure bandage should also be applied to slow the spread of any venom.

Dengue fever, Zika and malaria

The main mosquito-borne disease to be aware of – and the chief reason to take measures to avoid being bitten (see page 44) – is **dengue fever**. It is caused by a virus spread by the *Aedes aegypti* mosquito (identifiable by the white markings on its legs) and outbreaks occur. A new vaccine, not widely available, is recommended only to prevent reinfection

COMBATING LEECHES

Leeches are gruesome but pretty harmless creatures, related to earthworms, which almost all trekkers will encounter – especially after rain, when you can rely upon them to come out. Slender, muscular tubes with teeth at one end, they lie dormant in rainforest leaf litter until, alerted by footfalls and body heat, they make strange, darting movements towards you, latching onto your boot, then climbing until they find a way through socks and trousers and onto your skin. Their bites are painless, so you may not notice you've been bitten until you see a growing red stain on your clothes – formed by the trickle of blood that continues for several minutes. That said, the bite of the larger, orange-striped tiger leech can hurt or be felt as a slight itching sensation.

If you see one beginning to bite, you can use your fingernail or a credit card to gently dislodge its head end. Otherwise salt or a quick dose of mosquito repellent will cause it to let go rapidly, as will scorching it with a cigarette lighter.

Of course it's best to **avoid being bitten** in the first place. Some nature guides recommend simply wearing open shoes and shorts, so that you can see any leeches – an approach that requires an advanced jungle mentality. Most people prefer, at the very least, to wear trousers tucked into their socks. Better still, tuck your trousers into **leech socks**. The size of Christmas stockings and made from calico, they have a string at the top that you tie tight at the knee; you can buy them in specialist stores and at some Malaysian nature parks. For an additional deterrent, spray socks and boots with insect repellent.

---

in those who have already had dengue. Symptoms include severe headaches, pain in the bones, fever and often a fine rash over the body. There's no specific treatment, just plenty of rest, an adequate fluid intake and painkillers when required.

The **Zika** virus is spread by the same mosquito species and a number of cases have been reported in Malaysia and Singapore. Symptoms are mild, flu-like and can involve rashes, but the infection can affect foetal development so pregnant women should postpone travelling or seek medical advice on the latest risks.

Although the risk of catching **malaria** is fairly low, you should consider taking antimalarial tablets if you think you might be staying in remote jungle areas of **Borneo** for some time. Bear in mind you have to start taking the tablets before you arrive in a malarial zone – ask your doctor for the latest advice. Try to avoid getting bitten at all, by wearing long clothes.

Altitude sickness

Altitude sickness (or acute mountain sickness) can occur if you ascend above around 3500m. In Malaysia it's only likely to be relevant to those climbing **Mount Kinabalu** (4095m), and those affected usually report only mild symptoms at this altitude. Those symptoms include dizziness, headache, shortness of breath and nausea; severe cases can be life-threatening. Painkillers and other over-the-counter drugs may bring symptomatic relief in mild cases, but you must descend to lower altitude if symptoms drag on after a day or two or are severe.

Pharmacies, clinics and hospitals

Medical services in Malaysia, Singapore and Brunei are excellent; staff almost everywhere speak English and use up-to-date treatments. Details of pharmacies and hospitals are in the "Directory" sections of the Guide for cities and major towns.

Pharmacies stock a wide range of medicines and health-related items, from contraceptives to contact lens solution; opening hours are the same as for other shops. The two big local chains are Watsons and Guardian, found in most towns. Only the largest pharmacies have **pharmacists**. If you need a **prescription drug**, you should see a doctor at a clinic, at whose discretion the clinic's own dispensary may be able to provide it. That said, in Malaysia at least, lax regulation means some pharmacies will sell such drugs over the counter.

Private **clinics** can be found even in small towns – your hotel or the local tourist office will be able to recommend one. In Malaysia a consultation will incur a very small fee, though one obviously not including the cost of any treatment or medication; keep the receipts for insurance-claim purposes. Finally, the emergency department of each town's general hospital will see foreigners for a small fee, though obviously costs rise rapidly if continued treatment or overnight stays are necessary.

The media

Both Malaysia and Singapore boast plenty of newspapers, TV channels and radio stations serving up lively reportage of events, sports and entertainment, though don't expect to come across hard-hitting or healthily sceptical coverage of domestic politics. The major media organizations in each country are at least partly owned by the establishment; in Singapore, most newspapers have actually been herded into a conglomerate in which the state has a major stake.

Furthermore, the media are kept on their toes by a legal requirement that they must periodically renew their licence to publish. Thus the Sarawak Tribune was suspended indefinitely in 2006 after it reproduced the controversial Danish cartoons of the Prophet Muhammad; only in 2010 did it resume publication as the New Sarawak Tribune.

Given these circumstances, it's no surprise that the **Press Freedom Index** issued annually by the pressure group Reporters Without Borders, regularly puts Malaysia and Singapore in the bottom half of the world's nations. Brunei, also languishing low down in the table, has a much less well-developed media sector, and its newspapers are packed with anodyne stories about the latest deeds of the sultan and other royals.

Foreign newspapers and magazines are sold in the main cities, and international TV channels are available via satellite and cable. That said, issues of foreign magazines containing pieces that displease the authorities have occasionally been banned, while Singapore's leaders have a long history of winning defamation suits against foreign publications in the island's courts.

If this all seems a bleak picture, it should be said that coverage of Malaysia's opposition parties has increased since they have become more of a force to contend with in recent elections. Added to that, the advent of independent domestic **news websites** and **blogs** has been a breath of fresh air in both Malaysia and Singapore. It's also possible to turn up **YouTube** clips of discussion forums and interviews with activists, offering an alternative take on local issues.

Newspapers, magazines and online news

Both Malaysia and Singapore have English, Malay, Chinese and Tamil newspapers, while Brunei's papers appear in English and Malay. Though Malaysia's national dailies are available in towns in East Malaysia, locally-published English-language papers such as the Borneo Post in Sarawak (http://theborneopost.com) and the Daily Express in Sabah (http://dailyexpress.com.my) are more popular there.

MALAYSIA

Aliran Monthly http://aliran.com. Campaigning magazine with an avowed pro-human-rights stance.
Free Malaysia Today http://freemalaysiatoday.com. Non-partisan coverage of Malaysian politics and society, with a dedicated East Malaysia section.
Malaysia Insight http://themalaysianinsight.com. Considered more moderate than some of its online counterparts, the Insider provides intelligent news and commentary.
Malaysiakini http://malaysiakini.com. Invigorating reportage and opinion with an anti-establishment slant.
New Straits Times http://nst.com.my. Closely linked to the UMNO party, this offshoot of Singapore's Straits Times was created after the island separated from the Federation.
Sarawak Report http://sarawakreport.org. Not a Malaysian site – it's run out of London, and became the first blog to be blocked in Malaysia on the basis of "national security" – but worth a look for its hard-hitting coverage of issues such as logging, native peoples' rights and the probity of Sarawak's government.
The Star http://thestar.com.my. Founded by the MCA party, The Star is Malaysia's best-selling English daily and carries a broad range of local news, arts reviews and so forth.

SINGAPORE

The Online Citizen http://theonlinecitizen.com. An alternative and rather less sanguine view of Singapore affairs than you find in the island's mainstream media.
Straits Times http://straitstimes.com. This venerable broadsheet was founded in 1845, though sadly its pedigree isn't matched by the candour of its journalism; it's not bad on foreign news, however.
Today http://todayonline.com. Online-only paper from the state-owned broadcaster Mediacorp, Today is generally less blandly pro-establishment than the Straits Times and carries worthwhile commentaries at the weekend.
TR Emeritus http://tremeritus.net. Formerly the Temasek Review, this website offers independent-minded (though occasionally ranty and/or childish) reporting of the island's affairs.

BRUNEI

Borneo Bulletin http://borneobulletin.com.bn. Pleasant enough, but hardly the most challenging of reads.

Television

TV and radio in Malaysia, Singapore and Brunei are dominated by the state-owned broadcasters **RTM**, **Mediacorp** and **RTB** respectively, putting out programmes in several languages. Terrestrial **television** features an unexceptional mix of news, documentaries and dramas made locally and abroad,

FESTIVALS **BASICS** | 47

cookery and talk shows, Islamic discussions and so forth. Various foreign TV channels, including CNN, BBC World, National Geographic, ESPN Sports and Al-Jazeera (which has its East Asian base in KL), are available on cable and satellite in Malaysia, and on cable in Singapore (where ownership of satellite dishes is banned). Note that Malaysian broadcasts are easily picked up in Singapore, and Singapore broadcasts in southern Johor.

Festivals

With so many ethnic groups and religions represented in Malaysia, Singapore and Brunei, you'll be unlucky if your trip doesn't coincide with some sort of festival. Religious celebrations range from exuberant family-oriented pageants to blood-curdlingly gory displays of devotion. Chinese religious festivals are the best times to catch free performances of Chinese opera, or *wayang*, featuring crashing cymbals, clanging gongs and stylized singing. Secular events might comprise a parade with a cast of thousands, or just a local market with a few cultural demonstrations laid on.

Bear in mind that the major festival periods may play havoc with even the best-planned travel itineraries, and that some festivals are also public holidays (see page 56).

A festival and events calendar

The dates of many festivals change annually according to the lunar calendar. The Islamic calendar in particular shifts forward relative to the Gregorian calendar by about ten days each year, so that, for example, a Muslim festival that happens in mid-April one year will be nearer the start of April the next. We've listed rough timings; actual dates can vary by a day or two in practice depending on the sighting of the new moon.

JANUARY & FEBRUARY

Ponggal (mid-Jan) A Tamil harvest and New Year festival held at the start of the Tamil month of Thai. *Ponggal* translates as "overflow", and the festival is celebrated by boiling sugar, rice and milk together in a new claypot over a wood fire till the mixture spills over, symbolizing plenty.

Thaipusam (late Jan/early Feb) Entranced Hindu penitents carry elaborate steel arches (*kavadi*), attached to their skin by hooks and skewers, to honour Lord Subramaniam. The biggest processions are at Kuala Lumpur's Batu Caves and from Singapore's Sri Srinivasa Perumal Temple to the Chettiar Hindu Temple.

Chinese New Year (late Jan/early to mid-Feb) At which Chinese communities settle debts, visit friends and relatives and give children red envelopes (*hong bao/ang pao*) containing money; Chinese operas and lion- and dragon-dance troupes perform in the streets, while markets sell sausages and waxed ducks, pussy willow, chrysanthemums and mandarin oranges. Singapore and the major towns of west coast Malaysia see Chingay parades, featuring stilt-walkers, lion dancers and floats. Food plays a big part of the festival, with plenty of food stalls lining the streets.

Chap Goh Mei (Feb) The fifteenth and climactic night of the Chinese New Year period, and a time for more feasting and firecrackers; women who throw an orange into the sea at this time are supposed to be granted a good husband.

Brunei National Day (Feb 23) The sultan and tens of thousands of Bruneians watch parades and fireworks at the Sultan Hassanal Bolkiah National Stadium, just outside Bandar Seri Begawan.

MARCH–MAY

Easter (March/April) Candlelit processions are held on Good Friday at churches.

Qing Ming (April) Ancestral graves are cleaned and restored, and offerings made by Chinese families at the beginning of the third lunar month, signifying the start of spring and a new farming year.

Ramadan (late-March to mid-April in 2023) Muslims spend the ninth month of the Islamic calendar fasting in the daytime, and breaking their fasts nightly with delicious Malay sweetmeats served at stalls outside mosques.

Vesak Day (May) Saffron-robed monks chant prayers at packed Buddhist temples, and devotees release caged birds to commemorate the Buddha's birth, enlightenment and attainment of Nirvana.

Kaamatan (May 30 & 31) The Kadazan/Dusun version of Sarawak's Iban *gawai* rice-harvest festival, Kaamatan is marked all over Sabah (and Labuan Island), most notably with week-long festivities at the Kadazan/Dusun Cultural Association in Kota Kinabalu.

JUNE–AUGUST

Hari Raya Puasa/Aidilfitri (late-April in 2023) Muslims celebrate the end of Ramadan by feasting and visiting family and friends; this is the only time the region's royal palaces are open to the public.

Gawai Dayak (June) Sarawak's people, especially the Iban and Bidayuh, celebrate the end of rice harvesting with extravagant longhouse feasts. Aim to be in a longhouse on the Rejang or Batang Ai rivers, or around Bau.

Feast of St Peter (June 24) Melaka's Eurasian community decorate their boats to honour the patron saint of fishermen.

Dragon Boat Festival (June/July) Rowing boats, bearing a dragon's head and tail, race in Penang, Melaka, Singapore and Kota Kinabalu, to commemorate a Chinese scholar who drowned himself in protest against political corruption.

George Town Festival (July/Aug) One of the best arts festivals in Malaysia sees the historic streets and buildings of Penang given over to music recitals, art exhibitions and the like, over a month.

Sultan of Brunei's Birthday (July 15) Starting with a speech by the sultan on the padang, celebrations continue for two weeks with parades, lantern processions, traditional sports competitions and fireworks.

Singapore National Day (Aug 9) Singapore celebrates its independence with a huge show featuring military parades and fireworks.

Hari Raya Haji/Aidiladha (late-June to early-July in 2023) Muslims gather at mosques to honour those who have completed the hajj, or pilgrimage, to Mecca; goats are sacrificed and their meat given to the needy.

Festival of the Hungry Ghosts (late Aug) Held to appease the souls of the dead released from purgatory during the seventh lunar month. Chinese street operas are staged, and joss sticks, red candles and paper money are burnt outside Chinese homes.

Merdeka Day (Aug 31) Parades in KL's Merdeka Square and other cities mark the formation of the state of Malaysia.

SEPTEMBER–DECEMBER

Moon Cake Festival (Sept) Also known as the Mid-Autumn Festival, this is when Chinese people eat and exchange moon cakes, made from sesame and lotus seeds and sometimes stuffed with a duck egg. Essentially a harvest festival.

Yang di-Pertuan Agong's Birthday (Sept) Celebrates the birthday of Malaysia's king, elected every five years by the Peninsula's nine sultans from among their number.

Malaysia Day (Sept 16) Commemorates the establishment of Malaysia in 1963, when Singapore, Sabah and Sarawak joined with already-independent Malaya.

Navarathri (Sept–Oct) Hindu temples devote nine nights to classical dance and music in honour of the consorts of the Hindu gods, Shiva, Vishnu and Brahman.

Thimithi (Oct/Nov) Hindu firewalking ceremony in which devotees prove the strength of their faith by running across a pit of hot coals; best seen at the Sri Mariamman Temple in Singapore.

Deepavali (Oct/Nov) Also known as Diwali, this Hindu festival celebrates the victory of Light over Dark: oil lamps are lit outside homes to attract Lakshmi, the goddess of prosperity, and prayers are offered at all temples.

Christmas (Dec 25) Shopping centres in major cities compete to create the most spectacular Christmas decorations.

Sports and outdoor activities

With some of the world's oldest tropical rainforest and countless beaches and islands, Malaysia offers plenty of opportunities for trekking, snorkelling and scuba diving, and rafting, tubing, abseiling and paragliding – among others – are available in certain locations.

If you intend to take up any of these pursuits, check that they are covered by your insurance policy.

Watersports

The crystal-clear waters and abundant tropical fish and coral of Malaysia make snorkelling and diving a must for any underwater enthusiast. This is particularly true of the islands of southeast Sabah – Sipadan, Mabul and their neighbours boast some of the world's best dive sites – and the Peninsula's east coast, with islands like the **Perhentians**, **Redang**, **Kapas** and **Tioman**.

Dive shops offer all-inclusive, internationally recognized certification courses, ranging from a beginner's open-water course, right through to the dive-master certificate. If you're already qualified, diving will obviously come a lot more cheaply, although prices vary depending on the locality.

Most beachside guesthouses rent snorkelling equipment for a nominal fee. Some popular **snorkelling** areas mark out lanes for motorboats with buoy lines – stay on the correct side of the line to avoid a nasty accident. If you're not sure where it's safe to swim or snorkel, always seek local advice. Never touch or walk on coral as this will cause irreparable damage – besides which, you risk treading on the armour-piercing spines of sea urchins, or a painful encounter with fire coral.

Jetskiing and **parasailing** are also on offer at many popular beaches. **Windsurfing**, however, has yet to take off except at a few, usually pricey, resorts, as well as at Cherating on the east coast, where the open bay and shallow waters provide near-perfect conditions during the northeast monsoon.

Whitewater rafting and tubing

Whitewater rafting has become a popular activity in Sabah, where there are several rivers in the vicinity of Kota Kinabalu that tour operators organize regular trips to, notably the Padas River. Opportunities for rafting in **Peninsular Malaysia** are limited and hard to reach, with the notable exception of Gopeng (see page 118); here, it's best to go with an operator such as Nomad Adventure (http://nomadadventure.com) or River Bug (http://riverbug.asia). Prices vary depending on the location. A few nature parks also offer the chance to go **tubing** down jungle rivers.

Trekking

The majority of **treks** in Malaysia require forethought and preparation. In addition to the fierce sun if you're not in the jungle, the tropical climate can unleash torrential rain without warning, which rapidly affects

CHECKLIST OF CAMPING AND TREKKING EQUIPMENT

As camping and trekking are not especially popular with Malaysians, you need to bring your own **gear** if possible – especially core items like tents and sleeping bags – or take your chances with locally sold products, which are generally inexpensive and sometimes correspondingly short-lived. Hiking boots and shoes may not be that easy to find, especially in larger sizes, though local people, including trekking guides, often swear by plain, slip-on **rubber shoes** (kasut gatah), sold everywhere. Available in a variety of sizes for a very modest outlay, they are surprisingly versatile, offering a decent grip on the forest floor and suitable for fording streams as they can't soak up water. That said, you may find them less suitable for multiday trekking in difficult terrain.

There are small (and very expensive) "proper" outdoor gear stores in major cities; you might also be able to rent some of what you'll need on site, especially at Taman Negara, or have it supplied as part of a hiking package.

ESSENTIALS

- Backpack
- Breathable shirts/T-shirts
- First-aid kit (basic)
- Insect repellent
- Lightweight, quick-drying trousers
- Pocket knife
- Poncho or rainproof coat
- Sandals or rubber shoes (for wading through streams)
- Sun block
- Toilet paper
- Toiletries
- Torch (and/or head torch)
- Trekking shoes/boots
- Water bottle

OTHER USEFUL ITEMS

- Binoculars
- Compass
- Emergency snack food
- Fleece jacket (if at altitude)
- Hat, cotton, with brim (for exposed terrain)
- Heavy-duty refuse bag (to rainproof your pack)
- Insulation mat
- Leech socks
- Lip balm
- Mosquito net
- Sewing kit
- Sleeping bag
- Sunglasses (UV protective)
- Tent (if sleeping out)
- Towel, small
- Water purification tablets

---

the condition of trails or the height of rivers – what started out as a ten-hour trip can end up taking twice as long. That said, the time of year is not a hugely significant factor when planning a trek, although in the rainy season (Nov–Feb) trails can be slow going (or even closed for safety reasons) and the parks and adventure tours will be less busy.

Treks in national parks almost always require that you go in a group with a **guide**; solo travellers can usually join a group once there. Costs and conditions vary between parks; each park account in the Guide contains details, while tour operators in Kuala Lumpur, Kuching, Miri and Kota Kinabalu (listed throughout the relevant sections in the Guide) can also furnish information on conditions and options.

For inexperienced trekkers, **Taman Negara** is probably the best place to start, boasting a good range of walks, many of which can be done without a guide, while **Bako National Park** in southwest Sarawak offers fairly easy, day-long hikes. For more experienced walkers, other parks in Sarawak, especially **Mulu National Park**, should offer sufficient challenges for most tastes, while Sabah's **Maliau Basin** is at the demanding end of the scale. **Kinabalu Park** in Sabah is in a class of its own, the hike to the top of the mountain a demanding but highly rewarding combination of trekking and climbing. Equally challenging, although lesser in stature, is **Mount Trus Madi**, also in Sabah.

Culture and etiquette

Despite their obvious openness to influences from around the globe, Malaysia,

Singapore and Brunei remain fairly conservative and conformist places. Behaviour that departs from cultural norms – basically, anything that draws attention to the individuals concerned – is to be avoided.

Foreigners are generally cut some slack, but until you acquire some familiarity with where the limits lie, it's best to err on the side of caution. Get the balance right and you'll find locals helpful and welcoming, while respectful of your need for some privacy.

Dress

For both men and women, exposing lots of bare flesh is generally a no-no, and the degree to which you should **cover up** can seem surprisingly prim. Islamic tradition suffuses the dress code for locals, Muslim or otherwise, and dictates that both men and women should keep torsos covered; shirt sleeves, if short, should come down to the elbow (for women, long-sleeved tops are preferable), while shorts or skirts should extend down to the knee (long trousers are ideal). Figure-hugging clothes are often frowned upon, particularly for women. All of this said, dress codes are more liberal in most cities (especially Singapore), on the beach, and when doing sports or other activities.

Note that in Muslim tradition, the soles of **shoes** are considered unclean, having been in contact with the dirt of the street. Thus before entering any home (Muslim or otherwise), it's almost universal practice to remove footwear at the threshold or before stepping onto any carpeted or matted area.

Body language

Two things to **avoid** are public shows of affection (holding hands is OK, kissing is not) and drinking alcohol in the street, ie. outside the confines of a bar or hawker centre. In a situation where you need to make a **complaint**, the most effective approach is not to raise your voice, but to go out of your way to appear calm while stating your case.

As for body language, note that **touching someone's head**, be they Muslim or otherwise, is to be avoided as the head is considered sacred. Handshakes are fairly commonplace when meeting someone; Muslims often follow this by touching the palm of the right hand to their own chest. Some Muslims may be reluctant to shake hands with the opposite sex; however, in this case a smile, nod and that same right-hand-palm gesture will suffice. Muslims and Indians also avoid using their left hand for human contact or eating.

Visiting places of worship

It's common to see various temples and mosques happily existing side by side, each providing a social as well as a religious focal point for the corresponding community. Some shrines are among the oldest structures you're likely to see in the region and are worth a look around.

In theory all **mosques** are open to visitors outside prayer times, though in conservative areas they may not welcome tourists. Male visitors should wear long trousers and a shirt or top with sleeves coming down to the elbows (long sleeves are even better); women will also have to don a long cloak and headdress, which is provided by most mosques. You'll be required to remove your shoes before entering. Most Chinese and Hindu **temples** are open from early morning to early evening; devotees go in when they like, to make offerings or to pray. Hindu temples also expect visitors to remove shoes.

Even if there are no signs barring **photography**, staff and worshippers at some temples don't take kindly to it; if in doubt, ask.

Women travellers

Women who respect local customs and exercise common sense should have few problems travelling alone or with other women, though some Western women have been known to find the atmosphere in largely **Muslim areas**, such as Kelantan or Tereng-

---

THE STATUS OF MALAY WOMEN

Malay women are among the most **emancipated** in the Islamic world. They often attain prominent roles in business, academia and other areas of public life, and are very much the lynchpin of the family.

Although the more conservative tide running through the Islamic world has had relatively little impact on this situation, many Malay women now wear a *tudung* (headscarf). Sometimes this merely indicates an acceptance of the trappings of the religion – it's not unusual to see Malay women at a gig or club partying away in headscarf, T-shirt and jeans.

ganu, off-putting. Arriving there from Thailand or from a more cosmopolitan part of Malaysia, you may be stared at or subjected to wolf-whistles or lewd gestures, even if you are dressed more conservatively than some local Chinese or Indian women. If it's any consolation, this sort of thing is quite random, and the reason local non-Muslim women might get away with a bit more is that there is an unspoken understanding as to how Malaysia's various communities can behave in public.

Shopping

Southeast Asia can offer bargain shopping, with electrical equipment, cameras and fabrics all selling at competitive prices. What's more, the region's ethnic diversity means a range of unusual souvenirs and handicrafts to choose from.

One point to be aware of is that a lot of the crafts on sale in Malaysia are in fact made elsewhere in the region, particularly in Indonesia. Worthwhile buys, especially domestically made ones, are highlighted throughout the Guide. Also be aware that prices in small outlets such as family-run shops tend to be negotiable, and **bargaining** is expected. Asking for the "best price" is always a good opening gambit; from there, it's a question of technique, though be realistic – shopkeepers will soon lose interest if you offer an unreasonably low price. If you buy any electrical goods, it can be worth ensuring you get an international guarantee, endorsed by the shop.

Fabrics

Batik cloth is made by applying hot wax to a piece of cloth with either a pen or a copper stamp; when the cloth is dyed, the wax resists the dye and a pattern appears, a process that can be repeated many times to build up colours. Note that some vendors try to pass off printed cloth as batik. Make sure the brightness of the pattern is equal on both sides – if it's obviously lighter on one side, it is likely the cloth is printed.

Batik is used to create shirts, skirts, bags and hats, as well as traditional **sarongs**. The exquisite gold-threaded brocade known as **songket**, used to make sarongs, headscarves and the like, is a big step up in price from batik; prices soar for the finest pieces.

Unique to Sarawak is **pua kumbu** (in Iban, "blanket"), a textile whose complex designs are created using the *ikat* method of weaving (see page 309). The cloth is sold in longhouses as well as in some souvenir outlets. Sabah's Indigenous groups have their own woven fabrics, some of which are sold by Sabah Tourism's Kadaiku subsidiary (http://kadaiku.com).

> ### DUTY-FREE GOODS
> Malaysia has no duty on cameras, watches, cosmetics, perfumes or cigarettes. Labuan, Langkawi and Tioman are duty-free islands, which in practice means that goods there (including alcohol) can be a third cheaper than on the Malaysian mainland, though it's not as though a particularly impressive range of products is on sale. Duty-free products in Singapore include electronic and electrical goods, cosmetics, cameras, clocks, watches, jewellery, precious stones and metals.

Woodcarving

Woodcarving skills, once employed to decorate the palaces and public buildings of the early sultans, are today used to make less exotic articles such as mirror frames. However, it's still possible to see statues and masks created by the Orang Asli. As animists, Orang Asli artists draw upon the natural world – animals, trees, fish, as well as more abstract elements like fire and water – for their imagery. Of particular interest are the carvings of the Mah Meri of Selangor, which are improvisations on the theme of *moyang*, literally "ancestor", the generic name for all spirit images. In Borneo, look out for Indigenous face masks and rectangular shields adorned with intricate motifs. It's also possible to buy hardwood blowpipes, though these are drilled rather than carved.

Metalwork

Of the wealth of metalwork on offer, **silverware** from Kelantan is among the finest and most-intricately designed; it's commonly used to make earrings, brooches and pendants, as well as more substantial pieces. Selangor is known for its **pewter** – a blend of tin, antimony and copper – which can be used in elegant vases, tankards and ornaments.

Other souvenirs

Rattan, cane, **bamboo** and *mengkuang* (pandanus) are traditionally used to make baskets, bird cages, mats, hats and shoulder bags. The best items make surprisingly impressive accessories, and in Borneo it's possible to find baskets and bags bearing traditional motifs, too. Another unusual raw material is **breadfruit bark**; in Sarawak it's pressed to produce a "cloth" that makes excellent hats and jackets, as well as a canvas for paintings.

Malay pastimes throw up some interesting purchases: leather *wayang kulit* (shadow play) **puppets**, portraying characters from Hindu legend, are attractive and light to carry; equally colourful but impractical to cart around are Malay **kites** (*wau*), which can be a couple of metres long.

Pottery, though sometimes mass-produced, can be a worthwhile decorative acquisition. Examples include the Malay *labu*, a gourd-like slender-necked water jug (it's made in Perak, among other places) and Sarawak pots and jars bearing Indigenous motifs. Finally, it's possible to buy some fine examples of **beadwork** – from pricey Peranakan beaded slippers to Kelabit jackets from the northern highlands of Sarawak.

Travel essentials

Accessible travel

Of the three countries covered in this guide, **Singapore** is the most accessible to travellers with disabilities; tax incentives are provided for developers who include disabled access features into new buildings. In contrast, Malaysia and Brunei make few provisions.

Across the region, life is made a lot easier if you can afford to stay in the more upmarket hotels, which usually have disabled provisions, and to shell out for taxis and the odd domestic flight. However, few tour operators in the region are similarly accommodating.

SALES TAXES AND SERVICE CHARGES

Top-end and many mid-range hotels and restaurants in Malaysia and Singapore levy two surcharges: a **service charge** (usually ten percent) and a **goods and services tax** (GST; six percent in Malaysia, seven percent in Singapore). Always check if prices quoted – including those on online booking sites – include these charges (they are "nett" prices, in local parlance) or exclude them; the presence of "**++**" after a price indicates that you need to add them. GST also applies to goods sold in shops.

Singapore is certainly making a concerted effort to improve: the **MRT** metro system has lifts on most, if not all, of its stations, and many bus routes have wheelchair-accessible vehicles, though these operate only at certain times of day (see http://smrttrains.com.sg for details). Most major **taxi** companies have accessible vehicles available to book, too.

In Malaysia, wheelchair users will have a hard time negotiating the uneven pavements in most towns and cities, and find it difficult to board buses, trains, ferries and the LRT system in Kuala Lumpur, although the new MRT is meant to be accessible. The situation is similar if not worse in East Malaysia and Brunei, with little (sometimes zero) provision for disabled travellers.

CONTACTS FOR TRAVELLERS WITH DISABILITIES

Caring Fleet http://caringfleet.com. Transport services in Singapore for people with disabilities.
Disabled People's Association Singapore 6791 1134, http://dpa.org.sg. Nonprofit organization whose website has an FAQ section for tourists, with details of accessible taxis and local buildings.
Handicaps Welfare Association http://hwa.org.sg. Transport services for people with disabilities in Singapore.
Malaysian Confederation of the Disabled 03 7931 9038, http://facebook.com/MayasianCDisabled. A member of Disabled Peoples International, working for equal opportunities for disabled people in Malaysia.
Strides Mobility http://stridesmobility.sg. Transport services for people with disabilities in Singapore; also has a bus for tours within the city.

Costs

Anyone entering Malaysia from Thailand will find that costs are noticeably higher. Travelling in a group naturally helps keep costs down. The region affords some savings for senior citizens, and an ISIC student card (http://isic.org) might occasionally pay dividends.

Note that **bargaining** is routine throughout Malaysia and Singapore when buying stuff in markets or small shops, though you don't haggle for meals or accommodation.

Malaysia

In **Peninsular Malaysia** you can scrape by on under £22/US$30/RM125 per day staying in dorms, eating at hawker stalls and getting around by bus. Double that and you'll be able to exist in relative comfort without worrying about occasionally treating yourself. Over in **East Malaysia**, everything tends to cost that little bit extra – partly due to archaic regulations that require imported goods to be sent via Peninsula ports rather than arriving directly; here, expect to spend about ten percent more. Of course, if you do any ticketed sightseeing or book tours – especially pricey to reach remote nature parks – then costs will shoot up, wherever you are.

Singapore and Brunei

Costs in **Singapore** are at Western levels, with a minimum budget of around £35/US$47/S$60 per day. Upgrading your lodgings to a private room in a guesthouse, eating one daily meal in a cheap restaurant, and having a beer or two could require £52/US$70/S$90 per day.

Like-for-like costs in **Brunei** are perhaps ten to twenty percent less than in Singapore, though note that budget accommodation in the capital is limited. Otherwise, costs can spiral as you'll have to rely on taxis or package trips to reach outlying places of interest, notably Ulu Temburong National Park.

Crime and personal safety

If you lose something in Malaysia, Singapore or Brunei, you're more likely to have someone run after you with it than run away. Nevertheless, don't become complacent, as petty crime is an issue in Malaysia at least. Sensible **precautions** include carrying your passport and other valuables in a concealed money belt, and using the safety deposit box provided by many guesthouses and hotels. Take a photocopy of the relevant pages of your passport, too, in case it's lost or stolen. If you have to report a crime, be sure to get a copy of the police report for insurance purposes.

It's worth stating here on no account should you have anything to do with **illegal drugs** of any description in Malaysia, Singapore and Brunei (see page 31).

Malaysia

Pickpockets and **snatch-thieves** can be a problem in Malaysian cities, although violent crime is relatively rare.

Restrictions on contact between people of the opposite sex (such as the offence of *khalwat*, or "close proximity") and eating in public during daylight hours in the Ramadan month apply to Muslims only.

Singapore

Singapore is known locally as a "fine city". Substantial **fines** can be levied to punish misdemeanours like littering, jaywalking – defined as crossing a main road within 50m of a designated pedestrian crossing – and so forth, though these penalties are seldom enforced as the populace has become compliant over the

> ### EMERGENCY NUMBERS
>
> #### MALAYSIA
> Police/Fire/Ambulance 999
> From mobile phones 112
>
> #### SINGAPORE
> Fire/Ambulance 995
> Police 999
> From mobile phones 112 or 911
>
> #### BRUNEI
> Ambulance 991
> Fire 995
> Police 993

years. Bear in mind that **chewing gum** – despite what you may hear – is not illegal in Singapore, though it certainly is against the law to import or sell it; you're unlikely to have too much bother in practice, unless you're spotted throwing used gum on the ground (in which case you can be in trouble).

Electricity

Mains voltage in Malaysia, Singapore and Brunei is **230 volts**, so any equipment using 110 volts will need a converter. The plugs in all three countries have three square prongs, like British ones, though many hotel-room sockets will accept several different forms of plug; you can find adapters on sale for next to nothing (try 7-Eleven, Family Mart or other convenience stores, and if that fails go to a grocery store; those on sale at dedicated electrical stores are going to be more expensive).

Insurance

A typical travel insurance policy usually provides cover for the loss of bags, tickets and – up to a certain limit – cash or cheques, as well as cancellation or curtailment of your journey. Some policy premiums exclude dangerous sports; in Malaysia, for example, this can mean scuba diving, whitewater rafting or paragliding. Always ascertain whether medical coverage will be paid out as treatment proceeds or only after return home, and whether there's a 24-hour medical emergency number. When securing baggage cover, make sure that the per-article limit will cover your most valuable possession. If you need to make a claim, you should keep receipts for medicines and medical treatment, and in the event you have anything stolen, you must obtain an official statement from the police.

ROUGH GUIDES TRAVEL INSURANCE

Looking for travel insurance? Rough Guides partners with top providers worldwide to offer you the best coverage. Policies are available to residents of anywhere in the world, with a range of options whether you are looking for single-trip, multi-country or long-stay insurance. There's coverage for a wide range of adventure sports, 24-hour emergency assistance, high levels of medical and evacuation cover and a stream of travel safety information. Even better, roughguides.com users can take advantage of these policies online 24/7, from anywhere in the world – even if you're already travelling. To make the most of your travels and ensure a smoother experience, it's always good to be prepared for when things don't go according to plan. For more information go to http://roughguides.com/bookings/insurance.

Internet

Wi-fi is pretty widespread in Malaysia, though you'll find yourself off the grid – so to speak – at a number of places in remote Borneo. For details of internet access in Brunei and Singapore, see the relevant chapters of this Guide.

If you like being online constantly, it's worth buying a local **SIM or eSIM card** and getting a data plan with it (see page 56).

Laundry

Most Malaysian towns have laundries (*dobi*) where you can have clothes washed cheaply and quickly, according to weight, picking them up later in the day or early the next day. Some hostels and guesthouses have washing machines that guests can use for a small charge. Coin-operated **laundries** are becoming increasingly common, too, and are less tricky to use than might appear at first, with machines that dispense change and detergent. Dry-cleaning services are less common, though any hotel of a decent standard will be able to oblige.

LGBTQ+ travellers

Though Malaysia's largest cities, plus Singapore, have long had a discreet LGBTQ+ scene, its public profile was until recently still summed up by the old "don't ask, don't tell" maxim. However, cyberspace has helped galvanize LGBTQ+ people by providing a virtual refuge within which to socialize and campaign. Hitherto strait-laced **Singapore** now permits exploration of gay themes in the arts, hosts the hugely successful annual rally Pink Dot (see page 518) and for a time even played host to popular outdoor rave parties. Although the environment in **Malaysia** is always going to be more conservative, the Malaysian government has no obvious appetite, Islamically inspired or otherwise, to clamp down on the existing, yet limited, LGBTQ+ nightlife.

For all the general loosening up over the years, it's very much a case of two steps forward and one step back, however. In 2007, following an extraordinary parliamentary debate, Singapore MPs finally agreed to repeal **colonial-era laws** criminalizing anal and oral sex; they retained the injunction on such activity between men, though in 2022 this disappeared too. The same colonial legislation remains on the statute book in Malaysia, and what LGBTQ+-related campaigning exists tends to be channelled into the relatively uncontentious issue of HIV and AIDS. Although Singapore gave some tacit official recognition to Pink Dot in 2022, with the first-ever attendance by a governing MP, the 2023 edition of Malaysia's Good Vibes festival drew global attention when The 1975's frontman Matty Healy kissed his (male) bassist on stage, after criticising local LGBTQ+ laws; the festival was cancelled, and the band fined heavily. All in all, legal recognition of LGBTQ+ partnerships remain a distant prospect in either country.

This mixed picture shouldn't deter LGBTQ+ visitors from getting to know and enjoy the local scene, such as it is. A small number of LGBTQ+ establishments are reviewed in this Guide.

Living in Malaysia and Singapore

Opportunities for non-residents to find short-term **employment** in Malaysia and Singapore are few and far between. Helpers are often required in guesthouses; the wages for such tasks are low, but board and lodging are often included. On a more formal level, both Singapore and KL in particular hold large communities of skilled expats with work permits, secured by their employer. In Malaysia expats might still expect elevated salaries, but this perk is increasingly rare in Singapore, where pay is already at Western levels.

English-teaching qualifications are in demand by language schools in both countries, while qualified **diving instructors** can also find work in Malaysia. There are also a few **volunteer schemes**, mainly focusing on nature conservation fieldwork, though some require you to pay to join.

STUDY AND WORK PROGRAMMES

AFS Intercultural Programs http://afsmas.org. Community service schemes in Malaysia.

Ape Malaysia http://apemalaysia.com. Opportunities to do wildlife conservation work, and not just with orangutans – they have projects at the Sun Bear Conservation Centre near Sandakan, for example.

Camp Borneo http://campsinternational.com. Blurs the distinction between ecotourism and volunteering, with a range of trips that take in Sabah's top nature sights with stints spent doing conservation or community projects.

Fulbright Program http://macee.org.my. Regular opportunities for US citizens to spend several months teaching English in rural Malaysia, without requiring teaching experience.

Turtle Conservation Society http://turtleconservationsociety.org.my. Lists organizations offering volunteer conservation work schemes in Peninsular Malaysia.

Workaway http://workaway.info. Voluntary work – maintenance, gardening, sometimes language teaching – at guesthouses, farms and even art galleries, in return for free or discounted accommodation.

Maps

Online mapping of Malaysia offered by the usual internet giants sometimes contains **inaccuracies**, especially when it comes to road names, though this is becoming less and less of an issue. Many travellers are now using the Maps.me app to get around – it's less busy and energy-sapping than web-based apps, can be used offline, and often features walking trails that are not marked on (for example) Google Maps, as well as very handy subway-route overlay option in KL and Singapore.

Most Malaysian **tourist offices** have their own free maps of the local area, but these are often of poor quality and offer little that the maps in this Guide don't already include. Whichever maps you use, be aware that the high rate of road construction and development in rural and urban areas alike means that maps can be a little out of date as soon as they appear. Singapore maps are covered in the Singapore chapter of this Guide (see page 500).

Money

Malaysia's currency is the **ringgit** (pronounced ring-git and abbreviated to "RM", and sometimes informally called "dollar"), divided into 100 sen. Notes come in RM1, RM5, RM10, RM20, RM50 and RM100 denominations. Coins are currently minted in 5 sen, 10 sen, 20 sen and 50 sen denominations. At the time of research, the **exchange rate** was around RM4.25 to US$1 and RM5.75 to £1.

Singapore's currency is the **Singapore dollar**, written simply as $ (or S$ in this book to distinguish it from other dollars) and divided into 100 cents. Notes are issued in denominations of S$2, S$5, S$10, S$20, S$50 and S$100, with a couple of larger notes, rarely seen; coins come in denominations of 1, 5, 10, 20 and 50 cents, and S$1. At the time of research, the **exchange rate** was around S$1.30 to US$1, S$1.70 to £1. Confusingly, some coins in Singapore are very similar in size and appearance to some of their Malaysian counterparts, so it's best to keep them separate.

Brunei's currency, the **Brunei dollar**, is divided into 100 cents; you'll see it written as B$, or simply as $. The Brunei dollar has parity with the Singapore dollar and both are accepted by banks and larger businesses in either country. Notes come in B$1, B$5, B$10, B$50, B$100 and rare larger denominations; coins come in denominations of 1, 5, 10, 20 and 50 cents.

Banks

Major banks in **Malaysia** include Maybank, HSBC, Citibank, Standard Chartered, RHB and CIMB, most with ATMs; those of Maybank and HSBC, to name two, seldom have problems with foreign bank cards, but other banks' machines vary. In rural parts of Malaysia – for example, in the interior of Sabah or Sarawak, plus some coastal areas – banks and ATMs can be scarce, so here it's a wise idea to carry a fair amount of cash, in smallish denominations.

Licensed **moneychangers**' kiosks, found in bigger towns all over the country, tend to open later than banks, until around 6pm; some open at weekends and until 9pm, too. Some hotels will exchange money at all hours. Exchange rates tend to be more generous at moneychangers, though anyone still depending on travellers' cheques should note that moneychangers don't generally exchange them.

Singapore banks are detailed in the relevant chapter of the Guide (see page 523). Banks represented in **Brunei** include the International Bank of Brunei, Citibank, Standard Chartered Bank and the Overseas Union Bank.

Card and contactless payments

Credit and debit cards are only accepted by larger businesses in Malaysia and Brunei – you won't, for example, be able to use your Visa card at a *kedai kopi*, though a café chain in a big city may well accept it. In Singapore many companies accept card and contactless payments, but small firms may only do so for larger payments.

Opening hours and public holidays

In **Malaysia**, shops are open daily from around 9.30am to 7pm, though outlets in shopping centres and malls are typically open later. Government offices tend to work Monday to Friday from 8am to 4.15pm or 9am to 5pm, with an hour off for lunch, except on Friday when the break lasts from 12.15 to 2.45pm (or 11.45 to 2pm in East Malaysia) to allow Muslims to attend prayers. Banking hours are generally Monday to Friday 9.30am to 4pm and Saturday 9.30 to 11.30am (closed on every first and third Saturday of the month), except in the states where Friday is the day off: Kedah, Perlis, Kelantan, Terengganu and to a lesser extent Johor. In these states, the working week runs from Sunday to Thursday, with Friday and Saturday as days off.

In **Singapore**, offices generally work Monday to Friday 8.30am to 5pm and sometimes on Saturday mornings. Shop hours vary, but malls are typically open from 10am to 10pm.

Brunei **banking hours** are Monday to Friday 9am to 3pm and Saturday 9 to 11am.

Opening hours for temples and mosques are given in the text of the Guide where they keep to a formal schedule (often not the case).

Public and school holidays

The list of public holiday dates (see page 56) is a guide only – government websites issue new lists for each year a few months in advance. Note that Muslim holidays (marked with an asterisk) move earlier by ten or eleven days each year, and that precise dates depend on the sighting of the new moon, which determines when each month of the Muslim calendar begins. Note also that each Malaysian state has its own additional holidays, which could be to do with its sultan's birthday or an Islamic (in states with a largely Muslim population) or Indigenous cultural event, such as the *gawai* in June in Sarawak. Some holidays below are marked by special festivities (see page 47).

It pays to be aware of not just public holidays, but also local **school holidays**, as Malaysian accommodation can be hard to come by during these periods. In Malaysia, schools get a week off in mid-March and late August, and two weeks off at the start of June, with a long break from mid-November to the end of the year. Singapore school breaks are almost identical, except that the June holiday lasts the whole month, and kids get a week off in early September rather than late August.

MALAYSIAN PUBLIC HOLIDAYS

Jan 1 New Year's Day
Jan/Feb Chinese New Year
April Hari Raya Puasa/Aidilfitri*
May 1 Labour Day
May/June Vesak Day
June/July Hari Raya Haji/Aidiladha*
Aug 31 National Day
Sept 9 Yang Dipertuan Agong's Birthday
Sept 16 Malaysia Day
Aug Awwal Muharram (the Muslim New Year)*
Oct/Nov Deepavali
Nov Birthday of the Prophet Muhammad*
Dec 25 Christmas

SINGAPORE PUBLIC HOLIDAYS

Note that Singapore has designated dates for Islamic festivals and does not adjust them to fit sightings of the new moon.

Jan 1 New Year's Day
Jan/Feb Chinese New Year
March/April Good Friday
April Hari Raya Puasa (Hari Raya Aidilfitri)*
May 1 Labour Day
May/June Vesak Day
June/July Hari Raya Haji (Eid-al-Adha)*
Aug 9 National Day
Oct/Nov Deepavali
Dec 25 Christmas

BRUNEI PUBLIC HOLIDAYS

Brunei observes the same Muslim festivals as Malaysia, plus New Year, Chinese New Year, Christmas and the following:
February 23 National Day
February Israk Mikraj (the night when the Prophet ascended to heaven)*
March First day of Ramadan*
April Anniversary of Revelation of the Koran*
May 31 Armed Forces' Day
July 15 Sultan's Birthday

Phones

Malaysia, Singapore and Brunei all have a comprehensive **mobile network**. There are many outlets selling mobiles (known locally as "hand phones"), even in the smallest of towns. Your own phone is likely to work on roaming, or you can invest in an eSIM. If your phone is unlocked, you can also use a local SIM card from phone shops and *7–Eleven* stores. You can top up your balance at the same outlets; you either get a receipt with a pin number on it for you to dial and activate the recharge, or the shop staff will do this for you. It's worth looking out for low-priced SIMs aimed at tourists, loaded with a small amount of credit for voice calls and a data balance that should be good for a week or two of moderate online use.

Malaysia

The two big players in the **mobile phone** market are Maxis (maxis.com.my) and Celcom (http://celcom.com.my). Cellular coverage in Peninsular Malaysia is fairly good, though expect it to be patchy or non-existent in rural areas. Sabah and Sarawak coverage is variable, focusing on urban areas, major roads and populated river valleys. Tariffs can be complex, though you can expect calls made to other Malaysian numbers to cost very little.

Singapore

Three companies, Singtel (http://singtel.com), Starhub (http://starhub.com) and M1 (http://m1.com.sg) dominate the mobile phone market in Singapore. Their **SIM cards** are available from post offices and 7–Eleven stores, though note that your passport will be scanned as a form of registration of any SIM purchase. Two more things to note are that you pay not only to make mobile calls but also to receive them, and old **2G phones** do not work in Singapore.

The island has no area codes – the only time you'll punch more than eight digits for a local number is if you're dialling a toll-free (1800) or special-rate number.

Brunei

SIM cards can be obtained from outlets of the mobile provider DST Communications (http://dst.com.bn).

Time

For administrative convenience, Malaysia, Singapore and Brunei are all **eight hours** ahead of Universal Time (GMT), all year. This close to the equator, you can rely on dawn being around 6.30am in the Peninsula and Singapore, dusk at around 7.30pm; in Borneo both happen half an hour to an hour earlier. Not taking into account daylight saving time elsewhere, the three countries are two hours behind Sydney, thirteen hours ahead of US Eastern Standard Time and sixteen hours ahead of US Pacific Standard Time.

Tipping

Tipping is seldom necessary in Malaysia, Singapore and Brunei. That said, when eating out at a proper restaurant, it's customary to tip if a **service charge** isn't included, though you are never required to tip in *kedai kopis* or *kopitiams*. It's not necessary to tip taxi drivers either, unless they have gone out of their way to be helpful. Otherwise you might want to offer a modest tip to a hotel porter or hairdresser, or a tour guide who has been exceptional.

Tourist information

Most Malaysian state capitals have a tourist office run by the national agency **Tourism Malaysia** (http://malaysia.travel) and may boast a second tourist office, sometimes called the **Tourism Information Centre**, run by the state government; details are given in the Guide. Where these state-level tourist offices exist, they are generally better informed than the local Tourism Malaysia branch.

Whichever tourist office you deal with, bear in mind that staff always have plenty of glossy brochures to hand out, but their practical knowledge can be patchy – reflecting the hopelessly incoherent way information circulates in Malaysia. To find out about out-of-the-way attractions, you may be better off contacting local accommodation – calling is best, as emails often elicit slow responses.

Singapore is another proposition altogether. A huge amount of generally reliable information on everything from bus times to museum exhibitions is available in print and online. Tourist information is put out by the **Singapore Tourism Board**, which has a comprehensive website (http://visitsingapore.com), and operates several downtown **Visitor Centres**. Brunei's official tourism website is http://bruneitourism.com.

Travelling with children

Malaysia, Singapore and Brunei are child-friendly countries in which to travel. Disposable nappies and powdered milk are easy to find (fresh milk is sold in supermarkets), and bland Chinese soups and rice dishes, or bakery products, are ideal for children unaccustomed to spicy food. Many restaurants and the slicker *kedai kopis* have highchairs, though only upmarket hotels provide cots or baby-sitting services. However, rooms in the cheaper hotels can usually be booked with an extra bed for little extra cost. Children under 12 get into many attractions for half the price and enjoy discounts on buses and trains.

Kuala Lumpur and around

63 Kuala Lumpur
100 Around Kuala Lumpur

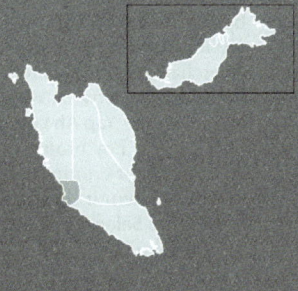

KUALA LUMPUR SKYLINE AT NIGHT

Kuala Lumpur and around

Founded at the head of the Klang Valley in the mid-nineteenth century, Kuala Lumpur – widely known here as KL – has never had a coherent style. The earliest grand buildings around Merdeka Square, dating from the 1890s, are an eccentric fusion of influences from across the British Empire, now overshadowed by soaring modern landmarks (notably the Petronas Towers and Merdeka 118) that wouldn't look out of place in Hong Kong or New York. This melange extends to the people too, as you could spend a visit to KL simply soaking up its excitingly diverse Malay, Chinese and Indian cultures: the conversations heard on the street, the huge range of food and the profusion of onion-domed mosques, incense-infused Buddhist temples and colourful Hindu shrines.

A stay of a few days is enough to appreciate the best of KL's attractions, including the colonial core around **Merdeka Square** and the adjacent enclaves of **Chinatown** and **Little India**, plus, to the east, the restaurants, shops and nightlife of the so-called **Golden Triangle**, the modern heart of downtown KL. It can be equally rewarding just to take in the street life, in particular the boisterous **markets**, ranging from fish and vegetable stalls stuffed into alleyways, via clothes and accessories vendors, to stands selling cooked food of every shape and description. Indeed, the capital offers some of the most exciting **cuisines** in the country, not only in the street markets but also in a plethora of restaurants to suit all tastes and budgets.

KL's hinterland has a number of worthwhile sights, too, among them the rugged limestone **Batu Caves**, which contain the country's most sacred Hindu shrine; **Kuala Selangor** and its magical fireflies; and the hard-to-reach birding hotspot of **Fraser's Hill**.

Brief history

KL was founded in 1857 when the ruler of Selangor State, Rajah Abdullah, sent a party of Chinese to prospect for **tin** deposits around the junction of the Gombak and Klang rivers. The pioneers duly discovered rich deposits 6km from the confluence near **Ampang** (east of the present-day city centre), which grew into a staging post for Chinese mine labourers. Unusually, the settlement acquired the name Kuala Lumpur ("muddy confluence") rather than, as convention dictated, being named after the lesser of the two rivers – KL should, by rights, have been called "Kuala Gombak".

At first, KL was little more than a wooden shantytown; small steamers could approach within 30km along the Klang River, but the rest of the trip was either by shallow boat or through the jungle. Yet settlers poured in, seeking to tap the wealth of this unexplored region: British investors, Malay farmers, Chinese *towkays* (merchants) and labourers. The Chinese also formed two **secret societies**, the fierce rivalry between which restrained the township's growth until the influential former miner **Yap Ah Loy** was appointed as Kapitan Cina, or Chinese headman, in 1869. Ah Loy brought law and order to the frontier town by ruthlessly making an example of criminals, parading them through the streets on a first offence and executing them if they reoffended. He led the rebuilding of KL after it was razed during the **Selangor Civil War** (1867–74) and personally bore much of the cost of a second rebuilding after a devastating fire in 1881.

The British Resident of Selangor State, **Frank Swettenham**, had most of KL's remaining wooden huts demolished in the 1880s, and he imported **British architects** from India to design solid, grand edifices suitable for a new capital. By 1887 the city

ARULMIGU MURUGAN STATUE

Highlights

❶ REXKL One of the first theatres in the land, and gutted by fire twice, the old Rex is now home to a trendy hawker centre. See page 69

❷ Petronas Towers Come to gawp at these surprisingly serene twin structures, then browse in one of KL's best shopping malls just beneath. See page 72

❸ Menara KL Tower Forget the Petronas Towers' Skybridge – this is the place for bird's-eye views of KL in all its glory. See page 76

❹ Islamic Arts Museum One of the most sophisticated museums in the capital, documenting Muslim cultures through arts and crafts. See page 79

❺ Eating around Jalan Alor The street food around Jalan Alor is some of the most memorable that you'll find in KL. See page 91

❻ Rooftop bars and clubs KL is Malaysia's party capital, and many of its bars and clubs enable you to party with a view. See page 94

❼ Shopping in KL's malls and markets Whether you prefer the bright lights of malls or the bustle of endless markets and bazaars, KL is a city made for bargain-hunting. See page 98

❽ Batu Caves Equal parts spiritual destination and theme park, these limestone caves on the edge of KL house a Hindu temple complex and offer subterranean adventures. See page 102

HIGHLIGHTS ARE MARKED ON THE MAP ON PAGE 62

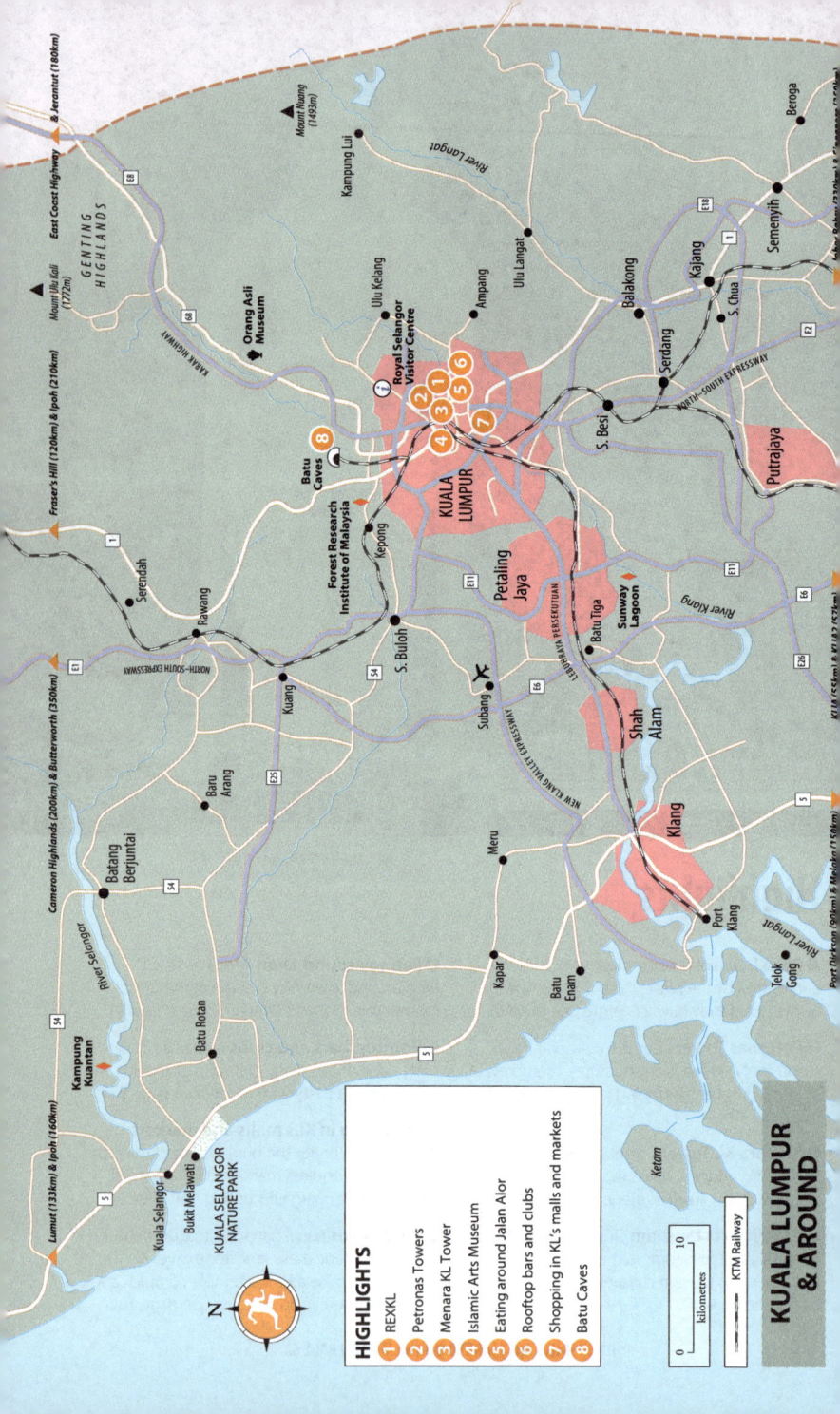

had five hundred brick buildings, and eight times that number in the early 1900s, by which time KL had also become capital of the **Federated Malay States**.

The early twentieth century
Development continued steadily in the first quarter of the twentieth century, during which time Indians mainly from Tamil Nadu swelled the population. Catastrophic floods in 1926 inspired a major engineering project that straightened the course of the Klang River, confining it within reinforced, raised banks. By the time the **Japanese invaded** the Peninsula in December 1941, the commercial zone around Chinatown had grown to eclipse the original colonial area, and the *towkays*, enriched by the rubber boom, were already installed in opulent townhouses along today's Jalan Tuanku Abdul Rahman and Jalan Ampang. While the city suffered little physical damage during World War II, the Japanese inflicted terrible brutality on their historic enemies, the Chinese – at least five thousand were killed in the first few weeks of the occupation alone – and sent thousands of Indians to Myanmar (Burma) to build the infamous railway; very few survived, as noted in Pierre Boulle's book, *The Bridge on the River Kwai*. At the same time, the Japanese ingratiated themselves with certain Malays by suggesting that loyalty to the occupiers would be rewarded with independence after the war.

Following the **Japanese surrender** in September 1945, the British found that nationalist demands had replaced the Malays' former acceptance of the colonizers, and many Chinese felt alienated by talk that a future Malay government would deny them full citizenship. The ensuing Communist-inspired **Emergency** (see page 535) left KL relatively unscathed, but the atmosphere in the city was tense. These issues finally came to a head in KL's May 1969 **race riots**, in which at least two hundred people lost their lives – though things calmed down rapidly after the imposition of a state of emergency.

Recent times
In 1974 KL was plucked from the bosom of Selangor State and designated **Wilayah Persekutuan** (Federal Territory), an administrative zone in its own right; **Shah Alam**, west along the Klang Valley, replaced it as Selangor's capital. After a period of consolidation, KL and the rest of the Klang Valley, including KL's satellite town of **Petaling Jaya**, became a thriving conurbation in the 1990s. That decade, and the early part of the new millennium, saw the realization of several huge infrastructural ventures that are part and parcel of local life today – KL's international **airport** and the **racetrack**, both at Sepang in the far south of Selangor; the **Petronas Towers** and the attendant **KLCC** shopping development; the various urban **rail systems** across the city; and **Putrajaya**, the government's administrative hub off to the south (though KL remains the legislative centre and seat of parliament). The transformation of swathes of KL and much of Selangor is less dramatic today, but still proceeds apace – not least in the ongoing extension of the **Klang Valley MRT rail network** – and concerns are being voiced over the potential strain on water resources and other environmental repercussions.

While KL is a noticeably sociable and safe place for visitors today, many Malaysians have mixed feelings about their capital. The city is second only to Singapore in regional economic clout, but it's undeniable that rapid development has bequeathed many featureless buildings, follies and terrible traffic snarls, which some locals tolerate only because KL offers them good money and experience before they retire to a cherished provincial village. Conversely, others feel that it has been their salvation, the one city in the country where they can explore their artistic or spiritual identity.

Kuala Lumpur

Rather than a discernible city centre, Kuala Lumpur has several hubs of activity. Close to the original "muddy confluence" of rivers that KL was named after, the former

colonial district and its distinctive architecture surrounds **Merdeka Square** – don't miss the informative **Textile Museum** here – with the busy tourist hub of **Chinatown** just southeast. In between the two lie the attractive **Jamek Mosque** and the craft cornucopia that is **Central Market**. Worthwhile forays can be made north to **Little India's** more locals-oriented shops and the altogether grittier **Chow Kit Market**.

Some 2km east, the **Golden Triangle** presents the city's modern face, with lively **Bukit Bintang** packed with upmarket hotels, restaurants and designer shopping malls. Overlooking it to the north are the tall, strikingly modernist **Petronas Towers**; visitors flock to the Skybridge here, though in fact the westerly **Menara KL Tower**, poking out of wooded Bukit Nanas, has better views.

Southwest of the centre – and tricky to reach on foot across one of KL's many pedestrian-unfriendly traffic flows – a clutch of worthwhile sights surrounds the green and airy **Lake Gardens**, notably **Masjid Negara**, one of the country's largest mosques, and the excellent **Islamic Arts Museum**. Below here, the **National Museum** is not as good as it could be, while **Brickfields** is another strongly Indian district, worth a peek for its day-to-day residential street life.

Colonial district

The city's small **colonial district**, which developed around the confluence of the Gombak and Klang rivers in the 1880s, is the area of KL that best retains its historic character. At its heart on the west bank of the Klang, the beautifully tended open padang (field) of **Merdeka Square** is where on 31 August 1957, Malaysia's first prime minister, Tuanku Abdul Rahman, hauled down the British flag and declared *merdeka*, or independence. The 95m-high **flagpole** to the south is one of the tallest in the world, and the tiled square below makes a popular spot for people to gather in the evenings.

Royal Selangor Club
Masjid Jamek station

On the western side of Merdeka Square, the **Royal Selangor Club**, founded in 1884, was the British elite's favourite watering hole, popularly known as the "Spotted Dog" after a former Dalmatian mascot. It was here, on 30 November, 1938, that **Albert Gispert** and fellow drinkers at the club's *Hash House* bar organized a weekly cross-country run; thus the now-international **Hash House Harriers** were born. The original KL group, formed in 1938 and respectfully regarded as the mother of all hashing groups, is still in existence (see page 99). Closed to non-members, the club's history outweighs the appeal of its facade, an oversized 1970s mock-Tudor affair that replaced a 1910 structure built by A.B. Hubback after the original burned down.

To the north, the Anglican **St Mary's Cathedral** (1894), usually open in the daytime, welcomed the city's European inhabitants every Sunday before they retired to the club.

KUALA LUMPUR'S MOORISH STYLE

KL's colonial look originated with **Charles Edwin Spooner**, the state engineer, and architect **Anthony Norman**, who in the 1890s fused a Neoclassical Renaissance style – then the standard for government buildings throughout the British Empire – with "Eastern" motifs, which were felt to be more appropriate for an Islamic country. This **Moorish style**, however, characterized by onion domes, cupolas, colonnades, arched windows and wedding-cake plasterwork, owed more to Indian Moghul architecture than wooden Malay structures. Buildings by Norman in this mould include the **Sultan Abdul Samad Building**, the Old Post Office next door, and the National Textile Museum further south. Norman was succeeded in 1903 by **A.B. Hubback**, who had lived in India and smoothly continued the Moorish theme in the **Jamek Mosque**, old Kuala Lumpur train station and elsewhere.

National Textile Museum

26 Jalan Sultan Hishamuddin • Free • http://muziumtekstilnegara.gov.my • Masjid Jamek station

Housed in an elegant Moghul-Islamic building dating back to 1905, KL's **National Textile Museum** traces the trends and development of textiles that have characterized and shaped the lifestyles of the people of Malaysia. As there are **four galleries** on two floors, it takes more than an hour to do the fairly informative collection justice – though the highlights can be skimmed over in far less time.

On the ground floor, the **Pohon Budi Gallery** focuses on the evolution of textiles from prehistory to modern times and the different weaving techniques adopted in Malaysia. Displays include fine double *ikat* textiles, made with a technique introduced from India in the eighteenth century, along with traditional equipment and paraphernalia for weaving, embroidery, batik making and beadwork.

The adjacent **Pelangi Gallery** displays textiles from Malaysia's multiethnic communities, including Chinese and Baba Nyonya silk and brocades, the elaborate embroidered textiles of Sabah and handwoven *ikat* and *songket* of Sarawak. Look out for Sarawak's Iban *pua kumbu* blankets, decorated with motifs of crocodiles and wild plants.

Upstairs, the **Teluk Beranti Gallery** is dedicated to Malay textiles, especially iridescent *songket* and *limar* cloth, which incorporates fine gold thread into its patterns. There are several pieces of splendid *berayat*, or scripted cloths, with brocade woven into the design in Arabic.

The final **Ratna Sari Gallery** departs into ceremonial metalwork for jewellery and personal adornments, including finely chased filigree tobacco boxes, golden anklets worn by Malay and Peranakan women in the early nineteenth century, and a small case of flame-bladed *kris* daggers and Iban head-hunting machetes from Sarawak.

Jamek Mosque (Masjid Jamek)

Entrance on Jalan Tun Perak • Free • Masjid Jamek station

East of Merdeka Square, across the river, Lebuh Pasar Besar connects the colonial district with the more frenetic life of the old commercial district. Just north of the river bridge is the **Jamek Mosque** (or more officially the Sultan Abdul Samad Jamek Mosque), on a promontory at the confluence of the Klang and Gombak rivers – pretty much where the first tin prospectors built their shacks in the 1850s. Part of the second great period of expansion in KL, the mosque was completed in 1909 by Hubback, its attractive pink brick walls and arched colonnades topped by oval cupolas and squat minarets. There's an intimacy here that's lacking at the modern, much larger Masjid Negara to the south, and the grounds, bordered by palms, are a pleasant place to sit and rest – though the best view of the mosque is from over the Klang at the base of the HSBC building on Jalan Benteng.

Chinatown and around

Spreading out southeast from the Central Market, **Chinatown** was KL's original commercial kernel, dating from the arrival of the first traders in the 1860s. Bordered by Jalan Sultan to the east, Jalan Tun Perak to the north and Jalan Maharajalela to the south, the area had reached its current extent by the late nineteenth century, with southern Chinese shophouses, coffee shops and temples springing up along narrow streets such as Jalan Tun H.S. Lee and Jalan Petaling. Though the shophouses today are fairly workaday, it is encouraging that many period buildings are being refurbished in the face of recurrent threats of redevelopment; in 2011, public outcry saved a row of old shophouses on **Jalan Sultan** from demolition during construction of the ongoing Klang Valley railway.

Although Chinatown scores more on atmosphere than essential sights, it's a hub for **budget accommodation**, and holds a wealth of inexpensive places to shop, eat and go out, so it's likely that you'll spend some time here.

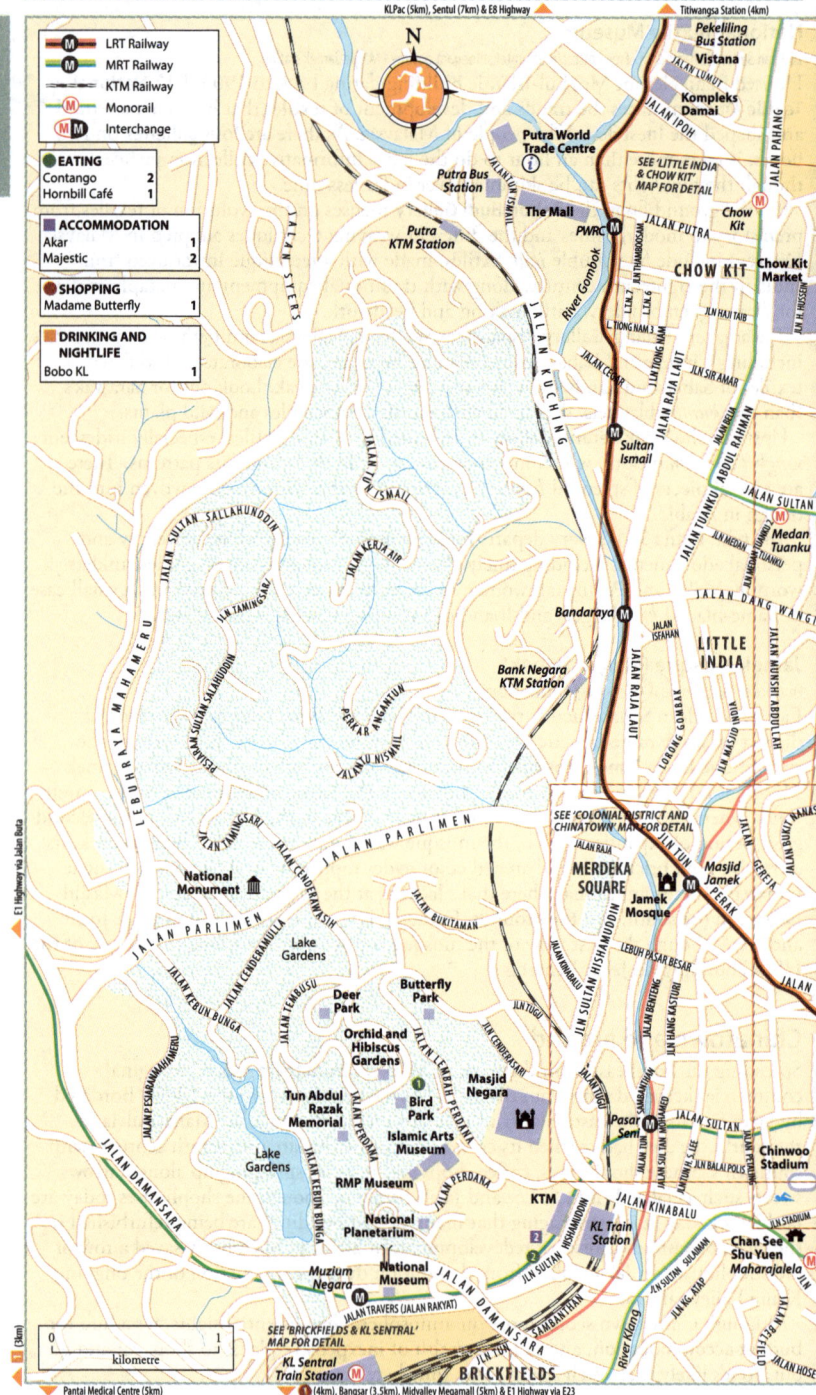

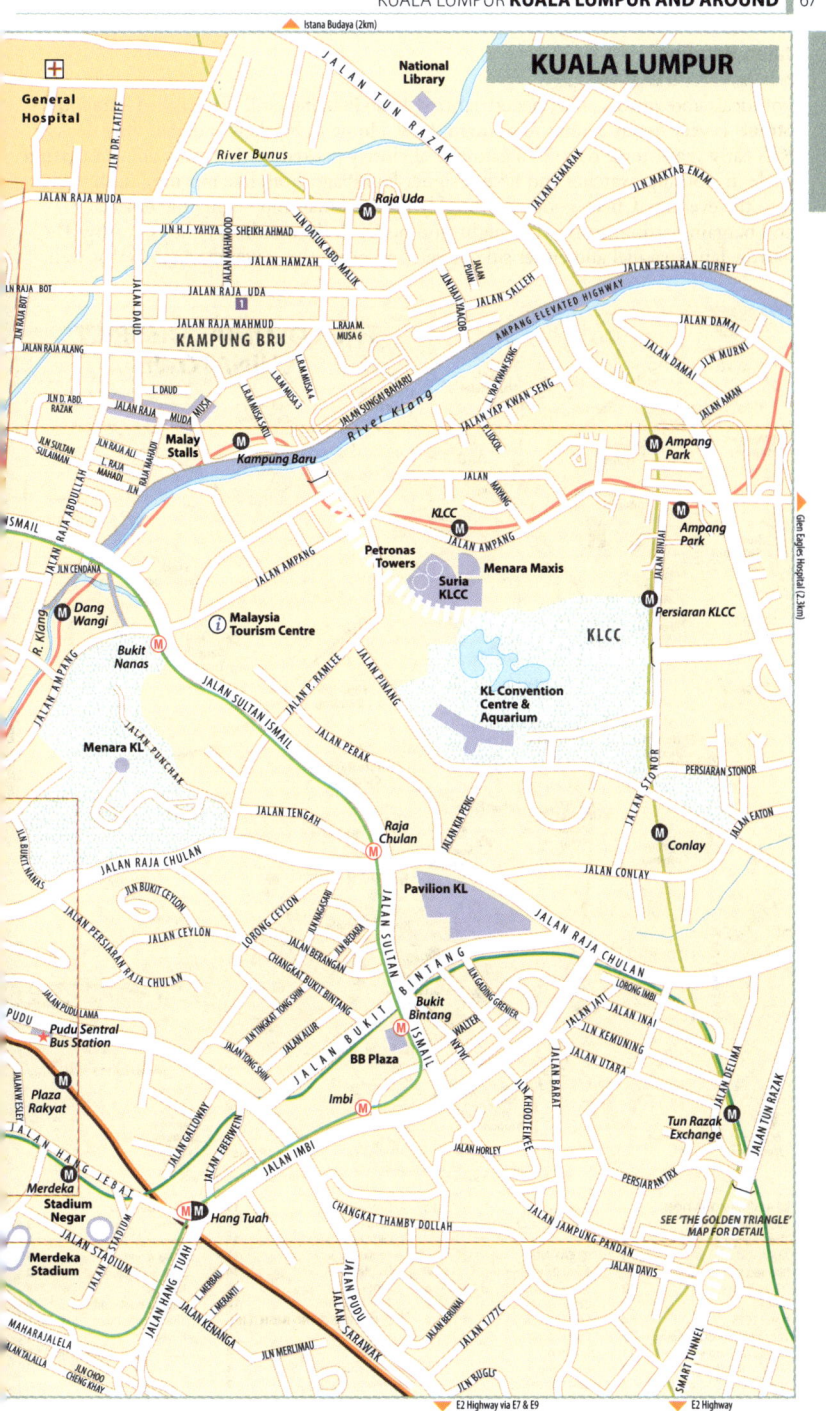

Jalan Petaling

Pasar Seni, Merdeka or Masjid Jamek stations

For locals and visitors alike, pedestrianized **Jalan Petaling** (still often called **Petaling Street**) is very much Chinatown's main draw. Home to brothels and gambling dens in KL's early years, these days it's a gauntlet of closely packed market stalls doing a roaring trade in clothing, watches and fake designer handbags, from late morning until well into the evening. Check goods thoroughly for workmanship – stitching especially – and bargain hard; in truth, you might find better deals in ordinary shops nearby. The narrow lanes parallel and either side of Petaling host grittier **wet markets** too, as well

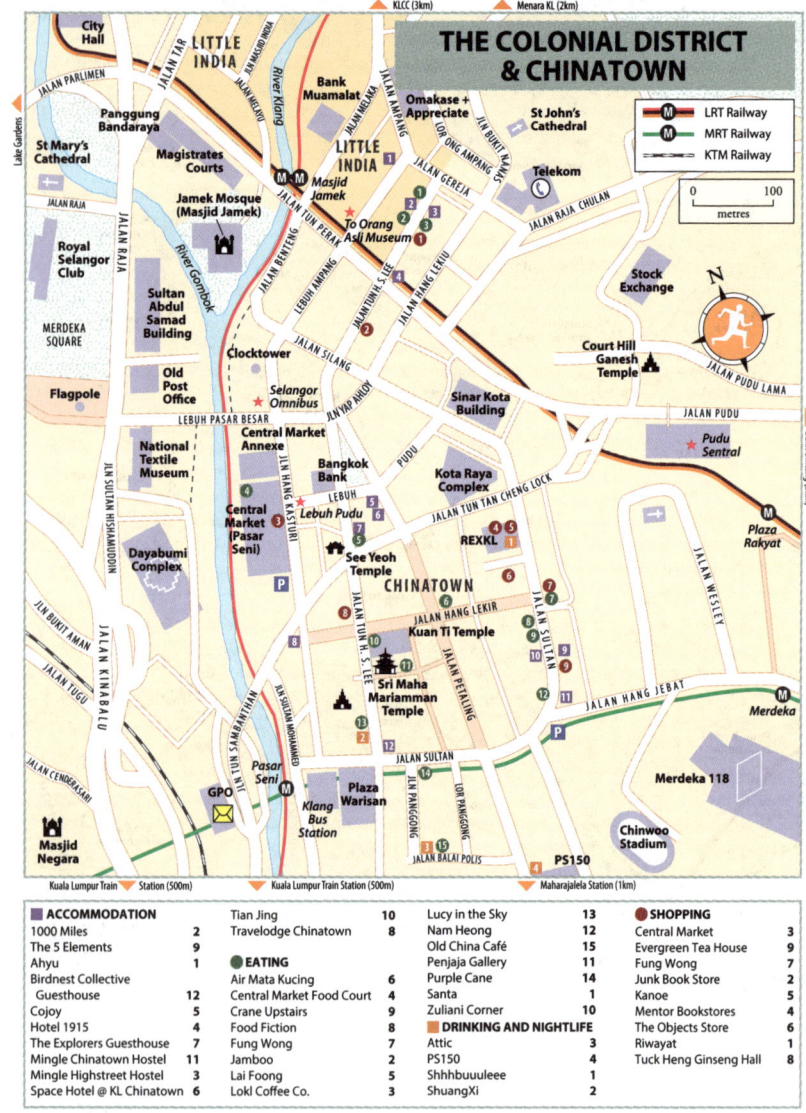

ACCOMMODATION		EATING		Lucy in the Sky	13	SHOPPING	
1000 Miles	2	Air Mata Kucing	6	Nam Heong	12	Central Market	3
The 5 Elements	9	Central Market Food Court	4	Old China Café	15	Evergreen Tea House	9
Ahyu	1	Crane Upstairs	9	Penjaja Gallery	11	Fung Wong	7
Birdnest Collective Guesthouse	12	Food Fiction	8	Purple Cane	14	Junk Book Store	2
Cojoy	5	Fung Wong	7	Santa	1	Kanoe	5
Hotel 1915	4	Jamboo	2	Zuliani Corner	10	Mentor Bookstores	4
The Explorers Guesthouse	7	Lai Foong	5	DRINKING AND NIGHTLIFE		The Objects Store	6
Mingle Chinatown Hostel	11	Lokl Coffee Co.	3	Attic	3	Riwayat	1
Mingle Highstreet Hostel	3	Tian Jing	10	PS150	4	Tuck Heng Ginseng Hall	8
Space Hotel @ KL Chinatown	6	Travelodge Chinatown	8	Shhhbuuuleee	1		
				ShuangXi	2		

as a popular early-morning bric-a-brac market, selling everything from old clothes to mobile phones.

Crossing Petaling at right angles, the eastern end of **Jalan Hang Lekir** hosts a slew of good, inexpensive restaurants and stalls selling *ba kwa* (slices of pork, given a sweet marinade and grilled), local fruits, and molasses-like herbal brews in tureens.

Chan See Shu Yuen
Southern end of Jalan Petaling • Daily 8am–5pm • Free • http://cssykl.com • Maharajalela station

The largest of Chinatown's numerous Chinese shrines, **Chan See Shu Yuen** was founded at the turn of the twentieth century. It's not actually a temple (though it looks like one), but rather a clan hall for families with the very common name of Chan – also transliterated Chen and Tan. A classic of southern Chinese architecture, the eaves are decorated in a riot of three-dimensional ceramic friezes depicting events in Chinese history and mythology; inside the green walls are a series of courtyards and halls, with the inner shrine covered in scenes of lions, dragons and mythical creatures battling with warriors. Most engaging of all are the two gentleman figurines on the altar, representing ancestors of the clan or possibly their servants – and wearing Western top hats to indicate their link with the colonial past.

Sri Maha Mariamman Temple
Jalan Tun H.S. Lee • Free; small donation appreciated • Pasar Seni station

Oddly perhaps, one of KL's main Hindu shrines, the **Sri Maha Mariamman Temple**, is located in the heart of Chinatown. The earliest shrine on the site was built in 1873 by Tamil immigrants, so this is the oldest Hindu temple in the city. It was named after the Hindu deity Mariamman, whose intercession was sought to provide protection against sickness and "unholy incidents". In the case of the Tamils, who had arrived to build the railways or work on the plantations, they needed all the solace they could find from the appalling rigours of their working life.

Significant rebuilding of the temple took place in the 1960s, when sculptors from India were commissioned to design idols to adorn the five tiers of the multicoloured, 22.9m-high gate tower – these now shine with gold embellishments, precious stones and exquisite Spanish and Italian tiles. Garland-makers sell their wares outside the entrance, while above it is a hectic profusion of Hindu gods, painted in realistic colours and frozen in dozens of scenes from the *Ramayana*.

During the Hindu **Thaipusam** festival, the temple's golden chariot is paraded through the streets on its route to the Batu Caves, on the city's northern edge (see page 101). The rest of the year, the chariot is kept in a large room in the temple; you might be able to persuade an attendant to unlock the door and let you take a peek.

Central Market
Jalan Hang Kasturi • http://centralmarket.com.my • Pasar Seni station

The Art Deco **Central Market** is housed in a baby blue-and-white brick hangar, initially built in the 1920s as the capital's wet market. However, the butchers and fishmongers have long since left for places like Chow Kit and the back alleys of nearby Chinatown, and the market was converted in the mid-eighties into what's now known as **Pasar Seni** (which translates as "art market"). Most of the shops now sell souvenirs: Royal Selangor pewter, specialist antiques, Malay regional crafts, carvings and batiks, plus clothes, sarongs, silverware and T-shirts; there's also a decent food court upstairs. Most artists, in fact, have moved into the newer **Central Market Annexe** immediately north, and the pavement in between is clogged with their canvases. Blatantly touristy, it is also enjoyable, with a lively atmosphere in the evenings.

REXKL
80 Jalan Sultan • http://rexkl.webflow.io • Pasar Seni station

The Rex became one of the first theatres in the land on opening in 1947, but was gutted by fire in 1972, and then again in 2002. Its latest incarnation as the **REXKL** will hopefully be around for a while – you'll find a hip mix of places to eat and drink here, most notably the modern hawker centre *Food Fiction* (see page 93), a branch of *Licky Chan* ice cream (see page 93) and the rooftop *Shhhbuuuleee* bar-restaurant (see page 94), while there are some cool shops, plus regular creative programmes.

Court Hill Ganesh Temple
9 Jalan Pudu Lama • Free • Masjid Jamek station

East of the Maybank Building and hidden up a small lane, **Court Hill Ganesh Temple** is KL's second-most-important Hindu shrine, dating to 1897 and reputedly founded by a gardener – which may explain why there's a **tree** growing beside the building. As it is dedicated to the elephant-headed Lord Ganesh, who specializes in the removal of all obstacles to prosperity, peace and success, the temple was understandably popular with visitors on their way to KL's original law courts, which were once located nearby.

Little India and Chow Kit
On foot from Chinatown, it takes around 45min to reach Chow Kit via Little India along Jalan TAR

Running north from Chinatown, **Jalan Tuanku Abdul Rahman** – commonly abbreviated to **Jalan TAR** – brings you within reach of a series of small-scale, local neighbourhoods, which are somewhat unexpected in such a large city. First is **Little India**, a bustling commercial district renowned for its fabrics, especially saris and *songket*s, as well as jewellery. The clothing theme persists immediately west, where Gulati's Silk House and the SOGO department store stock everything from saris to brand-name outdoor gear. There are also some fine 1920s Neoclassical and Art Deco buildings, including the dove-grey **LFS Coliseum Cinema** (see page 97), screening Bollywood releases – actually it's almost entirely Kollywood, the term for Tamil cinema. Beyond here, **Chow Kit Market** is the place to find bargain clothing and local produce, while **Kampung Bahru**, off to the east of Jalan TAR, is a low-key enclave of Malay housing. There are no major sights, but a visit adds depth to KL's character, and all three have excellent eating opportunities.

Little India
Masjid Jamek or Bandaraya stations

East off the lower end of Jalan TAR, **Little India** is still a commercial centre for KL's Indian community, though these days it's eclipsed by Brickfields (see page 80). Only a few steps north from the Masjid Jamek LRT station, **Jalan Melayu** holds Indian stores, some selling excellent *burfi* and other sweet confections; its name derives from the former Malay community here. Approaching **Jalan Masjid India**, you'll encounter a popular covered market, smaller but otherwise similar to Chinatown's Jalan Petaling. Further up is **Masjid India** itself, an Indian-influenced affair dating from the 1960s and tiled in cream and brown.

A few minutes further along the street, you'll come to a little square, to the right (east) off which you'll find plenty of *kedai kopis* and, come evening, street vendors selling food; turn off to the left to reach Lorong Tuanku Abdul Rahman, whose northern end is dominated by a **night market** which gets going at around 6pm and is busiest at weekends. Mainly Malay-run, the stalls sell both food and eclectic bits and pieces, from T-shirts to trinkets. Just past here, Madras and Semua House are two huge haberdasheries, packed to their roofs with **Indian textiles**.

Chow Kit
Chow Kit station is best for Chow Kit Market

Chow Kit district, 1.5km north of Little India, is mostly known for the sprawling, busy **Chow Kit Market**, which fills the lanes east off Jalan TAR. It's one of KL's busiest, most in-your-face fresh produce markets, a tight, overcrowded grid of alleyways under low-slung awnings. Stalls sell everything fit to put in your mouth: bulk tropical fruits at bargain prices, live and prepared fish and poultry, hunks and haunches of various animals, and piles of fresh or dried vegetables and spices. Hawkers around the edge sell freshly cooked snacks too, many with a definite Indonesian slant.

Chow Kit is also a good place to buy **secondhand clothes** (sometimes called "*baju* bundle"). The best deals are west of Jalan TAR along Jalan Haji Taib, where you may chance upon items like Levi's 501s in reasonable condition, and at prices that are almost too good to be true. The market runs for much of the day and into the evening, but note that some locals prefer to give Chow Kit a wide berth after dark, as it's also something of a red-light area; even during the day, the area can be pretty sketchy.

Kampung Baru
Kampung Baru station

If you've time on your hands and enjoy a wander, head 1km east from Chow Kit (along either Jalan Raja Bot or Jalan Raja Alang) into **Kampung Baru** (one of at least three similar spellings used widely), one of Malaysia's several designated Malay reserve areas – land that only people whose ID defines them as ethnic Malays can own, and indeed with its own status in law, not under the direct control of the KL city council. In 1969, this was one of the epicentres of widespread racial violence between Chinese and ethnic Malays; even today, it's often a hub of political protest. Though the Petronas Towers are visible off to the south, Kampung Baru's quiet lanes and painted wooden bungalows with gardens – not to mention chickens wandering the pavements – lend it a distinct village feel. Sadly, plans to "redevelop" the district may well involve wholesale demolitions,

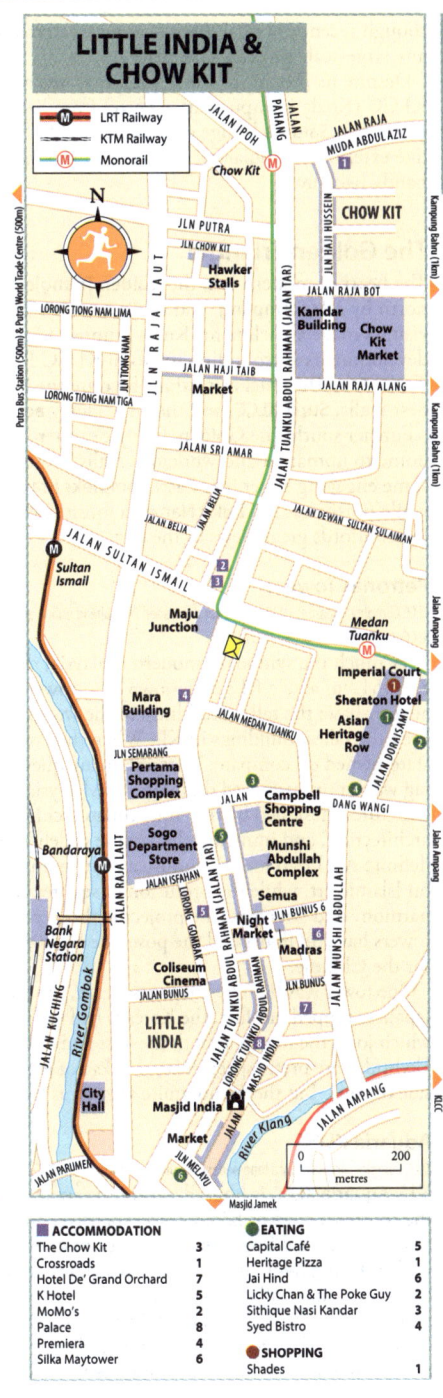

ACCOMMODATION		EATING	
The Chow Kit	3	Capital Café	5
Crossroads	1	Heritage Pizza	1
Hotel De' Grand Orchard	7	Jai Hind	6
K Hotel	5	Licky Chan & The Poke Guy	2
MoMo's	2	Sithique Nasi Kandar	3
Palace	8	Syed Bistro	4
Premiera	4		
Silka Maytower	6	SHOPPING	
		Shades	1

though recent political utterances have referred to "retaining the area's identity" should any large-scale projects take place.

Despite its proximity, until recently it was almost impossible to walk southeast to KLCC (Kuala Lumpur City Centre) from here, owing to the riverside expressway – the pedestrian **Saloma** bridge opened up in 2020 for just this purpose, and its snakeskin-like exterior is popular for dusktime photographs, with the Petronas Towers making a handy backdrop.

The Golden Triangle

The heart of modern KL, the **Golden Triangle** is a sprawling area bounded to the north by **Jalan Ampang**, and to the west by Chinatown and the Klang River. Many visitors make a beeline for Kuala Lumpur City Centre (**KLCC**), a group of huge developments surrounding the focal KLCC Park, on a site once home to the Selangor Turf Club. The chief attractions here are the **Petronas Towers**, soaring above one of KL's best malls, **Suria KLCC**, and the city's glossy **aquarium**.

Further south, the Golden Triangle's other magnet is **Bukit Bintang** ("Star Hill"), home to upmarket and workaday malls, many of KL's best hotels and restaurants, and some engaging street life. East, **Kompleks Kraf** is the city's largest handicrafts gallery, while northwest lies **Bukit Nanas**, a forested hill where the **Menara KL** communications tower affords great views of the city.

Petronas Towers

KLCC Complex • Charge; 1000 passes per day issued 24hr ahead online and at the base of Tower 2 • www.petronastwintowers.com.my • KLCC station

Very much the symbol of modern Malaysia, the twin columns of the **Petronas Towers** rise 451.9m above KL's downtown area, towering over the enormous **Suria KLCC mall** at their base; the tallest buildings in the world from 1998 to 2004, they're now not even the tallest buildings in KL. When they were completed as the headquarters of the state-owned oil company Petronas, many questioned whether the US$1.6 billion price tag was an unwarranted drain on the Malaysian economy, but the tapering, steel-clad structures (designed by the Argentinian architect Cesar Pelli) are a stunning piece of architecture, and immediately became widely recognized across the world. Despite a definite Art Deco feel, the unusual eight-pointed cross-sectional profile obviously draws on Islamic art, while the profusion of squares and circles on the interior walls symbolize harmony and strength. The project is also permeated by Chinese numerology, in that the towers have 88 floors and the postcode is 59088 – eight being a very auspicious number for the Chinese.

One tower was built by a Japanese team, the other by rivals from Korea; while the Japanese topped out first, the Koreans had the honour of engineering the **Skybridge**, which joins the towers at both the 41st and 42nd floors. The **views** of KL's sprawl from the Skybridge are pretty spectacular, thanks not least to the blue, glassy towers soaring either side of you – but they're not quite as good as from the **Observation Deck** on the 86th floor.

Aquaria KLCC

KLCC Complex, accessed by a long pedestrian underpass from Suria KLCC • Charge • http://aquariaklcc.com • KLCC station

KL's **Aquaria KLCC** is housed within the sizeable **KL Convention Centre**, which sits on the southern edge of KLCC. It's expensive, and labelling is occasionally lost thanks to the muted lighting, but some sections are wonderful. Prime examples include the well-lit **Living Reef** tank, which is packed with multicoloured, multiform anemones and corals, and will help you make sense of the riches on view at the Perhentian Islands and elsewhere, and the **Flooded Forest** tank, with its pair of hefty, 2m-long Amazonian arapaima freshwater fish. It also holds electric eels, otters and even piranhas, but the *pièce de résistance* is the vast **Living Ocean** tank, which is traversed on a moving walkway through a transparent tunnel, replete with sand tiger sharks, octopuses and huge rays. There's a raised pedestrian walkway from here to Pavilion KL mall.

Ilham Gallery
Ilham Tower, 8 Jalan Binjai, east of KLCC • Free • Ampang Park station

An excellent contemporary gallery that's one of KL's most modern, both in terms of age and focus, the **Ilham Gallery** is worth going out of your way for. Most of the works here were created by contemporary Malaysian artists, though the odd piece of work from wider Southeast Asia also peeks through. The building that the gallery is set in is also a work of art, in its own way – the **Ilham Tower**, whose distinctively edgy exterior can be seen from across the city.

Kompleks Kraf
63 Jalan Conlay, south of KLCC • Charge, plus extra for batik painting • http://kraftangan.gov.my • Conlay station

The sprawl of Malay Terengganu-style buildings housing **Kompleks Kraf** offers a good opportunity to see excellent examples of Malaysia's crafts in one place – including carved wooden boxes, modern textiles and woven baskets – and to do some serious souvenir shopping. Their small, well-presented **museum** is also worth a quick browse to explore the intricacies of the weaving, tie-dyeing and batik processes, *keris* casting and Malay kite construction. For a hands-on experience, try the batik-painting workshop, where you can make a handkerchief to take home.

Badan Warisan
2 Jalan Stonor • Guided tours (45min) available • Free; charge for tours • http://badanwarisanmalaysia.org • Conlay station

Badan Warisan, Malaysia's architecture conservation trust, campaigns to preserve the rich heritage of shophouses, temples and colonial buildings that developers and many municipal authorities seem intent on destroying. It's housed close to Kompleks Kraf in a 1925 colonial mansion that contains a gift shop, good for books on local architecture, and hosts occasional temporary exhibitions, focusing on anything from colonial furniture to restoration work.

In the grounds is the beautifully restored **Rumah Penghulu Abu Seman**, a traditional timber house that once belonged to a Malay chieftain. Moved here from Kedah, it can only be visited on a guided tour.

Bukit Bintang
Bukit Bintang station

For tourists and locals alike, **Bukit Bintang** – the broad corridor either side of Jalan Bukit Bintang – is one of the best spots in town for a wander, and it's absolutely teeming with people through the day (and much of the night). There's a **mall** here to suit everyone: the gigantic, massively modern Pavilion KL, packed with international chains and designer outlets; posh Starhill Gallery, with an exclusive, snazzy Art Deco feel; the more modest Berjaya Times Square, Lot 10 mall and BB Plaza, and casual Fahrenheit 88; and the behemoth tech mall Low Yat. The southwestern end of Jalan Bukit Bintang is lined with royal palms and inexpensive clothing shops – and a few too many touts hissing "massage, nice lady, young lady" at passers-by – while the pavement around Lot 10 has evolved into a parade of buzzing, smart cafés and shops. By night the centre of attention, at least for dining, switches to nearby **Jalan Alor**, which boasts some great alfresco Chinese eating. Close by, Changkat Bukit Bintang and Tengkat Tong Shin hold even more excellent bars and restaurants, serving differing cuisines.

Bukit Nanas
Bukit Nanas station

The western side of the Golden Triangle is dominated by forested **Bukit Nanas** (Pineapple Hill), where you can follow an easy forty-minute **walking trail** from the

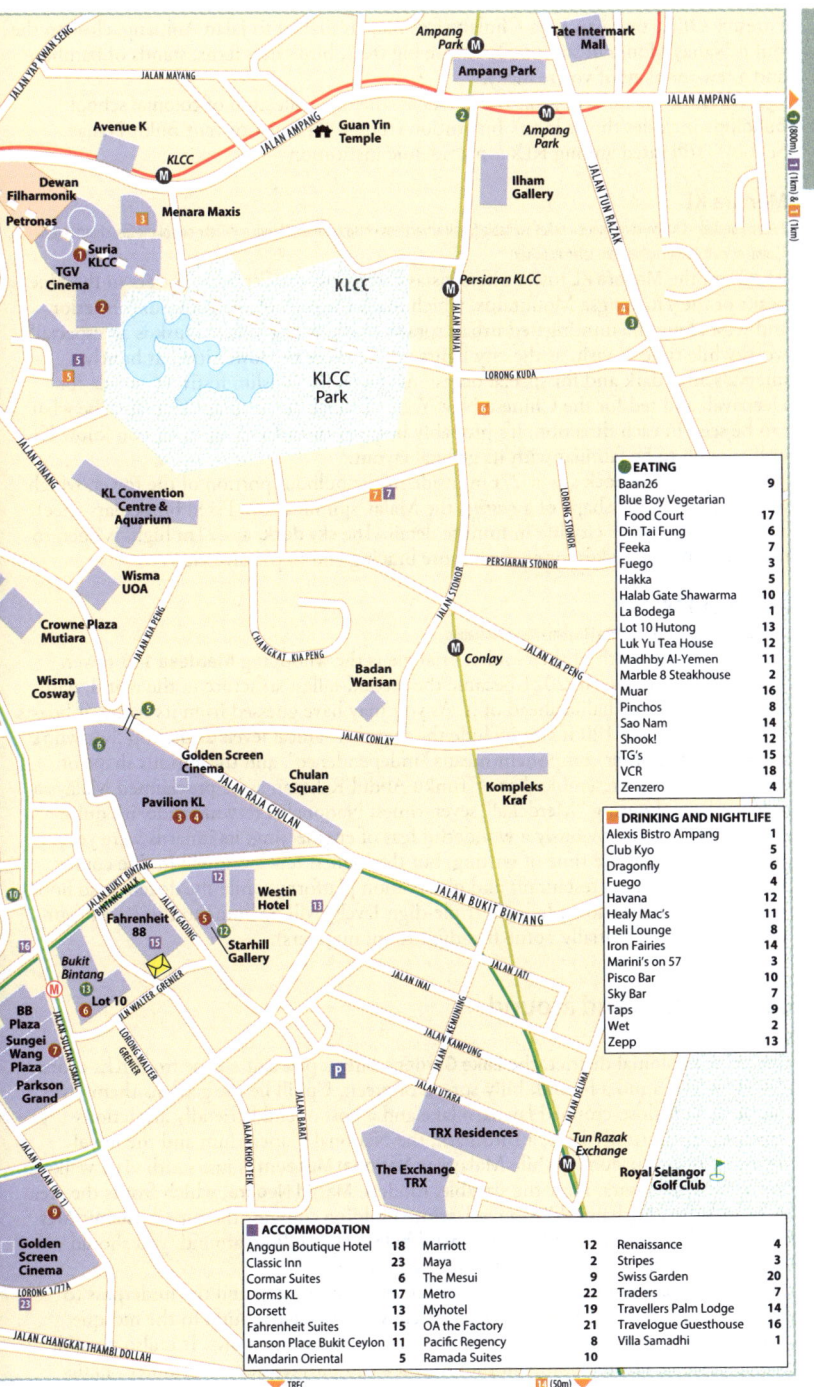

Forestry Office on Jalan Raja Chulan (free map available) to Jalan Ampang, close to the Bukit Nanas Monorail station. There are big trees, bird's nest ferns, stands of bamboo and a few monkeys if you're lucky.

Just west of the hill, on Jalan Bukit Nanas, the fine collection of **colonial school buildings** includes the St John's Institution from 1904 and Convent Bukit Nanas School – still rated among KL's top academic institutions.

Menara KL

2 Jalan Punchak • Charge, combination ticket available for all attractions • http://menarakl.com.my • Take one of the free shuttles (every 15min) or walk 15min uphill from Jalan Punchak

At 421m, the **Menara KL** tower offers vistas east across the Petronas Towers to the blue peaks of the Titiwangsa Mountains, which mark the start of the Peninsula's interior, and west along the unmitigated urban sprawl of the Klang Valley. Dusk is an especially worthwhile time to visit, as the city lights up – as does the tower itself at hourly intervals after dark and for special occasions (green for Muslim festivals, purple for Deepavali and red for the Chinese New Year). Though free audioguides describe what can be seen in each direction, it's probably best to hold off visiting until you know KL well enough to be familiar with its general layout.

The **observation deck** sits at 276m inside in the bulbous portion of the tower, which was designed in the shape of a *gasing*, the Malay spinning top. Fixed binoculars (free) allow you to observe city life in minute detail. The **sky deck**, at 421m high, is open to the elements and makes for an even more bracing and impressive view.

Merdeka 118

Jalan Hang Jebat • http://merdeka118.com • Merdeka station

Looming to the south of the Golden Triangle is the whopping **Merdeka 118** tower, which on topping out in 2021 became the second-tallest structure in the world, with only Dubai's Burj Khalifa ahead of it. As you may have guessed from its name, it boasts 118 floors (actually 120 if you include the two mechanical levels at the top ,but who's counting?); the other component means "independence", and the curious shape of the tower is said to resemble that of Tunku Abdul Rahman as he proclaimed Malaysia independent, shouting "Merdeka!" seven times. Nationalist fervour aside, it's quite a pretty tower, and obviously a wonderful feat of engineering; its innards were yet to be completed at the time of writing, but the highest few levels will in due course feature a VIP lounge, restaurant and observation platform, while the dozen or so floors immediately further down (all still triple-digit levels) will be home to the *Park Hyatt* (and therefore, potentially, some five-digit room numbers).

Lake Gardens and around

Kuala Lumpur train station

West of the colonial district, the **Lake Gardens** offer a pleasant escape from KL's more frenetic streets amid a humid, hilly spread of green. Uphill lie the gardens themselves, complete with close-cropped lawns, a lake and a host of child-friendly attractions – including a Butterfly Park, a Bird Park, the National Planetarium and the **Royal Malaysia Police Museum** – while Malaysia's **National Museum** is just south via a walkway over Jalan Damansara. Near the sizeable, modern **Masjid Negara**, which fronts the area on Jalan Sultan Hishamuddin, a cool, white building contains the superb **Islamic Arts Museum**. Although you could easily spend half a day strolling around, you should focus on the three museums if you're pushed for time.

The easiest **access** on foot is via Kuala Lumpur train station and the underpass to the KTM building (see page 79), from where you can edge around to the mosque – otherwise you have to risk crossing the usual furious traffic flows. It is also possible to access the area from Pasar Seni station, via a complicated series of tunnels, paths and elevated walkways. As smaller roads run through the gardens, however, it's perhaps easiest to get here by taxi.

Lake Gardens
Walkable from Pasar Seni station, though it's not a very enjoyable route

KL's **Lake Gardens** (Taman Tasik Perdana) were laid out in the 1890s by the British state treasurer to Malaya, Alfred Venning. Not quite parkland or gardens in the usual sense, they're probably best seen as a pleasant setting for various attractions, all connected by paths and sealed roads; at the time of writing, the southern section was quite a mess, due in equal parts to ongoing redevelopment work and general neglect. If you're out this way in the afternoon, consider dropping into KL's most exclusive hotel, the colonial mansion **Carcosa Seri Negara**, off to the west. Their oh-so-English **high tea** is a fitting reward for a hot day's wander around the gardens – as long as you don't mind dressing smartly (it can get hot on the verandah) and paying a hefty price for the privilege.

Butterfly Park
Jalan Cenderawasih • Charge • http://klbutterflypark.com

The beautiful **Butterfly Park** is an unexpected delight. Enclosed in invisibly fine netting, this garden of tropical vines, shrubs and ferns nurtures 120 species of gorgeous butterflies – some with 15cm wingspans – flitting about amid the undergrowth and feed stations baited with pineapple and banana. There are also tranquil ponds full of giant koi, and a small but informative insect museum.

Bird Park
Jalan Cenderawasih • Charge • http://klbirdpark.com

Billed as the world's largest, KL's popular **Bird Park** features a well-designed network of ponds and streams underneath a huge mesh tent, all linked together by a looped walkway. There are free-flying egrets, storks, African starlings, nutmeg pigeons and parrots all over the place, and there's a flock of flamingoes living in one of the ponds, as well as cages of indigenous species that you might well encounter in Malaysia's wilder corners – hornbills, birds of prey such as the Brahminy kite, and the sizeable argus pheasant. Give yourself an hour and a half to look around and take in a show; the only real downside is the park's high cost, relative to any other attraction in town (you can get a sneaky peek inside from *Hornbill Café* for the price of a drink; see page 93).

Orchid and Hibiscus Gardens
Jalan Cenderawasih • Charge

If you're into tropical plants, you'll love the **Orchid and Hibiscus Gardens**. There are said to be more than eight hundred Malaysian orchids alone, all lining paved walkways in brightly coloured, formal arrangements. The hibiscus collection is laid out along terraces and includes Malaysia's national flower, the bright red *bunga raya*. There are also groves of South American **heliconias** in the gardens, which look a bit like ginger plants, but with brightly coloured, strikingly shaped flowers.

Tun Abdul Razak Memorial
Jalan Perdana • http://arkib.gov.my

The main road through the Lake Gardens weaves south past a field of deer to the **Tun Abdul Razak Memorial**, a house built for the second Malaysian prime minister. He's commemorated with assorted memorabilia inside, while his motorboat and golf trolley are ceremonially positioned outside. Behind here is the **lake** itself, which takes nearly an hour to walk around.

National Planetarium
Uphill from Jalan Perdana • http://planetariumnegara.gov.my

Set on a forested hill east of the lake, the **National Planetarium** is reachable on foot using the steps opposite the RMP Museum (see below). Its blue dome and geometrically latticed walls make this an unlikely example of the city's Islamic-influenced architecture. As well as model rockets, info boards and statues pertaining to Gagarin and the like, there's a "space theatre" and a rocket cockpit simulator (which presumably doesn't quite match the real experience), plus a **viewing platform** upstairs – long a hidden gem of a lookout spot. A **pedestrian bridge** runs south from the planetarium to the National Museum.

Royal Malaysia Police Museum
5 Jalan Perdana • Free • http://facebook.com/RoyalMalaysiaPoliceMuseum

The **Royal Malaysia Police Museum** covers the vivid history of the Royal Malaysian Police (RMP) force. Fascinating photographs include a shot of British officers and their local charges on patrol on buffaloes, around 1900. The museum also displays **weapons** confiscated from the Communists during the Emergency of the 1950s, including a vicious assortment of *parangs* and a curved, bladed implement known as a Sarawak or Iban axe, all presented in a jungle-themed exhibition space. Once you've had a look around, you can, if you're feeling energetic, continue up Jalan Perdana into the Lake Gardens or head up the flight of steps opposite the museum to the hill where the National Planetarium is located (see page 77).

National Museum
Jalan Damansara • Charge • http://muziumnegara.gov.my • Accessible via signed pedestrian walkways from KL Sentral station

Built in 1963, the **National Museum** (Muzium Negara) has a sweeping roof characteristic of northern Malay architecture, and **four galleries** that focus perhaps a bit too much on the Malay side of things, giving relatively little space to the Orang Asli, Indians, Chinese and Europeans who have also left their mark on the nation's history and culture. Despite this, the museum is definitely worth an hour, especially if you've seen the Textile Museum's complementary exhibits.

On the first floor, **Gallery A** offers a stroll through prehistory, with human skeletal remains from Kelantan that prove that settlers were present on the Peninsula around 6000 BC. **Gallery B** covers early Malay kingdoms, in particular the Melaka Sultanate, with a particularly good collection of finely chased *kris* daggers and items recovered from sunken Chinese trading vessels. The pace accelerates upstairs, where **Gallery C** covers the colonial era, from reconstructions of Melaka's Portuguese fortifications to intricate models of trading ships to a fine seventeenth-century German Bellarmine jug depicting a bearded face – characteristic of such jugs – on the neck of the vessel. There's also ungenerous coverage of the British "interference" in the Malay States, including a diorama of the signing of the Pangkor Treaty (see page 531). Tin, the metal that opened up Malaysia to development, dominates the final part of the gallery; mining equipment sits alongside animal-shaped coinage – including a 30cm crocodile – once used in Selangor and Perak.

Gallery D parcels modern Malaysia into a triumphant photo parade of the nation's founding fathers, of various races, whose names you see on street signs downtown – though there's only cursory coverage of broader history, such as the Emergency during the 1950s (see page 535). Finally, don't miss the open-air courtyard at the back, which features an excellent run-down of the Peninsula's **Indigenous groups**, alongside fantastic totem-pole-like objects and grotesque face masks such as the one-fanged *moyang melor*, which were used in rites of ancestor worship.

Masjid Negara
Jalan Sultan Hishamuddin • http://masjidnegara.gov.my • Kuala Lumpur station

Opened in 1965, **Masjid Negara** (National Mosque) features an unusual theme: the 73m-high minaret resembles a folded umbrella, and the imposing blue 16-point dome looks like an open one. Surrounding it are paved courtyards and colonnades, all rectangles of white marble bisected by pools of water. The prayer hall can hold up to fifteen thousand worshippers, though size gives way to decorative prowess in its finely detailed stone archways and engravings of the Koran, inspired by Istanbul's Blue Mosque. To enter as a visitor (outside of prayer times), you must be properly dressed: robes can be borrowed for free at the mosque entrance.

Islamic Arts Museum
Jalan Lembah Perdana • Charge • http://iamm.org.my • Kuala Lumpur station

The ultramodern **Islamic Arts Museum** is housed in an elegant open-plan building with gleaming marble floors. This well-documented collection is a real standout; allow around ninety minutes to do it justice, and bear in mind that there's an excellent on-site Middle Eastern restaurant (open Tuesday to Sunday during museum hours). If you're arriving by taxi, you may find that the driver will know only the museum's Malay name, which is Muzium Kesenian Islam – if that doesn't work, just ask for the Masjid Negara, which is just a short walk away.

Level 1

The **first level** begins with a large collection of dioramas of Muslim holy places, including that of the Great Mosque of Xi'an in central China that draws attention to the neglected subject of Islam in the Far East, a theme continued elsewhere on this level. In the **India gallery**, devoted to the Moghuls, look for an intricately carved wooden locking mechanism, designed to cloister the harem away from the rest of the world; the **China gallery** features porcelain and scroll paintings bearing Arabic calligraphy. Best of all is an impressive three-metre-high archway in the **Malay gallery**, once part of a house belonging to an Indonesian notable, with black, red and gold lacquering and a trelliswork of leaves as its main motif. An equally fine trunk below it was used as a travelling box by Terengganu royalty. Built of the much-prized *cengal* hardwood, it's decorated in red and gold and bears the names of Islam's revered first four caliphs.

Level 2

On the **second level**, richly embroidered textiles and marquetry back up unusual examples of Western European ceramic crockery, influenced by the Islamic world in their design – and sometimes produced for that market. Most interesting here is the terrace containing the museum's main **dome**, a blue-and-white affair with floral ornamentation. Built by Iranian craftsmen, it's the only one of several similar examples in the building that's intended to illustrate the exterior of a grand mosque. Finally, look out for the bizarre, reversed-dome ceiling, bulging downwards from above – it's the last thing you see as you make your way back to the foyer from the area containing the excellent **gift shop**.

Old Kuala Lumpur train station
Reachable from Central Market along Jalan Tun Sambanthan, over the river and past the post office (Poslaju), then via the footbridge • Kuala Lumpur station

Old Kuala Lumpur train station, one of the city's best-known colonial buildings and now a stop on the KTM train lines, was completed in 1911 by A.B. Hubback. As with the Jamek Mosque, its meshing spires, minarets and arches reflect his inspiration from North Indian Islamic architecture. Inside, the main platforms sit under an airy, light vault of fine ironwork, reminiscent of pre-renovation Victorian stations in London.

Although the station is architecturally linked to similar-vintage buildings around Merdeka Square, feverish traffic makes it difficult to reach on foot from there; a system of tunnels and elevated walkways makes it just about possible to do so without risking life and limb, but don't expect decent signage. For the best view of the station facade, you'll need to get across to the western side of Jalan Sultan Hishamuddin. Conveniently, a pedestrian subway enables you to do just this, since it links the station with the **KTM**

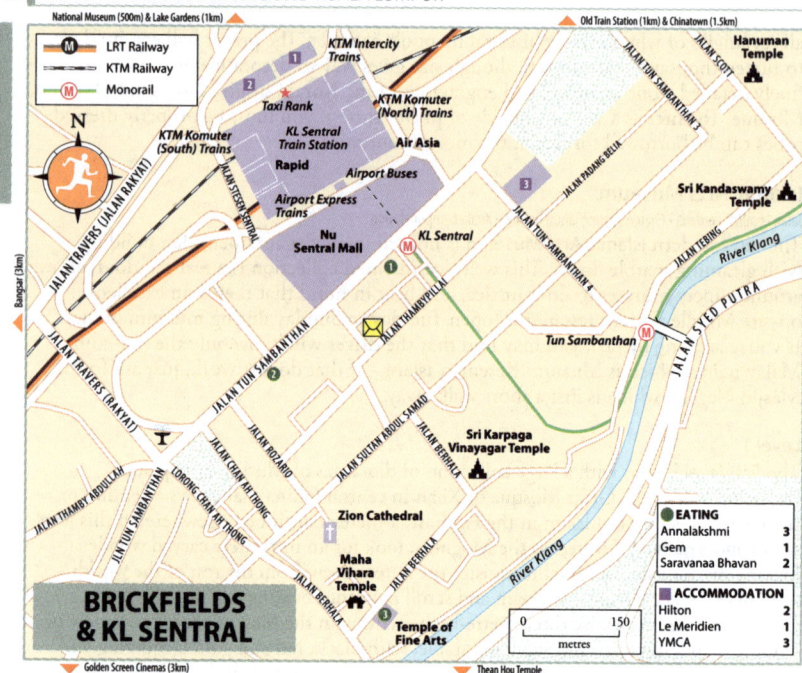

headquarters opposite – yet another attractive Moorish structure designed by Hubback, finished around the same time as the station and actually more imposing than its counterpart. From the KTM headquarters it's a few minutes' walk to either Masjid Negara or the National Museum.

Brickfields

The laidback residential neighbourhood of **Brickfields**, 2km south of the city centre near **KL Sentral** station, was first settled by Tamils employed to build the railways, and named after the brickworks that lined the rail tracks. Even today, the area retains a strong South Indian presence along **Jalan Tun Sambanthan** – the main thoroughfare – especially the western stretch beyond the huge pink fountain marking the intersection with Jalan Travers; the road has flowers painted on it, buildings are pastel-hued, and Indian pop tunes blare out of sari shops and grocers. This is one of the city's corners to visit for local ambience rather than monumental sights, though there are two wonderful temples and the area is also home to some good places to eat (see page 92).

Sri Kandaswamy Temple

3 Lorong Scott • http://srikandaswamykovil.org • Tun Sambanthan station

The Hindu **Sri Kandaswamy Temple** was founded by the Sri Lankan Tamil community in the 1900s, though the present structure was consecrated in 1997. Its facade, a riot of brightly coloured statues reminiscent of Chinatown's Sri Maha Mariamman Temple, is all the more appealing for being little visited by tourists; just don't expect to find anyone who can explain the layout, which includes, in the far-right corner of the entrance wall, a collection of nine garlanded deities representing the planets.

Thean Hou Temple

65 Persiaran Endah • Daily 8am–9pm • 03 2274 7088 • MidValley station

A stone's throw southeast from Brickfields proper, the six-tiered **Thean Hou Temple** is dedicated to the Chinese sea goddess Mazu and affiliated with Buddhism, Taoism and Confucianism. Built by local Hainanese communities and opened in 1989, it remains one of the largest Chinese temples in Southeast Asia. The building is illuminated with hundreds of lanterns on the birthdays of goddesses Tian Hou, Kuan Yin and Mazu (all of whom have shrines inside along with Chinese zodiac symbology) and looks particularly good at Chinese New Year – it's spellbinding stuff.

Bangsar

Bangsar station, then a 15min walk or the #T850 bus

West of Brickfields lies the trendy, relatively chilled-out neighbourhood of **Bangsar**. For most tourists, this will be the westernmost periphery of their interest in KL, but for the millions living in the city's western suburbs, it's the most accessible place with a decent dining, shopping and nightlife scene, so it makes a common compromise meeting spot, even though it's still some way from the city centre. While there are no actual sights to detain the average tourist here, it's certainly worth popping by to see a different side of contemporary KL life – even though, for

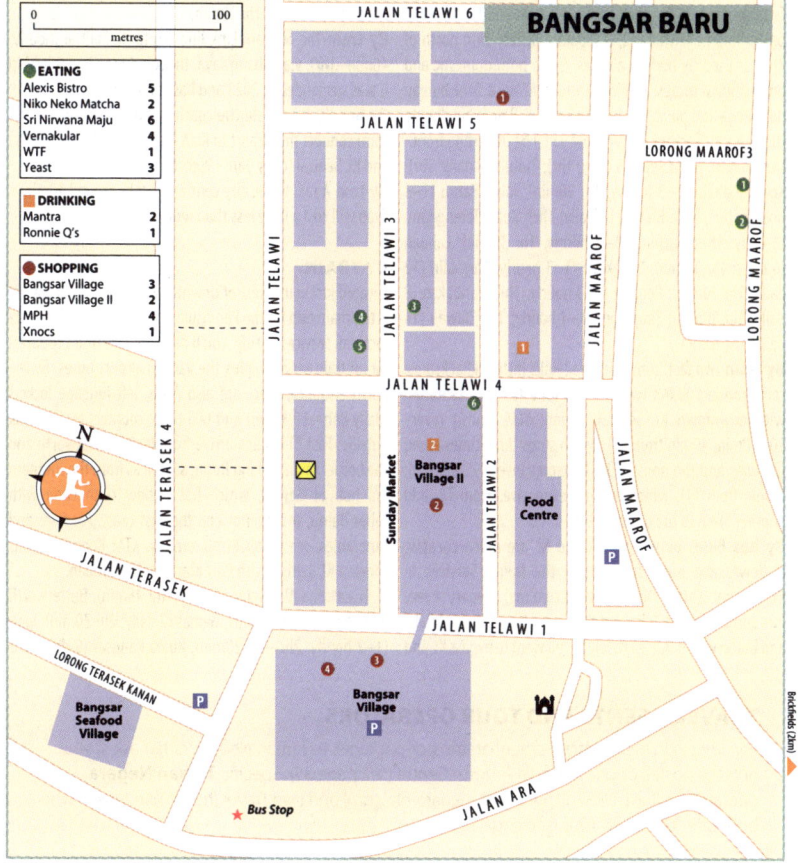

now, there's been no real effort to create a whole look or feel cooler than the sum of its constituent restaurants, cafés and shops.

ARRIVAL AND DEPARTURE — KUALA LUMPUR

KL's airports cover all major destinations across Malaysia, as well as Singapore, Brunei and many Southeast Asian and international airports. Arriving by train, you'll stop at KL Sentral, the main station, while buses are likely to stop at TBS (Terminal Bersepadu Selatan), 12km south of the centre.

BY PLANE

If you're coming to KL by plane from anywhere outside of Southeast Asia, you'll arrive at KLIA, while some low-cost regional flights arrive at Subang Skypark.

KUALA LUMPUR INTERNATIONAL AIRPORT

Kuala Lumpur International Airport (KLIA; http://klia.com.my), the main long-haul airport, is some 50km south of KL and serves all major international flights. The arrivals hall contains a visitor centre (daily 8am–11pm), 24hr exchange facilities, and desks representing car rental outlets and KL's pricier hotels. Terminal 2, a separate facility 2km north of KLIA, is used by budget airlines, flying both domestic and international routes; facilities include ATMs, a 24hr bureau de change and plenty of duty-free shops. Before heading to the airport, check which terminal you'll be departing from.

Destinations Alor Setar (5 daily; 1hr); Bintulu (8 daily; 1hr); Kota Kinabalu (1–3 hourly; 1hr 30min); Johor Bahru (1–3 hourly; 1hr); Kota Bharu (14 daily; 1hr); Kuala Terengganu (6 daily; 1hr); Kuching (1–3 hourly; 1hr 30min); Labuan (6 daily; 1hr 30min); Langkawi (1–3 hourly; 1hr); Miri (12 daily; 1hr 30min); Penang (1–3 hourly; 1hr); Sandakan (8 daily; 1hr 30min); Singapore (1–4 hourly; 1hr); Tawau (11 daily; 1hr 30min).

By train Two fast, convenient rail links (http://kliaekspres.com) connect KLIA's two stations (one for each terminal) with downtown KL Sentral station: KLIA Transit (every 20–30min; 40min from T1), which stops three times along the way; and the nonstop KLIA Ekspres (every 15–20 min; 28min from T1), which is more expensive. From T2, add another 5min to the duration times.

By bus Buses between KLIA and KL are much cheaper, if slower and more fiddly, than the trains. Services to KL Sentral (http://theairportbus.com.my) depart every 20–30min, almost 24hr, and there are also buses to Melaka and Butterworth. Alternatively, if you want to bypass KL and catch a bus to another part of the Peninsula, catch a train from KLIA to Terminal Bersepadu Selatan (see page 83).

By taxi The taxi ride to downtown KL takes about 1hr, and you can buy a fixed-fare ticket from the counter near the arrivals exit. Alternatively, get a Grab (usually a bit cheaper) to meet you at one of the airport doors.

SULTAN ABDUL AZIZ SHAH AIRPORT (SUBANG SKYPARK)

KL's small second airport, known as both Sultan Abdul Aziz Shah Airport and Subang Skypark (http://subangskypark.com), lies 25km west of the city, covering a few domestic destinations, plus Singapore, and Koh Samui in Thailand.

Destinations Johor Bahru (3 daily; 1hr); Kota Bahru (6 daily; 1hr); Kuala Terengganu (3–4 daily; 1hr); Langkawi (2–3 daily; 1hr); Penang (7 daily; 1hr); Singapore (mostly Seletar, not Changi; 7 daily; 1hr 20min).

By train The Skypark Link line ran to KL Sentral (hourly; 40min–1hr), via Subang Jaya, though due to low ridership it was suspended in 2023 and has yet to return.

By bus KL Airport shuttle coaches (http://subangskypark.com) connect the airport to KLIA (daily 5am–11pm; hourly) and KL Sentral (daily 9am–9pm; hourly).

By taxi A taxi to the city centre will take around 40min; a Grab will cost a little less than regular cabs.

BY TRAIN

Located just southwest of downtown KL, KL Sentral station is the main hub for the Peninsula's trains, and also for many local rail services. Inside, you'll find separate ticket counters for all train services, plus the various airport buses. By the north entrance, there are also ATMs, left-luggage lockers (daily 8am–10.30pm) and taxi ticket counters for the rank outside. Fast ETS trains arrive from Ipoh, Butterworth and the border town Padang Besar, as well as from the southern rail hub of Gemas, which has a slow connection with Johor Bahru, the interior and the east coast. For fares and timetables, see http://ktmb.com.my. KTM Komuter trains connect KL Sentral with Port Klang and Seremban.

Destinations Alor Setar (5 daily; 4hr 45min); Butterworth (6 daily; 3hr 35min–4hr); Gemas (2 daily; 2hr 30min); Ipoh (1–2 hourly; 2hr–4hr 20min); Kuala Kangsar (9 daily; 2hr

---

TRAVEL AGENTS AND TOUR OPERATORS

For advice on local **tours**, Perhentian trips, or packages to Taman Negara, either ask at your hotel or hostel, or visit Malaysia Tourism Centre (see page 85). Specific **Taman Negara** operators include NKS (http://taman-negara-nks.com) and Han Travel (http://han.travel), who both offer three-day trips (see page 187).

50min); Padang Besar (5 daily; 4hr 50min–5hr 30min); Port Klang (every 15–30min; 1hr); Seremban (every 15–20min; 1hr 20min); Sungai Petani (5 daily; 4hr 25min); Taiping (11 daily; 2hr 45min–3hr 15min).

ONWARD TRANSPORT
By rail There are a myriad of options from KL Sentral: the KLIA Transit and Ekspres services to KLIA airport; Komuter services to the Batu Caves, Port Klang or the second airport; or the Rapid KL and Monorail lines to downtown stations.
By taxi There's a taxi rank on the northern side of KL Sentral station, open until around 1am. You can negotiate a price with the driver; of course, this becomes unnecessary if using Grab or a similar ride-hailing app.

BY BUS
Buying tickets is generally best done online through services such as Redbus (http://redbus.my) or Easybook (http://easybook.com). Even if you've pre-purchased a ticket online, you'll most likely have to queue and print it out at the ticket counters, though this is usually a speedy process.

PUDU SENTRAL
KL's most central bus station, Pudu Sentral (Puduraya), occupies a multistorey complex on Jalan Pudu, just east of Chinatown; for decades a major hub, it now deals almost exclusively with services to Genting (every 30min; 1hr) and KLIA (hourly; 1hr 15min). You can walk to Chinatown in a flash from here, and it's also connected to Plaza Rakyat station, and by walkway to Merdeka station too; together, these will get you all over KL.

PEKELILING
Pekeliling bus station (sometimes known as Jalan Pekeliling), 3km northwest of central KL and just off Jalan Tun Razak, is used mainly by buses from Pahang including Taman Negara, along with some services to the Genting Highlands. The separate Titiwangsa stations on the Monorail and the LRT are just to the north.
Destinations Jerantut (for Taman Negara National Park; 3 daily; 3hr 30min); Kuala Lipis (5 daily; 3hr 30min).

TERMINAL BERSEPADU SELATAN (TBS)
Gargantuan TBS (http://tbsbts.com.my) has increasingly become by far the most important bus hub for the city, and is the closest bus station to KLIA. It's inconveniently located 10km south of KL, though adjacent Bandar Tasik Selatan station is served by all manner of rail transit, including KLIA Transit airport shuttles (see page 82), Komuter trains heading north and south, and the Sri Petaling LRT line to the city centre and/or transfers with other lines.
Destinations Alor Setar (2–5 hourly; 6hr 30min); Butterworth (1–3 hourly; 5hr 15min); Cameron Highlands (Tanah Rata; 9 daily; 3hr 30min–4hr 30min); Hat Yai (Thailand; 6 daily; 9hr); Johor Bahru (every 15min; 4hr 30min); Kuala Kangsar (11 daily; 4hr); Kuala Perlis (1–3 hourly; 7hr 30min); Ipoh (1–3 hourly; 3hr 15min); Kangar (1–2 hourly; 7–9hr); Kuantan (2–4 hourly; 4hr); Lumut (1–2 hourly; 4hr 30min); Melaka (2–5 hourly; 2hr–2hr 30min); Penang (3–4 hourly; 5hr); Singapore (1–3 hourly; 5hr); Sungai Petani (1–2 hourly; 5hr 30min); Taiping (2–3 hourly; 4hr).

BERJAYA TIMES SQUARE
From this central location, Transtar (http://transtar.travel) sends luxury buses to and from Singapore (7 daily; 5hr 30min). It's convenient, as it's practically in the heart of Bukit Bintang, and avoids the trek down to TBS; prices are higher, mind.

BY LONG-DISTANCE TAXI
Long-distance taxis leave from Pudu Sentral bus station; these can be good value if you're in a group heading to Cameron Highlands, Kuala Tahan (the main entrance for Taman Negara) or Kuala Terengganu.

BY CAR
Leaving KL by car onto the Peninsula's main highways is hampered by confusing road signage, one-way systems and countless express bypasses – this is only recommended for confident drivers.
E1 The North–South Expressway, northbound, is signed from Jalan Duta, which branches off Middle Ring Rd I west of the Lake Gardens. Major towns on the route include Tanjong Malim, Kuala Kangsar, Bukit Mertajam (for Penang Island) and Butterworth.
E2 The North–South Expressway, southbound, starts at Sungai Besi 2km south of Chinatown, and is most quickly reached using the long underground SMART tunnel on the eastern section of Jalan Tun Razak. This passes notable destinations like Seremban, Alor Gajah (for Melaka) and Yong Peng, on the way to Johor Bahru.
E8 To reach the E8 (Karak Highway), which is linked to the East Coast Highway to Kuantan, and Route 8 into the interior, get onto Jalan Tun Razak (or Jalan Raja Laut if starting from Chinatown) and head northwest to Jalan Ipoh; proceed up this for a short distance, then turn right onto Jalan Sentul and follow signs for the highway.

GETTING AROUND

Downtown KL isn't that large, so it's tempting to do a lot of your exploring **on foot**, but it's likely you'll soon find yourself wilting thanks to the combined effects of humidity and traffic fumes from the vehicle-choked roads. Thankfully, the light rail transit (**LRT**) and mass rapid transit (**MRT**) lines and the **Monorail**, along with **KTM Komuter** train services and taxis, are efficient and inexpensive. The services did not always coordinate well, though much of this has been rectified. The main governing body is **RapidKL** (http://myrapid.com.my), which runs the LRT, MRT and Monorail lines, plus many of the city's buses; its website includes network maps and details of monthly transport passes. If you're in KL for a while, consider investing in a prepaid Touch 'n Go pass (see page 85).

BY TRAIN

Tickets for all of the following can be purchased from station booths and automatic machines (both cash only) at the stops; weekly and monthly passes for designated journeys are also available.

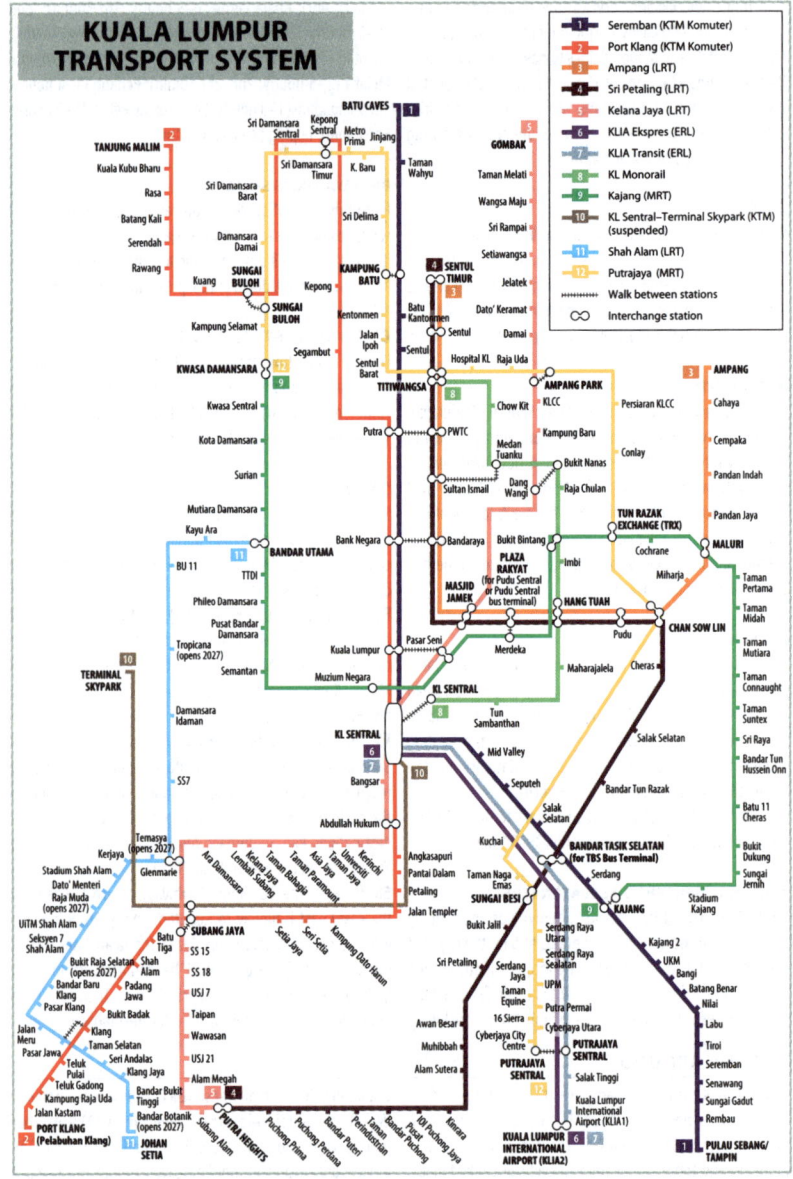

TOUCH 'N GO CARDS

As if literally named after KL's not-yet-realized dreams of a fully integrated transport system, the **Touch 'n Go card** (http://touchngo.com.my) is a useful **stored-value card** that you simply touch across the sensors at KTM Kommuter, LRT and Monorail stations, and when you board RapidKL buses; there's also the associated **TNG eWallet app** for touchless phone use. You will also need one of these to pay Expressway tolls on the Peninsula, and can use them in various car parks and fast-food joints around KL. Cards can be purchased at many stations (look for the blue and yellow logo); ticket office staff at the same places can recharge them (cash only), as can 7-Eleven stores and highway toll stations (*plaza tol*). As the cards save time queuing, rather than money, they're of most use if you are in the city a good deal, or plan to drive yourself around the Peninsula.

LRT AND MRT
The Klang Valley Integrated Transit System (daily 6am–midnight; every 5–10min) features four operational Light Rail Transit (LRT) lines, plus two Mass Rapid Transit lines (MRT, http://mrt.com.my). The LRT network comprises lines #3–5 and #11, and the MRT lines #9 and #12. They're very convenient for travel around KL and out to the main bus terminal, and you'll probably end up using them at least once.

MONORAIL
Trains on this elevated rail system (#8; daily 6am–midnight; every 5–10min; http://myrapid.com.my) have a noticeable tilt as they camber around bends. It has numerous interchanges with the LRT lines, sometimes via lengthy elevated walkways.

KTM KOMUTER
Run by national rail operator KTM (http://ktmb.com.my), trains travel on two lines: #1 from Pulau Sebang/Tampin, north of Melaka, to Batu Caves via Seremban, and #2 from coastal Port Klang (Pelabuhan Klang in Malay) north to Tanjung Malim in Perak. Both of them connect downtown at four stations: Putra, near the Putra World Trade Centre; Bank Negara, near Little India; the Kuala Lumpur train station, in the colonial district; and KL Sentral. Trains run every 15–20min during the day, but only every 30min after 8pm. Note that Komuter trains all have a central women-only carriage.

BY BUS
KL has a comprehensive city bus network, with Metrobus and RapidKL as the two main operators, but the lack of clearly marked terminuses and bus stops can make it baffling for outsiders to use. Services start up around 6am and begin winding down from 10pm onwards. Given KL's frequent traffic snarl-ups, do allow plenty of time for your journey – or just go by rail.

BY TAXI
KL taxis are cheap and convenient, though drivers used to be notorious for negotiating inflated prices rather than using the meter – a problem that has decreased drastically since the advent of competition from Grab (http://grab.com/my). There are two ways to deal with this: ask if they use the meter before getting in, and flag down another cab if they don't; or buy a prepaid coupon for your journey from booths attached to designated cab ranks or at the airport. A few drivers don't speak much English, so you may want to have the address of your destination, or a well-known landmark nearby, written down in Malay. There are numerous taxi ranks around the city, usually close to bus stops or outside shopping malls and tourist attractions. Fares are generally low; expect to pay a bit more for downtown journeys in the smarter (often blue) taxis. To book a taxi, which costs an extra couple of ringgit, call Sunlight Taxis (1300 800 222, http://sunlighttaxi.com).

INFORMATION

Bear in mind that, given the chaotic nature of KL city planning, **maps** and listings tend to go out of date fairly quickly; don't be surprised if roads, venues and buildings have sprung into existence or ceased to be.
Tourism Malaysia The national tourist board has branches across the city (http://malaysia.travel), handing out brochures and general advice. You can also book accommodation, local tours and packages to Taman Negara and the like through in-house travel agents. The main office is at Malaysia Tourism Centre (MaTiC), 109 Jalan Ampang, not far from the Bukit Nanas Monorail stop (daily 8am–10pm; 03 9235 4900). Other branches include: Sultan Abdul Samad Building on Jalan Raja (daily 9am–6pm; 03 2602 2014); KL Sentral Station, Level 1 (daily 9am–6pm; 03 2272 5823); KLIA international arrivals hall (daily 8am–11pm; 03 8776 5647); and KLIA 2 (daily 8am–11pm; 03 8778 7080).
Listings To keep an ear to the ground on happenings around town, check out the monthly *Time Out KL* (http://timeout.com/kuala-lumpur).

TOURS

Food Tour Malaysia 013 227 1505, http://foodtour malaysia.com. Offers excellent "off the eaten track" and KL walking tours both during the day and in the evenings, which are perfect for getting acquainted with Malaysia's many cuisines. Tours last around three hours.

Go KL City Buses There are numbered free buses that stop off at major sights around the city (Mon–Fri 6am–11pm, Sat & Sun 7am–11pm; every 5–10min); you can use the services as often as you please, and hop on and off as many times as you fancy. Pick up a detailed map at the tourist office, and board the bus right outside MaTiC on Jalan Ampang.

KL Hop-on Hop-off 1 800 885546, http://myhoponhopoff.com. The KL Hop-on Hop-off bus service, which loops around two set circuits via a string of tourist sights (daily 9am–8pm; every 20–30min). Buses are open-top double-deckers, and audio commentaries are available in a handful of languages.

ACCOMMODATION

Chinatown has traditionally been the favourite location for budget travellers, with its surfeit of backpacker-oriented guesthouses and budget hotels (not all of which will have windows in their rooms) augmented by inexpensive places to eat, drink and shop. However, the area faces growing competition from Bukit Bintang, a 15min walk east, part of KL's **Golden Triangle**, where you'll find plenty of excellent guesthouses, some in nicely restored old shophouses. Even though places here are usually more expensive than in Chinatown, they're often better value, less cramped and noisy, with slicker facilities and self-service breakfasts included in the rate. More upscale hotels can be found in the area, along with excellent serviced apartments offering a lot more space than you'd get in a similarly priced hotel room. All other parts of KL pale in comparison when it comes to accommodation, though **Little India** also features several mid-and upper-range options. Lastly, note that you can score some pretty decent Airbnb apartments here, so it's worth taking a look to compare and contrast with hotels of similar price.

Bookings Although it's almost inconceivable that you'd be unable to find somewhere to stay in your price range here, it always makes sense to book ahead, especially during busy periods – July to August and November to December, plus school and public holidays. As well as individual accommodation websites, you can try http://hostelworld.com, http://airbnb.com or http://booking.com, and other similar sites and apps.

Breakfast All high-end, international-brand hotels include breakfast in their rates, and this is usually a buffet spread featuring Asian and Western cuisine. Mid-range hotels and guesthouses tend to offer a more modest meal of toast or *nasi lemak* and a drink. For hostels, breakfast is rarely complimentary, but there is often an on-site café or *mamak* that offers discounts to residents.

HOSTELS AND GUESTHOUSES

CHINATOWN AND AROUND, SEE MAP PAGE 68

Birdnest Collective Guesthouse 210 Jalan Tun H.S. Lee; http://birdnestghouse.com. Friendly place dotted with birdcages (some made into quirky lamps) that the owner has picked up from various flea markets; the furniture is all recycled, and you'll doubtless make some use of it in the pleasantly airy common space. The little rooms, with fan or a/c units, have also been decorated along avian lines. $

The Explorers Guesthouse 128 & 130 Jalan Tun H.S. Lee; http://facebook.com/theexplorersguesthousekl. An oasis of calm in the hubbub of Chinatown, this guesthouse features a pleasant communal area with a water feature, decorative fans, dangling dreamcatchers and pebble tiles in the bathrooms. The rooms are on the smallish side but are kept immaculate, as are the bathrooms, and staff will happily advise on what to see and do in the area. $

★ **Mingle Chinatown Hostel** 53 Jalan Sultan; http://instagram.com/mingle_hostel. When it comes to city-centre hostels, there are two little words that can elevate a place way above its competitors – "swimming", and "pool". There's no doubt what the main draw of this cool hostel is, but they've got more or less everything else right too, from the shabby-chic decor (which quite suits the colonial building the place is set in) to dorms with personal lights and power sockets. The only real issue is various forms of noise, which for some proves a little too much. They've a sister hostel just to the north in Little India (see page 87). $

Space Hotel @ KL Chinatown 5 Jalan Petaling; http://spacehotel.com.my. Capsule-berth hostel with a great location right on Petaling; they've another branch near KL Sentral. The berths alone do justice to the hostel's name, with their futuristic, spaceship-like lighting, while here and there you'll find astronauts in painted or model form, robot butlers, and a "space laundry" – it's good to know that astronauts and aliens wash their clothes in a manner very similar to puny humans. $

LITTLE INDIA AND CHOW KIT, SEE MAPS PAGES 66, 68 AND 71

1000 Miles 17 Jalan Tun H.S Lee; http://1000mileshotel.com. A cheap and surprisingly trendy-looking place to stay. The dorms are nice and clean, though the private rooms (some of which have no windows) don't always cost too much more if you're travelling in a pair – well worth investigating. $$

Akar 31 Jalan Raja Uda; http://akarhotels.com.my. For the

THE BEST PLACES TO STAY IN KL

Best for views Lanson Place Bukit Ceylon (see page 89)
Best for luxury Mandarin Oriental (see page 88)
Best for colonial grandeur Majestic (see page 89)
Best for old-school charm The Chow Kit (see page 88) or Tian Jing (see below)
Best hostel Mingle Highstreet (see below)

rare chance to stay in the highly atmospheric Kampung Baru area, give this place a try – it looks quite modern from the outside, but rooms are large and decorated with tones of pleasing pastel and soothing magnolia. Wi-fi can be sketchy. $

★ **Mingle Highstreet Hostel** 22 Jalan Tun H.S Lee; http://facebook.com/minglehostel. One of surprisingly few decent hostel-guesthouses in the wider Little India area, this is a winner – set among a newly trendy row of shophouse cafés and eateries (of which this guesthouse is also one), it has spacious, pine-lined dormitories, as well as minute singles (seriously small!) and duplex-like doubles. There's also a small swimming pool… sold yet? $

THE GOLDEN TRIANGLE, SEE MAP PAGE 74

Classic Inn 36 Jalan 1/77a, Changkat Thambi Dollah; http://classicinn.com.my. Don't be put off by the anonymous backstreet location, nor the word "inn"; this pleasant guesthouse with wooden corridors and little piles of decorative pebbles has modern en-suite rooms with a/c and TV, and there's a peaceful café area with rustic wooden stools. A sister building a few doors down offers backpacker accommodation with travellers' notes plastered over the walls; the dorms are probably the tiniest you will ever come across. $$

Dorms KL 10 Tengat Tong Shin; http://instagram.com/dormskl. This is the owners' *third* stab at a hostel, this time with some singles and doubles added to the dorm options (all 12-bed); it's pretty basic, but still a very decent backpacker roost, with tidy (if plain) rooms and a couple of areas in which to socialize. $

OA the Factory Jalan Bukit Bintang; 012 230 8866. Relatively recent addition to the area's hostel roster, and one that has proven immensely popular with visiting backpackers. It's mainly about the little things – hairdryers to use, soft lighting and small hangers in each dorm berth, that sort of thing. Even though said dorm berths can be described as small things themselves, guests are usually busy socialising; they throw occasional parties. $

Travellers Palm Lodge 10 Jalan Rembia. This gorgeous little guesthouse – with just seven rooms – is located down a lane off Tengkat Tong Shin and fronted by two travellers' palms in the tiny front garden. The colour-coded rooms are on the smallish side, although they are secure – only guests have a front gate key. The smiley owner makes guests feel right at home. $

Travelogue Guesthouse Jalan Bukit Bintang; 03 2110 0628. Ace hostel with spacious dorms and affordable private rooms, plus a handy location right next to Bukit Bintang station – which makes things a little noisy from some rooms, though they do provide earplugs on request. It's a shoes-off place, which keeps things clean, and there's free hot and cold water, plus good hang-out areas. $

BRICKFIELDS, SEE MAP PAGE 80

YMCA 95 Jalan Padang Belia; http://ymcakl.com. This institutional place has been here since 1931, though rooms have been recently upgraded and there are plenty of facilities including a café, laundry and even tennis courts (you'll need your own gear, though). Rates include breakfast. $

HOTELS

CHINATOWN AND AROUND, SEE MAP PAGE 68

The 5 Elements 243 Jalan Sultan; http://the5elements hotel.com.my. Rooms are clean and comfortable at this fourteen-storey hotel, which has great views of Chinatown and beyond; the twelfth- to fourteenth-floor rooms will set you back extra. Some rooms are in better shape than others, so it's wise to take a look at a couple before settling in. $$$

★ **Cojoy** 3 Jalan Petaling; http://cojoyhotel.com. A wonderful reworking of a semi-decrepit hotel – now given a fresh lick of paint inside, outside and metaphorically, it's a trendy co-working space where guests tend to kick around for a while. From the outside, you'll notice that all rooms seem to have balconies, though none are actually accessible. An excellent find, anyway. $

Hotel 1915 49 Jalan Lebuh Ampang; 03 2022 0026. Just walking into the lobby of this hotel, located in a beautifully renovated building that dates back to 1915, is a welcome respite from the hubbub of Chinatown. The lobby features bare brick walls, black-and-white prints and Chinese stone sculptures and vases, while the contemporary rooms are equipped with modern amenities, en-suite facilities and in-room safes. $$

★ **Tian Jing** 66 Jalan Sultan; http://tianjinghotel.com. One of the breed of classy, shophouse-style accommodation and dining options now taking root in the area, this has been a very welcome addition to Chinatown. The place has been exquisitely designed, from the teal-coloured window frames to the almost monochrome rooms, via common areas kept shaded and cool by bamboo shutters. The bathrooms are adventurous (you'll see), and it's quite tempting to sit in the lobby café – which has some wonderful wooden furniture – and have a pot of tea. $$$

Travelodge Chinatown 7 Jalan Hang Kasturi; http://travelodgehotels.asia. Just a few steps from the Central Market, this great-value hotel offers well-kept, monochrome rooms with flashes of yellow and snazzy walls. The lobby certainly feels like that of a far more expensive place, and can come as a relief to return to if you've been walking around the busy nearby area. $$

LITTLE INDIA AND CHOW KIT, SEE MAPS PAGES 68, 71 AND 74

Ahyu 34 Leboh Ampang; http://facebook.com/ahyuhotel. There's good value to be had at this cheapie, which has small but pleasant rooms (many with no window; you'll pay a fair bit more for those with a view), and some good, old-fashioned style in the common areas (not to mention the vintage exterior). $$

★ **The Chow Kit** 1012 Jalan Sultan Ismail; http://thechowkit.com. If you're going to replace a so-so hotel, you might as well do so in style and this hotel doesn't disappoint. The lobby, decked out with quality local art, exudes old-time class, while the rooms are the same with a modern twist – brass fittings, with splashes of emerald green. Views are wonderful from the upper levels, and there's a small rooftop space for morning coffee, or perhaps a sundowner. $$$

Crossroads 1 Jalan Raja Muda Abdul Aziz; http://oyorooms.com. A stone's throw away from Chow Kit's market, this excellent budget hotel – now under the ever-more ubiquitous OYO umbrella – offers immaculate rooms kitted out with dark furnishings, in a pleasant interior with bare brick walls and funky orange chairs at reception. The area of Chow Kit, however, is known for prostitution and it's also wise to watch your wallet at all times. Breakfast is extra. $

Hotel De' Grand Orchard 81–83 Medan Bunus; http://oyorooms.com. Not to be confused with its sister hotel *Grand Orchard*, this budget place, just off Jalan Masjid India and also affiliated to the ever-growing OYO franchise, features welcoming rooms with chocolate-brown furnishings, faux wooden floors and smallish, albeit very clean, bathrooms. Rates increase at the weekends. $

★ **K Hotel** 142–146 Jalan TAR; http://khotel.com.my. This is a super little place, right from the ground-floor lobby, which passers-by will be forgiven for assuming to be a genuine cinema ticket counter. The carpeted rooms can be smallish, but they're all lovingly designed and sparklingly clean. $$

MoMo's 316 Jalan TAR; http://stayatmomos.com. A sister property to *The Chow Kit*, though different in almost every way – here they've gone for a younger, trendier aesthetic, which manifests itself in the design of the rooms and bar-like lobby, but also in the regular events popular with local influencers (DJ nights, art-themed speed dating, and the like). Their rooms can be a little on the wee side, as evidenced by the names of the two main types – "Crashpad" and "Bunkies" – but they're well designed. $$

Palace 40a Jalan Masjid India; 03 2698 6122. The simple rooms at this 1960s-style hotel are decorated in beige and olive green and have benefitted from a recent zhuzh; all have a/c, and the hotel is in a lively location. $$

Premiera 232 Jalan TAR; http://premiera.com.my. In the heart of Little India and just a short walk from Chinatown, this is a great independent option offering spacious rooms with modern amenities, and wonderful views of the city from the higher floors. Note that most out of the hotel's rooms are twins, so if you're after a double make sure you book ahead, or be prepared to do the whole squashing-the-beds-together thing. $$$

Silka Maytower 7 Jalan Munshi Abdullah; http://silkahotels.com/maytower. This international-standard hotel, set over 32 floors, offers modern rooms and apartments with earthy tones, equipped with flat-screen TVs and safes; the deluxes are more spacious, with sofas and bathtubs, and there are also two pools – one for adults, one for kids – on the eighth floor, along with a sauna and gym. $$$

Stripes 25 Jalan Kamunting; http://marriott.com. A relatively new choice in the area, its stylish rooms feature beds backed by black-and-white photo-panels depicting local life in bygone times. The rooftop swimming pool is a lovely place to relax, while you're bound to take a few photos of the hotel's exterior, especially during dusk, when it looks quite glorious. $$$$

THE GOLDEN TRIANGLE, SEE MAP PAGE 74

★ **Anggun Boutique Hotel** 7 & 9 Tengkat Tong Shin; http://anggunkl.com. This welcoming boutique hotel aims to recreate a Peranakan house from yesteryear; rooms are set around an airy central courtyard with a little fishpond and a lovely antique Chinese medicine cabinet, plus ginger tea available through the day (though this is largely aimed at those coming to use the massage facilities). Some rooms have four-poster beds, while the three suites have balconies overlooking the street; bathrooms feature beautiful Chinese sinks with lotus and fish motifs. $$$

Cormar Suites 10 Jalan Perak; http://cormarsuites.com. Right by the Petronas Towers and KLCC, these stylish, excellent-value suites are located between the ninth and thirtieth floors of a retail and office complex. All rooms feature floor-to-ceiling windows boasting wonderful city views, and facilities include a well-equipped gym and eighteenth-floor infinity swimming pool. $$$

Dorsett 172 Jalan Imbi; http://dorsetthotels.com. Within a lofty tower block lies this great-value mid-range hotel, some of whose modern rooms boast superb views of the Petronas Towers; facilities include a small outdoor pool. The central location is a real plus – it's just a couple of minutes' walk from Starhill Gallery and Pavilion mall, while the bars and clubs of Changkat Bukit Bintang are a 15min walk away. $$$$

Mandarin Oriental Kuala Lumpur City Centre (KLCC);

http://mandarinoriental.com. Enormous hotel – it only looks small by virtue of being conveniently next to the Twin Towers – that's as sumptuous as they come, with its own luxury spa, swimming pools, tennis courts and tiptop restaurants. Rooms are spacious and feature lovely KLCC Park or Petronas Towers views. $$$$
Marriott 183 Jalan Bukit Bintang; http://marriott.com. In the heart of Bukit Bintang and with direct access to chic Starhill Gallery from the lobby, this branch offers well-appointed rooms with modern amenities, a huge pool, spa facilities and well-equipped gym. $$$$
Maya 138 Jalan Ampang; http://hotelmaya.com.my. This stylish boutique hotel is sandwiched between two office blocks in the heart of KL's commercial district; the contemporary rooms with wooden floorboards feature modern amenities and floor-to-ceiling glass panels overlooking the city. There's an inviting hydrotherapy pool with massage jets, a welcome treat after a long day in the hustle and bustle of the capital, along with a gym and access to yoga classes. $$$$
★ **The Mesui** 9 Jalan Mesui; http://themesuihotel.com. Located in a unique building with a design that reflects the 1970s – porthole windows and retro furnishings – this contemporary hotel offers tasteful rooms decorated with fun wall designs; "loft" rooms are substantially larger than those in the entry-level "lush" category, but all are inviting and spick-and-span. $$
Metro 208 Jalan Pudu; http://metrohotels.com.my. This budget business hotel offers clean, carpeted rooms with crisp linen, just a few steps from Imbi monorail station and Berjaya Times Square. Breakfast is extra. $$
Myhotel 120 Jalan Pudu; 03 2143 5000. Budget business hotel, offering the usual value-conscious, low-frills rooms: trim modern furnishings, en-suite bathrooms and a/c, with little space for anything else. Pay a little extra, and you'll even get a window to look out of. $$
Ramada Suites 1 Lorong Ceylon; http://ramadaklcc.com. The elegantly furnished family rooms and studio suites feature modern designs; the higher floors boast terrific city views from the floor-to-ceiling windows. All rooms are equipped with kitchenettes, and there's a particularly inviting pool, well-equipped gym and comfy TV lounge, too. Discounts and deals can make this place a steal too. $$$$
Renaissance Junction of Jalan Sultan Ismail and Jalan Ampang; http://marriott.com. Part of the Marriott group, this sumptuous hotel overlooking the Petronas Towers features two wings of well-appointed rooms, an Olympic-sized swimming pool, spa and fitness centre, along with a number of dining outlets. $$$$
Swiss Garden 117 Jalan Pudu; http://swissgarden.com. This substantial modern hotel, which also features good-value serviced apartments, is conveniently located at the edge of Bukit Bintang and halfway to Chinatown. Facilities include satellite TV and a couple of restaurants, plus a pool, gym and spa. $$$

Traders Kuala Lumpur City Centre (KLCC); http://shangri-la.com. This great four-star hotel offers direct access to Suria KLCC mall – hotel buggies shuttle customers across the park to the mall. The well-appointed rooms feature modern amenities, and some have exceptional views of the Petronas Towers. The real draw is the hotel's *SkyBar*, on the 33rd floor, with its 360-degree views of the capital. The hotel has four food outlets, including a steakhouse. $$$$
★ **Villa Samadhi** 218 Jalan Ampang; http://samadhi retreats.com. This luxurious villa has been converted into a sumptuous boutique hotel. The rooms, decorated with Asian furnishings, brim with individual character – the Sarang rooms feature their own private plunge pools, while the cosy Loft room, with its slanted ceiling, has its own shallow lap pool. Lower-ground floor rooms have direct access to the lagoon pool from their private balconies. $$$$

LAKE GARDENS AND AROUND, SEE MAP PAGE 66
★ **Majestic** Jalan Sultan Hishamuddin; http://majestickl.com. Opposite the old Moorish-style railway station, this hotel, set in a wonderfully restored 1930s building, houses exquisitely furnished suites with butler service, the fifteen-storey Art Deco Tower Wing with deluxe rooms and suites, along with a swimming pool and gym. Other facilities include a bar, spa, barber and screening room. $$$$

BRICKFIELDS, SEE MAP PAGE 80
Hilton 3 Jalan Stesen Sentral; http://kuala-lumpur.hilton.com. Overlooking the National Museum and just a few steps from KL Sentral, this stylish hotel with a lavish lobby offers rooms as modern and comfortable as you'd expect from this reputable international chain. Facilities include ten opulent dining outlets, and a tropically styled pool with stunning views. $$$$
Le Meridien 2 Jalan Stesen Sentral; http://lemeridien kualalumpur.com. This 35-storey business hotel houses contemporary rooms; most of them boast panoramic views. Facilities include a freeform outdoor swimming pool with deckchairs partly immersed in water, a gym, spa and a handful of restaurants serving international cuisine. $$$$

SERVICED APARTMENTS

THE GOLDEN TRIANGLE, SEE MAP PAGE 74
Fahrenheit Suites Fifth floor, Fahrenheit 88 Mall, 179 Jalan Bukit Bintang; http://fahrenheitsuites.com. Modern serviced apartments, including some sleeping up to six, with their own pleasant lounge, kitchenette, and use of swimming pool. Parking is available. Occasional excellent online rates. $$$
★ **Lanson Place Bukit Ceylon** 10 Jalan Ceylon; http://lansonplace.com/bukitceylon. Seventy-odd floors high, these serviced apartments are popular with executive types and long-term visitors, and no wonder – the suites

are absolutely huge and boast all the conveniences guests could need, as well as jaw-dropping floor-to-ceiling views from most floors. There's also a sky-high gym and billiards room, plus a gorgeous, extremely lengthy swimming pool surrounded by towers. $$$$
Pacific Regency KH Tower, Jalan Punchak, off Jalan P. Ramlee; http://pacific-regency.com. Luxury apartments with kitchenettes, huge bathrooms, satellite TVs and, on the roof, a swimming pool. Ample parking too, though undergoing a major renovation at the time of writing. Check the website to verify that it has reopened, and also for promotional rates. $$$$

EATING

Without doubt, a highlight of any visit to KL is the city's **food**. There are more opportunities to enjoy high-calibre cooking here, in assorted local and international styles, than anywhere else in the country, and whether you dine in a chic bistro-style restaurant or at a humble roadside stall, prices are almost always very reasonable. Despite plenty of scope for cosmopolitan, upmarket dining, eating for many locals is still fundamentally about Malay, Chinese and Indian **street food**. Stalls, whether on the street or collected into **food courts** (found in or close to major office blocks and shopping malls), are your best bets for inexpensive, satisfying meals, as are *kedai kopis*, though these are a little scarce in the Golden Triangle. The best-known food stalls are held in the same kind of reverence as a top-flight restaurant might be in a Western city, and people will travel across KL just to seek out a stall whose take on a particular dish is said to be better than anyone else's; if you find customers lining up to partake of some stall's spring rolls or *laksa*, it's a sure-fire indicator of quality. Ranging from small affairs in beautifully refurbished shophouses to banqueting halls in five-star hotels, KL's **restaurants** are an equally vital part of the food experience. Be aware, however, that price and decor are not a watertight indicator of consistency or quality, and that service can be unhurried, even in big hotels.

RESTAURANTS

CHINATOWN AND AROUND, SEE MAP PAGE 68

Crane Upstairs 78 Jalan Sultan; http://cranekl.com. Gorgeous restaurant with exposed brick walls, hanging paper lanterns, foliage aplenty, and a good general mix of the modern and classic. The menu is largely Western but with local elements; it's perhaps best used as a brunch spot, though the weekday lunches are great value. $$$

Nam Heong 56 Jalan Sultan; 03 2022 3818. Original Hainanese chicken rice is rustled up in front of your very eyes as you enter this popular, spick-and-span restaurant, which attracts those in the know in Chinatown. The recipe won't have changed all that much since the place started way back in 1938. $

★ **Old China Café** 11 Jalan Balai Polis; http://oldchina.com.my. Wonderfully atmospheric restaurant set in a pre-World War I shophouse with old-world charm; much of the decor, including the saloon-style swing doors at the entrance, is original and lovingly preserved. Must-trys include the classic Peranakan dish *pie tee* (rice flour cones stuffed with minced chicken and vegetables), and *ikan asam* (mackerel cooked in tamarind). $$

Purple Cane 11 Jalan Sultan; http://tearestaurant.com.my. This calm and peaceful retreat from Chinatown's hubbub serves a range of speciality Chinese teas, but is of more note, and popularity, as a restaurant – the menu features dishes such as simmered black tea giant drumstick rice, among many other things to have been boiled in tea. $$

LITTLE INDIA AND CHOW KIT, SEE MAP PAGE 71

★ **Heritage Pizza** 26g Jalan Doraisamy; http://instagram.com/heritagepizza_kl. Even Italians approve of the divine pizzas fired out at this industrial-chic restaurant, hugely popular with affluent locals and the expat set. They've a good range of wines and aperitivo drinks to wash your pizza down with. $$$

Jai Hind 13 Jalan Melayu; 03 2692 0041. Friendly *kedai kopis* which, besides an impressively wide-ranging spread

---

KUALA LUMPUR'S TOP PLACES TO EAT

Best for dumplings Din Tai Fung (see page 91)
Best for colonial atmosphere Old China Café (see above)
Best for luxury Fuego (see page 91)
Best for coffee Feeka (see page 93) or Vernakular (see page 93)
Best for pizza Heritage Pizza (see above)
Best for ice cream Licky Chan & The Poke Guy (see page 93)
Best for vegetarians or vegans Blue Boy Vegetarian Food Court (see page 94)
Best for smoothies or salad bowls Jamboo (see page 93)
Best for that local hipster feel Food Fiction (see page 93)
Best for "cat's eyes" Air Mata Kucing (see page 92)

of curries and stir-fries, also has an extensive menu of North Indian savouries and sweets, as good as you'll get in smarter restaurants but at half the price. $

THE GOLDEN TRIANGLE, SEE MAP PAGE 74

Baan26 26 Changkat Bukit Bintang; http://baan26.com. Excellent, award-winning Thai restaurant right in the thick of the nightlife area – come by day if you want a little more peace and quiet, or in the evening as a prelude to some drinking. Dishes are well made, and beautifully presented. $$$

Din Tai Fung Level 6, Pavilion KL mall; http://dintaifung.com.my. This superb Michelin-starred Taiwanese light-meal chain specializes in Shanghainese *xiao long bao* – little pork dumplings served in a bamboo steamer, eaten dipped in ginger vinegar. You can watch the chefs at work at the open kitchen, painstakingly cutting out and stuffing each dumpling with minced pork and shrimp. $$$

Fuego Level 23A, Tower B, The Troika, 19 Persiaran KLCC; http://troikaskydining.com. This swanky South American restaurant, on the top floor of KL's swish Norman Foster building, offers fine dining and a bird's-eye view of the city. Many come for the barbecued meat, with servings designed to be shared – they'll happily pack any remainders for you to take back to your roost. Some linger longer than they'd planned to, on account of their excellent drink selection (see page 95). $$$$

★ **Hakka** 90 Jalan Raja Chulan; http://hakkakl.com. Excellent Chinese restaurant serving top-notch Hakka cuisine. The seafood is particularly good, although there are plenty of other dishes on offer including vegetables and even ostrich. $$$

La Bodega 222 Jalan Ampang; http://bodega.com.my. This well-liked tapas chain attracts a loyal expat following for its tapas, paella and wine buffets; this branch is augmented by a lounge and deli that serves imported Spanish produce. $$$$

Luk Yu Tea House Basement, The Starhill, 181 Jalan Bukit Bintang; http://thestarhilldining.com. Shaped like a teapot, this welcoming place is more of a restaurant than a teahouse, with excellent Hong Kong-style pork-free dim sum and other Chinese favourites; needless to say, there are plenty of fine teas too, including silver needle jasmine and ginseng oolong. $$$

Madhby Al-Yemen 83 Jalan Berangan; 03 2110 0015. Once an Iraqi street-food restaurant, this has now changed ownership and been renamed after a different Middle Eastern nation. In reality the offerings at this modern, modestly stylish venue are typical Middle Eastern fare, but really well done; special shout out to the mixed *meze* platters, which with the free bread will probably fill two. The outdoor area is also a pleasant place to sit and suck on a shisha. $$

Marble 8 Steakhouse Level 56, Persiaran KLCC; http://marinisgroup.com. Exceptional upmarket steakhouse serving fine cuts of wet-aged Wagyu and Black Angus beef, with unparalleled views out over the city. The *Privé* lounge offers a fine collection of whiskies and cigars, and a

> ### EATING IN KUALA LUMPUR: WHICH AREA?
>
> Area by area, there are quite a few differences when it comes to what you might end up eating. **Chinatown** is obviously good for Chinese food, but has a growing number of trendier options at all budget levels. Likewise, **Little India and Chow Kit** are primarily places in which to sample Indian cuisine, although there are now some great alternatives, particularly in the hugely trendy area just south of Medan Tuanku monorail station. You'll still find most choice in the wider **Golden Triangle** area, especially if you're after non-local cuisine. Heading southwest, **Brickfields** is another area dominated by Indian food, and slightly distant **Bangsar** is a popular choice for affluent or adventurous locals.

JALAN ALOR: KL'S OUTDOOR FOOD HAVEN

Along with numerous restaurants, the Golden Triangle also boasts one of KL's best alfresco experiences in **Jalan Alor**. The street actually has a double layer of food outlets: the open-fronted restaurants that line the street, and the food stalls arranged in front of them. The food is predominantly Chinese, with a strong seafood bias – and some of the city's tastiest Hokkien noodles, comprising egg noodles fried in lard, seasoned with dark soy sauce and garnished with prawn, pork and fishcake slices, and greens – but there are plenty of Thai and Malaysian options too, plus fresh fruit and drink vendors. It all fires up from 6pm, and the stalls stay open well into the small hours. Some menus omit prices, so fix them when ordering to avoid nasty surprises when the bill arrives. Cheaper dining options are easy to find, but the experience is worth the extra spend; you can usually order small, medium or large portions.

selection of pre-or post-prandial cocktails. Note that there's a dress code here – don't come in flip-flops. $$$$

Muar 6g Tengkat Tong Shin; http://facebook.com/restoran muar. This great restaurant in the heart of bustling Bukit Bintang offers a chance to try specialities from Muar, a little town renowned for its tasty variations of Chinese and Malay dishes. The menu includes the likes of butter *kalian* (deep-fried vegetables with butter and evaporated milk), and crispy fried egg. $

Pinchos 18 Changkat Bukit Bintang; http://pinchoskl.com. Authentic tapas and *pinchos* are served at this bustling Spanish tapas bar, which gets packed in the evenings. The atmosphere is warm and cosy, with seating at the bar or at wooden tables, and service is friendly and efficient. The dates wrapped in bacon are to die for. $$$

Sao Nam 25 Tengkat Tong Shin; http://saonam.com.my. Welcoming Vietnamese restaurant that actually feels a bit like old-school Hanoi – colonial lemon walls (check), wooden ceilings (check), tiled flooring (check, even if it's mock tiling). The dishes are still very good, with the likes of deep-fried chicken spring rolls and house speciality mangosteen and prawn salad, all served beneath wall posters extolling the collectivist life. $$$

Shook! Basement, The Starhill, 181 Jalan Bukit Bintang; http://thestarhilldining.com. Attracting celebrities and moneyed Malaysians and expats, this interactive restaurant with four show kitchens offers Japanese, Chinese, Italian and Western grill dishes. There's an extensive wine list (the walk-in cellar holds more than three thousand bottles), and the daily live jazz adds a nice touch to the restaurant's already appealing ambience. The crunchy snow-white dancing prawn starter (lightly wok-fried prawns coated in a hot mayonnaise and honey-glazed walnut sauce) is an absolute must. $$$$

Zenzero Harvard Residence, 6 Jalan Puncak; http://zenzerogroup.com. Understated casual-chic interior and refined cuisine, prepared by an experienced Italian chef. The menu changes seasonally, and the wine list includes an excellent selection from Italy and beyond. $$$$

LAKE GARDENS AND AROUND, SEE MAP PAGE 66

Contango Hotel Majestic, Jalan Sultan Hishamuddin; http://majestickl.com. Within the *Majestic*, this contemporary restaurant features a lively open kitchen with an incredible selection of cuisines on offer: Indian, Chinese, Japanese and Western, including Italian and grilled dishes. The buffet (breakfast, lunch or dinner) includes a delectable selection of desserts, and can feature a free flow of wine (for extra, obviously). $$$$

BRICKFIELDS, SEE MAP PAGE 80

★ **Annalakshmi** Temple of Fine Arts, 116 Jalan Berhala; http://annalakshmi.com.my. This community-run South Indian vegetarian restaurant, with a warm and welcoming ethnic interior, offers a stupendous eat-all-you-want lunchtime buffet; in the evenings it's a la carte only, and the profits go to support various projects. There's a small, informal canteen in the car park beneath the building, where you pay what you feel the meal is worth. Smart-casual dress; no shorts, sports clothes or open shoes. $$

Gem 124 Jalan Tun Sambanthan; 03 2260 1373. Reliable, moderately smart restaurant serving South Indian chicken, mutton and seafood curries. Conveniently close to the monorail station. $

Saravanaa Bhavan 196 Jalan Tun Sambanthan; http://saravanabhavan.com. One of a slightly eccentric Madras-based chain of inexpensive vegetarian restaurants that's spread as far afield as London and New York. Concentrate on the South Indian dishes – *dosai*, *idli*, *uthapam* and so forth – or one of their Special Meals, and be warned that spicing can be incendiary. $$

BANGSAR, SEE MAP PAGE 81

Alexis Bistro 29 Jalan Telawi 3; http://alexisbistro.cargo.site. This sleek café, bistro and wine-bar is worth visiting for its delectable cakes alone, although the menu includes Asian and Western dishes, along with hearty breakfasts; it's popular among expats and well-heeled Malaysians, especially for live music. $$$

Sri Nirwana Maju 43 Jalan Telawi 3; http://srinirwanamanju.com. This hugely popular banana-leaf curry house with canteen decor stands out in the swanky Telawi area of Bangsar, and attracts crowds for its excellent dishes such as mutton *varuval* and fried squid. Be prepared to queue. $

★ **WTF** 98 Lorong Maarof; http://wtfrestaurants.com.my. It actually stands for What Tasty Food (though plenty of other iterations of the acronym are printed across the walls here), and so it is – this place serves excellent Indian vegetarian dishes. Consider perusing their menu to add something you'd find harder to get at home, such as burst-in-your-mouth *pani puri* balls, or *jaljeera* (which can only truly be described as "curry juice"). $$

Yeast 24g Jalan Telawi 2; http://yeastbistronomy.com. A boulangerie, bistro and bar all in one, this is a great spot for a morning coffee and croissant, home-made granola or for more substantial dinners. The experienced French chef rustles up exceptional dishes including *boeuf bourguignon* and steak tartare. $$$$

CAFÉS, TEAROOMS AND DESSERTS

CHINATOWN AND AROUND, SEE MAP PAGE 68

★ **Air Mata Kucing** 15 Jalan Hang Lekir. Keep your eye out for this little stand, tucked away off Jalan Petaling, which serves take-away bottles of "cat-eye" tea (that's what *air mata* means); made with medicinal herbs, longans and other goodies, they're a great (and slightly weird) pick-me-up on a hot day. $

★ **Fung Wong** 85 Jalan Sultan; http://fungwong.my. The area's best place for local sweet treats, which can be purchased as souvenirs (see page 99) or enjoyed at the pretty, open-air space shaded with yellow parasols. They specialize in moon cakes (they've even made one with Marmite in the past), but plenty of baked goods are on offer here, including sesame rolls and coconut tarts. $

Lucy in the Sky 167 Jalan Tun H.S. Lee; http://facebook.com/lucyintheskykl. Located in a former warehouse, this café has pleasant staff and a minimalist interior, featuring bare brick walls and spotlights, and offers Western dishes including pastas, burgers and all-day breakfast choices such as French toast. $$

LITTLE INDIA AND CHOW KIT, SEE MAPS PAGES 68 AND 71

★ **Jamboo** 19g Jalan Tun H.S. Lee; 012 891 9159. Charming, chilled little place serving local takes on hipster health food – the smoothie bowls are just smoothie bowls (and they're great), but savoury ones feature satay sticks, *gula melaka*-infused chicken and the like; you can piece your own together using a cute colour-block system. There are more colours in the alley outside, where the outdoor seats are photogenically shaded by a kaleidoscopic "ceiling" of dye-filled plastic bottles. $$

★ **Licky Chan & The Poke Guy** 24 Jalan Yap Ah Shak; http://lickychan.com. Epitomising the ever-increasing trendiness of southern Chow Kit as well as anywhere, this ice cream parlour (that's Licky Chan; the "Poke Guy" is an on-site tattoo artist) looks a bit like a schoolroom pimped out in gentle neon, then set to a pulsing soundtrack that mainly seems to revolve around the 1980s. Their roster of ice cream changes all the time, though there are always plenty of boozy choices (sake and mezcal often feature), and curious concoctions created with the likes of banana bread, ghost pepper or silver-tip tea. Don't miss this place if you're anywhere nearby; they also have a branch in REXKL. $$

Lokl Coffee Co. 30 Jalan Tun H.S. Lee; http://loklcoffee.com. Small and welcoming café, a great spot for a mid-morning snack or light lunch as you explore Chinatown and Little India – it's between the two. The interior is cosy with wooden tables and bare brick walls, and the menu offers a selection of Western dishes including burgers; over coffee it's hard to look past desserts such as crème brûlée or burnt cheesecake. $$$

THE GOLDEN TRIANGLE, SEE MAP PAGE 74

★ **Feeka** 19 Jalan Mesui; http://facebook.com/feekacoffeeroasters. Pleasant coffee house in a renovated shophouse, serving locally-roasted beans and home-made pastries, as well as a smattering of light meals including omelettes and French toast – though sadly no Swedish desserts, despite what the name of the place may suggest. It's also a great spot to refuel for the morning after a long night out. $$

VCR 2 Jalan Galloway; http://vcr.my. Super-popular brunch spot for young, moneyed locals (not to mention guests from the nearby hotels). Reuben sandwiches, eggs all ways, and great coffee too; head to the upper level for a more chilled atmosphere, with greenery visible on all sides. Service can be slow, unfortunately. $$

LAKE GARDENS AND AROUND, SEE MAP PAGE 66

Hornbill Café 920 Jalan Cenderawasih; http://klbirdpark.com. If you don't feel like paying full whack for the bird park (see page 77), but *do* feel like paying far less to see some birds *and* have a sit down and a cold coconut shake, this is your spot. Its outdoor balcony is part of the bird park, and cheeky egrets pop by regularly to beg for food; you're almost guaranteed to see hornbills too. $$

BANGSAR, SEE MAP PAGE 81

★ **Niko Neko Matcha** 82a Lorong Maarof; http://nikonekomatcha.com. After clambering up its narrow entrance staircase, you may get a bit of a shock on entering this minimalist, almost forensically white café. They've plenty of teas to choose from (mostly sourced from Japan), plus desserts made with matcha powder – try the delectable cheesecake. $$

Vernakular 33 Jalan Telawi 3; 018 912 0733. Part store for watches and glasses, part café – a good example of the pleasing way that Bangsar is heading. The coffee's excellent, too. $$

STREET FOOD AND HAWKER CENTRES

CHINATOWN AND AROUND, SEE MAP PAGE 68

Central Market Food Court Jalan Hang Kasturi; http://centralmarket.com.my. The Central Market has plenty of excellent outlets specializing in food from different corners of the Peninsula and beyond, from traditional Nyonya food to Japanese crepes. $

★ **Food Fiction** 80 Jalan Sultan; http://rexkl.webflow.io. Part of the old Rex cinema has been converted into a fascinating modern take on the whole hawker centre thing – think luxury burgers, ribs, pizza and veggie/vegan takes on local staples. You can come here for a drink, too. $$

Lai Foong 138 Jalan Tun H.S. Lee; 03 2072 8123. The six stalls at this historic *kopitiam* rustle up all manner of local delicacies including noodle and rice dishes – try the Hainanese beef noodle, flavoured with herbs and served with not only beef slices, but also tripe. $

Penjaja Gallery Jalan Tun H.S. Lee & Jalan Petaling. It's worth heading into the alleyway that connects Jalan Petaling with Jalan Tun H.S. Lee to get a feel for life in Chinatown – vendors here display all manner of meats, vegetables and other foods, and there are a handful of great stalls where you can sample local dishes such as curry *laksa* as a morning snack. $

Zuliani Corner Jalan Hang Lekir & Jalan Tun H.S. Lee; 016 663 3548. This little stall churns out excellent Muslim Indian *rojak* – fried dough fritters with potatoes, bean curd, egg and shredded cucumbers mixed with a sweet and spicy peanut sauce. $

LITTLE INDIA AND CHOW KIT, SEE MAPS PAGES 68 AND 71

Capital Café 213 Jalan TAR; 012 854 5046. Locals flock to this endearing and enduring family-run *kedai kopis*, which first opened its doors in 1956, for morning *nasi lemak* or toast with *kaya* (coconut jam) or honey; plenty of other dishes are offered at lunch, including beef *rendang* and fried noodles, while the sizzling satay (evenings only) is said to be one of the best in town. $

Santa 11 Jalan Tun H.S. Lee; 019 269 9771. This laidback restaurant hums with activity at lunchtime, when locals flock here for the freshly made *chapatti* and *kimma mutton*, which are undoubtedly among the best in town. $

★ **Sithique Nasi Kandar** 237 Jalan Tuanku Abdul Rahman. One of a handful of popular *kedai kopis* specializing in *nasi kandar* with chicken or fish; fluffy *roti canai* and *dosai* are made on the spot, along with pretty tasty *mee goreng*. Watching the addition of so many different sauces to the rice – each a slightly different shade of orangey brown – is quite mesmerising. You'll have to queue at mealtimes. $

Syed Bistro 57 Jalan Dang Wangi; http://syedbistro.com. This laidback place proudly boasts they have "the one and only *biriyani*" and in all fairness it's pretty tasty – there's chicken, mutton and lamb, as well as a selection of fiery curries and freshly baked *roti canai* to choose from. $

THE GOLDEN TRIANGLE, SEE MAP PAGE 74

Blue Boy Vegetarian Food Court Lorong Pudu 4, Jalan Tong Shin. A hawker centre just for vegetarians – great stuff, but do note that this is (quite pleasingly) a simple, local-vibes place, not the sanitised hipster venue that you may expect. $

Halab Gate Shawarma 51 Jalan Sultan Ismail; http://halabgate.com. Shawarma place that's popular through the day, and for much of the night, since they're often still open when people are pouring out of bars and clubs and in the mood for something nice and greasy. Cheese options available. $

★ **Lot 10 Hutong** Basement, Lot 10 Mall, Jalan Bukit Bintang; http://lot10hutong.com. This evocative, modern take on heritage food, located in the basement of Lot 10 mall, offers a plethora of authentic Malay and Chinese meals. With over 900 dishes on offer, there's plenty of choice, from *hokkien mee* noodles to freshly made *siew bao*. $

TG's 3 Tengkat Tong Shin; http://facebook.com/tgsbistro. Offers simply the best naan breads in Bukit Bintang, within walking distance of Changkat. They also do a range of delicious north Indian specialities like chicken *kadai*, and *murtabak* (a savoury pancake with meat and/or cheese), plus fresh juices and a self-service curried vegetable counter. $

DRINKING AND NIGHTLIFE

KL's most fashionable **bars** and clubs are concentrated in the Golden Triangle, though Bangsar (see page 95) also plays host to a few slick bars, and Chinatown boasts a fair few speakeasy-style operations. Only during Ramadan are both bars and clubs distinctly quiet. Beer in KL is available on draught, though bottles and cans are more common; it'll cost a couple of ringgit less during the **happy hours** that most places offer. Note that it's common for tax to be added to alcohol, so be prepared for a larger bill than you first thought. If the drinking scene seems to tick over healthily enough, KL's **clubbing** scene appears surprisingly buoyant for its size. It largely focuses around the junction of Jalan Tuz Razak and Jalan P. Ramlee in the Golden Triangle. The music policy at each venue tends to change with alarming frequency, but as a rule weekends feature more serious dance sounds, while weekdays offer retro hits and fairly accessible R&B. To keep up with the latest news, including which big-name DJs might be in town, check out the Friday **club listings** in the *Star* newspaper, *Juice* magazine (http://juiceonline.com) or the clubs' own websites. The usual cover charges rise if well-known DJs are playing. Unfortunately, **live music** in KL is much less happening than in Singapore, partly because of Malaysia's old reputation as a centre for music piracy, which has caused many international bands to choose not to play here in the past. Religious conservatives have also protested when the likes of Avril Lavigne, Selena Gomez and Gwen Stefani have performed. Consequently, most concerts have tended to involve safe big-name pop, soul or country artists, plus occasional indie bands; there does seem to have been a shift towards the progressive in recent years, so keep your fingers crossed that this tangent continues.

BARS

CHINATOWN AND AROUND, SEE MAP PAGE 68

Attic 15 Jalan Balai Polis; http://atticbarkl.com. Spider your way up a dimly-lit spiral staircase, and you'll be up on the "hidden" third level, gazing out at the roofs of Chinatown. Cocktails are the name of the game here.

★ **PS150** 150 Jalan Petaling; http://ps150.my. Hidden down a dark back alley not too far from Petaling Street, this speakeasy bar's setting is as dark as the building's history – it's a former brothel. Drinks designed by Angel Ng, who is well known in the industry, include the Pandan Flip (with rum and coconut), and Red Poison Princess (absinthe, tequila and mezcal).

Shhhbuuuleee 80 Jalan Sultan; 012 612 0786. Sitting atop the old Rex cinema, this is a restaurant in theory, but is mainly used as a bar in practice – slightly overpriced, but there's a good selection of canned craft beer, and a cool atmosphere.

ShuangXi 177 Jalan Tun H.S. Lee; 010 238 7588. One of the area's more established speakeasy bars, beautifully dolled up in red neon, with images projected onto one of the walls. Guests are required to remove their footwear, and many of them end up sitting on the floor. Negatives are that there aren't that many cocktails to choose from, and that it's only open on (and around) weekends.

THE GOLDEN TRIANGLE, SEE MAP PAGE 74

Fuego Level 23A, Tower B, the Troika, 19 Persiaran KLCC; http://troikaskydining.com. As you'd expect from a 23rd-floor location, this tapas bar with open-air seating boasts stunning views of the cityscape; it's a great spot for a sundowner as you watch the sun set – the views don't get much better than this, although the view of the Twin Towers is now obscured. They've excellent cocktails (including some from, or influenced by, South America) and a worthy wine list, plus a good roster of single malts.

Healy Mac's 38 Changkat Bukit Bintang; http://healymacs.com. Quintessential Irish pub in the middle of Changkat with good Guinness and well-made cocktails. The quiz on Monday nights is usually a raucous and entertaining affair that's popular with Westerners and locals alike, and all major sports matches are shown on the multiple TV screens. It has sister branches elsewhere.

Heli Lounge Level 34, Menara KH, 1 Jalan Sultan Ismail; http://facebook.com/Heliloungebar. Hidden gem turned talk of the town, this aeronautics-themed venue features an active helipad that becomes a sprawling rooftop bar in the evenings and is perhaps the best place to watch the sunset over KL. Expect good cocktails and happy hour promotions, but be prepared to queue for drinks as the evening goes on.

Marini's on 57 Level 57, Petronas Tower 3; http://marinisgroup.com. As you'd expect, the capital's highest rooftop bar boasts spectacular views of the city and close-ups of the Petronas Towers. Award-winning mixologists shake up classic and signature cocktails such as the White Dame, with bourbon, cointreau, grapefruit juice, lemon, honey and egg white. Smart attire (trousers for gents) only, or you will be refused entry.

Sky Bar Traders Hotel, Kuala Lumpur City Centre (KLCC); http://shangri-la.com. 33rd-floor hotel cocktail bar, and one of the city's most prestigious places to drink – great drinks, a 360-degree views of the capital, and a swimming pool that people *could* use if they weren't so busy trying to look cool.

★ **Taps** Lion Office Tower, 1 Jalan Nagasari; http://tapsbeerbar.my. Still the best place to enjoy craft beer in Kuala Lumpur, despite increased competition. There's a regularly rotating selection of beers from Belgium, the UK, France and beyond – the staff claim to have served the best part of 1000 unique beers since opening. Live music on Thursday

KUALA LUMPUR'S BEST PLACES TO DRINK

Best for views Fuego (see page 91)
Best rooftop pool parties Wet (see page 96)
Best hotel bar Sky Bar (see below)
Best for high-class opulence Marini's on 57 (see below)
Best for international live music Zepp (see page 96)
Best for jazz Alexis Bistro (see page 92)
Best for old-school tunes Havana (see below)
Best for craft beer Taps (see below)
Best speakeasy PS150 (see page 94)
Best club Club Kyo (see below)

to Saturday, often the talented house band playing classic rock, and surprisingly good food.

BANGSAR, SEE MAP PAGE 81

Mantra Bangsar Village 2, 2 Jalan Telawi 1; http://mantrabarkl.com. On the rooftop of a shopping centre, this venue is where young expats and Chinese Malaysians go to see and be seen. The music ranges from house to heavier dance later in the evening, and there's a huge balcony space, which looks back towards Bukit Bintang, plus whiskey and innovative cocktails.

Ronnie Q's 32 Jalan Telawi 2; http://facebook.com/BangsarRonnieQ. The focus at this watering hole, with its four TVs and a projector, is very much on sport – not just soccer, but also cricket and rugby. Offers plenty of drinks including Guinness and Tiger beer.

CLUBS

THE GOLDEN TRIANGLE, SEE MAP PAGE 74

Club Kyo Mandarin Oriental, KLCC; http://clubkyokl.asia. Big club where the tunes are mostly hip-hop and R&B, though they have regular house, trance and EDM nights too.

Dragonfly Level 50, Naza Tower, Platinum Park; http://facebook.com/DragonflyKualaLumpur. They got rid of Zouk from Singapore, but this offshoot of a Jakarta club is still going strong – expect regular theme nights, superstar DJs, and awesome sound and light systems.

Havana 2 Changkat Bukit Bintang; http://havanakl.com. Located just above the bustling steak-and-grill restaurant of the same name, this place has been attracting punters for decades. At weekends locals and expats alike hang out over beers and stomp about to old school and retro hits. There's also a lounge and rooftop terrace bar for those who want to natter away over a few drinks.

KL'S SPEAKEASY CULTURE

In many ways surprisingly relevant for a still conservative Muslim country, the recent rapid rise of **speakeasy bars** in Greater KL has caught the attention of well-off Chinese locals and Western visitors, and has attracted superstar bartenders from Japan, Hong Kong and Europe to Malaysia.

Some of the first venues were concentrated around the still derelict (from the outside) shophouses in the south end of **Chinatown**, where swanky surroundings and plush furnishing lurk behind worn walls and dark windows. Increasingly, posh upmarket suburbs such as **Damansara** and **Mont Kiara** are stashing away trendy venues behind bookcases in stairwells or above newsagents. By their very nature, speakeasy bars may not be around for more than a season, but some such as *PS150* (see page 94) and *ShuangXi* (see page 95) have been around for a while, and show no sign of closing – still, keep your ear to the ground.

Iron Fairies Hive, Jalan Tun Razak; http://ironfairieskl.com. The design of this bar is absolutely insane – a highly detailed rendition of a fantasy involving an iron mine. It's best to swing by on weekends, when a section becomes a club of sorts. Music covers everything from African, Latin, Indian, K-Pop, to strong beats such as dancehall, hip hop, R&B, reggaeton, moombahton, G-house, Brazilian bass, house and pop mashups.

Pisco Bar 29 Jalan Mesui; http://piscobarkl.com. A range of excellent Peruvian/Spanish tapas are to be had at this trendy nightlife spot, where pisco sours are the drink of choice – though if you've been to Peru or Chile, or worse still are from one of those countries yourself, you're likely to be disappointed. Walls are adorned with blown-up photographs of pop icons and other celebrities, while upturned buckets serve as bar lamps. The dancefloor gets busy as the night goes on.

Wet Level 12, W Hotel, 121 Jalan Ampang; http://wkualalumpur-wetdeck.com. About as good a view of the Petronas Towers as you can find – actually two views (making a full four towers), since they're reflected in a swimming pool. This bar is a great place to be even when they don't have events on, but weekends see DJs spinning anything from chill to afro beats, through disco and techno; at other times, give *Wicked* (on the same level) a try.

LIVE MUSIC VENUES

Note that some venues listed in the Bars section also have regular live music, such as *Taps* (see page 95).

THE GOLDEN TRIANGLE, SEE MAP PAGE 74
Alexis Bistro Ampang Great Eastern Mall, 303 Jalan Ampang; http://alexisbistro.cargo.site. Under the same management as *Alexis Bistro* in Bangsar and elsewhere, this upmarket bistro and wine bar hosts excellent local and international jazz acts on Friday and Saturday nights.

★ **Zepp** 2 Jalan Hang Tuah Bukit; http://zepp.co.jp. Something KL has badly needed – a mid-sized music venue, catering to the vast chasm between mega-acts and your-mate-with-a-guitar. Part of a Japanese chain, since opening in 2022 it has already hosted the likes of Cigarettes After Sex (if the authorities understood the lyrics, then things are *really* changing in Malaysia), Jack White and Rex Orange County, plus similar acts from across Asia.

BANGSAR, SEE MAP PAGE 66
Bobo KL 65-2 Jalan Bangkung; http://facebook.com/BoboKualaLumpur. Intimate piano bar-style venue that has stood the test of time (the test of fairly recent time, anyway).

ENTERTAINMENT

The modest local **performing arts** scene is split between KL and its satellite town Petaling Jaya, which, with its complex system of numbered roads that even residents don't understand, is best accessed by taxi. **Theatre** is probably the strongest suit, with concerts, musicals and so forth throughout the year, by local as well as international performers and troupes. There's also a dedicated community of people working in the visual arts. For **listings**, check the national press and *Time Out* (http://timeout.com/kualalumpur). *Kakiseni* (http://kakiseni.com) is also worth consulting, not only for listings but also for an intelligent look at how the performing arts can find a balance with the Asian and Muslim values that hold sway in Malaysia.

THEATRE AND CLASSICAL MUSIC

Aside from the Actors Studio (see page 96), other drama companies worth making time for include the Five Arts Centre (http://fiveartscentre.org) and the satirical Instant Café (http://instantcafetheatre.com). There are two home-grown orchestras, namely the Malaysian Philharmonic Orchestra (http://mpo.com.my) and the Dama Asia orchestra (http://dama.asia), the latter specializing in Chinese classical music and musicals. Besides the venues listed here, there are occasional concerts at the KL Convention Centre.

Actors Studio http://theactorsstudio.com.my. The most prominent of KL's theatre companies, this studio mounts several productions each year, ranging from Malaysianized

versions of foreign classics to works by local playwrights, and has been instrumental in the creation and running of one of the city's more impressive independent arts centres, KLPac.
Dewan Filharmonik Level 2, Tower 2, Petronas Towers, Golden Triangle box office; http://dfp.com.my. The home of the Malaysian Philharmonic, this venue also hosts concerts by other performers, not just in the classical domain.
Istana Budaya (National Theatre) Jalan Tun Razak, east of the junction with Jalan Pahang and south of Titiwangsa Gardens, Titiwangsa; http://istanabudaya.gov.my. Besides providing a spacious modern home for the National Theatre Company and the National Symphony Orchestra, this venue sees performances by visiting international orchestras and also stages pop concerts, plays and ballets. Just over 1km from Titiwangsa or Chow Kit stations.
KL Performing Arts Centre Jalan Strachan, off Jalan Ipoh, Sentul; http://klpac.org. A joint project of the stalwart Actors Studio company and the construction conglomerate that's redeveloping the area, the KL Performing Arts Centre (KLPac) is housed in a former rail depot revamped to look like a Frank Lloyd Wright doodle. It hosts jazz, indie and dance events plus, of course, plays by various companies. The location couldn't be more awkward, in the depths of the old Sentul Raya Golf Club, but it's accessible via the nearby Sentul Komuter station, although far easier by taxi or Grab.
Panggung Bandaraya Sultan Abdul Samad Building, Jalan Tuanku Abdul Rahman, Colonial District; http://dbkl.gov.my. Occasional performances of Malay drama (*bangsawan*) take place in this historic theatre with a Moorish facade.

CULTURAL SHOWS

Traditional dance can be seen at the cultural shows put on by the Malaysian Tourism Centre and by a couple of restaurant theatres, though what's on offer is inevitably touristy. Indian dance is better catered for, thanks to the Temple of Fine Arts.
Malaysia Tourism Centre (MaTiC) 109 Jalan Ampang, Golden Triangle; http://matic.gov.my. Produces 45-minute cultural shows, featuring performers from Borneo as well as the Peninsula.
Temple of Fine Arts 116 Jalan Berhala, Brickfields; http://tfa.org.my. Community-run cultural centre set up to preserve Tamil culture by promoting dance, theatre, folk, classical music and craft-making. Probably the best place in KL to see traditional Indian dance.

CINEMA

Golden Screen Cinemas Third floor, Mid Valley Megamall, Mid Valley City; http://gsc.com.my. Cinema chain with branches also in Pavilion KL and Berjaya Times Square in Bukit Bintang; their Mid Valley Megamall screen is your best bet for occasional foreign art-house films.
LFS Coliseum Cinema Jalan TAR, Little India; http://lfs.com.my. As a total contrast to the main chains, this cinema is worth a trip for its 1930s Art Deco character, even if Kollywood (the Tamil-language subsection of Bollywood) films aren't your thing.
TGV Suria KLCC mall, Golden Triangle; http://tgv.com.my. A conveniently located multiplex.

SHOPPING

There's no city in Malaysia where **consumerism** is as in-your-face as KL. The **malls** of the Golden Triangle are draws for youths and yuppies alike, while street markets attract everyone, offering goods of all sorts. Jalan Petaling in Chinatown (see page 68) is where you'll find fake watches and leather goods; some of these have started to creep into the **covered market** on Jalan Masjid India and the nearby Lorong Tuanku Abdul Rahman *pasar malam* (see page 70), but their mainstays remain clothes and fabrics, plus a few eccentricities such as herbal tonics. Chow Kit Market (see page 70) has some clothing bargains but little else of interest to tourists except photo opportunities. A great just-out-of-town **flea market** for knick-knacks and general bric-a-brac happens every weekend inside the Amcorp Mall in Petaling Jaya, close to Taman Jaya station on the LRT.

ANTIQUES

Antiques can be extremely expensive in Southeast Asia, and are often fake; the dealers listed below are sound but even experts can be fooled, so don't fork out unless you know what you're doing. The biggest market is for Chinese and Peranakan (Nyonya) porcelain, woodcarvings and artefacts, though there are also some Malaysian and Asian specialists in town.

CHINATOWN AND AROUND, SEE MAP PAGE 68
Central Market Jalan Hang Kasturi; http://centralmarket.com.my. At various stalls on the ground level of this intriguing market (see page 69), you'll find a range of genuine antiques from Tibet, China and Central Asia, plus a few pieces from Sarawak. The real ones can be pricey; the replica ones sometimes look almost as good.

FURTHER AFIELD, SEE MAP PAGE 66
Madame Butterfly Second floor, Mid Valley Megamall, Mid Valley City; 03 2282 8088. Antiques and antique-style arts and crafts; best for gemstone jewellery and Nyonya porcelain.

BOOKS AND MUSIC

The larger KL bookshops are pretty impressive, divided into Chinese-, English- and Malay-language sections, and carrying a good range of publications. They tend to be strong in literature about Malaysia and the rest of Southeast Asia – everything from historical monographs and classics-in-translation, to Manga, cookbooks and coffee-table tomes on architecture and garden design. Unfortunately, as this country has long been famous for rampant piracy, the music shops are nothing to write home about.

CHINATOWN AND AROUND, SEE MAP PAGE 68
Junk Book Store 78 Jalan Tun H.S. Lee; http://facebook.com/JUNK.bs. Ancient establishment, jammed to its dusty rafters with secondhand books, most in English, covering every conceivable topic from pulp fiction to gardening.
Mentor Bookstores REXKL 80 Jalan Sultan; http://bookstore.mentor.com.my. On the mezzanine level of the old Rex cinema, you'll find this photogenic bookstore; most of the second-hand books are local, but there are a few in English too.

LITTLE INDIA AND CHOW KIT, SEE MAP PAGE 68
Riwayat 34 Jalan Tun H.S. Lee; http://riwayat.my. Small shop selling new, used and rare books, many of which are in English.

THE GOLDEN TRIANGLE, SEE MAP PAGE 74
★ **Kinokuniya** Fourth floor, Suria KLCC; http://kinokuniya.com.my. Huge and efficient Japanese chain, with the broadest selection of books in KL – and by far the biggest selection of Rough Guides, too.

BANGSAR, SEE MAP PAGE 81
MPH Bangsar Village, Jelan Telawi 1; http://mphonline.com. This veteran survivor of the local book trade is resting on its laurels somewhat, though it still carries a decent mix of novels and nonfiction titles.

CLOTHING

CHINATOWN AND AROUND, SEE MAP PAGE 68
★ **Kanoe** REXKL, 80 Jalan Sultan; http://kanoewear.com. Boutique batik clothing, on the first floor of the old Rex cinema. While the technique may be traditional, the designs here suit the modern day, and offcuts are sold as accessories, coasters and the like.

HANDICRAFTS

KL is a good place to stock up on handicrafts, though they tend to be available a little more cheaply in the provincial areas where they originate, and some here might even have been imported from overseas. For a broad range – everything from Royal Selangor pewter models of the Petronas Towers to bright batik, textiles and original paintings or sculptures – visit Chinatown's Central Market and Kompleks Kraf.

CHINATOWN AND AROUND, SEE MAP PAGE 68
The Objects Store REXKL, 80 Jalan Sultan; http://theobjects.store. Set on an upper level of the old Rex cinema, this cool spot is almost more of a gallery space than a shop, but they do indeed sell some of the "exhibits" – mainly homeware, and all quite pricey. You can get an idea of what they sell from their website.

LITTLE INDIA AND CHOW KIT, SEE MAP PAGE 71
Shades First floor, The Row KL, Jalan Doraisamy; 012 334 7123. Shop selling a range of arty-crafty soft furnishings, knick-knacks, textile bags and so forth, with a Southeast Asian flavour. There's also a pleasant café within the shop.

THE GOLDEN TRIANGLE, SEE MAP PAGE 74
Ana Tomy Fifth floor, Pavilion KL; http://ana-tomy.co. Stationary shop selling notebooks and the like, with sleeves designed by local artists – you can even do the designing yourself, if you like (details on their website).

MALLS

Locals and visitors alike come to KL's shopping malls to seek refuge from the heat as much as to shop; for local young people, the malls are also important places to socialize. Mostly located outside the old centre, particularly in the Golden Triangle, the malls divide into two categories – gargantuan affairs in the manner of Western malls, featuring international chains and designer names, and smaller, denser Southeast Asian-style complexes, basically indoor bazaars with row upon row of tiny independent retailers. The simpler malls tend to be much more popular than their more sophisticated, pricier counterparts, and can be atmospheric places to wander. Many malls house a supermarket or department store of one sort or another.

THE GOLDEN TRIANGLE, SEE MAP PAGE 74
Berjaya Times Square Jalan Imbi, opposite the Monorail's Imbi stop; http://berjayatimessquarekl.com. Enormous mall with several shops and even an indoor theme park plus entertainment attractions, though not as buzzing as it really ought to be considering its size, and living somewhat in the shadow of Pavilion KL and Suria KLCC.
Lot 10 Bintang Walk; http://lot10.com.my. Specializes in designer clothes and accessories, with many Western brands such as H&M.
Low Yat Off Jalan Bukit Bintang; http://plazalowyat.com. The best place in KL for electronic and digital purchases, from laptops to cameras.
Pavilion KL Between Jalan Bukit Bintang and Jalan Raja Chulan; http://pavilion-kl.com. One of the very largest malls in the city – and that's saying something – with a parade of big-name designer outlets on Jalan Bukit Bintang. There are branches of Singaporean department stores and Malaysia's own Parkson chain, present here in an especially upmarket version. There's also a cinema and a plethora of eating and nightlife outlets.
Starhill Gallery Next to the Marriott, Bintang Walk; http://thestarhill.com.my. Expect more designer names than is healthy, orbiting a suitably grand atrium. Just as

noteworthy is the maze of top-notch restaurants and bars in the basement of the building.
Sungei Wang Plaza Jalan Sultan Ismail; http://sungei wang.com. KL's first mall offers everything from clothes and a Giant brand supermarket to souvenirs and consumer electronics, all of which are generally keenly priced.
Suria KLCC At the base of the Petronas Towers; http://suriaklcc.com.my. A mall so large it's subdivided into sub-malls for ease of reference, Suria KLCC's oval atriums are home to UK department store Marks & Spencer, Isetan and Cold Storage supermarkets, plus numerous restaurants, the Petrosains science museum, and a TGV multiplex cinema.

BANGSAR, SEE MAP PAGE 81
Bangsar Village and Village II Bangsar Baru; http://bangsarvillage.com. The boutiques tend to play second fiddle to the restaurants in these two malls, joined by a bridge above street level. Shopping highlights include an MPH bookshop.

OUTDOOR GEAR

BANGSAR, SEE MAP PAGE 81
Xnocs 34 Jalan Telawi 5, Bangsar Baru; http://ufl.com. my. This small but serious outdoor shop features hiking boots, waterproofs, sleeping bags, water purifiers, camping stoves, packs, water bottles, tents, trekking clothing and accessories. Also good for small, low-tech essentials – seam sealer, plastic water bottles, small nylon bags and the like. Some decent snorkelling, gymnastics and even archery gear, too.

FOOD AND DRINK

CHINATOWN AND AROUND, SEE MAP PAGE 68
Evergreen Tea House 62 Jalan Sultan; 03 2026 8608. There's an excellent range of teas sold at this charming little store, as well as tea-drinking paraphernalia.
Fung Wong 85 Jalan Sultan; http://fungwong.my. This cute café (see page 93) also makes a great shop, since many of their sweet treats are available in beautiful packaging – ideal souvenir fodder.
Tuck Heng Ginseng Hall 133 Jalan Tun H.S. Lee; 017 348 4820. Worth entering for the smell alone, this shop sells not just ginseng and ginseng products, but all manner of roots, fungi, beans, berries and bark – go on, give your nose a treat.

SPORTS AND ACTIVITIES

Public sports facilities in downtown KL are limited, but there are a few places to get the pulse racing here and there.
Golf The Kuala Lumpur Golf & Country Club is at Bukit Kiara, 8km west of the city centre (klgcc.com).
Gyms Private health clubs, with gyms and other facilities, include Fitness First (http://fitnessfirst.com), with central locations at Avenue K mall, Jalan Ampang, next to the KLCC LRT station.
Rock climbing Batuu Climbing (http://batuuclimbing.com) runs excursions for novices or experienced climbers to sites around Batu Caves and Bukit Tabur. Guides and all equipment supplied; hotel pick-ups upon request at extra cost.
Running Join the original Hash House Harriers for a run (http://motherhash.com); guests are welcome for a charge, and it's male-only.
Swimming The most convenient pool is at Chinwoo Stadium, uphill south off Jalan Hang Jebat in Chinatown (Mon–Fri 2–8pm, Sat & Sun 9am–8pm). The pool is well maintained but the showers and changing facilities are basic, and baggy swimwear is not allowed (men can purchase appropriate swimming trunks if required). Some hotels let non-guests access their pools for a fee.

DIRECTORY

Banks and exchange Banks with ATMs are located throughout KL. Maybank is usually your best bet for foreign exchange – there are several branches across the centre of town. You may get better rates from official moneychangers, which can be found in shopping malls and in and around transport hubs.
Casino The casino at Genting Highlands (http://rwgenting.com) attracts both vacationing locals and tourists as it offers several resorts, a theme park and shopping malls. It's 30km out of town, best reached via the Karak Highway (E8); express buses head there from Pudu Sentral and Pekeliling bus stations, and there are also share taxis from Pudu Station.
Cultural centres Alliance Française, 15 Lorong Gurney (http://alliancefrancaise.org.my); British Council, West Block, Wisma Selangor Dredging, Jalan Ampang next to the Maya hotel (http://britishcouncil.my); Goethe-Institut, 374 Jalan Tun Razak (http://goethe.de).
Embassies and consulates Australia, 6 Jalan Yap Kwan Seng (03 2146 5555, http://malaysia.highcommission.gov.au); Brunei, 2/5 Jalan Diplomatuk (03 8888 7777, http://mofat.gov.bn); Cambodia, 46 Jalan U Thant (03 4257 1150); Canada 207 Jalan Tun Razak (03 2718 3333, http://international.gc.ca); China, Plaza OSK, 25 Jalan Ampang (03 2164 5250); India, 442 Jalan Pahang (03 4024 0990, http://hcikl.gov.in); Indonesia, 233 Jalan Tun Razak (03 2116 4016); Ireland, The Amp Walk, 218 Jalan Ampang (03 2161 2963, http://embassyofireland.my); Laos, Jalan Damai and Jalan Mesra (03 2148 7059); New Zealand, Level 21, Menara IMC, 8 Jalan Sultan Ismail (03 2027 8998, http://mfat.govt.nz);

Philippines, 1 Changkat Kia Peng (kualalumpurpe.dfa.gov.ph); Singapore, 209 Jalan Tun Razak (03 2161 6277, http://mfa.gov.sg/kualalumpur/); South Africa, Menara HLA, 3 Jalan Kia Peng (012 260 2213); Thailand, 206 Jalan Ampang (http://kualalumpur.thaiembassy.org); UK, Level 27 Menara Binjai, 2 Jalan Binjai (03 2170 2200, http://gov.uk); US, 376 Jalan Tun Razak (03 9212 6000, http://my.usembassy.gov); Vietnam, 4 Persiaran Stonor (http://mofa.gov.vn).

Emergencies Police and ambulance 999, fire and rescue 994. From mobile phones, dial 112.

Hospitals and clinics General Hospital, Jalan Pahang (03 2615 5555, http://hkl.moh.gov.my); Gleneagles Hospital, Jalan Ampang (03 4141 3000, http://gleneagles.com.my); Pantai Medical Centre, 8 Jalan Bukit Pantai (03 2296 0888, http://pantai.com.my); Tung Shin Hospital, 102 Jalan Pudu (03 2037 2288, http://tungshin.com.my).

Left luggage Luggage can be stored at KL Sentral station and Pudu Sentral bus station (look out for a couple of counters at the back of the passenger level). At KLIA, the service costs more.

Police KL has its own Tourist Police station, where you can report stolen property for insurance claims, within the same complex as MATIC tourist office at MTC, 109 Jalan Ampang (8am–midnight; 03 9235 4999).

Visa extensions The Immigration Office is at Kompleks Kementerian, Dalam Negeri, 69 Jalan Sri Hartamas 1 (Mon–Fri 7.30am–5pm, counter closes at 4pm; 03 6205 7400, http://sto.imi.gov.my).

Around Kuala Lumpur

The most obvious attraction worthy of an excursion from KL is 13km north, where limestone peaks rise up from the forest at the Hindu shrine of **Batu Caves**, one of Malaysia's main tourist destinations. Nearby, the **Forest Research Institute of Malaysia** (FRIM) encompasses a small but surprisingly thick portion of primary rainforest, where you can see birds and a few animals within an hour of downtown KL.

Further northwest of KL, the quiet town of **Kuala Selangor** offers the chance to observe the nightly dance of **fireflies**, while northeast, **Fraser's Hill** is one of Malaysia's many hill stations, set up in colonial times to allow government officials an escape from lowland heat. The most surreal day-trip you can make from KL is to the very Chinese fishing village on **Ketam Island**, off the coast near southwesterly Port Klang, which hardly feels like Malaysia at all.

Batu Caves and Ketam Island are easy to reach on **public transport**, but you'll need a rental car or taxi to reach FRIM. About the only package trip widely offered by KL's accommodation and tour agents goes to see the fireflies; you can do this on public transport, but it's bit of a slog and really requires an overnight stay at Kuala Selangor.

Forest Research Institute of Malaysia

16km northwest of KL • Free • http://frim.gov.my • KMT Komuter train to Kepong station (20min), then taxi for the final 5km (10min)

The **Forest Research Institute of Malaysia** (**FRIM**) sits amid a fifteen-square-kilometre reserve of rainforest and parkland, threaded with sealed roads and walking trails. It's a popular spot for weekend picnics, appealing to birdwatchers, joggers and anyone after some greenery and fresh air; its main attraction, the canopy "skywalk", was closed in 2017 due to concerns over safety and the health of the trees that supported it, but has since reopened. A couple of hours here is plenty of time for a walk around, and this makes a good warm-up for wilder affairs at Taman Negara (see page 178); for a full day out you could always continue to the Batu Caves and Orang Asli Museum (see page 103).

Taxis can drop you off at the gates; once there, pick up a **map** and follow the main road 1km into the park, past open woodland and rolling lawns, to the **One Stop Centre** for advice. A small **museum** nearby, which is strongly biased towards the timber industry, gives thumbnail sketches of the different types of tropical forests and the commercial uses of various woods.

For a good walk, follow the clear Rover **walking track** past the mosque and uphill into the forest; there are some huge trees, birds and butterflies here, and a single-plank suspension bridge across a deep gully – you may also see monkeys, if you're lucky.

You'll also have the option of joining up with a couple of other trails along the way, which will bring you back to the One Stop Centre in around ninety minutes.

Sunway Lagoon

15km southwest of KL • Charge • http://sunwaylagoon.com • KTM Komuter line from KL Sentral to Setia Jaya (hourly; 25min) then a taxi (5min)

Though it's not a must-see, **Sunway Lagoon** is Malaysia's most famous, and one of Asia's most popular, water parks, and is certainly worth a visit if you're spending a few weeks in KL. One of its main draws, the Vuvuzela ride, sees participants boarding a chute from an eleven-storey-high tower and plummeting into a huge horn-shaped waterslide. It's not all about slides and pools, however, as there's a total of ninety attractions, and the site also includes an amusement park, wildlife park and the Lost Lagoon, Asia's first Nickelodeon-themed attraction. The *Sunway Resort Hotel & Spa* is also based on site, which is handy if you find yourself too worn out to return to KL at the end of the day.

Putrajaya

30km south of KL • KLIA Transit from KL Sentral to Putrajaya Sentral (every 30min; 20min); there are also buses from KL and KLIA

Though it's generally viewed as a soulless admin hub, the city of **PUTRAJAYA** does in fact have some seriously impressive architecture and a wealth of gorgeous green areas, so it's more than suitable for an enjoyable daytrip from KL – or, given its proximity to the airport, potentially a useful place to spend a first or final night in Malaysia. The city is the Federal Government's administrative centre, though the main sights for tourists include the bright pink **Putra Mosque** at Putra Square and the nearby **Tuanku Mizan Zainal Abidin Mosque**, plus the **Botanical Gardens** and

---

THAIPUSAM AT THE BATU CAVES

The most important festival in the Malaysian Hindu calendar (along with Deepavali), **Thaipusam** honours the Hindu deity Lord Subramaniam. It's held during the full moon in the month of "Thai" (which in the Gregorian calendar always falls between mid-January and mid-February), when huge crowds arrive at the Batu Caves. Originally intended to be a day of penance for past sins, it has now become a major tourist attraction, attracting Malaysians and foreigners alike each year.

The start of Thaipusam is marked by the departure at dawn, from KL's Sri Maha Mariamman Temple, of a **golden chariot** bearing a statue of Subramaniam. Thousands of devotees follow on foot as it makes its seven-hour procession to the caves. As part of their penance – and in a trance-like state – devotees carry numerous types of **kavadi** ("burdens" in Tamil), the most popular being milk jugs decorated with peacock feathers placed on top of the head, which are often connected to the penitents' flesh by hooks. Others wear wooden frames with sharp protruding spikes, which are carried on the back and hooked into the skin, while trident-shaped skewers are placed through some devotees' tongues and cheeks. This rather grisly procession has its origins in India, where most of Lord Subramaniam's temples were situated on high ridges that pilgrims would walk up, carrying heavy pitchers or pots. At Batu Caves, the climb up to the main chamber expresses the idea that you cannot reach God without expending effort.

Once at the caves, the Subramaniam statue is placed in a tent before being carried up to the **Temple Cave**, where devotees participate in ceremonies and rituals to Subramaniam and Ganesh. Things climax with a celebration for Rama, which involves milk from the *kavadi* vessels being spilt as an offering; incense and camphor are burned as the bearers unload their devotional burdens.

Extra buses run to the caves during Thaipusam – make sure you get there early (around 7am) for a good view. Numerous vendors sell food and drink, but it's a good idea to take water and snacks with you, as the size of the crowd is horrendous.

Putrajaya Wetlands Park. The enormous lake, popular for watersports, is also well worthy of a wander or a bike ride (there is bicycle rental desk inside the Botanical Gardens), and you can take in the Millennium Monument along the way – inspired by the Washington Monument in Washington DC, it is 68m tall and depicts various milestones in Malaysia's history.

Botanical Gardens

Persiaran Sultan Sallahuddin Abdul Aziz Shah • Free • http://facebook.com/tamanbotaniputrajaya

Putrajaya's **Botanical Gardens** house a wealth of beautifully maintained green spaces and structures, including a Moroccan pavilion with exquisite *zellige* (Moroccan mosaics), the Sun Garden with its enormous sundial and the short but worthwhile canopy walk. Avoid visiting in the middle of the day, as it'll be unbearably humid. The views out across the lake to the Putra Mosque and beyond are fabulous. Look out for the *Putrajaya Seafood Restaurant* on the shore of the lake, which is a good place to settle down at sunset for a decent dinner and a visual treat.

Putra Mosque

Persiaran Persekutuan • Free • http://masjidputra.gov.my

The gleaming **Putra Mosque** is said to be one of only four **pink mosques** in the world. Not luridly pink like some of the others (such as Dimaukom Mosque in the Philippines), it was made with rose-coloured graite, and its various domes look quite beautiful on their lakeside perch.

Putrajaya Wetlands Park

Persiaran Persekutuan • Free • http://ppj.gov.my

Constructed in 1998, the two-square-kilometre Putrajaya Wetlands Park transformed an oil palm plantation into a thriving ecosystem – the first man-made wetland in Malaysia and the largest constructed freshwater wetland in the region. The site has a few informational displays at the Interpretive Centre, but the main draw here is the flamingo lake, where you can spot egrets and cinnamon bitterns.

ARRIVAL AND DEPARTURE PUTRAJAYA

By train Putrajaya Sentral, on the KLIA Transit line, is the main form of access to Putrajaya. From here there are trains every 30min north to KL (26min), or south to KLIA (16min).

ACCOMMODATION

DoubleTree by Hilton Putrajaya 2 Jalan P5; http://hilton.com. Lakeside accommodation that can be quite affordable for this branch of the Hilton chain. Pleasant pools will allow you to admire the lake while swimming in cleaner water, while the rooms and on-site restaurants are also top notch; it's also a great place from which to take an early-morning walk around the lake. $$$

Batu Caves

13km north of KL on Jalan Batu Caves, roughly midway between the junctions with Jalan Ipoh and the E8 • Free • KTM Komuter train from KL Sentral to Batu Caves (every 15–30min; 30min)

The **Batu Caves** sit right on the northern edge of Greater KL, where forested limestone thumbs poke out of a ridge of hills in the suburb of Gombak. In 1891, ten years after the caves were brought into the limelight by American explorer William Hornaby, local Indian dignitaries convinced the British administration that the caves were ideal places in which to worship (probably because their geography was reminiscent of the sacred Himalayas). Soon ever-increasing numbers of devotees were visiting the caves to pray at the shrine established here to Lord Murugan, also known as **Lord Subramaniam**; later the temple complex was expanded to include a shrine to the elephant-headed deity **Ganesh**. Although the caves are always packed with

> **THE FRIM–BATU CAVES–ORANG ASLI MUSEUM CIRCUIT**
>
> The proximity of FRIM, the Orang Asli Museum and the Batu Caves to **Middle Ring Road II** (also known as Jalan Batu Caves) makes it feasible for drivers to visit all three in a day. From KL, either take the E8 highway, which intersects Jalan Batu Caves, or use Jalan Ipoh, which starts at Chow Kit and meets Jalan Batu Caves 4km west of the E8. FRIM is west of Jalan Ipoh, the Orang Asli Museum close to the E8, and the caves are in between the two.
>
> Unfortunately, no buses connect the three, but you could use taxis or Grab to reach FRIM and the Orang Asli Museum from Batu Caves.

visitors, by far the most atmospheric way to visit is to join the thousands of devotees attending the annual three-day **Thaipusam festival** in late January or early February (see box, page 101).

Arriving at the site, you can't miss the immense staircase leading up into the limestone crags, and the gigantic golden statue of **Lord Murugan**, the Hindu god of war, to one side; it's claimed to be the tallest such statue in the world. A number of minor temples stand at ground level, but most visitors head straight up the 272 steps to the caves, pausing only to catch their breath or take photos of the marauding macaques who make their presence all too known.

Ramayana Cave
Charge

A minute's walk west of the Lord Murugan statue, past a blue 15m statue of Hanuman, lies the elaborately decorated and vividly illuminated **Ramayana Cave**, which depicts the story of the life of Lord Rama. The tale includes Rama's fight to rescue his wife Sita from Ravana, the demon king; one of the focal points of the temple is an enormous statue of a sleeping Kumbhakarna, brother of Ravana and a famous warrior in the battle. As the cave is still a relatively recent addition – the temple was only consecrated in 2001 – it's much less busy than the main cave complex, though it's perhaps more impressive thanks to its intricate carvings and absorbing storyline.

Subramaniam Swamy Temple
Free

At the top of the main staircase, there's a clear view through to the **Subramaniam Swamy Temple**, devoted to Lord Subramaniam and another deity, Rama. It's set deep in a cave (known today as **Temple Cave**) that's around 100m high and 80m long, the walls of which are lined with idols representing the six lives of Lord Subramaniam. In a chamber at the back, a statue of Rama, adorned with silver jewellery and a silk sarong, is said to watch over the wellbeing of all immigrants. If you want to look closely at this inner sanctum, the temple staff will mark a small red dot on your forehead, giving you the spiritual right to enter.

Royal Selangor Visitor Centre

11km northeast of central KL on Jalan Usahawan 6, Setapak Jaya • Free • http://royalselangor.com • LRT Kelana Jaya line from Dang Wangi to Wangsa Maju (every 20min; 25min), then a taxi (5min)

Pewter is something of a souvenir cliché in Malaysia, though the platters, mugs and other objects found in the **Royal Selangor Visitor Centre** still make elegant gifts. You wouldn't have been able to call this place a visitor centre a few years ago, but following a revamp it now offers the whole package, with exhibits on the origins of pewter and smithing, hands-on craft workshops and free guided tours. If you're tempted to buy something but don't fancy carrying it back from Setapak Jaya, the centre also has stores in Pavilion, Bangsar and Suria KLCC malls.

Orang Asli Museum

20km north of KL on Jalan Pahang Lama, Gombak • Free • http://jakoa.gov.my • Best to take a taxi or Grab (35min)

Run by the government's Department for Orang Asli Development, the **Orang Asli Museum** aims to present a portrait of the various groups of Orang Asli, former nomadic hunter-gatherers in the jungle who are now largely resident in rural settlements. A large map of the Peninsula in the foyer makes it clear that the Orang Asli can be found, in varying numbers, in just about every state, and that surprises some visitors, who see little sign of them during their travels. Besides collections of the fishing nets, guns and blowpipes the Orang Asli use as part of their traditional lives, the museum also has photographs of Orang Asli press-ganged by the Malay and British military to fight Communist guerrillas in the 1950s. Other displays describe the changes forced more recently on the Orang Asli – some positive, like the development of health and school networks, others less encouraging, like the erosion of the family system as young men drift off to look for seasonal work.

Hidden in an annexe to the rear of the building, examples of traditional handicrafts include the **head carvings** made by the Mah Meri Indigenous group from the swampy region on the borders of Selangor and Negeri Sembilan, and the Jah Hut from the slopes of Gunung Benom in central Pehang. Around 50cm high, the carvings show stylized, fierce facial expressions, and are fashioned from a strong, heavy hardwood. They still have religious significance – the most common image used, the *moyang*, represents the spirit of the ancestors.

Kuala Selangor

70km northwest of KL • Buses to Kuala Selangor leave from KL's Pudu Sentral station daily every 30min (2hr; last bus back at 7.45pm), and also from the TBS terminal (2 daily; 2hr)

Coastal **KUALA SELANGOR** lies close to the junction of routes 5 and 54 on the banks of the Selangor River. A former royal town, today it's a small, sleepy affair; the chief reason visitors continue to come here is to see the river's **fireflies**, which glow spectacularly in the early evening.

This natural spectacle appeared at one stage to be in terminal decline: the fireflies' mangrove habitat was rapidly being cleared away, and the river was becoming more and more polluted. Government intervention seems to have stabilized things, and you stand a reasonable chance of enjoying a decent light show, **weather** permitting – the flies don't perform in rain. It's easiest to see Selangor's highlights on an evening firefly

> ### FIREFLY TRIPS
>
> Kuala Selangor's **fireflies**, known as *kelip-kelip* in Malay, are actually 6mm-long beetles of a kind found between India and Papua New Guinea. During the day, the fireflies rest on blades of grass or in palm trees behind the river's mangrove swamps, and after sunset they move to the mangroves themselves, the males attracting mates with **synchronized flashes** of light at a rate of three bursts per second. Females flash back at males to indicate interest and initiate mating. Typically, the most successful males are those that flash brightest and fly fastest.
>
> Boats leave on 30min evening firefly-spotting trips from two locations several kilometres from town: **Bukit Belimbing**, where you'll find fibreglass boats run by *Firefly Park Resort*, on the north bank across the river bridge; and **Kampung Kuantan**, where you can hop on a manually steered wooden boat from the south bank. There are no buses to either of the jetties, so taxis from Kuala Selangor get away with inflated prices. It's important to remain quiet when watching the firefly display and not to use flash photography, as it scares the insects away.
>
> It's possible to take firefly tours all the way from KL with Han Travel (http://han.travel), or you can combine the fireflies trip with a **tour** that takes in the Batu Caves, a batik factory, a pewter factory, and a chocolate outlet, including return transport, all fees and a seafood dinner.

package tour from KL (see box), though you can visit independently if you're prepared to stay overnight.

Fort Altingsburg
Free

All that remains of Kuala Selangor's glorious past are the remnants of two forts overlooking the town. The largest, **Fort Altingsburg**, recalls an era when this part of the country changed hands, bloodily, on several occasions. Originally called Fort Melawati, Altingsberg was built by local people during the reign of Sultan Ibrahim of Selangor in the eighteenth century, and later captured by the Dutch (who renamed it) as part of an attempt to wrestle the tin trade from the sultans. The fortress was partly destroyed during local skirmishes in the Selangor Civil War (1867–73). Within its grounds is a cannon, reputed to be from the Dutch era, and a rock used for executions. **Bukit Melawati**, the hill on which the fort is based, also holds a **lighthouse** and a British colonial resthouse, and has hundreds of (mostly) friendly monkeys on the hunt for fruit.

Kuala Selangor Nature Park
Below Fort Altingsburg • Charge • http://kuala-selangor.com • The park is a 500m walk from Bukit Melawati (follow signs for Taman Alam); you can also get here on the buses that run up Route 5 from Klang – ask to be let off at the park, and you'll be dropped at a petrol station, from where the park is 200m up Jalan Klinik

The **Kuala Selangor Nature Park**, which encompasses mud flats, mangroves and a small patch of forest, is host to around 150 species of birds, with thirty more migratory species passing through, as well as silverleaf monkeys, which live in the forest, and crabs and fish in the mangroves. Clearly marked trails take between 30min and 1hr 30min to walk.

ACCOMMODATION AND EATING — KUALA SELANGOR

Firefly Park Resort Jalan Haji Omar, Kampung Bukit Belimbing; http://facebook.com/FireflyParkResort. Slick accommodation with simple, modern, a/c en-suite chalets for four. There's a BBQ area and Chinese seafood restaurant, with breakfast upon request (weekends only). Rates drop Mon–Thurs. $$

Jetty Seafood Restaurant Pasir Penambang, off Jalan Feri Lama; 01 7349 7713. Situated amid a group of similar waterside seafood restaurants, this one stands out for its bright red seating and fresh seafood, including crab in a variety of sauces. $$

Nature Park Chalets Taman Alam, Kuala Selangor Nature Park; 03 3289 2294. A mix of basic chalet and hostel accommodation. Book in advance, as school groups can fill the place up. There's nowhere to eat nearby, so it's best to bring everything you think you'll need. $

Ketam Island
50km west of KL • From KL Sentral, take a KTM Komuter train to Klang (1hr 15min); boats to Pulau Ketam Village via Sungai Lima leave from Klang's Terminal Penumpang South Port, opposite the train station

The moment you set foot aboard ferries to **KETAM ISLAND** (Crab Island), you'll find yourself in a kind of parallel universe: this is Chinese day-tripper land, with videos of Chinese karaoke clips and soap operas blaring from the on-board screens. The majority of Ketam's five thousand inhabitants are Teochew and Hokkien Chinese, who traditionally live almost entirely by fishing from their low, flat, mangrove-encrusted island. Every house is built on stilts above the sand, and practically every street is a concrete walkway or boardwalk raised in the same fashion. Aside from the chance to eat tasty, inexpensive seafood, you'd visit Ketam mainly for a slightly surreal break from KL's pace, and a couple of good places to stay if you like peace and quiet.

From the jetty, walk past the mosque towards Jalan Tepi Sungai and Jalan Besar, which are lined with grocers, general stores, and stalls and restaurants selling **seafood** – including, of course, crab. Beyond a shop selling Buddhist paraphernalia is a central square, where you'll find the **Hock Leng Temple**, as well as a small grotto containing a representation of Kwan Yin, the Goddess of Mercy, looking decidedly Madonna-like with a halo of red electric lights. Beyond, you'll come to a residential area of concrete and wooden houses, nearly all with their front doors left wide open. There's lots of refuse littering the mud flats beneath unfortunately, but you'll still get to see plenty of shrines outside the homes as well as netting containing seafood that's been left out to dry.

ARRIVAL AND TOURS   KETAM ISLAND

By ferry Ferries (every 45min; 45min) depart Klang Mon–Fri 8.45am–6.30pm, Sat 8.45am–7.10pm and return Mon–Fri 8.45am–6.30pm, Sat 8.45am–6pm.

By tour Not far from the jetty, Greenway (012 322 5333) offers packages including daytime fishing trips, and an overnight stay at a floating fish farm (minimum three people).

ACCOMMODATION AND EATING

Jia Jia Near the river. This place is similar to other places to eat nearby, but is just that little bit livelier. It offers excellent seafood omelettes, prawns, crab, noodles soups and generic stir-fries. $

Sea Lion S3 Jalan Merdeka; http://sealion.com.my. Near the jetty, in a distinctive yellow and white building, this simple establishment has a nice deck overlooking the water. The cheapest rooms are windowless with fans, while the others have a/c and a bit more space. You can book good-value packages here, such as one night's accommodation, an evening meal and a fishing trip. $

Fraser's Hill
98km northeast of KL

Set 1500m up in the forested Titiwangsa mountains, the collection of colonial bungalows comprising **FRASER'S HILL** was established after World War I as one of Malaysia's earliest **hill stations**, a retreat for administrators seeking relief from the torrid lowland climate. Though less visited than the much larger Cameron Highlands to the north, Fraser's Hill boasts excellent **nature trails** and superb **birdwatching**; some 250 species have been recorded here, and the Fraser's Hill International Bird Race each June (http://facebook.com/fhintbirdrace) sees teams competing to clock up as many as possible within a day. Even if you don't have the slightest interest in twitching, the hill remains a good getaway from the heat and hubbub of KL, and at weekends (when accommodation prices shoot up) it draws families from as far away as Singapore.

Sprawling amid a handful of wooded slopes, the hill station focuses on a T-junction at the south end of a **golf course**. *Puncak Inn* (see page 107) is located here, along with a distinctive **clock tower**, a post office and a bank, and the roads and trails head off in all directions from here to clusters of hidden bungalows and cabins.

Trails

The easiest targets for a stroll are **Allan's Water**, a small lake less than 1km from the clock tower, and **Jeriau Waterfall**, 4km north via *Ye Olde Smokehouse*, where the convincing English country decor and **cream teas** are a strong inducement to pause for a breather. Another good walk involves taking Jalan Lady Guillemard east to the loop road, Jalan Girdle; this leads to the most remote section of the hill station, bordering

---

COMMUNISTS ON THE HILL

During the Emergency in the 1950s, the mountainous jungle at Fraser's Hill provided perfect cover for some of the Communist guerrillas' secret camps, from where they launched strikes on British-owned plantations and neighbouring towns.

If you approach Fraser's Hill via Kuala Kubu Bharu (known as KKB), due north of KL, roughly halfway up you'll see a sign, "Emergency Historical Site", marking the spot where **Sir Henry Gurney**, the British High Commissioner for Malaya at the height of the communist insurgency in 1951, was ambushed and killed. The guerrillas hadn't known how important their quarry was: their aim had been only to steal guns, ammunition and food, but when Gurney strode towards them demanding that they put down their weapons, they opened fire.

Ulu Tramin Forest Reserve, though completing the entire circle only takes around ninety minutes. Even most of the **longer trails** can be covered in less than two hours; indeed it would only take a couple of days to cover them all. Signage, however, can be spotty – it's best to talk to the tourist office about your route before you set out, and consider hiring a guide. The trails can get slippery in wet weather, so be sure to wear proper footgear; leeches (see page 45) have also been known to be a problem.

The **Hemmant trail** begins on Jalan Genting close to the mosque, and snakes along the edge of the golf course just within the jungle. At its far end, you can turn left and either walk on to Jalan Lady Maxwell, or continue as far as the Bishop's House, where you can pick up the **Bishop's trail** en route to the **Maxwell trail**, at which point you can either leave the trail by turning right up the hill and returning to town via Jalan Lady Maxwell, or continue another hour until it reaches Jalan Quarry.

ARRIVAL AND INFORMATION FRASER'S HILL

By car Fraser's Hill is reached by a single-lane road that branches off Route 55, which connects Kuala Kubu Bharu (KKB, on Route 1) and Raub (Route 8) at a spot called the Gap. In theory, this road takes summit-bound traffic only, while downhill traffic uses a road that joins the KKB–Raub road 1km northeast. When either one is closed by landslips, however, traffic alternates hourly in each direction on the other. The entire journey to or from KL typically takes 2hr or so. There is no fuel station at Fraser's Hill (the nearest is out east on the highway), so be sure to fill up in KL.

By train and taxi Catch a Komuter train (blue Seremban line north) from KL to Kuala Kubu Bharu (KKB; 1hr 15min); note that not all trains stop here, so make sure you ask before boarding. From KKB, you'll have to take a taxi to Fraser's Hill (45min) – it might be better to simply take a Grab from the centre of KL.

Tourist information The tourist office is based inside the *Puncak Inn* at the centre of the hill station (daily 8am–11pm; 09 362 2007); they can provide maps, advise on current trail conditions and put you in touch with local guides. For up-to-date information on hotel and guesthouse accommodation plus the local attractions and a handy rundown of all the trails, check http://fraserhill.info.

ACCOMMODATION

Accommodation in Fraser's Hill is mostly motel-like and geared towards families and groups, though some **bungalows** – either detached single-storey houses or small apartment blocks – are also available. Always book in advance, and expect rates quoted here to rise by as much as fifty percent at weekends and during holidays.

★ **Puncak Inn** Jalan Gap; http://puncakinn.com. The block of this tourist-office-run hotel is not the most inspiring in town, but this is one of the best places to stay in Fraser's Hill, featuring neat and tidy rooms with flowery curtains, heating and en-suite facilities. There is free wi-fi at reception, but not in the rooms. $$

Shahzan Inn Jalan Lady Gullemard; http://shahzaninn fraserhill.com. Located in a large white concrete block, this bland hotel consists of tiers of rooms ascending a terraced hillside. Rooms are a bit dated and don't have much personality, although they are spacious and pretty comfortable, and either look onto the garden or the town's golf course. $$

★ **The Smokehouse** Jalan Jeriau; http://thesmokehouse.my. Founded in 1937 as a resort for British servicemen who fought in World War I, this stereotypical English country inn offers fireside chairs and spacious rooms with four-poster beds, guaranteed to make the cool nights pass all the more blissfully. There's a good restaurant too (see below). Rates drop by around thirty percent on weekdays (though it still doesn't hurt to ask about discounts on weekends) and include a full English breakfast. $$$

EATING

Fraser's Hill doesn't offer much choice for eating: aside from the restaurant below, there's a central **food court** offering a mix of Malay, Indian and Chinese staples.

The Smokehouse Jalan Jeriau; http://thesmokehouse.my. This quaint hill resort is the epitome of British country living, with its charming conservatory and log fire lit on colder days. English afternoon tea is served in the garden, and includes freshly baked scones and home-made strawberry jam. The restaurant menu features traditional British staples such as roast beef and Yorkshire pudding, and chicken and mushroom pie. Things are fairly informal during the day, but it's best not to turn up in a T-shirt and shorts in the evening. $$$$

DIRECTORY

Banks There is a small branch of Maybank at the *Shahzan Inn*, where you can change money (Mon–Thurs 9.15am– 4.30pm, Fri 9.15am–4pm); there is also an ATM.

The west coast

110 Perak
130 Cameron Highlands
139 Penang
161 Kedah and Perlis

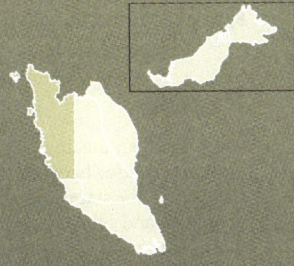

CHAIYA MANGALARAM THAI BUDDHIST TEMPLE

The west coast

It was on the west coast that the British got their first toehold in the Malay Peninsula, and long exposure to colonial influence has made it in many ways the most historical, multicultural and well-developed part of Malaysia today. Nowhere epitomizes this better than the island of Penang, whose capital, George Town, is arguably the most endearing city in the country, a fascinating conglomeration of century-old temples, museums and shophouses that set the backdrop to a modern and thriving art and café scene. Aside from Penang, the west coast's other major attraction is Langkawi, an island best known for its pricey resort hotels, although it also has plenty of budget places to stay along its southwestern beaches. The only other significant island off this coast, Pangkor, pales in comparison, but offers a more down-to-earth seaside experience.

Over on the mainland, the largest city is **Ipoh**, an excellent base for visiting **Cameron Highlands** (also easily reached from Kuala Lumpur), once a British hill station and still a popular refuge from the stifling heat of the plains. Ipoh's hinterland encompasses a number of attractions, including opportunities to take in Malay royal architecture or indulge in a spot of **white-water rafting**. Points of interest thin out inland, but it is possible to see the rainforest at the **Ulu Muda Eco Park** and the **Royal Belum State Park**, both bordering Thailand, and explore Malaysia's newest World Heritage Site, the archeologically important **Lenggong Valley** – though all are tricky to reach without your own transport.

GETTING AROUND — THE WEST COAST

By plane Penang has frequent flights to and from many other Malaysian and Southeast Asian cities, notably Singapore. Flights from KL, Singapore and Kuching, among others, serve Langkawi.

By car The west coast's major artery is the North–South Expressway (also referred to as "NSE", and north of KL, as the E1). Access to the east coast is mainly via Route 76, which links up with Route 4 (the East–West Highway) to Kelantan state in the northeast.

By bus Frequent express buses link the west coast with KL, the south and Singapore, and the east coast.

By train The West Coast Line operates frequent ETS (Electric Train Service) metre-gauge fast trains between Padang Besar on the Malaysia–Thai border and Gemas in Negeri Sembilan, where the line connects with the East Coast Line to Kota Bharu. Most trains stop at all major destinations, including Alor Setar, Butterworth, Taiping, Kuala Kangsar, Ipoh and Kuala Lumpur. There are also two convenient and cheaper KTM Komuter services between Butterworth and Padang Besar, and Bukit Mertajam (15min from Butterworth) to Taiping and Padang Rengas (for Kuala Kangsar).

By boat Langkawi is linked with southern Thailand by ferry, and there are also boat services between Langkawi and Penang, Kuala Kedah and Kuala Perlis.

Perak

Perak is still an unsung part of the country, but deserves to be more than just a pleasant corridor between the capital and the well-oiled tourist facilities of Penang and Langkawi. The state's topography is surprisingly diverse – monotonous coastal plains of mangrove and oil palm giving way inland to jagged limestone hills and the Titiwangsa mountain range – and so, in fact, are its attractions, not least its history. This was where the British began branching out from the Straits Settlements to open up the rest of the Peninsula, and consequently Perak's towns have relatively deep roots and more than a veneer of prosperity. Much of that wealth was founded on **tin** – a little ironic given that

DATARAN LANG (EAGLE LAND)

Highlights

❶ **Ipoh** Fast-gentrifying mining city of old, surrounded by intriguing attractions including cave temples and the bizarre Kellie's Castle. See page 113

❷ **Gopeng** This former mining town packs in history, nature, caving and excellent white-water rafting. See page 118

❸ **Pangkor Island** Laidback tropical island with some of the best beaches on the west coast. See page 119

❹ **Taiping** Traditional town with tranquil gardens and a mini hill station; Malaysia's largest mangrove reserve lies nearby. See page 124

❺ **Royal Belum State Park** Bordering Thailand, this unexpectedly fine nature reserve is a great place to spot *Rafflesia* flowers. See page 129

❻ **Cameron Highlands** Cool down amid the tea plantations and jungle trails of this former colonial hill station. See page 130

❼ **George Town** In Penang's capital, rows of old shophouses, elaborate temples and clan houses perfectly set the scene for an eclectic art and café culture. See page 141

❽ **Langkawi** This upmarket resort island on the Thai border features white-sand beaches and a cable car over the forested interior. See page 166

HIGHLIGHTS ARE MARKED ON THE MAP ON PAGE 112

perak is Malay for "silver". Malaysia was the world's biggest tin producer as recently as the 1970s, but a collapse in prices in the mid-1980s led to the country turning away from the metal. The old mining centres now offer inducements to visit that are anything but obviously linked to mining: grand Malay buildings at **Kuala Kangsar**, lush gardens and hill hiking at **Taiping**, and **whitewater rafting** at **Gopeng**. One hub for all these is the state capital, **Ipoh**, a likeable city with colonial architecture, a widely respected food scene and unique cave temples. In contrast are the laid-back resort island of **Pangkor** (Perak's most mainstream draw) and the **Royal Belum State Park** in the interior, which is an excellent place to spot stinky *Rafflesia* blooms. The most overlooked attraction is the UNESCO World Heritage Site at **Lenggong Valley**, also in the interior, with two clusters of archeological sites spanning 1.83 million years, and the oldest evidence of hominids outside of Africa.

Ipoh and around

IPOH was founded on the back of the great tin rush that kicked off in the 1880s, when major deposits were found in the area. The new settlement was sited at the highest navigable point on the **Kinta River**, a tributary of the Perak River – the Peninsula's second longest river – so was well placed for the ores to be collected for export. In common with the rest of the state, the city has seen a mini-exodus with the decline in mining, but in recent years people have been returning to invest in their hometown. Some three quarters of a million live here, making Ipoh the third-largest city in the country, its centre an architectural snapshot of how the tin boom helped create the diverse Malaysia of today, with the bonus of nearby sights such as outlying **Chinese cave temples**, set in dramatic surroundings, and the eccentric, anachronistic ruin of **Kellie's Castle**. With excellent places to stay and eat, Ipoh is also a good springboard for the rest of Perak, plus the Cameron Highlands.

Old town

Ipoh began on the west bank of the Kinta, an area still known as the **old town**. The padang and the colonial core lie in the northwest, the centrepiece being the grand **train station**, another Anglo-Moorish effort by A.B. Hubback (see page 64), completed in 1917. A plaque at the front of the station marks the spot where an old specimen of an upas tree (*pokok ipoh*) used to stand, until it collapsed in 2017. Once abundant in the area, the upas – which gave the city its name – produces a toxic sap that the Orang Asli used on blowpipe darts. Opposite the station and nearly as handsome is the old **City Hall** (another Hubback creation), restored but used only for receptions and functions. Just east, the elegant **Birch Memorial Clock Tower**, commemorating the first British Resident of Perak (see page 531), takes some of the sting out of the jarringly ugly 1960s **Masjid Negeri** nearby on Jalan Sultan Iskandar.

South of the colonial area is what might be deemed Ipoh's historic **Chinatown**, a tight grid of streets lined with pastel-coloured shophouses that are starting to gentrify as new cafés and restaurants spring up. Amid the still-mainly-Chinese shops selling dried goods and textiles, look out for narrow **Panglima Lane**, which was nicknamed Concubine Lane, as this back alley was where wealthy merchants kept their mistresses. There are some worthwhile **museums**, too.

Ho Yan Hor Museum

1 Jalan Bijeh Timah • Book tour on site • Free • http://hyhmuseum.com

The gorgeous little **Ho Yan Hor Museum** has features and displays pertaining to the most famous creation of Ipoh local, Dr. Ho Kai Cheong – Ho Yan Hor Tea, a herbal concoction still consumed today. It was invented in 1941, originally to help battle a local flu epidemic, and you'll get to try a free sample towards the end of the tour (and maybe buy a little to take home).

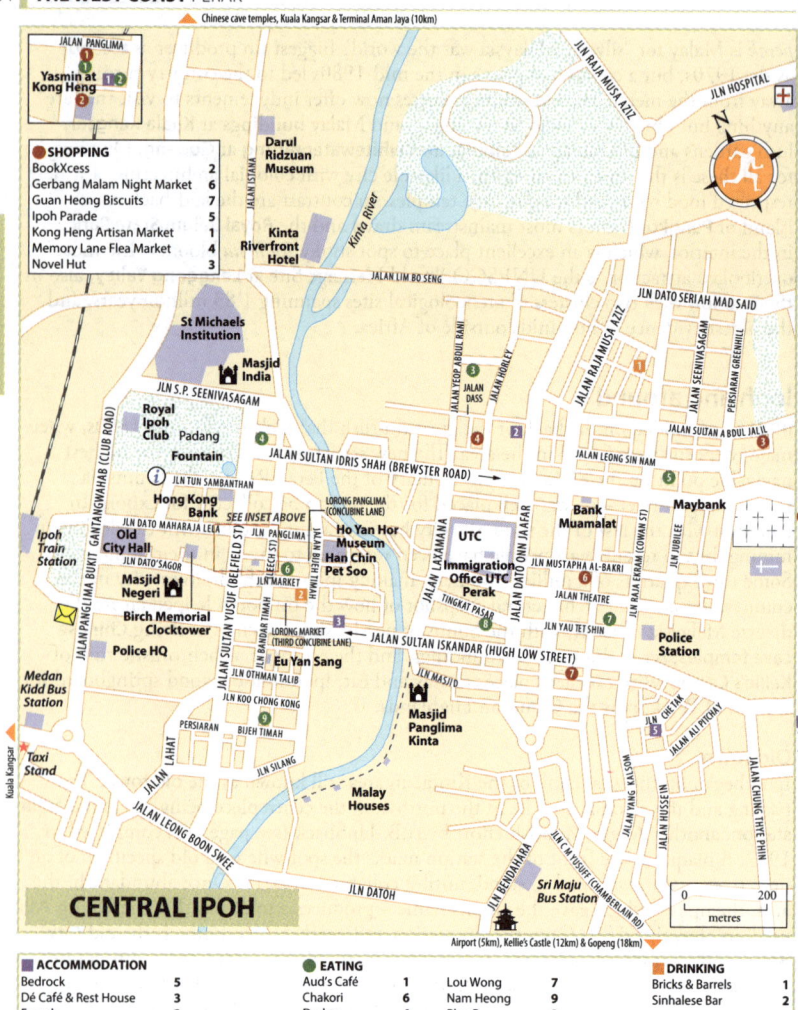

Han Chin Pet Soo

3 Jalan Bijeh Timah • Free, but donations welcome • http://ipohworld.org

Next door to the Ho Yan Hor Museum, and resplendent within a cream-coloured, Art Deco exterior, the three-storey **Han Chin Pet Soo** shophouse houses a reconstruction of a former mining tycoon's club; to visit, you'll have to book a tour online, though you may also be able to join tours at immediate notice if there are still places available. The guides are informative, and the Hakka antiques quite interesting.

Yasmin at Kong Heng

91 Jalan Sultan Yusof • Free • http://store.yasminahmad.com

At the very western end of Lorong Panglima, and tucked into the basement level of the highly interesting BookXcess (see page 117), the small **Yasmin At Kong Heng** gallery commemorates the legacy of legendary Malaysian film director Yasmin Ahmad, a voice for liberal and multicultural values.

New town

The tin boom had been under way for barely a decade when the cramped, wooden old town was devastated by fire in 1892. It underlined the pressing need for Ipoh to expand across the river, where hundreds of new shophouses were built on land once devoted to pig farms. But the tin price had slumped by the time this **new town** was completed in 1909, and the buildings remained vacant for some time – only to pick up when the old town's brothels were moved here.

Today there's little sense of a transition upon crossing the Kinta, except that the new town has some modern high-rises, almost totally absent in the old town. The only sight here is the pretty blue-and-white **Panglima Kinta mosque**, close to the river and named after a prominent line of local Malay chieftains.

Chinese cave temples

Caves begin 6km north of Ipoh • Free • Bus #35 from Medan Kidd to Perak Tong; bus #66 from Kampar or #T34 from Medan Kidd to Sam Poh Tong

Ipoh's sprawling suburbs and noisy outer roads are overlooked by craggy limestone peaks, some riddled with **caves** where Chinese workers established popular shrines. On the Kuala Kangsar Road, 6km north of Ipoh, **Perak Tong Temple** has a huge first chamber dominated by a 15m-high golden statue of the Buddha. At the back, a steep flight of 385 steps climbs up to a sort of balcony, with views over the Kinta valley. **Sam Poh Tong Temple** starts small, but opens into a beautiful tropical garden with turtle pond and a bright red-and-yellow pagoda encased by four lush limestone walls. Next to it, smaller **Ling Sen Tong** and **Nam Then Tong temples** have quirky and colourful statues, including characters from *Journey to the West*. From here it's 1.7km north off the main road and right into a housing area to **Kek Look Tong**. The massive cave entrance filled with statues and huge stalagmites leads to a large landscaped garden, bizarrely spoilt by a red-and-white transmission tower.

Kellie's Castle

Kinta Kelas Rubber Estate, 12km south of Ipoh • Charge • 010 505 4817 • Best to organise a taxi from Ipoh, including waiting while you look around; alternatively, take Perak Transit #T36 or #T35a from Medan Kidd to Batu Gajah (30min), from where you can either walk the remaining 4km on the clearly signposted A8 road, or take a taxi

Kellie's Castle symbolizes the prosperity achieved by many enterprising foreigners in the rubber and tin industries in the early 1900s. One of these was **William Kellie Smith**, a Scot who celebrated his success – and the birth of a long-desired son – by designing this extraordinary mansion. A flu epidemic in 1920 killed many of the Tamil workers; when work resumed, Smith embarked on a trip to Britain, but fell ill and died in Portugal, and the building was never completed.

Far from being a ruin, however, the mansion is a sort of tropical palace in apricot-coloured bricks, with a rectangular, off-centre tower. It incorporates a lift (the first in the Peninsula), underground tunnels only rediscovered in 2003, and rows of arched colonnades in Moorish style. Heavily influenced by Indian culture, Smith imported many of the bricks from Chennai (Madras) and even constructed an adjacent **Hindu temple** in thanks for the birth of his son.

ARRIVAL AND DEPARTURE — IPOH

Ipoh's compact **centre** has two major thoroughfares: Jalan Sultan Idris Shah, taking eastbound traffic, and westbound Jalan Sultan Iskandar. The **suburbs** are anything but compact, and the main bus station, Terminal Aman Jaya, is far north of the centre.

BY PLANE

Sultan Azlan Shah airport The airport is 5km southeast of the centre (http://ipoh.airport-authority.com). In theory, Perak Transit Bus #T37 and #T30 connect Terminal Aman Jaya to the airport and Medan Kidd bus station hourly

from 6am–9pm (30min); in reality, these buses stop at the airport roughly every 2hr, and only until 6.30pm. It's generally best to go by taxi.
Destinations Johor Bahru (1–2 daily; 1hr 20min); Singapore (2–3 daily; 1hr 20min).

BY TRAIN
Train station Ipoh station is on Jalan Panglima Bukit Gantang Wahab, at the western end of the centre (05 254 7987), an easy hop from most hotels by taxi, and quite walkable from some.
Destinations Alor Setar (5 daily; 2hr 20min); Butterworth (6 daily; 1hr 40min); Gemas (2 daily; 5hr); Kuala Kangsar (9 daily; 30min); Kuala Lumpur (16 daily; 2hr–2hr 30min); Padang Besar (5 daily; 3hr); Sungai Petani (5 daily; 1hr 50min); Seremban (2 daily; 4hr); Taiping (11 daily; 45min).

BY BUS
Ipoh's main bus station, Terminal Aman Jaya, is inconveniently located nearly 10km north of the centre. From here, hourly Perak Transit (http://peraktransit.com.my) buses #T37 and #T30a run to Medan Kidd bus station (40min), a 10min walk south of the train station in the centre, where local buses service Perak's satellite towns and the airport. Note that most services dwindle after 6.30pm.
Medan Kidd destinations Gopeng (#T34; every 1hr 30min; 45min); Kuala Kangsar (#35; every 20–30min; 1hr 15min); Taiping (every 45min; 1hr 45min).
Terminal Aman Jaya destinations Alor Setar (8 daily; 3hr 30min); Butterworth (at least 8 daily; 2hr 30min); Cameron Highlands (3 daily; 2hr 30min); Johor Bahru (4 daily; 8hr); Kangar (5 daily; 4hr); KLIA (8 daily; 3hr 30min); Kota Bharu (2 daily; 8hr); Kuala Lumpur (1–3 hourly; 2hr 30min–3hr 15min); Kuala Perlis (3 daily; 3hr 45min); Kuantan (3 daily; 8hr); Lenggong (hourly; 1hr 45min); Lumut (8 daily; 1hr 15min); Melaka (at least 6 daily; 5hr); Penang (every 2hr; 2hr 30min); Seremban (several daily; 4hr); Singapore (4 daily; 9hr 30min); Taiping (hourly; 1hr 30min); Sungai Petani (4 daily; 3hr).

GETTING AROUND AND INFORMATION
By taxi Grab (http://grab.com/my) is available in Ipoh, and better value than the regular taxis, many of which park opposite the Medan Kidd bus station.
Tourist office Ipoh City Council runs an information centre at Jalan Tun Sambanthan, by the Padang (Mon–Thurs 8am–1pm & 2–5pm, Fri 8am–12.15pm & 2.45–5pm; 05 208 3155). Although staff dispense brochures liberally, their practical knowledge is variable and they may not keep to their opening hours.

ACCOMMODATION   SEE MAP PAGE 114

★ **Bedrock** 13–15 Jalan Che Tak; http://bedrockhotelipoh.com. Extremely amiable place offering ten stylish and larger-than-life en-suite rooms, with coffee machines and water purifiers, housed in a dark-hued boutique hotel with a unique Chinese Scholar's Rock theme. The breakfasts are great too. $$$

Dé Café & Rest House 35 Jalan Sultan Iskandar; http://instagram.com/decafeandresthouse. Shabby-chic hostel with giant dorms – the female one has ten beds, and the mixed one a whopping eighteen capsule berths, and none of them are as cheap as you might expect. However, the beds are pretty plush, and they've thought of the little things – a hairdryer in the female toilets, for example. $

French 62 Jalan Datuk Onn Jaafar; http://frenchhotel.com.my. Simple mid-budget place, set in a pleasant area east of the river. It's an unusual hotel, one which may initially look like a shop, and has café-like elements too; the rooms are hotel-like enough, though some have the dreaded modern frosted glass bathrooms. $$

RPGC Garden Off Route 1; 05 547 3299. If you're prepared to stay out of the centre, this is an intriguing budget choice – a golf club hotel with large rooms, a modicum of class, and prices that are usually set within backpacker range. Plus, of course, you can go out and whack a few balls around. $$

Sekeping Kong Heng 75 Jalan Panglima; http://sekeping.com. Once a hostel for travelling troupes of Chinese opera performers, *Sekeping Kong Heng* seeded the old town's gentrification when it was artfully restored in shabby-chic style. Rooms are charming, and the new wing next door boasts a swimming pool overlooking the old town. $$$

EATING   SEE MAP PAGE 114

Although most of Ipoh's incredible range of restaurants and bars are in the burgeoning **suburbs**, there's a reasonable choice in the low-key centre as well. The numerous *kopitiam* joints of the **old town** are pretty foolproof for decent, cheap meals, though few are open at night.

★ **Aud's Café** 97 Jalan Sultan Yusof; http://helloaudscafe.wixsite.com. A whole row of places here have tried to nail the modern-meets-old school look, but this has done it best of all. Housed in an old merchant house (some of the old painted writing is still on the window), they serve a variety of caffeinated drinks, plus mains such as kimchi rice, eggs benedict, pulled pork sandwiches and smoothies – hipster heaven. $$

Chakori 35 Jalan Market; http://facebook.com/chakori2. Gorgeously decorated inside and out, this is just the spot if you're need of a sugar fix – croiffles, cakes and the like, plus

delicious gelato (try the black sesame flavour). $\overline{\$\$}$
Durbar 2 Jalan Sultan Idris Shah; http://facebook.com/DurbarAtFMS. If you'd like something non-local, consider heading to this pale yellow building of 1906 vintage. Meals include fish and chips, oxtail soup, and Chateaubriand steak, though there are plenty of Malay and Chinese choices too; some just pop in for dessert, and some of them are excellent. $\overline{\$\$\$}$
Foh San 51 Jalan Leong Sin Nam; http://fohsan.com.my. On two open-sided floors, this palatial restaurant is a fun place to come for a *dim sum* breakfast – order from counters packed with dumplings, *pow*, steamed sticky rice, custard tarts and other morsels. Some dishes are cooked to order, especially from noon when the lunch menu kicks in. $\overline{\$\$}$
Haji Yahaya Jalan Dato Onn Jaafar. Marvellous Malay joint serving fried chicken and fish, curries, stews, noodles and rice – choose from *nasi kunyit* (turmeric rice), or the purplish Kelantan-style *nasi kerabu*. $\overline{\$}$
Lou Wong 49 Jalan Yau Tet Shin; 05 254 4199. Ipoh residents wax lyrical over – of all things – local bean sprouts, supposedly plumper, crunchier and sweeter than any elsewhere in the country. The favoured way to have them is stir-fried, with a separate plate of steamed sliced chicken and a bowl of noodles; this is the most popular of a cluster of restaurants serving it, though some opt for the delicious meatballs instead of chicken. $\overline{\$}$
Nam Heong 2 Jalan Bandar Timah; 012 588 8766. A no-frills local institution, packed with Chinese customers who come to its various stalls for the delicious white coffee, egg tarts, *chee cheong fun* and freshly baked Portuguese egg tarts. $\overline{\$}$
★ **Plan B** 75 Jalan Panglima; http://thebiggroup.co/plan-b. Part of *Sekeping Kong Heng* hotel, this glossy restaurant/café revels in high ceilings and glass panelling. It's especially busy at weekends, when people come for brunch, but just as worthwhile are the fusion-inspired mains, excellent pastries and cakes, and the decent selection of beers, ciders and wines. $\overline{\$\$\$}$
Thin Hei 22 Jalan Dass; 011 2152 4866. The best bet in town for vegetarians, serving up Chinese stir-fries and lots of fake soy/gluten "meats", including an excellent spicy mock-mutton. $\overline{\$\$}$

DRINKING
SEE MAP PAGE 114

Bricks & Barrels 28–30 Jalan Lau Ek Ching; http://facebook.com/BricksAndBarrels. The city centre's pioneer bar, where the decor is themed around exposed-brick walls and beer barrels, offers a wide range of draught beers. Bench seating ensures everyone can have a convivial chinwag, and there's live music most nights from 10pm.

★ **Sinhalese Bar** 2 Jalan Bijeh Timah; 05 241 2235. There's no better place in the old town for a drink than this boxy institution, opened in the 1930s, with saloon-style doors, lace curtains and what look like bathroom tiles on the extremely pink walls. Come for cheap, cold beer to a backdrop of Tamil pop music and the whirring of fans overhead.

SHOPPING
SEE MAP PAGE 114

MARKETS
Gerbang Malam Night Market Jalan Dato Tahwil Azar. This market sells a bit of everything from clothes to trinkets, and it's all dirt-cheap. Daily 6pm–midnight.
Kong Heng Artisan Market Jalan Panglima; http://bit.ly/KongHeng. An old-town market offering handmade crafts and trendy trinkets. Daily 10am–5pm.
Memory Lane Flea Market Jalan Lim Bo Seng. Full of memorabilia, this morning market is a treasure trove for those looking for bargain antiques. Sun 6am–1pm.

MALLS
Ipoh Parade Eastern end of Jalan Sultan Idris Shah; http://ipoh.parade.com.my. One downtown mall worth browsing for its many shops and restaurant chains, and a Cineplex.

BOOKSHOPS
★ **BookXcess** 91 Jalan Sultan Yusof; http://bookxcess.com. This place was once a bank, as evidenced by the vaults in the basement (which is also home to the Yasmin at Kong Heng exhibition; see page 114). The whole place has been decorated with great attention, and there are plenty of English-language books to look through too.
Novel Hut 87 Jalan Abdul Jalil; http://bit.ly/NovelHut. Good selection of new and secondhand books and magazines.

GIFTS
Guan Heong Biscuits 160 Jalan Sultan Iskandar; http://guanheong.com. Century-old traditional Chinese shop, good for chicken floss and lotus-paste biscuits.

DIRECTORY

Banks There are Maybank and Bank Muamalat ATMs on Jalan Sultan Idris Shah.
Hospital Jalan Hospital (05 208 5000, http://hrpb.moh.gov.my).
Police Jalan Panglima Bukit Gantang Wahab, south of the train station (05 245 1562).
Visa extensions The Immigration Department is on the third floor of the UTC market complex on Jalan Laxamana (05 241 3524).

Gopeng

On Route 1, some 20km southeast of Ipoh, **GOPENG** was one of the first of the Kinta Valley rubber and tin boomtowns. Today it's a charming village set around a compact central square, and backed by a swathe of forest. Gopeng draws visitors for the nearby **Gaharu Tea Valley**, though **whitewater rafting** down the **Kampar River** (rated Grade I–III depending on how rainy it's been) is also a popular, with a cluster of accommodation close by. Although it's possible to see Gopeng on a day-trip, many visitors stay at least a night, combining rafting with a jungle hike or a visit to the nearby **caves** of **Tempurung** and **Kandu**, the latter featuring a 90m-long in-cave zipline.

Gopeng Heritage House and Gopeng Museum

House 6 Jalan Sungai Itek, main square • **Museum** 28 Jalan Eu Kong, main square • Free, but donation expected • http://facebook.com/MuziumGopengOfficial

Gopeng Heritage House, a beautiful three-storey wooden shophouse with a charming café, all choreographically furnished in the way of old, offers a feel for the town's past. On the opposite side of the main square, the exhibits at **Gopeng Museum** tell a lot about the impact of tin and rubber on local history.

Gaharu Tea Valley

About 3km east of the town centre along Jalan Sungai Itek • Free

A few kilometres east of town, the **Gaharu Tea Valley** is best approached by car. This impressive, though touristy, agarwood tea plantation is encased by an odd 3m-high replica of the Great Wall of China.

ARRIVAL AND ACTIVITIES — GOPENG

By bus Bus #66 from Ipoh's Medan Kidd bus station drops you on Jalan Pasar in the heart of the old town. Although you could attempt to trudge to the river (where all the rafting operators and accommodation are) from here, it's far better to arrange for your hotel or tour company to collect you. Alternatively, take a Kampar-bound bus from Medan Kidd station and get off at the Sungai Itek junction along Road 1 (look out for the Nomad Adventure signboard), from where it's about 2km to the river. Gopeng's small long-distance bus station, in walking distance from the Heritage House, has useful connections to Kuala Lumpur and the south; hopping on a bus from here can save you backtracking 30km to Terminal Aman Jaya in Ipoh.

Destinations Ipoh (every 1hr 30min; 45min); Johor Bahru (5 daily; 9hr); KLIA (several daily; 4hr); Kuala Lumpur (9 daily; 3hr); Kuantan (2 daily; 7hr); Melaka (2 daily; 5hr); Seremban (2 daily; 5hr); Singapore (5 daily; 10hr).

Activities Most visitors come on combined accommodation/activity deals, for which it's best to book in advance. Nomad Adventure (http://nomadadventure.com), Gopeng's first and most established operator, is recommended. Book ahead to organize pick up in town, as their headquarters is 7km away next to the river. Rafting trips take around 4–5hr; a full-day package adds a second activity (minimum five people), such as a visit to one of the caves, or abseiling down a waterfall. From Nomad Adventure, it's a 2km walk to Tempurung Cave, with paths branching off to the riverside and into the surrounding jungle.

ACCOMMODATION

Gopeng's hotels are, inconveniently, 7km away in the river valley, reached by an informally signed narrow country road via Kampung Sungai Itek. If you are not driving, your accommodation should be able to pick you up in Gopeng town, connected to Ipoh by regular buses, or you can catch a taxi or Grab from Ipoh.

Adeline Villa Along Jalan Sungai Itek, before Kampung Ulu Geruntum; http://adelinevilla.com. *Adeline* offers slick timber-and-glass solar-powered "villas", with a/c and en-suite rooms and dorms, alongside a "rest house" complex of shared-bathroom dorms in bamboo and rattan buildings. Everyone eats together in the restaurant, where meals can be basic or fancy depending on the chef's mood. You can add on rafting and other activities, or go for a package. Rates are full board per person. $$$

★ **Nomad Earth Camp** Off Route 1, roughly 2km inland along Jalan Hussin; http://nomadadventure.com. Nomad Adventure's headquarters offers a collection of eco-friendly en-suite chalets, simple treehouses and dorms next to the river. Meals are consumed in a convivial common area, next to which are the shared bathrooms. Groups can rent out full units. Rates include dinner and breakfast. $$

Pangkor

The laidback island of **Pangkor**, barely 10km long, is known to every student of Malaysian history as the place where the **Pangkor Treaty** was signed, leading to the creation of the Resident system by which the British gradually brought every sultanate in the Peninsula under their wing (see page 531). Now it's a popular, affordable weekend beach retreat for families, taking advantage of the ease of getting here from cities like KL and Ipoh: there are frequent ferries from **Lumut**, a small port and naval base 80km southwest of Ipoh.

Visitors mostly stay on the beaches of the island's west coast, at **Pasir Bogak** or **Teluk Nipah**. The islanders are concentrated in a town and villages on the east coast, and the interior is hilly and forested. Things are pretty quiet except during holidays and the annual Hindu festival of **Thaipusam**, centred on the Sri Pathirakaliaman Temple in the

east coast village of **Sungai Pinang Kecil**. There's also a community-run **arts festival** with outdoor film screenings and concerts (Sept).

Pangkor Town
Ferries from Lumut dock at **PANGKOR TOWN**, the island's principal settlement. The town has a few shops, banks and places to stay, but most people get straight on a minibus taxi to one of the beaches.

Galeri Pangkor
178 Jalan Besar • Free

Just a couple of minutes' walk northeast of the jetty, **Galeri Pangkor** is a small museum with nineteenth-century photos of the Pangkor Treaty signatories, a few fish traps and pieces of Chinese porcelain. From the terrace, you can survey the boats docked at wooden wharves in **Kampung Sungai Pinang Besar**, then descend to the mainly Malay village itself and take a signed road 1km inland to **Foo Lin Kong**. This Taoist complex is a riot of red and gold decorations and bright sculptures of animals – real and imaginary. There's a semi-wild garden behind, with a fishpond inhabited by enormous arapaima, and a miniature version of the Great Wall of China snaking up the hillside above.

Kampung Teluk Gedong and around
The wooden stilt houses at **Kampung Teluk Gedong** stand 1.5km south of Pangkor Town along the coastal road. Set back from the road is **Kota Belanda**, or Dutch fort, founded in 1670 to store tin supplies from Perak and keep a check on piracy in the Straits. Destroyed twenty years later, it was rebuilt in 1743 but abandoned again in 1748; the half-built structure you see today is a recent reconstruction. About 100m south, **Batu Bersurat** is a huge granite boulder under a canopy. Look here for carvings of the Dutch East India Company logo, an intertwined "VOC", and a **tiger** – a warning after a Dutch child was taken by one while playing nearby in 1743.

Pasir Bogak
It's just 2km from Pangkor Town to the west coast and the southern end of **Pasir Bogak**, one of the island's two main tourist beaches. This initial stretch is as busy as Pangkor gets, clustered with mid-range resorts popular with Malaysian Chinese. The beach itself is a lovely 2km arc of sand, looking out over a placid bay to the much smaller, privately owned **Pangkor Laut island**, and largely tranquil even though there is accommodation scattered across its length.

Teluk Ketapang
Around 2km north of Pasir Bogak and 1km south of Teluk Nipah is **TELUK KETAPANG** ("Turtle Bay"), named after the leatherback turtles that once nested here. The beach is worth a look, wide and attractively backed by forested hills, and quieter than it ought to be – perhaps because there are no facilities apart from a jetty and a lookout tower, or because a certain amount of debris can wash up on a bad day.

Teluk Nipah
In complete contrast to Pasir Bogak, **TELUK NIPAH** beach has a more Malay character and plenty of budget places to stay. It's also teeming with **hornbills**; every day at 6.30pm they come in droves for a feeding session at *Sunset View Chalet* (see map, page 119; http://bit.ly/SunsetViewChalet). The beach is slightly narrower than at Bogak, especially at its north end – the busiest part of the strip – where the embanked road and a profusion of stalls encroach; at high tide there's barely sand to stroll on without the water rushing around your ankles. Views over the bay are beautiful at sunset, with hunchbacked **Mentagor Island** rising darkly against the dusk.

PANGKOR WATERSPORTS AND ACTIVITIES

Malaysian holidaymakers at Pangkor are particularly keen on **banana boat** rides, with four people being towed around one of the bays astride an elongated float, culminating in an obligatory dunking at the end. Rides on other bizarrely shaped floats are available too, as is **jetskiing**. Much more worthwhile than any of these is a 45-minute **island-hopping tour** (negotiable, groups of up to four; make sure operators have a license and insurance), taking you out to Mentagor, Pangkor Laut and other islets for views of odd rock formations, after which you can swim and snorkel (no time limit – just arrange to be collected). For serious **fishing** or **snorkelling**, you'll need to charter a boat out to the Sembilan Islands, well west of Pangkor. For jetskiing and banana boats it'll depend where on the island you are; for snorkelling you're best off going out west to *Lie Pang Water Sport* (012 501 9756).

You can also ride all-terrain vehicles (ATVs) from Teluk Nipah along the Bukit Merah trail, a jungle path that goes beyond the airport strip and ends close to Teluk Dalam. **ATV Adventure Pangkor** (http://facebook.com/ATVAdventurePangkor) at the northern end of Teluk Nipah is a reliable operator.

The northern extension of Teluk Nipah, sometimes called **Coral Bay**, is a quieter, pleasant cove with a couple of eating places right on the beach, making this a great spot for a sundowner. Amid the rocks at its far end is a bizarre shrine, **Lin Je Kong**, replete with concrete toadstools and animal statues, including Mickey Mouse.

ARRIVAL AND INFORMATION   PANGKOR

By bus Lumut's bus station is 100m from the ferry terminal. Destinations from Lumut Alor Setar (at least 2 daily; 3hr 30min); Butterworth (7 daily; 2hr 30min); Ipoh (Medan Kidd; every 1hr 30min–2hr; 2hr); Ipoh (Amanjaya; 3 daily; 1hr 15min); Johor Bahru (at least 5 daily; 9hr); Melaka (3 daily; 5hr 30min); KLIA (5 daily; 5hr); Kota Bharu (3 daily; 9hr 30min); Kuala Kangsar (2 daily; 2hr); Kuala Lumpur (hourly; 4hr); Kuala Perlis (1 daily at 7.30am; 4hr 30min); Kuala Terengganu (at least 3 daily; 6hr); Kuantan (at least 1 daily; 9hr); Penang (1 daily at 3pm; 3hr); Seremban (2 daily; 5hr); Singapore (at least 5 daily; 10hr); Sungai Petani (at least 2 daily; 3hr); Taiping (3 daily; 1hr 10min).

By ferry Ferries run between Lumut and Pangkor Town daily from around 7am to 8.30pm (every 45min; 35min), calling at the village of Sungai Pinang Kecil en route. The Lumut ferry terminal has ATMs, with a moneychanger and food court close by.

By taxi Lumut's taxi rank is outside the bus station. A cab from Ipoh can be one option, despite the duration (1hr 30min).

Tourist office None on Pangkor itself; in Lumut, Tourism Malaysia occupies a traditionally styled wooden building close to the ferry terminal (Mon–Thurs, Sat & Sun roughly 9am–12.30pm & 1.30–5.30pm, Fri 9am–noon & 3–5.30pm; 05 683 4057).

GETTING AROUND

An 18km coast road, steep in places, loops around Pangkor, cutting inland only between Pangkor Town and Pasir Bogak. There are no buses.

By minibus taxi Pink minibus taxis park outside Pangkor's ferry terminal and at the southern end of both Pasir Bogak and Teluk Nipah. A sign at the ferry terminal displays fares, for up to four passengers.

By bicycle/motorbike Renting a motorbike in Pangkor Town or via your hotel is pretty simple; some guesthouses have bikes to rent.

ACCOMMODATION   SEE MAP PAGE 119

Pangkor has plenty of accommodation, all rather hit-and-miss. Most budget places are at **Teluk Nipah**, which has a bustling neighbourhood feel and is cluttered with cheap restaurants and shops. Mid-range hotels, meanwhile are concentrated at **Pasir Bogak**, which is more upmarket and more dispersed, with few shops and restaurants outside the resorts (it can be worth taking a full-board package). The rates we quote here are typical outside holidays and weekends, when prices can rise by ten to fifty percent depending on the establishment.

PASIR BOGAK

Puteri Bayu 300m inland from the beach along the main road; http://puteribayu.com. Pleasant complex of not-bad rooms and some quite attractive chalets. Breakfast is included.

Sandy Beach Resort Off the right end of Pasir Bogak's access road; http://pangkorsandybeach.com. Low-key buildings curling around a snazzy freeform pool. Rooms have all the customary conveniences, including fridges and safes, but are a little plain for the rate, which includes breakfast. $$$

TELUK NIPAH

Anjungan Beach Resort North end of Teluk Nipah; http://anjunganresortpangkor.com. The only mid-range resort in Teluk Nipah, comprising four-storey buildings surrounding a boat-shaped pool, with a popular restaurant. The rooms are comfortable enough, if rather plain; still, the overall tone is relaxed and the place is competently run. $$
Budget Beach Resort Southernmost turning off the main road; 05 685 3529. The densely packed chalets here aren't anything special at first sight, but they are in above-average condition, each with balcony and bathroom, and helpful staff keep the whole place shipshape. A sound choice. $
Nazri Nipah Camp Second turning off the main road; http://facebook.com/nazrinipahcamp. Laid-back to a fault, with slightly frayed fan chalets and poky A-frames, some with bathrooms, around a pleasant communal garden area. A/c chalets are available too. $
Nipah Bay Villa Second turning off the main road; http://pulaupangkornipahbayvilla.blogspot.com. Behind the shaded restaurant at the front is a tall, institutional block of rooms as well as rather better chalets, all with a/c, TV and bathroom. $
★ **Nipah Guesthouse** Southernmost turning off the main road; http://facebook.com/Nipah.Guesthouse. This wonderful guesthouse has four spick-and-span A-framed huts surrounding a pleasant pool area with loungers, and a cluster of mini-apartments for families. The included breakfast consists of a continental buffet in the breezy dining area, where guests are encouraged to rustle up eggs and pancakes themselves. $$
Ombak Inn Southernmost turning off the main road; http://oyorooms.com. Like a little kampung in the woods, this is a homely collection of chalets in grounds overgrown with bougainvillea. Rooms have a/c, TV and slightly cramped bathrooms. $

ELSEWHERE

Tiger Rock Inland of Kota Belanda; http://tigerrock.info. *Tiger Rock* is almost a mini country estate, but set in the tropics. There's a huge, wooden main house and various other buildings, all in colonial-era styles, lovingly decorated by the owner, artist Rebecca Duckett-Wilkinson. There's a total of eight tasteful rooms, a beautiful infinity pool facing a wild jungle slope, and a tennis court. Wi-fi in the lobby only; round-island trip included in rates. $$$$

EATING　　　　　　　　　　　　　　　　　　　　　　　　　　　　　　　　SEE MAP PAGE 119

There are few restaurants but plenty of street stalls on **Teluk Nipah's main road**, mostly dishing up simple Malay food and snacks such as BBQ sweetcorn and *lempeng pisang* (a banana and coconut pancake grilled inside a banana-leaf wrapping). At **Pasir Bogak**, a few stalls cluster on the road to the *Sea View* hotel, but most visitors eat at their resort.

PASIR BOGAK

★ **Sea View** Sea View Hotel, Pasir Bogak; seaviewpangkor.com. With tables on a beachside verandah, this perennially popular restaurant has an all-round menu of Chinese food – try standbys like tangy chicken in lemon sauce or the curry fish with *asam* (tamarind) – plus Western mains and snacks including black pepper steak. $$

TELUK NIPAH

★ **Daddy's Café** A 5min walk north from Teluk Nipah; http://facebook.com/daddyscafepangkor. This beachside restaurant-bar has tables on the sand overlooking the bay, a nice setting for a candlelit dinner. The menu covers a range of Western dishes, including steak and fish and chips, but the jumbo grilled prawns are spectacular. Beer is frosty-cold. $$
Nipah Deli Teluk Nipah, before Daddy's Café; 05 685 1416, http://facebook.com/NipahDeli. The Chinese resident chef here makes his steamboat spicy – and delicious. Other menu items include hot-off-the wok, unusual green-curry chicken noodles, Nyonya seafood *laksa* and seafood-based rice dishes. Vegan and vegetarian versions on request. $

Kuala Kangsar

A bustling country town, **KUALA KANGSAR** is Perak's **royal seat**, playing a similar role opposite Ipoh as Pekan on the east coast (see page 248) does for Kuantan, Pahang's capital. For Malaysians, Kuala Kangsar is best known as a centre for the production of **labu** – water pitchers with a pumpkin-shaped base (*labu* means "gourd" in Malay), excellent as souvenirs – and as the home of the **Malay College**. Founded in 1905 as a British-style boarding school, it began educating the most promising or well-connected Malay boys, thus bringing the community least involved in the colonial project into the Western intellectual fold; many of its students have gone on to achieve greatness in Malaysian public life, notably the prominent opposition politician and former deputy prime minister, Anwar Ibrahim. For visitors, the town is worthwhile for its royal and Islamic buildings, foremost among which is the newly reopened **Perak Royal Museum**.

Royal quarter

What passes for the town's **royal quarter** is **Bukit Chandan**, the hilly area south of the little Kangsar River, spanned by a road bridge close to the golden-topped clock tower in the town centre. The most prominent sight is the hilltop **Sultan Azlan Shah Gallery**, a colonially styled former palace (closed for long-term repairs at the time of writing; check website for more details: http://bit.ly/SASGallery). Some 500m beyond, **Masjid Ubudiah** sports a splendid array of golden onion domes amid a thicket of striped minarets.

Perak Royal Museum

Jalan Istana • Free • http://muzium.perak.gov.my

Around 1km beyond Masjid Ubudiah, past the marble 1930s **Istana Iskandariah**, the sultan's palace, lies the former palace, the **Istana Kenangan**. Now the **Perak Royal Museum**, it was built in the 1920s as a modest temporary residence while the present palace was being finished, and is of interest not for its exhibits but as a beautiful example of a traditional Malay mansion. Fashioned from wood without a single nail being used, the house is adorned with friezes and geometric-patterned panels. It was recently reopened after long-term renovation; though some visitors think there's little to actually see inside, it's a very pretty place nonetheless.

Sayong

Head east from the clock tower and you come almost immediately to the **estuary** of the **Kangsar** and the wide **Perak River** that the town is named for. Visible on the east bank of the latter is the village of **Sayong**, where the production and sale of *labu* is a major cottage industry. Boats shuttle across the river sporadically for a nominal sum; once across you can ask around for the location of *labu* makers, no more than a fifteen-minute walk away.

ARRIVAL AND INFORMATION — KUALA KANGSAR

The town centre is on the north bank of the Kangsar River. Although Route 1 runs through town, skirting the train station, the historic main street is Jalan Kangsar.

By train The train station (05 776 1094) is on the outskirts,

ANTHONY BURGESS' HERITAGE

It's a little-known fact that British writer Anthony Burgess, author of *A Clockwork Orange* (1962), taught in Kuala Kangsar from 1954 to 1956. His debut novel *Time for a Tiger* (1956), which became the first book in his *Malayan Trilogy*, is set in **Kuala Hantu**, a fictional Kuala Kangsar. Some of the locations described in the book still exist today: besides the **Malay College** there's the **Idris Club** (now a social club), the watering hole where protagonist Victor Crabbe – and possibly Burgess himself – would drink himself silly. A twenty-minute walk southeast of the Malay College is a girl's school, **SMK Raja Perempuan Kelsom**, formerly the **King's Pavilion**, where Burgess and his wife lived.

a 20min walk from the clock tower.
Destinations Alor Setar (5 daily; 2hr); Butterworth (6 daily; 1hr 15min); Ipoh (11 daily; 30min); Gemas (4 daily; 5hr 45min); Kuala Lumpur (11 daily; 3hr); Padang Besar (5 daily; 2hr 30min); Seremban (2 daily; 4hr 40min); Sungai Petani (5 daily; 1hr 25min); Taiping (11 daily; 15min).
By bus The bus station is on Jalan Bendahara, a few minutes' walk from Jalan Kangsar; it's served mainly by local buses, although some express buses call here too.

Destinations Butterworth (at least 4 daily; 1hr 30min); Ipoh (#35; every 20–30min; 1hr 15min); Kota Bharu (2 daily; 7hr); KLIA (2 daily; 4hr 40min); Kuala Lumpur (several daily; 3hr 30min); Lenggong (#99; every 90min; 75min); Lumut (2 daily; 2hr); Sungai Petani (2 daily; 2hr 45min); Taiping (every 45min; 1hr).
Tourist office The tourist office, by the clock tower, has plenty of leaflets (Tues–Thurs & Sat 9am–1pm & 2–6pm, Fri 9am–12.30pm & 3–6pm, Sun 9am–1pm; 05 777 7717).

ACCOMMODATION
SEE MAP PAGE 123

Casurina Jalan Bukit Kerajaan; http://casurinahotelkk.com.my. Quite a large hotel by the standards of Kuala Kangsar, with good rooms, though the common areas are already looking a bit dated – except, notably, for the river-facing infinity pool, which feels like by far the best place to be for miles around, especially when evening encroaches. $$$

★ **The Shop** 1 Persiaran Seri Delima, about 1km east of the train station; http://facebook.com/TheShopHotel. Kuala Kangsar's first boutique hotel has its own hipster café, where young locals sit on vintage chairs, surrounded by exposed brick. Upstairs is a series of retro-chic en-suite rooms, most with windows. The rooms are quite small, but in this town at this price, you can't ask for more. $

EATING
SEE MAP PAGE 123

If you're in Kuala Kangsar at the weekend, consider checking out the wide range of sweet and savoury snacks available at the **night market** around the main market off Jalan Kangsar, and at the **craft market** close to the jetty (Sat & Sun 7.30am–noon).

Laksa & Cendol Food Court Riverside. This breezy food court, by the river, is an ideal escape from the stifling heat; as you might guess, stalls here specialize in *laksa* and *cendol*, but they're not the only things to eat. $

Laksa Pak Ngah Jalan Dato Sagor, behind Tsung Wah secondary school; http://bit.ly/LaksaPakNgah. This mini chain started dishing up their signature *laksa* in 1955, before independence, and while Anthony Burgess was still in town. Unfortunately, it's quite a hike from the centre, but not too far from the train station if you're arriving or departing by rail. $

Yut Loy Jalan Kangsar; 05 776 6369. A gloriously antiquated, Chinese-owned, Malay-run *kedai kopi* – look out for the ancient notice from the days when Malay was still written in Arabic script, imploring people not to spit or beg, and some fascinating black-and-white photos taking during the 1967 floods. It's famous nationwide for its signature *char siew pow* (steamed pork buns), served from mid-afternoon; they also serve, sometimes glacially slowly, simple rice and noodle dishes, plus attempts at steak and scrambled egg. $

SHOPPING
SEE MAP PAGE 123

Craft market Close to the jetty. Kuala Kangsar isn't a bad place to buy crafts and souvenirs. Here you'll find a good range of basketry, wickerwork (including bags), some textiles and of course the obligatory *labu*. Daily 9am–7pm.
The Store 71 Jalan Kangsar. Useful mini mall, good for sundries.

Taiping and around

Set against the mist-laden Bintang Hills, **TAIPING** is one of few big towns in Malaysia with a Chinese name – one that means "everlasting peace", though it's somewhat ironic given the **clan wars** here between rival Cantonese and Hakka factions during the town's early days. Relaxed and mostly low-rise, it doesn't look like it was once one of the most important towns in the Peninsula. Yet the great **tin boom** in the second half of the nineteenth century, to which Taiping owes its existence, meant that by the 1890s it was in a race with Kuala Lumpur to be chosen as capital of the newly constituted Federated Malay States. Taiping evidently lost. Within a few years it suffered a second ignominy as Ipoh outgrew it, usurping even its role as state capital in 1937.

Today's Taiping is a discreetly prosperous affair, regarded as a desirable place to retire. Few foreign visitors come, which is a pity as it's one of the nicest provincial towns to relax in for a day or two. As you'd expect from its Chinese heritage, much of **central Taiping** comprises old shophouses, some being restored, centred on an unusual old **market** housed inside two huge, century-old wooden hangars. In addition to its **museums** there's the 1933 **Antong Coffee Mill**, the oldest coffee factory in the country, and the house where Sun Yat-sen stayed when he visited Taiping. The green **Lake Gardens** on the eastern edge of town, and the nearby former hill retreat of **Maxwell Hill (Bukit Larut)** and the lush **Matang Mangrove Forest Reserve** are also worth exploring.

Antong Coffee Mill

8a Jalan Assam Kumbang, under the flyover next to the train station • Free • http://antongcoffeemill.com.my

The oldest coffee factory in Malaysia, opened in 1933, **Antong Coffee Mill** still uses traditional wood-fire roasting techniques. You can sample a wide variety of brews, but the main reason to come here is visiting the enterprise's office, set in the historical house where founding father of the Republic of China, Sun Yat-sen, stayed with his Hong Kong-born concubine, Chen Chui Fen. Look out for the exquisite original Peranakan woodcarvings on the partition walls.

Telegraph Museum
Jalan Stesen • Charge

Another old building, this time of 1885 vintage (though heavily remodelled since), houses the city's modest **Telegraph Museum**, which is just about worth popping into on your way to or from the train station. There's not all that much to look at (old typewriters, morse code machines and the like), though information is presented well and relayed in English.

All Saints' Church
Jalan Taming Sari

Founded in 1887, **All Saints' Church** is the oldest Anglican church in what would become the Federated Malay States. It's built in a lightweight English Gothic style – though the roof is tiled in very Malaysian wooden shingles – and is also noteworthy for having one of the very few pipe organs in the country. The tiny churchyard contains the graves of some of the earliest British and Australian settlers.

Perak Museum
Jalan Taming Sari • Charge • jmm.gov.my

Housed in a purpose-built colonial building, the state-run **Perak Museum** is another Taiping "first" – it's the oldest museum in the Malay Peninsula, opened in 1883 at the instigation of the Resident Hugh Low. The three collections portray Malaysia's anthropology, zoology and local history, with displays of stuffed local fauna, as well as an extensive collection of ancient weapons and Orang Asli implements and ornaments. Incidentally, the grim, grey wall opposite the museum is the outside of Taiping's **prison**, built in 1879 and used by the Japanese during World War II.

Lake Gardens
Pedal boats can be rented from the gardens' south side Mon–Thurs 10am–7.30pm, Fri–Sun 9am–7.30pm

Taiping's extensive **Lake Gardens**, at the eastern edge of the centre, were created in 1880 when Hugh Low decided that the mess left by two tin mines should be landscaped and turned into a park. Today it's an inviting expanse of lawns, clumps of bamboo and mature trees covered in moss and ferns. At the time of writing, works were underway to turn part of it into **botanic gardens**. The view from the town side is particularly impressive on bright evenings, when the gardens seem to merge with the sunlit forested hills to the east, though the goofy duck-shaped **pedal boats** can mar the most meticulously composed photos.

Taiping Zoo and Night Safari
Zoo Charge • Night safari Charge • http://zootaiping.gov.my

A big magnet for Malaysian visitors, the **zoo** on the Lake Gardens' far side houses plenty of local wildlife, including *siamang* (a type of gibbon), civets, orangutan, tigers, elephants and bearded pigs. It also boasts the **Night Safari** – a modest copy of Singapore's – showcasing nocturnal animals illuminated using artificial moonlight.

Taiping War Cemetery
On the Bukit Larut Rd, 1.2km from the start of the Lake Gardens • Open access • http://bit.ly/TaipingWarCemetery

A serene memorial to the casualties of World War II, the Taiping **War Cemetery** contains the graves of 866 men, more than five hundred of whom are unidentified.

PERAK THE WEST COAST

Split in two by the road, it's divided between Hindu and Muslim Indians on one side and Christian British and Australians on the other.

TAIPING AND AROUND

ARRIVAL AND INFORMATION

By train Taiping station is on Jalan Stesen, just north of the centre (05 807 2591).

Destinations Alor Setar (5 daily; 1hr 40min); Butterworth (6 daily; 1hr); Gemas (2 daily; 6hr); Ipoh (11 daily; 45min); Kuala Kangsar (11 daily; 15min); Kuala Lumpur (11 daily; 3hr 15min); Padang Besar (5 daily; 2hr 15min); Seremban (2 daily; 5hr); Sungai Petani (5 daily; 1hr).

By local bus The local station in Taiping is off Jalan Masjid; for Ipoh or Kuala Kangsar, you're far better off taking the train.

Destinations Kamunting (#10A/B; every 40min; 30min); Kuala Sepetang (#77; every 1hr 20min; 30min).

By express bus The nearest express bus station to Taiping is Kamunting Raya Express Bus Terminal, 7km north, in the industrial town of Kamunting; confusingly, some bus firms advertise services for Taiping when they mean this station. Rapid Kamunting buses #10A/B run between Taiping's train station and the Kamunting Long Distance Bus Terminal; a taxi won't cost much. Given the far-flung location, you're best off buying tickets online.

Destinations Butterworth (hourly; 1hr 15min); Johor Bahru (several daily; 8hr 30min); Kota Bharu (1–2 daily; 7hr); Kuala Lumpur (hourly; 3hr 30min); Singapore (3 daily; 9hr 30min).

Tourist office Run by volunteers, inside the old clock tower on Jalan Kota (Mon–Sat 10am–5pm; 05 805 3245).

GETTING AROUND

Although Taiping is built on a grid layout, it's easy to lose your bearings thanks to patchy street signage (note that many of the north–south streets change their name across Jalan Kota). **Jalan Taming Sari** is the main street, busy by day but dead at night.

By bus Rapid Taiping Buses 20A/20B leave every 40min from the bus hub on Jalan Iskandar, stopping at the Taiping KTM Station, the Perak Museum, Maxwell Hill's foothills, the Taiping Zoo and the Lake Gardens. Buses 10A/10B shuttle passengers between Jalan Iskandar and the Kamunting Raya Express Bus Terminal, stopping at both Kamunting and Taiping KTM Stations.

By taxi Taxis await next to the bus hub on Jalan Iskandar.

By bike The pedal-boat rental outlet at the Lake Gardens also rents bikes – useful, given how scattered some of the town's sights are.

ACCOMMODATION   SEE MAP PAGE 125

Flemington Jalan Samanea Saman; http://flemingtonhotel.com.my. A modern hotel with a rooftop pool offering great views out over the Lake Gardens and east to the mountains (pricier rooms also have good vistas). The rooms could be a little more distinctive for the price, although breakfast is thrown in. $$$

Legend Inn 2 Jalan Long Jaafar; http://legendinn.com. The best of the mid-range hotels in the centre, and convenient for local buses. A modest extra fee pays for buffet breakfast in the coffee house. $$

Louis 129 Jalan Pasar; 05 808 2333, http://facebook.com/louishoteltaiping. This four-storey boutique hotel next to the old market has pleasant en-suite rooms with full facilities – hairdryers, safety boxes and ironing boards. Great value, despite the somewhat boxy toilets. $

Sentosa Villa In the Taman Sentosa residential estate off the Bukit Larut Rd, 2km from the Lake Gardens; http://facebook.com/SentosaVillaResort. The reward for staying this far from town is being in a sort of back-to-nature motel, the buildings styled like jumbo treehouses in a leafy compound with a stream-fed pool to swim in and ducks and geese waddling around. There's a café where you can buy breakfast. $$$

★ **Sojourn Beds & Cafe** 54 Jalan Kota; http://facebook.com/SojournBC. Taiping earned another first with this top-notch backpacker hostel. Renovated from a central shophouse that's walking distance to most sights, *Sojourn* is lovingly tendered by a local-Aussie team of backpacking aficionados. Their enthusiasm seeps into the many well-thought-out details – such as free desktop computers for guest use – and the spotless rooms and dorms (all with shared bathrooms). Simple breakfast is included. $

EATING   SEE MAP PAGE 125

+90 Specialty 71 Jalan Barrack; http://facebook.com/90specialty. Pared-down spot that's great if you'd like an espresso-based coffee, a tea, or a flavoured soy-milk latte; various snacks are also available. The name of the place sounds kind of cool, but it's actually sort of the opposite – it refers to the maximum time patrons are allowed to stay before ordering something else. $$

★ **Ansari Famous Cendol** 92 Jalan Barrack; 012 562 9440. Just about the best *cendol* that money can buy – and you don't need much money at all for these scrumptious dessert bowls. They also do *rojak* and other fried matter. $

Prima Jalan Kota, opposite Jalan Maneksha. Two *kopitiam*-type places on opposite street corners, with tables out on the street come evening, *Prima* runs the gamut of Malaysian hawker food: *laksa*, *rojak*, *nasi lemak* and more, plus some Western options too. $

Sri Annapoorana Curry House Corner of Jalan Taming Sari and Jalan Yusof; http://facebook.com/SriAnnapooranaCurryHouse. The friendliest eating place in Taiping's Indian quarter, with *roti* and *dosai* made to order, noodles, more substantial meals with or without meat, plus starchy South Indian breakfasts like *terrac* – almost a lightly spiced risotto. $$

Taman Tasik Food Court Western side of the Lake Gardens. Excellent, inexpensive Chinese food at all hours, including seafood noodles, rice with chicken *rendang* and, more unusually, century-egg porridge (rice gruel with gelatinous pickled eggs). Locals rate the stalls on the outside edge, facing the gardens, as the best. $

DRINKING
SEE MAP PAGE 125

Sky Bar Top of Flemington Hotel; http://flemingtonhotel.com.my. Set on the terrace of the *Flemington*, this is a good place for a sundowner as the light changes over the mountains and the Lake Gardens.

Maxwell Hill (Bukit Larut)

Charge • 05 807 7241 • Summit Rd begins 1.5km beyond the Lake Gardens – turn right at the Coronation Pool for Ranger Station; Rapid Kamunting Bus #20A/B shuttles between the Hab Bus on Jalan Iskandar and Jalan Air Terjun

Bukit Larut, still widely known by its colonial-era name, **Maxwell Hill**, is Malaysia's smallest and oldest hill station, its summit a mere 6km east of Taiping as the crow flies. The climate is wonderfully cool; when it isn't raining – this is one of the wettest places in the country – you can be treated to good views down to the coast. Local visitors prefer to ride the Land Rovers up and down (at the time of writing they'd been out of service for some time, due to landslide damage on the road), but the long, often steep hike up offers the chance to do some **birdwatching** or spot unusual **pig-tailed macaques** (the name makes sense when you come across one) which live in the forests lower down.

Walking to the summit

The **summit road** (10km to the top) twists and turns round some 72 terrifying bends; walking, allow at least three hours up, two hours down if you only take short breathers. About halfway up, the Tea Garden House, once part of an extensive tea estate but now little more than a shelter, makes an ideal rest stop, with a view of Taiping and the mirror-like waters of the gardens visible below. The main **hill station area** (1036m) has a few minor trails and circuits in the vicinity. Ambitious walkers continue a further 3km through groves of evergreens to the 1250m-high summit of **Mount Hijau**, although it's as well to seek advice from the rangers if you want to attempt this.

ACTIVITIES
MAXWELL HILL (BUKIT LARUT)

ATV tours It's possible to ride ATVs from the Lake Gardens up the hill to a waterfall, have lunch and return, or camp overnight (minimum six). ATV Adventure Park Larut (http://facebook.com/atvadventureparklarut) is an established and reliable operator.

Matang Mangrove Forest Reserve

16km west of Taiping, 2km before Kuala Sepetang (Port Weld) • Charge • http://kualasepetang.com • Bus #77 from Taiping bus station (every 1hr 20min) to Kuala Sepetang

More than a century old, the **Matang Mangrove Forest Reserve** is Peninsular Malaysia's largest surviving spread of mangroves, most of which have been extensively cleared for development or for **charcoal production** (still practised, sustainably, in the nearby town of **Kuala Sepetang**).

After the 2004 Indian Ocean tsunami, local interest in the mangroves increased; the trees' mesh of aerial support roots can absorb some of the force of tsunamis, and thus protect coastlines. They're also breeding grounds for small marine creatures, from fiddler crabs to mudskippers and archerfish. Extensive **boardwalks** at the reserve lead through a forest of tall, thin trunks and mangrove ferns; keep your eyes peeled for dusky-leaf monkeys.

Lenggong Valley

The one-horse town of **LENGGONG**, 77km north of Ipoh in the midst of Perak's jungle, hosts Malaysia's lesser-known fourth UNESCO World Heritage site. Inscribed in 2012, the town's open-air and cave sites span from the Paleolithic to the Neolithic and Bronze Age up to 1700 years ago. Hand axes found in nearby **Bukit Bunuh**, the site of a meteorite impact from 1.8 million years ago, are among the oldest outside Africa, and suggest that the Lenggong Valley was an extremely early site of hominids' presence in Southeast Asia. Both this and nearby **Bukit Jawa**'s workshop site, with tools dating back to 200,000 BC to 100,000 BC, are open to the public and are best visited with your own set of wheels. A tour should include stops at **Lata Kekabu**, 7km south of Lenggong off Route 76, a 50m-high waterfall, passing over three consecutive rock pools; and at **Tasik Raban**, 5km further south, a shimmering man-made lake popular with local holidaymakers.

Lenggong Valley Archaeological Gallery

Signed off Route 76, 6km south of Lenggong town near the village of Kota Tampan • Free • 05 767 9700 • Board a Kuala Kangsar-bound bus and get off at the turnoff on the main road, then walk the 2km to the site; alternatively, try to find an unofficial taxi in Lenggong (the *Soon Lee* hotel may help) • Temporarily closed at time of writing, call ahead

The main focus of this gallery is on 10,000 year-old **Perak Man**, Southeast Asia's most complete early human skeleton. His bones appear jumbled and inscrutable to the untrained eye, although it has deformities that indicate he had a congenital disease. He was buried in a cave called **Gua Gunung Runtuh**, 4km north of Lenggong, together with shells and tools, making him one of few known examples of ancient people with disabilities given a ceremonial burial; archaeologists believe he was considered a shaman by his community.

ARRIVAL AND TOURS — LENGGONG

By bus The bus station is by the central market off Jalan Besar, Lenggong's main road, where you will find everything from ATMs to grocery shops, a post office and a hospital. Some Kuala Lumpur buses leave from Dataran Lenggong, a parking lot along Route 76, 1.5km north of Lenggong's bus stand. Destinations Ipoh (7 daily; 1hr 30min); Johor Bharu (via Kuala Lumpur; daily at 10am; 8hr); Kuala Kangsar (hourly till 6.15pm; 45min); Kuala Lumpur (3 daily; 4hr); Gerik (roughly every 2hr; some continue to Betong, in Thailand; 1hr).

By car Lenggong is on Route 76, between Kuala Kangsar and Gerik. From the E1, exit at Kuala Kangsar toll and proceed north. A more interesting rural route from Penang goes through Road 136 between Kulim and Selama, in Kedah, before joining road A6, which connects to Route 76 about 7km north of the Lenggong turnoff.

ACCOMMODATION AND EATING

Chat Sook Back Lane West, 10m to the right of the bus station; http://bit.ly/ChatSook. Try Lenggong's famous fish balls and riverfish belly, cooked in sweet-and-sour sauce and garlic, at this no-frills place that sets the standard for most to follow. $

★ **Loh Dee** Jalan Besar. Look for the signboard over a red metallic awning to try juicy *char siew*-covered *wan tan mee*, roasted over charcoal, a rarity nationwide. Come very early for breakfast, and you will still have to compete for a table with dozens of hungry locals. $

MasBro Hidden Village On a hill west of Lenggong, only reachable by 4WD; 012 377 5005. A series of timber huts, built acceptably far from urbanity – hidden they may be, the compound is surprisingly attractive, with natural-water swimming holes, plus very decent toilets and washing facilities. The only slight downside is that the huts aren't often cleaned, putting you at the mercy of whoever stayed there before you. $$

Soon Lee 31 Jalan Besar; http://facebook.com/SoonLee Hotel. Basic yet clean en-suite rooms, in a homestay residence in the heart of town. The amiable owners are a fountain of local knowledge. $

Royal Belum State Park

Perak's last outpost before Kelantan is the underrated **Royal Belum State Park**, a pocket of rainforest and lakeland snuggled up against a Thai national park across the border. The lake here, **Temenggor**, was created in the 1970s as a hydropower project, although locals say it was also intended to frustrate infiltration by Communist insurgents from the Emergency days (see page 535), who had taken refuge in Thailand. Whatever the truth of that, the park itself and the adjoining Temenggor forest reserve to the south offer an excellent taste of Malaysian nature: the area is home to all ten of the country's indigenous **hornbill** species, plus the odd elephant, gaur and other wildlife. **Rafflesia** flowers bloom year-round too.

ARRIVAL AND INFORMATION   ROYAL BELUM STATE PARK

Visitors reach the park via the **Banding jetty**, on a lake island just off Route 4. Some 40km away on Route 76 is the nearest town, **Gerik** (or Grik), which is 65km east of Butterworth and 95km north of Ipoh as the crow flies.

By bus and taxi Local buses from Ipoh head to Gerik via Lenggong (5 daily; 3hr), from where you can take a taxi to the jetty. Express buses travelling between Penang (or other west coast cities) and Kota Bharu should call at Gerik and may be able to drop you at the access road for the jetty.

By car From Penang, take the E15/Route 67 to just before Kupang, where you turn right on to a minor road that eventually links up with Route 4 near Gerik. From points south, join Route 76 at the Kuala Kangsar exit on the North–South Expressway.

By boat Without a permit, you can still see some of the park by chartering a boat at the Banding jetty.

Permits To access the park, visitors need to apply for permits at least a week in advance and through a licensed operator. In practice, given that travellers must also hire guides and a boat to enter the reserve, the easiest way to come is on a pricey package (usually for 3 days/2 nights, including full board, accommodation and one day in the reserve) offered by the resorts.

ACCOMMODATION

Privately run lodges and houseboats are outside the park on Banding Island, in the **Temenggor** reserve. Book a week in advance so they can sort out your park permits.

Belum Eco Resort Banding Island; http://belumecoresort.com. Affordable, well-run place with simple chalets that have built-in showers, although toilets are shared. There's also a Malay-style houseboat that sleeps up to six. Packages include boat rides, kayaking, trekking to salt licks and a visit to an Orang Asli community. Three-day full-board stays available, including activities and permits. $$$$

Belum Rainforest Resort Banding Island; http://belumrainforestresort.com. The slickest accommodation in the area, offering big-city creature comforts and style in a range of spacious rooms and chalets. They price activities separately: a day's worth of boat rides and trekking can cost more than a night's stay. Breakfast included. $$$$

Cameron Highlands

On the western fringes of Pahang state, the **CAMERON HIGHLANDS** takes its name from William Cameron, a colonial surveyor who stumbled across the area in 1885, though not until forty years later did civil servant Sir George Maxwell propose it be turned into what would become the Peninsula's largest hill station. Indian planters, Chinese vegetable farmers and wealthy landowners in search of a weekend retreat flocked in, establishing **tea plantations** and leaving a swathe of what can only be called mock-mock-Tudor buildings in their wake.

The Camerons remain one of the most publicized attractions in Malaysia, although very much trading on past glories. Don't come expecting the pastoral idyll of the brochures – this is a major agro-industrial area, producing not only tea but also flowers, vegetables and fruit that are exotic for Malaysia (notably **strawberries**), much of it under unsightly plastic. What's more, it gets packed out during weekends, holidays and school breaks, when there can be long tailbacks on the main road, and then there's the din of building work wherever hotels and holiday apartments are springing up. Many from the Camerons bemoan the commercialization, but as ever in Malaysia, the real problem is the haphazard and unsustainable way in which it happens. (If you want to know more about the **environmental challenges** facing the area, contact the local campaigning group REACH: http://reach.org.my). All that said, many visitors have a perfectly pleasant time here. Lying more than 1000m above sea level, the area offers **cool relief** from the sultriness of just about everywhere else in the country, which is

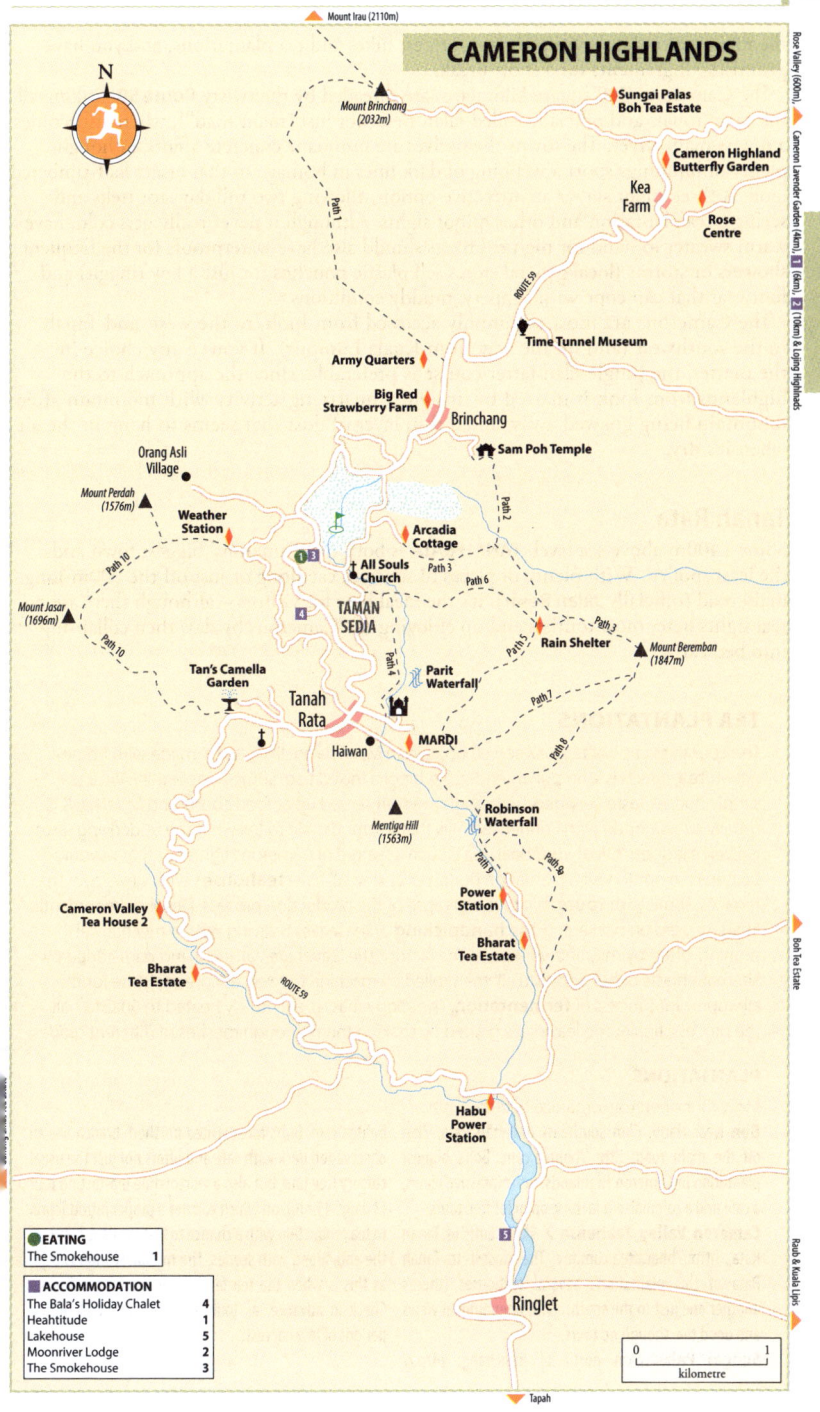

the main reason locals visit. Throw in forest hikes and tea plantations, and you have promising ingredients for a short break.

The Camerons' 700 square kilometres are threaded by the twisty **Route 59**, linking all the main towns and officially called Jalan Besar (or just "main road"), where it becomes a town's main street. The towns themselves are mundane concrete affairs, although plenty of buildings sport a webbing of dark lines in homage to that ersatz half-timbered look. A three-night stay is an attractive option, allowing two full days for treks and seeing a tea plantation and other minor sights. Although it never really gets cold, have a warm sweater to hand for nights. Hikers should also have waterproofs for the frequent showers or storms (local general stores sell plastic ponchos for just a few ringgit) and footwear that can cope with slippery, muddy conditions.

The Camerons are most commonly accessed from Ipoh, to the west, and Tapah, to the southwest (and on the way from Kuala Lumpur). If you've any choice in the matter, the jungle-clad latter course is preferable, since the approach to the highlands from Ipoh is marred by unsightly quarrying activity, with mountain after mountain being gnawed away, and a thin layer of dust that seems to hang in the air when it's dry.

Tanah Rata

Some 1400m above sea level, **TANAH RATA** is both the Camerons' biggest town and the least spoiled. With plenty of places to stay and eat along or just off the 500m-long main road (officially **Jalan Besar**), it's the ideal base for visitors – although there are no real sights here, most tourists end up enjoying the Camerons by day, then collapsing into bed early.

TEA PLANTATIONS

The countless cups of *teh tarik* served up daily in Malaysia are likely to be made with home-grown **tea**, which is – no pun intended – a bit of a mixed bag. Some people think local tea simply doesn't taste very good, although the stuff served up at food courts and *kedai kopis* is usually so swamped with condensed milk that it's impossible to tell what the underlying taste is. Even if it doesn't float your boat, tea is such a feature of Cameron Highlands that it would be perverse not to visit a plantation during your stay: all have **teahouses** with views over the terraces, some with **tours** that give a glimpse of the production process. Despite the romantic imagery used on packaging, the **handpicking** of tea leaves is giving way to mechanical pruning, often by migrant workers. At the factory, the leaves are withered and partly dried by alternate blasts of hot and cold air, then rolled by machine to release more moisture for the all-important process of **fermentation**. The soggy mass is eventually heated to 90°C to halt the process; finally, the leaves are graded by shaking them through meshes of different grades.

PLANTATIONS

Most tour operators organize half-day visits.

Boh Near Habu, 6km southeast of Tanah Rata, 7km off the main road; http://bohtea.com. Boh's biggest plantation in Cameron Highlands has impressive views, a café and a colonial-era factory, open for free tours.

Cameron Valley Teahouse 2 4km south of Tanah Rata; http://bharattea.com.my. The closest to Tanah Rata of this plantation's several teahouses (there's another one just to the south), with phenomenal views and good tea, though no tours.

Sungai Palas 6km north of Brinchang; http://bohtea.com. Boh's most visited northern branch has an observation deck with café and offers not just the usual cursory free tour, but also a worthwhile tea-tasting tour (3 daily; 45min), on which you get a proper introduction to tea production with a chance to taste various brews at the end, along with scones. The middle session is best, as this is when the tea tends to arrive for processing. Check in advance, as tours may be cancelled during periods of low harvest.

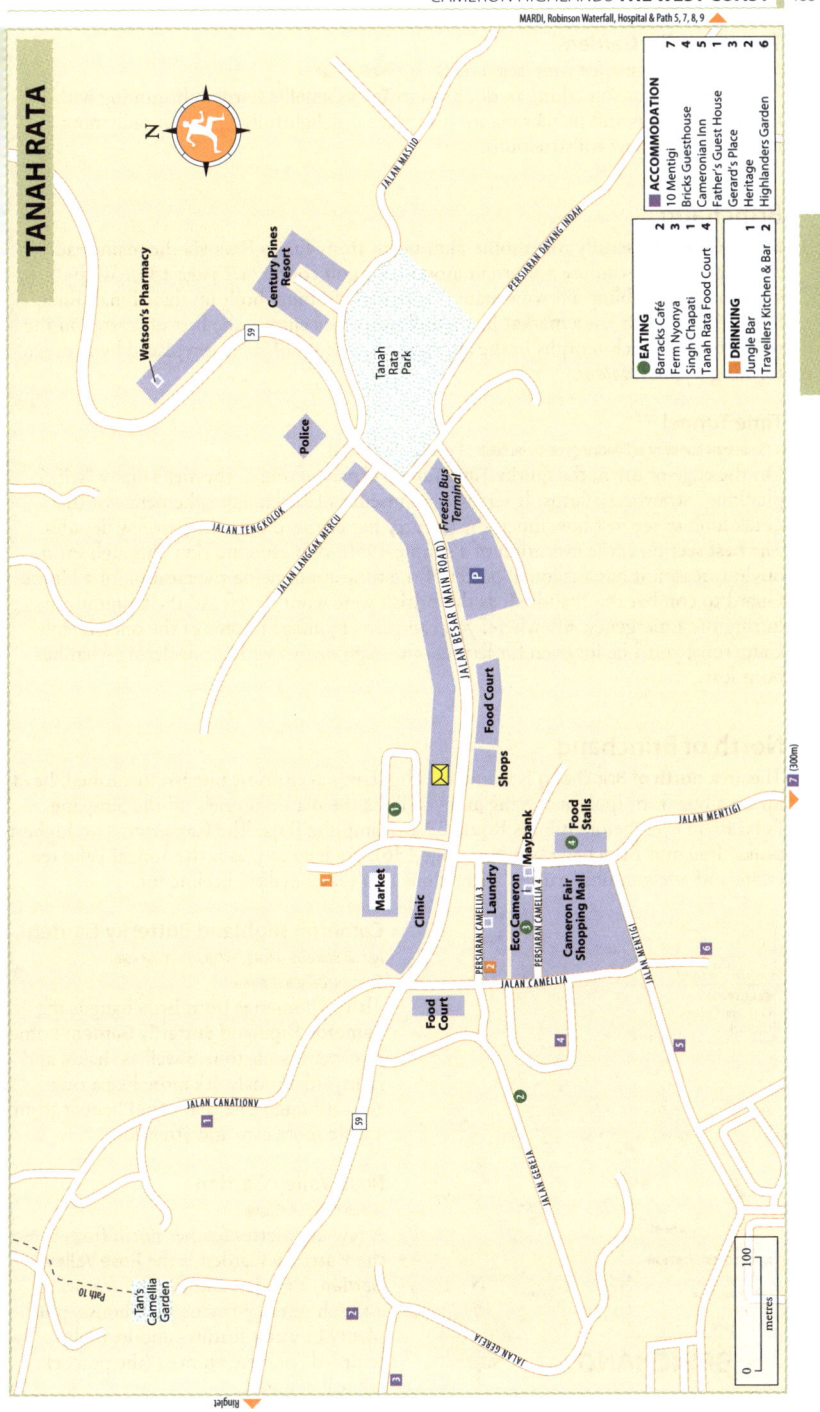

Tan's Camellia Garden

A 10min walk west of the town centre · Free · http://facebook.com/camelliagarden

If you're stuck for something to do, head to **Tan's Camellia Garden**, brimming with lilies, agapanthus and pitcher plants. The place is delightfully wild, but sadly now hemmed in by new constructions.

Brinchang

BRINCHANG is a scruffy town some 5km north from Tanah Rata via the main road, although walkers can use a shortcut around the golf course (see page 135). With something resembling a town square, it's denser and more built up than Tanah Rata, but in its favour it has a **market** just uphill from the centre – the first of several on the road north – which morphs in the afternoon as one set of stalls is replaced by another, forming a *pasar malam*.

Time Tunnel

A 15min walk northeast of Brinchang's centre on Route 59 · Charge · 05 491 4481

On the edge of town, the quirky **Time Tunnel** is part of one of the area's many "self-plucking" strawberry farms. It serves as a museum of Malaysian ephemera, worth a quick look to see just how much the country has changed over the past few decades. The best section is the evocation of a simple 1950s domestic interior, although for no obvious reason it has a colonial poster of the time announcing the creation of a Home Guard to combat the "bandits", as the British were wont to refer to the Communists during the Emergency. Elsewhere, you can gaze at vintage photos of the once-bucolic Camerons; you'd be forgiven for letting out a sigh or two while considering what has been lost.

North of Brinchang

The area **north of Brinchang** is Cameron Highlands at its most intensively farmed; head up on a bus from Ipoh or Penang and you'll see the plastic tunnels off the Simpang Pulai Road even before it joins Route 59 at Kampung Raja. The Camerons' two highest peaks, Irau and Brinchang (see box, page 136), are here too, as is the Sungai Palas tea estate and a few minor "garden" attractions that locals make a beeline for.

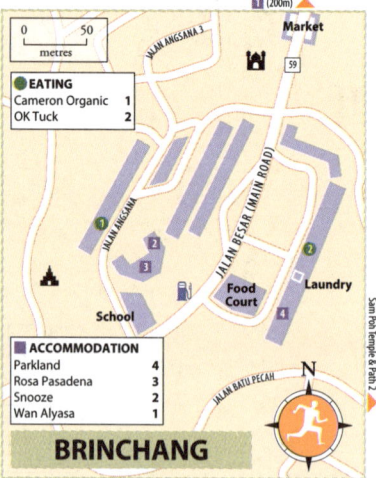

Cameron Highland Butterfly Garden

Just off Route 59 · Charge · http://facebook.com/ZoomaniaDeButterflyFarm

Three kilometres from Brinchang is the **Cameron Highland Butterfly Garden**; home to other insects too, as well as snakes and farmyard animals, it's more like a tiny zoo, although one that could benefit from a little more care and attention.

Rose Valley Garden

Just off Route 59 · Charge

A few kilometres further north from the Butterfly Garden is the **Rose Valley Garden**, a garden and nursery featuring a kitsch nursery-rhyme shoe house, plus plenty of water features and lovingly-sculpted concrete animals (the peacocks are real enough).

Cameron Lavender Garden

Just off Route 59 • Charge • http://facebook.com/cameronlavendergarden

Pressing on north from Rose Valley Garden, and 9km from Brinchang in total, you'll come to the **Cameron Lavender Garden**, by far the most popular sight in the area (as evidenced by cars double-parking on the road close by, causing tedious jams). The sizeable nursery is home to lavender and other plants, while the shop sells lavender-scented gifts and lavender-themed food.

Lojing Highlands

10km east of Kampung Raja on Route 185 • Self-drive, or catch a taxi from Tanah Rata or Brinchang

Technically in Kelantan but more like a northern extension of Cameron Highlands, the **LOJING HIGHLANDS** are a lesser-known, virtually unvisited part of the Titiwangsa Range. The fact that busloads of tourists haven't arrived here yet, however, doesn't mean that farmers haven't. The place has a couple of perks, primarily one well-organized eco-farmstay (see page 138), and the chance to see the elusive *Rafflesia* plant, almost ubiquitous in this region.

ARRIVAL AND DEPARTURE CAMERON HIGHLANDS

By bus Cameron Highlands' Freesia bus station is located at the east end of Tanah Rata, and is used by both local Perak Transit and express buses. Express services have dwindled in number in recent years, but backpacker minivans and tour vehicles also operate to and from the Highlands.

Destinations Butterworth (3 daily; 4hr); Ipoh (3 daily; 2hr 30min); KLIA (3 daily; 4hr 30min); Kuala Lumpur (at least 5 daily; 3hr 30min–4hr); Perhentian Islands (2 daily; 7hr); Raub (3 daily; 3hr 30min); Singapore (2 daily; 10hr); Taman Negara (2 daily; 6–8hr).

By car The Camerons can be easily reached off the E1, the North–South Expressway; use the exits at Tapah (if arriving from the south) or Simpang Pulai near Ipoh (from the north). If coming from Tapah, stop at Lata Iskandar, a waterfall 25km south of Ringlet. The Simpang Pulai Rd meets Route 59 at Kampung Raja before continuing to Musang Cave and Route 8 to Kota Bharu. A minor road links up with Route 8 via Sungai Koyan in the heart of the Pahang interior, connecting Ringlet on Route 59 with Raub and Kuala Lipis. Remember to top up your tanks: there are petrol stations in Ringlet and Brinchang, and one just west of the junction with Route 185 to Ipoh.

GETTING AROUND

By bus Local services from Tanah Rata's bus station run north to Kampung Raja via Brinchang (every 2hr, 6.30am–6.30pm) and south to Tapah via Ringlet (two in each direction daily).

By taxi Taxis park next to Tanah Rata's bus station (05 491 2355) and on the main road in Brinchang. Fares for intercity charter are clearly written at the taxi park in Tanah Rata.

By motorbike Renting motorbikes is increasingly popular; it's sometimes possible at Tanah Rata's bus station, and more reliably from most guesthouses.

On foot You can easily walk directly between Tanah Rata and Brinchang (40min) via Taman Sedia, the Malay village in the little depression in between. Signs on Route 59 outside both towns point the way to the village, the walk taking you past the Anglican All Souls' Church and skirting the golf course.

INFORMATION AND TOURS

Pahang Tourism used to run a tourist office at the western end of Tanah Rata, now occupied by a **tour agency** that still advertises itself as an information point – as does just about every other tour agency in town. The only reason to deal with an agency is if you want to arrange a guided **trek** or a taste-of-everything day **tour**. The standard ingredients for the latter include a drive up Mount Brinchang to see the mossy forest, visits to a tea plantation and an Orang Asli settlement (although the latter might be modern and charmless), and a foray to find *Rafflesia* flowers if in bloom.

Cameron Secrets Father's Guest House, Tanah Rata (see page 136); http://cameronsecrets.com.

Eco Cameron 72A Jalan Persiaran Camellia, Tanah Rata; http://ecocameron.com.

ACCOMMODATION

Both Tanah Rata and Brinchang have a fair amount of mid-range **accommodation**, although the former's hotels tend to be better run. Tanah Rata is also where you find most of the Camerons' budget **guesthouses**; all have hot water. Some places also have **apartments** to rent, listed on their websites. The rates given below rise by ten to fifty percent at

WALKING IN CAMERON HIGHLANDS

A network of **walking trails** makes it possible to take in Cameron Highlands' forests, packed with ferns, pitcher plants, orchids, thick moss and even *Rafflesia*. But despite the presence of mammals such as sun bears, you're unlikely to see interesting fauna other than insects and the odd wild pig.

Unfortunately, the trails are often poorly marked and maintained, and seem to have little immunity from being bulldozed to make way for development. The account below should be treated as a snapshot and is certainly not meant to provide turn-by-turn directions. *Father's Guest House* in Tanah Rata is a good place to get current trail information, and produces maps that mention lots of useful landmarks as well as wrong turns to avoid on each trail. It is also one of several tour operators offering guided treks – again, a good option given the state of the trails.

If **hiking independently**, tell staff at your accommodation where you intend to go and when you expect to be back. On longer hikes, take warm clothing and ample water. If you do get lost and can get a cellular signal, call your accommodation for them to alert the authorities.

TRAILS

The paths here are numbered according to local convention. Timings are one-way, for people going at an average pace. Note that at the time of writing, paths 9, 9B and 10 were **not recommended**, as several solo hikers had been assaulted and mugged here. Go in a group, or stick to the other paths. Some sections require a **permit** from the Forestry Department (http://forestry.gov.my); ask your guesthouse to obtain one, or risk a big fine.

Path 1 (2hr 30min) The trail to Mount Brinchang's summit (2000m) was closed for conservation at the time of research. You can still walk the trail from just north of Brinchang's street market – look for a track opposite the police headquarters – until the boardwalk through the ethereal Mossy Forest, where the trees are covered in a spongy, soft coat of green. But to climb further, you must get a permit. There is a road – the highest in Peninsular Malaysia – up to the forest, so you can cheat by taking a taxi up from Brinchang and walking down. The road begins close to Kea Farm, passing a turning for the Sungai Palas tea estate.

Path 2 (1hr 30min) Starting just before the Sam Poh Temple below Brinchang, it's not clearly marked and is often a bit of a scramble. The route undulates severely and eventually joins Path 3.

---

weekends, and can double during school breaks and public holidays, when it's best to book ahead.

TANAH RATA, SEE MAP PAGE 133

10 Mentigi Jalan Mentigi; http://staycameronhighlands.com. This mid-range hotel, set on top of a hill has smart and spacious rooms with balconies overlooking the town. There's a homely lounge with TV and a quiet garden outside. $\overline{\underline{\mathbf{\$\$\$}}}$

Bricks Guesthouse 65b Persiaran Camelia 3; https://www.facebook.com/people/Bricks-Guesthouse. What started off as a hostel has moved and turned into an attractive guesthouse. The dorms are gone, and there's nowhere left to socialise, but the management are friendly, and tours available. $\overline{\underline{\mathbf{\$\$}}}$

Cameronian Inn 16 Jalan Mentigi; http://thecameronianinn.com. This guesthouse serves up scones and offers plain but airy dorms and doubles (some en suite) in spotless bungalows, surrounded by a bougainvillea trellis and small garden. Classier family rooms are in the new wing. $\overline{\underline{\mathbf{\$}}}$

★ **Father's Guest House** Off Jalan Carnation; http://fathersguesthouse.net. *Father's* is the best-run budget guesthouse in the Camerons, and the best-informed place when it comes to trekking. Occupying a modern house with a small garden, they offer a range of pleasant rooms and a dorm. There's a relaxed, backpackery feel to proceedings here, and guests often congregate around the indoor tables in the evenings to drain a beer or two. $\overline{\underline{\mathbf{\$}}}$

Gerard's Place C9 Block Carnation, opposite the Heritage Hotel, 10min walk from Tanah Rata; http://fathersguesthouse.net. Run by *Father's*, this sleek B&B in a quiet block of flats has only eight rooms, most en suite, set around a homey TV lounge, with a leafy terrace out back. Free coffee and tea are provided 24hr, as well as a simple breakfast, and excellent information on treks. $\overline{\underline{\mathbf{\$}}}$

Heritage Jalan Gereja; http://heritage.com.my. A 10min uphill walk from town, this hotel is the closest Tanah Rata has to a resort-style complex, with "heritage" dating all the way back to the 1990s. Besides tidy, unexceptional rooms, it has a choice of restaurants plus indoor recreational facilities, such as snooker, for those inevitable wet spells. Breakfast is included. $\overline{\underline{\mathbf{\$\$\$\$}}}$

Highlanders Garden 17A Jalan Mentigi, behind the

Path 3 (2hr 30min) Starts at Arcadia Cottage southeast of the golf course, crossing streams and climbing quite steeply to reach the peak of Mount Beremban (1841m). Once at the top, you can retrace your steps, or head down via paths 5, 7 or 8.

Path 4 (20min) Paved in stretches and well marked, this walk starts south of the golf course and goes past Parit Waterfall, then on to the Forestry Office (Pejabat Hutan), where a sealed path leads back to the main road.

Path 5 (1hr) Branches off from Path 3 at the rain shelter – a little gazebo – and ends up at the Malaysian Agriculture Research and Development Institute (MARDI). From here the road, Persiaran Dayang Indah, takes you into Tanah Rata just north of the bus station.

Path 6 (2hr) From the Forestry Office on Path 4, this branches away to the rain shelter.

Path 7 (2hr) Starts near MARDI and climbs steeply to Mount Beremban; an arduous and overgrown hike better done as a descent from Path 3.

Path 8 (2hr 30min) Another route to Mount Beremban. From Tanah Rata, head up Persiaran Dayang Indah, ignore the MARDI turning on the left, and then turn right up a paved path for Robinson Waterfall. Just before the waterfall, turn left and you're on Path 8. Even more taxing than Path 7.

Path 9 As Path 8 initially, except that you head all the way to Robinson Waterfall (20min). You then descend to the access road to the Boh tea plantation, although there's a choice of routes. **Path 9B** (45min) is the direct, steep option via the hydropower station, where you may have to ask staff to let you through for the Boh road. **Path 9A** (1hr) curls away from it and descends more gently, though note that the last part is overgrown, so many people turn right here onto an easier trail to a vegetable farm, after which the track joins the path down to the Boh Road.

Path 10 (3hr) Beginning at the back of Tan's Camellia Garden in Tanah Rata (see page 132), this involves a fairly strenuous climb to Mount Jasar (1696m). It's best to turn back here, as the original path to Route 59 no longer has a clear exit.

Mount Irau (sometimes called **Path 14**; 6hr) The demanding ascent of Irau, the Highlands' highest peak (2110m), requires asking a permit at least one month before the climb. The trail commences at the end of Mount Brinchang's Mossy Forest walkway (take a taxi up rather than attempting this as an extension of Path 1). You return the way you came. It's best not to go alone, and an early start is advisable, as people often get lost when the light fades in the late afternoon.

Hillview Inn; http://facebook.com/highlandersguesthouse. Spick and span en-suite guesthouse rooms with hardwood floors, housed in a converted bungalow by a patch of forest that guarantees peaceful stays. The garden, filled with tropical flowers, is quite atmospheric. $$$

BETWEEN TANAH RATA AND BRINCHANG, SEE MAP PAGE 131

The Bala's Holiday Chalet Route 59, about 1km north of Tanah Rata; http://balasholidaychalet.com. Also known as *Planters*, this former colonial school still oozes old-world charm, doing a passable impression of English cottages with the lushest gardens imaginable, complete with country-pub-style dining room and a lounge with chintzy sofas. It's a bargain, if you can cope with the slightly wayward management. Free lifts to and from town. $$

★ **The Smokehouse** Route 59, midway between Tanah Rata and Brinchang; http://smokehousehotel.com. If ever a 1930s building could capture that mythical English country look, it's this one. Long the classiest place to stay in the Camerons, it boasts fifteen individually decorated suites, some with four-poster beds, others more modern in feel, as well as some more affordable rooms. Throw in the leaded windows, roast-beef meals (see page 138) and private garden with immaculate lawns, and you could pretend it's Surrey. Full English breakfast is included. $$$

BRINCHANG, SEE MAP PAGE 134

Parkland 45 Jalan Besar; http://staycameronhighlands.com. The friendly *Parkland* has uncluttered rooms that are good value midweek. The snag is that there's no lift, although you can pay fifteen percent more to stay at their more upmarket *Express* branch next door. Online bookings get discounted rates. $$

Rosa Pasadena 1 Bandar Baru Brinchang; http://hotelrosapsdn.com.my. Gargantuan hotel packing in more than a hundred rooms which, though slightly tatty, are quite comfortable and bigger than average, plus there are two restaurants. Breakfast is included. $$

★ **Snooze** 4 Jalan Besar; http://facebook.com/SnoozeCH. *Snooze* is a boutiquey homestay on two floors, with thirteen en-suite rooms. Everything is well set for traveller comfort, from the common lounge areas equipped with couches, writing desks and TVs, to the cute choice of bedsheets and wall coatings – part of which are plastered with guests' praise and comments. $$

Wan Alyasa Jalan Brinchang Sq; 05 491 4578. Set in a stripey line of mock-mock-Tudor buildings, this is a fair choice, with comfortable rooms (the cheapest don't have windows, but you can get a modest view for a little more) accessible by lift, and decorated along "natural" lines. $$

NORTH OF BRINCHANG, SEE MAP PAGE 131

Heahtitude 84 Kampung Kuala Terla; http://facebook.com/heahtitude. A great choice for those who don't want to be in one of the Camerons' main towns, this colourfully, funkily-decorated guesthouse sits by a small river in a relatively quiet village. The back patio offers wonderful views over your tea or coffee. Young children not allowed. $$

RINGLET, SEE MAP PAGE 131

Lakehouse 15km south of Tanah Rata; http://lakehouse-cameron.com. With your own transport, it's worth staying at this retro boutique hotel in Ringlet. Stone fireplaces and old-fashioned furniture meet plasma-screen TVs in the rooms; there's a suitably pub-like restaurant and bar, and a reading lounge, too. Breakfast is included. $$$$

LOJING HIGHLANDS, SEE MAP PAGE 131

★ **Moonriver Lodge** 12km east of Kampung Raja; http://moonriverlodge.wordpress.com. Next to a vegetable farm on a lush hillside, *Moonriver Lodge* is a relaxed cluster of wooden buildings, connected by walk paths and flanked by manicured tropical gardens and ponds. They have futon-style dorm beds, simple doubles or bunks, each wing with its own shared bathrooms. Pay for kitchen usage and bring provisions, or buy meals cooked on site. Multi-day packages include hiking activities; check the website for details. $$

EATING

Two things sum up Cameron Highlands cuisine – **steamboats** (see page 40) and **scones**. The former is highly popular with locals (there's usually a minimum of two diners, though solo travellers can always just order two portions); many restaurants still heat the stock using old-fashioned charcoal vessels with a central chimney. Plenty of hotels, and even curry houses, bake fine scones as part of their take on English cream teas – if only they weren't marred by the artificially pink local strawberry jam and "cream" with the colour and consistency of toothpaste.

TANAH RATA, SEE MAP PAGE 133

★ **Barracks Café** 1 Jalan Gereja; http://facebook.com/TheBarracksCafe. Quirky yet original, and housed in the original zinc barracks used by the British army during World War II, this café sits just downhill from the school once used as a military hospital by the Japanese. The outdoor seating area, in a manicured garden, is very pleasant, and the menu appealing: besides tea and scones, there are curries, chicken chops, breadbowl curries, cakes and mocktails. $$$

Ferm Nyonya 78a Persiaran Camelia 4; 05 491 5891. This authentically tatty and boisterous old timer serves the best-value steamboats in town (minimum two diners), along with hearty portions of juicy noodles. Packed and happening on most nights. $$

Singh Chapati Bangunan Brij Court, opposite Bird's Nest Hotel; http://facebook.com/SINGHCHAPATI. Excellent Punjabi food, somewhat expensive for the category, but always freshly made – and usually packed in the evenings. Long waits are accompanied by Indian music, constantly blaring from the TV. $$

Tanah Rata Food Court Jalan Camellia 1. Locals and backpackers alike absolutely love this food court. Not only is it open from early morning (ideal for breakfast if you've an early bus or tour), but it's atmospheric in a special way that can only be described as "highland-ey". It would be unfair to single out any particular stand, but the *roti canai* spots are awesome for breakfast, and the Chinese ones are good for later in the day. $

BETWEEN TANAH RATA AND BRINCHANG, SEE MAP PAGE 131

The Smokehouse Route 59, between Tanah Rata and Brinchang; 05 491 1215. If you feel a visit to the Camerons isn't complete without pukka English food, head here for roasts (such as beef Wellington) or cream teas (with quality jam and cream). They also do a full breakfast, with pork bacon and sausages. There's an atmospheric pub section too. $$$$

BRINCHANG, SEE MAP PAGE 134

Cameron Organic Jalan Angsana; 05 491 4807. Down-to-earth place popular for its steamboats which, unusually, come with either chicken or vegetable stock, and really do use organic local produce. $$$

OK Tuck 26 Jalan Besar; http://facebook.com/oktuck restaurant. Busy Chinese restaurant with an extensive menu, including excellent black vinegar spare rib and fried prawns. $$

DRINKING

TANAH RATA, SEE MAP PAGE 133

Jungle Bar Daniel's Lodge, 9 Lorong Perdah; 018 298 3429. With a pool table and fireplace, this backpackers' watering hole is a great hangout when busy, although it can be dead

some nights – perhaps because it's so discreetly tucked away at the back of a crummy guesthouse.
Travellers Kitchen & Bar 68a Persiaran Camellia 3; http://facebook.com/TravellersBistroPub. Tanah Rata's sole attempt to emulate a city bar doesn't exactly nail it, but it still attracts a (predominantly Western) crowd to compare travel stories over imported beers.

DIRECTORY

Banks It's easy to find banks with ATMs on and just off the main road in both Tanah Rata and Brinchang.
Hospital Sultanah Hajjah Kalsom (05 491 3333). There's also Klinik Ayob, a clinic on the main road (012 505 9220).
Pharmacy There's a branch of Watsons just a 5min walk from the centre of Tanah Rata, beyond the *Century Pines Resort*.
Police The police station is on Jalan Besar (05 491 1222).

Penang

In the far northwest of Peninsular Malaysia, **PENANG** is the most ambiguously named part of the country: depending on context, the moniker may refer to the **island** (Pulau Pinang in Malay; *pinang* is what Malays call the betel-nut palm), or the state (the island plus a chunk of mainland opposite, around the town of Butterworth), or even just the state capital – properly **George Town**. This was where the British established their first port on the Peninsula in the late eighteenth century, laying the foundations for the George Town of today, a fascinating blend of colonial, Indian, Malay and – especially – Chinese and Peranakan heritage. (At forty percent of the total population, Penang has the highest proportion of Chinese residents of any Peninsular state.) The city has seen a renaissance since its central old quarter, along with that of Melaka (see page 258), were jointly made a UNESCO World Heritage Site in 2008, and makes a wonderful base to see all of Penang from. Elsewhere on the 285-square-kilometre island are a coastal national park where you might see **nesting turtles**, a couple of unusual temples and a rather overdeveloped beach at **Batu Ferringhi**.

Pretty though Penang and George Town are, it's important to note that Penang island has a population not that far off one million, and the **population density** on its eastern flank is very high indeed – so much so that it's soon due to be home to a metro line. Set to open in 2030, it should make the ferries to Butterworth redundant, and hopefully alleviate some of Penang's occasionally dreadful **traffic congestion**.

Brief history

Penang Island was ruled by the **sultans of Kedah** until the late eighteenth century. But increasing harassment by Thai and Burmese raiding parties encouraged Sultan Abdullah to seek help from **Francis Light**, a British "country trader" searching for a regional trading base to counter the Dutch presence in Sumatra. A deal was struck: Light would provide military aid through the **British East India Company** and the sultan would receive 30,000 Spanish dollars a year. There was one snag – the East India Company's Governor-General, **Charles Cornwallis**, refused to get involved. Concealing the full facts from both the sultan and Cornwallis, Light went ahead anyway and took **possession** of Penang on 11 August 1786, then spent five years assuring the sultan that the matter was being referred to London. The sultan finally caught on but failed to evict the British, ending up with a modest annuity and no role in the island's government.

Penang thus became the **first British settlement** in the Malay Peninsula. Within two years, the population had reached ten thousand, swollen largely by Indian and Chinese traders. Light was made superintendent and, renaming the place Prince of Wales Island after the British heir apparent, declared it a **free port**. George Town took its name from the British king, George III.

For a brief time all looked rosy, with George Town proclaimed capital of the **Straits Settlements** (incorporating Melaka and Singapore) in 1826. But Singapore, founded

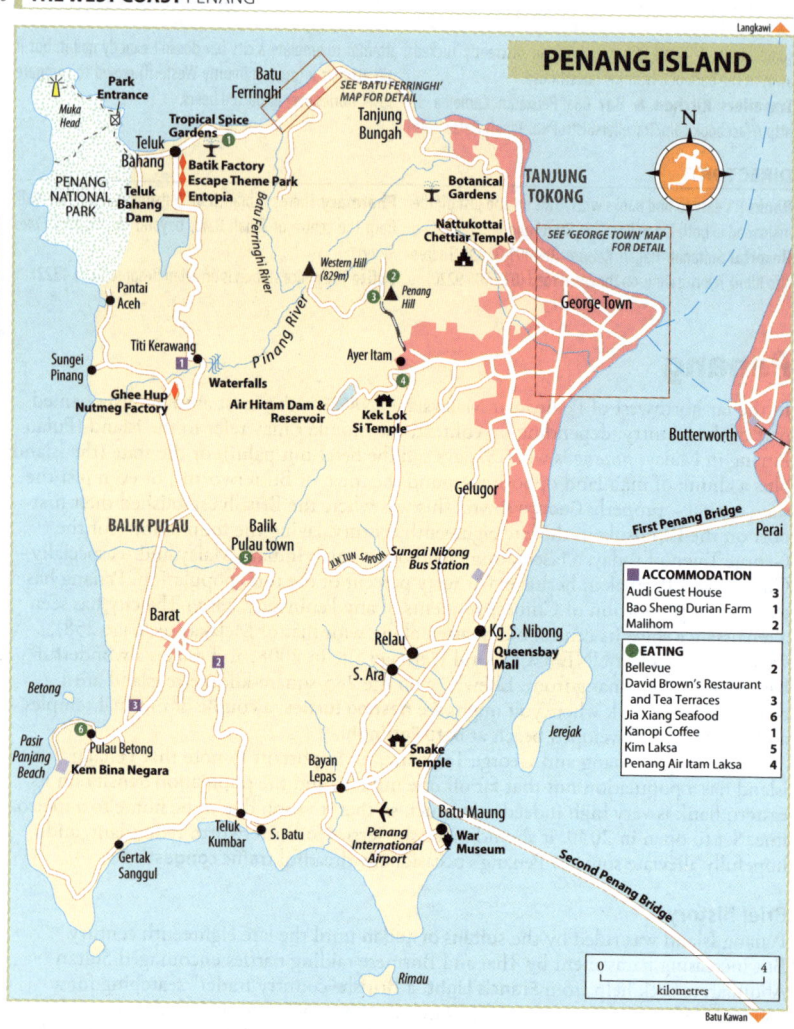

in 1819, would soon overtake George Town in every respect. Post-independence, even while Penang as a whole generally prospered through manufacturing, George Town itself had languished – which, ironically, helped preserve its historic core, rendering it ripe for UNESCO recognition (see page 146).

Butterworth

Some 70km north of Taiping and 40km south of Sungai Petani, the industrial port of **BUTTERWORTH** is home to **Penang Sentral**, the transport hub of northwest Malaysia. There's no need to linger, but with some time between connections, check out **Butterworth Art Walk**, an interesting attempt to keep up with George Town's artsy rebrand. It's a narrow lane 1.8km north of the ferry terminal, beside the Dewan Dato Haji Ahmad Badawi Field, and right next to business hotel *Lodge 18*. The alley is adorned with around twenty murals in diverse artistic styles.

ARRIVAL AND DEPARTURE

The bus station, ferry pier and train station are in a cluster, called **Penang Sentral** (http://penangsentral.com.my).

By train Fast ETS trains head south from Butterworth, down to KL and beyond. If heading north or into Thailand, you'll have to catch the slower KTM Komuter services.

Destinations Alor Setar (hourly; 1hr 10min); Ipoh (6 daily; 1hr 40min); Gemas (1 daily; 7hr); Kuala Kangsar (6 daily; 1hr 10min); Kuala Lumpur (6 daily; 4hr 10min); Padang Besar (hourly; 1hr 45min); Seremban (1 daily; 6hr); Sungai Petani (hourly; 35min); Taiping (7 daily; 50min).

By bus Tickets for bus journeys from Butterworth can be bought online, at the stations, or through agents at George Town's KOMTAR building (see page 149).

Destinations Alor Setar (hourly; 1hr 30min); Cameron Highlands (3 daily; 4hr); Hat Yai (Thailand; 5 daily; 4hr); Ipoh (9 daily; 2hr 30min); Johor Bahru (several daily;

BUTTERWORTH

10hr); Kangar (several daily; 2hr 15min); Kota Bharu (at least 2 daily; 6hr 30min); KLIA (3 daily with a change at Kamunting; 7hr); Kuala Besut (for Perhentian islands; daily at 9.30pm; 7hr); Kuala Kangsar (4 daily; 2hr 45min); Kuala Lumpur (at least hourly; 5hr); Kuala Perlis (4 daily; 3hr); Kuala Terengganu (1 daily; 8hr); Kuantan (4 daily; 9hr); Lumut (for Pangkor; at least 4 daily; 4hr); Melaka (at least 3 daily; 8hr); Padang Besar (2 daily; 3hr); Seremban (6 daily; 6hr); Singapore (several daily; 11hr); Sungai Petani (several daily; 45min); Taiping (Kamunting bus station; hourly; 1hr 15min).

By ferry The ferry to George Town leaves every 20min–1hr (6am–12.30am; 20min), and costs peanuts.

By taxi If catching a taxi across to Penang Island, check whether the bridge toll is included in the fare.

George Town

Visiting **GEORGE TOWN** in 1879, stalwart Victorian traveller **Isabella Bird** called it "a brilliant place under a brilliant sky", a description that's hard to improve. Filling a triangular cape at the island's northeastern corner is George Town's centre, the UNESCO-listed core of which is essentially the area south and east of Lebuh Farquhar, Love Lane and Lebuh Melayu. It's a surprisingly harmonious maze of lanes lined with **shophouses** in various states of repair, and liberally sprinkled with religious buildings, impressive **clan associations** or *kongsi* – a blend of Chinese welfare organization, social club and temple (see page 547) and other monuments. The obvious comparison is with Singapore, but it's as if the same ingredients have created an altogether mellower dish, without the slickness, crowds and incessant din of its former Straits Settlements partner. If time is short, make a point of seeing the **Khoo Kongsi** and **Cheong Fatt Tze mansion**; otherwise simply enjoy the relaxed pace and stroll at will.

The main arteries are **Jalan Penang**, **Jalan Masjid Kapitan Kling** and **Lebuh Pantai**, which run roughly west–east, along with traffic-clogged **Lebuh Chulia**, which runs northwest–southeast. Note that parts of Lebuh Chulia and Jalan Penang are distinctly seedy at night. George Town's northern fringes and the rugged, forested hills of the island's centre are home to a few interesting **temples** and the attractive **Botanic Gardens**.

Colonial district

Clustered around historic **Fort Cornwallis** are a motley collection of colonial buildings, including the former Town and City halls, St George's Church and some of George Town's oldest and most prestigious schools. A useful landmark, at the eastern end of Lebuh Pantai (Beach Street) and close to the tourist offices, is the graceful Moorish-

> ### GEORGE TOWN'S CAT SHUTTLE
> George Town's centre is served by the **CAT shuttle bus** (also signed as #5; every 15–30min; free), which can be useful, especially if you're flagging in the heat. Operated by Rapid Penang, it sets off from the Pengkalan Weld terminal, heading north to Little India and the colonial district, then Lebuh Muntri. It then turns southwest along Jalan Penang to the KOMTAR building, meandering in the vicinity before returning east via Lebuh Carnarvon, Jalan Masjid Kapitan Keling and the colonial district to the bus terminal.

style **clock tower**, with onion-dome roof and scalloped Arabesque windows. Presented in 1897 to mark Queen Victoria's Diamond Jubilee, it's 60ft (20m) high, a foot for each year of her reign.

Fort Cornwallis
Entrance in the northwest of the site, via the Padang • Charge

At the very eastern tip of the island, overpriced **Fort Cornwallis** marks the spot where Francis Light landed to take possession of Penang on 16 July 1786. The fort, named after Lord Charles Cornwallis, Governor-General of India, dates from 20 years later. Square in shape with redoubts at each corner, it's all a bit forlorn nowadays, the mildewed, lightly vegetated brickwork conveying little sense of history. The **statue** of Light by the entrance was cast in 1936 for the 150th anniversary of the founding of Penang, his features copied from a portrait of his son, Colonel William Light, founder of Adelaide in Australia. (Francis Light's **grave** is in the cemetery on Jalan Sultan Ahmad Shah, 1km west). Inside the walls, look for the early nineteenth-century chapel, powder magazine and bronze **Sri Rambai cannon**, sited in the northwest corner – local belief was that infertile women could conceive by laying flowers in its barrel.

Padang Kota Lama

The expanse of green that borders Fort Cornwallis, the **Padang Kota Lama**, was once the favourite promenade of the island's colonial administrators. The **Esplanade** here offers a vista of mainland hills and, to the left, the distant high-rise apartments of Tanjung Tokong in the northwest. Bordering the padang are a slew of grand buildings, including the early nineteenth-century **Dewan Undangan Negeri** (State Legislative Hall) to the south and, to the west, the yellow-and-white old **town hall** (1879) and the more ornate but less attractive former **city hall** (1903).

Penang Museum
57 Macalister Rd • Free • http://penangmuseum.gov.my

The **Penang Museum** is a worthwhile introduction to life on the island. Among the memorabilia are rickshaws, Peranakan furniture, clothing and ceramics, faded black-and-white photographs of early Penang's Chinese millionaires, and a panoramic photograph of George Town taken in the 1870s (note how many buildings survive to this day). Also on site is the **Penang State Art Gallery**, which focuses on modern and contemporary art; this may be the only thing you get to see, since the museum was undergoing a major renovation at the time of writing.

St George's Church
1 Lebuh Farquhar • Free • http://facebook.com/TheOfficialStGeorgesChurchPenang

As simple and unpretentious as anything built in Neoclassical style in Asia can be, **St George's Church** is one of Penang's oldest buildings, having been completed in 1818 by the East India Company using convict labour. Its construction marked the arrival of the Anglican Church in Southeast Asia, and early congregations must have found the airy interior a welcome reprieve from the heat.

Eastern & Oriental Hotel (E&O)
10 Lebuh Farquhar • http://eohotels.com

Though a little overshadowed by its recently added annexe, the **Eastern & Oriental Hotel** – built in 1885 by the Armenian Sarkies brothers, who also launched Singapore's even more famous *Raffles Hotel* – still epitomizes colonial elegance. Behind the grand, waterfront facade is an interior of cool marble floors, airy, dark timber and plasterwork, with a domed ceiling crowning the lobby; Rudyard Kipling, Somerset Maugham and Herman Hesse were among the guests, taking tiffin on the terrace and enjoying the sea breeze. The Victory Annexe is built on the site of the original annexe, unveiled

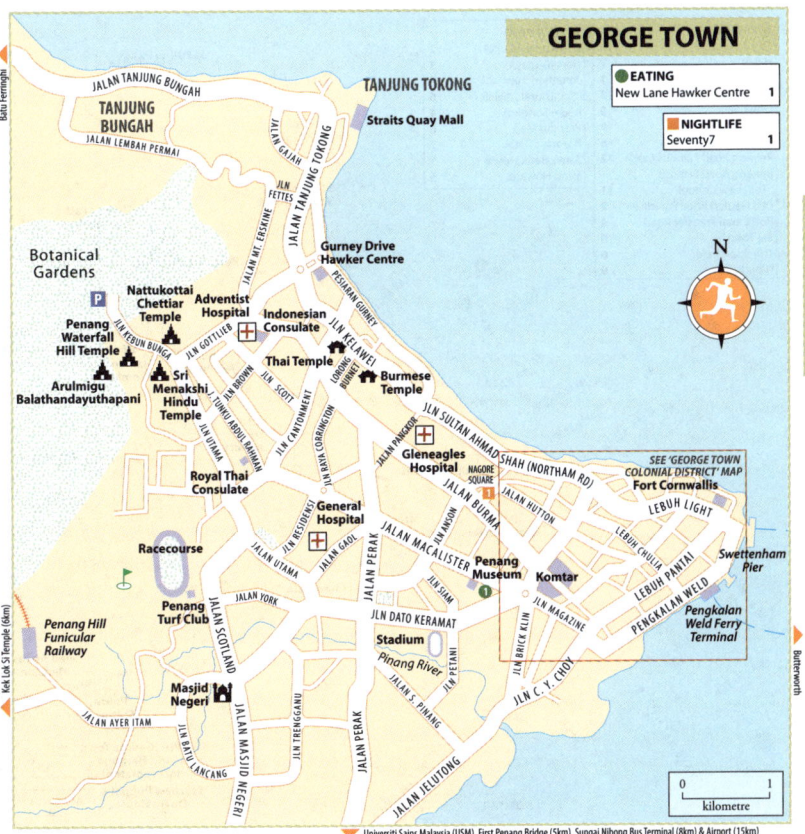

by Arshak Sarkies in 1923. If the hotel rates are beyond your budget, get a peek by treating yourself at its *Sarkies* restaurant.

Cheong Fatt Tze Mansion

14 Lebuh Leith • Compulsory tours: daily 11am, 2pm & 3.30pm; 1hr • Charge • http://cheongfatttzemansion.com

Leith Street was once lined by a gaggle of villas belonging to Hakka Chinese tycoons, one such being the **Cheong Fatt Tze Mansion**, the local home of a nineteenth century Dutch East Indies tycoon, and a splendid example of Penang's eclectic late nineteenth-century house design. Now trading mainly as *The Blue Mansion* hotel (see page 151), it's broadly southern Chinese in form, with good-luck motifs and complex decorative mouldings along the tiled roof, though its **arches** and **shutters** are definitely European touches, as are the Art Nouveau stained glass and the sweeping interior staircase, even if the delicate iron tracery and balconies might owe a nod to wooden Malay verandas. Note that you can get away with taking a tour (and the fee) if dining at one of the hotel's eateries – the *Indigo* restaurant isn't cheap (see page 153), but drink prices are fair at the café.

House of Yeap Chor Ee

4 Lebuh Penang • Charge • http://houseyce.com

The **House of Yeap Chor Ee**, a southern Chinese merchant who made his fortune becoming a sugar magnate and a banker, nestles within George Town's historical

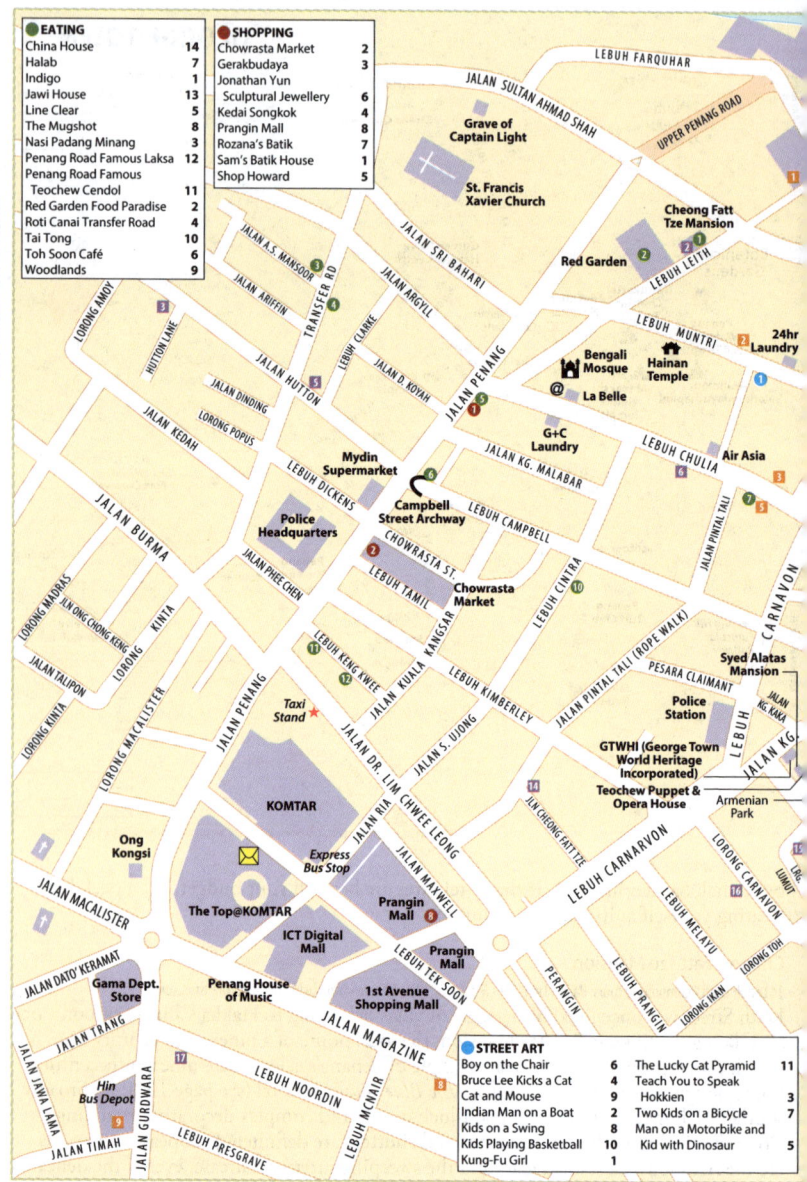

business district, dominated by the banks of Lebuh Pantai. Look for it next to the bright yellow former Chinese Chamber of Commerce building. Slicker than most of the country's state-owned museums, it's privately run. Many of the artefacts are transplants from the vast mansion that Yeap Chor Ee later acquired on Jalan Sultan Ahmad Shah. It was temporarily closed at the time of writing, however, with no date set for reopening.

PENANG **THE WEST COAST** | 145

Peranakan Mansion

29 Lebuh Gereja • Charge • http://pinangperanakanmansion.com.my

A sprinkling of Peranakan restaurants aside, George Town's one nod to Baba-Nyonya culture (see page 528) is a museum, the **Peranakan Mansion**. Painted pastel green, the house was built in the 1890s for Kapitan Cina Chung Keng Kwee, a Penang personality and secret society leader. Chinese wooden doors, gorgeous

> ## UNESCO AND GEORGE TOWN
>
> It might be hard to believe today, but George Town was in a bad way when the new millennium arrived. This was a classic case of inner-city decay: the centre, its shophouses shabby and unloved, was a place to make a hasty exit from once the day's work was done.
>
> Then came the idea of putting George Town forward for consideration as a **UNESCO World Heritage Site**. So it would become, though not in the form Penangites envisaged. George Town was perhaps too Chinese a city in the context of the country's politics, and Malaysia wound up lobbying for a joint ticket comprising George Town and Melaka, the other former British Straits Settlements' port in Malaysia (see page 258). It was this two-headed entity that was honoured as a single World Heritage Site in 2008. Watershed elections that same year saw, among other surprises, Penang taken over by the opposition. Suddenly the state was being run along pragmatic, less racially focused lines, and had a UNESCO listing to boot. The scene was set for the city's regeneration.
>
> The results are obvious for anyone to see. Properties all over the centre are being restored, some as boutique hotels and slick restaurants; young people are back in George Town, lounging in wannabe hipster cafés or cycling around checking out street art (see page 147); and the city has a real sense of its own heritage and creativity, celebrated in a slew of festivals and cultural events (see page 154).
>
> However, as gentrification compels old businesses and community organizations to relocate, conservation groups are worried that George Town is losing its **intangible heritage** – a key ingredient in its UNESCO status. Rapid social change is also an important factor, of course, and it may be that even with principled management, central George Town could one day become like Singapore's Chinatown: immaculate, thriving, but with little sense of deep-rooted neighbourhoods and traditions.

inlaid furniture and carved screens are everywhere, alongside more European touches including florid glass light fittings. The **display cases** are full of trinkets and heirlooms: green-and-pink Chinese-made porcelain painted with phoenixes and peonies, snuffboxes, embroideries and shoes. Upstairs, a **bedroom** with a four-poster bed has been left pretty much intact. There's also a section devoted to traditional **jewellery**, an adjoining shrine holding ancestral tablets, and a small **gift shop** selling Peranakan-themed souvenirs.

Jalan Masjid Kapitan Kling

For some locals, **Jalan Masjid Kapitan Kling** will always be **Pitt Street**, named after William Pitt the Younger, British prime minister when Francis Light founded Penang. It's also nicknamed the **Street of Harmony**, as, if you include the compound of St George's Church at its eastern end, it's home to places of worship representing all of Malaysia's major faiths.

Goddess of Mercy Temple (Kuan Yin Teng)

Jalan Masjid Kapitan Kling, close to the start of Lebuh China • Free

The oldest and liveliest of George Town's Chinese temples, **Goddess of Mercy Temple (Kuan Yin Teng)** is a down-to-earth granite hall dating to 1801, and where dragon-carved pillars and wooden roof beams are blackened by incense smoke. As Kuan Yin is the goddess of mercy, the temple is perpetually jammed with devotees, mostly beggars down on their luck and women praying for children, grandchildren and safe childbirth. The huge bronze bell in the first hall is rung by those who have made a donation; the flagstone forecourt features performances of **Chinese opera** during festivals.

Sri Mahamariamman Temple

Lebuh Queen, with a second entrance on Jalan Masjid Kapitan Kling • Free

The **Sri Mahamariamman Temple**, founded in 1833, is the chief sight in George Town's small but characterful **Little India**, centred on Lebuh Pasar. Recently renovated, its pale green and red entrance tower is a riot of sculpted deities, among which four **swans** represent incarnations of the goddess Mariamman.

Kapitan Keling Mosque (Masjid Kapitan Keling)
Western end of Jalan Masjid Kapitan Kling · Free

The oldest and largest mosque in Penang, **Kapitan Keling Mosque (Masjid Kapitan Keling)** dates back to 1801, when Indian Muslim migrants built a mosque here on land granted them by the East India Company. *Keling* is an old term – now regarded as derogatory – said to originate from the sound of clinking chains tied on the legs of British colonial Indian enslaved people– and Kapitan Keling was one Cauder Mohudeen, a successful businessman appointed by the East India Company to speak for the community. The present mosque was refashioned in Anglo-Moorish style at the start of the last century, and its dark onion domes, arched portico and minaret are especially attractive at night, when the whole place is subtly lit.

Lebuh Armenian (Armenian Street)

Short and curved at one end, **Lebuh Armenian (Armenian Street)** offers good value for visitors, packing in a number of minor sights along its highly gentrified length, including at its southern end the popular *Two Kids on Bicycle* street art. The narrow house at the street's northern end is the **Syed Alatas mansion**, which was named after a merchant and arms dealer from Aceh, in northern Sumatra, who lived here in the 1870s.

Teochew Puppet & Opera House
122 Lebuh Armenian · Charge; puppet shows (1hr) also available, including museum entry · http://teochewpuppet.com

The **Mor Hun Club** is one of George Town's surviving traditional social clubs, its entrance distinguished by colourful tilework and gorgeously carved gilt doors; walk past at night and you may hear the clacking of a game of mahjong from the upstairs windows. Downstairs is the **Teochew Puppet & Opera House** with displays on Chinese opera and metal rod puppetry, only preserved in Penang. Try to catch one of their occasional **puppet shows**, with some English explanations.

GEORGE TOWN'S STREET ART

Street art is a recent phenomenon in George Town but has already become a big draw for local visitors, who wander around the centre tracking down the murals and cartoons executed in steel wire on shophouse walls. The **wire pieces** – some fifty of them – were commissioned in 2009 from KL studio **Sculpture at Work** as a whimsical way of marking out the UNESCO-listed parts of the city.

In 2012, Lithuanian artist Ernest Zacharevic sketched a series of mural installations entitled **Mirrors of George Town** for the George Town Festival. Ever since, Penang has taken off as one of Southeast Asia's street art capitals. In 2013, Zacharevic's piece depicting two children on a bicycle was selected by *The Guardian* as among the best street art in the world, consolidating the position of the city's murals as a tourist draw. In the wake of George Town's success, Zacharevic has also sketched in Ipoh, Kuala Lumpur, Johor Bahru and Singapore.

As well as Zacharevic's pieces, George Town hosts work by local and international artists such as Kenji Chan (Sandakan), Fritilidea (KL), Rone (Melbourne), Elle (New York) and Julia Volchkova (Russia). You'll spot their art as you walk around town (see map, page 144).

The gallery **Hin Bus Depot** (31A Jalan Gurdwara; http://hinbusdepot.com) has long promoted street art in Penang, and today is still the best place to meet local artists and creative types, who organize rotating art exhibitions and the weekly **Sunday pop-up market** (http://instagram.com/hinmarket).

Sun Yat-sen Museum

120 Lebuh Armenian • Charge • http://sunyetsen.my

The **Sun Yat-sen Museum**, located in a beautifully restored shophouse, offers a permanent exhibition and guided tour of the Penang base of one of Asia's most important historical personalities, Sun Yat-sen. He led the revolution that overthrew the last Chinese emperor, drawing on support from the overseas Chinese.

Yap Kongsi

Corner of Lebuh Armenian and Lebuh Cannon • Free • 04 261 0679

It's hard to imagine two more contrasting shrines than the pair that make up the most obvious sight on Lebuh Armenian, the **Yap Kongsi**. On the left of the clan house compound is the conventionally styled **Ciji Temple** (also called **Choo Chee Keong**), its roof photogenically bedecked with dragons; next door, built in the 1920s on land furnished by the tycoon Yeap Chor Ee, the green-and-white **Yap Temple** looks like a European-style villa and holds the clan's ancestral tablets.

Hock Teik Cheng Sin Temple

57 Lebuh Armenian • Free

Just south of the corner with Lebuh Cannon, a passageway beneath a Chinese facade gives access to the gaudy, two-storey **Hock Teik Cheng Sin Temple**, with altars on both levels. It's dedicated to **Tua Peh Kong**, sometimes described as the god of prosperity and one of the most popular Chinese deities in Malaysia – many cities have at least one Tua Peh Kong shrine. In the mid-nineteenth century the temple and surrounding area was a stronghold of the Kean Teik secret society, which became embroiled in the Penang Riots of 1867. For nine days, George Town was shaken by gang fights around Armenian, Church and Chulia streets, where the groups were holed up. A bricked-up passageway can still be seen that once allowed a surreptitious escape to the street or to the Khoo Kongsi compound.

Khoo Kongsi

18 Cannon Square • Charge • http://khookongsi.com.my

Khoo Kongsi is the best known of Penang's clan associations, and no wonder: this is practically a gated community in its own right, reached by an alleyway off Lebuh Cannon. It brings you into an overpoweringly gaudy complex that includes shrines, opera stage, ancestral hall and residences. The *kongsi* represents Khoos from a particular village in southern China; one such was Khoo Thean Teik, the ringleader of the Kean Teik secret society during the Penang Riots, although he later rehabilitated himself and became a very wealthy pillar of local society.

The two-storey **main building** looks ready to collapse under the weight of the multicoloured ceramic sculptures, woodcarvings and shining gold leaf adorning its roof. Finished in 1906, this is a lesser version of an even more extravagant original that had just burned down – some say destroyed by jealous deities, angered by its ostentation.

The building opposite was the **opera stage**, beside which is the slightly incongruous administration building, a colonial-styled affair which houses some ancestral tablets. A former kitchen next to the main building is now a little **museum** explaining the evolution of the complex.

Chinese clan jetties

Pengkalan Weld

They're not as atmospheric as the water villages at Pulau Ketam near Kuala Lumpur or in the capital of Brunei, but the seven **Chinese clan jetties** of George Town still make for a good wander. Communities of stilt houses built over the water, they were set up by Chinese immigrants before George Town properly got going, and are so named because six of them are inhabited by individual clans whose roots are in specific villages in Fujian province, southeast China. The houses are connected by wooden boardwalks and dotted with temples. The **Chew jetty**, smack in the middle, is the largest and, as the target of most tourists, though thankfully it only has a few tacky souvenir shops; if you take the right fork immediately after entering the jetty, you'll see far fewer visitors and more "real" life. It's best to try one of the other jetties too, especially in the early evenings, when a myriad of red lights create a truly cinematic scene, though do be sensitive in these cramped residential environments – they're not ideal for loud conversations and incessant photography.

KOMTAR

the Top@KOMTAR Charge (wine and dinner options available) • http://thetop.com.my • **Penang House of Music** Charge • http://penanghouseofmusic.com

George Town's most prominent landmark, the **Kompleks Tun Abdul Razak** (**KOMTAR**) is a 68-storey cylindrical tower at the western end of the city centre. It languished for years, only partially filled with local government offices and malls clustered beneath and around it, and serving mainly as a transport hub. In 2015, three new levels were added to the existing 65, increasing the structure's height to 249m. Rebranded as **the Top@KOMTAR**, the extension has a 360-degree panoramic observatory, several restaurants and, at the very top, a bistro next to the open-air glass **Rainbow Skywalk**, Southeast Asia's first thrilling walk into the clouds.

Among KOMTAR's other (forgettable) theme-park-styled attractions and museums, don't miss **Penang House of Music**, on the fourth floor of ICT Digital Mall, next to Pranging Mall. The exhibits in this interactive museum span Penang's rich pop-music history from the 1940s to the 1960s. Their performance space has live jazz and other musical events and workshops.

Thai Temple

Lorong Burma, in the Pulau Tikus area on the northern edge of town • Free • Bus #101, #103 or #304; get off on Jalan Kelawei

The Buddhist **Thai Temple** (Wat Chaiya Mangkalaram) dates to the 1900s and is noticeably very different to the Chinese equivalents elsewhere in Penang. Brightly painted, it has flame-edged eaves and a huge, gilded pagoda, all soft curves. The main hall's entrance is flanked by *nagas* – fierce serpents painted gold and bright green – and guarded by two hefty demons wielding swords. The aircraft-hangar-like interior is a stark contrast to the exterior; in it lies a 33m-long **reclining Buddha** statue, draped in a gold sarong and with his aura flaming about him.

Burmese Temple

Lorong Burma, Pulau Tikus • Free • 04 226 9575 • Bus #101, #103 or #304; get off on Jalan Kelawei

The guardians of the **Burmese Temple** (Dharmikarama Temple) are two snarling white and gold lions, with scales, claws and fiery trim. The Buddha inside stands, smiling mysteriously into the gloom, one oversized white hand pointing up, and one down. The grounds are a bit nicer than those over the road at Wat Chaiya Mangkalaram, with more greenery and less concrete, and a few naturalistically painted statues.

Nattukottai Chettiar Temple

Jalan Kebun Bunga • Free • 04 227 1322 • Bus #10 from Pengkalan Weld

The **Nattukottai Chettiar Temple** (more formally the **Arulmigu Thandayuthapani Temple**) is the focus of the riotous three-day Hindu **Thaipusam** festival, in honour of Lord Subramanian (January or February). One of the crowning moments is the arrival of a silver chariot carrying the statue of Lord Murugan, and a golden chariot, introduced in 2017 to carry the statue's spear. The temple itself has an unusual wooden colonnaded walkway with exquisite pictorial tiles, leading up to the inner sanctum, where a life-sized solid-silver peacock bows its head to the deity, Lord Subramanian.

Botanic Gardens

Jalan Kebun Bunga, 6km west of central George Town • Free • http://botanicalgardens.penang.gov.my • Bus #10 (every 45min; 45min)

Dating to 1884, George Town's **Botanical Gardens** boast extensive lawns, a stream and little jungly waterfall, and several (rather paltry) plant houses. It's often packed with groups of exercising Malaysians, who storm around the circuit trail.

You can walk to **Penang Hill** (see page 156) from here using the so-called jeep track, but it's a tough uphill hike (3hr) – better to head down this way. A much easier hike just outside the gardens begins at the circular Chinese **moon gate arch** easily spotted on the main road; from here a wooded trail leads uphill, with views back over George Town. Most people head back down once they've reached the signed "Station 3" (allow 30min to get here).

ARRIVAL AND DEPARTURE — GEORGE TOWN

Unless you're on a plane or ferry, you'll reach or leave Penang island by one of two mammoth bridges linking it with the mainland part of the state: the 14km **Penang Bridge** (from Seberang Prai, just south of Butterworth) and the 24km **Second Penang Bridge** (from Batu Kawan, 15km south of Butterworth). Also note that 2030 is due to see the opening of the **Mutiara Line**, an elevated LRT that will run along the east coast of the island from the airport to George Town, and then across the Butterworth – hopefully a real game-changer in this extremely congested part of the country.

BY PLANE

Penang International Airport One of the busiest in the country, and boasting flights to Cambodia, China, Indonesia, Myanmar, Taiwan, Thailand, Vietnam and even Dubai, the airport (http://penangairport.com), 19km south of George Town at Bayan Lepas, has two tourist information counters (daily: Tourism Malaysia 8am–10pm; Penang Global Tourism 9am–5pm), a few ATMs, and car rental kiosks. Buses #401 and #401E (both every 30min) run from outside the building to the terminal at Pengkalan Weld (1hr), via the KOMTAR building in the west of the city centre (see page 149); bus #102 (hourly) also serves KOMTAR and then heads out to the beach at Batu Ferringhi (almost 2hr total). The fact that buses take forever makes Grab especially popular in Penang, and it beats the taxi prices between the airport and George Town (25min, if you're lucky; more than double that, if you're not). The airport operates a coupon system for unmetered taxis – buy a ticket from inside the airport building.

Destinations Johor Bahru (6–7 daily; 1hr 10min); Kota Bharu (3 weekly; 1hr); Kota Kinabalu (3–5 daily; 2hr 45min); Kuala Lumpur (KLIA: 1–4 hourly; Subang: 7 daily; 1hr); Kuching (2–4 daily; 2hr); Langkawi (4–5 daily; 35min); Singapore (11 daily; 1hr 25min).

BY TRAIN

Penang's train station is in Butterworth (see page 140). From here, you can either catch a Grab or a cab to George Town (20min) or follow the signed footbridge to the ferry. There is also a train ticket office at George Town's ferry terminal, or you can just buy online (http://kmtb.com.my).

BY BUS

In addition to online purchase methods (such as http://redbus.my and http://easybook.com), there are bus company kiosks on the ground floor of the Prangin Mall close to the KOMTAR building; informal travel agents on Lebuh Chulia (plus some hostels) sell train, bus and Langkawi ferry tickets.

Express bus station At Sungai Nibong, 8km southwest of George Town on Jalan Sultan Azlan Shah, the express bus station is served by several local buses, including #102 (for the airport, the KOMTAR building and Batu Ferringhi, hourly), plus #307 and #401 (both serve KOMTAR and the Pengkalan Weld terminal; every 30–45min). Departures from the bus station often head first to Butterworth, although a few southbound buses bypass it. In general, though, Butterworth still has more frequent services and a wider range of destinations, so it may pay to catch the ferry to the mainland and pick up a bus there.

Backpacker minibuses Run by tour agencies, minivan shuttles serving the east coast, Cameron Highlands and southern Thailand, among other destinations, pick up and drop passengers at hostels and the Prangin Mall, with tickets sold at both of these.

BY FERRY

Butterworth Ferries shuttle between Butterworth and Pengkalan Weld (every 20min–1hr; 20min; tiny fare to George Town, free to Butterworth), docking at a terminal close to the local bus station at the end of Chulia Street.

BY CAR

Driving to George Town Whichever bridge you use, tolls are payable only on the journey over from the mainland, and only using a local Touch 'N Go Card (http://touchngo.com.my) – you won't be able to go through the turnpike without one. Arriving on the island, bear right (north) up the coast for George Town. There's a reasonably central car park in the KOMTAR building on Jalan Penang.

GETTING AROUND

By bus Rapid Penang (http://rapidpg.com.my) operates buses across Penang state, though on the island they're far from rapid. Many island routes originate at their station on Pengkalan Weld, with a station beneath the KOMTAR building serving as a secondary hub. The website gives a breakdown of routes, operating times (daily roughly 6am–9.30pm, although some services wind down much earlier or later) and frequencies (every 15min–1hr depending on the route). Fares climb with distance travelled. A seven-day pass, Rapid Passport, offers unlimited travel and is available at the bus station, KOMTAR and the Penang Global Tourism tourist office (see page 151). Remember that drivers don't give change. The overpriced double-decker Hop-On Hop-Off (http://myhoponhopoff.com/pg) plies a city route (13 stops) and a beach route (15 stops), connecting all major tourist sites.

By taxi It's most convenient to use Grab (http://grab.com/my), as taxi drivers don't use their meters much and tend to overcharge, but there are ranks on Pengkalan Weld, on Penang Rd near the *Cititel* hotel, and on Jalan Dr Lim Chwee Long, around the Prangin Mall. To book a taxi in advance, call Penang Taxi Drivers Association (04 262 5721).

By trishaw The humble trishaw (*beca*) clings on in George Town, mainly for the benefit of tourists. You'll find the vehicles parked up on Lebuh Penang at the corner with Lebuh Muntri, and on Lebuh Armenian close to the Yap Kongsi, among other places.

By bike Bike sharing system LinkBike (http://linkbike.my) has 25 docking stations scattered around George Town, Straits Quay and Queensbay. Download the app, purchase credit and scan the QR code to get your bike. Some guesthouses and shops rent bicycles out too.

By motorbike Most guesthouses in Chulia St have motorbikes for rent.

By car Hawk, at the airport (http://hawkrentacar.com.my); Hertz, 38 Lebuh Farquhar (http://hertz.com); Mayflower, at the airport (http://mayflowercarrental.com.my).

INFORMATION AND TOURS

Penang Global Tourism Ground floor, The Whiteaways Arcade, Lebuh Pantai; 04 263 1166, http://mypenang.gov.my. Penang state's tourist office can provide maps and leaflets on various aspects of local history and culture, some of which can be downloaded from their website, where you can also get e-coupon twenty percent discounts for several tours and many of George Town's hit-and-miss museums.

Tourism Malaysia 10 Jalan Tun Syed Shah Barakbah; 04 262 2093, http://malaysia.travel. Close to Fort Cornwallis, this is one of the more knowledgeable Tourism Malaysia offices.

Tour guides If you have a special interest in, for example, architecture or history, or want to get off the beaten track, it can be worth engaging a professional guide at the Penang Tourist Guides Association (7 Lebuh Cannon; Tues–Sun; http://ptga.my).

ACCOMMODATION   SEE MAP PAGE 144

There's such a vast choice of hotels and guesthouses in George Town that there's little reason to base yourself further afield. That said, it's feasible to stay at the Batu Ferringhi beach or Balik Pulau and see George Town on day-trips.

HOTELS

★ 23 Love Lane 23 Love Lane; http://23lovelane.com. Step through the square gateway hung with lanterns and it immediately feels like you've arrived at a private villa. Set around a lush garden of frangipani trees are ten spacious rooms, eclectically done out in snazzy hues. Besides doubles, there's also a two-level family unit and a glorious three-bedroom shophouse. Breakfast and afternoon tea are included. $$$

The Blue Mansion 14 Lebuh Leith; http://cheongfatttzemansion.com. An expensive choice, but there are few more characterful places to stay in Penang. Cheong Fatt Tze's former villa (see page 143) now offers eighteen stylish suites plus a swimming pool, spa, reading room and its own restaurant (*Indigo*; see page 153) and bar. Noise from the adjacent *Red Garden* food court can be a little annoying at night, though. Breakfast is included. $$$$

Chulia Mansion 413 Chulia St; http://qanova.om.my. If you must stay on busy Chulia St, this tall, refurbished concrete hotel is a reliable option, with good-value rooms and a sheltered rooftop with open-air bar and a free jacuzzi. They also serve free-flowing wine, coffee, tea and ice cream to guests. $$

Citadines Connect 202 Lebuh Noordin; http://discoverasr.com. It might seem a pity to come to George Town and end up sytaying at a chain hotel, but this one's pretty good, and usually very fair value for money. It is at least housed in what looks like a trendy take on a colonial mansion, though everything else is very modern, and there's a lovely swimming pool with a jacuzzi tub at the end. $$$

Le Dream 139 Jalan Pintal Tali; https://le-dream-boutique-hotel.viue.com. The snazziest in an endless series of central George Town's gentrifying refurbishments, *Le Dream* has an attractive neo-noir decor and smart rooms with Japanese-style bathrooms. A perk is the panoramic rooftop with bar and mini swimming pool, great for sunsets and city views. On the ground floor, upmarket restaurant *Le Vie* is popular for French-fusion mains and inch-thick

Aussie-style ribeye steaks. $$$

★ **Eastern & Oriental (E&O)** 10 Lebuh Farquhar; http://eohotels.com. Some rooms at Penang's historic hotel (see page 142) are set in the original colonial building, while many more are in a fifteen-storey newer wing. But you'll pay hardly much more to stay in the former, where you can immerse yourself in what feels like a period mansion right on the seafront. The new wing has an infinity pool, and the original wing has a pool within a couple of metres of the sea. Breakfast is included. $$$$

East Indies Mansion 25 Lebuh China; http://eastindieshotel.com. Converted from a recently restored private residence, this boutiquey hotel was once a tycoon's home set around two adjacent Chinese courtyards. Some of the ten suites have mezzanines (with an extra queen bed) and a pretty spiral staircase. Breakfast is extra, but there's a huge kitchen and dining hall for guest's use. $$$

Jawi Peranakan Mansion 153 Jalan Hutton; http://georgetownheritage.com. Swish boutique hotel whose design conjures a legacy of opulent Muslim-Indian colonial traders. The eight mansion rooms and six family suites, some with elevated wooden mezzanines, maintain the mansion's original fittings, accompanied by a drizzle of authentic touches sourced directly from South India. Breakfast is included. $$$

Penaga Corner of Jalan Hutton & Lebuh Clarke; http://hotelpenaga.com. A block of 45 elegant rooms and several family villas set around a pool and garden in walking distance to all the main sites. Each of the spacious and naturally well-lit suites has a unique design, warm wooden floors and original beams. *Penaga* also runs an artist residency programme, and guests are invited to socialize with whoever is working in-house at the moment. Breakfast costs extra. $$$$

★ **Ren I Tang** 82a Lebuh Penang (entrance on Lebuh China); http://renitang.com. This imposing three-storey colonial building originally housed a Chinese apothecary, its name now given to the mid-range hotel that has emerged following a splendid conversion – although they've deliberately retained plenty of elements from the old herbalist's shop. There's a vast range of rooms, including a family unit, a self-contained apartment and assorted doubles, some with distressed paintwork for that aged look. Note that there's no lift, but they can winch your luggage to the top floor, on request. Breakfast is included. $$$

Spices 29 Lebuh China; http://spiceshotel.com. Tucked in behind Armenian Park, *Spices* feels more like an upmarket guesthouse. The rooms are large, with high ceilings and tall windows, and believe it or not, there's a living Bodhi tree on the premises. $$

HOSTELS AND GUESTHOUSES

Carnarvon House 28 Lorong Carnarvon; http://facebook.com/carnarvonhouse. Not to be confused with nearby *Carnarvon Suites*, you'll enjoy the old-school vibes are you enter this guesthouse – and then get surprised when things take a turn for the modern once you pass through the lobby. Rooms are likewise furnished in a fresh manner, though many have windows and ceilings that remind guests of the building's vintage. $$

The Frame Guest House 168 Lebuh Chulia; http://theframeguesthouse.com. Another in a series of cookie-cutter industrial shabby-chic George Town guesthouses, which are so popular with young flashpackers. Rooms have all the bells and whistles the standard demands, but lack distinctive character. This said, the long and airy common kitchen is a nice touch. $

House of Journey 47 Lorong Seckchuan; http://facebook.com/houseofjourneyspenang. Inspiring backpacker hostel with large and airy dorms, a sociable vibe, and hundreds of comments and travel tips scribbled on the walls. The hairdryers and individual mirrors in the shared bathrooms are a welcome touch in this price category. $

Li's Inn 19 Lorong Soo Hong; 012 456 6066. Boasting a pretty design and pretty low prices, this is a good budget choice, with rooms (mostly with shared facilities) and common areas alike given a pared-down look. One of the only regular complaints is about the early call to prayer from the nearby mosque. $$

Red Inn Court 35c Jalan Masjid Kapitan Keling; http://redinncourt.com. A nicely converted shophouse with polished wooden floors, although the dorms are basic and unremarkable. The doubles are far better value, though sadly the free breakfast offerings have also gradually become worse over the years. $

Roommates Penang 17b Lorong Chulia; http://bit.ly/RoommatesPenang. This tiny hostel has just two eight-bed dorms, and feels all the homelier for it. They're cosy, too, with privacy curtains and built-in lights for each bunk bed. $

EATING

SEE MAPS PAGES 143 AND 144

Despite lacking the glitz of KL's eating scene, Penang has earned a solid international reputation as the jewel in Asia's street-food crown. Rightly or not, people the world over come to relish local specialities such as **asam laksa**, a fishy rendition of *laksa* with the tang of tamarind; and **nasi kandar**, Muslim–Indian curries served with rice. The latter is ubiquitous in Malaysia now, of course, but originated, so the story goes, with Penang street vendors who carried their dishes in pots hanging from a shoulder pole (*kandar*).

RESTAURANTS

Halab 381 Lebuh Chulia; http://halab.my. The hugely popular Penang offshoot of a Middle Eastern restaurant chain from KL. You'll probably have to queue to get in at

dinnertime, but those that do can expect to be rewarded with delectable dips, grilled meats and the like. $$$
Indigo 14 Lebuh Leith; http://cheongfatttzemansion.com. By far the most refined place to dine in Penang, the main restaurant of the *Blue Mansion* hotel (see page 151) is a typically fancy affair, with inventive three-course lunch and dinner meals showcasing a fusion of Eastern and Western tastes, and all consummately prepared. There's a terrific wine list to boot. $$$$
Jawi House 85 Lebuh Armenian; http://jawihouse.com. A celebration of the Jawi Peranakan culinary heritage, cultivated by Middle Eastern and northern Indian spice traders who came to Penang and married local Malay women. Try specialities such as herbal *lemuni* rice, Jawi *biriyani*, or the highly recommended house signature *bamieh* – spice-rich tomato and lamb stew served with crusted Bengali bread. $$$
★ **Nasi Padang Minang** 92 Transfer Rd. A feast of tangy Padang food cooked by Indonesian residents and housed in a Chinese *kopitiam*. Take your own rice and dishes, and elbow your way to a table, as it's always packed with local workers on lunch break. The *ikan sumbat* (deep fried fish stuffed with shallots), is recommended. $
Tai Tong 45 Lebuh Cintra; http://facebook.com/taitong restaurantpenang. This dim sum restaurant has plastic chairs, wall fans and utilitarian metal trolleys groaning with food. The dim sum – only mornings and evenings – is excellent, including standards such as yam puffs and prawn dumplings; at lunchtime and at night the kitchen does à la carte orders, with dishes such as victory chicken (crisply roasted) and veg stir-fries. $$
Woodlands 60 Lebuh Penang; 04 263 9764. Run by two brothers, this a/c place is a tad smarter than the other Indian veg places in the area, and the cooking is a cut above, too. Come here for the usual *dosai* and South Indian snacks, plus North Indian dishes such as *malai kofta* (cheesy potato dumplings in a creamy sauce). $$

CAFÉS AND DESSERTS

★ **China House** 153 & 155 Lebuh Pantai, with another entrance at 183b Lebuh Victoria; http://chinahouse.com. my. This café-restaurant-gallery led the charge of Western-style venues setting up shop in George Town. It's famed for its enormous range of luscious cakes – more than two dozen at any time, including their signature tiramisu – though it also serves great meals (pies, pasta, etc) and breakfasts. Also a fun place to drink in the evening (see page 154). $$
The Mugshot 302 Lebuh Chulia; http://facebook.com/ TheMugshotCafePenang. This little café does excellent sesame bagels, baked in their own wood-fired oven. Wash them down with excellent coffee or freshly squeezed juice;

there's also homemade yoghurt in exotic flavours such as jackfruit and *gula melaka* (palm molasses). The artisan bakery next door is run by the same people, offering focaccia, poppy seed bloomers and the like. $$
Penang Road Famous Teochew Cendol 29 Lebuh Keng Kwee; http://chendul.my. Penang's quintessential ice-and-sugar-based sweets, *cendol* and *ais kacang*, have been dished up here for fifty-odd years, and they're absolutely delicious. Queues can be prodigious, but they go down fast, and you can often cheat them by sitting inside (if there's room) and being served more quickly. $
Toh Soon Café Off 184 Campbell St; 017 427 9327. Tucked up a side lane full of tables under a metal awning, this street-side *kopitiam* is perfect for coffees and all-day breakfast of *roti bakar* with *kaya* and boiled eggs. Constantly packed, but worth the wait. $

STREET FOOD AND HAWKER CENTRES

Line Clear In an alleyway by 177 Jalan Penang, 04 261 4440. The origins of the name are lost, although it may have been a cry related to cleaning drains or settling the bill. What isn't in doubt is the decades-long popularity of the *nasi kandar* in this unprepossessing joint. $
New Lane Hawker Centre Lorong Baru. An alternative to touristy Gurney Drive, yet increasingly popular with foreigners, New Lane's cluster of open-air hawker stalls has a bit of everything Penang is famous for, all within walking distance of town. $
★ **Penang Road Famous Laksa** 5 Lebuh Keng Kwee; http://instagram.com/penangroadfamouslaksa. Overly basic though it may look (barely a thing seems to have changed since they first opened up in 1970), this is the best place in town, bar none, for *asam laksa* – these steaming bowls of goodness really, *really* hit the spot, and were recently recognized with a Michelin bib gourmand (many years after they were first recognized by *Rough Guides*, of course). $
★ **Red Garden Food Paradise** 20 Lebuh Leith; http:// redgarden-food.com. Though locals often regard this place as touristy, it's quite possible that their parents or grandparents are here, grooving to the sound of extremely cheesy live bands. It's all quite entertaining, and this food court also offers an excellent range of hawker dishes, even stretching to Japanese and Filipino cuisine. $
Roti Canai Transfer Road Transfer Rd, between Jalan Hutton and Jalan Koyah. Sit at the roadside among chatty locals to enjoy Penang's *roti canai*, *mamak*-style at this eighty-year-strong powerhouse. Famous for *roti* and curry, frothy *kopi*, and boiled eggs on *roti bakar* – toasted bread smeared with coconut jam and butter. $

DRINKING AND NIGHTLIFE

Besides our selection, the pedestrianized eastern end of Jalan Penang, aka **Upper Penang Rd**, has two rows of

A YEAR OF PENANG FESTIVALS

For its size, Penang hosts an impressive number of **cultural events**, from religious celebrations to international arts festivals. Timing your visit with one of these can be the highlight of any trip; keep up with schedules on Penang Tourism's website (mypenang.gov.my).

JANUARY–APRIL

Thaipusam (Jan–Feb) Devotees carry *kavadi* from George Town to the Waterfall Hilltop temple.

Chinese New Year (Jan–Feb) Celebrated with fervour in George Town, with lion dances and fireworks, especially on the ninth day at the Clan Jetties on Weld Quay.

Chap Goh Meh (Jan–Feb) On the fifteenth day of Chinese New Year, unmarried girls throw oranges into the sea, traditionally an auspicious omen to get a good husband.

Penang Hot Air Balloon Fiesta (Feb) Huge hot-air balloons fill up the sky at Padang Polo in George Town, close to the Botanical Gardens.

MAY–AUGUST

George Town World Heritage Site Celebration (7–9 July) Three days of cultural events and pop-up stages to celebrate George Town's UNESCO status (http://facebook.com/GeorgeTownCelebrations).

George Town Festival (weekends in Aug) A month-long celebration packed with local and international art, music, drama, film and dance – most of it free of charge (http://georgetownfestival.com).

Hungry Ghost Festival (Aug–Sep) Quirky Chinese religious festival celebrated with pop-up stages to appease the return of demanding dead ancestors.

SEPTEMBER–DECEMBER

Nine Emperor Gods (Sept–Oct) A parade of chariots to welcome the arrival of the Taoist gods, with some light acts of self-injury.

Mid-Autumn Festival (Sept–Oct) Chinese festival celebrated eating moon cakes, which were used in ancient China to carry secret messages.

Deepavali (Nov) The Indian festival of lights enlivens the streets of Little India, George Town.

George Town Literary Festival (last weekend of Nov) Increasingly significant Southeast Asian literary event (http://georgetownlitfest.com).

Penang Island Jazz Festival (early Dec) Annual summit of international jazz musicians and fans, held at Batu Ferringhi.

Penang International Dragon Boat Festival (Dec) Dragon boats from all over Asia race on Teluk Bahang.

---

cookie-cutter pubs and a few dance clubs. Several discos also line **Beach and Chulia St** – expect trendy techno and R&B, and a predominantly well-heeled Chinese crowd. **Nagore Square**, a 10min walk from Chulia St up Hutton Rd, is a more interesting entertainment strip, packed with open-air bars, restaurants, cafés and a largely local crowd. The middle part of **Chulia St** and down along Love Lane and Muntri St has turned, for better or worse, into a blander version of Bangkok's Khaosan Rd.

BARS AND CLUBS

★ **Antarabangsa Enterprise** 21 Lorong Stewart. This place may bring back memories for Southeast Asia veterans – a Thai island or Lao village, perhaps, or back-in-the-day Myanmar. It's basically a shop selling cheap booze, which turns into a bar of sorts since people often want to consume their drink immediately; when there's no room inside, people spill onto the road, and when there's no room at the plastic tables, people use the tops of nearby cars instead, which is pretty funny if you're not the owner. It's all quite wonderful, and a good way to meet locals.

China House 153 & 155 Lebuh Pantai, with another entrance at 183b Lebuh Victoria; http://chinahouse.com.my. Though primarily a café-restaurant (see page 153), this also makes a highly atmospheric place to drink, with a decent list of cocktails and craft beer, plus bottles of soju that barely cost any more than in the shops.

★ **Good Friends Club** 39 Jalan Gurdwara; http://

facebook.com/goodfriendsclubpenang. Packed with local artists and hipsters, this shabby-chic cocktail bar has a tiny, dimly lit backroom filled with low tables. The bar out front serves drinks and snacks, and more chairs spill on the kerb under a bright-pink neon sign – you can't miss it.

Hong Kong Bar 371 Lebuh Chulia; 04 261 9796. You can't miss this Chinese-run dive, adorned with military insignia – if you're over forty, this will feel like a haven compared to other venues on Chulia.

Magazine 63 63 Jalan Magazine; http://facebook.com/ magazineM63. Hidden behind a wooden partition inside an apparently empty corner shophouse, George Town's first speakeasy relies on the element of surprise. Once you push the right wooden panel, the glamorous interior, fitted like an old Chinese opium den, complete with smartly attired waiters, will take you back a couple of centuries. Alas, the overpriced cocktails won't, but the well-choreographed concept is a mark above the competition. DJs play most nights. Reservations recommended.

Mish Mash 24 Muntri St; http://facebook.com/mm2 penang. Fairly upmarket bar with a large menu of not-so-cheap cocktails, an obsession with whisky, a good selection of tobacco and cigars, and a largely local crowd.

Seventy7 54 Jalan Chow Thye; http://seventy7bar.com. Penang's main LGBTQ+ venue is a friendly affair in a chic refurbished shophouse, drawing a crowd of mainly twenty- and thirty-somethings.

Three Sixty Degree Sky Bar Bayview Hotel, 25a Lebuh Farquhar; http://360rooftop.com.my. This open space around the *Bayview* revolving restaurant is a good spot for cocktails, Nyonya snacks and a bird's-eye view of the *E&O Hotel*, St George's Church and the dimly lit expanses of shophouses, dwarfed by the cylindrical KOMTAR building and more modest towers beyond the conservation zone.

Tipsy Cow 324 Lebuh Chulia; http://facebook.com/ tipsycowchuliapenang. Sometimes you just want a cheap, tacky bar to sit down at – this is that bar. Cocktails aren't that good; stick to beer and super-cheap soju.

LIVE MUSIC

Soundmaker Second floor, 62 Pengkalan Weld; http:// facebook.com/SoundmakerStudio. One of a rare breed in Malaysia, *Soundmaker* is a countercultural rock venue specializing in indie, punk, metal and so forth, with the occasional shot of hip-hop for good measure. Check their Facebook page for a list of gigs.

SHOPPING   SEE MAP PAGE 144

George Town has a mixture of old shops selling traditional goods, cheap-and-cheerful touristy outlets, and several pricier galleries and souvenir shops, generally rather chichi.

MARKETS

Chowrasta Market Jalan Chowrasta. Even if it now looks like a shopping mall, Chowrasta is one of the city's oldest markets, mainly selling produce, although there are some secondhand book stalls upstairs. Proceedings spill over colourfully into Jalan Kuala Kangsar behind; note too the traditional spring-roll-wrap maker on Jalan Chowrasta. Daily 7.30am–noon.

MALLS

Prangin Mall Jalan Dr Lim Chwee Leong; http://prangin-mall.com. The most popular of the malls around KOMTAR, unpretentious Prangin proves yet again that in Malaysia upmarket isn't usually best. There's something for everyone – a Parkson department store, a supermarket, bargain clothes shops, electronics and phone shops (fourth floor) and a food court (fifth floor).

BOOKSHOPS

Gerakbudaya 226 Beach Street; http://gerakbudaya penang.com. The best bookshop in town is a radical upstart with hard-to-find titles on Malaysian society and politics, Asian-focused coffee-table books, as well as English paperbacks. A great starting point to find out about George Town's many art events, too.

CLOTHES, TEXTILES AND SHOES

Kedai Songkok Corner of Chulia St & Lebuh King; 04 263 1290. The last remaining traditional Malay skullcap artisan in Penang still makes *songkoks* to order.

Rozana's Batik 81b Lebuh Aceh; http://bit.ly/Rozanas Batik. Small, family-run shop specializing in hand-painted textiles on cotton or silk, with some clothing available to buy. They also run walk-in batik classes.

Sam's Batik House 183 & 185 Jalan Penang; http://sams batikhouse.com. This shop has mounds of slightly garish batik and silk, including tops and dresses galore; there's more like this a few doors south at the Penang Bazaar.

SOUVENIRS, CURIOS AND GIFTS

Jonathan Yun Sculptural Jewellery 152 Jalan Masjid Kapitan Keling; http://jonathanyunjewelry.com. Bespoke pieces of fine jewellery, mainly in silver, that draw on Straits Chinese patterns and motifs by award-winning artist Jonathan Yun.

Shop Howard 154 Jalan Masjid Kapitan Keling; http:// studiohoward.com. Run by local shutterbug Howard Tan, this place sells artsy pictures and hip collectables.

DIRECTORY

Banks and exchange The major banks are on Lebuh Pantai, with ATMs also located on Jalan Penang and at the

KOMTAR development; moneychangers are easily found on Jalan Masjid Kapitan Kling and elsewhere.

Consulates Australia, 1c Hutton Ln (04 226 7285); Indonesia, 467 Jalan Burma (04 227 4686); Thailand, 1 Jalan Tuanku Abdul Rahman (04 226 8029).

Hospitals General Hospital, Jalan Residensi (04 222 5333); Gleneagles, 1 Jalan Pangkor (04 222 9111).

Internet access The island's Wireless@Penang service offers free wi-fi at malls, the KOMTAR building, the ferry terminal and even a few sights, including the top of Penang Hill. When connecting for the first time, you may need to register: just type in an arbitrary twelve-digit number in response to the question about your ID card/MyKad (you won't need it again).

Pharmacies Guardian and Watsons both have branches at KOMTAR and the Prangin Mall (both daily 10am–10pm).

Police The police headquarters is on Jalan Penang; emergencies 999.

Visa extensions The immigration office (Pejabat Imigresen) is on the corner of Lebuh Pantai and Lebuh Light (Mon–Thurs 7.30am–1pm & 2–5.30pm, Fri 7.30am–12.15pm & 2.45–5.30pm; 04 250 3410).

Ayer Itam (Air Hitam) and around

6km west of George Town • Bus #201, 203, 204 or #502 (45min)

The town of **AYER ITAM** amounts to little more than a 100m-long bottleneck, with the traffic squeezed between shops and the canvas awnings of a busy wet market. There are three reasons to visit: **Kek Lok Si**, a ludicrously overbuilt hilltop Buddhist complex; the colonial-era retreat of **Penang Hill** to the north; and the best-known *laksa* stall on the island. You could easily do all three, arriving at lunchtime for *laksa*, then spending a couple of hours at Kek Lok Si before heading up Penang Hill for views of the island lighting up at dusk.

Kek Lok Si

A 5min walk west from Jalan Pasar • Free; charge for climbing steps to top or using Sky Lift • http://kekloksitemple.com • From the market bus stop on Jalan Pasar, follow the road towards the temple and look out for a passageway on the left lined with trinket stalls; from here, steps ascend to the temple forecourt

Supposedly the largest Buddhist temple in Malaysia, **Kek Lok Si** was founded by the abbot of George Town's Kuan Yin Teng in the 1890s, when the initial bout of construction was bankrolled by Cheong Fatt Tze and other local tycoons. Today, the hill sprouts all sorts of fantastic shrines and pagodas, linked by multiple flights of steps, and bedecked with flags, lanterns and statues. The best time to visit is during Chinese New Year, when thousands of red lanterns and multicoloured LEDs illuminate the temple at night.

The two most prominent features of the temple are the white, seven-tier wedding-cake assemblage that is the **Ten Thousand Buddhas Pagoda**, capped by a golden Burmese stupa; and a 30m-high bronze statue of the goddess of mercy, **Kuan Yin**, sheltered from the elements by an open-sided pavilion, its pillars wreathed in carved dragons. Both can be reached either on foot (193 steps) or the easy way, using the **Sky Lift**, a sort of glass-sided funicular compartment that glides up and down the 45-degree slope.

Penang Hill

Jalan Stesen Bukit Bendera • Charge • http://penanghill.gov.my • Bus #204 from George Town; a 20min walk from Air Hitam and 25min from Kek Lok Si – turn left at roundabout signed "Bukit Bendera"

Once called Flagstaff Hill, when it was a retreat for British administrators, **Penang Hill** is now a mixed bag of gardens, woodland, shrines and colonial houses in various states of repair. The bus drops you at the foot of the hill close to the lower funicular station, where signs point the way to the **Bats Cave Temple**, worth a quick look for its colony of bats in a cave shrine at the back; they're regarded as auspicious because part of the Chinese term for "bat" sounds like the word for "luck". The **funicular**, a modern version of the original, built in 1923, can whisk you to the summit in just over five minutes. From here there's a great vista of the cape of George Town and across the straits to Butterworth.

For a decent couple of hours' **hike**, follow the main summit road round anticlockwise, heading towards the start of the path to Tiger Hill, then veer left on to Moniot Road. From here you can eventually join Viaduct Road, from where there are various routes back up to the summit. The sketch map on the leaflet given out with funicular tickets shows the options.

The Habitat
Bukit Bendera • Charge • http://thehabitat.my

Scattered around the hilltop park are a multicoloured Hindu temple, a mosque, an overpriced food court and numerous forgettable tourist traps. Worth visiting instead is **the Habitat**, an educational 1.6km guided hiking trail snaking along the course of an old British irrigation channel set above Penang Hill's best-conserved slope. The Habitat also operates a 230m-long **Canopy Walk**, as well as **Curtis Crest Treetop Walk**, Penang's highest, boasting 360-degree views that stretch all the way to Mount Jerai in Kedah.

EATING AND DRINKING   AYER ITAM, SEE MAP PAGE 140

Bellevue Summit of Penang Hill; 04 227 4006. Set in a dreary 1960s building, *Bellevue* is no colonial haven. Its saving grace is the terrace restaurant, which has good views, cream teas and highly regarded – though undeniably pricey – steamboat (for two people). $\overline{\$\$\$}$

David Brown's Restaurant and Tea Terraces On its own mound 100m from the upper funicular station, Penang Hill; http://penanghillco.com.my. A very English menu of cream teas, pies and steaks, plus a roast of the day and an excellent wine list, all in a smart country-pub-like setting – or as close to it as a house perched on a tropical hilltop can get. A few tables are set out on the immaculate lawn, and there's a separate *Sky Terrace* section for drinks and snacks. Tea and scones are recommended, or beef Wellington for a larger meal – when it's available. $\overline{\$\$\$}$

★ **Penang Air Itam Laksa** Jalan Pasar, Ayer Itam, where the bus sets down; http://facebook.com/penang.air.itam. laksa. Look for a small stall backed by a big red sign, and you'll find what many rate as the best *asam laksa* in Penang. The sauce is salty, sour and thick with *heh koh* prawn paste, all topped off with rice noodles, shredded vegetables, pounded fish and a handful of fresh herbs. Weekends only, unfortunately. $\overline{\$}$

Northwest Penang

An 18km-long road runs along Penang's northern coast, squeezed for much of the way between the sea and forests inland. The main settlement here, the dull beach resort of **Batu Ferringhi**, remains moderately popular as an alternative base to George Town and has a frequent (but slow) bus service to the city, though frankly you're not missing much if you simply shoot through to the **Tropical Spice Garden** or the coastal jungle of **Penang National Park** at **Teluk Bahang**, in the island's northwest corner. There's also a small clutch of minor sights along the road south of Teluk Bahang, en route to Balik Pulau.

Batu Ferringhi
Bus #101 from Pengkalan Weld/KOMTAR (every 20–30min) or #102 from the airport/KOMTAR (hourly)

To look at it now, you wouldn't think that **BATU FERRINGHI** was the standard-bearer for Penang tourism during the long years when George Town was in the doldrums. These days it distinctly plays second fiddle, thanks as much to its own ugly overdevelopment as George Town's successes.

Its centrepiece is some 2km of **beach**, not too narrow but with sand that, disappointingly, is the colour of milky tea. The whole beach is publicly accessible: either stride through the hotel compounds to reach it or, in the unlikely event staff are obstructive, use the path lined by beach-gear stalls that begins roughly opposite the McDonald's at the start of the strip. All that said, the beach still makes for a nice contrast with George Town and is decent enough for **watersports**, with multiple firms competing for custom. For a general look, turn up in the late afternoon when the

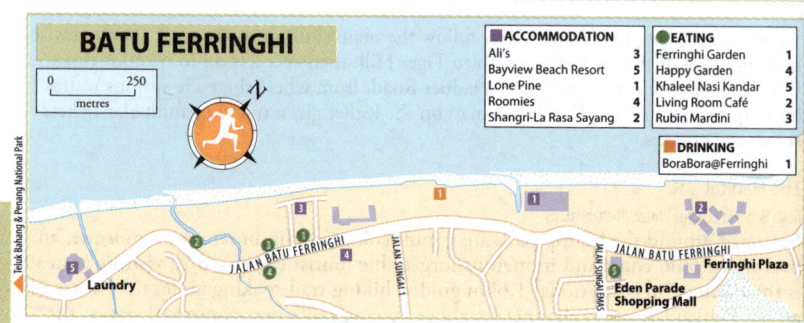

beach starts to get busy, and perhaps linger for an evening meal when the road comes alive with stalls selling batik, T-shirts and fake designer watches.

Tropical Spice Garden

Lone Crag Villa, Jalan Teluk Bahang • **Garden** Charge (inc audioguide); extra for guided tour (3 daily) • **Cooking classes** Charge • http://tropicalspicegarden.com • Bus #101 or #102

Between Batu Ferringhi and Teluk Bahang, the delightful **Tropical Spice Garden** has turned an abandoned rubber plantation into a cornucopia of herbs, spices and decorative flora, all set in a stylishly landscaped gully and shaded by former plantation trees. Three easy circuit trails loop between waterfalls and streams and introduce you to the plants and their commercial, culinary and traditional uses. There are **cookery classes**, a gift shop selling spices and products, and annexed **café** *Kanopi Coffee* (see page 159).

Teluk Bahang Road

Escape Charge • http://escape.my • **Entopia** Charge • http://entopia.com • Bus #101 or #102 both make a short detour here

Once it reaches the small town of **Teluk Bahang**, the **road** veers south and inland, passing two fairly major sights within the first kilometre before continuing to Balik Pulau. The first is **Escape** theme park, a series of obstacle-course-type challenges including zip lines and climbing ropes; to many visitors, these play second fiddle to the water park, whose longest slide is actually the **longest water slide in the world** – a whopping 1111m, meaning that you get to slide on your backside for more than a kilometre (if you're curious about the experience, many a video of the descent can be seen online). Right next to Escape is **Entopia**, a two-storey indoor landscaped park home to 15,000-odd free-flying butterflies, 200 species of plants, and all manner of frogs, snakes, stick insects and scorpions.

Penang National Park

At the end of a small coastal road 1.5km beyond the centre of Teluk Bahang • Free • **Nature guides** Half-day guided treks available for up to five people • **Boat rides** Trips to Monkey Beach and Kerachut available • http://bit.ly/PenangNationalPark • Bus #101 calls at the park (1hr from George Town) before doubling back to terminate at Teluk Bahang; bus #102 terminates at Teluk Bahang

PENANG NATIONAL PARK tends to fly under visitors' radar, but it's likeable all the same, a hilly chunk of old-growth forest, pandanus and mangroves. The trails lead to a handful of secluded, undeveloped **beaches**, where marine **turtles** nest throughout the year; the park also has some resident dusty-leaf monkeys in addition to the predictable long-tailed macaques.

At time of research, the **canopy walkway** was closed for maintenance. There are also two main trails, generally easy to follow, though steep and eroded in places. At the end of the initial 500m boardwalk, turn right for the 4.7km route to the **Muka Head Lighthouse**, where you might see sea eagles, passing **Monkey Beach** (3.4km), a good spot for a swim. Turn left for **Kerachut Beach** (3.4km), a cove with one of the only two neromictic lakes in the world (two layers of fresh and sea water that never mix), and a turtle hatchery at the far end; **Teluk Kampi** (4.9km) is yet another secluded beach.

At the park entrance is a booth staffed by **nature guides**, where you can book guided treks and buy useful gear. If you're short on time, talk to the various **boat operators** opposite the park entrance; they offer surprisingly cheap rides to the beaches.

ACCOMMODATION

NORTHWEST PENANG

BATU FERRINGHI, SEE MAP PAGE 158

Ali's 53 & 54b Jalan Batu Ferringhi; 017 500 7242. The best of a series of beachfront guesthouses, with bland, old-fashioned a/c rooms, some en suite, in a two-storey brick building surrounding a courtyard packed with pot plants. $

Bayview Beach Resort Western end of Batu Ferringhi; http://bbr.bayviewhotels.com. Rooms are arrayed around the impressive pyramid atrium at this reasonably priced hotel, with tennis courts and two swimming pools. Booking weeks in advance might bring discounts. $$$

Lone Pine 97 Jalan Batu Ferringhi; http://lonepinehotel.com. Now run by George Town's *Eastern & Oriental*, this boutique hotel was founded as a humble lodge in 1948. Completely renovated and extended since, it now comprises what might as well be a swanky apartment building behind the original, low-rise block with shuttered windows next to a well-tended sea-facing garden. The rooms are bright and contemporary, complemented by a spa, pool and several restaurants. Book online for discounts. $$$$

Roomies Fourth floor of the block opposite the Parkroyal Hotel, Jalan Batu Ferringhi; http://facebook.com/roomiespenang. The slickest guesthouse on the strip, with flashpacker capsule-style bunk beds plus two rooms, one sleeping three, the other a double with its own bathroom. $

★ **Shangri-La Rasa Sayang** Batu Ferringhi; http://shangri-la.com. One of the very first resorts at Batu Ferringhi is still recommendable today, a lush, sprawling complex topped by Malay-style roofs and with an excellent freeform pool. There's a garden wing for the hoi polloi and, for a premium of at least twenty percent, a boutique "Rasa" wing with its own pool, along with free cocktails and afternoon tea. $$$$

PENANG NATIONAL PARK

Campsites Penang National Park; http://wildlife.gov.my. There are free campsites at Monkey and Kerachut beaches, though bear in mind that either is a 75min trek from the entrance. Kerachut has basic bathrooms and a kitchen, but wherever you stay, bring your own tent, stove and kitchenware.

EATING

BATU FERRINGHI, SEE MAP PAGE 158

Eating in Batu Ferringhi is dominated by slightly overpriced restaurants, including an assortment of Middle Eastern places catering to the steady stream of Saudi and Gulf tourists.

Ferringhi Garden 34 Jalan Batu Ferringhi; http://facebook.com/ferringhigarden. The most elegant of the strip's restaurants, the outdoor tables drowning in potted orchids, ferns and pitcher plants, with plenty of stylish wood panelling and screens inside. There are two parts to the place: the *Coffee Garden*, serving light meals and snacks by day, and the main restaurant, with a more ambitious menu of Western/fusion dishes. $$$

Happy Garden Western end of Batu Ferringhi; 016 490 3543. *Happy Garden* looks more like a residential bungalow, in a lovely garden planted with bougainvillea, than a Hainanese restaurant. There's plenty of seafood on the menu, plus predictable Western-inspired dishes such as chicken chop. Breakfasts include oats, pancakes or sausage and egg. $$

Khaleel Nasi Kandar Ground floor, towards the rear of the Eden Parade Shopping Centre; 012 438 4146. A fine place to escape inflated prices and get your daily curry, *roti* and *teh tarik* fix – the food is genuinely above par, too. $

Living Room Café 43c Batu Ferringhi; http://facebook.com/LivingRoom11100. This informal place majors on Nyonya and other local cuisines, offering a limited number of dishes and doing them right. Locals tend to go for the beef *rendang*, although you can also take your pick from Western mains such as burgers and barbecued ribs. $$$$

Rubin Mardini 591 Jalan Batu Ferringhi; http://facebook.com/rubin.mardini. The best of a surprisingly large number of Middle Eastern restaurants hereabouts, with winning service, succulent grilled meat, and a simple yet amiable environment. $$

WEST OF BATU FERRINGHI, SEE MAP PAGE 140

Kanopi Coffee Tropical Spice Garden, 153a Jalan Batu Ferringhi; http://instagram.com/kanopicoffee. Part of the Tropical Spice Garden complex (see page 158), this place does indeed have a jungle feel to it, and it scratches a lot of itches – good Western brunch food for the peckish, excellent coffee for the caffeine-addicted, cold drinks and comfortable-enough seating for those brave enough to be on a bike ride in this part of Penang, and regular live music too. $$

DRINKING

SEE MAP PAGE 158

BoraBora@Ferringhi 72d Jalan Batu Ferringhi; http://borabora.com.my. Very decent beach bar and restaurant, with tables out on the sand and in the bar area under an atap roof. Food ranges from pizza to Malaysian staples; it's not haute cuisine, but the sunset compensates, as do the cocktails.

Balik Pulau

Stretching from the lower end of Teluk Bahang all the way to Pulau Betong in the far south, off-the-radar **BALIK PULAU** (literally "back of the island") roughly comprises one third of western Penang. It's by far the least developed part of the state, a paddy-field strewn coastal plain encased between the Andaman Sea and Penang Hill's western flanks, covered in viridian exotic fruit plantations, primarily coconut, banana, the endemic **nutmeg**, and the much prized, yet very smelly, **durian**. Roughly in the middle, Balik Pulau town is a 250m-long main street lined by old buildings, some recently tinted by Russian mural artist Julia Volchkova; though only **Fong Silversmith**, on the corner near the roundabout, is especially compelling. Its charming owner has been turning out simple, attractive jewellery for decades. At the other end of town there's a nineteenth-century convent and the **Sacred Heart Church**, a pale grey and cream tin-sided structure dating to 1854.

Balik Pulau is best experienced outside the town, pedalling through streams and paddies on a bicycle, or enjoying the fishing villages and beach at Pulau Betong, Penang's southwest corner, which also includes an islet of the same name. **Pantai Pasir Panjang** is one of the island's best and quieter beaches, on Penang's far southwestern headland, right in front of military base Kem Rimba Negara; watch out for the strong surf here. Uninhabited atoll Pulau Betong lies just north across the water; swimming here is prohibited, but it's a good spot for angling.

ARRIVAL AND GETTING AROUND

BALIK PULAU

By bus Bus #401, #401E or #502 runs to Balik Pulau Bus Hub (a 5min walk to the town's main strip) from George Town (#502 via Ayer Itam is the most direct service). It's also possible to catch the #501 from Teluk Bahang, hopping on and off en route to the sites. Bus #503 connects the Balik Pulau Bus Hub to Pulau Betong.

By bike Two reliable operators organize half and full-day bicycle tours (including return transfers from George Town). Explore Balik Pulau (http://facebook.com/explorebalikpulau) arrange tours in Balik Pulau's central area of Sungai Burong. Audi Dream Farm (http://audipenang.com) organize tours in the Pulau Betong area and also rent bikes.

ACCOMMODATION

SEE MAP PAGE 140

Audi Guest House 609 Jalan Pulau Betong, bus #503 stops nearby; http://facebook.com/AudiMTBClub. Charming Malay wooden kampung house, 6km from Pasir Panjang beach. Guests stay in fan dorms or simple tatami-style a/c rooms (sleeping up to seven; whole rooms are booked out) with spacious balconies overlooking the peaceful countryside. This is also Audi Dream Farm's headquarters, where you can rent bicycles or join tours. Breakfast costs extra. $

Bao Sheng Durian Farm Along the Balik Pulau–Teluk Bahang main road, close to Titi Kerawang waterfall; http://durian.com.my. Wake up and smell the durian in these two storeys of interconnected glass box rooms and private villas set around swimming pools on the slope of a durian farm. Mr "Durian" Seng, a true devotee of the spiky fruit, offers stay-and-eat packages in harvest season that include dinner, breakfast, and two durian tastings. Staying here off-season is no less charming, with good views over Penang and frequent burning-pink sunsets. Breakfast is included; dinner is extra. $$$

★ **Malihom** Up a steep hill off the main Balik Pulau–Teluk Kumbar main road; http://malihom.com. Pure high-class seclusion atop a private hill estate, with sweeping views over Penang's southeastern coast. The eight imported Thai wooden rice barns with en-suite bathrooms – some featuring sunken bathtubs with panoramic views, great for sunsets – are intimately clustered around the pool and restaurant-lobby. *Malihom*'s private 2km hiking trail passes through tropical fruit farms and woodland. Stays include one free transfer from the bottom of the hill. $$$$

EATING

SEE MAP PAGE 140

Jia Xiang Seafood 321 Mk 7 Pulau Betong, right at the village junction to Pantai Pasir Panjang; 019 746 8465. A popular no-frills *kampung* seafood restaurant dishing up fresh catch straight from the fish market nearby. You can bring in your own fish, which the chef will cook for you in lemongrass or homemade Thai-style sauce. Gets very busy on weekends. $\overline{\underline{\$\$\$}}$

Kim Laksa 67 Jalan Balik Pulau. The pineapple-tinged *asam laksa* and Thai curried *laksa* at this down-at-heel *kopitiam* in Balik Pulau town have people lining up some time before they start serving to make sure they get a bowl. $\overline{\underline{\$}}$

Snake Temple
Jalan Sultan Azlan Shah, close to the airport • Free • 04 643 7273 • Bus #102 from KOMTAR or #401 or #401E from George Town's Pengkalan Weld

Visible from the airport road, Penang's **Snake Temple** is a bright Buddhist affair, its forecourt guarded by two stone lions. Inside, the front altar – along with strategically placed shrubs in other halls – is draped in poisonous **green pit vipers** which, legend has it, mysteriously appeared upon completion of the temple in 1850. Pit vipers are naturally lethargic, but even so it's hard to account for quite how dozy the temple's specimens are – though you'd best not poke them to see if they're real.

Penang War Museum
Batu Maung • Charge • http://facebook.com/PenangWarMuseum • Bus #302

The **Penang War Museum** stands on the site of a 1930s British military fortress. You climb the hill to an area of bunkers, forts, underground tunnels and an observation tower, all designed to defend the position from a naval attack; unfortunately for the British, the Japanese stormed it from inland. The fort became a prison, abandoned after the war partly because it was believed to be haunted by those tortured to death here. It was recovered from the undergrowth and opened as a private museum during the 1980s.

Kedah and Perlis

The far northwest of Peninsular Malaysia is taken up by the states of Kedah and Perlis, which, in common with the northeast, were historically part of the Siamese sphere of influence. British rule this far north, in marked contrast to Penang and Perak, was relatively brief, kicking off in 1909 when the region was ceded to them by the Thais, who briefly reclaimed it during World War II courtesy of another treaty, this time with the invading Japanese.

    Kedah has long been billed as the Peninsula's *jelapang padi*, or rice bowl, and its landscape remains largely a mosaic of lustrous paddy fields. By far the best-known part of the state is the popular resort island of **Langkawi**, with good air links as well as ferry connections with Penang, Kuala Kedah, Kuala Perlis and southern Thailand. The mainland is easily bypassed, and the rewards for passing through are low-key, chiefly the **Ulu Muda Eco Reserve**, the odd **archeological remains** near the town of **Sungai Petani**, and the mosque-strewn capital, **Alor Setar**. **Perlis**, Malaysia's smallest state – at just 800 square km, it's ten percent larger than Singapore – is also the greenest and least visited. **Kelam Cave**, in a national park straddling the Thai border, is worth slowing down for between transport connections.

Sungai Petani and around

On the north bank of the Petani River, **SUNGAI PETANI** is the most populous town in Kedah, with bustling suburbs and industrial areas that thrive on its location in Penang's hinterland (Butterworth is just 35km away). There's nothing to see in the old town centre other than the Art Deco King George V **clock tower** on the main street, but the town is the jumping-off point for anyone travelling to the **Bujang Valley** archeological site by public transport.

Bujang Valley Archaeological Museum

15km northwest of Sungai Petani, 2km from Merbok's main street along a signed lane • Free • http://jjm.gov.my • Alor Setar-bound Maraliner buses from Sungai Petani's local bus station stop in Merbok (hourly; 45min), or charter a taxi (with a 1hr wait)

Just outside the town of **Merbok**, the **Bujang Valley Archaeological Museum** commemorates a significant Hindu-Buddhist kingdom that flourished here for hundreds of years, possibly from as early as the second century. That said, there's not very much to see; a brief visit of an hour or two is ample. First impressions are that you've arrived at the most surreal attraction in Malaysia, where a team of bricklayers has run riot on a landscaped hillside. What you're looking at are in fact the low, stepped remains of *candi* (temples) from various locations nearby, reassembled here in an unnaturally tight cluster.

The centrepiece, **Candi Bukit Batu Pahat**, is a 27m-long granite structure that was not moved, but restored *in situ*; the other *candi* are much smaller, some made of what look like worn, crimson-tinged brick, others suspiciously pristine. The on-site **museum** explains, somewhat incoherently, what little is known about the Bujang Valley kingdom, and how pre-war excavations brought its existence back to light. There are also some interesting finds from the various *candi*, including pots, gems and stone carvings of deities.

ARRIVAL AND INFORMATION SUNGAI PETANI

Sungai Petani lies on Route 1, which doubles up as the main street.

By train A couple of blocks south of the clock tower, a bridge up and over the railway line leads east to the train station (04 421 0703).

Destinations Alor Setar (hourly; 40min); Arau (hourly; 1hr); Butterworth (hourly; 35min); Ipoh (5 daily; 2hr); Kuala Kangsar (5 daily; 1hr 25min); Kuala Lumpur (5 daily; 4hr 20min); Taiping (5 daily; 1hr).

By bus The long-distance bus station is opposite the train station, in the UTC Building. The local bus station and taxi stand is on Jalan Petri, a further block south of the clock tower.

Destinations Alor Setar (every 45min–1hr; 1hr 30min); Butterworth (#EB60; every 45min, 6am–9pm; 45min); Ipoh (almost hourly; 4hr); Jerantut (for Taman Negara; 1 daily at 9.30pm; 8hr); Johor Bahru (at least 5 daily, all departing after 9pm; 10hr); Kota Bharu (2 daily at 11am and 8pm; 6hr); Kuala Besut (for Perhentian Islands; 1 daily at 10.50pm; 9hr); Kuala Kangsar (2 daily; 3hr); Kuala Lumpur (hourly; 5hr); Kuala Terengganu (2 daily; 5hr 30min); Kuantan (5 daily; 10hr); Lumut (for Pangkor; 3 daily; 4hr 30min); Melaka (4 daily; 7hr); Mersing (for Pulau Tioman; 1 daily at 10.15pm; 12hr); Seremban (3 daily; 5hr 30min); Singapore (4 daily; 10hr30min); Sik (en route to Ulu Muda; several daily; 2hr).

ACCOMMODATION AND EATING

There's no reason to stay in Sungai Petani unless you want to catch an early connection to Lembah Bujang. Eat at the Malay and Chinese stalls in food courts just north of Jalan Petri.

Big Banana Kampung Pengkalan; http://facebook.com. The best of several cheap, boutiquey hotels in Sungai Petani, with rooms that are a little bare but surprisingly stylish for this nondescript town; breakfast (usually included) is likewise served in a hall that could pass as a nice café, even in a far larger city. $$

Alor Setar

A largely Malay town, conservative in feel, **ALOR SETAR** (Alor Setar), Kedah's transport hub, is remarkably sleepy for a state capital, especially at night. Clustered around the padang are several historic buildings, including a prominent mosque and former **sultan's palace**, providing enough architectural and cultural interest that you might want to pause here for half a day en route to or from Langkawi, the Thai border or Ulu Muda Eco Park. **Orientation** is simple: the padang forms the heart of town, with the commercial centre to the east and what passes for Chinatown to the west across Route 1.

Padang

Balai Seni Negeri Free • **Galeri Sultan Abdul Halim** Charge

Alor Setar's **padang** and the open space on its north side are dotted with a mishmash of buildings, some associated with Kedah's ruling house. Within the padang itself, the

KEDAH AND PERLIS **THE WEST COAST**

long white-stucco **Balai Seni Negeri** is a courthouse-turned-gallery showcasing local artists. The curious octagonal tower topped by a yellow onion dome, on the western side of the open space, is the **Balai Nobat**, housing sacred instruments played only during royal ceremonies. At the north end is the low, Neoclassical facade of the former **High Court**, now the **Galeri Sultan Abdul Halim**, showcasing assorted royal regalia. The most refined building here, though, is the **Masjid Zahir** just across Jalan Pekan Melayu, which succeeds admirably despite being a mishmash of Moorish arches, a Turkish pencil minaret and weighty black bulbous domes.

Istana Balai Besar

The history of the padang's most important building, the elegant **Istana Balai Besar** (Royal Audience Hall), mirrors that of the town. Founded in 1735, it was badly damaged in 1770 by the Bugis (seafaring raiders from Sulawesi in Indonesia), and later by Thai armies in 1821. The present, late nineteenth-century version has a Malay multilayered shingle roof, supported by colonial-style iron columns and eave decorations, alongside a very European-influenced flowing staircase. One of its first functions was to host the **marriages** of Sultan Abdul Hamid's five eldest children in 1904: the celebrations lasted three months, and the cost bankrupted Kedah – forty buffaloes had to be slaughtered to feed the crowds each day.

Kedah Royal Museum (Muzium Diraja)

Behind the Balai Besar, northeast of the padang • Free • http://muziumkedah.gov.my

Guarded by a motley collection of bronze cannons (some stamped with the "VOC" of the Dutch East India Company), the **Kedah Royal Museum** was once the royal palace. Squat and compact, dating to 1930, it must have made a fairly modest palace, and though the cases of ceremonial *keris* daggers, silver dinner services, gold anklets and brass betel sets hint at wealth, there's no feeling of splendid indulgence – indeed, many exhibits (including a pair of binoculars used by one sultan on safari in Africa) are decidedly mundane.

Alor Setar Tower (Menara Alor Setar)
Route 1, north of the padang • Charge • http://menaraalorsetar.com.my

A mini-version of KL's similar Menara Tower, **Alor Setar Tower (Menara Alor Setar)** is a 165m-tall communications tower with an observation platform halfway up. Come here for views of pancake-flat paddy fields pierced by distant limestone outcrops, and the mostly low-rise, unprepossessing town below.

State Museum (Muzium Negeri)
Jalan Lebuhraya Darulaman (Route 1), 2km north of the centre • Free • http://kedahmuseum.gov.my • Any bus from Pekan Rabu bound for Shahab Perdana

The **State Museum (Muzium Negeri)** fills you in on Kedah's traditions and history, including background to the archeological finds at the Bujang Valley (see page 162). One noteworthy exhibit is the *bunga mas dan perak* ("the gold and silver flowers"), a pair of 1m-tall "trees", one in gold, one in silver – in the past, the Malay rulers would have despatched such items in tribute to their Thai overlords.

Pekan Rabu
Jalan Tunku Ibrahim

Pekan Rabu is the town's main market, three concrete floors of preserved, fresh and cooked food, clothes, handicrafts and household necessities, plus local farm produce. Look for stalls selling **dodol durian** (a sort of black, gooey jam made from the fruit) and "durian cake", a plain mix of pulp and palm sugar.

Tun Mahathir House (Rumah Kelahiran Mahathir)
18 Lorong Kilang Ais, southwest of the padang • Free

The life of the local doctor who became the most powerful Malaysian prime minister of modern times, Mahathir Mohamad, is documented at his birthplace and family home, **Tun Mahathir House (Rumah Kelahiran Mahathir)**, now a museum. Even if you're not interested in the brash former premier, it's worth dropping by to get an idea of what a traditional middle-class Malay home looked like in the middle of the last century.

ARRIVAL AND INFORMATION — ALOR SETAR

By plane The Sultan Abdul Halim Airport is 11km north of town, accessible by the hourly Kepala Batas bus from the express bus station, or by taxi.
Destinations Johor Bahru (4 weekly; 1hr 25min); Kuala Lumpur (6 daily; 1hr); Kuala Lumpur (Subang; 2 daily; 1hr).

By train The station is centrally located, just southeast of the centre on Jalan Stesyen (04 731 4045).
Destinations Arau (hourly; 20min); Butterworth (hourly; 1hr 50min); Gemas (1 daily; 7hr 40min); Ipoh (5 daily; 2hr 30min); Kuala Kangsar (5 daily; 1hr 50min); Kuala Lumpur (5 daily; 5hr); Seremban (1 daily; 6hr 30min); Sungai Petani (hourly; 30min); Taiping (5 daily; 1hr 35min).

By local bus A small number of firms, including HBR, MARA and Cityliner, run local buses to most parts of the state. They all use a central bus stop – with no ticket office or timetables – on the north side of Jalan Tunku Ibrahim, opposite the Pekan Rabu market. Some long-distance buses also call here en route to/from Shahab Perdana.
Destinations Kangar (hourly; 1hr 15min); Kuala Kedah (1–2 hourly; 20min); Naka (for the Ulu Muda Eco Park; hourly; 2hr); Sungai Petani (#2; every 45min–1hr; 1hr 30min).

By long-distance bus Long-distance buses use the Shahab Perdana station, annoyingly far away at 5km northwest of the centre, connected to town by local bus #2 and taxis. Some express buses pass through town first, setting passengers down at Pekan Rabu; some northbound local buses pass through Shahab Perdana en route to their destination.
Destinations Butterworth (8 daily; 2hr); Ipoh (10 daily; 4hr); Johor Bahru (4 daily; 12hr); Kota Bharu (daily at 10am and 10pm; 5hr); Kuala Kangsar (4 daily; 4hr); Kuala Kedah (every 30min; 15min); Kuala Lumpur (hourly; 6hr); Kuala Terengganu (2 daily; 8hr 30min); Kuantan (2 daily at 8.45am and 9.30pm; 9hr); Lumut (5 daily; 4hr 30min); Melaka (8 daily; 7hr); Mersing (for Pulau Tioman; daily at 8.45pm; 12hr); Penang (3 daily; 2hr 30min); Seremban (at least 2 daily; 6hr); Singapore (3 daily; 13hr); Taiping (daily at

9.45pm; 3hr 30min).

By ferry Langkawi ferries (langkawiferryline.com) dock at Kuala Kedah, 12km west of town. Local buses drop off and pick up on the main road outside the ferry terminal. Destinations Langkawi (Kuah; 14 daily, 7am–7pm; 1hr 45min).

By taxi Taxis can be found around Pekan Rabu.
Tourist office Tourism Malaysia occupies a yellow building behind the 1930s former courthouse on Jalan Raja (Mon–Wed, Sat & Sun 8am–5pm, Thurs 8am–3.30pm; 04 730 1322).

ACCOMMODATION   SEE MAP PAGE 163

With mainland Kedah seeing few visitors, Alor Setar's selection of hotels is quite dull.

38PC Boutique 38 Jalan Tunku Yaakub; http://38pc.my. Centrally located, with comfy and quirkily designed rooms, this would be a good choice even without the rooftop pool – small, but inviting, and with a lovely view. $\overline{\$\$}$

Urban Inn Off Sultanah Bahiyah Hwy; http://urbaninn.com.my. The best of the cheapies, though sadly a little distant from the centre – you may need a cab to get here and away. Rooms are a little bare but surprisingly modern, and there's a 7-Eleven on site, which can certainly come in handy. $\overline{\$}$

EATING   SEE MAP PAGE 163

Alor Setar's Chinatown (Pekan Cina), along a quiet bend of the Kedah River south of the Masjid Zahir, hasn't remained immune to street art and café gentrification, and is the best part of town for eating and drinking. At night, while the rest of the centre shuts down, the food courts around Jalan Putra and Jalan Cheah Toon Lok buzz with cheap Chinese street stalls.

★ Caffè Diem 44 Jalan Penjara Lama; http://facebook.com/DiemCaffe. This award-winning restored double-storey shophouse is a recent addition to Chinatown's hipster scene. Three original Kedah wooden fishermen boats dangle from the ceiling over exposed brick walls, maroon tiles and marble-topped wooden, retro-chic tables. Besides coffee and cakes, there's a wide array of pastas and burgers alongside Malaysian staples. $\overline{\$\$\$}$

Parrot Espresso 95 Pekan Cina; 016 400 3333. This tiny shophouse, with just a couple of tables and sofas as well as a delightful veranda over the Kedah River, is Alor Setar's attempt to imitate George Town's Western-style cafés. The coffee is more than tolerable, as are the cream cakes, but it's the views of Masjid Zahir soaring over the river that make it really worth a visit. Bottled beers and ciders available too. $\overline{\$\$}$

Ulu Muda Eco Park

Tucked up against the Thai border and enclosing three lakes, **Ulu Muda Eco Park** has similarities with Perak's Royal Belum. However, this isn't a state-level park, but a mere forest reserve which, in the context of Malaysia, confers little protection – indeed, logging remains an issue in an area that is, for now, still rich in **wildlife**. Due to its remoteness, the only practical way to see the park is on a pricey **package trip**, but the rewards can be substantial. Thick with salt licks that lure animals, the park offers a reasonable chance of encountering **elephants** and **wild boar**, as well as reptiles and birds, including the rare **spotted leopard** and, between May and September, the **plain-pouched hornbill**.

The park is accessed by boat from **Gubir**, not much more than a jetty 75km east of Alor Setar; a two-hour sampan ride from here lands you at the only accommodation, **Earth Lodge**. Hiking tracks link the lodge to limestone caves, hot springs (which many animals visit early in the morning or at night, when the temperatures drop) and wildlife hides.

ARRIVAL AND DEPARTURE   ULU MUDA ECO PARK

By bus and taxi The closest you can get to Gubir by public bus is either Sik, 30km southwest (buses from Sungai Petani), or Naka, 25km northwest (buses from Alor Setar). From either of these, you'll need to find a taxi (most likely, just a local with a car).

By car From Alor Setar, take Route 175/K8 through Langgar and on up the K11 to Kuala Nerang, where you turn southeast for Gubir. From Butterworth, take the North–South Expressway and exit at Gurun, taking route K10 to Sik, where you turn on to Route K8 to Gubir.

ACCOMMODATION

Earth Lodge Kuala Labua, inside the park; http://earthlodgemalaysia.com. Renovated cabins, managed by two committed conservationists. Book at least two weeks in advance. Rates offered are usually for a three-day package including full board, boat rides, various activities and park permits. $$$$

Langkawi

Situated 30km off the coast, just south of the Thai border, **LANGKAWI** is, at 500 square kilometres, the largest of an archipelago of mostly uninhabited islands. Once a haven for pirates, the island is now home to some of the priciest resorts in the country, taking advantage of **beaches** that are among the best on the west coast. Thankfully there's relatively little high-density development, and there is a sprinkling of budget and mid-range accommodation at two beaches, **Tengah** and **Cenang**. The island is also popular with international yachties for its **marinas**, which are relatively cheap – and Langkawi's **duty-free status** means that beer is ridiculously cheap. Many diversions are on offer beyond lazing around on the sand, including taking a **mangrove cruise** after sea eagles, snorkelling or scuba diving at the **Pulau Payar Marine Park** to the south, and riding the terrific **Langkawi Cable Car** and adventurous **zipline** over the interior forests to the top of **Mount Machinchang**.

Langkawi is sufficiently far north that, as at Phuket and other west-coast Thai resorts, the **southwest monsoon** can have some bite. From May to August, rainy days can be more frequent here than elsewhere in Malaysia, with a dampening effect on the crowds and room rates.

Kuah

If you fly in, chances are that you'll never glimpse Langkawi's forgettable main town, **KUAH**, in the southeast of the island; indeed, visitors off the ferries barely stay long enough to use the ATMs at the boat terminal and find a taxi to their accommodation. Just north of the ferry terminal, a separate section of the waterfront is home to **Dataran Lang** or Eagle Square, graced by the town's only landmark: an enormous sculpture of a sea eagle (*lang* being a contraction of *helang*, Malay for "eagle").

Cenang Beach

Around 18km west from Kuah, **Cenang Beach** is Langkawi at its most built-up, a 2km stretch that has seen an orgy of seemingly unrestrained get-rich-quick development in recent years, packing in numerous places to stay and eat as well as duty-free shopping malls. Whatever you think of the strip, you'll almost certainly warm to the beach – Langkawi's most popular – a long, broad strip of fine-white sand. There may be **jellyfish** in the water, so take local advice about swimming.

Laman Padi

At the northern end of Cenang Beach, opposite Meritus Pelangi Beach • Free • http://facebook.com/lamanpadilangkawiofficial

The **Laman Padi** rice garden and museum is home to an interesting collection of artefacts, photos and tools showing the history of rice cultivation in Langkawi and Kedah. There is a **Paddy Gallery**, a floating rice garden, and a viewing deck over a pretty, multi-tiered rooftop rice terrace. Things get more exciting at the **Herb Garden** and **Garden of Variety**, where you can don a straw hat and have a go at rice farming.

Underwater World

On the headland at the southern end of Cenang Beach • Charge • http://underwaterworldlangkawi.com

Although their Coco Valley duty-free emporium seems to be a significant reason for the enterprise, **Underwater World** is actually a substantial aquarium, with more than a hundred tanks housing thousands of marine and freshwater fish. The highlight is the obligatory walk-through tunnel where sharks, turtles and hundreds of other sea creatures swim around and above you. There are also penguin and seal sections, with daily feeding sessions.

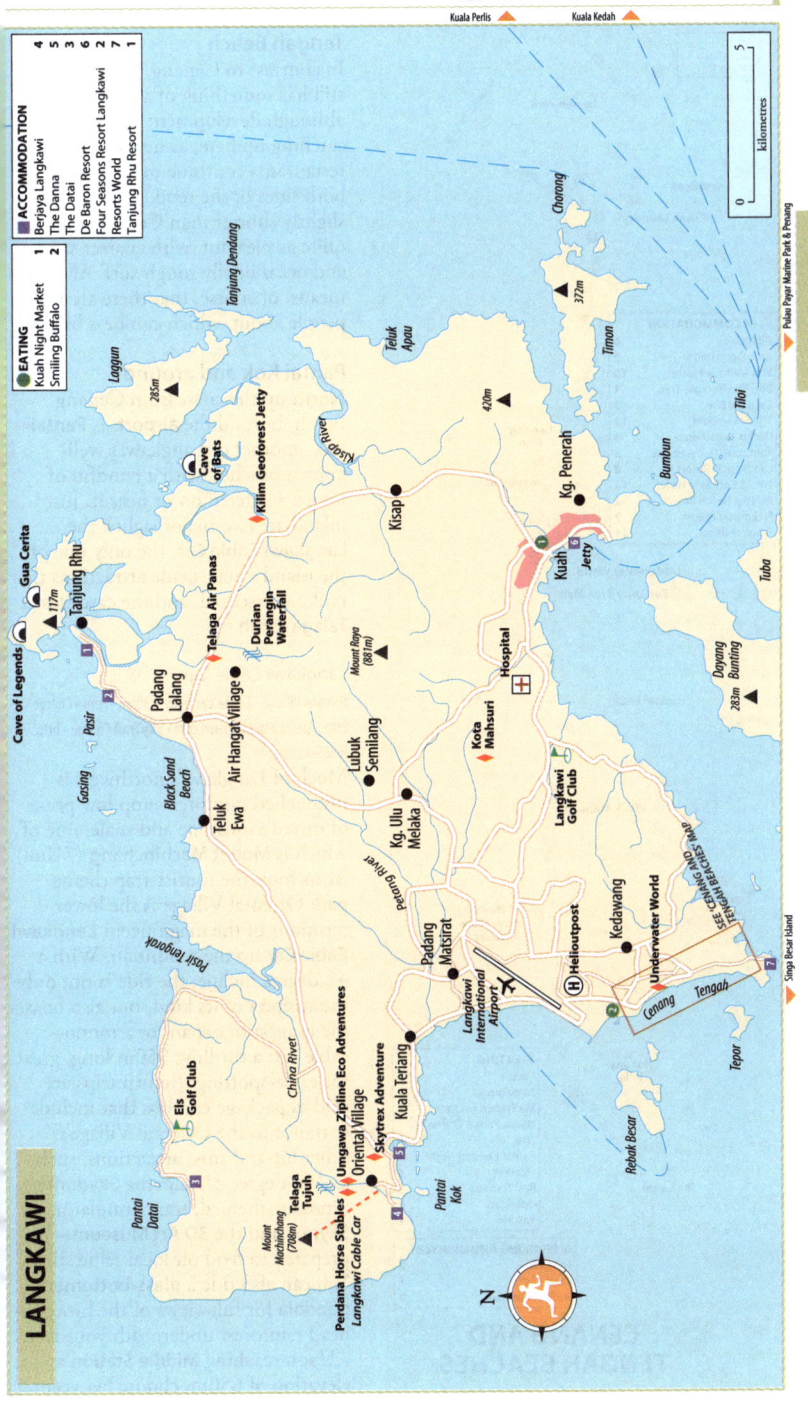

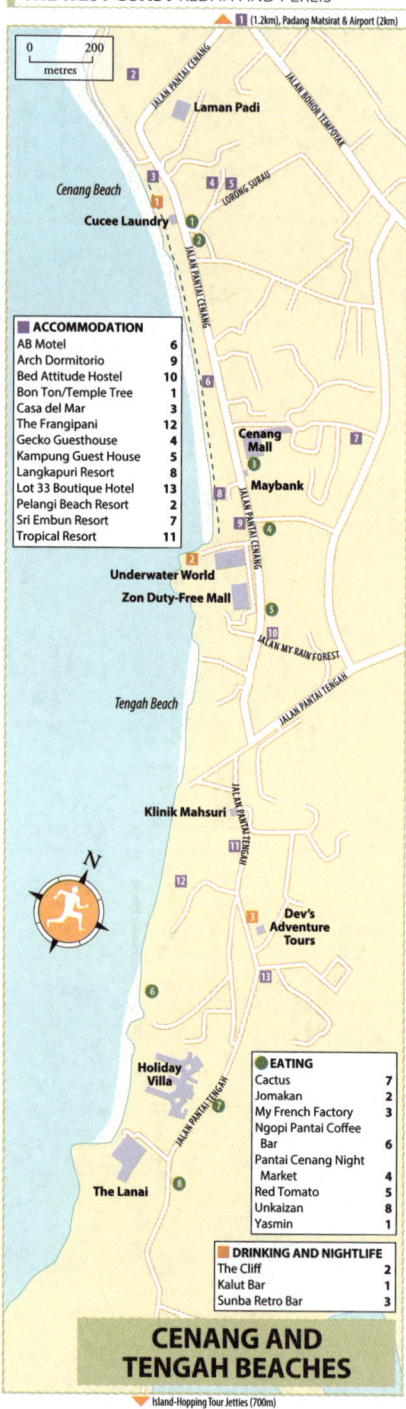

Tengah Beach

In contrast to Cenang, **Tengah Beach** still has something of a rural feel, although development is slowly catching up here, as new hotels and restaurants continue to sprout up on both sides of the road. The beach is slightly shorter than Cenang and not quite as pleasant, with coarser sand and occasionally rough surf. All this means, of course, that there are fewer people about, which can be a bonus.

Pantai Kok and around

North up the coast from Cenang Beach, beyond the **airport**, is **Pantai Kok**, another of Langkawi's well-known beaches, with a handful of resorts scattered on or near it. Just inland are two major sights: the **Langkawi Cable Car**, the only one of the island's man-made attractions that ranks as essential, and the cascades at **Telaga Tujuh**.

Langkawi Cable Car

Oriental Village • **Cable car** Daily 9.30am–7pm • Charge • http://panoramalangkawi.com • **SkyTrail** Charge • http://junglewalla.com

Much of Langkawi's northwest is untouched rainforest atop low peaks of mixed sandstone and shale, one of which is **Mount Machinchang** (710m). At its foot, the tourist-trap theme park Oriental Village is the lower terminus of the magnificent **Langkawi Cable Car** up the mountain. With a 42-degree incline, the ride is not only the steepest of its kind, but also boasts the longest free span for a mono-cable car: a thrilling 950m long, great for eagle-spotting. Return trips are sold as package combos that include entrance to the Oriental Village's other hit-and-miss attractions, such as 360-degree 3D cinema **Skydome**; dinosaur-themed, tram-simulator **Skyrex**; and the **3D Art Museum** – be prepared to fend off local selfie sticks. You can also ride a **glass-bottomed gondola** for full-views of the broccoli-head rainforest underneath your feet.

Upon reaching **Middle Station** at an elevation of 650m, choose between taking the **Skyglide** and walking the 900m to the **Top Station**, where a 125m-long **SkyBridge** spans a deep valley and gives a spectacular view over the Andaman Sea – not for those with a fear of heights. Keen hikers may consider walking the **SkyTrail** from Middle (900m; 45min), or even Base to Top Station (2.2km; 6–8hr return, with lunch and sightseeing breaks).

Seven Wells Waterfall (Telaga Tujuh)

About 1.5km beyond the Langkawi Cable Car turning, the main road terminates at the entrance to the **Seven Wells Waterfall (Telaga Tujuh)**, where a cascading freshwater stream has eroded the rock to form several pools down a slope. During the rainy season, the slipperiness of the moss covering the rock in between the pools helps you slide from one pool to another, before the fast-flowing water disappears over the cliff to form the 90m-high waterfall visible from below – it's only the depth of the water in the last pool that prevents you from shooting off the end. Legend as it that mountain fairies created the *sintuk*, a climbing plant with enormous pods, that grows around these pools; the locals use it as a hair wash, said to rinse away bad luck. The walk to the pools from the car park takes about 45 minutes, the last stage of which involves a steep 200m-high climb up from the inevitable cluster of souvenir stalls at the base of the hill. From the pools, you can climb further up to the top of the waterfall, where an ugly looking red metallic bridge offers unparalleled views over the Geopark and the Andaman Sea.

Umgawa Zipline Eco Adventures

Seven Wells Waterfall's Parking Lot • http://ziplinelangkawi.com

Umgawa Zipline Eco Adventures' zipline eco-tour features twelve zips, of up to 200m in length, which send visitors soaring over the Machinchang Cambrian Geoforest Park, offering a bird's – and monkey's – eye view of the Seven Wells Waterfall and the Andaman Sea. Unfortunately the facility had been closed for a while at the time of writing, but there's still hope that it will reopen eventually.

Skytrex Adventure

Opposite the Danna resort • Charge • http://skytrex-adventure.com

Skytrex Adventure sounds a discordant note amid the manicured resorts of Pantai Kok, and that's no bad thing. Here you can challenge yourself on three obstacle courses of varying levels of toughness, each taking two to three hours – expect lots of net and rope bridges and the odd spot of abseiling.

Black Sand Beach

Around halfway along Langkawi's north coast, **Black Sand Beach** (Pantai Pasir Hitam) is actually pale grey – said to have been caused by ash, after locals torched their rice fields during a war with the Thais in the eighteenth century. It's a pleasant place to pull up, with little craft hauled up on the gently sloping shoreline.

Tanjung Rhu

Langkawi's northernmost road runs to the tip of **Tanjung Rhu**, a 4km-long promontory fringed in casuarina trees, where you can join a **mangrove** cruise from the jetty. There's a good **beach**, sheltered and overlooking several islets – one of which, **Chabang**, can be reached on foot at low tide. Be sure to check tide times to avoid being stranded or swimming the 500m back to shore.

Kilim Geoforest Park

Taking up the northeastern part of the island, **Kilim Geoforest Park** showcases contorted limestone formations, some forested, others starkly beautiful, interspersed with valleys where mangroves thrive. There are no trails, however; most visitors make

LANGKAWI TOURS AND ACTIVITIES

Operators based at Cenang Beach and elsewhere offer a wide range of activities around Langkawi, perhaps the most popular being mangrove cruises and island-hopping trips. The price for non-beach activities often includes free pick-up from Cenang or Tengah beaches.

The standard itinerary for **island-hopping boat trips** (4hr) takes in forested Pregnant Maiden Island (Pulau Dayang Bunting), whose crater lake is good for swimming; Singa Besar for eagle feeding; and Beras Basah for beach and clear water. For something more luxurious, firms such as Crystal Yacht (http://crystalyacht.com) and Tropical Charters (http://tropicalcharters.com.my) offer sunset cruises with drinks and a barbecue dinner.

If it's **wildlife** you're after, your best bets are Junglewalla (http://junglewalla.com), run by expert naturalist Irshad Mobarak, and Dev's Adventure Tours (http://langkawi-nature.com). Both companies offer numerous excursions including cycling trips, birding tours, kayaking through mangroves and evening jungle treks, during which you might spot the bizarre flying lemur (colugo) – something like a cross between a fruit bat and a squirrel.

MANGROVE AND SEA SAFARIS

The Langkawi archipelago is a member of the Global Geoparks Network, a UNESCO-endorsed initiative to protect and promote "geological heritage of international significance". In Langkawi's case (http://langkawigeopark.com.my), that geology includes **karst** landscapes, and it's the limestone crags and peaks that add a special flavour to local **mangrove cruises**. In fact the mangroves themselves often play a mere supporting role, as these trips also involve a visit to a bat cave, a fish farm and **eagle-feeding** sessions.

Trips set off from the jetties at Tanjung Rhu (see page 169) and the Kilim Geoforest Park (see page 169) when enough people show up to fill them (rides usually 4hr); ideally turn up at 9 or 10am, although you can haggle to charter a boat privately (up to eight people). These cruises are essentially unguided as the fee just pays for the ride; for a professionally guided trip by boat or kayak (up to five people for a private boat, but also payable per person), with a restaurant meal along the way, try Dev's Adventure Tours (see above). Dev's also run the naturalist-guided **Sea Safari** (maximum eight people), an eco-adventure cruise through the lesser-visited southwestern islets of Langkawi's archipelago that includes jungle hiking and swimming at a secluded beach.

WATERSPORTS, SNORKELLING AND DIVING

On the beach, several watersports operators offer **parasailing** on the beach or around their bay, or half an hour on a **jet ski**, among other activities. It's even possible to do an island-hopping tour by jet ski (3hr; http://megawatersports.com).

Pulau Payar Marine Park is the place to head for **snorkelling and scuba diving**; south of Langkawi, it features seasonally clear water and colourful fish life including giant potato cod and blacktip reef sharks. A well-established operator is Scuba Club Langkawi (diving day-trips, snorkelling, and day-trips out of Penang; http://scubaclublangkawi.com), though other agents on Cenang Beach have cheaper deals.

---

a beeline for the **jetty** to sign up for a **mangrove boat** trip or **kayaking**. If you don't fancy either, you can simply survey the mangroves from a boardwalk, which ends at a cave populated by bats.

Mount Raya

Summit lookout tower • Charge

Reached off a road through the centre of the island, **Mount Raya** (881m) is Langkawi's highest point. It also happens to be driveable, although if you plan to head up in a rental vehicle, check with the agent that it can cope with the steep, twisting 7km access road. Once at the top, you're rewarded with views down over jungle to the coast that can rival those from the cable car. This is also one promising place on the island to spot **hornbills**.

ARRIVAL AND DEPARTURE LANGKAWI

Langkawi's excellent travel links with other parts of Malaysia, as well as with Singapore and southern Thailand, mean you don't have to return the way you arrived. Various **agents** at Cenang and Tengah beaches can assist with onward travel, including combined boat-and-van transfers to Thailand.

By plane Langkawi Airport is on the west coast at Padang Matsirat, 20km by road from Kuah and only 5km from Cenang Beach. There's a tourist information point and a taxi counter where you buy a coupon for your destination; you can also use Grab cabs.

Destinations Johor Bahru (3 weekly; 1hr15min); Kuala Lumpur (KLIA: 1–2 hourly; 1hr; Subang: 2–3 daily; 1hr); Penang (3–4 daily; 35min); Singapore (2–3 daily; 1hr 30min).

By ferry At the southeastern edge of Kuah, Langkawi's ferry terminal feels like a shopping mall with piers out the back. There are ATMs inside the building, while at the front is a separate building housing a tourist office and booths selling ferry tickets (schedules for most routes at http://langkawiferryline.com). It's worth booking Penang tickets a day in advance. To get to Koh Lipe, Thailand, in low season, buy a ferry and minivan combo ticket via Satun and Pak Bara at Kuah's Ferry Terminal.

Destinations Koh Lipe (Thailand; 1 daily; 1hr 30min); Kuala Kedah (6 daily; 1hr 45min); Kuala Perlis (6 daily; 1hr); Satun (Thailand; 2 daily; 1hr 15min).

GETTING AROUND

Langkawi has a reasonable network of country roads, with a veritable expressway between Kuah and Cenang Beach. Unfortunately, there are no buses, so you'll be using taxis at some point or renting a vehicle. As the island is barely 25km across at its widest point, even a comprehensive tour is unlikely to cover more than 100km.

By taxi Langkawi has Grab drivers – try the app (http://grab.com/my) first for the best fares. Taxis have set fares from the airport, ferry terminal and taxi stands, which can be found at *McDonald's* next to Underwater World at Cenang Beach, and *Tropical Resort* at Tengah Beach, among other places. If you think you're being overcharged, ask to see the official tariff sheet or check with tourist offices. For journeys that start elsewhere, you may need to haggle.

Vehicle rental Some car rental agents at Cenang soundly undercut the usual chains on price, but Kuah's ferry terminal is by far the best place for cheap rental vehicles. Don't be afraid to negotiate, and remember that a day should be counted as 24hr, not the date. Note that rates can rise by fifty percent or even double over busy holiday periods, at which time the chains may not be such a bad deal.

INFORMATION

Tourism Malaysia Both the counters at the airport (daily 9am–10pm; 04 955 7155) and at the back of the small building fronting the ferry terminal (daily 9am–5pm; 04 966 0494) have leaflets covering tours and activities and can help with practical advice on taxi fares and sightseeing.

LADA The authority that manages Langkawi runs a centralized tourist information website of varying usefulness (http://naturallylangkawi.my).

ACCOMMODATION SEE MAPS PAGES 167 AND 168

Practically all the worthwhile cheap places to stay are at Cenang Beach, all of the upmarket resorts are elsewhere, and you'll find a few mid-range options at **Tengah** and **Cenang**. If it's a toss-up between the last two, choose Cenang for buzz, cheap food and ready access to shops; Tengah if you'd prefer to pay a bit more for food and lodging in leafier surroundings. As ever, book a few days ahead over holiday periods, when rates can rise by ten to fifty percent.

KUAH

★ **De Baron Resort** Waterfront; 04 966 2222. Perhaps the cheapest resort in Langkawi, and just the treat if you have to arrive late or depart early by ferry. The swimming pool faces the bay and is hugely popular with kids; an excellent breakfast buffet is served in a covered outdoor area right alongside. Rooms are nothing special, and most are located in a separate building across the road, but you're within walking distance of the ferries, and also Kuah's fun night market (see below). Lastly, a little tip – if you book your Tanjung Rhu tour through the hotel, it's possible to be picked up here and then deposited by Cenang Beach at the end of the trip, which saves a taxi fare. $

CENANG BEACH

AB Motel Jalan Pantai Cenang; http://abmotel.weebly.com. This beachside motel isn't much to look at, but it's well established and popular. All rooms are a/c and en suite, some in the main block, others in single-storey rows. $$

Arch Dormitorio 1–2 Jalan Pantai Cenang, to the right of Underwater World; 013 810 1659. A good central choice,

2min walk from the beach, with clean and airy dorms with individual pods and private bathrooms, or bigger, luminous family rooms that are ideal for groups travelling together. $

★ **Bed Attitude Hostel** Jalan Pantai Cenang; 017 779 5658. Top dog in the local hostel stakes for some time now, with a large lobby that doubles as a bar, hangout zone and sports venue (there are dartboards and a pool table) all in one. Dorms can get a bit squeezy, but the bedding is comfortable, and there are kitchen facilities to use. $

★ **Bon Ton/Temple Tree** Coast road 2km north of Cenang Beach; http://bontonresort.com.my and http://templetree.com.my. Adjacent resorts run by the same team and both comprising vintage timber houses from all over the country that have been dismantled and rebuilt here using a harmonious mixture of period and contemporary fittings. *Bon Ton* is a collection of fine Malay kampung houses; *Temple Tree* features some quite substantial buildings from towns or plantations. Both have their own restaurants and pools, and *Bon Ton* overlooks a lagoon rich in birdlife. Every house is priced differently depending on how many it sleeps. Breakfast is included. $$$

Casa del Mar Northern end of Jalan Pantai Cenang; http://casadelmar-langkawi.com. With buildings in a terracotta hue, creating a faintly Moroccan feel, this boutique resort succeeds in screening out the general hubbub of the strip. It's slightly overpriced, but does boast spacious rooms and suites, a spa, beachside pool and two restaurants. Breakfast is included. $$$$

Gecko Guesthouse Off Jalan Pantai Cenang; http://bit.ly/GeckoGuesthouse. Pioneer rustic budget accommodation in kampung-style chalets as well as a boring concrete block, all set in a shady garden teeming with backpackers and their LCD screens. Paying a little extra will get you en suite, even a/c. $

Kampung Guest House 25 Jalan Madrasah, off Jalan Pantai Cenang; 017 425 3302. Well-staffed guesthouse for those on a budget. There's one dorm and six simple yet clean and inviting fan rooms, mostly en suite, all with small verandas. The only thing missing is breakfast. $

Langkapuri Resort Jalan Pantai Cenang; http://langkapuri.com. A motel-like collection of slightly faded rooms with tiled interiors, tiny balconies and satellite TV, comfortable enough but still in need of a refresh, even after a recent renovation. Breakfast is usually included. $$

Pelangi Beach Resort Jalan Pantai Cenang; http://pelangiresort.com. Top-notch resort with two-storey chalets, echoing traditional Malay architecture, in expansive gardens. There's a pool, spa, tennis and squash courts, and several restaurants. $$$$

★ **Sri Embun Resort** West of the beach, near the Park N' Ride; 04 955 3321. A motel-like concrete block, set some way back from the beach. Sounds great, right? Well, the walk to the beach is pleasant and over fast, and travellers of a certain disposition might prefer the slightly rural-feeling location of this "resort" (presumably so-called because it has a swimming pool) to the touristy main strip. Rooms do the job nicely, too, though breakfast usually costs extra. $$

TENGAH BEACH

The Frangipani Jalan Teluk Baru; http://frangipanilangkawi.com. A sprawling complex of buildings with roofs shaped like those of traditional Malay houses. There are rooms in two-storey buildings and a selection of "beach villas" (bungalows), as well as a spa, gym and jacuzzi. One of the two pools is salt water – odd, when the beach is just a minute away. Book directly on their website for the best deals. Breakfast is included. $$$$

★ **Lot 33 Boutique Hotel** Jalan Pantai Tengah, right next to the Turkish Bazaar; http://lot33boutiquehotel.com.my. Mekong-inspired glitzy boutique hotel in a leafy double-storey house filled with Buddha statues and Balinese-styled bamboo handicrafts. The seven rooms here are all huge, with jacuzzis, sofas, LCD screens and balconies. The swimming pool is hidden at the back, shaded by a tall wall of vegetation, and there's an equally classy Chinese-style seafood restaurant at the front where you can have your complimentary breakfast. $$$$

Resorts World Tanjung Malai; http://rwlangkawi.com. A perfectly good mid-range resort stuck out on its lonesome, at the island's southwestern tip; while not as fancy as some of its nearby brethren, it's a good spot with cosy rooms and a nice pool. $$$

Tropical Resort Jalan Teluk Baru; http://tropicalresortlangkawi.com. Just a 2min walk from the beach along a leafy path, this resort has a series of bungalows, each containing modern, blandly furnished rooms facing in different directions. Good value; breakfast is usually included. $$

NORTHWEST

Berjaya Langkawi Pantai Kok; http://berjayahotel.com. The resort for the hoi polloi, better value than much of the competition, with some newly refurbished chalets set inland among the trees or out over the sea. Facilities include watersports, tennis and the obligatory pool and spa. Breakfast is included. $$$$

The Danna Pantai Kok; http://thedanna.com. Generically grand, this place has a glut of marble and high ceilings, but it scores highly with its Olympic-sized infinity pool that's right by the beach, and its large, slick rooms overlooking the leafy courtyard, marina or ocean. Breakfast is included. Book online for big discounts. $$$$

The Datai Teluk Datai; http://thedatai.com. On the gloriously secluded Datai Beach, this is the quintessential luxury retreat, with self-contained mini-villas embedded in the woods or out on the beach, some with their own paddling pool or jacuzzi, as well as less extortionately priced rooms in the main building. Facilities include two pools, a

Malay-style spa, watersports and use of the adjacent golf course. Breakfast is included. $$$$

TANJUNG RHU
Four Seasons Resort Langkawi Tanjung Rhu; http://fourseasons.com. Close to the karst formations of Langkawi's northeast, this phenomenally expensive retreat doesn't so much have rooms as mini-apartments taking up a whole floor of their two-storey pavilions, as well as self-contained villas, all with outdoor showers in addition to their bathroom. Breakfast is included. $$$$

Tanjung Rhu Resort Tanjung Rhu; http://tanjungrhu.com.my. Well-designed rooms – all billed as suites and featuring wooden floors, teak furnishings and balconies – set this resort apart. Facilities include two pools, tennis courts and a spa, and they run their own short mangrove trips. Breakfast is included. $$$$

EATING
SEE MAPS PAGES 167 AND 168

The eating scene on Langkawi is predictably cosmopolitan and, away from the resorts, tends to focus on mid-range restaurants, although there are stalls and snack places to be found, especially at Cenang Beach.

KUAH
Kuah Night Market By the riverside. Twice a week (Sat & Wed) Kuah's riverfront gets lively with an excellent afternoon/night market; there are plenty of snacks to be had, and also some proper (though basic) restaurants, which are open daily. $

CENANG BEACH
Jomakan Off Jalan Pantai Cenang; http://facebook.com/jomakan.lgk. Simple local restaurant serving simple local food at simple local prices – sometimes, on Langkawi, that's all you really want. $

My French Factory Jalan Pantai Cenang, across from Underwater World; http://myfrenchfactorylangkawi.com. Tiny and friendly creperie, the first on Langkawi, serving up delicious savoury or sweet options. Most items can also be ordered gluten-free. $

Pantai Cenang Night Market Off Jalan Pantai Cenang. As soon as the sun even hints at moving in a downwards direction, the stalls at this popular market start to do their thing – a highly popular place with tourists and locals alike, while the vibe and the seating arrangements make it a good place to get yapping away to someone. $

Red Tomato Jalan Pantai Cenang, across from Underwater World; http://redtomatorestaurant.com.my. Middle-of-the-road, touristy restaurant easily spotted by virtue of the fuchsia VW Beetle usually parked outside (but don't confuse it with the *Red Sky* restaurant close by). Come here for Western cooked breakfasts, and a largely Italian menu of pizza and pasta meals. $$$

★ **Smiling Buffalo** Off Jalan Pantai Cenang; http://panji.com. Despite its out-of-the-way location, this large, jungle-styled venue is by far the most popular place in Langkawi for Western hipster fare – coffee, brunch, pasta dishes and so on. They do have some tasty local dishes if you want to remember where you actually are, and it has to be said that the coffee, decoration and ambience are all very good indeed. $$$

Yasmin Jalan Pantai Cenang; 019 449 5081. Many residents claim that this small Syrian-owned restaurant makes the best Middle Eastern food on the island. From creamy hummus and fresh *tabbouleh* to BBQ kebab sets and cheaper backpacker-tailored *shawarma*, falafel and *shish taouk*, the jovial chefs masterfully reproduce their region's flavours. $$

TENGAH BEACH
Cactus South end of the beach, across from Holiday Villa Resort; 012 482 8140. Humble yet popular open-air restaurant adorned with international customers' autographed T-shirts, and offering a wide selection of cheap Asian and Western breakfast favourites, coffees, tea and juices. $$

Ngopi Pantai Coffee Bar Beachside; http://facebook.com/ngopipantai.langkawi. Stuck in what feels like the middle of nowhere, this café will come as a lovely surprise if you're padding along the beach. The coffee and pastries are so-so, but the cakes are tasty, and you can sit and sip or gorge on cushions on the sand. $$

Unkaizan Far southern end of the beach; http://unkaizan.com. Up a jungly slope is this gem of a Japanese restaurant where you can dine out on the terrace or indoors. The range of sushi and sashimi offerings is impressive, although the set meals – chicken cutlet or tempura with rice, soup and pickles, say – are better value. There's Japanese ice cream too. $$$$

DRINKING AND NIGHTLIFE
SEE MAP PAGE 168

Langkawi has a more pragmatic attitude to **alcohol** than anywhere else in the four overwhelmingly Malay states of the north: many restaurants are licensed, and then of course there are the duty-free outlets where you can buy cheap spirits and beer.

CENANG BEACH
★ **The Cliff** Over the water at the south end of Cenang Beach; http://thecliffLangkawi.com. One of the priciest standalone restaurants in Cenang, *The Cliff* majors on fusion cooking (mostly spicy seafood), but it's the little bar that

stands out. Get here around 6pm, park yourself at one of the few beachside seats and watch parasails darting across the sea, silhouetted against a scarlet sky.

★ **Kalut Bar** Cenang Beach, behind Casa del Mar; http://facebook.com/KalutBar. Trendy beach shack without the scruff, set behind rows of colourful beanbags slung on the sand out front. The perk here is the daily fire juggling shows, starting after sunset and going on throughout the night, with an eclectic soundtrack of anything from R&B to reggae, trance and pop. Prime Aussie beef burgers, happy hours, "cheeky buckets" and free shots for ladies on Wed evenings all make it popular.

TENGAH BEACH

Sunba Retro Bar Slightly inland from Tengah Beach; 04 953 1801. Part of a modern complex but decked out in wood to simulate an old kampung house, this is a relaxed bar with pretensions of being a proper club. There's a live band most nights, otherwise DJs spin mainly mainstream oldies and some dance sounds.

SHOPPING

Langkawi's **duty-free status** can draw in even those not normally obsessed with cheap alcohol and cigarettes – don't be surprised if at some point you find yourself among the hordes at the **malls around Underwater World**, grabbing armfuls of beer, imported chocolates and the like. The **Cenang Mall**, also on the main drag, is a more orthodox and underwhelming shopping complex, best for branches of Western fast food and coffee chains.

DIRECTORY

Banks and exchange There are ATMs at Cenang Mall, the Zon duty-free mall, Underwater World (all at Cenang Beach), the airport and the ferry terminal. Cenang Mall also has a Maybank foreign-exchange counter.
Hospital The island's main hospital is on the main road (Jalan Padang Matsirat) midway between Kuah and Cenang Beach (04 966 3333). There's also Klinik Mahsuri, a clinic at Tengah Beach, next to Hummingbird Café.
Pharmacies Guardian has an outlet at Cenang Mall.

Kangar and around

As the fastest road to and from Thailand passes through Kedah rather than **Perlis**, it's easy to bypass the latter state completely. The few travellers who end up here do so to access Langkawi using convenient transport hub **Kuala Perlis**, or on visa runs to or from Penang via the border post at **Padang Besar**, which is much quieter than at Bukit Kayu Hitam in Kedah. Unremarkable **KANGAR**, Perlis's capital, sits immediately north of little **Sungai Perlis**. About 10km east of Kangar, **ARAU** is the least interesting of all Malaysia's royal towns; from the main road you can peek at the istana, looking like a small European stately home except that it sports two golden domes.

Kelam Cave

West of Kaki Bukit • Charge • Bus T11 from Kangar to Padang Besar stops very close to the park; alternatively, arrange a taxi including a 1hr wait

From Kangar, it's about 30km north to **Kelam Cave**, a 370m-long limestone tunnel that leads to a forest park at the foot of the Nakawan Range near **Kaki Bukit** village. You can camp (charge) at the nearby Hutan Hujan campsite (see page 175).

Wang Kelian

Nine kilometres north of Kelam Cave, over a mountain pass, is ghost town **Wang Kelian**, once home to a thriving border market, which closed down after the discovery of immigrant Rohingya workers' mass graves in 2015. The village is the entrance to the small state park of **Taman Negara Perlis** and an unorthodox **border crossing** to Satun, in Thailand, where boats depart for Koh Lipe. It's best to come here with your own transportation.

ARRIVAL AND DEPARTURE   KANGAR AND AROUND

Train station In the centre of Arau, off Road 176 (04 986 1225).
Destinations Alor Setar (7 daily; 20min); Butterworth (almost hourly; 1hr 30min); Ipoh (5 daily; 2hr 50min); Kuala Kangsar (5 daily; 2hr 15min); Kuala Lumpur (5 daily; 5hr); Sungai Petani (hourly; 50min); Taiping (5 daily; 2hr).
By bus Express and local services use the long-distance bus station on Jalan Bukit Lagi in Kangar, just south of the

river. Kuala Perlis' bus station has connections to all over the country; it's a 5min walk from the ferry terminal: turn left from the jetty, then right once you come to what's obviously a main street.

Destinations from Kangar bus station Alor Setar (local bus T14; 12 daily; 1hr 15min); Butterworth/Penang (at least 3 daily; 2hr 30min); Changlun (for Thailand border at Bukit Kayu Hitam; local bus T10; 12 daily; 1hr); Ipoh (3 daily; 4hr 30min); Johor Bahru (2 daily; 12–13hr); Kaki Bukit (local bus T11; 10 daily; 45min); Kota Bharu (daily at 9am and 9pm; 6hr 30min); Kuala Kangsar (3 daily; 3hr); Kuala Lumpur (almost hourly; 7hr); Kuala Perlis (local bus T12; 10 daily; 30 min); Kuala Terengganu (2 daily; 8hr); Kuantan (1 daily; 10hr); Melaka (8 daily; 11hr); Padang Besar (local bus T11; 10 daily; 1hr); Singapore (3 daily; 13hr).

Destinations from Kuala Perlis bus station Alor Setar (hourly; 1hr 15min); Ipoh (5 daily; 5hr); Johor Bahru (4 daily; 11hr); Kota Bharu (daily at 8pm; 7hr); Kuala Besut (for Perhentian Islands; daily at 8pm; 8hr); Kuala Lumpur (almost hourly; 7hr); Kuala Terengganu (daily at 7.30pm; 7hr); Lumut (5 daily; 5hr 30min); Melaka (daily at 9am and 9.30pm; 8hr).

By ferry Langkawi ferries (langkawiferryline.com) dock at Kuala Perlis (016 418 2539), 15km west of Kangar. Destination Langkawi (6 daily; 1hr).

TO THAILAND

The three border crossings (daily 6am–10pm) in this area are: Padang Besar, 30km north of Kangar, where the rail line enters Thailand; Bukit Kayu Hitam in Kedah, 30km northeast of Kangar as the crow flies; and Wang Kelian, 9km north of Kelam Cave. Bukit Kayu Hitam is overwhelmingly more popular, as it's on the North–South Expressway. Bear in mind that, since 2017, international travellers are only allowed two overland entries to Thailand per calendar year, and you may be asked to produce ten thousand Thai baht in cash as proof of sufficient funds for your stay in Thailand.

By train KTM operates a cheap and convenient hourly service between Padang Besar and Butterworth. At Padang Besar, change to one of the two daily services to Hat Yai in Thailand, clearing immigration directly on the platform before train departure. Otherwise, exit the station and walk 500m to Malaysian immigration, before proceeding 1km to the Thai checkpoint. You can catch onward bus or train connections from the Thai side of Padang Besar, where minivans to Hat Yai await.

By bus There are no buses through to Thailand, although tour-agency minivans service the Hat Yai route (you can book a place on 016 673 8082). From Kangar, it's also possible to take local bus T11 or charter a taxi to Padang Besar, where you have to get off before the border and cover the 2km to the Thai border post on foot or by motorbike taxi.

ACCOMMODATION AND EATING

Hujan Hujan Campsite Kelam Cave forest park; 019 358 6838. Well-equipped campsite in a superb location surrounded by huge trees right at the foot of the Nakawan range. Staff provide tents, four meals per day and a set of activities that includes hiking in the surrounding hills. Toilets are basic yet clean, and when it rains the tents are pitched under the protection of Malay-style open-sided hall. Camping with full board $

Kedai Khuan Bee Kaki Bukit's main junction; 04 945 7673. Friendly Chinese *kopitiam* famous for its strong coffee, handmade giant pork *pao* (steamed buns) and breakfast titbits. $

The interior

178 Taman Negara: Kuala Tahan

195 North through the interior

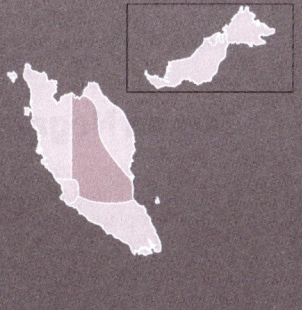

LONG-TAILED MACAQUES

The interior

Peninsular Malaysia's interior comprises a vast swathe of territory, stretching northeast of Kuala Lumpur all the way up to Kota Bharu on the east coast. Until relatively recent times, this was a remote region of steep, limestone peaks with knife-edge ridges and luxuriant valleys inhabited by Orang Asli groups. Colonial administrator Hugh Clifford described the terrain in the 1880s as "smothered in deep, damp forest, threaded across a network of streams and rivers". Indeed, rivers were the sole means of transportation until prospectors and planters opened the interior up through the twentieth century; roads and a railway arrived, helping to establish the towns of Temerloh, Gua Musang and Kuala Lipis.

Much of the interior has now been logged, settled and tamed, though Clifford's deep, damp forests survive in the dense chunk of undeveloped jungle that is **Taman Negara** (literally "National Park"). Gazetted as Malaysia's **first national park** in 1925 and covering 4343 square kilometres, Taman Negara forms the largest tract of rainforest in Peninsular Malaysia; it contains some of the **oldest rainforest** in the world, which has evolved over 130 million years as a home for a fabulous array of wildlife. Some of the Peninsula's 1500 **Batek** Orang Asli live here too, many as hunter-gatherers; the park authorities generally turn a blind eye to their hunting game.

Reached via the transport nexus of **Jerantut**, Taman Negara's main entry point, the riverside town of **Kuala Tahan** is the trailhead for jungle hikes. With so much to see here, it's easy to overlook the rest of the region, but outside the park you can ride the Jungle Railway north through the interior, touching on lesser-known sections of the wilds – caves and waterfalls at **Kenong Rimba State Park** and **Kota Gelanggi Cave Complex**; remoter areas of Taman Negara at **Merapoh** and **Kuala Koh**; the ancient Hakka settlement of **Kampung Pulai**; and more forest, waterfalls and views at **Gunung Stong State Park**.

GETTING AROUND THE INTERIOR

By bus Buses along Route 8 and the East Coast Highway can get you within range of all the main sights, but remoter corners require the help of your own vehicle, taxis or local tour operators.

By car Route 8, the interior's main artery, runs for 500km from Bentong near KL to Kota Bharu. It's a well-maintained road, though not a multi-lane highway, so expect to be periodically slowed behind ponderous lorries. The quickest way to reach Route 8 from KL is the E8 (Karak Highway), which careers northeast from KL through the foothills of the Genting Highlands. Expect a few thrilling, cambered descents – and be warned that there are often nasty accidents.

By train The "eastern" sector of peninsular Malaysia's rail network actually heads through the interior, and many of the area's larger towns are accessible in this manner.

Taman Negara: Kuala Tahan

The main gateway to Taman Negara, the town of **Kuala Tahan**, 250km northeast of KL, is where you'll find the **national park headquarters** and the pick of its visitor facilities. It's also the place to get your bearings and seek advice before crossing the Tembeling River and heading into the forest: well-marked **trails** include an easy boardwalk stroll to a popular **canopy walkway**; tougher day-treks out to waterfalls and hides overlooking salt licks in the jungle (for which you'll need to hire guides); or the seven-day return ascent of **Mount Tahan**, Peninsular Malaysia's highest peak, involving steep climbs and

TAMAN NEGARA NATIONAL PARK

Highlights

❶ Kota Gelanggi Cave Complex Right outside Jerantut, these little-visited caves make for the perfect prelude to – or conclusion from – Taman Negara. See page 181

❷ Taman Negara via Kuala Tahan The Peninsula's largest and oldest nature reserve offers river trips, hikes and wildlife spotting amid a swathe of ancient rainforest, best visited via the park headquarters at Kuala Tahan. See page 185

❸ Kenong Rimba State Park A barely developed reserve adjoining Taman Negara, offering its own trekking and animal spotting opportunities. See page 195

❹ Kampung Pulai Discover Malaysia's oldest Kuan Yin temple in this riverside Chinese Hakka village, set amid rubber plantations and limestone karsts. See page 201

❺ Gunung Stong State Park In the interior of Kelantan state, Mount Stong boasts a picturesque waterfall, good mountain trekking and a marvellous jungle camp. See page 202

HIGHLIGHTS ARE MARKED ON THE MAP ON PAGE 180

> **THE ORANG ASLI**
>
> The twentieth-century spread of the timber, rubber and palm oil industries through the interior had a huge impact upon the region's **Orang Asli**, who were traditionally nomadic peoples living by hunting and slash-and-burn agriculture. These days many have been forced to settle down, existing at the fringes of the cash economy. The mountain-dwelling **Temiar**, for instance, trade in forest products such as herbal medicines and, increasingly, **timber** (though their logging activities are minimal compared with those of the State Forestry Department and private companies). Some **Batek** do still live fairly traditional lives at Taman Negara, where you might meet shy groups walking in single file along trails, or come across their temporary vine-and-forest-brush shelters in jungle clearings.
>
> However, three-quarters of Orang Asli peoples (including many local Batek, **Senoi** and **Semang**) live below the poverty line, compared to less than a tenth of the population as a whole. That fact makes it all the harder for them to confront the many forces, from planning agencies to Christian and Muslim groups, who seek to influence their destiny. The issue of **land rights** is among their gravest problems, for while the country's Aboriginal People's Act has led to the creation of Orang Asli reserves, at the same time many Asli traditional areas have been gazetted as state land, rendering the inhabitants there, at best, tolerated guests of the government.

river crossings. Activities other than hiking include river swimming, low-key rafting and angling.

Listening to the sounds of the birds, insects and other animals, marvelling at the sheer size of the trees and peering into the tangled understorey of flowering lianas, luminous fungi and giant bamboo are memorable experiences. However, keep your expectations of spotting **wildlife** – particularly big game – low, as these days it's very rare to encounter any, even on the park's remotest trails.

Kuala Tahan is reached via the service town of **Jerantut**, or – increasingly – directly on minibuses from Cameron Highlands or the Pulau Perhentian jetty at Kuala Besut. It's also possible to enter Taman Negara further north at **Merapoh** (see page 199) and **Kuala Koh** (see page 201) – or even hike to either from Kuala Tahan in a week-long traverse of the park. Both require more effort to reach and have fewer facilities, but they're also less crowded than Kuala Tahan – though not necessarily easier places to see wildlife.

Jerantut

In tranquil **JERANTUT**, 70km south of Kuala Tahan, road, rail and river converge on a small grid of streets. Activity revolves around the main artery **Jalan Besar**, 200m east of the **train station**. The **Tembeling Jetty**, a short taxi ride north, sees traffic upriver to Kuala Tahan. For most, Jerantut is just somewhere to find last-minute supplies and top up with **cash**, as there are no banks at Kuala Tahan. However, it's worth lingering for an enjoyable half-day visiting the **Kota Gelanggi Cave Complex**, and if you're here on a Saturday, try some of the cheap local food at the bustling **night market** next to the bus station.

Kota Gelanggi Cave Complex

10km east of Jerantut city centre, along the main road to Maran • Charge; guides available for extra fee

Most travellers zip from Jerantut to Taman Negara, neglecting this remarkable limestone cave complex. A handful of the ten or so caves, including **Tongkat**, Terang Bulan and **Balai**, are scattered along the paved road that starts from the park's entrance. You will need a guide to hike further into the jungle to **Elephant's Head Cave**, a small tunnel that leads to the tiny **Portrait Cave**. The curious rock formation on the upper right-hand side of the rock face here resembles a female figure in the pose of Leonardo da Vinci's *Mona Lisa*. Hiking

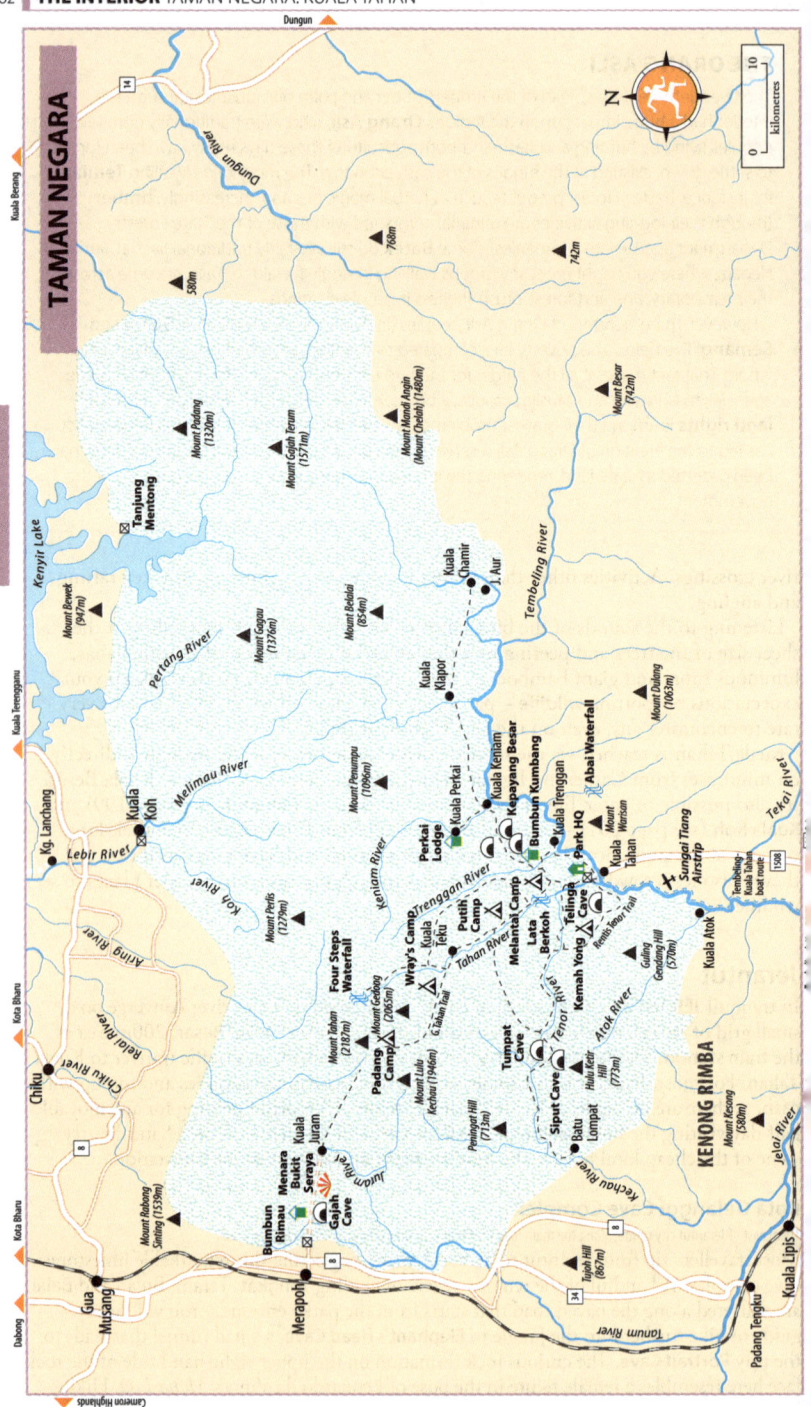

PLANNING A VISIT TO TAMAN NEGARA

Given that tropical rainforest is always sodden, the **driest** time of year is between February and mid-October, with the **peak tourist season** roughly from May to August – make sure you book ahead. Mid-November to mid-January is extremely **wet**, and movement within the park can be restricted as paths are submerged and rivers flood. Usually, however, most of the park's **trails** require no more than an average level of fitness, though of course longer trails require some stamina. Some essential **camping and trekking gear** is available to buy at Jerantut (see page 185), or to rent at Kuala Tahan, but take your own if possible.

Campsites are scattered through the park; they have absolutely no facilities at all, though most are close to rivers where you can wash. There's a small fee for hides and campsites (see below), payable at the national park office, where you can also reserve bunks in hides.

To **budget** for your trip, remember that for any trek involving overnighting in the forest (other than in a hide close to a park office or accessible by boat), you must hire a guide. It's generally more cost-effective to arrange guides through external operators than through the park headquarters, although the latter may be preferable if you would like a guide with a particular area of expertise. The fees for guides and boat excursions are the only substantial outlays you'll face, as inexpensive accommodation, eating and transport options are easy to find.

FEES AND CHARGES

Whichever section of Taman Negara you find yourself in, you'll have to pay nominal (tiny) fees for park entry and permits for camping or photography, plus a little more for fishing licences (Kenyam only) and the use of hides or fishing lodges. The only non-nominal expenses will be for your guide, and of course the transport getting there.

GETTING AROUND THE PARK

If you simply need to **cross the river** from Kuala Tahan, you can take one of the small wooden boats that cross on demand from Kuala Tahan's floating restaurants to the jetty below the resort and national park headquarters. Put your fare in the tin by the ferryman.

Aside from trekking, **wooden longboats** seating four to ten people are the only way to get around Taman Negara from Kuala Tahan; you can use them like a taxi service to reach distant trekking trails, or speed your return journey after a long hike. Boats might wait for you or, more likely, return at an agreed time; don't expect them to hang around indefinitely if you are late. Book through the national park office; prices are the same for single or return trips.

Destinations include the Blau/Yong hides, Canopy walkway, Kuala Keniam, Kuala Trenggan, Lata Berkoh, Lubok Lesong, Nusa Camp and the Tabing/Cegar Anjing hides.

---

for another fifteen minutes brings you to a clearing with six empty archeological digs and the entrance to **Wind Cave**, taking its name from its gale-battered upper chamber. Once inside, you reach the last two hollows, **Elephant** and **Wedding Cave** (Gua Sanding). It's actually a single hall divided into two chambers, each with its own rock formation shaped in the guise of an elephant, and of two human figures seated next to each other. From March to October, the sunlight that comes in through the huge hole in the chambers' ceiling casts spectacular light beams on the cave floor.

You can visit Kota Gelanggi independently, but hiring a guide (ask at hotels) saves you the hassle of organizing transportation and finding the park's elusive ticket seller.

ARRIVAL AND DEPARTURE JERANTUT

By train Jerantut is on the Jungle Railway (see box, page 193) but the main departures travel through the scenic jungle sections in the dead of night. Heading north, you can use more services with a change of train at Kuala Lipis, though the connections are almost never very convenient.

Destinations Dabong (1 daily; 4hr 30min); Gua Musang (1 daily; 2hr 40min); Johor Bahru (1 daily; 8hr 30min); Kuala Lipis (3 daily; 1hr); Gemas (for Kuala Lumpur; 3 daily; 3hr 40min–4hr); Wakaf Bharu (for Kota Bharu; 1 daily; 6hr 30min).

THE INTERIOR TAMAN NEGARA: KUALA TAHAN

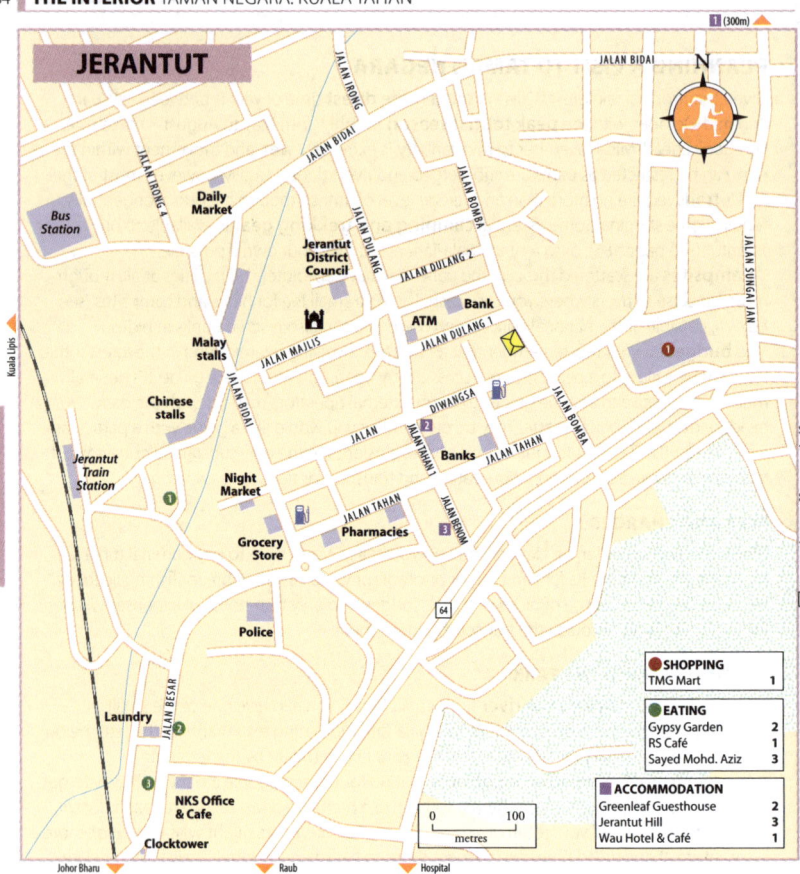

By bus The bus station is a 5min walk northwest of the Keris roundabout at the upper end of Jalan Besar. To catch buses to Ipoh, Butterworth, Alor Setar and Kangar you must travel first to Jengka Sentral and change there. For Tembeling Jetty, take a bus towards Kuala Lipis and ask to be let off near the jetty.

Destinations Jengka (7 daily; 1hr); Kota Bharu (2 daily; 7hr); Kuala Lipis (3 daily; 1hr 20min); Kuala Lumpur (at least 6 daily; 3hr 30min); Kuala Tahan (3 daily; 1hr 30min); Kuala Terengganu (5 weekly; 3hr 10min); Kuantan (2–3 daily; 3hr).

By taxi Taxis from the bus station run to Tembeling Jetty, Kuala Tahan and various east coast destinations.

By boat Boating up to Kuala Tahan on the muddy Tembeling River in motorized sampans is an essential part of the Taman Negara experience, though you may prefer to take the faster return trip downstream. Boats to Kuala Tahan (daily at 1.30pm; 3hr 30min) depart from Tembeling Jetty, 17km north of Jerantut; departures from Kuala Tahan are at 9am. You're best off booking through Han Travel (http://han.travel), who also run shuttles to the jetty; if you'd like to do it yourself, either catch a bus towards Kuala Lipis or take a taxi, then pray that there's still a spot on board for you.

ACCOMMODATION   SEE MAP PAGE 184

Greenleaf Guesthouse Jalan Diwangsa; http://greenleaf-tamannegara.com. A homely backpackers' place, with dorm beds and a variety of unexciting rooms with a/c and shared bathrooms. They also run package tours into the park, and non-guests can shower for a nominal fee. $

★ **Jerantut Hill** 27 Jalan Benom; http://facebook.com/jerantuthillhotel. A relatively new choice, with an extremely colourful frontage – they must have found a good multi-buy deal on paints. After this introduction, the rooms are almost disappointingly plain, though they do have coloured go-faster stripes on the walls; they're also comfortable and clean, and sport good bathrooms and large TVs. Currently the best value in Jerantut. $

Wau Hotel & Café Pusat Perniagaan Sungai Jan; http://

wauhotels.com. The closest Jerantut comes to a boutique hotel, with squeaky-clean, modern en-suite rooms with TVs, plus a café in the lobby. It's a 15min walk from the bus station: walk 500m east, take the third road on the left, and continue straight for another 600m. $

EATING
SEE MAP PAGE 184

During the day, open-air **food courts** serve inexpensive pan-Asian dishes either side of the train station access road. To stock up on supplies for the park, try the TMG Mart (see page 185).

★ **Gypsy Garden** 41 Jalan Besar; 016 460 4798. Surprisingly attractive for Jerantut, this is without doubt the most interesting place to eat in town, a quirky place with a largely Western menu (lamb chop, spag bol, burgers and the like). Veggies and vegans will find options here, and there's occasional "entertainment"; lastly, yes, they do have a garden, and it's a wonderful place to dine if the weather agrees. $$

RS Café 4b Jalan Stesen; 09 266 1230. This cool little Chinese-run café serves up the standard range of noodle and rice dishes, with ice-desserts and a range of beers on tap. $

Sayed Mohd. Aziz 36 Jalan Besar. Decent *roti canai*, curries and *nasi lemak*, all for extremely low prices. $

SHOPPING
SEE MAP PAGE 184

Numerous stores on Jalan Diwangsa sell day packs, rubber shoes, canvas track shoes and flashlights; check the quality before buying, especially stitching and straps on packs.

TMG Mart Off Route 64; http://tunasmanja.com. Well-stocked supermarket, good for snacks or loading up on supplies for the park.

Kuala Tahan

Around 70km north of Jerantut, **KUALA TAHAN** is a knot of guesthouses and floating restaurants facing a solid green wall of jungle across the turbid, 50m-wide **Tembeling River**. As a base, it has many virtues: reasonable transport connections, plenty of accommodation, a few stores selling (and renting) basics, and even mobile coverage, though there are **no banks or ATMs**. Most importantly, the **national park headquarters** – where you can pick up information, register and pay park fees – is a quick ferry ride over the river at the start of the park's **hiking trails**. Take a torch when wandering around the village after dark, as **electricity** can be flaky.

ARRIVAL AND DEPARTURE
KUALA TAHAN

By bus Buses drop at a roadside shelter on the edge of Kuala Tahan, a 5min walk from the river. Buses return to Jerantut three times a day (1hr 30min).
By minibus Several tour operators run minibuses between Kuala Tahan and regional tourist destinations. Prices vary little between operators, usually with a single morning departure.
Destinations George Town (9hr); Ipoh (7hr 30min); Jerantut (1hr 30min); Kota Bharu (8hr); Kuala Besut (for Perhentian islands; 7hr); Kuala Lumpur (5hr); Mersing (for Tioman

---

THE KUALA GANDAH ELEPHANT SANCTUARY

One attraction in the southern interior worth making a diversion for is the **Kuala Gandah Elephant Conservation Centre** (free, but donations appreciated; http://bit.ly/KualaGanda). Here, staff from the Wildlife Department care for elephants being relocated to reserves from areas of habitat destruction, or which had to be sedated while *mengamuk* – a Malay term that would be untranslatable were it not the origin of the English word "amok". The best time to turn up is mid-afternoon, when for a couple of hours visitors have the chance to get hands-on with the elephants, feeding or bathing them. Numbers are limited for bathing, though it's possible to book your spot (charge for guide fee per group, plus also fee per participant) up to three days in advance. The centre gets very crowded on weekends and holidays – visit midweek if possible.

If you're **driving** from KL via Route E8 (east), turn north at **Lanchang**, about 70km along, for the twenty-minute drive to the sanctuary. **Day-trips** are offered from Kuala Lumpur by Han Travel (http://han.travel), and **from Jerantut** through Greenleaf Holidays (http://greenleaf-tamannegara.com).

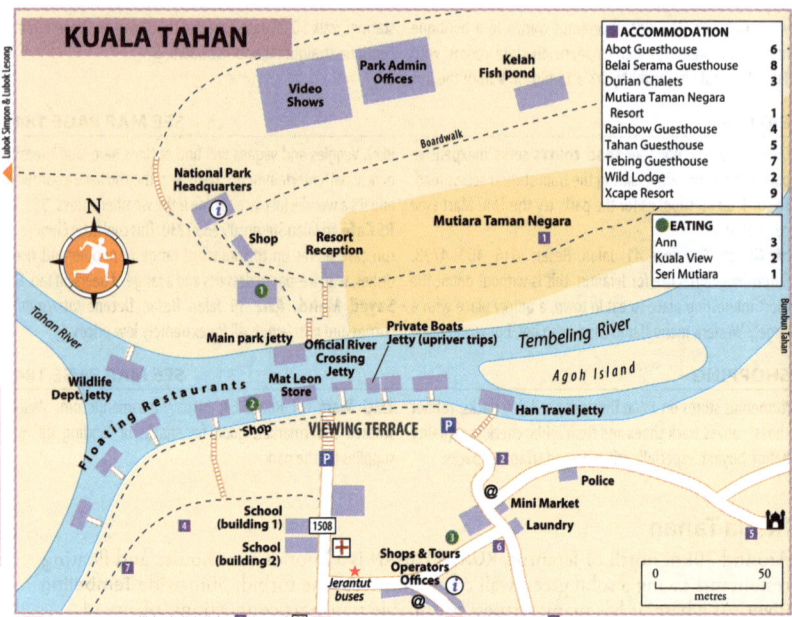

Island; 8hr); Tanah Rata (for Cameron Highlands; 6hr).
By boat Arriving boats deposit passengers at the park jetty, where steps lead up to the sprawling *Mutiara Taman Negara Resort* and park headquarters, or among the floating restaurants on the shingle beach opposite, with Kuala Tahan village on the bank above. Tickets downstream to Tembeling (daily at 9am; 2hr 30min) can be purchased the day before

your journey with Han Travel (http://han.travel). Once at the Tembeling Jetty, catch a bus, minibus or taxi to Jerantut.
By car The road to Kuala Tahan, Route 1508, branches north off Route 64 10km east of Jerantut. From KL, leave the East Coast Highway at Temerloh, heading up Route 98 for Jerantut, then pick up Route 64 eastwards for the Kuala Tahan Road. From Kuantan, pick up Route 64 at Maran.

INFORMATION

National Park Headquarters Stopping here, just north of the main park jetty, is an essential first port of call to pay the nominal entry fee, pick up a map and check the latest trail conditions (Mon–Thurs, Sat & Sun 8am–6pm, Fri 8am–noon & 3–6pm; 09 266 1122). You can also book hides and activity packages, charter boats and hire guides. Make sure you check the whiteboard, where the odd sightings of interesting creatures are listed; there are about sixty tigers in Taman Negara, with some three or four sightings per year, usually deep in the forest (many national park staff have never seen one).

Guides If you have a specialist interest, call the headquarters a week in advance to see if a guide with matching knowledge can be arranged. Trained by the Wildlife Department, the guides are generally better on fauna than flora, though many are experts on neither. They know the trails, but may fall short when it comes to more general skills, such as offering support in the event of a mishap.

ACCOMMODATION   SEE MAP PAGE 186

Almost all accommodation is in the village of Kuala Tahan itself, with the exception of the *Mutiara* resort on the opposite bank. Book in advance, especially during the peak season (May–Aug). Should you wish to **overnight in the forest**, the best option is to use one of five **hides** (see box, page 192); these sleep up to twelve people in bare wooden bunks (bring your own bedding), and some have tank water and toilets.

IN TOWN

Abot Guesthouse At the top of the hill from the bus stop; http://facebook.com/AbotGH. Low-set house with ten cosy en-suite rooms in two blocks, all with a/c. Light sleepers should avoid rooms facing the road from the bus stop. $$
Durian Chalets A 5min walk past Tahan Guesthouse, down a steep hill and through a small stand of rubber trees; 017 934 5180. Double rooms and chalets with mosquito nets and shack-like bathrooms, clustered around a pretty

hillside garden with a teeming fishpond – a great place to get away from it all. Breakfast is extra. $

Rainbow Guesthouse Walk left from the main view deck and beyond the kindergarten; 09 267 3519. A handful of homely and clean rainbow-coloured en-suite twins and doubles, set inside a Malay household, that offer a relaxing peek into Kuala Tahan's daily life. $

★ **Tahan Guesthouse** By the mosque; 017 970 2025. This old stalwart is a well-kept two-storey affair, brightly painted with wildlife murals, and set in a relaxing child-friendly garden where hornbills come to snag fruit. Accommodation comprises en-suite twins and doubles, all fan-cooled with mosquito nets and squat toilets; the double rooms have small balconies. The only downside is the early-morning call to prayer from the mosque. Walk uphill from the bus stop, following the main road for about 50m; turn right after the mini market, continue past the police station, and it's 3min along on the right. $

★ **Tebing Guesthouse** Down a side-street beyond the kindergarten; 013 584 3476. Guesthouse whose two floors of rooms are arranged in an L-shape, with their doors overlooking a small garden, and their windows facing the river beyond. Everything's immaculate and modern. $$

★ **Wild Lodge** On the river road; http://facebook.com/IAmWildTravellers. Attractive backpacker place with twenty-odd beds in a/c dorm rooms overlooking the river, all with plush mattresses and hot showers. The hostel runs its own treks, tours and onward minivan transport. The balcony is a popular evening hangout, with occasional live music. $

Xcape Resort Just south of Kuala Tahan; http://xcaperesort-temannegara.com. One of a handful of incongruous developments in this area, *Xcape* offers a pool and regimented rows of chalets with characterless but comfortable rooms, featuring a/c, TV, fridge and modern bathrooms. Breakfast is included. $$$

OUT OF TOWN

★ **Belai Serama Guesthouse** 4.5km south of town, Kampung Padang; http://balaiseramaguesthouse.com. If you're seeking a natural vibe and don't mind the inconvenience of being located out of town, this is your spot – rooms are a little plain, but this is more than compensated for by the views from the deck, which is where many guests seem to spend most of their time. All in all, a great place to chill out. $$$

★ **Mutiara Taman Negara Resort** In front of the national park headquarters, across the river from Kuala Tahan; http://mutiaratamannegara.com. Busy three-star resort occupying a strip of land between the river and forest, mostly comprising a/c chalets with spacious bathrooms, woven bamboo walls, cane furniture and jungle or river views. Boat transfers to and from Tembeling can be arranged for a fee. Buffet breakfast is included. $$$$

EATING   SEE MAP PAGE 186

Most visitors gravitate towards the row of ten or so floating, glorified **kedai kopis** moored beside the shingle beach. Opening around 8am and not closing until well into the evening, the restaurants offer the usual rice and noodle dishes, plus Western travellers' favourites including pancakes, sandwiches and milk shakes. The establishments we review are the most popular, but other places often serve similar food at lower cost. If you're in need of a drink, you could try the bar in the *Xcape Resort* car park; alcohol is also served at the *Seri Mutiara*.

★ **Ann** In the centre of town; 011 1299 6722. Perhaps the most reliable place to eat in town, and one of the cheapest too; the *roti canai* are great breakfast fodder, and fried rice or noodle dishes are made in a flash. Satay sticks and soups are available too, though for many the main draws are the banana or pineapple pancakes. $

Kuala View On the river; 011 6955 3694. The best of the river places, though this really isn't saying much – food is very hit or miss, though stick to the simpler dishes (or even just a drink) and you should be fine. Views are good, and the

---

TAMAN NEGARA PACKAGES

Besides a few short trails looping around the park headquarters, going anywhere beyond Bukit Indah requires hiring a guide, and thus many visitors prefer booking themselves on a convenient **package trip**. These typically comprise two or three nights at Kuala Tahan with a range of accommodation and meal options, and possibly activities such as walks and boat excursions as well.

The most established operator, **Han Travel** (http://han.travel), has offices in KL, Jerantut and at the Tembeling Jetty. Jerantut-based agents include **Greenleaf Holidays** (http://greenleaf-tamannegara.com).

If you're using one of the expensive but convenient minibus **transfers** to Kuala Tahan, your journey will typically feature a stop at the tour company offices. Despite what you may be told, there's no need to book park accommodation or day-trips through the same company; simply shop around once you've arrived or call ahead.

KUALA TAHAN ACTIVITIES

Most people who are in the park for just a few days sign up for various **activity packages** offered through Kuala Tahan guesthouses and tour operators. Many operators work together – you might book onto one company's trip, only to find yourself tagging along with another (often larger) group – if in doubt, clarify before you book.

SHORT TRIPS

Night jungle walks (1hr 30min). Easy and, despite being crowded and taking place along the park's most heavily used paths, can turn up everything from tapirs to scorpions; the sharp-eyed guides invariably spot camouflaged creatures you'd otherwise miss. Bring a torch.

Night safaris (2hr). These actually take place outside the park; you're driven around a plantation in a 4WD, and may get to see leopard cats, wild pigs, civets and the occasional snake.

Orang Asli village visit (2hr). Shows you how to use a blowpipe and fire-making using sticks at a semi-permanent Batek encampment; very touristy, but interesting too.

RIVER TRIPS AND FISHING

Rapids shooting trips (2hr). Taking place a few kilometres upstream, these are fairly tame, designed to appeal to families rather than hard-core rafters; you'll ride this stretch anyway if you catch a boat back from Kuala Trenggan (see page 191).

Night river safaris (2hr). Trips are run on a tamer stretch of water, where you often see larger animals along the riverside.

Fishing The most popular area is along the Keniam River, northeast of Kuala Tahan, where you can hope to catch catfish or snakehead; all fish must be returned. The very basic *Perkai Fishing Lodge*, around 2hr upstream from Kuala Tahan, is a popular base; most opt for 2 day/3 night packages including transport, guide and meals.

LONGER TRIPS

Guided forest walks The best operators arrange for you to stay overnight at a hide – Bumbun Kumbang is a favourite (see page 192) or a cave; you usually make your way down to the river on the second day and catch a boat back to Kuala Tahan. Prices depend on numbers, duration and destination.

---

service amiable; it's all about the location. $$
Seri Mutiara Beside the Mutiara resort; http://mutiara tamannegara.com. This smart, open-sided dining room in the jungle is well worth a splurge if you've been out in the wilds for a few days. The menu is geared to Taman Negara's better-heeled Malay and Western guests – pizza, *nasi lemak*, prawn *sambal*, T-bone steak, *rendang* – and the relatively steep prices reflect this, though you could just sneak in for a coffee and slice of black forest gateau. $$$

DIRECTORY

Banks There are banks with ATMs along Jalan Tahan and Jalan Dulang 1 – load up on cash here if you're going to Kuala Tahan.

Pharmacy Jalan Tahan has two well-stocked pharmacies.

Day treks

Cross the river (regular ferries from the jetty) and turn right at the national park headquarters, and you're at the start of most of the **hiking trails** that spread into the park. Popular and easy places to visit close to the park headquarters include **Bukit Teresek**; the **canopy walkway**, where you can observe treetop jungle life close up; and the waterfall at **Lata Berkoh** (following the first part of the trail there is a good way to kill a spare couple of hours). You could feasibly tackle two, perhaps three, of these in a day, and none of them require a guide.

Bukit Teresek

2.5km one-way from the park headquarters; 1hr

Although it's the most heavily used trail in the park, the route to the summit of **Bukit Teresek** (342m) is an excellent starter trek, taking about an hour in each direction along a boardwalk. Heading northeast away from the river, the trail passes an impressive stand of **giant bamboo** before ascending Bukit Teresek itself via a steep series of fibreglass **steps**; if you haven't already noticed the sauna-like conditions, you will now. The clanking of your shoes against the fibreglass is enough to scare off most wildlife, so content yourself with the promise of views – though the clearing at the top is partially screened by trees. Continue along the hilltop for another fifteen minutes to reach the so-called **second view**, where on clear days you can get marvellous vistas north over the valley to 2187m-high **Mount Tahan** (see page 193) and smaller Mount Gedong. Return the way you came and the canopy walkway will be just 300m to the south along a clearly marked path, or make the more challenging descent from the second view to the side of the Tahan River, from where you can loop back to the park headquarters (3km; 1hr 30min).

Canopy walkway

Closed during rain or if lightning is likely; numbers are limited, so waits possible • Charge

About thirty-minute walk from the national park office along the boardwalk, the **canopy walkway** is one of Taman Negara's highlights – though it's better for photos, and views down over the canopy to the Tembeling River, than wildlife spotting. Queues can form, so it's best to go early in the day, if possible. You climb a sturdy wooden tower and step out, 30m above the forest floor, onto a 330m-long swaying aluminium bridge, anchored to some suitably placed, 250-year-old *tualang* trees. Animals you may well see include the grey-banded leaf monkey, with a call that sounds like a rattling tin can, and the white-eyed dusky leaf monkey, with its deep, nasal "ha-haw" cry. At the end, you return to terra firma by another wooden stairwell.

Bukit Indah

3.5km from the park headquarters; 2hr

The route to **Bukit Indah** follows the boardwalk as far as the canopy walkway, before continuing along a rougher trail towards Kuala Trenggan and Bumbun Kumbang. After about 3km you'll see a signposted path leading to a 500m scramble. Use the fixed ropes to haul yourself up to the top of Bukit Indah, and enjoy views over the Tembeling River.

PICKING UP TREKKING GEAR AND SUPPLIES

CAMPING AND TREKKING GEAR

The only reliable places renting out decent trekking gear locally have recently closed down, or simply become less reliable. **Minimarts** around town sell torches, batteries, rubber ankle boots and day packs; a few places near the bus stop sell dry bags; and you'll probably get lucky somewhere with gas stoves and mosquito nets (though you may have to buy rather than rent these), as well as lower-quality backpacks, and sleeping bags and mats. Nevertheless, if you know exactly what you want, go shopping in KL instead, or contact your accommodation or tour agency to see what they can provide.

SUPPLIES

Kuala Tahan's **minimarts** sell water, biscuits and snacks, tinned sardines, soft drinks, ice cream, insect repellent and toothpaste. Across the river, the only store is a pricey one attached to the *Mutiara Taman Negara Resort*.

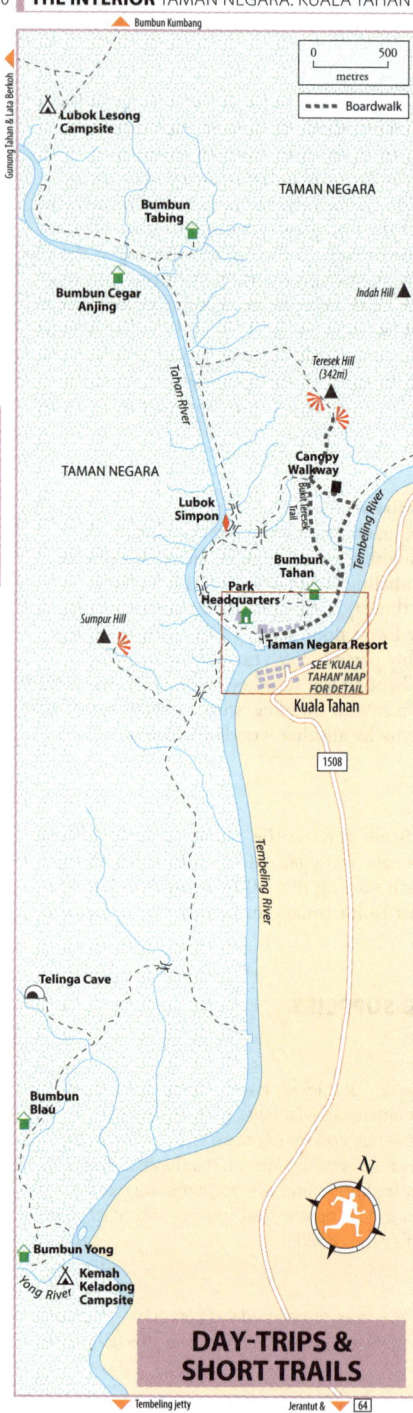

Kemah Keladong

5km from the park headquarters; 3hr

In the quiet **Kemah Keladong** area, 5km downriver from Kuala Tahan on the far side of the Tembeling River, trails link the Blau and Yong **hides** with a **campsite** at Kemah Keladong. They can be tackled either by catching a boat to drop-off points for the hides (15–20min), or by crossing by sampan to a trailhead just up the Tahan River from Kuala Tahan and hiking – in which case, allow a full day for the return trip. A major attraction of this route used to be **Telinga Cave**, but the cave – home to thousands of tiny **roundleaf bats** – is usually off-limits.

From the turn-off to Telinga Cave the trail continues for another 2km through beautiful tall forest, past the **Yong** and **Blau hides**, to where the trail divides. North is the track to Kemah Rentis (see page 194), while southeast it's just 500m to the tranquil **Kemah Keladong campsite** on the terraced bank of the Yong River. With an early start, it's possible to reach this point, have a swim in the river and get back before dusk.

Lata Berkoh

8.5km; 4hr from the park headquarters; a guide is compulsory if not travelling directly by boat

Most visitors catch a boat (at least in one direction) to the roaring rapids of **Lata Berkoh**, around 8.5km up the Tahan River; the return trip is a long way to walk in a day, and if water levels are high you may face a swim across the river near the end.

The trail from the park headquarters leads gently downhill. About fifteen minutes on is an excellent swimming spot, **Lubok Simpon**, a deep pool in the Tahan River next to a pebbled beach. After another 2km you pass the turning for **Bumbun Tabing** and then, 5km from the park headquarters, the **Lubok Lesong** campsite. The route to the waterfall veers west from the main trail, crossing gullies and steep ridges before reaching the river, which must be forded. The final part of the trail

> ### HIKING FROM KUALA TAHAN
>
> The shortest hiking trails from Kuala Tahan are clearly signposted and easy to follow, but to go any distance beyond Bukit Indah, hiring a guide is compulsory. Exposed to the elements and the passage of migrating elephant herds, the trails quickly deteriorate into slippery tangles of roots and leaf litter. If you're moderately fit, the hiking **time estimates** given out by the park authorities (and in the text of this Guide) are pretty reliable; expect to average 2km/hour.
>
> Even on the very simple day hikes, you should **inform** park staff of your plans so they know where to look if you get into difficulty. You won't be able to phone for help, as the mobile phone signal dies out just a little way from Kuala Tahan. Perhaps the most important advice is to **know your limitations** and not run out of time. Slipping and sliding along in the dark is no fun and can be dangerous – thus, if you start hiking **after 4pm**, you will still need a guide even before Bukit Indah.
>
> Don't be paranoid about encountering large **wildlife** – in fact, you could count yourself very lucky if you do, as most animals don't hang around after they hear you coming. Unfortunately, there's almost no way you can avoid getting bitten by a few **leeches**, whose numbers increase dramatically after rain; there are a few general guidelines, however, on keeping them at bay (see page 45).

runs up the west side of the Tahan River, passing the simple **Berkoh Lodge**, a small shelter in a clearing and a **campsite** before reaching the falls.

The **waterfall** itself drops into a deep pool with surprisingly clear water for swimming (tread carefully around the large rocks on the river bed). You can picnic here, too, overlooking the swirling water. Keep eyes peeled for kingfishers with their yellow-and-red wings and white beaks; large grey-and-green fish eagles; and, on the rocks, camouflaged monitor lizards.

Overnight trips

There are a number of possible guided **overnight trips**. The 24km-long, two-to three-day trail northeast of Kuala Tahan to **Kuala Keniam** involves overnighting in the jungle, either at **Bumbun Kumbang** or one of several **caves**, with the chance of seeing large animals, after which you could organize a **boat** back to base, rather than having to retrace your steps. If you're pushed for time or simply not so dedicated, hiking as far as Bumbun Kumbang (12km), staying the night there, then taking the alternative return trail – or again, catching a boat – is an excellent compromise. Note that you need to arrange any **boat transfers** before you head out, and that **guides** are compulsory.

Trails to Bumbun Kumbang
10–12km from the park headquarters; 5–7hr hike, depending on route

Both the two **trails to Bumbun Kumbang** are fairly damp and muddy. The longer, flatter, easier route initially follows the Lata Berkoh Trail (see page 190), then arcs northeast to the narrow **Trenggan River** – which has to be waded across, and may be impassable after heavy rain – beyond which you're just 1km from the hide.

The tougher, more direct route follows the Tembeling River upstream past the Bukit Indah turn-off (see page 189), crossing numerous **creeks**, each involving a steep, slippery descent and clamber up the far side. Eventually things settle down, and you will see a permanent settlement of the **Batek** people after crossing the small Trenggan River **bridge**. The path seems to peter out on the far side, but keep going and you soon come to a definite junction. Turn left and Bumbun Kumbang is a thirty-minute walk; right, and it's 1km to **Kuala Trenggan**, where some broken-down wooden cabins overlook the confluence of the Tembeling and Trenggan rivers.

> **KUALA TAHAN HIDES (BLINDS)**
>
> Spending a night in one of the park's **hides** (known as **bumbuns**) doesn't guarantee sightings of large mammals, especially in the dry season when the **salt licks** – where plant-eating animals come to supplement their mineral intake – are often so waterless that there's little reason for deer, tapir, elephant, leopard or seladang to visit, but it's an experience you're unlikely to forget. It's best to go in a group and take turns keeping watch, listening hard and occasionally shining a **torch** at the salt lick – if an animal is present its eyes will reflect brightly in the beam.
>
> Kuala Tahan's five hides are covered in the hiking trail accounts in this Guide. We have also listed details of time-saving boat rides to/from the hides (see box, page 183).

Bumbun Kumbang
Book bunks through the park headquarters

Raised high off the ground on concrete posts, the **Bumbun Kumbang** hide sits at the edge of a clearing, about 200m from a natural **salt lick** that attracts animals at wetter times of the year. As always, seeing anything is down to luck, though scan the muddy trails nearby and you'll often find three-toed tapir prints. Carrying binoculars and a powerful torch is a good idea.

Bumbun Kumbang to Kuala Keniam
8km one-way, 4–5hr

The superb hike between Bumbun Kumbang and Kuala Keniam forms the basis of most tour operators' shortest overnight treks, and combines the real possibility of seeing **elephants** with visits to three **caves**, one of which is big enough for an army to camp in. The trail is slow going, even in drier conditions, with innumerable streams to wade through, hills to circumvent and trees blocking the path. Most groups take two days, typically hiking this route in reverse and overnighting at **Kempayang Besar**.

Limestone caves

From Bumbun Kumbang, it takes around three hours on a boggy trail before you enter limestone cave country, first reaching **Kepayang Kecil**. A line of fig trees here drops a curtain of roots down the rock, behind which lies a small chamber, with a slightly larger one to the right, containing stalactites and stalagmites. A short way on is much larger **Kepayang Besar**, where the huge chamber at the eastern side of the outcrop makes an excellent place to spend the night, especially as you can dispense with tents. Despite its popularity with trekkers (on public holidays, the cave can see upwards of a hundred people overnighting here), civets and leopard cats are often seen after dark. Fifteen minutes north are **Luas Cave** and more impressive **Daun Menari Cave** ("Cave of the Dancing Leaves"), a breezy chamber inhabited by thousands of roundleaf bats.

Kuala Keniam

Once beyond the limestone band, the rest of the route to **Kuala Keniam** passes through a meranti forest of tall, straight trees with distinctive reddish-brown bark, much prized as timber. Finally, you reach the river at Kuala Keniam, where there's a **campsite** and **jetty** for boats back to Kuala Tahan.

Longer trails

For the two major **long-distance hiking trails** at Taman Negara, you'll need to hire guides and bring full camping and trekking gear, including food, cooking equipment and water-purifying tablets. The four-day **Mount Tahan Trail**, undoubtedly the toughest in the park, culminates in the ascent of Peninsular Malaysia's highest peak, after which you have to hike out again, perhaps via the alternative, shorter trail to Merapoh (see page 199);

you'll definitely need sleeping bags for a couple of nights spent at altitude. The other option is the three-to-four-day **Tenor Trail**, a lasso-shaped trek leading west from Kuala Tahan to Telinga Cave, then northwest to the campsite on the Tenor River. Either way, expect to see plenty of jungle, and to get soaked during river crossings and rain; allow a day extra either side of the trek to sort out arrangements.

Mount Tahan Trail

55km one-way, nine-day return from Kuala Tahan • Book in advance

To the Batek Orang Asli, **Mount Tahan** – Peninsular Malaysia's highest peak at 2187m – is the Forbidden Mountain, its summit the home of a vast monkey, who stands guard over magic stones. Though the Batek rarely venture beyond the foothills, ascending Mount Tahan is the highlight of any adventurous visitor's stay in Taman Negara. Although hundreds complete the trail every year, the sense of individual achievement after tackling the innumerable river crossings, steep hills and nights camping in the jungle – let alone the arduous ascent – is supreme.

Days 1–2

The **first day** involves an easy six-hour walk from Kuala Tahan to **Melantai**, the campsite on the east bank of the Tahan River, not far from Lata Berkoh. On the **second day** more ground is covered, the route taking eight hours and crossing 27 hills, including a long trudge up Bukit Malang ("Unlucky Hill"). This section culminates at **Mount Rajah** (576m), before descending to the Puteh River, a tiny tributary of the Tahan. Before the campsite at **Kuala Teku** you'll ford the Tahan half a dozen times.

THE JUNGLE RAILWAY

Riding the scenic **Jungle Railway** used to be one of Peninsular Malaysia's highlights and the best way to reach or leave Taman Negara. Sadly, in December 2014 the route – officially the less romantic "Sektor Timur–Selatan" (East–South Route) – was damaged by severe floods. Since resuming in 2016, the limited services have no longer been convenient either for seeing the jungle or reaching Taman Negara.

Nonetheless, the Jungle Railway maintains great historical significance: it took indentured Tamil labourers eight years to build the line's 500km-long section from **Gemas**, southeast of KL, to **Tumpat**, on the northeast coast near Kota Bharu. The first section from Gemas to Kuala Lipis opened in 1920, with the full extent of the line following in 1931. Initially it was used exclusively for freight – tin and rubber, and later palm oil – until a passenger service, originally known as the "Golden Blowpipe", opened in 1938.

At the time of writing, only two daily **overnight trains** – one in each direction – make the complete 700km journey between Johor Bahru and Kota Bharu, travelling mostly in the dead of night. However, if you're not just passing straight through, there are more daily services (up to five, between some stations) in the middle of the line; you're especially advised to travel in daylight between Merapoh and Wakaf Bharu, which is arguably the most pristine sector of the line. Note that by virtue of its existence, the line doesn't pass through virgin jungle; much of the route is flanked by regrowth forest and belukar woodland, as well as plantations of rubber, pepper and palm oil. None of this is to detract from the fact that as a way to encounter **rural life**, a ride on the jungle train can't be beaten, giving you the chance to take in backwater scenery in the company of cheroot-smoking old men in sarongs, and fast-talking women hauling kids, poultry and vegetables to and from the nearest market.

Buy **tickets** at the stations (you shouldn't need to book in advance except on express services during school holidays) or through KTM's website (http://ktmb.com.my) or Easybook (http://easybook.com). Don't expect luxury: the Jungle Railway's rolling stock is worn and fairly ordinary, with several classes of simple sleepers and seats available on all routes. Check current schedules on KTM's website before you set off.

If you're really enjoying the hike, consider a two-day detour from Kuala Teku to **Four-Steps Waterfall**, east of Mount Tahan. The trail up to it follows the course of the Tahan River for eight hours, right to the foot of the 30m-high falls.

Day 3

The **third day** on the trail to Mount Tahan sees you climb from 168m to 1100m in seven hours of steady, unrelenting legwork, leaving you on a ridge. Prominent among the large trees here is *seraya*, with a reddish-brown trunk, though as the ridge runs west these are replaced by montane oak forest, where **elephant tracks** are common. The night is spent at the Mount Tahan base camp, **Wray's Camp**, named after the leader of the first team to climb the mountain in 1905.

Day 4: to the summit

Day four involves six hours of hard climbing along steep gullies, ending up at **Padang Camp**, on the Tangga Lima Belas Ridge, sited on a plateau sheltered by tall trees. The summit is now only two and a half hours away, through open, hilly ground with knee-high plants, exposed rocks and peaty streams. The trail follows a ridge and soon reaches **Mount Tahan's summit**; provided it's clear, there's a stupendous view of around 50km in all directions. Weather conditions up here can't be relied upon, however: the **moss forest**, which dominates above 1500m, is often shrouded in cloud.

On from the summit

Most hikers make a straight return trip, spending the **fifth night** back at the padang, the **sixth** at the Puteh River, and reaching Kuala Tahan late on **day seven**. It's also possible to continue westwards from the mountain for a further two days, completing a **traverse** of the park and exiting Taman Negara at **Merapoh**. For more information about this route, contact a Merapoh-based tour operator (see page 199).

Tenor Trail

30km circuit from Kuala Tahan; 3–4 days

Shorter and not as tough as the hike to Mount Tahan, the mostly low-lying **Tenor Trail** is more likely to be flooded out during extra-wet conditions, but is otherwise an extremely satisfying trek, with a few easy ascents to viewpoints along the way.

Day 1

On **day one**, initially the **Tenor Trail** follows the track southwest from Kuala Tahan to Telinga Cave and the Yong hide (see page 190), before bearing northwest along the small **Yong River** and reaching the campsite at **Kemah Yong**, around 10km from the start.

A side trail from here ascends **Bukit Guling Gendang** (570m), a steep hour-and-a-half climb best undertaken in the morning. Towards the summit the terrain changes from lowland tropical to montane forest, where tall conifer trees allow light to penetrate to the forest floor and **squirrels** predominate, with the black giant and cream giant the main species. From the top, views reach north to Mount Tahan, west to Siput Cave and beyond that to Bukit Peningat (713m), the highest limestone outcrop in Peninsular Malaysia.

Day 2

From Kemah Yong campsite, the main trail continues on **day two** into the upper catchment of the Yong River, then over a low saddle into the catchment of the **Rentis River**. The path narrows through thick forest alongside the river, crossing it several times, until it joins the **Tenor River** three hours later, marked by a remote and beautiful riverside clearing, **Kemah Rentis**, where you camp, roughly at the halfway point.

Day 3

You can make it back to Kuala Tahan in one day from Kemah Rentis, though many people take it easy and rest up in one of the campsites along the way. Following the river downstream through undulating terrain on **day three** brings you first to rapids at **Lata Keitiah**, beyond which there's a campsite at **Kemah Lameh**. You're now in lowland open forest where walking is fairly easy; after four hours the trail leads to **Bumbun Cegar Anjing** (another possible overnight stop) from where it's a final 3km to Kuala Tahan.

North through the interior

North of Jerantut, Route 8 and the parallel **Jungle Railway** run around 350km to Kota Bharu, up on the east coast. Head this way if you want to spend time among the region's abundant forests and limestone hills at **Kenong Rimba State Park**, reach the alternative entrances to Taman Negara at **Merapoh** and **Kuala Koh**, or trek along forested waterfall trails at **Gunung Stong State Park**. Settlements along the way – including relatively substantial **Gua Musang** and **Kuala Lipis** – are more jumping-off points for nearby sections of wilds, rather than destinations in their own right. For a change from jungle trekking, experience southern Kelantan's unique Chinese culture at limestone-strewn **Kampung Pulai**, one of the oldest Hakka settlements in Malaysia.

ESSENTIALS · NORTH THROUGH THE INTERIOR

Banks The only regional banks are at Kuala Lipis and Gua Musang, though there is an ATM in Dabong, near Mount Stong.

Climate Conditions are damp throughout the year, though driest from April to Sept; you'll need to check in advance about access if heading here during the wet season (Nov–Jan).

Kenong Rimba State Park

Covering 128 square kilometres and backing onto the remote southwestern corner of Taman Negara, **Kenong Rimba State Park** offers jungle trails, riverside camping, mammal-spotting and excellent birdwatching, plus the likelihood of crossing paths with the nomadic **Batek** people. You can see the main sights in **five days**, on a 50km-long **loop** through the park past a series of caves, the seven-step **Lata Kenong waterfall** and limestone outcrops with **rock-climbing** potential. If you've only time for a brief visit, explore the **caves** strung out along the main trail, stop overnight at the Mount Kesong campsite and retrace your steps the following day.

The park is far less developed than the area around Kuala Tahan, and trails quickly get overgrown – arranging a **tour** from Kuala Lipis, or at least a guide, is mandatory to access the reserve. Make sure you bring everything you'll need with you.

ARRIVAL AND TOURS · KENONG RIMBA STATE PARK

TRAVELLING INDEPENDENTLY
By boat Kenong Rimba lies about 20km east of Kuala Lipis; the nearest village is Kuala Kenong, from where you can get a boat to the trailhead at Tanjung Kiara. All boats are by arrangement only, through your guide or an agent.

TOURS
Though it's possible to explore Kenong Rimba independently, this has become harder of late, and in any case it's much easier to visit on a tour from Kuala Lipis; guides, transport, meals and accommodation (in cabins or tents) are all part of the deal.

Endemic Tours http://endemicguides.com. Occasional two- to four-day excursions into the park; check their site for details.

Tuah Travel Tourist Information Centre, Kuala Lipis; http://facebook.com/tuahtravel. Staff here can arrange packages including transfers, meals and accommodation in tents, as well as rafting excursions.

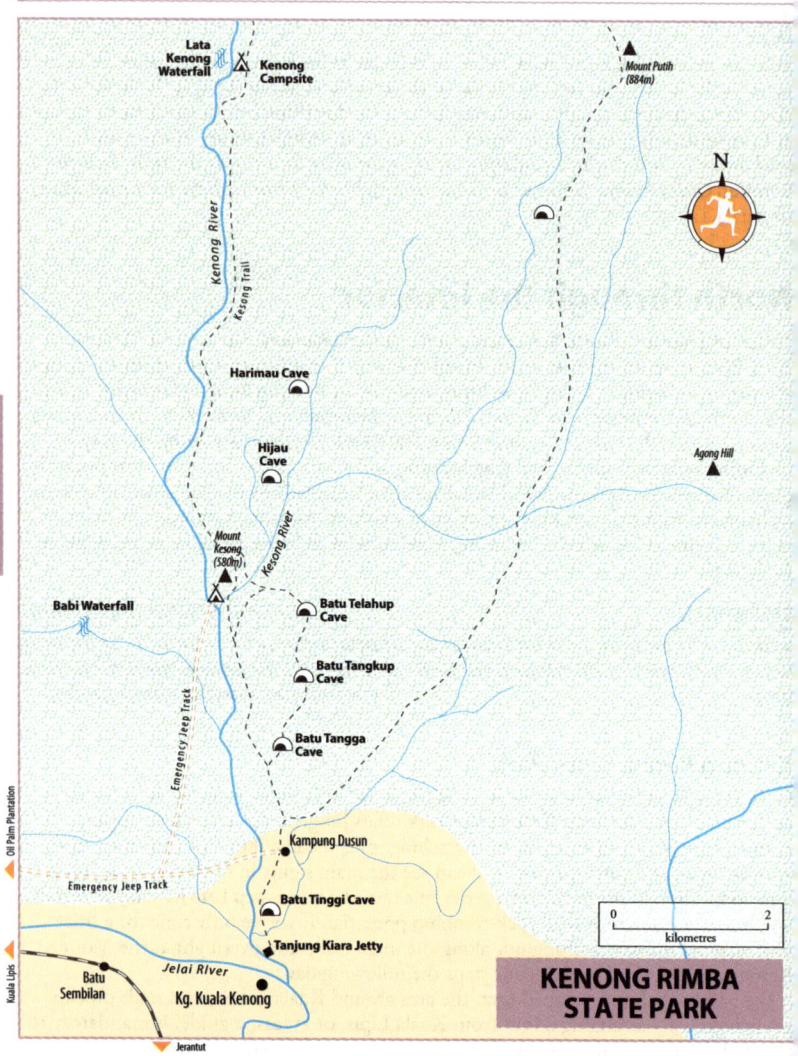

ACCOMMODATION AND EATING

To **camp** in the park costs a nominal fee per night; the most established campsite is at **Mount Kesong**, about 2hr in from the entrance, with the popular **Kenong campsite** another 5hr north of here at Lata Kenong waterfall. Some **chalets** are available, but your guide must book them through the Forestry Department at least one month before your visit, and their quality is not guaranteed.

Kuala Lipis

It's hard to believe that **KUALA LIPIS**, 50km northwest of Jerantut, was the state capital of **Pahang** from 1898 to 1955. Today, it's a sleepy, inconsequential place, situated at the confluence of the Lipis and Jelai rivers and surrounded by rolling hills and plantations. There are a few mementos from colonial days – many associated with the veteran administrator, **Sir Hugh Clifford** (the Pahang Resident 1896–1905), plus plenty of shops and places to eat, but Kuala Lipis's biggest draw is access to the relatively unvisited rainforest trails at nearby **Kenong Rimba State Park**. Here, wildlife abounds and you can expect to see monkeys, wild boar, squirrels and civets

Old town

Kuala Lipis started life as a **trading centre** for *gaharu* (a fragrant aloe wood used to make joss sticks) and other jungle products, collected by the Semiar and traded with Chinese *towkays*. The remnants of these origins survive in the **old town**, a busy grid of pastel-coloured **shophouses** squeezed between the railway and the Jelai River, where the jetty and steps still stand, though goods no longer arrive and depart by river. Overlooking the river to the west, the small, tin-roofed **Masjid Negeri**, dating from 1888, was reputedly founded by a trader from Yemen.

Pahang Club

Jalan Pahang Club

Incongruously hidden behind the huge new **hospital**, the **Pahang Club** dates to 1907. It's an archetypal tropical colonial building, a sprawling structure of whitewashed timber with black trim and wrap-around verandah, raised slightly off the ground on stumps as protection against damp and termites – which, given the lean on the building, clearly hasn't been entirely successful, and the club has fallen into disuse.

Lipis District Office

Kuala Lipis was chosen as a headquarters for the colonial government despite the town's relative isolation – the trip upriver from Singapore took more than two weeks, and there was no road out until the 1890s – though minor **tin deposits** brought short-lived prosperity. These boom days led to the construction of the surprisingly large **Lipis District Office**, which overlooks Kuala Lipis from a hilltop 1km southeast of town; a solid crimson-and-white Edwardian edifice, it now serves as local government offices.

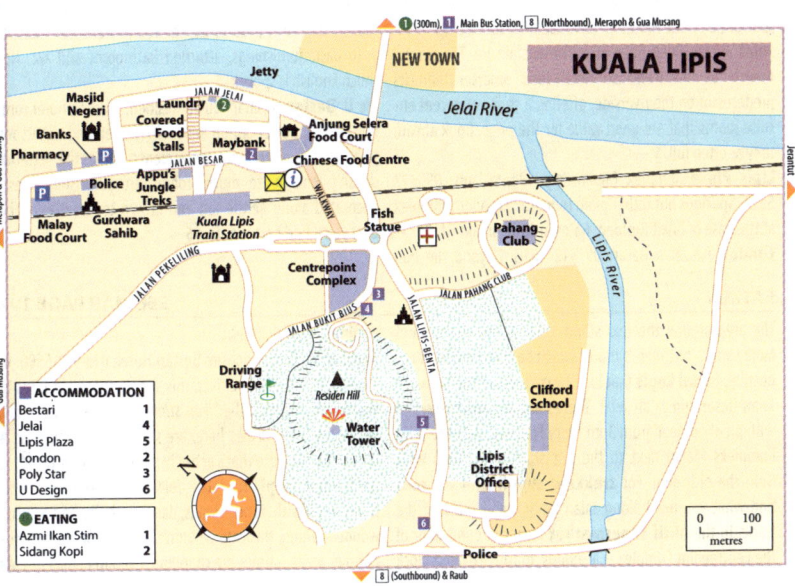

Clifford School

Below the District Office, at the back of green playing fields, **Clifford School** was built in 1913 and part-funded by Hugh Clifford; the original buildings are at the far end of the compound, visible from Jalan Pahang Club. The school is still one of a select group where the country's leaders and royalty are educated – though these days it's equally well known for being the alma mater of Malaysia's biggest-selling female pop star, Siti Nurhaliza.

Bukit Residen

A small rise just south of town is crowned by **Bukit Residen**, a graceful two-storey house built in the 1890s as Hugh Clifford's residence. Clifford arrived in Malaysia in 1883, aged seventeen, and worked his way up through the colonial administration, serving in Malaysia, Sri Lanka and West Africa before ending his career as the Malaya High Commissioner in 1930. The house's associations are more interesting than the building itself – it's now the *Government Rest House* – though it does enjoy great views over the surrounding hills.

ARRIVAL AND DEPARTURE KUALA LIPIS

By train Kuala Lipis's 1926-vintage train station is right in the old town (ticket office daily 9am–4.30pm; 09 312 1341), on the Jungle Railway line. Check http://ktmb.com.my for the latest times.
Destinations Dabong (2 daily; 3hr 40min–4hr 20min); Gua Musang (3 daily; 1hr 40min); Jerantut (3 daily; 1hr); Johor Bahru (1 daily; 9hr); Wakaf Bharu (for Kota Bharu; 2 daily; 6hr 30min–7hr).

By bus The main bus station, Terminal Anggerik, sits 1km north of the centre; cross the river, head up the hill and turn right into the small cluster of shops, where you'll see the open-sided barn of a station.
Destinations Jerantut (3 daily; 1hr 30min); Kuala Lumpur (hourly 6.30am–6.30pm; 4hr); Kota Bharu (via Gua Musang; 1 daily at 11.30am; 5hr 30min); Kuantan (2 daily; 6hr); Sungai Koyan (for Cameron Highlands; 4 daily; 2hr).

ACCOMMODATION SEE MAP PAGE 197

Bestari 42–43 Lorong BBKL, just north of town; http://hoteljelai.com. A 5min walk from the bus station on the opposite side of the main road, this modern, motel-like affair, owned by the Hotel Jelai group, is popular with travelling business people; they take credit cards and the spacious en-suite rooms all have cable TV and a/c. $$

Jelai 7 Jalan Bukit Bius; http://hoteljelai.com. The second branch of this franchise hotel feels smarter than its predecessor on the riverside, offering a series of decent en-suite rooms that are good value for the price. Book ahead; they're often full. $

Lipis Plaza Komplek Taipan Jalan Benta-Lipis; 09 312 5521. Spacious but rather plain rooms in a modern complex at the base of Bukit Residen. Rates include breakfast. $$

London 82 Jalan Besar; 09 312 1618. Beyond the dull facade, the orange-painted interiors here impress with an array of freshly renovated yet tiny rooms, and modern dorms with private curtains. This is the closest Kuala Lipis gets to a backpacker joint. $

Poly Star 5 Jalan Bukit Bius; 09 312 3225. Not as well looked after as it used to be, the rooms here are smallish, with basic furnishings, attached bathrooms and a/c. Not much English is spoken. $

★ **U Design** 7 Jalan Bukit Residen; http://uhotel.com.my. Decent, newer option above a 7-Eleven and a Watsons pharmacy – extremely convenient. While the exterior doesn't look up to much, rooms are surprisingly cosy, decorated along gentle tan and brown tones; they're the best you'll find hereabouts. $$

EATING SEE MAP PAGE 197

The area around the taxi stand holds a few despondent Malay stalls, but there's more atmosphere to be had in the bustling **kedai kopis** that line the covered arcade between Jalan Besar and Jalan Jelai. There's also a **night market** with plenty of food from 3pm every Fri in the purpose-built Kompleks Melati next to the bus station, a 15min walk from the old town. For **trekking supplies**, if you can't find what you need along Jalan Besar, head south of the tracks to the **Aktif supermarket** on the ground floor of the Centrepoint Complex – a shoddy, graffiti-covered block awaiting redevelopment.

Azmi Ikan Stim Opposite Bestari Hotel; 013 911 5500. In a great setting over the river, this simple spot specialises in steamed fish (that's the "*ikan stim*" from the name); this, and many other dishes here, are served with *tempoyak*, a durian-based sauce that's actually quite mild in taste. $$

★ **Sidang Kopi** 18 Jelan Jelai; http://facebook.com/sidangkopi. With its brick walls, dangling bulbs and painted wooden ceiling, this café wouldn't look out of place in KL's trendier areas – times are changing, even in Kuala Lipis. As well as good espresso coffee, they've fruit shakes, several types of cake and a few savoury meals too. $$

DIRECTORY

Bank There's a Maybank with ATM on Jalan Besar, and a couple of others in the vicinity.

Laundry A same-day laundry service is available on Jalan Jelai.

Merapoh

The tiny market town of **MERAPOH**, served by road and rail 80km north of Kuala Lipis, marks a 7km-long access road east to **Taman Negara's western entrance**, officially known as **Sungai Relau**. This is the only part of Taman Negara where a proper vehicle road runs deep into the park, providing access to the trails – most famously that to **Mount Tahan** (see page 193). There's not much point in turning up here with your own car, however, as the 14km-long park road is closed to private vehicles, and all trails – even the easiest strolls around the park's headquarters – require hiring a guide. What might make it worth stumping up for guide fees and official transportation is the chance of seeing elephants, as well as leopard cats, civets, otters and banting – a mix of buffalo and seladang. A new **tree-top walk** was nearing completion at the time of writing, with two circular routes joining to make a lofty figure eight.

Into the park

Charge • 09 915 0214

Beyond the park office and picnic ground, cross the little Relau River via a small **bridge** and you'll come to the narrow surfaced road that undulates through the jungle. Several trails lead off the initial few kilometres, including **Rentis Gajah** ("Elephant Trail"), leading south off the road to Gajah Cave, though you can't hike here independently; allow four hours for the return trip from the gate, plus an hour exploring.

Driving a few kilometres along the jeep track will take you to the 12m-high, red Menara Bukit Seraya, an **observation tower** with views of forested ridges and valleys to the north, and, on a clear day, east to Mount Tahan. Some 2km beyond Bukit Seraya is Air Terjun Sungai Kelam, a pretty **waterfall** in a secluded woodland setting.

The road ends at **Kuala Juram**, where trees overhang the Juram River, a stretch of which teems with *kelah* (mahseer), and where it's possible to kayak and fish. The suspension bridge over the river here is the gateway to the Mount Tahan mountain trail.

ARRIVAL AND DEPARTURE — MERAPOH

By bus There's no bus station, but the daily bus between Kuala Lipis or Kuala Lumpur and Gua Musang can drop you off; local tour operators can also deliver/collect from Gua Musang, just 30min north.

By train Merapoh train station is just west of Route 8. There is no local transport between the station and the park; if you can't get a ride, you can walk it: it takes 2hr to walk the rolling 7km through palm oil plantations.

Destinations Dabong (2 daily at 7.15am; 2hr 20min); Gua Musang (3 daily; 25min); Kuala Lipis (3 daily; 1hr 10min); Johor Bahru (1 daily; 10hr 30min); Wakaf Bharu (for Kota Bharu; 2 daily; 5hr 20min–5hr 50min).

TOURS AND GUIDES

You can ask at park headquarters for the prices of guides and jeeps; agencies are slightly more expensive.

Merapoh Adventure Along the main road; http://facebook.com/merapohadventure. Reliable local operator offering a wide range of tours, from multi-day caving explorations, canoeing and fishing inside and outside Taman Negara, and the five-day to week-long Mount Tahan hike. All prices include permits and insurance. They can also arrange accommodation in private homes where you can use the kitchen, an ideal option for self-catering groups.

SGI Outdoor 200m towards the park from Merapoh down the access road; http://natureguidemerapoh.webs.com. This operation arranges accommodation in Merapoh, plus tours and transport into the park; they also run multi-day caving trips in the surrounding area. Tents and sleeping bags are available to rent from their welcoming offices; there's also a decent range of gear (including boots and waterproofs) for sale.

ACCOMMODATION AND EATING

Unless you're camping in the park, it makes sense to base yourself 7km away in Merapoh to use the clutch of guesthouses and *kedai kopis* along the main road, as food and accommodation options are very limited in this part of Taman Negara. If staying at the park campsites, you'll need to bring all your own food and cooking gear.

Merapoh Adventure On the road leading to the access road from town; http://facebook.com/merapohadventureguesthouse. The main local tour operator (see page 199) also has a simple, though very popular, guesthouse, with good dorm rooms, common areas (one room including a Netflix-enabled TV), and cooking facilities. $

Gua Musang

GUA MUSANG ("Civet Cave"), 30km from Merapoh, is a former logging town strung thinly along a stretch of Route 8. A 100m-wide knot of scruffy buildings and shops surrounds the old **train station**, while a **new satellite town** coalesces 3km south. This being Kelantan, the Malay accent here displays a distinctive twang, and alcohol is available only at a few shops run by Chinese residents.

Gua Musang is fairly close to the **Taman Negara entrances** at Merapoh (see page 199) and Kuala Koh (see page 201). Time spent between connections can be filled with a day-trip to **Kampung Pulai** (see page 201) or exploring the **caves** that riddle a mass of limestone looming over the train tracks. Note that the path up to the caves is steep, crumbling and very overgrown, and particularly difficult after rain – it's best attempted with a local guide.

ARRIVAL AND INFORMATION   GUA MUSANG

By train The train station is just off Route 8, between the old and new parts of town.
Destinations Dabong (4 daily; 2hr); Gemas (1 daily; 6hr 30min); Kuala Lipis (3 daily; 1hr 30min); Merapoh (3 daily; 30min); Johor Bahru (1 daily; 11hr); Wakaf Bharu (for Kota Bharu; 4 daily; 4hr 40min–5hr 20min).
By bus Gua Musang's main bus station is 2.5km south of the train station in the new town. There are no direct buses to Cameron Highlands; take the train to to Kuala Lipis and then a bus to Sungai Koyan, from where three daily departures reach Tanah Rata.
Destinations Kota Bharu (3 daily; 4hr); Kuala Lumpur (5 daily; 4hr 30min).

ACCOMMODATION   SEE MAP PAGE 200

M Quality Just west of the train station; 09 913 4288. One of the newer, friendlier options in the town centre – not that there was much competition. The rooms, painted magnolia and occasionally with some splashes of emerald, are really quite comfy for the price, and guests can make use of a water fountain and free instant coffee through the day. $$

★ **Welcome Inn GM** PT 2870 Jalan Cengai, about 2km walk northeast of the train station along the main road; http://bit.ly/WelcomeInnGM. Not central but next to a supermarket in a new area of town, this is Gua Musang's best-value hotel, with squeaky clean and airy en-suite a/c rooms (some windowless). Contact them in advance for a free pick-up from either the bus or train station. $

EATING   SEE MAP PAGE 200

As well as the following, note that branches of several Western fast-food chains can be located around the three-way junction, just west of the train station – if you've made it as far as Gua Musang, you may well feel like partaking.
Kak Zah Restoran Jalan Besar; http://facebook.com/ KakZahRestoran. One of Gua Musang's most appreciated Malay restaurants serves an array of local curries and dishes, of which *nasi kerabu*, the quintessential Kelantanese blue-coloured rice served with crackers, dried fish and fried chicken, is highly recommended. $

Man Yek Pan Mee Kampung Baru; 014 228 1128. Chinese restaurant with a Chinese menu – unless you can read some basic culinary logograms, you may have to rely on pictures and a little mime. It's all good, cheap fare, with their signature *pan mee* (handmade noodles in soup) the highlight.

DIRECTORY

Banks There are several banks with ATMs on Route 8 near the train station.

Supplies Stores along Jalan Besar sell everything from food to batteries and umbrellas.

Kampung Pulai

KAMPUNG PULAI, 8km south of Gua Musang, may be southern Kelantan's best-kept secret. This traditional Hakka village lies in a beautiful riverside setting, where lush greenery is punctuated by karst formations rising dramatically from the earth. The Hakka first came here around six hundred years ago in search of gold. The continued prevalence of Hakka traditions today can be attributed to the village's isolation: the first tarred road to Gua Musang only arrived in 1988.

Life in Kampung Pulai revolves around the **Water and Moon Temple**, dedicated to goddess of mercy Kuan Yin, and said to be more than 400 years old. The centrepiece is an extremely rare Ming Dynasty painting of Kuan Yin as a maiden, brought here from China by the early settlers. On the nineteenth day of the second month of the Chinese lunar calendar, Kampung Pulai celebrates the goddess's birthday: the village fills up with devotees from all over Southeast Asia, rituals and parades are held in the main square, and free vegetarian food is served in the community hall next to the temple.

Princess Hill

Free • Ask for the guardian at the Water and Moon Temple for the key

From the courtyard outside the shrine, a suspension bridge crosses the **Galas River** joining a path to the foot of **Princess Hill**, a limestone karst housing a set of ancient meditation caves and a shrine with a statue of Kuan Yin carved out of a giant stalagmite. From the two viewing platforms at the top, the sunset views over the Galas River, snaking quietly through a carpet of untamed green jungle, are superb.

ARRIVAL AND DEPARTURE   KAMPUNG PULAI

By taxi There is no public transport between Gua Musang and Kampung Pulai, so you'll have to take a taxi from Gua Musang's bus station; don't forget to get your driver's number for the return journey.

By car From Gua Musang's bus station, turn right towards the hospital and then left at the main junction with Road D29. From here, it's a short drive along the D241.

ACCOMMODATION AND EATING

There's a series of inexpensive Malay restaurants along **Road D241**, all serving the usual Kelantanese staples – a mix of zesty Malay food with southern Thai influences, such as *tom yum* and *nasi kerabu*.

Chinese noodle corner store Next to the temple square, facing the river. This Chinese *kopitiam* dishes up a wide selection of cheap noodles and breakfast titbits. Note that it doesn't have an official name. The karaoke bar next door is the place to go for a beer.

★ **Pulai Holiday Village** 1km before the turn off to the Water and Moon Temple; 016 921 6652. Pulai's only guesthouse, occasionally masquerading online as *Pulai Vintage Resort*, has two blocks of smart en-suite rooms next to a secluded rubber estate. The older block, all decked out in wood, has slightly simpler but more picturesque rooms next to a private limestone cave, which you can explore at your leisure. Ample parking available, and there's also a small café on site.

Kuala Koh

With its jungle trails, boat trips and canopy walkway, **Kuala Koh**, Taman Negara's northern entrance, 85km east of Gua Musang, sounds like the ideal alternative to touristy Kuala Tahan. On the ground, however, the experience is dramatically different:

a lack of visitors, coupled with poor maintenance of both the canopy walkway and the trails after the 2014 floods, have left the place in a mess. At the time of writing, the canopy walkway was closed, pending repairs, and accommodation was only available in a campsite. Given that expensive private transport is the only way to get here, and guides are compulsory to venture anywhere beyond the bridge at the park's headquarters, it's strongly recommended that you contact the office (call rather than rely on the infrequently updated website) to enquire about the state of trails and facilities before you set off on a potentially disappointing journey.

Canopy walkway
Closed at time of research • Charge

Walk through park headquarters to reach the **suspension bridge** that leads over the Lebir River into the forest; turn left on the far side and it's 100m to the **canopy walkway**. The walkway is 20m up, over partially cleared forest with bamboo and barbed rattan palms below; from the top you can expect to see birds, insects and occasional troupes of monkeys.

Forest trails

Beyond the canopy walkway, several kilometres of **trails** weave through the forest and along the river. All hikes require arranging a guide in advance, either through the park headquarters or a tour operator. During the day, **listen** for wildlife – the zithering of cicadas, whooshing of hornbill wings, and staccato rustle of lizards amid the leaf litter. Pick of the routes are the **Rentis Ara** ("Fig Trail"), a 3km circuit, and the 1.5km-long **Rentis Bumbun**, ending at a pole-frame **hide** overlooking a salt lick – somewhere to sit still for an hour and see what turns up.

On the river

A pleasant **river trip** heads up the Lebir for half an hour to **Kuala Pertang**, passing a few sandy banks where you can camp, swim or fish; the river is home to *ikan kelah* and other freshwater denizens. The ride takes you under the overhanging boughs of leaning neram trees, some hung with the leafy tresses of **tiger orchids**, among the world's largest orchid species. You can also go **tubing** along the river, being carried downstream on an inflated rubber ring, or arrange a trip to a semi-permanent **Batek camp**, two hours upstream.

ARRIVAL AND INFORMATION   KUALA KOH

By car Turn off Route 8 at Simpang Aring (40km east of Gua Musang) and follow signs along a sealed, windy road through the Felda Aring palm oil plantation, looking out for plantation vehicles, before turning off onto an access road for the last 15km. The road passes an Orang Asli village just before entering the park, with the headquarters a short drive further on above the confluence of the Lebir and Koh rivers.
By taxi Taxis from Gua Musang are one way to go.
Park office Staff at the park office (09 741 6240, http://taman-negara-koh.blogspot.my) can give you a photocopied schematic map of Kuala Koh, and accept payment of the nominal entry and photography fees. Book guides and all river activities here too: tubing on the river is a popular choice (minimum four people), while you could also take an hour-long guided night walk, when you might see slow loris and civets.
Camping The only way to stay within the park is to camp. Keep in mind that you'll have to bring everything you'll need, including food, cutlery, plates and a stove, with you.

Gunung Stong State Park

Around 70km north of Gua Musang, **Gunung Stong State Park** (otherwise known as **Jelawang Jungle**) is based around 1420m-high **Mount Stong**, a prominent, forested granite mountain 7km outside the small rail township of **DABONG**. Current train schedules make it a great day stop, with a short but tough hike up through lush forest to a series of **waterfalls** and plunge pools, where you can have a swim and catch a late afternoon train out. However, it's also worth staying **overnight** on the mountainside for the magical sunrise views. Before heading to the park, you could also spend a few hours exploring the **Gua Ikan complex**, a system of five caves connected by an underground stream, roughly 3km out of Dabong. It's possible to visit independently, but hire a guide when the water level is high, when the main path becomes hard to follow.

Air Terjun Jelawang

The access road from Dabong ends at the foot of the mountain, where you buy your entry ticket. From the gate, follow a path that crosses a rickety suspension bridge into the forest, where the paving quickly gives way to a muddy path, tangled with tree roots. This is extremely steep, with ropes and chains to help you up – fortunately the gritty mud gives a decent grip. After about 1km, you'll reach a ramshackle pavilion where a side trail leads sharply down 300m to a pretty spot near the foot of the largest cascade.

As you continue along the main trail, *Baha's Camp* (see below) sits a sweaty 1.5km further up the hillside on the riverbank between the first and second tiers of **Air Terjun Jelawang**, also known as Lata Jelawang, Peninsular Malaysia's **highest waterfall**, which cascades a total of 540m down a bald granite rock face in seven steps. There's a pool that's great for swimming and a wonderful viewpoint – if you stay overnight, this is where you'll want to be at dawn to watch the **sunrise** over a sea of cotton wool clouds blanketing the plains. Do take care, though; the rocks are slick and people have slipped to their deaths.

Mountain trails

Baha's Camp is the trailhead for the **Elephant Trek**, which follows the main path up the mountain for two hours to the top of Mount Stong, before winding along the ridge and crossing over onto neighbouring **Mount Ayam** (1500m). Although it's possible to return to *Baha's* the same day, it's recommended to **camp** for the night on top of Mount Ayam – you'll need warm clothing and a good sleeping bag. Elephants are sometimes seen here, and there's a chance of encountering **tapir** and **deer** in the early morning or early evening.

ARRIVAL AND DEPARTURE — GUNUNG STONG STATE PARK

By train It's feasible to come on a day-trip, visit the caves and the falls and have a swim, if you arrive at Dabong on an early train from either direction, and leave the same evening (timetables on http://ktmb.com.my). Ask taxis at Dabong station for a lift to the caves or park entrance. Destinations Gemas (for Kuala Lumpur; 1 daily; 8hr 15min); Gua Musang (4 daily; 2hr); Jerantut (1 daily; 4hr 30min); Johor Bahru (1 daily; 13hr); Kuala Lipis (2 daily; 3hr 30min–4hr 20min); Merapoh (2 daily; 2hr 20min–3hr); Wakaf Bharu (for Kota Bharu; 3 daily; 3hr).

By car Dabong is just off Route 66, 70km north of Gua Musang; it's 40km west of the Sam River and Route 8. From Penang/Kedah and points north, follow the E4 to Jeli, then take the Route 66 turning and head south for 53km to the Dabong turning. Cross the river and drive north for 7km, before taking the signed road to the mountain.

ACCOMMODATION AND EATING

Simple meals are available from the restaurant at the **park gates** (daily 8am–7pm). Meals at *Baha's Camp* are by arrangement only. There are several *kedai kopis* around Dabong train station, but the closest place to buy supplies is Gua Musang.

Baha's Camp Inside the forest, 1hr 30min from the park gates, by the waterfall; 012 968 1554. A superb – if extremely basic – place to stay, with tents scattered around a jungle clearing. There's no electricity or running water, unless you count the nearby waterfall, and you might find yourself sharing the tent with some of the smaller forest creatures. If you can't contact the camp in advance (they're sometimes out of range), bring your own tent just in case their own are full, as well as your own food – they should be able to cook it for you. $

★ **Jelawang Dream Pipe Resort** http://facebook.com/Jelawangpiperesort. And now for something a little different – a resort where you sleep in coloured "pipes". All are horizontally arranged; some lie under trellis roofs, others under trees, and those staying in the green ones would be forgiven for doing a little *Super Mario* jump (noise optional) when on the way in or out. The pipes all have TVs, lighting and electrical sockets; essentially, it's a jungle version of a Japanese capsule hotel, with ATVs to ride outside. $$$

Rose House Down from the road bridge across the railway, Dabong; http://facebook.com/Rose.House.Dabong. With six rooms in two rose-pink blocks, this guesthouse is a great place to recuperate after a trip into the mountains. Clean rooms have fans, a/c and bathrooms, and the friendly owner may throw in *nasi kerabu* for breakfast. $

The east coast

- **209** Kota Bharu
- **218** From Kota Bharu to Kuala Terengganu
- **219** The Perhentian Islands
- **227** Redang Island
- **228** Lang Tengah Island
- **228** Kuala Terengganu
- **234** Tasik Kenyir
- **235** Marang
- **236** Kapas Island
- **238** Southern Terengganu
- **240** Cherating
- **243** Kuantan and around
- **248** Pekan

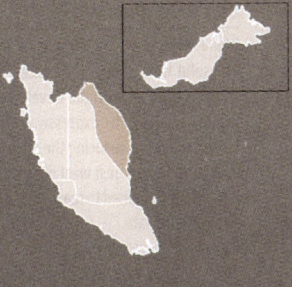

PULAU PERHENTIAN KECIL

The east coast

The 400km-long stretch from the northeastern corner of the Peninsula to Kuantan, roughly halfway down the east coast, draws visitors for two major reasons: the beaches and islands, and traditional Malay culture. Islands such as the Perhentians, Redang and Kapas offer great opportunities for diving and snorkelling; further south, the backpackers' coastal enclave of Cherating is a deservedly popular place simply to kick back for a few days. Among the cities, vibrant Kota Bharu, close to the Thai border, stands out for its opportunities to access Malay crafts and performing arts.

The east coast displays a different cultural legacy to the more populous, commercial western seaboard, from which it is separated by the mountainous, jungled interior. For hundreds of years, the Malay rulers of the northern states of **Kelantan** and **Terengganu** were vassals of the Thai kingdom of **Ayutthaya**, suffering repeated invasions as well as the unruly squabbles of their own princes. Nevertheless, the Malays enjoyed a great deal of autonomy, and both states remained free of British control until 1909. Only in 1931 did the railway arrive in Kelantan; previously, the journey from KL involved thirteen river crossings. In 1941 Kelantan saw the landing of the first Japanese troops, facilitated by the Thai government – who were rewarded by being given full control over Kelantan once more from 1943 until 1945.

While immigrants poured into the tin and rubber towns of the west during the twentieth century, the east remained rural. As a result, Kelantan and Terengganu remain very much **Malay heartland** states. There's a rustic feel to the area, the economy being largely based on agriculture and fishing, with the obvious exception of Terengganu's petroleum industry.

The country's religious opposition party, **PAS**, which was born in Kelantan in the middle of the last century, has governed its home state since 1990. For foreign visitors, the political backdrop distils down to the simple truth that the **social climate** of Kelantan and Terengganu is more obviously **conservative** than elsewhere in Malaysia: **alcohol** is harder to obtain than in other states; most restaurants, whatever cuisine they serve, are **halal**; and **dress** – for both men and women – needs to be circumspect, except at well-touristed beaches. You will also find that **English** is less understood in Kelantan and Terengganu than in most other parts of the Peninsula.

GETTING AROUND THE EAST COAST

While **flights** to Kota Bharu or Kuala Terengganu can be useful time-savers, road access to the east coast has really opened up with the development of the East Coast Expressway (E8). The expressway arrives on the coast just north of Kuantan, reducing the drive from KL to a 3hr whizz, then runs north to just west of Kuala Terengganu; the road is eventually planned to reach Kota Bharu, though progress has stalled of late.

By bus The express buses that ply the east coast's busy main roads are convenient for trips between the major towns, but if you're heading anywhere else often the only option is to take one of the slower, local buses that serve the smaller stops.

By car In addition to the E8 and East Coast Highway, the region's old backbone roads remain intact: the coast road (called Route 3 between Kuala Terengganu and Kuantan) and its shadow 10–20km inland (Route 14 south of Kuala Terengganu, Route 3 to the north). Unsurprisingly, the coast road, connecting a string of laidback towns and fishing kampungs, is the most interesting.

By train The only rail service is the atmospheric "Jungle Railway" through the interior (see page 193) to Tumpat, near Kota Bharu.

SITI KHADIJAH MARKET

Highlights

❶ **Kota Bharu** One of the Peninsula's most appealing cities, home to Malay crafts, traditional art forms and a popular night food market, with Buddhist temples within easy reach. See page 209

❷ **Perhentian Islands** Two of the most enticing islands the Peninsula has to offer, with excellent snorkelling and accommodation ranging from backpacker chalets to slick resorts. See page 219

❸ **Kapas Island** A delightful little island less than half an hour from Marang by speedboat with decent sands and opportunities for snorkelling, kayaking. There's also a good network of hiking routes – perfect for a couple of days' relaxation. See page 236

❹ **Cherating** Chill by the beach, watch fireflies or just enjoy the amiable, low-key nightlife in this long-established travellers' hangout. See page 240

❺ **Pekan** An appealingly quiet royal town, with a scattering of palaces, impeccable kampung houses and a newly renovated museum housed in a colonial building. See page 248

HIGHLIGHTS ARE MARKED ON THE MAP ON PAGE 208

THE EAST COAST IN THE OFF-SEASON

Many visitors give the east coast a wide berth during the **northeast monsoon**, which sets in during late October and continues until February. It's true that heavy rains and sea swells put paid to most boat services to the islands at this time, and most beach accommodation, whether on the mainland or offshore, is shut anyway. The rains will, however, usually be interspersed with good sunny spells, just as the so-called dry season can bring its share of torrential downpours. With luck, and a flexible schedule, you will find boats heading sporadically to and from the islands during the monsoon; some island accommodation opens year-round, although you should contact places in advance to be sure. While diving and snorkelling aren't great at this time of year, due to reduced visibility, the east coast comes into its own for **surfing** and **windsurfing**, with Cherating the prime destination. Away from the beaches, there's always reasonable sightseeing in Kota Bharu and Kuala Terengganu – just be prepared to take lengthy refuge in cafés or malls when yet another thunderstorm breaks.

Kota Bharu

The capital of Kelantan, **KOTA BHARU**, sits at the very northeastern corner of the Peninsula, on the east bank of the broad, muddy Kelantan River. Many visitors arrive across the nearby Thai border, and for most the city is simply a half-decent place to rest and get their Malaysian bearings. To breeze through Kota Bharu and the rest of Kelantan, however, would be to gloss over one of the country's most culturally fascinating states.

Kelantan has historically been a crucible for **Malay culture**, fostering art forms that drew on influences from around Southeast Asia and as far away as India. Kota Bharu is the ideal place to witness the region's distinctive heritage, on show at its **Cultural Centre** and in the various **cottage industries** that thrive in its hinterland – among them kite-making, batik printing and woodcarving. The city also boasts its share of historical buildings, now largely **museums**, plus some excellent **markets** and numerous **Buddhist temples** in the surrounding countryside.

The city centre is compact, with most of the **markets**, many of the **banks** and the biggest stores between Jalan Hospital and Jalan Pintu Pong, a few blocks north.

Around Padang Merdeka

West of the main markets, close to the river, the quiet oasis of **Padang Merdeka** marks Kota Bharu's historical centre. It was here that the British displayed the body of the defeated Tok Janggut (Father Beard), a peasant spiritual leader who spearheaded a revolt against colonial land taxes and tenancy regulations in 1915. Today the main attractions are a handful of historic buildings, several of which have been converted into **museums**.

One of the most obvious landmarks is the **Sultan Ismail Petra Arch**, beyond which is the **Istana Balai Besar** – a mid-nineteenth-century palace, closed to the public but still used for ceremonial functions – and the squat former **State Treasury**.

Istana Jahar
North of Sultan Ismail Petra Arch, Jalan Sultan • Charge • 09 748 2266

The well-preserved **Istana Jahar** was built in 1887 with a timber portico and pillars painted a regal shade of yellow. In 1911 Sultan Muhammad IV added an Italian marble floor and two wrought-iron spiral staircases. The palace now houses an exhibition on **royal ceremonies**, which can be seen in an hour (although you may want to linger on the breezy first-floor veranda). Rites illustrated include *istiadat pijak tanah*, a ceremony that marked the point when young royals – aged between five and seven years – were allowed to set foot on soil for the first time.

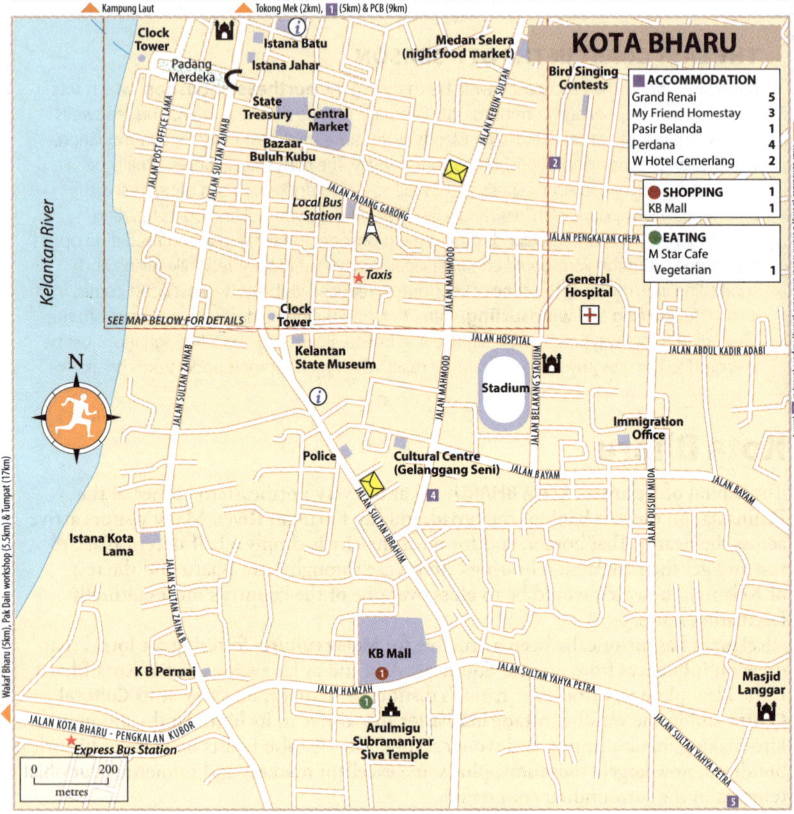
Kampung Laut
Tokong Mek (2km), 1 (5km) & PCB (9km)
KOTA BHARU
ACCOMMODATION
Grand Renai 5
My Friend Homestay 3
Pasir Belanda 1
Perdana 4
W Hotel Cemerlang 2
SHOPPING 1
KB Mall 1
EATING
M Star Cafe Vegetarian 1
Clock Tower
Padang Merdeka
Istana Batu
Istana Jahar
State Treasury
Central Market
Bazaar Buluh Kubu
Medan Selera (night food market)
Bird Singing Contests
Local Bus Station
Taxis
Clock Tower
SEE MAP BELOW FOR DETAILS
Kelantan State Museum
General Hospital
Stadium
Immigration Office
Police
Cultural Centre (Gelanggang Seni)
Istana Kota Lama
KB Mall
K B Permai
Arulmigu Subramaniyar Siva Temple
Masjid Langgar
Express Bus Station
Kelantan River
JALAN POST OFFICE LAMA
JALAN SULTAN ZAINAB
JALAN PADANG GARONG
JALAN KEBUN SULTAN
JALAN MAHMOOD
JALAN PENGKALAN CHEPA
JALAN HOSPITAL
JALAN ABDUL KADIR ADABI
JALAN BELAKANG STADIUM
JALAN BAYAM
JALAN DUSUN MUDA
JALAN SULTAN IBRAHIM
JALAN HAMZAH
JALAN SULTAN YAHYA PETRA
JALAN KOTA BHARU - PENGKALAN KUBOR
Wakaf Bharu (5km), Pak Dain workshop (5.5km) & Tumpat (17km)
N
0 200 metres

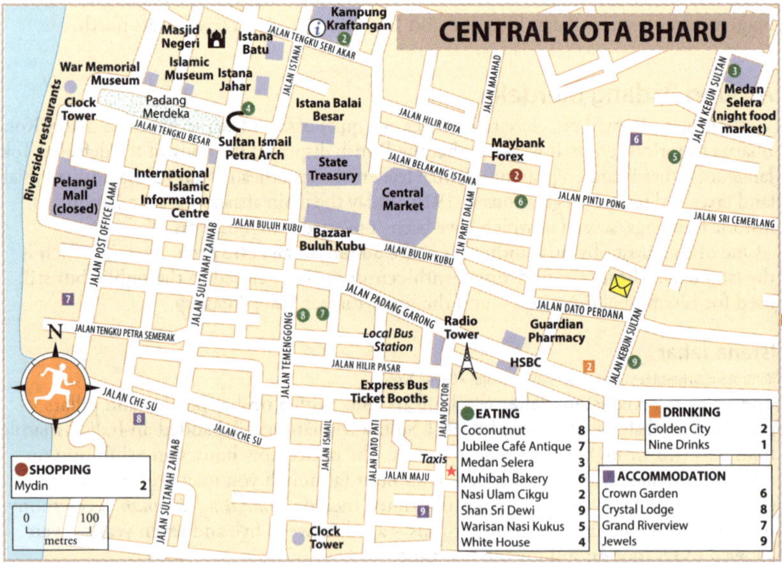
CENTRAL KOTA BHARU
Kampung Kraftangan
Masjid Negeri
Istana Batu
Islamic Museum
Istana Jahar
War Memorial Museum
Clock Tower
Padang Merdeka
Sultan Ismail Petra Arch
Istana Balai Besar
Riverside restaurants
Pelangi Mall (closed)
International Islamic Information Centre
State Treasury
Central Market
Bazaar Buluh Kubu
Maybank Forex
Medan Selera (night food market)
Radio Tower
Local Bus Station
Guardian Pharmacy
HSBC
Express Bus Ticket Booths
Taxis
Clock Tower
JALAN TENGKU SERI AKAR
JALAN ISTANA
JALAN MAAHAD
JALAN HILIR KOTA
JALAN TENGKU BESAR
JALAN BELAKANG ISTANA
JALAN PINTU PONG
JALAN SRI CEMERLANG
JALAN KEBUN SULTAN
JALAN POST OFFICE LAMA
JALAN SULTANAH ZAINAB
JALAN BULUH KUBU
JLN PARIT DALAM
JALAN PADANG GARONG
JALAN DATO PERDANA
JALAN TENGKU PETRA SEMERAK
JALAN TEMENGGONG
JALAN HILIR PASAR
JALAN CHE SU
JALAN ISMAIL
JALAN DATO PATI
JALAN MAJU
JALAN DOCTOR
EATING
Coconutnut 8
Jubilee Café Antique 7
Medan Selera 3
Muhibah Bakery 6
Nasi Ulam Cikgu 2
Shan Sri Dewi 9
Warisan Nasi Kukus 5
White House 4
DRINKING
Golden City 2
Nine Drinks 1
ACCOMMODATION
Crown Garden 6
Crystal Lodge 8
Grand Riverview 7
Jewels 9
SHOPPING
Mydin 2
N
0 100 metres

The **weapons gallery**, in a separate building just behind the palace, features an exhibit devoted to the *kris*, a dagger that has important symbolic value to Malays (see box, page 231).

Istana Batu
North of Istana Jahar, Jalan Istana • Charge • http://jmm.gov.my

An incongruous 1930s villa, **Istana Batu** was built as a wedding present for Muhammad IV's grandson. One of the first concrete constructions in the state (its name means "stone palace"), today it functions as the **Kelantan Royal Museum**.

Several rooms remain as they were when the royal family moved out, and a brief wander through is worthwhile if only to survey the tat that royals the world over seem to accumulate. Here it includes – among other treasures – tiger-skin rugs, a glass revolver and piles of imported crockery.

Kampung Kraftangan
Opposite Istana Batu, Jalan Hilir Kota • Free

In the **Kampung Kraftangan** (Handicraft Village), gift shops sell everything from tacky souvenirs to silverware, rattan baskets and other local products. You can try your hand at batik at Zecsman Design, and the complex is home to two branches of the excellent *Cikgu* restaurant (see page 217).

Handicraft Museum
Charge • 09 744 3949

The small **Handicraft Museum** upstairs in Kampung Kraftangan is worth a few minutes of your time; it displays traditional craft items including silverware, woven pandan, bamboo and rattan objects, woodcarving and *songket* (textiles woven with gold thread).

Masjid Negeri
Jalan Sultan • Permission required from International Islamic Information Centre on Jalan Sultanah Zainab (09 747 7824) • Free

The white **Masjid Negeri**, on the northern side of the padang, was completed in the late 1920s. Once you have permission and are inside the mosque – each gender sticking to their respective prayer halls – male visitors should keep an eye out for the enormous drum (*bedok*) that once summoned the faithful to prayer. The small and rather dull **Islamic Museum** is housed in a mint-green villa immediately west of the mosque.

THE MARKETS OF KOTA BHARU

Kota Bharu has a fine array of **markets**, reflecting its role as state capital and as a centre for Malay culture and handicrafts. There is also an excellent nightly **food market** (see page 217).

Bazaar Buluh Kubu West of the central market. Though lacking in atmosphere, this market does have a good range of batik, *songket* and other crafts on sale. Daily 9am–6pm.

Central market East of the historical centre. Kota Bharu's humming central market, Pasar Besar Siti Khadijah, is one of the city's focal points, and aptly named after the Prophet Mohamed's entrepreneurial first wife as most of its traders are women. The main building, an octagonal hall, has a perspex roof casting a soft light over the patchwork of the main trading floor – a mass of fruit, vegetables and textiles. The whole scene is worth contemplating at length from the upper levels, especially when it's busy in the mornings. Trading continues east of here in an extension to the original market; some brilliant first-floor food stalls make it a great place to sample Kelantanese flavours. Daily 8am–6pm.

Friday street market Jalan Ismail, south of Jalan Hulu Pasar. A visit to the informal, morning-only Friday market is recommended as a way to witness the rustic heart of Kelantan laid bare, as traders and shoppers pour in from the surrounding kampungs on their weekend day out in the city. Fri 8am–noon.

War Memorial Museum

Jalan Sultan • Charge • 09 748 2266

In a solid yellow building that once housed the Mercantile Bank of India, the **War Memorial Museum** commemorates the fact that Japanese troops first set foot in Malaya on Kelantan's beaches. They captured the entire state in December 1941, and Singapore fell just two months later. During the occupation, the bank was the local base for the Japanese secret police.

While the war artefacts are desultory (fragments of ordnance, ration pouches and the like), the accompanying text gives insight into the swiftness of the Japanese advance – aided by their use of bicycles – and the British collapse. The exhibition downstairs also covers the years leading up to independence, while upstairs there's an exhibit on Kelantan's peacetime history, the walls covered with fading photographs of colonial administrators.

Kelantan State Museum

Jalan Hospital • Charge

Much of the ground floor of the **Kelantan State Museum** is used for temporary exhibits, although it also includes a "time tunnel", where old photographs of locations in the city are paired with contemporary images taken of the same spots. It's fascinating to see what has – and hasn't – changed. The upper floor focuses on traditional local pastimes, with displays of kites, spinning tops, *wayang kulit* puppets and various musical instruments.

Cultural Centre

Jalan Mahmood • Free

A high point of any visit to Kota Bharu, the excellent **Cultural Centre** (Gelanggang Seni) holds demonstrations of Kelantan's cultural and recreational activities. Each day's session is different; check with the state tourist office if you have a particular interest. Performances might include a combination of *gasing* (spinning tops), *pencak silat* (martial arts), *rebana ubi* (giant drums), *kertok* (smaller drums formed from coconuts) and *congkak* (a game involving the strategic movement of seeds around the holes on a wooden board). Best of all, Wednesday evenings see **wayang kulit** (traditional shadow puppetry) performances.

Craft workshops

Most of Kota Bharu's **craft workshops** lie on the road to **PCB**, the uninspiring beach 11km north of the city. As they are quite spread out, the best way to see a variety of workshops (including kite-making, batik and more) is on a half-day tour, arranged either via your accommodation or through the state tourist office. The workshops listed here are not on the way to PCB, and are easier to visit independently.

K.B. Permai

5406 Jalan Sultanah Zainab, near Jalan Hamzah intersection • http://facebook.com/krafperak

Kelantanese **silverware** is well known throughout the Peninsula. At the **K.B. Permai** workshop, you can watch artisans shaping silver wire into fine filigree, and producing items such as embossed gongs and jewellery, and you can buy pieces here, or at their retail outlet in Kampung Kraftangan (see page 211), at much keener prices than in Kuala Lumpur.

Pak Dain workshop

5 impang 3 Morak, Wakaf Bharu • http://wayangpakdain.com.my

A *wayang kulit* **puppeteer** who also makes the tools of his trade, **Pak Dain** can be visited out on the west bank of the Kelantan River. His workshop holds examples of

THE PERFORMING ARTS IN KELANTAN

Kelantan has a rich artistic tradition, boasting two costumed dance/drama forms, **mak yong** and the Thai-influenced **menora**. Even more striking is **wayang kulit**, shadow puppetry, traditionally staged on a dais screened from the audience by a large sheet and illuminated from behind. The cast consists of a set of stencils made of hide and cut into silhouettes of the various characters; these are manipulated against the screen by a sole puppeteer, who also improvises all the dialogue. Reflecting India's historic influence in the region, the tales are taken from the Hindu epic, the *Ramayana*. In the past, *wayang kulit* functioned as a sort of kampung soap opera, serializing *Ramayana* instalments nightly during the months after the rice harvest. Performances are gripping affairs, with a hypnotic soundtrack provided by an ensemble of drums, gongs and the oboe-like *serunai*, whose players are seated behind the puppeteer.

Sadly, all three of the above traditional arts found themselves **banned** in Kelantan in the 1990s by the PAS-led state government. PAS cited issues of public morality, possibly connected to the fact that both *mak yong* and *menora* can involve an element of cross-dressing. PAS also objected to the non-Islamic nature of these performances, since they involve folk tales or Hindu mythology. Finally, the party also had a problem with the **spiritualism** permeating these arts. A *wayang kulit* performance begins with a *buka panggung* ceremony, in which the puppeteer readies the stage by reciting mantras and making offerings of food to the spirits, while *mak yong* can be staged for an individual as part of a folk-healing tradition called *main puteri*, in which the performers enter a trance to remove a spirit believed to be affecting that person.

The government's stance has softened somewhat in recent years. While menora is still prohibited, the **ban on mak yong** was lifted in 2019, so long as performances were sharia-compliant. Likewise, wayang kulit was allowed to be performed at two officially permitted venues.

Whatever the reasons for the ban, it effectively deprived a generation of Kelantanese of their own traditions – and continues to do so. A mere handful of *wayang kulit* troupes survive, performing outside Kelantan or, thanks to one **concession** from PAS, for the benefit of the largely tourist audience at Kota Bharu's Cultural Centre. On a brighter note, all three forms mentioned here are being passed on to a new generation outside their home state, at the National Academy of Arts, Culture and Heritage in KL (http://aswara.edu.my), which occasionally stages performances.

his distinctive puppets; short private shows are possible, as are hands-on activities for children, who may get the chance to make and colour their own puppets.

Buddhist temples

Tours (arranged via state tourist office or your guesthouse; charge); 4–5hrs, including visit to nearby craft workshops

The area **north of Kota Bharu** is dotted with **Buddhist temples**, many decorated with a striking combination of Thai and Chinese motifs. The temples can be visited using buses bound for the Thai border at **Pengkalan Kubor**. It's a slow process, getting from one to the next on public transport (though it can also be done using local taxis); if you're pushed for time, it's best to take a tour from the state tourist office or your guesthouse. The temples are especially worth visiting during **Vesak Day**, the festival (usually in May) celebrating the Buddha's birthday.

Wat Pracacinaram

Kampung Kulim, just outside Wakaf Bharu, on the road to Cabang Empat • Bus #19 or #27

The highly conspicuous main building of **Wat Pracacinaram** has an elaborate triple-layered roof decorated in gold, sapphire and red. The temple offers a herbal **steam bath** – with separate facilities for men and women – for a small fee.

Wat Phothivihan

Kampung Jambu • Bus #19 or #27; get off at Cabang Empat then walk 3.5km

The 40m-long reclining Buddha at **Wat Phothivihan** is the largest in Malaysia. The rather bland plaster statue was made by the monks themselves and contains ashes of the deceased who have been laid to rest here. Refreshments are available from *kedai kopis* inside the temple grounds.

Wat Machimmaram

Kampung Jubakar, 7km north of Cabang Empat • Bus #27

Topped by a 30m-high bronze-tiled seated Buddha, **Wat Machimmaram** contains bas-reliefs that depict the graphic punishments of hell – the corrupt are, for example, doomed to have molten tin poured into their mouths, while meat eaters are shown reincarnated as pigs on the carving block. Thai **massages** are available in a separate block.

Wat Mai Suwankiri

Around 4.5km southeast of Tumpat • Bus #43 stops outside the temple and #19 stops 500m away

The most striking construction at **Wat Mai Suwankiri** is a shrine built in the shape of a dragon boat, surrounded by a narrow moat to give the impression that it is afloat. The main temple hall is crowned by an elongated standing Buddha, its gorgeous interior decorated with hundreds of golden plaques.

Suri Island

Taxi to Kuala Besar (20–30min) then boat (15–20min); alternatively #43 bus to Jeti Kok Majid (1hr) then boat (40min)

One of many small riverine islands north of Kota Bharu, **Suri Island** is home to around five hundred people. Getting there is half the fun, requiring a trip down the tea-coloured Kelantan River in a motorized sampan, and the island itself has some pleasant paths for walking and a well-developed **homestay** programme (see page 217).

There are two ways to reach Suri from Kota Bharu. The most common route goes via **Kuala Besar** (not to be confused with Kuala Besut in Terengganu). While the second route, via **Jeti Kok Majid**, an hour's bus ride from the city centre, is considerably more scenic, it's also more time-consuming. If you're staying on the island, contact the homestay organizer in advance to arrange transport.

Arriving at Suri, you'll spot a boatyard next to the jetty where they mend traditional wooden craft. There's also a simple **café** or two for refreshments. From here you can head inland along a path lined with coconut trees.

ARRIVAL AND DEPARTURE — KOTA BHARU

BY PLANE
Sultan Ismail Petra airport The airport lies 9km northeast of the centre, and the #9 bus runs between town and airport until 7pm; official airport taxis can be pre-paid for at the counter before you exit customs, and Grab cabs can be used too.

Destinations Johor Bahru (3 weekly; 1hr 15min); Kota Kinabalu (3 weekly; 2hr 40min); Kuala Lumpur (International; 1–2 hourly; 1hr 10min); Kuala Lumpur (Subang; 4 daily; 1hr 5min); Kuching (3 weekly; 1hr 50min); Penang (1 daily; 1hr).

BY TRAIN
Train station The nearest station is 7km away in Wakaf Bharu (http://ktmb.com.my), a 20min ride on bus #19 (daytime only) from the local bus station – watch for the late-afternoon rush hour – or a taxi journey. Change at Johor Bahru for Singapore, and at Gemas for Kuala Lumpur. Destinations Dabong (5 daily; 2hr 45min–3hr 20min); Gemas (1 daily; 11hr); Gua Musang (4 daily; 4hr 35min–6hr 10min); Jerantut (1 daily; 7hr 15min); Johor Bahru (1 daily; 15hr 40min); Kuala Lipis (2 daily; 6hr 15min–7hr 15min); Merapoh (2 daily; 5–6hr).

BY BUS
Express bus station Between the AEON and Lotus's malls, near the Kelantan River bridge on the southern edge of town, and a short taxi ride from the centre. If you haven't booked online, bus tickets can be purchased from a row of cabins just south of the local bus station on Jalan Doktor. Most long-distance services leave between 8–10am and 8–10pm.

Destinations Alor Setar (4 daily; 7–8hr); Butterworth (4 daily; 7hr); Gua Musang (4 daily; 3hr); Ipoh (6 daily; 5hr); Johor Bahru (4 daily; 12hr); Kuala Kangsar (5 daily; 6hr 30min); Kuala Lumpur (1–2 hourly; 8hr 30min); Kuala Terengganu (12 daily; 3hr); Kuantan (10 daily; 7hr); Melaka (3 daily; 10hr 30min); Mersing (3 daily; 9hr 30min); Penang (3 daily; 7hr 15min); Seremban (4 daily; 10hr).

Local bus station Off Jalan Doktor in the town centre, and used by buses running to places within or just outside Kelantan – notably Wakaf Bharu (for trains), the Thai border crossings at Rantau Panjang and Pengkalan Kubor, and Kuala Besut for the Perhentians.

BY TAXI OR MINIVAN
Long-distance taxis Taxis depart from a yard on Jalan Doktor, south of the local bus station. Call 09 748 1386 to book. Note that you can't reach the Cameron Highlands and Taman Negara from Kota Bharu; minibuses to these destinations are now only available from Gua Musang or Kuala Besut.

TO THAILAND
There are two road crossings into Thailand – and none by rail – on the east coast. The closest large Thai town to either is Narathiwat, served by buses to other parts of southern Thailand and flights to Bangkok. Although the security situation in southern Thailand has improved slightly in recent years, it's worth checking online for the current situation – at the time of writing, Western governments were still advising against all but essential travel to the far south of Thailand. Visas for Thailand can be obtained from the consulate in Kota Bharu (see page 218) if required. Note that Thailand is one hour behind Malaysia.

Rantau Panjang The recommended crossing is at Rantau Panjang (daily 8am–9pm), 45km southwest of Kota Bharu; get there by local bus (if running; 1hr–1hr 30min) or taxi (45min). From Sungai Kolok, a short walk across the border on the Thai side, trains run to Bangkok, via Hat Yai and Surat Thani (2 daily; 20–22hr; http://dticket.railway.co.th), and frequent buses head to Hat Yai (hourly; 6am–4pm; 4hr).

Pengkalan Kubor The other crossing – slower to get through and with worse transport links – is at Pengkalan

Kubor (daily around 8am–7pm), 25km northwest of Kota Bharu; take local bus (if running; 30min), or a taxi then a car ferry. The small town of Tak Bai stands on the Thai side.

GETTING AROUND

By taxi Local taxis wait in the same yard as long-distance taxis. Drivers don't always use meters, so agree the price before you leave. Most accommodations can call for private taxis, which are around half the price of those hailed on the street. Taxis can also be arranged by the hour.

By trishaw A few tourist-oriented trishaws can be found around the central market for short hops within the centre; agree fares in advance.

Car rental Hawk (013 924 2455, http://hawkrentacar.com.my) and J&W (09 773 7312, http://jwcarental.com) have offices at the airport.

INFORMATION AND TOURS

Tourist information The state tourist office (Mon–Wed & Sun 8am–5pm, Thurs 8am–3.30pm; 09 748 5534, http://facebook.com/tic.kelantan) on Jalan Sultan Ibrahim can tell you about festivals and give you a timetable of events at the Cultural Centre.

Tours Any of the town's backpacker hostels can arrange city and craft tours, as well as the popular firefly tour along the Pengkalan River (8.30pm; 1hr). The state tourist office can also put together craft workshop tours (4–5hr).

ACCOMMODATION   SEE MAP PAGE 210

Kota Bharu has an excellent range of accommodation. Budget travellers will appreciate the good-value, if occasionally scruffy, **guesthouses**, many of which can arrange tickets for onward travel and offer packages to Taman Negara via Kuala Koh and Stong State Park (see page 202); unfortunately, Covid saw some of the best ones off for good, and acceptable alternatives have been thin on the ground, with some of the best budget options quite far from the centre (not necessarily a bad thing).

HOTELS

Crown Garden 302 & 303 Jalan Kebun Sultan; http://crowngardenhotel.com. At the upper end of the city's accommodation options, this 88-room hotel has marble floors and striking modern decor plus a seventh-floor bar. The cheapest rooms are cramped, but still nicely appointed, and price includes a breakfast buffet. $\overline{\$\$}$

Crystal Lodge 124 Jalan Che Su; http://crystallodge.my. Sleek mid-range hotel, with a café-restaurant, parking and satellite TV. The compact single rooms are good value, though the standard doubles and windowless twins are a bit disappointing. Breakfast is included. Singles $\overline{\$}$, doubles $\overline{\$\$\$}$

Grand Renai Jalan Sultan Yahya Petra; http://grandrenai.com. Some of the 298 rooms in Kota Bharu's first five-star hotel enjoy great views over the city, and they've all been given a thorough refresh of late. Facilities include two restaurants, a gorgeous semi-outdoor pool, spa and a 24-hour gym. Rates can often go down to three-star level. $\overline{\$\$\$}$

★ **Grand Riverview** 151 Jalan Post Office Lama; http://grv.com.my. You'll never guess what the main selling point of this hotel is… yup, a decent swimming pool and jacuzzi from which you can see the river, running almost right alongside. Their red-carpeted rooms have a touch of old-style class (you can also get a local newspaper delivered in the morning, which can be a charming experience even if you don't understand any of it), and there are a couple of very good on-site restaurants. $\overline{\$\$\$}$

Jewels Lot 1159–1162, Jalan Maju; http://jewelshotel.com.my. Friendly, centrally located and a solid mid-range choice, featuring squeaky clean rooms with flat-screen TVs. Deluxe rooms are more spacious, but otherwise identical to their cheaper counterparts. Price includes (a somewhat limited) breakfast. $\overline{\$\$}$

Perdana Jalan Mahmood; http://perdana.attanahotels.com. This Malaysian-owned five-star hotel is divided into two wings, "classic" and "executive", with slightly higher prices in the latter; both have the same comfortable rooms and psychedelic carpets. The multiple food outlets are alcohol-free. Breakfast is included. $\overline{\$\$\$}$

HOSTELS AND GUESTHOUSES

My Friend Homestay Kampong Panchor, 6km east of the city; http://facebook.com/myfriendhomestay. More of a guesthouse than a genuine homestay, this is a super-friendly little place east of town in a simple neighbourhood – experience some of the delights of rural Malaysia while staying a taxi-ride from city comforts. While the colours of the walls and bedding may induce migraines, rooms (including a dorm) are kept spick and span, and staff can assist with tours or onward travels. No breakfast, but there are some good basic places to eat nearby. $\overline{\$}$

★ **Pasir Belanda** Jalan PCB, Banggol district, 5km north of the city; http://pasirbelanda.com. This rural establishment consists of seven traditionally styled chalets, set in an immaculate garden with a swimming pool overlooking a creek. Activities include batik and Malay cookery lessons, and they offer kayak and bike rental. Catch #10 bus to Banggol mosque, then follow signs 1.5km east, or take a taxi. Two-night minimum stay. $\overline{\$\$}$

KOTA BHARU **THE EAST COAST** | 217

W Hotel Cemerlang Jalan Sri Cemerlang; http://oyorooms.com. The mammoth *OYO* franchise has absorbed most of the city's budget stays, which are accordingly "borderline acceptable" – seemingly the group's mantra. This is the best of a bad bunch, with rare thought put into the design of its rooms, corridors and lobby – not a bad place to stay by any means. $

EATING
SEE MAP PAGE 210

Kota Bharu has plenty of **restaurants** dotted around the centre, plus some excellent food options at the main market and the nightly **Medan Selera** (night food market); the city is great for budget eats, and there are a few Western fast-food places here and there, but few upmarket options. For a good spot to watch the sun set over the river, head for the line of restaurants behind the closed Pelangi Mall.

RESTAURANTS

Coconutnut 562d Jalan Temenggung; http://coconutnut.storehub.me. For something a bit different, try this industrial-chic Korean fast-food joint, which doles out Korean-style fried chicken, *budae jjigae* ("army" hotpot, long made by young Korean soldiers with beans, spam, kimchi, rice-cake and other stuff their mothers send them in the post; it tastes great), *bibimbap*, and simple sides. $$

M Star Cafe Vegetarian Jalan Hamzah; http://facebook.com/muhibahstarcafe. Excellent, inexpensive vegetarian establishment, once located above Muhibah Bakery, but now going it alone at a less convenient location. They put on a great veggie *nasi campur* spread, as well as à la carte dishes like "chicken" *rendang* and other Chinese and Malay favourites using the Chinese-style textured tofu instead of meat. $

★ **Nasi Ulam Cikgu** Kampung Kraftangan; 019 940 6066. Busy self-service lunch place, offering the classic Malay meal *nasi ulam* (a rice salad with blanched vegetables and herbs – some of them incredibly bitter). Dishes like fried chicken, vegetable curry and *asam pedas ikan patin* (catfish in spicy sauce) are laid out alongside rice and *ulam*. If you're feeling brave, have the dip made of *tempoyak* (fermented durian) and *budu* (fermented fish sauce), which to most people isn't as bad as it sounds. Cheap, and best enjoyed with a group. $

Shan Sri Dewi Jalan Kebun Sultan; http://facebook.com/shansridewi. Top-notch Malaysian-Indian *kedai kopi*, popular with locals but often with a scattering of foreigners, serving excellent banana-leaf *thalis* as well as light snacks such as *roti canai*, *masala dosai*, *idly* and *vada*. $

DRINKING
SEE MAP PAGE 210

Golden City 3950g Jalan Padang Garong; http://restoran-golden-city.business.site. For years the only central option for booze, it can still be worth swinging by this restaurant, which serves good (mostly fried) food, and a small range of beers.

Nine Drinks 27 Jalan Sri Cemerlang; 011 1229 3729.

HOMESTAYS

KB homestay programme Various locations. The state tourist office (see page 216) can arrange for visitors to stay with a local family whose members are expert in a particular craft. The prices are usually based on a standard two-night package for two people, including all meals and activities. $$$

CAFÉS AND DESSERTS

★ **Jubilee Café Antique** 3592 Jalan Ismail; 014 808 5000. You really have to see the zany decor of this place – they've stuck so many old signboards on the walls that it almost looks like demented wallpaper, while looking around you'll see an old rocking horse, a miniature Goodyear blimp, and whatever other eye-candy they've found. The coffee's good too. $$

Muhibah Bakery Jalan Pintu Pong; http://muhibahbakery.com.my. Basic little bakery café, serving pastries, cakes, donuts and ice-blended shakes, as well as more-than-acceptable coffee. $

White House Jalan Sultanah Zainab; http://facebook.com/Kedai-Kopi-White-House. No grand mansion (though next to one) but a ramshackle bungalow housing a *kedai kopi* that's a city institution. The trademark dish is humble *telur setengah masak* – soft-boiled eggs cracked into a saucer, seasoned with soy sauce and white pepper, and delicious scooped up with *roti bakar* (buttered toast). Washed down with *teh* or *kopi tarik*, it's great for breakfast or a late snack. $

STREET FOOD AND HAWKER CENTRES

Medan Selera (night food market) Off Jalan Pintu Pong. The few dozen stalls on the field here offer a great range of *murtabak* (savoury stuffed pancakes) as well as Kelantanese specialities such as *nasi kerabu* (rice tinted blue, traditionally using flower petals, and typically served with fish curry). Wash your meal down with *sup ekor* (oxtail soup) or *sup tulang* (made from beef bones), and round it off by sampling the colourful *kuih* (sweets). $

Warisan Nasi Kukus Jalan Kebun Sultan; 019 968 7878. This once-humble pushcart operation is very popular, renowned for fresh *sambal* fish, okra curry, *ikan bakar* (grilled fish) and the like. Your preferred toppings will be poured over steamed rice (*nasi kukus*), on a newspaper that's folded into a cone and wrapped for you to take away or eat at their plastic tables. $

Mainly a restaurant, but some of the patrons here occasionally seem quietly intent on obeying the tenets of nominative determinism – and with Guinness available on tap in this conservative part of the country, it's hard to blame them.

SHOPPING

In addition to its **markets**, Kota Bharu is also a good place to buy Malay **handicrafts**, with most of the workshops located outside town.

KB Mall Jalan Hamzah; http://kbmall.com.my. For general shopping, this mall is useful, housing the huge Pacific supermarket, several branded clothing stores, Western food chains, a branch of Watsons pharmacy and plenty more besides.

Mydin Jalan Pintu Pong; http://mydin.my. Useful supermarket selling food, toiletries and other essentials.

DIRECTORY

Hospital Jalan Hospital 09 745 2000.
Left luggage At the local bus station (daily 8am–8pm, Fri closed 12.30–2pm).
Pharmacies Central pharmacies include Guardian on Jalan Padang Garong and Watsons in KB Mall.
Police Jalan Sultan Ibrahim (09 748 5522).
Thai visas Many nationalities can get a visa at the border. Otherwise, visas can be obtained in advance from the Thai Consulate, 4426 Jalan Tok Guru (Mon–Thurs & Sun 9am–noon & 2–3.30pm; http://kotabharu.thaiembassy.org); they have been known to refuse entry to people in shorts, so dress smartly.
Visa extensions At the Pejabat Imigresen (Immigration Department), Wisma Persekutuan, Jalan Bayam (Mon–Thurs & Sun 8am–4pm; 09 748 2120).

From Kota Bharu to Kuala Terengganu

Though there are a few resorts by the shore, plus some interesting villages and wildlife in the **Setiu Wetlands**, few travellers linger on the coast south of Kota Bharu; most are simply waiting for a boat from **Kuala Besut** (for the Perhentian Islands) or **Merang** (to Redang or Lang Tengah islands; not to be confused with Marang further south). Whether you're staying or passing through, get money before you set out; there are **no ATMs** on any of the islands, or near the jetty in Kuala Besut, though some hotels accept cards, and you might be able to get a cash advance (at punitive rates).

Kuala Besut

The only reason to visit the mainland town of **KUALA BESUT** is to catch a boat to the Perhentian Islands. Kuala Besut comprises a few lanes lined with **hotel offices** and **travel agencies** selling Perhentians packages and boat tickets at similar prices, with most of the action concentrated between the peach-coloured **boat terminal** complex and the **express bus and taxi station**.

ARRIVAL AND DEPARTURE — KUALA BESUT

By bus There are express buses to KL and Penang directly from Kuala Besut Express bus station, but for other destinations you'll need to take a taxi (30min) to Jerteh, the closest transport hub.
Destinations Kota Bharu (5 daily; 2hr); Kuala Lumpur (8 daily; 8hr); Kuala Terengganu (5 daily; 2hr 30min); Penang (3 daily; 8hr).
By taxi The taxi stand is next to the bus station, but drivers will also swoop on new arrivals from the islands. Possible destinations include Jerteh, Kota Bharu, Kuala Terengganu, Marang and Merang.
By minibus Several travel agents arrange minibuses to a handful of major destinations, including Cameron Highlands, Penang and Taman Negara; all depart 10am.
By boat Boats sail from Kuala Besut Jetty to the Perhentians several times a day, leaving when full (daily 7am–5.30pm; 30min). Operators usually sell open-return tickets, with boats returning to Kuala Besut at 8am, noon and 4pm. Boat service is regular from March to October; at other times sailings are much reduced.

ACCOMMODATION AND EATING

88 Lucky Seafood Just north of the jetty on Jalan Besar; 013 997 9354. This place opens extra early for breakfast, offering dishes such as *nasi ayam* and noodles throughout the day, but it's the more expensive fresh seafood served later on that attracts most people.

Adam Cafe Jalan Pasar; 019 985 8222. "Toast and coffee", it says on the entrance sign, but though that's true, they also do a very pleasing local iteration of a fried English breakfast – scrambled eggs, beans, hash brown, sausage and toast, with a random slice of melon (which is probably a bit healthier than black pudding). All your Malay-style coffees and teas are available, as well as kaya toast and other light nibbles. $

Ila Homestay 422 Jala Hai Mohamad; 017 984 7974. A few rooms in a house which has gone for turquoise blue paint on the outside, and modern grey tones within; it's nice and central, and they sometimes throw in breakfast for free, though be warned that until they replace the curtains, you won't have an awfully high level of privacy from passers-by. $

IZ Village Resort Kampung Air Tawar; 019 308 9906. One of the only options hereabouts resembling a real hotel, resort or indeed anything that's not a guesthouse or homestay, located a few clicks to the east of town, across the river. The grounds have seen better days (or perhaps they were just designed to look neglected), but the colourful rooms are decent enough. *Malika Kitchen* is just down the road. $$

★ **Malika Kitchen** Kampung Air Tawar; 013 997 9354. The best place to eat in town (even though it's technically a few kilometres out of town), a seafood restaurant that has put some effort into its decor (gasp!), and even the presentation of its meals (double gasp!). Choose from dried chilli, butter cream or tom yam toppings for your fish or seafood mix, and follow it up with banana split for dessert. $$$

The Perhentian Islands

The name **Perhentian Islands** (Pulau Perhentian) actually covers two islands, **Perhentian Besar** and **Perhentian Kecil** (Big Island and Small Island are sometimes used instead, though Suitcase Island and Backpack Island might be more accurate descriptions). Both are textbook tropical paradises, which retain considerable appeal despite having been developed for tourism. The essentials of any idyllic island holiday – fantastic sandy beaches, great **snorkelling** and **diving** – are all in place. Both islands have jungly hills in their interior, with paths for **walking** and opportunities to spot flying foxes, monkeys and monitor lizards. All this is capped by a refreshingly laidback atmosphere that can make it difficult to tear yourself away.

For many years, large-scale development on the Perhentians was kept to a minimum. This was just as well, given that both islands have several **turtle nesting** sites, active from April to early August – the only organized viewing is through the *Bubbles* resort (see page 225) – and that the impact of the existing resorts on the environment is far from negligible. Shortages of **water**, for example, can be a hassle during peak season. The state government's attitude towards development has loosened in recent years, however, and a few larger resorts have been completed, with more in the works – particularly on Perhentian Kecil. **Alcohol** is sold openly at restaurants and bars on both islands, and there's even a modest party scene at Long Beach.

ARRIVAL AND DEPARTURE — THE PERHENTIAN ISLANDS

By boat All access to the Perhentians is from the mainland town of Kuala Besut (see page 218); boats depart several times a day (usually when full), regularly from March to October, with reduced sailings at other times. All will drop you at the bay of your choice, though at beaches without a jetty you may have to transfer to a smaller boat. The day before your departure, staff at your accommodation will arrange for you to be picked up, with boats usually leaving at 8am, noon and 4pm.

GETTING AROUND

By water-taxi Small speedboats operate a so-called water-taxi service around the Perhentians. It's even common to journey between adjacent bays (rocky obstructions often preclude walking), and you can of course travel from one side of Besar to the other, or even from one island to the other. Prices are clearly displayed in front of each water-taxi stand, with little room for bargaining, and it's usually possible to rustle up a boatman within a few minutes. The exception to this is after dark, when water-taxis can become scarce and you may have to pay double the usual fare. If you simply need to get to the next beach, you may be able to use a footpath instead (after dark a torch is essential).

ACCOMMODATION

Perhentian Kecil caters largely to the backpacker scene, and much of its accommodation is in low-priced chalets and resorts, many with restricted electricity supply. The construction of several **mid-range resorts**, however, has brought the same families, package tourists and better-heeled independent travellers that have traditionally gravitated to Perhentian Besar. Book in advance for the **peak season** – roughly June until the end of August – and

THE EAST COAST THE PERHENTIAN ISLANDS

ACCOMMODATION					
Abdul Chalets	27	Fauna Beach	24	Panorama	2
Alunan	23	Flora Bay	25	Perhentian Island Resort	15
The Barat Perhentian Beach Resort	18	Flora Bay 2	22	Perhentian Marriott	14
		Lemon Grass	5	Reef Chalets	17
B'First Chalets	21	Long Beach Camp	4	Senja Bay Resort	9
Bubbles	28	Mama's Chalet	19	Shari-La Island Resort	7
Bubu Long Beach Resort	13	Matahari Chalet	3	Tivoli Inn	6
Butterfly	10	Mimpi Perhentian	12	Tuna Bay Island Resort	26
Coral View	16	Oh La La	1	Villamas Perhentian Resort	20
D'Lagoon	11	Ombak Dive Resort	8		

DRINKING	
B'First Chalets	3
Cocteles Dani	4
Monkey Hut	2
Oh La La	1

EATING	
The Barat	5
Chillout Café	2
Crocodile Rock Bistro	4
Mama's Restaurant	6
Nia Café	7
Rosemary	3
World Café	1

at weekends, or you may have trouble getting a room. Many mid-range places offer full-board packages, typically for three days and two nights, and include boat transfers and some snorkelling or diving. B&B deals are also available, and unless you're on one of the more remote beaches, there's no shortage of places to eat. Outside peak season rates fall by at least a quarter. Many resorts begin closing in late October, sometimes earlier, and don't open again until February or March, but for a truly isolated island experience a few places stay open during the northeast monsoon. Note that internet service and phone reception on the islands can be spotty at best; many places don't bother with wi-fi due to the associated hassle, and those that have it sometimes charge for the privilege. If you do have internet access, it generally works best between 2–8am. For more details and listings, see the sections on the individual islands.

DIRECTORY

Banks There are no banks or ATMs on the islands; though some places take card, it's still prudent to bring enough cash to cover your stay.

PERHENTIANS DOS AND DON'TS

- Do bring more than enough **cash** – there are no banks or ATMs. Only mid-range places accept plastic for accommodation and food, often with a small surcharge. Several places offer cash advances for a significant fee.
- Do bring mosquito repellent.
- Don't leave **valuables**, even clothes, unattended on the beach – whether crowded or deserted – while you swim or snorkel. Thieves can appear seemingly from nowhere on snatch-and-grab raids, a particular problem on Perhentian Kecil. Also be aware thieves sometimes enter rooms, so keep your valuables with you if possible, and make sure your room is completely secured before you go out.
- Do **swim with care**: look out for boat lanes, marked by strings of buoys, and stay on the correct side to avoid being wiped out by a speedboat. Note also that Long Beach can have a significant **undertow** from February to April and in October; a few people get swept out every year and have to be rescued.
- Do be mindful of volleyball nets and sharp-pronged boat **anchors** sticking out of the sand as you walk along the beach at night – particularly if you're looking up at the stars.
- Don't touch the **coral** or disturb **marine life** when you snorkel or dive.

Perhentian Kecil

The small island of **Perhentian Kecil** has something to please most people. If you're looking for a laidback backpacker scene with the odd beach party, you've come to the right place, but several mid-range resorts cater for those who need a comfortable bed after a day snorkelling. The most popular beaches, **Coral Bay** and **Long Beach**, are only ten minutes' walk apart, along a woodland footpath.

Long Beach

For many visitors, east-facing **Long Beach**, boasting a wide stretch of glistening-white, deep, soft sand, is the prime attraction of Perhentian Kecil. The pretty beach is possibly over-busy, far from litter free, and lacks a view of the sunset, but somehow that really doesn't matter: the light gently fades away, leaving the illumination from the beach restaurants (and their Bob Marley or dance music playlists) to dominate the senses. Come nightfall there's a genuinely infectious buzz – in peak season expect pop-up bars and a party vibe on the beach.

Coral Bay and the west coast

While west-facing **Coral Bay** has become significantly more developed since the building of its huge and ugly jetty, it remains quieter and more relaxed than Long Beach. It also has sheltered waters, which make it a better bet than its eastern rival during the northeast monsoon, plus good snorkelling and sunset views, if you can ignore the jetty.

A couple of quieter and more secluded beaches lie south of Coral Bay, with accommodation in rustic campsites or guesthouses reached along a shady coastal footpath. **Mira Beach** has just one backpacker hangout, while **Petani Beach** has two resorts awkwardly jammed into its eastern end, and two smaller guesthouses enjoying the remaining stretch of beach.

ACCOMMODATION   PERHENTIAN KECIL, SEE MAP PAGE 220

Room rates on Perhentian Kecil – particularly on **Long Beach** – are rather fluid, varying from day to day with demand. Most of the cheaper accommodations are pretty poor value and badly maintained, mainly due to the scarcity of rooms during high season, so don't expect too much for your money – booking ahead is also highly recommended. The price codes below are at the higher end of the range for each property; ask about discounts if you visit midweek or either side of the July–August peak. Almost all accommodations now have attached dive shops, and rooms are much better value as part of a dive package. Due to the scarcity of rooms during high season there are now several places to camp; as well as

Long Beach camp (see below), there are campsites at *Awatif* on Long Beach, and also the *Rainforest Campground and Café* between Coral Bay and Mira Beach.

LONG BEACH

If you would rather a good night's sleep than party, don't stay anywhere near the beach.

Bubu Long Beach Resort Long Beach; http://bubu resort.com. With a motel-like complex of en-suite a/c rooms at one end of Long Beach, and a clutch of deluxe villas at the other, plus two spas and three restaurants (including the only Japanese one on the island), *Bubu* dominates the upper end of Perhentian Kecil's accommodation. The rooms and villas are perfectly nice, but it jars a little here. $$$$

Lemon Grass Long Beach; 012 956 2393. Splintery but sound chalets with fans, hammocks and mosquito nets; bathrooms in a separate shack. Three sea-view rooms are available for a modest extra charge. There's sporadic electricity and a two-night minimum stay in peak season. $

Long Beach Camp Long Beach; 016 893 2400. The best of the campsites hereabouts, right next to the beach and with decent tents to rent – you can even book them online on some of the major search engines. There are BBQ facilities, good toilets and showers, and hammocks to lie in, as well as a bunch of cats to play with. $

Matahari Chalet Set back from Long Beach; http://matahariperhentian.com. A hotel of two halves, with a collection of wooden chalets (fan and newer a/c ones) and A-frames, with an incongruous two-storey concrete dorm and fan room block – latter have been improved of late, with a/c and better furnishings. The largely en-suite chalets are a little rough around the edges, but pretty good value and popular. $$

Mimpi Perhentian Right at the north end of the beach; http://mimpiperhentian.com. Decent, slightly upper-end place, which comes across as more modern than most of its neighbours – largely because it is, though in all honesty it's already showing its age in certain parts. The wooden slats firing across the lobby ceiling are mirrored in the illuminated versions of the same poking down from the ceiling of the breakfast room, while there's artwork on many walls, and in the bedrooms themselves. A small swimming pool rounds off proceedings. $$$

Oh La La Long Beach; http://ohlalaperhentian.com. European-run dive resort with ten simple wood-partitioned fan rooms, a dorm and some tents, all with shared bathrooms. It's above one bar and beside another, however, so is quite noisy at night. There's a pleasant communal balcony with hammocks; most people staying here are doing dive courses, as room prices are halved if you're doing one. $

Panorama Set back from Long Beach; http://panorama perhentianisland.com. Overpriced chalets with fans or a/c, plus better-value dorms, all set around a messy hillside garden. There's a popular restaurant plus a dive shop; they offer all-inclusive diving packages. High-season rates often include one free meal. Electricity only at certain times. $

Tivoli Inn Midway between Long Beach and Coral Bay; http://perhentiantivoli.com. A compact development with rooms in neat, whitewashed bungalows, with budget and more upmarket sections. The good-value fan rooms and dorms (min 3 nights) are the stars here, being bright and far cleaner than their equivalents on Long Beach. $$

CORAL BAY

Butterfly At the end of Coral Bay; 019 346 9791. The tucked away, budget chalets strung out on the hill on the headland here are run-down but charming: popular with long-term guests, including dive masters. The further you get from reception, the better the sea views become. Electricity only in evenings and early morning. $

★ **Ombak Dive Resort** Coral Bay; http://ombak.my. A modern multistorey complex, with 24 fan and a/c rooms (extra charge for the latter) awkwardly shoehorned behind their popular seafront restaurant and dive shop. All have en-suite bathrooms, some with balconies too, though they're only decent value if you take a dive package. $$$

Senja Bay Resort Coral Bay; http://senjabay.com. This complex of en-suite chalets, built on a hillside and connected by decking, contains quite spacious and well-maintained rooms. There's also a restaurant and dive shop; snorkelling and diving packages are available. Breakfast is included, and there's 24-hour electricity. $$$

Shari-La Island Resort Northern end of Coral Bay; 09 697 7500. Fairly upmarket resort with dozens of chalets spread out over a well-manicured hillside, and overlooking its own private beach. The rooms are pretty good value for the island, though the cheapest are a bit small and have no hot water. $$$

THE REST OF THE ISLAND

★ **Alunan** Petani Beach; http://alunanresort.com. Splendid eco-resort which has spearheaded a drive to rehabilitate the local coral reef, with some success – guests can get involved too, should they choose to. The suites here are arranged higgledy piggledy, like an idealized version of a jungle village; each has its own rooftop "garden", with deckchairs for sun-lounging, morning coffee-drinking or evening wine-sipping; the on-site restaurant is very good too. $$$$

★ **D'Lagoon** Teluk Kerma; http://dlagoonchalet.com. Nestling in a secluded cove at the island's northeastern tip (which is also one of the island's best snorkelling sites), this friendly, family-run place makes for a great escape. Accommodation includes fan-cooled, en-suite cabins, a dorm, and an a/c treehouse. It's a long walk to the cove, but a water-taxi from Long Beach costs very little. Dive shop on site, as well as a short zipline. $

Perhentian Marriott Between Long Beach and Coral

Bay; http://marriott.com. Yes, it's a *Marriott*, with all that entails. However, it doesn't really feel like one, bar the sheer size of the complex, which spreads over a large stretch of the island north of Coral Bay and generally faces west, though can also be accessed from the east. Basically all of the rooms (and most of the bathrooms) have wonderful views, and the on-site facilities are top-notch too. $$$$

Villamas Perhentian Resort Petani Beach; http://facebook.com/villamasperhentianresort. Another small village, this time of cute-looking wooden huts with red roofs; given their location and the way they're laid out, you're almost bound to get a great sunset view. They do full-board packages including snorkelling excursions, meals and boat transfers. $$$

EATING

SEE MAP PAGE 220

Most places to **eat** are connected to accommodation – they're fine but rarely very exciting, and we've listed some worth seeking out below.

LONG BEACH

Chillout Café Long Beach; 017 979 2950. Towards the north of a beach, this laidback café serves some great breakfast sets along with pancakes, local-style meals and a fair stab at pizza. They also have a local crafts shop and a campsite ($), though no wi-fi. $$

World Café Long Beach; http://buburesort.com.my. This good-looking beach restaurant, part of Bubu Villa (sister property to *Bubu Long Beach Resort*) serves tasty but pricey Western food, from sandwiches and pasta to grilled lobster, with a buffet breakfast every morning. $$$

CORAL BAY

★ **Rosemary** North of Coral Bay. There's plenty of comfort food available at this tidy-looking shack of a restaurant – tall, juicy burgers, basic meat-and-rice dishes, fried noodles, veggie options, and some extremely sweet shakes. $$

THE REST OF THE ISLAND

★ **Crocodile Rock Bistro** On the path between Coral Bay and Long Beach; http://crocodilerockvillas.com. People boat here from all over the island for some great veggie and vegan food (there are a few meat dishes too). Dining takes place on a wooden deck, and there are appropriately green bean bags to slouch on before or after you've had your omelette, bruschetta, rice dish, burger or fish. Save room for the mango pana cotta dessert. $$$

SNORKELLING AND DIVING AROUND THE PERHENTIANS

Outside the monsoon, the waters around the Perhentians are superb with gentle currents and visibility up to 20m (although sea lice can sometimes be an irritant, inflicting unpleasant but harmless stings). A **snorkelling** foray around the rocks at the ends of most bays turns up an astonishing array of brightly coloured fish, including blacktip reef sharks, and an occasional turtle. The seas around the islands belong to a national park and the coral is protected, although as elsewhere in the region it suffered bleaching due to high sea temperatures in 2010, though patches of live coral still remain.

If you just want to explore around the main beaches, then snorkels and masks can be rented from accommodation, dive shops or shacks on the main beaches – most places can also arrange **snorkelling trips** to undeveloped coves, though they often take very large groups. Typical itineraries include Turtle Point (between the islands), Shark Point, Romantic Beach and the lighthouse; lunch, normally in the village on Perhentian Kecil, costs extra.

Some very good **dive sites** lie a short boat ride offshore, including the Pinnacle (or Temple of the Sea), T3 and Sugar Wreck (a boat that sank while carrying a cargo of sugar). Several of the islands' numerous dive shops organize night dives on the "Vietnamese" Wreck (actually a 1976 US landing craft, Advanced Open Water qualification required). In addition to fun dives, the shops also offer **courses**, including Open Water, Advanced Open Water and the introductory Discover Scuba Diving; a handful, including Flora Bay Divers, also offer specialist facilities such as Nitrox. Most places teach **PADI courses**, although Alu Alu (Perhentian Besar; http://alualudivers.com) offers both PADI and SSI.

RECOMMENDED DIVE SHOPS

Bubbles Dive Resort Tanjung Tukas; http://bubblesdc.com.

Flora Bay Divers Flora Bay; http://florabaydivers.com.

Octo Diver Petani Beach; http://octogroup.com.my.

Quiver Dive Team Coral Bay; http://quiverdiveteam.com.

Turtle Bay Divers Long Beach and Perhentian Besar Main Beach; http://turtlebaydivers.com.

DRINKING

SEE MAP PAGE 220

For nightlife, most people drink at guesthouse bars such as at *Oh La La*, or the *Monkey Bar* before decamping to the south of the beach where there are occasional fire shows in the evening at the likes of *Beach Bar* (one of many pop-up bars here); expect quite a party atmosphere. Coral Bay's only real bar is the pricey *Ombak Café*. Beers sold from coolers on the beach can be taken into most restaurants.

Monkey Hut Long Beach. A bar, a cafe and also a decent-enough place to stay, though as evening encroaches, most people have the booze on their minds. Cheap beer and cocktails, and a good vibe.

Oh La La Long Beach; http://ohlalaperhentian.com. The bar/restaurant at this dive resort sometimes sees its tables fill up with beer bottles – how busy it gets depends completely upon who's in town.

Perhentian Besar

The larger of the two islands, **Perhentian Besar**, has a more grown-up atmosphere. Although it holds a few relatively cheap options in addition to the mid-range resorts, it doesn't have the backpacker scene or nightlife of its neighbour. On the other hand, the beaches remain relaxed, despite some nearly continuous strings of development.

Western shore

The chain of attractive beaches on the **western shore** facing Perhentian Kecil are separated by rocks, though the southernmost ones are best avoided unless you like boats zipping past every few minutes, and the vibe gets better the further north you go. At high tide most **beaches** can be accessed along concrete walkways, with the notable exception of the path between *Mama's* and *Cozy Chalet*, which is essentially a fifteen-minute jungle trek – a boat taxi may be preferable, especially if you're carrying luggage. Most beaches are lined with resorts, but in a pleasingly organic way; the main beach has a good vibe after dark when the restaurants get busy. At the northern end of the main strip, the *Perhentian Island Resort* sits alone on one of the best stretches of sand, Teluk Pauh.

Flora Bay and the south coast

Flora Bay (Teluk Dalam) is less cramped than the western shore. Although it is home to several of the larger resorts, there are also some family-run businesses. The beach isn't the best on the island, especially when the tide is out, but it's more relaxed than the west coast ones. Further east, *Bubbles* resort sits on its own beach, only accessible by boat.

From the western shore, a steep **trail** (1km; 30min) to Flora Bay begins just past the second jetty south of *Abdul's*, behind the Teluk Keke beach restaurant. Another, prettier trail links Flora Bay with the *Perhentian Island Resort* (1.5km; 40min), starting behind the island's waterworks in Flora Bay.

Three Coves Bay

For the finest beaches on the Perhentians, take a water-taxi to **Three Coves Bay** (also known as Turtle Bay or Teluk Tiga Ruang) on the north of the island, a stunning chain of three beaches with crystal-clear waters, separated from the western shore by rocky outcrops. It's a great spot to spend the day, so get your boatman's telephone number or arrange a pick-up time for the return trip. This area also provides a secluded haven for green and hawksbill **turtles** to lay their eggs and as such may be off-limits during nesting season.

ACCOMMODATION

PERHENTIAN BESAR, SEE MAP PAGE 220

WESTERN SHORE

Abdul Chalets Further south from the main cluster; http://abdulchalet.com. Good value chalets with a/c and 24hr electricity, and those that don't boast views of the sea have views of the jungle instead. Come here for a peaceful, chilled ambiance. $$

★ **The Barat Perhentian Beach Resort** Main beach; http://baratperhentianisland.com. A series of charming huts set along the beach; though not huge they've been artfully decorated, and come with outdoor seating areas – the sunset views can be wonderful. $$

Coral View Northern main beach; http://coralview

islandresort.com.my. A range of wood-panelled rooms, mainly in steep-roofed chalets with small, attached bathrooms. They're connected by walkways through a pleasant garden, and the standard rooms in particular are good value. There's a restaurant, dive shop, minimart, batik shop, library and foreign currency exchange. $$$

Mama's Chalet Northern main beach; http://mamaschalet.com.my. Prim, decent chalets along a narrow stretch of beach, including a few sea-facing ones with multicoloured fanlights. All rooms have private facilities, and there's a popular restaurant, though things do feel a little slapdash. Wi-fi available in restaurant only. $

Perhentian Island Resort Teluk Pauh; http://perhentianislandresort.net. Set on a very appealing stretch of beach, this resort – known as *PIR* – has a veritable campus of bungalows and chalets, all spacious and boasting modern furnishings and verandas. There's even a swimming pool, tennis court and spa. $$$$

Reef Chalets Northern main beach; http://thereefperhentian.com. A semicircle of a/c chalets with hints of traditional Malay architecture in the design and spotless bathrooms. The interiors are simple, most rooms with mosquito nets and pleasant verandas, and the garden setting is very attractive. $$

★ **Tuna Bay Island Resort** Southern main beach; http://tunabay.com.my. This slickly managed collection of chalets gets it just right, combining the comforts of a mid-range city hotel (including beach towels for guests) with a cool informality that's perfect for a laidback beach holiday. The bar and restaurant are deservedly popular. Breakfast is included. $$$

FLORA BAY AND THE SOUTH COAST

★ **B'First Chalets** Flora Bay; 019 915 9871. This row of six concrete buildings is nothing special, but the large, clean fan rooms are good value and its friendly, family-run environment is far more pleasant than any of the resorts or hotels. There's a typical beach café at the front, and all-day electricity, but no wi-fi. $

★ **Bubbles** Tanjung Tukas; http://bubblesdc.com. A boat ride from Flora Bay, this family-friendly resort has a beach to itself, and combines isolation with good facilities, including a dive shop and in-house zoologist who looks after the resort's turtle hatchery. Rooms cost extra on Friday and Saturday nights. 24hr electricity. $$$

Fauna Beach Flora Bay; http://facebook.com/faunachalet.perhentian. Some of these 35 pleasant, unremarkable chalets are fan-cooled, and a couple of them enjoy Perhentian Besar's cheapest sea views. The remainder have a/c, but are shabby and overpriced. $

Flora Bay & Flora Bay 2 Flora Bay; http://florabayresort.com. En-suite accommodation ranging from inexpensive fan rooms to beachfront chalets, including some overpriced a/c units. *Flora Bay*, with its garden of frangipanis and oleanders, is marginally preferable for its location; its counterpart (where the fan rooms are located) features utilitarian two-storey blocks, and is better for the actual rooms. Breakfast is extra, and there's a good dive shop attached. $

EATING   SEE MAP PAGE 220

Almost all Besar's places to eat are affiliated with resorts. Most of the best options are on the **western shore**; the food on **Flora Bay** is generally less interesting, with a few open-air restaurants serving Western and Asian standards plus the odd barbecue.

The Barat Main beach; http://baratperhentianisland.com. One of the most adventurous kitchens on the islands, largely focused on seafood but also serving simple rice-or-noodle mains, plus nasi lemak or cereal for breakfast. Most fun are their evening seafood barbecues. $$$

Mama's Restaurant Northern main beach; http://mamaschalet.com.my. Your best bet for Malay food, served up with a lovely sea view – try the fish dishes, which can be particularly tasty. $$

Nia Café By Tuna Bay Island Resort, southern main beach; 011 2924 7932. Simple beach spot for breakfast toast sets, a confusingly long roster of fried rice dishes, noodles, juices, lassis and shakes. $$

DRINKING   SEE MAP PAGE 220

For drinking, it's largely a matter of choosing one of the **resort bars** that serves beer.

B'First Chalets Flora Bay; 019 915 9871. Probably your best bet for an evening vibe, with happy hour beer the tipple of choice; they've also a few spirits behind the bar, and as such cocktails are also an option.

Cocteles Dani By Flora Bay 2, Flora Bay. Cheap cocktails, lovingly served in little plastic cups – not everyone's idea of paradise, but the views and the vibe do all seem to fit.

Setiu Wetlands

As a breeding ground for the painted terrapin and green turtle, the **Setiu Wetlands**, between Kuala Besut and Merang, have been a focus for WWF projects since the early 1990s, but even now they attract only a trickle of tourists. Both the main settlements hereabouts, namely **Penarik**, on the T1 coastal road, and **Mangkok**, 4km to the north, are small villages with poor transport connections, so the easiest way to explore is on a tour organized by an operator in Kuala Terengganu (see page 232).

Pewanis

Pink House, Kampung Mangkok • Mon–Thurs & Sun 8.30am–5pm • 013 997 1195, but note that little English is spoken so you may need to get a Malay speaker to call for you

The **Pewanis** community project improves the financial position of local women, while working with the WWF on environmental projects. With advance notice, visitors can learn how to make banana chip snacks, help plant mangrove trees or take part in kite-making sessions. Staff can arrange bicycle rental and organize trips to the turtle hatchery.

ARRIVAL AND DEPARTURE — SETIU WETLANDS

By taxi Public transport is limited, so if you don't come on a tour it's best to rent a car or take a taxi (best from Kuala Terengganu).

By bus Buses between Kuala Besut and Kuala Terengganu (4 daily) can drop you at the turning for Mangkok, and you can walk the 3km from there.

Tours By far the best option is to come on an organized tour. Ping Anchorage (see page 232), for example, can arrange a trip including a visit to Pewanis, a turtle hatchery and a man raising *ayam serama* (chickens bred for competitions, which can sell for staggering prices).

ACCOMMODATION AND EATING

The women of Pewanis have started a homestay scheme (usually with full board) and the area has a couple of places to stay, including a stunning **resort**. There are few notable places to **eat** other than at accommodation or roadside *kedai kopis* – look out for local speciality *ikan celup tebung* (battered fish).

Pandan Laut 4km south of Penarik on Pantai Rhu Sepuluh; http://facebook.com/pandanlautbeachresort. Set in a leafy site, the tidy rooms here range from wooden chalets to a vast family suite; the on-site swimming pool is even bigger. You'll need to take your meals elsewhere, but turtle-watching is free and they can arrange snorkelling day-trips to Redang Island. $$

★ **Terrapuri Heritage Village** Kampung Mangkok; http://terrapuri.com. A labour of love, this site, sandwiched between wetlands and beach, features 29 traditional wooden buildings that have been saved from neglect elsewhere in Terengganu and carefully reconstructed. Staff can arrange day-trips or you can lounge by the pool; there's also a spa. Breakfast is included. $$$$

Merang

Most travellers who make it to **MERANG**, on the coastal road just south of the Sungai Merang creek, only glimpse the back of the village on their way to the jetty. The **beach**, accessible along a couple of side roads, is not exceptional, there's reasonable swimming and memorable views of the islands offshore – from left to right, the Perhentians, Lang Tengah, Redang and finally Bidung Laut, now uninhabited but once the site of a refugee camp for Vietnamese boat people.

ARRIVAL AND DEPARTURE — MERANG

By bus S.P. Bumi's buses between Kuala Besut and Kuala Terengganu (4 daily) stop close to Merang's school.

By taxi A taxi to Merang will be quite affordable from Kuala Besut, and also from Kuala Terengganu.

By boat Jetties for the resorts on Redang and Lang Tengah line the riverside, 500m walk from the bus stop (walk towards and past the traffic lights). Most packages include boat transfers, but tickets are also available from the boatmen. In peak season Nurul Boat Services (http://boattoredang.com) runs hourly return services to Redang Island (9am–3pm) and one to Lang Tengah Island (timing varies). They also do snorkelling trips to both islands for up to ten people (9am–3pm; snorkelling equipment and lunch not included) so you can save money by staying on the mainland.

ACCOMMODATION AND EATING

This quiet stretch of coast has a limited amount of beachfront accommodation, with one or two peeling resorts 4km south of the jetty. A handful of **food stalls** lie near the jetty, and a few *kedai kopis* line the road to Kuala Terengganu.

Villa Wanie Inn Jalan Merang, near Shell garage; 013 940 2536. More or less the only decent budget accommodation in Merang, with modern, tidy, a/c rooms (with tiny balconies on the upper level), and a small but inviting swimming pool. $$

Redang Island

Beautiful **Redang Island** is geared primarily toward visitors on resort-based scuba diving package trips. Don't expect a quiet island getaway; at weekends and in school holidays bars along the main beach have music or karaoke until midnight.

A **kampung** has been built inland for the two-thousand-strong fishing community who formerly lived in a traditional floating village here, which was removed in 2001 to make way for a jetty and other tourist developments. The highlight of the social calendar, April's **candat sotong** festival celebrates a pastime popular all along the east coast of the Peninsula, catching squid using small hand-held lures with hooks on one end.

Snorkelling and diving

For most visitors, the chief attraction of Redang is the abundant marine life. The **reefs** have endured a lot over recent decades, including a mid-1970s attack by the crown-of-thorns starfish, and silt deposition caused by development. More recently the coral has suffered from bleaching due to high water temperatures. Thankfully, coral reefs have remarkable properties for self-renewal, and Redang's marine environment appears to have stabilized.

Conservation has certainly been helped by the designation of the Redang archipelago as one of Malaysia's **marine parks**, and by the regulation of activities such as spearfishing, trawling and watersports. The best **snorkelling** is off the southern coast around the islets of Pinang and Ekor Tibu; the larger resorts take endless boats stuffed with tourists – and bags of fish food – to the main sites, so find a smaller group if you can. **Diving** is also excellent, with most sites off Redang's eastern shore – almost every resort has its own dive shop. Snorkelling day-trips are also available from Merang and Pandan Laut (see page 226).

ARRIVAL AND DEPARTURE — REDANG ISLAND

Regular transport to Redang only runs between **March** and **October**, when the resorts are open. A very small conservation fee covers three days' stay, and is included in your accommodation price.

By boat Most packages include a boat ticket to Redang. Departures are from Merang, or Kuala Terengganu's Shahbandar jetty; check with your accommodation.

ACCOMMODATION

Most of Redang's accommodation is on the island's **eastern shore**, on Pasir Panjang (Long Beach), the adjacent Shark Bay or, just to the south, Teluk Kalong. Pasir Panjang has a particularly gorgeous stretch of fine white sand; Teluk Kalong's beach is narrower and pebbly in places, but inviting nonetheless. Unless otherwise noted, the resorts have en-suite, a/c rooms and their own restaurants. Many also have dive shops and offer diving-specific packages.

Rates Given that packages tend to be the cheapest way to visit, price codes listed here are for the cost per night of a basic two-night package for two people, which typically includes buffet meals, a couple of snorkelling trips (but not equipment rental) and transfers. Not included are typical weekend/holiday surcharges; conversely, expect discounts of around 25 percent at the start or end of the season.

PASIR PANJANG/SHARK BAY

Coral Redang Pasir Panjang; http://coralredang.com.my. Located at the quieter end of the beach, this place has more character than most others on Redang. Rooms are arranged in quaint two-storey buildings, and there's a small swimming pool with a poolside bar. The food isn't great, so you may prefer the B&B option over the full board package. Scuba diving is available for an additional charge. B&B $$$, full board $$$$

Laguna Redang Shark Bay; http://lagunaredang.com.my. Huge, luxurious establishment, with more than two hundred rooms and a large free-form pool, famous while in Asia as the location of the Hong Kong comedy movie *Summer Holiday* (1999). A wide range of packages and rooms, all very comfortable and well equipped. Activities include snorkelling, canoe rental, archery and massage. Wi-fi only available for a fee, in the lobby. $$$$

Redang Beach Resort Shark Bay; http://redang.com.my. A sizeable collection of attractive wooden two-storey units with comfortable rooms, some of which have been recently remodelled. There's a tiny swimming pool and nightly entertainment, should you need either. $$$$

Redang Lagoon Chalet Pasir Panjang; http://redanglagoon.com. While the wooden chalets – arranged in two long rows – are nothing special, this is still good value, and

particularly popular with Malay families. $$$
Redang Reef Resort Shark Bay; http://redangreefresort.com.my. Perched on the headland at the southern end of Shark Bay, reached by a long wooden walkway, this good-value resort is less luxurious than its neighbours, with simply furnished rooms and a bar overlooking the sea. $$$

TELUK KALONG
Redang Mutiala Teluk Kalong; http://redangmutiara.com.my. Because this peaceful beach isn't as popular as Pasir Panjang, its only resort makes a blissfully calm place to kick back for a few days. The rooms and facilities aren't quite as good as some of the Pasir Panjang resorts, but for some this will be more than compensated for by the additional relaxation. $$$

FLORA BAY
The Taaras Beach & Spa Resort Flora Bay; http://thetaaras.com. This luxury resort is a cut above the rest in terms of service, facilities and prices, with golf buggies to help you get between the well-appointed rooms, spa, restaurants, dive shop, swimming pools and tennis courts. $$$$

Lang Tengah Island

Although **Lang Tengah Island** (Pulau Lang Tengah) is largely a package destination, it holds just a handful of spread-out places to stay and therefore offers a lower-key experience than its near-neighbour Redang Island. As well as attractive and quiet beaches, there's some good **snorkelling**, including a patch of blue coral (*Heliopora coerulea*) offshore from the *Sari Pacifica*. All the resorts, with the exception of *Lang Sari*, have **dive shops**.

Turtles lay their eggs on certain beaches; staff at *D'Coconut Lagoon* wake guests if any are spotted during the night on nearby Turtle Beach.

ARRIVAL AND DEPARTURE — LANG TENGAH ISLAND
By boat Most people visit on packages, which usually includes boat transfers (and the tiny visitor conservation charge) from Merang. Most boats leave before 10am, but afternoon charters are possible (contact resorts for details).

ACCOMMODATION
Lang Tengah holds just a few resorts, all of which can get very busy at weekends and public holidays (when prices rise). The **full-board** price codes listed below are per night, based on two people sharing on a two-night package (which includes boat transfers and a daily snorkelling trip, though not gear).

D'Coconut Lagoon Lang Tengah Island; http://dcoconutlagoon.com. Split into two wings a couple of minutes' walk apart. All rooms have a/c and hot showers; those in the much nicer west wing are more expensive than those in the east wing, quoted here. The resort gives out a very handy sketch map of the island. B&B $$$, full board $$$$

Sari Pacifica Lang Tengah Island; http://facebook.com/SariPacificaBeachResortSpaLangTengahIsland. Set on a lovely bit of beach and decorated in a traditional yet modern style, the cheaper rooms are far from luxurious, but the more expensive ones are worth the extra price, though all have a jacuzzi bath in the bathroom. $$$$

Summer Bay Resort Lang Tengah Island; http://summerbayresort.com.my. Packages at this resort, with simple wood-panelled, en-suite rooms in two-storey blocks, though the more expensive rooms are much more luxurious. The resort also has the only minimart on the island. $$$$

Kuala Terengganu

After a long spell as an important port trading with the Chinese, **KUALA TERENGGANU** (the capital of Terengganu state) had by the late nineteenth century been eclipsed by the rise of Singapore and other new ports in the Melaka Strait. Following the transfer of Terengganu from Siamese to British control in the early twentieth century, the state became the last in the Peninsula to take a British Adviser, in 1919. It continued to languish as a rural state with, unusually, most of its settlements at river mouths rather than on the lower reaches of rivers, as elsewhere in Peninsular Malaysia.

The discovery of oil in the 1980s transformed its fortunes; modern Kuala Terengganu is even more of a hotchpotch than most Malaysian cities, the remnants of its constituent kampungs sprinkled with oil-funded showpieces and construction sites. There is, nevertheless, a certain **austerity** about Terengganu state that's noticeable in

Kuala Terengganu. It lacks the commercial buzz of Kuantan or even Kota Bharu, partly because oil revenues have barely trickled down to ordinary people, but also because in some respects the state is more conservative and inward-looking than neighbouring Kelantan.

Many visitors use the city simply as a transit point for Terengganu's best-known attractions – the pleasant **beaches** that line most of the coastline, and glorious **islands** including the Perhentians, Redang, Lang Tengah and Kapas. Using the city as a base, you can also venture inland to the lake of **Tasik Kenyir**. Even in itself Kuala Terengganu holds enough to reward a day or two's sightseeing, in particular the **old town** with its lively **Central Market** and the adjacent historic **Chinatown**; the **State Museum**, among the best of such complexes in Malaysia; and **Duyong Island**, where the city's maritime heritage just about survives.

Old town

Kuala Terengganu's compact centre is built on a semicircular parcel of land that bulges north into the mouth of the Terengganu River, which flows past the western half of the city, where the **old town** is located. The eastern half of the city is flanked by the South China Sea, with ongoing land reclamation rapidly altering the shoreline.

Bukit Puteri
Off Jalan Pesar Besar Payang • Charge • 09 622 1444

A lovely little park with mature trees and chirruping cicadas, the steep hillock of **Bukit Puteri** ("Princess Hill") is crowned by a white tower that still serves as a lighthouse. You can access the hill via the escalators at the Bazaar Warisan (Heritage Bazaar) on Jalan Sultan Zainal Abidin.

Wide-ranging views take in the Terengganu River and the bell-shaped roofs of the blindingly white **Masjid Zainal Abidin** just to the south. Relics of the hill's time as an early nineteenth-century stronghold include a fort, its bricks once bound with honey (although it's now concrete), and several cannons imported from Spain and Portugal.

Central Market
Off Jalan Sultan Zainal Abidin • Daily 6am–5pm

Close to the lacklustre Bazaar Warisan with its assorted batik shops and jewellers, the ground floor of the much more rewarding **Central Market** (Pasar Payang) is occupied by a thriving wet market. Look out for stalls selling *keropok* (dried fish paste) and Malay confections in just about every conceivable hue. The upper floors comprise a maze of food stalls and outlets selling batik, *songket* and brassware.

Chinatown
Reached via Jalan Kampung Cina, south of the central market, Kuala Terengganu's **Chinatown** was established in the eighteenth century, when the trading links between Terengganu and China drew in early Chinese settlers. The main street is lined with pastel-coloured **shophouses**, one of the finest examples of which, the sky-blue **Teck Soon Heritage House**, is occasionally open to the public as a museum. A useful leaflet, *Chinatown Heritage Trail*, is available from the state tourist office.

Ho Ann Kiong Temple
183 Jalan Kampung Cina • Free

South of Chinatown, the photogenic **Ho Ann Kiong Temple** is dedicated to Mazu, the Goddess of the Sea. The current complex was reconstructed in 2010 after its predecessor burned down, but the temple has occupied the same spot since the late eighteenth century. A useful leaflet, *Chinatown Heritage Trail*, is available from the

THE KRIS

The **kris** (or *keris*) occupies a treasured position in Malay culture, a symbol of manhood and honour believed to harbour protective spirits. Traditionally, all young men crossing the barrier of puberty receive one that remains with them for the rest of their lives, tucked into the folds of a sarong; for an enemy to relieve someone of a *kris* is tantamount to stripping him of his virility. In the past, some weapons were reputed to have magical powers, able to fly from their owners' hand to seek out and kill an enemy.

The *kris* itself is intended to deliver a horizontal thrust rather than the more usual downward stab. When a sultan executed a treacherous subject, he did so by sliding a long *kris* through his windpipe, just above the collarbone, thereby inflicting a swift – though bloody – death. The distinguishing feature of the dagger is the hilt, shaped like the butt of a gun to facilitate a sure grip. The hilt can also be used to inflict a damaging blow to the head in combat, especially if there isn't time to unsheathe the weapon.

The daggers can be highly decorative: the iron blade is often embellished with fingerprint patterns or the body of a snake, while the hilt can be made from ivory, wood or metal. Hilt designs usually take the form of birds' heads.

---

state tourist office. Nearby, the **Peranakan Photo Gallery** displays black-and-white photographs showing the town's development.

Terengganu State Museum

Bukit Losong, 6km west of town centre • Charge • http://museum.terengganu.gov.my • Bas bandar service from city centre (45min) or taxi ride

Arriving at the **Terengganu State Museum**, you might think you've strayed into *Gulliver's Travels*. Visitors are confronted by a series of buildings modelled on the archetypal Terengganu village house, but absolutely Brobdingnagian in scale. Along with being Malaysia's biggest state museum, the buildings also house one of the country's best collections.

The ground floor of the **main building** holds exquisite fabrics from around Southeast Asia, while the next floor up displays various crafts. The top floor details the history of Terengganu. The **Petronas Oil Gallery**, in the building to the left, is sporadically interesting but predictably skewed. Behind it, the old-fashioned **Islamic Gallery** displays fine examples of Koranic calligraphy.

Allow time to see the rest of the site. Beside the river are two examples of the **sailing boats** for which Kuala Terengganu is famed – unique blends of European ships and Chinese junks. The small **Seafaring Gallery** and larger **Fisheries and Marine Park Gallery** are close by, as is a collection of smaller, beautifully decorated fishing boats. Five old timber buildings have been disassembled and reconstructed within the grounds. Among them, the **Istana Tengku Long** was originally built in 1888 entirely without nails, which to Malays signify death because of their use in coffins.

Duyong Island

Very sporadic water-taxis from moorings north of the Central Market; better to take a taxi

The proud home of a venerable **boat-building** tradition, **Duyong Island** (Pulau Duyong or "Mermaid Island") was once two islets in the Terengganu River; they were joined by reclamation to form what you see today. Although the northern end of Duyong was levelled to build a resort and a prestigious **yacht club**, the southeastern side of the island is essentially still a rustic kampung that's great for an hour's stroll.

If you want to visit one of the island's surviving **boatyards**, ask around for directions or head to the Sultan Mahmud bridge on the island's eastern shore.

ARRIVAL AND DEPARTURE

By plane The airport is 14km north of the city; take a prepaid taxi into the centre. MAS (http://malaysiaairlines.com) and AirAsia (http://airasia.com) fly to KLIA (6 daily; 1hr), and Firefly (http://fireflyz.com.my) operates flights to the capital's Subang airport (3 daily; 1hr).

By bus The spacious, modern bus station, smack in the centre on Jalan Masjid Abidin, is used by intercity and local buses.

Destinations Alor Setar (9.30pm daily; 9hr); Batu Pahat (3 daily; 8hr); Butterworth (1 daily; 8hr 30min); Cherating (hourly; 3hr 15min); Dungun (8 daily; 2hr); Johor Bahru (9 daily; 9hr); Kangar (1 daily; 10hr); Kemaman/Chukai (7 daily; 2hr 30min); Kota Bharu (10 daily; 3hr 40min); Kuala Besut (8 daily; 3hr); Kuala Lumpur (2–3 hourly; 6hr 30min); Kuantan (1–2 hourly; 3hr 15min); Marang (hourly until 5pm; 30min); Melaka (4 daily; 7hr 30min); Merang (4 daily; 1hr); Mersing (5 daily; 6hr 30min); Muar (3 daily; 8hr); Pekan (3 daily; 4hr); Rantau Abang (8 daily; 1hr 30min); Segamat (4 daily; 6hr); Seremban (4 daily; 7hr); Singapore (2 daily; 11hr 40min); Sungai Petani (1 daily; 8hr 25min).

By taxi Long-distance taxis depart for destinations across the Peninsula from outside an office (06 626 5150) just south of the bus station.

By boat The Shahbandar jetty on the seafront is used by a few resort boats to Redang Island, though public boats (3 daily; 2hr) are available too. You can also take faster, more frequent ferries (at least 4 daily; 40min) to Redang from Merang, 30km north of Kuala Terengganu; in addition, there are ferries from Duyong marina (1 daily). All can be booked online from various sites.

GETTING AROUND

By bas bandar Besides the city's standard bus services, an hourly "heritage bus" (*bas bandar*) service runs a hop-on, hop-off route to the main attractions. There are two different routes, each starting at the main bus station before going on to destinations including the State Museum and Noor Arfa. Enquire at tourist offices for schedules and fares.

By taxi Taxis are easily found near the bus station or around the Central Market; you'd be lucky to flag one down in the street.

By trishaw Trishaws can be found near the Central Market.

By car Car rental is available from booths in the airport arrivals hall.

INFORMATION

Tourist information The state tourist office is next to the GPO on Jalan Sultan Zainal Abidin (Mon–Wed & Sun 8am–5pm, Thurs 8am–3pm; 09 622 1553, beautifulterengganu.com). The Tourism Malaysia office is a little way south on Jalan Kampung Daik (Mon–Wed & Sun 8am–5pm, Thurs 8am–3.30pm; 09 630 9433). Ask at either about homestays in the city and its surroundings.

Travel agents Ping Anchorage Travel and Tours, 77a Jalan Sultan Sulaiman (daily 8.30am–7pm; 09 626 2020, http://pinganchorage.com.my), is efficient and well organized (if pricey), offering packages throughout the east coast and the interior. They also run the brilliant *Terrapuri Heritage Village* north of the city (see page 226).

ACCOMMODATION

SEE MAP PAGE 229

CITY CENTRE AND BEACH

Grand Continental Jalan Sultan Zainal Abidin; http://grandconkt.com. The fanciest place in town when it opened in 1997, this chain hotel is showing its age despite recent renovations. However, the spacious rooms have marbled bathrooms and satellite TV, and there's a gym, Western restaurant, pool and coffee shop; rates can be slashed quite heavily during slow times, when the place becomes quite a bargain. Breakfast is included. $$$

KT Beach Resort 548e Jalan Sultan Zainal Abidin; http://ktbeachresort.wordpress.com. This old-school hotel no longer enjoys a beachside position, thanks to ongoing land reclamation. The a/c rooms are squeaky clean if unexciting, and they also manage some surprisingly appealing, fully furnished apartments in the residential block across from the *Tian Kee* restaurant. Doubles $, apartments $$$

KT Mutiara 67 Jalan Sultan Ismail; 09 622 2655. While some fittings look worn and dated, these are comfortable rooms for a decent price. Some have no windows, though at least they're quieter. It also has a pleasant courtyard garden and discounts available midweek. $

Ming Paragon 219e Jalan Sultan Zainal Abidin; http://mingstarhotel.com. The deluxe room has a computer and complimentary minibar (no alcohol), but even the cheapest standard rooms have flat-screen TV, hairdryer, iron and kettle – all they're missing is windows, for which you have to pay extra. Breakfast is included, and there's a spa. $

Primula Beach Resort Jalan Persinggahan; http://primula-hotel.com. Behind the ugly facade is a decent 246-room hotel complete with pool, gym and two restaurants with a grand marbled lobby and a sea view. The a/c rooms are spacious and well kept, while the "Superior" rooms on the ground floor of an older block have patio doors leading to the beach. Ample parking, and free shuttle into the centre. Breakfast is included. $$$

Sentral 28 Jalan Tok Lam; 09 622 0318. Part of the *Redang*

BOAT-BUILDING ON DUYONG ISLAND

Historically, the boatyards of Duyong Island produced **schooners** that ranged from humble fishing craft to the hulking *perahu besar*, up to 30m in length. These days however, motorized, modern alternatives to the old-fashioned wooden boats, the increasing cost of timber, and the lure of other careers have all contributed to a steep decline in this traditional industry. Salvation for the handful of boatyards that remain has come from overseas, as clients from around the world place orders for all manner of bespoke craft.

The shipwrights of Duyong Island use the *pasat* technique that uses neither metal nails nor set plans. For hulls, their preferred material is **cengal**, a wood whose toughness and imperviousness to termite attack make it prized not only for boats but also the best kampung houses. After the hull planking is fastened with strong hardwood pegs, a special sealant – derived from the bark of swampland trees, and resistant to rot – is applied. Unusually, the frame is fitted afterwards, giving the whole structure strength and flexibility. As construction takes place in **dry docks**, the finished boats have to be manoeuvred on rollers into the water, an effort that often requires local villagers to pitch in.

Beach Resort group, this centrally located hotel has a range of bright, attractive, en-suite rooms at equally attractive prices. All fifty have a/c, though some lack windows. $

★ **Suite 18 Boutique** 71 Jalan Kampung Cina; http://suite18boutiquehotel.com. The only decent accommodation in Chinatown, this converted 1890s shop has retained some of its original features, with stylish and well-equipped (though small) en-suite, a/c rooms (most without windows), and three dorms. They also rent bikes, and there's a pleasant garden out back. $

Tanjong Vista 132d Jalan Sultan Zainal Abidin; http://hoteltanjongvista.com.my. The logo and uniforms may be bright pink, but the rooms in this business hotel are tastefully furnished and good value. The small semi-outdoor swimming pool on the fourth floor has views of the beach and sea; there's also a small gym. Breakfast is included. $$$

YT Midtown 30 Jalan Tok Lam; http://hotelytmidtown.com.my. While this convenient central hotel is neither fancy nor flashy, it does stand out for its comfortable beds and reasonable prices. All rooms have big TVs, a/c and en suite, breakfast is included and there's a car park. $$

DUYONG ISLAND

D'Sofia Homestay Duyong Island; http://facebook.com/dsofiahomestaypulauduyong. You'll feel far from the city (it's actually walkable, though most would take a taxi) at this no-frills complex, is one of several homestay options on Duyong Island, though one that elevates itself from the competition by simple virtue of being bookable online, and having a Facebook page. $

EATING   SEE MAP PAGE 229

Terengganu's signature dish, **nasi dagang**, consists of slightly sticky rice, steamed with a little coconut milk and chopped shallots, and often served with fish curry for breakfast. Other key dishes include **laksam** (rolled rice noodles in a thick fish and coconut milk gravy) and **keropok** – dried fish paste, served *lekor* (long and chewy), *losong* (steamed) or *keping* (crispy). There are a few decent **Malay restaurants**, and the Malay stalls at the Central Market, as well as just south of the junction of Jalan Sultan Ismail and Jalan Tok Lam, are worth trying. Chinatown is the obvious focus for **Chinese food** – especially after dark, when many other areas are quiet – with a hawker centre along Jalan Kampung Tiong 1 and several excellent restaurants on the main street. Chinatown is also your best bet for finding **alcohol** in this largely dry city.

Asia Signature Jalan Sultan Zainal Abidin; 011 1860 0818. This bright, airy spot is handy if you find yourself east of the town centre. The menu ranges from chicken *rendang* to *keropok* and dim sum (the salted egg buns come recommended) and they also offer vegetarian versions of a few Malay classics, including a tasty *nasi lemak* and a smattering of Western dishes. $

★ **Golden Dragon** Jalan Kampung Cina; 09 622 3034. One of the most established and popular Chinese restaurants in Chinatown, with a great *nasi campur* at lunchtime, and reliable seafood (try the steamed fish) and other stir-fried dishes in the evening. Portions are substantial. $

★ **KBB Burger & Steak** 4063 Jalan Sultan Zainal Abidin; http://kbbsteak.com. Swing by for the juiciest burgers in town, together with spare ribs, steak and other meaty meals; they really take care of their beef here, and the dishes are nicely presented too. $$$

Star Anise 82 Jalan Kampung Cina; http://facebook.com/staranisekt. Head to this funky café for excellent coffee, locally grown tea and a slice of cake. Outdoor seating on a quiet side street and plenty of decorative touches make this one of the nicest spots to take a break in Chinatown. $

Uncle Chua Signature Jalan Bandar. Pleasant restaurant

whose wide-ranging menu features pasta (with chicken meatballs or bolognese), fish and chips, grilled chicken chop and various forms of laksa, as well as sweet potato fries, chicken-rice, grilled salmon and more – no wonder it's so popular. $$$

DRINKING SEE MAP PAGE 229

Chinatown is your best bet for finding **alcohol** in this largely dry city.

The Vinum Xchange 221 Jalan Kampung Cina; http://facebook.com/thevinumXchange. With one wall covered by racks of spirits, pork chops on the menu and tinted glass in the windows, this bar feels downright subversive in straight-laced KT. Lavazza coffee and pastries are served in the daytime, but crowds congregate in the evening for beer and wine.

SHOPPING SEE MAP PAGE 229

Like neighbouring Kelantan, Terengganu is renowned for its **handicrafts**. At several places in and around the city, visitors can watch craftspeople at work and buy their products.

Noor Arfa Cendering Industrial Area, 7km south of the city; http://noorarfa.com. Large showroom with a more extensive choice of batik than the shops on Jalan Sultan Zainal Abidin, and occasional demonstrations. Take the *bas bandar* service to Cendering.

Wanisma Craft Near junction of Jalan Sultan Zainal Abidin and Kampung Ladang Sekolah; 019 983 7910. Local artisans have long been known for their brassware, working in a "white brass" alloy unique to the state. Containing at least forty percent zinc, with added nickel to make it less yellow, white brass is used for decorative items such as candlesticks. They have a largish shop selling metalware and batik and at their nearby workshop you can watch craftsmen using the traditional "lost wax" technique to make brass objects.

DIRECTORY

Hospitals and clinics The Hospital Sultanah Nur Zahirah is 1km southeast of the centre on Jalan Sultan Mahmud (09 621 2121). There are plenty of privately run walk-in clinics and the odd dentist's surgery along Jalan Tok Lam, some staying open well into the evening.

Left luggage At the bus station (daily 8am–10pm; 019 920 9679).

Pharmacy There are branches of Watsons and Guardian on Jalan Sultan Ismail.

Police The main police station is on Jalan Sultan Ismail (09 624 6222).

Visa extensions The Immigration Department is in Wisma Persekutuan on Jalan Sultan Ismail (Mon–Wed & Sun 7.30am–5pm, Thurs 7.30am–4pm; 09 622 1424).

Tasik Kenyir

More than three hundred square kilometres in area, **Tasik Kenyir** (Lake Kenyir) was created in 1985 by the building of the Kenyir hydroelectric dam across the Terengganu River. Much touted locally as a back-to-nature experience, the lake offers scope for **fishing**, waterborne excursions and wildlife-spotting – **elephants** are even glimpsed on the shore from time to time. It's possible to swim in **waterfalls** on the periphery, while at the lake's southern end you can visit the limestone **Bewah and Taat caves**. The lake is also Terengganu's gateway to Taman Negara, thanks to the park entrance at **Tanjung Mentong** that has recently received a much-needed renovation.

Sadly, due to poor transport connections and the fact that the attractions are so scattered, Tasik Kenyir remains something of a half-baked proposition. The government is in the process of jollying the lake up, creating – among other things – several botanical gardens and an aviary as well as plans for a **duty-free island**. What impact these will have remains to be seen, but for now, a lack of accommodation adds to the difficulty of visiting. Unless you plan to stay at a resort, your best bet is to book through a travel agent in Kuala Terengganu.

Kenyir Elephant Conservation Village

Off Route 185 • Charge • http://kecv.com.my

The lake has a small pachyderm population, thanks to the Department of Wildlife's policy of transporting wild elephants to the **Kenyir Elephant Conservation Village**

MARANG THE EAST COAST

from elsewhere in the country – and nearby, since elephants in the area are still killed for ivory, or by farmers angered at their crops being ruined. The beasts are kept well watered and fed, and there's also a café by the entrance, just in case you're in need of a bite yourself.

ARRIVAL AND GETTING AROUND   TASIK KENYIR

The jetty in the northeast of the lake, **Pangkalan Gawi**, can be reached by road and serves as the focal point for arrivals; a handful of tour operators have desks at the jetty and can arrange day-trips.

By bus No scheduled buses run to the lake from Kuala Terengganu, thanks to the demise of the Tasik Kenyir Express from KL.

By taxi A taxi to the jetty is your best option from Kuala Terengganu or its airport.

By boat Even if you do arrive independently, you can book trips on a per-person basis from *Kenyir Elephant Conservation Village*; packages from the main jetty are aimed at groups, so trips can end up costing quite a bit.

INFORMATION

Tourist office At the Gawi jetty (daily 8am–5pm; 09 626 7788, http://kenyirlake.com). Staff can hand out leaflets and advice, but cannot book you onto any tours – for that, speak to the companies with desks at the jetty, or contact Ping Anchorage Travel & Tours (see below).

Tours Most accommodation and packages are set up for groups of over eight people; the best bet for independent travellers is on a one-day tour from Kuala Terengganu with Ping Anchorage (see page 232; 6hr; min 2 people).

ACCOMMODATION

Most of the lake's official accommodation options have closed down in recent years, but other than the below one option is a homestay, which can be arranged through the tourist office.

RPP Tasik Kenyir Inside lake; http://bph.gov.my. More or less the only accommodation on or around Lake Kenyir, and it's quite a fun one, with a series of huts arrayed around an overlarge main building. Rooms are basic, though note that toilets are shared; unfortunately, given its remote location, meals are not available, and you'll have to come with all of your supplies. You'll be able to take banana boat trips, rent a jet-ski, or go on a wider tour of the lake. $\overline{\overline{\$\$}}$

Marang

The coastal village of **MARANG**, 17km south of Kuala Terengganu and not to be confused with Merang further north, is only visited by tourists as the departure point for the delightful islands of **Kapas** and **Gemia**, just 6km offshore. The islands have no banks or ATMs, so this is your last chance to withdraw money – there are a couple of ATMs opposite the mosque and around 400m from the jetty, though note they often run out of money by the end of the weekend.

ARRIVAL AND DEPARTURE   MARANG

By bus Local buses run between Kuala Terengganu and

Marang roughly hourly until 5pm (30min). It's also possible to reach Marang on the long-distance Kuantan–Kuala Terengganu buses that travel the coast road. To move on from Marang you can flag down a local bus, although southbound services go no further than Dungun or Kemaman. To catch an express bus further afield you'll need to make arrangements in Kuala Terengganu.

By taxi Taxis are pretty cheap between Kuala Terengganu and Marang.

By boat The two main boat operators for the trip to Kapas and Gemia islands, MGH (http://kapasisland.com) and Suria Link (019 983 9454), have their offices side by side at Marang's jetty. Both offer the same deal, and can book accommodation. Boats usually run every 2hrs from 9am–5pm, though cease from Nov–Jan when pretty much all the accommodation on Kapas is closed. Tell the boatman which resort you're staying at and they'll drop you on the nearest beach (you may have to wade a short distance), though it's generally easiest just to get off at the main jetty.

ACCOMMODATION
SEE MAP PAGE 235

Marang Guest House Bukit Batu Merah, 1367 & 1368 Kampung Paya; 09 618 1976. The rustic wooden cabins here are careworn but have pleasant porches and are a good choice if you're on a tight budget. Its location at the top of the hill means it gets a nice sea breeze. Only a/c rooms have Western toilets. $

Pelangi Marang Kampung Kijing; http://oyorooms.com. Budget-friendly and borderline acceptable, just like almost every place in the now-massive Indian *OYO* hotel chain; rooms are adequate if extremely plain, and the location is nice and central. $$

EATING
SEE MAP PAGE 235

D'Besi Ict Marang Waterfront By the market. Marang's best waterside dining is this basic food court opposite the main market, where a handful of stalls do a roaring trade in *roti canai* and *nasi goreng* until well into the evening. $

Maqburn Pizza Jalan Kijing; 014 294 9471. While its pizzas are far from Napoli level, this is the most notable eatery in town, with very cheesy pies available, as well as simple pasta dishes and even simpler coffee. $

Kapas Island

Diminutive **Kapas Island** (Pulau Kapas), less than half an hour from Marang by speedboat, boasts arcs of sandy beach the colour of pale brown sugar, and aquamarine waters that visibly teem with fish. It's a very appealing little island with a laidback charm, emphasized by the friendly approach of the best of the resorts. Just offshore, the even smaller **Gemia Island** (Pulau Gemia) is the site of just one resort. In theory it's possible to visit Kapas as a day-trip, by catching an early boat out and returning late in the afternoon, but this means dealing with the midday heat – and besides, it's really worth staying for at least a night or two.

The only **season** when things are not quite so idyllic is from June to August, particularly at the weekends, when the island can get pretty busy. The rest of the time it's a great place

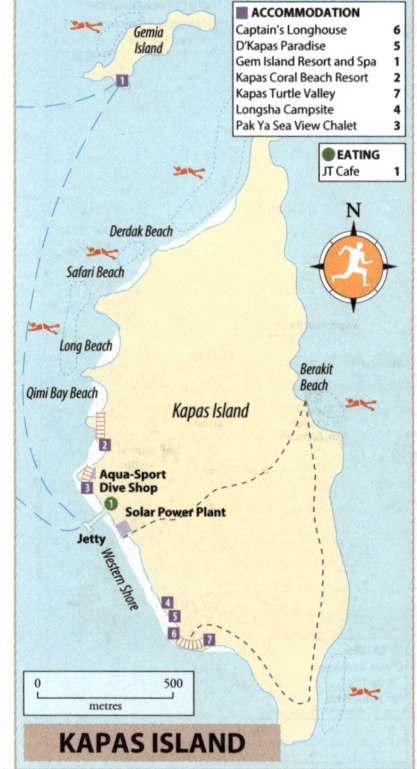

KAPAS ISLAND

ACCOMMODATION
- Captain's Longhouse 6
- D'Kapas Paradise 5
- Gem Island Resort and Spa 1
- Kapas Coral Beach Resort 2
- Kapas Turtle Valley 7
- Longsha Campsite 4
- Pak Ya Sea View Chalet 3

EATING
- JT Cafe 1

to do very little for a few days; the one notable highlight in the slim social calendar is the annual Kapas–Marang **swimathon** in April. During the northeast monsoon the island basically closes down.

A couple of marked trails make it possible to **hike** to the undeveloped eastern side of Kapas, ending up at the pebbly (and sadly far from litter-free) **Berakit Beach**, where you can take a dip. The longer but more interesting route (1.5km) starts close to *Kapas Turtle Valley*, the shorter (1km) from a spot inland from the jetty, running alongside a stream for most of the way. You can combine them to take a circular route; both include steep sections close to Berakit. Bring plenty of water and use insect repellent, and avoid being in the forest after 5pm, when the mosquitoes come out in force. The paths can be very slippery after rain.

ARRIVAL AND INFORMATION — KAPAS ISLAND

By boat Boats to Kapas leave from Marang (see page 235), while the return boats run every couple of hours from 9.30am–5.30pm; inform your accommodation when you want to leave and they'll arrange it for you.

Conservation fee As Kapas is a designated marine park, a small conservation fee applies for a stay of up to three days, though there isn't always an official present to collect it.

ACCOMMODATION — SEE MAP PAGE 236

For such a tiny island, Kapas has a surprising range of accommodation. Some mid-range places levy surcharges of twenty percent or more at weekends and during holidays, and all close down from November to February.

KAPAS ISLAND

★ Captain's Longhouse Southwestern shore; http://sites.google.com/view/captslonghouse. This rustic elevated longhouse of dark timber has seven decent fan rooms and a large, rather bohemian open dorm. All beds have mosquito nets and shared facilities. The driftwood beach-hut bar gives the impression that someone was shipwrecked here but made the best of it. Pretty over-priced, but pretty cool. $

D'Kapas Paradise Southwestern shore; 017 664 2711. A fairly extensive compound of wooden huts, inside which are some rather comfortable beds, and decent private facilities. The on-site restaurant is pretty good, too, and its sea views may make you want to linger. $$

Kapas Coral Beach Resort Western shore; http://facebook.com/KapasCoralBeachResort. Decent a/c rooms in a modern concrete building, plus more in huts fanning out onto the beach; all are en suite. Snorkelling equipment is free for guests. $

★ Kapas Turtle Valley Southwestern shore; http://kapasturtlevalley.com. Marvellously low-key family resort, set on a secluded cove a short but steep walk from the western shore – boats from Marang can drop you off here. It has just eight chalets, including two for families, featuring four-poster beds and swish bathrooms; the Western menu in the restaurant is sophisticated if pricey, and includes a decent range of wines. There's a two-night minimum stay, and booking is essential. Breakfast is included. $$$

Longsha Campsite Southwestern shore; http://longshacampingandboatservices.com. Located at the more laidback end of the beach, this campsite has a mess of two-person tents (mattresses extra), a kitchen for guests to use and copious amounts of hammocks overlooking the beach. Popular with large student/youth groups. $

Pak Ya Sea View Chalet Western shore; http://facebook.com/pakya.pulaukapas. Seven tidy A-frames behind a low protective wall on the beach, all with double beds, fans, lino floors and small but clean bathrooms. The beach café is quite popular and serves the usual gamut of Malay rice/noodle dishes and local specialities. $

GEMIA ISLAND

Gem Island Resort and Spa Southeastern tip; http://gemisland.com.my. This quiet spot is the only resort on Gemia, with chalets on stilts; the cheapest are in a long block, with better views away from the restaurant. Turtles land to lay eggs and the resort is involved in their conservation; facilities include a spa, small swimming pool and restaurant. A surcharge of is applied at weekends and during school holidays. Full board. $$$$

EATING — SEE MAP PAGE 236

Each guesthouse has its own **restaurant**, but the most popular backpacker places are the restaurant at *Pak Ya Sea View Chalet* and *JT Café*, right next to the jetty.

JT Cafe Western shore; 019 988 4034. More or less the only standalone place to eat on the island, serving up great local food such as sweet-and-sour fish, fried noodles, fish and chips, sandwiches and buttermilk chicken, all selectable from a cute chalkboard and updated every now and then according to what's available. The end results can be a mixed bag, and you might have to wait a while for them, but you're not exactly spoiled for choice on Kapas. $$

> ### SNORKELLING AND DIVING AROUND KAPAS ISLAND
>
> **Snorkelling** is of course a draw on Kapas; most places to stay can rent out gear, or arrange a boat trip out to a choice site. Visibility is best between May and August, but jellyfish can be a nuisance in June and July. Some of the most popular snorkelling spots are around rocky **Gemia Island**. If you're just renting equipment then try the rocks at the edges of the beaches beyond *Qimi Chalet* and the campsite.
>
> **Diving** isn't generally considered to be as good as on the Perhentians or Redang, but there are opportunities for it, particularly on the eastern side of the island. Popular sites include Berakit Reef, Octopus Reef and Coral Garden. Blacktip reef sharks are regularly seen, and you can find turtles at Coral Garden and near *Kapas Turtle Valley*. There's only one **dive shop**, Aqua Sport (http://aquasportdivers.biz.my), which offers PADI open water courses as well as regular dives.

DIRECTORY
Money There are no banks or ATMs on the island, so load up on cash in Marang.

Southern Terengganu

The stretch of **southern Terengganu** between Marang and the Pahang border offers fairly slim pickings for travellers. Pleasant **beaches** are the main draw, any of which make a good break during a drive along the coast road, though facilities at most amount to a mere straggle of food stalls.

Rantau Abang

Little more than a handful of guesthouses strung out along a dusty road 40km south of Marang, **RANTAU ABANG** used to reap a rich reward as one of a handful of places in the world where the giant **leatherback turtle** came to lay its eggs. No longer, thanks to overfishing, pollution and poaching – at the time of writing, the last officially recorded leatherback nesting was in 2010, though locals claim two or three a year still come. In the meantime, Rantau Abang has drifted into relative obscurity. It's still a pleasant enough way station though, offering a beach with fine, though plastic strewn, sand and superb 180-degree views of blue-green sea.

Turtle Conservation and Information Centre
Free • http://marinepark.dof.gov.my

The **Turtle Conservation and Information Centre**, or *Hentian Penyu*, holds informative, if dry, displays on turtle biology and conservation, plus a paddling pool full of hatchlings. If you want to spot nesting turtles, your best bets are elsewhere (see page 242).

ARRIVAL AND DEPARTURE — RANTAU ABANG

By bus Buses stop on the main road close to the Turtle Conservation and Information Centre. Local services from Kuala Terengganu, Marang and Dungun pass through Rantau Abang every 30min–1hr (8am–6pm) and are most regular in the mornings.

By taxi Ask at your accommodation about long-distance taxis to Kuala Terengganu or Dungun.

ACCOMMODATION AND EATING

The decline in tourism means that most places are now geared up for student groups and team-building sessions. The exception is the luxurious *Tanjong Jara Resort*, just south of Rantau Abang. Few accommodation options in Rantau Abang serve **food** other than for groups, but a handful of simple places to eat lie within walking distance.

Dahimah's Guesthouse 1km south of information centre; http://facebook.com/DahimahsGuestHouse. Located between the main road and a pretty lagoon, and run by Dahimah – originally from the UK – and her Malay husband.

Accommodation ranges from simple fan doubles to huge family rooms with TV, a/c and hot water. $
Tanjong Jara Resort 4km south of Rantau Abang; http://tanjongjararesort.com. One of the priciest east coast resorts, a complex of timber pavilions and houses almost fit for a sultan. Traditional treatments are on offer in the spa, and there's a diving and watersports centre. Activities range from waterfall treks and trips to Tasik Kenyir to cooking classes. $$$$

Dungun to the Pahang border

Driving south from **Dungun to the Pahang border** takes you through the heartland of Terengganu's oil industry, with refineries lining both side of Route 3 around the town of **Paka**. Most of the towns have little to detain tourists, but there are a few upmarket resorts along the coast.

Dungun

The backwater town of **DUNGUN** straggles for 9km along the coast south of Tanjong Jara. The bus station lies towards the northern end of town in a largely Chinese neighbourhood, with a handful of shophouses and a night market each Thursday. The only reason to stop here is because it's a **transport hub**; there's a taxi stand next to the bus station, with an ATM a few blocks north.

Tenggol Island

Further from the mainland than the popular islands further north, **Tenggol Island** (Pulau Tenggol; reached by boat from Dungun) is correspondingly less developed. While the few visitors who venture out here have to make do with rather run-down accommodation, there's beautiful, unspoiled scenery and arguably the best **diving** and snorkelling on the east coast. It's possible to arrange a diving trip from the mainland through *Tanjong Jara* resort (see below).

Ma'Daerah Turtle Sanctuary

Kerteh, 12km south of Paka • http://marinepark.dof.gov.my

Near the town of **Kertih**, on the road south of Paka, is the **Ma'Daerah Turtle Sanctuary**, with an information centre and hatchery on a quiet beach where green turtles lay their eggs. It's possible to volunteer here during the May to September hatching season.

Kemaman and Chukai

The southernmost settlement of significance in Terengganu is the fusion of **Kemaman** and neighbouring **Chukai**. The town, home of a major port, holds little attraction for visitors, but its two bus stations (Geliga Bus Station for express buses, and the local bus station in town) are useful, and it has the closest **banks** and ATMs to Cherating.

ARRIVAL AND DEPARTURE — DUNGUN TO THE PAHANG BORDER

By plane Although there have been flights to Kuala Lumpur in the past, at the time of writing no scheduled services were departing from tiny Kerteh airport.
By bus You may need to change at Dungun or Kemaman/Chukai if you are using local buses to travel the coast (7am–6pm roughly hourly).
By boat Speedboats run from Dungun to Tenggol Island (45min); transfers are normally included in accommodation packages.

ACCOMMODATION

The **resorts** along the coast are largely aimed at business travellers, so look for weekend discounts. Those on Tenggol are only open from February to November, and only when there are guests, so it is essential to book ahead.

DUNGUN
Pen'U Cottage Kompleks Perniagaan, Sura Gate; http://penucottage.weebly.com. Located 1.5km south of the bus station down a quiet side street towards the beach, this semi-homestay has small but clean rooms, all with a/c and bathrooms. There's a kitchen available for guest use. $

TENGGOL ISLAND
Tenggol Coral Beach Resort Pulau Tenggol; http://

tenggol.com.my. Pleasant, spacious rooms are linked by sandy paths facing Teluk Air Tawar ("Freshwater Bay") in the largest of Tenggol's three resorts. Rates are usually for two-night all-inclusive snorkelling packages; the diving equivalent, including five dives, costs around double. $$$$

Cherating

At first it can be hard to discern the enduring appeal of **CHERATING**, a laidback village 45km north of Kuantan. Its heyday as a tourist destination is clearly over, and many locals have long since moved out to the new settlement of **Cherating Baru**, 4km to the south. What's more, the **beach** is pleasant but hardly the best on the coast – it's best suited to windsurfing and kitesurfing (March to September), and **surfing** during the northeastern monsoon (October to December).

Nevertheless, at its best, Cherating Lama is still an appealing little travellers' community, chilled out yet warm-spirited, a place to share quality time with old companions and – chances are – to end up with a whole bunch of new acquaintances too. Local entrepreneurs have devised an array of **activities** to keep tourists coming, and it's well worth giving it a few days. Along the coast are a series of mid-range resorts that draw in families looking for a comfortable seaside break.

ACCOMMODATION	
Cherating Bay View	8
Holiday Villa Beach Resort	2
Ku Mimi Cablet	4
Matahari	3
Maznah's Guest House	1
Ranting Beach Resort	5
Royale Chulan	6
Tanjung Inn	7

EATING	
Café Marion	2
Don't Tell Mama	5
Duyong	1
Nabill Café	4
Ombok Surf Café	3

DRINKING	
Cherating Beach Bar	1

ACTIVITIES IN CHERATING

During the northeast monsoon – and especially mid-October to early January, when the waves are good and the rain is not too bad – **surfing** is the big attraction in Cherating. **Windsurfing** and kitesurfing are possible throughout the year, weather permitting, while there's also a range of **activities** and organized tours (see page 241).

CRAFTS CLASSES
Limbong Art Cherating Lama; 017 950 1281. Batik classes, in which you get your own designs onto T-shirts and sarongs. Classes take around two to six hours, depending on your project.

SURFING, WINDSURFING AND KITESURFING
There are only a couple of dedicated watersports schools, though surfboards and lessons are available from many guesthouses and cafés, the best being *Ombok* or *Cherating Beach Bar*.

Cherating Point Between Mazna's Guest House and Matahari; http://cheratingpoint.com. Surfboard rental and lessons (90min, plus 90min board rental afterwards), plus beginners' packages (including accommodation). Daily Nov–June.

Kam's Surf Shack On the beach; kamsurf.com. Surfing lessons in season; windsurfing and kitesurfing lessons, and equipment rental are available year-round.

Cherating beach

No trip to Cherating would be complete without time spent on the **beach**. While the shelter of the bay ensures calm waters, jellyfish and currents are occasionally a problem, and it's best to avoid swimming at low tide, when the sea recedes 100m or more. The headland obliterates any sunrise views, but in good weather it's still worth taking a dawn stroll on the beach, when only a few fishing boats disturb the stillness.

Turtle sanctuary

3.5km east of Cherating village • Free • 09 581 9087

Around the rocky headland at the eastern end of the bay sits Cherating's **turtle sanctuary** (signed from Route 3 as Santuari Penyu). Once a handy place to watch green and Hoxby turtles nesting on the beach, the development at *Club Med* nearby has caused the turtles to nest further north at Kemaman's Teluk Mak Nik Beach. Today the information centre has displays about the creatures, plus a few holding tanks at the back where you can see hatchlings and juveniles in season (May to September).

ARRIVAL AND DEPARTURE — CHERATING

By express bus Express buses on the coast road between Kuala Terengganu and Kuantan drop passengers on request at both Cherating Lama and Cherating Baru. However, they won't stop to pick up passengers, so reserve ahead for a seat from Geliga bus station near Chukai when you want to leave – taxis and local buses going north head there.

Destinations Ipoh (5 daily; 6hr 30min); Johor Bahru (8 daily; 6hr 30min); Kota Bharu (5 daily; 6hr); Kuala Lumpur (2–3 hourly; 4hr); Kuala Terengganu (hourly; 3hr 15min); Kuantan (4 daily; 1hr–1hr 30min); Marang (6 daily; 2hr 30min); Melaka (3 daily; 5hr 30min); Mersing (2 daily; 4hr); Rantau Abang (6 daily; 1hr 30min).

By local bus If you don't have a reservation on an express bus, wait on the main road for one of the sporadic local services to Kuantan or Dungun (roughly hourly; 7am–6pm).

By taxi It's possible to catch a taxi from Kuantan to Cherating (45 min), or to the nearest ATM and the Geliga bus station at Chukai.

TOUR OPERATORS AND GUIDES

Agencies along the main drag can book bus tickets and other travel arrangements, such as transfers to Taman Negara or islands off the east coast. All agencies and most guesthouses offer a range of **tours**, the selection and prices being similar wherever you go; night-time turtle-watching (usually including transport), firefly-watching (1hr) and morning snorkelling trips to Snake Island (2hr 30min) are the most popular options.

Cherating Firefly Cherating Lama; http://cheratingfirefly.com. This group not only run the firefly tours you might guess at from their name, but more besides, including night-time turtle-watching tours, ATV journeys, kayaking trips, and shuttle services.

Hafiz Cherating River Activities Lot 1156, Cherating Lama; http://facebook.com/dutakelipkelip. Magical evening firefly excursions (using an interesting way to attract the insects), although the trips can become busy; many other agencies book guests onto his trips. Snorkelling, fishing and kayak rental also available.

ACCOMMODATION

SEE MAP PAGE 240

The best places to stay are those by the river or towards the western end of the beach as they have the **best vibe**. Prices can drop by up to twenty percent on weekdays (the codes below are for weekend prices), with further **discounts** available during the northeast monsoon.

CHERATING LAMA

Cherating Bay View Cherating Lama; http://facebook.com. At the quieter end of the bay, this complex has a range of a/c chalets, the cheapest of them around a greenish swimming pool. While the standard seafront chalets lack the modern fixtures and fittings of the deluxe options, they

MARINE TURTLES

While four types of marine turtle lay their eggs on Malaysia's east coast, for years the sight of the largest – the giant, critically endangered **leatherback turtle** – was the star attraction, drawing visitors to Rantau Abang in Terengganu. In fact, all other kinds of marine turtle – **green** (nesting sites include the Perhentians, Redang Island, Cherating, Penarik and the Turtle Islands National Park in Sabah), **hawksbill** (Redang Island, Turtle Islands National Park, Tioman Island and Padang Kemunting near Melaka), **olive ridley** (rarely seen), and **Kemp's ridley** and **loggerhead** (neither of which nest in Malaysia) – are also at risk.

Harmful fishing methods, such as the use of **trawl nets**, kill thousands of marine turtles each year, and help explain the dramatic reduction in leatherbacks nesting on the Terengganu coast. In 1956, more than ten thousand were recorded; in 2000, just three; in 2002, there were no sightings of leatherbacks in Rantau Abang for the first time since records began; by 2005, leatherback, hawksbill and olive ridley statistics in Terengganu were all at zero, and green turtle figures were significantly down. On the rare occasions when a leatherback turns up – there was a lone turtle in 2010, and two nests were found in 2017 – their eggs often failed to hatch, probably because of the increasing rarity of male–female turtle encounters. In 2019, the Terengganu government declared the leatherback turtle extinct from Rantau Abang.

With a very meagre survival rate among hatchlings under ordinary conditions, any human pressure on turtle populations has drastic consequences for their survival. For the Chinese in Malaysia and Singapore, turtle soup is a classic delicacy, and while Malays eschew turtle meat, they do consume **turtle eggs**, which look like ping-pong balls and are sold at markets throughout the east coast. Their collection is licensed at certain sites, but there's no guarantee that anything on sale was collected legally. There appears to be no political will to outlaw this traditional food, a sad irony given Malaysia's general turtle conservation efforts: in many places, hatcheries pay licensed collectors for eggs rather than see them go to markets. At least the deliberate slaughter of turtles for their shells, once fashioned into bowls and earrings, has been banned since 1992.

TURTLE SPOTTING AND CONSERVATION

Nowadays, humans are excluded from various designated **sanctuaries** for nesting turtles. At these sites the eggs are dug up immediately after the turtle has laid them and reburied in sealed-off **hatcheries** on the beach. Burying the eggs in sand of the correct temperature is crucial as warm sand produces more females, while cooler sand favours males. When the hatchlings emerge, they are released at the top of the beach and their scurry to the sea is supervised to ensure their safe progress.

There are several officially sanctioned opportunities to watch nesting turtles on the east coast beaches and islands, including at Cherating, Perhentian Besar and Tioman Island (at Juara Beach). It is also possible to volunteer at turtle sites such as Ma'Daerah (see page 239). Be sure to avoid "turtle releasing" activities, however.

actually have better sea views.

Ku Mimi Cablet Centre of town; http://facebook.com/kumimicablet. A slightly overpriced, but really quite comfortable, clutch of white-painted wooden chalets. A good place to kick back, and despite its town-centre location, the beach is still only a short walk away. $$

Matahari Cherating Lama; 017 924 7465. A mishmash of units, from spartan A-frames to larger chalets, all arranged around a pleasant grassy area. Toilets and showers are in a separate block; while a few rooms have private bathrooms, only one has a/c. There's a communal kitchen. $

Maznah's Guest House Cherating Lama; http://maznahguesthouse.blogspot.com. Lovely family-run place with basic A-frames that share facilities, but you can hardly complain for the price. The spotless en-suite chalets are also good value, but the a/c ones are overpriced. Price includes breakfast and all-day hot drinks. $

Ranting Beach Resort Cherating Lama; http://facebook.com/rantingbeachresort. Spacious, well-kept garden rooms, plus pricier beach chalets; good views compensate for the generally uninspiring decor – some have breezy verandas. All options are en suite, some with a/c and TV. $$

Royale Chulan East end of town; http://royalechulan.com. If you prefer resort-style accommodation but want to stay in Cherating Lama, then this large complex of tidy en-suite rooms is the place to come. They've gone for warm, cosy decorations in the rooms, while guests tend to spend quite a bit of time in the lovely outdoor pool. Breakfast is included, and there's a very good on-site restaurant too. $$$

★ **Tanjung Inn** Cherating Lama; http://tanjunginn.com. Timber-built en-suite accommodation, ranging from simple chalets to brilliant, traditionally styled kampung houses boasting a/c, four-poster beds and slate-tiled bathrooms with hot water, which are set around two large ponds in a peaceful, pretty garden. The more basic rooms overlook the beach. $$$

CHERATING BARU

Holiday Villa Beach Resort Cherating Baru; http://holidayvillahotels.com. Twelve luxurious villas in traditional kampung houses from different Malaysian states. All have one or two beautifully appointed bedrooms, lounge and private outdoor jacuzzis; there's also a spa next door. Rates include turtle-watching trips and breakfast. $$$$

EATING
SEE MAP PAGE 240

Cherating Lama has a string of inexpensive **restaurants**, many emphasizing seafood including the *lala* – a sort of clam, which turns up in various sauces – but a couple of places also offer decent Western food. *Kedai kopis* serve reasonable Malay cuisine, with *roti canai* in the morning and *nasi campur* later in the day.

Café Marion Cherating Lama. A steady stream of locals and visitors pops into this café through the day, all sweet-tooth sorts itching to get one of their tasty treats – strawberry cheesecake, lemon meringue tart, pecan pie and more, all lined up and waiting at the counter. They can rustle up a coffee too, if you'd prefer to sit in rather than take away. $

★ **Don't Tell Mama** Cherating Lama; 010 900 5663. Open year-round, the beachside *Don't Tell Mama* is a great place to chill out with a beer and one of their excellent giant cheeseburgers, enjoying the relaxed playlist from a hammock/lounge chair or while playing with the dogs. The other, mostly Western dishes, such as pasta, are also good. $$

Duyong Cherating Lama; 09 581 9578. A popular old faithful, this large, airy place overlooking the river offers excellent Chinese and Thai dishes, plus a few Western standbys such as lamb chop and steak. Veggie dishes can be cooked to order. $$

Nabill Café Cherating Lama; 019 985 3302. Locals come here for their great *ikan bakar*, but if they've run out of fresh fish you can choose from a range of Chinese, Malay, Thai and Western dishes, including a long list of rice- and noodle-based standards. $

Ombok Surf Café Cherating Lama; 09 581 9274. Run by ecologically-minded Malaysian surfers, this very hip and funkily-decorated café serves up a mix of local and Western food, including satisfying breakfasts, pasta and sandwiches as well as espresso coffees and smoothies. They also can arrange surf boards and lessons, and have a small gallery, with evening musical jam sessions during high season. $$

DRINKING
SEE MAP PAGE 240

Cherating Beach Bar Cherating Lama; 017 674 7015. In a great spot in the middle of the beach, this atmospheric bar built partly from driftwood – often called *Mazlan's* after the very laidback owner – serves up cold beer, cocktails and simple snacks, though you're also welcome to make use of the barbecue.

Kuantan and around

The state capital of Pahang since 1955, **KUANTAN** is an undistinguished agglomeration of concrete buildings around an older core of shophouses close to the Kuantan River. While there's very little by way of historical or cultural interest in the city itself, Kuantan can be a breath of fresh air after a sojourn in Kelantan or Terengganu – it's closer in feel to the west coast cities than to Kuala Terengganu or Kota Bharu. If you're arriving from elsewhere in the country, however, Kuantan can seem mundane. With the creation of the **East Coast Highway** to Pelabuhan Kuantan, the port 40km north of the city, it's easy to bypass Kuantan altogether if you're travelling between KL and the east coast. Said coast is actually under threat in this area – though it has been an increasingly serious issue in recent years, a monsoon in 2021 saw much of the shoreline in these parts recede by up to four metres.

If Kuantan has a focus of sorts, it's the **padang**. The city's oldest streets, between there and the river, hold quite a few hotels and restaurants. The best reason to hang around for a night or two, though, is to take a day-trip to the cave temple of **Gua Charas** or the royal town of **Pekan**.

Masjid Negeri
Northeastern edge of the padang • Free

The town's main sight, the **Masjid Negeri**, was built in 1991, with a pastel exterior like a piece of fine Wedgewood – green for Islam, blue for peace and white for purity. It's distinctly Turkish in appearance, thanks to the pencil minarets at all four corners of the sturdy square prayer hall, topped with a looming central dome. Non-Muslims can visit outside of prayer times: men should wear long trousers, while women are advised to cover their hair and dress modestly.

Museum of Contemporary Art
Northeastern edge of the padang • Free

Housed in a lovely old British colonial administration building from 1910, the **Museum of Contemporary Art** features six galleries of Islamic art and calligraphy, traditional east coast crafts such as shadow puppets, and musical instruments – not exactly what you might expect, given the name of the place. It also has a gallery of abstract art, in addition to four abstract sculptures in the gardens depicting *raja sariman* (a Malaysian martial art), which are full of energy and movement. Temporary exhibits of international and local artists are also hosted here, and there are historic photos of the local people throughout.

Esplanade
Night cruises by advance booking only • Charge • 011 2575 8033

Down by the river, starting at the *Megaview Hotel*, an **esplanade** clings to the banks of the Kuantan River. Early evening is a good time to take a stroll, to see fishing boats returning with the day's catch and perhaps the occasional red eagle swooping on its prey. A small **night market** sets up here each evening, and boat trips depart from the jetty at the southwest end of the promenade.

Teluk Chempedak
5km east of centre following Jalan Besar, which becomes Jalan Teluk Sisek then Jalan Teluk Chempedak • Bus #200 from local bus station (every 20–30min; 30min); a shorter trip by taxi

Around the corner from a wooded headland, on an east-facing stretch of coast, **Teluk Chempedak** has long been a popular evening and weekend hangout for families and young people. The sands of the bay are encouragingly white, although undertows can render the sea off-limits (watch out for red flags). There is an appealing liveliness about the place, quite at variance from the langourous mood on the otherwise better sands of rural Terengganu. Bars, fast-food chains and restaurants line the main road as you arrive, before you reach the *Hyatt*, and there are more places to eat on the promenade.

KUANTAN AND AROUND THE EAST COAST

ARRIVAL AND INFORMATION

KUANTAN

By plane Sultan Ahmad Shah airport is 15km west of town, 20min by taxi. KL flights (2 daily; 55min) are operated by Malaysian Air (http://malaysiaairlines.com); there are also Singapore flights (3 weekly; 1hr) with Scoot (flyscoot.com).

By express bus Express buses depart from the lower level of Kuantan's modern Terminal Sentral bus station, 7.5km northwest of downtown Kuantan. It's a taxi ride away, or you can take the #303 bus.

Destinations Alor Setar (3 daily; 10hr); Butterworth (6 daily; 9hr); Dungun via Cherating (9 daily; 2hr); Ipoh (4 daily; 6hr); Jerantut (4 daily; 3hr); Johor Bahru (31 daily; 5hr 30min); Kota Bharu (13 daily; 6hr); Kuala Lipis (2 daily; 6hr); Kuala Lumpur (every 30min–1hr; 4–5hr); Kuala Terengganu (14 daily; 4–5hr); Melaka (3 daily; 4hr); Mersing (7 daily; 2-3hr); Seremban (10 daily; 6–7hr); Singapore (4 daily; 6hr 30min).

By local bus The local bus station is on Jalan Stadium, with regular #303 buses to the Terminal Sentral bus station (every 20–30min), Pekan, Sungai Lembing and Teluk Chempedak.

By taxi Local taxis can be found near the mosque; long-distance taxis arrive and depart from Terminal Sentral. Call 09 572 9892 to book.

By car For car rental, Avis (09 539 8768, http://avis.com), Hertz (09 538 4848, http://simedarbycarrental.com) and Mayflower (09 538 4490, http://mayflowercarrental.com) are all at the airport.

Tourist offices Tourism Pahang, the state tourism office (Mon–Thurs 9am–1pm & 2–5pm, Fri 9am–1pm & 2.45pm–5pm; 09 568 1623, http://pahangtourism.org.my), is at 33 ICT Hub, Jalan Putra Square 4, just south of the East Coast Mall, with the Tourism Malaysia office just a few doors north (Mon–Thurs 8am–1pm & 2–5pm, Fri 8am–12.15pm & 2.45–5pm; 09 567 7112).

ACCOMMODATION
SEE MAP PAGE 245

There's no shortage of places to stay in Kuantan, and you can also stay out of town at **Teluk Chempedak** or pleasant **Balok Beach**. For details of **homestays**, pick up the well-produced *Homestay Pahang* booklet from the state tourist office.

CENTRAL KUANTAN
Grand Darul Makmur Lorong Gambut, off Jalan Beserah; http://gdmhotel.com.my. This slick, central four-star hotel offers spacious rooms, several food outlets, a fitness centre and a pool complete with waterfall. The upper rooms in the twelve-storey Tower Block also provide great views. Breakfast is included. $$$

Mega View 567 Jalan Besar; http://megaviewhotel.com. You can't miss this place, sticking out like a sore thumb by the riverside. Rooms have been stylishly decorated, and feature splashes of lime green. Only rooms on the top two floors have balconies – you'll usually pay a bit more for these, but for the view, it can be worth it. $$

Seasons View A22 Lorong Haji Abdul Rahman 1; http://seasonsview-kuantan.com. A self-proclaimed "oasis of gracious hospitality", the rooms here are not exactly luxurious, but they're immaculate and easy to recommend for the price, though a window and breakfast will each cost extra. $

Spot On Kuantan Backpackers 39 Jalan Tun Ismail 1; http://oyorooms.com. An offering from the *OYO* behemoth's even-more-budget-than-budget subdivision, this is actually quite nice, with a backpacker vibe – painted world map and traveller musings on the wall, shared kitchen full of pots and pans, and dorms that are clean, if slightly regimental. $

TELUK CHEMPEDAK
Hyatt Regency http://kuantan.regency.hyatt.com. A long-established (though recently refurbished) beach retreat for well-heeled folk from KL and Singapore, with two swimming pools, a gym, tennis and squash courts, childcare facilities, multiple restaurants and a bar in a converted ship. Breakfast is included, and prices can be an absolute bargain at certain times of year – some of the cheapest *Hyatt* rooms you'll find anywhere, in fact. $$$$

BALOK BEACH
Some 15km north of Kuantan, Balok Beach can be reached by taxi, or by bus from the local bus station (45min).

Swiss Garden Resort http://swissgarden.com. Balconied rooms overlooking a landscaped garden or the South China Sea, plus a free-form swimming pool, spa and several restaurants. A large range of activity packages are available for adults and children. Prices rise on weekends. $$$

EATING AND DRINKING
SEE MAP PAGE 245

Laidback **kedai kopis** dot the streets west and south of the padang, while the area around Berjaya Megamall is packed with cafés and *mamak* joints. For inexpensive **Malay** food, try the places on and around the northern end of Jalan Haji Abdul Aziz or the area around the Central Market. International chain restaurants can be found at the East Coast Mall. Teluk Chempedak also holds plenty of eating choices, including many on the seafront, some open until as late as 2am. The **nightlife** in Teluk Chempedak is more lively than that in town, revolving around a handful of bars on the main road just before the beach.

CENTRAL KUANTAN
★ **Akob Patin House** Lorong Tun Ismail; 019 987 4463. The signature ingredient at this humble place is *patin* (silver catfish), served at lunchtime as *ikan patin tempoyak* – with chilli, tamarind and fermented durian – it's surprisingly tasty. $$$

Bombay Hamid Bros Jalan Teluk Sisek; 09 513 1945. Outstanding Indian food in a stylish a/c interior, serving very tasty banana leaf *thalis* either side of midday, and various Indian snacks and their highly-recommended *biriyanis* at other times. $

Chan Poh 52 Jalan Bukit Ubi; http://facebook.com. A good place for inexpensive dim sum, this earthy, no-frills place has a wide range of plates on display for you to choose from, which are then steamed for you. Beer is available too. $

Jelita Jalan Haji Abdul Aziz. Essentially a posh-looking metal hangar housing several food outlets, the star attraction among which is a branch of *Satay Zul*, Kuantan's best-loved satay house, offering beef, chicken, *kambing* (goat), *rusa* (venison) and even *perut* (stomach). Other stalls offer rice, noodles and doner kebabs. $$

Kula Cakes 96 Jalan Besar. An offshoot of *Lila Wadi*, this is a great little place to go for something sweet, especially their famous cheesecake. You can enjoy your treat, and perhaps a coffee too, in their leafy outdoor seating area. $

Lila Wadi Jalan Teluk Sisek; http://lilawadi.com.my. This great spot serves Japanese-style barbecue that's self-cooked at your table; you choose a main ingredient – beef, chicken or seafood – and receive a "set" (minimum two people) that includes side dishes. Leave space for a slice of their excellent cheesecake, which is so popular that they opened a spin-off shop, *Kula Cakes*. $$$

Sara Thai Kitchen Jalan Gambut; 012 937 9322. Thai food seems to be particularly popular in Kuantan, and this busy restaurant — part of a small chain, with another branch on Jalan Besar that may be worth considering if you're staying nearby — is one of several places specializing in dishes like green curry, *tom yam* and mango salad. $

★ **Tjantek** 46 Jalan Besar; 09 516 4144, http://tjantek.com. With soft lighting, chilled music and vintage artwork plastering the walls, this is one of Kuantan's most atmospheric dining spots. The pasta dishes are great, as are the sandwiches and salads, and the steak. There's no alcohol, but locals head here for their fresh juices and punches. $$

Ye Mi Won 236 Jalan Teluk Sisek; http://bit.ly/YeMiWon. A little way out of the centre, this traditional, family-run Korean restaurant is as good as you'll find anywhere, laying out an excellent spread of homemade *banchan* (side dishes) and *kimchi* with the barbecued *samgyeopsal* (pork belly), *bulgogogi* (marinated beef) and *galbi sal* (beef ribs). It's not cheap for the meat, however; the soups are slightly more affordable, and there are good-value rice-based lunch sets. $$$

SHOPPING   SEE MAP PAGE 245

Berjaya Megamall Jalan Tun Ismail; http://facebook.com/berjayamegamall. Central mall that's the most appealing of a motley selection across town; here you'll find plenty of cheap clothing, fast food, and even a bowling alley.

Hamid Bros 23 Jalan Mahkota; 09 516 2119. Decent little bookshop, which doubles as a money exchange facility.

DIRECTORY

Cinemas Two Golden Screen Cinemas (Berjaya Megamall and East Coast Mall; http://gsc.com.my) show some English-language films, as does Lotus Five-Star cinema in the Teruntum Complex (09 515 6881).

Hospital Hospital Tengku Ampuan Afzan (09 513 3333) is on Jalan Besar; the private Kuantan Medical Centre is next to the Berjaya Megamall (09 514 2828, http://kmc.tdmberhad.com.my).

Visa extensions The immigration office is out near the express bus station at Kompleks KDN, Bandar Indera Mahkota (Mon–Fri 7.30am–1pm & 2–5.30pm; 09 573 2200); take bus #302 from the local bus station.

Gua Charas

25km northwest of Kuantan on Route C4 • Entry by donation • Local bus #500 to Pekan Panching (30min) then 4km walk, or taxi from Kuantan

One of the great limestone outcrops close to Kuantan is home to **Gua Charas**, a **cave temple** that can be visited as a leisurely day-trip: if you charter a taxi from Kuantan then you can also visit the nearby Pandan River **waterfall**, where you can splash around in various pools. If you're taking the bus then you start at **Panching** village, where a sign to the cave points down a track through oil palm plantations. It's a long, hot 4km walk, so take plenty of water with you, though you may be able to hitch a lift from devotees.

Once you've reached the outer temple and paid your donation, you're faced with a steep climb to the cave temple itself. Halfway up, a flight of metal steps leads to the entrance of the main cave. The cave has been redeveloped to make it safer for worshippers to get inside, and concrete paths make access much easier than previously, though detract slightly from the atmosphere. Inside the echoing cavern, brightly illuminated shrines gleam from gloomy corners, guiding you past a phallic shrine dedicated to the Hindu god **Shiva** to the oldest shrine deep in the cave. Here a 9m-long reclining **Buddha** is almost dwarfed by its giant surroundings.

Sungai Lembing

42km northwest of Kuantan on Route C4 • **Muzium Sungai Lembing** Charge • http://bit.ly/SungaiLembingMuseum • **The Tin Mines Tunnels** Charge • Local bus #500 (roughly hourly; 1hr)

The small town of **SUNGAI LEMBING** retains an old-fangled, unhurried feel that's fading from the likes of Kuala Lipis and Pekan. Once the richest tin mining town in Pahang, the now sleepy town sits in a lush valley with steep forested hills on both sides, its main road planted with banyans and lined with 1920s **shophouses**. At the end of the main street is a **padang**, flanked by a dark timber building, once the **staff clubhouse** of the

Pahang Consolidated Company Limited (PCCL), which ran the nearby mines from 1905 until tin prices collapsed in the mid-1980s.

The history of the town and the PCCL are explored in the **Muzium Sungai Lembing** crowning the hill beyond the padang, formerly accommodation for PCCL's top managers. **The Tin Mines Tunnels** (some of the longest and deepest in the world) can also be toured, with a replica train taking you the first 100m, followed by recreations of working life for the old miners. Beyond the museum are several excellent **hikes** around the valley, the most popular of which is the 45-minute-long walk up **Panorama Hill**, signposted from the town. Sungai Lembing is popular with domestic tourists, who flock here on weekends for a hit of nostalgia so it's better to come on a weekday, when you'll find plentiful accommodation and few other visitors. Hiring a bike on the main street is also a good idea as there are several well-marked cycling routes through the surrounding countryside.

Pekan

Nearly 50km south of Kuantan lies the royal town of **PEKAN**, whose name literally means "small town". State capital of Pahang until 1898, Pekan still retains a measure of its charm and tranquillity, although this has been challenged in recent years with the growth of its modern centre. This is thanks in no small part – so locals say – to the fact that the town's MP is none other than prime minister Najib Tun Razak. Still, the town is definitely a worthwhile day-trip from Kuantan: you'll find unusually spruce **kampung houses** with pretty gardens, a few **museums** and a few wooden former **royal residences**. Highlights include the Sultan Abu Bakar Museum, housed in a 1920s British colonial building, and the wooden Chiefs' Rest House.

Muzium Sultan Abu Bakar

Jalan Sultan Ahmad • Charge; Waterfront Gallery free • 09 422 1371

At the edge of the commercial area, Jalan Sultan Ahmad faces the languid riverfront and holds the **Muzium Sultan Abu Bakar** – the State Museum of Pahang. It's housed in a well-proportioned Straits colonial building that has variously served as the sultan's istana, the centre of British administration, and the headquarters of the Japanese army during the occupation.

You'll need to take your shoes off to pad around the galleries, which cover a wide range of topics, from Sultan Abu Bakar's predilection for polo to the Orang Asli. Displays are nicely designed but poorly lit, and content is thin in places – the most informative gallery is dedicated to Pahang's traditional arts and crafts. The open-air **Watercraft Gallery**, part of the state museum but just across the river, houses a good selection of decorative boats that once plied Pahang's rivers and coast, the centrepiece being a boxy white houseboat built for Sultan Abu Bakar in the 1950s.

The palaces

At the intersection of Jalan Sultan Abu Bakar and Jalan Sri Terentang, an archway built to resemble elephants' tusks marks the way to the royal quarter of the town. The white timber building on the corner, once the **Istana Putih**, is now a centre for Koranic recitation. A few minutes' walk south, the squat **Istana Mangga Tunggal** is painted a dark blue. Continue and turn left at the archway to reach the expansive walled grounds of the **Istana Abu Bakar** – the gate flanked by a pair of fighter jets – current home of the royal family and closed to the public. The other side of the road holds some attractively colourful kampung houses. Follow the walls, and after nearly ten minutes you'll come to a vast **polo field**, home to a polo club founded in 1926. South of the padang sits **Istana Leban Tunggal**, an unusual wooden porticoed building with two octagonal towers crowned with yellow cupolas. Sadly,

PEKAN **THE EAST COAST**

the 1935 palace, once the only one of Pekan's istanas open to the public, is now locked up, its gardens slowly returning to the jungle.

ARRIVAL AND INFORMATION   PEKAN

By bus Cream-coloured rapid Kuantan bus #400 departs every 20-30min from Kuantan's local bus station for the hour-long journey to Pekan. If your main interest is the palaces, ask to be let off at the "Daulat Tuanku" arch on Jalan Sultan Abu Bakar, before the UFO-like water tower. Pekan's own bus station is in the modern centre, east of the padang. You'll need to head to Kuantan for most long-distance destinations.

Destinations Kota Bharu via Kuala Terengganu (4 daily; 7hr); Kuantan (every 20–30min; 50min); Johor Bharu (5 daily; 5hr 10min).

By taxi Taxis (09 422 2211) depart from close to the bus station, with fixed fares to Kuantan, Tasik Chini and other destinations.

ACCOMMODATION AND EATING   SEE MAP PAGE 249

The streets around the padang hold several places to **eat**, including a small row of stalls selling juice and snacks, with parasols providing a welcome break from the sun.

★ **Ancasa Royale** Over the river; http://ancasahotels.com.my. If you don't mind staying over the river (a few kilometres from the town centre), and also paying for the privilege, this is the nicest place to stay in the area, a gleaming hotel with very spacious rooms, and a delightful outdoor pool. There are spa facilities on site, as well as a very good restaurant. $$$$

Chief's Rest House Jalan Istana Permai; 09 422 6941. Occupying a spacious 1929 timber bungalow, and not unlike some of the istanas, this resthouse has nine high-ceilinged rooms, some with four-poster beds and bamboo blinds, with a/c and TV, as well as a dorm. Booking is essential. $

Farouk Maju 1 Jalan Engku Muda Mansor; 016 436 7129. As well as a decent *nasi campur* spread, this typical *mamak* restaurant serves tasty and cheap *biriyani*, curries and various Indian snacks such as *roti*, *poori*, *dosai* and *naan* to a constant stream of locals. Open around the clock, at least in theory – feel free to test their claim out in the wee hours. $

Kafe Belibis Muzium Sultan Abu Bakar, Jalan Sultan Ahmad; 010 358 1958. Something rather different, and quite a nice surprise out here in Pekan – a pretty-looking restaurant set by the old train tracks, and utilizing one not-actually-that-old carriage as a surrogate dining hall. The food doesn't quite match the setting, but it's still pretty good – mainly local dishes, plus some Western cakes and other snacks. $$

The south

- **252** Negeri Sembilan
- **258** Melaka
- **270** Around Melaka
- **272** From Melaka to Johor Bahru
- **274** Johor Bahru
- **279** The east coast
- **281** Tioman Island
- **290** Seribuat Archipelago: the other islands
- **292** Endau Rompin National Park

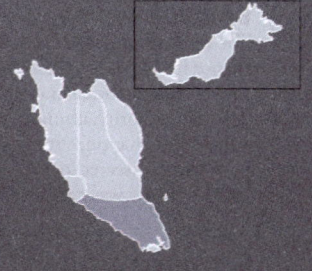

CHRIST CHURCH, MELAKA

The south

The south of the Malay Peninsula, below Kuala Lumpur and Kuantan, holds some of the country's most historically and culturally significant towns. Foremost among these is the west coast city of Melaka, founded in the fifteenth century and ushering in a Malay "golden age" under the Melaka Sultanate. For all its enduring influence, though, the sultanate was short-lived and its fall to the Portuguese early in the sixteenth century marked the start of centuries of colonial involvement in Malaysia. Today Melaka fascinates visitors with its historical buildings and cultural blend, including the Peranakan community (also called Baba-Nyonya), which grew from the intermarriage of early Chinese immigrant traders and Malay women.

Melaka is not, however, the only place in the region with historical resonance. Between KL and Melaka, what is now the state of Negeri Sembilan is where the intrepid **Minangkabau** Indigenous people from Sumatra settled, making their mark with architecture that can still be seen in **Seremban** and **Sri Menanti**. Both lie just over an hour south of the capital by road. Continuing down the west coast on the train line or the North–South Expressway (NSE), travellers soon reach the tip of the Peninsula and the thriving border city of **Johor Bahru** (JB) which dates back to 1855. Beyond it, over the Straits of Johor, lies Singapore.

Visitors tend to avoid the mountainous interior, where the road network is poor, but Route 3 on the east coast is a good deal more varied than the NSE, and winds for 300km through oil-palm country and past pleasant beaches. The biggest attractions along the east coast are **Tioman** and the other islands of the **Seribuat Archipelago**; havens for divers, snorkellers and anyone else in search of white sandy beaches, clear water and a tranquil atmosphere. Back on the Peninsula, and accessible from either east or west coast, the **Endau Rompin National Park** is a more rugged and less visited alternative to Taman Negara.

Negeri Sembilan

During the fifteenth century, the **Minangkabau** Indigenous peoples from Sumatra established themselves in what is now the Malay state of **Negeri Sembilan**. While the modern-day capital is **Seremban**, 70km south of Kuala Lumpur, the cultural heart of the state lies 30km east in the royal town of **Sri Menanti**. Both towns showcase traditional Minangkabau architecture, with its distinctive, saddle-shaped roofs.

Brief history

The modern state of Negeri Sembilan is based on an old confederacy of nine districts (hence its name – *sembilan* is Malay for "nine"). By the middle of the nineteenth century, the thriving **tin trade** and British control over the area were well established, with colonial authority administered from Sungai Ujong (today's Seremban). Rival Malay and Minangkabau groups fought several wars for control over the mining and transport of tin, with Chinese secret societies (triads) manipulating the situation to gain local influence, before a treaty was eventually signed in 1895.

Seremban

An hour south of the capital and just twenty minutes from KL International Airport, the bustling town of **SEREMBAN** is often overlooked by passing tourists. It

TIOMAN ISLAND

Highlights

❶ **Minangkabau architecture** The spectacular and distinctive architecture of this ancient Sumatran Indigenous group survives in Sri Menanti and Seremban. See page 257.

❷ **Melaka** The UNESCO World Heritage Site of Melaka has Portuguese, Dutch and British colonial buildings as well as unique Peranakan ancestral homes and some of Malaysia's best food. See page 258.

❸ **Johor Bahru** It may still be gritty by Malaysian standards, but this border city is smartening itself up with a combination of major public projects and small-scale entrepreneurship. See page 274.

❹ **Tioman Island** Palm-fringed, scenic and with great diving, this island is understandably popular but retains a laidback feel. See page 281.

❺ **Seribuat Archipelago** Tioman attracts all the attention, but the other islands of the Seribuat Archipelago offer even better beaches. See page 290.

❻ **Endau Rompin National Park** A little-visited lush tropical rainforest, rich with rare species of flora and fauna. See page 292.

HIGHLIGHTS ARE MARKED ON THE MAP ON PAGE 254

is, however, the access point for **Sri Menanti** and has good examples of Minangkabau architecture at the **Taman Seni Budaya Negeri** museum complex.

Lake Garden and around
State Library Free

The area around the **Lake Garden** – more lake than garden – holds the most appeal. Nearby is the white-stuccoed former **State Library** – built as the centre of colonial administration – with its graceful columns and portico. Beyond the black-and-gilt wrought-iron gates of the Istana (closed to the public), just north, a left turn leads to the **State Secretariat**, whose architecture (such as the layered, buffalo-horn roof) reflects the Minangkabau tradition.

Taman Seni Budaya Negeri
Near North–South Expressway, 3km northwest of the centre • Free • Bus from Terminal 1 (every 30min; 10–15min), or a short taxi ride

Although the small museum at the centre of the **Taman Seni Budaya Negeri** (State Arts and Culture Park) is unlikely to hold your attention for long, two reconstructed buildings in the grounds provide a good introduction to the principles of Minangkabau architecture. The 20m-long **Istana Ampang Tinggi** was built as a royal residence in the mid-nineteenth century. The interior of the veranda, where male guests were entertained, displays a wealth of exuberant and intricate leaf carvings, with a pair of unusual heavy timber doors. The other building was used for formal state events and also bears elaborate carving on the exterior.

ARRIVAL AND INFORMATION — SEREMBAN

By train Seremban's train station, just south of the centre, has regular Komuter connections from KL Sentral and the old Kuala Lumpur station.

Destinations Alor Setar (1 daily; 6hr 25min); Butterworth (1 daily; 5hr 50min); Gemas (2 daily; 1hr); Ipoh (2 daily; 4hr); Kuala Kangsar (2 daily; 4hr 30min); Kuala Lumpur (every 30min; 1hr 30min); Padang Besar (1 daily; 7hr).

By bus The bus station is just across the river west of the town centre on Jalan Sungai Ujong, connected to the handy Terminal 1 Shopping Centre (daily 10am–10pm) that houses a myriad of shops as well as a Golden Screen Cinema.

Destinations Alor Setar (2 daily; 8hr); Butterworth (3 daily; 5hr); Gua Musang (2 daily; 8hr); Hat Yai (Thailand; 3 daily; 10hr); Ipoh (3 daily; 5hr); Johor Bahru (every 1.5hr; 4hr); KLIA & KLIA2 (hourly; 1hr); Kota Bharu (2 daily; 8hr); Kuala Lumpur (every 10min; 1hr); Kuala Pilah (hourly; 45min); Kuala Terengganu (2 daily; 8hr); Kuantan (1 daily; 4hr 30min); Melaka (hourly; 1hr 15min); Mersing (1 daily; 6hr); Singapore (4 daily, 5hr).

By taxi Many choose to travel by taxi or Grab (http://grab.com/my) to/from KL Sentral.

Information Tourism Malaysia, Seremban Plaza, Jalan Dato' Muda Linggi (Mon–Fri 8am–5pm; 06 762 2388) about 3km east of the centre.

ACCOMMODATION — SEE MAP PAGE 256

★ **The Dusun** Kampung Kolam Air, Mukim Pantai; http://thedusun.com.my. This wonderful orchard retreat, 15km northeast of Seremban, offers accommodation in six classic kampung-style units dotted amid mangosteen, mango, durian and orange trees in twelve acres of land. Most units are open-fronted with unobstructed views of the rainforest, and each is equipped with kitchenette and BBQ sets. Note that meals are only available upon request, ordered well in advance, so you should bring your own food. Facilities include two inviting saltwater pools and a deer park; staff organize jungle treks and bird walks. Rates include breakfast. $$$$

Royale Chulan Jalan Dato' A.S. Dawood; http://royale chulan.com. This large establishment is Seremban's most upmarket option; rooms are spacious and comfortable, if a bit dated. Good facilities, including a large swimming pool, jacuzzi, gym, yoga studio and tennis court. There's also a spa on-site Rates can be slashed to very affordable levels outside busy times. $$$

SS Hotel 19 Jalan Tan Sri Manickavasagam; 06 767 1919. Most of Seremban's budget-level offerings are pretty poor, if not downright awful, so this is about as far down the price scale as you'll likely want to go – a presentable mini-hotel (with the fluttering flags outside to prove it) with tidy rooms, some of which have been designed with a little flair. $

EATING — SEE MAP PAGE 256

There's no shortage of **places to eat** in the town centre; Seremban is known for its *pao* (Chinese steamed buns) and

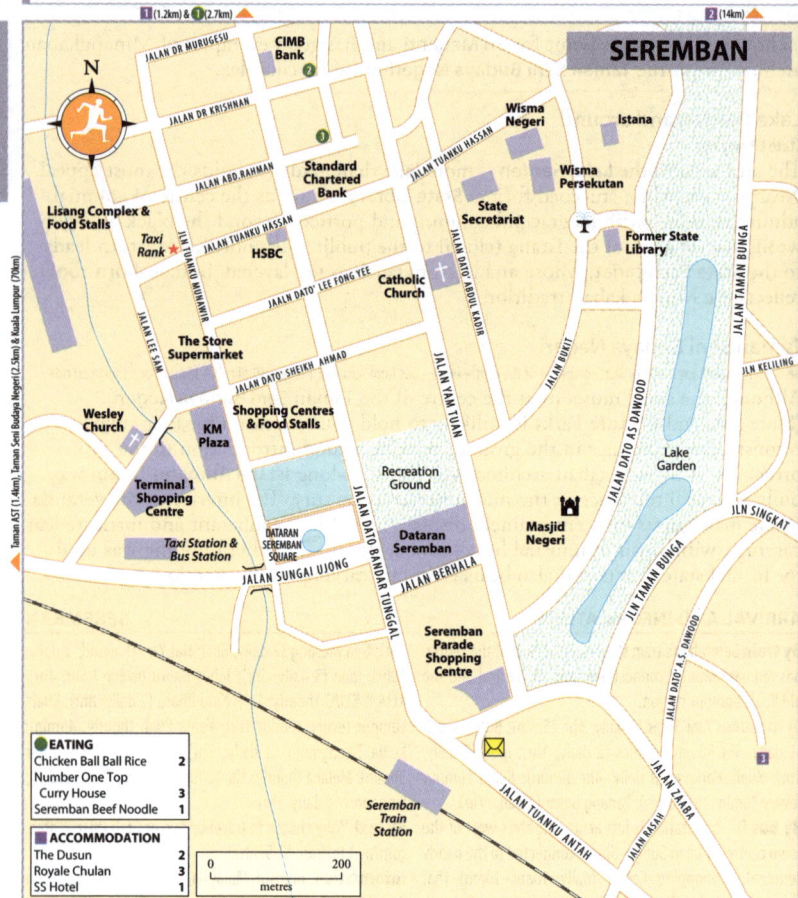

crab dishes.

Chicken Ball Ball Rice Jalan Dr Krishnan; http://facebook.com/cbbrseremban. Doing just what it says on the tin (perhaps with a superfluous ball) – great chicken rice, to be eaten with bean sprouts, with chicken balls as an alternative or addition. Some good noodle dishes too, plus yummy *cendol* and ABC for dessert. $

Number One Top Curry House Off Jalan Dato Bandar Tunggal; 019 542 4473. Who could argue with a name like that? Simple Indian eatery that doles out excellent banana-leaf biryanis, as well as some veggie-friendly *dosai*. $

Seremban Beef Noodle Upper floor of Pasar Besar (main market). It's a little out of the way, but the fantastic (and cheap) noodles here are a local favourite – make sure you get here early. Miraculously, the stall managed to survive a serious fire that devasted much of Pasar Besar in 2017. $

DRINKING AND NIGHTLIFE

Nightlife focuses on the Taman AST area west of the centre, particularly in the new **Era Square** development, connected to the bus station, though nowhere's particularly special.

Sri Menanti

The former royal capital of Negeri Sembilan, **SRI MENANTI**, is set in a lush, mountainous landscape 30km east of Seremban. The only reason to visit is to see a jewel of Minangkabau architecture, the **Istana Lama**. As you look for it, don't be misled by the sign for the **Istana Besar**, the current royal palace, which is topped by a bright blue roof.

Istana Lama
Free • http://lmns.ns.gov.my

A timber palace set in geometric gardens, the splendid **Istana Lama** was the seat of the Minangkabau rulers (see box). The sacking of Sri Menanti during the Sungai Ujong tin wars destroyed the original palace; today's four-storey version was designed and built in 1902 by two Malay master craftsmen, using no nails or screws. Until 1931, the building was used as a royal residence. Its tower, which once held the treasury and royal archives, offers a lovely view and can be reached by ladder from the sultan's private rooms. At its apex is a forked projection of a type known as "open scissors", now very rarely seen.

The whole rectangular building is raised nearly 2m off the ground by 99 pillars, 26 of which have been carved in low relief with complex foliated designs. Though the main doors and windows are plain, a long external veranda is covered with a design of leaves and branches known as *awan larat*, or "driving clouds". Above the front porch is the most elaborate decoration, a pair of Chinese-style creatures with lions' heads, horses' legs and long feathery tails.

ARRIVAL AND DEPARTURE   **SRI MENANTI**

By bus From Seremban, take a bus for the 45min journey to Kuala Pilah, then either wait for an infrequent local bus to Sri Menanti, or take a taxi (10 min).

By taxi A cab from Seremban will take around 45min.

THE MINANGKABAU

The **Minangkabau people**, whose cultural heartland is in the mountainous region of western Sumatra (Indonesia), established a community in Malaysia in the early fifteenth century. As they had no written language until the arrival of Islam, knowledge of their origins is somewhat sketchy; their own oral accounts trace their ancestry to Alexander the Great, while the *Sejarah Melayu*, or Malay Annals, tells of a mysterious leader, Nila Pahlawan, whose son, Sang Nila Utama, is said to have founded Singapore – originally "Singapura", Sanskrit for Lion City – after he saw a "lion" (more likely a Malayan tiger) in Temasek.

In early times the Minangkabau were ruled in Sumatra by their own overlords or rajahs, though political centralization never really rivalled the role of the strongly autonomous *nagari* (Sumatran for village). Each *nagari* was made up of numerous **matrilineal clans** (*suku*), whose members were descended from a common female ancestor and lived in a shared ancestral home. The household was also in control of ancestral property, which was passed down the maternal line. The *sumando* (husband) stayed in his wife's house at night but was a constituent member of his clan house, where most of his day was spent. Although the house and clan name belonged to the woman, and women dominated the domestic sphere, political and ceremonial power was in the hands of men; it was the *mamak* (mother's brother) who took responsibility for the continued prosperity of the lineage.

When and why the Minangkabau initially emigrated to what is now **Negeri Sembilan** in Malaysia is uncertain. Their subsequent history is closely bound up with that of Melaka and Johor, with the Minangkabau frequently called upon to supplement the armies of ambitious Malay princes and sultans. Evidence of intermarriage with the region's predominant Indigenous group, the Sakai, suggests some acceptance by the Malays of the matrilineal system. What is certain is that the Minangkabau were a political force to be reckoned with, aided by their reputation for supernatural powers. Today, the Minangkabau are very much integrated with the Malays, and their dialect is almost indistinguishable from standard Bahasa Melayu.

ACCOMMODATION

Sri Menanti Resort Kampung Buyau, next to the Istana Lama; http://mdkp.gov.my. Reasonable double rooms and chalets in Sri Menanti's only real accommodation option. There's also a pleasant pool where you can cool off. It doesn't hurt to ask about discounts. $\overline{\$\$\$}$

Melaka

When Penang was known only for its oysters and Singapore was just a fishing village, the influence of **MELAKA** (formerly spelled "Malacca") already extended beyond the Peninsula. Political and cultural life flourished in this trading centre under the auspices of the **Melaka Sultanate**, founded early in the fifteenth century, and helped to define what it means to be Malay.

The city subsequently suffered neglect from colonial rulers and fared little better after Independence, but in some ways this added to its faded charm. Recent years, though, have seen such developments as a land reclamation project that created the Taman Melaka Raya district and, in 2008, the gaining of UNESCO World Heritage Site status jointly with Penang. The latter has helped to encourage the development of a new wave of guesthouses and restoration projects, but has also brought some less welcome tourism schemes. Melaka remains, nevertheless, an undoubted highlight of any Malaysian itinerary.

Brief history

Melaka has its roots in the fourteenth-century struggles between Java and the Thai kingdom of Ayuthaya for control of the Malay Peninsula. The *Sejarah Melayu* (Malay Annals) records that when the Sumatran prince **Paramesvara** could no longer tolerate subservience to Java, he fled to the island of Temasek (later renamed Singapore), where he set himself up as ruler. The Javanese subsequently forced him to flee north to Bertam, where he was welcomed by the local community. While his son, Iskandar Shah, was out hunting near modern-day Melaka Hill, a mouse deer turned on the pursuing hunting dogs, driving them into the sea. Taking this courageous act to be a good omen, Shah asked his father to build a new settlement there and named it after the *melaka* tree (*Phyllanthus emblica*) under which he had been sitting.

A trading centre

Under its sultans, Melaka rapidly became a wealthy and cosmopolitan market town, trading spices and textiles with Indonesia and India. This meteoric rise was initially assisted by its powerful neighbours Ayuthaya and Java, both of which made good use of its trading facilities, but they soon found that they had a serious rival as Melaka started a campaign of **territorial expansion**.

By the reign of its last ruler, Sultan Mahmud Shah (1488–1530), Melaka's territory included the west coast of the Peninsula as far as Perak, the whole of Pahang, Singapore and most of east coast Sumatra. Culturally, too, Melaka was supreme – its sophisticated language, literature, hierarchical court structure and dances were all benchmarks in the Malay world.

The colonial era

It took a sea change in Europe to end Melaka's supremacy. The Portuguese were seeking to extend their influence in Asia by dominating ports in the region and, led by Alfonso de Albuquerque, conquered Melaka in 1511. They maintained their hold for the next 130 years, introducing Catholicism to the region through the efforts of the Jesuit missionary **St Francis Xavier**, after whom the main church in town is named.

The formation of the Vereenigde Oostindische Compagnie (VOC), or **Dutch East India Company**, in 1602 spelled the end of Portuguese rule. The primary objective was

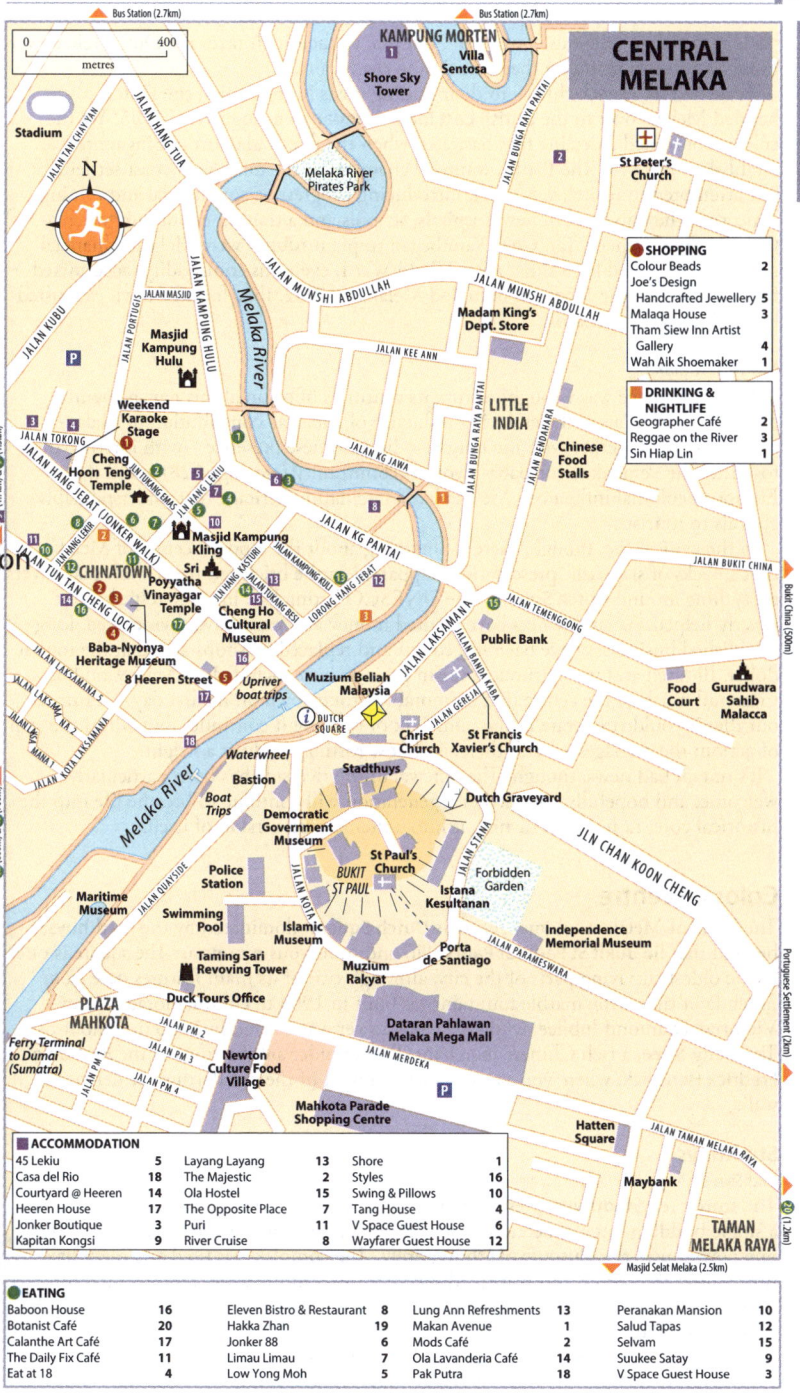

trade rather than religious conversion, but due to their high taxes the Dutch relied ever more on force to maintain their position in the Straits.

Weakened by French threats to their trading posts in the Indies, the Dutch handed Melaka over to the **British East India Company** on August 15, 1795. Yet the colony continued a decline that hastened when the free-trade port of Singapore was established in 1819. The British wanted Penang to be the main west coast settlement but attempted to revitalize Melaka, introducing progressive agricultural and mining concerns. They invested in new hospitals, schools and a train line, but only when a Chinese entrepreneur, Tan Chay Yan, began to plant **rubber** were Melaka's financial problems alleviated for a time. After World War I, even this commodity faced mixed fortunes – when the **Japanese occupied** Melaka in 1942, they found a town exhausted by the interwar depression.

Modern Melaka

Whatever damage was wrought during its centuries of colonial mismanagement, nothing can take away the enduring influence of Melaka's contribution to Malay culture. Taken together with the long-standing Chinese presence – with intermarriage fostering the Peranakan (or Baba-Nyonya) community (see page 528) – and the European colonial influences, Melaka has a fascinating heritage that understandably appeals to tourists.

To the cynical eye, though, there's something about the modern centre of Melaka that smacks of slapdash "preservation", apparent in the brick-red paint wash that covers everything around **Dutch Square**. The UNESCO listing has, in some respects, not exactly helped. As landowners have scented money and rents have skyrocketed, long-established businesses have been forced out and replaced by shops aimed at the tourist dollar. Ill-fated and incongruous tourism projects have included a RM15.9-million monorail north of the centre that memorably broke down on its first day – it turned out that it couldn't operate in the rain. Talk of reviving it continues, but with little sign of action; the carriages are still there, and now rotting gently at a height.

It's not all bad news, though. The renewal of the riverside has been particularly welcome, and hopefully any further regeneration will continue to breathe life into the historical core, rather than turning it into a theme-park version of itself.

Colonial centre

The heart of Melaka's colonial centre is **Dutch Square**, dominated by the **Stadthuys**; beyond that lie **Bukit St Paul (St Paul's Hill)** and numerous museums. The square is one of the oldest surviving parts of the city, although two of its main features date from much later times: the marble fountain was built in 1904 to commemorate Queen Victoria's Diamond Jubilee, while the clock tower was erected in 1886 in honour of Tan Beng Swee, a rich Chinese merchant. Rather older are the ruins of the **Bastion of Fredrick Hendrick**, where you can see the alignment of the old Portuguese defensive wall.

Stadthuys
Dutch Square • Charge • http://perzim.gov.my

The sturdy red **Stadthuys**, presiding over the entire south side of Dutch Square, is not a single building but a collection of structures dating from between 1660 and 1700; one now houses the **Museum of Ethnography**. The complex was used as a town hall throughout the Dutch and British administrations and the wide, monumental interior staircases, together with the high windows, are typical of seventeenth-century Dutch municipal buildings.

It's worth visiting mostly for the buildings themselves: the Museum of Ethnography displays an array of Malay and Chinese ceramics, weaponry, musical instruments and the like, plus a few dioramas and countless paintings depicting Melakan history. Several other **smaller museums** lurk behind the main buildings although they are mostly aimed at domestic visitors, covering topics such as the Malaysian education system.

Christ Church
Jalan Gereja • Free

Christ Church was built in 1753 to commemorate the centenary of the Dutch occupation of Melaka, making it the oldest functioning Protestant church in Malaysia. The simple design, with neither aisles nor chancel, is typically Dutch; the porch and vestry were nineteenth-century afterthoughts. The cool, whitewashed interior has decorative fanlights high up on the walls and elaborate, 200-year-old hand-carved pews, while the roof features heavy timber beams each cut from a single tree. The plaques on the walls tell a sorry tale of early deaths in epidemics.

Dutch Graveyard
East of Christ Church, along Jalan Kota • Free

Although the overgrown **Dutch Graveyard** was first used in the late seventeenth century, when the VOC was still in control (hence the name), British graves easily outnumber those of their predecessors. The tall column towards the centre of the tiny cemetery is a memorial to two of the many officers killed in the Naning War in 1831, a costly conflict which saw the nearby Naning region incorporated into Melaka's territory under the British.

Istana Kesultanan
Off Jalan Kota • Charge • http://perzim.gov.my

The **Istana Kesultanan** (Sultan's Palace) has played a central role in Malaysian history, although the current dark-timber palace is a contemporary reconstruction of the original fifteenth-century building. In the best Malay architectural tradition, its multilayered, sharply sloping roofs contain no nails. It was here that the administrative duties of the state were carried out, and also where the sultan resided when in the city (he mostly lived further upriver at Bertam, safe from attacks on Melaka). Remove your shoes to ascend the wide staircase to the ground floor, where you'll find a cultural museum housing several dioramas of scenes from Malay court life.

Porta de Santiago

At the time they conquered Melaka, the Portuguese used the forced labour of fifteen hundred enslaved people to construct the mighty **A Famosa** fort, completed in 1511. The Dutch East India Company later used the fort as its headquarters, but the British demolished it at the start of the nineteenth century when they relocated to Penang. All that's left today is a single gate, the crumbling **Porta de Santiago**, which was only saved thanks to a last-minute intervention from Sir Stamford Raffles, the founder of modern Singapore.

St Paul's Church
St Paul's Hill • Reached by climbing the steps behind the Porta de Santiago • Free

On the summit of St Paul's Hill (**Bukit St Paul**), and now no more than a roofless shell, **St Paul's Church** was constructed in 1521 by the Portuguese as Our Lady of the Mount. **St Francis Xavier** visited the church between 1545 and 1552, and his body was brought here for burial after his death in 1553, before being exhumed and transferred to its final resting place in Goa (India) the following year. The Dutch Calvinists changed the denomination of the church when they took over in 1641, renaming it St Paul's Church, and it remained in use until the construction of Christ Church at the foot of the hill. The British found St Paul's more useful for military than for religious purposes, storing their gunpowder here during successive wars. The 20-minute climb to the church is worth it, if only for the wonderful views over Melaka towards the sea.

Muzium Rakyat
Jalan Kota • Charge • http://perzim.gov.my

The **Muzium Rakyat** (People's Museum) is the most interesting of the museums that you pass as you skirt west around the base of St Paul's Hill from Porta de Santiago. Its ground and first floors house exhibits on such topics as the construction and competitive use of spinning tops. The third floor contains the much more interesting – and at times gruesome – **Museum of Enduring Beauty**. With the word "endure" here used in the sense of "to suffer", the exhibits show how people around the world have sought to alter their appearance: head deformation, dental mutilations, tattooing, scarification, corsetry and foot-binding and the like. The fourth floor is home to the Kite Museum, which speaks for itself.

Maritime Museum
Quayside • Charge • http://perzim.gov.my

The main part of the **Maritime Museum** (Muzeum Samudera) is housed in a towering replica of a Portuguese cargo ship, the *Flor de la Mar*, which sank in 1511 carrying treasure plundered from Melaka. Inside its hull, model ships, information boards and paintings chart the settlement's maritime history from the time of the Malay Sultanate to the arrival of the British in the eighteenth century.

It feels a little disjointed, rather than telling a single story, but there are some interesting facts in there. The same cannot be said of the drab displays across the road in the other section of the museum; the Royal Malaysian Navy patrol craft in the gardens is, however, popular with kids.

Taming Sari Revolving Tower
Jalan Merdaka • Charge

You can't miss the 80m-tall **Taming Sari Revolving Tower**, which offers a great (if relatively expensive for a five-minute tour) 360-degree view of the city and the sea. Its construction so close to the colonial district in 2008 was controversial, but it has nevertheless proved to be a popular attraction, with big queues at the weekend. Duck Tour tickets are sold next door (see page 266).

Chinatown

Melaka owed a great deal of its nineteenth-century economic recovery to its Chinese community: it was one Tan Chay Yan who first planted rubber here, and a Chinese immigrant called Tan Kim Seng established what became the great Straits Steam Ship Company. Most of these entrepreneurs settled in what became known as **Chinatown**, across the river from the colonial district. For many visitors, it's the most interesting part of town.

Jalan Hang Jebat

Chinatown's main street, **Jalan Hang Jebat** – popularly known as Jonker Street or Jonker Walk – runs parallel to Jalan Tun Tan Cheng Lock. It was formerly known for its antiques, but these days most shops sell souvenirs and cheap handicrafts. Still, its bars and restaurants continue to make it a centre of tourist activity.

The street is closed to traffic on weekend evenings for the **Jonker Walk Night Market**, when shops stay open late and the street is lined with vendors. Although very popular, quite atmospheric and often considered a must-do by visitors, it's nothing special by Malaysian street market standards – in particular, anyone looking for good street food is likely to come away disappointed.

Cheng Ho Cultural Museum
51 Lorong Hang Jebat · Charge · 06 283 1135

Dedicated to the life of Chinese Admiral **Cheng Ho** (also spelled Zheng He), who visited Melaka several times on his epic travels across Asia, the Middle East and Africa in the early fifteenth century, the **Cheng Ho Cultural Museum** provides an insight into early fifteenth-century Melaka, as well as trading and seafaring during the Ming Dynasty. Exhibits include a model of Cheng Ho's treasure ship and various navigational instruments; there's also a teahouse on the premises.

Jalan Tun Tan Cheng Lock

The elegant townhouses that line **Jalan Tun Tan Cheng Lock**, formerly Heeren Street, are the ancestral homes of the Baba-Nyonya community. The wealthiest and most successful of these merchants built long, narrow-fronted houses, minimizing the "window tax" by incorporating internal courtyards designed for ventilation and the collection of rainwater.

Several of the houses are now open to the public as shops, hotels and restaurants. You can't enter the **Chee Ancestral House** at no. 117, but it's worth checking out the exterior: an imperious Dutch building of pale green stucco topped by a gold dome, it's home to one of Melaka's wealthiest families. No less fascinating is the abandoned and overgrown property at no. 125, which once must have looked similarly impressive.

8 Heeren Street
8 Jalan Tun Tan Cheng Lock · Free (donations welcome) · http://badanwarisanmalaysia.org

Make time for a visit to the model conservation project at **8 Heeren Street**, where you can see how the building (dating from the 1790s) has been used and modified over the years. Printed information gives background on topics such as building materials and techniques, while the knowledgeable staff are happy to answer questions. Some commercial restoration projects in Melaka introduce inauthentic elements in the name of "heritage", but here the history of the building is laid bare.

Baba & Nyonya Heritage Museum
48 & 50 Jalan Tan Tun Cheng Lock · Charge · http://babanyonyamuseum.com

An amalgam of three adjacent houses belonging to a single family, the **Baba & Nyonya Heritage Museum** is an eclectic and ornate blend of Chinese and classical European architectural styles. Connected by a common covered footway, decorated with hand-painted tiles, each front entrance has an outer swing door of elaborately carved teak, while a heavier internal door provides extra security at night. Two red lanterns, one bearing the household name, the other messages of good luck, hang either side of the doorway, framed by heavy Greco-Roman columns.

The upper level of the building is the most eye-catching: a canopy of Chinese tiles over the porch frames the shuttered windows, with their glass protected by intricate wrought-iron grilles. The eaves and fascias are covered in painted floral designs. Inside, the homes are filled with gold-leaf fittings, blackwood furniture inlaid with mother-of-pearl, delicately carved lacquer screens and Victorian chandeliers. The guided tours, included in the entry price, add a great deal to the experience, revealing much about the Baba-Nyonyas themselves.

Jalan Tukang Emas

Jalan Tukang Emas (Goldsmith Street), continuing on from Jalan Tokong, is sometimes known as "Harmony Street" in reference to its buildings from different religions. A short way east from Jalan Hang Jebat, **Cheng Hoon Teng temple** – dedicated to the goddess of mercy – is reputed to be the oldest Chinese temple in the country. A little further along, the 1748 **Masjid Kampung Kling** displays an unusual blend of styles:

the minaret looks like a pagoda, there are English and Portuguese glazed tiles, and a Victorian chandelier hangs over a pulpit carved with Hindu and Chinese designs. Next door, the Hindu **Sri Poyyatha Vinayagar Temple** also has a minaret, decorated with red cows, and dates back to the 1780s.

Masjid Kampung Hulu
Jalan Kampung Hulu • Free

Thought to be the oldest mosque in Malaysia that remains in its original location, **Masjid Kampung Hulu** was constructed around 1728 in typical Melakan style. It's a large structure, surmounted by numerous pyramid-shaped roofs with red Chinese tiles, and has more than a hint of pagoda in its white minaret. Such architecture has its origins in Sumatra, perhaps brought over by the Minangkabau (see page 257) who settled in nearby Negeri Sembilan.

Northeast of the centre

From Christ Church, Jalan Laksamana leads north past the church of **St Francis Xavier**, a twin-towered, nineteenth-century, neo-Gothic structure. Further up from here on Jalan Bendahara you pass through the centre of Melaka's tumbledown **Little India**, a rather higgledy-piggledy line of incense and saree shops interspersed with a few eating houses.

Riverside walk
Melaka River Pirate Park Free; charge for rides • 06 288 1100

The redevelopment of Melaka's **riverside** has been a real success story, encouraging the opening of guesthouses and cafés where once there were dilapidated buildings. It's a pleasant 1.5km walk from Dutch Square to Kampung Morten (see page 264), and almost the whole stretch is illuminated at night. On the west side you'll find the **Melaka River Pirate Park**; not exactly in keeping with Melaka's heritage feel, this neon-lit entertainment park – which includes a ferris wheel and a pirate ship – should keep children occupied for an hour or two, but closes on rainy days.

St Peter's Church
Just north of the Jalan Bendahara and Jalan Munshi Abdullah crossroads • Free

The oldest Roman Catholic church in Malaysia, **St Peter's Church** was built by a Dutch convert in 1710 as a gift to the Portuguese Catholics, and has an impressive wooden, barrel-vaulted ceiling. The church really comes into its own at Easter as the centre of the Catholic community's celebrations.

Kampung Morten

The village of **Kampung Morten**, named after the British district officer who donated RM10,000 to buy the land, is a surprising find so close to the heart of Melaka. The wooden **stilt houses** here are distinctively Melakan, with their long, rectangular living rooms and kitchens, and narrow verandas approached by ornamental steps. It's easiest to explore on foot, and the riverside walk to get here is part of the experience.

Villa Sentosa
Lorong Tun Mamat 1 • Donation expected • 06 282 3988

The **Villa Sentosa**, with its miniature kampung house and mini-lighthouse, is a 90-year-old family home that now functions as a museum. The owner will gladly show you their artefacts, old family photographs and heirlooms, and there are a number of interesting newspaper articles on the wall near the entrance showing the news of the day from the 1930s.

Shore Sky Tower
Jalan Persisiran Bunga Raya • Charge • http://theshoremelaka.com

One of Melaka's more modern attractions and the tallest man-made structure in the city, the Shore Sky Tower provides unrivalled views of the area (billed as "50km in every direction") from the 43nd floor of the Shore Hotel and Residences. A visit starts with a walk along a stylish glass deck that's suspended above the hotel restaurant space, and which winds around to a staircase leading to a huge open rooftop where free telescopes allow for sight spotting. For the brave, the Sky Deck, projecting out beyond the building, has a glass floor so you can see the traffic moving down the road 140m beneath your feet.

Bukit China

East of the colonial heart of Melaka, **Bukit China** is the ancestral burial ground of the town's Chinese community – it's said to be the oldest and largest such graveyard outside China. Although Chinese contacts with the Malay Peninsula probably began in the first century BC, formal commercial relations were only established when the Ming Emperor Yung-Lo sent his envoy Admiral Cheng Ho here in 1409. Today, Bukit China is more an inner-city park than burial ground, where you're likely to encounter locals jogging, practising martial arts or simply admiring the view.

Sam Poh Kong temple
At the foot of Bukit China, at the eastern end of Jalan Temenggong

The **Sam Poh Kong temple** is a working temple dedicated to Admiral Cheng Ho. Accounts are vague as to the arrival of the first Chinese settlers, though it's said that on the marriage of Sultan Mansur Shah (1458–77) to the daughter of the emperor, Princess Hang Liu, the five hundred nobles who accompanied her stayed to set up home on Bukit China. It was supposedly these early Chinese settlers who dug the **Sultan's Well** behind the temple.

Portuguese settlement
Taxi or Grab from Dutch Square or Jalan Merdeka (15min)

The road east of Jalan Taman Melaka Raya leads, after about 3km, to Melaka's **Portuguese settlement**; turn right into Jalan Albuquerque, clearly signposted off the main road, and you enter its heart. Today you're likely to recognize the descendants of the original Portuguese settlers only by hearing their language, **Kristang**, a blend of Malay and old Portuguese. Note too the many Portuguese street names, including Fernandez, Rodriguez and Dominguez.

Medan Portugis

You could almost be forgiven for thinking that the whitewashed **Medan Portugis** (Portuguese Square), at the end of the road into the Portuguese settlement, is a remnant from colonial times. In fact, it dates only from 1985, but the local restaurateurs make an effort to conjure up a Portuguese atmosphere even if the food is Malay in character. A three-day **fiesta** – the feast of St Pedro – starts on June 29 every year, with traditional Portuguese food, live music and dancing. Just beyond the square is a row of waterfront seafood restaurants.

Masjid Selat Melaka, the Floating Mosque
Jalan Baiduri 8 • Taxi or Grab from Dutch Square or Jalan Merdeka (15min)

A little out of town, on Malacca Island, is the beautiful "Floating Mosque" – so-called because of its construction (which cost RM10 million) on stilts above the Strait of

Malacca. Although rarely open to foreigners, especially during times of prayer, make sure you pay a visit just before sunset. From the entrance, follow the waterfront to the left and around to the makeshift "viewing platform" to see the sun set into the sea behind the mosque as the building's neon lights come on; it's spellbinding (and nowhere near as gaudy as it sounds).

ARRIVAL AND DEPARTURE — MELAKA

By plane Melaka's airport (http://malaysiaairports.com.my) is 10km north of the city centre At the time of writing, the only flights available are to and from Singapore (4–5 weekly; 1hr). Irregular buses connect the airport to Melaka Sentral (every 30min; 40min), from where you'll have to change and catch a bus to the historical centre (every 30min; 20–30min). Taxi/Grab are options from the airport too.

By train Pulau Sebang/Tampin train station, with Komuter trains to KL, 38km north of Melaka (06 441 1034), is connected by irregular buses to Melaka Sentral, although the journey can take up to 1hr 30min as the bus stops frequently; it's much more convenient to catch a taxi (40min).
Destinations Alor Setar (1 daily; 7hr); Butterworth (1 daily; 6hr 20min); Gemas (for Jungle Railway; 6 daily; 35min); Ipoh (2 daily; 4hr 30min); Kuala Lumpur (hourly; 1hr 50min); Seremban (hourly; 30min).

By bus Melaka's bus station, Melaka Sentral, is just under 4km north of the centre, at the corner of Jalan Panglima Awang and Jalan Tun Razak, close to a large Tesco supermarket. The #17 bus (every 30min; 20–30min) from the domestic part of the station stops off at the Clock House as well as at Jalan Kabu at the western end of Jalan Hang Jebat; a taxi will take 15min or so to the centre, though you'll most likely save a bit by using Grab instead. Transnasional (http://transnasional.com.my) operates buses from Melaka Sentral to KLIA (12 daily; 3hr), with four daily services also departing from Mahkota Medical Centre, close to the Mahkota Parade Shopping Centre.
Destinations Alor Setar (4 daily; 7hr); Butterworth (6 daily; 6hr); Ipoh (5 daily; 4hr); Johor Bahru (1–2 hourly; 3–4hr); Kluang (11 daily; 2hr); Kota Bharu (2 daily; 10hr); KLIA (hourly; 2hr); Kuala Lumpur (1–2 hourly; 3hr); Kuala Terengganu (3 daily; 7hr); Kuantan (3 daily; 5hr); Mersing (5 daily; 4hr); Singapore (hourly; 4hr).

By ferry From the jetty on Jalan Quayside, ferries (http://indomalfastferry.com) head to Dumai in Sumatra (1 daily; 2hr). Tickets are best purchased at least a day in advance.

By car Melaka's streets are very narrow and the one-way system is awkward, so drivers should park at the first opportunity and get around the city by foot, bus, trishaw or taxi. One local car rental operator is Hawk, 34 Jalan Laksamana (Mon–Fri 8am–5.30pm; 06 283 7878, http://hawkrentacar.com.my).

GETTING AROUND

By bus There are several useful routes for visitors, departing from Melaka Sentral: #17 runs through the historical centre to Taman Melaka Raya and stops off at the entrance of the Portuguese Settlement.

By taxi or trishaw For longer journeys, taxis or the colourful disco trishaws are the best bet. Both cost roughly the same, and you can book trishaws for tours (see page 266). You should be able to get a trishaw around the Dutch Square or in front of the Taming Sari Revolving Tower; there's a taxi rank by the Mahkota Parade.

On foot Most places of interest lie within the compact historical centre, and so are best visited on foot.

INFORMATION AND TOURS

Tourist information The helpful Tourism Malaysia office is on the ground floor of Bangunan Surau Warisan Dunia on Dutch Square (daily 9am–6pm; 06 283 6220, http://malaysia.travel). There is a state tourist office at Melaka Sentral bus station (daily 9am–5.30pm; 06 288 1340; http://visitmelaka.com.my).

Duck Tours The Duck Tour uses an amphibious vehicle to explore Melaka on land and water. The main ticket office is by the Taming Sari Revolving Tower (daily 9am–6.30pm; 1hr; http://facebook.com/melaka.ducktours).

Trishaw tours A sightseeing tour by trishaw, covering the major sights, is easy to arrange.

Boat trips Boat trips up the river by Melaka River Cruise (http://melakarivercruise.my) set off from the jetty behind the Maritime Museum (daily 9am–11pm). Offering a good way to see the restored riverside area, the boat stops at numerous points along the river, taking you past the old Dutch quarter of red-roofed godowns (warehouses) as far as Kampung Morten.

ACCOMMODATION — SEE MAP PAGE 259

Melaka has a huge selection of **hotels** and guesthouses, including many that are good value and well kept, and a scattering of lovely boutique properties; there are even a couple of highly recommended **apartments**. Book ahead for Friday and Saturday nights, as Melaka is a popular weekend break destination – rates often rise by quite a bit too.

HOTELS

Casa del Rio 88 Jalan Kota Laksamana; http://casadelrio-melaka.com. This resort-style riverfront complex offers spacious well-appointed rooms with balconies, some with river views. The excellent restaurant (open to non-guests) serves traditional sweet and savoury Nyonya dishes at high tea, served in pretty tiffin boxes. $$$$

★ **Courtyard @ Heeren** 91 Jalan Tun Tan Cheng Lock; http://courtyardatheeren.com. The lobby of this boutique hotel sets the tone, with a soothing water feature, original marble floors and the owner's collection of antique wooden furniture. The welcoming rooms offer a delightful mix of old and new, with intricately carved bedsteads and flat-screen TVs, while the deluxe rooms feature heritage design with four-poster wooden beds and replica period tiles. $$$

★ **Jonker Boutique** 84 Jalan Tokong; http://jonkerboutiquehotel.com. Housed in a three-storey Art Deco building, the spacious rooms at this welcoming boutique hotel feature beautiful teak flooring and high ceilings. The central location, just a stone's throw from Jonker Walk, is a plus. Rates rise at the weekend. $$$

★ **Kapitan Kongsi** 53 Jalan KLJ 10, Taman Kota Laksamana; http://kapitankongsi.com. Set a little way west of town, this budget hotel is the star of a very interesting, redeveloped mock-colonial precinct. Rooms are a little small but quite lovely; make sure that you get one on the "street" side, so that you can see the charming, light-filled evening view, once you bang open your shutter windows. The town centre is a bit of a walk away (and one that gets boring fast), but staff can call you a Grab in no time; however, there are absolutely loads of places to eat and drink nearby, with an almost entirely tourist-free crowd, so you may well not want to go anywhere at all. $$

★ **The Majestic** 188 Jalan Bunga Raya; http://majesticmalacca.com. Located in a beautiful 1920s colonial mansion, the inviting rooms and hellishly expensive suites at this luxurious hotel feature polished timber floors, teakwood fittings and indulgent roll-top baths. The excellent spa offers therapies based on the healing heritage of the Peranakans, descendants of Chinese immigrants who intermarried with Malays; the restaurant offers traditional Nyonya cuisine, which combines Chinese cooking methods with Malay ingredients and spices. $$$$

The Opposite Place 18 Jalan Hang Lekiu; http://opposite-place.com. In a beautifully refurbished pre-World War II building, this boutique guesthouse features two sleek, individually designed suites – Opposite West has a living area with antique wooden furniture and a voyeuristic bathroom, while Opposite East has open-brick walls, hardwood floors and mock period armchairs. *Eat at 18 Café* downstairs (see page 268) serves excellent breakfast. $$$$

Puri 118 Jalan Tun Tan Cheng Lock; http://hotelpuri.com. Set in a beautifully restored Peranakan shophouse with a large foyer with polished marble floors, the rooms here are contemporary and stylish with hints of red and teak. The *Galeri Café*, open to non-guests, serves Peranakan and Western dishes to the soothing sound of the courtyard fountain. $$$

River Cruise 36 Jalan Kampung Pantai; http://rchotelmelaka.com. You know that you're staying somewhere fairly special when passers-by gaze up at your hotel. Acting as a large, old-school-institutional bookend to a riverside run of highly colourful buildings, this affordable hotel does look a little out of place, but its location couldn't be better, and *some* rooms (they're not all equal here) are quite pretty, too. $$

Shore 193 Jalan Persisiran Bunga Raya; http://theshorehotelmelaka.com. Part of Melaka's newest skyscraper development in the centre of town, this hotel has large rooms, suites and apartments in white with wooden finishes. Facilities include a sauna, steam room and pool, and numerous restaurants including the *SkyDeli* underneath the Sky Tower. Prices can absolutely plummet in quiet season, when this is up there with the best bargains in town. $$$

Styles 19 & 21 Lorong Hang Jebat; 06 288 1921. This spotless flashpackers' place features modern, vibrantly coloured rooms with cable TV, a/c and private bathrooms, set over four floors in the heart of town. There's a coffee and lounge area by the lobby, and a rooftop terrace. $$

HOSTELS AND GUESTHOUSES

Heeren House 1 Jalan Tun Tan Cheng Lock; 014 363 5218. Formerly a warehouse, a coffee shop, a family home and eventually a guesthouse, this is a pleasant choice right in the historical centre, offering spacious rooms with colonial and Peranakan furniture – some could do with a splash of paint here and there. Weekend surcharge applies. $$

Layang Layang 26 Jalan Tukang Besi; 06 292 2722. A lovely guesthouse with clean, welcoming rooms with parquet floors, set around a peaceful courtyard with a fishpond. The communal area is dotted with trinkets, including a guitar, the odd lantern and wooden giraffes; there are board games too. $

★ **Ola Hostel** 25 Jalan Tukang Besi; http://facebook.com/olalavanderia. Quirky hostel that's popular with travelling backpackers of a certain persuasion. Private rooms and dorms alike have some pretty interesting design elements – Christmas lights, brick barriers, dangling chains and the like, while there's bike rental, and a fantastic café too (see page 269). $

Swing & Pillows 28 Jalan Tukang Emas; http://swingandpillows.com. The excellent backpacker chain has opened up in Melaka, and instantly became hugely popular. Billing itself as a "co-living" space, it's inevitably fronted by a cafe-like space in which people can get their important laptop business done while draining something slowly. The rooms themselves are perhaps less interesting in design than one might expect, but they're comfortable enough. $

Tang House 88 Jalan Tokong; http://facebook.com. This welcoming, family-run guesthouse features very simple rooms with mattresses on the floor, as well as a/c rooms that are a steal; great rates for single travellers too. The nearby Jonker Walk karaoke stage means that it can get noisy on weekend evenings. $

V Space Guest House 94 Jalan Kampung Pantai; 019 289 1328. A relative newcomer (though set in a space previously used by other guesthouses) with a winning location, a great café space popular with guests and non-guests alike (see page 269), and a series of futuristic capsule berths – try to avoid those close to the door, unless you want passers-by on the street outside to see you dragging yourself out of bed. $

Wayfarer Guest House 104 Lorong Hang Jebat; 012 913 3992. Formerly a rubber trading house, this airy guesthouse offers spacious well-appointed a/c rooms with hardwood floors; room 6 has lovely views over the river and the Church of St Francis, while the large duplex room features a double bed and two twins on the mezzanine. Prices increase over the weekends. $$

APARTMENTS

45 Lekiu 45 Jalan Lekiu; http://45lekiu.com. This wonderfully restored Art Deco building is today a stylish two-floor apartment featuring bare-brick walls and sleek dark furnishings. There's a small yet inviting pool and a terrace with panoramic views over the city's rooftops. $$$$

EATING   SEE MAP PAGE 259

Melaka offers excellent dining, especially in **Chinatown**, where new and established restaurants, bars and cafés compete for the hungry tourists and locals. **Taman Melaka Raya** is fast catching up; it's also worth trying the area around **Jalan Kota Laksamana** southwest of Chinatown. For seafood, you could try the row of near-identical restaurants on the waterfront just beyond the Medan Portugis in the **Portuguese settlement**, where you can choose from the day's catch from around 7pm. Though it's rather overrated, you still shouldn't miss the chance to sample **Nyonya cuisine**; the emphasis is on spicy dishes using sour ingredients like tamarind, tempered by sweeter, creamy coconut milk. One particularly unusual ingredient is *buah keluak*, a nut that contains hydrogen cyanide (prussic acid), but which is harmless once cooked.

RESTAURANTS

★ **Baboon House** 89 Jalan Tun Tan Cheng Lock; http://facebook.com/thebaboonhouse. There are artworks and funky installations galore at this lovely art-café (the owner made most of them, and even the tables) with a courtyard dripping with greenery. The menu features seven types of burgers, made with chicken, lamb, beef or pork and served on home-made buns. Although the interior is as photogenic as Melaka eateries get (which is actually saying quite a lot), don't forget to check out the pretty gardens at the back. $$$

★ **Botanist Café** 41 Jalan Melaka Raya 8, Taman Melaka Raya; http://facebook.com/botanistveggie. Excellent, child-friendly, vegetarian café serving healthy organic dishes in a peaceful leafy interior. The Nyonya curry, made with cashew nuts instead of coconut cream, is a must, as is the *hoi lok feng*, a beautifully presented dish of brown rice with cabbage, beans, radish, ground nuts and other greens, accompanied by a healthy basil soup. $$

Eat at 18 18 Jalan Hang Lekiu; http://eatat18.com. Healthy, wholesome dishes are lovingly prepared at this little gem of a café, featuring open brick walls, chandeliers, books and artworks. Delicious home-made organic bread accompanies most dishes, from grilled salmon with salad to fresh roast chicken leg. Breakfasts are excellent, too, and there are sweet treats throughout the day such as home-made cheesecake and meringues with Häagen-Dazs ice cream and strawberry jam. $$$

Eleven Bistro & Restaurant 11 Jalan Hang Lekir; http://elevenbistro.com.my. This pleasant bistro serves a great mix of Portuguese and Malay dishes such as salted egg crab and Portuguese *sambal* prawns cooked with spicy chilli paste. It's also a good spot to grab a cocktail – in the evenings it morphs into a bar, with a house DJ after 10pm. $$$

Hakka Zhan 76 Jalan Laksamana 5; http://facebook.com/HakkaZhan. Genuine Hakka cuisine is served at this Chinese place just a short walk south of the historical centre, with a scarlet a/c interior featuring dangling Chinese lamps. Among the best sellers are *hakka* mutton and *hakka yong tau foo* (vegetables stuffed with pork paste). $$

★ **Pak Putra** 56 & 58 Jalan Kota Laksamana; 012 601 5876. Staggeringly good tandoori chicken is the main draw at this Pakistani restaurant, although all the dishes are exceptional, from the mutton *rogan josh* to the chicken curries, accompanied by fluffy *naan* bread prepared in front of you. It gets very busy on weekend evenings – make sure you arrive early. $$

Peranakan Mansion 108 Jalan Tun Tan Cheng Lock; 016 792 0000. One of the newer Nyonya restaurants in town, yet probably the best – it certainly looks the part, and service is very attentive too. Dishes can be surprisingly affordable, given the opulent, old-China look of the dining hall; unlike many other Nyonya places, they've gone for a modest roster of well-prepared meals, rather than an unwieldy please-everyone assortment. $$$

Salud Tapas 2 Jalan Tun Tan Cheng Lock; http://facebook.com/SALUDTAPAS. While we all know that outside Spain, the word "tapas" means "too small and too expensive", this is one of the better places to eat non-Asian food in town – a

fresh, funky setup that doubles as a cool bar. $$$$
Selvam 2 Jalan Temenggong; 06 281 9223. Consistently good Indian restaurant serving set meal banana leaf curries with rice, three types of vegetables and poppadums, and your choice of chicken, lamb, fish or seafood at very reasonable prices. $
V Space Guest House 94 Jalan Kampung Pantai; 019 289 1328. This guesthouse (see page 268) revolves around its café section, where the simple mains (chicken chop, spaghetti and assorted snack dishes) are thoroughly eclipsed by the drinks and desserts – decent coffee, a whole bunch of teas, and some delectable cakes and bakes. $

CAFÉS AND DESSERTS

Calanthe Art Café 11 Jalan Hang Kasturi; http://facebook.com/calanthe.melaka. Jam-packed with odds and ends from vinyl discs to recycled condensed milk tins, this laidback café is a great spot for a morning coffee (there are thirteen types, one from each Malaysian state) or a bite for lunch; the Baba chef rustles up a mean *laksa* and *ponteh chicken* (drumstick cooked with palm sugar and potatoes). The water feature, wicker chairs and soothing background tunes add to the place's easy-going atmosphere. $$
★ **The Daily Fix Café** 55 Jalan Hang Jebat; http://facebook.com/thedailyfixcafe. Not too obvious to spot, as it's located at the back of a shop, this relaxed, absolutely gorgeous café offers excellent home-made goodies including pancakes with maple syrup or honey, and plenty of home-baked cakes including cheesecake and brownies. Wash them down with a refreshing lemongrass drink, or coffee that's up there with the best in town. Recently, there has been a pivot towards actual meals here – if you're in the mood for a pasta or Western breakfast dish, you may well not want to limit yourself to coffee and dessert. $$
Limau Limau 9 Jalan Hang Lekiu; http://facebook.com/limaulimaucafemelaka. This itsy-bitsy café, playing mellow background tunes and with wooden stools lining the bar, serves great freshly squeezed juices (try the pineapple and passion fruit) and light lunches including toasted focaccia sandwiches and lasagne. There's also a cosy room upstairs featuring mismatched furniture and a motley range of lamps. $$
★ **Mods Café** 14 Jalan Tukang Emas; 012 756 4441. The decor of this café takes its inspiration from 1960s British mod culture; the music playing is often from this period too, though the owners have eclectic musical tastes and do like to mix things up, while occasionally there's live music too. As for what you can drink, the emphasis is on coffees, roasted and brewed on the premises, and served from a bright orange VW camper van; the cakes are also tempting. In general, a very cool place, though there isn't much room to sit. $$
Ola Lavanderia Café 25 Jalan Tukang Besi; http://facebook.com/olalavanderia. This cosy little minimalist café in the hostel (see page 267) also doubles as a laundry. It's a great spot to grab a morning coffee and a freshly baked croissant while you wait for your washing; light Western meals are served, including chicken and mushroom pies, Caesar salads and all-day breakfasts. $$

STREET FOOD AND HAWKER CENTRES

Jonker 88 88 Jalan Hang Jebat; http://facebook.com/jonker88. This well-established hawker-style restaurant is renowned for its tasty *laksa*, which comes in three main varieties: sour-spicy, coconut spicy or a mix of the two. The *baba cendol*, a popular Malaysian dessert made with coconut milk, jelly noodles, palm sugar and shaved ice, is a sweet tooth's delight. $
Low Yong Moh 32 Jalan Tukang Emas; 06 282 1235. This excellent little place just opposite the mosque rustles up outstanding prawn, pork and fish dim sum steamed in front of your very eyes; the buns stuffed with pork are also a real winner. Mornings only. $
Lung Ann Refreshments 91 Lorong Hang Jebat. This buzzing café and restaurant functions as a popular noodle stall in the morning, a hugely popular chicken satay hangout in the afternoons and a café throughout the day. The delicious *kaya* toast (with coconut jam) is worth trying for breakfast, the duck noodles and fish ball noodles are a real hit, and the crowds are drawn in the afternoons for the sizzling charcoal satay, traditionally dipped in a peanut and pineapple sauce. $
Makan Avenue 26 Jalan Kampung Hulu. Modern hawker centre with everything from clay pot to *kuay teow*, and popular with locals of all ages. Don't miss the outdoor stalls, selling fish and fruit juice by the riverside. $
Suukee Satay Perniagaan Complex; http://facebook.com/hainanesesuukeesatay. The best satay place in town – a Hainanese-style joint, tracing its origins back to the 1960s – is unfortunately a fair walk from the centre, but it's worth visiting. They don't re-use sauce or sticks here, and the *otak-otak* (fish cake grilled in a leaf) is just as good as the skewered meat. Unfortunately, it closes way too early for a satay-stick place. $$

DRINKING AND NIGHTLIFE   SEE MAP PAGE 259

Melaka's **nightlife** is no great shakes; most places tend to shut at around 1am. Cafés and bars spill into Jalan Hang Lekir, the liveliest street in **Chinatown**; more places are also opening up along the revitalized riverfront, and **Taman Melaka Raya** also holds some lively places for a drink, along with numerous seedy karaoke bars.
Geographer Café 83 Jalan Hang Jebat; http://geographer.com.my. A so-so restaurant by day, this turns into one of the town's better bars by night; grab a pint of draught Guinness and clamber up the stairs to the attractive upper level,

where you'll see lanterns and colonial architecture out of the window, instead of having Melaka's annoying traffic zip past your feet.

Reggae on the River 88 Lorong Hang Jebat; http://facebook.com/melakariverside. Both of the salient elements of this bar's name are proven correct as soon as you sit down. For a riverside spot, drinks can be affordable, though do note that cocktails (which have a couple of shots of spirit inside) cost more than bottles of soju (which are essentially small bottles of half-strength spirit) – seems like a no-brainer, and you might be a no-brainer too if you have more than three.

★ **Sin Hiap Lin** 5 Kampung Jawa. If you want a regular drink, go to the riverside – easy as. Here's a place to hunt down if you want something a little different, a little local, and don't mind a "bar" that shuts before 6pm. It's not officially a bar but a century-old shop at which you not only *can* drink, but are actively encouraged to do so; like a kindly, cheeky aunt, the owner will offer curious concoctions made from rose, bamboo and the like, served with ice if you please, and peanuts on the side, even if you don't please.

SHOPPING   SEE MAP PAGE 259

Melaka's Chinatown was once famed for its **antiques**, but these days you'll find few bargains. If the item you're thinking of buying is a genuine antique rather than a modern reproduction, check that it can be exported legally and fill in an official clearance form; the dealer should provide you with this. For more general shopping there are plenty of options along Jalan Bunga Raya and Jalan Munshi Abdullah; the **malls** – including Dataran Pahlawan, Mahkota Parade and Hatten Square – are concentrated in the south of the centre.

Colour Beads 80 Jalan Tun Tan Cheng Lock; http://colourbeads.com. Cute place selling Nyonya-style handmade beaded footwear, with designs across the spectrum from traditional to modern.

Joe's Design Handcrafted Jewellery 6 Jalan Tun Tan Cheng Lock; 019 656 5619. Handmade artisan jewellery produced by a Melaka native – is rather more interesting and imaginative than most of the city's mass-produced handicrafts.

Malaqa House 70 Jalan Tun Tan Cheng Lock; 013 363 5180. It describes itself as a museum but it's actually a shop and much of what is on sale – mostly furniture – is exquisite. Well worth a visit.

Tham Siew Inn Artist Gallery 49 Jalan Tun Tan Cheng Lock; http://thamsiewinn.com. This family-run gallery offers arts and crafts, including limited-edition prints, hand-crafted Chinese "chops" (seals for documents), impressionist watercolours and pencil sketches.

Wah Aik Shoemaker 92 Jalan Tun Tan Cheng Lock; 06 284 9726. This store was long renowned for making silk shoes, known as "lotus feet shoes", for the cruel Chinese tradition of foot binding. With the practice no longer legal, the shoes are lined up in the window as slightly macabre souvenirs.

DIRECTORY

Banks Banks include Maybank at 227 Jalan Melaka Raya 6, Public Bank at 60-68 Jalan Laksamana and HSBC, north of the centre at 777 Jalan Hang Tuah.

Cinema The Golden Screen Cinema on the top floor of Dataran Pahlawan Melaka Megamall shows English-language films.

Hospital Hospital Besar Melaka (General Hospital) is in the north of town on Jalan Mufti Haji Khalil (06 282 2344, http://jknmelaka.moh.gov.my). The well-equipped Mahkota Medical Centre is at 3 Mahkota Melaka, Jalan Merdeka (06 285 2999, http://mahkotamedical.com).

Police The police station is on Jalan Merdeka, near the Maritime Museum (06 284 2222).

Post office There is a post office branch on Jalan Laksamana just a few steps from Christ Church, while the GPO is inconveniently situated on the way to Ayer Keroh on Jalan Bukit Baru (both Mon–Fri 8.30am–5.30pm, Sat 8.30am–1pm).

Sport There's a public swimming pool in the shadow of the Taming Sari Revolving Tower on Jalan Kota.

Visa extensions The immigration office is out in Ayer Keroh, on floors 1–3 of Blok Pentadbiran, Kompleks Kementerian Dalam Negeri, Jalan Seri Negeri (Mon–Fri 7.30am–5pm; 06 232 2662).

Around Melaka

While there's more than enough to keep you occupied in Melaka, there are also a few popular getaways within day-trip distance. These include several opportunities to see animals: the tranquil coastal village of **Padang Kemunting** is a hatching site for hawksbill turtles, while **Ayer Keroh** has several wildlife parks and cultural attractions. Alternatively, the nearby island **Besar** provides an opportunity to feel some sand between your toes, even if the sea is fairly polluted.

Padang Kemunting Turtle Conservation and Information Centre

24km up the coast northwest of Melaka • Free • http://marinepark.dof.gov.my • Drive north towards Klebang Besar and proceed to Sungai Udang and then on to Masjid Tanah; from here take the junction to Padang Kemunting, commonly also referred to as Pengkalan Balak; or bus from Melaka Sentral to Masjid Tanah (every 30min; 1hr 30min), then taxi 8km; or taxi/Grab from Melaka Sentral

Padang Kemunting is one of the last nesting areas of the hawksbill turtle and the painted terrapin in southern Malaysia. Although open all year, it's only worth visiting the **turtle centre** during hatchling season (March–Sept). It's a friendly place with lots of information, including an introductory video about the turtle population of Melaka.

ACCOMMODATION AND EATING   PADANG KEMUNTING

There are a handful of places to stay near the sanctuary, plus several Malay **seafood restaurants** along the shore and a couple of convenience stores.

Ismah Beach Resort Next door to Padang Kemunting Turtle Sanctuary; http://ismahresort.com. This simple resort has a restaurant and swimming pool, and is very close to the turtle centre; if the turtles appear at night, the centre can let you know by prior arrangement. $$

Ayer Keroh

Despite its position adjacent to the North–South Expressway, 14km north of Melaka, **AYER KEROH** is a leafy recreational area with numerous attractions and a handful of places to stay. Although it's much cheaper to visit by bus, the attractions are quite spread out across both sides of the expressway so if you plan to visit several then it's better to rent a car or charter a taxi for the duration of the trip.

In addition to the attractions listed separately below, you may wish to pop into the **Botanical Gardens**, an open-all-hours tract of woodland set aside for walking and picnicking. Malaysia's oldest **zoo** (and second-largest) is also here, but since it prides itself on big cats, who almost always suffer in zoos, you might not want to bother.

Malaysia Heritage Studios

Lebuh Ayer Keroh • Charge • http://malaysiaheritagestudios.com • Bus #19 from Melaka Sentral (hourly; 45min) drops you off at the Melaka Zoo, from where it's a short walk; it's easiest, however, to take a taxi from Melaka

Ayer Keroh's most interesting attraction, **Malaysia Heritage Studios**, holds full-sized reconstructions of typical houses from all thirteen Malay states and the other members of the Association of Southeast Asian Nations – the complex was once known as "Mini Malaysia & ASEAN". Some buildings have displays inside and sell food, drink and souvenirs; cultural shows are also staged at the park's open-air arena.

World's Bees Museum

Jelan Taman Botanikal • Daily 9am–6pm • 06 293 0035

A quirky, well-designed little place, the **World's Bees Museum** is more like a shop than an educational facility, but it's still worth popping by if you have time; there are indeed a few exhibitions about honey production around the world, though for many it's the free honey samples, and an opportunity to buy more as souvenirs, that make the place worth visiting.

Melaka Wonderland

Lebuh Ayer Keroh, Hang Tuah Jaya • Charge • http://melakawonderland.com.my

The **Melaka Wonderland** water park can provide a welcome break on a hot day. Attractions include the Tornado Chaser (where you start in a giant bowl before passing through a darkened tunnel and into a pool) and a wide range of twisting and straight slides, as well as more sedate swimming pools. The place is quiet on weekdays outside school holidays.

ARRIVAL AND DEPARTURE   AYER KEROH

By bus Town bus #19 (hourly; 45min) from Melaka Sentral.
By taxi A taxi from Melaka won't cost much, and a Grab cab will usually be even less.

ACCOMMODATION AND EATING

INB Resort Lot 3169 Sempang Padang Keladi, Lebuh Ayer Keroh; http://inbresort.com. An affordable option, 15–20min on foot from the Malaysia Heritage Studios. With comfortable rooms in pink concrete buildings arrayed around a pool, it's very popular with local families. Breakfast is only served at the weekend, but there's a small place to eat outside. $\overline{\$\$}$

Philea 2940 Jalan Ayer Keroh, off Jalan Plaza Tol; http://philea.com.my. The stylish cabins at this site, built from Russian pine logs and with stone in the bathrooms, make great use of natural materials – although this does mean that ground-floor rooms can be a bit noisy. There's a spa, sauna and gym; the two Royal Villas have their own swimming pools. $\overline{\$\$\$}$

Besar Island

If you're looking for a beach getaway and don't have time to go further afield, then **BESAR ISLAND** ("Big Island", though in reality it covers just 16 square kilometres) may fit the bill. The island's beaches and hilly scenery are pleasant, although the waters are fairly polluted. Located 5km off the coast of Melaka, Besar Island was known as the burial ground of passing Muslim traders and missionaries; as a result, locals – particularly Indian Muslims – see the island as a holy place and visitors are asked to behave accordingly.

ARRIVAL AND DEPARTURE   BESAR ISLAND

By ferry Two jetties southeast of Melaka have boats to the island; neither are on any bus routes, but are within cheap taxi range. The Anjung Batu jetty sees regular ferries (6 daily, starting 8.30am, last boat back 7pm), while the Pengkalan Pernu jetty in Umbai has boats only on request.

ACCOMMODATION AND EATING

Putera Island Resort Besar Island; http://puteraislandresort.com. You are unlikely to want to spend much time in your room, but this resort might tempt you into doing so – the rooms are spacious and attractive, and sport little balconies from which you can admire the surrounding greenery. They also offer a range of water sport activities and boast a worthy on-site restaurant, which also makes it the island's best place to eat. $\overline{\$\$\$}$

From Melaka to Johor Bahru

The journey from Melaka southeast along **Route 5** to Johor Bahru covers just over 200km. The first 45km, as far as the town of **Muar**, passes through verdant countryside dotted with neatly kept timber stilt houses in some of Malaysia's prettiest kampungs. Further south, the towns of Batu Pahat and Pontian Kecil hold scant interest (the former, slightly inland, has a reputation as a red-light resort for Singaporeans). If you want to stop anywhere else before Johor Bahru and Singapore, aim instead for **Kukup**, right at the southern end of the west coast and terrific for seafood.

To get to Johor Bahru in a hurry, skip scenic Route 5 and use the **North–South Expressway** instead. From Melaka, you can head north to the expressway via Ayer Keroh; it's also straightforward to join the expressway from Muar (take the Bukit Pasir road for about 20km).

Muar

Also known as Bandar Maharani, the old port town of **MUAR** is a calm and elegant place that attracts few tourists, even though it rewards a day's exploration. Legend has it that Paramesvara, the fifteenth-century founder of Melaka, fled here from Singapore to establish his kingdom on the southern bank of the Muar River, before being persuaded to choose Melaka. The town later became an important port in the Johor empire (see page 274), as well as a centre for the sentimental Malay folk-pop called **ghazal music**, and its **dialect** is considered the purest Bahasa Malaysia in the Peninsula.

Today, Muar's commercial centre looks like any other, with Chinese shophouses and *kedai kopis* lining its streets. Turn right out of the **bus station**, however, following the river as the road turns into Jalan Peteri, and you'll find Muar's **Neoclassical colonial buildings**. The Custom House and Government Offices (Bangunan Sultan Abu Bakar) are on your right, and the District Police Office and Courthouse on your left; they still have an air of confidence and prosperity dating back to the town's days as a British administrative centre. Completed in 1930, the graceful **Masjid Jamek Sultan Ibrahim** successfully combines Western and Moorish styles of architecture. Further along Jalan Petri you'll pass a jetty on your right, from where irregular **river cruises** depart.

ARRIVAL AND DEPARTURE — MUAR

By bus The bus station, on Jalan Maharani, is served by buses from Melaka's Sentral station (every 30min; 1hr 30min).

By taxi You can conceivably, and affordably, get here by taxi from Melaka.

ACCOMMODATION

Muo Boutique 1 Jalan Petri; http://muoboutique.com. Fancy-looking new kid on the block, with a beautiful colonial exterior that you'll probably end up taking photos of; inside there's a shop and café/chillout area, and some very pretty, though slightly small rooms, while up on top you'll find a chillout terrace. $\overline{\$\$}$

Streetview 11 & 13 Jalan Ali; http://streetviewhotel.com.my. One of the town's oldest hotels, in a beautiful colonial building, featuring clean and comfortable a/c rooms. There are two more properties in the same chain, *Riverview* and *Townview*, both with equally well-kept rooms. $\overline{\$\$}$

EATING

Muar has a good reputation for its **coffee** and its **food**, particularly *otak-otak* (fish dumplings) and *mee bandung*. Another local speciality is satay (particularly satay *perut*, made from intestines) for breakfast.

Abu Bakar Hanipah 69a Jalan Abdullah. Up to 30kg of noodles are produced here every day; the speciality is *mee bandung* (noodles, beansprouts, egg, beef and tofu served in a sauce made from prawn, chillies and beef soup), which has been selling since 1961, and is regarded as the best in town. Closes before evening truly begins. $\overline{\$}$

Bentayan Hawker Centre Jalan Bentayan. Located at the end of the street, the stalls here – some of which have been operating for decades – serve up a wide range of dishes including Muar's famous colourful steamed rice cakes, dim sum, *otak-otak* and much more. $\overline{\$}$

Muar Soup House 47 Jalan Sisi. Another hugely popular spot, this time serving sup kambing, a hearty broth made with goat meat, celery, candlenut and lime leaf – come join the crowds, any time from noon until early morn. $\overline{\$}$

Kukup

The small fishing community of **KUKUP**, 60km southwest of Johor Bahru and 20km south of Pontian Kecil along Route 5, is a regular stop for the Singapore package-tour trade. Busloads of tourists arrive to see the old stilt houses built over the murky river and to sample Kukup's real attraction, the **seafood**: the town's single tumbledown street is packed with restaurants.

ARRIVAL AND DEPARTURE — KUKUP

By bus and taxi If you are travelling from Johor Bahru, there are no direct buses, so you need to catch a bus to Pontian Kecil (every 15min; 1hr) and then take a taxi.

By ferry The jetty at Kukup was, for many years, a little-known exit point from Malaysia to Indonesia, though services to Tanjung Balai on Karimun island had ceased at the time of writing – it might be worth checking to see whether they've resurfaced, but when ferry routes stop in South East Asia (or basically anywhere), they tend to stop for good.

ACCOMMODATION

Kukup is a small and compact town, and most travellers only stay for a few hours. If you do choose to overnight, you will easily find a bed; virtually all the **houses** double as basic guesthouses and restaurants. Accommodation is normally for groups of eight or more, but with a bit of bargaining you may well be able to persuade them otherwise – most people would rather their rooms didn't go empty.

Kukup Mangrove Floating Chalet Central Kukup, by the pier; 012 745 2452. One of the more oddball places to stay in the country, allowing you to stay not just by the sea, but over it. Rooms have been somewhat given somewhat racy designs (cushioned walls, and the like), while meals are usually included, as are mahjong tables and karaoke systems (in the rooms), and a trip to a fish farm. It's aimed at locals and visiting Singaporeans, and as such quite a fascinating peek into local life; you can forget about decent wi-fi for a while, though. $$$

EATING

New Kukup Seafood Restaurant 1 Kukup Laut; 07 696 0216. You are spoiled for choice for seafood restaurants in Kukup, but this large waterfront restaurant – complete with hanging lanterns – is one of the better ones. It serves some excellent Chinese-style seafood dishes – fresh crayfish, crab, baby squid and cuttlefish are accompanied by stir-fried vegetables including pak choi, bean sprouts and green tea shoots. $$$

Johor Bahru

The southernmost Malaysian city of any size, **JOHOR BAHRU** – or simply **JB** – is the main gateway into **Singapore**, linked to the city-state by a **causeway** carrying a road, a railway, and the pipes through which Singapore imports its fresh water. Every day around one hundred thousand vehicles travel across the causeway (the newer **second crossing** from Geylang Patah, 20km west of JB, is much less used because of its higher tolls), and the ensuing traffic, noise and smog affects most of downtown.

The city has been moulded by its proximity to Singapore, for better or for worse – it has the air of both a border town and a boom town. The vast majority of visitors are **day-trippers**, many drawn by the cheap shopping and the duty-free zone to the east of the city centre. JB's environs are also being transformed by **Iskandar Puteri**, a vast, Singapore-backed project to create, essentially, a new city west of the existing one. It boasts industrial zones, universities, leisure facilities (notably Legoland Malaysia), and a glut of expensive property developments.

Brief history

Johor Bahru stands with Melaka as one of the country's most historic sites. Chased from its seat of power by the Portuguese in 1511, the Melakan court decamped to the Riau Archipelago, south of modern Singapore, before upping sticks again in the 1530s and shifting to the upper reaches of the Johor River. There they endured a century of offensives by both the Portuguese and the Acehnese of northern Sumatra.

Stability was finally achieved by courting the friendship of the Dutch in the 1640s, and the kingdom of Johor blossomed into a thriving trading entrepôt. By the end of the century, though, the rule of the tyrannical and decadent **Sultan Mahmud** had halted Johor's pre-eminence among the Malay kingdoms, and piracy was causing a decline in trade. In 1699, Sultan Mahmud was assassinated by his own nobles while returning from prayers. With the Melaka-Johor dynasty finally over, successive power struggles crippled the kingdom.

Immigration of the Bugis peoples to Johor eventually eclipsed the power of the sultans, and though the Bugis were finally chased out by the Dutch in 1784, the kingdom was a shadow of its former self. The Johor-Riau empire – and the Malay world – was split in two, with the Strait of Malacca forming the dividing line, following the Anglo-Dutch Treaty of 1824. As links with the court in Riau faded, Sultan Ibrahim assumed power, amassing a fortune based upon hefty profits culled from plantations. He established his administrative headquarters in the fishing village of Tanjung Puteri, which his son Abu Bakar – widely regarded as the father of modern Johor – later renamed Johor Bahru ("New Johor").

Downtown

JB is a sprawling city, and many of the administrative offices have been moved out of the centre to **Kota Iskandar** in the west. Most places of interest to visitors, though, are still **downtown** or close to the **waterfront** near the Singapore causeway. The downtown area blends the scruffy with the modern: the claustrophobic alleys of the sprawling market are within a few paces of thoroughly contemporary shopping malls such as **City Square**. Close by, the huge **CIQ** (Customs, Immigration and Quarantine) complex – built to streamline travel between JB and Singapore – includes **JB Sentral** station, combining bus and train terminals.

Arguably the most interesting part of the area, though, is southwest of the CIQ complex, on and around **Jalan Tan Hiok Nee** and **Jalan Dhoby**. Formerly quite seedy, these streets have been tidied up and are now at the centre of a vibrant shopping and dining scene.

Sri Mariamman Temple

Jalan Tun Abdul Razak, south of City Square • Free

The **Sri Mariamman Temple** lends a welcome splash of colour to JB's cityscape. Underneath its *gopuram*, and beyond the two gatekeepers on horseback who guard the temple, stand vividly depicted figures from the Hindu pantheon. Shops outside the

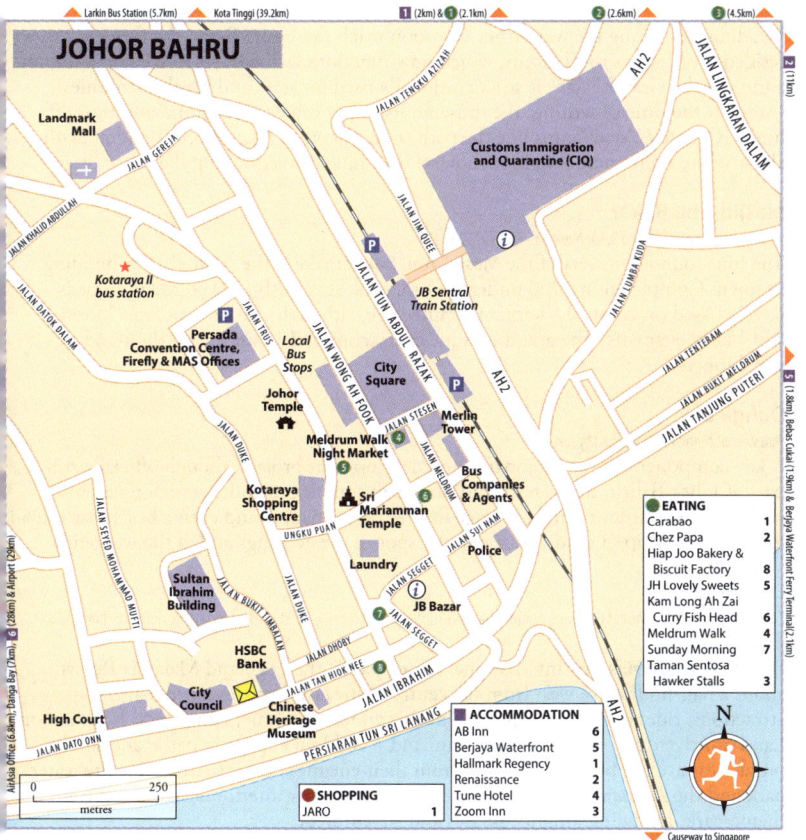

temple sell Bollywood movies and garlands of flowers used in worship, while on the street you can have your fortune told using cowrie shells.

Around the seafront

The views across to Singapore from the **seafront**, just a short walk from Sri Mariamman Temple, are doubly impressive after the cramped streets of the city centre. Several interesting attractions lie on or around Jalan Ibrahim, while just north of here is the fortress-like **Sultan Ibrahim Building**; formerly the home of the state government, which has been moved west to Kota Iskandar, the building is eventually scheduled to become a museum.

Chinese Heritage Museum
42 Jalan Ibrahim • Charge • http://jb-tionghua.org.my

As the name suggests, the **Chinese Heritage Museum** focuses on the Chinese contribution to the founding and development of Johor Bahru, and specifically on the production of gambier (a tropical shrub traditionally used in leather tanning and textile dyeing) and pepper, both of which were the economic lifeline of the Chinese community in the nineteenth century.

Royal Abu Bakar Museum
Jalan Tun Dr Ismail, the western continuation of Jalan Ibrahim

Heading west along the waterfront you soon reach the Istana Besar, the former residence of Johor's royal family, which now functions as the **Royal Abu Bakar Museum**, although the Grand Palace is still occasionally used for state and royal ceremonies – and, at the time of writing, the museum itself was under renovation, and thus off limits. Ornate golden lamps line the path to the Istana, a magnificent building with chalk-white walls and a low, blue roof, set on a hillock overlooking the Johor Straits.

Masjid Abu Bakar
5min walk west of Royal Abu Bakar Museum • Free • 07 223 4935

The four rounded towers of the **Masjid Abu Bakar** make it the most elegant building in town. Completed in 1900 under the orders of Sultan Abu Bakar, the mosque is largely based on colonial Victorian architecture, although also incorporates Moorish and Malay elements. The grand mosque can accommodate up to two thousand worshippers.

Danga Bay
5km west of centre • Best reached by taxi

A key component of the Iskandar Puteri development project, though officially still part of Johor Bahru, the waterfront **Danga Bay** complex includes several restaurants, stalls offering outdoor dining, a stage for live performances and even a beach bar (on an unappealing scrap of sand). It's a popular spot in the evenings and at the weekend.

Legoland
7 Jalan Legoland, 23km west of the centre centre • Charge • http://legoland.com.my • Best reached by taxi, though some hotels run shuttles

Billed as "Malaysia's first international theme park", the Legoland Malaysia Resort, about a half-hour drive west from the centre of the city, features more than 70 attractions, rides and shows. Split up into six zones – Technic, Kingdoms, Imagination, Land of Adventure, Lego City and Miniland – children engage in battle and solve puzzles to save the brick-shaped folk from their enemies. There's also an on-site water park and the *Legoland Hotel*, where the rooms take their interior design motif from the theme park, including knights, pirates and adventurers.

GETTING FROM JOHOR BAHRU TO SINGAPORE

There are several ways to head into Singapore from Johor Bahru, and vice versa. Oddly, facilities are generally far better on the Malaysian side.

BY TRAIN

The most obvious route to Singapore is to use the **train** from JB Sentral (5 daily; 5min); the problem is that this only takes you to Singapore's Woodlands station just across the causeway, and it's another's hour's journey to reach the city centre by bus and rail, since Woodlands station isn't on any MRT lines. Some find it a less stressful experience than travelling by bus, though carriages can be full (and tickets therefore sold out) at peak times. This will change in 2027, when the Johor Bahru–Singapore Rapid Transit System Link is scheduled to be up and running (though the date has kept slipping; initially it was supposed to be ready by 2019); this will connect Woodlands North (on Singapore's Thomson-East Coast MRT Line) to Bukit Chagar, a purpose-built station near JB Sentral.

BY BUS

It is easier and faster, though not always much fun, to get to downtown Singapore by bus. Starting from **Larkin bus station**, north of town, you can catch SBS #170X or #170 (daily 5am–midnight), or the faster yellow Causeway Link #CW1 and #CW2 services. All buses then proceed to the **CIQ** (Customs, Immigration and Quarantine) complex; at this point you need to get off the bus and clear customs, before getting on another to complete the journey to Singapore (take your luggage off the bus, keep your ticket and get on the same type of bus on the other side). If you're already in downtown Johor Bahru, simply board the bus at **JB Sentral**, which is part of the CIQ complex, and complete immigration formalities before you buy your ticket.

Once through customs, the Causeway Link buses run nonstop to Kranji MRT (#CW1) or Queen Street (#CW2); the SBS services go to Kranji MRT, with the #170 continuing to Little India and terminating at Queen Street, near Bugis MRT. There are also Transtar buses to **Changi Airport** from Larkin (hourly; 1hr 20min).

The problem with all of these services is that they can be absolutely rammed – long queues form at rush hour, and buses can end up with far more people than are legally allowed on board. This happens on the Singapore side, too, and it can be far worse there, since finding the right queue after the first border check can be a stressful experience – even a surprisingly dangerous one, with escalators disgorging crowds into pens that are already full, and frequently having to be shut down.

BY TAXI

Perhaps the best overall way to reach downtown Singapore is by **taxi** from outside JB Sentral station; shared cabs are often available too, though you'll have to ask around, since the situation keeps changing.

ARRIVAL AND DEPARTURE   JOHOR BAHRU

By plane Senai Airport (http://senaiairport.com) is 28km north of the city. Taxis connect with the city centre; bus #333 travels to Larkin bus station (45min), while the white Causeway Link airport shuttle bus (http://causewaylink.com.my) serves JB Sentral (5 daily; 35min).
Destinations Ipoh (1–2 daily; 1hr); Kota Kinabalu (2–4 daily; 2hr 20min); Kuala Lumpur (International; 13 daily; 1hr); Kuala Lumpur (Subang; 3 daily; 1hr); Kuching (5 daily; 1hr 30min); Langkawi (3 weekly; 1hr 20min); Miri (1 daily; 2hr); Penang (5–6 daily; 1hr 10min); Sibu (1–2 daily; 1hr 40min).

By train JB Sentral train station is part of the JB Sentral terminal on Jalan Tun Abdul Razak, just across the road from CIQ (Customs, Immigration and Quarantine complex). You'll have to arrive slightly early for trains making the short hop to Singapore, since you have to pass through customs and security; the process is far more pleasant on the Malaysian side.
Destinations Bekok (for Endau Rompin National Park; 3 daily; 3hr); Gemas (for northbound trains; 4 daily; 4hr

50min); Jerantut (1 daily; 8hr 40min); Kuala Lipis (1 daily; 9hr 40min); Wakaf Bharu (for Kota Bharu; 1 daily; 16hr); Singapore (Woodlands; every hour or so; 5min).

By long-distance bus Larkin bus station, on Jalan Geruda, 5km north of the centre, is used by most long-distance services. Buy tickets online (http://redbus.my and http://easybook.com are both recommended), or try the row of bus company offices running along the side of the Merlin Tower building in the city centre.

Destinations Alor Setar (4 daily; 10hr); Batu Pahat (every 15min; 2hr); Butterworth (8 daily; 12hr); Dungun (2 daily; 9hr); Ipoh (8 daily; 7hr); Klang (6 daily; 4hr 30min); Kota Bharu (3 daily; 9hr); Kuala Lumpur (every 15–30min; 5hr); Kuala Perlis (2 daily; 12hr); Kuala Terengganu (4 daily; 8hr); Kuantan (4 daily; 6hr); Melaka (every 30min; 3hr 30min); Mersing (10 daily; 2hr 30min); Muar (every 30min; 3hr); Segamat (hourly; 3hr); Seremban (hourly; 3hr); Singapore (every 10min; 1hr).

By local bus Buses heading east start from the JB Sentral combined bus and train terminal; local buses heading west run from around City Square.

By ferry Ferries from Tanjung Pinang (1–2 daily; 3hr) and Batam Island (6–9 daily; 2hr) in Indonesia arrive at ferry terminal, part of the Berjaya Waterfront Hotel complex 4km east of central JB; book tickets on http://berjayawaterfront.com.my, or the usual ticketing engines. Fuel taxes and seaport charges will be applicable.

By taxi Taxis are available at JB Sentral station. Shared taxis to Singapore are often the best way to travel between the countries.

Car rental Avis, 15 Jalan Dato Abdullah Tahir (07 331 7644, http://avis.com); Hertz is based in Menara Ansar at 65 Jalan Trus (07 223 7520, http://hertz.com) or at the airport.

INFORMATION

Tourist information JOTIC (Johor Tourist Information Centre; 07 222 3590) has branches at Senai Airport, JB Sentral and CIQ.

ACCOMMODATION SEE MAP PAGE 275

JB's manufacturing boom means the city attracts more business travellers than tourists, so **hotel** prices tend to be on the high side. The city's budget and mid-range hotels are mostly just outside the city centre; some of the cheapest (not listed here) double as brothels.

CITY CENTRE

Berjaya Waterfront 88 Jalan Ibrahim Sultan; http://berjayahotel.com. Enormous waterfront property with indoor spa and outdoor pool that stretches out into the Strait. The rooms are a little tired but the common areas are spick and span – and thanks to its position near the ferry terminal, the property is basically its own duty-free zone, so the hotel bars and mini nightclub with live band have some of the cheapest hotel drinks in Malaysia. $$$

Hallmark Regency 16 Jalan Harimau; http://hotelhallmark.com. Not exactly well located, and pretty old-fashioned (mostly in a good way), this tallish hotel is great value nonetheless, with large, carpetted rooms, free breakfast, and shuttle services to Legoland and elsewhere. $$

Renaissance 2 Jalan Permas 11, Bandar Baru Permas Jaya; http://marriott.com. Located just ten minutes from the Singapore–Malaysia border, this five-star hotel offers modern, tastefully furnished rooms and state of the art facilities, including an outdoor swimming pool, spa, fitness centre and business centre. $$$$

DANGA BAY

Tune Hotel Danga Bay, Jalan Skudai; http://tunehotels.com. This popular chain of budget hotels offers modern, clean and practical rooms, with add-ons such as TV and a/c. There's also a good-value restaurant, but the location – close to nothing in particular other than the bus terminal – is a major drawback. $

Zoom Inn Unit 7, 8 & 9, Block 7, Danga Bay, Jalan Skudai; 018 788 8802. Don't be fooled by the slightly drab exterior – this hotel in Danga Bay is a pleasant surprise. Rooms are neat and welcoming with quirky colourful wall drawings and modern bathrooms; there's also a small convenience store on the ground floor. $$

SENAI

AB Inn 22 Jalan Cyber 16, Senai; 018 766 6570. Large hotel near the airport, with rooms usually available for super-low rates – it's only really of use if you're flying in or out at a late hour, though given some of the flight times, being within walking distance of the terminal (there's also a bus stop) might be quite handy for some travellers. Rooms are just fine, the lobby is pleasingly fake-grand, and there are places to eat and buy groceries just steps away. $

EATING SEE MAP PAGE 275

There are scores of great international **restaurants** in JB, and some good street food on offer. The most interesting little cafés and restaurants are to the west of Jalan Segget, which also has its own **night market**.

RESTAURANTS

Carabao 16 Jalan Dato Abdullah Tahir; http://facebook.com/CarabaoThaiRestaurant. The setting of this Thai restaurant is particularly pleasant, with seating in an airy open-fronted area featuring natural materials and decorated with hanging lanterns, draped scarves and shell wind chimes singing in the breeze. The extensive menu includes a range of fish dishes (fried, steamed or curried), as well as seafood, chicken, and sweet and sour beef. $\overline{\underline{\$\$}}$

★ **Chez Papa** 38 & 40 Jalan Jaya, Taman Maju Jaya; http://chezpapa.com.my. This French bistro and wine bar offers traditional home cooking in a particularly welcoming interior that bursts with character; customers can sit at the bar lined with dangling wine bottle lamps, or at rustic wooden tables. There's a particular emphasis on hearty stews, and the menu includes French classics such as a dozen *escargots de Bourgogne*, *foie gras* and mussels. Good selection of wines from France and beyond. $\overline{\underline{\$\$\$\$}}$

Kam Long Ah Zai Curry Fish Head 74 Jalan Wong Ah Fook; 016 752 8372. Simple but highly popular place for fish head curry (you can get fish tail instead, for a slightly higher price), as well as fried dishes. $\overline{\underline{\$\$}}$

CAFÉS AND DESSERTS

Hiap Joo Bakery & Biscuit Factory 13 Jln Tan Hiok Nee; 07 223 1703. Opened in 1919, this historic bakery is one of the very few in the country that bakes in a wood-fired oven. The coconut buns and banana cake are the real winners, though be prepared to queue for your tasty trophy. $\overline{\underline{\$}}$

JH Lovely Sweets 418 Jalan Trus; http://facebook.com/jhlovelysweets. With a name like that, how could you refuse? If you've never tried Indian sweets before, this would be a good place to start; if you have tried them before, it's a good place to continue. $\overline{\underline{\$}}$

Sunday Morning 124 Jalan Trus; http://instagram.com/sundaymorning_sundaymorning. Sleek-looking cafe, hiding upstairs from the riff-raff, and selling simple meals (mostly Japanese, including curry rice, cheesy baked rice and slightly unauthentic *bento* trays), plus good desserts and tasty single-origin coffee. $\overline{\underline{\$\$}}$

STREET FOOD AND HAWKER MARKETS

Meldrum Walk Meldrum Walk. Colourful and vibrant market with a mouthwatering array of street food. Try the local speciality, *mee rebus* – noodles in a thick sauce garnished with bean curd, sliced egg, green chillies and shallots. $\overline{\underline{\$}}$

Taman Sentosa Hawker Stalls Jalan Sutera. A popular night food market where Chinese stalls line one side of the street and Malay places sit side by side on the other. Plenty of dishes on offer including prawn *mee* and *bak kut teh*. $\overline{\underline{\$}}$

SHOPPING   SEE MAP PAGE 275

Although JB has plenty of Western-style shopping malls, it's much more enjoyable to explore the **boutiques** around Jalan Tan Hiok Nee and Jalan Dhoby.

JARO 18 Jalan Sungei Chat; http://jaro.org.my. The Johor Area Rehabilitation Organisation (JARO) shop features handicrafts and artworks made by people with disabilities. Among the products on display are rattan baskets, picture frames and handmade cane furniture. Buying products here ensures the workers continue to have a source of employment, while also preserving traditional craft-making skills that have been passed down for generations.

DIRECTORY

Banks and exchange The main shopping centres hold ATMs and currency exchanges. There's also an HSBC on Jalan Bukit Timbalan; in JB Sentral there's a 24hr moneychanger at the main entrance.

The east coast

Without the patronage of neighbouring Singapore, the area around Johor Bahru would have quietly nodded off into a peaceful slumber. Most people heading to the **east coast** beat a hasty path along Route 3 to **Mersing**, a dusty little town that is the departure point for boats to **Tioman Island**.

Mersing

The industrious little fishing port of **MERSING**, 130km north of Johor Bahru, lies on the languid Mersing River. It serves as the main gateway to **Tioman Island** and most of the smaller islands of the **Seribuat Archipelago**.

ARRIVAL AND DEPARTURE   MERSING

By boat Mersing is the main departure point for Tioman Island – with Bluewater (http://bluewater.my) – and most of the other islands of the Seribuat Archipelago, although boats to Sibu Island leave from Tanjung Leman (see page 291). At the jetty there's a secure car park, while there and in the R&R Plaza nearby, assorted booths and offices

THE SOUTH THE EAST COAST

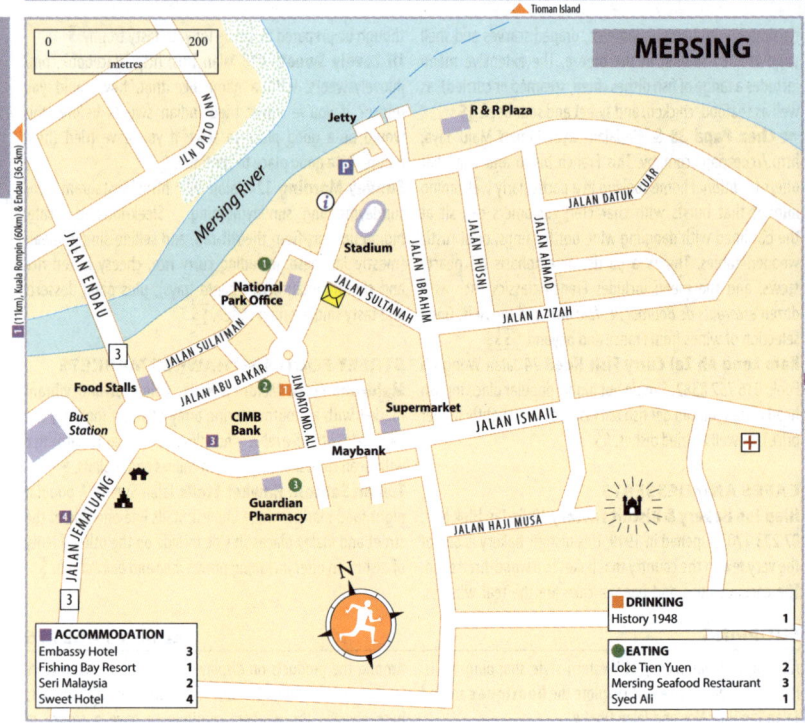

represent various islands, boats and resorts. Tioman Ferry (http://tiomanferry.com) also offers online booking for a little fee.

By bus Buses normally stop at the bus station on the western edge of town, and also at the R&R Plaza beside the jetty. The overnight bus from KL will arrive at around 5am in the morning, so if you're moving on to Tioman you may have to find a *mamak* to rest in for most of the morning. If you're leaving Mersing, for most destinations there is no need to walk to the bus station; buy tickets from SS International (http://ssinternational.com.my) on Jalan Abu Bakar by the jetty, or other online engines. They will make sure the bus picks you up at the plaza. Leaving by bus in peak season can be problematic; many are full. Buy express bus tickets in advance, at the station or online.

Destinations Alor Setar (1 daily; 12hr); Butterworth (1 daily; 9hr); Cherating (4 daily; 4hr 30min); Endau (hourly; 45min); Ipoh (1 daily; 8hr); Johor Bahru (9 daily; 2hr 30min); Kluang (5 daily; 1hr 30min); Kota Bahru (2 daily; 8hr); Kota Tinggi (hourly; 2hr); Kuala Lumpur (8 daily; 6hr); Kuala Perlis (1 daily; 12hr); Kuala Terengganu (5 daily, 9hr 30min); Kuantan (5 daily; 3hr 30min); Melaka (3 daily; 5hr 30min); Muar (3 daily; 5hr); Pengkalan Kubor (daily; 10hr); Singapore (5 daily; 4hr).

By taxi Taxis can be picked up either at the main bus station or at the jetty.

INFORMATION

Tourist information Mersing's neat tourist office is at Jalan Abu Bakar on the way to the ferry port (METIC; Mon–Fri 8am–5pm; 07 798 1979).

Travel agents Numerous agents, operators and resort offices in and around the jetty complex deal primarily with Tioman and the Seribuat Archipelago. Hotel Mersing Travel & Tours, 7 Jalan Abu Bakar (http://hotelmersing.com), also organize full-day tailor-made island-hopping trips, and trips to Endau Rompin National Park (see page 292).

ACCOMMODATION   SEE MAP PAGE 280

Embassy Hotel 2 Jalan Ismail; 010 665 9167. A rather soulless three-storey orange hotel building in the centre of town, featuring a selection of adequate rooms that will do the trick for the night if you're on a tight budget. $

Fishing Bay Resort 15km north of Mersing; http://fishingbaymersingresort.com. This good-value place has neat bungalows and rooms set around a beachside garden and small pool, and a restaurant serving excellent local and Thai food. Kayaks are available for a trip to Batu Gajah Island, just offshore. Cab it, or ask about transfers. Weekend rates rise by almost fifty percent. $

Seri Malaysia Jalan Ismail; http://serimalaysia.com.my. Just east of the centre, this is Mersing's best hotel, though don't expect *too* much. The grand-ish entrance and little welcome drink set the scene; rooms are carpeted but a bit drab, and there's a decent-enough swimming pool. Prices are usually quite a bit lower than the rack rates. $$

Sweet Hotel 5 Jalan Jemaluang; 07 799 2228. A short walk from the bus station, this friendly hotel is the safest mid-range bet in town; the clean, a/c rooms, all with TV and hot water, feature pleasant touches like mounted fabrics. $

EATING SEE MAP PAGE 280

Mersing is a good place to **eat** out, with seafood unsurprisingly topping the menu. The **market** serves the popular local breakfast dish *nasi dagang*: glutinous rice cooked in coconut milk, served with *sambal* and fish curry.

Loke Tien Yuen 55 Jalan Abu Bakar; 07 799 1639. The oldest and friendliest Chinese restaurant in town with a small, reliable menu. The sweet and sour pork is particularly good; seafood costs a fair bit more. Unfortunately, at the time of writing the owners had just retired, but hopefully someone will be continuing their legacy by the time you read this. $

Mersing Seafood Restaurant 56 Jalan Ismail. Great seafood dishes prepared Szechuan or Cantonese style in a slightly kitsch a/c interior, though some can be pricey; among the best sellers are deep-fried squid with salted egg yolk, BBQ squid, and fried prawns with butter and coconut. $$

Syed Ali 72–73 Jalan Sulaiman; 07 799 6336. This bustling place just a short walk from the jetty offers a good selection of tasty Indian and local grub that is considered by most to be the best in town. A meal can cost next to nothing. $

DRINKING SEE MAP PAGE 280

History 1948 10 Jalan Dato Mohd Ali; 016 758 9882. A second-floor restaurant-cum-bar that makes the most cordial place to drink in town; the selection isn't massive, but you'll most likely enjoy sitting up on the balcony with a beer in hand. There's not all that much "history" about (bar a Terracotta Warrior), but they do also dole out good pub grub.

Tioman Island

Shaped like a giant apostrophe, located in the South China Sea 54km northeast of Mersing, **TIOMAN ISLAND** is the largest of the 64 volcanic islands that form the **Seribuat Archipelago**. Ever since the 1970s – when *Time* magazine ranked Tioman as one of the world's ten most beautiful islands – sun worshippers and divers have been flocking to its palm-fringed shores, in search of the mythical Bali H'ai (the island in the Hollywood musical *South Pacific*, which was filmed on Tioman).

It could be argued that this popularity, and its **duty-free** status, have dented the romantic isolation that once made the island so desirable. Tioman Island does, however, display a remarkable resilience – and in part due to the lack of a decent road network, the greater part of the island retains something of its intimate, village atmosphere. Anyone in search of unspoilt beaches is likely to be disappointed, though superb exceptions do exist; divers and snorkellers will find plenty to enjoy, and there are also opportunities to take jungle hikes in the largely untouched interior.

Accommodation possibilities range from international-standard resorts to simple beachfront A-frames; it takes time and money to get from one beach to another, so choose your destination carefully. During the **monsoon**, from November to February/March, the whole island winds down dramatically; many places close until at least mid-January. July and August are the busiest months, when prices increase and accommodation is best booked in advance; visibility for divers is also at its lowest during these months.

ARRIVAL AND DEPARTURE TIOMAN ISLAND

By boat Blue Water Express (http://bluewater.my) has services from Mersing (3 daily; 2hr) to the island, with boats

THE SOUTH TIOMAN ISLAND

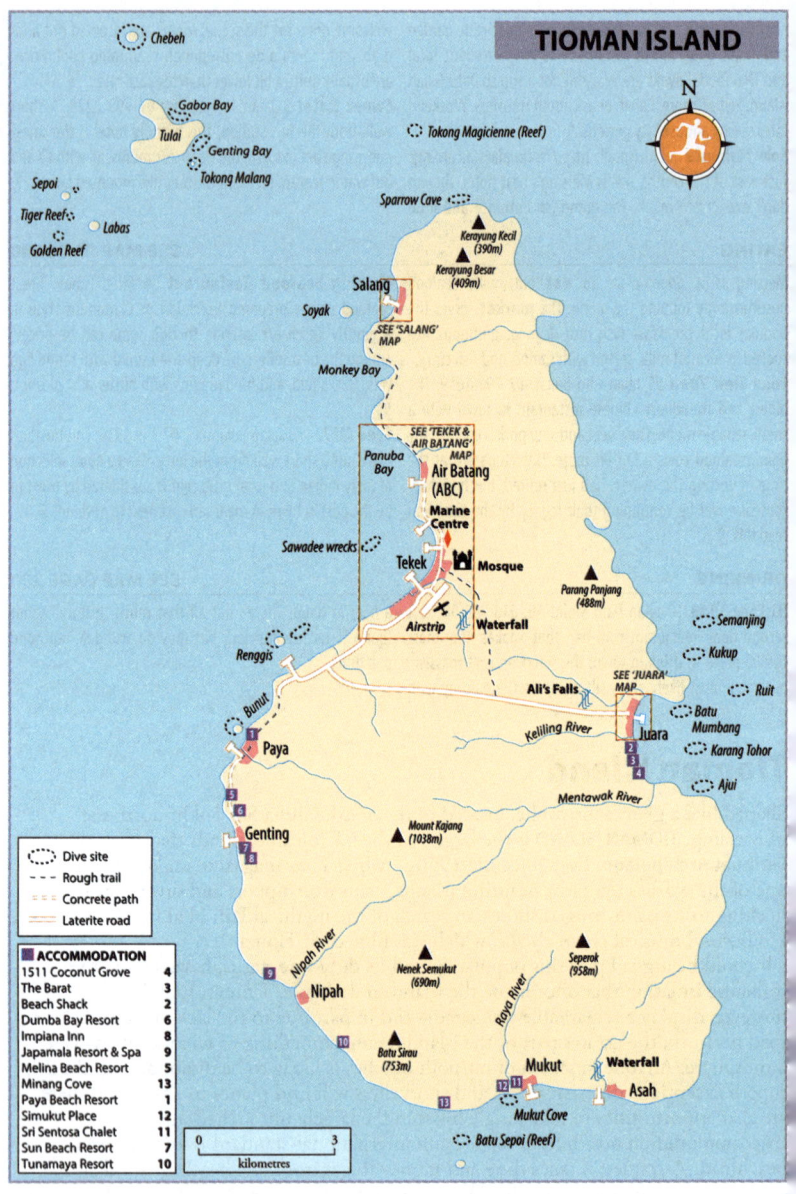

stopping off at Genting, Paya, Tekek, ABC and Sabang (in that order); note that when leaving the island, once the boats fills up, they travel directly to the mainland without picking up passengers at the remaining stops (although they always stop at Tekek, the main port). There are also ferries from Tanjung Gemok ferry terminal (1 daily; 2hr), about 40km north of Mersing. Allow extra time if you need to catch a flight from the mainland, as the boat services are not entirely reliable and are dictated by the tide. Boats are also often full, especially in high season, when ferries get booked up days or even weeks in advance. Tickets can be booked online, and also with Tioman Ferry (http://

tiomanferry.com) for a small fee; check the website for the latest schedules. Note that there is also an Tioman area entry fee, payable when buying your ferry ticket.
By plane *Tunamaya Resort* has a private eight-seater service from JB's Senai airport (1hr) and KL's Subang Airport; the flights can be booked by phone or on their website (07 798 8108, http://careluxuryhotels.com/tunamaya-tioman).

GETTING AROUND

On foot The best-connected stretch is on the west coast, between Tekek and Salang. A road runs from the *Berjaya* resort in the south, up through Tekek village and as far as the headland at the northern end of the bay, but it's an exposed and uninteresting walk – about 30min from the village to the headland. You're better off paying for a taxi from Tekek to the Marine Park Centre, from where steps lead over the headland to Air Batang. A narrow concrete path runs the length of the beach to the point where a jungle trail sets off to Penuba Bay, Monkey Beach and Salang. Other coastal trails include one that connects Genting with Paya, while you can walk across the island from Tekek to Juara (see page 289).

By bicycle Bicycle rental is a good option, but remember you'll have to carry the bike over the headlands at some point. The road to Juara is only for the resilient. Outlets in Tekek and Air Batang offer bikes by the hour or day.

By 4WD Only 4WD vehicles can safely drive the steep route between Tekek and Juara.

By boat The rented boats (known as water-taxis) that

SNORKELLING AND DIVING AROUND TIOMAN ISLAND

The waters around Tioman boast abundant **marine life**. Many nearby islets provide excellent opportunities for **snorkelling**, and most of the hotel operations offer **day-trips**. The relatively healthy coral and huge biodiversity in these temperate waters also make for great **diving, in areas well away from the ferry routes**. Dive centres offer a full range of PADI certificates, from a four-day Open Water course through to the Dive Master and instructor qualifications. For the already qualified, boat dives remain relatively cheap by international standards. The **dive sites** listed below are the most popular on the west coast, where most people dive.

DIVE SHOPS

B&J Diving Centre Air Batang; http://divetioman.com; see map page 284. Well-established shop with a second branch in Salang.

Blue Heaven Divers Air Batang; http://blueheavendivers.com; see map page 284. Offers a good-value Open Water package that lasts 3–4 days.

Eco-Divers Air Batang; http://eco-divers.weebly.com; see map page 284. Close to the jetty and with friendly staff. Half-day Discover Scuba courses available.

Freedive Tioman Tekek; http://freedivetioman.com; see map page 284. The island's first freediving school, offering introduction, beginner and advanced courses, including Apnea Total Freediver.

Ray's Dive Adventure Air Batang; http://raysdive.com; see map page 284. Small but highly experienced outfit at Air Batang offering a range of courses.

Tioman Dive Centre Tekek; http://tioman-dive-centre.com; see map page 284. A reliable outfit on Tekek, with popular night dives that are super-cheap if you have your own equipment.

DIVE SITES

Golden Reef (typical depth 10–20m). 15min off the northwestern coast; boulders provide a breeding ground for marine life, and produce many soft and hard corals. Known for nudibranchs and other macro life.

Chebeh Island (15–30m). In the northwestern waters, this is a massive volcanic labyrinth of caves and channels. Napoleon fish, triggerfish and turtles are present in abundance.

Labas Island (5–20m). South of Tulai Island, this island has numerous tunnels and caves that provide a home for pufferfish, stingrays and moray eels.

Sawadee wrecks (25–30m). Two wooden Thai fishing boats just offshore from Tekek airport attract scorpionfish and juvenile barracuda, as well as more common marine life.

Tiger Reef (10–25m). Deservedly the most popular site, southwest of Tulai between Labas and Sepoi islands. Yellow-tail snappers, trevally and tuna, spectacular soft coral and gorgonian fans.

Tokong Magicienne (Magicienne Rock) (10–25m). Due north of Tioman, this colourful, sponge-layered coral pinnacle is a feeding station for larger fish – silver snappers, golden-striped trevally, jacks and groupers.

travel along the shore are very expensive by Malaysian standards. To save money, you can join the Mersing ferry as it makes its scheduled stops, if there's room, although they will still charge you a fair bit.

INFORMATION

Tourist information There is no official information office on Tioman, despite the fact that many agencies tout themselves as tourist information points – your best bet is to ask your hotel or guesthouse for information.

DIRECTORY

Banks and exchange Be sure to change money in Mersing before you head out to Tioman, where the exchange rates are lousy; the only ATM on Tioman is the Bank Simpanan Nasional in Tekek, opposite the airport.

Tekek

The main settlement on Tioman, **TEKEK**, doesn't make a great first impression. The area around the airport, marina and public jetty has been rapidly developed, while coming from Air Batang you first pass a long stretch of deserted waterfront promenade. South of the marina, though, things start to get much better. Not only are there a handful of good resorts, but the beach is also attractive and has a dive shop as well as one of the island's best bars. Further south still is the high-end *Berjaya* resort.

Marine Park Centre

North of the main jetty, at the very end of the bay • Free • 03 8886 1111

The hefty concrete jetty and dazzlingly blue roofs of the government-sponsored **Marine Park Centre** make it hard to miss. Set up to protect the island's coral and marine life, and to patrol the fishing in its waters, the centre also contains an aquarium and displays about marine conservation.

ARRIVAL AND DEPARTURE
TEKEK

By plane and boat Whether you fly or come by boat, you're close enough to walk to most of the resorts within Tekek; although the *Berjaya* is a bit far, it offers a transfer. Services in and around the terminal complex next to the airstrip include an ATM, moneychangers and duty-free shops.

ACCOMMODATION
SEE MAP PAGE 284

Berjaya Tioman Resort Just south of Tekek; http://berjayahotel.com. This village-sized complex at the end of

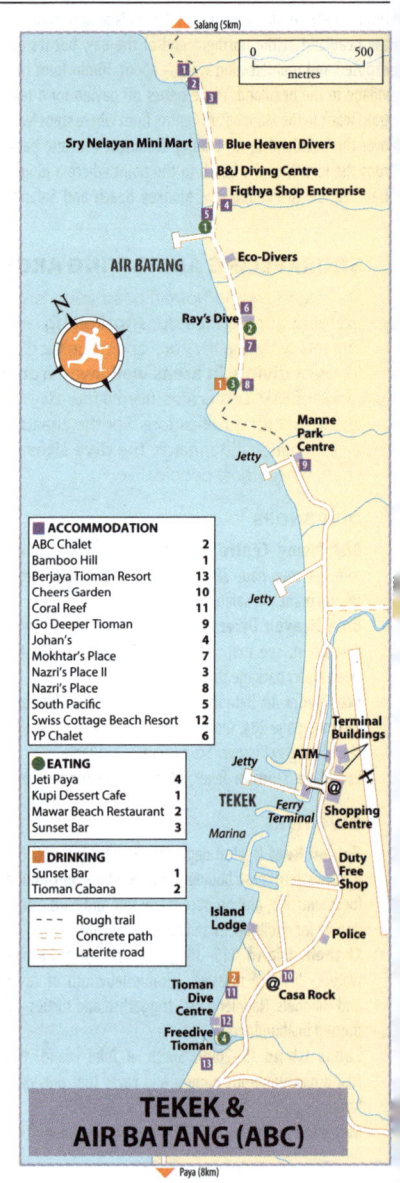

TEKEK & AIR BATANG (ABC)

Tekek Beach has a couple of great restaurants – including a gorgeous Thai place just off the beach – plus two pools, tennis courts, and facilities for watersports, golf and jungle trekking. Some of the rooms have been refurbished more recently than others; it's a good idea to stay in the newer ones, if possible. $$$$

Cheers Garden Tekek; 013 931 1425. Just a few hundred metres inland, this decent budget choice offers simple fan doubles aimed at backpackers, plus a/c rooms with hot showers giving onto a pleasant leafy garden with potted plants. Fish and meat barbecues can be rustled up upon request (minimum six people). Bike and motorbike rental available too. $$

Coral Reef Tekek; http://coralreeftioman.com. The crumbling fan rooms you walk past if coming from the main road are definitely worth a miss (overpriced and rather grotty), but the deluxe beachside rooms are a big step up, with decorative stonework on the walls, kettles, hot showers and hammocks slung between the trees just outside the rooms. $$

★ **Swiss Cottage Beach Resort** Tekek; http://swiss-cottage-tioman.com. Tekek's best all-round choice is a real winner – the clean and welcoming rooms feature tasteful individual furnishings, from pretty chests to sturdy wooden wardrobes. Fan-cooled bungalow rooms are in a shady beachside spot ensuring they don't get too warm, and the resort is located on a wonderful stretch of beach. The friendly, helpful owners can organize snorkelling trips, hikes to waterfalls and jungle tours. $$$

EATING   SEE MAP PAGE 284

Jeti Paya Just south of Tekek; 012 794 7979. Chinese restaurant, mainly for seafood, with meals that aren't all that pricey for a resort island. The restaurant's interior is as plain as they get, but you can sit outside under the illuminated tree, or on the beach itself. $$

DRINKING   SEE MAP PAGE 284

★ **Tioman Cabana** Tekek Beach; 013 717 6677. This quirky beach bar bursts with character, with its worn-out stools, mismatched wicker chairs, flags from the world over and a rusty anchor. It's a great spot to unwind over a drink or two, and the food's good too – including burgers and local dishes including chicken fried rice and curries. $$

Air Batang (ABC)

Despite its ever-increasing popularity, **AIR BATANG**, 2km north of Tekek from jetty to jetty, retains a sleepy charm and rivals Juara (which admittedly has a better beach) in its appeal for budget travellers. Larger than Salang or Juara, less developed than Tekek and well connected by boat services, Air Batang (or **ABC** as it's often called), is a happy medium as far as many visitors are concerned. What development there is has been sympathetically done and relatively low-key, and there's still a definite sense of community.

A jetty divides the bay roughly in half; the **beach** is better at the southern end of the bay, where there are fewer rocks, though the shallow northern end is safer for children. The cement path that runs the length of the beach is interrupted by little wooden bridges over streams and overhung with greenery; stretches are unlit at night. Between the guesthouses, a few small shops sell essentials such as shorts, T-shirts, sun cream and toiletries. Like the guesthouses, they also arrange snorkelling trips and boat taxis.

A fifteen-minute **trail** leads over the headland to the north. After an initial scramble, it flattens out into an easy walk and ends up at **Panuba Bay**, a secluded cove that holds just one resort and a quiet little beach, and offers some of the best snorkelling on the island. From Panuba Bay, it's an hour's walk to **Monkey Beach** and then a further 45 minutes to Salang. Heading south instead from ABC, steps lead over the headland to **Tekek**.

ARRIVAL AND DEPARTURE   AIR BATANG (ABC)

By boat Ferries from the mainland stop off at Air Batang along with other major stops including Genting and Tekek. There are also private taxi boats that connect the island's main beaches.

ACCOMMODATION   SEE MAP PAGE 284

As you get off the boat, a helpful signpost indicates the numerous **places to stay** in the bay. All but the most basic A-frames have fans and their own bathrooms, and mosquito nets are usually provided. The pricier options should have hot showers. Some places charge significantly more at peak times, such as during school holidays.

ABC Chalet At the far northern end of the bay; http://abcbeachtioman.com. A little quieter than most, due to its location, this is one of the area's best options, with chalets set in a garden. The cheapest are fair for the price, while the a/c doubles have great views, kettles and hot showers. $\overline{\$}$

★ **Bamboo Hill** On the northern headland of Air Batang; http://bamboohilltioman.com. Six beautiful wooden chalets perch on the headland, all with wonderful sea views. All rooms are fan only, although the location means there's a nice breeze anyway. The cosy reception area has a book exchange. $\overline{\$\$}$

★ **Go Deeper Tioman** Dindong Beach, south and around the corner from the jetty; http://godeeperchalets.com. Relatively new place with quirky tube-rooms arranged on two levels, like some kind of oversized insect experiment. You'll be the ant if staying here, and rooms certainly aren't large, but it's quite an experience; there's also a restaurant here (made out of containers, just because), and the secluded location away from the hubs is a real bonus. $\overline{\$\$\$}$

Johan's Just north of the jetty; 09 419 1359. A pleasant spot with chalets dotted around a leafy slope offering fan and larger a/c doubles, plus a four-bed fan dorm nestled at the top of the hillside. They arrange snorkelling trips, as well as trips round the island. $\overline{\$\$}$

Mokhtar's Place South of the jetty; http://facebook.com/MokhtarPlace. These rust-coloured chalets are clean and airy with little porches, although they face inwards, rather than out to sea. Staff can book buses on the mainland, snorkelling and fishing trips, and water-taxis. $\overline{\$}$

Nazri's Place II Northern end of Air Batang; 09 419 1375. Owned by the same family as *Nazri's Place*, below, this outfit boasts cottages dotted around a pleasant garden area with swings and shaded by palm trees. $\overline{\$\$}$

Nazri's Place Southern end of the bay; 017 490 1384. Clean a/c rooms in a series of red blocks that look onto a large courtyard. The rooms are some of the best on the beach, and often get booked up in advance. $\overline{\$\$}$

South Pacific Close to the jetty; 019 708 5647. Clean chalets with attached bathrooms and mozzie nets; those right on the beach are good value. There are also a few modern spacious chalets with hot showers and a/c; the beach just opposite is very rocky, though, so you're best off walking further south if you want to have a swim. $\overline{\$}$

YP Chalet South of the jetty; 019 419 1018. A basic place on this part of the island, with simple fan rooms that are very worn around the edges. It's best to scope out some of the other places first, but if you're on a very tight budget *YP* may be the answer, and it's a popular choice for scuba divers $\overline{\$}$

EATING SEE MAP PAGE 284

Kupi Dessert Cafe By jetty. Nothing all that special in appearance, though popular for its sweet treats – waffles with a scoop of ice cream plonked on top, slices of cake, or pre-prepared trays of sugary sustenance. $\overline{\$\$}$

Mawar Beach Restaurant Towards southern end of the beach; 09 419 1153. Cheap-enough, backpacker-friendly grub such as fried rice and chilli chicken burgers, with an immediate beach view – not a bad choice at all. $\overline{\$\$}$

★ **Sunset Bar** Southern end of the beach. Though of more note as a bar (see page 286), this is up there with the best places to eat hereabouts, thanks to the tasty pizzas they dole out – delivery also possible on the beach (ie, a few metres away). $\overline{\$\$\$}$

DRINKING SEE MAP PAGE 284

Air Batang is the only place on the island with significant **nightlife**; there are a handful of laidback beach bars open until the early hours. Most have a **happy hour**, usually from around 5–7pm.

Sunset Bar Southern end of the beach. The most popular bar on the beach, this laidback place is a great spot for a sundowner. They shake up excellent mojitos, and have a modest roster of beers.

Salang and around

Just over 4km north of Air Batang, **SALANG** is a smaller bay with a pretty stretch of beach at its southern end by the jetty. The bay has seen a lot of development, but it still retains its own charm. The southern end of the beach is the more scenic; swimming can be an ordeal at the northern end due to the sharp rocks and coral. Just off the southern headland a small island, **Soyak**, has a pretty reef for snorkelling. There are also several dive shops.

A rough trail takes you over the headland to the south for the 45-minute scramble to **Monkey Bay**. There are few monkeys around these days, but the well-hidden cove is more than adequate compensation. Walkers can carry on to **Panuba Bay** (which will take about 1hr) and Air Batang.

ARRIVAL AND DEPARTURE SALANG

By boat Ferries from the mainland stop off at Salang, along with other major stops including Genting and Tekek and is also served by served by private taxi boats (as is Monkey Bay).

ACCOMMODATION
SEE MAP PAGE 287

Ella's Place Northern end of the bay; 014 844 8610. This place brims with character and oozes a mellow vibe, with its chaos of potted plants, dangling buoys, small fishpond, and hammocks slung between palm trees. The little restaurant serves a handful of dishes for breakfast (which costs extra), including omelettes and pancakes. Fan rooms are pretty simple, while the larger a/c rooms all sleep three. $

Puteri Salang Inn Set back at the southern end of the beach; 013 796 6965. Offers seventeen pretty chalets, mostly A-frames, are set around a carefully landscaped garden with hammocks – the most peaceful spot in Salang. The cheaper rooms are pretty simple, but the friendly staff make up for it, and there's all-day tea and coffee, and a book exchange. $

Salang Indah Tioman North of jetty; http://salangindahresort.com. Offering a slightly more hotel-like air than most of the competition (though still a beach place; don't worry), with rooms featuring balconies in the main building, and huts laid out in a row up the hill. $$

Salang Pusaka Resort http://salangpusakaresorttioman.com. Set back from the beach, most of the chalets here give onto a spacious verdant garden. All rooms have a/c, and

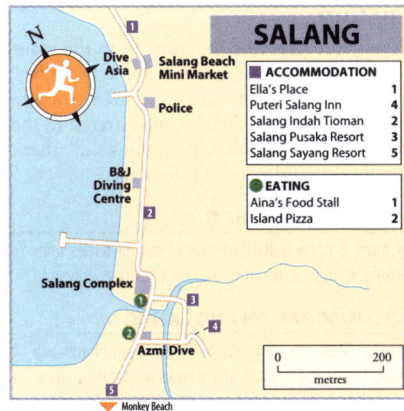

the basic rooms are pretty good value overall – some are in better shape than others, so it's wise to look at a few before settling in. $$

Salang Sayang Resort Southern end of the beach; http://resortsalangsayang.wixsite.com. At the southern end of the beach, this place offers a range of accommodation, from garden and seafront fan rooms to larger a/c hillside chalets on "banana hill", from where there are lovely views over the bay. The attached restaurant serves a range of Malay dishes, and a BBQ kicks off each evening. There are deckchairs for guests' use, too. $$

EATING
SEE MAP PAGE 287

Aina's Food Stall Salang Complex. The best place to eat in the large Salang Complex, doling out round after round of mains centred on rice, noodles or egg. $

Island Pizza South of the jetty; 019 955 8938. Unpretentious, feet-in-the-sand pizza place that has become the Salang area's most popular place to eat – the pies aren't amazing, but they're tasty enough and will fill you up. $$

Paya

Just 5km south of Tekek, the pristine stretch of beach in **PAYA**, only accessible by private boat transfer from Genting, has been developed but still seems peaceful when compared to Genting a little further south. **Jungle walks** are worth exploring here, where the island's greenery is at its most lush. The thirty-minute trail north to Bunut ends up at a fantastic deserted beach. From here it's a hot 45-minute walk through the golf course to the *Berjaya Tioman Beach Resort* and a further half-hour to Tekek.

ACCOMMODATION
PAYA, SEE MAP PAGE 282

Melina Beach Resort Between Paya and Genting; http://melinabeachresort.com. Appealing resort with its own beach, but accessible on foot from both Paya and Genting, which gives you more eating options. There's a good range of rooms, from the cheapest garden-view rooms with bunks (and sleeping four) to suites overlooking the forest canopy. $$$$

Paya Beach Resort Northern end of Paya Bay; http:// payabeach.com. Paya's best-value accommodation, with comfortable red-roofed chalets plus a good on-site restaurant, dive shop, swimming pool and spa. There's good snorkelling just in front of the resort, and staff can arrange excursions further afield, such as canoeing, trekking and adventure safaris. Two-night minimum stay in peak season. The resort also offers various packages which include accommodation, meals and activities. $$$

Genting

Usually the first stop for boats from the mainland, **GENTING** has been very heavily developed, especially around the jetty. Its beach is not as appealing as its neighbours', and as a result doesn't attract as many travellers – sadly, it's often littered, especially by the jetty, although there's a nice stretch to the north by *Dumba Bay Resort*, and towards the southern end too. On the plus side, there are several dive shops and the beach is usually very quiet during the week.

ARRIVAL AND DEPARTURE — GENTING

By boat Genting is the first port of call for ferries from Mersing; from here, private water-taxis take passengers to other beaches around the island.

ACCOMMODATION AND EATING — SEE MAP PAGE 282

Dumba Bay Resort http://facebook.com/dumbabayresort. This laidback place offers basic sea-facing chalets, although they are just on the main pathway, which means they can get quite noisy at night as mopeds scoot past. The draw is the pleasant stretch of beach with picnic tables and the odd hammock. Nightly fish and seafood BBQs, too. $$

★ **Impiana Inn** http://innimpian.weebly.com. Highly popular with divers, and for good reason: the rooms are the best in Genting and the common areas are well kept. The deluxe rooms with TV are worth the extra fee – they are attractively furnished with sturdy wooden beds and the slightly aging bathrooms are kept nice and clean. A couple of attractive wooden garden pavilions make a pleasant spot to unwind and read a book. $$

Sun Beach Resort http://sunbeachresort.com.my. Genting's widest range of rooms: the deluxe are mostly on the hillside; the cheaper ones on the beach. Overall, they are relatively clean, but take a look before deciding. $$$

South of Genting

The area **south of Genting** is home to a number of upmarket resorts on private stretches of beach, which tend to be busiest at the weekend and on holidays and are reachable only by private boat transfer from Genting. The exception is **Nipah**, which has a couple of laidback places and is accessible by water-taxi from Genting.

Nipah

There's no jetty, so access is by water-taxi from Genting

Located on the southwest coast, **NIPAH** is the closest you'll get to an idyllic beach hideaway on the island; once a backpacker hangout, it's now almost exclusively focused on the upper end. There is good **snorkelling** around a nearby islet, and although there's no proper dive shop, the local accommodation options can make arrangements. They also offer kayak rental and jungle trekking. Don't turn up at Nipah without having first made a booking.

Mukut

Private taxi boats take passengers to Mukut from different points around Tioman

Lying in the shadow of granite outcrops, the ramshackle little fishing village of **MUKUT** is shrouded by dense forest. It's a peaceful and friendly spot to unwind, with a fine beach, though note that locals are unused to Western sunbathing habits and frown upon the open consumption of alcohol.

One good reason to stay here is to hike up **Bukit Nenek Semukut**, whose twin peaks are known as the "dragon's horns"; guides can be arranged at *Tanjung Inn Adventure*.

ACCOMMODATION — SOUTH OF GENTING, SEE MAP PAGE 282

NIPAH AND AROUND

★ **Japamala Resort & Spa** On its own beach just north of Nipah; http://japamalaresorts.com. This eco-luxe resort offers thirteen Malay village-style villas and chalets tucked away amid lush tropical rainforest. No trees were felled in building the resort – the villas were built with reclaimed timber around their natural landscape. $$$$

Tunamaya Resort On its own stretch of beach south of Nipah; http://careluxuryhotels.com. This pleasant upmarket resort, with wonderful views of the twin peaks, features more than fifty villas set on both sides of a small leafy stream that is atmospherically lit up in the evenings. The well-appointed rooms feature modern amenities and there's an inviting swimming pool and spa. The restaurant serves great Asian dishes, with weekend seafood BBQs. The resort's private plane flies to and from Johor Bahru and Kuala Lumpur (see page 284). $$$

MUKUT AND AROUND
Minang Cove Standing alone on the southern end of the island, west of Mukut; http://tiomanislandresort.net. The rooms at this delightful resort have benefitted from a recent refresh, and its location and service have long raised it well above the average. Excellent snorkelling, and they also arrange round-island trips. Half-board for two $$$$

Simukut Place Western end of Mukut Cove; 011 2928 6306. One of the rare budget options hereabouts, with simple rooms in cheerily-painted buildings that feel like they're constantly trying to push back against the jungle – which, of course, enhances the natural, calm feel of the place. $$

Sri Sentosa Chalet West of jetty; 017 799 2672. Budget-friendly choice where everything seems to be on stilts. The wood-panelled rooms are quite charming, though the bathrooms could do with some work, and they'll be able to get you in the water on a vessel or with some snorkelling equipment. $$

Juara

With Tioman's western shore now extensively developed, those eager for a hideaway often head for **JUARA**. The only east coast settlement, it's a quiet and peaceful kampung with two excellent beaches – **Juara Beach**, aka **Barok Beach**, where you arrive from Tekek, and Mentawak Beach just south. The sand is cleaner and less crowded than on the other side of the island, and Juara is altogether more laidback – even than Air Batang.

The beaches here do, however, have a reputation for harbouring **sandflies** (see box, page 290), so take what precautions you can. The bay, facing out to the open sea, is also susceptible to bad weather. The constant sea breeze keeps the water choppy; it attracts **surfers** from November to March, with 3m-plus waves in February. The beach break is good for beginners, while more experienced surfers favour the point at the southern end of Mentawak.

A popular, clearly marked 45-minute walk leads from the south beach to a small **waterfall** with a big freshwater pond that's good for swimming.

Juara Turtle Project
Mentawak Beach • Tours 15–30min • Minimum donation • http://juaraturtleproject.com

The southern beach is home to the **Juara Turtle Project**, whose work takes several forms. They collect eggs from the eastern beaches, then hatch and release turtles, and also campaign for greater protection, with a small Visitor Centre to raise awareness. Volunteers are welcome to get involved for a payment of RM120 per day for a minimum of four days, which includes accommodation, breakfast and lunch.

ARRIVAL AND INFORMATION JUARA

By road A road starting just before the *Berjaya Tioman Resort* has given 4WD vehicles easy access to Juara, though you'll need to bargain hard for the 30min journey. If you've booked a place to stay, hotel staff will probably be able to organize transport for you from Tekek, which is likely to work out cheaper than sorting it yourself. Regular cars will struggle with the steep roads, but it's theoretically possible by motorbike or mountain bike (don't undertake either lightly). Several guesthouses in Juara can arrange transport back to Tekek.

On foot You can also reach Juara on foot through the jungle. The steep trek from Tekek takes about

> ### SANDFLIES
> **Sandflies** can be a real problem throughout the Seribuat Archipelago, including on Tioman Island. These little pests, looking like tiny fruit flies with black bodies and white wings, suck blood and cause an extremely itchy lump, which may become a nasty blister if scratched. The effectiveness of various treatments and deterrents is much debated; the general feeling is that, short of dousing yourself all over with insect repellent, covering up completely or hiding out in the sea all day long, there's not much you can do. You may find that Tiger Balm, available at any pharmacy, can reduce the maddening itch and help you sleep. If you are able to take them, antihistamines also provide some relief.

2hr 30min, not counting rest stops, and is definitely not recommended if you have luggage. Don't walk the less appealing vehicle road, and carry plenty of water. Starting as a concrete path a 5min walk away from the airstrip, the trail soon becomes rocky, running uphill with intermittent sections of concrete steps. After an hour or so you reach the highest point, and the route then tapers off into a smooth, downhill path, eventually joining the main road. There's a waterfall just off the main road that's a good spot for a refreshing dip; it's easy to miss – keep your eyes peeled for the little wooden hut on your right. Look carefully and you will see the words "waterfall" lightly inscribed on the side of the hut. It's just a couple of minutes' walk from there.

Information desk An unofficial information desk (daily 9am–6pm) by the jetty rents out motorbikes and snorkelling equipment, and arranges full-day boat tours.

ACCOMMODATION
SEE MAPS PAGES 282 AND 289

★ **1511 Coconut Grove** Mentawak Beach; http://1511 coconutgrove.my. This pleasant resort offers inviting chalets just a short walk from the beach, while along the seafront a couple of viewing towers have recently been converted into duplex rooms. Rates include breakfast and, unusually for the island, there's wi-fi throughout. $$$

The Barat Mentawak Beach; http://barattioman.com. One of the more adventurously-designed places on the strip, with rooms and common areas alike quite jazzy. A surprisingly large complex, you may need a map to locate your room, and they do indeed hand you such directions when checking in; you'll probably only need it once, since it's easy to use the central swimming pool as reference. $$$

★ **Beach Shack** Mentawak Beach; 012 696 1093. Ozzie/Malay-run place with a relaxed backpacker vibe, offering accommodation in simple colourful A-frame chalets along the beach; there's also an a/c deluxe room, made of recycled timber, with great sea views, plus a café and book exchange. Open all year. $

Bushman Tioman End of the northern bay; 09 419 3109. This friendly and easy-going option offers a handful of simple but gorgeous chalets at the northern end of the beach; all are clean, with hot water. There are a couple of a/c rooms, and meals can be cooked upon request. $$

Juara Beach Resort Close to the jetty; http://juarabeach resort.com. This is a good choice if you're looking for a/c and hot showers, and there's also an excellent Chinese restaurant. Spacious rooms, set around a verdant garden, all feature TV and fridge, and rates include breakfast. $$$

Juara Mutiara Resort Near the jetty; http://juaramutiara resort.com. Some of the rooms here are set on the beach, while others look onto a well-kept garden with palm trees and benches outside each room. There's a mini-market on-site and they can arrange fishing trips. Open all year. $$

Rainbow Tioman South of the jetty; 012 989 8572. Brightly painted in pastel shades, these chalets are on a pleasant stretch of beach, with their own bathrooms and mosquito nets. There are basic fan rooms on offer as well as more spacious a/c doubles with hot showers. They can organize a taxi service from Tekek. $

EATING
SEE MAP PAGE 289

De Sanosa Café South of the jetty; 019 933 8398. One of the only places to eat that isn't attached to accommodation, a simple affair that mainly serves rice dishes, fried food, and rice options. plus a modest selection of seafood. $$

Santai Bistro & Chalet Near the jetty; 013 333 3670. This accommodation option also features a good restaurant, mostly serving Malay dishes, and focusing on seafood. $$$

Seribuat Archipelago: the other islands

Tioman Island may be the best known and most visited of the 64 volcanic islands in the **SERIBUAT ARCHIPELAGO**, but a handful of other accessible islands hold beaches and opportunities for seclusion that outstrip those of their larger rival. For archetypal azure waters and table-salt sand, three in particular stand out: **Sibu**, **Besar** and **Rawa**. There are, however, a few resorts on other islands; Aur, for example, is popular among Singapore-based scuba divers. The tourist office in Mersing (see page 280) can advise on the various options. Wi-fi is supplied at most accommodation; however, the signal is unreliable, even in upmarket places, especially when the weather is poor.

Sibu Island

Closest to the mainland, accessible from the village of Tanjung Leman, 30km south of Mersing, **SIBU ISLAND** is actually a cluster of four islands that are collectively the most popular after Tioman. Most resorts are on **Sibu Besar**, which, although not as scenically interesting as some of its neighbours, does have butterflies and huge monitor lizards. The sand here is yellower and the current more turbulent than at some others; most of the coves have good diving spots with offshore coral.

Besar Island

Long, narrow **BESAR ISLAND**, (not to be confused with the island of the same name off Melaka) is about 13km from Mersing and measures 4km by 1km. It holds several resorts and sets of chalets, but you're likely to have the place pretty much to yourself outside weekends and public holidays.

Rawa Island

The tiny island of **RAWA ISLAND**, just 16km (a thirty-minute boat ride) from Mersing, holds a glorious stretch of fine, sugary-sanded beach. The only sure way to get there is by resort-owned speedboat, booked in advance, but if you're lucky then the Tioman-bound ferry might make a stop (on request).

Tengah Island

Approximately 16km from Mersing, **TENGAH ISLAND** has a 3km circumference with eight powdery white sand beaches. The island was the setting for Swedish reality TV show *Expedition Robinson*, the predecessor of the world-famous *Survivor* series. The private island is today home to only one resort.

ARRIVAL AND DEPARTURE   SERIBUAT ARCHIPELAGO: THE OTHER ISLANDS

By resort transfer People staying on the islands normally have to take a boat from Mersing supplied by the resort they are staying at. Note that Sibu is reached by resort boats from Tanjung Leman, a tiny coastal village 30km south of Mersing.

ACCOMMODATION AND EATING

Except where noted, resorts operate on package deals, and the prices given in the reviews below are for two people for one night; subsequent nights may be cheaper. All resorts offer watersport facilities, and most have dive shops, too.

SIBU ISLAND

Rimba Resort http://resortmalaysia.com. Friendly resort and spa with rustic, welcoming rooms on a lovely stretch of beach dotted with palm trees. There's an unspoilt reef just by the shore, which means you'll spot plenty of fish as you snorkel or dive. The tasty food is all home-made. Call ahead to book transfers from Singapore. $$$$

Sea Gypsy Village Resort East coast; http://siburesort.com. Set in well-manicured grounds in a 5-acre jungle clearing, this family-friendly resort offers accommodation in traditional Malay-style wooden chalets and A-frames; all are sea facing and feature private verandas. There are complimentary kids' clubs, and buckets of kids' activities throughout the day (extra charge), as well as plenty of activities including sailing. $$$

BESAR ISLAND

Aseania Beach Resort Middle of the bay, west-facing beach; http://pulaubesarjohor.com. Set on an appealing stretch of sand with decent chalets, a swimming pool and good service – a great place to relax. $$$$

★ **Mirage Island Resort** Just south of the jetty, west-facing beach; http://mirageislandresort.com.my. This is a great choice for its friendly service, well-appointed chalets and reasonable prices. Cheaper rooms are A-frames, but still clean and comfortable. Rates include breakfast and sometimes speedboat transfers too; all-inclusive packages are also available. $$$$

RAWA ISLAND

Rawa Island Resort West-facing beach; http://rawaislandresort.com. Sumptuous resort and spa with wooden chalets equipped with a/c and hot showers, and there's kayaking, snorkelling and scuba diving, as well as a water slide that's actually quite impressive for such a remote location. Rates include boat transfers, and decrease after the first night. $$$$

TENGAH ISLAND

Batu Batu http://batubatu.com.my. This luxurious private island resort, built in the style of a kampung village, comprises 22 villas sprinkled around lush grounds. Being the only resort means that guests have all the island's beaches to themselves – it's a wonderful spot to relax, and the resort welcomes families with young children – the Turtle Watch Camp with be especially popular. There are one or two scheduled boat trips to the resort each day. $$$$

Endau Rompin National Park

One of the few remaining areas of lowland tropical rainforest left in Peninsular Malaysia, the **ENDAU ROMPIN NATIONAL PARK** covers 870 square kilometres. Despite its rich **flora and fauna**, prized by conservationists, the area has only been adequately protected from logging since 1989. There's plenty on offer for nature lovers, from gentle **trekking** to more strenuous **mountain climbing** and **rafting**; for the moment, its trails remain refreshingly untrampled.

Surrounding the headwaters of the lengthy Endau River, and sitting astride the Johor–Pahang state border, the region was shaped by volcanic eruptions more than 150 million years ago. The force of the explosions sent up huge clouds of ash, creating the quartz crystal ignimbrite that's still very much in evidence along the park's trails and rivers, its glassy shards glinting in the light. Endau Rompin's steeply sloped mountains level out into sandstone plateaus, and the park is watered by three **river systems** based around the main tributaries of the Marong, Jasin and Endau rivers, reaching out to the south and east.

Visiting the park

As it can be hard to arrange transport, most people come on one- or two-night **tours**, although day-trips can be organized from Mersing. The **best time** to visit is between March and October, while the paths are dry and the rivers calm. Take loose-fitting, lightweight clothing that dries quickly – even in the dry season you're bound to get wet from crossing rivers – and helps to protect you from scratches and bites. Waterproofs will come in handy, and you'll need tons of insect repellent.

ARRIVAL AND DEPARTURE

ENTRY POINTS

The park has three entry points: one from the west at Selai via Bekok (Johor), and two from the east, at Kuala Kinchin via Kuala Rompin (Pahang) and Kampung Peta via Kahang (Johor). The best is Kampung Peta, where more activities are available; the least interesting, Kuala Kinchin, is often used for one-night tours, but is not recommended as you don't get enough time to get into the jungle proper. The useful Tourism Johor (07 922 2875, http://tourismjohor.my) office is at GPS coordinates Latitude 2.420260, Longitude 103.2611191, and would be a good place to start your planning.

ON TOURS

While it is possible, if tricky, to visit under your own steam, most visitors come on tours that include transport. Mersing see page 280) is the best place to approach from the east; tour agents in KL for the western Selai entry. Tour companies often offer one-night trips staying in Merekek, which include all fees, transport to and from the park office near Kahok (2.5hr from Mersing), and accommodation.

ARRIVING INDEPENDENTLY

Kampung Peta Approaching from the south on the North–South Expressway, take the Ayer Hitam exit and continue straight through Kluang to Kahang town (1hr from Mersing); the park's administrative office is located here, at 11 Tingkat Bawah, Jalan Bawal 1 (07 788 2812), where you'll have to register and pay the entrance fee – given 48 hours' notice, they can help organize 4WD transport into the park. From here continue 5km east, turn north at the park sign and follow logging tracks for 48km (2hr; 4WD is strongly advised) until you reach the Visitor's Complex at Kampung Peta (daily 8am–5pm, registration ends 3pm). There are fan dorms and chalets here, as well as licensed guides. You can also catch a boat to Kuala Jasin.

Kuala Kinchin From Kuala Rompin in Pahang, a road runs through paddy fields 20km to Selandang; continue another 15km to Kuala Kinchin (gate open 9am–5pm), on the park boundary. Although a 4WD is not required, there's no public transport; you can take a taxi to the park entrance from Kuala Rompin. Contact the Forestry Department in Kuala Rompin (09 414 5204). There are basic A-frame chalets to stay at here.

Selai Catch a train to Bekok from JB Sentral, then rent a 4WD to get to the park entrance. By road from the west, exit the North–South Expressway at Yong Peng and head for Chaah in Segamat (20min). After Chaah, follow signs for Bekok (15min) then Sungai Bantang (another 7km). Go past the Sungai Bantang turn-off and carry on for 20km, through an oil-palm estate and past several resettled Orang Asli villages. There is a Visitor Centre at Selai (daily 8am–5pm; 07 922 2875).

Sarawak

302 Southwestern Sarawak
327 Central Sarawak
340 The northern coast
349 The northern interior

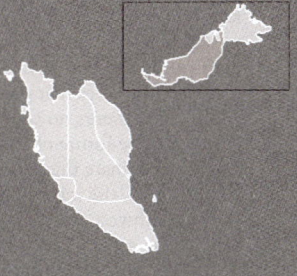

KUCHING, SARAWAK

Sarawak

With its beguiling Indigenous cultures and jungle highlands, Sarawak would seem to epitomize what Borneo is all about. By far the largest state in Malaysia, with an area almost equal to the whole of Peninsular Malaysia, it packs in a host of national parks that showcase everything from coastal swamp forest to vast cave systems, and help preserve some of the world's richest and most diverse ecosystems. There are numerous opportunities for short or extended treks both inside and outside these protected areas, and it's also possible to visit remote longhouse communities, some of which can only be reached by venturing far upriver.

For all its attractions, however, Sarawak is not quite the paradise it might seem on paper. The state encapsulates the bitter dichotomy between development and conservation more clearly than anywhere else in Malaysia. Many of its forests have been degraded by **logging** or cleared for oil palm, putting wildlife and the traditional lifestyles of Indigenous communities under severe pressure. The state government has repeatedly won electoral mandates for its policies, but critics complain it has opened up Sarawak's resources to corporate exploitation in a way that's at best not transparent and at worst mired in corruption. While much of this may have little practical impact on visitors as they travel through, it's good to be aware that the changes you will see throughout the state have a subtext in the ongoing struggle for Sarawak's soul (see page 552).

The lie of the land is complex on many levels, not least **demographically**. Malays and Chinese each make up almost a quarter of Sarawak's almost two and a half million people, but Indigenous peoples account for nearly half that figure. They're sometimes subdivided under three broad headings, though it's nowadays much more common to refer to the Indigenous groups by name. The largest group by far, the **Iban**, constitute nearly thirty percent of Sarawak's population. They, along with the Muslim **Melanau** and other groups, comprise the so-called **Sea Dyaks**, a slightly odd name given that these groups historically lived along river valleys. Then there are the **Land Dyaks**, who live up in the hills; chief among them are the **Bidayuh** of southwestern Sarawak, representing almost a tenth of the population. Finally, the **Orang Ulu** include disparate groups of the northern interior such as the **Berawan**, **Kenyah**, **Kelabit**, **Kayan** and the traditionally nomadic **Penan**. They're grouped together in that they live in the "ulu" or upriver regions of this part of the state.

While this cultural mosaic is a huge highlight of Sarawak, social and economic change, along with widespread conversion to **Christianity**, mean that the old ways are fast dying out. Classic multi-doored **longhouses** do survive and can be superb places to visit, and some peoples do still subsist semi-nomadically in the forest, but you'd be hard-pushed to find any Orang Ulu aged under fifty still sporting, say, the once-prized distended earlobes that previous generations developed by wearing heavy earrings. Meanwhile, there's no shortage of Indigenous people pursuing careers in Sarawak's cities, and the future of Indigenous languages appears under threat as Malay and English dominate the majority of state-run education.

For visitors, the most popular attractions are concentrated at either end of the state. In the southwest, **Kuching**, the understated, attractive capital, makes a perfect base to explore the superb **Bako National Park**, with its wild shoreline of mangrove swamp and hinterland of *kerangas* bush teeming with proboscis monkeys. The Kuching area also packs in lesser national parks, an **orangutan** sanctuary and substantial **caves**. Although Sarawak is not noted for its **beaches**, there are beautiful ones in Bako and decent

PROBOSCIS MONKEY, BAKO NATIONAL PARK

Highlights

Kuching One of Malaysia's most endearingly chilled-out cities, with a pretty waterfront, reasonable museums and great food. See page 303

Santubong Peninsula Lovely beaches hosting resort hotels and an impressive folk museum, all beneath the slopes of Mount Santubong. See page 316

Bako National Park This beautiful reserve has good trekking and sublime sea views and is home to proboscis monkeys. See page 318

Tanjung Datu National Park Little-visited national park on the Indonesian border featuring jungles and beaches, with homestays available at nearby Malay kampungs. See page 324

Niah National Park The superb caves here are not only a natural wonder, easily explored on foot, but also a workplace for men collecting edible swiftlet nests. See page 346

Gunung Mulu National Park Sarawak's top attraction, with astonishing caves and a popular three-day trek to see the shard-like Pinnacles. See page 350

Kelabit Highlands Trek to remote communities dotted around this cool upland backwater. See page 356

HIGHLIGHTS ARE MARKED ON THE MAP ON PAGE 298

options nearer Kuching at the family-friendly resorts of Santubong. A handful of **longhouses** are also worth visiting, notably south of Kuching at **Batang Ai** and around **Sibu**.

In terms of pulling power, Bako is exceeded only by **Gunung Mulu National Park** ("Mulu" to locals) in the far northeast. Most tourists fly in, either making the short ho from nearby **Miri**, Sarawak's second city, or direct from Kuching, to trek to the park's limestone Pinnacles and see its extraordinary caves. Miri itself, though a bland affair

AROUND KUCHING

HIGHLIGHTS
1. Kuching
2. Santubong Peninsula
3. Bako National Park
4. Tanjung Datu National Park
5. Niah National Park
6. Gunung Mulu National Park
7. Kelabit Highlands

that thrives on the proceeds of Sarawak's oil and gas industry, has good accommodation nd is the hub for Twin Otter flights to interior settlements, most notably **Bario** and a' **Kelalan** in the **Kelabit Highlands**. Here, close to the Indonesian border, you can ndertake extended treks through jungle and mountainous terrain, overnighting in Kelabit villages. Other Twin Otter flights head to settlements in the upper reaches of he **Baram** river system, from where it's possible to reach isolated **Penan villages** offering omestays and yet more treks. Another major draw, visitable on a day-trip from Miri,

> ### SARAWAK PLACE NAMES
> As you travel through Sarawak, you'll notice certain terms cropping up repeatedly in the names of places, longhouses and other features. You'll seldom encounter them elsewhere in Malaysia, so it pays to know what they mean:
> **Batang** "Trunk" or "strip"; used before a river name, it denotes that the river is the central member of a system of rivers.
> **Long** "Confluence"; used in town names in the same way as the Malay "Kuala".
> **Nanga** "Longhouse" in Iban; many longhouses are named "Nanga" followed by the name of the river they are next to.
> **Pa** or **Pa'** In the Kelabit Highlands – denotes a village.
> **Rumah** "House" in Malay; some longhouses are named "Rumah" followed by the name of the headman (if there's a change of headman, the longhouse name follows suit).
> **Ulu** From the Malay *hulu*, meaning "upriver"; when used before the name of a river, it indicates the region surrounding the headwaters of that river – for example, the Ulu Ai is the upriver part of the Ai River and its tributaries there.

is **Niah National Park**, its extensive caves a site of major archeological significance as well as a centre for the harvesting of swiftlet nests and bat guano.

Visitors who overland between Kuching and Miri tend to breeze through central Sarawak, but the region is worth considering for the state's most accessible river journey – the popular route along the **Batang Rejang**. The boat ride, beginning at the city of **Sibu**, is its own reward for making it up to nondescript Rejang towns such as **Kapit** and **Belaga**, though it's possible to arrange longhouse trips from either. Also noteworthy in this region is **Bintulu**, a coastal oil town like Miri that's conveniently placed for the beachside forests of **Similajau National Park**.

Brief history
Cave-dwelling **hunter-gatherers** were living in Sarawak forty thousand years ago. Their isolation ended when the first trading boats arrived from Sumatra and Java around 3000 BC, exchanging cloth and pottery for jungle produce. By the thirteenth century Chinese merchants were dominant, bartering beads and porcelain with the coastal Melanau people for bezoar stones (from the gall bladders of monkeys) and birds' nests, both considered aphrodisiacs. In time, the traders were forced to deal with the rising power of the Malay sultans including the Sultan of Brunei. Meanwhile, Sarawak was attracting interest from Europe; the Dutch and English established short-lived trading posts near Kuching in the seventeenth century, to obtain pepper and other spices.

With the decline of the Brunei sultanate, civil war erupted early in the eighteenth century. Local rulers feuded, while piracy threatened to destroy what was left of the trade in spices, animals and minerals. In addition, the Indigenous groups' predilection for **head-hunting** had led to a number of deaths among the traders and the sultan's officials, and violent confrontations between powerful groups were increasing.

The White Rajahs
Just when matters were at their most explosive, the Englishman **James Brooke** took an interest in the area. A former soldier, he helped the Sultan of Brunei quell a rebellion by miners and, as a reward, demanded sovereignty over the area around Kuching. The weakened sultan had little choice but to relinquish control of the awkward territory and in 1841 James Brooke was installed as the first White Rajah of Sarawak. He had essentially created a new kingdom, not formally part of the British Empire.

Brooke built a network of small **forts** – many are now museums – to repel pirates or warring parties. He also sent officials into the malarial swamps and mountainous interior to make contact with the Orang Ulu. But his administration was not without its troubles. In one incident his men killed dozens of marauding Indigenous people, while in 1857 Hakka Chinese **gold-miners**, based in Bau near Kuching, retaliated against his attempts to eliminate their trade in opium and suppress their secret societies. When they attacked Kuching, Brooke got away by the skin of his teeth. His nephew, **Charles Brooke**, assembled a massive force of warrior Indigenous people and followed the miners; in the ensuing battle over a thousand Chinese were killed.

In 1863 Charles Brooke took over and continued to acquire territory from the Sultan of Brunei. River valleys were bought for a few thousand pounds, the local Indigenous people either persuaded to enter into deals or crushed if they resisted. The sultan's territory had shrunk so much it was now surrounded on all three sides by Brooke's Sarawak, establishing the geographical boundaries that still define Brunei today.

Charles was succeeded by his son, **Vyner Brooke**, who consolidated his father's gains. However, the **Japanese occupation** of World War II effectively put an end to his control. Vyner escaped, but most of his officials were interned and some executed. Upon his return in 1946, he was compelled to cede Sarawak to the British government. The Brooke dynasty was effectively at an end, and a last link with its past was severed in 2011 when Vyner's nephew **Anthony Brooke**, his designated successor who had briefly run Sarawak before World War II while Vyner was in the UK, died.

To the present

With Malaysian independence in 1957, attempts were made to include Sarawak, Sabah and Brunei declined at the last minute to join the present-day **Federation of Malaysia**, inaugurated in 1963. Sarawak's inclusion was opposed by Indonesia, and the **Konfrontasi** broke out, with Indonesia arming communist guerrillas inside Sarawak. The insurgency continued for three years until Malaysian troops, aided by the British, put it down. To this day, many inhabitants of the interior remain displaced.

Since then, Sarawak has developed apace with the rest of Malaysia, though at considerable cost to the **environment**, with up to ninety percent of its primary rainforests having been logged. Politically, the state today is closely identified with the policies of **Taib Mahmud**, a Melanau, who was chief minister from 1981 to 2014, and who to an extent oversaw a time of infrastructural and economic growth, yet also passed laws that gave him control of the logging industry during that time. The support of his PBB party and allied parties has helped prop up the ruling coalition in general elections, and the PBB is often viewed as a proxy for UMNO. Sarawak is the only state where Malaysia's main Malay party has no presence.

There are signs of a backlash, however, brought on perhaps by the rising cost of living, economic disparity, and allegations from international environmental groups as well as Taib's opponents and the Malaysian media, that Sarawak's administration is tainted by **corruption** – the list of allegations is far too long to include here, but an internet search will return dozens of examples including damning leaked US embassy cables published by Wikileaks in 2011. In 2014, Taib resigned as chief minister (a role taken over by Adenan Satem, his former brother-in-law) to become **Governor of Sarawak,** although many feel that Taib is still a big influence in the government.

The 2016 local elections saw the PBB claw back the swing to the opposition that took place in the 2011 election, and this was consolidated further in 2021 – ironically enough, given what is happening to the state's natural resources, with the continued help of rural voters. Much of this may have to do with the fact that rural areas in support of the PBB still seem to see more infrastructure development than those that support opposition parties.

Taib's main environmental legacy is the project to construct twelve hydroelectric dams in the state, of which only the **Bakun** and **Murum** dams have so far been added to the Batang Ai dam (completed back in 1985); the Bakun dam is already showing worrying signs of having been poorly constructed by its Chinese contractors. The **Baram Dam** was all set for construction but local and international opposition to the project, which would have displaced over twenty thousand mainly Penan people, saw the plan shelved (but not cancelled) in 2015. Construction has already started on the newest dam, Baleh, scheduled for completion in 2027.

ARRIVAL AND DEPARTURE SARAWAK

By plane It's easy enough to fly into Kuching, Miri, Bintulu or Sibu from the Peninsula, and there are also decent connections with Sabah, Brunei and Singapore. There are also flights from Pontianak in Indonesian Kalimantan to Kuching. Note that Sarawak has its own immigration controls, so you will be stamped in and out even if flying between Sarawak and the other states of Malaysia.

By boat There's a boat from Labuan island, off the Sabah coast, to Lawas.

By bus A handful of buses connect Bandar Seri Begawan and Miri, and Kota Kinabalu and Miri via Lawas. The main official border crossing between Kalimantan and Sarawak is at Entikong/Tebedu (daily, roughly 6am–6pm), 100km south of Kuching by road; it's used by frequent buses plying between Pontianak and Kuching, with some continuing all the way to Miri. However, there are another two crossings at Serikin (southwest of Kuching) and Biawak (west of Kuching), with the latter possibly going to become the main crossing once various road and highway schemes have been completed.

GETTING AROUND

Sarawak covers pretty much the same area as England or the state of Mississippi, but with much of the state wild and thinly populated, there's not that much ground to cover unless you wish to visit remote communities or the interior's national parks, such as Mulu. As ever, it's essential to book **public transport** at least a week in advance if you want to travel around the time of a major festival, notably the two-day *gawai* harvest festival at the start of June, when huge numbers of Indigenous people return to their original longhouses.

By plane Flying is a useful timesaver between Kuching and Miri, and to reach Mulu from either Kuching, Miri. and Kota Kinabalu. However, the most memorable flights are on the tiny Twin Otter planes (see page 349), connecting the interior with Bario and Ba'Kelalan.

By bus Numerous buses ply the trunk road between Kuching and Miri, though thanks to slow-moving trucks journeys take a little longer than distances might suggest. Buses operated by MTC (http://mtcmiri.com) and BusAsia (no relation to AirAsia; http://busasia.my) are a cut above the rest in terms of comfort. Fares are reasonable, and more or less on par with Peninsular Malaysia. Local bus services also radiate from the main cities, mostly during daylight hours only.

By boat The only scheduled boat services you're likely to catch are those between Kuching and Sibu, and express boats along the Rejang River.

By taxi On some routes, buses are supplemented by *kereta sapu* (see page 34); any "taxis" mentioned in small towns here will usually be of this type. Useful in rural areas, such share taxi services are generally reliable – though, of course, their operators are neither licensed nor insured. Prices are comparable to bus fares, unless you're in a 4WD (see page 302). Grab is available in Miri and Kuching, and some smaller cities.

By car Sarawak's road network is simplicity itself. Given that signage is adequate and drivers' behaviour a little less manic than in the Peninsula, renting a car is worth considering. The state's one and only trunk road, part of the so-called Pan-Borneo Highway, runs between Kuching and Miri, via Sibu and Bintulu, and on into Brunei. It's a dual carriageway in an ever-increasing number of sections, though in parts it's still little more than a two-lane country road. Lengthy sections of the highway have few facilities or settlements, so fill up with petrol frequently and try to give yourself plenty of time to arrive before nightfall.

By longboat or 4WD Finally, in remote areas, you might need to charter a longboat for a river trip or a 4WD to gain access to the network of rough logging roads that have begun to supplant boat travel. As always in Malaysia, getting off the beaten track isn't cheap unless you're travelling in a small group – ideally of four people. Details are given in the text where relevant, but unless you're on a budget it's often more worthwhile to pay a tour operator to arrange things.

Hitchhiking Although we don't recommend it in general, for male travellers and couples, hitching can significantly reduce your travel costs and help you meet Sarawak people. It's also possible to hitch along logging tracks, though be prepared to spend the night at a basic jungle rest stop if you don't find a ride.

Southwestern Sarawak

Visitors flying in from Peninsular Malaysia or Singapore are treated to a spellbinding view of muddy rivers snaking their way through the jungle beneath lush peaks. It not only just about sums up Borneo, but also sets the tone for what the southwest of

Sarawak has in store. The area is home to several of Sarawak's national parks, notably **Bako**, with its proboscis monkeys and excellent trekking. It's also a good place to get a grounding in Borneo's Indigenous cultures, which you can do at the museums in the likeable state capital, **Kuching**. Among other top draws are the orangutans of the **Semenggoh Wildlife Rehabilitation Centre** and the **Sarawak Cultural Village**, a brilliant collection of Indigenous houses near the beaches of Damai. You can also see a proper longhouse at **Annah Rais**, or head east to the edges of **Batang Ai National Park**, home to many Iban communities, though they're very much maintained purely for the tourists, and whose inhabitants already seem a bit sick of hanging around.

Kuching

KUCHING, the state's oldest, largest city, is the perfect gateway to Sarawak. This is one of Malaysia's most charming and laidback cities, revelling in a picturesque setting on the Sarawak River, with Mount Santubong looming on the western horizon. Despite central high-rises, much of the recent development has been confined to the bland but burgeoning suburbs, and the historical core remains appealingly sleepy and human in scale, its colonial architecture redolent of a bygone era. Kuching's blend of contradictions – of commerce alongside a sedate pace of life, of fashionable cafés rubbing shoulders with old-fangled *kedai kopis* – makes it an appealing place to chill out for several days while exploring sights such as the **Sarawak Museum**, which showcases the state's ethnological heritage, and making excursions to the numerous national parks and other sights in the vicinity.

Most of Kuching lies on the south bank of the river, its core an easily walkable warren of crowded lanes. The area sandwiched between Jalan Courthouse to the west, Jalan Wayang to the east and Reservoir Park to the south, usually referred to as **old Kuching**, includes several colonial churches and administrative buildings. **Chinatown** occupies the same general area, incorporating what were once the main shopping streets of Main Bazaar, facing the river, and Carpenter Street, and Chinese businesses and restaurants also dominate Jalan Padungan to the east. The traditional **Malay district** is dominated by the domes of the **Masjid Negeri**, with several Malay kampungs north of the river too. The Chinese and Malays together make up nearly two-thirds of Kuching's population of just over 650,000, though there are also substantial communities of Bidayuh and Iban.

Brief history

When **James Brooke** came up the river in 1841, he arrived at a village known as Sarawak, on a small stream called Sungai Mata Kuching ("Cat's Eye"), adjoining the main river; he probably shortened the stream's name, which came to refer to the fast-expanding settlement. However, a much-repeated tale has it that the first rajah pointed to the village and asked its name. The Malay locals, thinking Brooke was pointing to a cat, replied – reasonably enough – "kuching" ("cat"; which explains the city's obsession with cat memorabilia). Either way, in 1872 Charles Brooke officially changed the settlement's name from Sarawak to Kuching.

Until the 1920s, the capital was largely confined to the south bank of the Sarawak River, stretching only from the Chinese heartland around Jalan Temple, east of today's centre, to the Malay kampung around the mosque to the west. On the north bank, activity revolved around the fort and a few dozen houses reserved for British officials. The prewar **rubber boom** financed the town's expansion, with tree-lined Jalan Padungan, running east from Chinatown, becoming one of its smartest streets. Kuching escaped relatively lightly during World War II, since Japanese bombing raids largely focused on destroying the oil wells in northern Sarawak.

In recent decades, the city has sprawled south and port facilities and warehouses in the centre closed as new shipping terminals and industrial estates were created downriver, to the northeast. Robbed of waterborne traffic, downtown's **riverside** was reinvented in the 1990s with partial success as a leafy, pedestrianized recreation area, its quaint panoramas spoiled only by the bizarre oversized hulk of the State Assembly building, completed in 2009 on the north bank, now joined to the south bank via a rather funky new bridge.

Kuching waterfront

Beginning along Jalan Gambier and continuing for just over 1km until it peters out close to the *Grand Margherita* hotel, Kuching's central **waterfront** is where most visitors begin exploring the city – almost everything of interest is within 500m of this esplanade. Sporting the odd fountain and several fast food kiosks, it has a somewhat sanitized feel, but a sprinkling of whitewashed colonial buildings, tranquil river views and the shophouses of Main Bazaar and Jalan Gambier make for a worthwhile wander.

KUCHING

SHOPPING	
Everrise	5
Greek's Outgear Discovery	2
Indah Café & Art Space	4
Plaza Merdeka	3
Sarawak Craft Council	1
Spring Mall	7
Wong San Hiup Pottery	6

SOUTHWESTERN SARAWAK SARAWAK

For views alone, the best time to turn up is around 6pm on a fine day, when you'll be treated within an hour to a fiery **sunset** behind Mount Serapi (one of the peaks of Kubah National Park), casting an orange glow over city and river. To get an aerial view, head up to the cinema on the top floor of the colourful Medan Pelita building on Lebuh Temple, where a large balcony offers a fine vista over old Kuching. It's possible to take **boat trips** on the river (see page 311).

Along the Main Bazaar

The fast-gentrifying **Main Bazaar** is home to a few guesthouses and tour agencies, plus a rash of souvenir shops and a gallery, the odd attempt at a posh café, and a handful of more traditional shops. At its junction with Jalan Tun Haji Openg lies the **Old Courthouse** that used to house many of the region's tourist facilities but has been now rented out to an assortment of high-end restaurants. Built in 1874, and sporting

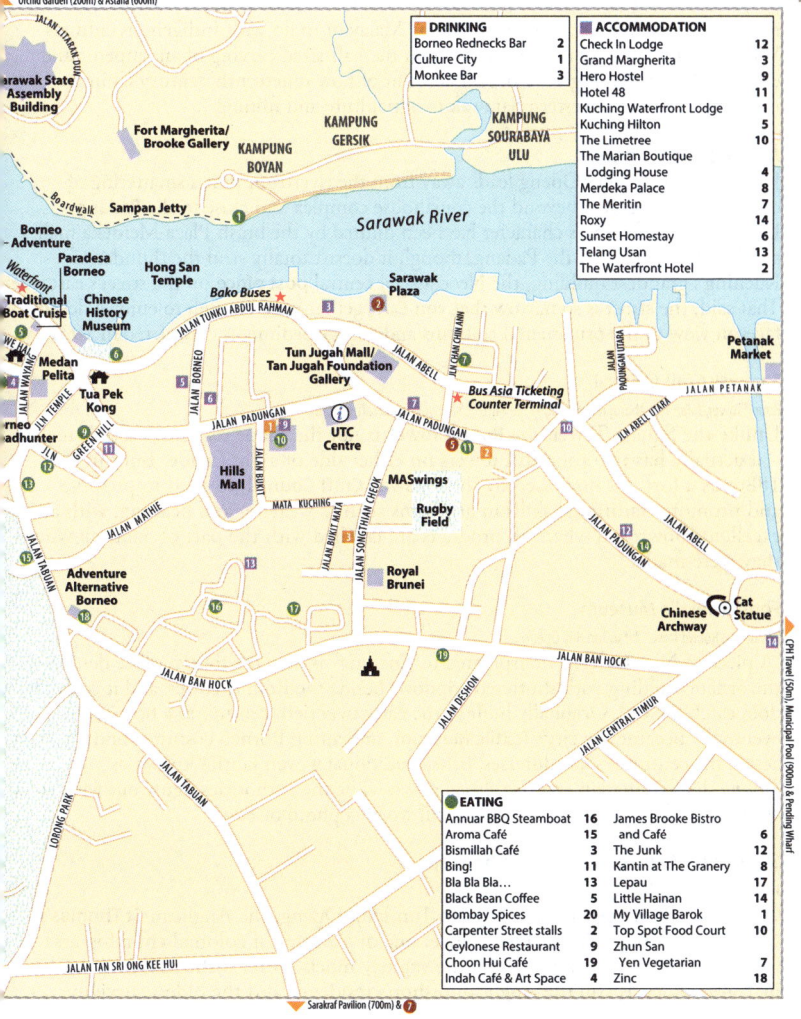

impressive Romanesque columns, the complex is fronted by the **Charles Brooke Memorial**, a 6m-high granite obelisk erected in 1924. Stone figures at its base represent the state's Chinese, Malay, Dayak and Orang Ulu communities.

Diagonally across, on the waterfront itself, the single-turreted **Square Tower** is all that's left of a fortress built in 1879. An earlier wooden construction burned during the 1857 gold-miners' rebellion. The trio of compact 1930s buildings next door, once belonging to the **Sarawak Steamship Company**, now house the so-called waterfront bazaar, a disappointing collection of souvenir outlets; you're better off checking out the touristy shophouses opposite.

Chinese History Museum
Eastern end of the Main Bazaar • Free; no photography allowed • 082 231 520

The squat, pale orangey-pink **Chinese History Museum** was built in the 1910s as a courthouse for the Chinese community, after which it became the Chinese Chamber of Commerce. It's a source of pride to the local Chinese in a country where state-run museums often snub traditions that aren't Malay or to do with Indigenous cultures. While the artefacts are modest, apart from the half-sized carving of an emperor and empress, the museum gives a decent account of how nineteenth-century Chinese migrants opened up western Sarawak to agriculture and mining.

Around the Padang

Jalan Tun Abang Haji Openg leads away from the riverfront past a smattering of colonial buildings just beyond the courthouse complex and close to the **Padang**. Unfortunately the area's character has been diluted by the brash Plaza Merdeka mall and hotel just north of the Padang, though it doesn't totally steal the thunder of Kuching's grandest building, the Neoclassical central **post office** on the street's east side. That said, the street is so narrow that you can't get far back enough to enjoy a decent face-on view of the ornamental columns and a huge pediment, completed in 1931.

Sarawak Craft Council
Round Tower, Jalan Tun Abang Haji Openg • Free • http://sarawakhandicraft.com.my

Unlike the Square Tower, the **Round Tower** is not the shape its name would suggest – it actually has two roundish towers on either side of a flat facade. Built in the 1880s as a fort, it's now used by the **Sarawak Craft Council**, formed to preserve and promote traditional skills in art forms such as weaving and beading, with an excellent showroom where all products are labelled with the part of Sarawak where they were made.

Former Textile Museum
Beside the Round Tower, Jalan Tun Haji Openg

"A piece of New Orleans transplanted to Kuching" is how the tourist office describes the ornate building with shuttered windows beside the Round Tower, and it certainly does catch the eye. Originally built in the early twentieth century as a hospital, it eventually became the city's **Textile Museum**, presenting Borneo costumes and artefacts across the centuries – headdresses, belts, traditional woven fabrics known as *pua kumbu*. Unfortunately, this has closed down while the authorities figure out what to do with the building, but the exterior is still worth a photo or two.

St Thomas's Cathedral and the Bishop's House
Jalan Tun Haji Openg • Free

On a hillock off the east side of Jalan Tun Haji Openg, the Anglican **St Thomas's Cathedral** is a tidy, plain 1950s edifice, one of a cluster of colonial churches and mission schools hereabouts. Only the vaguely mock-Tudor **Bishop's House**, built in 1849, which is still the Anglican bishop's residence and the oldest surviving building in the city, is worth a look, though the inside is not usually open to the public; reach it by turning left off Jalan McDougall and walking uphill for a couple of minutes.

Chinatown
East of the Old Courthouse complex, a gaudy Chinese archway marks the entrance to Kuching's historic **Chinatown** via **Carpenter Street** (the name is still used rather than the Malay "Jalan Carpenter"), which becomes Jalan Ewe Hai at its eastern end. Truth be told, the district's Chinese flavour is somewhat diluted by a rash of bars these days, but a few old-fashioned *kopitiams*, herbalists and snack shops still dot the shophouses of Carpenter Street and the tiny lanes running off it, and a handful of well-maintained temples merit a peek, the largest being **Tua Pek Kong** on Lebuh Temple, at the district's eastern end. Tua Pek Kong, one explanation has it, is a sort of patron saint of Chinese communities in Southeast Asia; temples throughout Malaysia and Singapore bear his name. Raised behind a gaudy retaining wall, Kuching's version was built in the mid-eighteenth century, though a rather plastic restoration has left it slightly charmless; you may find the Siang Ti (Northern Deity) temple on Carpenter Street and the Hong San (Phoenix Hill) temple on Jalan Ewe Hai more atmospheric. Any of these temples may play host to theatrical or musical performances during **festivals**, especially Chinese New Year.

Sarawak Museum
Jalan Tun Abang Haji Openg • http://museum.sarawak.gov.my

Borneo's oldest museum (previously known as the **Ethnology Museum**) and housed in a lovely nineteenth-century faux Normandy townhouse set in lush grounds, this used to be regarded locally as one of the country's finest museums, thanks largely to its former curator, **Tom Harrisson** (1911–76). Best remembered for discovering a 39,000-year-old skull at Niah in 1957, which led to a reappraisal of the origins of early man in Southeast Asia, he also frequently visited Indigenous peoples to collect the artefacts that comprised the museum's biggest attraction, though the bulk of these are now in the Borneo Cultures Museum across the road. At the time of writing, the Sarawak Museum was undergoing long-term renovation, though it had completed the initial phases – the building was largely empty inside, but open to visitors on limited tours, which did at least allow some appreciation of its architecture.

Borneo Cultures Museum
Jalan Tun Abang Haji Openg • Charge • http://museum.sarawak.gov.my

You can't miss the **Borneo Cultures Museum**, which is already up there with Borneo's most distinctive specimens of modern architecture – tall pillars, backed by a rattan-effect lattice of rhombus windows, split and join near a distinctive golden arched roof. It's a giant place, with exhibits strewn across five levels, including much of Tom Harrisson's hoard (see page 307). Level two features arts, crafts and displays pertaining to Borneo's many rivers; level three looks at the relationship between local communities and the environment; level four displays historical artefacts from across the centuries; while on the top level you can have a look at textiles and other local craft. They've really tried hard with the presentation, and the lighting really makes the ancient artefacts look evocative.

Islamic Heritage Museum
Jalan P. Ramlee • Free • http://museum.sarawak.gov.my

Just west of the Borneo Cultures Museum, the **Islamic Heritage Museum** is housed inside a former Malay college and religious school. Seven galleries in its cool, tiled interior hold unexpectedly fine examples of Islamic art and displays on architecture, coinage and textiles, which are all set around a pleasant central courtyard garden.

SARAWAK'S CERAMIC JARS

The status and wealth of members of Sarawak's Indigenous groups depended on how many **ceramic jars** they possessed, and you can still see impressive models in longhouses as well as in some museums. Ranging from tiny, elegantly detailed bowls to much larger vessels, more than 1m in height, the jars were used for such purposes as storage, brewing rice wine and making payments – dowries and fines for adultery and divorce settlements. The most valuable jars were only used for ceremonies like the Gawai Kenyalang (the rite of passage for a mature man of means, involving the recitation of stories by the longhouse bard), or for funerary purposes. When a member of the Kelabit people died, the corpse was packed into a jar in a foetal position to await rebirth from the jar, its "womb". The Berawan did the same, and as decomposition took place, the liquid from the body was drained through a bamboo pipe, leaving the individual's bones or clothing to be placed in a canister and hoisted onto an ossuary above the riverbank. It's said that the jars can also be used to foretell the future, and can summon spirits through the sounds they emit when struck.

West of the centre

The pocket of town immediately west of the Padang has a noticeably Islamic feel, with the golden-domed **Masjid Negeri** (Kuching Mosque) atop a hillock at its heart and nearby streets packed with Malay and Indian Muslim *kedai kopis*. The most colourful approach to the area is via pedestrianized **Jalan India**, named for the Indian coolies who arrived in the early twentieth century to work at Kuching's port; today it's packed with market stalls selling cheap shoes, clothing and household items. The mosque aside, the only specific sight is a popular **weekend market**, further southwest.

Sunday market

Just north of the Tun Abdul Rahman Bridge at Medan Niaga Satok • Fri evening until late, Sat mid-afternoon until late, Sun early morning until noon • City Public Link buses #K5 and #K7 leave every 30min or so from Jalan Mosque bus park office, though it's probably quicker to walk: head to Masjid Negeri, then down Jalan Haji Taha and under the flyover at Jalan Kulas, turning right into Jalan Satok at the second flyover, then follow Jalan Satok until reaching the bridges

Variously known as the **Sunday market** or night market, the weekend market on Medan Niaga Satok is not quite the spectacle it used to be when it was in the street – but for once, that's no bad thing. The bush meat trade of years gone by has been halted by better environmental enforcement; these days the most exotic thing you might see on sale are edible sago grubs, which live on thorny sago palms in the jungle. However, the market is certainly colourful and frenetic, selling a good range of snacks as well as a few souvenirs, jungle products including wild honey, and local vegetables such as the ubiquitous fern tops. When crossing the river, either use or at least keep an eye out for the **Satok Suspension Bridge**, built in 2021 in homage to an earlier bridge that carried water pipelines over the waters, and beautifully illuminated at night.

Sama Jaya Nature Reserve

Jalan Setia Raja, 8km southwest of the Padang • Free • http://sarawakforestry.com

Little-known to anyone other than from the joggers that frequent it, the **Sama Jaya Nature Reserve** is the closest you'll get to real wildlife in the city. Despite being entirely surrounded by the city, the reserve is home to both a boisterous troop of short-tailed macaques and a wide range of birds. Most people come here to use the jogging trail, though there are also four short nature trails that give you a bit of an experience of the jungle (if you can ignore the hum of traffic). Here you'll also find the **Sarawak Forestry accommodation booking office** (see page 311), and a couple of tiny tree-related museums, though you'll have to ask for the keys at the office if you want to look inside.

East of the centre

Downtown Kuching's commercial district, east of Chinatown, is home to most of the city's modern hotels, a handful of ordinary shopping malls and several banks. The easiest way to get there is to follow Jalan Tuanku Abdul Rahman, the continuation of Main Bazaar, east until it swings away from the river at the *Grand Margherita* hotel to join the area's other main thoroughfare, **Jalan Padungan**. This road feels like a natural extension of Chinatown, its shophouses still home to several largely Chinese restaurants and *kopitiams*, though Western-style cafés and bars have made their presence felt too.

The archway by the major gyratory further east on Jalan Padungan has a certain notoriety as the site of Kuching's original **cat statue**, a tacky 1.5m-high white-plaster effigy, paw raised in welcome. Though the location isn't at all prepossessing, the statue was regarded as a city icon for many years, so much so that more cat statues have since appeared elsewhere on Jalan Padungan and in other parts of town.

Tun Jugah Foundation Gallery
Level 4 (via lift), Tun Jugah Mall, 18 Jalan Tuanku Abdul Rahman • http://tunjugahfoundation.org.my

The excellent modern **Tun Jugah Foundation gallery**, the showcase for a charity set up to honour a long-serving Iban politician who died in 1981, showcases fine Iban weaving – around a dozen examples of **pua kumbu** cloth, wall-mounted or framed in sliding panels. The geometrical patterns are fascinating but bafflingly abstract to the untrained eye, though once you read the labelling you might be able to make out the animal and other motifs. Most are in shades of reddish brown and black, the colour applied through *ikat* (tie-dyeing) with a base brown pigment traditionally made from the bark of the *engkudu* tree (*Morinda citrifolia*); vegetable indigos are added on top, yielding black in areas already dyed brown. The depth of colour depends on the type of yarn and the number of times it's dipped in the dyes.

In a large **teaching room**, the arts of weaving are passed on to a new generation of local women, not just Iban; you may be able to sit in on some classes or talk to the instructors or participants. An additional side gallery is devoted to **beads**, as used in the jewellery of the Iban and other Indigenous people, and features examples in semiprecious stone and snazzy multicoloured glass.

The north bank

The leafy far side of the Sarawak River, views of which are the major part of the waterfront's appeal, has been redeveloped with the construction of the curvy new **Darul Hana Bridge**, and a riverside walk past the two important colonial buildings here, the **Astana** (closed to the public) and **Fort Margherita**, which holds a small museum. The shoreline, however, is dominated by the outlandish **State Assembly Building** (also called the DUN Building), a sort of giant espresso maker crossed with a spaceship that locals disdain as a waste of taxpayers' money. Still, it is worth crossing the water to look back at downtown Kuching and perhaps to wander through the Malay kampungs.

Sampans still shuttle across the river all day and into the evening, though they're a dying breed.

Fort Margherita/Brooke Gallery
600m east of the Astana • Charge • http://brookegallery.org

Dwarfed by the State Assembly Building, **Fort Margherita** is one of the best examples of the Brookes' system of fortifications, and named after James's wife Margaret – she must have been quite a woman, as one of Oscar Wilde's fairy tales, *The Young King*, is also dedicated to her. It's a fine, sturdy building; well preserved, too, since it never saw any action. The interior contains the three floors of the **Brooke Gallery**, explaining his extraordinary life and works as well as their effect on the Indigenous peoples. You can also visit the grassy courtyard, where the small antique cannons still point out, and the execution room on the ramparts, containing a hanging bag of "laughing" skulls.

Malay kampungs

Quite a few **Malay kampungs** are visible on the north bank from downtown Kuching; the cluster of three east of Fort Margherita are the most visited. The obvious target is **Kampung Boyan**, marked out by its waterside food court with its twin-humped roof, though the mixture of traditional clapboard dwellings and more modern houses is not particularly atmospheric. Look out for the local cottage industry, the manufacture of multicoloured *kek lapis* (layer cake); street traders all along Main Bazaar hawk examples. If you come in the evening, consider dining at *My Village Barok* (see page 313), a fine Malay restaurant.

ARRIVAL AND DEPARTURE — KUCHING

BY PLANE

KUCHING INTERNATIONAL AIRPORT
The airport (http://kuchingairportonline.com) is 12km south of the city, and plays host to most of the main regional airlines.
Facilities There's a small Tourism Malaysia desk (generally daily 9am–10pm) in the baggage hall, though the tourist office (see page 311) is much better. The arrivals hall also holds car rental agencies, ATMs and a foreign exchange counter.
Getting into town Booths sell pre-paid coupons for the taxi ride into town, though it usually works out about half the price if you use a Grab car instead. Alternatively, if you walk west to the main road (turn left at the car park; it's about 1.5km away), you can cross at the lights where there is a bus stop heading north, and flag down any local bus (6am–8pm; 25min), all of which end up at one of the stops in the Kuching mosque area – ask here for which buses head out to the airport too.
Destinations Bintulu (5 daily; 55min); Johor Bahru (3–5 daily; 1hr 25min); Kota Kinabalu (6 daily; 1hr 25min); Kuala Lumpur (2–3 hourly; 1hr 45min); Miri (6–7 daily; 1hr); Mukah (3 daily; 1hr); Mulu (1 daily; 1hr 30min); Penang (2 daily; 2hr); Sibu (5–6 daily; 40min); Singapore (3–4 daily; 1hr 20min).

BY BUS

If you're leaving by bus and want to avoid trekking out to the new bus station to buy a ticket in advance – advisable around the time of a festival – it's useful to book online, or travel with BusAsia, which has a ticket office just off Jalan Padungan.

KUCHING SENTRAL REGIONAL EXPRESS BUS TERMINAL
All the bus companies arrive and depart from Kuching's long-distance bus station, located a little way west of the airport.
Getting into town Taxi drivers may attempt to overcharge you to the city centre, and can be hard to bargain with. Alternatively, take a Grab or cross the main road and flag down any bus – all will take you to the centre, most likely to one of the stops in the Kuching mosque area.
Destinations Bintulu (9 daily; 11hr); Miri (9 daily; 15hr); Mukah (2 daily; 9hr); Pontianak (Indonesia; 2 daily; 8hr 45min); Sarikei (8 daily; 5hr 30min–6hr 30min); Sibu (5 daily; 7hr); Sri Aman (10 daily; 3hr 30min).

BY BOAT

Ferries Before Covid hit, there were regular passenger ferries to and from Sibu (4hr 30min), via Sarikei on the coast, using the Pending terminal 6km east of the centre. At the time of writing, these had not been operating for some time, but it's worth checking to see whether they've resurfaced, as many travellers found them preferable to the bus ride.

GETTING AROUND

By city bus and minivan You're unlikely to use Kuching's city buses in the easily-walkable downtown area, where bus stops offer practically no information or labelling. Also, while some services run two or three times per hour, many only go a few times a day, and local buses have in any case been in flux for years; ask at the Visitors' Information Centre (see page 311) for the latest schedules. All buses operate between dawn and dusk only, and most start out from the area just east of Masjid Negeri, where cramped minivans shadow many bus routes. Minivans leave when full – avoid if you value comfort.
By local bus Most bus services that start and end inside Kuching are run by Rapid Kuching (red vehicles) or City Public Link (largely green vehicles). Both firms, along with the Sarawak Transport Company (green and cream buses) and some minor operators, also provide handy services out into Kuching's hinterland; details are given in the relevant accounts. The city's new autonomous KUTS bus system is due to be in operation by the beginning of 2027, running along three colour-coded lines that will almost certainly be of use to tourists.
By taxi While Grab (http://grab.com/my) is the transport option of choice, there are taxi ranks near the mosque and in front of hotels along Jalan Tuanku Abdul Rahman.

By boat It's possible to take an expensive sunset river trip, the Sarawak River Cruise (1–2 daily, from the jetty near the Sarawak Steamship Company building; 1hr 30min; http://sarawakrivercruise.com), but the views are little better than those from dry land. Other options include the Royal Kuching Cruise (royalkuchingcruise.com), which goes out on sunset and night tours each evening; the former comes with a free flow of drink, and the latter with a beer or soft drink included.

By motorbike A couple of guesthouses along Jalan Carpenter rent motorbikes, but the best deals are to be had from Kuching Car Rental (kuching-carrental.com), who rent a variety of bikes by the day or week, and can arrange pick-up or drop-off at the airport; you'll need to show a licence.

By bike Paredesa and CPH Travel (see page 311) are among the places renting bikes, though prices can be outrageous. CPH also organizes bike tours of Kuching and the surrounding kampungs (see page 311).

By car Rental operators include Kuching Holidays (082 463 318, http://kuchingholidays.com) at the airport; Flexi (082 452 200, http://flexicarrental.com) at the airport and at Lot 7050, Jalan Sekama; Hertz at the airport (082 450 740; http://hertz.com).

INFORMATION

Visitors' Information Centre The state's tourism office is in the Old Courthouse complex at the western edge of the waterfront (daily 9am–6pm; 082 410 944, http://sarawaktourism.com). Staff are knowledgeable about Kuching and its environs as well as the rest of Sarawak.

Sarawak Forestry Corporation Located some way out of the centre at the Sama Jaya Nature Reserve (see page 308; Mon–Fri 8am–5pm; 082 248 088, http://sarawakforestry.com). It takes bookings for accommodation at many national parks, though not Mulu. The friendly and knowledgeable staff can also tell you where *Rafflesia* flowers (see page 558) are blooming, and in theory all relevant information and accommodation bookings (http://ebooking.sarawak.gov.my) are online; this is a great place to work out which parks would be best for you (and see monkeys).

Newspapers and Magazines English-language newspapers such as the *Borneo Post* (http://theborneopost.com), *Sarawak Tribune* (http://sarawaktribune.com) and *The Star* (which has a separate Sarawak edition) detail cultural and other happenings in town and around the state. There was also a local lifestyle magazine called *Kuching In & Out* (http://kuchinginandout.com), which no longer exists, though its website still has some decent information.

TOUR OPERATORS

Sarawak's tour operators come into their own for **longhouse stays**, typically around the Batang Ai area, and other trips off the beaten track – which could mean the less touristy national parks or a foray into an *ulu* area where local contacts are needed to ensure transport and accommodation. That said, if you're an experienced traveller, many of these destinations are perfectly easy to visit by organizing yourself using this Guide – and considerably cheaper, especially if you travel with companions.

★ **Adventure Alternative Borneo** Lot 37, Jalan Tabuan; http://adventurealternativeborneo.com. By far the best choice for interesting, off-the-beaten-track tours at reasonable prices. This outfit also has top ethical credentials, not only putting half their profits back into the communities they work in, but also treating them with a lot more respect than some of the larger agencies. They go to many locations in southern Sarawak that nobody else goes to, with some excellent trips to remote Iban longhouses and wildlife spotting in the area between Simujang and Sri Aman.

Borneo Adventure 55 Main Bazaar; http://borneoadventure.com. Award-winning, pioneering operation, particularly good on longhouse stays. Its jungle lodge along the Batang Ai at Nanga Sumpa (see page 327), is probably the best of the three companies that go to the region.

CPH Travel 70 Jalan Padungan; http://cphtravel.com.my. Especially good on boat trips, for example to the mouth of the Santubong River (4hr) to spot Irrawaddy dolphins (see page 317), though they also do longhouse tours on the Lemanak River (two days, one night).

Paredesa Borneo 1 Jalan Wayang; http://paradesaborneo.com. Offers a great one-day bike tours of Kuching, as well as one- and two-day kayaking, biking and trekking tours – or a combination of all three – out in the wild. Also one of your best bets if you'd like to go caving in the area, with regular day-trips on offer.

ACCOMMODATION   SEE MAP PAGE 304

There's plenty of choice when it comes to places to stay. **Guesthouses** are clustered in and around Chinatown (especially Carpenter Street); they all have pretty similar rooms and prices (though most are without en-suite bathrooms), and include a "simple breakfast" which invariably turns out to be toast and jam. Most **hotels** are in the commercial district to the east, although it's not as atmospheric as staying near Carpenter Street. To stay at or near the **beach**, consider the Santubong Peninsula, a 30min bus ride west (see page 317). As ever, you should book ahead to stay during a major **festival** – a month ahead if you plan to be here over the weekend of June's Rainforest Music Festival (see page 318).

GUESTHOUSES, HOSTELS AND B&BS

★ Check In Lodge 177 Jalan Padungan; 016 889 4896. Artsy in design from tip to toe, this is grand value for money, whether you're looking for a dorm or a private room. The common areas encourage mingling, while staff are knowledgeable and friendly, and there's a decent breakfast spread, plus coffee, tea and crackers 24hr. $

Hero Hostel 23 Jalan Bukit Mata; 011 5626 2579. Great, if slightly mucky, hostel option that's just about the cheapest place to stay in town – and that applies to the private rooms too. They've taken the superhero theme and run with it, and the end result is kind of fun, even if it may feel like you're waking up in a kid's bedroom, with blue-and-red bedspreads, and Captain America staring you in the face. A lot of rooms don't have windows, yet you can still hear noise from the nearby bars quite clearly. $

Hotel 48 13 & 14 Jalan Greenhill; http://facebook.com/48Room4Rent. Very clean, inexpensive but large a/c rooms and dorms. There's not a great deal of character, but it's efficiently run and fantastic value. The cheapest doubles are fairly spartan (though some have windows), but you'll have to pay more if you want a bathroom. Close to lots of places to eat and drink. $

Kuching Waterfront Lodge 15 Main Bazaar; http://kuchingwaterfrontlodge.com. Atmospheric and cosy lodge housed in a refurbished shophouse done out like a Chinese mansion with floor tiles, wooden beams and a chandelier in the foyer. Rooms are less slick and occasionally a bit tatty, but all are en suite, with a/c and TV, and some even have four-poster beds. $$

★ Sunset Homestay Off Jalan Bukit Mata; 016 859 8988. Hands down the best budget sleeps in Kuching, so long as you don't mind sleeping in a new-fangled "pod" – a win-win combination of dorm and private room (though still definitely a dorm). The furnishings are new, and the place is kept very clean by a professional team. $

HOTELS

Grand Margherita Jalan Tuanku Abdul Rahman; http://grandmargherita.com. Swanky top-end affair, with Cantonese restaurant, river-facing pool, and shuttle services to many local attractions and the airport. It's also pretty child-friendly, with a children's pool, playground and babysitting service. Rates can fall on Fri & Sat. $$$

Kuching Hilton Jalan Tuanku Abdul Rahman; http://kuching.hilton.com. As well organized as you'd expect a *Hilton* to be, with many large, modern rooms boasting comfortable beds; those on upper floors have great views. There is also a pool (with bar), mini-gym and six cafés and restaurants, but you may have to pay for in-room wi-fi – super annoying. $$$

The Limetree Jalan Abell; http://limetreehotel.com.my. Though lacking any character, this is a reliable and clean mid-range option. The *Limetree* boasts modern rooms with stylish minimalist decor, including some jumbo-sized executive suites, and a pleasant rooftop bar. Non-smoking throughout, and rates include breakfast. $$

★ The Marian Boutique Lodging House 25 Lebuh Wayang; http://themarian.com.my. Housed in an old girls' school on a hill overlooking the main bazaar, this boutique heritage hotel has retained many of the 1885 building's original features. The forty-odd rooms (named after previous headmistresses) have the dark timber or tiled floors, with faux nineteenth-century decor but modern fittings. Also has a pool and a very good Western restaurant. $$

★ Merdeka Palace Jalan Tun Abang Haji Openg; http://merdekapalace.com. Not quite the five-star it likes to think of itself as, but then again you won't be paying five-star prices – in fact, sometimes rooms here cost barely any more than a cheap guesthouse, on which occasions they're a real bargain. With a swanky lobby, pleasant pool and good service, plus fine views from the higher levels, it's worth a look to see what's on offer here. $$$

★ The Meritin 92 Jalan Padungan; http://meritinhotel.com. Elegant in a monochrome kind of style, this can be very fair value for money if you book in advance. Rooms score highly on the comfort front, breakfasts are bountiful, and the staff sharp and attentive – all in all, a lovely place to stay. $$$

Roxy Off Jalan Padungan; http://roxyhotel.my. Mid-ranger with a flashy exterior, but rooms that are perfectly normal, and mostly quite spacious and airy, with mood lighting and excellent bathrooms. The lobby and common areas look surprisingly refined for the price you may end up paying, and the breakfasts are great too. $$$

Telang Usan Off Jalan Ban Hock; http://telangusan.com. This pioneering hotel is Kayan-owned, hence the swirly

---

SARAWAK CUISINE

Popular **local dishes** in Sarawak include *manok pansoh* (or *ayam pansoh*), a Bidayuh/Iban dish of chicken and tapioca leaves stewed in bamboo tubes; *umai*, the state's answer to sashimi – raw fish or prawn shreds mixed with chilli and lime juice; *ambal*, delicious rubbery little clams, usually curried; and, as greens, the ubiquitous fern tops *paku* and *midin*. And, of course, Sarawak has its own variants of common Malaysian dishes, notably *laksa* – the Sarawakian variety uses rice vermicelli and is usually served in the morning – and *kuay teow*, often prepared in a tangy tomato gravy (outside the state people add a little vinegar to get the same sourness).

Orang Ulu motifs in its decor. Rooms are comfortable enough; on the downside, reaching the waterfront requires you to head south to Jalan Ban Hock and double back. Rates include breakfast. $\overline{\$\$}$

The Waterfront Hotel 68 Jalan Tun Abang Haji Openg; http://thewaterfrontkuching.com. Perched on top of Plaza Merdika, this high-rise, high-end hotel is far better located and has better views than those in the commercial district, and for a much better price. Decor of both rooms and public areas is "artrageous", painted in bright colours with artwork on the walls, and the hotel also boasts a pool, gym and restaurant. $\overline{\$\$\$\$}$

EATING SEE MAP PAGE 304

Kuching's lively and dynamic **eating** scene offers opportunities to sample Indigenous dishes (see box page 312), as well as decent international cuisine. Many top-end restaurants close for several days over the Gawai festival, when staff return to their "hometown" longhouses or jungle villages.

RESTAURANTS

Annuar BBQ Steamboat Close to the Telang Usan hotel, off Jalan Ban Hock; 019 886 7900. Among the best places in town for steamboat; for a small fee you get unlimited helpings from their spread of seafood, meat and other ingredients, which you then cook yourself at the outdoor tables. Their slogan is "you cannot go home if you are not full". $\overline{\$\$}$

★ **Aroma Café** 126 Jalan Tabuan; 082 417 163. This simple Bidayuh-run restaurant, on the ground floor of a dreary commercial block, is a fine place to sample Indigenous dishes such as *umai*, *ayam pansoh* and *midin* with garlic. Best value is the popular lunchtime *campur*-style spread (Mon–Fri only), but going à la carte is unlikely to cost much more. $\overline{\$}$

Bla Bla Bla... 27 Jalan Tabuan. Designer touches such as Oriental water features set the tone at this fusion restaurant where you can savour Chinese-style renditions of un-Chinese ingredients such as salmon, ostrich and lamb, and round off your meal with cheesecake. Their speciality is a tangy *midin* salad, but many main courses will set you back double that. $\overline{\$\$\$}$

Bombay Spices Lot 62, Lorang 4, Jalan Nanas; 010 972 7176. One of the best curry houses in town, serving excellent and authentic North Indian food. It's a little difficult to find unless you take a taxi – it's about 2km out from the centre just off Jalan Tun Ahmad Zaidi Adruce. The tandoori items are the speciality (including a fine chicken tikka masala), with great *naan* bread, and you can sit inside the a/c interior or outside if you want to smoke. $\overline{\$\$}$

Ceylonese Restaurant Jalan Greenhill; 012 891 5385. Open, spacious and clean restaurant with outdoor seating, serving a range of cuisines, from Sri Lankan *biriyanis* and curries to North Indian tandoori dishes and filling *naan* – the chef's special *naan* with cheese and meat is perfect for pre- or post-drinking. Also has a range of local Malay and Chinese standards. $\overline{\$\$}$

Choon Hui Café 34 Jalan Ban Hock; 082 243 857. This humble spot – and Sarawak *laksa* in general – exploded in popularity with travellers after a certain Anthony Bourdain came to visit (he actually ate here twice, ten years apart). Snobs will tell you that it's not the best *laksa* in town, but it's a very solid, near-the-top-of-the-pile effort nonetheless, and the place has a singular charm. $\overline{\$}$

James Brooke Bistro and Café Waterfront, near the Hilton; http://facebook.com/jamesbrookebistrocafe. It's very touristy, but this open-sided, greenery-surrounded building offers nice views, even if the food – a mixture of Western and local standards such as Sarawak *laksa* – is nothing special, and the prices on the high side. Unusually for this class of restaurant, they don't take plastic. $\overline{\$\$}$

The Junk 80 Jalan Wayang; http://facebook.com/thejunkkc. Part of a labyrinthine bar complex, this place has a higgledy-piggeldy junk-store look, serving hearty and good-quality plates of Western cuisine, such as lamb shank, steak, fish and chips and other standards. $\overline{\$\$\$}$

Kantin at The Granery Marian Boutique Lodging House, 23 Lebuh Wayang; http://facebook.com/kantingranary. Housed in a high-ceilinged, stylishly restored 1920s grain warehouse, this well-run bar-restaurant isn't cheap, but serves up very good Western favourites such as burgers, pizza, and meats such as steak, lamb shank and sausages, plus desserts like pineapple-vodka crumble. It's also got a decent bar with imported draft and bottled beers, and live acoustic lounge music at weekends. $\overline{\$\$\$\$}$

★ **Lepau** 99 Jalan Ban Hock; http://instagram.com/lepau restaurant. You'll certainly feel like you're in Borneo while dining at this open-air venue, styled – like the tablecloths and waitress clothing – along traditional lines. The food is excellent, too – think jungle dishes such as *jani tunu* (chargrilled pork longhouse style), and the tasty, veggie/vegan-friendly *ubi randau* (a type of fern), among plenty of others. $\overline{\$\$}$

Little Hainan 207 Jalan Pandungan. Your best choice for Chinese-Malay food, with a pleasingly old-fashioned setting – tiled floors, dangling upside-down parasols (okay, maybe these weren't used to this effect in Old China), lanterns and the like. Basically a *kedai kopi* at breakfast time, lunch and dinner see rice dishes come to the fore – try a Hainanese *nasi lemak* with pork curry. $\overline{\$}$

★ **My Village Barok** Kampung Boyan, down the lane from the jetty and then to the right; http://facebook.com/myvillagebarok. Here's that rare thing, an excellent Malay restaurant in interesting surroundings – a two-storey wooden building decorated with drapes and lanterns and meant to recall a *baruk*, or Bidayuh roundhouse. *Nasi ayam* *penyet* – chicken tenderized by pummelling and then grilled – is the speciality, but they also grill mussels and fish, plus (off-menu) *ayam pansoh*, emptied gloopily from bamboo tubes, and *nasi goreng dabai*, rice fried with the locally grown olive-like *dabai* fruit, when available. Service can be slow at busy times. $\overline{\$}$

Zhun San Yen Vegetarian Jalan Chan Chin Ann; 082 230 068. The best of a handful of Chinese vegetarian places in the area, this is a cafeteria-like place where you can choose from a spread of two dozen veggie stir-fries and soups (noodles dominate at breakfast). $\overline{\$}$

★ **Zinc** 38 Jalan Tabuan; 082 258 000. Smart and convivial, this well-run and stylish restaurant uses many imported ingredients to create delicious Mediterranean cuisine, such as imaginatively topped thin-crust pizzas (including a *laksa* variety), paella and risotto, plus a variety of main salads and even suckling pig. They also serve a range of tapas and have a decent wine list and other imported booze. Housed in a restored, century-old shophouse, it has bags of charm and also has a pleasant terrace bar, popular with the after-work crowd. $\overline{\$\$\$\$}$

CAFÉS

Bing! 84 Jalan Padungan; http://facebook.com/bingcoffee sarawak. Kuching's plushest, slickest independent café chain, with a stylish a/c interior and prices to match. Serves Illy coffee and tasty desserts (try the brownies), and it has a smoking terrace and free wi-fi. $\overline{\$\$\$}$

Black Bean Coffee 87 Carpenter St; http://facebook.com/BlackBeanCoffeeTea.Co. This tiny café and shop serves coffee grown in Sarawak and parts of Indonesia, made using *robusta* and the little-known *liberica* beans – certainly worth a try, though some people find it bitter or even "burnt". There's enough room to drink your cappuccino inside (just about), but most come to grab a takeaway, or just to buy a bag of ground beans to take home. $\overline{\$}$

★ **Indah Café & Art Space** 33 Upper China St; http://indahcafekuching.com. Funky little café just off Carpenter Street, this small, friendly place serves great espresso coffees, outstanding cakes (including lime cheesecake and their famous fruity "messy affair") as well as local dishes, sandwiches and a vegan menu. They also have a small gallery for local artists, and a couple of rooms, plus they run yoga classes (Sun), day-long cookery classes and village tours, and art and batik workshops upstairs. $\overline{\$\$}$

HAWKERS, FOOD COURTS AND KEDAI KOPIS

Bismillah Café Jalan Khoo Hung Yeang; 082 415 803. This little Malay place does a good range of rice and noodle dishes, plus *roti* and curries – its location makes it the best place to fill up before catching a bus. $\overline{\$}$

★ **Carpenter Street stalls** Opposite Siang Ti temple. A tiny, venerable clutch of Chinese-run stalls where the highlight is the Sarawak *laksa*, plus other popular favourites such as chicken rice and *kueh chap* (pork and pig offal in broth). As ever, stalls keep their own time; don't expect to find *laksa* after late afternoon. $\overline{\$}$

★ **Top Spot Food Court** Jalan Padungan. Forget the unpromising location – atop a blue multistorey car park, topped with a giant plastic prawn – this is a great place, featuring a dozen large stalls focusing on seafood. Sit near a stall you like the look of and they'll present you with their menu; try *ambal*, or crab and prawns done with garlic or chilli, or *oh jian* – the Sarawak version of this oyster omelette is like an enormous bowl-shaped crêpe. No pork served. Not super-pricey either. $\overline{\$\$}$

DRINKING AND NIGHTLIFE

SEE MAP PAGE 304

Kuching's **drinking** scene is pretty good in a low-key kind of way. Venues are intimate for the most part, and the locals are very approachable. Carpenter Street is now clogged with bars, all of which are pretty similar, catering to both tourists and locals, though they seem to open and close with alarming rapidity. For a city with a sizeable middle class, the entertainment on offer is surprisingly meagre, however, though *Culture City* has nightly shows of music and dancing. The Rainforest Music Festival is the highlight of the cultural year (see box, page 318), but otherwise a lack of performance venues means there's not that much on apart from bar bands and DJs.

Borneo Rednecks Bar 40–46 Jalan Pandungan; 082 521 844. Fun spot with bar seating, sports on TV, cheap beer and cider (cheaper by the bucket, of course), and occasional live music. Their food is pretty good too – more local dishes than pub grub, you'll be pleased/sad to hear.

Culture City 18 Jalan Green Hill; http://facebook.com/culturecitykuching. Currently the largest performance venue in the city, this large, mainsteam a/c bar features regular Dyak music and dance perfomances, mixed up with by cover bands and DJs. They have a wide range of beers on tap, as well as more pricey cocktails.

Monkee Bar Jalan Song Thian Cheok. Cosy, low-lit, foreign-owned bar, décorated with Dyak and Iban woodcarvings and dedicated to the orangutan rehabilitation centre at Matang – half of the profits are donated there. Fun and friendly, they serve a large range of imported beers, as well as wine, cocktails and of course local *tuak*.

SHOPPING

SEE MAP PAGE 304

Although Kuching offers the best **shopping** in Sarawak, that's not always obvious from a stroll around downtown,

IBAN TATTOOS

For the Iban, **tattooing** is not just a form of ornamentation, but also an indication of personal wealth and other achievements. Many designs are used, from a simple circular outline for the shoulder, chest or outer side of the wrists, to more elaborate motifs (highly stylized dogs, scorpions or crabs) for the inner and outer thigh. The two most important places for tattoos are the hand and the throat. The tattooing process starts with a carved design on a block of wood that's smeared with ink and pressed to the skin; the resulting outline is then punctured with needles dipped in dark ink, made from sugar-cane juice, water and soot. For the actual tattooing a hammer-like instrument with two or three needles protruding from its head is used. These are dipped in ink and the hammer is then placed against the skin and tapped repeatedly with a wooden block.

Kuching has become a magnet for people wanting to have a Bornean tattoo, and guesthouses may be able to introduce you to practitioners. The leading light of the scene, however, is the Iban-run **Borneo Headhunter** studio, is upstairs at 47 Jalan Wayang (best to make appointments two weeks in advance; http://borneoheadhunter.com). They offers traditional motifs done either the traditional way, or by machine (as in any Western tattoo parlour), and can also do modern designs (always by machine).

---

which is mostly devoid of huge modern malls. There are certainly more souvenir shops than anywhere else in Sarawak; outlets along Main Bazaar sell textiles, pottery, rattan mats, locally grown pepper and so forth. As ever, however, their handicrafts may well have been made abroad – especially in Indonesian Kalimantan. The listings here concentrate on places selling domestically made items; the Sarawak Craft Council is the obvious place to start. If you're heading out to longhouses, you may prefer to defer buying crafts until you get there, though what you'll be offered will probably vary considerably in quality.

ARTS AND CRAFTS
Indah Café & Art Space 33 Upper China St; http://indahcafekuching.com. This cool café (see page 314) also makes a good place to buy local art, which can be viewed in its little gallery; there are usually other nick-knacks on sale too.
Sarawak Craft Council Round Tower, Jalan Tun Abang Haji Openg; http://sarawakhandicraft.com.my. The Craft Council's shop showcases some of the best crafts made in the state, labelled by area of origin. Here you'll find beaded necklaces, hats made from breadfruit-tree bark and bags woven from *bemban* reeds, all costing several tens of ringgit, and the sun hats of the Orang Ulu, shaped like giant mushroom caps and sold for several hundred ringgit.
Wong San Hiup Pottery Jalan Penrissen (on the way to the airport); 082 456 675. Kuching has a cottage industry producing Chinese ceramics with Indigenous cultural influences, and this is probably the best of the potteries. Watch the potters in action at the wheel and firing kilns, and buy wares ranging from huge pots to coffee mugs or vases.

CAMPING GEAR
Greek's Outgear Discovery Second floor, Sarawak Plaza, Jalan Tuanku Abdul Rahman; 082 413 217. This oddly named store sells a range of high-end rucksacks, waterproofs, tents and so forth.

MALLS AND SUPERMARKETS
Everrise 199 Jalan Padungan; http://everrise.com.my. This well-established supermarket is a convenient (though pricey) place to load up if you're staying a while, or heading into the Bornean countryside.
Plaza Merdeka 88 Jalan Tun Haji Openg; http://plazamerdeka.com. The biggest and best of the downtown malls, with a good range of foreign and domestic shops and food outlets, including a Parkson department store, a decent supermarket, and pharmacies.
Spring Mall 3km south of the centre, Jalan Simpang Tiga; http://thespring.com.my. Kuching's biggest, busiest mall holds a Parkson department store, a supermarket and outlets selling electronic gadgets, clothes, household items and so forth. Buses #K8 and #K11 come here from the centre.

DIRECTORY

Consulates Australia (honourary), E39 Level 2, Taman Sri Sarawak Mall, Jalan Tunku Abdul Rahman (082 230 777); Indonesia, 53 Lot 86, Jalan Central Timur (082 460 734).
Cookery classes Of the various cooking classes on offer across town, the one at Indah Cafe & Art Space (see page 314) is the most reliable, and also the most fun – you'll need to set half a day aside, since the class begins with a trip to buy ingredients at the market, and then ends with a big pig-out session where students eat what they made.
Hospitals The main state-run hospital is the Sarawak

General Hospital, 2km south of the centre off Jalan Tun Abang Haji Openg (082 276 666). You can also try the private clinics at the Timberland Medical Centre at the southern end of Jalan Rock (082 234 466, http://timberlandmedical.com).

Massage The Alternative Therapy Centre in the basement of Sarawak Plaza offers excellent massage from blind people at very reasonable prices (daily 10am–7pm).

Pharmacy All of the shopping centres have either a Watsons, a Guardian, or both.

Police Jalan Khoo Hun Yeang, opposite the Padang Merdeka (082 241 222).

Visa extensions Immigration Office, first floor, Bangunan Sultan Iskandar, Jalan Simpang Tiga (Mon–Fri 8am–noon & 2–4.30pm; 082 245 661). Get there by 3pm to have your application processed on the day.

Around Kuching

One joy of visiting Kuching is the sheer number of potential excursions within the vicinity, including several worthy of an overnight stay. Within an hour's bus ride north are the beaches and resorts of the **Santubong Peninsula**, also known as **Damai** after the beach area at its tip. Nearby is the **Sarawak Cultural Village**, a showpiece community where model longhouses are staffed by guides from each ethnic group. **Bako** is the essential national park to visit nearby, but there's also decent trekking at **Kubah National Park**.

South of Kuching, the main attractions are the orangutans at the **Semenggoh Wildlife Centre** and the easily accessable Bidayuh longhouse at **Annah Rais**. Sarawak's remote western edge draws a trickle of visitors who mainly head to the **Gunung Gading National Park** to see *Rafflesia* blooms, though the beaches at **Sematan** and near **Lundu**, and the stunning **Tanjung Datu National Park**, further west, are also worthwhile.

Unless otherwise stated, all **buses** mentioned below are local services leaving from the area east of Kuching mosque.

Santubong Peninsula

Cut off from Kuching by the Santubong River to the south, the **Santubong Peninsula** has been inhabited since prehistoric times. Excavation in the 1960s and 1970s found tens of thousands of artefacts, including digging implements, across six neighbouring sites; they dated back to 3000 BC, when the Indian/Javanese Empire extended here, though little of any ancient civilization can be seen today.

Dominated by the 810m **Mount Santubong**, the area is dotted with oddly shaped geological formations amid patches of thick forest. The mountain is a **national park** (with the entrance 1km south of Damai Central) and the well-marked, moderately taxing trek to the top takes five to six hours return, with rope ladders to help where things get steep; if you're lucky you might see hornbills, or proboscis and silver leaf monkeys. There's also a shorter marked path past a small waterfall that takes just 45 minutes. Oddly, there is no charge to enter the park here, though if you enter via the privately-owned *Permai Rainforest Resort* you will be charged.

However, most visitors prefer to venture out to the **beaches** of **Damai**, 35km from Kuching at the Peninsula's northwest tip, or the excellent if pricey folk museum nearby, the **Sarawak Cultural Village**. Since the 1980s, stretches of the river and coastline have been developed as retreats for tourists and city-weary locals, though thankfully the resorts have left the tranquil, almost lonesome, nature of the area largely undisturbed. There are also two low-key villages, **Buntal** and **Kampung Santubong**.

Sarawak Cultural Village

33km north of Kuching • Charge; day-tours from Kuching available too • http://scv.com.my

After crossing onto the peninsula from Buntal, the main road continues west and then north past several resorts, ending at the modern leisure development of Damai Central. Not far from the end, the **Sarawak Cultural Village** features seven authentically styled, if rather too perfect, Indigenous dwellings of timber and thatch, close to a central lake, with the jungle escarpment of Mount Santubong looming dramatically behind. As folk

> **SPOTTING SANTUBONG WILDLIFE**
>
> The mouth of the Santubong River is a promising spot to see the rare **Irrawaddy dolphin**. With a rounded snout rather than a beak, these marine mammals live in brackish coastal waters and river deltas, as well as in fresh water further upriver – for example, along the Mekong in Indochina, where the population is dwindling. In fact the dolphin is considered vulnerable in many habitats due to human activity – they may get snared in nets or see their range whittled away by barrages, for example.
>
> Several tour operators can take you on dolphin-spotting cruises, though the specialist is **CPH Travel** (see page 311), which has its own launch; their trips leave in the late afternoon, taking you along the Santubong River in search of proboscis monkeys and fireflies as well as dolphins (3hr 30min). The odds of spotting dolphins aren't great during the rainy season if seas are rough; the rest of the time you have a fair chance of seeing them, though not necessarily close up.

museums go, it's worth the steep price of admission and doesn't feel forced; in fact, many of the staff you see kitted out in traditional finery live on site, and the place has become a community in itself.

Arguably the most impressive dwelling is the massive **Orang Ulu longhouse**, raised almost impossibly high off the ground, though the Melanau "tall house" also grabs the eye, with windows on two levels. You'll also see Iban and Bidayuh longhouses, a refreshingly simple Penan lean-to shelter, and – mundane by comparison – a Chinese kampung house and a formal Malay house in a style that only someone of status could have afforded to build.

Despite being out of context, the twice-daily 45-minute cultural shows are worth catching, striking the right balance between entertainment and education, and demonstrations of activities such as weaving, sago-processing and blowpipe-making are staged throughout the day.

Damai Beach

While the pleasant stretches of beige sand at Damai have individual names, such as Teluk Bandung and Teluk Penyuk, most people simply refer to the area as **Damai Beach**. The beaches don't belong to the resorts, though resort staff may levy a small fee if you try to access them via their compounds. One way to avoid this is to head to **Damai Central**, the shopping development opposite the Cultural Village, from where a path leads down to the beach. It's also possible to arrange activities in the area, such as trekking in the nearby **Kuching Wetland National Park** (which also has a birdwatching tower) or kayaking along the coast – you can arrange these at the *Permai Rainforest Resort* (see page 318).

ARRIVAL AND DEPARTURE — SANTUBONG PENINSULA

Transport from Kuching Private shuttles leave from the *Grand Margherita* hotel for Damai and the Cultural Village (every 2hr), and some Kuching guesthouses can arrange transport for the same price. Otherwise, unreliable minibuses leave when full from opposite the food stalls in the Kuching bus station area, near the mosque (and take a while to get there as they visit many of the villages on the way), while a taxi will be affordable if you're in a pair or small group.

ACCOMMODATION

Campsite Next to Damai Beach; 012 856 6557. You can rent a two-person tent here or pitch your own – though you'll have to make do with Damai Central's bathrooms. $

The Culvert South of Dumai; http://theculvert.com. Roll up for the most unique stay in the area – tiny rooms housed in little tubes. Bathrooms are shared (you'll be very glad of this, once you see your "room"), and the complex as a whole has been beautifully designed, also featuring a pretty pool. $$$

★ **Damai Beach Resort** Teluk Bandung beach, Damai, 1km north of Damai Central; http://damaibeachresort.com.

The rooms are mostly modern and not all that special, but the lovely freeform pool set back from the beach sets the tone beautifully at this huge complex, all the more homely for being one of the area's oldest resorts. Rooms near the reception and in the blocks stacked up on the lush hillside behind are cheaper, though you might feel like splashing out on a *baruk* suite, built to look like a Bidayuh roundhouse with a conical roof. There's also a spa plus a couple of restaurants and a bar, and staff can organize guided jungle walks and other activities. Rates include breakfast. $$$

Nanga Damai 2km from Santubong village, right of the road as you head north; http://nangadamai.com. Not a longhouse, as *nanga* might suggest, but a swish six-room "boutique homestay" in a substantial, beautifully decorated modern house. Good value, with rates including breakfast. They also have a dorm. Note that there's a two-night stay minimum, and no under-14s are allowed. Dorm $, doubles $$$

Permai Rainforest Resort Keep going north after Damai Central then follow the boardwalk; http://permairainforest.com. You could come to this place to laze by the beach, but the emphasis is on being active – they offer kayaking, Santubong climbs and even an obstacle course. Guests stay in individual en-suite cabins, mostly sleeping up to six and good value if you're in a group of three or more (a/c extra), or two-person treehouses; they also have a small campsite. Quite cheekily they'll charge you to enter and use their jungle paths and access the two pretty, small beaches along here, despite the fact that the whole place is built within the national park. Rates include breakfast but activities cost extra. Camping with own tent $, treehouses $$$, cabins $$$$

★ **The Village House** Kampung Santubong, 30m down the track to the beach from Santubong crossroads, http://villagehouse.com.my. This gorgeous timber-built development features en-suite rooms set around a long, narrow swimming pool. Many have four-poster beds, but otherwise the decor is elegant without being over the top. They also have two of the slickest six-bed dorms you'll ever see, each with its own bathroom. The restaurant serves Western, local and fusion food. No under-12s. Rates include breakfast. Dorms $$, doubles $$$

EATING

In addition to the places listed below, there's likely to be food available at your accommodation, or you can head for the inexpensive (if unexciting) stalls at Damai Central's food court.

Budaya Sarawak Cultural Village; 082 846 411. Authentic Indigenous cooking, with dishes from all over Sarawak served in an ethnic setting. The set menus are very good for a taster of a diverse range of dishes, and include *mamok pansoh*, chicken and rice cooked in bamboo in the firepit. You can eat at the restaurant without paying the entrance fee if you ask at the ticket office. The same menu is also served at a higher price at the outside *D'Sea* restaurant on Damai beach, which also has a big seafood menu. $$$

Escobar Bar and Grill Damai Central; http://facebook.com/escobarDC. This place by the beach offers Western bar food such as burgers and meat/fish with chips, (not so good) pasta and a few Indian and Malay dishes. It's a great place to watch the sunset, especially with a bottle of their *tuak*. $$$

Bako National Park

East of the Santubong Peninsula, and no further away from Kuching, a second peninsula is occupied by the fabulous **BAKO NATIONAL PARK**, named for its location at the mouth of the Bako River. Sarawak's oldest national park (once a timber reserve, it attained its current, fully protected status in 1957), it's also among its most memorable

---

THE RAINFOREST MUSIC FESTIVAL

Since 1998, the Sarawak Cultural Village has been home to the annual **Rainforest Music Festival** (http://rwmf.net), usually held during June or July. It would be hard to find a more appropriate and evocative setting for a major world music event, with the Village's beautiful Indigenous homes not far from the stages and Mount Santubong the perfect backdrop.

While the event attracts performers from across the globe, it's especially worthwhile for the opportunity to watch Indigenous Bornean musicians – some of whom can seem decidedly exotic even to city-dwelling Sarawakian youth, never mind audiences from further afield. With some noted performers having died since the festival was first staged, the sense that many traditions are living on borrowed time makes the chance to glimpse *sape* players (pronounced *sap-ay*, the *sape* is the Orang Ulu lute, shaped like a longboat), gong ensembles and the like that much more valuable (especially if you catch them in the intimate confines of a workshop). Beds are hard to come by in Damai and Kuching over this period, so book accommodation early. During the festival City Link provide late-running shuttle buses between Damai and Kuching.

its steep coastal cliffs, offering huge vistas over the South China Sea, are thrillingly different from the rest of the predominantly flat and muddy Sarawak coastline, and there are opportunities to spot proboscis monkeys, swim in jungle streams or at isolated sandy coves, and hike through terrain that takes in rainforest, mangrove and *kerangas* (see page 319), with pitcher plants easily visible on some trails.

Bako is such a gem that trying to pack it all into one day is not ideal, though you can make a go of it if you set out early from Kuching and pay a boatman at the park to take you out to a remote beach, then walk back to the park headquarters; this gives you a good taste of the park without having to do a trek in both directions. A stay of at least one night is still preferable, though, and there's a range of accommodation to choose from – this also gives you the chance to see many of the park's nocturnal animals.

Note that the entire eastern side of the park (east of the Tajor Waterfall) is **closed for path renovation** with no date set as to its completion.

Inside the park

First impressions of Bako, the coastal forest and craggy outcrops you see as you head here by boat, don't begin to do justice to its riches. The park boasts a multitude of different types of **vegetation**, including peat bog, scrub and mangrove; most trails run through a mixture of primary dipterocarp forest and *kerangas*, an Iban term referring to soil too poor to support rice, and now used to mean a type of woodland on poor soil characterized by fairly sparse, small trees and scrub, plus insect-eating plants such as pitcher plants. The *kerangas* stems from the unusual, largely infertile **sandstone** geology of the peninsula, eroded down to produce striking honeycomb weathering on some trails, and contorted rock arches rising from the sea. As for fauna, **proboscis monkeys** are top of most visitors' lists; there's a good chance of seeing them not far from the park headquarters itself, though silverleaf monkeys tend to be harder to spot. Less exotically, monitor lizards and assorted snakes are sometimes seen, along with bearded pigs (a group have even made themselves at home close to the park cafeteria) and the usual assortment of creepy-crawlies, best spotted on a guided night walk.

No special equipment is needed, but pay particular attention to **sun protection** – it's amazing how you can be walking through a jungle glade one minute and in baking hot *kerangas* the next.

VISITING SARAWAK'S NATIONAL PARKS

Sarawak's two dozen or so **national parks** vary enormously, not just in terms of terrain and habitats – some boast accommodation for various budgets, well-marked trails and other amenities, while many others have nothing more than a ranger post and require a minor expedition to reach. All are managed by the state-owned **Sarawak Forestry Corporation** (http://sarawakforestry.com) with the notable exception of Mulu, where tourist facilities have been privatized. You can pick up information about park conditions and accommodation at Sarawak Forestry's offices at the Sama Jaya Nature reserve on the outskirts of Kuching (see page 311) and at the desk inside the Sarawak Tourist Office in Miri (see page 343). Informal accommodation bookings can be made by calling the park concerned, while the Kuching office can confirm reservations with payment up front, and you can now also make reservations online (http://ebooking.sarawak.gov.my). Almost all parks have well-organized **campsites**, usually covered, with bathrooms and cooking facilities, as well as a basic canteen nearby.

Guides can be engaged at just a few parks, with prices depending on their level of experience and English ability. Many, but not all, know about the local wildlife. Knowledgeable, licensed guides for parks in the Kuching area can be contacted through the Tourist Guide Association (see page 311).

The trails

A free map from the park headquarters shows the **trails**, colour-coded and waymarked with splashes of paint on trees and rocks. Park staff can advise on what you can expect to complete in the time you have available, or whether to take a boat ride as a short cut (see page 321).

Most trails start from a spot north of the park headquarters, back towards the jetty and reached by a series of boardwalks through mangrove. You then ascend through steepish jungle, with the option of branching off left early on to **Teluk Paku**, a small, not particularly attractive cove where proboscis monkeys are often seen. Most people carry on to reach the **Padang** about 45 minutes from the start – here not a grassy colonial town square, but a rocky plateau of *kerangas* that's another hangout for proboscis monkeys.

At the Padang you're on the park's most popular trail, the looping **Lintang** trail that leads alternately through jungled slopes and *kerangas* via occasional stretches of boardwalk, and returns to the park headquarters from the south. Taking around four hours to complete if you don't pause frequently to rest or take photos, it can get monotonous after a while.

You may find it more interesting to branch off the Lintang trail at a clearly marked point only a few minutes' walk along the Padang. This two-hour side trail heads east to the **Tajor Waterfall**; a couple of low cascades in a jungled stream, the waterfall itself is no great shakes, but the pool just down from it is good for a swim. From here you can return to the headquarters the way you came, or continue east and south along a much bigger loop, the **Ulu Serait trail**, and returning along the southern part of the Lintang trail; allow at least six hours to do this.

Even more worthwhile may be to branch off the Tajor trail at another signed side trail, less than a quarter of the way towards the falls, which leads north towards two beautiful **beaches**, Teluk Pandan Kecil and Teluk Pandan Besar. Curiously, semi-dry stream beds seem to serve as the trail in some sections, eventually bringing you to viewpoints with superb views of the beaches and the South China Sea. The Pandan Kecil viewpoint also features bizarre hexagonal sandstone formations in the ground, where iron-rich rock has eroded less than the surrounding material. The steep descent to Pandan Kecil (15min) is rewarded with a swim at a secluded cove with whitish sand; unfortunately, no path leads down to Pandan Besar.

Other possible treks include heading to the remote Teluk Limau or Teluk Kruin beaches at the park's eastern end, taking at least eight hours (you'll probably want to travel one way by boat), or hikes off the main trails up to hills such as Bukit Gondol (260m) for great views.

ARRIVAL AND DEPARTURE — BAKO NATIONAL PARK

By bus Reaching the park from Kuching is straightforward: Rapid Kuching's red bus #1 heads east to Bako village roughly hourly from Jalan Khoo Hun Yeang, close to the Masjid Negeri, from 7am–5pm (1hr) with return buses running 6.30am–5.30pm. It stops en route at the Old Courthouse complex and along Jalan Tuanku Abdul Rahman, though given the lack of signage at bus stops, be sure to ask other commuters if the bus will call where you hope to flag it down. The bus stops at the Bako boat terminal for onward travel to the park.

By boat At the Bako boat terminal you can buy your park permit, register, and board a park-bound boat (25min). They leave when full, from early morning until 3.30pm; last boat back is 4.30pm.

INFORMATION

Park HQ Just a few minutes' walk from the jetty, where you can pick up a simple park map, hire a green-jacketed official guide (prices depending on group size and English ability) or book to go on a guided night walk (8pm; 1hr 30min), which takes you south along the Lintang trail to spot insects, spiders and, with luck, nocturnal mammals and birds.

Information Centre Close to the Park HQ, the excellent information centre holds displays on the park's geology and history, and plenty of photographs to help you get a handle on the plants and animals you may see on the trails.

Admission Park permits are purchased from the Bako boat terminal; day-tours from Kuching (including admission) are also an option.

Contact details 082 370 434, http://sarawakforestry.com.

GETTING AROUND

By boat Saving time by using a boat to reach one of Bako's beaches is well worth considering; park staff can give an idea of the going rate, though you'll still have to negotiate with the boatmen at the jetty once you've signed in at the headquarters. Long journeys are possible, but you're more likely to make the short hop to a popular beach such as Teluk Paku or Teluk Pandan Kecil; boats leave when full.

ACCOMMODATION AND EATING

It's much cheaper to buy provisions in town before you arrive than to eat at the park's sole café, though note that cooking is not allowed inside any of the accommodation.

Bako National Park accommodation http://sarawakforestry.com. The park's accommodations include a campsite; a recently renovated hostel with four-bed dorms; forest lodges, which are a little worn, where the three-bedded rooms share facilities; and en-suite doubles. Best are the newer a/c chalets, with two bedrooms that sleep up to six. Camping/dorms/en-suite doubles/lodge rooms $\overline{\$}$, chalets $\overline{\$\$\$}$

Kubah National Park

Some 20km west of Kuching, **Kubah National Park** is a rainforest reserve considered one of the world's richest sites for **palm** species: of the 95 types found, including coconut, sago and many rattans, eighteen are endemic to the region. Look out too for giant squirrels, which are bigger than a cat.

Three modest peaks, **Selang**, **Sendok** and **Serapi**, emerge out of the lush forest; they're crisscrossed by trails, waterfalls and streams. Marked hikes include the three-hour **Raya Trail**, a good walk to catch sight of the palms, and the **Waterfall Trail**, a ninety-minute uphill hike to impressive, split-level falls. Kubah's best views, however, come on the three-hour **Mount Serapi (Summit) Trail** – from the top of the peak, you can take in Kuching and much of southwestern Sarawak.

Also within the park is **Matang Wildlife Centre**, where injured, sick or orphaned wild animals such as orangutans, gibbons and hornbills are rehabilitated before being returned to the wild. There are many foreign volunteers working here, but it's fairly underfunded so you may find the conditions and state of the animals distressing – if you want to help with funding or volunteering, visit the *Monkee Bar* in Kuching (see page 314).

ARRIVAL AND INFORMATION	KUBAH NATIONAL PARK
By bus City Public Link bus #K21 runs to Kubah from Kuching (every 3hr – check timetable with the tourist office; 30–40min).	**Admission** The entrance ticket includes the wildlife centre. **Further details** http://sarawakforestry.com.

ACCOMMODATION AND EATING

Kubah National Park accommodation http://sarawakforestry.com. The park offers accommodation in either a hostel or a two-bedroom lodge. There's no canteen or anywhere to eat nearby, so bring supplies to cook meals yourself. Dorms $, lodges $$

Semenggoh Wildlife Centre

Off Sarawak's main trunk road, 25km south of Kuching • Charge; day-tours from Kuching available • 082 442 180 • City Public Link bus #K6 (45min) leaves Kuching to coincide with feeding times, and returns shortly after; it stops by the ticket office on the main road, a 1.5km walk from the centre along an undulating access road

The first forest reserve in the state, the **Semenggoh Wildlife Rehabilitation Centre** was set aside by Vyner Brooke in 1920. Today it's a sort of open zoo in a surviving pocket of forest, where tourists flock to watch orangutans being fed fruit by rangers, who have names for all of them. How many you're likely to see will depend on the time of year – when wild fruits are in season, fewer orangutans emerge from the forest to seek out the rangers.

Most of the action takes place at a clearing, with seating close by, reached by a short jungle trail from the car park. Don't be surprised if you see the orangutans roaming around the car park itself – and give them a wide berth if you do. Look out also for orangutan nests, which they build in the treetops using clumps of leaves and branches, for sleeping. The morning feeding is usually better, and arriving by 8.30am will give you a decent seat.

Annah Rais

Near the mountains that straddle the border with Kalimantan, 60km south of Kuching, the Bidayuh longhouse settlement of **ANNAH RAIS**, while occasionally touristy, makes a decent day-trip from Kuching, particularly if you don't have time to see longhouses elsewhere in Sarawak. It's easy to combine a visit with a trip to Semenggoh if you're driving, and not too hard by bus, though confirm bus times with the tourist office (see page 311).

The settlement of around 1300 feels like a hybrid of **longhouse** and **village** – assorted differently styled wooden "houses" are joined together in two long parallel rows and raised off the ground, with platforms of bamboo slats on planks serving as "streets". This higgledy-piggledy style is in part due to the fact that it is one of the oldest remaining wooden longhouses in Sarawak, with a written history of more than 175 years, and an oral tradition that goes back 500. Behind the facades, individual family quarters open off vast corridors, just as in a regular longhouse, and as ever there's a **river** nearby for bathing (a bridge brings you to a third longhouse). You'll probably be offered a small glass of *tuak* (or Borneo brandy) upon arrival, while depending on the season, you may see the rice harvest or longhouse-made latex sheets being dried. Be sure to pop into the **panggah**, or skull house, where skulls hark back to a martial tradition that only ceased a few generations ago – the villagers claim that they were actually used as part of a ceremony to bring peace.

ARRIVAL AND INFORMATION	ANNAH RAIS
By bus City Public Link bus #K6, which also serves Semenggoh, heads from Kuching to the small town of Kota Padawan (8 daily; 30min) from whose market you can catch a minivan (1hr) to Annah Rais. The longhouse homestay programme can arrange transfers from/to Kuching. Day tours are available from hotels and travel agents in Kuching.	**Admission fee** Small charge, payable at the information booth in front of the longhouse.

ACCOMMODATION

★ **Annah Rais Homestay Programmes** http://longhousehomestay.com. Several longhouse homes host homestay programmes, which are for the most part very basic but clean. Packages are available; these include food activities take place in the morning, so either get here early, or organise things so that you can enjoy them the morning after your arrival.

Bau and around

Nineteenth-century prospectors were drawn to **BAU**, half an hour's drive southwest of Kuching, by the gold that veined the surrounding countryside, but the modern-day market town is mundane in the extreme, though it does have a picturesque mining lake, **Blue Lake**, on its southwestern edge. Pretty though the lake is, it contains arsenic and is unsafe to swim in; the main reason to come to Bau is to visit the two nearby **caves**, around 4km apart to the west.

Bau caves

Charge • Sarawak Transport Company bus #2 goes from Kuching to Bau (3 daily), from where the Bau Transport Company #2 bus (2 daily) runs to the caves (catch the earlier service if you want to return to Kuching by bus the same day; check return times before you leave) – each cave has its own bus stop on the main road, at least 15min walk from its entrance; there are also taxis from Bau (get the driver's number for the return)

If you have to pick one of the two **Bau caves** – which you may well have to do if relying on public transport – choose the larger, **Fairy Cave**. Steps inside enable you to wander through the gloom towards a gaping maw at one end of the system, which lets in refreshing breezes and enough light for the cave floor to be blanketed in ferns and moss. The smaller **Wind Cave** is a little less impressive, with two dark tunnels inhabited by a colony of bats – you'll need to make sure you bring a decent torch with you to fully explore it.

ACCOMMODATION AND EATING	BAU

★ **Lan e Tuyang** 14km short of Bau and 23km from Kuching on the Batu Kawa Rd, parallel to and north of the main Bau Rd; http://facebook.com/Lanetuyanghomestay. Excellent homestay run by a Kenyah *sape* exponent and artist, who has created a sort of mini-longhouse decorated with Orang Ulu motifs and *sapes* built in his workshop below. He can teach you the rudiments of the lute-like instrument and how to build one, or you can try your hand at woodcarving. Five simple guest rooms have fans and mosquito nets, with toilets and showers in a separate block; take traditional meals (extra charge) in the house or they can give you a lift to the simple restaurants in the Chinese hamlet of Tondong a few minutes' drive away. Arrange ahead for pick-up from Bau town, Kuching or the airport.

Gunung Gading National Park

75km by road west of Kuching • Charge • http://sarawakforestry.com

The main claim to fame of **Gunung Gading National Park** is that it's home to the parasitic **Rafflesia** plant (see page 558), with its stinky blooms. However, when the buds are maturing the park can go for months without a single *Rafflesia* in flower; if you're coming specifically to see the plants (as the vast majority of visitors are), check with the park in advance.

The park can be visited as a day-trip from Kuching. With an early start, you can tackle the **Waterfall Trail**, on which it takes ninety minutes to reach the end at waterfall 7 – it really is the seventh waterfall en route – where you can have a good, refreshing swim. With more time, you can also climb Gading, one of the park's two hills. It's a full-on hike and a six-hour round trip, though it's a well-marked trail and a guide is not needed.

ARRIVAL AND INFORMATION	GUNUNG GADING NATIONAL PARK

By bus There are eight daily buses from Kuching's regional express bus terminal to the town of Lundu (1hr 30min), from where you can either walk 3km north along the main road to get to the park, or catch a minivan or taxi which congregate next to the bus station.

ACCOMMODATION

Gunung Gading National Park accommodation 082 735 144. The park has a campsite, a hostel where four rooms offer dorm beds (or can be let as four-bed rooms) and a lodge holding six-bed chalets. There's no canteen, but you can cook at the park's kitchens. Camping/dorms/doubles $\overline{\underline{\$}}$, chalets $\overline{\underline{\$\$}}$

Tanjung Datu National Park and around
40km by road west of Lundu • Charge • http://sarawakforestry.com

Some 40km west of **Lundu** town, and at the end of the road from Kuching (until the new section of the Pan-Borneo Highway opens), the seaside town of **Semantan** has a long, picturesque beach and reasonably clean almost-yellow sands. However, most foreign visitors are here to visit **Tanjung Datu National Park**, whose beaches are far superior to the wide flat beach in the town.

At the very western tip of Sarawak, this tiny park covers a mountainous region around a coastal spur close to the Kalimantan border. Although it offers splendid rainforest, swift, clean rivers and isolated bays, the main draws are its two dazzling **beaches**, with shallow, unspoilt **coral reefs** perfect for snorkelling only a short distance from the shore (bring your own equipment), and occasionally frequented by dolphins.

The park is also among the few destinations in Sarawak where green **turtles** come to lay eggs (April to October), while the jungle holds six species of primate, seven species of hornbill, elusive clouded leopards and much more easy-to-spot deer and wild boar. There are four marked **trails** too: the hardest, the Belian Trail, takes around an hour and a half, leading halfway up Mount Melano (542m) to where *Rafflesia* bloom, while the Pasar Antu Laut Trail (also 1hr 30min) leads almost 4km north through the jungle, ending up at the isolated and slightly surreal Golden Sand Beach.

ARRIVAL AND INFORMATION   TANJUNG DATU NATIONAL PARK

By road A new road links the park with Sematan, where it connects with the Pan-Borneo Highway – previously only accessible by boat, it's now possible to get to Tanjung Datu by bus or taxi – or, at least, as far as the village of Telok Melano, still a 90min walk from the park HQ. Getting to Sematan itself is fairly straightforward, with four daily express buses leaving from Kuching's regional express bus terminal, via Lundu (where you may have to change).
Package tours You can also come to the park on an overpriced package tour from Kuching, such as from CPH Travel (see page 311), or locally from *Telok Melano Homestay Program* (see page 324).
Admission fee Payable at the Park HQ.

ACCOMMODATION

There are several accommodation options in Sematan, including a couple of resorts along the coast, several homestays signposted from the main road near the bus station, and one grubby but cheap guesthouse.
Tanjung Datu National Park Accommodation 082 248 088. Basic accommodation is available at the park HQ, with four fan twin rooms, a six-person, dorm-like forest hut (bedding extra) and a campsite. There's no canteen, so for food you'll either have to walk to Telok Melano and back, or cook your own – cooking equipment can also be rented. $\overline{\underline{\$}}$
Telok Melano Homestay Program 082 711 101. This tiny Malay fishing village of fifty families, around a 90min walk from Park HQ, operates a local homestay programme, with over half the homes here offering rooms. It is used by tour operators (who massively overcharge for it), though you can contact them directly for one of their packages (up to five people), which includes transport from Sematan, full-board accommodation, cultural shows, park entrance, and other activities. It's also possible to stay on a nightly basis if you are travelling independently. The village has community wi-fi near the only restaurant on the beach. $\overline{\underline{\$\$}}$

Batang Ai – the Iban longhouses

The **Iban longhouses** of the Ai headwaters, both 150km due east of Kuching beyond the lake of the Batang Ai hydroelectric dam, and also to the north along the **Lemanak** river system, are the best excuse for anyone travelling between western and central Sarawak not to catch the fast Kuching–Sibu ferry. Despite being on the tourist trail, the longhouses offer a glimpse (if somewhat fake) of what used to be the semi-traditional lifestyle in this remote corner of the state, much of which is protected as a **national park** and wildlife sanctuary. Sadly, most locals now prefer to live nearer to the road, and many of the villages and longhouses you'll be taken to are only inhabited while tourists are there – unfortunately, the locals see little of the profits made by the agencies that run tours here, and you may get the impression that they're all rather weary of the whole thing.

Batang Ai dam and lake

Around three and a half hours' drive from Kuching, a couple of kilometres beyond the village of **Jelukong**, a signed 38km turning branches southeast off the main trunk road, passing a few modernish longhouses en route to the small border town of **Lubok Antu**. Some 12km short of that, another small road branches east (left) towards the **Batang**

THE IBAN

Easily the most numerous of Sarawak's Indigenous peoples, the **Iban** make up nearly thirty percent of the state's population. Their language is from the same family as Malay, and any Malay speakers will notice considerable overlap in vocabulary as well as predictable changes in word endings – *datang* (come) and *makan* (eat) in Malay, for example, become *datai* and *makai* in Iban.

ORIGINS AND CONFLICTS

Having outgrown their original home in the Kapuas river basin of west Kalimantan, the Iban migrated to the Lupar River in southwest Sarawak in the sixteenth century, and came into conflict with the Melanau and Malays. With the Brunei sultanate at its height, the Malays pushed the Iban back inland up rivers such as the Rejang, into interior areas dominated by the Kayan. Great battles were waged between the two groups; one source recorded seeing "a mass of boats drifting along the stream, [the combatants] spearing and stabbing each other; decapitated trunks and heads without bodies, scattered about in ghastly profusion". Although such interethnic conflict stopped as migration itself slowed, the Iban were still taking heads as recently as the 1960s during the Konfrontasi, when the Indonesian army came up against Iban who had thrown their lot in with Malaysia.

SOCIETY

The Iban figure prominently in the minds of visitors, thanks to their traditional communal dwelling, the **longhouse** (see page 326). Each has its own *tuai* (headman), who leads more by consensus than by barking orders. Traditionally, young men left the longhouse to go on **bejalai**, the act of joining a warring party – essentially a rite of passage for a youth to establish his independence and social position before marriage. Nowadays, to the extent that *bejalai* has meaning, it may translate into going to university or earning a good wage on offshore oil rigs or in a hotel or factory in Singapore.

Further complicating the *bejalai* tradition is the fact that **women** are now much more socially mobile, and can pursue education and their own careers. Traditionally, however, women had distinct duties, which is cited as a reason why a woman is not permitted to be *tuai*. They never went hunting, but were great weavers – an Iban woman's weaving prowess would once have determined her status in the community. The women are most renowned for their **pua kumbu** (blanket or coverlet) work, a cloth of intricate design and colour. The *pua kumbu* once played an integral part in Iban rituals, hung up prominently during harvest festivals and weddings, or used to cover structures containing charms and offerings to the gods.

DEVELOPMENT AND URBANIZATION

More than half of Sarawak's Iban have moved permanently to the cities and towns in the west of the state, or may spend the working week there and weekends back in their longhouse. Most rural Iban no longer live purely off the land, but also undertake seasonal work in the rubber and oil industries. By no small irony, logging – the business that most devastated their traditional lands – also long supplied plentiful and lucrative work; these days, oil-palm cultivation and production provide more employment.

Ai dam, a way station en route to the upper Ai. Built in the 1980s as Sarawak's first hydroelectric venture, the Ai dam created a lake covering 90 square kilometres. Though now dwarfed in scale, generating capacity and controversy by the Bakun dam (see page 336), it's an impressive sight nonetheless, and the road up gives good views of the narrow valley downriver.

No parts of the dam are open to tourists, though, and once you get there you'll head to one of the jetties to continue east by boat to an Ai longhouse or the *Aiman Batang Ai Resort & Retreat*.

Batang Ai National Park

Only accessible with an official guide, who can be hired in Lubok Antu; if you're on a tour, you have to pay a tour operator for a day-trip to be added onto a longhouse package • Charge • http://sarawakforestry.com

East of the lakeshore, an hour by boat from the dam, the little-visited **Batang Ai National Park** preserves an important area of rainforest that merges with the Lanjak Entimau Wildlife Sanctuary (LEWS; off-limits to visitors), which itself merges with another protected area across the border in Kalimantan. **Orangutans** are occasionally spotted on various trails in the national park, but a boat to these trails will set you back a fair whack from the HQ. The park holds no residential or other facilities, and all visitors must be accompanied by a guide.

Ai River

An hour east from the Batang Ai dam, longhouse-bound boats leave the lake and head up the **Ai River**. As is clear from the tall trees that come right to the water's edge, the initial stretch is still a drowned portion of the river. Further up you'll observe a transition to the true river banks, the vegetation more open and compact. Also visible sporadically to either side are the odd school and clinic in simple metal-roofed timber buildings, and areas of hillslope cleared for traditional rice cultivation. The Iban leave paddies to the jungle once the soil is exhausted and move on to clear new areas. As the river narrows, you also begin to see the occasional **longhouse** lurking in the vegetation. Among those that take tourists are **Nanga Delok** (also called Rumah Ipang, on the Delok, a tributary of the Ai) and the more distant **Nanga Sumpa** (the Sumpa being a tributary of the Delok). Wherever you stay, you will be offered opportunities for additional longboat trips to areas where you can make short treks or local beauty spots such as waterfalls.

Lemanak River

The **Lemanak River** is, like the Batang Ai dam, reached by the Lubok Antu Road, though you turn off earlier to head to the jetties. Several longhouses here regularly

---

LONGHOUSE ARCHITECTURE

Longhouses can be thought of as indoor villages, housing entire communities under one roof. Although several Indigenous peoples build dwellings that are sometimes called longhouses, the definitive article is the **Iban** longhouse. This has a long veranda or *tanju* at the front where rice, rubber and other produce can be laid out to dry; it's accessed by steps or sometimes a log into which notches are cut. Behind the front wall, running the entire length of the building, a corridor or *ruai* serves as a sort of main street where the community can socialize. Multiple doors (*pintu*) open on to the *ruai*, behind which lie each family's quarters (*bilik*); locals describe a longhouse not in terms of its length or the number of inhabitants, but by how many *bilik* or *pintu* it has. Above the living quarters, a loft space (*sadau*) is used for storage.

Traditionally longhouses were built of hardwood timber and bamboo, perhaps with ironwood shingles on the roof. Even though most longhouses now feature plenty of unsightly concrete, they still retain their characteristic *ruai* inside, and most continue to be sited close to rivers or streams, where people enjoy bathing even when piped water supplies exist.

host travellers, notably **Ngemah Ulu**, where guests are put up in the longhouse itself. Independent travel here is not easy. Coming on a two-night package offers the option of a great local trek.

ARRIVAL AND DEPARTURE   BATANG AI

By tour Most visitors book with a Kuching or Miri tour operator, which usually includes the road transfers, the journey in and out by longboat, plus all meals.

By travelling independently Roads have reached some longhouses north of the Ai, but since many longhouses aren't signposted, having your own car is little advantage unless you have local friends or hire a guide in Lubok Antu. That said, you can visit by public transport. If you get dropped at Jelukong Junction on the main road by any bus to or from Miri, then it's 39km to Lubok Antu (by taxi, often possible to share) where there is accommodation and you can ask around to find a guide. To get to the more remote settlements by boat (without hiring a whole one), there are usually "public" boats taking students back for the weekend from the dam; they'll most likely leave Friday afternoon, and return on Sunday afternoon. When leaving, there's no need to backtrack all the way to Kuching; to head on to Sibu and beyond, flag down a bus on the main road. There are at least a couple of buses per hour and tickets can be bought on board.

ACCOMMODATION

Unfortunately, two of the area's most prominent places to stay shuttered their doors in recent years, but this gap in the market can't stay closed forever, so do check to see whether anything new has popped up.

Nanga Sumpa Ai River, a 90min boat ride from the dam; only bookable as part of a package; borneoadventure.com. This longhouse deserves special mention as the site of an excellent purpose-built tourist lodge, sited at a discreet distance from the longhouse itself across a creek. Rooms have wooden platforms that hold a simple mattress and a mosquito net, but little else, though there's a pleasant open sitting/dining area and modern shared bathrooms. Prices vary; only bookable through tour operators based in Kuching (see page 311).

Central Sarawak

For travellers, central Sarawak offers rather slim pickings compared to Kuching's hinterland and the north of the state. Those visitors who venture here tend to be drawn by the prospect of travelling into the interior along the **Rejang** (also spelled **Rajang**), Malaysia's longest river. All such trips start from the bustling city of **Sibu**, some 50km inland near where another major river, the **Igan**, splits away from the Rejang. Express boats depart daily to zip up the Rejang to **Kapit**, beyond which, through the **Pelagus Rapids** and on to the sleepy town of **Belaga**, eight hours from Sibu, the Rejang becomes wild and unpredictable and the scenery spectacular. There's not much to do in either Kapit or Belaga, and while there are longhouse communities near both, almost all are made from concrete – the last easily accessible traditional wooden longhouse is east of Kapit along the Balui River. Public transport is thin on the ground, so it's best to regard the Rejang journey as an end in itself or else fork out for (pricey) local guides to arrange trips for you.

With Sibu being so far from the sea, and the coast here dominated by mangrove swamps, the main trunk road runs deep inland until it finally hits the coast again at Bintulu. Halfway along, a side road leads off through a chink in the vegetation to the coastal town of **Mukah**, which has an appealing museum-cum-guesthouse nearby. **Bintulu** itself is a nondescript but (thanks to oil and gas) prosperous town, whose main attraction is as a base for **Similajau National Park**, easily reached yet appealingly quiet.

Sibu

From its humble 1850s origins as a tiny Melanau encampment, **SIBU** has grown into Sarawak's third largest city and its biggest port. Nearly half its quarter-million population are ethnic Chinese. Unusually for Malaysia, many are Foochow, descended from migrants from what's now Fuzhou in southeast China. Their diligence is often

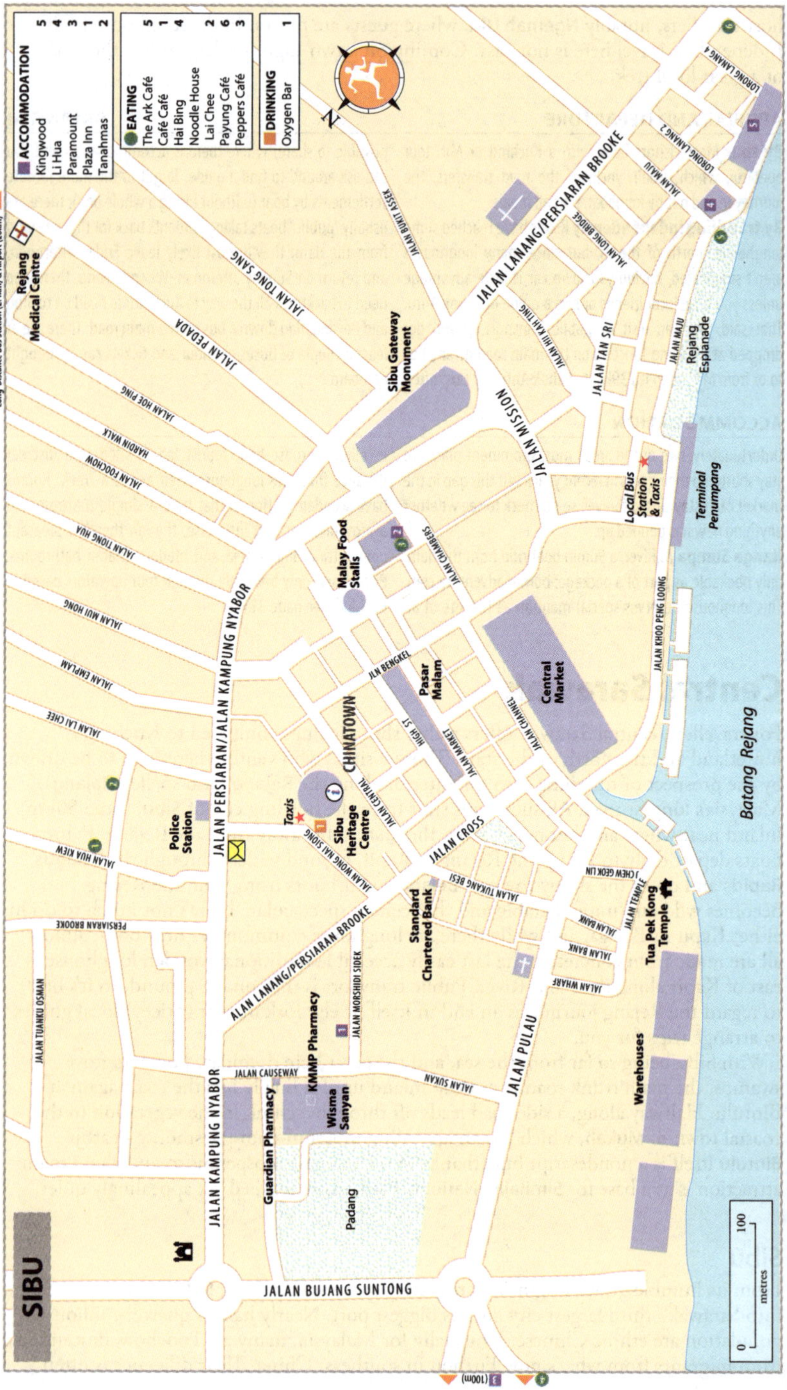

SIBU
ACCOMMODATION
Kingwood 5
Li Hua 4
Paramount 3
Plaza Inn 1
Tanahmas 2
EATING
The Ark Café 5
Café Café 1
Hai Bing 4
Noodle House
Lai Chee 2
Payung Café 6
Peppers Café 3
DRINKING
Oxygen Bar 1
N
Long-Distance Bus Station (2.4km) & Airport (20km)
Rejang Medical Centre
JALAN PEDADA
JALAN TONG SANG
JALAN BUNYI KASEK
JALAN LANANG/PERSIARAN BROOKE
JALAN LONG BRIDGE
JALAN MAJU
LORONG LANANG 2
LORONG LANANG 4
JALAN HOE PING
HARDIN WALK
JALAN FOOCHOW
JALAN TONG HUA
JALAN MUI HONG
JALAN EMPLAM
JALAN LAI CHEE
JALAN HUA KIEW
PERSIARAN BROOKE
JALAN TUANKU OSMAN
Police Station
JALAN PERSIARAN/JALAN KAMPUNG NYABOR
Sibu Gateway Monument
JALAN HII KAH TING
JALAN TAN SRI
JALAN MISSION
Rejang Esplanade
Local Bus Station & Taxis
Terminal Penumpang
JALAN CHAMBERS
Malay Food Stalls
JALAN KHOO PENG LOONG
JLN BENGKEL
Pasar Malam
HIGH ST
JALAN MARKET
JALAN CHANNEL
Central Market
CHINATOWN
Batang Rejang
Taxis
Sibu Heritage Centre
JALAN CENTRAL
JALAN WONG NAI SIONG
JALAN CROSS
JALAN TUKANG BESI
J CHEW GEOK LIN
JALAN TEMPLE
Tua Pek Kong Temple
JALAN BANK
JALAN WHARF
Standard Chartered Bank
JALAN LANANG/PERSIARAN BROOKE
JALAN MORSHIDI SIDEK
KMMP Pharmacy
JALAN CAUSEWAY
JALAN SUKAN
JALAN PULAU
Warehouses
JALAN KAMPUNG NYABOR
Guardian Pharmacy
Wisma Sanyan
Padang
JALAN BUJANG SUNTONG
0
100
metres
(100m)

credited with helping the city become the commercial centre it is today. Its Foochow flavour aside, Sibu is also identified with Sarawak's controversial **logging** industry, which helped the city recover from the Japanese occupation, when many Chinese were forced into slave labour. Sibu subsequently became, for a time, the centre for timber processing in Sarawak and investors, many drawn from long-established Chinese families, made large fortunes as a result.

Having experienced devastating fires in 1889 and 1928, plus serious damage during World War II, Sibu is characterized more by energy than visual appeal. However, boasting a huge **market** and a lively **waterfront**, it has enough sights to keep you occupied for half a day – just as well, as most travellers en route to or from the upper Rejang spend at least a night here.

Waterfront

If you arrive on the boat from Kuching, you'll find yourself on the **waterfront** on the Rejang's right bank, facing rows of dull modern shophouses and commercial buildings. Efforts have been made to landscape and beautify the **Rejang Esplanade** – the tiny riverside recreation area by the ferry terminal – but it's still a fairly humdrum spot. Look out, however, for a riverside marker indicating the Rejang's level during historic floods. Sibu's commercial lifeline is also a scourge; every few years the river overtops this area and inundates the city centre. Efforts are ongoing to tame the Rejang by dredging away sediment, some of which no doubt results from forest clearance.

Tua Pek Kong temple
Eastern end of Jalan Temple • Free • 082 312 005

A small wooden temple stood on the site of Sibu's Taoist **Tua Pek Kong temple**, at the northern end of the riverfront, as early as 1870. Soon afterwards it was rebuilt on a much grander scale, with a tiled roof, stone block floor and decorative fixtures imported from China. Two large concrete lions guard the entrance. The **statue** of Tua Pek Kong, the temple's most important image, survived both the fire of 1928 and Japanese bombardment. The pagoda at the back is, by contrast, Buddhist, and if you ask for the key you can walk up to enjoy the views from the top.

Central Market
Northern end of the riverside Jalan Khoo Peng Loong • Daily dawn–dusk; hawker stalls upstairs stay open into the evening

Sibu's modern and entertaining **Central Market**, one of the biggest in the country, is housed in a long, curved-roofed building. It's best to turn up on a Saturday, when it's at its busiest and the entire ground floor is taken up with vendors selling items such as bamboo tubes for stewing *ayam pansoh*, live roosters tied up in newspaper, slabs of what look like mummified bats but are in fact smoked fish, and, in the run-up to Indigenous cultural festivals, gongs – which prospective buyers have no qualms about trying out. Stalls at the edge offer a tasty Sibu speciality, *kongbian*, sometimes called Chinese bagels, but more like dainty versions of the sesame-seed breads sold in Turkey and Lebanon. An upstairs **food court** offers a few vantage points overlooking the colourful goings-on below.

Sibu Heritage Centre
Jalan Central • Free • 084 331 315

The **Sibu Heritage Centre** is a fine museum highlighting the city's history and cultural diversity. There's a good discussion of how Chinese pioneers, with the support of Brooke officials, founded the settlement and got it off the ground with crops such as rubber – logging didn't arrive until the 1930s – and of Foochow immigration, which only began in earnest at the start of the twentieth century. Among the basketware, beadwork and so forth you can see a striking nineteenth-century Kayan burial hut (*salong*) atop a 1m-high totem pole.

ARRIVAL AND DEPARTURE SIBU

By plane Sibu's airport (084 307 770) is 25km east of the centre. While you could walk 10min to the nearest major road junction and flag down a passing bus or van into town (roughly hourly), it's a lot easier to pay for a taxi (Grab cabs are available at the airport, and are usually a fair bit cheaper). Heading out to the airport, any bus from the local bus station bound for Sibujaya or Kanowit can drop you at the same junction.
Destinations Bintulu (1 daily; 35min); Johor Bahru (2 daily; 1hr 35min); Kota Kinabalu (2 daily; 1hr 15min); Kuala Lumpur (8 daily; 2hr 5min); Kuching (5–6 daily; 40min); Miri (2–3 daily; 55min); Mukah (3 weekly; 25min).
By boat Sibu's express-boat terminal on the esplanade, Terminal Penumpang, was used by fast boats between here and Kuching (4–5hr), via Sarikei downriver; these stopped during the Covid crisis and have yet to restart, but it's certainly worth you checking. The boats upriver to Kanowit and Kapit have been put paid to by new roads, and are far less likely to resurface.
By long-distance bus All express buses use the long-distance bus station, 5km northeast of the centre off Jalan Pahlawan. Hourly Lanang Bus Company services #20 and #21 go to the local bus terminus, which is in front of the express-boat terminal close to the centre.
Destinations Bintulu (every 1–2hr; 3hr 30min); Kapit (6 daily; 3hr); Kuching (7 daily; 7–8hr); Miri (10 daily; 7hr 25min); Mukah (4 daily; 2hr 30min–3hr 30min); Pontianak (Indonesia; 2 daily; 18hr).

INFORMATION AND TOURS

Tourist information Knowledgeable and helpful staff at Sibu's central Visitors' Information Centre, at the Sibu Heritage Centre (Mon–Fri 8am–5pm; 084 340 980), also cover the Rejang River towns, plus Bintulu and Mukah, which don't have tourist offices. They produce a very good guide to Sibu town and the region, with several maps included.

TOUR OPERATORS

Great Holiday First floor Pusat Pedada, eastern end of Jalan Pedada; http://ghtborneo.com. This agency does a one-day Sibu tour, and a half-day one to visit to the Bawang Assan longhouses (see box, page 326), as well as a Heritage walking tour around Sibu. A two-day, one-night trip to Gunung Mulu is also possible, with more advance warning.
Greatown Travel Behind the Rejang Medical Centre at 6 Lorong Chew Siik Hiong; http://greatown.com. Unusual one-day trips downriver to Sarikei, where you can do some trekking, see pepper being cultivated and visit a wooden Iban longhouse where you can also add on a homestay (full-board included). Even more unusually, they can take you north down the Igan River to Mukah (three days/two nights, also full board), which includes a visit to Lamin Dana (see page 336). Book a few days in advance.

ACCOMMODATION SEE MAP PAGE 328

Sibu has a couple of decent inexpensive **hotels**, plus loads of choice once you get to mid-range and above. The cheapest guesthouses are around Chinatown, though this area also hosts a couple of loud bars and is also frequented by prostitutes.
★ **Kingwood** 12 Lorong Lanang; http://kingwoodsibu.com. This huge hotel, with a gleaming extension back from the river, boasts a pool, gym, sauna and other amenities. Prices can be slashed when things are quiet, making the place an absolute steal. Rates include breakfast, though you can save yourself a bit of money if you get a rate without. $$
Li Hua By the river at the junction of Lorong Lanang 2 and Jalan Maju; http://lihuahotel.com.my. It's not the place to come for little refinements, and the sound of guests' chatter can echo around the small lobby, but this is a terrific budget hotel, efficiently run, with dated and plain, but well-kept, en-suite rooms. Reserve ahead. $
Paramount 3 Lorong, 9A Jalan Kampung Dato; http://paramounthotelsibu.com. Located a five-minute walk north of the market near the river, this ageing mid-range place is a little careworn but retains a certain style, like a glamorous great-aunt. The rooms are good value and, while not super modern, are spacious and have nice views of the river. The hotel's restaurant serves local food, including a lunchtime buffet. Avoid staying on the fourth floor, as this is where the karaoke room is. $$
Plaza Inn 2 Jalan Morshidi Sidek; 084 341 218. One of the only budget sleeps in the centre not to have affiliated itself to *OYO* (or its subdivision, *Spot On*), at least for now. And for the time being, it remains a slight cut above the rest, with friendly staff and rooms that are kept clean – sometimes that's more than you need. $
★ **Tanahmas** Off the eastern end of Jalan Chambers; http://tanahmas.com.my. This slick mid-range hotel boasts some of the nicest rooms in its class, fairly spacious with elegant modern furnishings, a swimming pool, mini-gym and a popular Chinese restaurant on the second floor. $$$

EATING SEE MAP PAGE 328

Local specialities include **Foochow noodles** – steamed and then served in a soy and oyster sauce with spring onions, chilli, garlic and dried fish; and *kang puan mee*, which literally translates as "dry-plate noodles" though it

LONGHOUSES NEAR SIBU

There are very few traditional wooden **longhouses** left along the Rejang, but there are a couple of semi-traditional ones within easy striking distance of Sibu that are excellent and well-established at hosting tourists.

Bawang Assan Longhouse Homestay 14km southwest of Sibu; 014 582 8105. Just 40min by road from Sibu by charter taxi or minivan, there are nine colourful longhouses here where Iban families take guests. The longhouses are a mix of traditional and modern, and prices include food, board and a range of activities such as paddy planting and fishing. The tourist office in Sibu can help you make the arrangements. $

Rumah Benjamin Angki Rantau Kemiding, 4km southwest of Kanowit, which is a boat stop or a 40min bus ride upriver from Sibu; 013 882 3076. Painted bright yellow, this venerable longhouse with more than 64 doors and a correspondingly vast *ruai* dates back to 1936. Being set in an agricultural area just uphill from the Kanowit River, it isn't a full-on outback experience, and is great for families with young children. Guests can stay in a purpose-built modern block with two a/c rooms, or in the longhouse itself, where some of the Iban speak good English. Call in advance to discuss prices and some kind of programme as well as to arrange a pick-up from Kanowit; potential activities, all costing extra, include guided walks through the woods, fishing trips and so forth. $$

---

is in fact *mee* fried in lard and garnished with pork slices.

The Ark Café Rejang Esplanade; http://facebook.com/thearkcafesibu. It may look like a designer home, but The Ark is actually a multi-cuisine restaurant that serves Thai, Western, Chinese, Korean and Malaysian dishes. The food, at best, is not bad (try the Emperor Pork Belly), but the contemporary decor compensates, and prices are reasonable, especially for simple rice and noodle dishes. Several outdoor tables, set around a courtyard that's nicely lit at night, have river views by day. $$$

Café Café Texas Inn, 1 Jalan Hua Kiew; 084 328 101. While not as swish as *The Ark*, for many middle-class locals this is the place for a smart night out. The food is mostly a mix of Chinese, Malay and Thai dishes (the Thai chicken salad is very popular), served in different portion sizes with rice, with set lunches even better value. $$

Hai Bing 59 Lorong La King Howe; 084 311 975. Well-established, earthy, and often busy Chinese restaurant known for its seafood, such as ginger crab (priced per kg), though the prawns and other options are a bit cheaper. If you stick with the meaty rice and noodle dishes you can eat for very little money indeed. $

★ **Noodle House Lai Chee** 1 Lorong Laichee; http://facebook.com/yourdailymeal. A new, fresher alternative to the *kopitiams* for those looking for Foochow noodles, though they've plenty more besides, from *nasi lemak* for breakfast to *cendol* for dessert – a one-stop shop for all your local cuisine requirements. $

★ **Payung Café** Jalan Lanang; 016 890 6061. This smart and stylish restaurant, smartened up with artefacts and a thatched awning, is one of the quirkiest in Sarawak, with a fusion menu that reflects enthusiasm rather than fancy culinary training. Their cooking often uses local herbs and could feature anything from Indochinese pomelo salad to prawns with starfruit and spaghetti. You can wash down your meal with, say, their brilliant home-made pineapple ginger soda, or even fresh durian milkshake, if the pongy fruits are in season. $$$

Peppers Café Tanahmas Hotel, off eastern end of Jalan Chambers; http://tanahmas.com.my. The usual hotel restaurant menu ranging from Western staples – including lamb chop and rump steak – to Malaysian fried rice and Chinese noodles, in plush surroundings and at somewhat elevated prices. It's the best Western grub in town, and not a bad option for a slap-up buffet breakfast. $$$

DRINKING   SEE MAP PAGE 328

Good **bars** are thin on the ground, but not for lack of trying; a few venues, such as along Jalan Tukang Besi, are beautifully done out, but lack finesse and descend into karaoke at the slightest opportunity – there is also quite a lot of prostitution.

Oxygen Bar 21 Jalan Wong Nai Siong; 012 808 9330. Your best target for a drink of an evening, far less seedy or karaoke-driven than its competition, and with a delightful courtyard to sit in, if the weather agrees. Guinness, Tiger and a few more on tap, and a range of potentially hazardous shooters.

DIRECTORY

Hospitals and clinics The Sibu Hospital is a taxi ride away at 5 1/2 mile on Jalan Ulu Oya (084 343 333); alternatively, try the Rejang Medical Centre, 29 Jalan Pedada (084 330 733).

Pharmacies Guardian is just outside Wisma Sanyan mall, and KKMP is just inside the mall (both daily 9.30am–10pm).
Police Jalan Kampung Nyabor (084 336 144).

Up the Batang Rejang

Even though much of the traditional culture and architecture of the region has been lost, a journey to the **upper reaches of the Rejang** should still engender a little frisson of excitement. This area was, after all, once synonymous with mysterious warring Indigenous people. Even a century ago, conflict persisted between the Iban and the Orang Ulu, particularly the Kayan. Things had been much worse before the arrival of the Brookes, who wanted to develop – and therefore subjugate – the interior. To that end, James Brooke bought a section of the Rejang from the Sultan of Brunei in 1853, while his successor, Charles, asserted his authority over the Iban and Kayan Indigenous people and encouraged the Chinese to open up the interior to agriculture and trade.

Thus began the gradual pacification of the Rejang. Even today, despite development and modern communications, it's possible to glimpse something of that pioneer spirit in these upriver towns, while forts at **Kanowit** and **Kapit** hint at the lengths taken by the Brookes to get the region under their thumb. Until very recently, the only way in was by boat, though new roads have simplified access, with obvious positives and negatives for locals (and, much less importantly, tourists). Boats are still the main route upriver from Kelit, as far as the nondescript town of **Belaga**, reached by a thrilling ride through the **Pelagus Rapids**. There is, however, another exciting route into or out of Belaga – by **4WD**, the road connecting up with the main trunk road near Bintulu (see page 337).

Unfortunately, **visits to traditional wooden longhouses** can be difficult to pull off. The vast majority are now made of concrete – notable exceptions are Bawang Assan near Sibu, the Rumah Benjamin Angki Longhouse near Kanowit (see box, page 326), the Rumah William Unchat longhouse near Kapit, and a few up the tributaries near Belaga or Kapit – easy enough to get to by "flying coffin" (see box).

Kapit

KAPIT is the main commercial centre upriver from Sibu, and it looks it too, trapped in an architectural no-man's-land between the modern town it could become and the rustic backwater it was a generation ago – the place feels like an utter jumble, despite a certain appealing energy. If you do end up here, you may well stay the night – either because you can't face the journey to Belaga in one go or because this is as far as you intend to get – and fortunately it has some good accommodation options. Although there are a couple of **museums** (plus several banks and a couple of cafés), there's not much else to do beyond wandering the river bank or having a look around the market.

> **REJANG BOATS**
>
> One explanation for the nickname "flying coffins" – formerly attached jokingly to the **Rejang express boats** – is that they are long and narrow, and feature aircraft-like seating. Otherwise they are serviceable, if not massively comfortable or user-friendly: boarding entails stepping off the jetty onto the boat's rim or gunwale and walking around until you reach the entrance hatch. You may also have to fling your luggage on the roof yourself, although sometimes staff are on hand to help load and unload.
>
> Unfortunately, they're a dying breed between Sibu and Kapit – the Covid crisis saw some boatmen leave the business, and then more did so when travel started to reopen, but with capacities reduced so greatly that turning a profit became almost impossible. And all this was happening while a new road to Kapit was being built – not quite the final nail in the (flying) coffin, but the end may well be nigh.
>
> Boats are still running to Belaga from Kapit, usually leaving in the morning, so with an early start it's quite possible to make it from Miri to Belaga in one day. Note that during the dry season, if the river level is low, Belaga boats are cancelled – ask at the jetty or tourist office in Sibu (see page 330) for the latest.

Fort Sylvia

Jalan Kubu (you may need to wait for the caretaker to show up with the keys) • Free • http://tunjugahfoundation.org.my

Fort Sylvia, the white, low-slung building a couple of minutes' walk upriver from the boat terminal, makes quite a grand first impression. Built in 1880 of tough *belian* (ironwood) timber, it was an attempt to prevent the marauding Iban attacking smaller and more peaceable groups, and to limit Iban migration along the nearby Baleh River, confining them to the Rejang below Kapit; note the diamond-shaped gun holes all along the facade.

The fort is now a small **museum** and conference venue, managed by the people behind Kuching's Tun Jugah Foundation gallery (see page 309). Evocative photographs depict great moments in the history of the Ulu Rejang, including the 1924 peace-making ceremony in Kapit between Brooke officials and the warring Iban and Kayan representatives. In addition, ceramic jars, *pua kumba* textiles and small cannon are on display.

Civic Centre and Museum

Jalan Hospital • 084 796 003 • Free

Also known by its Malay name, Dewan Suarah, Kapit's **Civic Centre and Museum** holds interesting exhibits on the Indigenous groups in the Rejang region, including a well-constructed longhouse and a mural painted by local Iban. Sketches and watercolours of Kapit, Belaga and Song portray a life that is slowly disappearing. The museum also describes the lives of the Hokkien traders who helped put towns like Kapit on the map.

Rumah William Unchat Longhouse

Yong River • Charge, including entry, photo permit and community donation; skull room extra • 084 796 903 • You can visit using a guide from Kapit, though it's not that difficult to organize yourself; take a minivan from Kapit's market square (45min), and if the driver speaks English, ask them to come in with you to help translate

Some 50km southwest from Kapit, the weather-worn **Rumah William Unchat Longhouse** is one of the last remaining traditional wooden longhouses in the region, and one of the few anywhere that still keep the skulls hanging outside the skull room, though most of today's inhabitants now live in the shiny new 34-door longhouse built next door. It's also possible to **stay** here, and although you'll have to bring your own food, they'll help you to cook it.

ARRIVAL AND INFORMATION   KAPIT

By bus Kapit hasn't yet got around to building a permanent bus terminal – they've only recently been connected to the road network, so perhaps a little delay is quite easy to understand – but buses are already arriving from Sibu (6 daily; 3hr), unloading (for now) at a temporary depot 2.5km west of town.

By boat Kapit's large boat terminal is far quieter these days than it used to be, though there's still a daily service to Belaga (5hr); these actually use a pier just a couple of minutes' walk downriver.

Guides If you want to visit Rumah William Unchat Longhouse, your accommodation can usually organize an English-speaking guide and an all-inclusive overnight stay. You can also ask them about destinations such as Nanga Pulang Longhouse, or the remote Horse Mountains. Make sure all the terms are clearly agreed before you set out.

ACCOMMODATION

Kapit has a few reasonable budget hotels (if the ones listed here are full, you'll easily stumble upon a handful more around town) and two mid-range options, though accommodation tends to be slightly overpriced. There is also the option of staying at the **Rumah William Unchat Longhouse** nearby. If you want to experience staying at one of the longhouses between Kapit and Belaga, or on the less-visited tributary between Kapit and the logging camp at Putai, residents often hang out around the docks looking for tourists.

Ark Hill Inn Jalan Penghulu Gerinang; http://facebook.com/hill.ark.5. Good-value budget place with spartan but quite serviceable and clean en-suite doubles, twins, triples and a couple of "single" rooms that hold a bed large enough for two; showers are pretty good. $

Loft Pals Urbanstay Jalan Teo Chow Beng; http://facebook.com/loftpals. Good choice, a cheap hotel at which they've tried to jazz things up with twee light fittings and the like, which has mostly worked a treat. The rooms are

just fine (wi-fi usually works too), and there's an on-site laundry. $
Meligai Jalan Airport; http://hotelmeligai.com. Just about the only proper "hotel" in town (it feels way more like a motel), with four floors of rooms (gasp!) It looks fine from outside, though the reality in the rooms are often less pleasing – be sure to check one out before you hand over your money. $$

EATING

Eating in Kapit is largely a matter of picking from the numerous **kedai kopis** and ordering from a fairly predictable range of dishes. Almost all eating places – apart from the *Taman Selera Empurau*, the *KFC*, and the *Sugarbuns* – close by 6.30pm.
Gelanggang Kenyalang One block south of Jalan Teo Cheow Beng. Popular with locals, this food market serves inexpensive and delicious Malay food at plastic tables – noodles, fried rice, excellent satay sticks and of course *nasi goreng*. Sadly, it closes up in the early afternoon. $
Good Taste Jalan Airport; 016 281 8981. This place opens up just after Gelanggang Kenyalang closes, and stays open until late evening, so between them you're covered (most days). Good for fried meat dishes, with a few seafood options, most of which are quite basic. $

Belaga

Belaga-bound boats make frequent stops upriver from Kapit, and some passengers decamp to the roof for views of longhouses as the Rejang narrows. Forty minutes from Kapit, the **Pelagus Rapids** is an 800m-long, deceptively shallow stretch of the river where large, submerged stones make the through passage treacherous, and although it might get your adrelalene pumping slightly, remember that the boatmen are well-practiced in traversing them. Further upriver, the population shifts from being largely Iban to featuring a mix of other Indigenous groups, including the Kayan and Kenyah.

Five hours beyond Kapit, the boat finally reaches tiny **BELAGA**, 40km west of the confluence of the Rejang and the Balui. The town started life as a small bazaar, and by 1900 pioneering Chinese *towkays* were supplying the Indigenous groups – both the Kayan and the then-nomadic Punan and Penan – with kerosene, cooking oil and cartridges, in exchange for beadwork and mats, beeswax, ebony and tree gums. The British presence in this region was nominal; Belaga has no crumbling fort to serve as a museum, as none were built this far upriver.

The town square and around

The first sight that confronts new arrivals climbing the steps from the river bank is Belaga's slightly shabby tennis and basketball court. Next door a small garden serves as the **town square**, with a hornbill statue atop a traditional-style round pillar bearing Indigenous motifs. There are just six streets and alleys in the centre, and while quite a few shops sell provisions, there's no market, though Orang Ulu traders may arrive at weekends to sell jungle produce in the streets. In the morning, picturesque mists settle on the Rejang.

Walks around Belaga

Having made it all the way here, the best thing you can do is luxuriate in Belaga's tranquillity, a welcome contrast from Kapit. Short walks lead through the **Malay kampung** just downriver (which includes the shanty town by the river for children from outlying villages attending the school here) or cross the river by boat (charge) and walk two hours along a red paint-marked path through the jungle to the **Sihan** (a semi-nomadic people) village – there are only a handful of sporadic inhabitants now, usually coming for harvest and festival times.

ARRIVAL AND DEPARTURE   BELAGA

By bus There is one daily boat to Kapit, which leaves around 7.30am. Boats use the jetty by the basketball court.
By 4WD Most days at least a couple of 4WD vehicles leave for Bintulu from the town square, usually in the early morning (3hr 40min). You may be able to pay less to reach the main trunk road, where you can flag down a long-distance bus; either way, you should ask around on the square to reserve a place (and, of course, figure out when the vehicles are departing). Alternatively, it's possible for men and groups to hitch the route (just stand by the bridge

THE KAYAN AND KENYAH

The **Kayan** and the **Kenyah** are the most populous and powerful of the Orang Ulu groups who have lived for centuries in the upper Rejang and, in the northern interior, along the River Baram. The Kayan are more numerous, with some (probably exaggerated) estimates running towards 200,000, while the Kenyah population is around fifty thousand (with about the same number over the mountains in Kalimantan). Both groups migrated from East Kalimantan into Sarawak roughly six hundred years ago; they were pushed back to the lands they occupy today during the nineteenth century, when Iban migration led to clashes between the groups.

The Kayan and the Kenyah have a fair amount in common: their language, though of the same family as the other Bornean tongues and Malay, has a singsong quality that sounds like Chinese, and they have a well-defined social hierarchy, unlike the Iban or Penan. Traditionally, the **social order** was topped by the **tuai rumah** (chief) of the longhouse, followed by a group of three or four lesser aristocrats or **payin**, lay families and slaves (slavery no longer exists). Both groups take pride in their **longhouses**, which can be massive.

KAYAN ART

Artistic expression plays an important role in longhouse culture. The Kayan especially maintain a wide range of **musical traditions** including the lute-like **sape**, used to accompany long voice epics. **Textiles** are woven by traditional techniques in the upriver longhouses, and Kayan and Kenyah **woodcarvings**, among the most spectacular in Southeast Asia, are produced both for sale and for ceremonial uses. One artist, Tusau Padan, originally from Kalimantan, became much revered. He used mixed media of vibrant colours to create the flowing motifs he applied to painting and textiles – adorning burial poles, longboats and the walls of many Ulu Sarawak chiefs' homes. Some Kayan still drink potent **rice wine**, although now that nearly all the communities have converted to Christianity, alcohol is harder to come by.

---

in Belaga or at the junction on the main road) – you may be asked to pay, so it may help clarify whether you're expected to do so before you get in.

INFORMATION AND TOURS

Tours and longhouse trips About the only entity seriously organizing tours in Belaga is Daniel's Corner (see page 335), who run trips to the small waterfall 20min away up a tributary, as well as an all-day tour to the Bakun Dam using 4WD and boat, which stops in various old and new longhouses on the way – this tour could drop you on the Bintulu–Miri highway. Although his guesthouse is very good value, the tours are pricey. However, if you bargain, prices may come down considerably.

ACCOMMODATION AND EATING

The town's Malay *kedai kopis* cluster on the main street, while there are a couple of decent Chinese places, which serve beer, a few doors down from *Daniel's Corner guesthouse*. None of them are bad, but none particularly good, and all close shortly after dark. This is when you can get the best food at the sociable **night food stalls** just north of the centre, which dish up inexpensive Malay foods including outstanding grilled meats and satay.

Belaga Main St; 086 461 244. The oldest of the main street's all-but-identical hotels (all more or less the same price), and it looks it too, with dated fittings. The simple en-suite rooms have a/c, and – this gives it an edge – there's a café below with wi-fi. $

Daniel's Corner Two blocks behind Main St; http://facebook.com/oranguluhomestay. More like a homestay, with two double rooms and a dorm that open up onto a nice and homely communal area, where there is also a small kitchen. A little dirty, the place has gone downhill of late. $

Sing Soon Huat At the end of a lane, just back from the Sing Soon Hing; 086 461 307. Sharing management with the nearby *Sing Soon Hing*, these are probably the best rooms in town; bigger and a little quieter than those on the main street, with a/c, TV and better en-suite bathrooms. $

DIRECTORY

Banks The town has a Bank Simpanan National, with ATM, three streets back from the river.

THE BAKUN DAM

The massive **Bakun hydroelectric dam**, 37km east of Belaga on the Balui tributary of the Rejang, has been dogged by controversy since the project got the go-ahead in the 1990s. The 200m-high dam was designed to generate 2400 megawatts – much more power than Sarawak could use – but construction would flood an area of rainforest the size of Singapore, displacing ten thousand Orang Ulu and destroying many thriving longhouse communities.

Furious environmentalists and human-rights campaigners asked what the point was, and for years their concerns seemed vindicated as the dam was beset by delays. First, the **Asian economic crisis** of 1997 put the project on hold, but even so the government continued to resettle local communities to Asap, two hours' drive along the logging road connecting Belaga with the coast. When construction resumed it lumbered on until, in mid-2011, the dam finally began operating. However, it still doesn't run at anything near capacity, since there is no obvious market for the **surplus power** (one idea, to lay a submarine cable to Peninsular Malaysia, would be technically challenging and prohibitively expensive, but is still a possibility). Despite this, yet another dam has been built just upriver on the Rejang at Long Murum – both that one and another proposed dam on the Baram have seen massive protests and blockades by local people, thanks to which the Baram dam was shelved (not quite cancelled) in 2015.

Attempts have already begun to create tourist facilities at the Bakun Dam lake, as has been tried with limited success at Batang Ai and Tasik Kenyir in Terengganu, though these have yet to bear fruit, and the hotel there is mostly used to house dam workers. Sibu's tourist office (see page 330) and guesthouses in Belaga have details of the enormous and quite swanky Kayan and Kenyah **longhouses** at Asap that accept guests, and whose inhabitants have a fishing lodge on the lake itself.

The coast from Sibu to Bintulu

The drive from Sibu to Bintulu is mundane, the roadscape lacking the grandeur of southwest Sarawak's mountains, though there are occasional glimpses of (usually modern) longhouses by the highway. The chief point of interest on this coastal stretch is **Similajau National Park**, a strip of forest with isolated beaches thirty minutes' drive beyond the industrial town of **Bintulu**. With plenty of time, you could also get a dose of the culture of the largely Muslim Melanau people by diverting off the trunk road to the small coastal market town of **Mukah**. While not of huge interest in itself, it's a potential base for the Melanau water village of **Kampung Tellian**, which has a heritage centre, **Lamin Dana**, that you can also stay at.

Kampung Tellian and around

The Melanau water village of **KAMPUNG TELLIAN**, 3km east of **MUKAH**, is a veritable spaghetti junction of ramshackle wooden houses connected by precarious crisscrossing boardwalks and bridges. It's an immensely atmospheric and peaceful spot, the kind of place where you might wish you were born so that you could always go back there. Some of the Melanau residents of its many stilt houses still process sago the traditional way – by pulverizing the pith in large troughs and squeezing the pulp through a sieve, then leaving it to dry.

Lamin Dana
Tellian Daya • Charge • http://lamindana.com

Aside from its picturesque appeal, Tellian's main attraction is its beautiful heritage centre and guesthouse, **Lamin Dana**, built in 1999 in the style of a traditional Melanau tall house, though not quite on the scale of the one at the Sarawak Cultural Village in Santubong (see page 316). Exhibits include a collection of betel-nut jars, once used to store heirlooms, finely woven textiles for ceremonial occasions, musical instruments – including the obligatory gongs – and handicrafts such as hand-woven rattan baskets for which the Melanau are well known. A short walk along the plankway to the front of the tall house reveals a Melanau burial ground, or *bakut*, amid a clump of bare, ancient trees.

ARRIVAL AND DEPARTURE

By plane No buses run between Mukah's airport, 7km west of town, and the town itself; best take a taxi. MASwings flies to both Kuching (2–3 daily; 1hr) and Miri (1 daily; 1hr 10min), plus less frequently to Bintulu (2 weekly; 35min) and Sibu (3 weekly; 25min).

By bus The bus station in Mukah lies off Jalan Setiaraja, on the southern edge of the old town. Destinations Bintulu (3 daily; 3hr); Miri (1–2 daily; 4hr 20min); Sibu (3 daily; 1hr 30min).

KAMPUNG TELLIAN AND AROUND

By taxi Taxis from Mukah's bus terminus can take you to Kampung Tellian. Note that most taxi drivers finish work at around 4 or 5pm.

ACCOMMODATION AND EATING

King Ing 1 Jalan Boyan, Mukah. Mukah's best hotel choice is a 20min walk from the bus station in the old town, with a bright and appealing foyer and clean, a/c rooms with sizeable bathrooms. The place was given a new lick of paint in recent years, both literally and figuratively, and rooms can be booked online. $

Lamin Dana Cultural Boutique Lodge Kampung Tellian; http://lamindana.com. This recreated tall house is an atmospheric place to stay, with ten variously sized, airy doubles and a couple of family rooms. Bathrooms are shared and there's no a/c. If you come on a package, you'll be taken on a boat trip through the mangroves, do a guided village walk, and see a sago-processing demonstration; contact for details and to customize an itinerary. Three-day, two-night full-board packages available. $$$$

Bintulu

Forty years ago, **BINTULU** was little more than a resting point en route between Sibu (220km to the southwest) and Miri (210km northeast). Since large **natural gas** reserves were discovered offshore in the 1960s, however, speedy expansion has seen Bintulu follow in Miri's footsteps as a primary resources boom town. Today some quite prosperous neighbourhoods can be seen on the outskirts, though the old centre remains as unassuming as ever. There are only two reasons why you might want to stop over: to use Bintulu as a base for the excellent **Similajau National Park** or, if you're heading south from Miri, as a springboard for **Belaga** and the Batang Rejang (see page 332). You can also reach **Niah National Park** (see page 346) from here (though it's easier to go on a trip with one of the Miri backpacker lodges), while any express bus to Miri can drop you at **Lambir Hills National Park** (see page 345).

The old centre

You could spend a couple of hours strolling around Bintulu's **old centre**, a grid of streets squashed between the defunct airfield to the east and the wide Kemena River

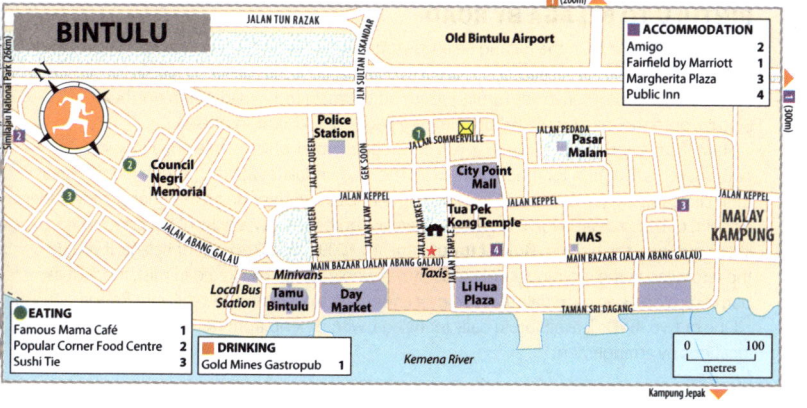

to the west. This is why the town feels so low-key: the centre simply hasn't been able to grow. It looks as though developers and road builders are finally being allowed to chip away at the unaccountably abandoned airfield, however, so the heart of Bintulu is changing rapidly.

The obvious place to start is on Main Bazaar in front of **Tua Pek Kong**, a grand Chinese temple that's really in too good a state of repair to impress. Redevelopment of the **riverfront** has created the open square here, as well as an esplanade and parkland area leading north towards the South China Sea – only 3km away, concealed beyond the Kemena's final bend.

Just downriver are the modern **day market** (*pasar utama*) and the more informal **Tamu Bintulu**, where locals still bring in goods and lay them on rough tables to sell. The jetties behind are a good place to observe life on the river: fishing boats bring their catch in every morning, barges laden with timber or building materials lumber past, while the opposite bank is dotted with rustic kampung houses.

ARRIVAL AND DEPARTURE — BINTULU

By plane The airport, 5km southwest of town (086 331 073), can only be reached by following a convoluted road route, detouring east and then south. A taxi into the centre takes 25min.
Destinations Kota Kinabalu (5 weekly; 1hr 15min); Kuala Lumpur (6 daily; 2hr 15min); Kuching (5 daily; 50min); Miri (1–2 daily; 35min); Mukah (2 weekly; 35min); Sibu (1 daily; 35min).
By bus Bintulu's long-distance bus station is 5km northeast of town in the lively suburb of Medan Jaya. You might be able to find an hourly local bus into the centre, but otherwise you'll have to pay for a taxi.
Destinations Kuching (7 daily; 11–15hr); Miri (13 daily; 4hr); Mukah (3 daily; 4hr); Pontianak (Indonesia; at least 2 daily; 19hr); Sibu (every 1–2hr; 4hr).
By minivan Minivans (which leave when full) ply the highway up to Miri and down to Sibu; the depot is in front of Tamu Bintulu. One route north passes the turning to Similajau National Park.
By taxi The main taxi rank (086 332 009) is next to the Tian En Ting temple.

ACCOMMODATION — SEE MAP PAGE 337

Central Bintulu holds a number of unexciting **budget hotels**, all with a/c, en-suite rooms. The cheapest are in the red-light district east of Li Hua Plaza, but are a bit unsavoury. Several business-oriented hotels, including some north of the centre towards the seafront, cater to visiting oil-industry executives.
Amigo Jalan Abang Galau; 019 750 4588. Relatively new hotel, set in a relatively new part of town – the Shahida Commercial Centre, out west. Like all of its immediate neighbours, it's a three-floor affair with white walls, blueish windows and a wave-like metal roof; with the river sliding past nearby, you could kid yourself that you're in Copenhagen (for a few seconds, at least). Some rooms are a little small, but all have a/c and modern bathrooms. $$
Fairfield by Marriott 1 Old Airport Place; http://marriott.com. The only upper-end hotel in town, and actually quite

BINTULU TO BELAGA BY ROAD

When the water level in the Batang Rejang is too low for boats to reach Belaga, the one sure way to get there – and an interesting drive through remote terrain – is by **4WD** from Bintulu. The four-hour journey involves turning south off the main trunk road, 50km northeast of Bintulu, onto the road for the Bakun dam (see page 336), 125km southeast.

After 80km, another right turn puts you on a logging road which, while not a classic boneshaker, is roughish for much of the way. The road undulates at first through jungle areas, then climbs steadily, snaking past isolated communities and through areas either already under oil palm or being cleared for it. Eventually there are gorgeous views of lushly forested peaks in the distance; the highest, **Bukit Lumut** at nearly 1000m, is 25km west of Belaga. If you do the return leg in the morning you'll probably see whole valleys blanketed in mist, too. Just as bumping along begins to pall, the road descends quite steeply, and you pull into Belaga.

One or two 4WDs leave Bintulu daily for Belaga, with pick-up from hotels or other central locations by arrangement.

affordable for what you get (if you can afford it, that is). Rooms are typically attractive (and some are colossal), and there's a gym and very decent restaurant; the only negative is a slightly out-of-the-way location. $$$
Margherita Plaza Jalan Abang Galau; http://margherita plaza.com. A business-oriented hotel with an opulent lobby, rooftop swimming pool, bar, restaurant (with Western lunches) and café – though the atmosphere can be a bit sterile. Rates are on the affordable side, though, and include breakfast. $$
Public Inn 47 Jalan Abang Galau (Main Bazaar); 019 815 5510. Very clean, safe, quiet and respectable guesthouse with good-value rooms that have comfortable beds, TV and a/c, as well as friendly staff. There's a food court next door. $

EATING
SEE MAP PAGE 337

Buoyed by oil and gas money and a small expat population, Bintulu boasts several decent restaurants, though many – along with a handful of bars – are in the suburbs. Still, quite a few **central eating places** are worth trying, and for evening snacks you can always try the *pasar malam* in the open space close to the airfield.

Famous Mama Café Jalan Somerville; 086 336 541. The closest thing you'll find to a West Malaysian *mamak*-style joint, this excellent Indian *kedai kopi* draws in people of all colours and faiths to socialize and stuff their faces from the great *nasi campur* spread (eaten with plain or *biriyani* rice) or various *roti* plates. $

Popular Corner Food Centre 50 Jalan Abang Galau. The size of four or five *kedai kopis* put together, this brilliant food court could hold its own in downtown KL. An endless range of stalls sell the likes of duck noodles, *yong tau foo* and dim sum, and there's a pastry stall doing custard tarts and local savouries including sweet potato or yam fritters. $

★ **Sushi Tie** Jalan Abang Galau; http://facebook.com/SUSHITIE. This place blew everyone's minds when opening – Bintulu had simply never seen anywhere this fancy before. It's nothing out of this world, just a very decent, and surprisingly attractive, Japanese restaurant, hiding out here in the Sarawak hinterlands. Sushi's the main draw, obviously, but there are good Japanese rice and noodle staples on offer too, including a tasty curry *udon*. $$$

DRINKING
SEE MAP PAGE 337

★ **Gold Mines Gastropub** 4 Jalan Tun Ahmad Zaidi; http://facebook.com/thegoldminesgastropub. Yet another example of the relative food-and-drink paradise that Bintulu is turning into – a gastropub, of all things, and quite a good one at that (or may it just feels better than it is, on account of the location). Cold drinks (including draught Kilkenny), good food, and a cool-looking space to boot.

DIRECTORY

Hospital Bintulu Jalan Nyabau (086 859 000, http://jknsarawak.moh.gov.my/hbtu) is 13km from downtown (a 15min taxi ride at least).
Pharmacies The Park City Mall has branches of Guardian and Watsons.
Police Jalan Somerville 086 332 004.
Visa extensions Immigration Department, 3km north of the centre on Jalan Tun Razak (086 331 441).

Similajau National Park

With its sandy beaches broken only by rocky headlands and freshwater streams, the seventy-square-kilometre **Similajau National Park**, 28km northeast of Bintulu by road, has something of the appeal of the highly popular Bako, near Kuching. Enjoyable trekking makes for a great day-trip, and there's even good accommodation. Though wildlife is not a major highlight, the park is well known for its population of saltwater **crocodiles** (signs along the creeks pointedly warn against swimming), with a few dolphins also sighted each year off the coast outside the rainy season. Birdlife includes black hornbills and, in the mangroves, kingfishers.

The main trail

The first stretch of the 10km **main trail** – which runs northeast, mostly just inland, from the park office – has you crossing a bridge over the mouth of the Likau, more of a large brown creek than a river, and heading into the jungle. Around 1km in, a short side branch leads west to a **viewpoint** – a wooden pavilion perched over a rocky beach, from where you can just spot Bintulu's oil and gas installations at Tanjung Kidurong, 15km north of town. Return to the trail and you eventually come to **Turtle Beach I** (6km along; allow 3hr to reach it), then **Turtle Beach II** (total 7.5km along) and finally **Golden Beach** (10km; 4hr). You can overnight at any of them in the hope of spotting turtles, who nest here from March to September, though there are no facilities and you should inform park staff of your intentions. Sadly, **swimming** at these beaches is not advised, because the sea is deep even close to shore and there's a strong undertow, though other smaller stretches of sand en route are okay for a dip.

ARRIVAL AND INFORMATION: SIMILAJAU NATIONAL PARK

By minibus The park lies 9km down an access road off the coastal road to Miri; minibuses heading along the coast road from Bintulu can drop you at the junction from where you can walk or hitch.

By taxi Taxis from Bintulu are the best way to get here, and the driver can either wait around, or come back at a set time if you're doing a hike or staying the night – so get their number.

Park HQ The friendly and helpful staff at the Park HQ (019 861 998, http://sarawakforestry.com), where you pay the admission fee, can provide a schematic trail map; find you a guide, or book you onto a night walk on which you just might see pangolins or wild boar; they can also arrange boat trips.

GETTING AROUND

By boat Boats are a useful timesaver – instead of trekking in two directions, you can pay for a boat (for up to five passengers) to head out to Golden Beach or either of the Turtle beaches, then trek back. You can also use boats to reach Batu Mandi ("bath rock" in Malay), a rock formation out at sea with large depressions that regularly fill with sea water, or do a so-called night cruise along the Likau to spot kingfishers and those notorious crocodiles (up to six people).

ACCOMMODATION AND EATING

Similajau National Park accommodation 019 861 0998. The park's generally under-utilized accommodation makes it a relaxing place to spend a night or two and has recently been refurbished. There's quite a range on offer, from two hostels that have rooms rather than dorms, each with one bunk bed and some with a bathroom too, to quite fancy a/c accommodation; check for the latest pricing. A simple canteen serves the usual rice and noodle dishes. Camping/hostel rooms $, a/c lodge rooms $$

The northern coast

North of Bintulu, the scenery along the main trunk road is increasingly dominated by oil-palm estates; if you're driving, the quiet coastal highway is a more scenic option for the 210km drive to **Miri**, Sarawak's second largest city. Though boasting no important sights, Miri is nearly as important a gateway to Sarawak as Kuching, thanks to good flight connections and its location amid the riches of northern Sarawak, mostly deep inland and requiring days to explore properly. A couple of national parks lie close to the coast south of Miri: **Niah** is noted for its formidable **limestone caves**, while **Lambir Hills** offers more predictable jungle trekking.

Sarawak's northern coastal strip is also home to **Lawas**, near the Sabah state boundary. It has an air connection to Ba Kelalan that's useful if you want to see the Kelabit Highlands immediately before or visiting Sabah.

Miri

Before oil was discovered in 1882, **MIRI** was a tiny, unimportant settlement. While production has now shifted offshore, the petroleum industry largely accounts for the thriving city of today, with a population of around 360,000. Some of Miri's earliest inhabitants were pioneering **Chinese** merchants who set up shops to trade with the Kayan longhouses southeast along the Baram River, and the city retains a strong Chinese flavour, though the Iban and Malays are also well represented, along with a significant number of Orang Ulu.

Now blandly modern for the most part, Miri makes a surprisingly pleasant base from which to see northern Sarawak; visitors generally wind up staying longer than expected, sometimes in several stints interspersed with trips into the interior. The

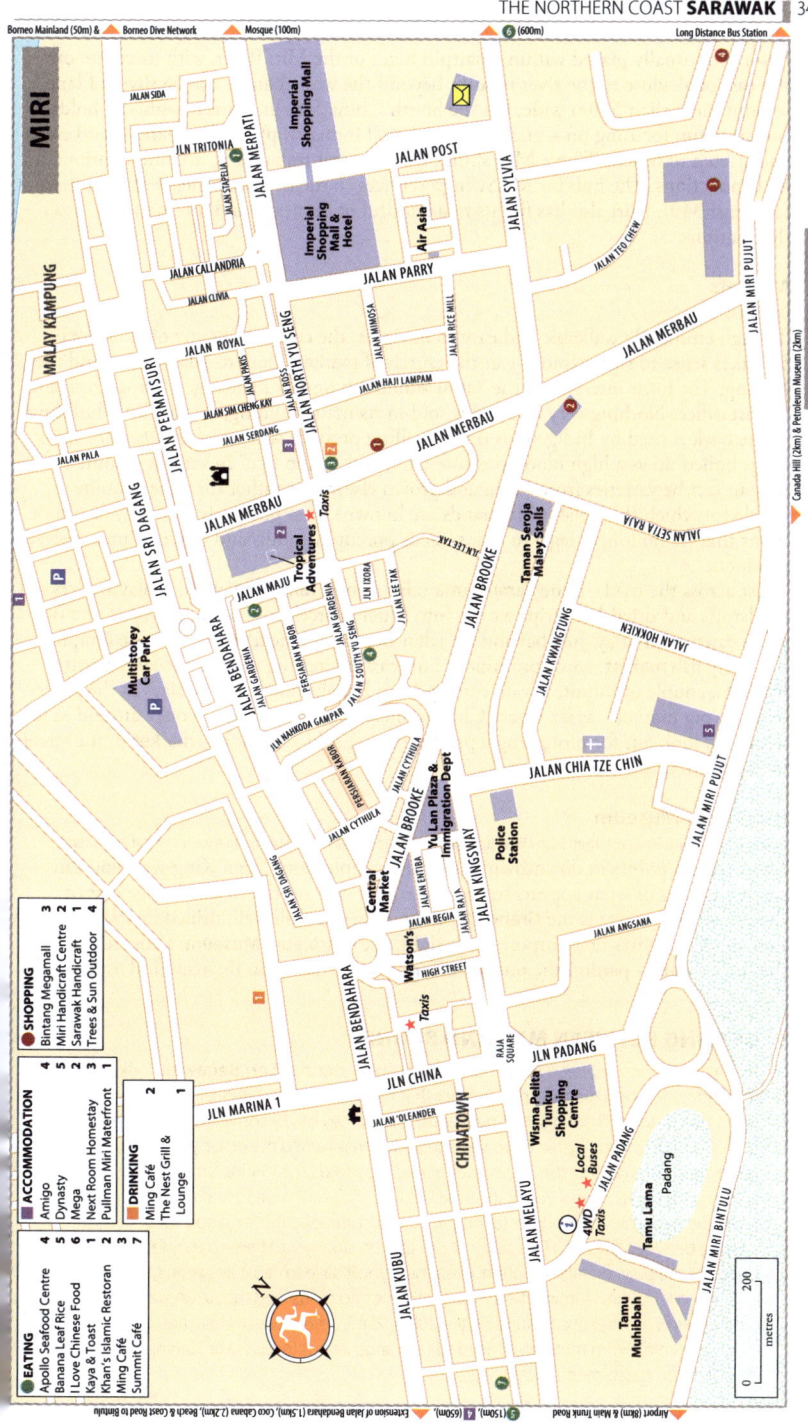

town is unusually placed within a hairpin bend of the Miri River, with its centre on the east bank close to the river mouth; beyond the west "bank", a mere sliver of land seldom more than 500m wide, lies the South China Sea. In terms of sights, it holds one museum focusing on – guess what – the oil industry, plus a few **markets** and not a bad stretch of beach. Where Miri shines is in its great restaurants, accommodation and **air connections**. The hub for MASwings' services to the tiny settlements of the interior (see page 349), Miri also has flights to a handful of domestic and international destinations.

Markets
Daily dawn–dusk

Though eminently walkable and easy to navigate, the centre lacks any obvious focus. It makes sense to start exploring at the clutch of **markets** close to Jalan China and the Padang. The most interesting, the **Tamu Muhibbah** on Jalan Padang, is across from the tourist office. Nothing very unusual is sold in its main building, but the little building at the back is used by Indigenous traders selling produce such as *akar bakawali*, spiny twigs boiled up as a high blood pressure cure, and "Bario rice" in various colours (it may in fact be varieties from Bario and grown elsewhere, rather than the genuine article for which the Kelabit Highlands are known). Less positively, you may also spot items that it's no longer legal to sell, such as porcupine quills and other animal-derived products.

Just across the road, in the **Tamu Lama** (also signed **Tamu Kedayan**), Malay traders sell foodstuffs and dried-leaf strips woven into square parcels for cooking *ketupat*, the rice cakes eaten with satay. Just beyond on Jalan Bendahara, next to the Chinese temple, is a lively **fish market**. Most prominent but least interesting of all is the large **Central Market** a couple of minutes' walk east on Jalan Brooke, known to Malays as the *pasar babi* or "pig market", as it's where Chinese meat traders operate. If you're around at the weekend, look out for more jungle produce being sold at a **Sunday market** in the streets to the south of the Tamu Lama.

Petroleum Museum
Canada Hill (aka Bukit Tenaga); turn off Jalan Miri Pujut opposite Jalan Setia Raja • Free • Taxi ride from town, or a stiff 20min climb

From certain points in downtown Miri, for example along Jalan Kingsway, you can catch glimpses of what appears to be a tapering tower on the wooded ridge east of the centre. The tower is the **Grand Old Lady**, Miri's first oil well, drilled in 1910 and now marking Miri's one purpose-built sight, the **Petroleum Museum**. Unfortunately, the displays are – pardon the pun – boring, concentrating on the technical aspects of

---

GETTING BETWEEN MIRI AND BRUNEI

The act of moving between **Miri** and Brunei's capital, **Bandar Seri Begawan**, looks straightforward on a map, despite the fact that it crosses an international border, but since direct buses stopped during the Covid crisis, this journey has become arduous, expensive, or both. Obviously, if you just want to see one and then return to the other, you can rent a car; if you're on a one-way trip, the easiest way across is by **taxi** (2hr 30min), though obviously this won't come cheap, even if you're in a small group, and you'll have to find a driver prepared to make the haul across the border (asking at your accommodation is a good start).

Flying between the two cities takes all day at best, since you'd have to transfer, which leaves **buses** as the only remaining option. Even then, you'll have to cab it between Miri and the Brunei border (28km; 40min), then walk 1km across no man's land (not a fun walk, either), before taking another taxi to Kuala Belait (20km; 25min), from which there are regular buses to Seria (30min). From there you'll need to take another bus (hourly; 1hr 30min, if you're lucky, though often much more) to BSB.

drilling and refining, with some historical context, but no tales of the human impact the nascent industry must surely have had.

The beach

Just over 3km southwest of the Padang • Taxis are your best bet, but you can walk it too

The coast road out of town (the extension of Jalan Bendahara) holds a stretch of public beach around 500m long. The sands are fairly narrow, but it's a relaxed enough spot and a fine place to watch the sun go down. The beach's proper name is **Tanjung Lobang**, though many locals call it **Taman Selera** as Malay stalls sell seafood at a simple evenings-only food court.

ARRIVAL AND DEPARTURE MIRI

By plane Miri's airport is 10km south of town (http://miriairport.com). To get a taxi into town, buy a voucher from the taxi counter. The number of destinations in Malaysian Borneo has been reduced in recent years, meaning that for some you may have to change planes in Lawas or Marudi. Destinations Bintulu (1–2 daily; 35min); Johor Bahru (1 daily; 1hr 55min); Kota Kinabalu (4 daily; 50min); Kuala Lumpur (8–9 daily; 2hr 10min); Kuching (6–7 daily; 1hr); Labuan (3–4 daily; 40min); Lawas (4 –5 daily; 45min); Limbang (2 daily; 35min); Long Akah (1 weekly; 40min; more via Marudi); Long Banga (1 weekly via Marudi; 1hr 25min); Long Lellang (2 weekly; 45min; more via Marudi); Long Seridan (2 weekly; 45min–1hr); Marudi (2–3 daily; 20min); Mukah (1 daily; 1hr); Mulu (2 daily; 30min); Sibu (2–3 daily; 55min); Singapore (4 weekly; 2hr).

By bus The long-distance bus station is at Pujut Corner, 4km northeast of the centre off Jalan Miri Pujut. Services to Bandar Seri Begawan in Brunei, via Kuala Belait and Seria, dried up during the Covid crisis and have yet to resurface; it's now a difficult, or expensive, journey (see box). The same is true of the buses through to Kota Kinabalu. Heading all the way to KK by road can be laborious in any case, though thanks to the new bridge it no longer entails four unpleasant border crossings and eight new stamps in your passport (it's now only two crossings and four stamps), so many people choose to fly direct, or via Mulu or Bario. To get into town from the bus station, you can either walk to the bus stop on the other side of the nearby shopping centre, and wait around for the infrequent #20 bus (every 60–90min), or simply take a taxi/Grab or *kereta sapu*. Destinations Bintulu (11 daily; 3hr 30min–4hr); Kuching (10 daily; 14–17hr); Mukah (1–2 daily; 6–7hr); Pontianak (Indonesia; at least 2 daily; 24hr); Sibu (10 daily; 8–10hr).

By kereta sapu Miri is one part of Sarawak where you might want to make use of informal taxis to head into the northern interior – most places can be reached by logging roads, although it can be a long and expensive slog. Some 4WD vehicles leave regularly from the streets close to the tourist office; others will need to be arranged in advance through you accommodation in Miri or Bario.

Car rental Hara Car Rental, 183 Jalan Permaisuri (085 422 227, http://haracar.com); Kong Teck, at the airport (085 313 219, http://kongteck.com.my).

GETTING AROUND

By local bus As Miri's centre is easily walkable, you're very unlikely to catch any of the very limited bus services, which only run to the main hospital.

By bicycle Bicycles (ideal for heading to the beach), can be rented from a number of hotels and guesthouses.

By taxi Miri Taxi Association (085 432 277) and Koperasi Teksi Miri (085 431 000) are both 24hr. Meters are not used, so agree the price beforehand. Grab cabs are easily available.

INFORMATION

Tourist office Miri's excellent Visitors' Information Centre, on Jalan Padang at the southern end of downtown (Mon–Fri 8am–5pm, Sat & Sun 9am–3pm; 085 434 181, http://sarawaktourism.com), covers all of northern Sarawak as well as Bintulu, and has good maps and leaflets. A Sarawak Forestry desk here (Mon–Fri) has up-to-date information on nearby national parks.

TOUR OPERATORS

A small number of tour operators offer Mulu and Kelabit Highlands packages, as well as, more usefully, genuinely imaginative trips to help you get off the beaten track in the upriver Baram and other parts of the interior. A couple of firms offer **dive trips** at the reefs off Miri's coast, which offer a few wreck dives; practically all sites are within an hour's boat ride.

Borneo Dive Network Lot 1084, First Floor, Jalan Merpati; http://borneodivenetwork.com. PADI courses plus guided and unguided dives, and other courses up to and including dive master.

Borneo Travel Network http://borneotravelnetwork.

com. Major operator offering the normal range of Sarawak tours, as well as a mammoth five-day deep-sea fishing trip, though things usually have to be organised well in advance, and they don't have an office in Miri.

Tropical Adventure Tours Across the road from Puma Sera restaurant on Jalan Maju; http://borneotropicaladventures. com. Well-thought-through packages from this excellent outfit include trips to Mulu, the Kelabit Highlands – usually easy four-day packages in and around Bario, and other much longer and more challenging trips of up to fourteen days. They're also good for excursions on the Headhunters' Trail (see page 354).

ACCOMMODATION   SEE MAP PAGE 341

Miri's accommodation is mostly used by **business travellers**, or tourists just passing through. It's not cheap, and although there are quite a few budget hotels in the backstreets around *Mega Hotel* they are pretty bad, with tiny, airless (though sometimes a/c) rooms, and the area is a bit of a red-light district.

Amigo Marina Bay; http://facebook.com/amigohotelmiri. So long as you don't mind being a little outside the centre, this is a fine, affordable option, set in a new precinct that features some old-fashioned buildings – mock shophouses, really. It's a relaxed place with comfy rooms, and there's a 7-Eleven right outside for all your convenience store conveniences. $\overline{\$\$}$

★ **Dynasty** Jalan Miri Pujut; http://dynastyhotelmiri.com.my. The good impression given by this hotel's sizeable marbled lobby is reinforced by the spacious, comfortable rooms; some have bathtubs and sea views too. Facilities include a mini-gym and sauna, though no pool; it's among the best-value places in its class. Breakfast is extra (note they add the B&B option automatically online). Book ahead. $\overline{\$\$}$

Mega 907 Jalan Merbau; http://megahotel.com.my. Highly popular choice, a tall block whose large lobby gives way to rooms that err towards the functional side. The outdoor pool offers some good views, while on site you'll also find a gym and restaurant. Nothing too special, but also nothing particularly bad. $\overline{\$\$}$

Next Room Homestay First Floor, 637 Jalan North Yu Seng; http://nextroomhomestay.blogspot.com. Even after its third name change (and owner), this guesthouse is still somewhat haphazardly run, though it partly makes amends through its informality and sociability, and the rooms are clean and comfortable enough. However, it's on a busy stretch for bars and restaurants and so the rooms by the street (which includes both dorms) can be very noisy till late. It's also big, with a rooftop area from where you can take in the nightlife below. $\overline{\$}$

Pullman Miri Waterfront Miri Waterfront Commercial Centre; http://all.accor.com. Set riverside with fresh, opulent rooms, this is the best higher-end choice in town – you'll certainly think so if lucky enough to plop into the pool, which has wonderful views of central Miri, and the river running alongside it. Not in the best area (as in interest, not safety), but the on-site bar and eateries are just fine, if pretty hotel-standard in terms of price and choice. $\overline{\$\$\$}$

EATING   SEE MAP PAGE 341

Miri's eating scene rivals Kuching's for quality, if not variety – it's a treat to taste genuinely delicious and interesting food after days spent hiking in the northern interior. **North and South Yu Seng roads** hold a particular concentration of restaurants, while along the riverfront you'll find a bunch of not-bad seafood places (no sea views, but occasional sightings of crocodiles in the Miri River). There's also a concentration of more mid-price restaurants and bars at Centrepoint on Jalan Kubu. For inexpensive **stalls**, try the Chinese options at the Central Market (also good for cheap beer) or the Malay outlets on Jalan North Yu Seng and at Taman Seroja, up the road from the *Miri Handicraft Centre*.

Apollo Seafood Centre 4 Jalan South Yu Seng; 085 420 813. Not much to look at, this old-fashioned Chinese place serves well-regarded standards such as fish-head curry. Affordable for sure, though you'll pay much more if eating fresh seafood. $\overline{\$\$\$}$

Banana Leaf Rice Centrepoint 2, Jalan Kubu; 016 583 3313. Serving just what you might expect from the name, and more besides – not just banana-leaf meals, but thali-style sets, noodle dishes and more. Portions are pretty large, so come with an appetite. $\overline{\$}$

I Love Chinese Food 810 Jalan Bintang Jaya; 085 320 993. Fun name (Monty Python merely *liked* Chinese food, didn't they?), and a suitably authentic Chinese feel, right down to the large, squeaky picture menus. Rarely for Malaysia, the food on offer includes offers from all of mainland China's main schools of cooking, such as the sizzling tofu and aubergine dishes, excellent *tudousi* (fried, vinegared strips of potato, with chilli), and all manner of rice and seafood meals. $\overline{\$\$}$

Kaya & Toast 1088 Jalan Zinnia. Continuing a theme of say-it-like-it-is eateries, this is your best bet *for* kaya toast and sugary coffee or tea, and they also pump out good bowls of *laksa*, and rice dishes. $\overline{\$}$

Khan's Islamic Restoran 233 Jalan Maju; http://facebook.com/Islamicrestoran. Though a little dreary, this is a central and well-established *kedai kopis* where the cheap-and-cheerful description really does apply. Offerings are predictable: *nasi campur*, a range of *biriyani* dishes, curries (veg and non-veg) and tandoori chicken, plus various *roti* and *murtabak* options. $\overline{\$}$

Ming Café Corner of Jalan North Yu Seng and Jalan Merbau; 085 422 797. Probably the most popular place in town with foreigners (largely because it also makes a good bar; see page

345), with an a/c indoor section and a prominent, more bar-like area outside with powerful ceiling fans. Separate menus feature Chinese stir-fries, Indian curries and sets, and some Western offerings such as fish and chips and thin crust pizzas – all pretty good, if a little overpriced. $\overline{\$\$}$

★ **Summit Café** Off Jalan Melayu; head up the lane with Maybank on the corner and you'll see it on the left; 010 464 0622. One of Sarawak's most interesting restaurants: run by a Kenyah woman whose husband is Kelabit, it serves Kelabit food of a sort you may struggle to turn up in Bario. Specialities include *labo senutuk*, smoked shredded pork or wild boar, and *kasam*, a sour/salty fermented combination of wild boar and rice. The latter is sold in tubs, but you order most dishes from a *nasi campur* spread to be eaten with rice or *nuba laya*, made by pounding rice till smooth and then steaming it wrapped in leaves. $\overline{\$}$

DRINKING   SEE MAP PAGE 341

Miri's **bars** aren't up to much, unfortunately. Some venues opposite the *Next Room Homestay* on Jalan North Yu Seng are your best bet for a drink; if you're really in luck, you won't even have to endure awful karaoke.

★ **Ming Café** Corner of Jalan North Yu Seng and Jalan Merbau; 085 422 797. This bar-restaurant is not a bad place for a drink, with a reasonable wine list and a massive selection of imported beers, with seven on draft and around twenty bottled. Daily happy hours.

The Nest Grill & Lounge Miri Times Square; http://thenestcafelounge.com. Walking distance from the centre, this looks for all the world like a cafe that's dressed itself up a bit for the evening – which is exactly what it is. For most of the day coffees, desserts and meals – quite varied, and mostly pretty good – rule the joint, though wine bottles on the walls watch in stealth mode, waiting for evening to encroach. And then when it does... the place still feels like a cafe, but with a few people drinking wine or cocktails.

SHOPPING   SEE MAP PAGE 341

Miri's shopping isn't especially distinguished, and it's disappointing when it comes to handicrafts, though the malls are lively.

Bintang Megamall Corner of Jalan Miri Pujut and Jalan Merbau; http://bintangmegamall.com. With two wings, this large mall houses a branch of the Parkson department store, a Giant supermarket and outlets of several Western fast-food chains. Numerous small shops sell phone chargers, memory cards and the like, while Chinese discount shops here stock endless camping paraphernalia.

Miri Handicraft Centre Corner of Jalan Brooke and Jalan Merbau. Some of the shops in the handicraft centre are worth a look, with woodcarving and Kenyah shields on show at the best – the other shops here are a little desultory, and many of their wares are from Kalimantan. All the items in the shops here are overpriced, unfortunately.

Sarawak Handicraft Block 9, 5B Ground Floor, Lot 96, Jalan Merbau; 085 430 086. All the same mass-produced souvenirs you'll find in the Miri Handicrafts Centre, but at a fraction of the cost.

Trees & Sun Outdoor Bintang Jaya Commercial Centre; http://tnsoutdoor.com. High quality but expensive torches, sleeping bags, tents and so forth.

DIRECTORY

Hospital Miri General Hospital, Jalan Lopeng (085 420 033).
Laundry Two excellent laundries stand practically side by side a couple of doors along from the *Next Room Homestay*.
Pharmacy Guardian and Watsons are both at Bintang Megamall.

Police HQ Jalan Kingsway (085 433 730).
Visa extensions First floor of the tall Yu Lan Plaza, unmissable on Jalan Kingsway (Mon–Fri 8am–5pm; 085 442 112).

Lambir Hills National Park

Charge, levied at park office • http://sarawakforestry.com

Popular with weekend day-trippers, **Lambir Hills National Park**, 35km out of Miri and the closest national park to the city, holds some pleasant trails – though leeches can be annoying – and good accommodation. Mixed dipterocarp forest makes up more than half the park, with giant hardwood trees such as *meranti*, *kapur* and *keruing* creating deep shadows on the forest floor; there's also *kerangas* forest, with its peat soils and scrubby vegetation.

Trails

The park's most popular trail, the short **Latak Trail**, passes three **waterfalls**. The furthest – Latak itself, 1.5km (or 30min) from the park office – is the nicest, its 25m cascade feeding an alluring pool, but is inevitably busy at the weekends. The **Inoue Trail** from the park office joins the **Lepoh–Ridan Trail** half an hour along, which leads after about an hour to three more falls, **Dinding**, **Tengkorong** and **Pancur**; swimming isn't allowed at the last two as their pools are deep. The end of the Lepoh–Ridan Trail marks the start of the trek to the top of **Bukit Lambir** (4–5hr one way from here; set off by 7–8am from the park office to be back by sunset). It's a tough, hot, but rewarding climb with a wonderful view across the park – take snacks and at least two litres of water.

ARRIVAL AND INFORMATION — LAMBIR HILLS NATIONAL PARK

By bus The park lies beside the main trunk road to Bintulu; any long-distance bus en route between Miri and Bintulu can drop you here.

By taxi A taxi from Miri won't cost too much; ask your driver to pick you up at a set time or take their number.

ACCOMMODATION

Lambir Hills National Park accommodation http://sarawakforestry.com. Though accommodation in the park is limited, few people stay so you shouldn't have trouble overnighting. Choose either a two-bedroom lodge, or take a room within a lodge, sharing facilities. There's also a campsite, and a canteen serving simple Malay and Chinese dishes. Wi-fi available in main building only. Camping/rooms $, six-person a/c lodges $$

Niah National Park

Charge, levied at park office • http://sarawakforestry.com

NIAH NATIONAL PARK, 110km south of Miri and 130km from Bintulu, is practically a compulsory visit even if you're already caved out from visiting Mulu. Yes, its main attractions are massive **limestone caves**, but there any similarity with Mulu ends. Whereas almost all excursions at Mulu are regimented and chaperoned, visitors at Niah simply wander the caves at will, in places stumbling along tunnels – lightless but for your own torch – like questers from *The Lord of the Rings*. Elsewhere the caves are alive, with not just bats but people, who harvest bat guano and swiftlet nests for much of the year. This potent combination of vast caverns, communities at work, the rainforest and Niah's archeological significance – it's famous for prehistoric cave paintings and early human settlement – makes even a day-trip to Niah a wonderful experience. It is indeed possible to see much of Niah in a day: allow two to three hours to get from the park offices to the most distant caves, with breaks along the way.

Niah Archaeological Museum

By boat jetty • Free; no photography

Before becoming a national park in 1974, Niah was made a National Historic Monument in 1958, after Tom Harrisson discovered that early man had been using it as a cemetery. Fragments of human skull, nearly 40,000 years old, were the earliest examples of *homo sapiens* found in Southeast Asia. For a sense of the park's history and archeological importance, spend half an hour at the newly revamped **Niah Archeological Museum** across the stream beyond the park headquarters. Fascinating photos, from a mere half-century ago, but seeming much older, show Harrisson at work, and Iban and other Indigenous people engaged in traditional dances or sporting activities, while video and interactive displays help you undestand the geology of the caves.

Caves

Trader's Cave, the nearest cave to the museum, is nearly 3km along a concrete path that soon becomes a jungle boardwalk. En route, you may stumble upon monkeys (including silverleafs and even gibbons), butterflies, snakes, skinks and odd scarlet millipedes. Twenty minutes' walk from the museum, a few traders sell refreshments and souvenirs at the start of a clearly marked path on the left that leads in ten minutes to a

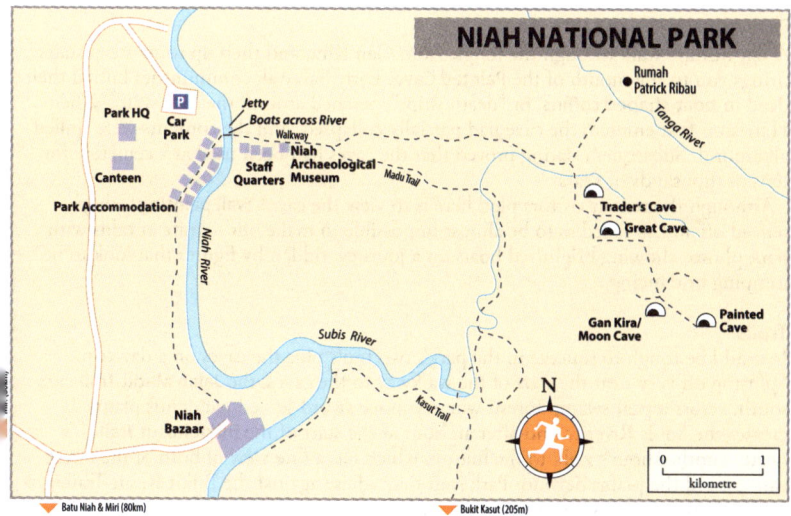

small, not all that enthralling, village, **Rumah Patrick Ribau** (often still signed Rumah Chang) where they have a homestay programme at the Sungai Tangap longhouse.

Trader's Cave

A 45-minute walk from the museum, a great metal grille crosses the entire boardwalk, with a small gate below marking the entrance to the cave area. Within a few minutes you reach the **Trader's Cave**, not so much a cave as a long, wedge-shaped gash in the rock, open to the jungle along the entire right-hand side. The wooden platforms here were used as shelters by nest-gatherers, who until the 1970s used to barter their harvests here for goods brought by the townsfolk.

Great Cave and Gan Kira (Moon Cave)

Labelled "Niah Cave" on some maps, the huge, 250m-wide west mouth of the **Great Cave** is not far beyond Trader's Cave. A fenced-off stretch to the left marks the site of Tom Harrisson's groundbreaking archeological **digs** in 1957. The dark, gradually ascending area of cave floor beyond is known thanks to its breadth and flatness as the **Padang**; bear left to begin a path that leads down into the depths of the cave, where you will certainly need your torch. The earthy smell of bat **guano** is pervasive; people you may see wandering off-path with sacks on their backs are harvesting it to sell as fertilizer.

Between September and March you'll also see **bird's-nest collectors**, who work in groups of three, shinning up bamboo poles and hanging from ropes dangling from the ceiling in search of the edible swiftlet nests so prized by the Chinese. At around 6 or 7pm, you can see the swiftlets fly in and vast numbers of bats stream out for the night, and from much closer up than at Mulu – arrange this with a boatman (see page 348) and remember it takes at least forty minutes to walk back to the river.

The path curls round and then branches, the right-hand track taking you back up and out towards the Padang. Head more or less straight on, past several cave mouths with jungle views on the left, to reach the pitch-black, stuffy tunnel out to Gan Kira at the southern end of the Great Cave system. It takes ten minutes to traverse, though it feels like years.

At the mouth of **Gan Kira**, a delightful spot nearly 4km from the park offices, the boardwalk ends at a shelter bathed in fabulous breezes. A blessed relief after the stuffiness of the preceding tunnel, it offers views of lushly forested hillside beyond.

Painted Cave

A ten-minute walk through the jungle from Gan Kira, and then up some steep stairs, brings you to the mouth of the **Painted Cave**. Early Sarawak communities buried their dead in **boat-shaped coffins**, or "death ships", perched around the cave walls. When Harrisson first entered, the cave had partially collapsed, and the contents were spilled all around. Subsequent dating proved that the caves had been used as a cemetery for tens of thousands of years.

Although the reason visitors plod here is to view the cave's **wall paintings**, they're fenced off and so faded as to be almost impossible to make out – quite at odds with park photos showing bright red boats on a journey, ridden by figures that look to be jumping or dancing.

Trails

It would be tough to squeeze in the park's two trails plus the caves on a day-trip. Splitting off very near the start of the walkway to the caves, the **Jalan Madu Trail** cuts south, across a peat swamp forest, where you see sword-leaved pandanus plants. It crosses the Subis River to end after an hour at the start of the **Bukit Kasut Trail**. It's nearly another hour's walk to the hilltop, which has a fine view of both of the forest canopy and the plains beyond. Park staff may advise against the Bukit Kasut Trail if it has recently rained, as it can be slippery when wet.

ARRIVAL AND INFORMATION — NIAH NATIONAL PARK

By road The park is accessible from both the main trunk road and the coastal highway. All Miri guesthouses organize trips, or catch any express bus between Miri and Bintulu and get off at the Batu Niah junction from Miri (slightly more from Bintulu), where buses use the food court as a rest stop. Catch a *kereta sapu* or Grab for the 15km drive to the park entrance; park staff can summon a vehicle for the return trip. Driving, following signs from either the main road for Batu Niah, Niah Bazaar or the park; after a few minutes take a signed turning east for Niah Bazaar, and then another turning north (left) for the park itself.

Ferry crossings To cross the stream just beyond the park headquarters to the museum and trails, you have to take a ferry ride. To see the bats flying out at the Great Cave, tell the boatman on your way out that you'll be back at 7.30pm – they won't leave before you come back if they know to expect you. It's best to leave the cave by 6.45pm at the very latest – a small gratuity may be appropriate if you're a bit late. You will need a torch to get back to the jetty at that time; if you get stuck in the park, you can stay the night at the Rumah Patrick Ribau village.

Equipment A reliable torch (flashlight) with fresh batteries is essential.

ACCOMMODATION

Niah National Park accommodation http://sarawakforestry.com. Though ageing, Niah's accommodation is in reasonable condition as it's little used – there are no park guides and thus no night walks, so there's little reason to stay except to see the dusk exodus of the bats and to enjoy a little quiet. Options include four-room lodges and fancier rooms with bathroom and a/c, plus a campsite. A simple canteen serves a limited menu of local food. $

Sungai Tangap Longhouse Patrick Libau village; 013 834 2461. Good homestay at a typical longhouse inside the park itself. Rooms are comfortable but tend to be a little small, and of course have shared bathrooms. Full board is advisable. $

Lawas

One of the eleven administrative **divisions** into which Sarawak is parcelled is a horseshoe-shaped territory named **Limbang**, whose western arm splits Brunei into two and whose eastern arm slots between Brunei and Sabah. This eastern prong was bought by Charles Brooke from the Sultan of Brunei in 1905 and is home to **LAWAS**, a bustling bazaar town on the Lawas River, with a **tamu** above the river. The only reason to visit is because Lawas has flights to Ba' Kelalan in the Kelabit Highlands, making it possible to reach the Highlands en route to or from Sabah. The town is known for its cultural diversity, with a mix of ethnic groups including the Lun Bawang, Malay, and Chinese communities

ARRIVAL AND DEPARTURE LAWAS

By plane Lawas' airport is 2km south of town; take a taxi into town, or walk it.
Destinations Ba' Kelalan (2 weekly; 35min); Kota Kinabalu (2 weekly; 45min); Miri (4–5 daily; 45min).
By bus The bus station is on Jalan Liaw Siew Ann, about 200m from the main junction and just behind the indoor market. At the time of writing, services to Sarawak destinations beyond Brunei (including Limbang) had not yet restarted, after shutting down during the Covid crisis.
Destinations Bandar Seri Begawan, Brunei (1 daily; 1hr 30min); Kota Kinabalu (2 daily; 4hr 30min).
By boat Boats leave from the Customs Wharf beside the old mosque, 300m east of town.
Destinations Labuan (1 daily; 2hr 30min); Limbang (1 daily; 2hr).

ACCOMMODATION

Mandarin Lot 466, Jalan Trusan; 085 283 222. Centrally located on the main street, and next to the excellent *Leeya Café*, this place isn't exciting, but the rooms are fairly large, clean, and have nice bathrooms – some even have windows. There is a handful of other budget options nearby. $
Seri Malaysia Jalan Gaya; http://serimalaysia.com.my. $$$ This enormous, modern hotel, just over the bridge as you enter town from the airport, is the plushest place to stay – which isn't saying much. There's a coffee house, restaurant and a pool, but the rooms are in need of a bit of TLC. Prices are highest at the weekend, and rates include breakfast.

The northern interior

For visitors who take the time and trouble to explore it, Sarawak's **northern interior** often ends up being the most memorable part of their stay. Some of the wildest, most untouched parts of the state are interspersed, sometimes in close proximity, with badly degraded patches, thus putting everything you may have read about the state's environmental problems into sharp relief. The timber industry has been systematically logging here since the 1960s, with tracts of land already under oil palm or being cleared to grow it, yet the rugged terrain still offers fabulous **trekking** – something most visitors only experience at **Gunung Mulu National Park**, with its extensive caves (including one of the largest in the world) and the razor-sharp limestone Pinnacles.

TWIN OTTERS

One entertaining aspect of travel in the northern interior is the chance to fly on **Twin Otters** – nineteen-seater propeller planes. More formally known as the de Havilland DHC-6, the Twin Otter can turn on the proverbial dime and take off from a standing start in seconds, making it ideally suited to the tiny airfields in Sabah and Sarawak. As such, the plane forms the backbone of the Rural Air Services operated by Malaysia Airlines subsidiary **MASwings**, mostly out of Miri (though it's not used for Mulu, where the airport can take larger aircraft).

As the Twin Otter isn't pressurized – you can see daylight around the door rim – it doesn't fly above 3000m, and affords great views of the north's mountain ranges. That MASwings' Twin Otters can be old and a bit shabby (though perfectly serviceable) only adds to the experience; the cabin will be fan-cooled (and probably boiling hot when you board) and the cockpit "door" will be open, letting you see what the pilots are up to.

On a practical note, passengers sit where they like, and luggage is limited to 10kg per person (you may well have to weigh yourself at check-in so staff know the laden weight of the plane). Prices are lower if booked well ahead, rising one week before and three days before travel; the most expensive tickets can be bought at the airport on the day. At some airfields, departing passengers are slapped with a "service fee" atop the taxes included in ticket prices. Levied by the small private concerns that run the airfields, these fees appear to be condoned by the authorities. Note that the planes get booked solid during public and school holidays and over Christmas and New Year, when you may have to reserve weeks in advance. Flights are seldom cancelled except in very gusty or stormy weather.

As central Sarawak has the Rejang, so the north has its major river system, the **River Baram** (Batang Baram). There the resemblance ends, for only the lowest part of the Baram – from **Marudi**, 50km southeast of Miri, to the river mouth at **Kuala Baram** near the Brunei border – has anything like a proper boat service, and that stretch is any case devoid of sights. Further upriver, the days of being able to just turn up and find a longboat and someone who can pilot it have long since gone. Much travel is therefore by small **aircraft** (see box, page 349) or **4WD**, using the spider's web of logging roads, which adds to the outback feel. Anyone wanting to get off the beaten track will most likely have to talk to the Miri tour operators (see page 343), who have contacts with boatmen and drivers and can arrange accommodation in towns with hardly any formal places to stay. That said, it is possible to visit remote **Penan settlements** in the upper Baram using a homestay programme called **Picnic with the Penan** (see page 363).

Mulu aside, the highlight is the lush **Kelabit Highlands**, accessible by air and an upgraded logging road, where the pleasant climate is ideal for long treks in the rainforest. Of much less significance unless you're an avid birdwatcher is **Loagan Bunut National Park**, some distance off the Miri–Bintulu road and difficult to visit independently.

Gunung Mulu National Park

GUNUNG MULU NATIONAL PARK, Sarawak's premier national park and a UNESCO World Heritage Site, is named after the 2376m mountain at its heart. Modern explorers have been coming here since Spenser St John in the 1850s, who didn't reach the summit but wrote inspiringly about the region in *Life in the Forests of the Far East*. A more successful bid in 1932 saw Edward Shackleton, son of the Antarctic explorer, get to the top during a research trip organized by Tom Harrisson.

The park's best-known features, however, are the mind-bogglingly big **Deer Cave** and, atop another mountain, Mount Api, the dozens of 50m-high razor-sharp limestone spikes known as the **Pinnacles**. Visitors stream into Mulu (as the park is generally known) year-round to catch sight of them – a three-day trek, there and back, from the park offices – and also to see the park's incredible network of **caves**. Mulu contains the largest limestone cave system in the world, formed when surface water eroded vast amounts of material, dividing the limestone belt that runs southwest–northeast across the middle of the park into separate mountains as well as carving cave passages within. Most people see some or all four of the dramatic **show caves**, though other caves are accessible on adventure packages and yet more are still being explored.

Mulu is unique in Sarawak for having been **privatized**. While the Sarawak Forestry Corporation remains in overall charge, most things to do with tourism, including the accommodation, are now run by Borsarmulu. This means that Mulu feels more like Singapore than Sarawak: **tours** are timetabled and formatted, and you can explore few parts of the park unaccompanied. The tours are well run, the guides are better communicators than at any other Sarawak park, and close supervision has helped prevent the poaching of valuable plants – but if it were possible to make the jungle somehow corporate, this is it. The only way to avoid taking the tours is by having your own registered guide, which enables you to book boat charter and accommodation on the trails separately, though this only makes sense if you are in a group.

The caves

The show caves – **Clearwater**, **Wind**, **Lang's** and **Deer** – are a must, though interest can begin to wane if you see all four. If you're doing a Pinnacles trek, the cost will usually include a tour of the Clearwater and Wind caves. If not, and you don't want to spend ages underground, opt for the Lang's and Deer caves – the last is the most impressive of the lot – then hang around for the incredible "**changing of the guard**", when the bats leave Deer Cave at sunset. Tours of these caves fill up quickly, so book as soon as your plans are fixed. It's also possible to do tours of **Lagang Cave**, where obscure cave-dwelling fauna is the highlight, plus more challenging caving trips.

Lang's and Deer caves
3km from the park office • Two tours daily • Charge

Lang's Cave, an hour's walk from the park office, is the smallest of the show caves. It makes an unremarkable appetizer for the splendid Deer Cave, though your guide will point out unusual rock formations, most interestingly the curtain stalactites and coral-like growths – helictites – gripping the curved walls.

Deer Cave, a few minutes' walk further, was once inhabited by deer that sheltered in its cavernous reaches. Dim artificial lighting helps you appreciate one of the world's largest cave passages, more than 2km long and up to 174m high, though what's really striking is how scenic it can be: silvery curtains of water plummet from the cave ceiling, while there's at least one chimney-like structure, formed by erosion of a weaker section of limestone, where rainwater jets down as though from a shower head. Elsewhere, your guide will point out the cave's Abraham Lincoln-in-profile rock formation and the entrance to the Garden of Eden.

Once the tour is over, walk back to the park offices unaccompanied or linger with the guide at a viewpoint – the so-called Bat Observatory, with snacks on sale and toilets –

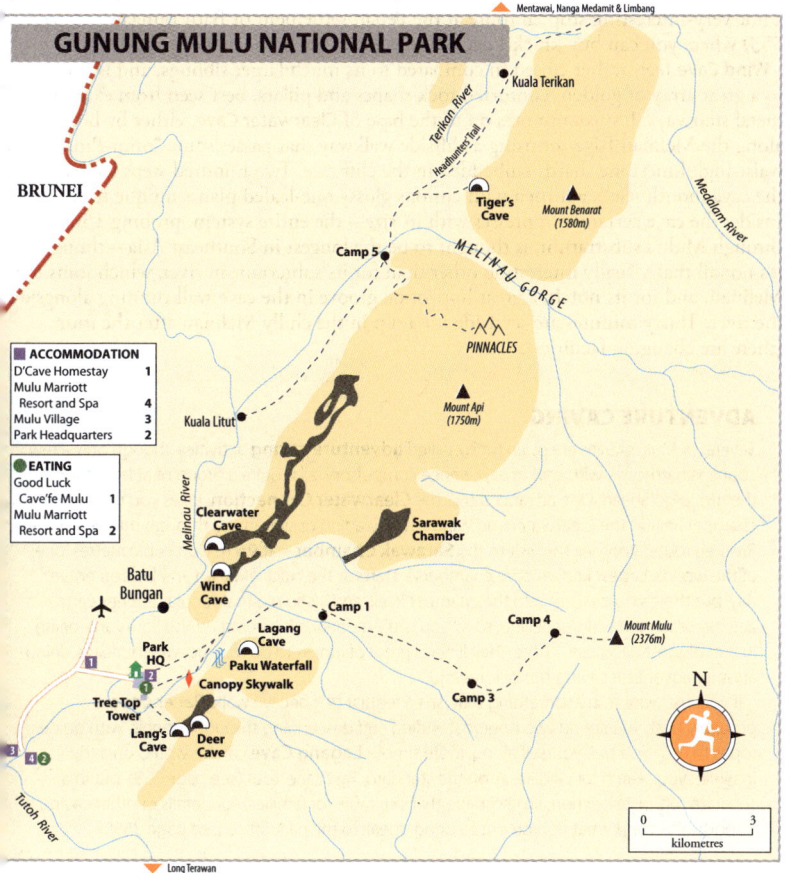

near the caves. As evening approaches, swiftlets fly into the caves for the night, which isn't necessarily easy to make out, but what you can't fail to notice is the **bats**. They emerge from various holes in the roof – there are about three million of them – at first in little cloud-like bursts, then in streams that can last for minutes at a time.

Garden of Eden
One tour daily (minimum three people) • Charge

A hole at one point in Deer Cave offers a glimpse of lush ferns in the so-called **Garden of Eden**, a veritable "lost world" penned in by the steep cliffs of Mulu's limestone formations. It was discovered by a Royal Geographical Society expedition in 1976 whose leader noted that "even the fish were tame and gathered in shoals around a hand dipped in the water". Today the park offers a trip to the area, reached by wading along a river that flows through a dark passage at Deer Cave. It continues through the jungle to small waterfalls and yet more pools (where you can swim), and ends with lunch in the wilds.

Wind and Clearwater caves
Two tours daily • Charge, including boat transport and a stop at Batu Bungan

As they lie upriver of the starting point for the Pinnacles trek, almost everyone heading to the Pinnacles sees these two caves as well. Most park trips include boat transport and a not-very-interesting stop en route at the Penan settlement of Batu Bungan (see page 353) where you can buy knick-knacks and watch a blowpipe demonstration.

Wind Cave feels rather closed in compared to its much larger siblings, and is home to a great array of golden, contorted rock shapes and pillars, best seen from extended metal stairways. It's five minutes on to the base of **Clearwater Cave**, either by boat along the Melinau River or using a cliffside walkway that passes some "mini-Pinnacles", waist-high limestone shards embedded in the cliff face. Two hundred steps lead up to the cave mouth itself, adorned with curious glossy one-leafed plants unique to Mulu. Inside, the cave certainly impresses with its size – the entire system, probing 150km through Mulu's substratum, is thought to be the longest in Southeast Asia – though it's not all that visually interesting other than for its subterranean river, which joins the Melinau, and for its **notch**, a great horizontal groove in the cave wall running alongside the river. Thirty minutes are set aside for a dip in the chilly Melinau after the tour (there are changing facilities).

ADVENTURE CAVING

Several of Mulu's caves are open for so-called **adventure caving** activities, though only a few count as hard-core, with caving experience compulsory; all require a group of at least three for the trip to go ahead. One advanced trip, the **Clearwater Connection**, takes you through a chamber linking the Clearwater and Wind caves, wading or swimming through the Clearwater River en route. Another, the visit to the **Sarawak Chamber** – at 9.5 million cubic metres, one of the world's largest known cave chambers – starts at the crack of dawn and lasts an entire day, but there's no descent into the chamber itself, and it's so big that regular torches can't actually reach the walls or ceiling, so all you can experience is turning off the lights and being in the "biggest darkness" – note, they'll need proof of fitness to do this trip, which means doing another adventure caving trip beforehand.

If you just want to try something that isn't a regular trek or cave walk, **Racer Cave** is probably best; you spend two hours ascending and descending through tunnels, with guide ropes to help you pull yourself along. More simply, **Lagang Cave** can be visited on a trip in which you search for wildlife, as on the standard "Fast Lane" tour (see page 353), but in a separate, "off-piste" section, an escapade that's suitable for families. For details of other caving opportunities and what equipment to bring, speak to the park office (see page 355).

Lagang Cave
Lagang "Fast Lane" tours leave daily 2pm from the park office; bring a torch • Charge, including boat rides

Animals rather than geology are the highlight in the **Lagang Cave**. The tour proceeds at a relaxed pace, the guide encouraging people to use their torches to spot the different beasties lurking in the darkness; the blue racer snakes who feed on the bats, the reflective eyes of cave spiders, and the blind white crabs in shallow pools. Of course there are no problems locating the many bats sleeping in little round holes in the ceiling along with mossy-nest swiflet nests (made of a mixture of moss and saliva). Later, as the cave widens, you'll also see some well-lit and interesting rock formations.

Batu Bungan
A stop on boat tours to Wind/Clearwater caves, or a signed 30min walk from the airport in the opposite direction from the park

Just outside the park boundary, a couple of kilometres northwest of the park entrance, is a somewhat desultory collection of concrete houses called **Batu Bungan** which, a worthwhile information display notes, is "probably the most-visited Penan settlement in Sarawak". Tourists indeed visit every morning en route to the caves, and the locals sell souvenirs, but the whole experience is rather artificial. The Penan here perhaps quite haven't got the hang of the whole living-in-houses thing, and the present concrete longhouses are there because previous two wooden ones burned down within ten years.

Canopy skywalk and Tree Top Tower
Six skywalk tours daily; 2hr • Charge; Tree Top Tower free (get key from the park office)

Mulu's **canopy skywalk**, 480m long and 20m up in the air, is reached by a side trail off the Deer Cave trail. The skywalk laces around six broad hardwood *kasai*, *betang*, *meranti*, *peran* and *segera* trees and takes around half an hour to complete. Though it's not that different to the canopy walkways at Taman Negara or at Temburong in Brunei, the tours are often full, so book promptly or try spotting birdlife from the elevated hide called the **Tree Top Tower**, just fifteen minutes from the park office.

The Pinnacles
The park offers a package for the trek, including accommodation but no food; tour operators offer similar packages, as well as to the Headhunters' Trail north of the Pinnacles (see page 354)

Five million years ago, the splatter of raindrops gradually dissolved Mount Api's limestone and carved out the **Pinnacles** – 50m-high shards, as sharp as samurai swords – from a solid block of rock. Erosion is still continuing, and the entire region is pockmarked with deep shafts penetrating far into the heart of the mountain: one third of Mount Api has already been washed away, and in another ten million years it might all be gone.

The chance to view the Pinnacles draws many visitors to Mulu, and the trek offers exactly that, by heading not to the Pinnacles but to a **ridge** across the way from where you can take everything in. It's a three-day, two-night hike, but only the ascent of the steep final ridge and the awkward descent are genuinely demanding. That said, if you're reasonably fit and suitably equipped, you should cope, and the guides put safety first and make allowances as appropriate for the slower members of their group. With whoever you arrange the trek with, book or make enquiries at least a week in advance; base camp, **Camp 5**, sleeps fifty people, so there's a firm ceiling on the number of climbers per day. Considering the tough journey, some people are a little disappointed when they arrive at the Pinnacles, but as with many things in life, the journey is everything, and the views along the way are terrific.

The hike
The itinerary is simple. **Day 1** usually sees trekkers visiting the Wind and Clearwater caves after which the boat takes them down the Melinau to **Kuala Litut**, the start of the 8km trek to Camp 5. Following a rough track of coarse stones embedded in the

ground, it's mostly flat and perfectly straightforward, and you can expect to arrive well before sunset.

Camp 5 itself is spruce and homely; all accommodation is dorm-style, and there's a large, reasonably well-equipped kitchen and communal eating area. If you book through the park office, you'll have to bring your own provisions (see page 355) and remember to ask to borrow a free mosquito net at the park HQ. It's close to the **Melinau Gorge**, across which nearby **Mount Api** (1750m) and **Mount Benarat** (1580m) cast long shadows in the fading afternoon light. A bridge straddles the river here, with a path disappearing into the jungle on the far side – the first stage of the Headhunters' Trail. It's possible to explore the gorge instead of tackling the Pinnacles; ask at the park office for details (see page 355).

Day 2 is the only time you are accompanied by a guide, setting off around 7.30am for the ascent. Departure may be delayed in heavy rain; if the weather fails to let up, and the climb has to be called off, you'll get half your money back if you booked through the park office. After two hours, a striking vista opens up: the rainforest stretches below as far as the eye can see, and wispy clouds drift along your line of vision. Eventually the trail reaches **moss forest**, where pitcher plants feed on insects, and ants and squirrels dart in and out among the roots of trees. The last thirty minutes of the climb is especially steep, with ladders and ropes to assist.

Parties usually arrive at the top of the **ridge** that overlooks the Pinnacles in late morning. The ridge is itself a pinnacle, sited across a ravine from the main cluster, and if you tap the rocks around you, they reverberate because of the large holes in the limestone underneath. After an hour it's time for the return slog, which can be more awkward on the legs and nerves, and takes longer, especially when the route is slippery. You'll probably arrive back at Camp 5 around 4pm.

On **day 3** trekkers retrace their steps to Kuala Litut for the boat ride back to the park office, usually arriving in plenty of time to catch an afternoon flight out.

Mount Mulu

Expect to find packages including accommodation and a guide, though you'll have to bring provisions and sleeping bags; a porter costs extra

The route to the summit of **Mount Mulu** (2376m) was first discovered in the 1920s by Tama Nilong, a Berawan rhinoceros hunter. Earlier explorers had failed to find a way around the huge surrounding cliffs, but Nilong followed rhinoceros tracks along the southwest ridge trail, and thus enabled Lord Shackleton to become the first

---

THE HEADHUNTERS' TRAIL

A wonderful way to start or end a Pinnacles trek, the **Headhunters' Trail** adds just one day to the total duration, but when you consider the itinerary it's clearly all but impossible to make the necessary arrangements independently. The 11km trail – which corresponds to a route once taken by Kenyah and Kayan warring parties – leads north from Camp 5 to **Kuala Terikan**, at the confluence of the Terikan and Medalam rivers on the park's northern boundary. From here it's necessary to find a longboat down the Terikan to reach **Mentawai**, also on the park's edge, where you sign out of the park at a **ranger post** (or sign in if doing the route in reverse). The boat then continues to a longhouse before **Nanga Medamit** where tour operators put visitors up for the night. From here you can drive to the coastal town of **Limbang**, in between the two lumps of Brunei, and pick up a flight to Miri or bus to Kota Kinabalu, Bandar Seri Begawan or Miri.

As a trek, the trail is similar to the path from Kuala Litut to Camp 5, but less well maintained and 3km longer. Some say it's therefore better for exiting the park than entering it, as there's a lot of ground to cover to reach Camp 5 from Nanga Medalan before dark. In practice, people continue to trek in both directions.

To tackle the route, contact a tour operator in Miri or Kuching (the park itself is not currently offering this service).

mountaineer to reach the summit in 1932. It's still an arduous climb, a 48km round trip that usually takes four days. Few visitors attempt it, but with enough notice, the park office can usually arrange it for groups of three or more.

Day 1, for most groups, is usually spent heading to **Camp 3** roughly midway along the route, passing Camp 1 en route (there is no Camp 2). The trek takes you from the limestone belt that most tourists associate with Mulu into sandstone terrain that dominates the southeast of the park. On **day 2** you spend the night 1800m up at **Camp 4**. Most climbers set off well before dawn on **day 3** for the hard ninety-minute trek to the **summit**, if possible arriving there at sunrise. Big clumps of pitcher plants dot the final stretch, though it's easy to miss them as by this point you are hauling yourself up by ropes onto the cold, windswept, craggy peak. From here, the view is exhilarating, looking down on Mount Api and, on a clear day, far across the forest to Brunei Bay. Once again you spend the night at Camp 4. **Day 4** is a very full day as the aim is to get right back to the park HQ by nightfall.

ARRIVAL AND GETTING AROUND — GUNUNG MULU NATIONAL PARK

By plane MASwings flies from Mulu's airport, 1500m from the park entrance, to Kota Kinabalu (1 daily, more via Miri; 50min), Kuching (1 daily; 1hr 40min) and Miri (2 daily; 30min). They're not Twin Otter services, but demand is high, so book a week or two in advance.

By bicycle Bikes are a useful way of getting to and from the park if you're staying outside. The *Mulu Marriott* (see page 355) rents bikes, to non-guests as well.

INFORMATION

Park office The office (daily 8am–6pm) stocks good listings of treks, cave tours and activities, as well as browsable reference books on the park and Borneo.

Discovery Centre The informative displays on cave formation and Mulu's topography and ecology in the excellent Discovery Centre, a small free museum alongside the park office, are worth at least half an hour of your time.

Entrance fee Charge is valid for five days.

Contact details 085 792 300, http://mulupark.com.

Equipment Unless you are climbing Mount Mulu itself or doing advanced caving, you will need the same gear that you would bring to other national parks. As people tend to do longer treks here than at most parks, however, items that may seem optional elsewhere become necessities. A poncho (or umbrella) is essential for extended downpours, while rubber shoes come into their own when paths and trails are flooded or waterlogged; carry bandages to deal with any blisters. If you are using regular shoes, they must have a good grip. Ponchos, rubber shoes and food you can cook on multiday treks are sold at the park gift shop, but it's much cheaper to buy these before you arrive.

Money Bring a reasonable amount of cash – there are no ATMs – though this is one park where you can pay for rooms and tours with plastic, and it's occasionally possible to take cash out on your credit card at the park office, though they often run out of cash.

Leeches Leeches are not a problem on trails near the park headquarters, though you might want to take precautions (see page 45) on the Pinnacles climb.

ACCOMMODATION — SEE MAP PAGE 351

Accommodation within the park is limited to a hostel – basically a twenty-bed dorm – and much more expensive private rooms and chalets; the dorm fills up, so enquire at least a week in advance. Other places to stay **nearby** range from hostel-type places and homestays (mainly along the road from the airport to the park entrance) to the *Mulu Marriott Resort and Spa*.

★ **D'Cave Homestay** 700m from the airport, at the turning to the park entrance; 011 1508 5990. By far the best of the homestays, with a basic ten-person fan dorm and a couple of double rooms, one of which has an en-suite. The friendly family is absolutely lovely, and the rate includes an astonishingly good breakfast served at a long table – they just don't stop bringing out food. $$

Mulu Marriott Resort and Spa 2km from the park entrance; http://marriott.com. The only upmarket place to stay at Mulu, well known for its swimming pool, which sticks out amid the jungle when viewed from the air, Balinese spa, and its sprawling collection of slick, longhouse-like blocks, raised on stilts. Rooms are spacious, and there's a vaguely smart bar and restaurant – although, unless you're having the buffet, it's quite overpriced, so many guests go to the cheaper restaurant just across the river. $$$$

Mulu Village 2km from the park entrance; 017 743 4763. Neighbour to the *Mulu Marriott Resort* across the bridge, this is a really good budget option. Set in spacious green grounds, it exudes a countryside feel, even though there's a café across the road and a supermarket just down the way – the best of both worlds. The riverside terrace is a fantastic place to hang out by day or night, and the fan rooms are

simple but just fine. Breakfast is available. $$
Park Headquarters http://mulupark.com. Clustered around the park office are various chalets and more luxurious bungalows, some recently built and all with a/c and bathroom, plus its hostel. All rates include breakfast. Dorms $, doubles $$$

EATING   SEE MAP PAGE 351

Most people simply **eat** where they're staying, but it can be worth moving around a bit for variety. For the Pinnacles and other long treks, the park gift shop sells sachets of instant pasta, canned beans and curries, biscuits, chocolate and so forth. If you want to save a few ringgit, use the shop for the locals on the way from the park to the *Mulu Marriott*.

Good Luck Cave'fe Mulu Next to park office. An airy affair, overlooking the Melinau River and serving pretty decent local food. Their highly spicy and creamy "Good Luck" *laksa* is their strongest suit, and they also do a tasty Indian platter, a limited range of stir-fries to be eaten with rice (including a good Indonesian beef *rendang*), and the odd dessert such as chocolate cake. Beer and spirits available too. $$

Mulu Marriott Resort and Spa 2km from park entrance; http://marriott.com. The hotel restaurant's buffet dinner – a grand spread of rice and pasta, salads and stir-fries, and *kuih* for dessert, plus a half-hour dance show – will set you back a fair bit, though you can eat more cheaply earlier in the day. *Tuak* is available too, and there's also a river bar serving alcohol, and reasonably priced light bites, at night. $$$

Loagan Bunut National Park

Charge, levied at park office • http://sarawakforestry.com

Some 80km south of Miri as the crow flies, **Loagan Bunut National Park**, best visited on an overnight trip, is a good spot for dedicated birdwatchers, boasting stork-billed kingfishers and hornbills among many other species. Many live around the park's lake, **Tasik Bunut**, tucked away on the upper reaches of the **Teru River**, a tributary of the Tinjar, which in turn flows into the Baram. During prolonged dry spells, when the lake level drops drastically, a peculiar form of fishing, which the local **Berawan** people call *selambau*, is carried out. Just before the lake dries out, fishermen use giant spoon-shaped wooden frames to scoop up any fish that haven't escaped down the lake's two watercourses.

For birds, these dry times are a perfect time to feed too, and in May and June the surrounding peat-swamp forest supports breeding colonies of such species as darters, egrets and bitterns. Initially the lake can appear huge, its edges hard to detect as the sunlight is often hazy; however, it's only around 500m wide and 1km long. Small cabins built on rafts house Berawan fishermen, while around them lies an intricate network of fishing plots, with underwater nets and lines tied to stakes pushed into the lake bed. The best times to drift by boat across the lake are early morning and dusk, when the birds are at their most active.

ARRIVAL AND INFORMATION   LOAGAN BUNUT NATIONAL PARK

By taxi There's no public transport to the park, but cars may head here in the morning (2hr 30min) from near Miri's tourist office; ask staff there where to wait; a Grab will be far less hassle. When you want to head back, park staff can usually arrange a vehicle.

By tour Miri tour operators (see page 359) offer one- to three-day trips to the park.

ACCOMMODATION AND EATING

If you're here on a trip with Borneo Mainland you have the option to stay at a nearby farm with which the company has links. Note that there are some **water** issues at the park accommodation and you should phone ahead to ascertain the situation.

Loagan Bunut National Park accommodation http://sarawakforestry.com. Located near the lake, the in-park accommodation is limited to a hostel and a so-called VIP chalet with two bedrooms, a/c and its own bathroom; a small canteen serves basic meals and snacks. Dorms $, chalet $$

Kelabit Highlands

Right up against the Kalimantan border, 100km southeast of Mount Mulu, the long, high plateau of the **Kelabit Highlands** has been home to the Kelabit people for hundreds of years. Western explorers had no idea this self-sufficient mountain community existed until the early twentieth century, and the Highlands were literally not put on the map until World War II, when British and Australian commandos, led by Major Tom Harrisson, used Kelabit settlements as bases during a guerrilla war against the occupying Japanese. Before Harrisson's men built an airstrip at Bario, trekking over inhospitable terrain was the only way to get here – it took two weeks from the nearest large town, Marudi, on the opposite side of Mulu. When missionaries arrived and converted the animist Kelabit to Christianity after the war, many traditions, like burial rituals and wild parties called *irau*s (where Chinese jars full of rice wine were consumed) disappeared. Many of the magnificent Kelabit **megaliths** associated with these traditions have been swallowed up by the jungle, but some dolmens, urns, rock carvings and ossuaries used in funeral processes can still be found, so the region draws archeologists and anthropologists from far and wide.

Nowadays the Kelabit (well certainly the males) seem to be the good ol' boys of Asia; cowboy hats are much in evidence and they are very keen on pick-up trucks, country music, hunting, and their dogs. The Kelabit are not the only inhabitants of this part of the state, however; there are also populations of **Penan** and **Lun Bawang** (formerly called the Murut).

Despite logging in the Bario area, the Highlands remain generally unspoiled, with occasional wildlife sightings and a refreshing climate – temperatures are only a few degrees lower than in Miri by day, but in winter at night they can drop to an untropical 15°C (60°F). As such the region is a great target for **walkers**, and it is easily accessible by air, with several villages served by plane.

Most visitors head to **Bario** as it has the main airport and well-established formal accommodation, but the real point of being here is to get out into the countryside, doing day-walks or longer treks through the jungle, on which you can be hosted in little settlements or longhouses en route such as at **Pa' Lungan** and **Pa' Dalih**. It's also possible to do more challenging treks up to the peaks of the **Pulong Tau National Park** (which currently has no facilities and no one to collect the entrance fee), notably **Mount Murud**. Another option is the **Picnic with the Penan** scheme (see page 363), further south along the Upper Baram region, which enables you to really get off the beaten track and explore the jungle with the Penan people.

There are **no banks** in the Kelabit Highlands, so bring enough cash to cover board and lodging plus guiding/trekking fees. If you're wondering why the 4WD prices are so high, it's because the region has no mechanics, so if they need repairs one must be flown in once to diagnose, then flown in again with spare parts to finish the job.

Bario and around

The short flight from Miri makes a thrilling introduction to this corner of Sarawak, the Twin Otter giving passengers amazing **views** (sit on the left on the way in, on the right on the way back) of serried ranks of blue limestone ridges at Gunung Mulu National Park and then of the double-humped **Batu Lawi** (see page 360) before landing at the settlement of **BARIO**. From the air, it's a sprawling jumble of little paths and houses, as well as fields planted with the **rice** for which the village is well known. There is a centre of sorts, a grassy space 2km northwest of the airfield, ringed by a few modern buildings housing a few shops, including one selling Penan baskets, uninteresting *kedai kopis* and a small hall with an exhibition on Kelabit culture, but much of the village is scattered around the fields 2km further northwest, along the main road and a couple of minor tracks off or parallel to it.

Between the village centre and the military base stands a **memorial to Tom Harrisson** in the shape of a *sape*, the Orang Ulu lute. Celebrating the enormous contribution Harrisson made to our understanding of Sarawak's history, as curator of the Sarawak Museum in Kuching and as a roving anthropologist and archeologist (notably at Niah), the memorial has an inscription that, besides paying tribute to the military work of Harrisson and his British and Australian comrades, also cites the "sacrifice of the tribal warriors of the Baram and Rejang basins" in helping liberate Sarawak from Japanese occupation.

The village's main street is named Jalan Penghulu Lawai, after the first English-speaking village spokesman appointed by the British in 1948. What the colonial authorities failed to realize, however, was that their appointee had learned English while in Marudi Prison, having been imprisoned by them a year earlier for headhunting – Lawai, however, didn't think he'd done anything wrong, so had escaped and walked all the way back to Bario through the jungle.

Situated on a plateau, with very little shade thanks to agriculture, Bario is visually dull in places but scenic in others, with vistas of rice fields and water buffalo against the lush mountains of the **Tama Abu Range** to the north and west. Although there are a few half-day walking opportunities, and a couple of things to look at in the village itself, it is only a taster of what you can experience on longer treks.

Bario Asal

While not the sole longhouse in the vicinity, **Bario Asal** is the oldest and close to the northern end of the main road – it was once the only settlement in the area and, technically speaking, they own all of the land in Bario. The unassuming timber building is unusual for effectively having two *ruais* – the second one, at the back, houses a communal kitchen with a long row of individual fireplaces for cooking. As a social venue, it's as important as the main *ruai* at the front. The longhouse also has a special area where travellers can stay (see page 360), and sells Kelabit beadwork, jackets and hats.

Walks around Bario

In addition to the popular trek to Ba' Kelalan and the Batu Lawi trek, a couple of shorter routes have been developed in the area for which you'll need the services

HIGHLANDS TREKS

Guesthouses and homestays in Bario (see page 360), and the tourist office in Miri (see page 343), are the best place to start when planning your trip to the highlands. Certified, English-speaking guides can be in short supply during the June–August peak season, so you should try and arrange them as far ahead as possible. Guides estimate the fitness of the group and set the pace accordingly. Trips may involve gathering wild vegetables, catching fish and cooking, Kelabit-style, on the campfire, as well as locating dolmens and visiting longhouses.

Guides' daily fees will go up if a little if you're jungle trekking, and more for overnight trips; the same goes for porters. For remote treks, you'll need a minimum of two guides (in case of an accident – one stays with the group and the other goes for help), though if you have a porter, you might be able to forgo the second. Fees generally do not include provisions, which will add to the cost. Where you overnight in villages, quotes usually include board and lodging; remember that if you don't return to where you started your trek, you'll have to pay your guide per day for their return journey.

As regards **equipment**, it's wise to travel light, bearing in mind the strict baggage limits on Twin Otters; in addition, slogging through the jungle with more than 10kg on your back is a real drag. On top of what you'd normally bring for a day-trek at a national park, it makes sense to have a thin sleeping bag and poncho, plus warmish clothing if you want to overnight outdoors or do any mountain trekking. A tent can be useful, though it obviously weighs down luggage; guides will usually stop overnight in villages or at shelters, though may have canvas sheets that will suffice for shelter at a pinch. For jungle trekking the best footwear is by far Wellington (rubber) boots as they not only make walking through mud and rivers less hassle but also help keep the leeches off (as does wearing thick, long trousers or anti-leech socks) – all are available in Miri or Lawas.

Leeches are quite common in this region, and although mostly harmless, they are not pleasant to have on you, or worse, biting you. There are a number of ways to discourage them, but they're not fail-safe (see page 45). If all else fails simply do as the locals do and use the sharp pinch and pull technique to get them off, and at least carry some salt, which dissolves them. A good way to deter them is to get some fresh tobacco leaves, grown locally, and rub them onto your exposed skin.

---

of a guide. The first, the **Aren Bario Trail**, is a half-day loop west of the village past Pa'Rumapu, via the **Bario Nature Site**, a newly constructed lookout (with café) that offers great views of the surrounding forest – especially of interest to birders. The trail then continues through the jungle and past five waterfalls before heading back to the village. In addition to birds, if you're very lucky you might spot the endangered Bay Cat, a wild feline only found in Borneo.

The overnight **Indigenous Trail** takes you into the jungle to the northwest of Bario, a moderate four to six hour walk to the Batu Buli camp, where there is a basic shelter for sleeping, though a mossy forest and past the 30m-high Batu Buli Waterfall, with a similar return leg the next day. It offers the chance to find the Spider *Rafflesia*, a smaller more arachnoid version of its famous cousin.

Prayer Hill

The best views of Bario are a short hike away up **Prayer Hill**, which will give you a great panorama across the village and to the mountains in the middle distance including Mount Murud. Coming from the village, turn right at Bario Asal and follow the stony path for ten minutes until you reach the end. Here there is a small house up the hill and you should follow the smaller path to the right of it. The path then climbs steeply (with ropes to help haul yourself up) for another twenty minutes until you reach a small wooden church, where services are occasionally held. The summit is another ten minutes up from here, where you'll find a small cross and magnificent views.

Batu Lawi

The most challenging local trek, apart from the one to Murud, is the climb up **Batu Lawi** (2044m), the strange double-horned peak that you may have seen on the flight in. The trek is an attractive prospect as it's less arduous and time-consuming than tackling Mount Murud, though as ever logging roads blight the landscape here and there, making it look as though the forest has been gnawed by rats.

The first day out from Bario (8–10hr) is a fairly easy trek past Pa'Ukat and the **Batu Buli camp**, then the **Batu Narut megalith** and a river sinkhole to where you camp at **Arur Bila Bigan**. On the more taxing second day you scramble to the lower and much blunter of the peak's two "horns" for an amazing view of the other, looking like a huge upright stone pillar, though ruder interpretations are possible. The descent has trekkers camping at **Kubaan camp** near a Penan village, and the fourth day, the descent to Bario. It's also possible to do the trek from Ba' Kelalan; contact Miri tourist office (see **Highlands Treks**, page 359) or see **Guides** in Ba' Kelalan (see page 361).

ARRIVAL AND DEPARTURE — BARIO

By land Perhaps the best way to enter the Kelabit Highlands is by using a car, which gives you a real sense of how remote it is, affords some lovely views (despite the logging) and offers the chance to stop off at villages along the way. It's 400km from Miri to Bario via the Lapok Junction (on the Miri–Bintulu highway, and from which you can hitch), from where a decent logging road heads inland through Kiloten, Long Supit (where there are some nice food stalls), Long Kerong, and Pa' Dalih, finally arriving in Bario some 10hr later – or many more hours if the roads are in worse condition than usual (which does happen). Every few kilometres there's a muddy bit where you really need a 4WD, and rain will slow you down considerably. Many visitors rent a car between them to/from Miri, Long Kerong or Long Banga, or Pa'Lungan.

By plane Passengers arriving by plane are met by Bario's guesthouse owners every morning, so you should be collected if you've booked to stay, and be able to arrange a room if not.

Destinations Marudi (1 daily; 40min); Miri (2 daily; 50min).

ACCOMMODATION AND EATING

There are several simple places to **stay** in and around Bario, and although some have 24hr electricity, some only have some solar-powered lighting at night. You may have trouble finding a place to stay over Christmas and New Year – when guesthouses may shut for lack of incoming tourists – and during the annual **Bario Food Festival** in July, when the village centre is transformed into a mini-fair. Rates all include meals, so people usually eat where they stay. Not spicy by Malaysian standards, **Bario cuisine** features ingredients such as wild boar and locally farmed fish such as carp, though guesthouses may not serve traditional staples unless you request them. If you're out for the day, you can request a packed lunch. The Y2K shop on the main road, nearly 10min walk north of the centre, sells drinks and snacks at steepish prices.

★ **Bario Asal** 4km northwest of the airport; 011 2508 1114. The longhouse has a nice guest area with four homely bedrooms with double beds, one reasonable bathroom (with hot water and washing machine) and a huge lounge area, plus a little balcony where you can take coffee and watch the longhouse's semi-tame hornbill flap around hoping for scraps. Sonarang and her family are excellent hosts, and occasionally host cultural shows. $

Nancy Harriss Next to the military base; 013 298 4007. Built next to the old British airstrip (there are the remains of a crashed Australian plane in the garden), this well-run homestay is fairly active, and often busy with groups. The rooms in the main building are pretty standard, but they've just built a row of two- and three-bedroom chalets – the most luxurious accommodation in the village. $$$

★ **Ngimat Ayu House** 3km from centre, reached by a signed path northeast off main road; http://bit.ly/NgimatAyu. Exactly what you might imagine a rural Borneo homestay to be – a charming wooden building, with delightful inhabitants living a simple, unhurried way of life. They put on occasional cultural shows, and make excellent food too – veggies will be very happy to hear that they'll be well catered for. $

Pa' Lungan

The lovely, tranquil village of **PA' LUNGAN**, around a four- to five-hour trek (or less by road) north from Bario, is made up of a group of detached houses on stilts built around a large rectangular field for buffalo, with a "new town" slightly higher up past the modern church. While for many it's just an overnight stay on the way to somewhere else, it actually makes a great trekking base as well as being a peaceful place to hang

THE BARIO TO PA' LUNGAN TREK

The five-hour **hike** from Bario to Pa' Lungan along the old path is fairly easy for the most part, although it becomes trickier if it's been raining. Otherwise the trail is pretty clear and a guide is not needed, though you will be getting your feet wet at some point. The first stretch involves heading northeast out of town along the main road. About 3km from the centre the road forks; take the left-hand branch to reach, 1km on, the settlement of **Pa'Ukat** – don't follow the obvious path here, but take a right at the church. From here, it passes through a very swampy part, after which it rises into mainly secondary jungle – the really swampy sections are crossed on log or bamboo "bridges" of up to 60m long. Using a stick to stabilize yourself while shuffling forward will make these crossings much easier. Along the way you may come across monkeys and other arboreal mammals, as well as **carvings** on a rock called Batu Narit, an hour out of Pa' Ukat, which shows a masked man and a hornbill, along with more than three hundred notches at the bottom which are thought to represent heads taken. Three or four hours on, you finally arrive at Pa' Lungan.

To save time, some trekkers opt to be taken part of the way to Pa' Lungan (or back) by **boat** (1–2hr), which Bario guesthouses can usually arrange. The boatman takes you to a point on the river called **Long Palungan**, and can point out the trail to follow uphill from the bank; from the right spot on the hilltop, a clear wide trail takes you on to Pa' Lungan (1hr). At this point you can also arrange kayaking to get back to Bario.

---

out for a few days. There are several **trails** from here for which you'll need guides: to the 20m-high Arur Waterfall (2hr each way); the Pa' Lungan River loop (three days) though the jungle; the gruelling trek up Mount Murud (see box, page 362); and the easier Kalimantan Loop (four days) via Long Pedit, which involves two nights sleeping in jungle camps and one at a homestay in one of the many villages along the way. It is advised that you arrange guides beforehand as the village only has a population of around a forty, and only two licensed guides.

Shorter walks that don't need guides include the two megaliths within a few minutes' walk of the village. One is leaning drunkenly, thanks to some sloppy archeology by Tom Harrisson, and the other has collapsed, damaged by villagers looking for foundation stones. There's also a hill to the north of the village, topped with a tin cross and offering fabulous views – it's a steep forty-minute hike through some nice jungle, but be warned there's little cover at the top. It's unclear as yet what effect the new Bario–Ba'Kelalan road will have on the village, but hopefully the economy will improve and its population will begin to increase.

ACCOMMODATION AND EATING   PA' LUNGAN

There are homestay options hereabouts, many in traditional stilted houses, with basic rooms; none are truly reliable, but asking around in Bario for information is likely to yield some results – remember to ask about the dining arrangements, too.

Pa' Lungan to Ba' Kelalan

It's currently possible to walk from **Pa' Lungan to Ba' Kelalan**, either via Mount Murud, which takes five days (see box, page 362) or less if you walk part of the way on the new road (which goes to Longbawan, over the border in Indonesia, so don't follow it too far). As things may well change significantly when the new road opens, it's best to check the situation first with the Miri tourist office (see **Highlands Treks**, page 359).

Ba' Kelalan (Bakelalan)

Apart from a few fruit orchards, **Ba' Kelalan** amounts to a mere smattering of houses in five settlements and places selling basic provisions. The chief reason to come here is to trek – you can head to Bario (on the new road, when it's finished, by foot or 4WD), Mount Murud or Batu Lawi, or, less ambitiously, do short walks into Kalimantan and then back within a day, or a four-hour round trip up to the **viewpoint** at Budukteudal. Note that the name is currently changing to Bakelalan, so you may see both spellings.

ARRIVAL AND INFORMATION — BA'KELALAN

By plane The airfield, right next to the village, has flights to Miri (3 weekly; 1hr 35min) via Lawas (3 weekly; 35min).
By 4WD A logging road runs from Ba'Kelalan to Lawas, and takes 6hr with 4WD; however, with upgrading this is likely to reduce significantly, and become possible with more regular forms of transport.
Guides Along with 4WDs and information, guides can be arranged for trips to Mount Murud, Bario, Batu Lawi, or Kalimantan, as well as the viewpoint at Budukteudal – you'll have to ask around in the village.

ACCOMMODATION AND EATING

Julia Sang Homestay 300m north of the airport "terminal"; 012 854 7041. Surprisingly large and well-maintained place with a gorgeous lounge, and an extremely spacious dining area – breakfast is usually included in the price, and lunch and dinner are available too. The rooms have been prettified with floral bedspreads, plastic flowers and the like, and make for a very pleasant place to stay. In the (unlikely) event that it's full, there are a couple of other homestay options nearby. $

Ulu Baram

The Baram River system so dominates northern Sarawak that you could consider virtually all the interior here, excepting Limbang division, to be the **Ulu Baram** – practically every river, including the Melinau and Tutoh at Mulu, the Tinjar at Loagan Bunut and the Dapur and Kelapang at Bario, ends up flowing into the Baram. The river itself, however, wends its way southwest from the town of **Marudi**, 80km from Miri, occasionally passing confluence towns such as **Long Lama** and **Long San**, before approaching the border with Kalimantan. Here it swings east to peter out beyond **Lio Matoh**, 200km southeast of Miri.

This Ulu Baram, due south of Mulu and southwest of the Kelabit Highlands, is definitely outback territory, rugged and lushly forested, with no specific sights; the reason you might venture here is to **trek** through virgin rainforest and stay in remote settlements as part of a **homestay** programme. The usual **caveats** about Malaysia

---

MOUNT MURUD

Barring the way between Bario to the south and Ba'Kelalan to the northeast, **Mount Murud** is the highest peak in Sarawak at 2423m, and is part of the Pulong Tau National Park. It presents a challenging but rewarding trek, with spectacular views across the Highlands to Batu Lawi and even Mulu. From Ba'Kelalan, it takes six days there and back; from Bario, allow one day extra.

Leaving Ba'Kelalan, trekkers head to Base Camp 1 at Lepo Bunga (8hr) on the first night, traversing some steep hills. If you need to save a day, you can take 4WD on this leg. On day two the target is **Church Camp** (4–5hr) – a wooden shelter built by local evangelical groups for a three-day Christian meeting held once a year. The next morning sees the haul up to the summit (3hr) via the **Rock Garden**, an exposed area of stunted trees and sharpish boulders. After another night back at Church Camp, you retrace your steps back to Ba'Kelalan.

If you're starting from Bario, the first day is spent reaching **Pa'Lungan**, where you stay the night. The next day brings a trek to a simple shelter at **Long Rapung** (7hr), with about half an hour's worth of climbing en route. On day three, some guides head to Church Camp (7hr), others to the slightly nearer Camp 2 at **Long Belaban**, with hammocks to sleep in (5–6hr), though you have to ford a few streams en route and climb for a couple of hours at the end of the day. If you start from Camp 2, day four is gruelling, the climb up to the summit beginning at dawn (5–6hr); the descent usually means heading to the Rock Garden and Church Camp (4hr). On day five you head back to Camp 2 for the night; it's then possible to get all the way back to Pa'Lungan on day six.

THE PENAN

For some, the **Penan** have a mystique beyond that of any of Sarawak's many Orang Ulu groups, as a kind of poster child for the ongoing struggle for native peoples' rights. That status is largely thanks to the campaign waged on their behalf by the Swiss activist **Bruno Manser** in the 1980s and 1990s. Manser lived with the Penan for years and became a thorn in the side of the Sarawak government, drawing the world's attention to the destruction of their traditional forest habitat, though his PR successes had little impact on Sarawak's logging industry. The Penan lost their champion when Manser disappeared in 2000, having trekked alone from Bario to meet the Penan in the jungle; he was never seen again, but the campaign he founded soldiers on (http://bmf.ch).

Most of Sarawak's twelve thousand Penan live in the upper reaches of the Baram, Tutoh and Belaga rivers, with only two or three hundred still following their nomadic lifestyle. Their language is of the same family as Iban and Malay. Traditionally they were nomadic hunter-gatherers, but these days the majority live in tiny villages – thanks not only to habitat loss but also to the embrace of the outside world and cash economy. Their staple of sago has often been supplanted by rice, which the Penan grow like the Iban, in clearings using shifting cultivation. Many Penan struggle to make ends meet, both in towns where they may be in poorly paid work, and in their villages, where food is in reasonable supply but cash hard to come by. Another problem is the lack of identity documents, without which many Penan cannot access services, education and jobs.

---

homestays apply here (see page 38). One key point is that villagers take turns to put up guests, so quite how adept your hosts will be is a matter of luck.

Ulu Baram trekking

It can be hard to get to Ulu Baram, but when you arrive the rewards can be considerable. There are ample chances to **trek** through jungle, using "trails" hacked out by your guide, spending the night perhaps in a hut of the type the Penan erect, or in a shelter that your guide might build using branches. From the Selungo River it's also possible to climb **Mount Murud Kecil** ("Little Murud"; 2112m), at the opposite end of the Tama Abu Range from its more famous sibling, and there are many interesting trips to caves and waterfalls.

Ulu Baram villages

Village life can itself be a highlight in Ulu Baram. Local people can teach crafts, and then there's the simple pleasure of bathing in the river with the villagers, or the spectacle of being at the simple village church on Sunday (many Penan belong to the evangelical Sidang Injil Borneo or SIB movement, which has churches throughout Sarawak); it's great to witness hymns sung in Penan with the village youths showing off their self-taught skills on guitar, keyboards and drums. After the rice is planted (June) or harvested (February), you can even accompany the men as they **hunt** wild pigs, aided by dogs and the odd gun.

ARRIVAL AND INFORMATION — ULU BARAM

Picnic with the Penan Though it's possible to visit independently, the best way to visit Penan settlements near Lio Matoh, such as Long Kerong and Ajeng close to the Selungo River, is by tour with one of the agencies based in Miri (see page 343) or Kuching (see page 311). The experience is similar to visiting villages in the Kelabit Highlands (see page 356), but much more cut off. It doesn't come cheap, as this area has better resisted the logging industry – logging roads and bridges are fewer and further between, so expensive boat charter is required. Currently, the typical trip is four days (three nights) and starts with a flight to Long Akah or Long Banga, followed by a 4WD drive, then a boat ride to your village. After this, a two-day trek takes you through the jungle, staying at camps and homestays, after which you boat and 4WD it back down, then fly out. Local guides may speak little English, so is this is essential to you make it clear to your agency, while porters are often a good added expenditure.

Sabah

- 371 Kota Kinabalu
- 380 Around Kota Kinabalu
- 383 The southwest coast
- 385 Labuan Island
- 389 The northwest coast and Kudat Peninsula
- 392 Kinabalu Park
- 399 Around Kinabalu Park
- 400 Eastern Sabah
- 419 The interior

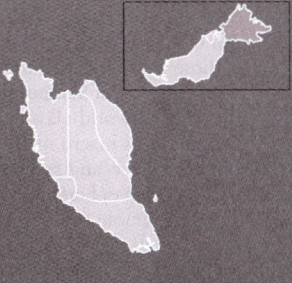

MOUNT KINABALU

Sabah

Sabah is, in many ways, Malaysia's "Wild East", a state with a frontier feel tinged by the influence of neighbouring Indonesia and the Philippines. It's markedly different to its western neighbour Sarawak, too, despite superficial similarities: both states are largely rural, and both encompass a bewildering number of ethnic groups (for more on Sabah's make-up, see page 550). But whereas Sarawak is prosperous, Sabah is often visibly poor, and – more pertinently for visitors – where Sarawak makes a big thing of its Indigenous cultures, in Sabah the focus is overwhelmingly on nature. Indeed, this is arguably the very best place in Malaysia for wildlife-spotting, a fact that has kept visitors coming despite the odd security scare (see page 370). Part of the reason for that focus on fauna is the paucity of Sabah's urban heritage; in few other parts of the country do the major cities exude such a sense of rootlessness, due largely to World War II bombing.

The **terrain** of "The Land Below the Wind" – a moniker that has clung to Sabah thanks to Agnes Keith's fine book of the same name (see page 559), although it really means anywhere equatorial outside the typhoon belt – ranges from wild, swampy, mangrove-tangled coastal areas, through the dazzling greens of paddy fields and pristine rainforests, to the substantial Crocker mountain range. It's home to Malaysia's highest peak, **Mount Kinabalu**, whose distinctively craggy summit is visible throughout much of western and central Sabah, and appears on the state flag. A plethora of state parks and forest reserves provide refuges for indigenous animals, although much of eastern Sabah is now given over to oil palm.

The state's most enjoyable city by far is the capital **Kota Kinabalu** (KK) in the northwest. With a fine selection of accommodation, restaurants and markets, it's a springboard for many of Sabah's attractions, notably the **Kinabalu Park** to the northeast and the whitewater rafting and wildlife cruises of the **Klias Peninsula** to the south. Also within reach of here is **Pulau Tiga Park**, for island solitude; the duty-free island of **Labuan**; and the beaches and coconut groves of the **Kudat Peninsula**, whose northernmost point, the **Tip of Borneo**, features windy shorelines and splendid isolation.

Across on the east coast is the mundane city of **Sandakan**, another springboard for major attractions, including the **Sepilok Orangutan Rehabilitation Centre**, **Bornean Sun Bear Conservation Centre** and **Labuk Bay Proboscis Monkey Sanctuary**. Deeper into the oil-palm plantations of east Sabah lies the protected **Kinabatangan River**, where visitors can take boat trips to see wild proboscis monkeys, elephants and orangutans.

Those who venture into the state's southeast corner are generally headed to the islands near the town of **Semporna**, which are the jewel in Sabah's crown for divers. **Sipadan Island** offers world-class diving off coral walls, while its neighbour **Mabul Island** is known for its macro marine life. These two are simply the best known, and the area can keep divers and snorkellers enchanted for days. There are also a couple of excellent wildlife reserves here, most notably the **Danum Valley Conservation Area**.

Sabah's remote interior is generally somewhere visitors bypass on a plane between coasts, or else grind through on an express bus, but there are things worth seeing here, too: the forested **Maliau Basin**, where the trekking overshadows the wildlife; and the village of **Sapulut**, home to an excellent community tourism project offering a mix of climbing, caving and trekking.

PULAU TIGA (SURVIVOR ISLAND)

Highlights

❶ **Tiga Island** With the TV crews long gone, "Survivor Island" remains largely undeveloped with attractive beaches, jungle walks and a natural mud bath for good measure. See page 383

❷ **Mount Kinabalu** The climb is arduous and expensive, but still one of the very best experiences in all of Malaysia. See page 393

❸ **Sepilok** This rural area outside Sandakan boasts sanctuaries for orangutans and sun bears, as well as a rainforest park. See page 405

❹ **Kinabatangan River** Home to a great diversity of animal life, including proboscis monkeys and the occasional pygmy elephant herd. See page 408

❺ **Danum Valley** A stretch of untouched rainforest with plenty of wildlife-spotting possibilities. See page 412

❻ **Sipadan and Mabul** Spectacular marine life makes these two islands a must for scuba divers; reefs off other nearby islands are also worth exploring. See page 415

❼ **Sapulut** This remote area is home to an excellent community tourism project, offering a dose of nature, Murut culture and the chance to climb limestone pinnacles. See page 422

❽ **Maliau Basin** A true taste of virgin jungle, with multi-day treks to take in pretty waterfalls. See page 422

HIGHLIGHTS ARE MARKED ON THE MAP ON PAGE 368

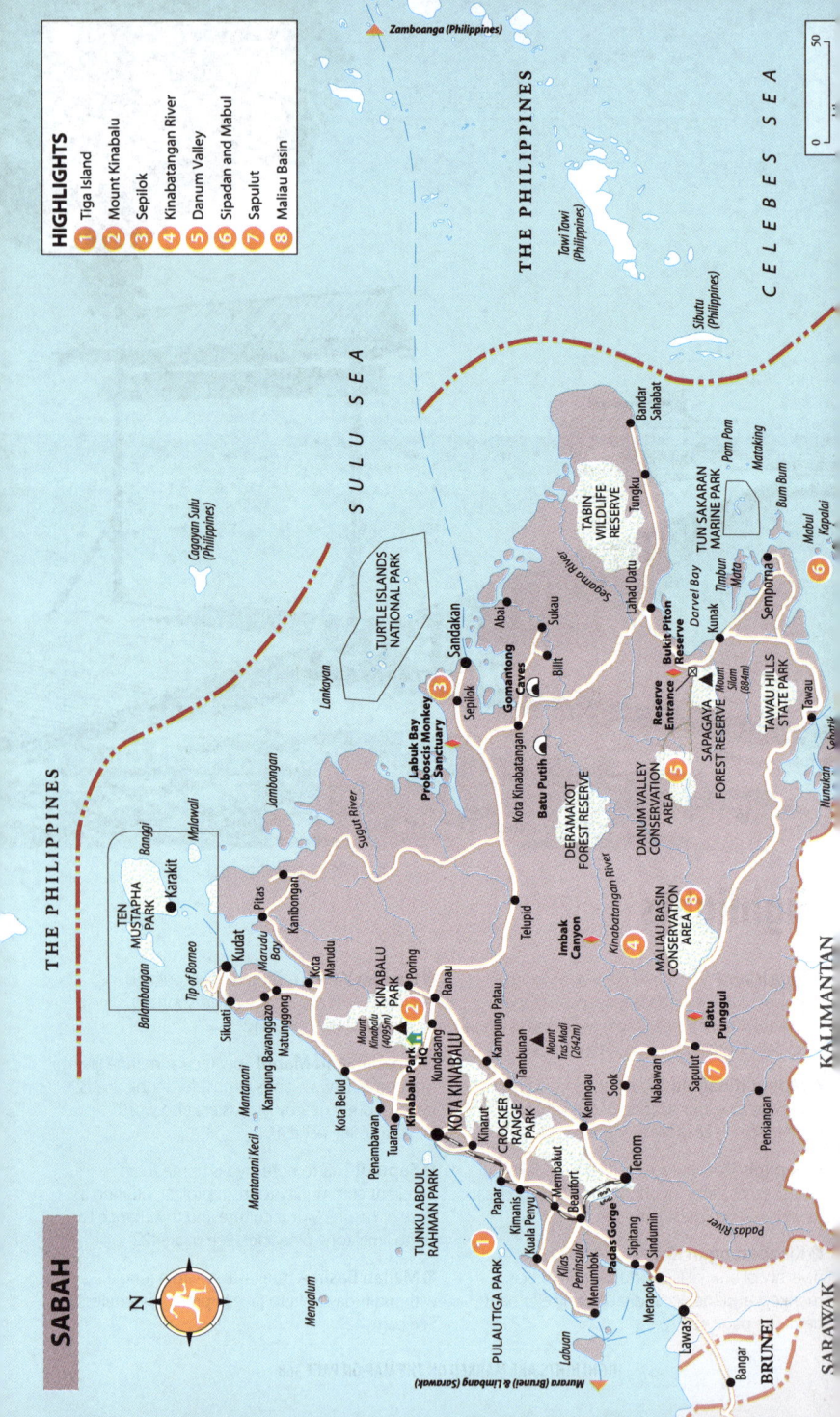

Brief history
Little is known of Sabah's **early history**, though archeological finds in limestone caves indicate that the northern tip of Borneo has been inhabited for well over ten thousand years. **Chinese merchants** were trading with local settlements by 700 AD, and by the fourteenth century the area was under the sway of the sultans of **Brunei** and **Sulu**.

Colonialism
Europe's superpowers first arrived in 1521, when the ships of **Portuguese** navigator Ferdinand Magellan stopped off at Brunei before sailing northwards. Almost 250 years later, in 1763, colonial settlement began when one Captain Cowley established a short-lived trading post on Balambangan Island, north of Kudat, on behalf of the **British East India Company**. Further colonial involvement came in 1846, when Labuan Island (at the mouth of Brunei Bay) was ceded to the British by the Sultan of Brunei. The 1870s were a pivotal decade: first the Sultan of Brunei signed over what is basically now western Sabah to the British in return for a yearly remittance, and soon after the **Sultan of Sulu** (the archipelago at the southern fringe of what's now the Philippines) struck a similar deal covering eastern Sabah. By 1881 the **British North Borneo Chartered Company** had full sovereignty over northern Borneo.

First steps were then taken towards making the territory pay its way: rubber, tobacco and, after 1885, timber were commercially harvested. By 1905 a **rail line** linked the coastal town of **Jesselton** (later Kota Kinabalu) with the resource-rich interior. When the company introduced taxes, the locals were understandably displeased and some resisted; **Mat Salleh**, the son of a Bajau chief, and his followers sacked the company's settlement on Gaya Island in 1897. Another uprising, in **Rundum** in 1915, resulted in the slaughter of hundreds of Murut Indigenous people by British forces.

World War II and independence
On New Year's Day 1942, Japanese imperial forces invaded Labuan Island; Sandakan fell less than three weeks later. By the time the Japanese surrendered on September 9, 1945, little of Jesselton and Sandakan remained standing (although the worst structural damage was inflicted by Allied bombing). Even worse were the hardships endured by civilians and captured Allied troops, the most notorious of which were the Death Marches of 1945 (see page 401).

Unable to finance the postwar rebuilding of North Borneo, the Chartered Company sold the territory to the British Crown in 1946, and Jesselton was declared the new capital of the **Crown Colony of North Borneo**. Within fifteen years, however, plans had been laid for an independent federation consisting of Malaya, Singapore, Sarawak, North Borneo and (it was intended) Brunei. The **Federation** was proclaimed at midnight on September 16, 1963, with North Borneo renamed Sabah.

Modern concerns
Kuala Lumpur feels very remote from Sabah, but federal politics have been gradually imposed ever since independence. Although local and Indigenous parties have ruled Sabah in stretches, since 2002 the state has largely remained firmly in the grip of the country's ruling BN coalition. One factor in this is **immigration** – both legal and undocumented – which remains a live issue. Around a quarter of Sabah's population is non-Malaysian, the highest proportion of any state in the federation, and in recent decades there has been a vast influx of largely Muslim migrants from the Philippines and Indonesia. Many Indigenous Sabahans view their requests for residency (and in some cases citizenship) with suspicion, seeing it as a creeping way of Islamizing the state, but their opposition has been unfocused and ineffective. The BN coalition was ousted in the 2018 state elections by an opposition coalition that, though unwieldy, managed to maintain power following the snap election in 2020; another election will have taken place by the time you read this.

Sabah was, for a time, the poster child for Malaysian tourism. It remains the state with the best environmental track record in the country (although critics might say it could be better managed still) and its wildlife attractions meant visitor numbers boomed in the first decade of the new millennium; for a while, Kota Kinabalu even enjoyed direct flights from Australia. Unfortunately things fell off a cliff after a spate of **security incidents** (see box), but are now back on the mend despite another sad event, the Mount Kinabalu **earthquake** in 2015 (see page 398).

ARRIVAL AND DEPARTURE

By plane Kota Kinabalu, Sandakan and the southeastern town of Tawau all have modern airports, but KK's is the only de facto international gateway, with connections to various Southeast Asian cities. Tawau barely counts as international, with a few short flights to Tarakan in Indonesian Borneo; Sandakan may attract flights from abroad now that a runway extension is complete.

By bus The only overland route into Sabah is from Lawas in Sarawak. Express buses follow this route to KK from Bandar Seri Begawan in Brunei – and, previously, even from Miri in Sarawak, though getting from Sarawak to Brunei is no longer simple.

By boat Ferries run between Labuan Island and Sipitang, Menumbok and KK; Labuan itself has connections with Limbang and Lawas in Sarawak, plus Brunei. Ferries also sail from Indonesian Borneo to Tawau, and from the Philippines to Sandakan.

GETTING AROUND

The relatively backward state of Sabah's roads can make driving or bus travel a bit of a bore – for many years, highway extension plans dragged on rather like the two-lane country roads everyone was forced to rely on. However, there have been substantial recent changes; allied with Sarawak's success in upgrading its own sectors of the Trans-Borneo Highway, travel on the northwestern coast of the island is becoming far more manageable. There is also a sealed road right through the southern interior to Tawau, and although it can be in a poor state between Sapulut and Maliau Basin, an ordinary car will cope; off the beaten track, you might need to rent a 4WD. Nevertheless, given the distances involved, it's worth considering internal flights as a timesaver.

By plane MASWings' nineteen-seater Twin Otters (http://maswings.com.my) serve the airfields at Kudat (near the Tip of Borneo) and Lahad Datu on the east coast. For more on these planes, see page 349.

SECURITY IN SABAH

Certain areas of Sabah are subject to official **travel advisories**, as a result of incidents blamed on Muslim militancy in the southern Philippines. Alarming though this may sound, some perspective is called for: such events are sporadic and, as in other countries that have witnessed random acts of violence of late, ordinary people are going about their lives as normal.

Sabah has witnessed **abductions** on and off over the years, most recently since 2010. Some have involved tourists, seized on the dive islands off Semporna; in Sandakan, two local people were kidnapped and one was subsequently killed, apparently because no ransom was paid. Undoubtedly the most serious event was an **incursion** by armed insurgents near Lahad Datu in 2013, ostensibly to revive the old Sulu Sultanate claim on eastern Sabah; several dozen people, mostly militants, died in the ensuing fighting as the authorities regained control.

In general, however, Sabah remains as calm as any other part of Malaysia, and the travel warnings reflect this. At the time of writing, for example, only the islands off the Tip of Borneo and off Semporna were included in a UK warning advising against "all but essential travel", while the US was recommending general caution in eastern Sabah. Things can change for better or worse at any time, of course, so it's best to keep abreast of the latest official advice.

Note that many local people avoid the **water villages** that still exist on the edges of many towns, as they may harbour undocumented migrants – the subtext here being because of petty crime and, perhaps, militancy. Such concerns may be overblown, but in any case most of these settlements aren't really sights (unlike the one in Brunei's capital) – the odd exception is mentioned in the text.

> **VISITING PARKS AND RESERVES**
>
> A range of organizations manage Sabah's wildlife sanctuaries. **Sabah Parks** (http://sabahparks.org.my; see page 375) runs the state's nine **state parks**, six of which are out at sea. There's usually a **conservation fee** to visit (typically quite low). Note that accommodation and other facilities at the most popular parks – including Kinabalu – are largely privatized and can be pricey. Then there are forest **conservation areas** such as Deramakot, which fall under the **Sabah Forestry Department** in Sandakan (entry permits priced per day; http://forest.sabah.gov.my). Some sites are wholly or partly run by other agencies; details are given in the text, along with information on how to sort out a visit, but given the complexities involved it can be preferable to pay one of the many tour operators in KK (see page 376) or Sandakan (see page 404) to sort out the paperwork and transport – in some cases this is the only option.

By long-distance bus Long-distance buses provide a fairly comprehensive service but may peter out towards evening, and adherence to timetables can be arbitrary. Fares are reasonable, though.

By shared minivans/taxis Shared taxis and minivans leave when full on routes of up to 150km, though most cover distances that are much shorter. Prices are at least twenty percent higher than bus fares for the same distance.

By train Sabah State Railway (http://railway.sabah.gov.my) provides a limited service that's of little use to most visitors. The main part of the line runs from Tanjung Aru, on the outskirts of KK, via several southwestern towns to Beaufort (2 daily; 2hr), where there's a branch line to Tenom in the interior (2 daily; 2hr 30min). It costs next to nothing to travel the entire network. Unless timetables change, there are no convenient connections between the two parts of the network at Beaufort, in either direction.

Kota Kinabalu

While first impressions of **KOTA KINABALU** (universally referred to as KK) may be of a glut of functional concrete, it does have a laid-back vibe and plenty of worthwhile amenities. In terms of sights, there's nothing to warrant staying more than a couple of nights – highlights include the **markets** and the islands of the **Tunku Abdul Rahman Park** – but the city's role as a hub for transport and tour operators means you might pass through more than once. Another appealing thing about the place is its manageability: the city centre is a mere 4km strip stretching from the resort area in the southwest to Likas Bay in the northeast, its grid of streets crammed in between the sea and the ridge of Signal Hill.

Brief history

Modern-day KK has its roots in a failed British settlement at Gaya Island, which was burned down in 1897 by followers of the Bajau rebel Mat Salleh. Starting anew, in 1899 the North Borneo Chartered Company founded a new town on a site on the mainland opposite. Named **Jesselton** after Sir Charles Jessel, the company's vice-chairman, the settlement soon prospered as the seaward terminus of the new railway line to Beaufort in the interior, allowing commodities to be brought efficiently to the coast for export.

The Japanese invasion of North Borneo in 1942 marked the start of three and a half years of **military occupation**; little of the old town survived subsequent Allied bombing. Soon after the war, Jesselton replaced Sandakan as Sabah's capital, and in 1968 it acquired its present name – an apt choice considering that on a clear day, Mount Kinabalu is actually visible from Likas Bay, the airport and elsewhere. Since then KK has grown rapidly, attracting a true cross-section of Sabah's population even though it sits in the Kadazan/Dusun heartland. In 2000 it finally gained official city status, and in terms of property prices, KK is now one of the most expensive cities in East Malaysia.

Gaya Street

There are echoes of the past in the names of the districts in KK's centre: Api-Api was a Bajau fishing village in the area, while Kampung Air ("water village") hints at the land reclamation that was necessary to flesh the centre out to its present size. For more tangible traces of the past, however, head to **Gaya Street** (Jalan Gaya), which still has the feel of a small-town main street even though all the architecture is postwar. The only two buildings of note are the whitewashed former General Post Office, which now houses the main **tourist office**, and the 1954 *Jesselton* hotel metres away, though this packs rather less old-world charm. Signage throughout reveals the presence of Chinese associations, and the odd hardware shop and picture framer can be found clinging on amid fairly obvious gentrification.

One of the very best **street markets** in Malaysia takes place here every Sunday morning, when the entire street gets packed out with stalls selling items as varied as tropical fruit trees, hats, basketry and live rabbits. Buskers are usually on hand too.

Australia Place and Signal Hill

A stone's throw south of the tourist office is **Australia Place**, so named because the Australian soldiers made camp here in 1945. From the back of the lane here, called **Lorong Dewan** (also known as Jalan Dewan), two sets of steps lead up the ridge behind

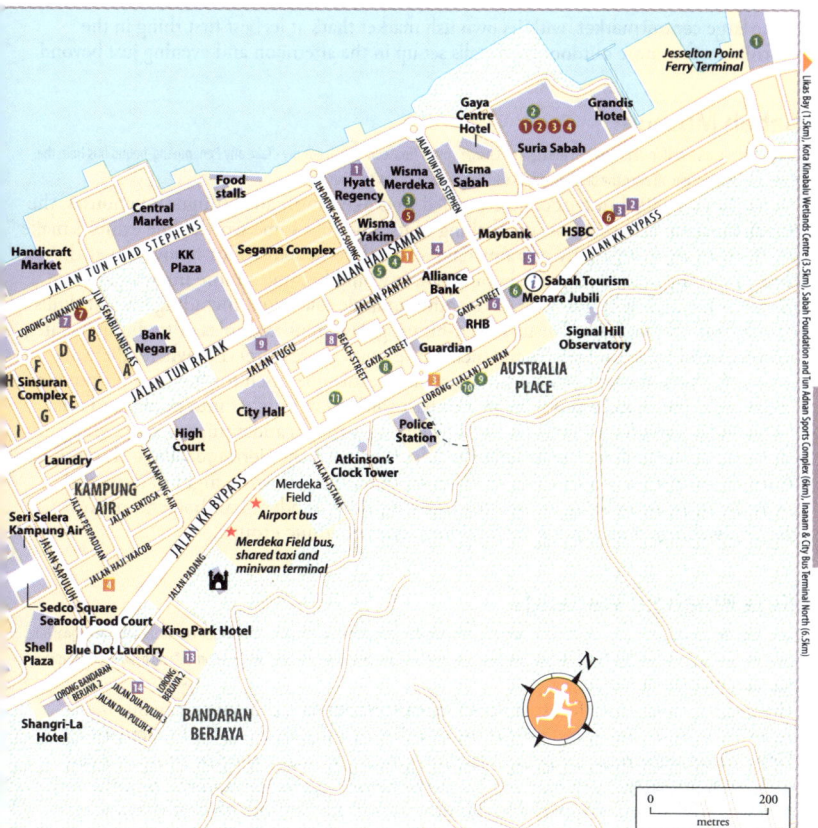

KK's centre to **Signal Hill** (Bukit Bendera), which is the highest point in town with a modern **observatory platform** for views over the centre and out to sea.

The oldest surviving structure in the city stands on a hillock just a couple of minutes' walk west of Australia Place: the wooden **Atkinson's Clock Tower**, built in 1903 to commemorate the first district official of Jesselton, Francis George Atkinson, who died of malaria at 28. Practically next door is **Merdeka Field**, where Sabah's independence and simultaneous union with modern Malaysia was declared.

The waterfront

Handicraft market Daily 7am–8pm, though hours vary · **Central market** Daily 6am–6pm

KK's **waterfront** is no grand promenade, but a series of nondescript modern buildings with some overpriced restaurants and bars at the southwestern end (when locals use the term "waterfront", they may mean this area specifically). The real highlights are its markets, most notably the **handicraft market** in the centre of the strip. Also known by its old name of the Filipino market, thanks to the ethnicity of some of its traders, it's a veritable warren of stalls mainly selling cheap clothes, with tailors doing alterations at antique sewing machines set up outside.

Next door to the southwest is the **night market**, a photogenic combination of fish market and stalls selling cooked food (see page 410). At the other end of the handicraft market is the large **central market**, with its own fish market that's at its best first thing in the morning; a few more outdoor food stalls set up in the afternoon and evening just beyond.

Sabah Museum

Jalan Muzium, on a hilltop 2km south of the centre • Charge • http://museum.sabah.gov.my • Take any Penampang-bound bus from the Marina Court stop; get off once the bus turns into Jalan Penampang, below the museum

Housed in a 1980s hunk of concrete styled to evoke Murut and Rungus longhouses, the **Sabah Museum** isn't the most compelling of its kind, but some worthwhile exhibits make it a decent target, especially on rainy days – the place was closed for renovation at the time of writing, and locals were hoping that it would become a more interesting place to visit. One highlight, however, is the **ethnographic collection**, including human skulls dating from the Kadazan/Dusun's head-hunting days, plus examples of traditional crafts, costumes and musical instruments such as the *turali* (nose flute). Elsewhere, there are various Chinese **ceramic jars**, including some sizeable ones used for funerary purposes as in Sarawak, plus **nature dioramas** that impart some fresh insights into rainforest fauna.

Outside the main building is a small gallery of carriages and equipment drawn from modern Sabah's dalliance with railways. Much better is the **Heritage Village** (Kampung Warisan) on the leafy north side of the compound; head down a flight of steps and cross the suspension bridge to reach a lake ringed by wooden, bamboo and palm-thatch dwellings representing the building styles of ethnic groups.

Kota Kinabalu Wetlands

Jalan Bukit Bendera Upper, east of Signal Hill • Charge • http://sabahwetlands.org • A 40min walk from the centre up and over Signal Hill; alternatively, any bus from Jalan Tunku Abdul Rahman (opposite Merdeka Field) signed "Likas" or "One Borneo" will head to Likas Square, from where it's a short walk south and west

The patch of mangrove forest at **Kota Kinabalu Wetlands** is the only remnant of an extensive system that once covered the coastline. Designated as a bird sanctuary in 1996, it's an important refuge and feeding ground for many species. From marked trails on **boardwalks**, you may catch sight of herons, egrets, sandpipers, pigeons and doves, as well as mudskippers and monitor lizards; for birdlife, it's best to come early in the morning or late in the afternoon. The wetlands are managed by a non-profit conservation group, which does its best to defend them against pollution and fast-encroaching development.

The beaches

Tanjung Aru Beach starts 4km southwest of the centre, and minivans from the Marina Court bus stop can drop you near the start; Likas Bay is only 1km on from the Jesselton Point ferry terminal – take bus #6 northbound from Jalan Tunku Abdul Rahman

They're nothing much to write home about, but the public beaches in KK are out at **Tanjung Aru** and in the opposite direction at **Likas Bay**. The former is preferable, a 2km stretch in three sections – "first beach" near the *Shangri-La* resort the most popular; Likas Bay has nice views, but can be a little dirty. Both beaches have basic showers and toilets. Jellyfish are an occasional problem, so it's worth asking the tourist office whether there have been any recent stinging incidents before diving in.

ARRIVAL AND DEPARTURE   **KOTA KINABALU**

BY PLANE

KK International Airport (KKIA) The airport (http://kotakinabaluairport.com) is 7km south of the centre in the Kepayan district. A shuttle bus (daily 8am–8.30pm; every 45min) runs from here to Merdeka Field, although getting a Grab cab is a useful alternative if you're travelling with others, as it may work out cheaper per person. Official taxis make the trip to the centre at fixed rates.

Destinations Bandar Seri Begawan (1–2 daily; 40min); Bintulu (1 daily; 1hr 15min); Johor Bahru (2–3 daily; 2hr

15min); Kota Baru (3 weekly; 2hr 30min); Kuala Lumpur (1–3 hourly; 2hr 30min); Kuching (6 daily; 1hr 25min); Kudat (3 weekly; 40min); Labuan (3 daily; 30min); Lahad Datu (4 daily; 55min); Lawas (2 weekly; 45min); Limbang (3 weekly; 45min); Miri (4–5 daily; 55min); Mulu (1 daily; 55min); Penang (3 daily; 1hr 40min); Sandakan (6–7 daily; 40min); Sibu (1–2 daily; 1hr 35min); Singapore (3 daily; 2hr 20min); Tawau (12 daily; 55min).

BY BUS

City Bus Terminal North (Inanam) In the Inanam suburb a whopping 11km east of the centre, this bus terminal is used by buses to the east coast. Note that for Tawau, there are also buses via Keningau and the interior from Merdeka Field, which are often quicker even with the variable state of the road. Bus #4 (approximately 2 hourly; 40min) runs south from the Shangri-La bus stop in the city centre and then east to Inanam (heading into town, it's a short walk south from the terminal to the main road). Taxis and Grab cabs are good options too.
Destinations Lahad Datu (14 daily; 8hr); Sandakan (at least 12 daily; 6hr); Semporna (6 daily; 11hr 30min); Tawau (via the east coast; 7 daily; 11hr); Telupid (frequent; 4hr 30min).
Merdeka Field The Merdeka Field car park right in the city centre is used mainly by shared minivans and taxis, although a handful of buses also operate from here.
Destinations Keningau (frequent; 2hr 30min); Kota Belud (1 daily; 1hr 30min); Kudat (1 daily; 3hr 30min); Tawau (via the interior; 2 daily; at least 10hr); Tenom (4 daily; 3hr).
KK Sentral Buses for the border town of Menumbok (for Labuan Island ferries) and as far afield as Miri in Sarawak (not running at the time of writing, but they may return) depart from a nice, modern terminal close to the City Hall. There's also a Brunei service from here run by Sipitang Express (daily 8am; http://sipitangexpress.com.my).
Destinations Bandar Seri Begawan (Brunei; 1 daily; 7hr 30min); Beaufort (5 daily; 2hr); Menumbok (roughly hourly until 3pm; 2hr 30min); Miri (1 daily; 11hr).

BY MINIVAN AND SHARED TAXI

Minivans and shared taxis serve towns within about 4hr of KK from Merdeka Field, in all directions; signs indicate where each cluster of vehicles is bound. Taxis may fill up more promptly and are quicker generally. The cost is similar, although minivans are generally slightly cheaper.
Destinations Beaufort (2hr); Keningau (2hr); Kinabalu Park (2hr); Kota Belud (2hr); Kuala Penyu (for Pulau Tiga Park; 2hr 30min); Kudat (4hr); Menumbok (for Labuan ferries; 3hr); Ranau (3hr); Tambunan (1hr 45min); Tenom (3hr).

BY FERRY

Jesselton Point Ferry Terminal The terminal (http://jesseltonpoint.com.my) is at the north end of Jalan Haji Saman. Services run to Labuan Island (3–7 weekly; 2hr 30min); if you're aiming to reach Brunei, departures will usually get you there in time for an onward ferry, though do check. In addition, the Island Hop Express makes shorter trips to islands near KK; these are usually used by locals looking for a beach escape and a spot of snorkelling.

BY TRAIN

Tanjung Aru station The train station is a gleaming affair just off the highway, 5km southwest of central KK (088 279300), and provides a limited service. Any bus from Marina Court bound for Kepayan, Petagas or Putatan will pass close by, and they may detour into the station on request.
Destinations Beaufort (2 daily; 2hr); Papar (2 daily; 45min); Kinarut (2 daily; 20min).

GETTING AROUND

By bus or minivan Within the centre itself, there are three looping city bus services (#A, #B and #C), though there's little reason to use them given the compactness of the place. Buses and minivans more often display the suburb where they terminate rather than a route number.
By taxi A journey within the centre won't cost too much at all; taxis park up in little clusters all over the area. Grab cabs are generally better value.
By car Companies include Extra Rent A Car, based at the Sabah Oriental Hotel off Jalan Kemajuan (088 251529, http://e-erac-online.com); Hertz, at the airport (088 413326, http://hertz.com); and Borneo Kinabalu Elegant Tours, on the ground floor of Wisma Sabah shopping mall (012 502 0608).

INFORMATION

Sabah Parks Ground floor, Block H, KK Times Square (Mon–Thurs 8.30am–1pm & 2–5pm, Fri 8.30–11.30am & 2–5pm; 088 523500, http://sabahparks.org.my). Information on Sabah's state parks, including nitty-gritty details of facilities and so forth.
Sabah Tourism Board 51 Gaya Street (Mon–Fri 8am–5pm, Sat & Sun 9am–4pm; 088 212121, http://sabahtourism.com). Pick the brains of the knowledgeable, well-organized staff here as much as you can, because Sabah Tourism has no offices in any other towns. Their free tourist map of KK, although sketchy, can be handy for the suburbs.
Tourism Malaysia At the airport (daily 8am–11pm; 088 413359, http://malaysia.travel).
Events KK can seem like a cultural desert most of the year, but towards the end of May there are performances for Kaamatan (see box, page 379). The city also hosts annual film (http://kkiff.com) and jazz (http://facebook.com/KKJazzFestival) festivals. For a list of cinemas, see page 380.

ACCOMMODATION

SEE MAP PAGE 372

KK has a great selection of hostels and hotels, though many long-established budget places found themselves forced to close during the Covid pandemic, and decent replacements have been thin on the ground so far. If it's hotels you're after, it's worth booking at least a couple of weeks in advance as hotels can be unpredictably packed out if there are lots of tour groups or a major conference in town. Note that practically all the **budget hotels** cluster in Kampung Air, a district local people consider seedy and possibly rough at night. It can certainly be rowdy into the small hours, which is as good a reason as any not to stay here, given the poor sound insulation of most cheap hotels. As for hostels, there are two

KOTA KINABALU TOUR OPERATORS

KK has plenty of handy **tour operators**, many based in Wisma Sabah shopping mall on Jalan Tun Fuad Stephens. Their offerings are usually pricey, but can be worthwhile for destinations that are tricky to arrange independently or if you want to see several places in a short space of time. The companies are also useful for arranging **day-trips** from KK, such as wildlife cruises or firefly-watching at the Klias Peninsula, and rafting on the Padas or Kiulu rivers; a few firms even run their own resorts or attractions.

Adventure Alternative Borneo Orangutan Tattoo Parlour, Lorong Dewan; http://adventurealternative borneo.com. Specializes in off-the-beaten-track destinations such as the Deramakot Forest Reserve and Imbak Canyon. You can also try contacting their Kuching office (see page 311).

Bike Borneo Second floor, Block C, City Mall, Damai, 4km southeast of the centre; http://bikeborneo.com.my. Offers mountain-biking escapades, including a three-day tour of the foothills of Kinabalu and another that combines a riverside ride with rafting.

Borneo Divers Ninth floor, Menara Jubili, 53 Gaya Street; http://borneodivers.com.my. Diving specialist with its own resort on Mabul (see page 416) and a dive school at the Tunku Abdul Rahman Park – they offer packages at both plus Sipadan Island.

Borneo Dream Tanjung Aru Plaza; http://borneo dream.com. A little bit of everything – unusually for a place without the word "diving" in its name, they specialize in undersea matters, though they also run trips up the Kinabatangan River, tours of the Danum Valley, excursions up Mount Kinabalu, and more besides.

★ **Borneo Eco Tours** Kolombong Jaya Industrial Estate, off Jalan Kolombong; http://borneoecotours.com. Inconveniently sited out towards Inanam, they run the excellent *Sukau Rainforest Lodge* on the Kinabatangan River and a "farmstay" at Kiulu, northeast of KK, where residents can combine trekking with a taste of rice cultivation. Otherwise, they cover all the standard destinations, with birding tours a forte.

Borneo Trails First floor, Wisma Sabah; http://borneo trails.com. Has an unusually wide range of day-trips, including mangrove cruises and visits to the Kota Belud Sunday *tamu*, plus standard packages elsewhere.

Like Scuba Center Nosoob Food Court, Penampang; likescubacenter.com. Rather bravely based nowhere near the sea, this outfit nevertheless offers a good range of dive courses, plus packages at Tunku Abdul Rahman Park, the islands off Semporna, Lankayan Island off Sandakan, and Labuan's waters.

Nasalis Larvatus Second floor, 56 Lorong Bandaran Berjaya 5; http://insabah.com. Titled after the scientific name for proboscis monkeys, this firm has its own accommodation at the Kinabatangan River, Sepilok and Libaran Island, and sells a full range of nature tours.

★ **River Junkie/Scuba Junkie** Ground floor, Wisma Sabah; http://river-junkie.com & scubajunkiekk.com. Sibling firms with a growing range of eco/nature tours, including the Maliau Basin, Mount Trus Madi climbs and the Sapulut community tourism project, plus rafting trips, and diving and snorkelling off Semporna.

Sticky Rice Travel Third floor, 134 Gaya Street; http://stickyricetravel.com. Ecotourism specialist offering the usual attractions plus lesser-known ones, including the Tabin reserve of eastern Sabah, a multi-day trek in Kinabalu Park, plus climbing and trekking in the Crocker range.

Sutera Sanctuary Lodges Ground floor, Wisma Sabah; http://suterasanctuarylodges.com.my. Offers climbing packages at Kinabalu Park, where they run much of the accommodation; that aside, they operate a resort at the Tunku Abdul Rahman Park.

Traverse Tours Second floor, Wisma Sabah; http://riverbug.asia. Has diving trips to Sepanggar Island just outside the Tunku Abdul Rahman park, where they run their own accommodation, with a similar offering at Mantanani Island much further north (see page 390). They operate the Mari Mari Cultural Village, too, while their Riverbug wing sells the usual rafting packages.

TYK Adventure Tours Second floor, Wisma Sabah; http://tykadventuretours.com. A lengthy roster of tours available, most notably a cycling tour that covers part of Sandakan's death-march route (see page 403).

little **backpacker enclaves** abutting the ridge of Signal Hill, at Australia Place and further south in the Bandaran Berjaya neighbourhood, both convenient for Merdeka Field.

HOSTELS

★ **Faloe Hostel** KK Times Square; http://facebook.com/faloehostel. One of the most modern hostels in town, and already up there with the most popular, on account of dorms as pretty as they are comfortable, good service and information, and nice hangout areas (including one that's good for beers, and another that's good for movies). The ideal hostel. $

★ **Homy Seafront Hostel** Warisan Square; http://facebook.com. Excellent choice by the seafront, with large windows gazing straight at the sea from the common room, which has been decorated almost along what you might call your-cool-mate's-lounge lines. There are dorm berths, but they have more private rooms than most hostels hereabouts; facilities are usually shared, in any case, including clean toilet and shower facilities, and a decent kitchen. $

Signel Poshtel 120 Jalan Gaya; signel.com.my. Calling themselves "The rare gem of North Borneo" is talking a big game, but this place isn't all mouth and no trousers – private rooms and common areas have been decorated in a manner that one might even call "posh", while even the dorms have been given a fun, fresh style. There's an on-site laundrette, and a TV room that might make you wonder why your own lounge doesn't look as appealing. $$

Step-In Lodge Block L, Sinsuran Complex; http://.com/stepinlodgekotakinabalu. A homely, buzzing hostel a stone's throw from the waterfront, with an airy lounge and a plant-decked balcony for a bird's-eye view of proceedings below in the bustling Sinsuran district. There's a choice of dorms and private rooms, all with a/c, though prices are a bit higher than at the competition. Dorms $, doubles $$

★ **Toojou** 12 Jalan Masjid Lama; http://toojou.com. Billing itself a "social" hostel, this is your best pick if you'd like to meet new travel companions – there are plenty of social areas both in the hostel and within its home building, including a café, bar and pool room. Things look fresh and modern throughout, with murals inside and on the outer wall, and a very sleek vibe. $

Vibrant Hostel KK Times Square; 011 2669 5665. One of KK's flashier, more modern hostels, eschewing the generic backpacker look for bare lightbulbs, a cosy lounge with a sofa and smart TV, and some very decent bedding. There's a kitchen for guest use, and a 24hr convenience store downstairs. $

HOTELS AND RESORTS

Eden 54 54 Gaya Street; http://eden54.com. "Stark opulence" is how staff have styled this place, but forgive them the oxymoron; rooms feature tasteful modern decor and there's a surprisingly large lounge, too. Note that the cheapest rooms, including the singles, are windowless. $$

Horizon Jalan Tun Razak; http://horizonhotelsabah.com. A massive block somewhat on its own and hard to miss, but a little disappointing inside, with a charmless lobby and rooms in often gloomy hues, some with old photos blown up across entire walls. The restaurants, gym, spa and sixth-floor pool make the rates half-bearable. $$$

★ **Hyatt Regency** Jalan Datuk Salleh Sulong; http://kinabalu.regency.hyatt.com. Five-star comforts just metres from the waterfront, boasting oodles of restaurants, a wonderful swimming pool with sunset views and well-appointed rooms. $$$$

Jesselton 69 Gaya Street; http://jesseltonhotel.com. The oldest hotel in town – not that it means much in a city like KK – with Lady Mountbatten and Muhammad Ali among former guests. The place is reasonably well run, but in truth it looks a little frumpy next to newer upstarts. $$$

Kinabalu Daya 9 Jalan Pantai; http://kinabaludayahotel.com. A well-established, serviceable affair with snug, en-suite rooms, a ground-floor café and street-side bar. $$

Klagan Warisan Square, Jalan Tun Fuad Stephens; http://theklagan.com. This mid-range hotel, part of a small local chain, offers a bit more character than much of the competition. Rooms have big, red designer chairs and swanky bathrooms, and there's also a rooftop restaurant (rates usually include breakfast). $$

Le Meridien Jalan Tun Fuad Stephens; http://lemeridien kotakinabalu.com. A convenient location and sumptuous facilities, including high-spec rooms, pool, spa and gym. The rooms here have been fitted out along sleek lines (the same goes for the lobby, which looks especially cool in the evening), and the bathrooms can be colossal. $$$$

★ **Little Gaya** 52 Gaya Street; 088 261838. Like its next-door neighbour, Eden 54, this just about counts as a boutique hotel and has a range of rooms, the cheaper ones windowless. There's a more spacious feel here, though, as the bathrooms are only half-walled off so the sink area blends into the rest of the room. $$

Maxim Bandaran Berjaya; 088 262811. A small, decent budget option, with blandly modern rooms (ones with windows cost extra). $

Shangri-La Tanjung Aru Tanjung Aru, nearly 4km southwest of the centre; http://shangri-la.com. Perched on the beach at the tip of the headland, this luxury resort has everything you'd expect of a *Shangri-La*: rolling, landscaped grounds, two pools, a gym, tennis courts, water sports, plus several high-class food outlets and bars. There's also the eleven-hole Kinabalu Golf Club just nearby. $$$$

Sixty3 63 Gaya Street; http://hotelsixty3.com. Opposite the tourist office, this newish, rather bland affair has the usual range of rooms around a narrow rectangular atrium, but no restaurant. Good value, so often full. $$$

Sutera Harbour Resort Sutera Harbour, right at the southwest end of the centre; http://suteraharbour.com. This development is so vast it has its own shuttle buses to whiz guests around. Besides a marina and golf course, it features two hotels: the palatial *Magellan* and the comparatively humble five-star *Pacific*; the latter is topped by a worthy bar (*Horizons Sky Bar*; see page 379), but both feature enormous pool complexes, water sports and a spa. $$$$

EATING SEE MAP PAGE 372

KK has a decent range of **restaurants** and *kopitiams*, although international cuisine is somewhat lagging. Some worthwhile places are tucked away in malls; by contrast, the glitzy ones at the Waterfront development tend to be overpriced and mediocre. Locally run **indie cafés** are popping up all over, but especially at Australia Place (Lorong Dewan), where quite a few have names reflecting the area's past association with the printing industry.

RESTAURANTS

Chilli Vanilla 35 Jalan Haji Saman; http://facebook.com. A truly eclectic restaurant, with Middle Eastern-ish tiles and a menu that takes in goulash and chicken schnitzel (the owner is Hungarian), tortillas, Moroccan lamb stew, burgers and more. With something for almost everyone, the place is popular with travellers and locals alike. The weekday set lunch is particularly good value. $$$

D'Malindo Café 205A, second floor, Wisma Merdeka, Jalan Tun Razak; http://facebook.com/dmalindokk. This hidden-away, no-frills place serves a terrific *nasi campur* spread of Malay and some Bornean food – such as "Sabah vegetable", vaguely spinach-like greens more properly called *sayur manis*. $

★ **El Centro** 32 Jalan Haji Saman; 014 862 3877. This compact restaurant and bar (see page 379) with multicoloured lights on the walls has become a favourite hangout for tourists and expats alike. There are ample portions of food from all over (Mondays feature Mexican specials, for example). $$$

Grazie Third floor, Suria Sabah Mall; http://facebook.com/graziekk. Authentic wood-fired, thin-crust pizzas, pasta and other dishes, plus a good range of Italian wines and liqueurs, all served in a winning location overlooking the sea – if the weather agrees, and you don't mind concrete underneath your feet, grab one of the tables on the outdoor patio. $$$

Jothy's Fish Head Curry G9, Lorong Api-Api 1, Api-Api Centre; http://facebook.com/JothysFishHeadCurry. Excellent South Indian establishment serving satisfying *dosai* and a variety of delicious curries, including a classic fish-head variety. Their filleted chicken 65 is also a hit. $$

Mamasita 15 Lorong Dewan; http://mamasita.my. Popular Mexican restaurant and tapas bar, whose sombrero lightshades are a nice touch. The interior is as fresh and colourful as you'd expect a Mexican restaurant to be, and the usual roster of tacos, burritos, enchiladas and quesadillas are all present and correct. Plenty of margaritas and tequilas to wash them down with too. $$$

★ **The Native Cafe** 8km south of the centre, off Route 500; http://facebook.com/mynative.sabah. Quite some way from the centre it may be (just take a cab), this marvellous Kadazan/Dusun restaurant is your best bet for Indigenous Sabah food. Come for the terrific buffets (lunch, or dinner with a cultural show) with dishes like pineapple chicken and samosas filled with *hinava* (raw fish salad). The accompaniments include reddish hill rice and *ambuyat*, the gluey sago staple also beloved in Brunei. Leave space for stodgy desserts such as stewed pumpkin in coconut milk, and perhaps imbibe some *lihing* (a rice brandy) too. If you're feeling really brave, try one of the *butod* (sago grubs), either eaten live and whole or baked into their *butod* pizza, in which case the cheese conveniently masks any larval flavours. $$$$

★ **Welcome Seafood** Ground floor, Star City complex, off Jalan Tunku Abdul Rahman; http://wsr.com.my. Massive Chinese restaurant that's a little out of the way, but better value than its more prominent rivals in Kampung Air. There are open-air and a/c sections, and plenty of live fish and crustaceans in dozens of tanks, priced by weight. If you eschew the seafood, a slap-up meal can be quite affordable, but otherwise you'd better bring plenty of cash. $$$$

Yee Fung 127 Gaya Street; 088 312042. One of several old-school Chinese *kopitiams* here with a devoted following, in this case for their claypot chicken rice and laksa – it's not uncommon to spot people lining up here at various times of day. $

CAFÉS AND DESSERTS

Mizumizu Coffee 115 Jalan Gaya; http://mizumizu.coffee. So good they named it twice, after the Japanese word for water ("*mizu*"); appropriately, as well as good coffee, you can get matcha here, in tea, latte or cake form, as well as *hōjicha* (another kind of Japanese green tea), loads of desserts, and more besides. $$

October 13 Lorong Dewan; http://instagram.com/octobercoffeegaya. This Korean-owned chain is among the best cafés at Australia Place. Go for the house blend (roasted by the boss himself) or a single-origin coffee to accompany one of the scrumptious cakes or (daytime only) snacks such as the Korean omelette toasted sandwich. $$

STREET FOOD AND HAWKER CENTRES

Akina Night Market Pasar Sinsuran, Jalan Tun Fuad Stephens. Next door to the handicraft market, dozens of stalls set up in the evening, either part of a frenetic seafood market or selling barbecued fish, grilled meat and other delights. You can have a full meal with accompanying rice and vegetables or just grab some chicken on a stick or even a Bajau snack like *koci* (conical rice dumplings). $

★ **Fook Yuen** Ground floor, Menara Jubili, 53 Gaya

KAAMATAN

Kaamatan is to Sabah's Kadazan/Dusun what *gawai* is to Sarawak's Iban, a rice harvest festival culminating in **public holidays** on 30 and 31 May. As ever people try to return to their longhouses or villages for the event, with much quaffing of the usual rice-based alcoholic drinks; inevitably, malls get into the spirit too, sporting decorations styled after steamed rice cakes and ears of grains. Most importantly, at the Kadazan/Dusun Cultural Assocation (**KDCA**; http://kdca.org.my) in the KK suburb of Penampang, there's a gradual build-up in festivities from mid-May, with arm-wrestling and cookery contests, and sometimes even buffalo races. The climax is a two-day jamboree of music and dance, kicking off on 30 May with **sugandoi**, a traditional singing competition. The following day sees the **Unduk Ngadau pageant**, with women in Indigenous costume vying to be chosen as the individual who embodies the qualities of Huminodun, a mythical figure; smaller versions of it are staged even in longhouses. The KDCA events aren't ticketed, so get the latest details from Sabah Tourism (see page 375) if you'd like to attend.

Street; 088 743406. A mini-food court and bakery rolled into one, this cafeteria chain deserves an award for sheer convenience. Noodles, rice, cooked dishes, dim sum, breads and cakes are all laid out at different counters; nearly everything is self-service apart from toast, eggs and drinks, which are made to order (watch for your order number to come up on the screen once you've paid the cashier). Only slightly more expensive than a standard *kedai kopi*. $

Jesselton Point Hawker Centre Jesselton Point, Jalan Haji Saman. These stalls – also known as the "Todak Waterfront" centre, roar to life in the evenings selling satay, fried fish and other popular dishes. There's even an Aussie steakhouse and the seating is pleasantly alfresco, looking out over the harbour toward the islands. $

DRINKING   SEE MAP PAGE 372

Although there are a few good **bars**, KK is not noted for its **nightlife**. However, there has been a recent glut of rooftop bars – as well as Horizons below, most five-star hotels have a bar with a view (and, occasionally, a pool).

999 Jalan Haji Yaacob; 088 283889. The most over-the-top club you'll ever see, in a converted cinema with Corinthian columns and statues of centurions outside. The interior is hangar-like and sometimes hosts live bands in addition to DJs. No dress code, but pricey drinks.

Biru-Biru 24 Lorong Dewan; http://instagram.com/birubirucafe. Informal venue with an old-fashioned Malay/Chinese signboard and quirky décor, including an old bicycle stuck to one wall. A good selection of beers and spirits, plus light bites, salsa sessions and acoustic and open-mic nights keep travellers and locals happy.

El Centro 32 Jalan Haji Saman; 014 862 3877. This restaurant (see page 378) also makes a great bar, with a good selection of well-priced beers, wine and cocktails. Keep an eye out for regular quiz nights.

Horizons Sky Bar Sutera Pacific Hotel, Sutera Harbour; http://suteraharbour.com. Twelfth-floor sky bar and sigar lounge that remains the best bar-with-a-view in town, despite increased competition. For a start, the views are excellent and unobstructed, and even those without edge seats will get to enjoy the vistas. Secondly, the drinks on offer are also of high quality, though of course they won't come cheap.

The Shamrock 1664 Jalan Tun Fuad Stephen. Fairly generic Irish-pub-in-Asia, though one that's located right by the sea – the outdoor seats make a wonderful place for a sundowner, since the sunsets can be magical.

SHOPPING   SEE MAP PAGE 372

BOOKS

The Borneo Shop Ground floor, Wisma Merdeka, Jalan Haji Saman; http://borneo.bio.link. Head to this shop for specialist books on Borneo, including titles published by the KK-based National History Publications.

Popular Bookstore Level 3, Suria Sabah Mall; http://popular.com.my. For general books and magazines, try this large bookstore.

CAMPING AND OUTDOOR EQUIPMENT

KK is a good place to stock up for a Kinabalu climb or exploits elsewhere in the country.

Montanic Adventure Basement level, Suria Sabah; http://montanic.com. Sells high-end branded rucksacks, anoraks and camping equipment. Also has a branch on the first floor of Imago mall.

Mr DIY Level 1, Imago mall; http://mydiy.com. Nationwide chain selling household items, also great for head torches, water bottles, cycling gloves and other basics.

Outdoor Gear Level 3, Centre Point; 088 260 585. Cheap but with a limited range of products.

MALLS

It's not hard to notice there's a glut of malls in KK, which means only a handful are thriving.

Centre Point Mall Jalan Tun Razak; http://centrepoint sabah.com. The busiest of the Asian-style shopping complexes, housing small stores.

Imago Mall Just beyond the KK Times Square office complex; http://imago.my. This enormous, Western-style mall is the very best of the lot, and it's packed with major stores and franchises.

Suria Sabah Mall Opposite Wisma Sabah; http://suria sabah.com.my. KK's second best mall, with the usual range of eating outlets and boutiques.

SOUVENIRS AND CRAFTS

Make a beeline for the Gaya Street Sunday market, offering a host of interesting local products including instruments such as the *sompoton* (like pan pipes stuck to a gourd) and handmade soaps containing unusual ingredients such as seaweed. Items sold at the handicraft market are of variable quality and may originate in the Philippines or Indonesia. Grocery shops on Gaya Street, plus Kadaiku and stalls at the central market, stock edibles made with local produce, including chocolate and Tenom coffee.

The Borneo Shop Ground floor, Wisma Merdeka, Jalan Haji Saman; borneo.bio.link. This bookstore also has some textiles and beadwork.

Kadaiku Block L, Sinsuran; http://kadaiku.com. Kitsch orangutan and proboscis monkey soft toys infest the wares of Kadaiku, a Sabah Tourism subsidiary, though they also sell handicrafts, including woven textiles; the tourist office has a small selection of these and other items.

SUPERMARKETS

Bataras Third floor, Suria Sabah; http://bataras.com.my. Has the widest range of local and imported produce, including alcoholic beverages. Other branches around the city.

Tong Hing 55 Gaya Street; 088 230 300. Specializes in imported products but is expensive, although many swear by its bakery's bread.

DIRECTORY

Banks Gaya Street and nearby streets are littered with banks, including HSBC and Maybank. Both Suria Sabah and Imago malls have ATMs.

Cinemas Some films are screened in English at the Growball Cinemax in Centre Point Mall (http://growball.com), and Golden Screen Cinemas (http://gsc.com.my) at Suria Sabah and in Imago Mall.

Consulates Indonesia, Lorong Kemajuan, off Jalan Kemajuan in the southwest corner of the centre (088 218600).

Hospitals and clinics The state-run Queen Elizabeth Hospital is beyond the Sabah State Museum, on Jalan Penampang (088 517555); closer in is the private Gleneagles (088 518888), just beyond KK Times Square. For a routine consulation, head to the private Permai Polyclinics, 4 Jalan Pantai (24hr; 088 232100); a doctor will usually see you within 30min.

Laundry Both Bandaran Berjaya and Lorong Dewan have laundries close to the hostels, and coin-operated affairs have popped up in various locations all over the centre.

Pharmacies In addition to the pharmacies in many malls, there's a handy branch of Guardian on Jalan Gaya.

Police The main police station is below Atkinson's Clock Tower (088 247111).

Visa extensions Immigration Department, UTC Building, Jalan Belia, off Jalan Tunku Abdul Rahman (Mon–Thurs 8.30am–5pm, Fri 8.30–11.30am & 2–5pm; 088 270 586); it's a walkable 1.5km from Merdeka Field.

Around Kota Kinabalu

There are a number of attractions and activities available around KK, including **Mari Mari Cultural Village** and **Monsopiad Cultural Village** for a dose of local culture; you could also consider a ride on the pricey **North Borneo railway** (see page 383). Most popular of all, however, are the beaches of **Tunku Abdul Rahman Park** just offshore.

Tunku Abdul Rahman Park

3km west of KK • Charge; extra for diving permit • http://sabahparks.gov.my

Named after Malaysia's first prime minister, **Tunku Abdul Rahman Park** contains five islands representing the most westerly ripples of the Crocker mountains. Their forests, beaches and coral reefs lie within 8km of KK, with marine park territory as close as 3km off the mainland; snorkelling, diving, watersports and more unusual **activities** are available. Such is the park's appeal that **Manukan Island** in particular is often overrun. This isn't to say you can't have an enjoyable day-trip either on one island or, as many people do, on one in the morning and another in the afternoon – but don't expect total calm unless you stay the night at one of the park's pricey **resorts**. Manukan aside, only **Sapi** and **Mamutik** islands are served by regular boats.

Manukan Island

Crescent-shaped **Manukan Island** is in the centre of the group. The most developed of the islands, it has become something of a victim of its own success, with tour-group parties hogging stretches of beach and departing day-trippers struggling to make their way through at the little jetty, assuming they can even spot the right boat. Among plus points, the island boasts a lengthy beach and there are upmarket meals, including buffet lunches, to be had at the *Manukan Island Resort*, although many settle for cheap food at the Sabah Parks co-op restaurant next door. If you tire of the beach, you could try the island's **marine education centre** or the **aquarium**, or hike wooded paths signed at the edge of the resort area; one heads up a ridge to the other side of the island, and the other goes 1.5km west along the island's length to Sunset Point.

Mamutik Island

Southeast of Manukan, tiny **Mamutik Island** is a snorkeller's delight. The island is surrounded by coral gardens, with the best stretch off the beach to the southwest towards the back of where the boat drops you, but to reach it it's necessary either to clamber over rocks or to swim right round. Borneo Divers (see page 416) has its own diving school on the island; head out early if you plan to dive, as it's much more cost-effective to do two or three dives than just one.

Sulug Island

Southwest of Manukan, **Sulug Island** is the quietest island in Tunku Abdul Rahman Park: hardly any public boats come, although the dive operators bring their customers here to spot the plentiful marine life, including turtles and moray eels among others, amid healthy corals.

Gaya Island

The largest island in the group is **Gaya Island**, a fifteen-minute boat ride north of Manukan. The site of the British North Borneo Chartered Company's abortive settlement before Jesselton was founded, the island initially seems a mass of jungle and anything but developed, but it actually holds three out of the park's four resorts. Although the closest island to KK, Gaya doesn't feature on standard island-hopping routes; visitors can simply take any boat to neighbouring Sapi and ask to be dropped off across the channel. If you do make it over, you'll find idyllic stretches of sand such as **Police Bay Beach**, as well as jungle **trails** where you might see proboscis monkeys and hornbills.

Sapi Island

Little **Sapi Island**, off the southwest tip of Gaya, has a very decent beach and so draws an equally decent crowd, meaning it has reasonable facilities without feeling quite as packed as Manukan. Beachside outfits offer diving (including taster sessions) as well as snorkelling gear for rent, and food is generally cheaper here than on Manukan, with a small café for basic meals (daily 8am–4pm). If you head generally rightwards from the jetty, you will come to a very short, gently uphill trail hugging the shore, where you might well see monitor lizards before the track halts at the end-point of the **Coral Flyer** zip line from Gaya (see page 382).

ARRIVAL AND DEPARTURE TUNKU ABDUL RAHMAN PARK

By boat A dozen or so operators run boats to Manukan, Mamutik and Sapi from the Jesselton Point Ferry Terminal (departures from around 8.30am, last boat back leaves around 5pm). Try to get there by 9.30am, if not earlier, as the first set of departures sell out quickly and you may not get your preferred outward (or return) slot if you're tardy.

Prices vary slightly between operators, and you can pay for one island, two or all three. The operator should explain the arrangements for island-hopping and returning. You might also be able to charter a boat for one island. Some boat firms and other companies at the terminal also arrange activities; rent your snorkelling gear at the terminal if you plan to go to more than one island.

ACTIVITIES

Jetskiing and parasailing Jetskiing (30min) and parasailing (10min) are among the watersports available at Manukan, Sapi and Mamutik islands, through operators like Sea Quest Tours (http://facebook.com/SeaQuestSabah).

Seawalking This peculiar activity has people donning what look like astronaut suits with air piped in from above, in order to spend half an hour wandering the sea floor. One operator has an office at the beach on Sapi, and Sea Quest Tours (http://facebook.com/SeaQuestSabah) can arrange this as well.

Snorkelling and diving Snorkelling and, to a lesser extent, diving are worthwhile around the islands, with a decent amount of marine life around though the health of the coral is variable. Beachside outfits rent snorkelling equipment; diving packages can be arranged in advance with tour operators in KK (see page 376) or on Manukan, Sapi and Mamutik.

Zip lining It's possible to descend, from high above the sea, from Gaya to Sapi using the Coral Flyer zip line, billed as the longest inter-island line of its kind (seek out the team near the Sapi jetty or enquire on http://sipadan.com). The experience is brief, but then it's the adrenaline rush you're really forking out for; unfortunately, the line was closed at the time of writing, with no word on when, or even if, it would reopen.

ACCOMMODATION

The price codes for **resorts** here represent the cost during high season if booked early, and include breakfast and boat transfers except where stated; discounts of around twenty percent may be available at other times. **Camping** is allowed on Gaya, Mamutik and Sapi (small charge for permits; tents may be available to rent, but it's better to have your own).

Bungaraya Island Resort Gaya; http://echoresorts.com/bungaraya. Offers luxurious timber villas hidden away within the forest; rooms are spacious and some feature their own jacuzzi or mini-pool. There's a gym and spa, and guests can partake of activities at their sister *Gayana Marine Resort*. $$$$

Gaya Island Resort Gaya; http://gayaislandresort.com. A lavish affair blending contemporary design with traditional elements, nestled neatly into a bay on Gaya's north shore. There's a spa, pool, dive shop and several restaurants of course, and the resort also has its own marine conservation centre. Price excludes boat transfers. $$$$

Gayana Marine Resort Gaya; http://echoresorts.com/gayana. This resort has attractive chalets, many built out over the sea, with its own dive shop and marine conservation centre where guests can get involved in simple projects. $$$$

Manukan Island Resort Manukan; http://sutera sanctuarylodges.com.my. Features small, somewhat characterless units resembling little houses. Unusually, the beach units are cheaper; the "hillside" ones are fancier and more removed from the noise of day-trippers. Price excludes boat transfers. $$$$

Monsopiad Heritage Village

13km south of KK on Jalan Putatan Ramayah, Penampang • Charge; extra for tour and cultural show • http://bit.ly/Monsopiad • Bus #13 (or minivan) south to Donggongon, then a Terawi-bound bus

Themed around the tale of a legendary head-hunter, the **Monsopiad Heritage Village** provides an introduction to the history and traditions of the Kadazan/Dusun people. The star attraction is a hut where Monsopiad's grisly harvest of 42 skulls is displayed, although you can also sample rice wine and test your blowpipe skills. If you've paid for the full experience, knowledgeable guides will explain traditions such as the rituals practised by the *bobohizan* (priestess), and there'll be a dance show to take in too.

Mari Mari Cultural Village

18km east of KK, Kionsom • Compulsory tours (3 daily; 2hr) • Charge (a little more in the evening); day-trips including transport plus one meal available, or in the evening with an additional fire-breathing show; book through Traverse Tours, which runs the village (see page 376), or other KK tour operators • http://marimariculturalvillage.my

Mari Mari Cultural Village has more of an orchestrated theme park feel than the Monsopiad Heritage Village, and unlike Monsopiad it tries to cover a broad sweep of

> **THROWBACK RAIL JOURNEYS**
>
> Sabah's tiny rail network features two contrasting journeys that might be worth considering. One uses a specially built **steam train** running from Tanjung Aru station (see page 375) to the small town of Papar (2 weekly; 4hr; price includes breakfast and lunch on board). Billed as the **North Borneo Railway**, this is a semi-luxurious 66km round trip using a wood-burning British Vulcan, plus five carriages constructed to a vintage design in the 1970s. In truth they're the most attractive thing about the trip, as the scenery isn't much to write home about; if you're keen, ask at KK's various travel agencies (see page 376) for ticketing and advice.
>
> The other noteworthy journey involves the branch line between the town of **Beaufort** and agricultural **Tenom** in the southern interior (see page 421). This is an ordinary passenger service (2 daily in each direction; 2hr 30min), distinguished by the antiquated, very basic carriages and the fact that the line shadows the **Padas river valley**; indeed rafting packages often include the train ride as a prelude. With endearingly rural scenes en route, there's something for non-railway buffs as well. Whichever direction you do it in, be aware that there were no sensible connections at Beaufort, so a day-trip will require two bus journeys at either end unless you stay the night (Tenom is far preferable to Beaufort).

several of Sabah's ethnic groups, with recreations of their traditional houses on site. It sometimes feels a little phoney, but if you take it in the right spirit, you will come away both entertained and educated. Activities and demonstrations include rice-wine tasting, starting a fire using bamboo, making the lacy sweet fritter *kuih jala* and using a blowpipe; for this option, a buffet lunch, tea or dinner is thrown in too.

The southwest coast

The coast southwest of KK, inhabited in particular by the Bisaya and Kedayan ethnic groups, is a largely mundane area. The **Klias Peninsula** here is prime country for **day-trips** organized by tour operators in KK, whether for rafting or wildlife watching. Offshore is **Tiga Island**, the setting for the first series of the TV show *Survivor*.

Kota Kinabalu to the Klias Peninsula

The first town of any size on the coast road is **Kinarut**, with a smattering of factories and a decent beachside resort; it's here, some 20km southwest of Kota Kinabalu, that you finally feel you've left the environs of the city behind. The scenery soon turns much more rural until at **Papar**, around 15km further on, you're treated to vistas of paddy fields with the Crocker mountain range constantly looming to the east. An old-fangled railway bridge spanning the Papar River is the most memorable thing about the town itself. Another 15km on, the otherwise scraggly **Kimanis** boasts a gleaming petrochemical facility, processing Sabah's offshore oil and gas, and also marks the start of the road up and over the Crocker range to **Keningau** and the southern interior (see page 420). Within another 15km, the coast starts veering ever further away as the road enters the Klias Peninsula.

ACCOMMODATION — KOTA KINABALU TO THE KLIAS PENINSULA

Langkah Syabas Beach Resort Kampung Kinarut Laut; http://langkahsyabas.com.my. Appealing, small-scale beachfront resort, started by an Australian/Malaysian couple and attracting plenty of Antipodean guests. The older chalets are set in a garden and encircle the swimming pool, while the newer ones facing the sea cost fifty percent more. The restaurant does a popular Sunday roast, and they make their own surprisingly good cheese on the premises. Rates include breakfast. $$$

The Klias Peninsula

The gateway to the **Klias Peninsula** is the forgettable Padas River town of **BEAUFORT**, on the main KK road some 40km southwest of Kimanis and 65km from the border with Sarawak. Named after an early governor of British North Borneo, the town itself is utterly forgettable, distinguished only being the hub of Sabah's puny rail network. The Padas, however, is a fine choice for **whitewater rafting**, arranged through tour operators in KK, while the peninsula offers an excellent chance of spotting **proboscis monkeys** on the Garama or Klias rivers, or at Weston near the mouth of the Padas, with **fireflies** also visible at night. Note that although these locations may be signposted nearby, you can't just fetch up and get on a trip, as the boatmen work for the tour companies; however, some firms may offer a discount if you get here under your own steam.

Kuala Penyu

Around an hour northeast of Beaufort, or 45 minutes from Menumbok, at the northern point of the peninsula, **KUALA PENYU** is the departure point for **Pulau Tiga Park**. It's a simple grid of streets with little more than a few basic stores and *kedai kopis*.

Menumbok

The most westerly settlement on the Klias Peninsula, tiny **MENUMBOK** is notable only for its frequent boat connections with Labuan Island.

ARRIVAL AND DEPARTURE   KLIAS PENINSULA

BEAUFORT
By bus and minivan Buses and minivans park up at a tiny station opposite a yellow-domed mosque less than a 10min walk away from the east bank of the Padas River. There are services to KK (hourly; 2hr) and more sporadic ones to Menumbok and Kuala Penyu (1hr), plus Keningau (at least 2 daily; 2hr 30min).
By train Beaufort train station is on the east bank of the river. At the time of writing there were no convenient connections between trains on the Tanjung Aru line (2 daily; 2hr) and Tenom line (2 daily; 2hr 30min), whichever direction you're heading in, but it's still possible to visit or depart in this manner.

MENUMBOK
By bus Buses for KK leave roughly hourly (2hr 30min), but often delay departures considerably to await arriving ferries. There are also a couple of daily buses for Keningau in the interior (3hr 30min).
By minivan or shared taxi Minivans and shared taxis leave sporadically for KK (3hr), Beaufort (1hr) or Kuala Penyu (45min). If you can't find a vehicle to Kuala Penyu, catch a Beaufort one to the junction (*simpang*) for Kuala Penyu and try to flag down onward transport there.
By boat Speedboats (1–2 hourly; 20min) and car ferries (5–6 daily between 8am–8.30pm; 1hr 30min; price per person, plus per car) travel daily between Menumbok and Labuan Island; note that there's also a small ferry terminal tax.

KUALA PENYU
By minivan It takes just over 2hr to travel by minivan to KK's Merdeka Field bus stand from Kuala Penyu, or you can get a minivan to Beaufort. These vehicles leave from one block back from the jetty.

Pulau Tiga Park

Charge • A 20min boat ride from Kuala Penyu – the Survivor Lodge provides boats at 10am & 3pm for guests (non-guests can use these for a fee if arranged in advance) • http://sabahparks.org.my

> ### CROSSING INTO SARAWAK
> Note that because Sarawak maintains its own immigration controls, passports will be stamped by the authorities of both Sabah and Sarawak at the **Merapok border post**; the Sarawak stamp still entitles most visitors to a ninety-day stay in Malaysia. There will be one more border checkpoint to negotiate if Bandar Seri Begawan in Brunei is your final destination – add yet another if heading for Miri.

Nestled in the South China Sea 12km north of Kuala Penyu, **Pulau Tiga Park** is a beautiful and peaceful place that acquired a degree of fame in 2001 as the paradise location for the first series of the American reality TV show *Survivor*. It used to consist of three islands, one of which has since been reduced to a mere sand bar by wave erosion. Of the remaining two – **Tiga** and **Kalampunian Damit** – only the former holds accommodation; the latter is normally visited as part of a morning snorkelling trip from the *Survivor Lodge*.

Most visitors content themselves with relaxing on the sandy beaches and **snorkelling** or **diving** in the azure sea. It's possible to hike right around the jungle-cloaked island in six hours, but the paths are poorly maintained so it's best to check at the park office which ones are passable. The best is the easy twenty-minute walk to the centre of Tiga, which leads to a couple of **mud volcanoes**.

ACCOMMODATION AND EATING   PULAU TIGA PARK

In addition to the resort (and more of these may be developed), camping is allowed with your own tent (small charge for camping permit).

Borneo Eagle http://echoresorts.com/borneoeagle. Luxurious eco-resort with a collection of charming wooden villas; some boasting their own pool, though all are surrounded by expansive gardens, and you're never more than a short walk from the beach. On site you'll find a spa, a gym and a delightful swimming pool, as well as a surprisingly large selection of places to eat and drink; resort can also organise trekking, snorkelling and other activities. **$$$$**

Labuan Island

A short distance west of the Klias Peninsula, the 15km-long **LABUAN ISLAND** is surprisingly appealing, with wide, clean streets planted with flowering shrubs and a relaxed pace of life. It's striking how unlike Sabah the place feels, which is half-explained by the fact that it isn't part of Sabah at all, being instead **Federal Territory** – meaning it has the same administrative status as Kuala Lumpur. The rest of the explanation lies in the wealth generated by Labuan's offshore oil and gas, although the island has lately fallen on hard times with the plunge in crude oil prices. For now, Labuan is keeping up appearances, with its eponymous main town still offering decent accommodation, eating, nightlife and **duty-free** shopping. With far fewer oil workers passing through, the authorities are desperate for tourists to keep things going, and in truth the island isn't a bad place to spend a day or two en route between Brunei and Sabah; there are a few minor sights and **beaches**, and **wreck diving** is possible in Labuan's own **marine park**. Most sights outside Labuan Town are a little too far away to walk. Labuan has a basic bus network and taxis, but it's worth considering **cycling** around the island – there are proper cycle lanes on long stretches of the coastal road, and traffic isn't that heavy outside of peak hours. For details of transport and bike rental, see page 388.

Labuan Town

The main urban centre, simply called **LABUAN TOWN**, lies on the island's southeastern side. Despite its nondescript modern appearance, the town dates back to the mid-nineteenth century, when the British – having newly prised Labuan from the Brunei Sultanate – established a free port called Victoria here. Centred on the padang, with older quarters to the west, the town is pleasantly walkable, with a couple of museums to visit and a beach not far away to the northeast. Labuan Town is one of Malaysia's duty-free centres, but the selection of goods is rather more limited than at, say, Langkawi. Once you've browsed the imported chocolates, alcohol, perfumes and cigarettes on sale at the ferry terminal there's little to be gained by exploring outlets elsewhere in town.

Labuan Museum
Behind the Padang • Free • http://bit.ly/LabuanMuseum

> **DIVING AROUND TIGA**
>
> Tiga's prime dive site is probably **Asmara Point**, close to the Sabah Parks jetty. With a maximum depth of 10m it's a nice, easy dive, albeit sometimes with a slight current, with good coral attracting lionfish, Moorish idols and groupers, plus sometimes sea turtles. Other good sites include **Phukat Point** (where they very occasionally see white-tip sharks) and **Larai Point** (notable for its excellent coral). The dive shop at *Borneo Eagle* charges decent rates for the first dive (minimum of two people), excluding equipment rental, and also does Discover Scuba courses.

Although lacking in artefacts, the small, yellow **Labuan Museum** is worthy of an hour's visit. Downstairs, display boards offer a decent account of the island's history and constantly evolving political status: shunted from Brunei to the East India Company, then the British North Borneo Chartered Company, then the Straits Settlements, then Sabah – which it left in the 1980s to become Federal Territory. Displays upstairs outline the customs of Labuan's various ethnic groups including the largest, the Kedayan.

Marine Museum

1.5km east of the centre at Labuan International Sea Sports Complex (Kompleks Sukan Laut), Jalan Tanjung Purun • Free • http://facebook.com/muziummarinlabuan • Bus #1, #3 or #4

Housed in a gleaming modern building at the eastern end of town, the **Marine Museum** contains various displays on coastal and deep-sea ecosystems, plus the environment around Labuan. Its main attraction, however, is its **aquarium**, with more than a dozen tanks plus a touch pool.

Labuan War Cemetery and Memorial

3km northeast of Labuan Town on Jalan Tanjung Batu • Free • http://cwgc.org • Bus #1

Containing the remains of approximately 3900 Allied soldiers, many of them unidentified, Labuan's **war cemetery** is Malaysia's largest by far (the one at Taiping in Perak is a distant second; see page 126). Many were victims of the Sandakan "death march" (see page 403); hundreds more were transferred here from Kuching, site of an infamous prisoner-of-war camp. Inside the compound, white stone markers are poignantly arrayed on manicured lawns. There's also a red-brick, columned memorial to one side, commemorating the 2300 Australian and other troops who died in Borneo and the Philippines during World War II, and have no known graves.

Chimney Museum

On the northeast tip of the island on Jalan Tanjung Kubong • Free • http://facebook.com/chimneymuseum • Bus #6

One of the most bizarre museums in the country must be Labuan Island's **Chimney Museum**, which celebrates the mysterious red-brick tower next door. Most of the museum is actually given over to a passable history of **coal-mining** in Labuan – under the British, the northeast of the island was a major centre for this until the early twentieth century. Dioramas and antique equipment attempt to spice up the story, but the great lacuna is just what role the square chimney itself – so heavily restored that you'd swear it was built a few years back, although it's thought to date from 1900 – actually played. Indeed, no one is even sure that the chimney had anything to do with mining at all.

The beaches

There are beaches dotted all around Labuan's coastline, the nearest to Labuan Town being **Tanjung Batu Beach**, 2.5km to the northeast; it's a so-so stretch, let down by brownish sand

and views of shipping and the odd oil rig. Rather better are the half a dozen or so beaches dotted all along the northwest coast, which all offer good sunset views. If you only have time for one, make it **Layang-Layangan Beach**, smack in the middle of the stretch and including **Surrender Point**, where Japanese troops acquiesced at the end of World War II. The adjoining **Peace Park**, built in the 1980s with Japanese funds, is a pretty spot to relax.

ARRIVAL AND DEPARTURE — LABUAN ISLAND

By plane Labuan Island's airport is 5km north of Labuan Town, served by all the local minibuses except #1; easy enough, but most still take a taxi into the centre.
Destinations KK (3 daily; 30min); Kuala Lumpur (3–5 daily; 2hr 20min); Miri (4–5 daily; 40min).

By boat Passenger ferries serving Sabah and Sarawak dock at Labuan Town's international ferry terminal on Jalan Merdeka (087 581006). Car ferries, which only serve Muara in Brunei and Menumbok in Sabah, leave from a jetty close by to the east. In addition, there are Menumbok speedboats, which use the international terminal (1–2 hourly). Schedules do change, so check to be sure.
Destinations KK (3–7 weekly; 2hr 30min); Lawas (1 daily; 2hr 15min); Limbang (1–2 daily; 2hr); Menumbok (speedboats hourly, 20–30min; car ferry 5–6 daily, 1hr 30min); Muara (Brunei; 6 daily; 1hr 15min).

GETTING AROUND

By minibus Labuan has six numbered local minibus services operating to an irregular timetable; details are given here where relevant. They leave between dawn and the early evening from the bus station to the northwest of Labuan Town.

By taxi Taxis park at the bus station.

By bicycle A counter at the ferry terminal offers bike rental by the hour/day.

By car If you'd like to rent a car, you can try Hertz at the airport (087 410 740), or LDA Travel & Tour at the ferry terminal (087 413 155).

INFORMATION

Tourist information Tourism Malaysia is at Jalan Merdeka, close to the Labuan Museum (daily 8am–5pm; 087 423445). The Labuan Corporation, the body that runs the island, also operates an information counter at the airport (Mon–Thurs, Sat & Sun 8am–1pm & 2–5pm, Fri 8–11.30am & 2–5pm; http://pl.gov.my).

ACCOMMODATION — SEE MAP PAGE 386

Hotels in Labuan Town are mostly geared towards **business travellers** and so are struggling somewhat in the face of the local economic slump. Price codes here reflect the resulting discounts, but you should expect some volatility. There are no hostels, and the handful of **budget hotels** are usually undone by one thing or another, such as being located close to the noisy nightlife of the Jati district. Elsewhere, there's a beach resort worth considering, and it's also possible to stay on the islands of **Rusukan Besar** (within the marine park, see page 388) and **Papan** (just to the southeast of Labuan Town).

Dorsett Grand Jalan Merdeka, Labuan Town; http://dorsetthotels.com. Fancy but modest hotel, with muted tones in the lobby and rooms – try to aim for as high a floor as possible, in which case the views will be great even if you're not looking directly at the sea (though obviously try to get one looking directly at the sea). A sweet little pool and good dining options round out a very pleasing picture. $$$

VISITING LABUAN'S MARINE PARK

Labuan's **marine park**, 5km southwest of Labuan, encloses three islands, **Kuraman** (the largest by far), **Rusukan Besar** and **Rusukan Kecil**, along with four **wreck dive** sites. With no regular boat service, however, the only way to visit is on a trip organized by an operator in Labuan – and unfortunately, these are very thin on the ground. It's possible to overnight here, though don't expect resort-style luxury; the only accommodation takes the form of simple A-frame chalets, with a/c and bathroom, on Rusukan Besar. Note there is a small conservation fee.

TOUR OPERATORS

Borneo Wreck Divers Dorsett Grand hotel, Labuan Town; 013 808 8678. This operator offers a basic diving package to the marine park, excluding food and the park conservation fee, while wreck diving costs a bit more. Snorkelling and Discover Scuba courses are also available.

★ **Labuan Avenue** Jalan OKK Awang Besar, Labuan Town; http://oyorooms.com. This budget option is a godsend, as it's quiet, homely and – unlike most of its peers – not bad to look at either, with a snazzy lobby and pantry where a self-service breakfast is available. Conveniently placed for just about everything in the centre. Rooms with windows cost about ten percent extra, and rates rise by ten percent at weekends. $\overline{\underline{\$}}$

Lazenda Lazenda Commercial Center; http://lazendahotel.com. There's some very fair value to be had here – the rooms and lobby look like they belong somewhere more expensive, although admittedly you only need to look out of the windows to realise that you're somewhere that an expensive hotel would never open up. $\overline{\underline{\$\$}}$

Palm Beach Resort & Spa Jalan Batu Manikar, near the island's northern tip; http://palmbeachresortspa.com. A tranquil, likeable affair where the rooms, in modern blocks, are unremarkable, but the leafy grounds and beachside pool really hit the spot. Rates can drop to bargain levels, if you're in luck (visiting at the right time helps). $\overline{\underline{\$\$\$}}$

EATING   SEE MAP PAGE 386

Labuan Town holds the usual mix of no-frills *kedai kopi*s plus more formal restaurants for Western basics or seafood (as ever, priced by weight).

Choice Restaurant Jalan Okk Awang Besar; 087 504 693. Spacious, inexpensive a/c place with a long à la carte menu, as well as a good *nasi campur* spread. The *roti* and *dosai* are excellent – try the *ghee masala dosa* for breakfast. $\overline{\underline{\$}}$

Mawilla Yacht Club Tanjung Batu Beach, just beyond the edge of town; 087 423 888. An unpretentious affair, despite the grand name, in an open-sided beach bungalow with a fairly standard menu of Chinese stir-fries and seafood – obviously, you're going to be paying more for the latter. $\overline{\underline{\$\$\$}}$

New Sung Hwa PCK Building, Jalan Hujong Pasir; 087 411 008. Hidden upstairs in a featureless concrete block, but highly popular for its reasonably priced Chinese seafood, including crispy squid. Some tables have views west across the channel to Labuan's two water villages. $\overline{\underline{\$\$}}$

Senkawa Tanjung Batu Beach, just beyond the edge of town; 087 453 668. Attractive Japanese restaurant out of town, oddly named after one of Tokyo's most boring neighbourhoods (although it technically means "thousand rivers" too), but worth going to for its *bento* boxes, noodle bowls and crispy tempura. The food isn't all that authentic, but it's tasty nonetheless. $\overline{\underline{\$\$\$}}$

DRINKING   SEE MAP PAGE 386

The town was once known for its **nightlife**, with oil-industry workers coming here to unwind. Things have quietened down somewhat, though you might not think so if you're anywhere near the raucous karaoke bars of Jati, with one or two more venues clinging on near the western edge of town – but nowhere is particularly appealing.

Murphy Bar Jalan Kemajuan; 014 282 8979. Just about the only reliable bar in town – nothing too special, but with beer on tap, a pool table and occasional live music, it's not too bad either. Pub grub available too.

DIRECTORY

Banks and exchange The ferry terminal has an ATM, while others aren't far away on the same street, Jalan Merdeka.
Clinic Permai Polyclinic, Jalan Kemajuan (Mon–Fri & Sun 9am–11pm; 087 423 100).
Left luggage You'll find facilities at the ferry terminal (daily 7am–5pm).

The northwest coast and Kudat Peninsula

Sabah's northwestern coast is relatively untarnished by oil palms; instead there are views of jewel-bright paddy fields and stilt houses, with Mount Kinabalu looming in the distance. The area tends to be overlooked by visitors, however, partly because it lacks a star attraction, though that could change if the extension of the highway all the way north to the town of **Kudat** gets under way as planned. Until then, the **beaches** of the northernmost **Tip of Borneo** will probably remain off the radar, as will Malaysia's largest marine protected zone, the **Tun Mustapha Park**. Closer to KK, and feasible as a day-trip, are the **Mantanani Islands**.

Kota Belud

Sixty-five kilometres northeast of KK, the main road reaches bustling **KOTA BELUD**, famed for its weekly *tamu* (market). Early on Sundays, the otherwise indistinguishable town springs to life as hordes of Rungus, Kadazan/Dusan and Bajau people are drawn together at Sabah's largest weekly market. Though a few visitors arrive on tours from KK, you won't see many souvenirs for sale; instead you're far more likely to come across dried fish, chains of yeast beads (used to make rice wine), buffalo and betel nut. If heading here independently from KK, set off by 8am at the latest. In late October, things scale up by an order of magnitude at Kota Belud's annual *tamu besar* (literally "big *tamu*"), which features cultural performances, Bajau men on horseback in traditional finery and handicraft demonstrations. Away from the town, the area is a less common target for proboscis monkey and firefly-spotting cruises run by KK tour operators.

Mantanani Islands

A further 9km drive north and west of Kota Belud is coastal **Kuala Abai**, the departure point for the **Mantanani Islands**, a pair of islands 30km offshore to the north. There's no transport other than that laid on by tour operators who offer it as a long day-trip, including diving or snorkelling, but you only get to spend just over four hours on the islands, so it's worth considering a night or two here.

ACCOMMODATION   MANTANANI ISLANDS

Nido Matanani Lodge 011 3163 6923. A collection of simple two-person *sulaps* (huts) on stilts, with a hammock and chairs under each one, plus a hostel. Rates usually include transfers from KK, breakfast plus one snorkelling session; extra nights cost much less. $$$$

Sutera at Matanani Island Eastern tip of island; http://suteraatmatanani.com. The main resort hereabouts, with absolutely gorgeous chalets, a modest-looking restaurant (food's still good, though), and a pristine beach running past the whole thing – quite idyllic, if you can afford it. $$$$

Sumangkap and Bavanggazo

Beyond Kota Belud, it's only half an hour's drive to the start of the road up the **Kudat Peninsula**, which is inhabited by the Rungus people, one of several subgroups of the Kadazan/Dusun and known for their beadwork. The first point of interest, signed some 140km from KK and 42km short of Kudat, is the village of **SUMANGKAP**, where gong-making is a cottage industry. Just about every house seems to be festooned with them, some looking like freakish saucepans, and villagers can be seen (and heard) in their front yards hammering away at them, listening closely to the tones they produce. Hardly anyone can explain their work in English, but that shouldn't prevent you haggling to buy a souvenir gong if you wish. Be sure to check out the field at the back of the village, where one monumental gong is as tall as a two-storey house.

Only a couple of kilometres beyond Sumangkap, a few traditional **Rungus longhouses** have survived the shift to modern housing in the village of **BAVANGGAZO**, where there are a couple where tourists can stay.

ARRIVAL AND DEPARTURE   SUMANGKAP AND BAVANGGAZO

By bus or shared taxi Sumanggkap and Bavanggazo are some 140km from KK and 40km short of Kudat; Sumangkap is near the main road, but Bavanggazo lies 2.5km off it. Any bus or shared taxi between KK and Kudat (see page 390) can drop you at the turning for either village.

ACCOMMODATION

Bavanggazo Longhouse The second of the two longhouses in Bavanggazo, further in off the main road; 019 842 6990. The better of the longhouse options here, the low sleeping platforms in one of 21 rooms have their own mosquito net; bathrooms are shared and there's no a/c. Rates include half board and a cultural show. $

Kudat

Dreary little **KUDAT** is the jumping-off point for the Tip of Borneo and for Banggi island in the Tun Mustapha Park (see page 392), and that's the best that can be said for it. The town centre sits on a tongue of land jutting into Marudu Bay. The main road in, Jalan Ibrahim Arshad, passes right by an orange-hued **Chinese temple**, with a couple of rows of old timber shophouses just beyond. The road then changes its name to Jalan Lintas, curling past the **harbour** to the southwest, with a new centre – holding a few banks – on its northeast side. The temple, the sea views and the **market** area on Jalan Lintas are the only things worthy of a few minutes of your attention.

ARRIVAL AND DEPARTURE KUDAT

By plane MASWings (http://maswings.com.my) call at Kudat's airfield, 9km northwest of town, three times a week en route between KK (40min) and Sandakan (50min). Taxis meet all arrivals at the airport.

By bus Salam Bumimas buses leave from a tiny station near the beginning of Jalan Lintas for KK (2 daily; 3hr 30min) and Sandakan (3 weekly; 5hr).

By boat Ferries to Karakit town on Banggi Island (2–3 daily; 1hr; buy tickets on board) leave from an easily-spotted jetty in the harbour area.

By taxi Shared taxis serving Kota Belud and KK park up northeast of Jalan Ibrahim Arshad in the old part of town.

ACCOMMODATION

Kinabalu Jalan Melor, off Jalan Lintas and opposite KFC; 012 788 1361. This place is good value and well kept for a budget hotel. While rooms are very dated, they do have a/c and private bathrooms. $

Ria Jalan Ibrahim Arshad; http://riahotel.blogspot.com. This mundane, squarish block towers over other buildings in Kudat and holds the best rooms in the centre. Suites cost more than double the ordinary rate, but they do have their own jacuzzis. $$

EATING AND DRINKING

It speaks volumes that the *KFC* is one of the slickest-looking restaurants in the centre, but many of the drab *kedai kopis* aren't too bad at all for cheap meals.

Kudat Curry House Jalan Ibrahim Arshad; facebook.com. The best place to head for a morning *roti canai*, or simple lunchtime curries – simple, but effective. $

Rainbow Kitchen Jalan Chin Sham Choi; http://facebook.com. Local favourite for tom yam soup, made with juicy shrimp and a spicy oil. Fish-head soup, *nasi goreng* and other local staples are on the menu too, as are all your *kopitiam* tea and coffee favourites. $

The Tip of Borneo

Most opt to charter a taxi to or from Kudat

Some 6km short of Kudat, a pair of northbound turnings give access to the triangular cape of the **Tip of Borneo** (Tanjung Simpang Mengayau), which is still fairly rustic and totally bypassed by public transport. The main draws include scenic vistas of azure waters and a good dose of calm, but on the downside, the **beaches** are of variable quality, some pristine, others periodically strewn with detritus.

All roads eventually funnel into the road to the tip itself, which first passes a lovely 2.5km arc of sand – the southern section is **Kosohui Beach**, the northern part **Kalampunian Beach**. At the tip just to the northeast, a small landscaped area is crowned by a globular **monument**, with Balambangan and Banggi islands, part of the Tun Mustapha Park, visible on the eastern horizon.

As for **activities**, mangrove trips, surfing, kayaking, snorkelling and diving are available, although seas can be rough from November to January, and you should be wary of currents at other times. Jungle and coastal walks are possible, for example to **Kelambu Beach** 6km south of Kosohui, where a spit of sand links a forested islet to the mainland, but the lack of bike rental can make for some sweaty treks along shadeless roads.

ACCOMMODATION THE TIP OF BORNEO

A handful of places to stay cluster around Kalampunian Beach and the tip itself, with other options scattered all over the area. The most distant of these is noteworthy as it's the only place offering trips to the Tun Mustapha Park.

Most of these places have at least a simple kitchen serving breakfast, if not a full restaurant. Wi-fi isn't commonplace, and even a phone signal can be hard to come by.

Hibiscus Villa 2.5km southwest of Kosohui Beach on Jalan

Marang Parang; http://hibiscusvillaborneo.com. Savour life in your very own seaside mansion at this immaculate two-storey, three-bedroom affair, set in lush gardens and with its own infinity pool. The place sleeps up to nine, with prices depending on group size. If your pockets aren't deep enough, ask about their neighbouring property with just two chalets, each rented separately. Rates include breakfast. $$$$

North Borneo Biostation Bak Bak Beach, some 20km southeast of the Tip of Borneo and 8km north of Kudat; http://borneobiostation.com. Part resort, part field station, with unusually spacious A-frame chalets complete with a/c and open-air bathrooms, plus a huge range of activities and trips. Rates include breakfast. $$$

Secret Place Signed off Jalan Marang Parang about 3km south of Kosohui; http://secretplaceborneo.jimdo.com. A no-frills outfit offering camping on a secluded stretch of sand, with communal toilets and showers as well as a simple restaurant. $

★ **Simpang Mengayau Chalet** Tip of Borneo; http://facebook.com/SimpangMengayauChalet. This competently run outfit is set above a secluded cove and has a range of a/c, en-suite chalets, from very plain ones along a terrace to quite striking bamboo units and substantial timber ones. All have two or even four double beds, apart from the basic chalets. Lastly, just look at its location on a map – you couldn't be any more tip-of-Borneo if you tried. $$$

★ **Tampat Do Aman** Jalan Marang Parang, 2.5km from Kosohui Beach; http://facebook.com/tampatdoaman.my. This place offers a kind of back-to-basics experience. It's true there are some quite comfortable *sulaps* and chalets, all with bathrooms though no a/c, but many guests go for the basic longhouse rooms with shared showers and composting toilets. A small museum of Rungus culture is a noble feature. The fly in the ointment is the distance from the beach, something several daily free shuttles doesn't quite overcome. Rates exclude meals (only breakfast is served on site – or at their all-day beach restaurant, depending on your taste). $$

Tommy's Place Just south of Tip of Borneo; 013 823 8148. Surprisingly attractive rooms (a/c and en suite) all lined up alongside each other, right next to the Tip of Borneo, with a relaxed, secluded vibe pervading through the evening. Also a good place to eat. $$

EATING

Ayeena Amor Cafe 1km south of Tip of Borneo. Simple *kopitiam* fare near the Tip of Borneo, made well and served in a relaxed space. $

Secret Place About 3km south of Kosohui Beach on Jalan Marang Parang; http://secretplaceborneo.jimdo.com. The restaurant at this beach campsite does simple Malay meals, and best of all, they offer evening seafood barbecues on request. $

Tommy's Place Just south of Tip of Borneo; 013 823 8148. A great spot for a beer, or a simple meal, overlooking the waves – don't expect anything too fancy (or too efficient), but they'll be able to rustle up something tasty. $$

Tun Mustapha Park

No conservation fee or permits at the time of writing • http://sabahparks.org.my

The waters north and northeast of the Kudat Peninsula form the **Tun Mustapha Park**, Sabah's newest state park, which was created to try to protect sea life following years of overfishing and general neglect. Covering 9000 square kilometres, the park extends all the way to the Tip of Borneo, encompassing dozens of small islands plus three major ones – none of them have been set up for tourism, however. In principle, it's possible to do a half-day trip by ferry to the largest island, **Banggi**, which is 40km northeast of Kudat. The sights there aren't anything special, though: a **beach** on the northeast coast a couple of hours from the main settlement, **Karakit**, and the 529m **Mount Sinambung**, where the 70m-high **Sinambung Waterfall** nestles in the jungle.

Taxis are the only way to get around independently, so it's far better to visit on a **package trip** run by the *North Borneo Biostation* resort (see above). The main draw is, of course, the marine life, but in addition to diving and snorkelling they offer an excursion to **Balambangan Island**, west of Banggi, where there are limestone caves to explore.

Kinabalu Park

Charge • http://sabahparks.org.my

The journey to **Kinabalu Park** is one of the most scenic anywhere in Malaysia, traversing a classic, winding mountain road with views of mist-shrouded valleys and the jagged spectre of its eponymous mountain constantly arresting the eye. The mountain is revered as *aki nabalu* (home of spirits of the dead) by the Kadazan/Dusun, and dominates the park's 750 square kilometres, a UNESCO World Heritage Site renowned for its ecology and geology. All other hikes within the park pale in comparison with the prospect of reaching the summit at Low's Peak (4095m), but climbing slots can be tricky to get, and the climb itself obliges you to **stay** one night on the mountain – an expensive affair, given the logistics of running facilities at altitude.

In view of those downsides, not every visitor is here to tackle the mountain, and the park has other temptations lower down. **Trails** loop the montane forest around the **park headquarters**; for great views, try either the 1082m-long Bukit Burung Trail or the 465m Bundu Tuhan View Trail. There's also the chance to visit **Poring Hot Springs**, reached by another park entrance to the east.

Mount Kinabalu

Charges for climbing permit, guide and insurance (all compulsory; groups of up to five); optional charges for porter, summit certificate and left luggage

Hugh Low, then British colonial secretary on Labuan, made the first recorded ascent of **Mount Kinabalu** in 1851, though he baulked at attempting its highest peak, considering it "inaccessible to any but winged animals". Seven years later, Spenser St John, British consul-general to the native states of Borneo, found his progress blocked by Kadazan/Dusun "shaking their spears and giving us other hostile signs". The peak, subsequently named after Low, was finally climbed in 1888 by John Whitehead.

Things are much easier now, of course, with a **main trail** to follow – actually an exhausting 8.7km-long series of steps and rocky tracks that weaves steeply up through forest on the south side to the bare granite of Low's Peak in the northwest. Its existence is one of the joys of Kinabalu, as **no climbing skills or special equipment** are needed. Indeed, every two years, elite runners **race** from the park HQ to the summit and back down again, with winners covering the 26km in five hours or less.

Even so, Kinabalu deserves respect: conditions can be miserably cold and blowy up top, and you need to watch out for cramping and altitude sickness. Take care as you go, as you really don't want to be stretchered down by porters – which takes hours – because you twisted your ankle high up. At the same time, don't overthink the challenge; this is a mountain that can be climbed by anyone of **reasonable fitness**.

The **Timpohon Trail** is the main route up, and the only one available following the Kinabalu earthquake (see page 398). It's possible to set off for the park from KK on the morning of your climb, but staying the previous night in the area is a lot more restful. Allow half an hour at the park office to register, meet your assigned **guide**, and sort out porters and any luggage you want to store. Note that the guides' main job is to chaperone you up and back down in one piece – consider knowledge of flora and fauna or advanced linguistic skills a bonus.

Timpohon Gate to Panar Laban (around 6km; typically 5–7hr)

The whole climb operates to a timetable, with climbers setting off from the park HQ (1564m) from 8am until about 10.30am; many save time and avoid the tiresome 4.5km trudge up the road to **Timpohon Gate** (1866m) by using park transport (15min; for up to four people). Beyond the gate, the trail skirts Carson Waterfall around 500m on and, via countless steps, passes six **rest huts**, with toilets and water supplies, en route to the accommodation at **Panar Laban** (often called **Laban Rata** after the accommodation of that name; 3272m). From the outset you're in **montane rainforest**, with its delicate ferns, mosses, rhododendrons and orchids, and it's worth making time to appreciate the vegetation and vistas – the South China Sea is visible at times – rather than plod on. Many climbers pause for a lunch break at Layang-Layang hut (2700m), beyond which the vegetation becomes noticeably sparser, dominated by withered *sayat-sayat* trees occasionally decked with blond strands – a type of lichen. Look out for **pitcher plants**,

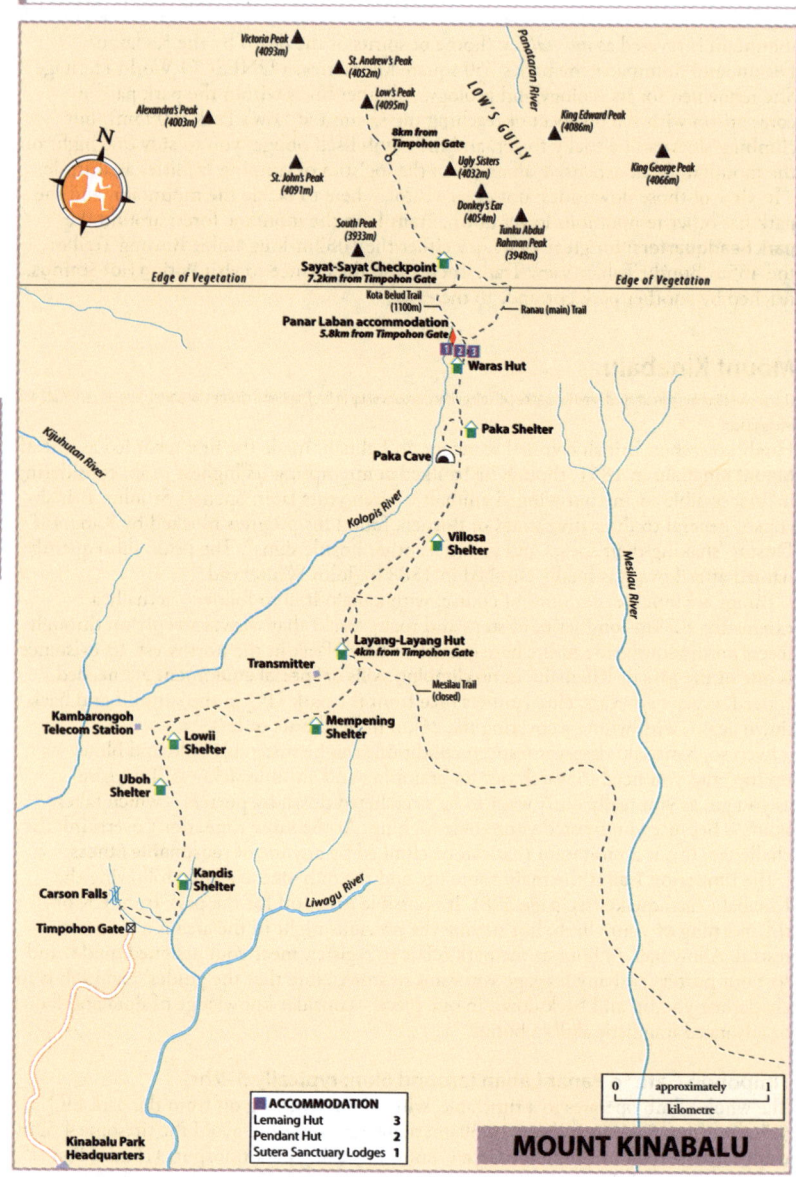

notably *Nepenthes villosa*, its sizeable pitchers ribbed at the rim. If fatigue hasn't struck yet, it may well bite hard now, turning the last kilometre or so into a grind.

Panar Laban to the summit (2.7km; 2hr 30min–4hr)

After dinner, served from late afternoon, there's time to sleep until 2am (the electricity may be turned off around 8pm), when there's another meal before climbers resume. There's a choice of routes at this point: either the standard **Ranau Trail** or the shorter, steeper **Kota**

Belud Trail (the latter must be arranged beforehand at the park HQ). They reunite at the **Sayat-Sayat Checkpoint**, which is 1.2km from Panar Laban via the Ranau Trail. Stragglers must make this checkpoint by 5.30am or will be turned back without reaching the top.

On the Ranau Trail everyone gets bunched together at first like a huge caterpillar, but when the stairs end the faster ones break free to tackle the granite slopes of the mountaintop, with ropes on the steeper sections. The aim is to arrive at Low's Peak shortly before taking in the **sunrise** around 5.40am, to avoid lingering at the exposed summit longer than need be (although you may have to line up to have your picture taken at the summit signboard).

The descent

Heading down in daylight, you can finally take in the breathtaking scenery: the horned **South Peak**, seldom climbed; the curving granite rock face that seems to funnel up towards Low's Peak; and, on a clear day, views of green plains and distant ranges. Back at the Sayat-Sayat Checkpoint, climbers who booked with Mountain Torq head off to tackle the **via ferrata** (see page 397); the rest continue down to Panar Laban for a late breakfast and then retrace their steps to Timpohon Gate. The whole descent might take a quarter less time than the climb, although you might be hobbled by aching legs – stairs may be difficult for a couple of days afterwards.

ARRIVAL AND DEPARTURE   MOUNT KINABALU

If you're heading to the park from KK, the best option is to get a shared minivan or taxi from the central Merdeka Field

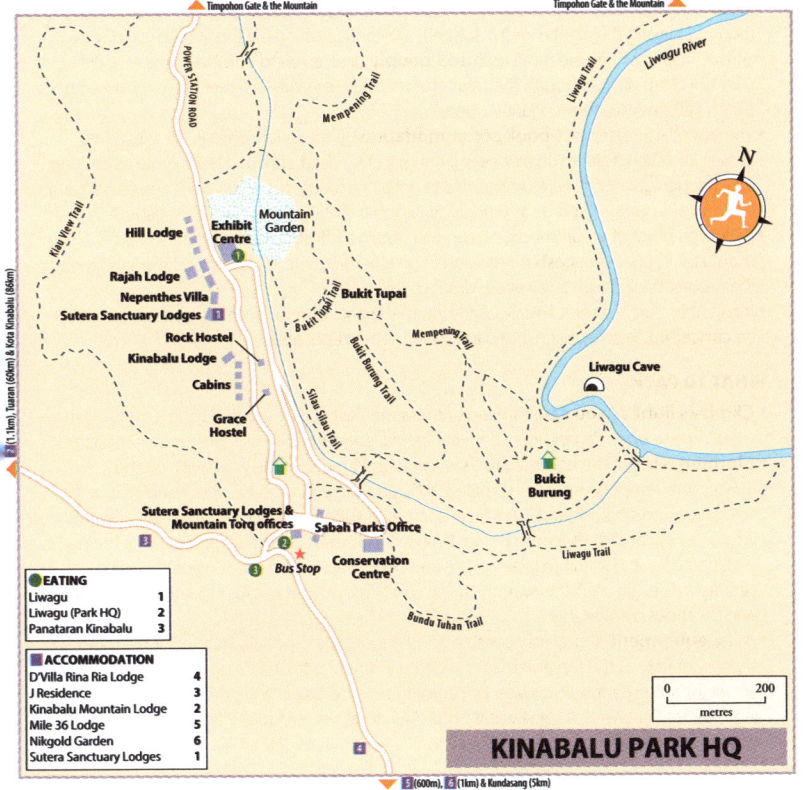

terminal. Returning to KK, however, you may find that these are full, so catching a bus for the inconveniently located Inanam terminal is the better option.

By bus In daylight hours, it's often possible to flag down buses travelling between KK and the east coast, but you may need to be patient as some will be practically full. Also, the fare may be calculated from the last town the bus called at.
Destinations KK (frequent; 1hr 30min); Lahad Datu (14 daily; 7–8hr); Sandakan (at least 12 daily; 6hr); Semporna (6 daily; 9–10hr); Tawau (7 daily; 10–11hr); Telupid (frequent; 3hr).

By shared taxi and minivan Shuttling between KK and Kundasang/Ranau, shared taxis and minivans are a convenient way to reach the park. If you intend to set off for the park on the morning of your climb, aim to be at Merdeka Field no later than 7.30am.

INFORMATION

Tourist information Clustered very near the gates are the park HQ (daily 7am–7pm), a Mountain Torq office and a Sutera Sanctuary Lodges counter and shop with a left luggage service. The park office, which is swarming with climbers in the morning, can provide maps and general information, and also find specialist birding guides if contacted in advance.

Internet access Depending on your phone network, you can either get online for much of the mountain trail or not at all. There's usually coverage at Panar Laban.

ACCOMMODATION

Park accommodation at the **HQ** is run by Sutera Sanctuary Lodges (SSL) and is overpriced; there are better deals within 2km of the park entrance. Up the mountain at **Panar Laban**, however, climbers have three outfits to choose from: SSL, Mountain Torq (for via ferrata packages) and Sabah Parks itself. One snag other than sheer demand is

---

CLIMBING KINABALU: KEY POINTS

- The ascent and descent via the main trail takes **two days** in total, with hikers setting off in the morning, staying the night near the summit, and then reaching the top at dawn on day two.
- At the time of writing, no more than **163 people** (a nice, round number) were allowed to start the climb daily, although this might return to the pre-quake figure of two hundred once Sabah Parks' new accommodation opens.
- The essential first step is to **book accommodation** up the mountain at Panar Laban (see above). You should aim to do so weeks, if not months, ahead, although last-minute places pop up if people cancel. If it seems impossible to get a bed for the dates you want, consider paying more for a via ferrata package as *Pendant Hut* is more likely to have spaces (see page 397).
- Only with proof of accommodation can you obtain a **climbing permit** at the park HQ. You should bring adequate **cash** for this and to pay for the guide, transport and everything else; the nearest bank is 5km away in Kundasang.
- If conditions are very wet and/or windy when the final summit push is meant to start, it will be **cancelled**. Rescheduling and partial refunds aren't possible.

WHAT TO PACK

- **Climb as light as you can**, carrying only essentials. It can be worth paying a porter to lug anything else up to Panar Laban, but you should leave those items there for the final ascent.
- **Clothing** is tricky. The daytime hike is warm to mild much of the way, while on the pre-dawn climb temperatures can dip below 10°C and there may be a vicious wind chill; at the same time, the slog will work up a bit of a sweat. A suitable compromise for many people is to don regular clothes for the tropics (trousers, not shorts) and pack a sweater or thermal vest, plus a light to medium jacket and warm headgear. A cheap plastic poncho will keep you dry in the rain and adds warmth. Bring sports gloves, not just for insulation but also to grip the ropes comfortably.
- As for **equipment**, sturdy shoes with a good grip will be especially helpful for the moist, slippery granite at the top. You must have a head torch as the trail is unlit (check the batteries are fresh). Many people also swear by climbing poles to take the pressure off your knees and leg muscles in general. A small water bottle will do, as you can refill it at rest huts along the way. Sugary snacks are handy to refuel.

THE VIA FERRATA

If the huge trek up to the summit doesn't sound like enough of a challenge, then you might want to book your climb with Mountain Torq (Level 2, MAA Building, Lorong Api-Api 1, KK; http://mountaintorq.com), who offer two-day full-board packages and operate the **via ferrata** – pathways of rungs, bridges, rails and planks running along Kinabalu's cliffsides. Their introductory Walk The Torq route is suitable for anyone over 10 (2–3hr), while the alternative Low's Peak Circuit has a minimum age of 17 (4–5hr). It's exhilarating stuff, with some incredible views and the assurance of being tethered or hooked to something all the time; it's also even more tiring as it slots in soon after you've conquered Low's Peak. With either route, you will still be back at Timpohon Gate by late afternoon. If that sounds too rushed, consider a longer package, possibly with an **abseiling** course thrown in. In all cases you'll stay in dorms at the firm's own *Pendant Hut* at Panar Laban.

It's also possible to add the via ferrata **last-minute** to an ordinary climbing package: pay on day 1 of your climb (credit cards accepted) at Mountain Torq's office at the Park HQ or at *Pendant Hut*.

---

that SSL normally steers climbers into buying a three-day package, with the extra night spent at its accommodation at either the park HQ or Poring Hot Springs; the two-day package is on sale only if they have unsold Panar Laban beds with a month to go. The Sabah Parks alternative is **Lemaing Hut**, where foreigners can only get beds if there are vacancies with a few days to go (to register your interest, call the park office or just turn up and ask). The good news, however, is that Sabah Parks' new accommodation at Panar Laban promises to be a game changer and should be open by the time you read this, although no prices were available at the time of research. All the options listed here have their own simple restaurant unless otherwise stated.

PARK HQ AND AROUND, SEE MAP PAGE 395

D'Villa Rina Ria Lodge On the main road 750m southeast of the park entrance; http://facebook.com. This place is not much to look at, but isn't a bad choice, with a twelve-bed dorm as well as standard rooms with balconies offering valley views. The restaurant is better than average. Breakfast is included. Dorms $, doubles $$

★ J Residence 300m west of the park entrance; http://jresidence.com. Offers eleven rooms spread over six units on the mountainside among the pines, including three in a villa with a kitchen. The design and furnishings are much slicker than most places around here, though there are no mountain views and no meals. Prices leap by half at the weekend. $$

Kinabalu Mountain Lodge At the end of a steep, winding 800m road that starts 1.2km west of the park entrance; 018 238 1010. Popular with backpackers, this peaceful wooden building on a spur of the mountain has a lovely view from the terrace, but the trek from it to the park is a drag. Rooms are fairly basic, and en-suite ones cost quite a bit more. Meals aren't included, but don't cost much. Dorms $, doubles $$

Mile 36 Lodge On the main road 1.5km southeast of the park entrance; 08 888161. A real hotchpotch of chalets and rooms, ranging from rather bare affairs to genuinely comfy units that are suitable for groups and cost two to three times as much. The best thing about it is the view of Kinabalu from the edge of the sprawling, leafy grounds. Breakfast is included. $

Nikgold Garden Signed 1.5km southeast of the park HQ, then another 500m down a steep valley road; http://nikgoldkundasang.com. An imposing set of two-storey timber buildings staggered up a slope, with spacious modern bedrooms and the mountain towering close by. No meals. $$

Sutera Sanctuary Lodges On the road to Timpohon Gate; http://suterasanctuarylodges.com.my. Sprinkled inside the park north of the HQ are several cosy "lodges", which range from plain-looking chalets to quite plush bungalows that sleep two, four or six people, plus the *Grace Hostel* (which has dorms). Rate includes breakfast at the park's *Balsam* restaurant. $$$$

ON THE MOUNTAIN, SEE MAP PAGE 394

Lemaing Hut Panar Laban. Tiny hostel aimed at Malaysians with two cramped 20-bed dorms and basic bathrooms – it's clean but unmemorable. This is a bargain for foreigners who are able to get a last-minute place. Book through Sabah Parks (see page 375). Full board per person $$$

Pendant Hut Panar Laban; http://mountaintorq.com. White-painted wooden lodge that looks as though it might get skittled by a stiff breeze. It's cheap, which is the best thing most have to say about it, though climbers will find the buffet meals gloriously satisfying, though anything ordered off the menu is pricey – if you're tempted to moan, remember the porters plodding up the trail laden with eggs, melons and other supplies. $$

Sutera Sanctuary Lodges Panar Laban; http://sutera sanctuarylodges.com.my. As well as their place down below, *Sutera* have a lodge up on the mountain too – wrapped in the embrace of muscular cliffs, it looks quite something from a distance. The rooms and dining area don't exude luxury, however, so if that's what you're after, stay down the mountain instead – what we have here is a simple (though rather expensive) place with an old-school Alpine feel. $$$$

EATING   SEE MAP PAGE 395

Liwagu At the park HQ; 088 303 900. Run by SSL, the park's restaurant offers predictably expensive yet satisfying buffets with local and Western dishes; and breakfast and lunch are quite affordable, but dinner costs a fair bit more. $$$$

Liwagu On the road to Timpohon Gate; http://sutera sanctuarylodges.com.my. Run by the *Sutera* (the lower one, that is), this is the best place to eat for many a mile around, serving a mix of local and Western dishes, plus steamboat meals that are particularly popular with domestic tourists. $$$$

Panataran Kinabalu On the main road opposite park turning; 088 889 117. Sabah Parks' co-op restaurant is the best spot for inexpensive food close to the park, with a menu of largely Chinese dishes. $$

7 Poring Hot Springs

North of Ranau and some 40km east of the main park entrance • Daily 7am–5pm • Charge, including use of outdoor tubs; extra for indoor tubs and/or canopy walkway; also charge for conservation fee (not payable if you have visited the park HQ the same day) • http://sabahparks.org.my

The **Poring Hot Springs** were developed during World War II by the Japanese, who installed wooden tubs that have since been replaced by tiled versions. Don't come expecting natural pools, luxury or solitude, but it can still be a good place to relax aching muscles after descending from Mount Kinabalu. It's least crowded early or late in the day.

There are also a few other attractions within the site, including an orchid garden, a butterfly farm, a **canopy walkway** and a few walking trails. Outside the gates, households occasionally advertise that they have **Rafflesia flowers** to see in their grounds; expect to pay to see them.

ARRIVAL AND DEPARTURE   PORING HOT SPRINGS

By bus or minivan Park shuttles run between Poring Hot Springs and the park HQ (1hr). For long-distance travel, you can hop in a minivan from outside the park gates to get to Ranau (see page 399), where you'll find plenty of options for onward transport.

ACCOMMODATION

Besides accommodation run by SSL, this part of the park has a campsite and some homestay-style arrangements.

THE 2015 KINABALU EARTHQUAKE

It struck at 7.15am on June 5, 2015 – an unprecedented **magnitude 6 quake** with its epicentre at Kundasang, close to Kinabalu Park. In KK, 50km to the southwest, the tremors sent people scurrying into the street, but it was on the mountaintop that the impact was terrible. Eighteen people died, including six Singaporean schoolchildren on the via ferrata, as well as several guides; in many cases, the victims were crushed by falling rocks.

Mount Kinabalu had been in the **headlines** just days earlier, when a group of foreign climbers partially disrobed for a photo at the summit. Flaunted on social media, the image caused some outrage locally, and when the quake hit some pointed to vengeful spirits. A few of those involved in the stunt were soon charged in court.

Extensive repairs kept the park closed for several months after the quake. The scars are still easy to see, with slopes still partially denuded by landslides and boulders strewn on valley floors; at the summit, Kinabalu's "donkey ears" rock formation is now one ear and a stump. The once-popular **Mesilau Trail**, starting several kilometres east of the main park gate and joining the main trail 2800m up, is out of commission, as is its *Mesilau Nature Resort*, with no date set for their reopening. Signs at the park now warn against "unethical acts (including nude)" and, in the same spirit, notify visitors that **drones** are banned.

Kinabalu Poring Vacation Village Within the park; 012 829 6923. Large place that looks almost like a tropical countryside school, at first glance. On closer inspection it's still a tiny bit institutional, but the rooms are comfortable, and you'll eat well enough too. $$

Sutera Sanctuary Lodges Within the park; http://suterasanctuarylodges.com.my. The official accommodation includes a slick dorm, a handful of mid-range doubles and very pricey lodges sleeping up to six. Breakfast is included. $$$

EATING

Poring Station On the main road, opposite Sutera; 019 308 4903. Nothing special, but the most reliable cheap eats – appetizing Western, Malay and Chinese food, served in a somewhat unappetising environment. $$

Rainforest Restaurant Just inside the park; 088 877 215. The restaurant at *Sutera Sanctuary Lodges* serves buffet lunches and dinners, if they have enough guests staying, but otherwise you have to order off the menu and prices are steep. $$$

Around Kinabalu Park

The area southeast of Kinabalu Park is known for its agriculture, the fruits of which can be glimpsed in tiny **Kundasang**, where simple stalls sell local produce – although the town is also on the tourist trail for its **war memorial**. Further east there's a **tea plantation** with tours and accommodation. In between, the mundane town of **Ranau** is known for paragliding.

Kundasang War Memorial

Just off the main road in Kundasang • Charge • Buses and minivans stop close to the main junction on the highway, though for onward travel you will have to flag them down

Five kilometres southeast of the main entrance to Kinabalu Park, the **Kundasang War Memorial** commemorates the victims – although no soldiers are buried here – of the Sandakan Death Marches of 1945, when Japanese troops force-marched POWs from Sandakan to Ranau (see page 401). There's an information centre that shows an Australian documentary about the death marches, plus three peaceful and well-tended memorial gardens (Australian, British and Bornean).

ACCOMMODATION AND EATING   KUNDASANG

Blue Mountain Lodge East of the centre; http://facebook.com. Excellent value, though it doesn't look all that great – like a two-storey motel from an American horror movie, with a couple of shipping containers stapled to the side. Rooms are basic, but they do the job, and there are hammocks outside from which to test the theory that wonderful views get even better when you're swinging gently. $$

Kinabalu Pine Resort Southwest of the centre; http://kinabalupineresort.com. The rooms here are overpriced, for sure, but this is the nicest place to stay hereabouts, in a structure with some charm and great views. They also have a good restaurant on site. $$$

Ranau and around

RANAU is an undistinguished transport hub, where the main road between the west and east coasts is joined by the interior road for Tambunan and other points east of the Crocker Range. The town hosts a large and lively *tamu* on the first Sunday of the month, based 1km out of town towards Sandakan, and there's also a smaller *tamu* there every Saturday.

Ranau Paragliding Park

6km northeast of Ranau • Tandem flights possible • http://facebook.com/ranauparagliding

The valleys and consistent winds around Mount Kinabalu make the area a good site for **paragliding**, and novices can come here to try a thrilling tandem flight starting at 700m; with an early start, it's feasible as a day-trip from KK. There are multi-day paragliding courses on offer, too.

Sabah Tea Resort

18km east of Ranau in Nalapak • Charge for factory tours • http://sabahtea.com.my • Long-distance buses between KK and the east coast will drop passengers here on request; local buses from Ranau can drop you at the start of the turning, from where it's a 15min walk

The **Sabah Tea Resort** is a well-run organic tea plantation and factory that makes a worthwhile place to stay for a night or two, but may also be worth a daytime visit if you're just passing through. Make sure you also ask about getting a **fish massage** at nearby Luanti, where surprisingly large river fish converge to nibble at customers' feet.

ARRIVAL AND DEPARTURE — RANAU AND AROUND

By bus Long-distance buses stop on the main road beside the turning into town.
Destinations KK (frequent; 2hr); Lahad Datu (14 daily; 7hr); Sandakan (at least 12 daily; 5hr 30min); Semporna (6 daily; 9–10hr); Tawau (7 daily; 10–11hr); Telupid (frequent; 2hr 30min).
By shared minivan and taxi Shared transport parks up at the eastern edge of town and heads to Merdeka Field in KK (2hr) plus the interior town of Tambunan (1hr 15min).

ACCOMMODATION AND EATING

Sabah Tea Resort Nalapak, 18km east of Ranau on the road to Sandakan; http://sabahtea.com.my. This plantation has a campsite and longhouses that are popular with student groups, as well as cosy cottages that include breakfast. Batik-painting sessions are available, as are organized jungle treks, although for the latter there must be a minimum of ten people. Camping costs half the price if you bring your own tent. There's also a restaurant on site, one that won a local award for its environmental credentials – and, of course, there's excecllent tea on offer too. Camping $, longhouses $$, cottages $$$

Eastern Sabah

Despite being seemingly engulfed in tracts of oil palm trees, eastern Sabah is still a superb place for animal encounters. In the vicinity of the northeastern city of **Sandakan** alone, it's possible to see orangutans and sun bears in **Sepilok**, proboscis monkeys at **Labuk Bay Proboscis Monkey Sanctuary** and turtles at the **Turtle Islands Park**. Heading further south, the **Kinabatangan River** features prominently and various jungle lodges offer cruises to seek out pygmy elephants, proboscis monkeys and more. Then there's **Danum Valley**, a verdant rainforest area with a majestic canopy walkway, and the equally appealing **Tabin Wildlife Reserve**, both in the southeast. In the same area, the bustling coastal town of **Semporna** is the gateway to superb diving around world-famous **Sipadan**, **Mabul** and numerous other islands.

Sandakan

Situated at the northern edge of Sandakan Bay, facing the Sulu Sea, the town of **SANDAKAN** was all but destroyed during World War II; postwar reconstruction has created a cramped centre of indistinguishable concrete blocks, now plagued by the worst case of inner-city decay anywhere in Malaysia. It is possible to see most of the surrounding wildlife attractions and the **Sandakan Memorial Park** without really setting foot in town, and many visitors do just that, though there's nothing rough or seedy about the centre and it's still worth a visit to see the echoes of the **colonial past** so absent in KK – notably the **Agnes Keith House**, a shrine to the American writer who once brilliantly chronicled Sabah. The town also has a visitable **water village** where you can dine, as well as a sprinkling of tour operators.

Brief history

Although eighteenth-century accounts mention a trading outpost called Sandakan within the Sulu Sultanate, the town's modern history really begins in 1879, when a settlement named **Elopura** got going thanks to the efforts of the Englishman **William**

Pryer. By 1884, it was the **capital** of British North Borneo. Its natural harbour and proximity to sources of timber, rattan and edible birds' nests would transform it into a thriving centre, one that lured so many Chinese settlers it was nicknamed "Little Hong Kong". In January 1942 the Japanese seized what was now known as Sandakan, establishing the POW camp from which the **death marches to Ranau** began (see page 403). What Allied bombing failed to destroy, the Japanese burned down, and the end of the war saw Sabah's administration shift to Jesselton (KK). Nevertheless, by the 1950s the rebuilt town was profiting from the **timber boom**, so much so that by the 1970s it was said to have the world's greatest concentration of millionaires. Business then faltered due to the overexploitation of the forests, forcing Sandakan to look to cocoa and **oil palms**; today, tourism aside, much of the town's prosperity hinges on servicing the oil-palm industry.

The old town and waterfront

Sandakan's **old town centre** is squeezed between the sea and Trig Hill (Bukit Bendera) to the north, but has been extended slightly thanks to land reclamation south of Jalan Pryer. The modern **waterfront** area, including a large development called **Harbour Square** to the northeast, has tried its best to breathe some life into the town, but the shops and restaurants are, by and large, a bit mundane. Just beyond here is the sizeable **central market**, which is unusually tidy and well laid out. The rest of the old centre is lively enough by day but tends to peter out by nightfall, when many of the shops close up.

The Agnes Keith House

Jalan Istana, Trig Hill • Charge • http://museum.sabah.gov.my

In *The Land Below the Wind* (1939), Agnes Keith wrote: "When we sat in that house and looked out through its open doors the harbour of Sandakan with the dark mangrove swamps in the distance became a background to our entire world. I knew then that was where I wanted to live".

Today, Trig Hill – reached by the so-called **hundred steps** leading up from Lebuh Empat – still has the feel of a leafy colonial refuge, and offers views out across the sea to the far side of Sandakan Bay. Its showpiece is the **Agnes Keith House**, a shrine to the American writer whose works (see page 559) introduced many in the West to the peoples of Borneo. The building isn't the actual one Keith wrote about, but a spacious two-storey postwar replacement where she and her husband stayed on their second stint in Sabah. Over-restoration and air conditioning have rendered the museum rather sterile, and the vintage furnishings, including a writing desk that sports a sewing machine, are unconvincing – but if it gets you to seek out Keith's three books, on sale all over Sabah, it will have done its job.

Around the Padang

Sam Sing Kung Temple Free • Church Charge

Close to the **Padang** are a couple of the oldest buildings in town. On the northern side, the Taoist **Sam Sing Kung Temple** (daily 7am–3pm; free), completed in 1887, is dedicated to three deities – Liu Bei, Guan Yu and Zhang Fei – who were the heroes of the fourteenth-century *Romance of the Three Kingdoms*. On a hilltop west of here and reachable by steps off Jalan Singapura, the Anglican **St Michael's and All Angels Church** still has something of the feel of an English country church. Although it dates back to 1893, its most notable features are the lurid stained-glass remembrance windows, commemorating Allied war dead, and the POW chapel dotted with regimental plaques.

Sim-Sim Water Village

Jalan Buli Sim-Sim • Look for minibuses signed "Sim-Sim" from Jalan Coastal or take a taxi

The **Sim-Sim Water Village** is split into a sprawling Muslim section starting 1km east of the centre, and a Chinese one 2.5km away; their numbered boardwalks are

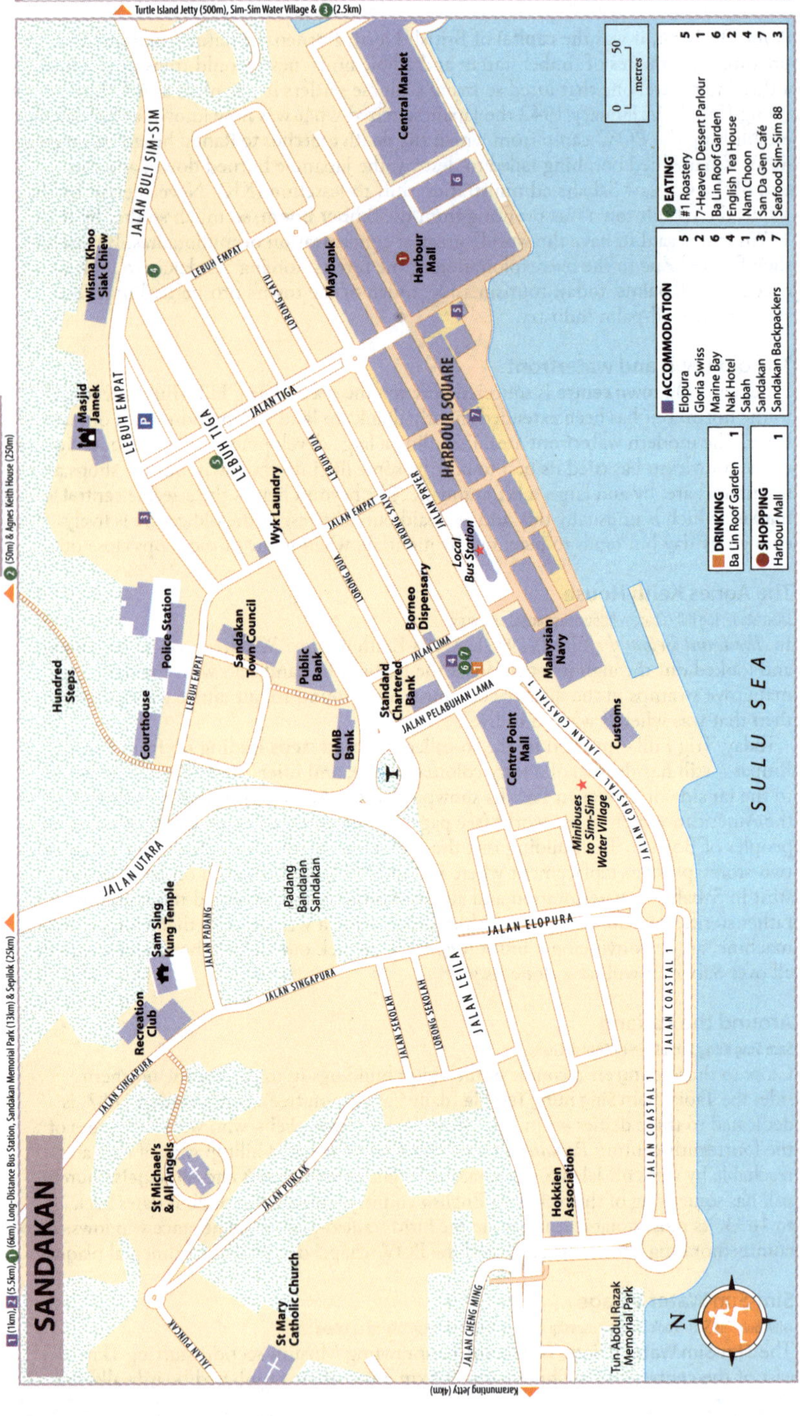

402 ❘ SABAH EASTERN SABAH

SANDAKAN

ACCOMMODATION
Elopura	5
Gloria Swiss	1
Marine Bay	6
Nak Hotel	4
Sabah	2
Sandakan	7
Sandakan Backpackers	3

EATING
#1 Roastery	5
7-Heaven Dessert Parlour	1
Ba Lin Roof Garden	6
English Tea House	2
Nam Choon	4
San Da Gen Café	7
Seafood Sim-Sim 88	3

DRINKING
Ba Lin Roof Garden	1

SHOPPING
Harbour Mall	1

SULU SEA

respectively signed *jambatan* (bridge) and *lorong* (lane). Most visitors are here for the seafood served up by several restaurants in the Chinese section (see page 404). The set-up feels not dissimilar to Penang's clan jetties (see page 148), with a grid of boardwalks laid out over the sea, flanked by largely timber houses. If your aim is to wander around and take pictures, be sensitive about residents' privacy, as the lanes take you right past their windows.

Sandakan Memorial Park

Mile 7, 11km west of Sandakan • Free • Any bus displaying 7 or higher; taxis also possible from the town centre

Sandakan Memorial Park marks the site of the World War II POW camp where the infamous **death marches** began. In 1942, around 2700 British and Australian soldiers were sent from Singapore to Sandakan and set to work building an airstrip. They were kept in appalling conditions and around three hundred had already died by early 1945, when the decision was made to relocate them to Ranau (260km away through mud and jungle). Around five hundred prisoners died on three forced marches, while many more perished after they arrived in Ranau or – if ill or injured – were left behind to die in Sandakan. In the end only six soldiers, all Australian, survived.

Signboards provide explanations for the few scattered remnants of the camp, while a small but moving museum covers the harsh conditions in the camp and the actual marches. If you are interested in a cycling tour that covers part of the death-march route, contact **TYK Adventure Tours** in KK (see page 376).

ARRIVAL AND DEPARTURE SANDAKAN

By plane Sandakan's airport is 11km north of town, and it's best to take a taxi into the centre from here. Buses hardly serve the airport, although occasional shared minivans do set off for the main road into town, where you can pick up onward transport or hop on a minibus bound for Sepilok (any vehicle displaying the number 14 or higher; see page 403).

Destinations Kota Kinabalu (6–7 daily; 45min); Kuala Lumpur (7 daily; 2hr 45min); Lahud Datu (1 daily; 30min); Tawau (1 daily; 30min).

By bus The transfer of the long-distance bus station to a new terminal at Mile 3 ran several years overdue, and finally took place in 2023; clearly a rush-job, the station looked old and dirty mere months after opening. It's a taxi or bus ride from pretty much everything of note; even more annoyingly, it can be frustratingly hard to book tickets to or from Sandakan using the regular websites.

Destinations Kinabalu Park (at least 12 daily; 5hr); Kota Kinabalu (at least 12 daily; 6hr 30min); Kudat (3 weekly; 5hr); Lahad Datu (at least 4 daily; 3hr); Semporna (at least 4 daily; 5hr); Tawau (at least 4 daily; 5hr); Telupid (at least 12 daily; 2hr 30min).

By minivan The only out-of-town service of interest to travellers is a daily private minivan to Sukau (019 536 1889), leaving from Lorong Satu.

By ferry Aleson Shipping (http://aleson-shipping.com) operates services to the Phillippines from the Karamunting Jetty, 4km southwest of town via any Pasir Putih-bound minivan.

Destinations Zamboanga (Philippines; 1 weekly; 16–20hr).

GETTING AROUND

By shared van or minibus Shared vans depart from Lebua Dua, and are much faster than the ageing minibuses that use the bus station on Jalan Pryer. As ever, transport grinds to a halt around dusk.

By taxi It's not hard to find a taxi on the main streets or outside hotels; Grab cars (http://grab.com/my) are, as ever, better value.

INFORMATION

Addresses As there's only one main road out of town (Jalan Utara), most suburban addresses include a distance along it – in miles (*batu*). Likewise, the numbers displayed by many minibuses and vans aren't routes, but how far in miles they go up that main road before turning off into one suburb or another. To reach a Mile 6 suburb, you should catch any vehicle numbered six or higher – but make sure you know the right spot on the main road to get off. To avoid what might be a long walk, it's safest to ride only a Mile 6 bus that also displays the name of the suburb you want.

Tourist information The *San Da Gen Café* (see page 405) has an informal information point with leaflets, and staff can also offer basic transport and sightseeing tips.

SANDAKAN TOUR OPERATORS

Sandakan's tour operators tend to focus on **packages** involving resorts that they run, notably around the Kinabatangan River (see page 408) or Sepilok (see page 405), but they usually offer other trips too.

Borneo Sandakan Tours Harbour Square; http://borneosandakan.com. Offers trips to all the key attractions of eastern Sabah and elsewhere across the state.

Pulau Sipadan Resort and Tours Mile 6, on the main road opposite the Giant supermarket; http://divemalaysia.com. Besides the nearby *Sepilok Nature Resort* and the *Lankayan Island Dive Resort* off the coast here, they also run resorts at Sipadan and Kapalai islands off Semporna.

Sepilok Tropical Wildlife Adventure Eastern end of Lebuh Tiga; http://stwadventure.com. Well-established operator that runs *Bilit Adventure Lodge* on the Kinabatangan River, plus *Sepilok Jungle Resort*.

SI Tours Block Harbour Square; http://sitoursborneo.com. Runs *Kinabatangan Riverside Lodge* and a second lodge on the Kinabatangan River, as well as offering tours.

Sukau Greenview Block Harbour Square; http://sukaugreenviewtravel.com. Runs the inexpensive *Sukau Greenview B&B* on the Kinabatangan River.

ACCOMMODATION   SEE MAP PAGE 402

Central Sandakan has several worthwhile places to stay, although it's feasible to base yourself at Sepilok instead (see page 405) and take a day-trip into town.

Elopura Eastern end of Harbour Square; http://elopurahotel.my. You'd usually expect to pay a premium price to be by the sea, but rates here are very fair indeed. Rooms can be a little on the small side, but it's worth enduring this minor discomfort; breakfasts are decent and the service also better than you'd expect at this price level. $\overline{\$\$}$

Gloria Swiss Jalan Letat Jaya, Bandar Letat Jaya; http://gloriaswisshotel.com. A good choice when (or possibly still "if") the new bus terminal comes on stream, since it will (possibly "would") be within walking distance, at least with light luggage. Cheerfully painted outside, and with rooms resembling those of proper hotels on the inside, it's a comfortable place – it may be worth shelling out extra on a suite, since they're pretty huge. $\overline{\$\$}$

Marine Bay Harbour Square, opposite the Central Market; http://oyorooms.com. This is a cheapish hotel with predictably unexciting rooms, but it's clean, well kept and fairly snug. Pay a bit extra for a sea view. $\overline{\$\$}$

Nak Hotel Jalan Pelabuhan Lama; http://oyorooms.com. If there's a glimmer of a revival in the town centre, this wannabe boutique hotel is it – though don't expect Penang-style slickness. There are some vintage Chinese touches such as the colourful chests in the lobby and blue-and-white porcelain sinks in the rooms, and the café and rooftop restaurant are excellent. $\overline{\$\$}$

Sabah On the main road, 1.5km north of the centre; http://sabahhotel.com.my. Venerable hotel with restaurants, a swimming pool and various sports facilities, all set within lush grounds spread up a low hill. The walk into town isn't that convenient, though. $\overline{\$\$\$}$

Sandakan Off Lebuh Empat; http://hotelsandakan.net. A solid, mid-range choice (almost upper end for Sandakan), peering down over the town. The breakfast area is really rather funky, and the rooms are supremely comfortable; try to get one on as high a floor as possible. $\overline{\$\$}$

★ **Sandakan Backpackers** Harbour Square; http://sandakanbackpackershostel.com. Snazzy wall art added by past guests aside, the decor here isn't particularly vibrant, though there's a leafy terrace with great bay views, and the owners are friendly and really know their city – you will genuinely feel right at home. Pay a little extra for an en suite or sea view. $\overline{\$}$

EATING   SEE MAP PAGE 402

There are a handful of worthwhile restaurants and *kedai kopis* in Sandakan's centre, but it's out in the **suburbs** – especially at Mile 4 and Mile 6 – that you'll find the full range of outlets you'd expect in most large Malaysian towns. There are also a few seafood places out over the water in the Chinese section of the **Sim-Sim Water Village**, east of town, plus two **markets** mainly selling cooked meals and snacks: one in Kim Fung (a Mile 4 neighbourhood; Sat 5–9pm, with a cultural performance by a school group most weeks), the other at Lebuh Dua in the centre (Sun 7am–1pm or so).

#1 Roastery Lorong 21 Lebuh Tiga; http://instagram.com/no.1roastery. The best of several decent cafes in this part of town – not only does the place smell great (somewhat inevitable, with a real roastery), but it looks fresh and has a lively vibe, plus Western comfort food to eat if you're peckish. $\overline{\$\$}$

7-Heaven Dessert Parlour In the grid of blocks about 200m up Jalan Cicely North, Bandar Indah, Mile 4; 089 220 326. This place isn't worth a special trip unless you have a very sweet tooth, but there's a huge range of ice cream and frozen yoghurts in flavours like green tea, as well as sinful sundaes and cakes. $\overline{5}$

★ Ba Lin Roof Garden Nak Hotel, Jalan Pelahuban Lama; http://facebook.com/Balinrooftop. Hearty quantities of inventive Western cuisine in stylish surroundings – this rooftop restaurant and bar (see page 405) ticks all the boxes. The pizzas, with unorthodox toppings such as pumpkin and pine nuts or salmon and crab, are terrific, as are the daily specials such as stewed lamb shank. There's an extensive brunch menu. $\overline{555}$

English Tea House Jalan Istana; http://englishteahouse. org. Sited near *Agnes Keith House* and with a lawn crying out for croquet, this bungalow restaurant majors on English favourites including shepherd's pie and tea for two with sandwiches, scones, jam and cream. The service can spoil the fantasy. $\overline{555}$

Nam Choon Northern end of Lebuh Tiga. One of not that many surviving old-school *kedai kopis* in the centre, serving four dishes: chicken rice; *nasi paha-paha atas* (the same, with chicken on the bone), *nasi* fish balls and *nasi ikan* (with fish). Each dish is brilliant and costs just a few ringgit. $\overline{5}$

★ San Da Gen Café Nak Hotel, Jalan Pelahuban Lama; http://facebook.com/TasteSanDaGen. With its marble tables and pristine floor tiles, *San Da Gen* blends the best of the old *kedai kopis* with modern decor. The menu concentrates on hawker standards with veggie variants. It's also one place to try a Sandakan speciality whose Chinese name literally means "cowdung tart" – more attractively branded here as the UFO tart, with a disc-shaped sponge topped with a "cabin" formed of a meringue ring enclosing custard. $\overline{5}$

Seafood Sim-Sim 88 Lorong 8, Sim-Sim Water Village; 089 226 558. One of the most popular of the various restaurants in the Sim-Sim Water Village, with lots of open-air tables and colourfully lit tanks of marine creatures awaiting an encounter with the wok. $\overline{55}$

DRINKING
SEE MAP PAGE 402

Ba Lin Roof Garden Nak Hotel, Jalan Pelahuban Lama; http://facebook.com/Balinrooftop. As well as good food (see page 405), this bar-restaurant boasts a range of beers and cocktails, too. Happy hours are nice and long, and the atmosphere convivial.

SHOPPING
SEE MAP PAGE 402

Harbour Mall The waterfront; http://harbourmall sandakan.com. This mall is admittedly a bit of a letdown, but has the usual necessities plus a Mr DIY outlet with a few basic camping/outdoor goods.

DIRECTORY

Banks Maybank is on Jalan Pryer at the northern end of Harbour Square, and there's a handful of other banks dotted about the centre.

Hospital Try the Duchess of Kent, on the main road 2km north of the centre (089 248 600).

Laundry Wyk Express at the start of Lebuh Empat is coin-operated and open 24hr.

Pharmacy You can find Guardian and Watsons at Harbour Mall.

Police The main police station is on the main road 1.5 km from town (089 211 222) with a smaller one on Lebuh Empat.

Visa extensions Immigration Department, Wisma Persekutuan, Mile 7 (089 668 328).

Sepilok

SEPILOK, 22km west up the main road from Sandakan, is a rural, partly forested area that clings on to some of Malaysia's most celebrated **wildlife**, among them rhinoceros hornbills and, famously, orangutans. A 3km turning south off the main road gives access to three fine attractions: the **Sepilok Orangutan Rehabilitation Centre** is the most well-known, but also worthwhile are the **Bornean Sun Bear Conservation Centre**, devoted to the world's smallest bear species, and the **Rainforest Discovery Centre**, part very wild town park, part forest reserve. There's also plenty of accommodation in Sepilok, so it's no wonder many visitors base themselves here rather than Sandakan.

Sepilok Orangutan Rehabilitation Centre
At the end of the Sepilok road • Charge • http://wildlife.sabah.gov.my

Occupying a 43-square-kilometre patch of lowland rainforest, the **Sepilok Orangutan Rehabilitation Centre** is one of just a few such sanctuaries and a standard stop on Sabah's tourist trail. Most of the orangutans here are victims of forest clearance; many have been orphaned, injured or traumatized in the process. Some have been illegally kept as pets, so their survival instincts remain undeveloped. The training the centre gives them in fending for themselves has led to many successful reintroductions to the wild.

There are several chances to observe these animals, designated as critically endangered in 2016: at a glass-fronted viewing gallery as they hone their climbing skills on a rope course; on trails through the trees (where their nests, at least, can be seen) and at the **feeding station** where they are offered only bananas to ensure they keep foraging. Don't be alarmed by a poor turnout: it can point to the health of the forest and its food sources.

Bornean Sun Bear Conservation Centre
Opposite the Orangutan Rehabilitation Centre • Charge • http://bsbcc.org.my

Like orangutans, sun bears are vulnerable – either because their adorable, teddy-like appearance makes them attractive as pets, or because traditional medicine calls for their body parts – and rescued ones need to relearn life skills. This is where the **Bornean Sun Bear Conservation Centre** comes in, housing some forty animals in woodland enclosures, a small number of which the public can view. Spotting scopes on the elevated boardwalks capture great close-up footage of the bears if you let staff hold your camera up against the eyepiece.

Rainforest Discovery Centre
2km down the Sepilok road and then 700m west along Jalan Fabia • Charge; extra fees for Kabili trail permit and night walk • http://rainforestdiscoverycentre.com

At first sight, the **Rainforest Discovery Centre** is a disappointingly landscaped version of the jungle, with an all-too-immaculate lake in the middle. The **canopy walkway** is, however, pretty impressive, a 347m series of substantial aerial bridges from where you might spot brightly coloured trogons and other birds, and perhaps giant squirrels. Take the lake anticlockwise (bear right towards the café from the entrance) to complete the circuit at the nicely air-conditioned visitor building, which has exhibits on rainforest ecology and a mini botanical garden close by. If you sign up for the guided **night walk**, you might just see flying squirrels, slow lorises and (rarely) tarsiers.

It's worth venturing beyond these core sights if you've time. Instead of turning left at the café for the canopy walkway, turn right for a series of signposted trails where the star attraction is the **Sepilok giant**, a 65m *Shorea* tree (allow 40min one-way). A full-scale trek is also possible on the **Kabili trail** (permit required), which terminates 8km from the lake.

ARRIVAL AND DEPARTURE   SEPILOK

By bus Sepilok is at Mile 14 on the Sandakan road, so any bus numbered 14 or higher from Sandakan can drop you at the start of the turning; express buses bound for Sandakan will do the same on the north side of the main road. Only the sporadic Mile 14 bus (5–6 daily) travels the full 3km of the Sepilok road. To flag down express buses for the rest of Sabah (routes are as for Sandakan, see page 403), wait at the start of the turning.

By taxi Taxis are on hand between Sepilok and Sandakan.

ACCOMMODATION

Keen competition means that Sepilok's accommodation is generally good value. Rates include breakfast except where stated.

My Nature Resort Very west end of Jalan Fabia; http://sitoursborneo.com. One of the area's newer places to stay, beautifully designed throughout, and with rooms that might make you feel like you're staying in a cosy wooden cube. It's even more tranquil than most of the competition, and the outdoor pool is a grand place to cool off after a day padding around the sights (or, it has to be said, sitting on a bus); late-evening swims are particularly blissful here. There's also a decent restaurant on site. $$$

★ **Paganakan Dii Tropical Retreat** Taman Hiburan Jalil Alip, a private forest track 2km northwest of the Sepilok turning; http://paganakandii.com. A brilliant jungle hilltop haven, this timber and bamboo complex boasts slick chalets with a/c and open-air bathrooms, plus cheaper longhouse-style fan rooms and dorms. Facilities include an elevated open-air lounge area, a lookout tower and zip line. Breakfast is included; other meals available too. Dorms $, doubles $$

★ **Sepilok B&B** Jalan Fabia; http://sepilokbednbreakfast.com. A friendly place with timber lodges and chalets set in sprawling grounds. The decor isn't the most lavish, but some units come with sizeable living rooms and kitchens that more than compensate. There's also a campsite (own tent required) and dorms (though you'll have to pay a bit extra if you want a/c and hot water). Only campers pay for breakfast. Camping/dorms $, doubles $$

Sepilok Forest Edge Resort 700m up Jalan Rambutan, a turning 2.5km from the main road; http://sepilokforestedgeresort.com. This place has small dorms and a series of appealing chalets, some boasting open-air showers, all dotted around a multilevel landscaped garden with a plunge pool. Their *Nest* restaurant serves up sophisticated takes on local cuisine, plus fusion creations such as lamb shank in a Thai curry sauce. Dorms $, chalets $$$

Sepilok Jungle Resort 200m up Jalan Rambutan; 089 533031. A large complex with its own lake, somewhat dated faux timber dorms and rooms, and a pool (open to non-guests for a fee). If you take a double room, a/c will cost you extra. Dorms $, doubles $

Sepilok Nature Resort Jalan Sepilok, close to the Orangutan Rehabilitation Centre; http://facebook.com/SepilokNatureResort. The plushest place to stay in Sepilok, with spacious and eco-aware chalets nestled amid lush jungle. The restaurant, looking out on to the resort's lake, is predictably on the pricey side. Rates exclude breakfast. $$$$

Tanini Sepilok 1.5km south of the main road; http://taninihotel.com. On its own little hillock, this assembly of buildings – formerly known as the *Nature Lodge*, and still referred to that way by some locals and on some maps – has surprisingly slick rooms, some with open-air bathrooms at the back opening onto private patches of greenery. There are four-bed dorms, too. Dorms $, doubles $$

Labuk Bay Proboscis Monkey Sanctuary

Near Samawang, a kampung 15km up a signed turning 30km (i.e. at Mile 19) up the Sandakan road • Charge • http://proboscis.cc • Shuttle minibus leaves Sandakan 8am, Sepilok 10.30am, returning at 3pm & 5pm • Taxi from Sandakan; asking your driver to stick around for the return trip won't cost that much more than two cab rides

Set amid mangrove forest and reached via a track through an oil-palm plantation (under the same ownership, which is a bit disappointing), **Labuk Bay Proboscis Monkey Sanctuary** functions as a companion to the more famous orangutan sanctuary at Sepilok. Most visitors come on a **day-trip** from Sandakan – or from Sepilok, which is significantly closer. It's no longer possible to stay the night in Labuk Bay.

Two large observation platforms offer perfect vantage points from which to view the monkeys (see page 433); you might also see silverleaf monkeys scavenge fruit left behind, and there's some fantastic birdlife including hornbills. On a day-trip you could see all four feedings if you like, or even leave after just one, but it's more usual to see one from each platform. Using the shuttle bus makes sense as the site is quite spread out, and it will take you to two feedings and the restaurant at lunchtime.

Lankayan Island

Ninety minutes' boat ride north of Sandakan in the Sulu Sea lies the **Sugud Islands Marine Conservation Area**, managed by a Sandakan nonprofit organization. Only one of its three islands, **Lankayan Island**, is visitable, with a delightful resort and an active turtle-hatching programme; that said, **diving** and **snorkelling** are the real pull. Hard and soft corals surround the island and are in very good condition, and the macro life in particular is excellent. Divers may see whale sharks in April and May.

ACCOMMODATION — LANKAYAN ISLAND

Lankayan Island Dive Resort c/o Pulau Sipadan Resort and Tours (see page 404 for details); http://lankayan-island.com. This is a delightful resort with large, comfortable chalets, helpful staff and a competently run dive shop. Most plump for a two-night package, including transfers from Sandakan and the conservation fee – bring along plenty of extra cash if you'd like to try your hand at diving here. $$$$

Turtle Islands National Park

Trips operated by Crystal Quest (http://turtleisland.com.my); check for latest prices and to book, or book through a travel agent

Peeping out of the Sulu Sea 40km north of Sandakan is the **Turtle Islands National Park**, where green and hawksbill turtles haul themselves laboriously above the high-tide mark to bury their clutches of eggs most nights. Although all three of the islands – Selingan, Bakungan Kecil and Gulisan – hold **hatcheries**, tourists can only visit **Selingan**; full-board overnight packages offer accommodation in 25 double rooms, all en suite and with air conditioning.

Before dark (when a beach curfew kicks in) there's plenty of time for **swimming**, **snorkelling** and **sunbathing**. At night, besides seeing a mother turtle laying her eggs, you can watch as the park wardens release hatchling turtles that waddle, Chaplin-like, into the sea.

Along the Kinabatangan River

Sabah's longest waterway, the 560km **Kinabatangan River**, ends its journey to the Sulu Sea southeast of Sandakan Bay. Whereas logging has had an impact on the river's ecology upstream, the area covered by the **Lower Kinabatangan Wildlife Sanctuary** offers some of the state's best opportunities for seeing wildlife – days of trekking in Sabah's jungle reserves may yield paltry rewards by comparison.

Day-trips from Sandakan and Sepilok are possible with some tour operators (see page 404), but tend to offer just one river trip bookended by meals – it's far better to book at least a one-night package to get an evening and a morning crack at the river or a trek. With a few exceptions, most lodges are located either in or around the villages of **Sukau** or **Bilit**, from either of which you can visit the **Gomantong Caves**, where edible swiftlet nests are harvested. Note that from November to February, rainy-season floods can disrupt trips or close some lodges.

Lower Kinabatangan Wildlife Sanctuary

The last 70km or so of the Kinabatangan River forms the **Lower Kinabatangan Wildlife Sanctuary**, a large forested floodplain, peppered with oxbow lakes and mangrove swamps. The designation of 260 square kilometres of land close to the river as the reserve in 2005 was commendable, but it is still broken up into eleven pockets interspersed with villages of the local **Orang Sungai** (literally "river people") and oil-palm plantations. Policing remains a headache: in 2013 a plantation was illegally extended, and there have been sporadic discoveries of dismembered sun bear carcasses, the handiwork of poachers. At least there was one success in 2017 when, following opposition from conservationists – including David Attenborough – the state government scrapped a planned road bridge over the river at Sukau that would, opponents argued, have seriously impeded the movement of animals.

For now, the sanctuary offers visitors a half-decent chance of seeing **mammals** such as pygmy elephants, orangutans, proboscis monkeys, macaques and gibbons; dolphins are occasionally seen near the river mouth (away from most lodges). The resident **birdlife** is as impressive, including hornbills, brahminy kites, crested serpent eagles, egrets, exquisite blue-banded and stork-billed kingfishers, and oriental darters, which dive for food and then sit on the shore, their wings stretched out to dry. Some lodges offer **night cruises** with opportunities to photograph owls and sleeping birds using floodlights.

Gomantong Caves

Reached by a 4.7km turning off the Sukau road, 19km east of the main road • Charge • http://wildlife.sabah.gov.my • Without your own transport, take a Sukau-bound minivan from Sandakan to the start of the turning and walk/hitch the rest of the way

The **Gomantong Caves** are inhabited by swiftlets whose nests, formed of hardened saliva, are harvested for the bird's-nest-soup trade (usually February to April and July to September). There are nineteen limestone caves in all, and they're also home to a huge number of **bats** that emerge at dusk in sinewy streams – although visits as part of Kinabatangan packages are never timed for this.

Tourists usually visit **Simud Hitam**, the "black cave", which gets its name because it mostly contains dark nests produced by the black-nest swiftlet. It's quite an impressive chamber, and of scientific interest because recent laser- and drone-mapping suggests that the acidic bird and bat guano has substantially enlarged the cave over millennia by speeding erosion. That said, the stinky guano attracts hordes of cockroaches that crunch underfoot or crawl on your feet, so sandals aren't a good idea; some visitors don ponchos, in addition to the helmets provided, to keep extra-clean. The even larger **Simud Putih** beyond, from where the bats emerge, is generally closed to all but nest collectors, who head there for the more valuable constructions of the white-nest swiftlet.

Sukau and Bilit

SUKAU, 134km from Sandakan, was where the first tourist lodges on the Kinabatangan opened. Linked to the main road by its own sealed one, the village sits on the north bank of the river and is a particular target for independent travellers. By dint of its popularity, however, Sukau is not the place to seek solitude, with dozens of boats on this stretch of river at peak times. If this doesn't appeal, **BILIT** lies a little further upriver and remains a quiet place to stay – it can be reached by a turning off the Sukau road.

ARRIVAL AND DEPARTURE

By tour Tour operators generally arrange transport to their respective lodges from Sandakan and Sepilok, as well as boat transfers – sometimes all the way from Sandakan – for lodges on the right bank.

By bus If you're travelling independently or arriving from somewhere other than Sandakan or Sepilok, you can reach Sukau by public transport. Any express bus plying the main east-coast road – en route between KK/Sandakan and Lahad Datu and beyond – can drop you at the Sukau turning, 89km from Sandakan, from where Sukau minivans travel the remaining 45km to the village (45min). For Bilit, arrange with your accommodation to be picked up at the Sukau turning. If you're departing, you'll need to ask around about the best time to be back at the main road, as buses tend to leave in clusters – there's usually a group of southbound buses departing daily between 9 and 9.30am, for example.

ALONG THE KINABATANGAN RIVER

ACCOMMODATION

Kinabatangan package accommodation ranges from swanky **timber lodges** with eco-friendly credentials to fairly basic affairs, and this is one part of Malaysia where **homestays** (see page 38) are worth considering – many are bookable online, using the regular sites and apps. Single-night packages always offer an evening boat ride plus a short trek or a second cruise at dawn the next day, and can be totally satisfying if a bit rushed. Two-night packages may only cost thirty percent more and generally include three boat rides, plus a trek and sometimes the Gomantong Caves. Independent travellers can save money by choosing a B&B or homestay and then adding boat trips and activities as desired. Don't expect cheaper places to serve **alcohol**, and make sure you dress conservatively if you choose a homestay – the local Orang Sungai are largely Muslim. Unless otherwise stated, all **prices** are for two people sharing and include all meals and transport to/from Sandakan.

SUKAU AND AROUND

Borneo Nature Lodge http://borneonaturelodge.com.my. This mid-range option, attractively surrounded by tall trees, has its own observation tower and a/c restaurant – a rarity in these parts. $$$$

Kinabatangan Riverside Lodge www.sitoursborneo.com. A slick timber affair whose bougainvillea-laden decking adds a splash of colour to the river. The two-night package includes trips to see the orangutans and sun bears in Sepilok and boat transfers to/from Sandakan. $$$$

Sukau Greenview Lodge At the end of the Sukau road; http://sukaugreenviewtravel.com. This place, once cheap and cheerful, has gone upmarket in recent years – it's thus no longer as popular with independent travellers, but the hefty prices do usually include transport to and from the airport, plus full board, and a minimum of three boat rides (including one in the dark of evening), even if you're only staying one night. $$

Sukau Rainforest Lodge http://sukau.com. This has been a sound choice for many years, as it has its own spa and a range of recreational activities including batik painting. Their boats are some of the speediest, giving them an edge whenever wildlife heaves into view. Two-night packages are the basic option, but given that they are run by birding specialist Borneo Eco Tours, there's also a three-night birdwatching package. $$$$

BILIT AND AROUND

Bilit Adventure Lodge http://stwadventure.com. This was the first lodge to open in Bilit and is still popular, with two dozen fairly simple en-suite rooms, some with a/c. The owners have a sense of humour: if you get bitten by a leech,

you'll be awarded a blood donor certificate. Rate is for a one-night package including the Gomantong Caves. $$$$
Borneo Jungle Adventure http://borneojungleadventure.com. Given their price, the rooms here are fairly simple en-suite affairs, minus a/c, but they do offer specialist birding and photographic tours in addition to the usual trips. $$$$
Borneo Natural Sukau http://kinabatanganriver.com.my. This place offers an attractive clump of chalets and slightly cheaper longhouse rooms nestled amid the forest, as well as an airy restaurant and a huge range of add-on activities, including cycling and night walks. Price is for a one-night package including the Sepilok Orangutan Rehabilitation Centre and the Gomantong Caves. $$$$
★ **Last Frontier** http://thelastfrontierresort.com. This chic guesthouse is set on a jungle-swathed hill, only accessible via 538 steps (ask about porters if you need help with your luggage). There are just four rooms, which all offer excellent views over the surrounding plains. Packages include river trips (only one on the one-night option); transfers from Sandakan cost extra. $$$$
Tanini Kinabatangan On the eastern bank near Bilit; insabah.com. This good-value option has one wing of dorms and another of quite pleasant chalets, a few with a/c. If you're staying two nights, you can enjoy an optional jungle trek to an oxbow lake an hour away, and you can also do a spot of kayaking (free). Transfers from Sandakan or Sepilok cost extra. Dorms $$$, chalets $$$$

OTHER LOCATIONS
Tanjung Bulat Jungle Camp At the Tanjung Bulat oxbow lake, west of the main road and south of Kota Kinabatangan; http://lamagborneo.com. A basic timber lodge with a dorm consisting of mattresses on a raised platform, plus some private rooms. They do the usual two- and three-night deals, with Gomantong Caves as an option, and can pick guests up near the town of Kota Kinabatangan. $$$$
★ **Tungog Rainforest Eco Camp** North of the Kinabatangan River; http://tungoglakeecocamp.com. Basic rainforest camp with the usual boat trips plus a trek, and optional trips to funerary caves nearby. $$$$
Uncle Tan's Wildlife Camp Beside the Lokan River, a Kinabatangan tributary; 016 824 4749, http://uncletan.com. "The camp is not exactly the *Hilton*" is the owners' own description of their camp in the wilds, where the huts are elevated against floods and lack doors and windows. Electricity is by night only. Still, this is as close as you'll get to a back-to-nature experience here, and they also offer morning and evening river trips and treks. Rates are for a one-night package. $$$$

Lahad Datu and around

Tiny **LAHAD DATU** is a bland but pleasant enough seaside town on the northern shore of **Darvel Bay**, 173km from Sandakan by road. The town has been a magnet at times for Indonesian and Filipino migrants, often undocumented, who come to work on plantations and in the construction industry, and in 2013 the place hit headlines when the worst of Sabah's recent security incidents took place (see page 370).

The few visitors who come to Lahad Datu usually pass through en route to the **Danum Valley** and the **Tabin Wildlife Reserve**, though it's often necessary to stay at least one night and the town has a few nice diversions to help pass the time – nearby **Mount Silam** offers a much cheaper taste of the jungle than its celebrated counterparts, for one.

The waterfront market
The main road through town is Jalan Teratai, one block south of which is the seafront Jalan Pantai and the **waterfront market**, which is divided across three buildings: the *pasar ikan* (fish), *pasar rakyat* (meat and vegetables) and *pasar kain* (cheap clothes and bags). The most entertaining of these is undoubtedly the fish market, where tourists are still something of a novelty for the traders who sit within circular enclosures amid the day's catch.

Kwan Tee Temple
Jalan Dahlia • Free • Look for the police post on Jalan Teratai then head north a short distance from there

It isn't anything grand, but the Chinese **Kwan Tee Temple** is worthy of a brief look for its colourful wall reliefs showing a green-robed figure on horseback. Often seen toting a halberd, this is none other than Kwan Tee, a semi-mythological character who may have lived circa 200 AD. Deified as the Chinese god of war, he takes pride of place on the central altar, with his halberd-bearer immediately to his right.

ARRIVAL AND DEPARTURE

By plane Lahad Datu's airport has MASwings flights to KK (4–5 daily; 55min) and Sandakan (1 daily; 30min). It's only 1km or so from Jalan Teratai, the main road – head uphill onto Jalan Kastam Lama from the roundabout at the southern end of the runway, and you will shortly arrive in the centre. A taxi into town costs very little.

By long-distance bus The express bus station is located at First Palm City Centre, a relatively new development 800m northwest of the centre.

Destinations Kinabalu Park (14 daily; 7hr); Kota Kinabalu (14 daily; 8hr); Sandakan (4 daily; 3hr); Semporna (3–4 daily; 2hr); Tawau (7 daily; 1hr 30min).

By shared taxi, minivan and local bus Shared taxis and minivans leave from a few points around the centre, although most use a station at the corner of Jalan Pantai and Jalan Bunga Raya, towards the eastern end of the centre, which is also used by slow local buses to Tawau and Sandakan. The only vehicles here you might want to use are for Semporna.

INFORMATION AND TOURS

Danum Valley information Three offices linked with the Danum Valley (see page 412) stand side by side, facing the airport runway. The Danum Valley Field Centre office (closed weekends; 089 880441) takes bookings for their accommodation, issues permits and can provide general information on the conservation area. Next door you'll find Borneo Nature Tours (http://borneonaturetours.com), which runs the *Borneo Rainforest Lodge*, as well as an office run by Borneo Refugia.

Tours Bike and Tours has some distinctive offerings alongside its accommodation (see page 411), including – as their name suggests – a combination tour and bike ride to Mount Silam (see page 411), plus diving at Darvel Bay. They as well as the owner of *Tabin Lodge* (see page 411) run trips to the Bukit Piton reserve (see page 412), where there's a decent chance of spotting orangutans. Make bookings in advance as time is needed to secure permits and other necessities.

ACCOMMODATION

Bay Hotel Western end of Jalan Teratai; 016 826 3801. Offers surprisingly pleasant rooms in an otherwise mundane four-storey block. No breakfast and no lifts. $$

★ **Bike and Tours B&B** 2km northwest of the centre in Taman Hup Heng, near the northern end of the airport runway; http://bikeandtours.com. Simply furnished but very comfortable a/c double rooms in a sprawling suburban home, which has its own little garden pool at the back. The cheapest rooms are on the cosy side and share bathrooms. Free guest pick-ups; breakfast costs extra, and other meals available on request. $$

Grace Jalan Kastam Lama; http://facebook.com/gracehotelld. This place initially looks a little different, with its budget-sleek facade forming quite a contrast with its workaday surroundings. Inside it's a bit more basic, but still very fair value for the price, with spacious rooms, some with very partial sea views. $

Tabin Lodge Jalan Urusetia Kecil, near the eastern end of Jalan Teratai; http://oyorooms.com. This must have been quite a guesthouse in its heyday, but some fittings now look like museum pieces. Still, the rooms are perfectly serviceable and come with optional a/c and en-suite bathrooms, though the latter are sometimes simply half-walled off from the rest of the room. $

EATING

★ **Auliah** Down a lane opposite the Executive Hotel on Jalan Teratai, close to the RHB Bank; 089 880 266. Featuring a dazzling selection of inexpensive curries and *roti* and rice variations, including the bright yellow local speciality *nasi kuning*, this is a classic *mamak* place, busy even late in the evening and popular with the entire cross-section of Sabah society. The upstairs tables have a/c. $

Unicorn Vegetarian Down a lane just south of the airport; 089 882 467. Decent veggie restaurant a short walk away from the airport – very basic, but to some it will feel like heaven. Simply get in line and scoop your chosen edibles onto your plate. $

Mount Silam

15km southwest of Lahad Datu · Charge; guides extra · 089 881560 · Any southbound local bus from Lahad Datu or express bus can call here

The tallest peak in the vicinity of Lahad Datu is the 884m **Mount Silam**, within the Sapagaya Forest Reserve. From the entrance on the main road, a 10km lane snakes its way up the mountain; en route is an elevated viewpoint, the 33m **Tower of Heaven** (Menara Kayangan), with terrific vistas out to the islands in Darvel Bay and, in the opposite direction, the jungle centred around the Danum Valley. Besides the lookout tower, there are also several jungle **trails** of varying lengths – you may see sambar deer, Bornean gibbons, pig-tailed macaques, the arboreal loris, pitcher plants, and, if you're very lucky the small and orange-red **silam crab**, unique to this mountain.

Tabin Wildlife Reserve

Some 40km northeast of Lahad Datu • http://tabinwildlife.com.my • Take the daily minivan (departs 8am, returns 1.30pm; 1hr 30min) from the resort's office at Lahad Datu airport

Tabin Wildlife Reserve, twice the size of Singapore, combines primary and secondary forest with excellent opportunities to see wildlife. Pygmy elephants, macaques, wild boar and orangutans can be spotted, as can the rare clouded leopard if you're lucky. Birdwatchers can look out for more than three hundred kinds of birds, with endemic species such as the Bornean bristlehead, blue-headed pitta and all eight local species of hornbills. You can take a walk to a **mud volcano**, used by animals as a mineral lick, or head off on a hike (the longest trail is 2.8km) or a night drive. The reserve also houses Malaysia's last two known **Sumatran rhinos**, cared for by the Borneo Rhino Alliance, although this particular sanctuary isn't open to the public. It's difficult to have a proper taste of Tabin with a one-night stay, so it's worth budgeting for at least two.

ACCOMMODATION   TABIN WILDLIFE RESERVE

Tabin Wildlife Resort http://tabinwildlife.com.my. This place offers a range of chalets with high ceilings, half of them by a river and the other half spread up a hillside; all of them come with nice private balconies, and buffet meals and transport to/from Lahad Datu are provided in the rates. Rates are for two nights. $$$$

Danum Valley

About 90min from Lahad Datu by 4WD • Charge; camera and vehicle permits extra • http://searrp.org • Reached by a signed turning 15km southwest of Lahad Datu

The **Danum Valley** is "perhaps the last area of primary lowland forest in Southeast Asia which remains truly pristine". That glowing description isn't from a tour operator brochure, but from the South East Asia Rainforest Research Partnership, an international scientific collaboration that's been based here since the 1980s – and you can meet their biologists if you stay at the field centre. **Wildlife** includes bearded pigs, orangutans, proboscis monkeys, elephants and more than 320 species of bird, and the area is also home to the world's tallest known rainforest tree, a 94m *Shorea*. Be aware that, as ever, spotting animals in dense jungle is a challenge.

RESERVES AROUND THE DANUM VALLEY

The Danum Valley is the brightest star in a constellation of forest reserves covering thousands of square kilometres in southeast Sabah, all belonging to the non-profit **Sabah Foundation**, which uses the proceeds of logging to fund scholarships. There are two nearby reserves, reached via the Danum Valley turning, that are also worth visiting.

   Kawag reserve, 36km in from the coast road, offers a "jungle-lite" experience in secondary forest northeast of Danum, which has now been restored after logging. The vegetation is noticeably more open here. Wildlife includes gibbons, pig-tailed macaques, elephants, martens, flying squirrels and the usual range of creepy-crawlies. An upgraded former research station here also offers short treks up to 1.5km, including one to a stream where you can swim and try tubing. Most go for a two-night all-inclusive package, with transport to and from Lahad Datu included.

   Further east and quite different is the **Bukit Piton reserve**. The big draw in this badly logged region, which is being slowly reforested, is the orangutans, which were unfortunately marooned here between oil-palm plantations to the north and the Segama River to the south. Day-trips run from Lahad Datu are the only way to visit (see page 411).

There are just two (very different) places to stay here, located apart from each other. Packages at the slick, pricey **Borneo Rainforest Lodge** include the services of professional guides who accompany you on a 300m canopy walkway, a 3km trek to a burial cliff and a night drive, for example. At the prosaic **Danum Valley Field Centre**, it's possible to trek to waterfalls up to three hours away, and rangers can be hired as guides – though their skills in this area vary.

ACCOMMODATION — DANUM VALLEY

Borneo Rainforest Lodge 77km from the Danum Valley turning; http://borneonaturetours.com. Resort-style accommodation in the heart of the jungle in hardwood chalets, all naturally ventilated rather than with a/c. The more expensive units face the Danum River and have a private outdoor tub or even an infinity pool. Book through Borneo Nature Tours in KK or Lahad Datu. Think about choosing a two-night package, including transport. $$$$

Danum Valley Rainforest Lodge Beside the river, 63km from the Danum Valley turning; http://danumvalley.rainforestlodge.com. The place where researchers and most travellers stay, featuring a campsite (tents provided), dorms (bunk beds in cubicles for two), en-suite doubles and two chalets with upmarket doubles. Meals cost extra, payable by the day. 4WDs. Try to book at least a month and a half in advance; packages usually include a 4WD ride from the office in Lahad Datu. Camping/dorms $, doubles $$$, chalets $$$$

Semporna

Fringed by water villages on either side, **SEMPORNA** is inhabited largely by the **Bajau Laut** (sometimes dubbed sea gypsies) who once lived nomadically on houseboats (*lepa*) – although only a fifth of those in the area now do. As a prelude to the marine marvels of Sabah's southeastern islands, the town is pretty unappealing. The only tourists who seem to relish being here are the ubiquitous groups from China, who saved the local dive industry when security scares (see page 370)

kept Westerners away – it's worth **booking** dive packages a few weeks in advance whenever there's a holiday in China.

Most visitors avoid the grubby centre and stick to the area around **Bandar Baru** (the "new town"), the tiny grid of modern seafront blocks southeast of the **Ur-Rahman mosque** (look for its silvery dome) and beyond the main market. There's little to see except during the touristy **Regatta Lepa** in April, a pageant contested by *lepa* with colourful sails.

ARRIVAL AND DEPARTURE   SEMPORNA

By plane Tawau airport (see page 418) is the gateway for many visitors to Semporna, and is about 110km away. A taxi between the two obviously won't be cheap, but neither should it break the bank.

By bus The main bus terminal is off the coast road about 50m west of the mosque, although one company, Dyana Express, uses a space 100m inland from here. Most buses leave before 9am or after 6pm.

Destinations Kota Kinabalu (6 daily; 10hr); Lahad Datu (3–4 daily; 2hr); Sandakan (at least 4 daily; 5hr); Tawau (5 daily; 1hr 30min).

By minivan Most minivans leave from just beside the main bus terminal, though Tawau services set off from close to *KFC* a little further inland.

Destinations Lahad Datu (2hr); Tawau (1hr 30min).

ACCOMMODATION   SEE MAP PAGE 413

★ **Best Bunk Beds** Northern corner of Bandar Baru; 019 851 8039. The bunk beds are crammed together and the management is somewhat bureaucratic, but the whole place is immaculate. The free breakfast – eggs, noodles, cake, toasted sandwiches – is about as good as it gets for a hostel. $

★ **Cube Bed Station** Bandar Baru; http://facebook.com/cbshostel. Swanky capsule beds with privacy drapes and a handful of double rooms with beds on wooden platforms; roughly rendered walls lending an industrial chic touch throughout. An en-suite sea view room costs nearly twice the standard rate. Dorms $, doubles $$

Scuba Junkie Dive Lodge Bandar Baru; http://scuba-junkie.com. This is a functional affair with dorms and double rooms (a few with private bathrooms), but a real bargain if you're diving or snorkelling with them as accommodation prices halve. Dorms $, doubles $$

Seafest Hotel Jalan Kastam Extension; http://seafesthotel.com. This is the smartest hotel in town, with a pool and gym, plus a newer "boutique" wing across the road where rooms are actually around twenty percent cheaper. Buffet breakfast is included for the more expensive room types, otherwise it's extra. $$$

EATING   SEE MAP PAGE 413

Mukbang Lab Cafe Jalan Causeway; 089 788804. This simple Korean restaurant at least brings some variety to proceedings – instead of seafood, you can have Korean comfort fare such as fishcake in broth, *ramyeon* noodles, fried chicken, or an iteration of *bibimbap* (veggies and egg on rice), all served with a miniature armada of *banchan* (side dishes). $$$

★ **Thien Wang** Bandar Baru; 016 881 8677. This place is deservedly popular among Chinese visitors, who flock here for the excellent fresh seafood. The menu is extensive, with simple one-plate meals such as rice and butter squid alongside sizzling tofu, lemon chicken and a dozen noodle variations. $$

DIRECTORY

Bank There's a Maybank near one of the two filling stations in the centre, just one block back from the mosque.
Clinic Permai Polyclinics is around the corner from the Dyana Express bus depot (24hr; 017 763 8393).
Pharmacies Bandar Baru has branches of both Guardian and Watsons.

DIVING AND SNORKELLING AROUND SEMPORNA

Many of Semporna's **dive shops** focus on selling packages at their own accommodation on the islands (see page 414), but also sell diving and snorkelling day-trips from town.

★ **Scuba Junkie** Bandar Baru; http://scuba-junkie.com. This impeccably organized firm runs courses from Discover Scuba right up to instructor level, and takes a strong conservation-oriented stance. They use their Semporna branch for trips to Tun Sakaran Marine Park and their Mabul one as a base for Sipadan trips.

Scubaholics Bandar Baru, above the Century store; http://scuba-holics.com. This is a popular indie operator covering all of the usual diving destinations in the area.

Islands around Semporna

Two marine parks lie off the coast of southeast Sabah. Most famed is **Sipadan Island**, a park in its own right and the prime destination for experienced divers, although nearby **Mabul Island** and **Kapalai Island** (which don't lie within a park) are also renowned for marine life – all three lie south of Semporna. North and east of the town in Darvel Bay are the eight islands of the **Tun Sakaran Marine Park**.

Sipadan Island
Charge for visitor permit

Acclaimed by Jacques Cousteau as "an untouched piece of art", **Sipadan Island** is mindboggling, its waters teeming with turtles, moray eels, sharks, barracuda and vast schools of colourful tropical fish, as well as the occasional dolphin and pilot whale. The diversity of coral found here is also comparable to that of Australia's Great Barrier Reef. Only 120 visitor permits are available for Sipadan daily, so it's likely you'll spend a day here with your dive operator and then a few around the nearby islands.

Most of the dozen-plus commonly visited dive sites around Sipadan offer the chance to see abundant turtles and white-tip sharks. The most popular spot, **Barracuda Point**, is a drift dive where divers hold onto rocks while shoals of barracuda pass by. Another great site is the **Drop-off**, close to the jetty, where you often find large schools of barracuda, bumphead parrotfish and Napoleon wrasse. Close to here is the entrance to **Turtle Cave**, where you'll find the skeletal remains of turtles that have strayed in and become lost.

Mabul Island

Mabul Island is split between dive accommodation and the shanties of the Bajau Laut. There are beaches on the north shore, but refuse is a problem in some areas, and while it's possible to stroll round the entire island in 45 minutes, most visitors focus on the attractions offshore. Visibility is less reliable than at Sipadan, and the **muck diving** – seeking out creatures in the sediment – is famous here. Among the marine life close to the island are many turtles of all sizes, seahorses – including the rare pygmy seahorse – frogfish, cuttlefish, mimic octopuses, lionfish, stonefish and ribbon eels.

Kapalai Island

Really a sandbar, tiny **Kapalai Island** is exquisite and otherworldly. The house reef has five minor wrecks, and divers are drawn by macro life such as pygmy seahorses, harlequin ghost pipefish and mandarinfish. There's one pricey resort, although Kapalai is accessible from Mabul, too.

Tun Sakaran Marine Park
Conservation fee applies

The most interesting islands at **Tun Sakaran Marine Park** are **Sibuan Island**, with a breathtaking beach, shallow reefs and calm waters, making it suitable for inexperienced divers and learners; and **Mantubuan Island**, where you can dive to see rare black (actually multicoloured) coral, resembling a forest of underwater Christmas trees. Accommodation lies just east of the park on two immaculate little islands, namely **Pom Pom Island** and teardrop-shaped **Mataking Island** – the latter has a wall dive where you might see turtles, rays and sharks.

ACCOMMODATION   ISLANDS AROUND SEMPORNA

All accommodation lies outside the two marine parks (the lion's share of it on Mabul Island), and is mostly sold in **packages** including boat transfers and meals, with diving and snorkelling either charged separately or with a fixed number of dives included. Pricing is often quoted per person – unless noted, **room rates** used here are for two people for one night (though longer stays are better value), excluding diving. Details of booking offices in Semporna are given where relevant.

MABUL

Mabul has resorts and a few basic guesthouses of variable

quality; all places on the south shore are on stilts out at sea amid the scruffy water villages, although guests are largely insulated from that by dint of arriving and leaving by boat.

RESORTS

★ Borneo Divers North shore of Mabul; http://borneo divers.com.my. A great mid-range choice, with two-room chalets in well-kept grounds centred around a freeform pool. There's a nice restaurant, a bar and spa, too. Two-night diving packages available. $$$$

★ Mabul Beach Resort North shore of Mabul; 089 785 372. The perfect middle ground between resort and guesthouse, with dorms as well as en-suite rooms equipped with rain showers and outdoor hammocks (although only some rooms have a/c and hot water). There are decent buffet meals and there's an upstairs bar, too. Given Scuba Junkie's conservation stance, they run a small turtle hatchery and don't serve seafood. You can either book an all-inclusive package or pay for everything separately, in which case you'll get a twenty percent discount on accommodation if you're a diver. The one-night diving package is a good deal; book through Scuba Junkie in Semporna (see page 414). Dorms $$$, doubles $$$$

Mabul Water Bungalows North shore of Mabul; http:// mabulwaterbungalows.com. The ultra-luxurious sibling of the *Sipidan-Mabul Resort*, with Balinese-style chalets perched on stilts over the sea. VIP rooms have glass panels in the floor and jacuzzis. Dive packages available. $$$$

Seaventure Off the north shore of Mabul; http:// seaventuresdive.com. It looks like a levitating ship from afar, but this is really a former oil rig with good rooms and buffet meals. The best deal is for a three-night dive package. $$$$

Sipadan-Mabul Resort (aka SMART) Eastern shore of Mabul; http://sipadanmabulresortcom. Taking up much of the southeast of Mabul, this fine resort has more than forty wooden en-suite chalets, a pool, a large restaurant and jacuzzis in the grounds. Five nights' stay needed for Sipadan. $$$$

Sipadan Water Village North shore of Mabul; http:// swvresortmabul.com. A less grand version of *Mabul Water Bungalows* next door, with a range of standalone and two-roomed chalets supposedly built according to Bajau design. Dive packages available. $$$$

GUESTHOUSES

Arung Hayat South shore of Mabul; http://sipadan. com. Compact, very plain rooms, some with a/c, in a sort of longhouse on stilts. Try their one-night diving package (with or without Sipadan). $$$$

Seahorse Sipadan Scuba Lodge South shore of Mabul; 019 803 0428. This is the most visually arresting guesthouse, with chalets lining two boardwalks connected by elevated bridges, to allow boats to enter. There are also cheaper longhouse rooms. Packages exclude diving, which is available at nearby Billabong. Two-night snorkelling packages are best value here. $$$$

Uncle Chang's Dive Lodge South shore of Mabul; http:// facebook.com/UCbackpackers. "Reasonably spartan" is how this veteran backpacker place styles itself, so don't come with high expectations. The centrepiece is the restaurant/ lounge with a ping-pong table; dorms and rooms are basic and a bit shabby, but some rooms have a/c. Book through the office on Jalan Kastam, Semporna. Divers pay less for the first night's accommodation. Dorms $$, doubles $$$

KAPALAI

Sipadan-Kapalai Resort Kapalai; http://sipadan-kapalai.com. A little taste of the Maldives, right here in Sabah. Spectacular chalets built on stilts, surrounded by shallow azure water that's perfect for snorkelling. Boats take divers to Mabul (as well as Sipadan if spare permits become available), and there is good diving around the artificial reef. Rates are for a two-night package, and diving is extra. $$$$

POM POM

Pom Pom Island Resort Pom Pom; http://pompom island.com. Chalets are either out over the water or on (or behind) the beach at this tip-top resort, which also has its own spa. Diving and snorkelling are charged separately (dives cost less if booked in advance, though you'll still have to add gear rental). Book through the office on Jalan Kastam Extension in Semporna. $$$$

MATAKING

Makating Reef Resort Mataking; http://mataking.com. This is a luxury development kept in splendid isolation, with swanky beach villas featuring patios and rear jacuzzis. Dive packages include three boat dives/day and free access to the house reef, where an artificial wreck has an underwater mailbox. $$$$

Tawau and around

Most travellers bypass **TAWAU** altogether, which now rivals Sandakan in size, although it's not a bad idea to overnight here if you're travelling between interior sights like the Maliau Basin and east coast. There are some pleasingly aged timber shophouses on and around Jalan Chester in what passes for an old town centre, and the breezy seafront promenade has views out to Sebatik Island (which is shared with Indonesia). The only

real sight in the vicinity is the **Tawau Hills Park**, half an hour's drive away. Smartish hotels and restaurants tend to cluster in the **Fajar** neighbourhood north of **Jalan Dunlop**, the main street.

Tawau Hills Park

25km north of Tawau • Charge; extra for climbing permits and guides • http://sabahparks.org.my • Taxi from Tawau; vehicles back can be scarce, so ask for a return price including waiting time, or get the driver's number

The 280-square-kilometre **Tawau Hills Park** is a stretch of rainforest and cloud forest, with the Tawau River cutting through its centre. The thirty-minute trail up **Bombalai hill** from the park HQ offers some great views; also worthwhile is the hike up **Gelas Hill** to a waterfall that's perfect for swimming (2hr one-way). For the ambitious, there are multi-day treks to mounts Magdelana, Lucia and Maria, all just over 1000m; contact the park or Sabah Parks in KK in advance for more details.

ARRIVAL AND DEPARTURE — TAWAU AND AROUND

By plane Tawau's airport (089 950 777) is 32km east of the centre; as well as the following domestic destinations, there have at times been services to Tarakan in Indonesia, as well as Hong Kong. Minibuses run from the airport to town (hourly 7am–8pm; 30min), and it doesn't cost much by taxi. Buses and minivans also run east from here to Semporna.
Destinations Johor Bahru (4 weekly; 2hr 35min); Kota Kinabalu (6–7 daily; 50min); Kuala Lumpur (6–7 daily; 2hr 45min); Sandakan (1 daily; 40min).

By long-distance bus Tawau has two long-distance bus terminals. The bus park on Jalan Chen Fook has services to KK via both Lahad Datu and the interior (via Keningau). Sandakan-bound buses use the station at the eastern end of Jalan Dunlop.
Destinations Keningau (4 daily; 6hr 30min); Kota Kinabalu, via the interior (2 daily; at least 10hr); Kota Kinabalu, via the coast (7 daily; 11hr); Lahad Datu (7 daily; 2hr); Sandakan (4 daily; 5hr); Sapulut (4 daily; 4hr 30min); Semporna (5 daily; 1hr 30min).

By shared minivan or local bus Services for Tawau's airport, Lahad Datu and Semporna use the Jalan Dunlop long-distance terminal. Most other local transport uses the station at the west end of Jalan Stephen Tan, although you're unlikely to make use of this.

By ferry Ferries to Nunakan and Tarakan in Indonesia, run by a variety of companies, use the terminal south of the market. Buy tickets early (the terminal opens at 8am and shuts at night) as counters may close irregularly later in the day.
Destinations Nunakan (around 5 daily; 1hr); Tarakan (3 weekly; 3hr).

ACCOMMODATION — SEE MAP PAGE 417

★ **City Garden** Jalan Chen Fook; http://citygardenhotel.net. Although new and characterless, this hotel has beautifully maintained and seriously soundproofed rooms. It's well located too, directly opposite the food court and near both of the bus terminals. $$

LA Hotel Jalan St Patrick; http://lahotel.com.my. The slickest hotel in town, with a range of plush rooms, a spa and two restaurants (including one that's superbly perched atop the building). $$

Shervinton Jalan Bunga; http://shervintonhotel.com. A wannabe business-class hotel (as if you couldn't tell by the name; they could also have called it the Hiltarriott) with a few stylish flourishes, including all-metal sinks in the bathrooms. There's also a rooftop restaurant and bar. Rates include breakfast. $$

TAWAU HILLS PARK

Tawau Hills Park HQ 25km north of Tawau; 089 925 719. The Park HQ's facilities include a hostel with a choice of a/c or fan dorms, as well as chalets. An on-site canteen serves up simple dishes. Dorms $, chalets $$$

EATING — SEE MAP PAGE 417

★ **Jalan Chen Fook Food Court** Jalan Chen Fook. There's no official name for this expansive place, which is dominated by a large Chinese seafood restaurant (*Good View*) and draws crowds every evening. Also worthwhile is *1st Drink and Food Centre* for cheap noodle and dim sum breakfasts; for very cheap Malay/Indonesian food, try the stalls at the western end of the site. $

Nasi Lemak Guru Besar Jalan Kelapa; 019 811 5144. Down-to-earth, open-air restaurant with a self-explanatory name, serving *nasi lemak* in several slightly different forms, as well as deep-fried fish, soups, and some really good *cendol* for dessert. $

The Peaky Barista Off Jalan Baru; http://facebook.com/thepeakybarista. Fun name, fun place, and as good a caffeine fix as you'll find in Tawau. Most guests seem to go for iced concoctions, but they have good hot ones too, as well as nitro cold brew. $\overline{\underline{\mathsf{S}}}$

Roof Garden Lounge Tenth floor, LA Hotel, Jalan St Patrick; 089 777 557. One of the nicest restaurant-bars anywhere in Sabah, this rooftop place offers 360-degree views out to the Tawau Hills Park and the sea – get here before sunset to pick a good table. The extensive menu covers everything from steak to satay. $\overline{\underline{\mathsf{SSS}}}$

DRINKING   SEE MAP PAGE 417

★ **Roof Garden Lounge** Tenth floor, LA Hotel, Jalan St Patrick; 089 777 557. As well as being a good place to dine, you can drink in the views here with an alcoholic beverage or two, with Strongbow cider and plenty of cocktails on hand.

The interior

The Crocker mountain range marks the start of the transition from the western coastal plains to Sabah's geographical **interior**, which covers a vast swathe of terrain south from here to the Indonesian border. The isolation of this sparsely populated region ended at the start of the twentieth century, when a rail line was built between Jesselton (now KK) and Tenom to transport the raw materials being produced by the region's thriving rubber industry. Today, the region is known for the cultivation of coffee, rice, cocoa and, lately, even avocados. The mountains themselves are a major attraction, largely wrapped up within the **Crocker Range Park** – the notable exception is **Trus Madi**, part of a forest reserve. To the east and southeast, lowland rainforest reasserts itself at the wildlife haven of **Deramakot** and the **Maliau Basin**, where there are superb opportunities for trekking. Another draw is the excellent Murut cultural tourism project at **Sapulut**, where visitors get to scale the limestone pinnacle of **Batu Punggul**. The three main towns – **Tambunan**, **Keningau** and **Tenom** – have little to offer in themselves, but you may find yourself passing through en route to nearby attractions.

Crocker Range Park

Main entrance 12km northwest of Keningau • Charge • http://sabahparks.org.my • Transport between Kota Kinabalu and Keningau or Tambunan can drop you at or close to the entrances, and can be flagged down for onward travel

Covering 1400 square kilometres, the **Crocker Range Park** is the largest of Sabah's terrestrial state parks with, unusually, a road – between Kimanis on the coast and Keningau – slicing right through it. Largely uncommercialized, the park offers cool mountain air, montane forest, birdlife and occasional sightings of *Rafflesia* flowers. The one part of the park that's easily explored independently is reached via the **main entrance**, close to where the road exits the park on its eastern side – here there's a collection of ferns, an insectarium, a lookout tower and a couple of short forest trails.

Two **substations** – as alternative gates are named – are also worth a visit. The **Mahua** substation, 14km north of Tambunan and reached off the Tambunan–Ranau road, gives access to the chilly waters at the Mahua Falls, 500m from the gate. Even better is the **Alab** substation close to **Mount Alab** (2000m) and some 15km northwest of Tambunan, off the KK road – here the 12km **Minduk Sirung Trail** makes an excellent day trek downhill to Mahua, but you will need a guide and permits (contact the park office for details).

ACCOMMODATION   CROCKER RANGE PARK

Utan Paradise Where the Kimanus–Keningau road meets the western edge of the park; http://facebook.com/utanparadise. This rustic camp has a lodge with dorms and A-frames that are comfy for two, all with palm-thatch roofs. There are kitchens, but no meals are included unless you come on a package including trekking and a night walk. Dorms/A-frames $\overline{\underline{\mathsf{S}}}$, chalets $\overline{\underline{\mathsf{SSS}}}$

Tambunan and around

The northernmost of the interior's small towns is **TAMBUNAN**, amusingly billed as "the Switzerland of the East" in tourist leaflets, with Mount Trus Madi looming to the southeast and two entrances to the Crocker Range Park to the north. The best thing about the town itself is its lively *tamu* (Wednesday evening and Thursday morning).

Tambunan Rafflesia Information Centre
On the main road 20km north of Tambunan • Charge • http://forest.sabah.gov.my • Tambunan minivans and shared taxis from Merdeka Field in Kota Kinabalu pass by

Prospects of seeing a *Rafflesia* (see page 558) in flower are decent at the **Tambunan Rafflesia Information Centre**, a small forest reserve often visited as a day-trip from Kota Kinabalu. It's worth calling ahead to find out if there are blooms, but as it can be hard to get hold of staff here, you might just have to chance it. Assuming that one is flowering, expect a trek of up to an hour to reach it.

Mount Trus Madi
20km southeast of Tambunan • Charge; climbing permit extra

At 2642m, **Mount Trus Madi** is the second tallest mountain in Sabah, but is still totally overshadowed by Kinabalu as far as tourists are concerned. It's a pity: Trus Madi is a good place to find **pitcher plants**, and there are wonderful views of Kinabalu from the summit. Three trails (*wayaan* in local dialect) with different starting points lead up Trus Madi; the easiest is the Kaingaran trail, reached by 4WD from Tambunan, which is a two-day round trip and has basic accommodation halfway up. Several KK tour operators offer the climb, including TYK Adventure Tours, which has been doing it longer than most (see page 376).

ARRIVAL AND DEPARTURE — TAMBUNAN AND AROUND

By shared minivan and taxi Shared transport to and from KK (1hr 30min), Ranau (1hr 15min) and Keningau (45min) stops in Tambunan's main square.

ACCOMMODATION

Padi View Resthouse Jalan Kampung Lintuhun, 600m northwest of town; http://padiview.com. This relatively new cheapie has pleasant rooms, some with views of paddy fields and Mount Trus Madi – try to get one on the upper floor, or else you'll probably have to make do with viewing the guesthouse garden instead. $\overline{\underline{\$}}$

Tandarason Resort 2km north of Tambunan; http://facebook.com/Trcctbn. Also known as TVRC (the initials of its old name), this place has a holiday camp feel, and is set around a lake where you can kayak. There are basic en-suite "motel" rooms, plus fancier chalets costing double, and a campsite. Some rates include breakfast. Camping $\overline{\underline{\$}}$, doubles $\overline{\underline{\$\$}}$

Keningau

Just north of the Pegalan River, **KENINGAU** is the largest of the interior towns, with a mainly Kadazan/Dusun, Murut and Chinese population. It's also a minor transport hub, as it's 1km east of where the main road up the eastern side of the Crocker Range meets the road between Kimanis on the coast and Tawau. The only things to see are the night market, which sells produce and snacks in a hangar-like building off the eastern end of the main street, plus the Sunday morning *tamu* in the centre. All worthwhile shops and facilities, including some decent hotels and restaurants, are on the north side of the main street or a block further north around Jalan OKK Sodomon.

ARRIVAL AND INFORMATION — KENINGAU

By long-distance bus The Tung Ma Nui Lok company runs the bulk of the town's bus services from a little depot on Jalan Masjid, the road on the western edge of the centre where the mosque is located. Salam Bumimas buses, which

only serve KK, Sapulut and Tawau, call at a car park by the post office and night market.
Destinations Beaufort (2 daily; 2hr 15min), KK (hourly during the day; 2hr 30min); Menumbok (2 daily; 3hr 30min); Sapulut (4 daily; 2hr), Tawau (4 daily; 6hr 30min); Tenom (4 daily; 1hr).

By shared taxi and minivan Shared transport uses at least three locations in the centre, so ask around to find the right spot for your destination. Routes of use to tourists are the same as for buses, though it's also possible to find vehicles for Tambunan (45min).

ACCOMMODATION

Juta 100m north of the main street; http://hoteljuta.com. Impossible to miss – it's one of the tallest buildings in town – this is the closest thing the town has to a business hotel, with surprisingly modern rooms and a restaurant. Breakfast is included. $$

Kristal Northern end of Jalan OKK Sodomon; http://oyorooms.com. The best budget option, with antiquated but sound a/c, en-suite rooms. $

Mee Woo Resort Off Jalan Bariawa, 1km north of the centre; http://facebook.com/MeWooResortandSpa. Keningau just isn't the sort of place where a glorified holiday camp like this ought to thrive, but this place's swimming pools and water slides draw weekending families from KK. Rooms galore are stacked up the side of a small valley, and there's a restaurant and a café/bar too. Half-board; weekdays (add 20 percent at weekends) $$$

EATING

Maimunah Off the main street, close to the Juta hotel. Basic but reliable *mamak* place with a good *nasi campur* selection and the usual *roti* and noodle favourites. $

Uncle Pepper Look for the RHB Bank beyond the Kristal hotel, then follow the road round to the north; 087 337 005. Its walls plastered with images of Western celebs, this vaguely hip café is the best place in town for burgers, grills and fish and chips. $$

Tenom

Named after Ontoros Antanom, a Murut warrior, **TENOM** is a backwater on the north bank of the Padas River, with tasteful wooden shophouses and a blue-domed mosque. The closest most visitors get is Pangi station, 10km to the west, which is the starting point for **rafting** trips booked in KK (see page 376). Locally, Tenom is best known for growing **coffee**, and there are opportunities to taste the local product and to stay on a small plantation. The town's *tamu* takes place on Sunday morning.

Sabah Agriculture Park

On the east bank of the Padas River, 15km northeast of Tenom • Charge • http://sabah.net.my/agripark • Shared minivan from Tenom to Lagud Seberang, then walk 1km

The **Sabah Agriculture Park** is a crop research station known for its **Orchid Centre**, which has four hundred species, and there's a **Living Crop Museum** with tropical plants. Other attractions include the **Bee Centre**, planned gardens, mini zoo and lakes.

ARRIVAL AND DEPARTURE TENOM

By train The train station is on the east side of the padang, just off the main Keningau road; for more details on the journey, see box, page 383.
Destinations Beaufort (2 daily; 2hr 30min).
By bus Buses call at the padang, with tickets sold across from the train station.
Destinations Keningau (4 daily; 1hr); Kota Kinabalu (4 daily; 3hr 30min).
By shared minivan and taxi Minivans congregate close to the padang – the ones heading north to Keningau generally circle around Tenom, looking for passengers. Shared taxis wait at the southern edge of the padang.
Destinations Beaufort (2hr 30min); Keningau (1hr); Kota Kinabalu (3hr).

ACCOMMODATION AND EATING

Fatt Choi Coffee Cabin Fatt Choi coffee plantation, 1.5km west of town; http://fccoffee.com. The four- and six-person cabins here, based in the hills outside town, come with a/c and en-suite bathrooms. If you need help finding it, ask directions at their *Tenom Fatt Choi (TFC)* café on the main road in the centre, where you can sample their coffee for free. $$

Sri Perdana Jalan Tun Mustapha; 087 734001. A reliable budget choice, just west of the padang across the main road. $

Sapulut and Batu Punggul

Two hours' drive south of Keningau, **SAPULUT** is a district of hamlets in the heartland of the Murut people. Only 30km from the Indonesian border, the area is also home to one of Sabah's most intriguing challenges, **Batu Punggul**; unlike the limestone pinnacles at Sarawak's Mulu National Park, this is one you can climb. It looms like a misshapen brick above the jungle, and the journey to reach it requires a longboat trip followed by a steep half-hour trek up. From the base, most visitors take around twenty minutes to get to the top of the 100m-high mound, where there are views of pristine forest.

On a physical level, Batu Punggul is something any reasonably fit and agile person can manage, with no rock-climbing experience needed. It's like using a series of ladders, with the limestone fiendishly eroded into jagged pockets, providing hand- and footholds; ropes assist on a few sections. It is psychologically testing, however, in that there are **no safety harnesses**; this is a climb you do **at your own risk**, and there is no shame in skipping it at the last minute. The Murut guides are assiduous about safety and will even drag your hands and feet to the right spots if you're stuck. It's worth wearing trousers as the limestone will cause bad grazes or worse if you briefly miss your footing.

ACTIVITIES AND ACCOMMODATION — SAPULUT AND BATU PUNGGUL

★ **Orou Sapulot** http://orousapulot.com. Once the logistics of climbing Batu Punggul were as tricky as the feat itself, but now it's the highlight of the multi-day trips organized by this Murut community tourism project. Activities include caving, Murut dancing and a rapids-shooting trip starting near the Indonesian border (only an option on longer stays). Accommodation is in purpose-built longhouses and lodges with shared toilets. Bear in mind that you will stay in a different place every night and that there are some very early starts. Two-night full-board packages available, including transport to and from Keningau. $$$

Maliau Basin Conservation Area

Off the Sapulut–Tawau road, reached by a turning 63km east of Sapulut • http://maliaubasin.org

Billed as Sabah's "Lost World", the **Maliau Basin Conservation Area** superficially resembles Danum Valley (see page 412). There's a centre for visiting biologists who come to study, among other things, its impressive roster of large mammals, including the Borneo pygmy elephant, clouded leopard, banteng and sun bear. Unlike at Danum, however, here the aim is to range far and wide, with lower montane, heath and dipterocarp forest to explore on extended **treks**, which could mean covering 12km in a day through dense jungle – needless to say, they shouldn't be attempted lightly. Highlights include several waterfalls, notably the seven-tiered **Maliau Falls**. You'll need to book through a tour operator to visit (expect to pay heftily for an all-inclusive package). Standard itineraries include only one night at the studies centre, where a canopy walkway and night drive provide diversion; the remaining two to four nights are spent at field stations ranging from basic campsites to wooden lodges with hammocks and proper bathrooms.

Deramakot Forest Reserve

Reached by a rough 70km road starting 20km east of Telupid and 105km from Sandakan • Charge; extra for car, guides and night drives • http://deramakot.sabah.gov.my

Cradled by the Kinabatangan River, south off the road between Ranau and the east coast, the 555-square-kilometre **Deramakot Forest Reserve** is heralded by the Forestry Department and conservationists alike. In the heart of Sabah, it is the only one of the state's forests with FSC certification, covering not just logging but also **wildlife** – the reserve is a good place to spot sun bears, orangutans, pygmy elephants, marbled cats and the vulnerable clouded leopard. Treks tend to be short, although new trails are being developed; **night drives** are when much of the action takes place. Although it's possible to visit independently, you're far better off booking with a tour operator in KK or Sandakan, who will take care of transport, meals and perhaps take you on unofficial trails.

ACCOMMODATION — DERAMAKOT FOREST RESERVE

Forestry Department Accommodation Reserve HQ; 089 278800. The reserve's accommodation is fairly new and in good shape, with a/c and bathroom. There's no restaurant, however, so if you aren't here on a package you must arrange catering in advance with the Forestry Department and budget extra. Dorms $\overline{\underline{\$}}$, doubles $\overline{\underline{\$\$}}$, chalets $\overline{\underline{\$\$\$}}$

Brunei

431 Bandar Seri Begawan
440 Muara district
442 Temburong district
443 Belait district

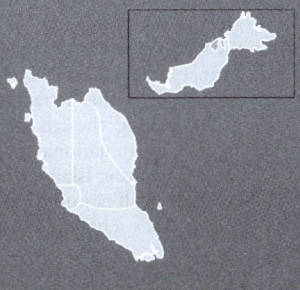

KAMPONG AYER

Brunei

A tiny, oil-rich monarchy that seems, superficially, more Middle Eastern than Southeast Asian, the enigmatic country of Brunei often intrigues visitors. Its official title is Negara Brunei Darussalam, Darussalam meaning "Abode of Peace" – and tranquil it certainly is, with little crime and a sense of calm, bordering on ennui, thanks to the income generated by massive offshore oil and gas deposits. The 460,000 inhabitants – two-thirds Malay, almost a tenth Chinese, nearly a quarter expatriates and foreign workers, and just a few percent Indigenous peoples – enjoy a cosseted existence. While the genuinely wealthy elite form a select few, there's a large middle class; education and healthcare are free, and houses, cars and even pilgrimages to Mecca are subsidized. Despite this, it doesn't feel like a rich country – don't go expecting to see sports cars or glitzy malls, rather potholed roads and a general air of neglect.

Brunei's sultan, **Hassanal Bolkiah** (see page 429), is famously one of the world's richest people. Ruling as an absolute monarch, he is not only prime minister, but a one-man cabinet – he's also the country's defence minister, finance minister and minister of foreign affairs. His extended family, the Bolkiahs, control virtually all government departments and the vast majority of the nation's wealth; it's said that nothing of any real importance is decided without the thumbs-up from a family member.

This is, however, no glitzy Gulf sheikhdom. Brunei is basically low-rise and low-key, feeling not unlike Malaysia's oil-rich state of Terengganu (see page 228), only more torpid and with more discernible signs of wealth. Primary and secondary tropical forest still covers seventy percent of the land area; indeed the country's boundaries are easily discerned from the air, as Sarawak's logging roads and oil-palm plantations halt as if by magic at the border. Most of Brunei is less than 150m above sea level, its rainforest, peat swamp and heath forest running down to sandy beaches and mangrove swamps. The country is divided into four districts: **Muara**, which contains the capital, **Bandar Seri Begawan**; agricultural **Tutong**; oil-rich **Belait**; and **Temburong**, a sparsely populated enclave severed from the rest of Brunei by Sarawak's Limbang district.

For most travellers, Brunei is simply a transit zone on the long bus ride between Miri and Kota Kinabalu. Those who stay seldom do so for more than two or three nights, long enough to glimpse the main sights and the way of life without the cost of living – much higher than in Malaysia – creating too much of a dent in their bank account. Conveniently, the capital is home to many of the key attractions, notably the fascinating **Kampong Ayer**, a rambling collection of houses built over the wide Brunei River, and offers one of the best chances to see **proboscis monkeys** in all of Borneo. The other attraction is the pristine rainforest in **Ulu Temburong National Park** in Temburong, though this is a much more controlled and sanitized experience than any Malaysian national park, with few trails to explore. Otherwise, the sultanate holds some interesting Islamic architecture; a clutch of moderately interesting museums, beaches, small nature parks and modern longhouses; and one solitary nod to Dubai-style excess – a hotel/country club, the *Empire*, that's worth seeing for its ludicrous grandiosity.

Visitors may find aspects of the country – not least its use of Sharia law and *hudud* punishments (see page 430) – uncomfortable and oppressive; it remains hard to see how the Sultan will fulfil his aim of making tourism a major part of the nation's GDP by 2035.

ROYAL REGALIA MUSEUM

Highlights

❶ Proboscis monkeys Just minutes from the city centre by boat, a group of these curious-looking creatures can usually be seen foraging by the Brunei River. See page 433

❷ Kampong Ayer This scenic collection of wooden houses, built out over the Brunei River, offers a glimpse of traditional life. See page 433

❸ The Royal Regalia Building One of Brunei's most entertaining museums, housing processional chariots, ceremonial paraphernalia and offbeat official gifts. See page 434

❹ The Empire Hotel Come to witness how a royal folly with a cavernous marble atrium now functions as a successful hotel, then hang around for a bite to eat. See page 441

❺ Ulu Temburong National Park Brunei's premier nature reserve holds a heart-stopping canopy walkway and opportunities for river rafting and tubing. See page 442

HIGHLIGHTS ARE MARKED ON THE MAP ON PAGE 428

Brief history

The Brunei of today is just the rump of a vast, powerful sultanate that was gradually gobbled up by the Brookes' regime in Sarawak in the nineteenth century. Trade was the powerhouse behind its growth. Tang and Sung dynasty coins and ceramics, found a few kilometres from Bandar Seri Begawan, suggest that China was trading with Brunei as early as the seventh century. Brunei subsequently benefited from its strategic position on the **trade route** between India, Melaka and China, and exercised a lucrative control over merchant traffic in the South China Sea. As well as being a staging post, where traders could stock up on supplies and off-load cargo, Brunei was commercially active in its own right by the fourteenth century; the *nakhoda*, or Bruneian sea traders, traded local produce such as camphor, rattan and brassware for ceramics, spices, wood and fabrics.

The Brunei Sultanate

Islam had begun to make inroads into Bruneian society by the mid-fifteenth century, a process accelerated when wealthy Muslim merchant families decamped to Brunei after Melaka fell to the Portuguese in 1511. Brunei was certainly an Islamic sultanate by the time its first **European visitors** arrived from Spain in 1521. Commonly acknowledged as the sultanate's golden age, this period saw its territory and influence stretch as far as the modern-day Philippines.

However, things turned sour towards the close of the sixteenth century. Following a sea battle in 1578, Spain took the capital, only to relinquish it days later due to a cholera epidemic. The threat of piracy caused more problems, scaring off passing trade. Worse still, factional struggles loosened the sultan's control at home. With the arrival of **James Brooke** (see page 532) in 1839, the sultanate was to shrink steadily as he siphoned off its territory to neighbouring Sarawak. This trend culminated when Charles Brooke's capture of the Limbang region split Brunei in two. By 1888, the British had declared Brunei a **protected state**, meaning responsibility for its foreign affairs lay with London.

THE SULTAN OF BRUNEI

Brunei's head of state, **Sultan Hassanal Bolkiah** (whose full title is 31 words long), is the 29th in a line stretching back six hundred years. Educated in Malaysia and Britain, he has been sultan since 1967, following the voluntary abdication of his father, Omar.

Hassanal Bolkiah was once deemed the world's richest person, though today a conservative estimate of his net worth, at a mere US$28 billion, would barely squeak him into the top fifty of *Forbes*' list of billionaires. Tales of his extravagance are legion – of private jets festooned with gold bathroom fittings, for example, or the thousands of luxury cars that, many never having been driven, now sit rotting in huge garages. However, the sultan takes pains to live down that persona by cultivating an image of accessibility. Brunei's highly compliant press is full of stories of his majesty's presence at community events – the launching of a new school, say – and for two days a year, at Hari Raya Aidilfitri, the sultan throws open the Istana Nurul Iman to the public, with tens of thousands standing in line for hours to meet him and other members of the royal family. Despite the pious nature of the regime, there have been many accusations of corruption and debauchery within the palace, though these tend to be settled out of court.

The sultan defined the philosophy underlying his rule when, in the 1990s, he introduced an ideology called Melayu Islam Beraja, essentially that the monarchy is founded on the twin pillars of Islam and Malayness. There are few signs of participatory democracy, however. In 2004 the sultan reconvened Brunei's **legislative assembly**, two decades after it was suspended, with sixteen appointed members. They voted to enlarge the assembly to include up to fifteen elected members, but no elections have so far taken place. In 2006 the sultan amended Brunei's constitution to make himself infallible under Bruneian law, and in 2014 he took the controversial step of introducing harsh traditional punishments under Islamic law (see page 544).

The twentieth century and beyond

The start of the twentieth century was marked by the **discovery of oil**, which drove the British to set up a Residency in 1906. By 1931 the **Seria oil field** was on stream, but the Japanese invasion of 1941 temporarily halted Brunei's path to prosperity. As in Sabah, Allied bombing during the occupation that followed left much rebuilding to be done.

While Sabah, Sarawak and Labuan became Crown Colonies in the early postwar years, Brunei remained a British protectorate. The British Residency was finally withdrawn in 1959, and a new constitution established, with provisions for a democratically elected legislative council. At the same time, Sultan Omar Ali Saifuddien (the present sultan's father) was careful to retain British involvement in defence and foreign affairs – a move whose sagacity was made apparent when, in 1962, an attempted coup led by Sheik Azahari's pro-democratic **Brunei People's Party** was crushed by British Army Gurkhas. Ever since the failed coup, which stemmed from Omar's refusal to convene the first sitting of the legislative council, the sultan has ruled by decree in his role as an unelected prime minister, and emergency powers have been in place. Despite showing interest in joining the new Malaysian Federation in 1963, Brunei chose to opt out rather than risk losing its oil wealth and compromising the pre-eminence of its monarchy; not until 1984 did it cease to be a British protectorate and become fully independent.

Little scrutinized by the outside world, modern Brunei charts an unruffled course, though there's no clear sense how the country plans to cope when its oil runs out in a couple of decades, and even fairly well-educated young people find it hard to find jobs. The sultanate retains close ties with the UK and, regionally, especially with Singapore and Malaysia. Following the seventy percent slump in the price of oil from 2014–15, the country spiralled into debt (reaching around sixteen percent of GDP in 2017), though this declined substantially when oil prices rose again.

In May 2014, to international and some local consternation, **Islamic hudud punishments** were brought in at the sultan's behest (see page 429). In theory, this could mean people convicted of adulterous or homosexual acts being stoned to death, and thieves having a hand amputated, but at the time of writing none of these punishments had been carried out.

SHARIA LAW IN BRUNEI

At the sultan's behest, Brunei introduced **sharia law**, and **Islamic hudud punishments** in 2014, and it took full effect in 2019. Such law had long been called for by the country's religious leaders, who form Brunei's second-largest power base after the sultan and his family. In theory, the code could mean people convicted of adulterous or homosexual acts being stoned to death, and thieves having a hand amputated. However, at the time of writing none of these punishments had been carried out, and it mainly seems to be "for show". In addition, many rules (but certainly not all) apply only to Muslims. However, to be prudent, you're advised to check online for the latest situation before visiting.

Some of the more minor sharia laws have, however, already impacted the country's minority peoples and foreign residents. Celebrating Christmas is banned in public (a Muslim could get five years in prison if they appear in public in a Santa outfit); Chinese festivals were banned too, but Chinese New Year has since made a creeping return. In 2017 an Australian expat faced twelve months in prison for "containment" (being in the same house as a non-related member of the opposite sex), though he was eventually allowed to leave the country after a costly legal case. One injunction it's as well to adhere to is the ban on consuming food and drink (even water) in public during daylight hours throughout **Ramadan** – you could be fined heavily for not adhering to it. Blasphemy is also a serious crime, so exercise caution over anything you might say about religion in public.

ARRIVAL AND DEPARTURE

By plane Bandar's airport has flights from Kota Kinabalu, Kuala Lumpur, Jakarta and Singapore (see page 436 for details), and reasonable connections with cities elsewhere in the region and further afield. A departure tax is payable at the check-in desk on departure, and as with many such matters card payment is not allowed, so it's wise to make sure that you still have a little cash at the end of your trip.

By bus Reaching Brunei by bus from Malaysia is possible. A couple of daily services run to Bandar from Miri in Sarawak, via the coastal towns of Kuala Belait and Seria, and from Kota Kinabalu in Sabah. Daily buses also run all the way from Pontianak in western Kalimantan (Indonesia). See page 29 for more details.

By boat Muara, Bandar's port, is served by boats from the Malay island of Labuan (see page 385).

GETTING AROUND

By car Brunei is small enough that you can visit most towns as day-trips from the capital. However, the bus system is indifferent, so renting a car is the ideal way to explore. It's not overly expensive, and fuel is cheap, though you may not be allowed to go to Temburong district as you have to leave the country to do so.

ESSENTIALS

Alcohol, tobacco and drugs Brunei is famously dry, though tourists are permitted to bring two bottles of liquor and twelve cans of beer into the country for private consumption, but this must be declared to customs and consumed in private. The sultan is also very anti-smoking (although he himself smokes cigars), but you are permitted to bring one packet of nineteen cigarettes through customs; smoking is not permitted in any public space and doing so carries a fine. You will also see many signs in customs making it clear that being found with drugs is an executable offence.

Money The Brunei dollar (B$; also called the ringgit in Malay) has the same value as the Singapore dollar, widely used in Brunei.

Opening hours Brunei has a split weekend as far as government bodies are concerned: Fridays and Sundays are days off. Some private businesses follow government hours, others work Monday to Friday with a half-day on Saturday.

Entry visas Most Western nationalities are allowed to enter visa-free for 30–90 days, except for New Zealand (30 days) and Australia (visa required, but 30-day one issued on arrival). South Africans need to apply for a visa in advance.

Bandar Seri Begawan

BANDAR SERI BEGAWAN (known locally as **Bandar** or **BSB**) feels more like a provincial town than a capital. It is also a newish, largely postwar city, dominated by drab concrete – until comparatively recently, the seat of power and main settlement was Kampong Ayer, the picturesque water village visible from all along Bandar's river bank. The commercial centre, built on reclaimed land after the British Resident arrived in 1906, comprises a mere handful of riverside streets and is surprisingly tranquil, not to say dull; recent development has been concentrated in the suburbs.

Despite its underwhelming air, Bandar packs in a surprising amount for visitors. **Kampong Ayer** is the obvious sight (see page 433), but perhaps even more memorable are the **proboscis monkeys** that live in a mangrove forest just a twenty-minute boat ride upriver from the centre. Not many tourists glimpse them, though, whereas virtually everyone heads to the **Omar Ali Saifuddien mosque** – an iconic building that turns out not to be all that spectacular up close. At their best, the city's **museums**, whether glorifying the sultanate or documenting local history and culture, are genuinely enlightening.

The waterfront

Following the middle-class flight to the suburbs, efforts to bring life back to the centre (thus far not entirely successful) have culminated in the revamp of the city's **waterfront** along Jalan McArthur. The 0.5km esplanade is a good place to get your bearings – from here you can see **Kampong Ayer**; a golden onion dome and white saddle-roofed

BRUNEI BANDAR SERI BEGAWAN

ACCOMMODATION
Badi'ah	5
Brunei	6
Minilen Guesthouse	2
Pusat Belia (Youth Centre)	4
Qing Yun Rest House	7
Radisson	3
Rizqun International	1

EATING
Fratini's	2
Gadong Pasar Malam	1
Kaizen Sushi	9
Phongmun	8
Syazwan Café	5
Taman Selera	7
Tarindak d'Seni	10
Thiam Hock	4
TT Blues Café	3
Yelo Café	6

BANDAR SERI BEGAWAN

SHOPPING
Arts and Handicrafts Centre	3
Gadong Mall	1
Yayasan Complex	2

> **PROBOSCIS MONKEYS**
>
> For many visitors, a trip to Borneo would not be complete without an encounter with a **proboscis monkey**, found only in riverine forests and coastal mangrove swamps. The reddish-brown monkey derives its name from the adult male's enlarged, drooping nose; females and young animals are snub-nosed. The role of the male's oversized member, which seems to straighten out when the animal is issuing its curious honking call, is likely to do with establishing dominance within a group and, by doing so, attracting a mate.
>
> The monkeys specialize in eating hard-to-digest mangrove leaves, an adaptation that has enlarged their stomachs and left them with distinctive pot-bellies – and limited their distribution. Entirely arboreal, they're capable of making spectacular leaps across the river channels that cut through mangrove forests, arms thrown wide to catch foliage on the far side – though, in case they miss, they're also proficient swimmers, with webbed toes.
>
> As well as the Brunei River near Bandar Seri Begawan, good places to spot proboscis monkeys include the Kinabatangan (see page 408) and Labuk Bay (see page 407) sanctuaries of Sabah, and Bako National Park (see page 318) in Sarawak.

building that forms part of the sultan's palace; and the tower of the **Arts and Handicraft Centre**.

At the heart of the esplanade, a couple of buildings with pointed white tent-shaped roofs are home to several attempts at smart **cafés**, but they've still not really become part of the city's fabric and are frequented mainly by foreigners. At night families arrive for a quick stroll, admiring the myriad lights of Kampong Ayer across the dark river, before scooting off elsewhere for refreshments.

Kampong Ayer Tourism and Culture Gallery
Across the water from the esplanade • Free • 220 0874 • Water taxi from main waterfront

The **Kampong Ayer Tourism and Culture Gallery** is the obvious place to start exploring Kampong Ayer. It houses the **tourist office** (see page 437), though its small museum is sadly not as interesting as the 600-year-old history of Kampong Ayer it charts, though there are English captions. A little **observation tower** offers good views over the colourful wooden houses and back towards the city centre. From here you can simply head off into the water village via assorted meandering walkways, though the maze-like character of the place and lack of signage make it difficult to identify specific sights. A few homes may have crafts for sale, and you may be lucky enough to chance upon, say, cottage industries involving rattan weaving.

Omar Ali Saifuddien Mosque
Jalan Masjid Omar Ali Saifuddien

Though modest in size, the **Omar Ali Saifuddien Mosque** must have been a marvellous sight when completed in 1958. Topped by a 52m-high dome, it would have dominated what was then very much a small town, and is beautifully located on the edge of a circular lagoon. The decision to plonk the modern Yayasan Complex of shops just southeast has done it no favours, however, and the mosque is now at that awkward in-between age where it looks neither gleaming new nor venerable, though this is disguised when the lights come on at night. Still, commissioned by and named after the father of the present sultan, it makes tasteful use of opulent fittings – Italian marble, granite from Shanghai, Arabian and Belgian carpets, and English chandeliers and stained glass. The lagoon holds a replica of a sixteenth-century royal barge, or *mahligai*, used on special religious occasions.

KAMPONG AYER

While neighbouring Malaysia still holds a few water villages, notably in Kota Kinabalu, none can match Bandar's **Kampong Ayer** for size. Practically a small town by itself, it snakes downriver for 2km beyond the city centre and upriver for another 1km or so. Until recently it also stretched up the Kedayan tributary of the river to the Edinburgh Bridge, but these areas have now been cleared. Timber houses built on stilts and piles have occupied this stretch of the Brunei River for hundreds of years, and Kampong Ayer's historical significance cannot be underestimated. A census in 1911 showed that nearly half Brunei's population lived here, including the sultan, whose long-vanished palace was a suitably souped-up wooden affair.

Today the main six component bodies of Kampong Ayer are together home to more than 10,000 inhabitants; villages have their own shops, clinics, mosques, schools and fire services (minus the fire engines, of course). They also have electricity and mains water, but many houses remain unconnected to the sewerage system, which doesn't seem to deter the boys who swim in the river. While residents are content with their lot, insofar as they have stayed put rather than move to dry land, the authorities are intent on tinkering with Kampong Ayer. They have embarked on a project to build several dozen non-timber homes in the area, boasting solar panels and billed as eco-friendly, and they continue to extend sanitation to the villages. There's also talk of action to arrest the decline in village traditions, notably crafts; one plan is to market Kampong Ayer as an "artisanal village" to showcase the trades that linger on, for example silversmithing and boatbuilding, though it's not clear when this might be put into effect. Most tour operators (see page 437) offer half-day **boat trips** that include the water village.

Royal Regalia Building

Jalan Sultan • Free • http://museums.gov.bn • Outdoor shoes must be removed at entrance

In addition to a handful of uninteresting museums, downtown Bandar holds one that is simply essential – the **Royal Regalia Building**, easy to pick out as its roof is shaped like a strange domed helmet. While the name might lead you to expect a dry costume collection, it's actually a hilarious collection of regal paraphernalia whose subtext is to serve as a massive paean to the sultan. Perhaps the most significant objects are those used during his coronation, including the *tongkat aja* – a model of a human arm in gold, used to support the royal chin during the ceremony, which took place just across the road in the grand-looking Lapau Diraja building. Most visitors get an even bigger kick out of two massive **chariots**, one used for the coronation, the other for his highness's silver jubilee in 1992, the throng on the day recreated by dozens of mannequins in aristocratic Malay dress. Elsewhere there's an eccentric display of gifts the Brunei royals have been lumbered with, courtesy of blue-blooded intimates and world statesmen – replica temples made of crystal, and the like. The countries that the gifts hail from make for an interesting collection – mostly places in which the power of the leadership is absolute (or was, in the case of South Korea and certain former communist states). Plenty of gifts have arrived from the Philippines, mainly depicting or in the form of jeepneys, as if to say "we're still poor; share some wealth".

Tamu Kianggeh

Jalan Sungai Kianggeh • Daily dawn–dusk • Free • 224 1909 • Bus #37

The central produce market, **Tamu Kianggeh**, alongside the canalized Kianggeh creek sells everything from machetes to *midin* – nothing you can't see in markets in Sarawak or Sabah, but entertaining all the same. Friday morning is the busiest, and thus the best time to turn up.

Arts and Handicrafts Centre

Jalan Residency, just over 5min walk east of Tamu Kianggeh • Free • http://instagram.com/pusatkesenianbrunei • Bus #39

Bandar's **Arts and Handicrafts Centre** is a substantial complex where young Bruneians are taught traditional skills such as weaving, brass-casting and the crafting of the *kris*, the traditional Malay dagger. Unfortunately, classes are not generally open to public view without prior arrangement, so you'll have to make do with browsing the overly pricey **gift shop** (see page 440). The other reason to visit is to enjoy classic Bruneian food at their restaurant, *Tarindak d'Seni* (see page 439).

Kota Batu

It's fitting that Brunei's main **museums** should be a little way east of the centre at **Kota Batu**, the site of the capital when the Brunei sultanate was at its height. The area was excavated in the early 1950s by Tom Harrisson, who was instrumental in uncovering so many aspects of Sarawak's history and culture. A few old walls aside, however, this largely wooded area, close to the river, holds scant signs of former habitation.

Malay Technology Museum

Jalan Kota Batu, 4km east of the centre • Free • http://museums.gov.bn • Bus #39 • No photography allowed inside

Right by the Brunei River, the endearingly misnamed, but surprisingly good **Malay Technology Museum** focuses not on kampung-built MP3 players, but on traditional lifestyles and architecture, with – despite Brunei's tiny population of Indigenous groups – some creditable ethnographic exhibits that are sorely lacking in northern Sarawak. The first hall has a thought-provoking display on different styles of kampung house and their bewildering roof shapes; another is devoted to activities such as fishing using traditional traps. Best of all is the third hall, with scaled-down replicas of a Lun Bawang longhouse, a Penan shelter and a hut for trampling sago pith to make flour, among other structures.

Maritime Museum

Jalan Kota Batu, 4km east of the centre • Free • http://museums.gov.bn • Bus #39 • No photography allowed inside

If you're interested in ships, you may want to trek from the Malay Technology Museum to the nearby **Maritime Museum**, a modern affair dating back to 2015. Its badly-lit interior displays the recovered contents – mostly ceramics – of a sixteenth-century Chinese trade ship discovered in Brunei waters, as well as models of other historic craft that sailed in the region.

Istana Nurul Iman

By the Brunei River 4km west of the centre, off Jalan Tutong • Open two days a year during the Hari Raya Aidilfitri festival marking the end of Ramadan • Bus #42, #44, #46, #48 or #56

Unless you are in town at the right time of year, the closest you're likely to get to the sultan's palace, the **Istana Nurul Iman**, is on a river trip to spot Bandar's proboscis monkeys. Even viewed from afar, the palace impresses with its scale: it's bigger than London's Buckingham Palace, the main buildings stretching for nearly 0.5km.

Needless to say, it's also a monument to sheer self-indulgence (it cost over US$1.5 billion to build in the mid-1980s), with nearly eighteen hundred rooms – including 257 toilets – and at least five hundred chandeliers. The design, by Filipino architect Leandro Locsin, tries to incorporate Islamic motifs such as arches and domes, plus a traditional saddle-shaped roof, though many might say it fails on all counts. There's said to be a secret passage connecting the palace with the sultan's former home, the considerably more modest Istana Darul Hana, also by the river about 1km closer to the centre of town.

Jame 'Asr Hassanal Bolkiah

3km northwest of the centre, on the northern edge of Kiarong suburb • Free • Bus #1 or #22

With sky-blue roofs, six golden domes and pleasant grounds with fountains, the **Jame 'Asr Hassanal Bolkiah** is a grander sibling to the Omar Ali Saifuddien mosque downtown. Built in the 1990s to mark the sultan's silver jubilee, it's also the largest mosque in Brunei, though some of the neat mosaic decoration has a slightly plastic appearance. The mosque is conveniently close to the malls and restaurants of the suburb of Gadong, 1km north, but getting there on foot means traversing some fearsome highways; unless you're Muslim, you won't be allowed in on Thursdays or Fridays. If you happen to pass this way at night, look out for the evocative lighting, which gives the building an air of serenity despite the fast-moving traffic.

Gadong

5km northwest of the centre • Bus #1 or #20 runs along the main drag, right past the Abdul Razak Complex, or it's a short hop by taxi

If you spend much time outside the centre while in Bandar, it's likely to be in the most thriving suburb of **Gadong**. The place isn't much to look at: a collection of mundane concrete blocks and traffic-clogged streets surrounding the multiple blocks of the **Abdul Razak Complex**, which includes two hotels and the **Gadong Mall**, where despite the grandiose exterior the shopping is unmemorable. Gadong is, however, a good spot for **eating**, with decent restaurants and a terrific **pasar malam** where they sell all manner of Bruneian Malay goodies (see page 440).

ARRIVAL AND DEPARTURE — BANDAR SERI BEGAWAN

By plane Brunei International Airport (233 1747) is 8km north of the city, and has a decent range of facilities. A taxi into town takes 20min and can be booked and prepaid from the airport taxi counter; during daylight hours, buses #11, #23, #24, #36, #38 and #57 run to the bus station. The Dart app can get you into town a little cheaper. In addition to the following Singa-Malay flights to destinations covered in this book, there are plenty more heading further afield, including intercontinental services to London (seasonal) and Melbourne.

Destinations Kota Kinabalu (1–3 daily; 40min); Kuala Lumpur (3–5 daily; 2hr 30min); Singapore (2–3 daily; 2hr).

By bus All domestic buses use the bus station on Jalan Cator, while international services – which currently run

BRUNEI RIVER TRIPS

Most Bandar tour operators (see page 437) offer guided half-day trips on the Brunei River that take in **Kampong Ayer**. Unfortunately the tours tend to be pricey, starting at B$85/person, and, in Kampong Ayer at least, they show you little that you can't see on your own, though most include tea and cakes at one of the houses. Where such trips come in handy is in combining Kampong Ayer with the chance to see **proboscis monkeys**. If you were in Kuching or Kota Kinabalu, the nearest groups of the monkeys would be a long excursion away in Bako or the Garama River, so it's incredible that here in Bandar they can be found a mere twenty minutes' boat ride upriver from the centre, beyond the royal palace in a sliver of woodland and mangrove hemmed in between a residential neighbourhood and the river. The best time of day to see them is around 8am or 5pm, when it's cooler and the monkeys come out to forage.

It's perfectly possible to arrange a river trip **independently**: village boatmen hang around at the jetty area at the western end of Jalan McArthur, close to *Kaizen Sushi* restaurant, which is also where the tour boats leave from. The boatmen won't proffer life jackets or slick commentary (and may not speak that much English), but they charge much less than a tour company. Note that it will take at least an hour to have a reasonable go at spotting the monkeys (depending if there's a queue to enter the mangroves) and enjoy a quick spin around Kampong Ayer. Another advantage of arranging your own trip is that you can ask to be let off elsewhere along the river later – after monkey-spotting first thing in the morning, possible places to visit include the Handicrafts Centre (see page 435).

BANDAR SERI BEGAWAN **BRUNEI** | 437

to Sabah alone – park on Jalan Sungai Kianggeh by a conspicuous modern glass tower. The Jesselton/Sipitang Express (http://sipitangexpress.com.my) heads to Kota Kinabalu (7hr) via Lawas (1hr 30min), Sipitang (3hr) and Beaufort (4hr) daily at 8am (the return from KK is also at 8am). You seldom need to buy tickets in advance, but can do so from bus conductors before departure, or if you're in luck, from http://easybook.com. Going south to Sarawak and Indonesia has been fraught with difficulty since services stopped during Covid; you'll need to minibus it to Seria, and then take another to Kuyala Belait, then taxi to and from the border.

Intertown buses Public minibuses (hourly) serve Tutong and Seria, though they can take an absolute age to travel what isn't exactly a great distance.

By boat The only boats that serve Bandar itself, to and from Bangar in the Temburong district, use a jetty on Jalan Residency close to the Kianggeh food court (around hourly 6am–4.30pm; 45min). All international ferries use the terminal in Muara (see page 440).

GETTING AROUND

Nowhere in Bandar's compact centre is more than a 20min walk from anywhere else, but you'll probably use the city's modest **bus** system to reach outlying attractions and the suburbs.

BY BUS

Bus station On the ground floor of Kompleks Darussalam on Jalan Cator.
Routes Most domestic buses are compact, 22-seater vehicles, with brightly-coloured liveries varying by route; they all only run between 6am and 6.30pm. There is a bus map in the tourist office guide, and on http://jpd.gov.bn and the TransportBN app (don't expect Google Maps to be of any use), though it's perhaps more useful to ask at the bus station (or your accommodation) about the route number for your destination. On average there are two buses an hour on each route (popular services such as #1A to Gadong and #39 to Muara via the Kota Batu museums might run every 15–20min). Fares are dirt cheap.

BY TAXI

Ranks and companies Taxis come into their own at night, when the bus network has shut down, but are relatively rare – most people can afford cars so there are only around fifty taxis in the whole country, though more cars can be hailed on the Dart app (http://dartbrunei.com) – Uber and Grab have been useable in the past, but were not at the time of writing. While there are a couple of taxi cooperatives (222 2214 or 222 6853), most drivers work independently and can only be summoned by mobile phone; hotels keep lists of favourites, and you're likely to receive a business card from every driver you use. In the centre of Bandar, there's a taxi rank outside the Jalan Cator bus station. Taxis show up sporadically at suburban malls too, though they can be so scarce in Gadong that you may have to ask a hotel there to book one.
Fares Taxis aren't always metered, so get an idea of current fares from your hotel. Hourly rates can be negotiated, and prices rise by fifty percent after dark.

BY WATER-TAXI

Routes and access Little speedboats plying the Brunei River, known as water-taxis, are fun for whizzing around the river, but bar the trip across the river to Kampong Ayer, they are of limited use, since most of the few waterside attractions are perfectly walkable. You can attract the attention of a boatman at numerous jetties and steps leading down to the river and Kianggeh canal (near the *Brunei Hotel*).

BY CAR

Car rental Avis, at the *Radisson* hotel (222 7100); Hertz, at the airport (233 2983); Qawi in Gadong on Jalan Penghubung Berakas Lambak Kanan (265 5550).

INFORMATION

Tourist offices Brunei Tourism (http://bruneitourism.com) runs offices at the airport and the Kampong Ayer Tourism and Culture Gallery (both Mon–Thurs & Sat 9am–5pm, Fri 9–11.30am & 2–5pm; 220 0874). Both supply maps and brochures, but little else. Tourism Malaysia (Mon–Thurs & Sun 9am–5pm, Fri 9–11.30am & 2–5pm, Sat 10am–5pm; 238 1575) is on the first floor of the *Rizqun International* in Gadong (see page 438).
Newspapers Since the closing of *Brunei Times* in 2016, the only English-language newspaper is the *Borneo Bulletin* (http://borneobulletin.com.bn), inevitably filled with news about the royal family, though it offers useful leads on events and new venues.

TOUR OPERATORS

Although Bandar's expensive tour operators major in rather predictable city tours, Ulu Temburong trips, and river excursions to see the monkeys and floating village, they also offer a few destinations that are awkward to visit independently, notably **Selirong Island** in Brunei Bay – a great spot for birding – and the **Bukit Peradayan Forest Reserve** on the eastern edge of Temburong (the latter is also sometimes included in Temburong packages). Brunei is also a good spot for diving – although much more expensive than in Malaysia, there are several worthwhile wreck dives in Brunei waters.

Borneo Guide Unit 5, second floor, Plaza Al-Abrar, Simpang 424a, Gadong; http://borneoguide.com. Fairly standard offerings, with two notable exceptions: the Countryside Tour is a day-trip out to Mukim Amo (3hr) for a slice of rural Brunei, including a visit to the rice paddies and a bee farm. The other is a longhouse visit near Labi that includes a walk into primary rainforest (7hr).

Freme Travel 403b Wisma Jaya, Jalan Pemancha; http://freme.com. The usual destinations, plus two-night dedicated bird-watching trips and another two-night trip that includes the Seria oil field (see page 430).

Intrepid Tours http://intrepid.com. This agency has plenty of Borneo trips on offer, and some duck into Brunei.

Poni Divers Simpang 287, Serasa; http://ponidivers.com. Located just east of Bandar, this group will have you making a splash in a flash; the most appealing options, for many, are the wreck dives. And lastly, how many people do you know who got their PADI licence in Brunei? Eternal bragging rights await.

Sunshine Borneo 2 Simpang 146, Jalan Kiarong; http://instagram.com/sunshinetours.bwn. This veteran company has a comprehensive portfolio of packages, and they can do tailor-made trips such as to Bukit Peradayan Forest Reserve, combined with visits to nearby modern longhouses.

ACCOMMODATION　　　　　　　　　　　　　　　　　　　　　　　SEE MAP PAGE 432

Brunei not being backpacker territory, Bandar holds few great **budget** options, though the city has an adequate array of hotels, and higher-end Airbnb rooms are also available (plus some cheaper ones in Kampung Ayer). Some visitors prefer to stay outside Bandar, commuting in for the sights – certainly feasible, though it won't save you any money and you'll have to head out well before sunset if you're using public transport. The obvious out-of-town place to stay is the lavish *Empire* (see page 441), and there's a good guesthouse in Muara, though it's possible to base yourself in **Seria** or even Bangar in **Temburong** if you have your own transport.

DOWNTOWN

★ **Badi'ah** Jalan Tutong; http://badiahhotel.com. If you don't mind being just outside the centre, this is the best choice at this price level, with perfectly comfortable rooms, a cute swimming pool (though one too small to actually swim in), and cheery, professional staff. Some of the floating village is within easy walking distance, and it's also pleasant getting to the city centre on foot across the pedestrian bridge. $$

Brunei 95 Jalan Pemancha; http://thebruneihotel.com. The best-value place in the centre, transformed from a dowdy lump of 1960s concrete into a well-run business-oriented hotel. All rooms have beautiful timber flooring and stylish modern fittings, though there's no discount for singles. Free shuttle transport to and from Gadong for the shops and night market. Rates include breakfast. $$$

Pusat Belia (Youth Centre) Jalan Sultan Kianggeh; 222 2900. Used for student conferences, Bandar's youth centre features various dorms – single-sex, in line with local values – that take travellers. Facilities include a small pool, but no wi-fi, and cleanliness can be an issue. Awkwardly, reception keeps standard office hours, with a break for lunch; at other times, call the manager using the number on display or hope to bump into a staff member. $

Qing Yun Rest House Third floor, Jalan McArthur; http://facebook.com/qingyunresthouse. Archetypal Chinese-run flophouse, of a kind that's vanishing elsewhere. Rooms are spacious enough and have a/c and decent flooring, but the common areas can stink of goodness-knows-what. The wi-fi is slow, and their website comically bad; it may be best to What's App them if you'd like to book. $

★ **Radisson** Jalan Tasek Lama; http://radisson.com. Brunei's first top-notch hotel, with a pool, spa, fitness centre and other amenities, and the rooms are modern and clean and the service excellent. Deluxe rooms don't cost that much more and come with free breakfast, which you probably won't regret. Free shuttle-bus service to the shopping malls. $$$

GADONG

★ **MiniInn Guesthouse** Off Simpang 137; 837 3727. What a lovely addition to the Bandar area's accommodation scene this has been – almost like a homestay, the rooms here have hot showers, fast wi-fi, and are fairly priced. One small negative – the glass doors to the bathrooms don't afford much privacy. $

Rizqun International Southeastern end of Abdul Razak Complex, off Simpang 137; http://rizquninternational.com. The priciest hotel in town, adjoining the Gadong Mall, with an ostentatious lobby featuring lots of marble and gaudy

---

ACCOMMODATION PRICE CODES

All accommodation reviewed in this Guide is accompanied by a price category, based on the cost of a basic room for two (or two dorm beds, in the case of hostels) in high season. Price ranges don't include breakfast, unless stated otherwise. For camping, prices are given per pitch. The codes for **Brunei** are as follows:

$ = under BND50
$$ = BND50–100
$$$ = BND100–200
$$$$ = over BND200

stained glass. Facilities include a pool and gym, and forty percent discount is sometimes available at weekends, including breakfast. $$$$

EATING
SEE MAP PAGE 432

In a country where eating and shopping count as the main pastimes, Bandar has a good sprinkling of venues catering for both. There are inexpensive stalls downtown at **Tamu Kianggeh** and a stone's throw away at the so-called **Kianggeh food court** on Jalan Residency, the latter good for river views at dusk – however, both pale in comparison to those at Taman Selera and at **Gadong's pasar malam**. If Brunei has a national dish, it's **nasi katok**. Widely sold at stalls and in a few cheap diners, it's a more substantial answer to *nasi lemak* – featuring plain rather than coconut rice, topped with a large joint of chicken or sometimes a helping of beef. Various tales explain the name (meaning "knock rice"), the most common being that hawkers devised it as a breakfast for people working night shifts, and used to knock on workplace doors in the morning to announce its arrival. Malay food doesn't dominate the culinary scene, however – there are plenty of Chinese and a few Indian options as well, plus a smattering serving Japanese and other international cuisines.

DOWNTOWN

Kaizen Sushi Jalan McArthur; 224 6336. Highly attractive and very popular sushi restaurant, with a prime location on the riverfront. As well as good sushi, they have other Japanese meals and treats, including curry udon, bento boxes and breaded katsu. Book ahead, especially on weekends. $$$$
Phongmun Second floor, Teck Guan Plaza, Jalan Sultan; http://facebook.com/phongmunrestaurant. The city centre's best Chinese restaurant, overlooking the river and predictably done out with temple-style red arches and dragons. Cantonese food is the order of the day, including dim sum in the mornings; otherwise the house specialities are braised pork leg eaten with buns, and claypot chicken. The full menu runs to several pages, but you'll probably be given a cut-down version. $$$
★ **Syazwan Café** 30a Jalan Sultan; 233 0727. A cut above the area's other Indian Muslim *kedai kopis*, frying a full range of rice or noodle dishes to order, plus a good *nasi campur* spread, *dosai*, *murtabak*, very good *roti* and *naan* bread, and even Chinese-style stir-fries. $
★ **Tamu Selera** Off Jalan Tutong, close to the Terrace hotel. The most atmospheric downtown place for dinner, bar none, is this open-air food court, where dozens of stalls sell Malay food. *Ayam penyet* – tender barbecued chicken – is especially popular, and a couple of vendors sell satay and *nasi katok* too. For something a little pricier, head to the Mizu Seafood Village, where they have live lobster in tubs

EATING PRICE CODES

Throughout the Guide, every dining option reviewed is accompanied by a price category, based on the cost of a basic two-course meal for one (or similar, at cafés and hawker centres), without drinks. The codes for **Brunei** are as follows:
$ = under BND10
$$ = BND10–15
$$$ = BND15–20
$$$$ = over BND20

and other seafood, all sold by weight and cooked to order. Cheaper seafood stir-fries, fried rice and noodles are also available. Sit close to the stall you're ordering from. $
Tarindak d'Seni Eastern end of the Arts and Handicrafts Centre complex, Jalan Residency; 224 0422. Despite the bland modern decor, this buffet restaurant serves a very impressive Malay spread; as well as lunch and dinner options, Sunday sees breakfast and high tea come into play. Tables groan with dishes such as beef *rendang*, stir-fried *keladi* (yam greens) and *ikan kicap* (fish stewed in soy sauce), all eaten with plain or *biriyani* rice. They also serve a classic Bruneian staple, *ambuyat* – sago starch, looking and smelling like congealed glue; tease it out of the bowl with chopsticks and eat it with sauces such as *tempoyak* (fermented durian). More palatably, they have Western salads and oodles of local and European cakes. $$$
Yelo Café Brunei Hotel, 95 Jalan Pemancha; http://thebruneihotel.com. The *Brunei Hotel's* coffee house is great for a Western-style breakfast – a buffet of chicken sausage, beans, hash browns, cereals and so forth, with eggs and pancakes cooked to order, plus the usual local rice or noodle options. At other times they serve up a mixture of Western and Malaysian food. $$

GADONG

Fratini's Gadong Centrepoint, Simpang 37; http://facebook.com/fratinis.restaurant. Highly popular, *Fratini's* is an upmarket Italian chain with several branches around the country. The food tends to be average rather than great, but the breadth of the menu compensates: the best option is their wide range of pizzas, but they also have similarly-priced pasta options and more expensive mains such as sea bass with ratatouille in a lemon sauce. $$$$
Gadong Pasar Malam Just east across the canal from the Rizqun hotel. Many tourists trek out to Gadong for this entertaining night market. Besides a section selling fruit and vegetables, it has a few dozen stalls selling all manner of local snacks, including grilled chicken and fish, *kelupis* (glutinous rice, often stuffed with minced beef or prawns and steamed in the leaves of the *irik* plant) and the sweet crêpe *apam balik*.

Annoyingly though, there's nowhere to sit. $\overline{\$}$

★ **Thiam Hock** 5 Yong Siong Hai Building; 244 1679. Clean and stylish, and revered by locals for its excellent fish-head dishes – curried, cooked in a spicy tamarind sauce, or chopped up with noodles. There's also a wide range of other seafood, plus the usual pork, veg and tofu; mornings are dominated by noodles. To find the building, head south out of the Gadong Mall. $\overline{\$\$}$

TT Blues Café 12 Yong Siong Hai Building; 242 4527. This informal café-restaurant has big-screen football, and is good for a cholesterol-raising mixed grill and Western snacks, though they also have Malay options ranging from *rojak* to *cendol*. Especially busy at lunch and on weekends. $\overline{\$\$}$

SHOPPING SEE MAP PAGE 432

Despite the population's healthy disposable incomes and attachment to shopping, Brunei's **malls** are disappointingly devoid of glitz – plenty of people drive across the border to **Miri** to shop, while the genuinely rich jet off to Singapore or Kuala Lumpur on a regular basis. **Opening hours** are curtailed during Ramadan, and individual shops in shopping centres keep their own hours.

Arts and Handicrafts Centre Jalan Residency; http://facebook.com/pusatkesenianbrunei. The gift shop here is a great place to browse a wide selection of crafts, though anything really worth having – notably silverware and brocade – is priced in the hundreds of Brunei dollars. Annoyingly, you can't pay with card.

Gadong Mall Abdul Razak development. While the sheer size of the Gadong Mall is impressive, its shops, mostly selling trinkets, phone accessories, cheap clothes and so on, are nothing special; the big name, such as it is, is the Utama Grand department store. Otherwise, it's more of a place where young people turn out to see and be seen. The paltry selection of English-language books in the ground-floor magazine shop is the best you can get anywhere close to central Bandar.

Yayasan Complex South of Omar Ali Saifuddien mosque. A much earlier attempt to revive downtown Bandar than the revamped waterfront, this multi-building mall is rapidly losing ground to its out-of-town rivals and the top floors are deserted. The only outlet worth much of a look is the Hua Ho supermarket, but you can make use of free wi-fi, and there are a few cafés.

DIRECTORY

Cinemas Your best bet is the The Mall Cineplex at Gadong Mall (http://mall-ticket.com).

Embassies, consulates and high commissions (Note that all embassies are shut from Fri lunchtime or afternoon till Mon morning) Australia, 6F DAR Takaful IBB Utama, Jalan Pemancha (222 9435, http://bruneidarussalam.embassy.gov.au); Canada, 2203 Jalan Tesek (222 0043, international.gc.ca); Indonesia, Lot 4498, Simpang 528, Sungai Hanching Baru, Jalan Muara (233 0180); Malaysia, 61 Simpang 336, Kampong Sungai Akar, Jalan Kebangsaan (238 1095); Philippines, Simpang 336, Diplomatic Enclave, Jalan Kebangsaan (224 1465); Singapore, 8 Simpang 74, Jalan Subok (226 2741); Thailand, 2 Simpang 682, Kampung Bunut, Jalan Tutong (265 3108); UK, Unit 2.01, Block D, Kompleks Yayasan Sultan Hassanal Bolkiah (222 2231, http://gov.uk); US, Jalan Kebangsaan, Simpang (238-7400, http://bn.usembassy.gov).

Hospital The RIPAS Hospital is near the centre on Jalan Tutong (224 2424). For an ambulance, call 991.

Pharmacies Guardian Pharmacy has outlets on Jalan Sultan and on the ground floor of Gadong Mall.

Police Central Police Station, Jalan Stoney (222 2333), or call 993.

Visa extensions The Immigration Office is out towards the airport on Jalan Menteri Besar (Mon–Thurs & Sat 7.45am–12.15pm & 1.30–4.30pm; 238 3106, http://immigration.gov.bn; bus #1 or #24).

Muara district

As most of Brunei's natural attractions are in Temburong and Tutong, there's little to detain you in the capital's surrounding district, **Muara**. However, no visit to Brunei would be complete without checking out two eccentric attractions in **Jerudong** – the **Empire Hotel & Country Club** and the **Jerudong Park Playground**. Also worth a visit is **Muara Beach** and the **Bukit Shahbandar Forest Recreation Park**, a nature reserve with only the most basic facilities for visitors.

Muara

MUARA, Brunei's main port, 25km northeast of Bandar, has nothing else to recommend it other than **Muara Beach** 3km north, which boasts an adequate stretch of sand and a small food court; it's a long hot walk out here unless you want to wait for the erratic local minibus. You can wear your bikini on the beach, so long as it's under all your other clothes – everybody in the sea is fully clothed.

ARRIVAL AND DEPARTURE   MUARA

By ferry Brunei's international Serasa Ferry Terminal, a couple of kilometres south of what passes for the town centre, is served by bus #39 (hourly; 1hr), which stops on the main road at the green mosque, just under 1km from the terminal. The #33 minibus runs from Maura Beach via Maura town centre to the port, but it's request-only for the ferry terminal and so only really useful when departing. Ferries only run to Labuan (1 daily; at least 1hr 30min, depending on weather), and you should arrive at least an hour before your departure. From Labuan, boats run to both Lawas in Sarawak, and Kota Kinabalu in Sabah.

By bus From Bandar, the most reliable buses for Muara are #38, which heads north to the airport and then east to Muara, and #39, which goes east to the Kota Batu museums and then north to Muara. The only bus to the beach is the #33 from Maura town centre. All go round the houses and take around an hour.

ACCOMMODATION

★ Poni Homestay 1km west of the ferry terminal, Jalan Serasa; http://ponihomestay.com. The only accommodation in Brunei to have anything resembling an international hostel vibe – it's a homestay run by Poni Divers (http://ponidivers.com), but the common room, kitchen and bunk beds exude that classic backpacker vibe. Occasional BBQ nights, and they can also get you on a diving tour. Breakfast is included. $\overline{\underline{\text{S}}}$

Jerudong and around

The fishing village at **JERUDONG**, 15km northwest of Bandar, is a simple place where you can see the fishing boats pulled up on the beach, and sample smoked fresh fish in the wet market. Walking west along the beaches and through the car park will bring you to the **Empire Hotel & Country Club**, the big sight around here, while the **Bukit Shahbandar Park** is across the highway, and the **Jerudong Park Playground** is just 4km southwest.

Empire Hotel & Country Club

Close to Jerudong, 15km northwest of Bandar, off the Muara–Tutong Highway • http://theempirebrunei.com • Bus #57 from Bandar may on request call at the hotel itself; if the driver refuses, get off on the highway and walk in (around 10min), or take a #55 to the fish market at Jerudong and walk in through the back entrance; alternatively, take a taxi from Bandar

It might seem odd to traipse out of Bandar just to see a hotel, but then the **Empire Hotel & Country Club** is no ordinary hotel. A personal project in the 1990s of Prince Jefri, the wayward and discredited former finance minister, the complex cost US$1 billion to build and put such a drain on the state's coffers that the government had to take a stake in what had been intended as a private development.

The result, benefiting from the skills of thousands of craftsmen from assorted artistic traditions, is jaw-dropping. Just to stroll through the lofty central atrium with its 25m-high marble columns, is striking enough. Then there are the gold-plated balusters of the lobby staircase, laden with 370 tiger's eye gemstones, and the handrails coated with mother-of-pearl. While the hotel doesn't really throw open its doors as a tourist attraction, it's vast enough that no one minds neatly dressed visitors who come to gawp and then, more often than not, eat at one of the restaurants.

Bukit Shahbandar Forest Recreation Park

Along the Muara–Tutong highway, directly south of the Empire Hotel & Country Club • Free • Bus #57

The **Bukit Shahbandar Forest Recreation Park**, a compact area of acacia, pine and heath forest equipped with trails, carpets a hilly area with lookout points over the *Empire Hotel* complex, Bandar and the South China Sea. Marking the entrance to the park is an information centre with displays on the surrounding terrain. The trails are well signposted and popular with joggers, and there are a few rest huts for shade and shelter.

Jerudong Park Playground

Jerudong, south off the Muara–Tutong highway, 4km southwest of the Empire Hotel & Country Club • Charge; foreigners must bring ID • http://jerudongpark.com • Bus #57

In its 1990s heyday, the **Jerudong Park Playground** was the wonder of Brunei, almost like the country's answer to the Tivoli Gardens in Copenhagen. Built by the government as an amusement park for the sultan's subjects, it was an essential stopover for visitors, the rides all totally free; famously, Michael Jackson and Whitney Houston played the park's theatre. Like all extravagances the place inevitably became uneconomic to maintain, even with Brunei's oil revenues, and it slowly descended into moribundity. Relaunched in 2014, albeit on a diminished scale, the park is worth a visit if you're in the area – but even the kids might think it a bit dated. It's most atmospheric in the evening; if using public transport, be sure to arrange a taxi in advance to collect you after the buses stop at sunset. Note that all rides close for thirty minutes during prayer times.

ACCOMMODATION AND EATING — JERUDONG AND AROUND

Empire Hotel & Country Club Near Jerudong; http://theempirebrunei.com. The great thing about staying here is that while the high-ceilinged rooms, unlike the public areas, aren't exceptional for a five-star-type resort, rates can be very reasonable. Amenities include a golf course, spa, cinema, swimming pools and a private lagoon. $$$$

Pantai Empire Hotel & Country Club; 241 7783, http://theempirebrunei.com. Housed in a separate building – look for the red lanterns outside – this is the best known of the *Empire*'s restaurants, serving halal Cantonese food, with dim sum available at lunchtime over the weekend. $$$$

Temburong district

With a population of just ten thousand, including some Iban and Lun Bawang (Murut), **Temburong district** is the wilds of Brunei. Forested and hilly, it contains Brunei's best-known attraction, the 500-square-kilometre **Ulu Temburong National Park**, with its entrancing canopy walkway. The park has limited possibilities for walks though, so some people visit on a short day-trip from Bandar, while most opt for two-day packages.

Bangar

The starting point for all Ulu Temburong trips is the district's only town, **BANGAR**, normally reached by speedboat from Bandar. The boats head downriver through narrow mangrove estuaries before shooting off into the open expanse of Brunei Bay and then curling back south to head up the Temburong River. It's also possible to drive here via Limbang in Sarawak, or catch the Kota Kinabalu bus from Bandar, which passes through at about 10am. The town itself is nothing to write home about; its main street, running east from the jetty to the town mosque, holds a handful of *kedai kopis* and general stores. However, it is the nearest town to the Ulu Temburong National Park, with much cheaper accommodation, and tour operators that charge around half of what you'll pay in Bandar to visit it.

ACCOMMODATION — BANGAR

Stone Ville Jalan Pekan Bangar, just north of town; 522 2252. The best place to stay in Bangar, with simple though tidy rooms, and a good location near the creek. It's also a decent place to eat, with a roster of local and Chinese staples, plus a few Western choices for breakfast (not included with accommodation). $

Ulu Temburong National Park

Park HQ daily 8am–6.30pm • Prebooked tours compulsory, park fees included in package price

Contained within the Batu Apoi Forest Reserve, which constitutes a tenth of the area of Brunei, the **Ulu Temburong National Park** undoubtedly impresses as a pristine nature area. There isn't that much to do – the only trails are simple and short – but there are some activities on offer (tubing down the river, for one) and the park is great for peace and quiet.

Canopy walkway

The park's main attraction, the **canopy walkway**, is reached by an hour-long trek (or longboat ride) taking in two hanging bridges and a plankway, followed by a giddying climb up the stairs around a near-vertical, 60m-high aluminium structure. The view from the top, of Brunei Bay to the north and Sarawak's Gunung Mulu National Park to the south, is breathtaking. At this height (on a good day) you can see hornbills and gibbons in the trees, as well as numerous squirrels and small birds. Fifty species of birds have been sighted on the netting around the walkway, while flying lizards, frogs and snakes feed regularly at ground level.

And now for the slightly bad news. The walkway was never built as a tourist sight, but as a bird-watching post for park rangers; it's an extremely simple structure whose four constituent towers get wobbly at the top, especially on the walkway between the middle two. It has often found itself closed for extended periods when things got just that little too unsafe (usually remedied with a few more ropes tethered to nearby trees), and in a similar vein, one of the hanging bridges heading there was closed down in 2018 after it flipped and dumped a few tourists way down in the river. Lastly, the popular Ulu-Ulu Resort, the only one in the national park itself, closed its doors in 2020, finished off by Covid troubles after years of underinvestment. Ulu Temburong being Brunei tourism's pride and joy, it makes you wish that someone nearby had, say, hundreds of luxury cars lying idle, and had instead been able to cash in a few to provide some much-needed funding... if only.

ARRIVAL AND INFORMATION ULU TEMBURONG NATIONAL PARK

From Bandar On a standard two-day package, the first day is spent reaching your accommodation from Bandar, and much of the second day given over to the park before you zip back to Bandar in the late afternoon. Tour operators also offer somewhat rushed day-trips.

From Bangar You may find you pay slightly less if you make your own way to Bangar and join a tour there, though you still need to book in advance. From Bangar, van transport is laid on to the jetty at Batang Duri, 15km south. The final leg is via longboat, with dense jungle cloaking the hills on either side and birds and monkeys bustling around in the trees. Though lasting less than an hour, the journey sets the tone for the park itself. You can also take day-trips from Bangar.

Activities Besides the climb up to the canopy walkway, activities in and around the park include night walks, rafting or tubing down the river and treks to a nearby waterfall.

ACCOMMODATION

As well as the following, it's probably worth checking to see whether anything has been done with the once-popular *Ulu-Ulu Resort*, which closed down in 2020 – a lovely property, destined to be taken over either by a new owner, or the surrounding jungle.

Freme Rainforest Lodge Batang Duri, 30min by longboat from Temburong National Park; http://freme.com. A substantial, comfortable place (though pretty basic considering the price) with a/c dorms and a large, open-air dining area. Rates include one night's stay, meals and transfers from Bandar. $$$$

Sumbiling Eco Village Sumbiling Lama, the penultimate village before Batang Duri; http://sumbiling.com. This is a fairly simple jungle encampment with tents and three basic huts, though proper toilets are provided. In keeping with the eco theme, meals are eaten off leaves rather than plastic plates. Packages include a night walk in the vicinity. Rates include one night's stay, meals and transfers. $$$

Belait district

West of Muara, beyond the noticeably agricultural Tutong district, is **Belait district**, whose coastal section is oil and gas country, and has been the economic heart of the sultanate ever since the Seria oil field was established in 1931. The oil boom led directly to the rise of the region's two main towns, **Seria** and **Kuala Belait**, both still fairly sleepy, with generally ugly concrete centres that contrast with suburbs that have quite a rural feel. Inland, though, it's a much more rural story: down the 50km-long road to **Labi** are a few modern Iban **longhouses** and forest reserves to visit.

The Labi Road
No public transport, though tour operators such as Borneo Guide and Sunshine Borneo in Bandar offer trips here

More or less midway between Tutong and Seria, a turning south off the highway marks the start of the Labi Road. Just 500m on, the thick lowland forest of the **Sungai Liang Forest Reserve** can be explored by following various walking trails from the lakes. Twenty kilometres further along, at the **Luagan Lalak Forest Recreation Park**, a freshwater swamp swells into a lake with the onset of the monsoon rains. A little further on and you reach **LABI** itself, a small agricultural settlement where durian and rambutan are cultivated.

The road beyond turns into a laterite track; around 300m along, a trail off to the east leads, after two hours' walk, to **Wasai Rampayoh**, a large waterfall. Continue south on the track to reach **Mendaram Longhouse**, the first of four Iban communities here, and home to a few dozen people. Like most Iban architecture in Brunei, it's a modern structure, with electricity and running water, though it does have an informal homestay programme. From here a well-marked path leads past **Teraja Longhouse** to **Wasai Mendaram**, a tiny waterfall thirty or so minutes' walk away with a rock pool perfect for swimming.

Seria

SERIA, 65km southwest of Bandar, stands at the epicentre of Brunei's oil and gas wealth. Before oil was discovered here at the start of the twentieth century, this was nothing more than a malarial swamp, known locally as Padang Berawa, or "Wild Pigeon's Field". Once S1, the sultanate's first oil well, began to deliver commercially in 1931, Seria expanded rapidly, with offshore drilling following in the 1950s. As you approach from Tutong, you may see small oil wells called "nodding donkeys" because of their rocking motion. Around the town are numerous bungalows, constructed by petroleum companies for their employees, while on the seafront nearly 2km west of the centre the interlocking arches of the **Billionth Barrel Monument** celebrate the huge productivity of the first well. Bandar's tour operators can organize trips to oil-related sights, including the Oil and Gas Discovery Centre. It's not all oil, though – BSP (a joint venture between the Brunei government and Shell, and the sultanate's largest employer) attempted to diversify its power production with the addition of a major solar power plant in Seria, which is expected to be fully open in 2026. However, if you have no great interest in energy production, you'll still probably want to avoid this soulless town.

Seria Energy Lab
750m northwest of the bus station • Tues–Thurs & Sun 8.30am–5pm, Fri 2.30–7pm, Sat 8.30am–7pm • Charge • http://seriaenergylab.com • From the bus station, head 500m north up Jalan Sultan Omar Ali, the road running west of the Plaza Seria mall, then 250m west; alternatively, take a taxi

Seria's only specific sight is the **Oil and Gas Discovery Centre**, a museum created by Brunei Shell to bolster understanding of technology in general and the petroleum industry in particular. With its hi-tech interactive exhibits, it's marginally more entertaining than the similar museum not far away in Miri, though you still need more than a passing interest in oil extraction to get much out of it. It's somewhere that all Brunei school kids are forced to visit at least once. There is also a small "town" where kids can zoom around in pedal cars, though it would be more apt (and fun) if the cars were petrol-driven.

ARRIVAL AND INFORMATION

SERIA

By bus Seria's bus terminus is diagonally across from the bank, south of the mall.
Destinations Bandar Seri Begawan (hourly; 1hr 30min or more); Kuala Belait (every 30min–1hr; 45min).

Services There are banks and ATMs in the drab Plaza Seria shopping mall, which dominates Seria's small centre.

ACCOMMODATION AND EATING

Koperasi Jalan Sherif Ali; http://facebook.com. A dark green building just a couple of minutes walk up Jalan Bunga Kemantin from the bus terminal, the *Koperasi* is old-fashioned in a somehow restful way, its simple rooms equipped with a/c, TV, fridge and bathroom. $\overline{\$\$}$

Roomz Jalan Sultan Omar Ali; http://roomz.com.bn. Not cheap, but by far the snazziest place around. Rooms are decorated in pleasing brown tones, and more homely than the modern office block-like exterior might suggest. $\overline{\$\$\$}$

Zuki Café Below the Koperasi hotel, Jalan Sherif Ali; http://facebook.com. A decent local choice, with a good range of simple Chinese and Malay specialities, including *laksa* and *char kway toew*. $\overline{\$}$

Singapore

- **452** Downtown Singapore
- **486** Central Catchment Nature Reserve
- **489** Kranji and Sungei Buloh
- **490** Geylang and Katong
- **492** Changi
- **493** The Southern Ridges and Pasir Panjang
- **495** Jurong and Tuas
- **496** Sentosa Island

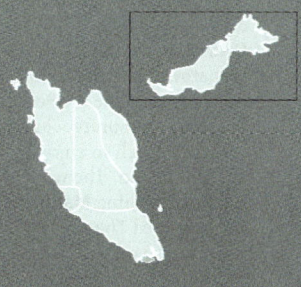

THE MARINA BAY SANDS HOTEL

Singapore

Singapore is certainly the handiest city I ever saw, as well planned and carefully executed as though built entirely by one man. It is like a big desk, full of drawers and pigeon-holes, where everything has its place, and can always be found in it.
William Hornaday, 1885

Despite the immense changes since wrought upon the tiny island of Singapore, natural historian William Hornaday's appraisal is as valid today as it was in 1885. This absorbing city-state, just one degree north of the Equator and only 720 square kilometres in size – if all the outlying islands are included – has evolved from a colonial port into a slick shrine to wealth and consumerism.

Singapore's rise began in 1819, when Sir Stamford Raffles took advantage of its natural harbour and strategic position on the maritime route between China and India to set up a British trading post. The port thrived from the word go, and remains one of the world's busiest. The country's coffers were boosted by **industrialization** following independence, and when in the 1980s Singapore grew too successful to remain a cheap sweatshop for multinationals, it maintained its competitive edge by developing a super-efficient infrastructure and work ethic, and diversifying into technology and finance.

Lacking any significant welfare system, Singapore appears to be a paragon of capitalism. However, much of its economy is dominated by conglomerates set up by the state, which retains a controlling interest. Regulations govern everything from flushing public toilets after use to jaywalking, and, less benignly, there's a low tolerance of **dissent**.

This unwritten, paternalistic contract underlies what visitors see today: kampungs and slums have long been cleared, with people resettled in bland, though well-planned, new towns. Even today the island is dogged by a sense of impermanence, its buildings scarcely bedding down before being replaced by something even grander. But while Singapore is the most westernized of Southeast Asia's cities, it would be unfair to dismiss it as sterile. As with Malaysia, much of Singapore's fascination springs from its **multicultural population**, the main groups being the Chinese (around 75 percent), Malays (15 percent) and Indians (under 8 percent). This diversity can turn a short walk across town into what seems like a hop from one country to another.

Getting a decent taste of the island requires at least three days. Old Singapore is looking better than ever thanks to belated conservation work, and each of the original ethnic enclaves boasts neatly restored shophouses and its own distinct flavour: **Little India** has its garland-sellers and curry houses, **Chinatown** its calligraphers and fortune-tellers, while **Arab Street** is home to cluttered stores selling fine cloths and curios. At the core of downtown Singapore are historic public buildings and the lofty cathedral of the **Colonial District**. It also has a clutch of fine **museums**, something rarely on offer in Malaysia; the **Chinatown Heritage Centre** evokes the harsh conditions endured by Chinatown's earlier inhabitants, while the **Peranakan Museum** and **Baba House** celebrate Singapore's Baba-Nyonya community – just as important as that of Penang and Melaka.

There's much to enjoy by way of modern and, perhaps surprisingly, nature-oriented attractions too. The wings of reclaimed land at the mouth of the Singapore River, together forming **Marina Bay**, hold the striking **Marina Bay Sands** hotel and casino and the bug-eyed **Theatres on the Bay**. Huge investment in the **arts** means that even on a short visit, you may well catch world-renowned performers in town. North of the city, there's primary rainforest to explore at **Bukit Timah Nature Reserve** and the splendid **Singapore Zoo**, which you can even tour at night. The best offshore day-trip is south to **Sentosa**, the island amusement arcade that features Singapore's other casino resort.

BUDDHA TOOTH RELIC TEMPLE

Highlights

❶ National Gallery Singapore's National Gallery is certainly an architectural showpiece, uniting two of the island's grandest colonial buildings. See page 455

❷ Little India Old Singapore's most atmospheric district is a sensory overload of temples and spice shops. See page 464

❸ The Buddha Tooth Relic Temple One of the island's newest temples is also one of its grandest, housing thousands of Buddha figurines. See page 470

❹ The Baba House Singapore's answer to the fine showpiece Peranakan residences of Melaka and Penang. See page 476

❺ The Botanic Gardens This park boasts an immaculate orchid collection. See page 483

❻ Bukit Timah Nature Reserve A pocket rainforest for a decent taste of the jungle. See page 487

❼ Singapore Oceanarium This gargantuan affair revels in the marine life of Southeast Asia's maritime trade routes. See page 497

❽ Hawker food centres Cut costs at these lively, stall-packed eating venues. See page 515

❾ The arts scene Get a taste of the best cultural life in the region, with international performers constantly passing through. See page 519

HIGHLIGHTS ARE MARKED ON THE MAPS ON PAGES 450 AND 453

Brief history

Little is known of Singapore's ancient history. Third-century Chinese sailors could have been referring to the place in their account of Pu-Luo-Chung, or "island at the end of a peninsula". In the late thirteenth century, Marco Polo reported seeing a place called Chiamassie, which could also have been Singapore; by then the island was known locally as Temasek and was a minor trading outpost of the Sumatran Srivijaya Empire.

Throughout the fourteenth century, Singapura felt the squeeze as the Ayuthaya and Majapahit empires of Thailand and Java struggled for control of the Malay Peninsula. Around 1390, a Sumatran prince called **Paramesvara** threw off his allegiance to Majapahit and fled to Temasek. There he murdered his host and ruled the island until a Javanese offensive forced him further north, where he and his son, **Iskandar Shah**, subsequently founded the Melaka Sultanate.

The country's present name is derived from one first recorded in the sixteenth century, when a legend recounted in the *Sejarah Melayu* (Malay Annals) told of how a Sumatran prince saw what he thought was a lion while sheltering on the island from a storm. He then founded a city here and named it **Singapura**, Sanskrit for "Lion City".

The British colony takes shape

By the late eighteenth century, with China opening up for trade with the West, the British East India Company felt the need to establish outposts along the Straits of Melaka. Enter **Thomas Stamford Raffles** (see page 456), lieutenant-governor of Bencoolen in Sumatra. In 1819, he alighted on the north bank of the Singapore River accompanied by William Farquhar, former Resident of Melaka. Raffles quickly saw the potential of what was then an inconsequential fishing island to provide a deep-water harbour and struck a deal to establish a British trading station with **Abdul Rahman**, the *temenggong* (chieftain) of Singapore and a subordinate of the Sultan of Johor. The Dutch, however, were furious at this British incursion into what they considered their territory. Realizing that the pro-Dutch sultan would not implement the deal, Raffles simply recognized the sultan's brother, **Hussein**, as the new ruler, then concluded a second treaty with both Hussein and the *temenggong*. The Union Jack was raised, and Singapore's future as a trading post was set.

As early as 1822, Raffles set about drawing up the demarcation lines which can still be perceived in the layout of modern Singapore. The area south of the Singapore River was earmarked for Chinese migrants; Muslims were settled around the sultan's palace in today's Arab Street area. In 1824, Hussein and the *temenggong* were bought out, and Singapore was ceded outright to the British. Three years later, the new port was united with Penang and Melaka to form the **Straits Settlements**, which became a British Crown Colony in 1867.

Singapore consolidates

Thanks to its **strategic position** at the gateway to the South China Sea, Singapore grew meteorically. By 1860 it had eighty thousand inhabitants; Arabs, Indians, Javanese and Bugis all settled here, but most numerous of all were southern Chinese. The opening of the Suez Canal and advent of the steamship consolidated the island's position, a status further enhanced as the British drew all of the Malay Peninsula into their clutches, allowing Singapore to profit from its hinterland's tin- and rubber-based economy.

By the 1920s, Singapore's communities were starting to find their voice: in 1926, the Singapore Malay Union was established; as was the Malayan Communist Party four years later, largely backed by local Chinese. But rumblings concerning greater self-rule were barely audible when an altogether more immediate problem reared its head.

World War II

In December 1941, the **Japanese** bombed Pearl Harbour and invaded the Malay Peninsula; less than two months later they were at the Causeway between Johor and Singapore. On February 15, 1942, the **fall of Singapore** was complete. Winston Churchill called the surrender "the worst disaster and the largest capitulation in British history". Three and a half years of brutal Japanese rule ensued, during which upwards of 25,000 Chinese men were shot dead at Punggol and Changi beaches as enemies of the Japanese, and Europeans were either herded into **Changi Prison** or marched up the Peninsula to work on Thailand's infamous "Death Railway".

Independence

After the war, Singaporeans demanded a say in the island's administration, and in 1957 the British agreed to an elected legislative assembly. Full internal self-government was achieved in 1959, when the **People's Action Party** (PAP) emerged on top in elections. Cambridge law graduate **Lee Kuan Yew**, Singapore's first prime minister, quickly sought security via a merger with newly independent Malaya (now Peninsular Malaysia). In 1963 Singapore joined with Malaya, Sarawak and British North Borneo (Sabah) to form the **Federation of Malaysia**, but within two years it was asked to leave (see page 537). Things looked bleak for the tiny island. But Lee's personal vision and drive transformed Singapore into an Asian economic heavyweight, and enabled his party to utterly dominate Singapore politics to this day. Much of the media was taken under the state's wing and opposition politicians were harassed through the courts or even detained without trial.

New leaders, new maturity

Goh Chok Tong became prime minister in 1990 upon Lee's retirement – though many felt that Lee still called the shots. In 2004, Goh was succeeded by **Lee Hsien Loong**, Lee Kuan Yew's son, and on the very same day the elder Lee was named "minister mentor", a new position that gave him an official high horse from which to influence affairs. However, while the younger Lee has a sternness reminiscent of his father, Singapore was already becoming less uptight before his tenure, with a more open stance towards artistic expression and gay issues, for example, and the trend has continued. Perhaps the most startling expression of this maturing character came in the **2011 polls**, when the opposition won nearly forty percent of the popular vote and six out of 87 elected parliamentary seats – its best showing ever.

Although the PAP rebounded in the 2015 polls – held soon after the republic's **golden jubilee** and the **death of Lee Kuan Yew** – and maintained its share of the vote in 2020 and 2025, it seems clear that Singapore is capable of greater critical thinking than its media would suggest. Issues that continue to rankle include rising **healthcare** and **housing** costs, and the PAP's open stance on **immigration** – foreign workers on short-term contracts make up thirty percent of the population.

Downtown Singapore

Taking up the southern part of the diamond-shaped main island, **downtown Singapore** is essentially the historic city centre. Although it's easy to navigate, given the excellent transport network, individual districts are best explored on foot. You need two days to do justice to the main areas, namely the **Colonial District**, **Chinatown**, **Little India** and the **Arab Quarter**, although you could just about squeeze in a trip to **Marina Bay Sands** too, or go shopping in **Orchard Road**.

The Colonial District

On the north bank of the Singapore River is what might be termed the **Colonial District** – although locals might refer to it as the Civic District or use the names of landmarks, notably the **Padang**. This rectangular green expanse is flanked by dignified reminders of

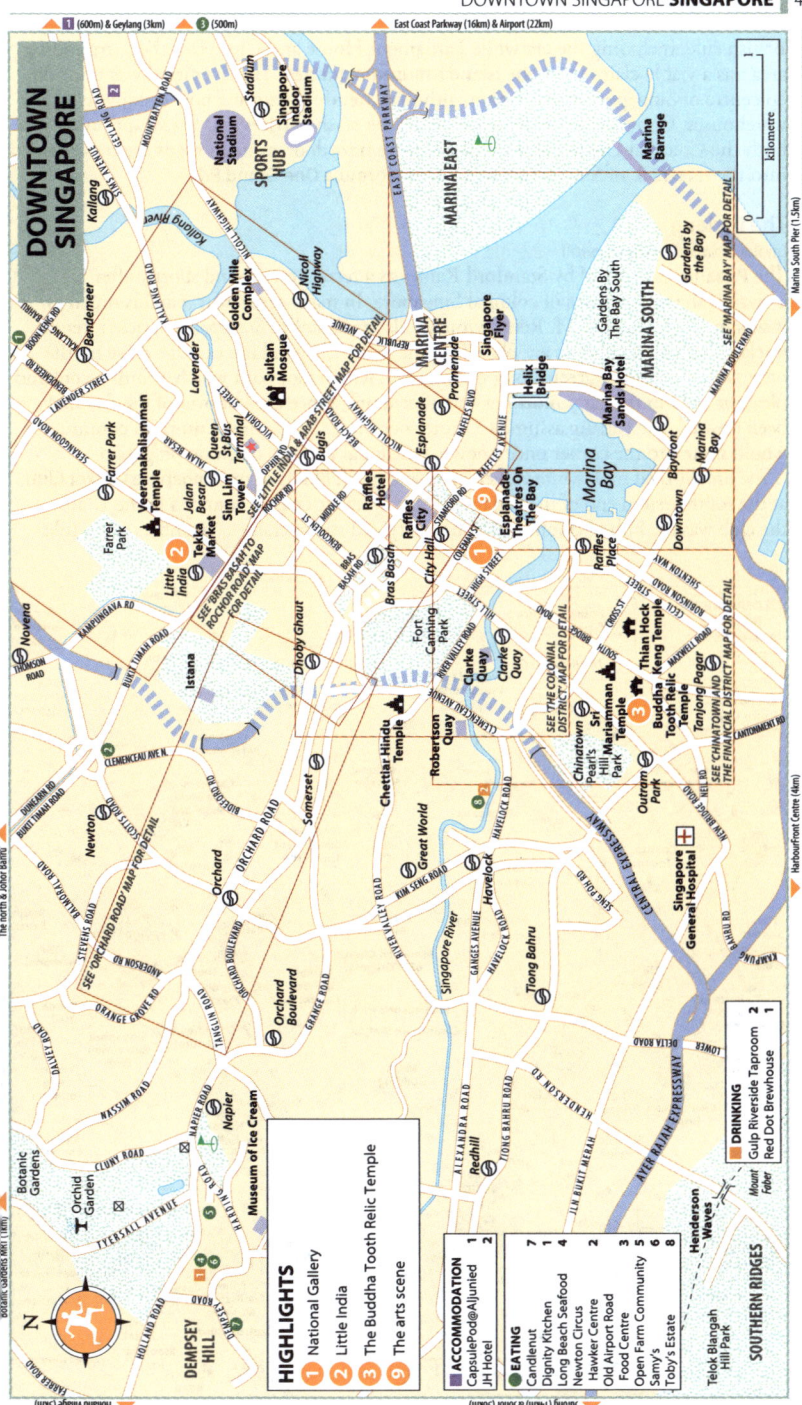

British rule, including the erstwhile Parliament House and City Hall; the surrounding area has a viable claim to be the island's **museum quarter**. The river itself was once the epicentre of Singapore's trade boom, although trendy nightspots now occupy its old warehouses. Come in September, and you'll see crash barriers and fences sprouting in both the Colonial District and Marina Centre next door, as main roads are transformed into the racetrack of Singapore's night-time **Formula One Grand Prix**.

The Padang
City Hall, Esplanade or Raffles Place MRT

The **Padang**, earmarked by Stamford Raffles as a recreation ground shortly after his arrival, is the very essence of colonial Singapore. In many respects it remains much as it was in 1907, when G.M. Reith wrote in his *Handbook to Singapore*: "Cricket, tennis, hockey, football and bowls are played on the plain…beyond the carriage drive on the other side is a strip of green along the sea-wall, with a foot-path which affords a cool and pleasant walk in the early morning and afternoon". Once the last over of the day had been bowled, the Padang assumed a more social role: Singapore's European community would hasten to the corner once known as Scandal Point to catch up on gossip.

The brown-tiled roof, whitewashed walls and green blinds of the **Singapore Cricket Club**, at the southwestern end of the Padang, have a nostalgic charm. Founded in the 1850s, the club was the hub of colonial British society and still operates a "members only" rule.

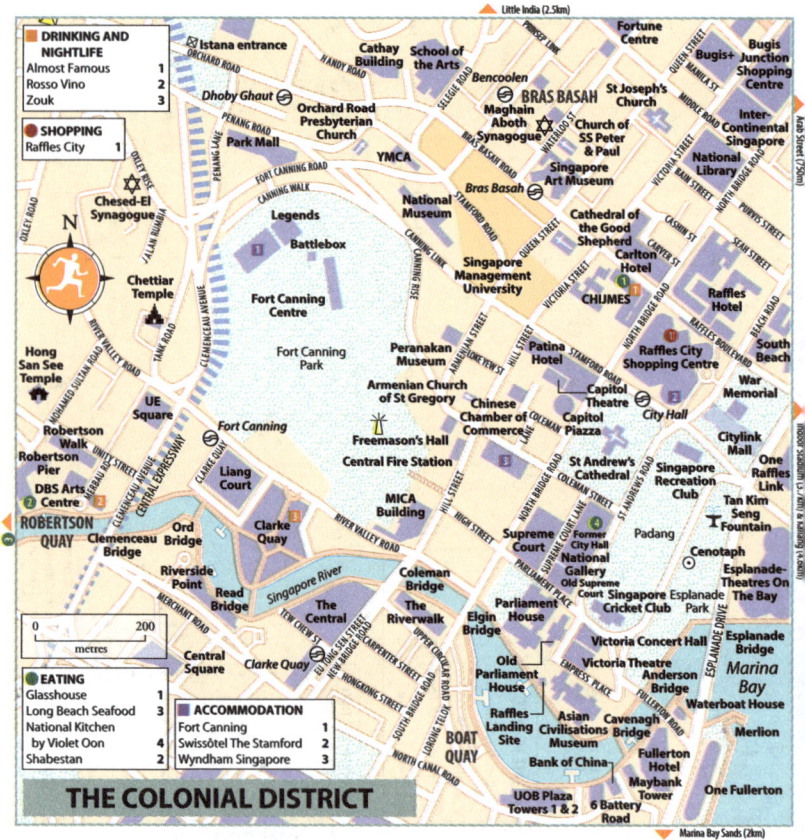

(Eurasians, formerly ineligible for membership due to the prejudices of the time, founded their own establishment in 1883: the **Singapore Recreation Club**, at the opposite end of the Padang.) These days, the Padang plays occasional host to open-air music, night-time light shows and the like, though for locals it's of more use as a pedestrian short-cut.

National Gallery
St Andrew's Rd (main entrance Coleman St) • Charge • http://nationalgallery.sg • City Hall or Raffles Place MRT

Taking up the entire west side of the Padang, Singapore's prestigious **National Gallery** is redolent with history, formed as it is out of two of the island's most imposing colonial buildings. On the right as seen from the Padang is the old **City Hall**, its steps backed by grandiose Corinthian columns; it was here that Louis Mountbatten, supreme allied commander in Southeast Asia, announced Japan's surrender in 1945. Fourteen years later, Lee Kuan Yew chose the same spot for his address at a victory rally celebrating self-government for Singapore. On the left, the domed former **Supreme Court** was built in Neoclassical style in the 1930s and served its judicial functions until 2006.

DBS Singapore Gallery
Housed inside the old City Hall is the three-roomed **DBS Singapore Gallery**, which showcases work by artists who were either born in Singapore or lived here for a time. There's a notable emphasis on the **Nanyang style** (*nanyang* being the Mandarin term for the South China Sea), an umbrella term for art featuring a fusion of Western and Chinese techniques. One exemplar is Georgette Chen, whose elegant *Lotus in a Breeze* bears the hallmarks of Neo-impressionism, yet was only painted in 1970. Look out also for Chua Mia Tee's *Epic Poem of Malaya* and Tan Tee Chie's *On Strike*, both stirring depictions of the restive 1950s and yearnings for independence, and Tan Choh Tee's 1981 *Singapore River*, proof – if any were needed – that today's river is but a shadow of its former fetid self (see page 457).

UOB Southeast Asia Gallery
At the opposite end of the National Gallery, former courtrooms now house the **UOB Southeast Asia Gallery**, which attempts to put a hotchpotch of modern, often conceptual, art from the region into some kind of context. Although the exhibits may not grab you, the architecture probably will: this is the most lovingly conserved part of the National Gallery, retaining its original black-and-white marbled floors and wooden ceilings; an internal domed rotunda still houses a collection of legal books.

The roof garden
It's worth heading up to the National Gallery's **roof garden** for a fine panorama out over the Padang, with *Marina Bay Sands* directly opposite; you can even peer down to City Hall's foyer through the glass-floored decorative pools. Turn around and face west to take in the flying-saucer-like crown of the Norman Foster-designed **New Supreme Court** on North Bridge Road, which opened in 2006.

The parliament buildings
The Arts House 1 Old Parliament Lane • http://theartshouse.com.sg • **New Parliament House** 1 Parliament Place • http://parliament.gov.sg • Raffles Place or City Hall MRT

Probably the island's oldest surviving building, the **Old Parliament House** was built in 1827 as the home of a rich merchant, with Singapore's pre-eminent colonial architect, the Irishman George Drumgoole Coleman, as its creator. The bronze elephant at the front was a gift to Singapore from King Rama V of Thailand (upon whose father *The King and I* was based) after his visit in 1871. Relieved of its legislative role in 1999, the building now holds a contemporary arts centre called **The Arts House**. Backing onto it and facing North Bridge Road is the rather soulless new **Parliament House**, where parliamentary business is now conducted.

Victoria Concert Hall and Victoria Theatre

11 Empress Place • http://vtvch.com • Raffles Place or City Hall MRT

Opposite the Singapore Cricket Club are two more fine examples of colonial architecture, the **Victoria Theatre**, and to the right, the **Victoria Concert Hall** (also called the Victoria Memorial Hall). The former was completed in 1862 as Singapore's town hall, while the concert hall was added in 1905; both now boast extensive glass panelling after a refit.

During the Japanese occupation, the concert hall's clock tower was altered to Tokyo time, while the **statue of Raffles** that stands in front of it narrowly escaped being melted down. It was sent to the National Museum, where the newly installed Japanese curator valued it enough to hide it instead of destroying it. A copy can be seen staring towards the Financial District at Raffles' **landing site**, where the great man apparently took his first steps on Singaporean soil in January 1819.

Asian Civilizations Museum

1 Empress Place, north side of Cavenagh Bridge • Daily 10am–7pm, Fri until 9pm • Charge • http://nhb.gov.sg/acm • Raffles Place or City Hall MRT

A robust Neoclassical structure, the **Empress Place Building** was named after Queen Victoria and completed in 1865. Once government offices, it now houses the fine **Asian Civilizations Museum**, tracing the origins and growth of Asia's many cultures.

The museum's newer glassy riverside extension is also its highlight, housing the **Tang Shipwreck Gallery**, a dazzling trove of ninth-century Chinese goods controversially salvaged from a sunken Arab dhow discovered off the coast of Sumatra in 1998. There's a profusion of ceramic bowls, but the few specimens of

---

SIR STAMFORD RAFFLES

Fittingly for a man who was to spend his life roaming the globe, Thomas Stamford Raffles was born at sea on July 6, 1781, aboard the *Ann*, whose master was his father Captain Benjamin Raffles. By the age of 14, the young Raffles was working as a clerk for the **East India Company** in London, his schooling curtailed because of his father's debts. Even then, Raffles' ambition and self-motivation were evident: he studied through the night with a hunger for knowledge that would spur him to learn Malay, amass a collection of natural history treasures and write his two-volume *History of Java*.

In 1805 he was chosen to join a team going out to Penang, then being developed as a British entrepôt. Once in Southeast Asia, he enjoyed a meteoric rise and by 1807 he was named chief secretary to Penang's governor. In 1810, Raffles was appointed secretary to the Governor-General in Malaya, then **governor of Java** in 1811. Raffles' rule there was libertarian and compassionate, but short-lived – to his chagrin, Java was handed back to the Dutch in 1816. Transferred to the governorship of **Bencoolen** in Sumatra, he arrived there in 1818 and found time to study its flora and fauna, including the incredible *Rafflesia arnoldii*. By this time, Raffles strongly believed that Britain should establish another base in the Straits of Melaka. In 1819 he sailed to the southern tip of the Malay Peninsula, where he secured Singapore early that year in the face of local and Dutch opposition.

For a man inextricably linked with Singapore, Raffles spent remarkably little time there. His last visit was in 1822; by August 1824, he was back in England. Hoping for a pension from the East India Company, he busied himself founding **London Zoo** and setting up a farm in what is now northwest London. But the new life he had planned never materialized, as days after he heard that the Calcutta bank holding his savings had folded, his pension application was refused; worse still, the Company was demanding he return an overpayment of £22,000. Then on July 4, 1826, the brain tumour that had caused him headaches for several years took his life. He was initially buried with no memorial tablet; only in 1832 was Raffles commemorated, by a statue in Westminster Abbey.

THE SINGAPORE RIVER

Little more than a creek, in the nineteenth century the **Singapore River** became the main artery of Singapore's growing trade, and was clogged with **bumboats** – houseboat-sized vessels with eyes painted on their prows. The boats ferried coffee, sugar and rice to warehouses called **godowns**, where coolies loaded and unloaded sacks. In the 1880s the river itself was so busy it was practically possible to walk from one side to the other without getting your feet wet. Of course, **bridges** were built across it as well, most endearingly old-fangled to look at now, apart from the massive new Esplanade Bridge at the river's mouth.

Walking beside the river today, all sanitized and lined with trendy restaurants and bars, some occupying the few surviving godowns, it is hard to imagine that in the 1970s this was still a working river. It was also filthy, occasioning a massive clean-up campaign that moved the river's commercial traffic west to Pasir Panjang within the space of a few years; it contributed to the river's current status as one of the leading nightlife centres of Singapore.

RIVER TOURS

You can get a view of the city at river level on the **Singapore River Experience**, trips taking in Clarke Quay, Boat Quay and Marina Bay in souped-up versions of bumboats (3–4 hourly; 40min; buy tickets and board at any of several ticket booths along the route; http://rivercruise.com.sg). Tickets cost more for certain evening sailings, which take in the laser light show at Marina Bay (see page 480). More prosaically and much more cheaply, it's also possible to ride the company's **river taxi** service (see page 503).

---

gold and silverware are the most memorable: cups, dishes decorated with swastikas or birds, and flasks for wine. Upstairs in the main building is an assortment of artefacts, including Muslim gravestones, Sumatran lacquerware and some fine examples of *ikat* dyed textiles from Borneo.

Cavenagh Bridge
Raffles Place or City Hall MRT

Cavenagh Bridge, with its elegant suspension struts, is one of the Singapore River's antiquated bridges, linking the Padang with Boat Quay and Raffles Place in the Financial District. Named after Major General Orfeur Cavenagh, governor of the Straits Settlements from 1859 to 1867, it was built in 1869 by Indian convict labourers using imported Glasgow steel. A sign still maintains: "The use of this bridge is prohibited to any vehicle of which the laden weight exceeds 3cwt and to all cattle and horses" – which is just as well, as nowadays the bridge takes only pedestrians.

St Andrew's Cathedral
11 St Andrew's Rd; Visitor Centre on North Bridge Rd • Free • http://cathedral.org.sg • City Hall or Esplanade MRT

The Anglican **St Andrew's Cathedral** is the most distinguished of a clutch of nineteenth-century churches north of the Padang, their steeples dwarfed by most buildings around them. Built in high-vaulted Neo-Gothic style using Indian convict labour, it was consecrated on January 25, 1862.

The exterior walls were plastered using Madras *chunam* – an unlikely composite of eggs, lime, sugar and shredded coconut husks which shines brightly when smoothed – while the small cross behind the pulpit was crafted from two fourteenth-century nails salvaged from the ruins of England's Coventry Cathedral after it was razed during World War II.

The middle stained-glass window in the nave was dedicated to Raffles in the 1960s and bears his coat of arms. Note that tours of the cathedral were available pre-Covid; they'd yet to restart at the time of writing, but it's certainly worth asking.

CHIJMES
30 Victoria St • http://chijmes.com.sg • City Hall, Bras Basah or Esplanade MRT

Two venerable Catholic institutions lie almost immediately north of St Andrew's Cathedral, although one of them no longer serves its original purpose. What was the Convent of the Holy Infant Jesus is now a complex of bars and restaurants named **CHIJMES** (pronounced "chimes"). Its Neo-Gothic husk, complete with courtyards, fountains and a sunken forecourt, appeals particularly to expats and tourists, although it still irks some locals that planners allowed a historic convent school to be repurposed like this. Look out for the **Gate of Hope** on its Victoria Street flank, where foundlings were once taken in by the nuns.

Cathedral of the Good Shepherd
Corner of Queen St and Bras Basah Rd • http://cathedral.catholic.sg

Opened on June 6, 1847, the **Cathedral of the Good Shepherd** is more modest in scale than its Anglican rival, and more refined. Neoclassically styled, the building has regained its lovely chequerboard flooring and white, cream and gold colour scheme, thanks to restoration works that took place 2013–2016. Upstairs, the 1912 organ is similarly immaculate, having been completely overhauled by specialists from the Philippines.

War Memorial
Esplanade or City Hall MRT

The open plot north of the Padang is home to four 70m-high white columns. Often referred to as "the chopsticks" by locals, these are actually the country's **Civilian War Memorial**, commemorating those who died during the Japanese occupation. Beneath it are bodily remains, reinterred from unmarked wartime graves around the island.

Church of St Gregory the Illuminator
60 Hill St • Daily 9am–6pm • http://armeniansinasia.org • City Hall or Bras Basah MRT

A couple of blocks west of the Padang, **Hill Street** holds one of the most delightfully intimate buildings in downtown Singapore. The Armenian **Church of St Gregory the Illuminator** was designed by George Drumgoole Coleman and completed in 1835. The white circular interior, fronted by a marble altar and a painting of the Last Supper, includes a framed photo of the few dozen Armenians who lived in Singapore in 1917, for whom the tiny church would have been room enough. Among the handful of graves in the tranquil garden is the tombstone of Agnes Joaquim – a nineteenth-century Armenian resident of Singapore – after whom the national flower, the delicate, purple *Vanda Miss Joaquim* orchid, is named; she discovered it in her garden and had it registered at the Botanic Gardens.

Central Fire Station
Junction of Coleman and Hill streets • Free • http://scdf.gov.sg • City Hall or Bras Basah MRT

The splendid red-and-white-striped **Central Fire Station**, built in 1908, sports a central watchtower that was once the tallest structure in the area, a perfect vantage point for spotting blazes early. Today it's partly given over to the **Civil Defence Heritage Galleries**, tracing the history of firefighting in Singapore. Of more interest than the displays – restored vintage fire engines and the like – are the accounts of historic fires in Singapore. At Bukit Ho Swee, in 1961, a blaze ripped through a district of *atap* huts and timber yards, destroying sixteen thousand homes. The disaster led directly to a public housing scheme that would ultimately spawn the island's numerous new towns.

Freemasons' Hall
23A Coleman St, directly behind the Central Fire Station • http://fmhbsg.org • City Hall or Bras Basah MRT

Kept immaculate with regular fresh licks of paint, Singapore's compact **Freemasons' Hall** features a proud Palladian facade bearing the masonic compass-and-square motif.

The building dates from the 1870s and remains in use. It's worth noting that Stamford Raffles himself was apparently a mason.

Peranakan Museum
39 Armenian St, just west of Hill St • Charge • http://nhb.gov.sg/peranakanmuseum • City Hall or Bras Basah MRT

A beautifully ornamented three-storey building that started out in 1910 as the Tao Nan School – Singapore's first school to cater for new arrivals from China's Fujian province – now houses the **Peranakan Museum**. It honours a culture which, in its own way, is to Singapore, Malaysia and Indonesia what Creole culture is to Louisiana. The museum should whet your appetite for not only the Baba House (see page 476) but also the Peranakan heritage of the Katong area (see page 491).

The diversity of the Peranakans comes through in the first gallery, which includes video interviews with members of Melaka's small **Chitty** community, a blend of Tamil, Chinese and Malay. Thereafter the galleries concentrate on the **Baba-Nyonyas**, the Peranakans of Singapore, exploring their possessions – theirs was always largely a material culture – and customs, in particular the traditional twelve-day **wedding**. Memorable displays include the classic entrance into a Peranakan home: a pair of *pintu pagar* (tall swing doors), overhung with lanterns; look out also for artefacts such as beautiful repoussé silverware, including "pillow ends", coaster-like objects used for some reason as end-caps for bolsters.

National Museum of Singapore
93 Stamford Rd • Charge • http://nhb.gov.sg/nationalmuseum • Bras Basah, Dhoby Ghaut or City Hall MRT

An eye-catching dome on Stamford Road, seemingly coated with silvery fish scales, marks the **National Museum of Singapore**. The museum has been revamped twice this century, most recently to tie in with the island's 50th anniversary of independence celebrations in 2015, and the results are a mixed bag. A lack of significant artefacts is always going to be an challenge for such a young country, but the main issue is a lack of academic weight – its scale aside, this feels more like a provincial museum with a parochial mindset.

Level 1

Almost the entire lower level of the museum is taken up by the **Singapore History Gallery**. Look out early on for the mysterious **Singapore Stone**, all that survives of an inscribed monolith which once stood near where the *Fullerton* hotel is today, though more memorable is the beautiful gold **jewellery** excavated at Fort Canning in 1928 and thought to date from the fourteenth century. With the colonial era come **portraits** of Stamford Raffles, his sidekicks and later officials, most notably one of Frank Swettenham, governor of the Straits Settlements in the 1900s, by the American artist John Singer Sargent. There's also a look at the lives of colonial housewives, including an amusing Malay phrasebook for transacting with servants, with phrases such as "I want to inspect the kitchen to-day" and "This meat is tainted!"

A replica Japanese tank heralds what's perhaps the most interesting section for foreigners, dealing with the British collapse during **World War II**, and the massacres of Operation Sook Ching (see page 470). Also interesting are the displays on postwar politics, including the abortive marriage with Malaysia. From today's perspective it seems hard to believe that up until around the early 1970s, much was still up for grabs in Singapore politics, and the museum deserves credit for devoting space to former opposition figures.

Level 2

The spaces upstairs have gone through many changes in recent years, but exhibitions here have always been of varying quality, in any case. The only permanent fixture on this level is **Wings of a Rich Manoeuvre**: essentially a moving chandelier, created by local artist Suzann Victor. At the time of writing, the museum was preparing to open the permanent **Singapore Odyssea** gallery, a "multimedia experience" blending light, artistic and interactive elements to tell the history of Singapore – a story already told on the lower level, then, but with some gadgetry.

Fort Canning Park
Numerous entrances, including steps on Hill St or via the back of the National Museum • Free • nparks.gov.sg • Fort Canning, Bras Basah, Dhoby Ghaut or Clarke Quay MRT

When Raffles first caught sight of Singapore, **Fort Canning Park** was known as Bukit Larangan (Forbidden Hill). Malay annals tell of the five ancient sultans of Singapura who ruled the island from this site, and unearthed artefacts prove it was inhabited as early as the fourteenth century. The last of the sultans, Iskandar Shah, reputedly lies here, and it was out of respect for – and fear of – his spirit that the Malays decreed the hill forbidden. Singapore's first Resident, William Farquhar, displayed typical colonial tact by promptly erecting a bungalow on the summit. It was replaced in 1859 by a fort named after Viscount George Canning, Governor-General of India, but only a gateway, guardhouse and adjoining wall remain today.

The park has plenty of entrances, though most notable is the "Tree Tunnel" linking to Dhoby Ghaut station, which brings visitors into the park via a picturesque spiral staircase. Also note that you can even stay here, at the aptly named *Fort Canning* (see page 505).

Fort Canning Heritage Gallery
Cox Terrace • Charge

The surprisingly grand building up the slope from the National Museum is the **Fort Canning Centre**, a former British barracks. It has been used on and off as an art or history centre – and, for years on end, shuttered up while the relevant bodies decided what to do next with the place. Its current guise is as the **Fort Canning Heritage Gallery**, which tells the story of the hill and its importance to the nation, and contains assorted historical artefacts, some dating back to the 14th century.

Battlebox
Cox Terrace • Compulsory tours • Charge • http://battlebox.sg

Just west of the Fort Canning Centre, a path leads to the 1939 bunkers from which the Allied war effort in Singapore was masterminded. Now restored and called the **Battlebox** (a strange name for what's basically a war museum), it contains dioramas bringing to life the events leading up to the British surrender in February 1942. Visits are only possible by prebooking a guided tour; after which you can explore the bunker further on your own.

Raffles Terrace
South side of Fort Canning Park

South of the Fort Canning Centre, there is a *keramat* (auspicious place) on the supposed site of Iskandar Shah's grave, which attracts a trickle of local Muslims. Continue round the hill and you'll meet the staircase from Hill Street at **Raffles Terrace**, where there are replicas of a colonial flagstaff and a lighthouse – the hill was the site of a working lighthouse that functioned up until the middle of the last century.

Along River Valley Road
Fort Canning Park's southern boundary is defined by **River Valley Road**, which skirts below the park from Hill Street. At the corner with Hill Street is the **Old Hill Street Police Station**, with shuttered windows in bright colours. Once, indeed, a police station, it is now home to two government ministries, and its central atrium houses several galleries majoring in Asian artworks.

Clarke Quay
3 River Valley Rd • http://clarkequay.com.sg • Clarke Quay or Fort Canning MRT

Painted in gaudy colours and housing flashy eating and nightlife venues, the nineteenth-century godowns of **Clarke Quay** feel about as authentic as the translucent plastic canopy that shelters them, and the area feels eerily quiet during the daytime; nearby Boat Quay (see page 477) feels homelier even when at its busiest. Further up River Valley Road is **Robertson Quay**, offering more of the same, although generally quieter.

Sri Thendayuthapani Temple
15 Tank Rd • Daily 8.30am–12.30pm & 5.30–8.30pm • Free • http://sttemple.com • Fort Canning or Dhoby Ghaut MRT, or bus #143 from Orchard Rd or Chinatown

Just west of Fort Canning Park and close to Robertson Quay is the **Sri Thendayuthapani Temple**, still often known as the **Chettiar Temple**. The shrine, with a large, attractive *gopuram*, was built in 1984 to replace a nineteenth-century temple constructed by Indian *chettiars* (moneylenders) and is dedicated mainly to the Hindu deity Lord Murugan. It's also the destination of every participant in the procession that accompanies the annual Thaipusam Festival (see page 47).

Bras Basah Road to Rochor Road
Bras Basah, City Hall, Dhoby Ghaut or Bencoolen/Rochor (when open) MRT

Bras Basah Road – the main thoroughfare between Orchard Road and what would have been the seafront – is so named because rice arriving on cargo boats used to be brought here to be dried (*beras basah* means "wet rice" in Malay). The zone between it and **Rochor Road** at the edge of Little India has a transitional sort of feel, sitting as it does between the Colonial District and two of Raffles' ethnic enclaves to the northeast. The aptly named Middle Road, running smack through the centre of the grid, was originally meant to mark the Colonial District's northern edge.

Despite modernization, the area still boasts some long-established places of worship and is another focus for the **arts**, home to institutions such as the School of the Arts in a striking new building next to the Cathay cinema, and to several creative organizations occupying distinguished old properties on and around **Waterloo Street**.

Raffles Hotel
1 Beach Rd • http://raffles.com/singapore • Esplanade or City Hall MRT

The area's most famous occupant is the legendary **Raffles Hotel**, almost a byword for the colonial era; Somerset Maugham once remarked that it "stood for all the fables of the exotic East". With its gleaming white facade and location by the sea – that is, until land reclamation intervened – it very much recalls its former sister hotel, the *Eastern & Oriental* in Malaysia's George Town (see page 152). Liveried doormen, largely Sikh, still greet arriving guests, and the inner courtyard is a true haven, fringed with palm and frangipani trees. If you're not staying here, the best way to glimpse the place is by dining at one of its restaurants or treating yourself to a Singapore Sling in the *Long Bar* (for a rather princely sum).

History of the hotel
Oddly, for a hotel whose name is now shared with others as part of an international chain, the *Raffles* started out as a modest seafront bungalow belonging to an Arab trader. In 1886, the property was bought by the Armenian Sarkies brothers, who had only just launched the *E&O*; the *Raffles* opened the following year, and over the next twenty years it was gradually extended to something approaching its present scale. In 1902, according to an apocryphal tale, the last tiger to be killed on the island was shot inside the building. Bartender Ngiam Tong Boon created another *Raffles* legend, the **Singapore Sling** cocktail,

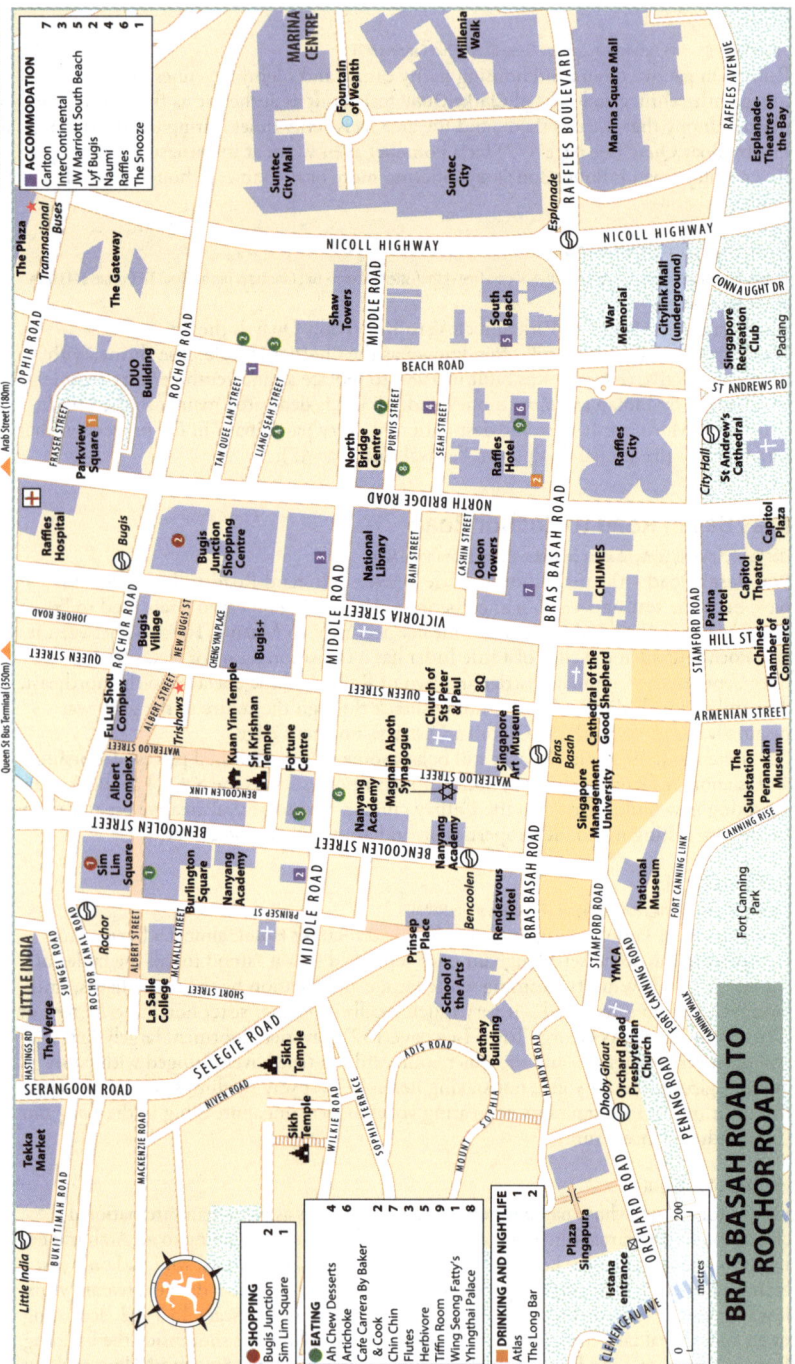

in 1915. Over the years, the hotel has hosted many a politician and film star, but it is proudest of its **literary connections**. Hermann Hesse, Rudyard Kipling, Noël Coward and Günter Grass all stayed here, and Somerset Maugham is said to have written many of his Asian tales under a frangipani tree in the garden.

Following the Japanese conquest in 1942, the hotel became a Japanese officers' quarters, then briefly a transit camp for liberated Allied prisoners in 1945. Postwar decay earned it the affectionate but melancholy soubriquet "the grand old lady of the East", and the hotel was little more than a shabby tourist diversion when the government declared it a national monument in its centenary year. An expensive and contentious four-year facelift and extension followed, which restored the air of bygone elegance, but also added a mundane shopping arcade on North Bridge Road; another major refit was completed in 2018.

Waterloo Street
Bras Basah, Bencoolen or Bugis MRT

The presence of a large synagogue hints at the fact that the area surrounding Waterloo Street was once something of a Jewish enclave – another building midway along nearby Selegie Road also bears a prominent Star of David – though the Jewish community, largely of Middle Eastern origin, never numbered more than about a thousand.

Maghain Aboth Synagogue
24/26 Waterloo St • Free • http://singaporejews.com

Head up Waterloo Street from the Art Museum and you'll almost immediately come to the peach-coloured **Maghain Aboth Synagogue**, which looks like a colonial mansion despite the Stars of David on the facade. Dating from the 1870s, the synagogue can be visited by prior arrangement – see the website for details.

Sri Krishnan Temple
152 Waterloo St • Free • 6337 7957

In 1870 the **Sri Krishnan Temple** was nothing more than a thatched hut containing a statue of Lord Krishna under a banyan tree. The present-day shrine is a good example of Southeast Asian religious harmony and syncretism in action, with worshippers from the nearby Buddhist Kwan Im Temple sometimes praying outside.

Kwan Im Temple
178 Waterloo St • Free • 6337 3965

The best-known sight on Waterloo Street is the **Kwan Im Temple**, named after the Buddhist goddess of mercy. The current version dates only to the 1980s – hence its rather slick, palatial appearance – and draws thousands of devotees daily; it can be filled to overflowing during festivals. Fortune-tellers and religious artefact shops operate in a little swarm just outside.

Albert Street
Northern end of Waterloo St, close to Rochor Rd • Rochor, Bugis or Jalan Besar MRT

Intersecting Waterloo Street is **Albert Street**, which half a century ago looked quite like Jalan Alor in KL (see page 91), lined with hugely popular street food stalls. All of that is now gone, although the street is still worth a stroll to gaze at the zigzagging glass facades of the **Lasalle College of the Arts** near the street's northern end, or to check out the **market** that stays open into the evening around the junction with Waterloo Street, selling everything from potted plants to mobile phone cases. Albert Street is also the starting point for touristy **trishaw** excursions (see page 503).

Bugis Village and Bugis Junction
Bugis MRT

Bugis Street (pronounced "boogis"), the southern extension of Albert Street, was one of the most notorious places in old Singapore, crawling with rowdy sailors, prostitutes and ladyboys by night. The street was duly cleared, partly to build the Bugis MRT station and partly because it was anathema to the government. In its place today is **Bugis Village**, a bunch of stalls and snack vendors lining a few covered alleyways. It's hardly the Bugis Street of old, though it does recapture something of the bazaar feel that the island's markets once had.

Across Victoria Street from here is another throwback to the past, the **Bugis Junction** development. Entire rows of shophouses have been gutted, scrubbed clean and then encased under glass as part of a modern shopping mall and hotel, the *Intercontinental*.

Little India
Little India, Farrer Park or Jalan Besar MRT; note that buses up Serangoon Rd return via Jalan Besar

Of all Singapore's historic quarters, the most charismatic has to be **Little India**. Indian pop music blares out from speakers outside cassette shops; the air is perfumed with incense, curry powder and jasmine garlands; Hindu women parade in bright saris; and a wealth of restaurants serve up excellent, inexpensive curries.

That Little India has kept its identity better than any other old quarter is in no small way down to the migrant Tamil and Bengali men who labour to build new MRT stations, shopping malls and private villas. On Sundays they descend on Little India in their thousands, making the place look like downtown Chennai or Calcutta after a major cricket match. The district's backbone is **Serangoon Road**, one of the island's oldest roadways, dating from 1822; the account here starts from Tekka Market, next to Little India MRT, and then covers the side roads off Serangoon Road in stretches. The best time of year to visit is in the run-up to **Deepavali** (October or November) when much of Serangoon Road is festooned with festive lighting and special markets are set up in the open space beyond the Angullia Mosque (opposite Syed Alwi Road) and on Campbell Lane, which sell decorations, garlands and Indian sweets.

Tekka Centre
Southwestern end of Serangoon Rd · Daily 6am–11.30pm · Free · Little India MRT

The **Tekka Centre** is a must-see, combining many of Little India's commercial elements under one roof. It's best to arrive in the morning when the wet market is at its busiest. Halal butchers push around trolleys piled high with goats' heads, while live crabs, their claws tied together, shuffle in buckets on seafood stalls. Look out also for a couple of stalls selling nothing but banana leaves, used to serve up the curry meals you'll probably enjoy at some point during your stay. Talking of food, the hawker centre here is excellent (see page 515), and although the same can't be said of the mundane outlets upstairs selling Indian fabrics and household items, there are great views over the wet market to be had from above.

Buffalo Road
Buffalo Road, along the northern side of Tekka Market, sports a few provisions stores with sacks of spices and fresh coconut, ground using primitive machines. Its name, and that of neighbouring Kerbau ("buffalo" in Malay) Road, recall the latter half of the nineteenth century when **cattle and buffalo yards** opened in the area, luring more Indians in search of work and swelling the population.

Kerbau Road
Kerbau Road, like Waterloo Street 1km south, is a designated "arts belt", its shophouses home to a couple of creative organizations. Curiously, the road itself has been split into two by a pedestrianized bit of greenery. At no. 37, you can't miss the gaudily restored **Chinese mansion**, built by one Tan Teng Niah, a confectionery magnate, in 1900 and

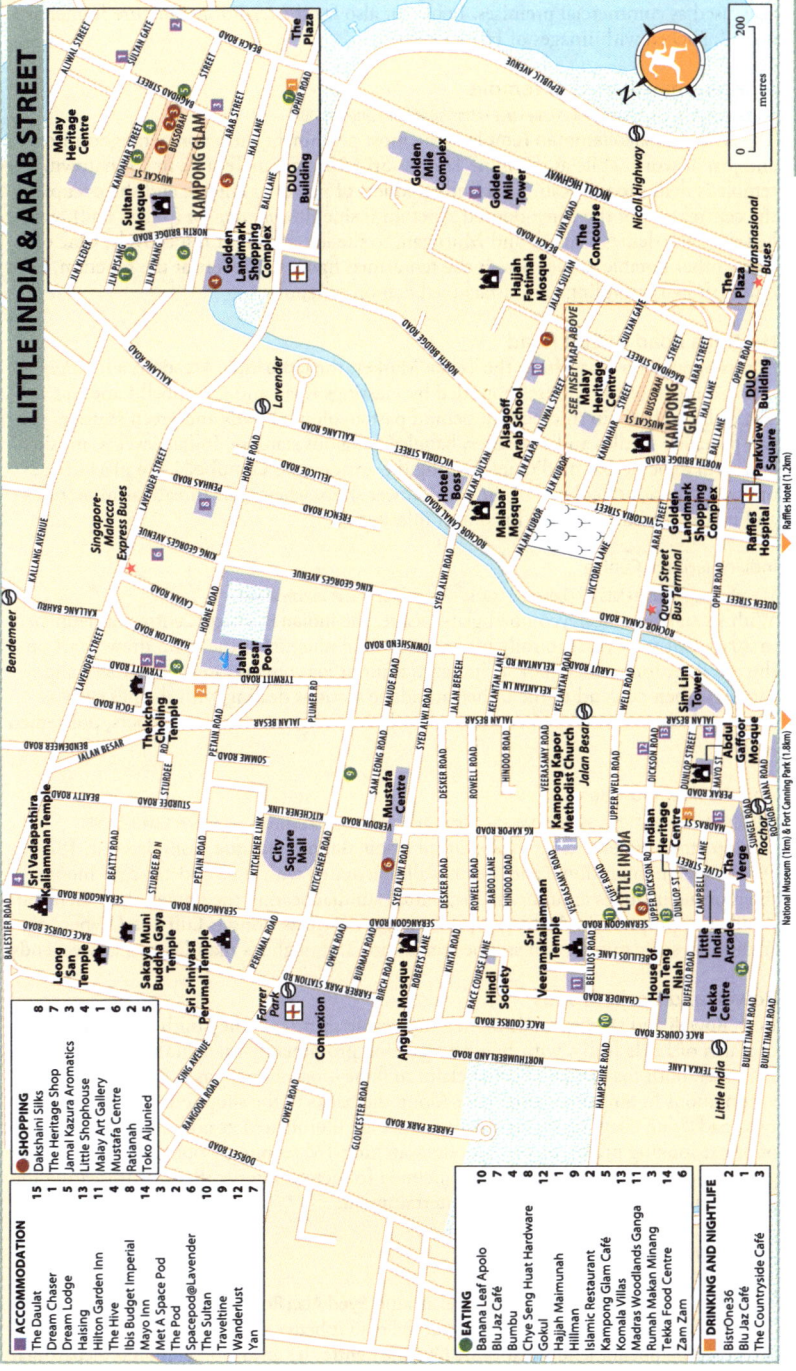

now used as commercial premises. Look out also for the traditional picture framer at no. 57, packed with images of Hindu deities.

Sri Veeramakaliamman Temple
141 Serangoon Rd, just beyond Belilios Lane • Free • http://srivkt.com • Little India MRT

The **Sri Veeramakaliamman Temple** is the most prominent shrine on Serangoon Road and just as worthwhile as the more famous Sri Mariamman Temple in Chinatown. The temple is dedicated to Kali, the Hindu goddess of power or energy, and she occupies the central part of the three-doored sanctum inside the *mandapam* (prayer hall), with her sons, the deities Ganesh and Murugan, to the left and right respectively. One of many other notable deities here is the ten-armed figure to the left of the sanctum, Lord Shiva, shown trampling a moustachioed demon of ignorance.

Hastings Road to Cuff Road
Across Serangoon Road from the Tekka Market, the **Little India Arcade** is a lovingly restored block of shophouses bounded by Hastings Road and Campbell Lane. It's a sort of Little India in microcosm: behind pastel-coloured walls and green shutters you can purchase textiles and tapestries, bangles, religious statuary, Indian sweets, music and Ayurvedic herbal medicines. Exiting the arcade onto **Campbell Lane** places you opposite the riot of colours of the Jothi flower shop, where staff thread jasmine, roses and marigolds into garlands for prayer offerings.

Indian Heritage Centre
5 Campbell Lane • Charge • http://indianheritage.gov.sg • Rochor, Little India or Jalan Besar MRT

With its startling, honeycombed glass facade, the **Indian Heritage Centre** was launched in 2015, but took years to fully hit its stride. The museum is the main draw. Start on the top floor for a broad look at Indian traditions via some impressive statuary and carvings, then descend to the rather mundane sections dealing with themes such as stereotypical occupations once pursued by Indian migrants (rubber tappers, policemen and so on).

Abdul Gafoor Mosque
41 Dunlop St • Mon–Fri 1–9pm, Sat 9am–1pm • Free • http://facebook.com/masjidabdulgafoor • Rochor or Jalan Besar MRT

Dunlop Street is defined by the beautiful **Abdul Gaffoor Mosque**, completed in 1907. With a green onion dome and cream walls decorated with stars and crescent moons, the mosque includes an unusual 25-pointed sundial bearing the names of an identical number of prophets in Arabic script. A couple of streets along is **Cuff Road**, where a traditional spice grinder can still be seen at no. 2, though it's mainly open at weekends.

Rowell and Desker roads
Both **Rowell** and **Desker roads** mark a noticeable shift from the South Indian flavour of much of Little India, with Bengali featuring prominently on some shop signs. However, both roads have another claim to fame – or infamy – as they have long been synonymous in Singapore with vice. Along the backs of the shophouses between the two roads is an alleyway where the doorways are illuminated at night. Here gaggles of bored-looking prostitutes sit indoors watching TV, seemingly oblivious to the men gathered outside who mostly appear inclined to merely observe them, as if treating the whole thing as some kind of street entertainment.

Syed Alwi Road to Petain Road
Farrer Park MRT

Little India takes on a more Islamic feel around **Syed Alwi Road**, across from which is the Angullia Mosque at its northern end, but the road is better known for being the hub of the shopping phenomenon that is the **Mustafa Centre**. It's an agglomeration of department store, moneychanger, travel agent, jeweller, fast-food joint and supermarket, mostly open 24 hours. You'll probably find it more interesting than most places on Orchard Road, as you rub shoulders with Indian families seeking flown-in confectionery from Delhi, Chinese and Malay shoppers wanting durian fruit or pots and pans, and even African businesspeople buying consumer goods that are hard to find at home.

Sam Leong Road is home to some surviving **Peranakan shophouses** decorated with stags, lotuses and egrets. There's more of the same a few blocks north on **Petain Road**, where the shophouses have elegant ceramic tiles reminiscent of Portuguese *azulejos*.

Sri Srinivasa Perumal Temple
397 Serangoon Rd • Free • http://sspt.org.sg • Farrer Park MRT

Little India more or less comes to an end at Rangoon and Kitchener roads, but it's worth continuing up Serangoon Road to see two very different temples. Dating from the late nineteenth century, though rebuilt in the 1960s, the **Sri Srinivasa Perumal Temple** has an attractive five-tiered *gopuram* with sculptures of the various manifestations of Lord Vishnu the preserver. On the wall to the right of the front gate, a sculpted elephant trumpets silently, its leg caught in a crocodile's mouth. But the temple's main claim to fame is as the starting point for the annual **Thaipusam** festival (see page 47), when devotees leave the temple in procession, pausing only while a coconut is smashed at their feet for good luck, and parade all the way to the Chettiar Temple on Tank Road (see page 461).

Sakaya Muni Buddha Gaya Temple
366 Race Course Rd • Free • Farrer Park MRT

Just beyond the Sri Srinivasa Perumal Temple, a small path leads northwest to Race Course Road, where the slightly kitsch **Sakaya Muni Buddha Gaya Temple** betrays a strong Thai influence – which isn't surprising as it was built by a Thai monk. On the left of the temple as you enter is a huge Buddha's footprint, inlaid with mother-of-pearl, and beyond it a 15m-high Buddha ringed by a thousand electric lights. Twenty-five dioramas depicting scenes from the Buddha's life decorate the pedestal on which he sits. It is possible to walk inside the statue, through a door in its back; inside is one more diorama, depicting the Buddha in death. One wall of the temple features a sort of wheel of fortune, decorated with Chinese zodiac signs. To discover your fate, spin it (for a small donation) and take the numbered sheet of paper that corresponds to the number at which the wheel stops.

Arab Street (Kampong Glam)
Bugis or Nicoll Highway MRT

The area of Singapore south of the now canalized Rochor River once held a Malay village known as Kampong Glam, possibly named after the *gelam* tree that grew there. After signing the dubious treaty with his newly installed Johor sultan, Raffles allotted the area to him and designated the land around it as a Muslim settlement. Soon the zone was attracting Malays, Sumatrans and Javanese, as well as Hadhrami Arabs from what's now eastern Yemen. Now the Arab community, descended from those Yemeni traders, is thought to number around 15,000, though they are something of an invisible minority, having intermarried into Singapore society and being resident in no particular area.

Today, the area is still referred to as **Kampong Glam** or just **Arab Street**, and is akin in some ways to London's Brick Lane – part Islamic, part hipster, with an all-pervasive aroma of spices. Gentrification seems to be winning out, though, with slick upstart restaurants, many serving alcohol (to the chagrin of some locals), displacing old textiles stores and curry houses. Nevertheless it's worth spending an hour wandering the area's lanes, with the **Sultan Mosque** and the **Malay Heritage Centre** being the two obvious sights. The little shophouses on Arab Street itself and the surrounding lanes have a cosiness and intimacy that's more George Town than Lion City. Textile and carpet stores are most prominent, and you'll also see leather, basketware, gold, gemstones and jewellery for sale.

Haji Lane and Bali Lane

South of Arab Street, **Haji Lane** and tiny **Bali Lane** – the latter petering out into the wide walkway next to Ophir Road – have traditional shops rubbing up against trendy boutiques; in the evenings and on weekends DJs set up informally to spin dance music on Haji Lane.

Incidentally, it's worth taking a brief look at the **Parkview Square** office building just across from here on North Bridge Road. Though the tower is only a decade old, its styling just screams 1930s Art Deco (à la Gotham City), and there's a stunning ground-floor bar in the same vein, *Atlas* (see page 517). When it was built, the need to ensure good feng shui meant it had to be sited dead between the two razor-blade-like towers of **The Gateway** one block south (designed by the Chinese-American architect I.M. Pei – the man behind the glass pyramid fronting the Louvre in Paris).

Sultan Mosque
3 Muscat St · Free · http://sultanmosque.sg · Bugis or Jalan Besar MRT

The **Sultan Mosque** is the beating heart of the Muslim community in Singapore. An earlier mosque stood on this site, finished in 1825 with the help of a donation from the East India Company. The present building was completed a century later to a design by colonial architects Swan and Maclaren. Look carefully at the base of the main dome and you'll see a dark band that looks like tilework, though it actually consists of the bottoms of thousands of glass bottles. The prayer hall is decked out in green and gold, but non-Muslims must look on from just inside the entrance.

Bussorah Street to the south offers the best view of the mosque, and is also home to some worthwhile souvenir outlets. During the Muslim fasting month, the area around the mosque is thronged with stalls of the **Ramadan bazaar** from mid-afternoon, selling *biriyanis*, *murtabak*, dates and cakes for consumption by the faithful after dusk.

The Malay Heritage Centre (Istana Kampong Glam)
Sultan Gate · Charge · http://malayheritage.gov.sg · Bugis or Nicoll Highway MRT

Between Kandahar and Aliwal streets, the colonially styled **Istana Kampong Glam** was built as the palace of Sultan Ali Iskandar Shah, son of Sultan Hussein who negotiated with Raffles to hand Singapore over to the British. Until just a few years ago the house was still home to the sultan's descendants, though it had fallen into disrepair. Then the government acquired it together with the similar, smaller yellow house in the same grounds, which belonged to the heirs of a wealthy merchant.

The yellow house now hosts an attempt at a posh Malay restaurant, while the istana has mutated into the overly slick **Malay Heritage Centre**, a hit-and-miss museum. The best displays celebrate the rural boatbuilding and fishing lifestyle of yore, plus Singapore's unjustly overlooked Malay literary and pop-culture scene of the postwar period. But there's a deafening silence on the building of new towns – a mixed blessing for all who experienced upheaval and relocation, especially for the Malays, who saw practically all their kampungs razed and communities broken up. The centre was closed for renovation at the time of writing, but should have reopened by the time you read this.

North of Sultan Mosque

The stretch of **North Bridge Road** between Arab Street and Jalan Sultan has a less touristy feel, and although gentrification is evident here, too, the shops and restaurants tend to be geared more towards locals, stocking items such as alcohol-free perfume and the black, fez-like *songkok* traditionally worn by Malay men.

Several roads run off the western side of North Bridge Road, including Jalan Kubor (literally "Grave Street"), which takes you to an unkempt **Muslim cemetery**, where it's said that Malay royalty are buried. Turn right here up Kallang Road to reach Jalan Sultan and the blue **Malabar Mosque**, built for Muslims from the South Indian state of Kerala and a little cousin of the Sultan Mosque, with similar golden domes. Its traditional styling belies its age – the mosque was completed in the early 1960s.

Hajjah Fatimah Mosque
4001 Beach Rd, just east of the junction with Jalan Sultan • Free • http://masjidhajjahfatimah.sg • Nicoll Highway or Lavender MRT

Beach Road's chandlers and fishing-gear shops betray its former proximity to the sea, until land reclamation created Nicoll Highway and the Marina Centre district. One quirky sight here is the **Hajjah Fatimah Mosque**, its minaret looking strangely like a steeple (perhaps because its architect was European). The minaret also visibly slants at six degrees to the vertical – locals call it Singapore's Leaning Tower of Pisa. Completed in 1846, the building is named after a wealthy Melaka businesswoman who, having moved out of her home on this site, funded the mosque's construction.

Chinatown and around
Chinatown, Telok Ayer, Outram Park, Tanjong Pagar or Clarke Quay MRT; buses run southwest along North and South Bridge roads and New Bridge Rd, returning along Eu Tong Sen St

Bounded roughly by Eu Tong Sen Street to the northwest, Neil and Maxwell roads to the south, Cecil Street to the southeast and the Singapore River to the north, **Chinatown** is somewhat misnamed. Never really an enclave – Singapore has long had a Chinese majority, after all – it was more the focus of Chinese life and culture. Within its two square kilometres, newly arrived migrants found temples, shops with familiar goods and, most importantly, *kongsis* – clan associations that helped them find lodgings and work.

This was one of the most colourful districts of old Singapore, but after independence the government tackled its tumbledown slums by embarking upon a drastic **redevelopment** campaign. Not until the 1980s did surviving shophouses and other period buildings begin to be conserved. Furthermore, gentrification has led to *kongsis* and religious and martial arts associations being turned into boutique hotels, new media firms and bars. Getting a taste of the old ways now often means heading off the main streets into the concrete municipal housing estates.

Even so, as in Little India, the character of the area has had a bit of a shot in the arm of late courtesy of recent immigrants. As regards sights, the **Thian Hock Keng**, **Buddha Tooth Relic** and **Sri Mariamman** temples are especially worthwhile, as is the **Chinatown Heritage Centre** museum, and there's enough shophouse architecture to justify a leisurely wander.

Chinatown Heritage Centre
48 Pagoda St • Charge • http://chinatownheritagecentre.com.sg • Chinatown MRT

One exit from Chinatown MRT brings you up into the thick of the action on Pagoda Street, where the **Chinatown Heritage Centre** stands in marked contrast to the tacky souvenir stalls. Occupying three whole shophouses, it's a museum enshrining the difficult experiences of Chinatown's inhabitants over the past couple of centuries.

Things kick off with a recreation of a comparatively spacious postwar tailor's shop; note the cloth ring dangling down from the ceiling, meant for holding a baby's cot, as still happens in rural Malaysia. Soon you're into the claustrophobic living cubicles, recreating conditions in shophouse slums, where you'd find trishaw drivers, clog-makers and prostitutes living cheek by jowl. Landlords once shoehorned as many as forty tenants into a single floor; if you think it couldn't possibly happen today, spare a thought for the thousands of migrant workers on building sites all over Singapore, many of whom are crammed into very basic dormitories. Other sections revisit the sadly vanished nightlife of postwar Chinatown and, commendably, the area's Indian minorities.

Along South Bridge Road

Head down Pagoda Street from the Chinatown Heritage Centre and you come to **South Bridge Road**, one of Chinatown's main thoroughfares, carrying southbound traffic. At no. 218, on the corner of Mosque Street, stands the pastel green **Jamae Mosque** (also called the Chulia Mosque), established by South Indian Muslims in the 1820s. Its twin minarets appear to contain miniature windows while above the entrance stands what looks like a tiny doorway, all of which makes the upper part of the facade look strangely like a scale model of a much larger building.

One street northeast, at the junction with Upper Cross Street, roadblocks were set up during the Japanese occupation, and Singaporeans were vetted for signs of anti-Japanese sentiment in the infamous Sook Ching campaign. That tragic episode is commemorated by a simple signboard in the Hong Lim Complex, a housing estate whose walkways are lined with herbalists and stores selling dried foodstuffs and so forth.

To top up your blood-sugar level while wandering the area, pop into the **Tong Heng pastry shop** (see page 515) at no. 285, which sells various Chinese sweet treats.

Sri Mariamman Temple

244 South Bridge Rd • Free • http://smt.org.sg • Chinatown or Telok Ayer MRT

Singapore's oldest Hindu shrine, the **Sri Mariamman Temple**, has its roots in a wood and palm-thatch hut erected here in 1827 on land belonging to Naraina Pillay, a government clerk who arrived on the same ship as Stamford Raffles on the latter's second trip to Singapore. The present temple was finished around 1843, though it has been extended and overhauled several times since.

Inside, walk around the courtyard to admire the temple's roof friezes depicting a host of Hindu deities. The main sanctum is devoted to Mariamman, a goddess worshipped for her healing powers. Smaller sanctums include one dedicated to the goddess Periachi Amman, portrayed with a queen lying on her lap, whose evil child she has ripped from her womb; it's odd, then, that Periachi Amman is the protector of children, to whom babies are brought when one month old.

Once a year, during the festival of **Thimithi** (October or November), a patch of sand to the left of the main sanctum is covered in red-hot coals that male Hindus run across to prove their faith. The participants, who line up all the way along South Bridge Road waiting for their turn, are supposedly protected from the heat by the power of prayer.

Buddha Tooth Relic Temple

288 South Bridge Rd • Free • http://buddhatoothrelictemple.org.sg • No shorts, vests or non-vegetarian food • Chinatown or Tanjong Pagar MRT

The imposing **Buddha Tooth Relic Temple** is arguably the most in-your-face of Chinatown's shrines. The place simply clobbers you with its opulence – even the elevators have brocaded walls – and the thousands upon thousands of Buddhist figurines, each with its own serial number, arrayed along various interior surfaces.

With gently curving roofs featuring tiles and other ornaments made in Japan, the temple has its origins in the discovery, in 1980, of what was thought to be a tooth of Buddha inside a collapsed stupa at a Burmese monastery. The monastery's chief abbot visited Singapore in 2002 and decided the island would make a suitable sanctuary for the relic, to be housed in its own temple if there were a chance of building one. A prime site in Chinatown was duly secured, and the temple opened in 2007.

The main hall

The focus of the main hall is **Maitreya**, a Buddha who is yet to appear on Earth. Carved from juniper wood said to be 1000 years old, his statue has a yellow flame-like halo around it. But what really captures the attention are the Buddha figures covering the entirety of the side walls. There are a hundred main statuettes, all individually crafted, interspersed with thousands of tiny figurines embedded in a vast array of shelving. Behind the main hall, another large hall centres on the **Avalokitesvara Bodhisattva**.

The **mezzanine** affords great views over proceedings and chanting ceremonies in the main hall, while **level 2** contains the temple's own **teahouse**.

Buddhas of the World Museum

On **level 3** are some seriously impressive examples of Buddhist **statuary** in brass, wood and stone, plus other artworks from all over Asia, some dating back as far as the 2nd century. They're all part of the **Buddhas of the World Museum**, with panels telling the story of Gautama Buddha in the first person. At the back, the relic chamber displays what are said to be the cremated remains of Buddha's nose, brain, liver etc, all looking like fish roe in different colours.

Sacred Buddha Tooth Relic Stupa

On **level 4** you finally encounter what all the fuss is ultimately about – the **Sacred Buddha Tooth Relic Stupa**. Some 3m in diameter, it sits behind glass panels and can't be inspected close up, though there is a faithful scale model at the front. The Maitreya Buddha is depicted at the front of the stupa, guarded by four lions, with a ring of 35 more Buddhas below; floor tiles around the stupa are said to be made of pure gold.

The roof garden

The temple's lovely **roof garden** has walls lined with twelve thousand tiny figurines of the Amitayus Buddha, but its centrepiece is "the largest cloisonné prayer wheel in the world", around 5m tall. Each rotation (clockwise, should you wish to have a go) dings a bell and represents the recitation of one sutra.

Sago Street

The tight knot of streets west of South Bridge Road between Sago Street and Pagoda Street is Chinatown at its most touristy, packed with souvenir sellers and foreigner-friendly restaurants. However, in bygone days these streets formed Chinatown's nucleus, teeming with trishaws, food stalls, brothels and opium dens. Until as recently as the 1950s, **Sago Street** was home to several **death houses**, rudimentary hospices where citizens nearing the end of their lives spent their final hours on rattan beds.

Smith Street

Smith Street is perennially being promoted as Chinatown Food Street, after several half-cocked attempts to repackage it and Trengganu Street as a hub for street eating – ironically, the very thing Singapore abolished decades ago – and the latest involves a slew of phoney-looking hawker "pushcarts". Chinatown's **old trades** can occasionally be seen clinging on for dear life, including stores where they make shirts, watches, mobile phones and laptops out of paper for burning at funerals, to ensure the deceased don't lack creature comforts in the next life. The ugly, concrete **Chinatown Complex** at the end of the street is a workaday place housing outlets selling silk and household goods, and has some excellent food stalls above.

The Bukit Pasoh conservation area

Outram Park MRT

In the southernmost corner of Chinatown is an area packed with restored shophouses, worth a look for their beautifully painted facades, some in Art Deco style, and tilework. **Clan houses** were once the claim to fame of **Bukit Pasoh Road**, but while some have survived with their character intact, many more have morphed into boutiques or boutique hotels; the Gan Clan's building at 18–20 Bukit Pasoh Rd now rents out space

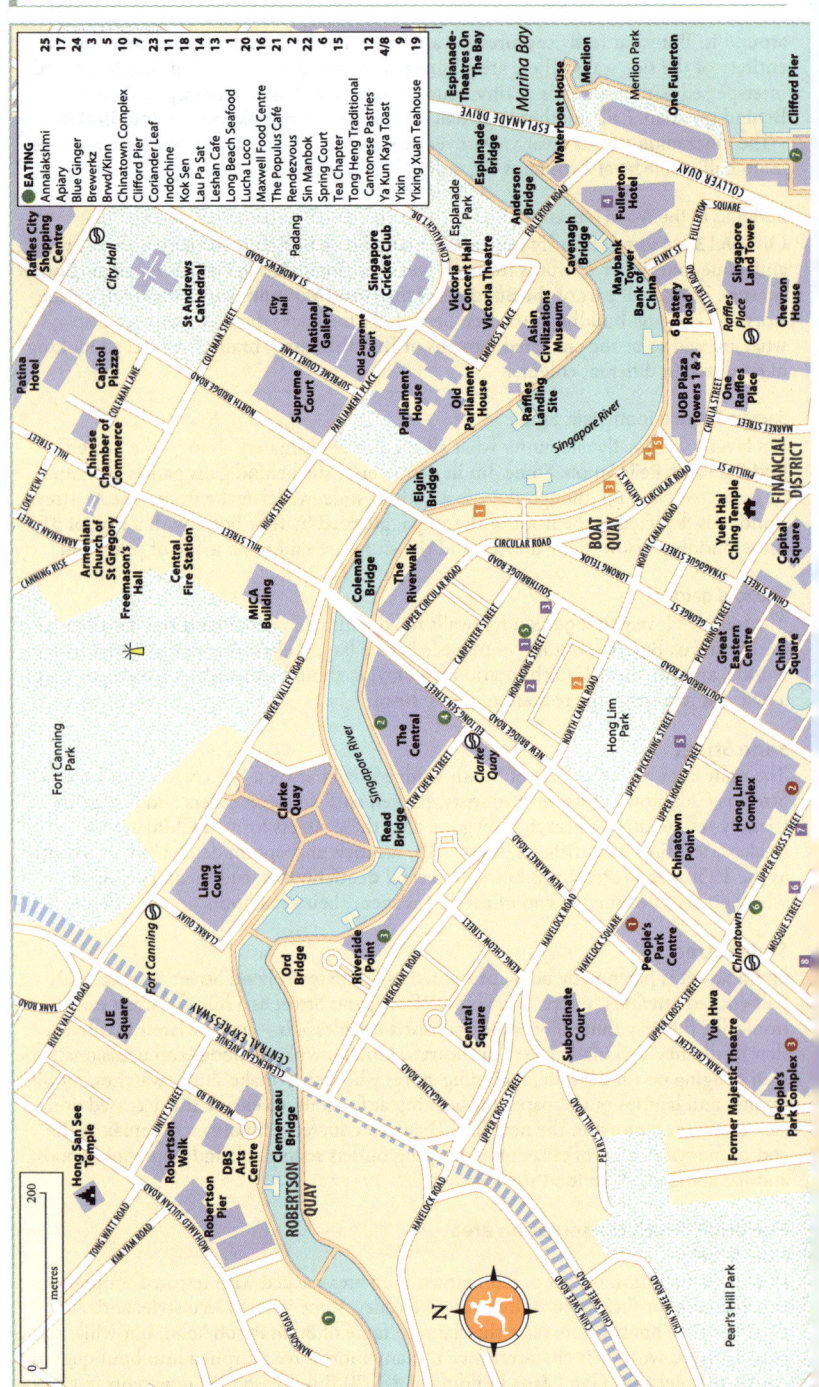

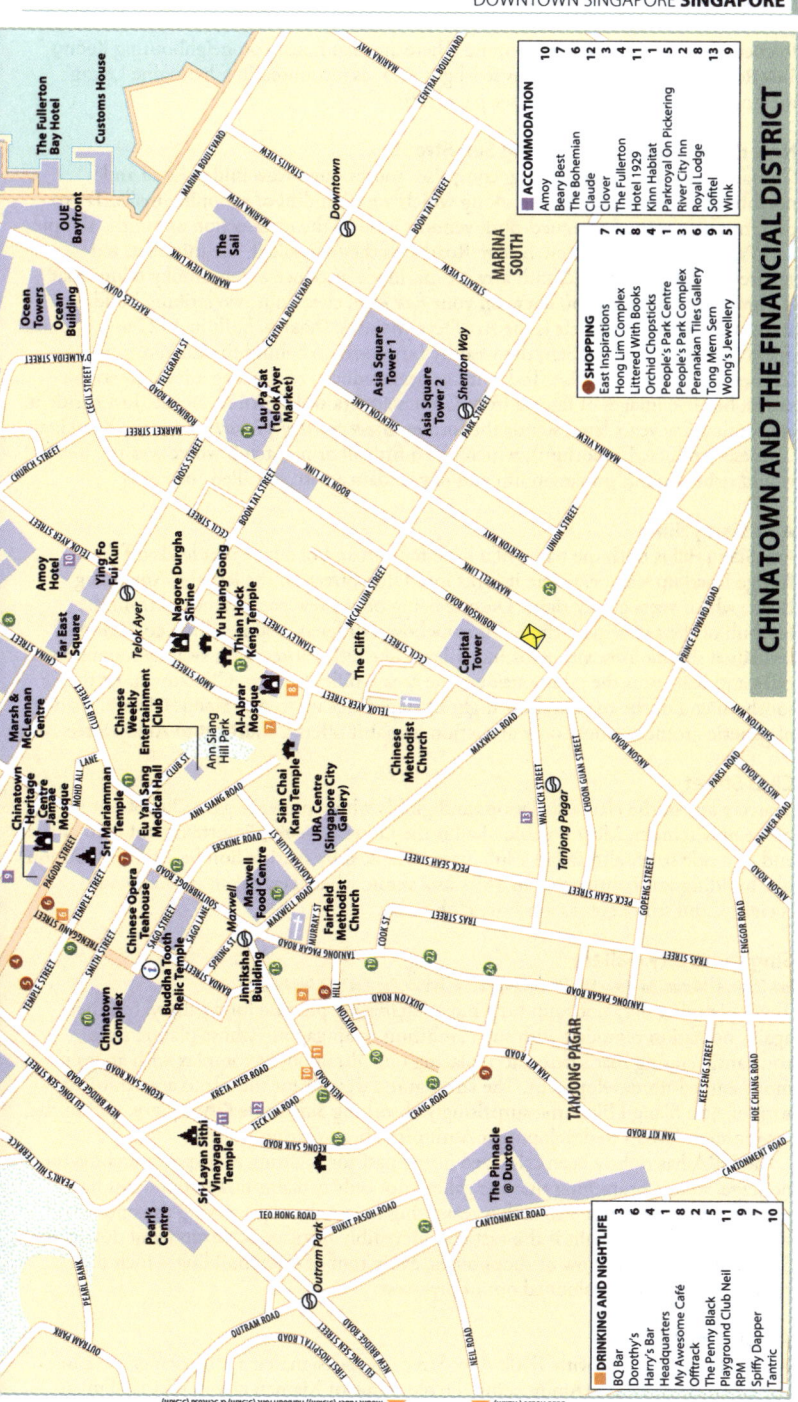

to cocktail bars and a posh restaurant. There are clan houses on neighbouring **Keong Saik Road** too – once a notorious red-light area, as recounted in Charmaine Leung's memoir, *17A Keong Saik Road* (see page 560).

New Bridge Road and Eu Tong Sen Street

Chinatown's main shopping drag comprises southbound **New Bridge Road** and northbound **Eu Tong Sen Street**, along which are a handful of shopping malls. Try to pop into one of the barbecued-pork vendors around the intersection of Smith, Temple and Pagoda streets with New Bridge Road – as they're cooked, the thin, flat, red squares of *bak kwa*, coated with a sweet marinade, produce a rich, smoky odour that is pure Chinatown. As you chew on your *bak kwa*, check out two striking buildings across the road. On the left is the Art Deco **Majestic Theatre**, built in 1927 as a Chinese opera house by Eu Tong Sen, the wealthy businessman behind the Eu Yan Sang Chinese medicine franchise. Today it has been reduced to housing a few forgettable shops, but five images of figures from Chinese opera still adorn its facade. Just beside it, and built a few years later, stands the former *Great Southern Hotel* (today the Yue Hwa Chinese Products Emporium), which had a fifth-floor nightclub where wealthy locals would drink liquor, smoke opium and pay to dance with so-called "taxi girls".

Ann Siang Hill

Ann Siang Hill is both the name of a little mound and of a lane that leads off South Bridge Road up a slope, where it forks into Club Street on the left and Ann Siang Road, which veers gently right. Despite being only a few paces removed from the hubbub of the main road, the hill is somehow a different realm, a little collection of gentrified shophouses with a distinct village-like feel. Packed with swanky restaurants, cafés and bars, plus the odd boutique, the area typifies the new Chinatown. At the southern end of the road, a short flight of steps leads up to **Ann Siang Hill Park**, a sliver of generic greenery whose only attraction is that it offers a **short cut** to Amoy Street.

Club Street

Scarcely any of the clan associations and guilds whose presence gave **Club Street** its name now remain. Most notable of all is the **Chinese Weekly Entertainment Club** at the end of a side street also called Club Street. Flanked by roaring lion heads, this mansion-like building was constructed in 1891 as a venue where Peranakan tycoons could socialize, and still serves as a private club today.

Singapore City Gallery

URA Centre, 45 Maxwell Rd • Free • http://ura.gov.sg/gallery • Tanjong Pagar or Telok Ayer MRT

Town planning may not sound the most fascinating premise for a gallery, but then again, no nation remodels with such ambition as Singapore, whose planners are constantly erasing roads here and replacing one ultramodern complex with an even more souped-up development. The latest grand designs for the island are exhibited west of Ann Siang Hill at the surprisingly absorbing **Singapore City Gallery**, within the government Urban Redevelopment Authority's headquarters.

The URA has rightly been criticized in the past for slighting Singapore's architectural heritage, so it is heartening that the gallery not only explains how shophouses have evolved stylistically, but also makes reassuring noises about preserving the ones that remain. But the highlight is the vast and incredibly intricate **scale model** of downtown Singapore, with every row of shophouses, every roof of every building – including some not yet built – fashioned out of plywood.

Amoy Street

Amoy Street, together with Telok Ayer Street, was designated a Hokkien enclave in the colony's early days (Amoy being the old name of Xiamen city in China's Fujian province). Long terraces of smartly refurbished shophouses flank the street, all featuring characteristic **five-foot ways**, or covered verandas, so called because they jut five feet out from the house. If you descend here from Ann Siang Hill Park, you'll emerge by the small **Sian Chai Kang Temple** at no. 66. With the customary dragons on the roof, it's dominated by huge urns, full to the brim with ash from untold numbers of burned incense sticks. Two carved stone lions guard the temple; their fancy red neck-ribbons are said to bring good fortune and prosperity.

Telok Ayer Street

One street removed from Amoy Street is **Telok Ayer Street**, its name, meaning "Watery Bay" in Malay, recalling the mid-nineteenth century when the street would have run along the shoreline. Thanks to land reclamation, it's no closer to a beach than Beach Road is, but some of Singapore's oldest buildings cling on between the modern towers – temples and mosques where newly arrived immigrants and sailors thanked their god(s) for their safe passage.

The first building of note you come to if you walk up from the station is the square 1889 **Chinese Methodist Church**, whose design – portholes and windows adorned with white crosses and capped by a Chinese pagoda-style roof – is a pleasing blend of East and West. Just beyond McCallum Street, the blue-and-white **Al-Abrar Mosque** is built on the spot where Chulia worshippers set up a makeshift thatched mosque in 1827.

Thian Hock Keng Temple and around

158 Telok Ayer St • Free • http://thianhockkeng.com.sg • Telok Ayer or Chinatown MRT

With ornate dragons stalking its broad, low-slung roofs, the immaculately restored **Thian Hock Keng Temple** feels marooned in a sea of commercialization, and with much of Chinatown's community uprooted, it is something of a museum piece, one that schoolkids are taken to so they can glimpse life in "the old days".

A statue of the goddess Mazu, shipped in from southern China in time for the temple's completion in 1842, stands in the centre of the main hall, flanked by the martial figure of Guan Yu on the right and physician Bao Sheng on the left. Against the left wall, look out for an altar containing the curious figures of General Fan and General Xie. The two are said to have arranged to meet by a river bridge, but Xie was delayed; Fan waited doggedly and drowned in a flash flood, which supposedly accounts for his grimace and dark skin. When Xie finally arrived, he was filled with guilt and hanged himself – hence his depiction, with tongue hanging down to his chest.

Incidentally, the **pagoda** visible to the left from Telok Ayer Street, called **Chongwen Ge**, formed part of an adjacent school, a site that now hosts a Peranakan café. It's also worth walking around to Amoy Street to see the back-wall **mural** by Yip Yew Chong, an accountant who does street art in his spare time; it kicks off on the right with the Chinatown of old in sepia and ends with a full-colour fantasy in which both existing and demolished towers in the Financial District loom over a river still busy with cargo-filled bumboats.

Nagore Durgha Shrine

140 Telok Ayer St • Free

It's a testament to Singapore's multicultural nature that Thian Hock Keng's next-door neighbour is the charming brown-and-white **Nagore Durgha Shrine** to the Muslim ascetic, Shahul Hamid of Nagore. It was built in the 1820s by Chulias from southern India, as was the Jamae Mosque (see page 470), so it's not surprising that the buildings appear to be cut from the same architectural cloth.

Part of the shrine now houses a fine little **museum** dedicated to the history of Telok Ayer Street. The few simple artefacts and photographs do a good job of unpacking the nuances of Muslim Indian identity in Singapore, a country where Hindu Indians are referred to by the part of India they emigrated from, yet their Muslim counterparts are lumped together under the banner of their faith.

Ying Fo Fui Kun
98 Telok Ayer St, beyond the junction with Cross St • Telok Ayer or Chinatown MRT

Among the smartest of Chinatown's surviving clan houses, the **Ying Fo Fui Kun** was established in 1822 by Hakkas from Guangdong province. It has narrowly avoided being swallowed up by the adjacent Far East Square complex, but in its present orderly state, with an immaculate altar boasting gilt calligraphy and carvings, it's hard to imagine it having been the hub of an entire community. Periodic membership drives try to stop it turning into a senior citizens' club, given that provincial dialects – traditionally used as a marker of identity among the Chinese – have been on the decline since the 1970s following an aggressive state campaign to standardize on Mandarin.

Fuk Tak Chi Street Museum
76 Telok Ayer St • Free • Telok Ayer or Chinatown MRT

Far East Square is a sort of heritage development, engulfing the shophouses of what would have been the northernmost part of Amoy Street. Also co-opted into the complex, indeed into a hotel, is the **Fuk Tak Chi Street Museum**. This was once Singapore's oldest temple, having been founded by Hakka and Cantonese migrants in 1824; now its altar holds a model junk crewed by sailors in blue shorts. A diorama depicts Telok Ayer Street in its waterfront heyday, with a stage set up in front of the temple and opera performers getting ready to strut their stuff.

Tanjong Pagar
Tanjong Pagar or Outram Park MRT

The district of **Tanjong Pagar**, south of Chinatown, was once a veritable sewer of opium dens and brothels. Then it was earmarked as a conservation area and dozens of shophouses were refurbished as bars, restaurants and shops, notably on Neil Road and Duxton Hill. A grander example of the area's architecture can be found right where South Bridge Road flows into Neil and Tanjong Pagar roads: here you'll easily spot the arches and bricked facade of the **Jinrikisha Building**, constructed at the turn of the last century as a terminus for rickshaws.

Tanjong Pagar's most interesting attraction is the **Baba House**, though as an architectural attention-grabber it's rivalled by the seven interlinked towers of **Pinnacle@Duxton**, a showpiece municipal housing development on Cantonment Road, dominating Chinatown's southern skyline.

Baba House
157 Neil Rd • Free • http://babahouse.nus.edu.sg • Outram Park MRT (Cantonment Rd exit), or bus #174 from Orchard Rd or Bras Basah Rd to its terminus

The **Baba House** is one of Singapore's most impressive museums, partly because it isn't really a museum: what you see is a late nineteenth- or early twentieth-century Peranakan house, meticulously restored to its appearance in the late 1920s, a particularly prosperous time in its history. Like Penang's Cheong Fatt Tze Mansion, the place is easily spotted as it's painted a vivid blue. Note the **phoenixes** and **peonies** on the eaves above the entrance, signifying longevity and wealth respectively and, together, marital bliss. Even more eye-catching is the **pintu pagar**, the swing doors with gilt and mother-of-pearl inlays. Note that it's compulsory to visit on a guided tour, unless you can nab of of the "self-guided" slots on Saturday – either way, try to book at least a week in advance.

Beyond the *pintu pagar*, the altar here – among the last of its kind in Singapore – is backed by an exquisitely carved wood screen, behind which the women of the household could eavesdrop on proceedings. Beyond it is the **family hall**, with an air well open to the sky in its midst. Note the original tilework depicting roses and tulips, indicating European influence, and the gilt bats on the walls – bats, *bianfu* in Mandarin, are considered lucky because *fu* is a homonym for the Chinese character meaning "good fortune".

Upstairs at the front end of the house, the centrepiece of the **main bedroom** is an ornate wooden four-poster bed with gilt and red lacquer decorations, bearing carved motifs such as musical instruments and yet more bats. Your guide will almost certainly open up the **peephole** in the floor, exposing a small shaft down to the main hall. The **third storey**, a later addition, is used for temporary exhibitions.

The Financial District
Raffles Place, Telok Ayer or Downtown MRT

If Singapore's **Financial District** (or **Central Business District/CBD**; map page 472) figures in the popular imagination at all, it would be because of the rogue trader Nick Leeson, whose antics here brought about the **Barings Bank collapse** of the 1990s. The area, south of the mouth of the Singapore River, has few specific sights but makes a reasonable prelude to nearby Boat Quay (see below), Telok Ayer Street (see page 475), the Colonial District (via Cavenagh Bridge; see page 452) or the southern part of Marina Bay (see page 479).

Boat Quay and around
Close to the old mouth of the Singapore River, the pedestrianized row of waterfront shophouses known as **Boat Quay** is one of Singapore's most commercially successful bids at urban regeneration. Derelict in the early 1990s, it's since become a thriving hangout, sporting a huge collection of restaurants and bars; to many visitors, it's far more appealing than mall-like Clarke Quay, just up the way, and having a drink with boats gliding past and umpteen towers in the background can be quite something. The area's historical significance can sometimes be appreciated through its street names – Synagogue Street nearby, for example, was the site of the island's first synagogue.

Hong Lim Park
Between Upper Pickering St and North Canal Rd • Clarke Quay MRT

A few minutes' walk southwest from the Singapore River, **Hong Lim Park** is not much more than a field ringed by trees, but it's of symbolic significance as the home of **Speakers' Corner**, at its northern edge. Since its designation in 2000, citizens have, in theory, been able to speak their minds here, just as people do at its famous exemplar in central London. This being Singapore, regulations require you to register your intention to speak and prohibit discussion of religion or anything that could be deemed to provoke racial discontent. Despite this, the site has regained some of its historic role as a site for political meetings and also hosts the annual gay pride event, Pink Dot.

Yueh Hai Ching Temple
30B Philip St • Free • Telok Ayer or Raffles Place MRT

The twin-shrined **Yueh Hai Ching Temple** (also called **Wak Hai Cheng Bio**) feels a little isolated, nestling as it does among the towers where Chinatown merges into the Financial District. Completed in the 1850s, it is another of the area's temples built on the old coastline, and was a magnet for newly arrived migrants who, once ashore at Bullock Cart Water (the translation of the Chinese name, used to this day, for what would become Chinatown), would come here to give thanks for their safe arrival. Hai Ching means "calm sea" and an effigy of Tian Hou or Mazu, the queen of heaven and protector of seafarers, is housed in the right-hand shrine. Be sure to look up at the roof, crammed with scenes from Chinese folklore built up using the traditional *jiannian* technique, involving multicoloured porcelain shards.

Raffles Place and around
What is now the Financial District was a swamp until land reclamation in the mid-1820s rendered it fit for building. Within just a few years, it was home to the colony's busiest business address, Commercial Square, boasting the banks, ships' chandlers and warehouses of a burgeoning trading port. The square later became the island's main shopping area until Orchard Road overtook it in the late 1960s; today known as **Raffles Place**, it's the heart of Singapore's high-profile banking sector.

Surfacing from Raffles Place MRT, follow the signs for Raffles Place itself to feel like an ant in a canyon of skyscrapers; many of the worker ants hereabouts are heading to or from the Kenzo Tange-designed One Raffles Place complex to the west of the square; until 2022 there were truly stunning views on offer from its rooftop bar, but this has been closed, with no replacement yet in the works at the time of writing. The three roads that run southwest from Raffles Place – Cecil Street, Robinson Road and Shenton Way – are all chock-a-block with more high-rise banks and financial houses.

Battery Road
Heading towards the river from Raffles Place, you reach **Battery Road**, its name recalling the days when Fort Fullerton (named after Robert Fullerton, first governor of the Straits Settlements) and its attendant battery of guns stood to the east on the site of the elegant **Fullerton Building** – the main attraction today. This was one of Singapore's tallest buildings when it was constructed in 1928 as the General Post Office, a role it fulfilled until the mid-1990s. These days, it serves as the luxury *Fullerton* hotel; head inside to plunge into the Neoclassical and Art Deco splendour of the atrium, with a Y-shaped marbled staircase surmounting a carp-filled fishpond, and enormous columns reminiscent of Egyptian temples.

Collyer Quay
Collyer Quay runs south along the western shore of Marina Bay from what was the mouth of the Singapore River, linking the Colonial District with Raffles Quay and Shenton Way further south, both of which mark the former line of the seafront. Just east of Collyer Quay, the Merlion Park is home to a cement statue of Singapore's national symbol, the **Merlion**. Half-lion, half-fish and wholly ugly, the creature reflects the island's maritime connections and the old tale concerning the derivation of its present name, derived from the Sanskrit "Singapura", meaning "Lion City".

Clifford Pier
80 Collyer Quay

South of the park, the Art Deco **Clifford Pier** building, long the departure point for boat trips out to Singapore's southern islands, was rendered defunct by the barrage that seals Marina Bay off from the sea. The building, along with the **Customs House** building a minute's walk on, have been transformed into restaurant complexes, run by

---

> ### TAKING CHINESE TEA
>
> At two Tanjong Pagar teahouses – Tea Chapter (see page 515) and Yixing Xuan (see page 515) – visitors can glean something of the deep Chinese connection with tea by taking part in a **workshop** lasting up to an hour. Participants are introduced to different varieties of tea and talked through the history of tea cultivation and the rituals of brewing and appreciating the drink. The water, for example, has to reach an optimum temperature that depends on the type of tea being prepared; experts can tell its heat by the size of the rising bubbles, described variously as "sand eyes", "prawn eyes", "fish eyes", etc. Both venues also stock an extensive range of tea-related accoutrements such as tall "sniffer" cups used to savour the aroma of the brew before it is poured into squat teacups for drinking.

THE MERLION

Even if you haven't yet been to Singapore, you've doubtless seen images of its famed **Merlion** statue, which regularly appears on "around the world" montages on international news bulletins and the like, as well as pretty much all of the country's tourism images and literature. As with certain other national icons, it can be a little disappointing to see in the flesh, though at almost nine metres in height, the Merlion is at least a little bigger than, say, the Manneken Pis in Brussels, or Copenhagen's Little Mermaid.

Before you try to get the perfect photographic angle of the **lion-fish** squirting water, a little history lesson may be in order. It was constructed in 1972, though had to make a short – but technically difficult – journey to its present location in 2002, after the Esplanade Bridge (built in 1997) blocked its view of the River Singapore. In 2009, the statue's ear was blown off in a lightning strike, which in 2011 the small park area surrounding the Merlion became a hotel suite of sorts, for the duration of the Biennale. A far larger Merlion, standing at 37m in height, was built on **Sentosa**; with a viewing deck in the head and lasers shining out of its eyes, it actually became more famous and popular than the original, though it was closed in 2019 as part of a major redevelopment plan, and has since been demolished.

the firm that owns the *Fullerton* hotel; part of Clifford Pier forms the entrance to the hotel's pricier new sibling, the *Fullerton Bay*.

Lau Pa Sat
18 Raffles Quay

Arguably the best place for refreshments in the Financial District is the charmingly old-world **Lau Pa Sat**, literally meaning "old market" – it was built in 1894 as a place for traders to sell produce. Also known by its original name, **Telok Ayer Market**, Lau Pa Sat has served as a hawker centre since the 1970s, except for a hiatus in the 1980s when tunnelling for the MRT required the octagonal cast-iron structure to be dismantled, then reassembled piece by piece. Aficionados of **satay** should turn up in the evening, when vendors set up in a row outside on Boon Tat Street, and the immediate area finds itself under a photogenic fug of smoke.

Marina Bay
Bayfront, Downtown or Promenade MRT

It's hard not to be awed by the audacity of **Marina Bay**, the project that has transformed downtown Singapore's seafront over the last several decades. An exorbitantly ambitious piece of civil engineering, it entailed the creation of three massive expanses of reclaimed land, as well as a barrage to seal off the basins of the Singapore and Kallang rivers from the sea. The result is a seaside freshwater **reservoir** that now plays a crucial role in reducing Singapore's dependence on Malaysian water supplies.

Although the bay's southern "jaw", **Marina South**, now sprouts a host of bank buildings to rival Raffles Place, the area is dominated by the **Marina Bay Sands** resort, with its casino, museum and rooftop restaurants; it is inevitably the focus of any visit to the bay, along with the extravagant **Gardens by the Bay** next door. Close to the Padang, the **Theatres on the Bay arts complex** is worth a detour for its skyline views, with more of the same available from the oversized Ferris wheel of the **Singapore Flyer**.

Marina Bay Sands
10 Bayfront Ave • http://marinabaysands.com • Bayfront MRT

Rarely does a building become an icon quite as instantly as the **Marina Bay Sands** hotel and casino, a major development consisting of three 55-floor towers topped and connected by a vast, curved-surfboard-like deck, known as the SkyPark. Even if you have no interest

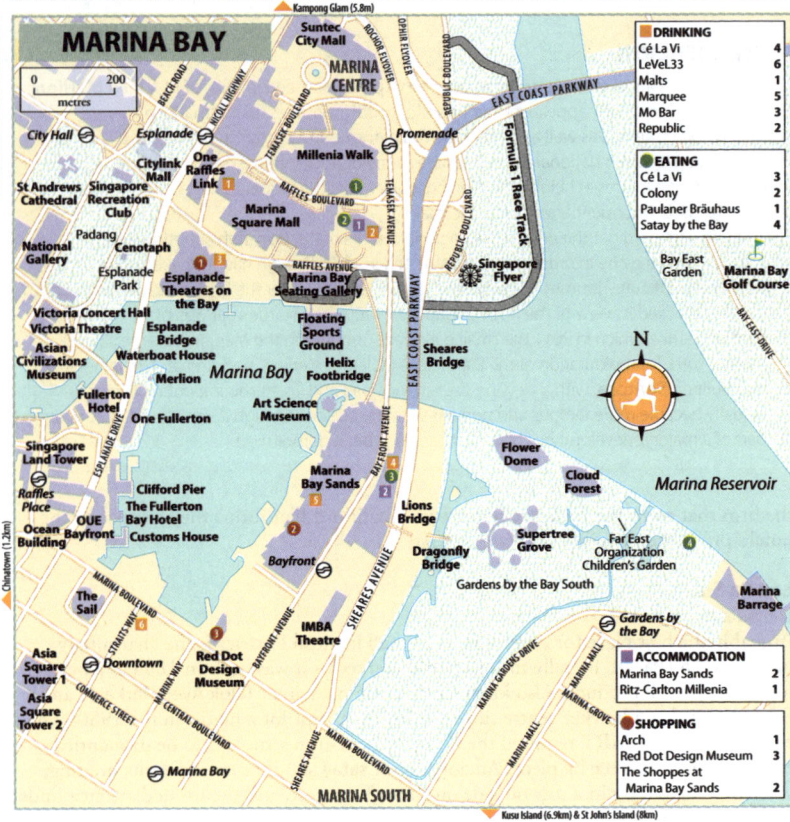

in the casino – open 24/7, naturally – the complex, which includes a convention centre, a shopping mall, two concert venues, numerous restaurants and its own museum, is well worth exploring. The hotel atrium, often so busy with people gawping that it feels like a train station concourse, is especially striking, the sides of the building sloping into each other overhead to give the impression of being inside a narrow glassy pyramid.

In the evening, the free **Spectra** sound-and-light show (2–3 daily, in the evening; 15min) takes place outside the hotel, with illuminated fountains and lasers. Visible from the Padang and surrounding areas, it's quite adventurous by the standard of such displays, and especially captivating if you're at the hotel itself.

In 2025, construction started on a new Marina Bay Sands tower. Though set apart from the other three and largely similar in design, some locals are understandably wary about this tampering with a national icon – time will tell as to whether the new addition will add to, or detract from, the majesty.

SkyPark

Charge • Tickets and access via the basement ticket office of tower 3, at the northern end of the complex

From what would have been an impossible vantage point, high above the sea, before the creation of Marina Bay, the SkyPark's observation deck affords superb views over Singapore's Colonial District on one side and the conservatories of **Gardens by the Bay** on the other. Unfortunately, tickets are overpriced and don't allow you up close to the most famous feature, the 150m **infinity pool**. On the other hand, there's effectively no charge to visit if you eat or drink at either of the two SkyPark venues, such as *Cé La Vi* (see page 513) – you can effectively get a cocktail, plus a better view and more interesting environment, for just a few bucks more than you'd pay for the observation deck, which for many constitutes a no-brainer.

ArtScience Museum
At the northern end of the complex, close to the helix footbridge for the Singapore Flyer and Theatres on the Bay • Charge

The **ArtScience Museum** is easily spotted: its shape is supposed to represent a stylized lotus blossom, though from certain angles it looks far more like a stubby-fingered Transformer hand, or perhaps even a landing pad for visiting spacecraft. The museum aims to decode the connections between art and science, but in practice it puts on world-class travelling exhibitions, some only tenuously linked to the supposed remit: highlights to date have included items salvaged from the *Titanic*, and exhibitions focusing on Harry Potter and Studio Ghibli. There's only one permanent gallery, Future World, in which children (and grown-ups) can interact with colourful multimedia installations by, for example, crafting and scanning objects that then pop up in a large-scale animation.

Gardens by the Bay South
18 Marina Gardens Drive • Free admission to gardens; charges for OCBC Skyway, observatory & conservatories • http://gardensbythebay.com.sg • Bayfront or Gardens by the Bay MRT

Two vast conservatories, roofs arched like the backs of foraging dinosaurs, are the most eye-catching features of the southern section of **Gardens by the Bay**. Intended to be a second botanic garden for Singapore, the gardens are split into three chunks around Marina Bay; the southern area, next to *Marina Bay Sands*, is very much the centrepiece.

One conservatory houses Mediterranean and African flora, the highlight being the stands of bizarrely shaped **baobab** trees. The neighbouring conservatory nurtures **cloud forest** of the kind found on tropical peaks like Kinabalu, and includes a 35m "mountain" covered in ferns, rhododendrons and insect-eating butterworts.

The gardens' other big draw is the **Supertree Grove**, an array of towers resembling gigantic golf tees and sheathed in a sort of red trelliswork, from which climbers, ferns and orchids poke out. More exciting by day is the slightly wobbly **OCBC Skyway**, an aerial walkway connecting the tops of the two tallest supertrees and providing good views; you can go even higher at the newer **Supertree Observatory**, to observe goings-on from 50m up. At night, though, the supertrees come into their own when they are illuminated in free evening **light shows**; if you want to kill time, rest up or have a meal, there's a decent hawker centre on site (as well as plenty of cheesy or overpriced restaurants).

IMBA Theatre
Shears Ave • imbaglobal.com

At the time of writing, the **IMBA Theatre** was gearing up for its grand opening. Squeezed into the space between Marina Bay Sands and the Gardens by the Bay, it's not really a theatre at all, but a cutting-edge visual arts space, centred on the "Black Box", a large hall in which projects on the walls can make visitors feel like they're somewhere else entirely; multi-sensory and interactive exhibitions are on the cards.

Red Dot Design Museum
11 Marina Boulevard • Charge • http://museum.red-dot.sg • Downtown or Bayfront MRT

Housed in a futuristic glass building, the **Red Dot Design Museum** focuses on international product design and the creative use of illustration, following the process from conceptualization all the way through to the realized work – be it a sports car or art installation. It's at its best during the monthly **crafts market**, MAAD, when local artists and designers showcase their work (one weekend per month). The gift shop stocks quirky designer items that make good gifts (see page 522).

Marina Centre
Promenade or Esplanade MRT, or City Hall MRT via the subterranean CityLink Mall

The large triangle of reclaimed land east of the Padang and the *Raffles Hotel*, robbing Beach Road of its beach, is officially called **Marina Centre**, though locals invariably invoke the names of the Marina Square or Suntec City malls when referring to it. This is the oldest part of the Marina Bay project, open since the early 1990s, but still feels quite disconnected from the historical neighbourhoods to the west.

Esplanade – Theatres on the Bay
1 Esplanade Drive • Free; charge for tours (45min; check online for latest schedule) • http://esplanade.com

Opinion is split as to whether the two huge, spiked shells that roof the **Esplanade – Theatres on the Bay** project, just east of the Padang, are peerless modernistic architecture or indulgent kitsch. They have variously been compared to hedgehogs and even durians (the preferred description among locals), though "two giant insect eyes" is perhaps a more apt description. Facilities include a concert hall, theatres and gallery space. It's possible to do a guided tour of the site, but what lures most casual visitors are the **views**, particularly fine at dusk, across the bay to the Financial District and *Marina Bay Sands*.

Singapore Flyer
30 Raffles Ave • Charge • http://singaporeflyer.com

Standing a lofty 165m high, the **Singapore Flyer** is actually slightly taller than the summit of Bukit Timah, the island's highest natural point, and about 30m taller than the London Eye. The downside is that from its location, the remaining rows of shophouses are largely obscured by clumps of towers; better views can be had from some hotels and rooftop bars.

The pricey ride – billed as a **flight** – initially has you looking east over the Kallang district, home to the new Sports Hub stadium complex. Beyond the shipping lanes, Indonesia's **Riau archipelago** appears very close. Looking north, it's more exciting to pick out the golden domes of the Sultan Mosque and the shophouses of Arab Street beyond the twin Gateway buildings on Beach Road. As your capsule reaches maximum height, you might just make out the low hump of **Bukit Timah**, topped with a couple of radio masts, on the horizon beyond Theatres on the Bay.

The descent affords good views of **Marina Bay Sands** and the **Financial District**. Originally the ride began with these, but the wheel had to be reversed due to feng shui concerns (apparently the old direction was channelling good luck up and away from the area).

Orchard Road and around

It would be hard to conjure an image more at odds with the present reality of **Orchard Road** than historian Mary Turnbull's description of "a country lane lined with bamboo hedges and shrubbery, with trees meeting overhead". In the early part of the last century, merchants taking a constitutional here would have strolled past rows of nutmeg trees, followed at a discreet distance by their manservants. Today, the area is synonymous with **shopping** – huge, often glitzy malls now line the road (see page 521).

Orchard Road begins as the continuation of Tanglin Road and channels traffic east for nearly 3km to Bras Basah and Selegie roads, near the Colonial District. The bucolic allure of the area of old survives 1km beyond Orchard Road's western end, where you'll find Singapore's excellent **Botanic Gardens**.

Dhoby Ghaut
In the **Dhoby Ghaut** area, at the eastern end of Orchard Road, Indian *dhobies* (laundrymen) used to wash clothes in the Stamford Canal, which ran along Orchard

and Stamford roads. Those days are long gone, though something of the past survives in the **Cathay Gallery**, home to the company behind one of Singapore's and Malaysia's oldest cinema chains.

Cathay Gallery
2 Handy Rd • Free • http://thecathay.com.sg

Boasting a 1939 Art Deco facade, the Cathay Building houses a multiplex cinema and the **Cathay Gallery**, displaying memorabilia – costumes, promotional materials and vintage photos – from decades upon decades in the movie business, including its 1950s and 1960s heyday, when the company made its own Chinese- and Malay-language films.

The Istana
Istana and grounds only open four or five holidays a year, with a nominal entrance fee (see website for details) • http://istana.gov.sg • Dhoby Ghaut MRT

A short walk west along Orchard Road from Dhoby Ghaut MRT takes you past the **Plaza Singapura** mall, beyond which stern soldiers guard the main gate of Singapore's **Istana**, built in 1869. With ornate cornices, elegant louvred shutters and a high mansard roof, the building was originally the official residence of Singapore's British governors; now it's home to Singapore's president, a ceremonial role for which elections are held nonetheless. The first Sunday of the month sees a **changing of the guard** ceremony at the main gate at 5.45pm.

Emerald Hill
Somerset MRT

A number of architecturally noteworthy houses have survived the bulldozers at **Emerald Hill**, behind the Centrepoint mall and a five-minute walk west of the Istana. Granted to Englishman William Cuppage in 1845, the hill was for some years afterwards the site of a large nutmeg plantation. After his death in 1872, the land was subdivided and sold off, much of it to members of the **Peranakan** community. Walk up Emerald Hill Road today and you'll see exquisite houses from the era, in the so-called **Chinese Baroque** style, typified by the use of coloured ceramic tiles, carved swing doors, shuttered windows and pastel-shaded walls with fine plaster mouldings. Unsurprisingly, quite a few now host trendy restaurants and bars.

ION Orchard
2 Orchard Turn • Charge for viewing gallery • http://ionorchard.com • Orchard MRT

The most striking of the area's malls, **ION Orchard** has a bulging glass frontage vaguely reminiscent of Theatres on the Bay, and is topped by a tower of luxury apartments that also boasts a 55th-floor viewing gallery, ION Sky.

Goodwood Park Hotel
22 Scotts Rd • http://goodwoodparkhotel.com • Orchard MRT

A few minutes' walk north up **Scotts Road** off Orchard Road stands the impressive **Goodwood Park Hotel**, with gleaming walls and a distinctive squat, steeple-like tower. Having started out in 1900 as the Teutonia Club for German expats, it was commandeered by the British with the outbreak of war across Europe in 1914, and didn't open again until 1918. In 1929 it became a hotel, though by 1942 it and the *Raffles* – designed by the same architect – were lodging Japanese officers. The *Goodwood Park* was later used for war-crimes trials. Today the hotel remains one of the classiest in town and is a well-regarded venue for a British-style tea.

Botanic Gardens
Several entrances, including 1 Cluny Rd • Free, with free weekend tours of some sections plus free concerts • http://nparks.gov.sg • Napier or Botanic Gardens MRT

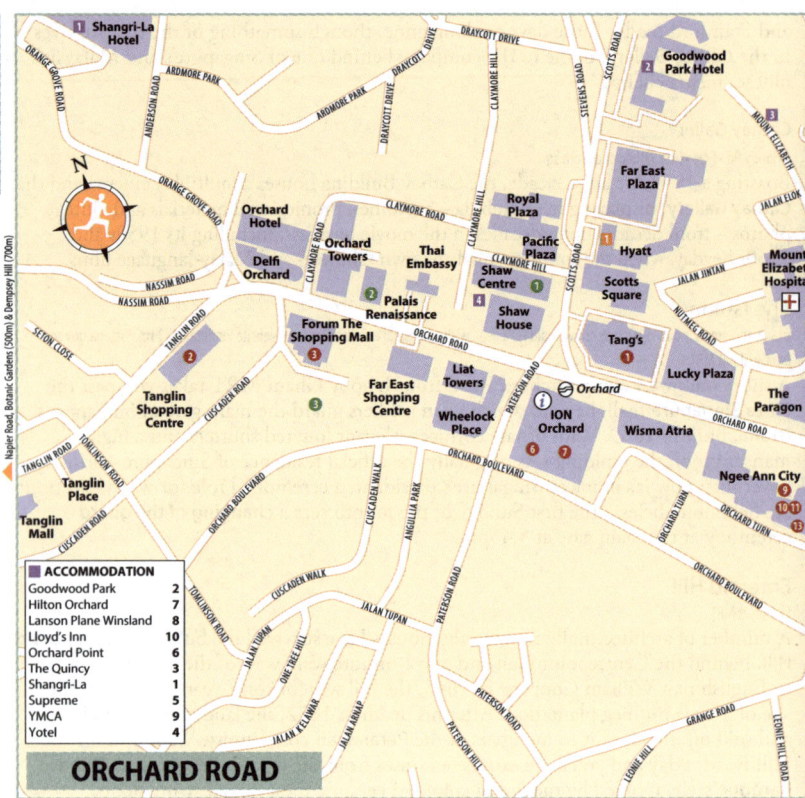

Singapore has long made green space an integral part of the island's landscape, but none of its parks come close to matching the refinement of the **Botanic Gardens**, the island's sole UNESCO World Heritage Site. Founded in 1859, the gardens were where the Brazilian seeds that gave rise to the great **rubber plantations** of the Malay Peninsula were first nurtured in 1877. Henry Ridley, named the gardens' director the following year, recognized the financial potential of rubber and spent the next twenty years persuading plantation-owners to convert to this new crop, an obsession that earned him the nickname "Mad" Ridley. In later years the gardens became a centre for the breeding of new **orchid** hybrids. Recent additions have extended the park all the way north to Bukit Timah Road, where the Botanic Gardens MRT station offers a route to the newer, less interesting part of the gardens; the itinerary that follows assumes the classic approach up Tanglin and Napier roads to the **Tanglin gate** at the start of Cluny Road.

Into the gardens

The path from the Tanglin gate, lined with frangipanis, casuarinas and the odd majestic banyan tree, soon reaches the tranquil **Swan Lake**, nearly as old as the gardens themselves. Veer to the left and you reach the newest additions to the gardens, the Walk of Giants (a tree-canopy elevated walkway) with a wetland area at the far end. Both are still bedding down, so it's more interesting to keep to the right side of the lake, following signs for the **ginger garden**, packed with flowering gingers as exotic and gaudy as anything you could hope to see in the tropics.

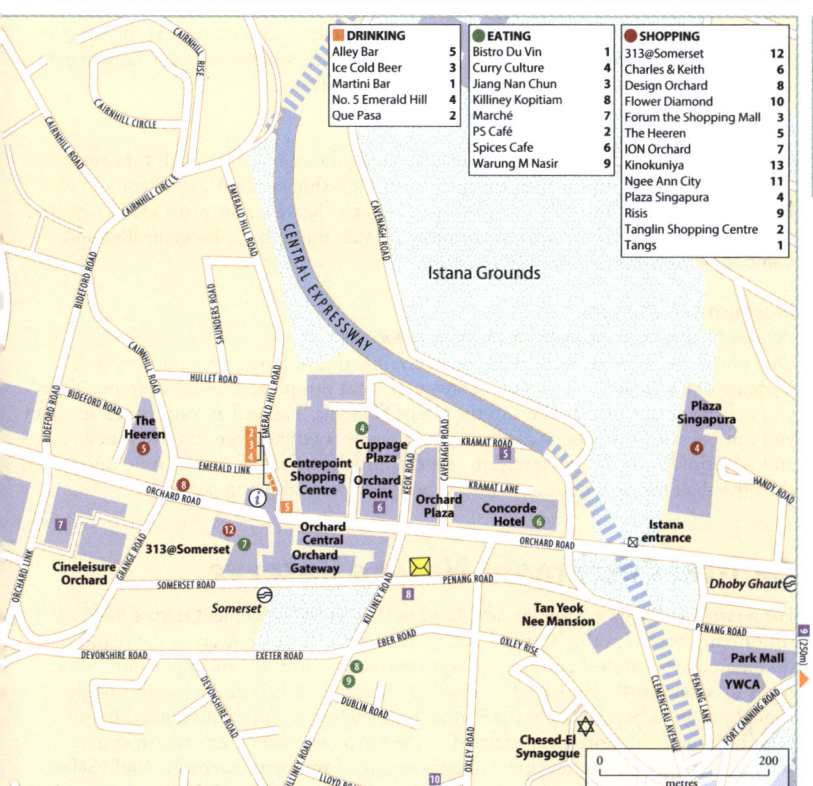

National Orchid Garden

Charge

A feast of blooms of almost every hue are on show at the **National Orchid Garden**. There's an entire section of orchids named after dignitaries and celebrities who have visited; *Dendrobium Margaret Thatcher* is a severe pink with a couple of petals twisted like pasta spirals, while *Vandaenopsis Nelson Mandela* is a reassuring warm yellowy-brown. Looking slightly out of place is the black-and-white **Burkill Hall**, exemplifying the so-called Tropical Tudor style, few examples of which now survive in Singapore; the gardens' director once lived here. The gift shop at the exit stocks an incredible range of orchid paraphernalia, including blossoms encased in glass paperweights or plated with gold.

Back to the Tanglin gate

Exiting the orchid garden, head up the boardwalk to enter the central **rainforest** with a trail past numbered highlights, including a spectacular banyan tree that's a mass of aerial roots. The trail and forest end above **Symphony Lake**, where occasional concerts are staged.

By now you've seen much of the best of what the gardens have to offer, and there's not that much to be gained by continuing north. Heading back towards the Tanglin gate, look out for the park's loftiest tree, a stunning 47m *jelawai* on the edge of the rainforest tract; this and several other exceptionally tall trees are fitted with lightning conductors. Close by, to the right, is one of the loveliest spots in all of Singapore, a grassy area centred upon a 1930s **bandstand**, encircled by eighteen rain trees for shade.

Head downhill from here through the **sundial garden** to end up back at the lake, or bear left to reach **Holttum Hall** – only a couple of minutes' walk from the Tanglin gate – a 1920s house that hosts a museum of the gardens' history.

North to Bukit Timah Road

Continue northwards from Symphony Lake, and you soon reach the **Visitor Centre** – marooned in the middle of the gardens – with a gift shop and café. Next comes the **Evolution Garden**, where fake petrified trees help to illustrate how plant life has evolved over millennia. From here, it's several minutes' walk through the **bougainvillea and bamboo garden** to reach the MRT station.

Museum of Ice Cream

100 Loewen Rd • Charge • http://museumoficecream.com/singapore • Napier MRT

One of the area's newest attractions, and certainly one of Singapore's pinkest, is the **Museum of Ice Cream**. You can probably guess what this place is all about (especially if you've been to one of the others in the US or Shanghai); as well as more ice cream than you can eat, there's a bouncy castle of sorts (maybe try this before you overindulge), and a "sprinkle pit". Visitors seem to spend approximately half of their time eating, and the other half taking pictures; it's pricey, but good for families in particular.

Central Catchment Nature Reserve

For a taste of Singapore's wilder side, head to the **Central Catchment Nature Reserve** (informally known as the "Central Nature Reserve"). The lush heart of the island is dominated by **rainforest** and several large **reservoirs**, and there are opportunities for **hikes** up **Bukit Timah**, the island's tallest hill. The interest isn't limited to the jungle though: close to Bukit Timah, the **Former Ford Factory** is a museum housed in the building where the British surrendered to the Japanese, while the northern end of the nature reserve holds Singapore's highly regarded **zoo**, with a separate **Night Safari** section open from dusk, and the zoo's newest offshoot, the **River Safari,** presenting the fauna of rivers as diverse as the Mekong and the Mississippi.

The Peirce Reservoirs

The bulk of the Central Catchment Nature Reserve is located in the surprisingly wide area around the **Peirce Reservoirs**, divided into "upper" and "lower" bodies by a 300m-long dam, whose innards also function as a water treatment plant. There are plenty of small parks to visit hereabouts, and umpteen hiking trails joining the dots; for many, the main draw is the lovely **TreeTop Walk**.

TreeTop Walk

30 Venus Drive • Free • http://nparks.gov.sg • A 2km walk west of Windsor Nature Park

A good target if you're on a walk through the area is the **TreeTop Walk**, a free-standing suspension bridge providing some majestic views. It's only 250m long, though at points you'll be a full 25m above the ground; access is only from the eastern end (ie, from Windsor Nature Park), and it's one-way traffic until you get to the other. From here, you can retrace your steps at ground level, or even press further west to MacRitchie Reservoir Park, 4.5km further on (1hr 30min–2hr, making the whole walk 3–5hr in total from Windsor Nature Park).

Windsor Nature Park

30 Venus Drive • Free • http://nparks.gov.sg • Bright Hill MRT, then a short walk west up Sin Ming Ave

While it's not exactly a jungle experience, **Windsor Nature Park** makes a great place to do some nature walking. Trails are well signposted, with various paths and boardwalks winding their way around the marshes, with rare native plants visible on the way around; you may well come across **wild boars**. You'll need fairly decent footwear, especially given Singapore's fickle weather.

Bukit Timah

Bukit Timah Road shoots northwest from Little India, passing leafy suburbs en route to Johor Bahru (it was the main road to the Causeway until superseded by the Bukit Timah Expressway). Some 9km on from Little India, the road becomes Upper Bukit Timah Road and arrives at **Bukit Timah** itself, often called "Bukit Timah Hill" by locals – a deliberate tautology as the surrounding district is also known as Bukit Timah.

Bukit Timah Nature Reserve

Hindhede Drive • Free • http://nparks.gov.sg • Beauty World MRT, then a short walk north up Upper Bukit Timah Rd

One of Singapore's last pockets of primary dipterocarp forest can be experienced in the **Bukit Timah Nature Reserve**, established in 1883 by Nathaniel Cantley, then superintendent of the Botanic Gardens. **Wildlife** abounded in this part of Singapore in the mid-nineteenth century, when the natural historian Alfred Russel Wallace came here to do fieldwork; he later observed that "in all my subsequent travels in the East I rarely if ever met with so productive a spot". Wallace also noted the presence of tiger traps, but by the 1930s Singapore's tigers had met their end. **Long-tailed macaques** haven't dwindled in number, however; some can be seen wandering around the houses at the base of the hill, usually peeking in bins for food.

The trails

Don't expect a full-blown jungle-trekking experience, as the four colour-coded **trails** consist largely of family-friendly boardwalks, steps and stretches of proper road. Three share a very steep start up a sealed road; the exception, the green trail, meanders along the side of the hill before rejoining the others. Most people tackle the red trail (30min), which is the road up to the summit at a paltry 164m; a flight of narrow steps halfway along – the Summit Path – offers a shortcut to the top.

Former Ford Factory

351 Upper Bukit Timah Rd • Charge • http://nlb.gov.sg • Hillview MRT, then three stops south on bus #67, #170, #171 or #184

The Art Deco **Former Ford Factory** at Bukit Timah was the first car-making plant of its kind in Southeast Asia when it opened in October 1941. But in early 1942 the Japanese invaded, and on February 15 Lieutenant General Percival, head of the Allied forces in Singapore, surrendered to Japan's General Yamashita in the factory's boardroom. Today the scene is recreated as part of a worthwhile museum

---

LONG-DISTANCE HIKING IN SINGAPORE ON THE RAIL CORRIDOR

Singapore wouldn't usually be the first country that would come to mind if someone happened to mention long-distance hiking, but the opening of the **Rail Corridor** (http://railcorridor.nparks.gov.sg) has given rise to just such a possibility. **24km** in length, the corridor runs from Kranji MRT in the north to Tanjong Pagar down south, mostly along tracks that aren't just hiking trails, but also double as a means of movement for local wildlife – facilities are kept deliberately minimal, with no lighting at night (so it's best to be off before the sun goes down). Though it's quite possible to do the whole thing in one day, there are dozens of entry points, and visitors can enter or exit wherever they choose; the central 4km section is most popular, though the 10km-long northern section is also very pretty.

focused on the occupation and, less successfully, its aftermath and the beginnings of decolonization. Being run by Singapore's National Archives service, it leans heavily on documents and ephemera – everything from Japanese textbooks and the notorious wartime "banana money" (bananas were depicted on one Japanese-issued banknote) to sketches by POWs at Changi and watercolours commissioned by the occupying administration.

Singapore Zoo

80 Mandai Lake Rd • Charge • http://mandai.com • Bus #138 from Ang Mo Kio MRT, #927 from Choa Chu Kang MRT or the special Mandai Express bus from Khatib MRT (every 40min; 1hr); slightly faster private buses to/from downtown available (details on website)

Singapore's main wildlife attractions cluster in woodland around the tranquil Seletar reservoir: the **Singapore Zoo** and its offshoots, **Night Safari** and **River Wonders**. They consistently draw crowds, which is partly down to their "open" policy: many animals are kept in spacious, naturalistic enclosures behind moats, though creatures such as big cats still have to be caged.

The zoo

Charge; combination tickets available including Night Safari, River Wonders or Jurong Bird Park • http://mandai.com

Home to more than 300 species, the **zoo** could easily occupy you for half a day if not longer. A tram (small charge applies) does a one-way circuit of the grounds, but as it won't always be going your way, be prepared for some legwork.

Highlights include the **Fragile Forest** biodome, a magical zone where you can actually walk among ring-tailed lemurs, sloths and fruit bats, and **Frozen Tundra** featuring, naturally enough, polar bears. The **white tigers** are a big draw too, not actually white but resembling Siamese cats in the colour of their fur and eyes. Primates are something of a strong point, too: orangutans swing through the trees overhead close to the entrance, and at the **Great Rift Valley zone** you can espy the communal life of a hundred Hamadryas baboons, including some rather unchivalrous behaviour on the part of males, who bite females to rein them in. There are animal shows and feeding displays throughout the day.

Night Safari

Charge; combination tickets available • http://mandai.com

Many animals are nocturnal, and the **Night Safari** presents them so well that you'll wonder why similar establishments aren't everywhere. It's true that the Borneo-style show at the entrance is tacky, and there can be queues for the free tram tours (40min), but these are mere niggles at what is the most popular strand of the zoo.

The trams take you around two-thirds of the site. You can forgo them and simply walk around the leafy grounds – an atmospheric experience in the muted lighting. But if you do this, you'll miss out on some enclosures, notably those for large mammals such as elephants and hippos, and the **Indo-Malayan trail**, featuring Asiatic black bears and an artificial waterfall. Areas you can only visit on foot include the **Fishing Cat Trail**, with the *binturong*, sometimes called the bearcat (you'll understand why when you see it); and the **Leopard Trail**, where you may spot the clouded leopard and slow loris.

It's worth catching the **Creatures of the Night** show, which touches on the importance of conservation and recycling, and stars otters, raccoons, civets and owls, among others.

River Wonders

Charge, extra for Amazon River Quest; combination tickets available • http://mandai.com

The **River Wonders** safari spans the divide between aquarium and zoo, trying to do justice to the fauna of seven of the world's great rivers and the lands they flow through. There are too many tanks for comfort at the start, presenting badgers, various alligators and crocs, catfish and other creatures of the Congo, Mississippi, Ganges, Nile and

Mekong. Much better is the hangar-like **Giant Panda Forest**, housing two giant pandas and the raccoon-like **red panda**, with white ears and a stripy orange tail. The second half of the park is given over almost entirely to what's billed as **Amazonia**, and much of that is taken up by one 10min ride, the so-so **Amazon River Quest**, in which your "boat" is carried along a sluiceway past enclosures of scarlet ibises and spider monkeys, among others. Saved for last is the most humongous tank of all: the **Amazon Flooded Forest**, home to manatees, giant arapaima fish, otters and piranhas.

Bird Paradise
20 Mandai Lake Rd • Charge; combination tickets available • http://mandai.com

One of Singapore's newest sights, and a direct replacement for the hugely popular Jurong Bird Park (which closed in 2023), **Bird Paradise** is home to more than 3500 winged creatures, from over 400 avian species, altogether constituting one of the world's biggest bird collections. You'll need at least a couple of hours to have a good look around the grounds, though you can save a little time using the park's shuttle trains (small fee applies).

The new facilities are broadly similar to those that once existed in Jurong Bird Park. One of the main highlights is **Penguin Cove**, which also has a fun restaurant in which you may get to see the creatures while they're busying themselves underwater. A little further on are sections pertaining to birds from Africa, South East Asia and the Aussie Outback, plus the **Lory Loft**, a giant aviary under netting, packed with multicoloured, chattering lories and lorikeets. At the back of the complex, the **Crimson Wetlands** section sends many visitors into a photo-taking frenzy, featuring as it does range of mostly red- or pink-coloured birds (flamingoes, scarlet ibises, and so on), with a large waterfall functioning as a scenic backdrop.

The park also puts on various bird **shows**, the most exciting being Predators on Wings, in which eagles, hawks, falcons and owls show off their predatory capabilities.

Rainforest Wild Asia
20 Mandai Lake Rd • Charge; combination tickets available • http://mandai.com

Even newer than Bird Paradise is **Rainforest Wild Asia**, which opened up to great fanfare in 2025. Instead of birds or fish, this park focuses on the rainforests of South East Asia, having created a safer, more sanitised form of such an environment with the aid of over 7000 trees and shrubs from across the region. There's even the chance to take a rainforest "trek" – not quite the wilds of Borneo, but enjoyable nonetheless.

Kranji and Sungei Buloh

While land reclamation has radically altered the east coast, and industrialization the west, the **northern** expanses of the island up to the Straits of Johor still retain pockets of the **rainforest** and mangrove swamp that blanketed Singapore on Raffles' arrival in 1819. Though thickets of state housing blocks are never far away, something of rural Singapore's agricultural past clings on by way of the odd prawn- or poultry-farm or vegetable garden. Two sights make it worth considering coming this far: the **Kranji War Cemetery and Memorial**, and the wetland reserve at **Sungei Buloh**.

Kranji War Cemetery
9 Woodlands Rd • Free • http://cwgc.org • Kranji MRT then a 10min walk, bus #170 from opposite Little India MRT/Bukit Timah, or #927 from the zoo to the junction of Woodlands and Mandai rds and a 15min walk north

Kranji War Cemetery is the resting place of many Allied troops who died in the defence of Singapore. Row upon row of graves slope up the manicured hill, some identified only as "known unto God". Beyond the simple stone cross that stands over the cemetery is the **memorial**, around which are recorded the names of more than twenty thousand soldiers (including personnel from Britain, Canada, Australia, New Zealand, Malaya and South Asia) who died in this region during World War II. Two unassuming **tombs** stand on the wide lawns below the cemetery, belonging to Yusof bin Ishak and Dr B.H. Sheares, independent Singapore's first two presidents.

Sungei Buloh Wetland Reserve

301 Neo Tiew Crescent • Free • http://nparks.gov.sg • Bus #925 from Kranji or Choa Chu Kang MRT to the Kranji reservoir car park, then a 15min walk; on Sun the bus becomes #925C from Kranji MRT and goes direct

A coastal reservoir runs through the western part of Kranji, beyond which is the **Sungei Buloh Wetland Reserve**, the island's only nature park of its kind. Expanses of mangrove and mud flats are crisscrossed by embanked trails and walkways, with views across the strait to Johor Bahru. The vegetation rapidly gets monotonous, but then **birdlife** is the main reason to come. There's a reasonable chance of spotting sandpipers, egrets and kingfishers, and between September and March, migratory birds from around Asia roost and feed here, especially in the early morning. Several **hides** dot the landscape, and you can get an elevated view over the reserve from the tallest of them, the oversized-treehouse-like **Aerie**. It's worth gazing down at the creeks, too, harbouring mudskippers, banded archerfish – which clobber insect prey by squirting water at them with their mouths – and even the occasional saltwater crocodile.

Geylang and Katong

The eastern suburbs of **Geylang** and **Katong** may seem mundane at first sight, but both have deep roots and character of the sort absent from the island's new towns.

Malay culture has held sway here since the mid-nineteenth century, when Malays and Indonesians arrived to work first in the local *copra* (dried coconut kernel) processing factory and later on its *serai* (lemongrass) farms. The eastern part of Geylang, called **Geylang Serai**, retains quite a strong Malay feel and is worth checking out for Malay food or merchandise, though there are no specific sights. Katong was once a beachfront district popular with the wealthy, including many Peranakans, who built their villas here in pre-war times. That **Peranakan heritage** lives on to some degree, and provides the main lure for visitors. You can sample what both districts have to offer by heading south from Geylang Serai to Katong via **Joo Chiat Road**, as described below. It's also quite possible that you'll end up staying in wider Geylang, since it's home to many of Singapore's more affordable places to bed down.

Geylang Serai

Paya Lebar MRT, then a short walk south and east, or bus #2 or #51 (from Chinatown) and #7 (from the Botanic Gardens and Orchard Rd), which pass through Victoria St and will drop you on Sims Ave, the main eastbound drag

Geylang has acquired a certain notoriety as something of a **red-light district**. Arrive by bus, and you'll spot numerous numbered lorongs (lanes) on the way, mainly to the right of Sims Avenue; brothels along them are recognizable by the coloured lights outside. However, Geylang is also home to the recently rebuilt **Geylang Serai Market**, which is very much the focus of the area's Malay life. A two-storey complex, it's easily spotted on the side of Sims Avenue, with sloping roofs reminiscent of certain styles of kampung house. The stalls are predominantly Malay, selling textiles, *kuih* (sweetmeats) and snacks such as *rempeyek*, delicious fried flour rounds encrusted with spices and peanuts.

Joo Chiat Road

Languid **Joo Chiat Road** is where Geylang shades into Katong, the latter now a middle-class residential area, though a little of the former's seediness spills over here after dark. The 1.5km stroll southeast into Katong proper at East Coast Road is hardly a chore thanks to several distractions, including some old businesses amid ever fancier shops.

At the northern end of the road, opposite the Geylang Serai market, the **Joo Chiat Complex** has a notable Malay/Islamic feel, the shops selling batik, rugs and silk, and Malay *jamu* – assorted herbal remedies. Occasionally a stage is set up behind for people to partake of impromptu bouts of old-fangled *joget* dancing.

The immaculate **Peranakan shophouses** on Koon Seng Road are the architectural highlight of the area, with their restored multicoloured facades, French windows, eaves and mouldings.

Katong

Bus #12 from Lavender MRT, or #14 from Dhoby Ghaut MRT; both call at Mountbatten MRT en route

From the Koon Seng Road intersection, Joo Chiat Road runs 600m on to **East Coast Road**. The beach hinted at by that name has long since gone – pushed further south by the creation of the East Coast Park on several kilometres of reclaimed land. However, the area is worth visiting thanks to a pocket of outlets celebrating its Peranakan traditions – it's not hard to find places serving Nyonya food, and there's Rumah Bebe at 113 East Coast Rd, selling clothing and jewellery (see page 523).

Katong Antiques House

208 East Coast Rd • Free entry, usually by appointment only • 6345 8544

East of the junction with Joo Chiat Road is the **Katong Antiques House**, whose former owner, Peter Wee, was a spokesman for the Peranakan community until his passing in 2018. He amassed a treasure trove of artefacts, from wedding costumes to vintage furniture and, more prosaically, old books in Baba Malay, a blend of Malay and Hokkien Chinese. Call ahead and you'll be able to take a tour of the traditionally decorated shophouse, which – as with all such buildings – stretches on for a surprising distance behind the narrow facade.

Changi

Even in the 1970s, eastern Singapore still looked the way the outskirts of some Malaysian towns do today, dotted with kampungs, low-rise housing estates and coconut palms. It's hard to visualize that landscape as you scoot out through new towns like Bedok (once a quiet seaside suburb) on the way to **Changi**, at the eastern tip of the island – home, of course, to the eponymous **airport**, justly revered around the world (see box). Flights aside, the main reason to head this far east is to see **Changi Museum**, commemorating the internment of Allied troops and civilians by the Japanese during World War II. In the Singaporean consciousness, Changi has long embodied a beachside idyll; just a bit further afield from the museum is the **beach**, which is great for a dip or bask on a hot day.

Changi Museum

1000 Upper Changi Rd North • Free • http://nhb.gov.sg • Tanah Merah or Upper Changi MRT, then a 15–20min ride on bus #2

Changi Prison was the site of an infamous World War II POW camp, where Japanese jailers subjected Allied prisoners, civilians included, to the harshest of treatment. Those brutalities are movingly remembered in the **Changi Museum** – which was once housed within the prison itself, but later moved wholesale just up the road when the prison was extended.

Novelist James Clavell drew on his experience of Changi in *King Rat*: "the stench was nauseating… stench from a generation of confined human bodies", he wrote. The museum does a reasonable job of picking over the facts of the Japanese occupation and the conditions prisoners endured. Memorable exhibits include artworks by internees, with pride of place given to reproductions of Stanley Warren's so-called **Changi Murals**, depicting New Testament scenes (the originals are housed within an army camp nearby, where Warren was held). Towards the end, there's a recreation of an improvised theatre where internees put on entertainments to amuse fellow inmates.

In the museum courtyard is a simple **wooden chapel**, typical of those erected in Singapore's wartime camps; the brass cross on its altar was crafted from spent ammunition casings. The messages on its board of remembrance are often touching and worth a read (ask staff for pen and notepaper to add your own).

Changi Point and the beach

Bus #2 from Tanah Merah MRT to Changi Point, or #19 from Tampines East MRT to the beach

Beyond Changi Museum, the tower blocks thin out and the landscape becomes a patchwork of fields, often a relic of colonial-era military bases still used by Singapore's forces. Ten minutes on via the #2 bus is the coast at **Changi Point**, with a cluster of eating places and shops called Changi Village, mainly serving the beach-going public.

Just beyond the #2 bus terminus is the **beach**, reached by a footbridge over a canalized inlet. Once you're past a stretch of manicured grass and trees, you'll reach a narrow strip of brownish sand fronting greenish-blue water – actually not uninviting (unless you were expecting something out of coastal Terengganu). The sight of aircraft rumbling in low every few minutes on the Changi flight path soon ceases to be a distraction.

> ### CHANGI AIRPORT – HOW TO DO THE PLACE JUSTICE
>
> Rarely does an airport count as a sightseeing must-see, but then again, **Changi Airport** is no normal airport by any means. A serial winner of major airport awards since its opening in 1981 (frankly, any other airports that scoop the big prizes must be paying for them somehow), it's not just a pretty airport that functions well and has affordable places to eat and drink, but something that makes many a visitor stay on a little longer than they ordinarily would.
>
> The airport's most notable, or at least most-photographed, sight is the **Jewel Rain Vortex** in T2 (land side, so you don't have to be flying to see it) – that's the official name, anyway, but more people probably know it as "that massive fountain falling from a glass roof into a jungle or something", or words to that effect. Images of the cascade are probably quite familiar to anyone who's used Instagram, TikTok, Tinder or similar apps, and it really is quite something to behold.
>
> Then, of course, there's the famed **Butterfly Garden** in T3; this one is, sadly, on the airside, so be sure to visit after landing, or before your departure (passengers can move between most terminals quite freely on the airside, as you'll notice). After passing through the double doors, you'll see colourful butterflies all over the place – some of these questing lepidopterans even choose to alight on visitors, and they're a real treat for anyone experiencing a bout of pre-flight anxiety (entomophobes aside, perhaps).
>
> Lastly, if you're staying a while at the airport by choice or necessity, many of its **eateries** are surprisingly affordable (shame on you, most other airports!), and you can have a hot meal for next to nothing by using the microwaves at branches of 7-Eleven. Not only that, but there are **massage** facilities, and loads of places in which to have a nice little **sleep** – the proper reclining chairs aside, there are plenty of patches of clean-enough carpet, plus a secret little space at the back of the **cinema** in T3 (airside), which screens films around the clock, and is thus also worthy of a special mention.

The Southern Ridges and Pasir Panjang

While no less endowed with new towns and industrial estates than the east of the island, western Singapore retains a leafier, more open feel. An unusually verdant example of this is at the **Southern Ridges**, an umbrella term for the coastal ridge that runs 9km northwest from the southern tip of the island. The ridge is lined by parks and greenery, and the whole thing can be walked using a series of ingenious footbridges and walkways.

Two minor attractions en route are **Reflections at Bukit Chandu**, a museum commemorating the wartime defence of that hill by Singapore's Malay Regiment; and **Mount Faber**, with views over downtown Singapore and cable-car rides across to Sentosa Island (see page 496). Down on the coast, **Pasir Panjang**, once a sleepy district of kampungs and still a relatively quiet residential area, is home to the entertainingly tacky Buddhist theme park of **Haw Par Villa**.

The account here takes the Southern Ridges in an easterly direction, ending at Harbourfront MRT beneath Mount Faber – a sensible choice as this avoids a steep climb up the hill and allows you to finish at the massive VivoCity mall, which has plenty of places for refreshment. Haw Par Villa is really an optional extra as far as the walk is concerned. The links between parks on the walk often offer little shade, so be assiduous about **sun protection** and bring a reasonable supply of water.

Haw Par Villa

262 Pasir Panjang Rd • Free • http://hawparvilla.sg • Haw Par Villa MRT

Delightfully unmodernized, **Haw Par Villa** is an unexpected star among Singapore's lesser-known sights. Featuring a gaudy parade of statues of people and creatures from Chinese myth and legend, it was once the estate of the brothers Aw, Boon Haw and

Boon Par, who made a fortune early in the last century selling Tiger Balm – a cure-all ointment their father devised. The grounds held their villa and private zoo, but when the British wanted to license the owning of large animals the brothers ditched the zoo for statuary; the park then gained a new moniker, a mishmash of the brothers' names.

The main path curls up and around a hill past one kitsch tableau after another. One of the best shows titanic combat as the Eight Immortals of Taoist mythology attack the Dragon King's undersea palace. Elsewhere, look out for a curious folkloric scene in which a deer and a goat, the latter talking into a bakelite telephone, take tea with a rabbit and a rat, who are newlyweds.

The centrepiece, housed in its own tunnel, is the **Ten Courts of Hell**. Here, tax dodgers and late rent-payers are pictured being "pounded with a stone mallet", while prostitutes are drowned in the "filthy blood pool"; in one tableau someone appears to be being gored to death by a giant brush. Finally, the dead are shown having their memories wiped by drinking a cup of "magic tea" prior to reincarnation.

Reflections at Bukit Chandu

31K Pepys Rd • Free • http://nhb.gov.sg • Pasir Panjang MRT, then a 10min walk north uphill

The defence of Pasir Panjang against the Japanese by the 1st and 2nd Battalion of the Malay Regiment is remembered at the tiny **Reflections at Bukit Chandu** museum. It's housed in a lone colonial building that once served as officer accommodation, though it became a food and munitions store during the war. Here "C" company of the Malay Regiment's second battalion made a brave stand against the Japanese on February 13, 1942 – two days before the British capitulation – and sustained heavy casualties.

The displays, given a thorough refresh in 2020 and now including "immersive" experiences, bring home the human toll of the conflict, as well as highlighting British ambivalence about working with the Malays: the regiment was begun as an experiment to see "how the Malays would react to military discipline", and only when they proved themselves were members sent to Singapore for further training.

Brass Lion Distillery

40 Alexandra Tce • Charge • http://brassliondistillery.com http://nhb.gov.sg • Between Pasir Panjang and Labrador Park MRTs

While the once-popular Tiger Brewery tours out west have bitten the dust, Singapore can offer a slice of something more modern, and perhaps also more tasty, at the **Brass Lion Distillery**, where some of the island's best gin is made. Here they pride themselves on using local botanicals – their Butterfly Pea gin is a slightly shameless attempt to ride South East Asia's ongoing butterfly pea bandwagon, but ingredients in this and other creations include star anise, torch ginger flower and chrysanthemum.

The canopy walk

Bear left along the ridge from the Reflections at Bukit Chandu for your first taste of the Southern Ridges trail; it also happens to be where the **canopy walk** begins. Soaring above the actual trail, the walkway takes you east through the treetops, with signs pointing out common Singapore trees such as cinnamon and *tembusu*, and views north across rolling grassy landscapes, the odd mansion poking out from within clumps of mature trees. After just a few minutes, the walkway rejoins the trail leading downhill to some nurseries and the west gate of the rather mundane **Hort Park** on Alexandra Road.

From Alexandra Arch to Mount Faber

The Alexandra Road end of Hort Park is very close to one of the huge, purpose-built footbridges on the Southern Ridges trail, the white **Alexandra Arch**, which is meant to resemble a leaf. On the bridge's east side, a long, elevated metal walkway zigzags off into the distance; it's called the **forest walk**, though it passes through nothing denser than mature woodland on its kilometre-long journey east. The walkway zigzags even more as it rises steeply to the top of **Telok Blangah Hill**, whose park offers good views of Mount Faber and Sentosa Island to the southeast.

Proceed downhill, following signs for **Henderson Waves**, and after 750m you will come to a vast footbridge of wooden slats over metal. High up in the air over broad Henderson Road, the bridge has undulating parapets – its "Waves" – containing built-in shelters against the sun or rain.

Mount Faber
On the east side of Henderson Waves and north of the VivoCity mall • Free • http://nparks.gov.sg • A stiff walk up from Harbourfront MRT

In bygone years, leafy **Mount Faber**, named in 1845 after government engineer Captain Charles Edward Faber, was a favourite recreation spot for its **views** over downtown. These days, you'll have to look out for breaks in the dense foliage for vistas over Bukit Merah new town to Chinatown and the Financial District, or head to the one of the restaurants at the very summit. The complex is also the departure point for the deluxe **cable car** to the HarbourFront Centre and on to Sentosa Island (see page 496). To descend, follow signs for the **Marang trail**, which eventually leads down a steep flight of steps on the south side of the hill to VivoCity, with the HarbourFront Centre next door.

HarbourFront Centre and VivoCity
Harbourfront MRT

On Telok Blangah Road, the **HarbourFront Centre** is nothing more than a glorified ferry terminal from where boats set off for Indonesia's Riau archipelago (see page 500), as well as a departure point for **cable cars** heading to Mount Faber and Sentosa Island. Much more worthwhile is the **VivoCity** mall, housing three good food courts (in particular *Food Republic* on level 3; see page 516), a slew of restaurants, a cinema and other amenities; from here Sentosa is just a 10min walk away.

Jurong and Tuas

Occupying a sizeable slab of southwestern Singapore, sprawling **Jurong** was notoriously dubbed "Goh's folly" in the 1960s when Goh Keng Swee, then the finance minister, decided it was vital to create a major industrial town here on unpromising swampy terrain. To the surprise of not just the avowed sceptics, the new town took off, and today the area, including neighbouring **Tuas**, boasts a diverse portfolio of industries, including pharmaceuticals and oil refining – in which Singapore is a world leader, despite having nary a drop of black gold of its own. Jurong's most significant attraction – the mammoth bird park – closed its doors in 2023 and reopened near Singapore Zoo as the Bird Paradise (see page 489), but there's still the **Singapore Science Centre** to be going along with.

Singapore Science Centre
15 Science Centre Rd • Charge • http://science.edu.sg • Jurong East MRT, then a 10min walk or bus #66 or #335

Interactivity is the watchword at the **Singapore Science Centre**, on the eastern edge of the parkland around the artificial Jurong Lake. Galleries here hold hundreds of hands-on displays focusing on genetics, space science and other disciplines, allowing you to understand fire, test your ability to hear high-pitched sounds and be befuddled by optical illusions. It goes down well with the kids on school outings, who sweep around the place in deafening waves.

> **SENTOSA'S CABLE CARS**
>
> Eight-seater **cable cars**, each with glittering lighting inside and out, shuttle between Mount Faber (see page 495) and Imbiah Lookout on Sentosa Island, calling at the HarbourFront Centre en route. The best time for **views** is at dusk, when you see Singapore lighting up from Jurong in the west to the Financial District closer by, to the northeast. The service is complemented by a branch line within Sentosa, from near the Imbiah station to Siloso Point (for Fort Siloso; same times). For more details and prices of tickets valid on both lines, see mountfaberleisure.com.

Omni-Theatre

21 Jurong Town Hall Rd • Charge; observatory free • http://science.edu.sg

Just north of the Science Centre but under the same management, the **Omni-Theatre** shows IMAX movies about the natural world, and houses an **observatory** that offers free stargazing sessions on Fridays. Being almost on the equator, Singapore enjoys views of both the northern and southern skies, though light pollution and puffy clouds can put a dampener on things.

Sentosa Island

http://sentosa.com.sg • Harbourfront MRT, then a 10min walk using the Sentosa Boardwalk footbridge from the VivoCity mall; for more on transport to/on Sentosa, see page 499

Nearly forty years of rampant development have transformed **Sentosa Island** into the most built-up of Singapore's southern islands, so it's ironic that its name means "tranquil" in Malay. The island has certainly come a long way since World War II, when it was a British military base and known as Pulau Blakang Mati ("Island of Death Behind"). Contrived but enjoyable in parts, Sentosa today is a hybrid of resort island and theme park, with **Resorts World** on its northern shore as the showpiece attraction – incorporating a Universal Studios theme park, a fabulous aquarium and casino. Just about every patch of Sentosa that isn't a beach, hotel, golf course or a home for the super-rich is a diversion of some kind, ranging from a Merlion replica, whose inside you can walk around, to a vertical wind tunnel that replicates the sensation of skydiving. The selection here covers a few of the more interesting and sensibly priced offerings.

If you want to visit, avoid the weekends and school breaks unless you don't mind the place being positively overrun, with long waits to get into the main sights. Booking tickets in advance is a good idea, not only to save time lining up but also because discounts may be available and some attractions can sell out on certain days.

Resorts World Sentosa

Close to Waterfront station on the island's north shore • http://rwsentosa.com

The **Resorts World Sentosa** casino development looks plastic, like something out of a Silicon Valley corporate headquarters, but it boasts some of Sentosa's biggest attractions.

Universal Studios Singapore

Resorts World Sentosa • Charge; combo tickets available with Singapore Oceanarium; many rides have minimum height requirements and may not be suitable for young children

The ersatz character of Resorts World becomes rather entertaining at the **Universal Studios** theme park, where fairy-tale castles and American cityscapes rear bizarrely into view in the sultry heat. The park is divided into seven themed zones, encompassing everything from ancient Egypt – the least convincing of the lot – to the newest attraction: Minion Land, which opened in 2024. Standard tickets offer unlimited rides, but there's much more to do than get flung around on cutting-edge roller coasters or, in the case of the Jurassic Park Rapids Adventure, on a circular yellow raft. Street performers regularly strut their stuff, and one particularly memorable special-effects show creates an indoor hurricane. Try to book well ahead of your visit.

Singapore Oceanarium
Resorts World Sentosa • Charge; combo tickets available with Universal Studios Singapore

A like-for-like replacement for the former SEA Aquarium, the **Singapore Oceanarium** was preparing to open its doors at the time of writing. Three times the size of its predecessor, attractions are split across 22 zones, focusing on everything from shallow waters to the deep sea – go spotting sea jellies in Ocean Wonders, local marine life in Singapore Coast, and sharks and manta rays in the Open Ocean section. In total, a whopping 10,000 sea creatures will live in this facility, including some endangered axolotls.

Adventure Cove Waterpark
Resorts World Sentosa • Charge

The Adventure Cove Waterpark is the best water-themed play park in Singapore, and by no means just for kids. The magic ingredient is actual sea life: **Rainbow Reef** lets you snorkel in the presence of thousands of fish, while at **Adventure River** you float down a channel past surreal marine-themed statues, ending up inside a glass tunnel within an aquarium tank, where the fish gawp at you drifting by. Of the rides and slides, **Riptide Rocket** is the star, a roller coaster which magnetically hoists passengers' dinghies on the upward legs.

Imbiah Lookout and around

The bulk of Sentosa's other major sights are clustered around **Imbiah Lookout**, and easily accessible from Imbiah station – or, indeed, on a simple walk from Resorts World Sentosa to Siloso Beach.

Madame Tussauds
Imbiah Lookout • Charge; book online for discounts • http://madametussauds.com/singapore • Imbiah station

The inevitable **Madame Tussauds** waxwork franchise features a sprinkling of local and East Asian figures, including Malaysian actress Michelle Yeoh, amid the usual cast of celebrities from the worlds of showbiz and sport. Its unique feature, however, is a magical illuminated boat ride down a fake river, past miniaturized Singapore scenes such as Gardens by the Bay, an Indian temple *gopuram* and a Chinese opera. From there, it heads on to **Images of Singapore Live**, which covers Singapore history using a mixture of life-sized dioramas and costumed actors.

Skyhelix Sentosa
Imbiah Lookout • Charge • http://mountfaberleisure.com • Imbiah station

The newest attraction in the area is the **Skyhelix Sentosa** tower, which affords great views, reaching 79m above the ground at its highest point. The "flight", as it's billed, takes place in an open-air gondola that rotates gently; the ride takes around 12min, though you'll most likely have to queue for longer than that, even though bookings are all timed.

Luge and Skyride
Charge • http://skylineluge.com • Beach station for Skyride, Imbiah station for Luge

Surprisingly good fun, the **Skyride**, akin to a ski lift, takes you up the hill behind Siloso Beach, after which you ride your **Luge** – a sort of small, unmotorized go-kart – and coast down one of several curving tracks back to your starting point.

> **WATERSPORTS ON SENTOSA**
>
> Siloso Beach offers a range of (often pricey) watersports. Near the start of the beach, **Ola Beach Club** (http://olabeachclub.com) has everything from kayaking to a water-based jetpack – like something out of a sci-fi movie – that allows you to hover several metres above the sea. They'll also be able to get you on a banana boat or SUP.

Megazip Adventure Park
A 5min walk west of Imbiah station • Charge • http://sg.megaadventure.com

Megazip is a zip-line or flying-fox ride, in which you slide, suspended from a steel cable, from a hilltop down to an islet beyond Siloso Beach. Other offerings include an obstacle course that's all ropes and netting, and a climbing wall.

Siloso Beach and around

The best that can be said about Sentosa's three **beaches**, created with vast quantities of imported beige sand, is that they're decent enough, with blue-green waters, the odd lagoon and facilities for renting canoes, surfboards and aqua bikes. You also get treated to a view of one of the world's busiest shipping lanes – expect a parade of container ships and other vessels, passing by all day long.

    Siloso Beach, extending 1500m northwest of Beach station, is the busiest of the three. **Palawan Beach**, in the opposite direction from Beach station, is meant to be the most family-oriented and boasts a children's play area centred on a mock galleon. It also features a suspension bridge leading out to an islet billed as the "Southernmost Point of Continental Asia" – though a sign concedes that this is so only by virtue of three artificial links, namely the bridge itself, the bridge from HarbourFront to Sentosa, and the Causeway. Beyond Palawan, **Tanjong Beach** tends to be slightly quieter than the other two as it starts a full kilometre from the station.

Skypark Sentosa
Siloso Beach, a 5min walk west of Beach station • http://skyparkglobal.com

New Zealand bungy pioneer **A J Hackett** arrived in Singapore with the 50m-tall **Skypark Sentosa** bungy tower – actually two towers, linked by a narrow bridge meant as a challenge for people with a fear of heights. You can also pay to stride down the side of one of the towers (harnessed, of course), and there are also two massive swing rides to choose from.

Fort Siloso
At the northwest tip of the island, beyond Siloso Beach • Free • 6736 8672 • Bus A from Beach station

Sentosa's one bona fide historical attraction is the sprawling **Fort Siloso**, which guarded Singapore's western approaches from the 1880s onwards; today, though, only uniformed dummies man the observation posts and gun emplacements. The **Surrender Chambers** are the focus, re-enacting the British and Japanese surrenders of 1942 and 1945, respectively, using waxwork figures. Other chambers offer a deeper analysis of British military failings in the region than anything at the National Museum, although the history can be confused: some panels spin the old story that Singapore's guns were pointing the wrong way as they were meant to deter a naval attack from the south, while others present the revisionist idea that the guns could turn to fire northwards, but were ineffective. Oddly, Japanese labelling is almost ubiquitous, as if sending a none-too-subtle "don't try that again" message.

Wings of Time
At the start of Siloso Beach • Charge • http://mountafaberleisure.com • Beach station

The minority of visitors who hang around Sentosa after dusk are either heading to one of the beach bars (see pages 518 and 518) or to **Wings of Time**, a kids' fable cast as a lavish sound-and-light show, featuring pyrotechnics, lasers and live actors. Most of the action takes place on a series of offshore platforms, as well as aerial screens of water and mist, with seating right at the beach to take it all in.

ARRIVAL AND DEPARTURE   SINGAPORE

Most visitors fly into Changi International Airport, in the east of the island, or arrive by bus via the 1km-long Causeway that links Johor Bahru to the island (although some buses use the Second Link bridge into Tuas in the west). Unbeknown to most visitors, there is actually a second airport in Singapore, though precious few use it.

BY PLANE

CHANGI AIRPORT

Singapore's multi-award-winning airport (http://changi airport.com), 16km from downtown at the eastern tip of the island, is well laid out and runs like clockwork – the country in microcosm – and is deemed by many to be the best on the planet. There are four terminals, connected by free Skytrains. Chances are you'll not linger long – baggage comes through so swiftly that you can be heading to the city centre within twenty minutes of arrival – but with a butterfly park, massage rooms and a great choice of places to eat within the terminals (not to mention the world's tallest indoor waterfall just outside), it can certainly be tempting to stay a while (see box page 493). Connections with Malaysia and Brunei include:

Destinations Bandar Seri Begawan (2–3 daily; 2hr); Ipoh (2–3 daily; 1hr 30min); Kota Kinabalu (3 daily; 2hr 20min); Kuala Lumpur (KLIA; 1–4 hourly; 55min); Kuala Lumpur (at least 6 daily; 1hr); Kuching (3–4 daily; 1hr 20min); Langkawi (2–3 daily; 1hr 30min); Miri (4 weekly; 2hr); Penang (11 daily; 1hr 20min).

Onward transport Between 6am–11.15pm, the easiest way to get into the city centre from the airport is on an MRT train (change to adjacent platform at Tanah Merah; 30min); the station is beneath terminals 2 and 3. Alternatively, bus #36 (same hours, every 10min) heads to the Orchard Rd area via Marina Centre and the Colonial District, though it takes far longer. Transport desks at each terminal can also book you onto the 24hr airport shuttle buses, which serve most downtown hotels and hostels. A taxi downtown costs takes

TRANSPORT FOR SENTOSA

There are multiple ways to reach the island other than walking, the most popular of which is the **Sentosa Express** monorail. Note that all the options here include the island entry fee in the fare, and that **taxi** journeys to and from the island incur a small surcharge, with price dependent on the time of day.

An **information point** at the end of the Sentosa Boardwalk where you arrive dispenses free **maps** (also available at monorail stations and from http://sentosa.com.sg), which are especially handy given that new venues and sights seem to replace others every few months. Alternatively, download the **MySentosa app**.

GETTING TO SENTOSA

By monorail The Sentosa Express operates every 5min from level 3 of the VivoCity mall. See below for details of stops on the island. Note that the ride back to VivoCity is free; the one out incurs a charge.

By bus Bus #123 heads to Resorts World from Orchard Rd. At weekends there are one-way night buses #NR1 and #NR6 from Resorts World to Marina Bay, the Colonial District, Clarke Quay and Orchard Rd, with NR#6 continuing to Little India.

TRANSPORT ON THE ISLAND

All transport on Sentosa itself is free.

By bus The island has two buses that run on loop routes until midnight, plus a so-called beach tram running the length of the southern beaches; all services are charted on the free island maps.

By monorail The Sentosa Express calls at Waterfront station on the northern shore (for Resorts World), Imbiah station a little further south, and Beach station on the southern shore, for the three beaches. While rides are free on the island, you'll have to pay for tickets when arriving or departing in this manner.

up to half an hour. You can also head straight to Johor Bahru on Transtar buses (daily every 2hrs 8.15am–11.15pm from terminal 2; 1hr 45min; http://transtar.travel).

SELETAR AIRPORT
Singapore's lesser-known second airport (http://seletarairport.com), around 25km north of the CBD, is mainly used by prop planes and private jets, but to help you avoid the shame of turning up at the wrong airport (which never feels great), there is one service to KL's Subang Airport with Firefly, plus occasional charter flights. From the airport, bus #102 runs to Sengkang MRT, though it's often far faster to get off at Thanggam LRT station and proceed from there.
Destinations Kuala Lumpur (Subang; 7 daily; 1hr 20min).

BY TRAIN
Malaysian trains run a shuttle service a dozen times a day between Woodlands station near the Causeway checkpoint and Johor Bahru – a 5min journey. If you arrive at Woodlands station, you can catch bus #170 to Bukit Panjang MRT. For those wanting to head to KL or the east coast by train, it's sometimes easier to get a bus to the Causeway and walk through immigration, then continue to JB's train station on foot, though crowding and queuing can make this a stressful journey at peak times.

BY BUS
In the absence of a long-distance bus terminal, most buses terminate at, and leave from, the Beach Rd area. Heading to Malaysia, note that you don't have to buy a ticket from Singapore; it's cheaper to catch a local bus from the Queen St terminal to Johor Bahru's Larkin bus station, where you can pick up the very same buses for much less money (with additional routes to the east coast too). With so many companies to choose from, it's often better to look for tickets on websites such as Redbus (http://redbus.my) or Easybook (http://easybook.com). For details on crossing the Causeway, see page 277.
Golden Mile Complex/Golden Mile Tower Most bus companies serving west coast destinations beyond KL and also Hat Yai in Thailand are based at these two neighbouring shopping/office complexes (5001/6001 Beach Rd), including Grassland Express (6292 1166), Sri Maju (http://srimaju.com) and Starmart Express (http://starmartonline.com). Any westbound city bus from outside the complex will take you to City Hall MRT station, while Nicoll Highway station is a 10min walk away.
Destinations Alor Setar (2 daily; 12hr 30min); Cameron Highlands (1 daily; 10hr); Gopeng (3 daily; 8hr); Hat Yai (Thailand; 3 daily; 14hr); Ipoh (7 daily; 8hr 30min); Kamunting (for Taiping; 2 daily; 9hr 30min); KLIA (7 daily; 5hr); KLIA2 (4 daily; 5hr); Kuala Kangsar (2 daily; 9hr); Kuala Lumpur (at least hourly; 6hr); Lumut (for Pangkor; 1 daily; 9hr 30min); Melaka (at least 8 daily; 3hr 30min); Penang (5 daily; 10hr 30min); Seremban (9 daily; 5hr); Sungai Petani (1 daily; 11hr); TBS (9 daily; 5hr).
Queen St Terminal Johor Bahru buses use this terminal near Bugis MRT, including #170 (daily 5.30am–12.30am; every 15min; 1hr–1hr 30min) and two nonstop services, the Singapore–Johor Express (6am–10pm; every 10min) and the Causeway Link #CW2 (6am–11.45pm; 2–4 hourly; http://causewaylink.com.my). Hang on to your ticket at immigration so you can use it to resume your journey (on the same service, though not necessarily on the same vehicle) once you're through. These buses terminate at JB's Larkin bus station; if you want to reach the town centre, leave the bus at the Causeway. There's also a rank for shared taxis to JB (6296 7054). One long-distance bus company, 707-Inc, uses Queen St for services to Melaka (10 daily; 3hr 30min; http://707-inc.com).

BY FERRY
Indonesia Ferries serving Batam, Bintan and Karimun in Indonesia's Riau archipelago use either the HarbourFront Centre on Telok Blangah Rd ("RFT" in some timetables; HarbourFront MRT) or Tanah Merah ferry terminal in the east of Singapore, linked by bus #35 to Tanah Merah and Bedok MRT stations. For timetables and ferry companies see http://singaporecruise.com.sg; note that to Batam there are several choices of route, with Harbour Bay usually the most

---

SINGAPORE ADDRESSES AND MAPS

Addresses linked to high-rise towers, shopping complexes and other buildings are generally written using two numbers preceded by #, as in #XX-YY. Here XX is the floor (ground level is 01, the next floor up 02, the first basement B01, and so on) while YY is the unit number – thus a restaurant whose address includes #04-08 can be found in unit 8 on the building's fourth storey. All buildings within municipal housing and industrial estates have a **block number** displayed prominently on the side, rather than a number relating to their position on the street.

The usual **online mapping** services cover Singapore pretty well, and they can come in handy as restaurants, shops and even hostels sometimes move their premises because of rent hikes downtown.

> ### USEFUL BUS ROUTES
>
> A few handy **bus routes** are listed below. One-way systems downtown mean that services using Orchard Road and Bras Basah Road in one direction return via Stamford Road, Penang Road, Somerset Road and Orchard Boulevard; buses up Selegie and Serangoon roads return via Jalan Besar and Bencoolen Street; and services along North and South Bridge roads and New Bridge Road return via Eu Tong Sen Street, Hill Street and Victoria Street.
>
> **#7** From the Botanic Gardens to Orchard Road, Bras Basah Road and Victoria Street (for Kampong Glam), then on to Geylang Serai.
>
> **#36** Loops between Orchard Road and Changi airport via the Marina Centre and the Singapore Flyer.
>
> **#65** Orchard Road to Little India and on up Serangoon Road.
>
> **#170** From the Queen Street terminal to Bukit Panjang MRT (shadowing the MRT's Downtown line), then all the way to the Larkin terminal in Johor Bahru. Note that #170A runs the same route but terminates just before the Causeway.
>
> **#174** Between the Botanic Gardens and the Baba House in Neil Road, via Orchard Road, the Colonial District, Boat Quay and Chinatown.

suitable target.

Malaysia From the Changi Point terminal near Changi Beach, humble bumboats sail when full to Pengerang, just east of Singapore in the Straits of Johor (daily 7am–4pm; 45min). There are also ferries to Tanjung Belungkor, just northeast of Singapore (2–4 daily; 30min). In the unlikely event you arrive on one of these routes, catch bus #2 to pick up the MRT at Tanah Merah station.

GETTING AROUND

Just about all parts of Singapore are accessible by **bus** or the **MRT** (Mass Rapid Transit) metro system. **Fares** are eminently reasonable and usually rise in tiny steps depending on the distance travelled. Two companies run most of the public transport network: **SBS Transit** (http://sbstransit.com.sg) and **SMRT** (http://smrt.com.sg). Their websites can help with journey planning, but more comprehensive advice is available on the (rather flawed) MyTransport app, and the Google Maps site and app work pretty well here too.

TICKETS

These days, most city passengers aren't using tickets at all anymore – in 2019, Singapore introduced the **SimplyGo** system, which means that you can tap in and out of metro stations or buses using a **bank card** (foreign ones too), or **mobile wallet**. One downside of this is that you don't always get to see how much journeys are costing you (or that you're not actually paying to change between trains and buses). You can still use **cash**, at least for now, though it's slowly being phased out of operations – it's already buses only, and with no change given.

EZ-link card Some still prefer to get around using stored-value EZ-link cards (http://ezlink.com.sg). You can buy these at most MRT stations, post offices and 7-11 stores, with stored credit equal to the purchase price (minus a bit for the card itself). The cards, which also work as debit cards in some shops and taxis, can be topped up at ticket offices or using ticket machines, and remain valid for at least five years.

Singapore Tourist Pass For short-stay visitors, Singapore Tourist Passes (http://thesingaporetouristpass.com.sg) can save money. Sold in visitor centres (see page 504) and a few MRT stations, including the one at the airport, they grant 1/2/3 days of unlimited travel (excluding special services such as night buses), for a refundable deposit. Once the pass expires, it can be topped up and used like an ez-link card. To reclaim the deposit, return the card within five days of purchase.

THE MRT

Using Singapore's MRT network (map page 502) is straightforward, although note that you're not allowed to eat, drink or smoke on trains. Signs in the stations appear to ban hedgehogs as well, but actually signify "no durians". Using mobile phones (quietly) is okay, though – and they even work in the tunnels.

Hours Trains run every five minutes, on average, from 6am until midnight downtown.

Payment No cash – contactless payments only, including stored-value cards, international bank cards, and mobile wallets.

LRT Three LRT (Light Rail Transit) networks connect suburban estates with the MRT. As a tourist, you're unlikely to make use of any of them.

BUSES

Singapore's bus network is so comprehensive that the sheer profusion of routes can be confusing. Many bus stops do,

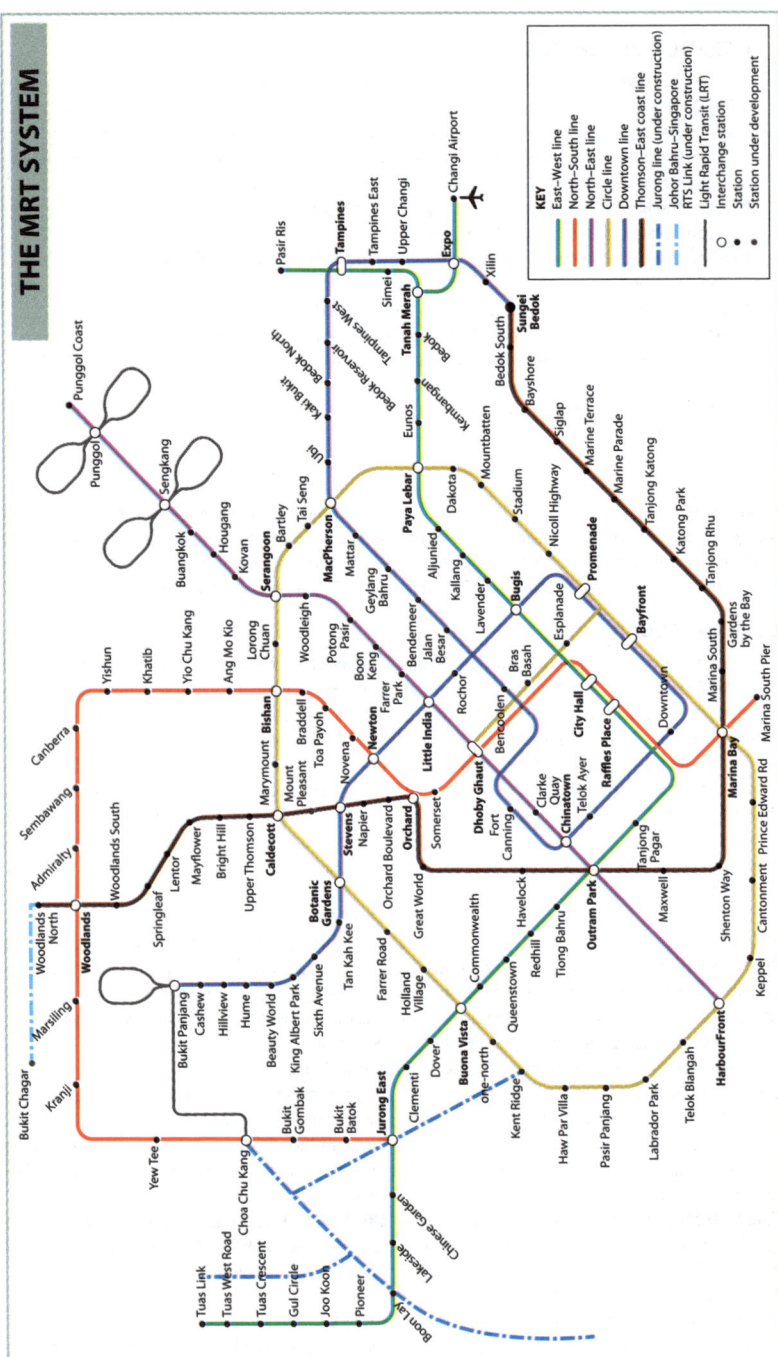

however, display lists of destinations served by each route.

Hours Buses start running around 6am and wind down from 11.30pm; the very last regular buses leave downtown around 12.30am. Between midnight and 2am a few Night-Rider (prefixed "NR") and Nite Owl (suffixed "N") buses are available. They are one-way services that cross the downtown area and then run as express services to the outlying new towns.

Fares As with the MRT, fares are usually cheap, but a bit more if paying by cash (which some buses no longer accept; those that do no longer give change). If paying by card, remember to tap the reader both after getting on *and* before disembarking.

TAXIS

Thousands of taxis roam the streets of Singapore, so you'll seldom have trouble hailing a cab – except late at night, or when demand soars during a tropical downpour. This being the modern day, you've a choice of regular taxis, or app-based alternatives.

Ride-hailing apps Now Uber has stopped operating in Singapore, Grab (http://grab.com/sg) is the most-used app, with Gojek and Ryde also alternatives; all will continue to be pretty useful if you're on a wider South East Asia trip (Grab especially so in Malaysia).

Regular taxis All drivers use their meters, the fare rising every 400m or so (classier limousine taxis cost 30 percent more). There are annoying surcharges: an extra 25 percent is payable Mon–Fri 6–9.30am & 6pm–midnight, Sat & Sun 6pm–midnight, and 50 percent extra nightly between midnight and 6am. Journeys involving Changi airport or the casinos incur a surcharge of several dollars, as do phone bookings. Fares also factor in road usage tolls on journeys along expressways and within the downtown area. You can pay using your card. On the whole, drivers are friendly, but their English isn't always good; if you're heading off the beaten track, be aware of a landmark they can aim for. Note that in the downtown area, queuing at a taxi rank is supposed to be compulsory Mon–Sat 7.30am–8pm, though some drivers will ignore this rule to pick up passengers on quieter roads.

RIVER TAXIS AND CRUISES

Shuttling between Robertson Quay and Marina Bay, river taxis are pricey but still a lot cheaper than Singapore River cruise trips (Mon–Thurs 1–10am, Fri–Sun 10am–10pm; every 10min; http://rivercruise.com.sg); the latter are quite appealing, though, especially after dusk descends and the city lights turn on.

DRIVING

Car rental Given the excellent public transport, there's hardly any reason to rent a car in Singapore, especially considering it's a pricey business. Major disincentives to driving are in place to combat traffic congestion: a permit just to own a car costs more than many cars themselves. If you were thinking of driving up into Malaysia, it's far cheaper to rent a car in JB. If you must rent in Singapore itself, contact Avis (http://avis.com.sg) or Hertz (http://hertz.com); both have offices at Changi airport.

Tolls Drivers have to pay tolls to enter a restricted zone encompassing Chinatown, Orchard Rd and the Financial District, and to use many of the island's expressways. This being Singapore, it's all done in the most hi-tech way using Electronic Road Pricing (ERP) – all cars have a gizmo that reads a stored-value CashCard, from which the toll is deducted as you drive past an ERP gantry.

Parking Generally expensive, though at least many car parks offer the convenience of taking the fee off your CashCard, failing which you have to purchase coupons from a booth, post office or shop, or the Parking.sg app.

Driving to or from Malaysia To drive a Malaysian car into Singapore, you need to buy a stored-value Autopass card and rent a card reader; both are available at the Causeway or Second Link. Thus equipped, you can pay your vehicle entry toll and road tolls in Singapore. For more on this and other matters to do with driving in Singapore, see http://lta.gov.sg. To use expressways in Malaysia, you're

---

ORGANIZED TOURS

Singapore is so easy to navigate that there's little reason to do an **organized tour**, which is perhaps why the range of offerings tends to be uninspired. Many seem to feature transport as a key element, whether that be a dedicated tourist bus, a Singapore River boat (see page 457 for more on river trips), a novelty vehicle, or the **trishaw**, which at least hearkens back to the island's past.

DuckTours http://ducktours.com.sg. Tour the Colonial District and Marina Bay on an amphibious vehicle (daily 10am–6pm).

The Original Singapore Walks http://journeys.com.sg. Guided walks of historic downtown areas and Changi (the latter with a wartime focus), generally lasting 2hr 30min.

Singapore Nature Society http://nss.org.sg. If your stay in Singapore is an extended one, consider taking out annual membership of this conservation group, which conducts guided nature walks, birdwatching trips and so forth.

likely to need a Touch N' Go card.

CYCLES AND SCOOTERS

Despite the clammy heat, tropical downpours and furious traffic, cycling is starting to take off in Singapore, with a handful of bike lanes now in existence and the government publicly committed to making the island more cyclist-friendly in future. Even so, cycling downtown can be tricky unless you have some familiarity with the roads, and bicycles aren't allowed on expressways.

Parks and beaches Bikes come into their own in recreational areas and nature parks, which are linked by a park connector network; see http://nparks.gov.sg. The East Coast Park, on the southeast shore of the island, has a popular cycle track with rental outlets along the way (bring along some form of ID). You'll also find bike rental at Changi and Siloso beaches (the latter on Sentosa).

Rental apps Numerous bike-sharing schemes have come and gone in Singapore; Hello Ride (http://helloride-global.com) and Anywheel (http://anywheel.sg) were the main players at the time of writing. You'll see locals zipping around on e-scooters, though as a visitor it's a little hard to do likewise – banned outright in 2019, they're now only allowed on dedicated cycle paths, and even then only to those who pass a theory test.

INFORMATION

Heritage trails Although targeted at a local audience, leaflets describing Singapore neighbourhoods and a few walking trails can be viewed on, and downloaded from, http://roots.gov.sg.

Internet access There's a nationwide free wi-fi network, Wireless@SGx, available in shopping malls and some MRT stations and public buildings.

Listings The best of several publications carrying entertainment listings and restaurant reviews is *SG Magazine* (http://sgmagazine.com).

Visitor centres The Singapore Tourism Board (STB; helpline Mon–Fri 9am–6pm; 1800 736 2000, http://visitsingapore.com) bills its tourist offices as visitor centres. Their main downtown location is at 216 Orchard Road (daily 8.30am–9.30pm; Somerset MRT). Much smaller are their counter on the ground floor of the ION Orchard mall (daily 10am–10pm; above Orchard MRT), and their Chinatown office at 2 Banda St, behind the Buddha Tooth Relic Temple (daily 9am–9pm; Chinatown MRT).

ACCOMMODATION

If one thing leaves a nasty taste in the mouth in Singapore, it's the price of **accommodation**; even a lower-mid-range double room now nudges S$140 a night. On the plus side, most accommodation is of a high standard for the price, and rates have been drifting lower in recent years. Budget travellers have a plethora of centrally located **hostels** and **guesthouses** to choose from, often with upmarket decor and fittings, and increasingly offering capsule berths to sleep in rather than bunk beds; Chinatown and Little India are the best areas for these (see page 506 for more by-area advice about where to stay in Singapore). Most **hotels** are blandly modern, but there are plenty of **boutique hotels**, usually characterful or quirky affairs in refurbished shophouses. One thing to note is that any hotel advertising hourly or "transit" rates tends to be used by locals for illicit liaisons – normally only obviously seedy hotels stoop to this, though the ubiquitous and otherwise well-managed budget chain *Hotel 81* was tainted by this in the past, and *K Hotel* still very much is. Most establishments, even hostels, adjust prices year-round in line with demand, and those that do not will offer **promotional rates** most of the time, except during the Formula One race in the third week of September. The prices here are meant to be typical starting prices, including taxes, if you reserve reasonably early. Besides contacting places directly, you can also book through the usual online search sites, such as http://agoda.com, http://booking.com and http://hostelworld.com.

HOSTELS AND GUESTHOUSES

LITTLE INDIA, SEE MAP PAGE 465

★ **Dream Lodge** 172 Tyrwhitt Rd; http://dreamlodge.sg. This comfy, superbly run hostel boasts plush capsule beds with privacy drapes and lockers beneath. There's a cosy lounge with a quirky wall drawing of Singapore landmarks by a young student, and bike rental is on offer. $

The Hive 624A Serangoon Rd; 8168 4337. While a little far out, this is a delightful little place, with space-pod berths (de rigeur in Singapore for years; where was that idea in the early 2000s?) with good bedding, and a hang-out area that, while not terribly cosy, does make a good place in which to meet new travel buddies. $

Spacepod@Lavender 111J King George's Ave; 6683 2924. Way up by Lavender, this is one of the best picks in an area full of hostels, serving (relatively) generous breakfasts, and providing the space-age capsule berths that seem to be de rigeur at Singapore hostels these days. $

ARAB STREET (KAMPONG GLAM), SEE MAP PAGE 465

★ **Dream Chaser** 38 Sultan Gate; http://dream-chaser.sg. "Boutique capsule hostel" that has put some admirable effort into making itself look the part, from rattan curves on the dorm berths (not really necessary, but kinda cool-looking) to funk floor tiling. Even the reception looks

ACCOMMODATION PRICE CODES

All accommodation reviewed in this Guide is accompanied by a price category, based on the cost of a basic room for two (or two dorm beds, in the case of hostels) in high season. Price ranges don't include breakfast, unless stated otherwise. For camping, prices are given per pitch. The codes for **Singapore** are as follows:
$ = under SGD100
$$ = SGD100–200
$$$ = SGD200–350
$$$$ = over SGD350

pretty; it's one of those places to which you look forward to returning in the evening. $
Met A Space Pod 56 Arab St; http://metaspacepod.com.sg. This hostel has hi-tech capsule beds which can give you the impression of climbing into a washing machine drum, if not your own personal cylinder on a spaceship. Each bed has a built-in control panel, TV and safe. The kitchen, bathrooms and breakfasts are much more down to earth; however, it's not quite as good as its predecessor in Clarke Quay, and not just in terms of location. $
★ **The Pod** 289 Beach Rd; http://thepodcapsulehotel.com. Ultra-slick designer place where you check yourself in using an electronic kiosk. Their slogan is "pay for the stay, everything else is free" – and that includes use of their laundry facilities and laptops, plus a cooked breakfast. As the name suggests, all beds are capsule-style, and there are even "suites", rooms with one or two solitary pods. Prices rise by twenty percent at weekends. $$

CHINATOWN AND AROUND, SEE MAP PAGE 472

Beary Best 16 Upper Cross St; http://bearybesthostel.com. A spick-and-span hostel decorated in bright colours and, as the name suggests, bears – ursine stuffed toys litter the place. Beds come with individual reading lights, there's a self-service laundry, and the management offers bike rental and tours. $
★ **The Bohemian** 40 Mosque St; http://facebook.com/bohemianhostelsingapore. Not truly Bohemian, but appealingly quirky, with glittery masks like something from a Baroque-era ball lining one wall in the lounge. No dorm has more than eight beds (choose from capsules or cheaper double-deckers), and breakfast includes sandwiches in additional to the self-service basics. $
Royal Lodge 66A/B Pagoda St; http://royalhostel.com.sg. An unexciting but competently run place with ten- or twelve-bed dorms and lots of pastel colours, just footsteps from the MRT station. Good value for Chinatown. $
★ **Wink** 8A Mosque St; http://winkhostel.com. One of the best designer hostels in town, with capsule beds (including some doubles), each inside flower-themed rooms with colour-coded lighting to match. Facilities include an upstairs kitchen and lounge, and free use of a tablet computer for every guest. They have three other branches elsewhere. $$

THE FINANCIAL DISTRICT, SEE MAP PAGE 472

★ **Kinn Habitat** 5 Hongkong St; http://staywithkinn.com. Marginally the more appealing of two almost-adjacent *Kinn* properties, with highly attractive, pine-lined dorms, affordable private rooms, and just about every possible place painted a fetching pastel pink. This is also true of the room that looks for all the world like a trendy cafe – oh wait, that's because it is a trendy cafe (*Brwd/Kinn*; see page 515). $$
River City Inn 33 Hongkong St; http://rivercityinn.com. Family-run hostel that's surprisingly homely, given its location by the Financial District tower blocks. Old-school bunks, rather than capsule berths, remain the way of things here; breakfast is free, and they'll let you use showers and other hostel facilities until 10pm on your checkout date. $

ORCHARD ROAD AND AROUND, SEE MAP PAGE 484

YMCA 1 Orchard Rd; http://ymcaoneorchard.org.sg. This place is predictably staid and the rooms are plain, but nowhere downtown do you get amenities like a pool and gym at the prices charged here (except, as it happens, at the *YWCA* nearby). $$

GEYLANG AND KATONG, SEE MAPS PAGES 453 AND 490

Betel Box 200 Joo Chiat Rd; http://betelbox.com. Styling itself as Singapore's socially committed hostel, *Betel Box* tries to highlight the island's heritage by organizing tours of interesting neighbourhoods. A 15min walk from Paya Lebar MRT, or bus #33 from Kallang, Kembangan or Dakota MRT. $
CapsulePod@Aljunied 76A Lorong 27; 9025 1453. One of the most popular of Singapore's many, *many* capsule hostels, despite its lack of a website and out-of-the-way location. It's hard to pin down exactly why it's so popular, but mainly it seems to stem from a ticking of all the little boxes – clean bathrooms, good showers, winning staff, and proximity to an MRT station. $

HOTELS

THE COLONIAL DISTRICT, SEE MAP PAGE 454

Fort Canning 11 Canning Walk, northern side of Fort

ACCOMMODATION BY AREA

There are major differences in price level, as well as atmosphere and proximity to the sights you'd like to visit. Here's a little run-down of what to expect accommodation-wise, area by area.

THE COLONIAL DISTRICT

The area immediately north and east of the Singapore River has surprisingly few places to stay, all higher-end hotels; needless to say, the extra bucks put you right in the thick of the action.

BRAS BASAH ROAD TO ROCHOR ROAD

The grid of streets between Bras Basah Road and Rochor Road (and a bit beyond, uphill from Selegie Road) has been rendered a bit sterile by redevelopment, but remains a good choice if you can afford it; it's within easy walking distance of the Singapore River, Little India and the eastern end of Orchard Road.

LITTLE INDIA

Little India proper and beyond – the zone extending up to Lavender Street, reachable via Farrer Park or Lavender stations – has some decent budget accommodation, although hotels can be hit and miss. There's also a knot of cheapies (often rivalling Geylang for price) on Balestier Road, near Novena, though it's a bit of a walk from the nearest MRT station.

ARAB STREET (KAMPONG GLAM)

The area around Arab Street doesn't have as many places to stay as Little India proper, but there are some good budget options here, and it's in more or less the same part of town.

CHINATOWN AND AROUND

Chinatown runs a close second to Little India and Lavender Street in its selection of guesthouses, and also boasts a good many upmarket and boutique hotels.

THE FINANCIAL DISTRICT

There are only a few hotels amid the office towers of the Financial District. It's an interesting place to stay in, in its own way, and proximity to Chinatown and the Colonial District make it worth considering. Boat Quay, right on the south bank of the Singapore River, is dominated by restaurants and bars but also has a few worthwhile options.

MARINA BAY

Marina Bay accommodation is synonymous with modern four- and five-star affairs, all located at the rather bland Marina Centre district next to Beach Road.

ORCHARD ROAD

You generally pay a premium to stay in the Orchard Road shopping area, which is modern and great for the malls, though it's hardly the most interesting part of downtown. It's also where most of Singapore's best serviced apartments are located.

GEYLANG AND KATONG

With the range of accommodation available downtown, there are few compelling reasons to stay in the suburbs – except to save a little money, which is obviously not to be sniffed at. Katong, with its Peranakan heritage and good restaurants, is as good a choice as any, though note that some of neighbouring Geylang's seediness can spill over into Joo Chiat Road after dark.

SENTOSA

Staying on Sentosa isn't such a bad idea, especially if you have young children. Note that prices can rise by twenty percent over weekends and holidays.

Canning Hill; http://hfcsingapore.com. A plush boutique hotel housed in a former British military building; rooms are spacious, immaculately decorated and boast bathtubs that are, curiously, often smack in the middle of the room or out towards the window. There are pools on two levels and lush gardens. The one snag: it's a bit of a trek up flights of steps from Dhoby Ghaut MRT and Orchard Rd. $$$

Swissôtel The Stamford 2 Stamford Rd; http://swissotel.com. The upper-floor rooms, restaurants and bars aren't for those with vertigo, though the views are as splendid as you'd expect from one of the tallest hotels in the world, with over 1200 rooms tucked into its 60-plus floors. Perhaps even more impressive is the fact it has a MRT station (City Hall) in the basement, and a big sports facility with two pools and several tennis courts. $$$$

Wyndham Singapore 3 Coleman St; http://wyndhamsingapore.com. Formerly the *Peninsula Excelsior*, this was recently given a major revamp and rebranded as a *Wyndham* property. It's really two hotels fused together – as hinted at by the presence of two swimming pools at either end, one of which abuts the current lobby – and nicely modernized, unlike the 1970s shopping arcades below. $$$

BRAS BASAH ROAD TO ROCHOR ROAD, SEE MAP PAGE 462

Carlton 76 Bras Basah Rd; http://carltonhotel.sg. Boasting a lobby dominated by a spidery glass artwork suspended from the ceiling, this towering four-star hotel has elegant rooms in two wings, plus a pool, spa and gym – and good rates for what's on offer. $$$

InterContinental 80 Middle Rd; http://ihg.com. Like the adjoining Bugis Junction mall, the *InterContinental* incorporates some of the area's original shophouses, here converted into "heritage rooms" designed along Peranakan lines, though this largely amounts to dark wood floors and paintings of tropical fruit. Still, the hotel is luxurious and has all the amenities you could want; breakfasts can be a real treat. $$$$

JW Marriott South Beach 30 Beach Rd; http://marriott.com. Dominating the northern Padang skyline, the box-grater-like towers of the South Beach development incorporate some colonial buildings and this impressive hotel. The lobby – all individually styled chill-out spaces, certainly makes a statement, as do the 600-plus über-chic rooms, the work of French designer Philippe Starck. One of the two pools has glorious views out over the Padang. Nearest stations are Esplanade or City Hall MRT. $$$$

★ **Lyf Bugis** 200 Middle Rd; http://discoverasr.com. This co-living hotel occupies a converted office building, which is perhaps why there's a touch of post-industrial chic about the rooms; all are well soundproofed and feature pale wood floors and furniture. The entire ground floor is taken up by two restaurants, and note that this ASR brand usually spells "Lyf" (pronounced as "leaf") with a small L, which looks rather like an I, and can confuse matters when searching for the place on your phone. $$

Naumi 41 Seah St; http://naumihotels.com. The slate-grey exterior with what look like vines creeping up doesn't inspire, but inside is a fine boutique hotel where rooms are kitted out like a slick apartment. The rooftop infinity pool looks out over the *Raffles* hotel, with the Financial District's towers beyond. Rooms on one floor are reserved for women only. $$$$

Raffles 1 Beach Rd; http://raffles.com. Though the modern extension is a mixed bag, the *Raffles* remains refreshingly low-rise and still has colonial-era charm in spades, especially evident in the opulent lobby and the courtyards fringed by frangipani trees and palms. Amenities include oodles of restaurants and bars, a rooftop pool and a spa. All rooms are suites, and there's a round-the-clock butler service – plus, of course, the world-famous *Long Bar* (see page 517). $$$$

The Snooze 103 Beach Rd; http://snooze-inn.com. This simple hotel is surprisingly comfortable, the rooms done out in soothing tones, which is a nice surprise given how colourful the building's exterior is. A good deal, and breakfast can be added for very little extra. $$

LITTLE INDIA, SEE MAP PAGE 465

The Daulat 16 Madras St; http://hotelcalmo.co. This tiny hotel has an equally tiny rooftop pool, a sliver of water that's 10m long but barely wide enough for two to pass; it still provides welcome relief from the heat. Rooms can be boxy, but some have unusual touches, including upstairs bathrooms in the suites. Rates include breakfast. $$

Haising 37 Jalan Besar; http://haising.com.sg. Friendly, secure Chinese-run cheapie offering simple, a/c en-suite rooms with TVs; rather boxy, but not bad for the price. $

Hilton Garden Inn 3 Belilios Rd; http://hilton.com. Towering over Little India, this representative of *Hilton*'s mid-range brand offers understated contemporary decor, a small outdoor pool and some great vistas out over the surrounding shophouses from rooms higher up. Good value. $$$

Ibis Budget Imperial 28 Penhas Rd; http://all.accor.com. Despite the drab, yellow exterior, this is a cut above fellow members of the budget chain, with slick if smallish rooms, a café and rooftop swimming pool. Rates include breakfast. $$

Mayo Inn 9 Jalan Besar; http://facebook.com/mayoinnsg. There are just two dozen rooms in this cosy budget hotel, some featuring what's billed as a Japanese-style "bed" – a wooden dais with a mattress on top. Breakfast included. $$

★ **The Sultan** 101 Jalan Sultan; http://thesultan.com.sg. A pleasant, relatively low-key hotel occupying a series of tastefully refurbished shophouses. Take your pick from, among others, a handful of cosy singles plus so-called attic rooms on the top floor, which are a little quieter than the rest. Excellent value, with breakfast included. $$

Traveltine 700 Beach Rd; http://hoteltraveltine.com. A decent mid-range option with bland but nicely soundproofed rooms, in a modern tower. The rooftop pool has good views out towards Marina Bay. $$

Wanderlust 2 Dickson Rd; http://oakwood.com. Appealingly wacky, *Wanderlust* has an "industrial glam" lobby with barber's chairs, and many rooms are colour-themed, some even with multicoloured lighting you can program. Facilities include a jacuzzi and French restaurant. Rates include breakfast. $$$

Yan 162 Tyrwhitt Rd; http://hotel-yan.com. Industrial-chic to the max at this hotel, whose rooms often showcase an inventive use of space – others might call them stylishly cramped, and the bathrooms often offer little privacy, but otherwise it's a good-value place to stay in an interesting area. $$

CHINATOWN AND AROUND, SEE MAP PAGE 472

Amoy 76 Telok Ayer St; http://fareasthospitality.com. Entered via the Fuk Tai Chi Museum, this hotel manages to squeeze the best out of every nook and cranny of its shophouse conversion. Rooms are on the small side, but feature the odd unusual touch such as slat-floored bathrooms through which water drains away. $$$

Claude 12 Teck Lim Rd; http://claudehotel.com. Not bad for the price and location, this trendy little hotel has rooms that are comfortable enough, even though the glass-fronted bathrooms in some may make goings-on a little too visible for some tastes. Be sure to check out the snazzy bar. $$

Clover 5 Hongkong St; http://hotelclover.com. Functional, contemporary rooms in a six-storey building crowned by a small rooftop pool. Their sister hotel, round the corner, offers slightly bigger rooms with funky murals and access to the same pool, for about ten percent more. $$

Hotel 1929 50 Keong Saik Rd; http://hotel1929.com. This shophouse hotel looks genuinely 1929 on the outside, but the interior has been renovated to look like a twenty-first-century version of the early 1960s, all very retro chic. $$

Parkroyal On Pickering 3 Upper Pickering St; http://panpacific.com. Looming over Hong Lim Park, this is one of Singapore's most architecturally striking hotels since *Marina Bay Sands* and likewise has three towers, linked by curvy-sided rice-terrace-like structures overflowing with vegetation. The use of wood and glass throughout emphasizes the natural theme, in part by allowing plenty of sunlight in. Another garden crops up at the open-sided central tier that serves as a "wellness floor", home to the infinity pool, spa and gym. $$$$

★ **Sofitel** 9 Wallich St; http://sofitel.accor.com. The Sofitel has moved away from its previous location amongst staid bank buildings to a slightly more lively location closer to Chinatown. They've certainly gone all in on their decor – described as "Art Deco meets Prohibition" by Conde Nast – and also on little luxuries; in your room you might find anything from Russian dolls to adult colouring books on the tables, while even the drinks in the minibar are sourced from Singapore or someplace close by. $$$$

THE FINANCIAL DISTRICT, SEE MAP PAGE 472

★ **The Fullerton** 1 Fullerton Square; http://fullertonhotels.com. Nearly as impressive as the *Raffles*, with a stunning Art Deco atrium; rooms and bathrooms are spacious and feature contemporary styling. Amenities include a gym, spa and pool, plus of course the simple feeling of being in such an enviable location – note that this does *not* come cheap. $$$$

MARINA BAY, SEE MAP PAGE 480

Marina Bay Sands 10 Bayfront Ave; http://marinabaysands.com. Not just one of the island's most famous buildings but also the largest hotel in Singapore, with an astonishing 2500 rooms. Frankly they're no better than those in most of its five-star competitors unless you shell out for, say, one of the Straits suites, with two en-suite bedrooms, a baby grand piano and butler service – costing thousands a night. Otherwise, stay here for the architecture and the infinity pool. $$$$

★ **Ritz-Carlton Millenia** 7 Raffles Ave; http://ritzcarlton.com. Arguably king of the pricey hotels in Marina Centre, with magnificent views across to the towers of the Financial District – even from the bathrooms, where you have the option of getting a butler to fill the bath for you. The on-site eateries and bars are all top-notch, as are the fitness centre and other facilities – all in all it's one of the most luxuriant places to stay in Singapore. $$$$

ORCHARD ROAD AND AROUND, SEE MAP PAGE 484

Goodwood Park 22 Scotts Rd; http://goodwoodparkhotel.com. Built on a leafy hillock and designed by the architect responsible for the *Raffles*, this is a genuine landmark in a cityscape characterized by transience. It still exudes the refinements of a bygone era and boasts a variety of rooms and suites, plus several highly rated restaurants and two pools. $$$$

Hilton Orchard 333 Orchard Rd; http://hilton.com. Female staff at this old favourite wear kitsch quasi-oriental uniforms, but don't let that put you off; this towering hotel with more than 1000 rooms is still at the top of its game, luxurious to a fault, and has its own high-end mini-mall too. $$$$

Lloyd's Inn 2 Lloyd Rd; http://lloydsinn.com. Less than a 10min walk from Orchard Road, this low-rise, recently modernized establishment has rooms where the beds are raised on platforms with storage space beneath. Some bathrooms are open to the outside air (with a privacy curtain, of course). There's a garden, too, largely taken up by a water feature intended for foot-dipping. Breakfast is included. $\overline{\$\$\$}$

★ **The Quincy** 22 Mount Elizabeth; http://quincy-hotels.com. One of Singapore's more endearing boutique hotels, melding contemporary aesthetics with comfort. Features include glass-walled bathrooms in some rooms, and a pool near the top of the building. Note that it's a 10min, slightly uphill walk off Orchard Road. Rate includes breakfast. $\overline{\$\$\$\$}$

Shangri-La 22 Orange Grove Rd; http://shangri-la.com. A 10min walk west of Orchard Road, the oldest member of what's now a global hotel chain still epitomizes elegance, with 750 rooms set in oodles of landscaped greenery. Facilities include tennis courts, gym, pool and spa. $\overline{\$\$\$\$}$

Supreme 15 Kramat Rd; http://supremeh.com.sg. This 1970s concrete box has basic, predictably dated rooms, though they're not too cramped; rates are a steal for the area, and include breakfast. $\overline{\$\$}$

Yotel 366 Orchard Rd; http://yotel.com. This upstart international hotel chain wants to emulate the experience of flying first class, but in reality it's more like a smart home: beds, TV and lighting in your room can be controlled by your phone or tablet, and you can even check yourself in with their app. Everything's ultramodern in the blandest way, and the cheapest rooms are windowless, but a pool and gym are available. $\overline{\$\$\$}$

GEYLANG AND KATONG, SEE MAPS PAGES 453 AND 490

★ **Classic by Venue** 12 Joo Chiat Rd; 6881 3131. Cheap option in seedy Geylang. That said, it's really quite a nice place; set, indeed, inside a classic building, what we have here are tidy rooms – note that the cheapest have no windows – with some thought put into their design in terms of decor and function, and a lobby and common space that would be the envy of anyone staying at one of the many nearby *Hotel 81*s. $\overline{\$\$}$

Hotel 81 Sakura 181 Joo Chiat Rd; http://hotel81.com.sg. Perhaps the best of Singapore's many branches of the budget *Hotel 81* chain; locals may sniff at them, but pickings are slim if you're on a budget and want a private room, and in all honesty they're not that bad at all. This one doesn't quite know what it wants to be – a faux-colonial baby-blue exterior, yet Japanesey flourishes on the inside – but that's part of the admittedly dubious charm. $\overline{\$}$

JH Hotel 8 Lorong 10; 6513 7922. One of the better budget digs in seedy Geylang, on a quiet street that has a modest dole of vice come evening time – but this being Singapore, you're more likely to view it as free entertainment than anything remotely threatening, and that's if you notice it at all. The rooms are fine, with powerful a/c and decent wi-fi. $\overline{\$}$

Santa Grand East Coast 171 East Coast Rd; http://santagrand.sg. One of the nicer offerings from this mid-priced chain, partly housed in a conservation building. Rooms are more than adequate, and the secluded rooftop pool is a bonus. Bus #14 from Dhoby Ghaut/Mountbatten/Bedok MRT. $\overline{\$\$}$

SENTOSA

Hotel Michael Resorts World; http://rwsentosa.com. The main reason to stay at Resorts World is to tap into packages that throw in discounted or free admission to Universal Studios and so forth. *Hotel Michael* is more interesting than the rest, with fittings, wall paintings and other decorative touches by American architect and designer Michael Graves. $\overline{\$\$\$}$

Oasia Resort Sentosa 23 Beach View, near Imbiah station; http://oasiahotels.com. A splendid hotel housed partly in former British barracks dating from 1940. All rooms have elegant contemporary fittings, but the most impressive are the pricey suites with their own large outdoor hot tubs. $\overline{\$\$\$}$

Rasa Sentosa Resort Western end of Siloso Beach; http://shangri-la.com. One of the best pre-casino-era hotels, and now under the *Shangri-La* wing; family-friendly, it boasts a large freeform pool with water slides, a kids' club with purpose-built play areas, and activities such as treasure hunts and beach walks, plus a spa. $\overline{\$\$\$\$}$

Siloso Beach Resort 51 Imbiah Walk; http://silosobeach resort.com. The central swimming pool is a stunner, its curvy fringes planted with lush vegetation and featuring a waterfall and slides; it far outshines the slightly tired rooms. Still, the resort is tranquil enough (the music from the nearby beach bars generally stops around 10pm) and breakfast is included in the rates, which can dip to surprisingly low levels on weekdays. $\overline{\$\$\$}$

ELSEWHERE

Mandai Rainforest Resort 60 Mandai Lake Rd; http://banyantree.com. Opened in 2025, this offering from the luxury *Banyan Tree* group is already up there with the most distinctive places to stay in Singapore. Set in verdant tropical grounds – yes, basically a swathe of rainforest

---

COOKERY CLASSES

There are two venues with half-day courses in the rudiments of Southeast Asian and other cooking. **Food Playground** (24A Sago St, Chinatown; http://foodplayground.com.sg) is an unusual set-up where senior citizens, among others, get a chance to teach local recipes, including ones for many hawker favourites. For a broader culinary palette, try the courses at **Coriander Leaf** (see page 511), which cover Singaporean, Indochinese and Middle Eastern cookery.

– near the zoo, this eco-resort has beautifully appointed rooms, as well as two dozen "seed pods" on stilts. Most of the latter have prime views of the lake. $$$$

SERVICED APARTMENTS

ORCHARD ROAD AND AROUND, SEE MAP PAGE 484

★ **Lanson Plane Winsland** 167 Penang Rd; http://lansonplace.com. Excellent serviced apartments, all well appointed and pretty huge (especially by Singapore standards), right in the thick of things near Orchard Rd. As well as all the facilities you'd expect, there's a 24hr gym, plus a generously-sized pool on the roof. There's usually a six-night minimum stay. $$$$

Orchard Point 160 Orchard Rd; http://opsa.com.sg. Spacious apartments with cooking facilities, washing machines and the like; they can be quite an affordable splurge if you're in town for a week or more. $$$

EATING

Along with shopping, **eating** ranks as Singapore's national pastime. Walk along any street downtown and just about every other building seems to be overflowing with food outlets, from restaurants to corner kiosks serving snacks. It's not just local food on offer, of course: the island's restaurants truly run the gamut of Asian and international cuisine. As in Malaysia, food is both a passion and a unifier across ethnic divides. Certain foods are largely or uniquely Singaporean: **chilli crab**, a sweet-spicy dish pioneered at long-gone rural seaside restaurants and now served all over the island; and **bak chor mee**, ribbon noodles with minced pork and chilli vinegar – to name but two. Some Chinese restaurants and *kopitiams* are popular for **zichar** food – essentially informal, done-to-order cooking that isn't hung up on classical traditions or fancy presentation.

ESSENTIALS

Booking It's worth booking a table at weekends, when many restaurants are packed out – either contact the venue directly, or try http://chope.co or the Chope app.

Costs When it comes to costs, by far the cheapest and most fun places to eat are hawker centres/food courts, housed either within shopping malls or in their own open-air premises. Old-fangled *kopitiams* (the same as *kedai kopis* in Malaysia) are also inexpensive, though increasingly rare downtown. Prices for non-Asian food are always noticeably more expensive, although many places do have good-value weekday set lunch specials. As with hotel bills, there's also the matter of the ten percent service charge and seven percent tax, levied by all the pricier restaurants and cafés.

Opening hours Singapore is one of those places where you may have to do a little legwork if you've plans to eat somewhere particular – at all budget levels, many eateries close up during the window between lunch and dinner, and some have different opening hours on weekends. In addition, it's common for them to take a day or two off each week, which may come as a surprise to those who've been travelling through Southeast Asia. However, this still being Asia after all, many places are open from early until late, and some stay open round the clock.

RESTAURANTS

ARAB STREET (KAMPONG GLAM), SEE MAP PAGE 465

Blu Jaz Café 11 Bali Lane; http://blujaz.net. Easily spotted thanks to its gaudy decor, this venue led the gentrification of the area, and now runs two other similarly garish venues close by. The menu combines Turkish, East Asian and European food – anything from chicken kebab to fish and chips – at affordable prices. Live jazz nights too. $$

★ **Bumbu** 44 Kandahar St; http://bumbu.com.sg. An

STREET ICE CREAM

A couple of generations ago, ice cream in Singapore often meant stuff sold by hawkers from pushcarts, in **exotic flavours** like sweetcorn, red (aduki) bean and yam. This was so-called *potong* ("cut" in Malay) ice cream because it came in brick shapes and the seller would use a cleaver to slice it into slabs, to be served either between wafers or even rolled up in white bread – giving a new dimension to the term "ice cream sandwich".

The general elimination of street stalls put paid to that trade, but in recent years the ice-cream vendors have made a comeback. They're often to be seen at Cavenagh Bridge, on Orchard Road, outside Bugis MRT and at other downtown locations. The **bread option** (these days often using colourful "rainbow" slices) complements the ice cream surprisingly well, serving as a sort of neutral sponge cake. As for the **weird flavours**, they're all more than palatable; you can also find red-bean ice cream on a stick in supermarkets and convenience stores, sold under the name "Potong".

entire shophouse festooned with antique Peranakan tiles and carved wooden screens hosts this restaurant serving a terrific mix of Thai and Indonesian cuisine, all fragrantly spiced. Standouts include the inky stir-fried squid, chilli basil chicken and bean sprouts with salted egg yolk, plus traditional desserts such as sago with palm molasses. $\overline{\underline{\$\$\$}}$
★ **Hajjah Maimunah** 11 & 15 Jalan Pisang; http://hjmaimunah.com. A handily located branch of a Geylang restaurant that's one of very few places in Singapore for authentic, inexpensive Malay meals; snacks and Malay dessert also available. Closed during Ramadan. $\overline{\underline{\$\$}}$
Islamic Restaurant 745 North Bridge Rd; http://islamic.sg. The modernized premises don't hint at this restaurant's heritage – make sure you check out the photos of functions they catered for in the 1920s. *Biriyanis* are their speciality, though they also do a huge range of North Indian chicken, mutton, prawn, squid and veg curries, with good-value set meals. $\overline{\underline{\$}}$
Zam Zam 697 & 699 North Bridge Rd; http://zamzam.sg. Staff at this venerable Indian Muslim *kopitiam* have the annoying habit of touting for custom even though the place draws crowds, especially on Fridays, with its *murtabak* and *biriyani* offerings (there's even a venison version of the latter). Avoid the house speciality drink, *katira* – it's like one of the local sickly ice desserts, only melted. $\overline{\underline{\$\$}}$

BRAS BASAH ROAD TO ROCHOR ROAD, SEE MAP PAGE 462

★ **Artichoke** 161 Middle Rd; http://artichoke.com.sg. Inspired Middle Eastern-tinged fusion food. For weekend brunch, there are mains such as the superbly rich lamb *shakshouka*, lamb shoulder alongside spicy baked eggs; in the evenings, choose from meze and sharing platters, including quirky offerings such as beetroot tzatziki and pork with a coffee and date sauce. The only desserts are their wonderful "neh neh pop" – homemade stick ice creams in flavours such as chocolate baklava. Weekend reservations advised. $\overline{\underline{\$\$\$}}$
Chin Chin 19 Purvis St; http://chinchineatinghouse.com. This likeably old-fangled Chinese shophouse diner with a cheap and cheerful menu of Hainanese standards like breaded pork chops and more generic faves, including chicken sautéed with cashew nuts and spicy *mapo* beancurd. $\overline{\underline{\$}}$
Flutes 120 Beach Rd; http://flutes.com.sg. Newly exiled here from its previous location in the National Museum, this is an upmarket choice for modern European and fusion cuisine. It's pricey unless you go for the set lunch – or, even better, the Sunday lunch of roast beef with the usual trimmings, plus dessert. $\overline{\underline{\$\$\$\$}}$
★ **Herbivore** #01–13 Fortune Centre, 190 Middle Rd; http://herbivore.sg. There's a cluster of vegetarian restaurants near Waterloo St's Kwan Im Temple, particularly at the Fortune Centre building, where the star is this

EATING PRICE CODES

Throughout the Guide, every dining option reviewed is accompanied by a price category, based on the cost of a basic two-course meal for one (or similar, at cafés and hawker centres), without drinks. The codes for **Singapore** are as follows:
$\overline{\underline{\$}}$ = under SGD10
$\overline{\underline{\$\$}}$ = SGD10–20
$\overline{\underline{\$\$\$}}$ = SGD20–40
$\overline{\underline{\$\$\$\$}}$ = over SGD40

excellent place serving tasty tempura, "chicken" teriyaki and so forth. Good-value sets with noodles or rice plus accompaniments like soya sashimi, pickle and salad, plus dessert. $\overline{\underline{\$\$\$}}$
Tiffin Room Raffles Hotel, 1 Beach Rd; http://tiffinrooms.com.sg. High tea (afternoon only) at this Anglo-Indian-themed restaurant is a genuinely scrumptious buffet of English scones, pastries, cakes and sandwiches, plus pies with a chicken curry filling and even dim sum – a real treat. $\overline{\underline{\$\$\$\$}}$
Wing Seong Fatty's #01–31 Burlington Square, 175 Bencoolen St; http://wingseongfatty.com. Run by an avuncular chubby cook in bygone decades, *Fatty's* was an institution on the now-vanished foodie paradise that was Albert St. Today it's a touristy restaurant that maintains the original's no-frills *zichar* approach, and also does standards such as chicken rice. $\overline{\underline{\$}}$
Yhingthai Palace #01–04, 36 Purvis St; http://yhingthai.com.sg. A smart Chinese-influenced Thai restaurant, where you can't go wrong with the deep-fried pomfret with mango sauce or deboned chicken wings stuffed with asparagus and mushroom. $\overline{\underline{\$\$\$}}$

CHINATOWN AND AROUND, SEE MAP PAGE 472

Annalakshmi #01–03 Downtown Gallery, 6A Shenton Way; http://annalakshmi.sg. Come here for excellent Indian vegetarian buffets served up by volunteers, with no price specified; you pay what you feel the meal was worth. Profits go to an association promoting South Indian culture. Note that they take a dim view of people helping themselves to more than they can finish. $\overline{\underline{\$}}$
Blue Ginger 97 Tanjong Pagar Rd; http://theblueginger.com. In a smartly renovated shophouse, this trendy Nyonya restaurant has become a firm favourite thanks to such dishes as *ikan masal asam gulai* (mackerel in a tamarind and lemongrass gravy), and that benchmark of Nyonya cuisine, *ayam buah keluak* – chicken braised in soy sauce together with savoury Indonesian black nuts. $\overline{\underline{\$\$\$}}$
Coriander Leaf 20 Craig Rd; http://corianderleaf.com. Pan-Asian and Mediterranean food in elegant premises,

encompassing everything from Lebanese meze to Vietnamese spring rolls, with a menu of mix-and-match options. They also serve an astonishing range of Asian liqueurs and whiskies. $$$$

Indochine Upstairs at 47 Club St; http://indochine-group.com. Classy Vietnamese, Lao and Cambodian cuisine in chic surroundings sums up this chain, and their Club Street venue is no exception. The Vietnamese *chao tom* (minced prawn wrapped round sugar cane) and deep-fried spring rolls are mouth-watering starters, while the Lao *larb kai* (chicken in lime juice with salad) is one of many excellent main dishes. $$$

★ **Kok Sen** 4 Keong Saik Rd; http://facebook.com/koksen foryou. Open to the street at the front and back, with the odd pigeon loitering between basic tables, this *zichar* place serves food as exemplary as the decor is plain: try their *har cheong kai* (fried chicken seasoned in fermented prawn paste), black bean beef *hor fun* noodles, or even the very spicy *kung pao* frog. Note that the English name on their sign is hard to spot, though you'll doubtless spy the multiple Michelin bib gourmand stickers. $$

Sin Manbok 81 Tanjong Pagar Rd; http://sin-manbok.shop. This stretch of Tanjong Pagar Rd is teeming with Korean restaurants, but they're much of a muchness, and few succeed on the authenticity front for either food or atmosphere. This BBQ house does so better than most – the meat (which you grill yourself) and *banchan* (side dishes) are excellent, and tables often groan under the weight of umpteen beer or soju bottles. $$$

★ **Spring Court** 52–56 Upper Cross St; http://spring court.com.sg. With a pre-war pedigree, *Spring Court* is now a mammoth occupying multiple floors of adjacent shophouses. Its popularity hasn't blunted the quality of the cooking; must-tries include the excellent if expensive *popiah* (steamed spring rolls, hand-wrapped by staff at a counter outside) and steamed chicken with Chinese ham and greens. Plenty of seafood options, and dim sum too. $$$

THE COLONIAL DISTRICT, SEE MAP PAGE 454

★ **National Kitchen by Violet Oon** National Gallery, St Andrew's Rd; http://violetoon.com. Award-winning restaurant giving a fresh yet dedicated take on the Indian, Chinese and Malay cuisines that dominate Singapore's culinary tapestry. The decor is old-school glam, with polished dark surfaces, flowers and fancy lighting everywhere you look. $$$$

Shabestan 80 Mohamed Sultan Rd; http://shabestan.sg. The best Persian restaurant for miles around (okay, so there aren't that many to choose from), and one of the more interesting places to eat in Clarke Quay. Their portions of tender kebabs and stews, served with mounds of fluffy, aromatic saffron rice, are massive, as are the lunch deals – you can dine for far less if you're not super hungry. $$$

THE FINANCIAL DISTRICT, SEE MAP PAGE 472

Brewerkz #01–05/06 Riverside Point, 30 Merchant Rd; http://brewerkz.com. Popular for its highly rated beers, brewed on site, and American food including excellent burgers and sandwiches, plus barbecued ribs, pizzas, nachos and the like. It's on the pricey side, but there is a three-course lunch deal. $$$

Clifford Pier 80 Collyer Quay; http://fullertonhotels.com. An upmarket restaurant majoring on a sort of nouvelle cuisine take on Southeast Asian street food: *bak chor mee*, *sup kambing* (Malay mutton soup), plus Hokkien *kong bak bao* (soy sauce pork eaten with steamed buns). There's also a posh afternoon tea. Everything costs about four times what you'd pay at a food court, but then food courts don't feature marble floors, a pianist tinkling away and the lofty, arched ceiling of the former boat terminal. $$$$

Long Beach Seafood 60 Robertson Quay; http://longbeachseafood.com.sg. The best-located branch of a small Singaporean chain, serving delectable black pepper crab and chilli crab, among other pricey seafood options. It's touristy, yes, but nowhere near the level of similar restaurants around Clarke Quay and Boat Quay. $$$$

Lucha Loco 15 Duxton Hill; http://super-loco.com. Popular with young expats, this Mexican joint does tacos and burritos at lunchtime, with the burritos dropped in favour of quesadillas and sharing platters in the evenings. Portions are on the small side, but they make amends with a buzzing garden drinking area where you can enjoy their vast range of margaritas. $$

Rendezvous #02–72 The Central, 6 Eu Tong Sen St; http://rendezvous-hlk.com.sg. For decades *Rendezvous* has been dishing out its revered *nasi padang*. Its current location in a mediocre mall doesn't suit at all, but thankfully the curries have stayed the course, in particular the superb chicken korma – a mild curried stew of just the right degree of richness, derived from coconut milk rather than cream or yoghurt. $$

LITTLE INDIA, SEE MAP PAGE 465

★ **Banana Leaf Apolo** 54 Race Course Rd; http://thebananaleafapolo.com. Banana-leaf-type restaurant with a wide selection of Indian dishes, including fish-head curry, plus chicken, mutton and prawn options. Come at mealtimes and you'll most likely have to queue – a good sign that the food will be worth it. $$$

Gokul 19 Upper Dickson Rd; http://gokulraasvegeterian.com.sg. Although they mainly serve standard Indian vegetarian dishes, this restaurant – boasting a tucked-away feel, though it's just steps from central Little India – also does great meatless versions of local street food classics such as *mee rebus*, the Malay noodle dish with a spicy/tangy gravy. $$

Hillman 135 Kitchener Rd; http://hillmanrestaurant.com. This little Chinese restaurant is oddly popular with Japanese businessmen, though don't let that put you off. They come, as you should, for the tip-top *zichar* food. The claypot dishes are a particular speciality, ranging from noodles to, for the adventurous, sea cucumber – not a vegetable, but a marine relative of starfish that, for many, is not just an acquired taste, but a taste they'll never acquire. $$$

★ **Komala Villas** 76–78 Serangoon Rd; http://komalavilas.com.sg. In business since 1947 and still hugely popular, this pleasingly cramped vegetarian establishment has more than a dozen variations of *dosai* – this is what they're best at, although they also have more substantial rice meals, as well as super tasty *kothu parotta* (shredded flatbread fried in a curry sauce, varieties of which are popular in Southern India, as well as Sri Lanka and the Maldives). Wash it all down with some fresh coconut water. $

Madras Woodlands Ganga 1 Cuff Rd; 6295 3750. This simple vegetarian restaurant serves up great-value Indian buffets, featuring several curries, rice, *naan* and a dessert, with the option of ordering à la carte as well. $

MARINA BAY, SEE MAP PAGE 480

Cé La Vi SkyPark at Marina Bay Sands; http://celavi.com. If you find that SkyPark admission charge hard to stomach, you can get round it by eating at this restaurant, serving Asian-influenced fusion food. Best to go for the set lunch, as it can be very pricey otherwise. No shorts or vests in the evenings. $$$$

★ **Colony** Ritz-Carlton Millenia, 7 Raffles Ave; http://ritzcarlton.com. A modern beaut designed along old British colonial lines, this is perhaps the pick of the Ritz-Carlton's various fancy places to eat (though it's not the one with the Michelin star). No fewer than seven open-air kitchens whip up food from all over Asia, and guests enjoy their meals under an ornate glass-tunnel ceiling. Take your pick from buffet or à la carte options; there's also daily afternoon tea, except for Sunday, when there's vintage champagne brunch instead. $$$$

Paulaner Bräuhaus #01–01 Millenia Walk, 9 Raffles Boulevard; http://paulaner-brauhaus-singapore.com. The cavernous ceiling with a maypole sticking up into it is impressive, as is the menu of Bavarian delights such as the bitty *spätzle* pasta, but the best reason to come is the terrific Sunday brunch spread, including superb pork knuckle, sausages and salads, and desserts like strudel and cheesecake. Pay a little more, and you can "pair" it with unlimited beer from their microbrewery. $$$

ORCHARD ROAD AND AROUND, SEE MAPS PAGES 453 AND 484

Bistro Du Vin #01–14 Shaw Centre, 1 Scotts Rd; http://bistroduvin.com.sg. Informal French restaurant that does an exceptional duck leg confit, plus standards such as escargot and French onion soup – and none of that nouvelle cuisine presentation-over-substance nonsense either. The two-course weekday lunch deals are reasonable value; mains ordered à la carte cost just about as much. $$$

Candlenut Block 17A, Dempsey Rd; http://comodempsey.sg. It doesn't look especially upmarket, but this restaurant lofts Peranakan food towards haute cuisine, with dishes like barramundi *asam pedas* (with chilli and turmeric). Everything still tastes recognizably Peranakan, just with all the flavours cranked up to eleven. Prices are correspondingly on the high side too. $$$$

Curry Culture 31 Cuppage Terrace; http://thecurryculture.sg. The options on Cuppage Terrace may be touristy, but it's a pleasant, traffic-free outdoor area, and sure beats eating in one of the nearby malls. This is the best place to eat on the strip; the menu's a little more like you may see in your own country rather than Little India, but it's extensive enough to cover some of the subcontinent's more interesting treats. $$$

Jiang Nan Chun Four Seasons Hotel, 190 Orchard Bvd; http://fourseasons.com. A hugely stylish Cantonese restaurant, decked out with turquoise tiling and calligraphic artwork. The consummately prepared food isn't cheap, especially if you're after seafood, although their simpler rice dishes – and even the dim sum – can be quite affordable. $$$

Long Beach Seafood Block 25, Dempsey Rd; http://longbeachseafood.com.sg. Once you had to trek to the beaches to find Singapore's best Chinese-style seafood, but no longer, now that this beachside stalwart has set up here. The best dishes really are magic, including treacly crisp baby squid, chunky Alaska crab in a white pepper sauce, steamed *soon hock* (goby) and, of course, chilli crab. An expensive but worthwhile blowout, and they've a newer branch in Robertson Quay if you'd like to stay more central. $$$$

Marché Ground floor and basement, 313@Somerset, 313 Orchard Rd; http://marche-movenpick.sg. Never mind that Mövenpick's *Marché* restaurants are formulaic when you can have *rösti*, sausages or crêpes cooked to order in front of you, or help yourself to the superb salad bar. In addition, the bakery counter does takeaway sandwiches, bread sticks and Berliners – doughnuts with a range of fillings (or certain former presidents of the US). $$

Open Farm Community 130E Minden Rd; http://openfarmcommunity.com. Appropriately situated just south of the Botanic Gardens, this eco-friendly, urban-farm-style restaurant has myriad veggie, vegan and gluten-free options, all served beautifully. The only negative is that there are few options for diners on a budget. $$$

★ **PS Café** Level 2, Palais Renaissance, 390 Orchard Rd; http://pscafe.com. Marvellous restaurant set in something resembling a giant greenhouse and offering an inventive, constantly revised menu of fusion fare and great desserts. Brunchtimes are popular; take your pick from Western staples like eggs benedict to spaghetti crab *mee goreng*. $$$$

Samy's Block 25, Dempsey Rd; http://samyscurry.com.

Housed in a colonial-era hall with ceiling fans whirring overhead, *Samy's* is an institution that's been serving superb banana-leaf meals for decades. Choose from curries of jumbo prawn, fish head, crab or mutton, and either plain rice or the delicate, fluffy *biriyani*. $$

Spices Cafe Concorde Hotel, 100 Orchard Rd; http://concordehotelsresorts.com. Buffets galore: an evening seafood feast, afternoon tea, and best of all, a great-value spread of Peranakan and other local cooking for lunch on weekdays. $$$$

GEYLANG AND KATONG, SEE MAP PAGE 490

Guan Hoe Soon 38/40 Joo Chiat Place; http://guanhoesoon.com. Open in one form or another for more than half a century, this restaurant turns out fine Nyonya cuisine in home-cooked style, including yummy *ngoh hiang*, in which minced prawn is rolled up in a wrapper made from bean curd, and satay *babi* – not a Malay satay, but a sweetish red pork curry. $$$

★ **Hajjah Maimunah** 20 Joo Chiat Rd; http://hjmaimunah.com. Inexpensive Malay diner serving good breakfasts (*nasi lemak* etc) and a fine *nasi campur* spread, featuring the likes of *ayam bakar sunda* (Sundanese-style barbecued chicken), with assorted *kuih* for afters. $$

Sandwich Saigon 93 East Coast Rd; http://sandwichsaigon.com. Katong has both gentrified and become a little Vietnam, eating-wise, in recent years. This restaurant stands out for its yummy *banh mi*, using bread baked on the premises and with fillings such as garlic chicken or pork chop. Also well-executed spring rolls and noodle dishes, plus drip coffee. $

SENTOSA AND AROUND

★ **Soup** #02–141 VivoCity; http://souprestaurant.com.sg. So-called *samsui* women once sailed from China's Guangdong province to work on Singapore building sites. This fine little restaurant celebrates the cuisine of these redoubtable women, most famously their ginger chicken; steamed, it comes with a gingery dip and iceberg-lettuce leaves to roll it up in. $$$

Trapizza Siloso Beach; 6376 2662. *Trapizza* stands out from the many eating places here, for its excellent pizzas and pasta dishes. $$

CAFÉS, TEAROOMS AND DESSERTS

THE COLONIAL DISTRICT, SEE MAPS PAGES 453 AND 454

Glasshouse #01-03 CHIJMES, 30 Victoria St; http://theglasshousesg.com. Gorgeous little café, festooned with plants and looking a bit like your richest friend's kitchen. The coffee's great, as are the sandwiches, salads and other Western brunch fare. Other branches can be found around the city. $$

Toby's Estate 8 Rodyk St; http://tobysestate.com.sg. Spacious roastery with a prime riverside location – good enough reason to stop by and sate your caffeine fix, though the food's pretty good too. $$

BRAS BASAH ROAD TO ROCHOR ROAD, SEE MAP PAGE 462

Ah Chew Desserts #01–11, 1 Liang Seah St; http://ahchewdesserts.com. Taking up two shophouses, *Ah Chew* confronts you with strange local sweets containing beans or other unexpected ingredients. The cashew-nut paste is not bad if you like the sound of a broth made of nut butter; also available are the likes of *pulot hitam*, made with black sticky rice. Cautiously sample a few items by ordering the small servings. $

Cafe Carrera By Baker & Cook 130 Beach Rd; http://bakerandcook.com. By far the most central branch of a small domestic café chain, Kiwi-run and featuring New Zealand coffee, with great croissants and brownies, plus quiches, open sandwiches and salads. At this one, you also get to admire some fancy cars – it's set inside a Porsche studio, and car prints and Porsche badges often worm their way onto the sweet treats and coffee foam. $$

LITTLE INDIA, SEE MAP PAGE 465

★ **Chye Seng Huat Hardware** 150 Tyrwhitt Rd; http://cshhcoffee.com. Part of the slow gentrification that's converting the area's hardware shops into restaurants and hostels, *CSHH* is a hip café-bar with all-day breakfasts and varied mains that include linguine with bacon or Japanese curry rice. Marvellous light bites too, like *soon kueh* (savoury bamboo shoot dumplings) and *cempedak* (a jackfruit relative) crumble, with coffee blended and ground on the premises. In the evening the focus shifts to their craft beer stall in the courtyard. $$$

CHINATOWN AND AROUND, SEE MAP PAGE 472

★ **Apiary** 84 Neil Rd; http://apiary.sg. Hugely popular place for craft ice cream, which can be enjoyed in the normal ways, or served with hot brownies or freshly made waffles. Their divine produce is on rotation, but local flavours are likely to stand out most, whatever the season – think lychee and yuzu sorbet, or blue pea flower milk and salt. Great coffee and a good range of teas round out a pleasing picture. $$

Leshan Café 168 Telok Ayer St; http://instagram.com/leshancafe. Next to Thian Hock Keng, this museum-like little place has a short menu of spicy Peranakan classics, but the food took a bit of a dive after a change of ownership – though things seem to be on the mend again, it's best to stick to cold drinks and sweet treats. $$

The Populus Café 146 Neil Rd; http://thepopulus. cafe. This slick, contemporary café is popular with young professional types for its gourmet coffee blends and fusion meals such as Korean beef with quinoa salad. $\overline{SS}$

★ **Tea Chapter** 9–11 Neil Rd; 6226 1175; http://teachapter.com. Hands down the best place for tea in Chinatown, and perhaps all Singapore: a hugely atmospheric, multi-level place (the ground level is a teashop) where guests sit drinking from beautiful crockery, it's almost like an old opium den that's been through detox and taken up yoga. They also do tea appreciation sessions (served with snacks), or expensive, full-blown four-session courses, for two or more people. $\overline{S}$

Tong Heng Traditional Cantonese Pastries 285 South Bridge Rd; http://tongheng.sg. Great for a sugar fix while you're wandering Chinatown, this long-established pastry shop sells custard tarts, lotus seed-paste biscuits and other Chinese sweet treats. $\overline{S}$

Yixing Xuan Teahouse 78 Tanjong Pagar Rd; http://yixingxuan-teahouse.com. Homely, almost kitchen-like tearoom, where as well as great brews you can take part in hour-long workshops (for groups of at least five). $\overline{S}$

THE FINANCIAL DISTRICT, SEE MAP PAGE 472

Brwd/Kinn 5 Hongkong St; http://staywithkinn.com. One of few affordable cafes in the Financial District, and part of the excellent *Kinn Habitat* hostel (see page 505), this is a simple, yet attractive, spot for decent coffee; they also do matcha shakes and other specials on a rotating basis. $\overline{S}$

ORCHARD ROAD AND AROUND, SEE MAP PAGE 484

Killiney Kopitiam 67 Killiney Rd; http://killineykopitiam.com. If you find yourself in need of a Singapore-style (ie. very sweet and very strong) coffee or tea near Orchard Rd, this always-crammed place has decades of custom to recommend it – it started life here in 1919, and has since spawned several other branches. $\overline{S}$

STREET FOOD AND HAWKER CENTRES

LITTLE INDIA, SEE MAPS PAGES 453 AND 465

Dignity Kitchen 69 Boon Keng Rd; http://projectdignity.sg. A small hawker centre whose seven stalls are staffed by the disadvantaged and differently-abled; they also act as a training centre, teaching senior citizens how to garden. The food is largely excellent, and even cheaper than at most of the island's hawker centres; note that they also offer you the chance to feed this price difference back into the community by buying a meal for someone in need. $\overline{S}$

★ **Tekka Food Centre** Alongside Tekka market at start of Serangoon Rd. One of the best old-school hawker centres on the island, always steamy, hot and busy. The Indian and Malay stalls are especially good; look out for exceptional Indian *rojak* – assorted fritters with sweet dips. There's a decent selection of Chinese stalls too, but they pale by comparison. $\overline{S}$

ARAB STREET (KAMPONG GLAM), SEE MAP PAGE 465

★ **Kampong Glam Café** 17 Bussorah St; http://kgglamcafe.ec-platform.net. Fantastic roadside *kopitiam* serving inexpensive Malay rice and noodle dishes, cooked to order, plus curries. Come not just for the food, but for a good chinwag with friends over *teh tarik* late into the evening. $\overline{S}$

Rumah Makan Minang 18 Kandahar St; http://minang.sg. A street-corner place serving superb *nasi padang*, including the mildly spiced chicken *balado* and more unusual curries made with *tempeh* (fermented soybean cakes) or offal. For dessert you might get freshly made sweet pancakes stuffed with peanuts and corn – much better than they sound. $\overline{S}$

CHINATOWN AND AROUND, SEE MAP PAGE 472

Chinatown Complex 335 Smith St. The hawkers upstairs are much preferable to anything on the ersatz "food street" of Smith Street, and one of their number shot to fame in 2016 as one of the island's first two Michelin-starred stalls: Hawker Chan (at #02-126). If you don't fancy lining up for half an hour, then eat at their pricier, fast-food-style outlet at 78 Smith Street. $\overline{S}$

Maxwell Food Centre 1 Kadayanallur St. One of Singapore's first hawker centres (which, amazingly, means that once upon a time there somehow weren't any), and home to a clutch of popular Chinese stalls, including the well-known *Tian Tian* for Hainanese chicken rice, plus others that are good for satay or *rojak*. $\overline{S}$

Ya Kun Kaya Toast 18 China St; http://yakun.com. Now a ubiquitous chain, *Ya Kun* started out in the pre-war years as a Chinatown stall offering classic *kopitiam* breakfast fare – *kaya* toast (the same as *roti kahwin* in Malaysia) plus optional soft-boiled eggs eaten with white pepper and soy sauce, and strong tea or coffee, both normally served with condensed or evaporated milk. Of the many branches in Singapore, this is the most old-school, and surely more true to the original than the mall-based alternatives. $\overline{S}$

Yixin 43 Temple St; 9366 6002. Workaday vegetarian place turning out dishes such as mock Peking duck, plus rice and noodle standards like *lor mee* (noodles in a tangy, gloopy sauce). It must also be said that their veggie laksa is absolutely divine – maybe even up there with the best on the island, veggie or otherwise. The good news for visitors is that they've added some English to the sign outside – you'd previously have had to recognise the Chinese characters (meaning "one heart"). $\overline{S}$

THE FINANCIAL DISTRICT, SEE MAP PAGE 472

★ **Lau Pa Sat** 18 Raffles Quay; http://laupasat.sg. The food court at this historic market building (see page 479) offers a real panoply of Singapore hawker food, including satay – vendors set up their barbecues just outside on Boon Tat St in the evenings, and these are by far the most popular choices for Singaporeans. Pricier outlets offer cooked-to-order seafood such as chilli crab, but tourists are the main focus. $

MARINA BAY, SEE MAP PAGE 480
Satay by the Bay Gardens by the Bay, 18 Marina Gardens Dr; http://sataybythebay.com.sg. A hawker centre in Gardens by the Bay – just what the Marina Bay area needed. In all honesty the food's not always up to scratch, but the atmosphere is cheery, and you can see the waters of Marina Bay itself from some tables. $

ORCHARD ROAD AND AROUND, SEE MAPS PAGES 453 AND 484
Newton Circus Hawker Centre Corner of Clemenceau Ave North and Bukit Timah Rd, near Newton MRT. A venerable open-air place with a wide range of hawker food. It's especially noted for its seafood, for which you can end up paying through the nose; prices are on the high side for stalls anyway, as the place is very much on the tourist trail. $
★ **Warung M Nasir** 69 Killiney Rd; 6734 6228. Tiny but well-respected Indonesian *nasi padang* joint, with standards such as fried chicken *balado*, beef and chicken *rendang* and tofu or beans fried with *sambal*. The food's great, and cheap as chips, but the staff do seem to make up the prices as they go – it won't amount to much, anyway. $

GEYLANG AND KATONG, SEE MAP PAGE 490
328 Katong Laksa 51 East Coast Rd, at the corner of Ceylon Rd; http://328katonglaksa.com. Just as different parts of Malaysia have their own take on *laksa*, so does Katong: here the noodles are cut into short strands for easy slurping off a spoon. This café is regarded as one of the original purveyors of the dish, using seafood and without the meat of more modern variations. $
★ **Old Airport Road Food Centre** 51 Old Airport Rd. A really decent hawker centre that's notable in two significant ways – firstly, it's almost entirely free or tourists; secondly, it's within walking distance of many of Geylang's budget sleeps, which means that for many visitors it'll be their nearest spot for cheap noodles, kaya toast and the like. $

SENTOSA AND AROUND
★ **Food Republic** Level 3 VivoCity; http://foodrepublic.com.sg. Perhaps the best example of this upmarket food court chain, where the stalls are "curated" for their culinary calibre and styled to resemble something out of pre-war Chinatown. Try the scissors-cut curry rice – mixed rice/*nasi campur* but with the hawker slicing up the rice serving with scissors and heaping curry gravy onto it. Avoid at peak times, though, as the place will be rammed. $

DRINKING AND NIGHTLIFE

Singapore supports a huge range of watering holes, from elegant colonial chambers through hip rooftop venues with skyline views to slightly tacky joints featuring Chinese karaoke or middling bands covering Western hits. Chinatown is particularly good for **bars**, though anywhere expats hang out won't be short of options. There are also a handful of glitzy **clubs** that spin cutting-edge sounds, all minus – this being Singapore – any assistance from illicit substances. Although the scene has come off the boil in recent years, one or two venues still lure world-leading DJs.

ESSENTIALS
Bars Some surveys deem Singapore one of the world's most expensive cities for drinking. It's true that beers at bars can be very pricey, but hawker centres usually charge only half the amount (often less), and some bars thrive on selling keenly-priced drinks. A glass of house wine usually costs much the same as a beer, and spirits a bit more. During happy hour, which can last half the evening, you'll either get a considerable discount off drinks or a "one-for-one" deal (two drinks for the price of one), and some bars also have a "house pour", a discounted cocktail, wine or beer on offer all night. Note that some bars close on Sundays, and that more upmarket venues, including hotel bars, often have a "smart casual" dress code: generally no shorts, vests or sandals after 6pm.

Clubs Most clubs have a cover charge, if not all week then at least on Friday and Saturday; the charge almost always includes your first drink or two (weekends are pricier, and men pay slightly more than women). Where women get in free on ladies' night (often midweek), they have to pay for their first drink but may get unlimited refills of the "house pour" at certain times.

Opening hours Bars often open their doors when evening is already underway, though those that double as restaurants or cafés – or those in noted drinking areas – are often open through the day. Clubs follow regular club hours, and plenty of places of either stripe are closed on Sundays.

Drinking laws Following an extraordinary riot in Little India in 2013, which the government saw as fuelled by alcohol (although it was sparked by a fatal road accident involving migrant workers), restrictions were placed on drinking in public. In practice, this means anywhere on the street beyond the premises of restaurants, hawker centres, bars and clubs, plus beaches and parks, and applies nightly from 10.30pm to 7am. Within Little India and Geylang, an additional ban applies throughout the weekend and until 7am on Mondays. Shops and supermarkets are also unable to sell alcohol when the ban is in force. However, this all disguises the fact that you *can* drink in public in Singapore – until a certain, Cinderella-like hour, you'll see locals (mainly young, though not exclusively so) drinking in groups on the banks of the Singapore River, and around Marina Bay, with 7-Eleven the usual fuelling station. Read Bridge, in Clarke Quay, was once the epicentre of such activity, but has had its "seating areas" fenced off for a while now.

BARS

THE COLONIAL DISTRICT, SEE MAPS PAGES 453 AND 454

Almost Famous #01-06 CHIJMES, 30 Victoria St; http://almostfamous.sg. Simple craft beer bar, where the brews and nibbles (and, of course, the drinkers) often represent the only flashes of colour in a monochrome space. Prices are pretty good by Singapore (and international craft beer) standards.

Gulp Riverside Taproom 7 Rodyk St; http://gulpbeer.co. This small, cafe-looking venue isn't quite as riverside as the name might suggest, but has proven popular with young locals and budget travellers for its affordable craft beer; as well as a selection on tap, they've plenty more in the fridges, plus some wines to drink too.

Rosso Vino 15 Merbau Rd; http://rossovinosingapore.com. Though a decent Italian restaurant in its own right, this riverside venue is perhaps of even more appeal as a bar, especially when they have happy-hour Aperol spritz on offer (as often seems to be the case). The smells from the kitchen may tempt you into eating here too.

BRAS BASAH ROAD TO ROCHOR ROAD, SEE MAP PAGE 462

★ **Atlas** Ground floor, Parkview Square, 600 North Bridge Rd #03-07; http://atlasbar.sg. Aptly located at the Gotham-esque Parkview Square, *Atlas* is a palatially opulent evocation of Jazz Age glamour, all gilt Art Deco-style fittings. Cabinets stretching to the lofty ceiling hold a veritable library of wines and spirits, including some fiendishly expensive vintages. If you don't feel like indulging, just come for a daytime coffee and a gawp.

The Long Bar Raffles Hotel, 1 Beach Rd; http://raffles.com. It's still just about mandatory to have a Singapore Sling amid the old-fashioned elegance of the bar where Ngiam Tong Boon invented it in 1915 – not at all cheap, but you only need to do it once.

LITTLE INDIA, SEE MAP PAGE 465

BistrOne36 121 Tyrwhitt Rd; http://bistrone36.co. Decent restaurant that tries hard to be a jack of all trades – all-day breakfasts, pasta dishes, coffee, Pop Art on the walls. However, it's perhaps most notable for their "cocktail buffet" deals – you need to drink three or so to make it worth your money, but some stagger out having had a fair few more than that.

The Countryside Café 71 Dunlop St; http://thecountrysidecafe.sg. A low-key, convivial establishment, with middle-of-the-road oldie sounds and five dozen different bottled beers at reasonable prices. The menu of bar snacks and food – partly Indian, partly Western – is nearly as impressive.

CHINATOWN AND AROUND, SEE MAP PAGE 472

My Awesome Café 202 Telok Ayer St; http://myawesomecafe.com. This verging-on-hipster place, housed in a former Chinese shophouse clinic, is a café in theory but much more of a bar in practice, with people drinking on the outer seats most of the day. Its jumbo salads, sandwiches and wraps are also decent draws.

★ **RPM** 16 Duxton Rd. Cool cocktail and *shochu* bar with a vinyl-only music policy, though said music can be anything from soul to jazz via rock and World. They occasionally rope along DJs for live sets.

Spiffy Dapper Upstairs at 73 Amoy St; http://spiffydapper.com. This tiny indie cocktail bar must be the darkest venue in town, its thick drapes keeping out any extraneous lighting. There are at least fifteen standard cocktails on offer, and the mixologists can talk through these and other options based on your tastes.

THE FINANCIAL DISTRICT, SEE MAP PAGE 472

BQ Bar 39 Boat Quay; http://bqbar.com. One of Boat Quay's cooler venues, thanks to the friendly staff, memorable views of the river from upstairs and diverse sounds, anything from dance to rock. Kebabs available too from a nearby outlet run by the same management. Happy hours each evening.

Harry's Bar 28 Boat Quay; http://harrys.com.sg. Singapore's most ubiquitous chain of bars started out here, and now has some twenty branches island-wide. Popular with locals as well as foreigners, it does half a dozen draught beers and ciders, plus light meals and snacks; happy hour is until 8pm.

The Penny Black 26 & 27 Boat Quay; http://pennyblack.com.sg. Hardly a convincing evocation of a "Victorian London pub" but pleasant enough, with one table built around a red pillar box, Strongbow cider on draught, plenty of pub grub – steak pie, ploughman's lunches, etc – and live UK football matches on TV.

MARINA BAY, SEE MAP PAGE 480

★ **LeVeL33** Level 33, 8 Marina Boulevard; http://level33.com.sg. One of Singapore's "it" places to drink, perched way up – hence the lofty-sounding name – in the Marina Bay Financial Centre. The views out are almost as good as those from Marina Bay Sands, and of course from here you can see (rather than sit on) the towers themselves. They claim to be the world's highest microbrewery (in a building, at least... there are several microbreweries in Bhutan, after all), and perhaps thanks to the rarefied air, the beers are excellent, as are the meals on offer. A top pick in more ways than one.

Malts #01-07 Marina Square, 6 Raffles Blvd; http://facebook.com/malts.sg. Well-stocked whisky bar whose outdoor tables fill up each and every evening – many patrons are on corporate jollies, but plenty simply choose to relax with mates here after work. Prices are fairly reasonable, considering the location, and the drink in question.

Mo Bar 5 Raffles Ave; http://mandarinoriental.com. This bar makes a big thing of its huge range of cocktails, which emphasize fresh fruit and herbs, but the views of the spires of the Financial District sell themselves.

Republic Ritz-Carlton Hotel, 7 Raffles Ave; http://republicbar.com.sg. Often ranked among Asia's most exclusive bars, this has taken the 1960s as its cue, and gone all-in with its decoration – and the cocktails it serves. These are expertly whipped up, and the mixologists occasionally add their own creations to what's already an extensive menu.

ORCHARD ROAD AND AROUND, SEE MAPS PAGES 453 AND 484

Quite a few of Orchard Rd's most interesting drinking spots occupy restored Peranakan shophouses at the start of Emerald Hill Rd, close to Somerset MRT.

Alley Bar Peranakan Place, corner of Orchard Rd and Emerald Hill Rd; http://alleybar.sg. Less touristy than its neighbours, *Alley Bar* slots into a narrow, high-ceilinged space and does a good range of cocktails and spirits. The food menu is extensive, too, with lots of sandwiches and more substantial meals.

Ice Cold Beer 9 Emerald Hill Rd; http://ice-cold-beer.com. Noisy, happening place where the beers are kept in ice tanks under the glass-topped bar. Leffe Blond and Fuller's London Pride on tap, among others. Shares a kitchen with *No. 5 Emerald Hill*. Happy hour daily 5–9pm.

Martini Bar Grand Hyatt Hotel, 10 Scotts Rd; http://hyatt.com. Choose from several dozen martini variations at this plush bar, ranging from their trademark lychee martini to options that include local ingredients such as sugar cane. At the time of writing, it was yet to reopen after a Covid-induced slumber, so check ahead.

★ **No. 5 Emerald Hill** 5 Emerald Hill Rd; http://emerald-hill.com. Set in one of Emerald Hill Rd's restored houses, *No. 5* is not only an opulent feast for the eyes, but also offers speciality cocktails plus great chicken wings and thin-crust pizzas. Tetley's on tap, some outdoor seating and a pool table upstairs.

Que Pasa 7 Emerald Hill; http://quepasa.com.sg. A wine bar with a creaky wooden staircase and plenty of tapas, yet at the base of one of Singapore's most charming roads.

Red Dot Brewhouse 25A Dempsey Rd; http://reddotbrewhouse.com.sg. Many of Singapore's slicker bars are expat-run, but not the *Red Dot Brewhouse*, the brainchild of one local who got bitten by the homebrew bug many years ago. Among their range of beers and ales, the most radical is the Monster Green Lager, rich in blue-green algae regarded by some as a superfood.

SENTOSA

Rumours Beach Club Siloso Beach, opposite Siloso Beach Resort; rumoursbeach.club. Fancy yet friendly establishment where you can imbibe sundowners at outdoor tables clustered around the freeform pool, with the sea just metres away. Seafood bites and pizzas, too. Hours can vary.

CLUBS

THE COLONIAL DISTRICT, SEE MAP PAGE 454

Zouk The Cannery, Clarke Quay, 3C River Valley Rd; http://zoukgroup.com. Still going decards after it first opened its doors way back in 1991, *Zouk* is Singapore's pre-eminent club, specializing in house and other dance sounds. Its new home at Clarke Quay, oozing post-industrial chic, is four venues in one, including two bars and its little-sister club *Phuture*, where the emphasis is more on hip-hop and R&B.

THE FINANCIAL DISTRICT, SEE MAP PAGE 472

★ **Headquarters** 66A Boat Quay; http://thugshopsg.com. "The Council" seem to run the club scene in Singapore, and this is their de facto home – a dingy lair pulsing to the sounds of DJs, both resident and guest.

MARINA BAY, SEE MAP PAGE 480

Cé La Vi Marina Bay Sands SkyPark; http://sg.celavi.com. The bar/club at the SkyPark is one way to bypass the 57th-floor admission fee and enjoy fabulous views over downtown Singapore. There's an entry charge until 9pm, redeemable against food and drink (meaning that you may effectively be paying just a few dollars for a cocktail, versus the price of admission to the observation deck), and a post-midnight cover charge certain days.

Marquee #B1-67 The Shoppes at Marina Bay Sands, 10 Bayfront Ave; http://marquee.com. Claiming to be the biggest nightclub in Singapore – though notably not claiming to be the best, or even the best-organised – this is a fun enough place to let your hair down.

SENTOSA

Tanjong Beach Club 120 Tanjong Beach Walk; http://tanjongbeachclub.com. If you needed a reason to schlep to the furthest of Sentosa's beaches, this would be it. Styled like a luxury beach bungalow, it boasts an incongruous infinity pool, a pricey restaurant and a bar that hosts weekly beach parties.

LGBTQ+ VENUES

Singapore's LGBTQ+ scene, while modest, is among the best in Southeast Asia, and in recent years the country has seen the annual Pink Dot rally (June or July; http://pinkdot.sg) – an LGBTQ+ event, although this being Singapore it's all tame and family-friendly – grow into one of the best-attended mass meetings on the island. That said, attitudes toward homosexuality remain contradictory. In 2022, the government repealed colonial-era legislation banning sex between men (though it had not been enforced for some time). However, as recently as 2017, the government ordered multinationals to stop sponsoring Pink Dot and banned tourists from participating. This is why gay venues still keep a low profile, functioning largely unhindered, but scarcely using the word "gay" in advertising. The scene centres on Chinatown and Tanjong Pagar, where there are some half a dozen bars and clubs; note that they only really get busy at weekends, and only after 10pm. Two sources of information are the Pelangi Pride Centre (a small gay library project near Commonwealth MRT; http://pelangipridecentre.org) and, for lesbian events, http://facebook.com/twoqueensasia.

CHINATOWN AND AROUND, SEE MAP PAGE 472
Dorothy's 13A Trengganu St; http://instagram.com/dorothysbar. Entered through a side door in Temple Street (look for the discreetly placed rainbow flag), this tiny bar offers a view over the souvenir stalls of Trengganu Street.
Playground Club Neil 47 Neil Rd; 6610 6271. Not specifically a gay bar, though very LGBTQ+ friendly, and good for mingling whatever your persuasion.
Tantric 78 Neil Rd; http://homeofthebluespin.com.

Pleasant enough shophouse bar with a clientele slightly more reflective of Singapore's multi-ethnic make-up than the largely Chinese crowd elsewhere. There's outdoor seating on a slick terrace, and upstairs, a nominally separate bar that's a mini-shrine to the pre-war American Chinese actress Anna May Wong.

LIVE MUSIC VENUES
As well as these live-music bar listings, see page 520 for more info on the country's music festivals.

ARAB STREET (KAMPONG GLAM), SEE MAP PAGE 465
Blu Jaz Café 11 Bali Lane; http://blujazcafe.net. Live jazz on Wednesday, Friday & Saturday evenings.

THE FINANCIAL DISTRICT, SEE MAP PAGE 472
Offtrack 34 North Canal Rd; http://offtrack.sg. Brought to you by Darker Than Wax and Ice Cream Sundays, two doyens of the local music scene, this is surprisingly sedate-looking for a party venue. Regular DJ nights change all that, though.

ELSEWHERE
Timbre+ One North 73A Ayer Rajah Cres; http://timbreplus.sg. Sets by local musicians in a new location out west – a good excuse to get out of central Singapore.

ENTERTAINMENT
Even on a brief visit, it's hard not to notice how much state money has been poured into the **arts**: prime property has been turned over to cultural organizations in areas like the Waterloo Street "arts belt", and prestigious venues such as Theatres on the Bay host world-class performers. Cynics might say this cultural push is mainly about keeping Singapore attractive to expats, while others raise the important issue of whether world-class art can bloom where **censorship** is very much alive. Nonetheless, the cultural scene is streets ahead of anything in Malaysia, so it would be a shame not to catch a performance of some kind, whether one drawing on Asian traditions or a gig by a big-name Western band.

ESSENTIALS
Festivals Major cultural festivals include the Singapore International Festival of the Arts (calendar online; http://sifa.sg), running the gamut from concerts to theatre through dance and film; and the Singapore Fringe Festival (Jan or Feb; http://singaporefringe.com), which concentrates on theatre, dance and the visual arts. There's also the annual Singapore Writers' Festival (http://singaporewritersfestival.

STREET THEATRE
Walk around Singapore long enough and you're likely to stumble upon some sort of streetside cultural event, most usually a **wayang** – a Malay word used in Singapore to denote **Chinese opera**. Played out on outdoor stages next to temples and markets, or in open spaces in the new towns, *wayangs* are highly dramatic and stylized affairs, in which garishly made-up characters enact popular Chinese legends to the accompaniment of the crashes of cymbals and gongs. They're staged throughout the year, but the best time to catch one is during the **Festival of the Hungry Ghosts** (late August), when they are performed to entertain passing spooks. Another fascinating traditional performance – lion-dancing – takes to the streets during Chinese New Year, and puppet theatres may appear around then, too. Downtown, Chinatown and the Bugis/Waterloo Street area are where you're most likely to stumble upon performances.

com), featuring international as well as local writers working in all four of the country's official languages.

Tickets You can buy tickets directly from venues or through the SISTIC ticket agency, with outlets in downtown malls (http://sistic.com.sg).

FILM

As well as the latest Hollywood blockbusters, Singapore's cinemas show a range of Chinese, Malay and Indian movies, all with English subtitles. Although international cinema features year-round in one-off screenings and mini-film festivals, the main event for cineastes is the Singapore International Film Festival (usually Nov; http://sgiff.com). If you're watching a hot new release, it's worth turning up early or buying tickets in advance. Tickets are fairly cheap, but can cost two or three times more for blockbuster films or screenings at the fanciest multiplexes. Be prepared for a certain amount of chattering during shows.

MULTIPLEX CHAINS

Cathay Cinemas include: Cineleisure Orchard, 8 Grange Rd (near Somerset MRT), cineleisure.com.sg; Cathay Cineplex, 2 Handy Rd (near Dhoby Ghaut MRT), http://cathaycineplexes.com.sg.

Golden Village Cinemas include: Level 7, Plaza Singapura, 68 Orchard Rd; Levels 2 & 3, VivoCity, Harbourfront; http://gv.com.sg.

Shaw Cinemas include: Lido 8 Cineplex, Shaw House, 350 Orchard Rd (IMAX-equipped); Bugis Cineplex, Bugis Junction, 200 Victoria St; http://shaw.sg.

INDEPENDENT VENUES

Alliance Française 1 Sarkies Rd; http://alliancefrancaise.org.sg. Weekly French-language films with English subtitles. A 10min walk from Newton MRT.

CozyPlace 316 Jalan Basar; http://cozyplace.sg. Not really a cinema so much as a clutch of what could be termed private Netflix-and-chill rooms. You can sign in to your own accounts (other apps available too), or be signed in on the house ones.

National Museum National Museum, 93 Stamford Rd; http://nationalmuseum.sg. Intermittent screenings of vintage classics, some free.

★ **The Projector** Level 5, Golden Mile Tower, 6001 Beach Rd; http://theprojector.sg. Lurking within a concrete parking deck is the island's best cinema, an unmodernized 1970s affair lovingly revived with just some fresh coats of paint and cool murals. Devoted to films from around the world, it also sports two bars, one with views of Marina Centre.

THEATRE

A surprising number of small drama companies have sprung up over the years, performing works by local playwrights that dare to include a certain amount of social commentary; watch out for productions by The Necessary Stage (http://necessary.org), the Singapore Repertory Theatre (http://srt.com.sg) and Theatreworks (http://theatreworks.org.sg). Foreign companies visit occasionally, too, and a lavish musical is usually staged at least once a year.

CLASSICAL AND TRADITIONAL MUSIC AND DANCE

At the heart of Singapore's healthy Western classical music scene is the Singapore Symphony Orchestra, whose concerts often feature stellar guest soloists, conductors and choirs from around the world. Dance is another thriving art form, with several active local troupes and regular visits by international companies.

COMPANIES AND ORCHESTRAS

Chinese Opera Teahouse 5 Smith St; http://ctcopera.com. A touristy show of Chinese opera excerpts; weekends only, and you can arrive early and more more to have dinner included.

Singapore Ballet http://singaporeballet.org. Contemporary and classical works at various venues, sometimes by moonlight at Fort Canning Park.

Singapore Chinese Orchestra Singapore Conference Hall, 7 Shenton Way, Financial District; http://sco.com.sg. Traditional Chinese music concerts, with occasional free shows.

Singapore Lyric Opera http://singaporeopera.com.sg. Western opera and operetta, at various venues.

Singapore Symphony Orchestra http://sso.org.sg. Performances at Esplanade – Theatres on the Bay and the Victoria Concert Hall. Occasional free concerts at the Botanic Gardens and hour-long daytime shows for children.

Siong Leng Musical Association http://siongleng.com. A body dedicated to preserving *nanyin* (literally "southern sound") – the distinctive music and opera of southeast China, sung in dialect. A few shows each year at various locations, sometimes in the exceptional temple surroundings of Thian Hock Keng.

Temple of Fine Arts http://tfasg.org. This Indian cultural organization puts on occasional concerts and exhibitions.

POP, ROCK, BLUES AND JAZZ

Singapore is firmly on the East Asian gig circuit for Western stadium-rock outfits as well as indie bands, though some gigs can be a bit staid, with locals wary about letting their hair down. Local bands do exist and some aren't at all bad, but these are more likely to perform in community centres than decent venues. Music festivals include the Singapore Jazz Festival, which spans world music as well (March/April; http://sing-jazz.com) and Baybeats, an Esplanade event focused on Asian indie (dates vary). Canto- and Mando-pop (both bland hybrids of Chinese lyrics and Western pop) and K-pop are hugely popular, too. See page 519 for live music bar listings.

SHOPPING

Choice and convenience make the Singapore shopping experience a rewarding one, but the island's affluence and strong currency mean most things are priced at Western levels; Kuala Lumpur can be a better hunting ground for bargains. **Orchard Road**, of course, is home to the biggest and swankiest malls; more interesting are those in **Chinatown**, which are often like multistorey markets and house more traditional outlets stocking Chinese foodstuffs, medicines, instruments and porcelain. Chinatown also has a few antique and curio shops along South Bridge Rd, and more knick-knacks are on sale around **Arab St**, where you'll also find textiles and batiks, robust basketware and some good deals on jewellery. **Little India** has silk stores and goldsmiths as well as the **Mustafa Centre**, a department store that's known all over the island for being open 24/7. Shopping complexes, malls and department stores are almost all open daily from 10am–9pm, some until 10pm.

ESSENTIALS

Complaints In the unlikely event that you encounter a problem with a retailer that you cannot resolve mutually, you may be able to recover your money by initiating proceedings online with Singapore's Small Claims Tribunal; see http://judiciary.gov.sg for more information.

Tax refunds When leaving the country by air or sea, tourists can claim a refund of Singapore's goods and services tax (GST; nine percent at the time of research) on purchases over S$100, provided the shop in question is a member of one of three tax refund schemes. You will either have to complete a form which must be signed by the retailer, and then present the goods, forms and receipts to the customs authorities when you leave, or else ask the shop to link your purchases to one of your debit or credit cards, in which case you claim the tax back by, for example, scanning a barcode at a booth at the airport. It's a bureaucratic headache; for detailed guidance, have a look at the GST section of http://iras.gov.sg, or pick up the appropriate leaflet from a tourist office or participating outlet.

MALLS AND DEPARTMENT STORES

THE COLONIAL DISTRICT, SEE MAP PAGE 454

Raffles City 252 North Bridge Rd (above City Hall MRT); http://rafflescity.com.sg. Home to a branch of Robinsons department store with a Marks & Spencer within it, plus numerous fashion chains.

BRAS BASAH ROAD TO ROCHOR ROAD, SEE MAP PAGE 462

Bugis Junction Victoria St, above Bugis MRT; capitaland. com. Mall encasing several streets of restored shophouses, and featuring the Japanese/Chinese department store BHG.

Sim Lim Square 1 Rochor Canal Rd; http://simlimsquare.com.sg. Cameras and electronic goods.

LITTLE INDIA, SEE MAP PAGE 465

Mustafa Centre Syed Alwi Rd; http://mustafa.com.sg. Totally different in feel to the malls of Orchard Rd, Mustafa is a phenomenon, selling electronics, fresh food, luggage, you name it – and it never closes.

CHINATOWN AND AROUND, SEE MAP PAGE 472

Hong Lim Complex 531–531A Upper Cross St. One of several Chinatown shopping centres where ordinary people buy ordinary things – dried mushrooms, cuttlefish and crackers from provisions shops, for example.

People's Park Centre 101 Upper Cross St. Chinese handicrafts, electronics, silk, jade and gold.

People's Park Complex 1 Park Rd. A venerable shopping centre that, like the Hong Lim Complex and adjacent People's Park Centre, is among the most entertaining places to browse in Chinatown because it's so workaday. Also here is the Overseas Emporium on level 4, selling Chinese musical instruments, calligraphy brushes, lacquerwork and jade.

MARINA BAY, SEE MAP PAGE 480

The Shoppes at Marina Bay Sands 10 Bayfront Ave; http://marinabaysands.com. Beneath the iconic hotel (see page 479), this mall actually has its own "canal" for boat rides, as well as the usual designer names.

ORCHARD ROAD AND AROUND, SEE MAP PAGE 484

313@Somerset 313 Orchard Rd (above Somerset MRT); http://313somerset.com.sg. Muji and Zara are the star names here.

Forum the Shopping Mall 583 Orchard Rd; http://forumtheshoppingmall.com.sg. Plenty of items to please the most pampered of children– upmarket kids' clothes, toys and so forth.

The Heeren 260 Orchard Rd; http://heeren.com.sg. There's really only one reason to come here – it's home to the flagship outlet of Robinsons, Singapore's oldest department store.

ION Orchard 2 Orchard Turn (above Orchard MRT); http://ionorchard.com. Despite the impressive hyper-modern facade, 55th-floor viewing gallery and sprinkling of designer names, by far the most popular section of this cavernous mall is *Food Opera*, its excellent food court on basement 4.

Ngee Ann City 391A Orchard Rd; http://ngeeanncity.com.sg. A brooding twin-towered complex, home to the Japanese Takashimaya department store and the excellent Kinokuniya bookstore, plus several jewellers.

Plaza Singapura 68 Orchard Rd; http://plazasingapura.com.sg. Veteran mall with a bit of everything, including sports equipment, musical instruments and electronic equipment.

Tanglin Shopping Centre 19 Tanglin Rd; http://tanglinsc.com. Good for art, antiques and curios.

Tangs Corner of Orchard and Scotts rds; http://tangs.com. Tangs is a department store dating back to the 1950s, and the only one to have its own building on Orchard Rd, topped by a pagoda-style construction occupied by a *Marriott* hotel. The store itself sells a wide range of reasonably priced clothes and accessories.

SENTOSA AND AROUND

VivoCity Next to HarbourFront Centre and above HarbourFront MRT; http://vivocity.com.sg. A humdinger of a mall, containing a branch of Tangs department store, a cinema, three food courts and many restaurants.

ART, ANTIQUES, CURIOS AND SOUVENIRS

ARAB STREET (KAMPONG GLAM), SEE MAP PAGE 465

The Heritage Shop 93 Jalan Sultan; facebook.com/theheritageshopsg. An incredible range of bric-a-brac, from antique radios to beautiful enamelware tiffin carriers – little pots for cooked food, stacked and held together within a metal frame for easy carrying.

Jamal Kazura Aromatics 21 Bussorah St; http://facebook.com/JKASingapore. Veteran maker and seller of alcohol-free perfume, using various essential oils.

Little Shophouse #03-49 Golden Landmark Shopping Centre, 390 Victoria St. Recently exiled from Bussorah St to a lame mall, this small outlet boasts some fine but pricey examples of Peranakan beaded slippers, plus replica Peranakan crockery. Contact them via Facebook prior to your visit, as the place is usually closed.

Malay Art Gallery 31 Bussorah St; http://themalayartgallery.com. Stocks *songket* and *kerises* from Malaysia and Indonesia. Another one of those places that's best contacted in advance of a visit.

CHINATOWN AND AROUND, SEE MAP PAGE 472

East Inspirations 256 South Bridge Rd; http://east-inspirations.com. The classiest of several antique shops here, offering Asian furniture, porcelain lamps and vases.

Orchid Chopsticks 65 Pagoda St; 6423 0488. You'd never have thought chopsticks could be this interesting: here they come in just about every material and hue, some fairly plain, others lustrous and ornamented.

Peranakan Tiles Gallery 37 Pagoda St; http://asterbykyra.sg. This little shop sells Peranakan-style scarves and porcelain, but its mainstay is lovely shophouse tiles.

Tong Mern Sern 51 Craig Rd; http://facebook.com/tongmernsern. "We buy junk and sell antiques", proclaims the banner outside this great little establishment. The owner is quite a character and can tell you all about the crockery, old furniture and other bric-a-brac he has amassed – if he decides to let you in.

MARINA BAY, SEE MAP PAGE 480

Arch #02-07 Esplanade Mall; http://archsingapore.com.sg. Their secretive production process works magic on thin slices of wood, transforming them into intricately carved and etched pieces of artwork, often Singapore-themed, that can be framed for your wall or worn as jewellery.

Red Dot Design Museum 11 Marina Boulevard; http://museum.red-dot.sg. A good place for quirky, ergonomically designed items, including household gadgets, plus jewellery and paper artworks for self-assembly.

GEYLANG AND KATONG, SEE MAP PAGE 490

Katong Antiques House 208 East Coast Rd; 6345 8544. Peranakan artefacts and Chinese porcelain. Also counts as a sight in its own right (see page 491).

ORCHARD ROAD AND AROUND, SEE MAP PAGE 484

★ **Design Orchard** 250 Orchard Rd; http://dors.com.sg. There's always plenty to catch your eye in this shop, which focuses on the works of local artists and artesans – everything from couches to shampoo, via fans and cushions.

JEWELLERY

CHINATOWN AND AROUND, SEE MAP PAGE 472

Wong's Jewellery 62 Temple St; wongsjewellery.com. Chinese-style outlet, good for jade, gold and pearls.

ORCHARD ROAD AND AROUND, SEE MAP PAGE 484

Flower Diamond #03–02 Ngee Ann City, 391B Orchard Rd; http://flowerdiamond.com. Contemporary designs as well as more traditionally styled bling, at sensible prices.

Risis B1 Ngee Ann City, 391 Orchard Rd; http://risis.com. Singaporeans tend to view gold-plated orchids – available as brooches, pendants, earrings, even on tie clips – as clichéd, but tourists snap them up here in Takashimaya. They also have a couple of other outlets nearby, as well as one at Changi Airport.

FABRICS AND FASHION

LITTLE INDIA, SEE MAP PAGE 465

Dakshaini Silks 13 Upper Dickson Rd; http://dakshainisilk.com. Indian embroidered silk textiles and clothes.

ARAB STREET (KAMPONG GLAM), SEE MAP PAGE 465

Ratianah 23 Bussorah St; instagram.com/ratianahtahir. Friendly Malay shop offering Nyonya- style fabrics and blouses, plus bangles and brooches.

Toko Aljunied 91 Arab St; facebook.com/TokoAljunied. Quality batik cloth and *kebaya* – the blouse/sarong combinations traditionally worn by Nyonyas. Bespoke clothes too, by appointment.

ORCHARD ROAD AND AROUND, SEE MAP PAGE 484
Charles & Keith #B3–58 ION Orchard; http://charleskeith.com. Singapore's answer to Malaysia's Jimmy Choo, the brothers Charles and Keith Wong design stylish, affordable women's shoes and handbags too.

GEYLANG AND KATONG, SEE MAP PAGE 490
Rumah Bebe 113 East Coast Rd; http://rumahbebe.com. This delightful place sells beaded shoes and handbags, costume jewellery and the traditional garb – *kebaya* and sarong – of Nyonya women. They also offer courses in beading and Nyonya cookery.

BOOKS
Singapore bookshops are reasonably stocked; all the larger ones carry a good selection of Western and local fiction and nonfiction titles, plus a range of magazines.

CHINATOWN AND AROUND, SEE MAP PAGE 472
Littered With Books 20 Duxton Rd; 6220 6824. Despite its name, this indie outlet has a neatly laid out, though somewhat random, selection of literary fiction, thrillers and travel writing. Hours can be irregular, sometimes open longer Fri–Sun.

ORCHARD ROAD AND AROUND, SEE MAP PAGE 484
Kinokuniya Level 3, Ngee Ann City, 391 Orchard Rd; http://kinokuniya.com.sg. Singapore's best general bookshop, with titles on every conceivable subject and some foreign-language literature too, plus loads of magazines, and also plenty of Rough Guides.

DIRECTORY

Banks and exchange There's no shortage of ATMs – practically every MRT station has one, as do all malls. Licensed moneychangers, offering slightly more favourable exchange rates than the banks, aren't hard to find, particularly in Little India (eg. at Mustafa, see page 466) and on Orchard Road.
Embassies and consulates The "missions" section of the Singapore Ministry of Foreign Affairs website http://mfa.gov.sg carries a full list.
Emergencies See page 53.
Gyms Fitness First (http://fitnessfirst.com.sg) operate downtown gyms, though you will need to take out membership to use them.
Hospitals The state-run Singapore General Hospital, Outram Rd (SGH; 6222 3322; http://sgh.com.sg; Outram Park MRT), has a 24hr casualty/emergency department, as does the privately run Raffles Hospital, 585 North Bridge Rd (6311 1111, http://rafflesmedicalgroup.com).
Pharmacies Both Guardian and Watsons are ubiquitous downtown, with branches in shopping malls and even in a few MRT stations, though only the largest outlets handle prescriptions.
Phones For details of mobile phone providers, see page 56.
Police In an emergency, dial 999; otherwise call the police hotline 1800 225 0000.
Swimming Singapore has some of the world's best state-run swimming facilities; just about every new town has a well-maintained 50m open-air pool, open from early morning until well into the evening, while a fair proportion of the island's population also lives in apartment complexes that have communal swimming pools. The best-located downtown pool with public access is the Jalan Besar Swimming Complex on Tyrwhitt Rd, near Lavender and Farrer Park MRT station. Have coins available for the ticket gates and lockers.
Vaccinations Tan Tock Seng Hospital, across the road from Novena MRT, has a Travellers' Health & Vaccination Centre (Mon–Fri 8.30am–5pm; http://ttsh.com.sg).
Women's helpline AWARE 1800 774 5935, http://aware.org.sg.

CELEBRATING MALAYSIA INDEPENDENCE DAY

Contexts

525 History
542 Religion
546 Peoples
551 Development and the environment
555 Wildlife
559 Books
563 Language
573 Glossary

History

The modern-day nations of Malaysia, Singapore and Brunei only became independent in 1963, 1965 and 1984 respectively. Before that, their history was inextricably linked with events in the larger Malay archipelago, from Sumatra across Borneo to the Philippines.

Unfortunately, little hard archeological evidence in the region pertains to the prehistoric period, while events prior to the foundation of Melaka are known only from unreliable accounts written by Chinese and Arab traders. For an understanding of the formative fourteenth and fifteenth centuries, there are two vital sources: the **Suma Oriental** (Treatise of the Orient), by Tomé Pires, a Portuguese emissary who came to Melaka in 1512 and used his observations to write a history of the region, and the seventeenth-century **Sejarah Melayu**, the "Malay Annals", which recount oral historical tales in a poetic style. Portuguese and Dutch **colonists** who arrived in the sixteenth and seventeenth centuries supplied written records, though these tended to concern commercial rather than political or social matters. At least there's a wealth of information from **British colonial** times that, despite an imperialistic bias, gives detailed insights into Malay affairs.

Beginnings

The oldest remains of *Homo sapiens* in the region, discovered in the Niah Caves in Sarawak, are thought to be those of hunter-gatherers, dating back some 40,000 years; other finds in the Peninsular state of Kedah are only 10,000 years old. The variety of **ethnic groups** now found in both east and west Malaysia – from small, dark-skinned Negritos through to paler Austronesian Malays – has led to the theory of a slow filtration of peoples through the Malay archipelago from southern Indochina. That theory is backed by an almost universal belief in animism, celebration of fertility and ancestor worship among the various peoples.

The Malay archipelago acquired a strategic significance thanks largely to the **shipping trade**, which flourished as early as the first century AD. This was engendered by the two major markets of the early world – India and China – and by the richness of its own resources. From the dense jungle of the Peninsula and northern Borneo came aromatic woods, timber and nipah palm thatch, traded by the forest-dwelling Orang Asli with the coastal Malays, who then bartered or sold it on to Arab and Chinese merchants. The region was also rumoured to be rich in **gold**, leading to its being described by contemporary Greek writers as "The Golden Chersonese" (*chersonese* meaning "peninsula"). Although gold was never found in the supposed quantities, ornaments made of the metal helped to develop decorative traditions among craftsmen, and survive today. More significant, however, were the **tin fields** of the Malay Peninsula, mined in early times to provide an alloy used for temple sculptures. Chinese traders were also attracted by the medicinal properties of various sea products, such as sea slugs, collected by the Orang Laut (sea people), as well as by pearls and tortoise shells.

c.35,000 BC	200 AD	7th c.	c.14th c.
Human settlement at Niah in what is now northern Sarawak	Malay Peninsula comes under Indian cultural and religious influence	The Sumatran Sriviyajan empire, encompassing the Malay Peninsula, rises to prominence	Srivijaya is challenged by the Majapahit empire of Java and declines

For their part, the Indigenous peoples acquired cloth, pottery, glass and absorbed the beliefs of those with whom they traded. From as early as 200 AD, **Indian traders** brought their Hindu and Buddhist practices, and archeological evidence from later periods, such as the tenth-century temples at Lembah Bujang (see page 162), suggests that the local population not only tolerated these new belief systems, but adapted them to suit their own experiences. Perhaps the most striking contemporary example of such cultural interchange is the traditional entertainment of *wayang kulit* (shadow plays), whose plots are drawn from the Hindu *Ramayana*.

While trade with India developed very early, contact with **China** was initially less pronounced due to the pre-eminence of the Silk Road, further north. Only in the eighth and ninth centuries did Chinese ships first venture into the archipelago. By the time Srivijaya appeared on the scene, a number of states – particularly in the Kelantan and Terengganu areas of the Peninsula – were sending envoys to China.

Srivijaya

The inhabitants of the western Peninsula and eastern Sumatra were quick to realize the geographical advantage afforded by the Strait of Malacca, which provided a refuge where ships could wait for several months for a change in the monsoon winds. From the fifth century onwards, a succession of **entrepôts** (storage ports) were created to cater for the needs of passing vessels. One such entrepôt eventually became the mighty empire of **Srivijaya**, eminent from the start of the seventh century until the end of the thirteenth, and encompassing all the shores and islands surrounding the Strait of Malacca. Its exact location is still a matter for debate, although most sources point to **Palembang** in southern Sumatra. Srivijaya's stable administration attracted commerce when insurrection elsewhere frightened traders away, while its wealth was boosted by extracting tolls and taxes from passing ships. Srivijaya also became an important centre for **Mahayana Buddhism** and learning. When the respected Chinese monk I Ching arrived in 671 AD, he found more than a thousand monks studying the Buddhist scriptures.

Political concepts developed during Srivijayan rule were to form the basis of Malay government in future centuries. Unquestioning **loyalty** among subjects was underpinned by the notion of *daulat*, the divine force of the ruler (called the Maharajah), which would strike down anyone guilty of *derhaka* (treason) – a powerful means of control over a deeply superstitious people.

The decision made around 1080 to shift the capital, for reasons unknown, north from Palembang to a place called **Melayu** seems to have marked the start of Srivijaya's decline. Piracy became almost uncontrollable, and even the Orang Laut, who had previously helped keep it in check, turned against the Srivijayan rulers. Soon both local and foreign traders began to seek safer ports, and the area that's now Kedah was a principal beneficiary. Other regions were soon able to compete by replicating the peaceable conditions and efficient administration that had allowed Srivijaya to thrive.

Srivijaya's fate was sealed when it attracted the eye of foreign rivals. In 1275, the Majapahit empire of Java invaded Melayu and made inroads into many of Srivijaya's peninsular territories. Sumatra and Kedah were raided by the Cholas of India, while the Thai kingdom of Ligor was able to extract **tributes** of gold from Malay vassals, a practice that continued until the nineteenth century. Moreover, trading

Early 15th c.	**15th c.**	**1511**
Paramesevara, a Srivijayan prince, establishes a kingdom at Melaka, which soon flourishes as a Muslim sultanate	The Brunei Sultanate rises to prominence, exercising power over most of northern Borneo	The Portuguese capture Melaka

restrictions in China were relaxed from the late twelfth century onwards, making it more lucrative for traders to bypass the once mighty entrepôt and go directly to the source of their desired products. Around the early fourteenth century Srivijaya's name disappears from the records.

The Melaka Sultanate

With the collapse of Srivijaya came the establishment of the **Melaka Sultanate**, the Malay Peninsula's most significant historical period. Both the *Sejarah Melayu* and the *Suma Oriental* document the tale of a Palembang prince named **Paramesvara**, who fled the collapsing empire of Srivijaya to set up his own kingdom, finally settling on the site of present-day Melaka.

As well placed as its Sumatran predecessor, with a deep, sheltered harbour and good riverine access to lucrative jungle produce, Melaka set about establishing itself as an international marketplace. The securing of a special agreement in 1405 with the new Chinese emperor, Yung-lo, guaranteed trade to Melaka and protected it from its main rivals. To further ensure its prosperity, Melaka's second ruler, Paramesvara's son **Iskandar Shah** (reigned 1414–24), took the precaution of acknowledging the neighbouring kingdoms of Ayuthaya and Majapahit as overlords. In return Melaka received vital supplies and much-needed immigrants, which bolstered the expansion of the settlement.

Port taxes and market regulations were managed by four **shahbandars** (harbour masters), each in charge of trade with certain territories. Hand in hand with the commodities trade went the exchange of ideas. By the thirteenth century, Arab merchants had begun to frequent Melaka's shores, bringing with them **Islam**, which their Muslim Indian counterparts helped to propagate among the Malays. Melaka's prestige was enhanced both by its conversion to Islam, making it part of a worldwide community with profitable trade links, and by territorial expansion which, by the reign of its last ruler **Sultan Mahmud Shah** (1488–1528), included the west coast of the Peninsula as far as Perak, Pahang, Singapore, and most of east coast Sumatra.

The legacy of **Melaka's golden age** reaches far beyond its material wealth. One significant development, the establishment of a hierarchical **court structure**, was to lay the foundations for a system of government lasting until the nineteenth century. According to Malay royal tradition, the ruler, as head of state, traced his ancestry back through Paramesvara to the maharajahs of ancient Srivijaya; in turn Paramesvara was believed to be descended from Alexander the Great. The ruler also claimed divinity, a belief strengthened by the kingdom's conversion to Islam, which held sultans to be Allah's representatives on earth. To further secure his power, always under threat from the overzealous nobility, the Melaka sultan embarked on a series of measures to emphasize his "otherness": no one but he could wear gold unless it was a royal gift, and yellow garments were forbidden among the general population.

The Melaka Sultanate also allowed the **arts** to flourish; the principal features of the courtly dances and music of this period can still be distinguished in traditional entertainments today. Much more significant, however, was the refinement of **language**, adapting the primitive Malay that had been used in the kingdom of Srivijaya into a language of the elite. Such was Melaka's prestige that all who passed through the

c.1530	**1641**	**1786**
Alauddin Riayat Shah, son of the deposed Melaka sultan, establishes the Johor Sultanate	The Dutch East India Company seizes Melaka from the Portuguese	Francis Light establishes a port at Penang – the first British settlement in the Malay Peninsula

entrepôt sought to imitate it, and by the sixteenth century, Malay was the most widely used language in the archipelago. Tellingly, the word *bahasa*, although literally meaning "language", came to signify Malay culture in general.

The Portuguese conquest of Melaka

It wasn't long before Europe set its sights on the prosperous sultanate. At the start of the sixteenth century, the **Portuguese** began to take issue with Venetian control of the Eastern market. They planned instead to establish direct contacts with the commodity brokers of the East by gaining control of crucial regional ports. The key player in the subsequent conquest of Melaka was Portuguese viceroy **Alfonso de Albuquerque**, who led the assault on the entrepôt in 1511, forcing its surrender after less than a month's siege. Aloof and somewhat effete in their high-necked ruffs and stockings, the Portuguese were not well liked, but despite the almost constant attacks from upriver Malays, they controlled Melaka for the next 130 years.

There are few physical reminders of the Portuguese in Melaka, apart from the gateway to their fort, A Famosa, and the small **Eurasian** community, descendants of intermarriage between the Portuguese and local women. The colonizers had more success with religion, however, converting large numbers of locals to **Catholicism**; their churches still dominate the city.

The Dutch in Melaka

Portuguese control over Melaka lasted for well over a century, until it was challenged by the Vereenigde Oostindische Compagnie (VOC), or **Dutch East India Company**, who were already the masters of Indonesia's valuable spice trade. Melaka was the VOC's most potent rival, and the company's bid to seize the colony succeeded in 1641 when, after a five-month siege, the Dutch flag was hoisted over Melaka.

Instead of trying, like the Portuguese, to rule from above, the Dutch cleverly wove their subjects into the fabric of government. Each racial group was represented by a *kapitan*, a respected figure from the community who mediated between his own people and the new administrators – often becoming wealthy and powerful in his own right. The Dutch were also responsible for the rebuilding of Melaka, much of which had turned to rubble during the protracted takeover of the city; many of these structures, in their distinctive Northern European style, still survive today.

By the mid-eighteenth century, conditions for Melaka's trade with China were at their peak: the relaxation of maritime restrictions in China itself had opened up the Strait for their merchants, while Europeans were eager to satisfy the growing demand for tea. The Chinese came to Melaka in droves and soon established themselves as the city's foremost entrepreneurs. Chinese settlement in the area and, in some cases, intermarriage with local Malay women, created a new cultural blend, known as **Peranakan** or Baba-Nyonya – the legacies of which are the opulent mansions and unique cuisine of Melaka, Penang and Singapore.

A number of factors prevented Dutch Melaka from fulfilling its potential, however. Since their VOC salary was hardly bountiful, Dutch administrators found it more lucrative to trade on the black market, taking backhanders from grateful merchants, a situation that severely damaged Melaka's commercial standing. High taxes forced

1795	**1819**	**1824**
The British East India company captures Dutch possessions in Southeast Asia, including Melaka	Exploiting a succession dispute in Johor, Stamford Raffles negotiates the creation of a British settlement in Singapore	The Anglo-Dutch treaty leaves the British firmly in control of the Malay Peninsula and Singapore

> **THE BUGIS AND MINANGKABAU**
>
> Through the second half of the seventeenth century, a new ethnic group, the **Bugis** – renowned for their martial and commercial skills – trickled into the Peninsula, seeking refuge from the civil wars that wracked their homeland of Sulawesi (in the mid-eastern Indonesian archipelago). By the start of the eighteenth century, they were numerous enough to constitute a powerful court lobby, and in 1721 they took advantage of factional struggles to capture the kingdom of Johor, now based in Riau. Installing a Malay puppet sultan, the Bugis ruled for over sixty years, making Riau an essential port of call on the eastern trade route; they even almost succeeded in capturing Melaka in 1756. But when Riau-Johor made another bid for Melaka in 1784, the Dutch held on with renewed vigour and finally forced a treaty placing all Bugis territory in Dutch hands.
>
> In spiritual terms, the **Minangkabau** (see box, page 257), hailing from western Sumatra, had what the Bugis lacked, being able to claim cultural affinity with ancient Srivijaya. Although this migrant group had been present in the Negeri Sembilan region since the fifteenth century, it was in the second half of the seventeenth century that they arrived in the Malay Peninsula in larger numbers. Despite professing allegiance to their Sumatran ruler, the Minangkabau were prepared to accept Malay overlordship, which in practice gave them a great deal of autonomy. Although the warrior Minangkabau were not natural allies of the Bugis or the Malays, they did occasionally join forces to defeat a common enemy. In fact, over time the distinction between various migrant groups became less obvious as intermarriage blurred clan demarcations, and Malay influence, such as the adoption of Malay titles, became more pronounced.

traders to more economical locations such as the newly established British port of **Penang**, whose foundation in 1786 heralded the awakening of British interest in the Straits. In the end, Melaka never stood a chance: the company's attention was distracted by other centres such as Batavia (modern-day Jakarta), the VOC "capital", and by the kingdom of Johor.

Johor and Brunei

When Melaka fell to the Portuguese, the deposed sultan, Mahmud Shah, made for Bintan island in the Riau archipelago, just south of Singapore, where he established the first **court of Johor**. When, in 1526, the Portuguese attacked and razed the settlement, Mahmud fled once again, this time to Sumatra, where he died in 1528. It was left to his son, Alauddin Riayat Shah, to found a new court on the upper reaches of the Johor River, though the kingdom's capital was to shift repeatedly during a century of assaults on Johor territory by Portugal and the Sumatran Sultanate of Aceh.

The **arrival of the Dutch** in Southeast Asia marked a distinct upturn in Johor's fortunes. Hoping for protection from its local enemies, the court aligned itself firmly with the Dutch, and was instrumental in their successful siege of Portuguese Melaka. That loyalty was rewarded with trading privileges and assistance in securing a treaty with Aceh, which at last gave Johor the breathing space to develop. Johor was the supreme Malay kingdom for much of the seventeenth century, but by the 1690s its

1826	1841	1846	1851
Singapore joined administratively with Penang and Melaka to form the Straits Settlements	With the Brunei Sultanate in decline, James Brooke is installed as the first rajah of Sarawak	Brunei cedes Labuan island to the British	Hugh Low makes the first documented ascent of Gunung Kinabalu

empire was fraying under the despotic rule of another Sultan Mahmud. Lacking strong leadership, Johor's Orang Laut turned to piracy, scaring off trade, while wars with the Sumatran kingdom of Jambi, one of which resulted in the total destruction of Johor's capital, weakened it still further. No longer able to tolerate his cruel regime, Mahmud's nobles stabbed him to death in 1699. Not only did this change the nature of power in Malay government – previously, law deemed that the sultan could only be punished by Allah – but it also marked the end of the Melaka dynasty.

During Melaka's meteoric rise, **Brunei** had been busily establishing itself as a trading port of some renown. The Brunei Sultanate's conversion to **Islam**, no doubt precipitated by the arrival of wealthy Muslim merchants fleeing from the Portuguese in Melaka, also helped to increase its international prestige. When geographer **Antonio Pigafetta** visited Brunei with **Ferdinand Magellan**'s expedition of 1521, he found the court brimming with visitors from all over the world. This, indeed, was Brunei's "golden age", with its borders embracing land as far south as present-day Kuching in Sarawak, and as far north as the lower islands of the modern-day Philippines. Brunei's efforts, however, were soon curtailed by Spanish colonization in 1578, which, although lasting only a matter of weeks, enabled the Philippine kingdom of Sulu to gain a hold in the area – and thus put paid to Brunei's early expansionist aims.

The arrival of the British

At the end of the eighteenth century, Dutch control in Southeast Asia was more widespread than ever, and the VOC empire should have been at its height. Instead, it had somehow become **bankrupt**. Defeat in the Fourth Anglo-Dutch War (1781–83) lowered Dutch morale still further, and when the British, in the form of the **East India Company** (EIC), moved in on Melaka and the rest of the Dutch Asian domain in 1795, the VOC barely demurred; it was dissolved five years later.

Initially, the British agreed to a caretaker administration whereby they would assume sovereignty over the entrepôt to prevent it falling under French control, now that Napoleon had conquered Holland. By the time the end of the Napoleonic Wars in Europe put the Dutch in a position to retake Melaka, between 1818 and 1825, the EIC had established the stable port of **Penang** and – under the supervision of **Sir Thomas Stamford Raffles** – founded the new settlement of **Singapore**. The strategic position and free-trade policy of Singapore – backed by the impressive industrial developments of the British at home – threatened the viability of both Melaka and Penang, forcing the Dutch finally to relinquish their hold on Melaka to the British, and leaving Penang to dwindle to a backwater. In the face of such stiff competition, smaller Malay rivals inevitably linked their fortunes to the British.

The British assumption of power was sealed by the **Anglo–Dutch Treaty of 1824**, which apportioned territories between the two powers using the Strait of Malacca and the equator as the dividing lines, thereby splitting the Riau-Johor kingdom as well as putting the brakes on centuries of cultural interchange with Sumatra. This was followed in 1826 when Melaka, Penang and Singapore were unified into one administration, known as the **Straits Settlements**. Singapore replaced Penang as its capital in 1832.

Raffles had at first hoped that **Singapore** would act as a market to sell British goods to traders from all over Southeast Asia, but it soon became clear that **Chinese**

1874	1881	1887
Perak becomes the first Malay state to take a British adviser or Resident after the signing of the Pangkor Treaty	The British North Borneo Company takes control over all of what is now Sabah	Having launched Penang's *Eastern and Oriental* hotel two years earlier, the Sarkies brothers create Singapore's *Raffles*

merchants, the linchpin of Singapore's trade, were interested only in Malay products such as birds' nests, seaweed and camphor. But passing traders were not the only Chinese to come to the Strait. Although settlers had trickled into the Peninsula since the early days of Melaka, new **plantations** of pepper and gambier (an astringent used in tanning and dyeing), and the rapidly expanding **tin mines**, attracted floods of workers eager to escape a life of poverty in China. By 1845, half of Singapore's population was Chinese, and likewise principal towns along the Peninsula's west coast (site of the world's largest tin field) and, for that matter, Kuching, became predominantly Chinese.

The Pangkor Treaty

Allowed a large degree of commercial independence by both the British and the Malay chiefs, the Chinese formed **kongsis** (clan associations) and triads (secret societies). The **Malays**, too, were hardly immune from factional conflicts, which frequently became intertwined with Chinese squabbles, causing a string of **civil conflicts**: in Penang in 1867, for example, the triads allied themselves with Malay groups in a bloody street battle that lasted several days.

Such lawlessness was detrimental to commerce, giving the British an excuse to increase their involvement in local affairs. A meeting involving the chiefs of the Perak Malays was arranged by the new Straits Governor, Andrew Clarke, on Pulau Pangkor, just off the west coast of the Peninsula. In the meantime, Rajah Abdullah, the man most likely to succeed to the Perak throne, had written to Clarke asking for his position as sultan to be guaranteed; in return, he offered the British the chance to appoint a **Resident**, a senior British civil servant whose main function would be to act as adviser to the local sultan, and who would also oversee the collecting of local taxes. On January 20, 1874, the **Pangkor Treaty** was signed, formalizing British intervention in Malay political affairs.

Perak's first Resident, J.W.W. Birch, was not sympathetic to the ways of the Malays; his centralizing tendencies were opposed by Abdullah when he became sultan. Fearful of a Malay rebellion, senior British officials announced that judicial decisions would from now on be in the hands of the British. This went against the Pangkor Treaty, and furious Malays soon found a vent for their frustration: on November 2, 1875, Birch was killed on an upriver visit. Only with the appointment of the third Resident of Perak, the respected Hugh Low, did the system start to work more smoothly.

Other states soon saw the arrival of a Resident, and agreements along the lines of the Pangkor Treaty were drawn up with Selangor, Negeri Sembilan and Pahang during the 1880s. In 1896, these three and Perak became bracketed together under the title of the **Federated Malay States**, with the increasingly important town of **Kuala Lumpur** as the capital.

British Malaya

By 1888 the name **British Malaya** had come into use – a term that reflected the intention to extend British control over the whole Peninsula. Over subsequent decades, the economic and administrative powers of the Malay sultans were eroded, while the introduction of rubber estates in the first half of the twentieth century made British Malaya one of the world's most productive colonies. The rapidity and

1890	**1890s**	**1896**
Charles Brooke, second rajah of Sarawak, captures Limbang from Brunei, splitting the sultanate in two	Henry Ridley, director of Singapore's Botanic Gardens, works out how to tap rubber commercially	The Federated Malay States are created, encompassing the four states that have a British Resident, with Kuala Lumpur as capital

extent of the British takeover in the Peninsula was unprecedented, aided by advances in communications.

The extension of British power brought further unrest, particularly in the east coast states, where the Malays proved just as resentful of British control as in Perak. A set of skirmishes took place in Pahang in the early 1890s, when Malay chiefs protested about the reduction of their privileges. After one powerful chief, Dato' Bahaman, was stripped of his title by Pahang's Resident, Hugh Clifford, the Dato' led a small rebellion that soon became the stuff of legends. One fighter, **Mat Kilau**, earned a place in folklore as a hero who stood up to the British. From this time, Malays would interpret the uprisings as a valiant attempt to safeguard their traditions and autonomy.

By 1909, the northern Malay states of Kedah and Perlis had been brought into the colonial fold. In 1910, Johor accepted a British general-adviser; a 1914 treaty between Britain and Johor made his powers equal to those of Residents elsewhere. Terengganu, which was under Thai control, was the last state to accept a British adviser, in 1919. These four states, together with Kelantan, were sometimes collectively referred to as the **Unfederated Malay States**, though they shared no common administration.

By the outbreak of World War I, British political control was more or less complete. The Peninsula was subdivided into groups of states and regions with the seat of power split between Singapore and Kuala Lumpur.

The expansion of British interests in Borneo

The Anglo-Dutch Treaty did not include **Borneo**, where official expansion was discouraged by the EIC, which preferred to concentrate on expanding its trading contacts rather than territorial control. The benefits of Borneo did not, however, elude the sights of one British explorer, **James Brooke** (1803–68). Finding lawlessness throughout the island, Brooke persuaded the Sultan of Brunei to award him his own area – **Sarawak** – in 1841, becoming the first of a line of "**White Rajahs**" who ruled the state until World War II. Brooke quickly asserted his authority by involving formerly rebellious Malay chiefs in government, although the interior's Indigenous groups proved more of a problem. Subsequently Brooke and his successors proved adept at siphoning more land into the familial fiefdom.

Though the association between the British and James Brooke was informal (Brooke was careful not to encourage European contacts that might compromise his hold), trade between Singapore and Sarawak flourished. By the mid-nineteenth century, however, the British attitude had altered; they chose Brooke as their agent in Brunei, and found him a useful deterrent against French and Dutch aspirations towards the valuable trade routes. Eventually, in 1888, Sarawak, North Borneo (Sabah) and Brunei were transformed into **protectorates**, a status that entailed responsibility for their foreign policy being handed over to the British.

The legacy of James Brooke was furthered by his nephew **Charles Brooke** in the second half of the nineteenth century. Like his uncle, Charles ruled Sarawak in paternalistic fashion, recruiting soldiers, lowly officials and boatmen from the ranks of the Indigenous groups and leaving the Chinese to get on with running commercial enterprises and opening up the interior. **Vyner Brooke**, Charles's eldest son, became rajah in 1917; his reign saw no new territorial acquisitions, though there was a steady

1917	**1933**	**1941**	**1942**
Vyner Brooke becomes the third and, as it turns out, last White Rajah of Sarawak	The first Malay-language feature film, *Laila Majnun*, is made in Singapore	Japan lands forces in Kelantan and captures Miri in Sarawak	Singapore falls to the Japanese

development in rubber, pepper and palm-oil production. The Indigenous peoples mostly continued living a traditional lifestyle in longhouses along the river, while the end of their practice of head-hunting was followed by some degree of integration among the area's varied racial groups.

By way of contrast, the **British North Borneo Chartered Company**'s writ in what became Sabah encountered some early obstacles. The company's plans for economic expansion involved clearing the rainforest, planting **rubber** and **tobacco** over large areas, and levying taxes on the Indigenous groups. Resistance ensued, with the most vigorous action, in 1897, led by a Bajau chief, **Mat Salleh**, whose men rampaged through the company's outstation on Pulau Gaya. Another rebellion by **Murut** Indigenous people in 1915 resulted in a heavy-handed response from British forces, who killed hundreds.

By the start of the twentieth century, the majority of the lands of the once-powerful **Sultanate of Brunei** had been dismembered – the sultanate was now surrounded by Sarawak. But the sultan's fortunes had not completely disappeared and with the discovery of oil, the British thought it prudent to appoint a Resident. Exploitation of the small state's oil fields gathered pace in the 1930s following investment from British companies.

Development and ethnic rivalries

In the first quarter of the twentieth century, the British encouraged hundreds of thousands of **immigrants** from China and India to come to Peninsular Malaysia, Sarawak, North Borneo and Singapore. They arrived to work as tin miners or plantation labourers, and Malaya's population in this period doubled to four million. This bred increasing resentment among the Malays, who believed that they were being denied the economic opportunities advanced to others.

A further deterioration in Malay–Chinese relations followed the success of mainland Chinese revolutionary groups in Malaya. Malayan Chinese joined the **Malayan Communist Party** (MCP) from 1930 onwards and also formed the backbone of postwar Chinese movements that demanded an end to British rule and what they perceived as special privileges extended to the Malays. At the same time, Malay nationalism was gathering its own head of steam. The **Singapore Malay Union**, which held its first conference in 1939, advocated a Malay supremacist line. A year earlier, the first All-Malaya Malays Conference, organized by the Selangor Malays Association, had been held in KL.

The Japanese occupation

Landing in Kelantan in December 1941, Japanese forces took barely two months to sweep down the Peninsula and reach Singapore. The **surrender** of the British forces there in February 1942 ushered in a Japanese regime that brutalized the Chinese, largely because of Japan's history of conflict with China; at least 25,000 people were tortured and killed in the two weeks immediately after the surrender of the island by the British military command. Allied POWs were rounded up into prison camps; many of the troops were subsequently sent to build the infamous "Death Railway" in Burma.

In **Malaya**, towns and buildings were destroyed as the Allies attempted to bomb strategic targets. But with the Japanese firmly in control, the occupiers ingratiated

1945	1946	1946	1946
Japanese forces in Southeast Asia formally surrender in Singapore	Britain introduces the Malayan Union, turning Malaya into a full colony rather than a protectorate	Despite local protests, Vyner Brooke cedes Sarawak to the British government, bringing the White Rajahs' dynasty to an end	The British North Borneo Company cedes Sabah to the British government

themselves with some of the Malay elite by suggesting that after the war the country would be given independence. Predictably, it was the Chinese activists in the MCP, more than the Malays, who organized resistance during wartime.

December 1941 also saw the Japanese invade **Sarawak**, beginning with the capture of the Miri oil field. Although the Japanese never penetrated the interior, they quickly established control over the populated towns along the coast. The Chinese in Miri, Sibu and Kuching were the main targets: the Japanese put down rebellions brutally, and there was no organized guerrilla activity until late in the occupation. What resistance there was arose from "Z Force", namely Major **Tom Harrisson** and a team of British and Australian commandos, who in 1945 parachuted into the remote Kelabit Highlands to build a resistance movement.

In **North Borneo**, the Japanese invaded Pulau Labuan on New Year's Day, 1942. Over the next three years the main suburban areas were bombed by the Allies, destroying most of Jesselton (modern-day KK) and Sandakan. Captured troops and civilians suffered enormously – the worst single outrage being the "Death March" in September 1944, when 2400 POWs were forced to walk from Sandakan to Ranau (see page 401).

In September 1945, just prior to a planned Allied invasion to retake Singapore, the **Japanese surrendered** following the dropping of atomic bombs on Nagasaki and Hiroshima. The surrender led to a power vacuum in the region, with the British initially having to work with the MCP's armed wing, the **Malayan People's Anti-Japanese Army** (MPAJA), to maintain order in many areas. Violence occurred between the MPAJA and Malays, particularly against those accused of collaborating with the Japanese.

Postwar upheaval

Immediately after the war, the British introduced the **Malayan Union**, in effect turning the Malay States from a protectorate into a colony and removing the sovereignty of the sultans. Another effect was to give the Chinese and Indian inhabitants citizenship and equal rights with the Malays. This quickly aroused opposition from the Malays, the nationalists among whom formed the **United Malays National Organization** (UMNO) in 1946. Its main tenet was that Malays should retain special privileges, largely because they were the first inhabitants, and that the uniquely powerful position of the sultans should not be tampered with.

UMNO's resistance led to the Malayan Union idea being replaced by the **Federation of Malaya**. Established in 1948, this upheld the sultans' power and privileges and brought all the Peninsula's territories together under one government, apart from Chinese-dominated Singapore, whose inclusion would have led to the Malays being in a minority overall. Protests erupted in Singapore at its exclusion, with the **Malayan Democratic Union** (MDU), a multiracial party, calling for integration with Malaya – a position that commanded little support among the Chinese population.

After the Japanese surrender in **Borneo**, the Colonial Office in London made Sarawak and North Borneo **Crown Colonies**, with Vyner Brooke offering no objection. Sarawakians were torn over the change in arrangements, however: while the ruling assembly, the Council Negeri (composed of Malays, Chinese, Iban and British), had voted to transfer power to Britain, some Malays and prominent Iban in Kuching

1948	**1948**	**1957**
Malay opposition to the Malayan Union leads to its replacement by the Federation of Malaya, which respects the status of the sultans	The Malayan Community Party launches an insurgency from the jungle, which comes to be called The Emergency	The Federation of Malaya – the Malay Peninsula, minus Singapore – gains independence

THE EMERGENCY AND THE ORANG ASLI

The impact of the Emergency on the **Orang Asli** of the interior was dramatic. All but the most remote Indigenous groups were subject to intimidation and brutality, from guerrillas on one side and government forces on the other. In effect, the Orang Asli's centuries-old invisibility had ended; the population of Malaysia was now aware of their presence, and the government of their strategic importance.

The Orang Asli had no choice but to grow food and act as porters for the guerrillas, as well as – most important of all – provide intelligence, warning them of the approach of the enemy. In response, the government implemented a disastrous policy of removing thousands of Orang Asli from the jungle and relocating them in new model villages in the interior, which were no more than dressed-up prison camps. Hundreds died in captivity before the government dismantled these settlements. By then, not surprisingly, active support for the insurgents among the Orang Asli had risen – though allegiances switched to the security forces when it became clear the guerrillas were heading for defeat. Government attempts to control the Orang Asli during the Emergency turned out to be the precursor to initiatives that persist to the present day, drawing the Orang Asli away from their traditional lifestyle and into the embrace of the Malaysian nation-state.

opposed the move. Protests reached a peak with the assassination in Sibu in 1949 of the senior official in the new administration, Governor Duncan Stewart. But on the whole, resentment at the passing of the Brooke era was short-lived as the economy expanded and infrastructure improved. Britain also signed a Treaty of Protection with the Sultan of Brunei, who remained the chief power in the state while Sarawak's high commissioner took on the purely decorative role of governor of Brunei.

The Emergency

Many Chinese in the Peninsula were angered when the country changed status from a colony to a federation, effectively making them second-class citizens. According to the new laws, non-Malays could only qualify as citizens if they had lived in the country for fifteen out of the last twenty-five years, and they also had to prove they spoke Malay or English.

Following the communist takeover in China in 1949, most Malayan Chinese ceased to look to China; the more political among them founded a new political party, the **Malayan Chinese Association** (MCA). Some local Chinese, however, identified with the MCP, which under its new leader, **Chin Peng**, declared its intention of setting up a Malayan republic. Peng fused the MCP with the remains of the MPAJA, and, using arms supplies that the latter had dumped in the forests, from June 1948 he launched sporadic attacks on rubber estates, killing planters and employees as well as spreading fear among rural communities. This civil conflict, which lasted until 1960, was euphemistically called **the Emergency** for insurance purposes; planters would have had their policies cancelled if war had been officially declared. At its peak, around ten thousand of Chin Peng's guerrillas were hiding out in jungle camps, using a support network of Chinese-dominated towns and villages in the interior. In many cases inhabitants were cowed into submission by means of public executions, though many poor rural workers identified with the insurgents' struggle.

1959	**1962**	**1963**
Singapore gains full self-government under Lee Kuan Yew, while remaining a British colony	President Sukarno of Indonesia uses military incursions – the Konfrontasi – to agitate against Sabah and Sarawak joining Malaya	The Federation of Malaya becomes the Federation of Malaysia, augmented by Singapore, Sarawak and Sabah; Brunei opts out

Although the Emergency was never fully felt in the main urban areas, British rubber-estate owners would arrive at the *Coliseum Hotel* in KL with harrowing stories of how "communist terrorists" had hacked off the arms of rural Chinese workers who refused to support the cause, and of armed attacks on plantations.

The British were slow to respond to the threat, but once Lieutenant-General Sir Harold Briggs was put in command of police and army forces, Malaya was on a war footing. Briggs' most controversial policy was the **resettlement** of 400,000 rural Chinese – mostly squatters who had moved to the jungle fringes to avoid the Japanese during the war – as well as thousands of Orang Asli. Although these forced migrations were successful in breaking down many of the guerrillas' supply networks, they alienated many Chinese and Orang Asli who had previously been sympathetic to the British.

The violence peaked in 1950 with ambushes and attacks near Ipoh, Kuala Kangsar, Kuala Lipis and Raub. The most notorious incident occurred in 1951 on the road to Fraser's Hill, when the British high commissioner to Malaya, **Sir Henry Gurney**, was assassinated. Under his replacement, Sir Gerald Templer, a new policy was introduced to win hearts and minds. "White Areas", perceived as free of guerrilla activity, were established; communities in these regions had food restrictions and curfews lifted, a policy that began to dissipate guerrilla activity over the next three years. The leaders were offered an amnesty in 1956, which was refused, and Chin Peng and most of the remaining cell members fled over the border to Thailand where they received sanctuary.

Towards independence

The Emergency had the effect of speeding up political change prior to independence. UMNO stuck to its "Malays first" policy, though its president, **Tuanku Abdul Rahman** (also the chief minister of Malaya), won the 1955 election by cooperating with the MCA and the Malayan Indian Association. The resulting bloc, the **UMNO Alliance**, swept into power under the rallying cry of **Merdeka** (Freedom). The hope was that ethnic divisions would no longer be a major factor were **independence** granted.

With British backing, *merdeka* was proclaimed on August 31, 1957 in a ceremony in Kuala Lumpur's padang – promptly renamed Merdeka Square. The British high commissioner signed a treaty that decreed that the **Federation of Malaya** was now independent of the Crown, with Tuanku Abdul Rahman the first prime minister. The new **constitution** allowed for the nine Malay sultans to alternate as king, and established a two-tier **parliament**, comprising a house of elected representatives and a senate with delegates from each state. Under Rahman, the country was fully committed to economic expansion, with foreign investment actively encouraged – a stance that has survived to the present.

Similarly, in **Singapore** the process of gaining independence acquired momentum throughout the 1950s. In 1957, the British gave the go-ahead for the setting up of an elected 51-member assembly, and full **self-government** was attained in 1959, when the People's Action Party (PAP) under **Lee Kuan Yew** won most of the seats. Lee immediately entered into talks with Tuanku Abdul Rahman over the notion that Singapore and Malaya should be joined administratively. Tunku initially agreed, although he feared the influence of the far left in the PAP.

In 1961, Tuanku Abdul Rahman proposed that Sarawak and North Borneo should join Malaya and Singapore in an enlarged federation. Many in Borneo would have preferred the idea of a separate Borneo Federation, although the Konfrontasi (see

1965	1969	1971	1981
Singapore leaves the Federation and goes it alone as an independent country	Deadly race riots scar Kuala Lumpur	The Malaysian government introduces its New Economic Policy, including positive discrimination in favour of Malays	Mahathir Mohamad, to become Malaysia's long-serving prime minister, takes office

below) was to make clear how vulnerable such a federation would be to attack from Indonesia. Rahman's suggestion was, however, not fuelled by security concerns but by **demographics**: if Singapore were to join the federation, the country would acquire a Chinese majority. This made the two Borneo colonies useful as a counterweight to Singapore's Chinese.

Although Abdul Rahman had wanted **Brunei** to join the Malaysian Federation, Sultan Omar refused when he realized Rahman's price – a substantial proportion of Brunei's oil and gas revenues. Brunei remained under nominal British jurisdiction until its **independence** on January 1, 1984.

Federation and the Konfrontasi

In September 1963, North Borneo (quickly renamed Sabah), Sarawak and Singapore joined Malaya in the **Federation of Malaysia** – "Malaysia" being a term coined by the British in the 1950s when the notion of a Greater Malaya had been propounded. Both Indonesia, which laid claim to Sarawak, and the Philippines, which claimed jurisdiction over Sabah as it had originally been part of the Sulu Sultanate, reacted angrily. Border skirmishes with Indonesia known as the **Konfrontasi** ensued, and a wider war was only just averted when Indonesian President Sukarno backed down from taking on British and Gurkha troops brought in to bolster Sarawak's small armed forces.

Within the federation, further differences surfaced in Singapore during this period between Lee Kuan Yew and the Malay-dominated Alliance over the lack of egalitarian policies; many Chinese were concerned that UMNO's overall influence in the federation was too great. Tensions rose on the island and racial incidents developed into full-scale **riots** in 1964, in which several people were killed.

These developments were viewed with great concern by Tuanku Abdul Rahman in Kuala Lumpur, and when the PAP subsequently attempted to enter Peninsular politics, he decided it would be best if Singapore left the federation. This was emphatically not in Singapore's best interests, since it was an island without any obvious natural resources; Lee cried on TV when the expulsion was announced and Singapore acquired full **independence** on August 9, 1965. The severing of the bond between Malaysia and Singapore has led to a kind of sibling rivalry between the two nations ever since.

Racial issues and riots

Singapore's exit from the Malaysian Federation was not enough to quell ethnic tensions. Resentment grew among the Malaysian Chinese over the principle that Malay be the main language taught in schools and over the privileged employment opportunities offered to Malays. After the Alliance lost ground in elections in May 1969, Malays in major cities reacted angrily to a perceived increase in power of the Chinese, who had commemorated their breakthrough with festivities in the streets. Hundreds of people, mostly Chinese, were killed and injured in the **riots** that followed; KL in particular became a war zone with large crowds of youths on the rampage. Rahman kept the country under a state of emergency for nearly two years, during which the draconian **Internal Security Act** (ISA) was used to arrest and imprison activists, as well as many writers and artists, setting a sombre precedent for authoritarian practices still followed today.

1984	**1987**	**1997**	**1998**
Brunei becomes independent	The Malaysia government launches Operation Lalang, a major crackdown against its critics and sectors of the press	The Asian economic crisis envelops the region	KL's Petronas Towers become world's tallest buildings

> ### THE BUMIPUTRA POLICY
>
> Provisions in the New Economic Policy (NEP), introduced in the wake of the 1969 race riots, became known as the **Bumiputra policy** as they were intended to provide a more level economic playing field for Malays, Orang Asli and the Indigenous peoples of east Malaysia (*bumiputra* means something like "sons of the soil" in Malay). In terms of wealth, these communities (as well the Indians) were lagging far behind the Chinese. This was partly the result of colonial policy: the immigrant Chinese made strides as businesspeople in the towns, while the Malays were either employed as administrators or left to get on with farming and fishing in rural areas, while the Indians toiled on the railways and the plantations.
>
> The policy has been moderated, renamed and rejigged over the years, but basically awards *bumiputras*, in particular the Malays, privileges such as subsidized housing and easier access to higher education and civil-service jobs. The *bumiputra* policy has undoubtedly achieved a reasonable degree of **wealth redistribution**, though a less laudable consequence has been the creation of a super-rich Malay elite. What's more, the policy is deeply resented by the non-beneficiaries. The Indians are especially aggrieved, having never been wealthy; the Chinese have continued to rely on their own devices in business while shunning the public sector, where they feel the odds have been stacked against them.
>
> Despite the policy's undoubted popularity among Malays, successive leaders have questioned the wisdom of allowing the system to continue indefinitely, fearing that it has fostered complacency in the very communities it is meant to help. The difficulty for all UMNO leaders is that any meaningful retreat from the policy requires political daring. Only the opposition, which generally wants to reform Malaysian politics in a non-racial mould, has attempted to make progress in this regard, though it is just as risky an enterprise for them.

Abdul Rahman never recovered full political command and resigned in 1970. That September, the new prime minister, **Tun Abdul Razak Hussein**, initiated a form of state-orchestrated positive discrimination called the **New Economic Policy** (NEP), which gives ethnic Malays and members of Borneo's Indigenous groups favoured positions in business and other professions. Also under Razak, a crucial step was taken towards Malaysia's current political map with the formation in 1974 of the **Barisan Nasional** ("National Front", usually abbreviated to **BN**), comprising UMNO plus the main Chinese and Indian parties and – since the 1990s – parties representing Indigenous groups in Sabah and Sarawak. This multiethnic coalition has governed the country ever since.

The Mahathir era

The dominant figure in Malaysian politics since independence has been **Dr Mahathir Mohamad**, prime minister from 1981 until 2003. Even Malaysians not generally favourably disposed towards the BN credit him with helping the country attain economic lift-off; under Mahathir, industrialization changed the landscape of regions like the Klang Valley and Johor, manufacturing output eclipsed agriculture in importance, and huge **prestige projects** like the Petronas Towers and KLIA were completed. Mahathir meanwhile kept his supporters happy with a raft of populist pronouncements, including railing against the West for criticizing Malaysia's human-rights record (he claimed that by what he

2003	2004	2004	2009
Abdullah Badawi succeeds Mahathir as Malaysian prime minister	Lee Hsien Loong, Lee Kuan Yew's son, becomes prime minister of Singapore	Penang and Kedah in Malaysia are struck by the Indian Ocean tsunami, though with only modest loss of life	Najib Tun Razak becomes Malaysian prime minister

termed "Asian values", prosperity was valued more highly than civil liberties). Less well remembered is the fact that Mahathir's tenure also saw the extensive use of the ISA in what became known as **Operation Lalang** when, in 1987, more than a hundred politicians and activists were detained following tensions between UMNO and Chinese political parties over matters to do with Chinese-language education. These arrests were bad enough, but more durable in its effects was state action to curb press freedom. Especially notable was the government's closure of the pro-MCA English-language *Star* newspaper for several months; when it reopened, many of its senior managers had been replaced.

In 1997, the economy suffered a major setback when Malaysia was sucked into the **Asian economic crisis**, which began in Thailand and Korea. Mahathir took personal charge of getting the economy back on track, sacking his deputy and finance minister **Anwar Ibrahim** in 1998. A former student leader and once an espouser of progressive Islamic policies, Anwar had enjoyed a meteoric rise upon joining UMNO and had been groomed to succeed Mahathir, though relations between the two subsequently soured. The nation was stunned when, within a week of his dismissal, Anwar was arrested on corruption and sexual misconduct charges; a succession of mass demonstrations in his support ensued. Anwar's treatment in detention became the subject of much concern when he appeared in court on the corruption charge sporting a black eye. He was eventually found guilty – leading many observers to question the independence of the judiciary – and sentenced to six years in jail. In 2000, he was also found guilty of sodomizing his driver and sentenced to nine years in prison.

Meanwhile, Anwar's wife, Wan Azizah Wan Ismail, formed a new party, **Keadilan** ("Justice", sometimes also called **PKR**), which has contested subsequent elections in alliance with other opposition parties, including the Chinese-dominated Democratic Action Party (**DAP**) and the Islamist **PAS**.

Malaysia under Abdullah Badawi

Momentously, in 2003, Mahathir resigned and handed power to Anwar's replacement as deputy prime minister, **Abdullah Badawi**. Hailing from Penang, Abdullah (often referred to as Pak Lah) is a genial man, in marked contrast to his abrasive predecessor, and he asserted himself effectively, winning a landslide general election victory in 2004. Soon after, Anwar's sodomy conviction was overturned and he was released, though he remained barred from standing for parliament until 2008 as his corruption conviction was not quashed.

As a relatively new broom, Abdullah enjoyed much goodwill early on; it was hoped he would make good on his promises to sweep cronyism and corruption out of Malaysian politics. But as time wore on, authority seemed to ebb away from his government in the face of crises and scandals.

The most sensational of these was the affair of **Altantuya Shaariibuu**, a Mongolian woman who went missing in the KL area in 2006. Her remains, which had been blown to bits with explosives, were soon discovered, and it transpired that she was an associate of a defence analyst with links to **Najib Tun Razak**, Abdullah's deputy. The case created a stink around the government, and two policemen, members of an elite unit protecting politicians and other senior authority figures, were subsequently sentenced to death for her murder.

2013	2014	2014
The Malaysian opposition wins the popular vote in the general election, although the BN coalition remains in power	Two disasters hit Malaysia Airlines, with flight MH370 vanishing and flight MH17 destroyed by a missile	First World Hotel, in Genting, becomes the largest hotel in the world, with 7351 rooms

The 2008 elections

In February 2008, Abdullah called a **snap general election** for the following month – when Anwar Ibrahim was still barred from standing. If the timing was maximally convenient for Abdullah, the result was anything but: the BN was duly returned to power, but on its **worst showing** since its formation in 1974. This time, the BN failed to win more than two-thirds of seats in parliament, which had hitherto afforded it the right to tinker with the constitution. To make matters worse, the opposition alliance unseated the BN in an unprecedented number of **state assemblies**, not just in largely Malay Kedah, where voters had previously flirted with PAS, but also in cosmopolitan, prosperous Selangor, Penang and Perak.

In the wake of the election, amid euphoria and recrimination, everything in Malaysian politics seemed to be up for grabs. Perhaps the worst news for Abdullah was how badly the BN fared in the Peninsula, home to three-quarters of the population: its majority there was wafer-thin, and it took just one out of eleven seats in KL. Only victories by the BN-allied parties of Sabah and Sarawak had secured the coalition a working majority.

Testing times

Unfortunately for Abdullah, things got no better for the BN in the aftermath of the polls, as the various affairs that had come to light beforehand played themselves out like a tragicomic drama. Against this turbulent backdrop, **Anwar Ibrahim** made a triumphant return to parliament in August 2008, his wife resigning her seat so that he could stand in a by-election. Just prior to all this, however, Anwar was sensationally arrested once again on a charge of sodomy, this time involving a young aide of his. Allowed bail, Anwar took up his new role as leader of the opposition coalition, **Pakatan Rakyat**, while having to make appearances in court. Then in 2009 Abdullah Badawi stepped down, to be replaced by his deputy **Najib Tun Razak**.

In 2012, Anwar was cleared of the second sodomy charge, freeing him to play a frontline role in the impending polls, which took place in May 2013. It proved to be another watershed election, though not quite as the opposition would have liked. For the first time, the combined opposition parties won more than half the popular vote, but the first-past-the-post voting system meant the BN achieved a workable majority in the federal parliament, as well as recapturing the state assemblies in Kedah and Perak. The opposition's next significant move was an attempt to shoehorn Anwar into the chief minister's job in **Selangor**, the most developed state in the Federation and their one true showcase. But that was thwarted when, in March 2014, his acquittal on the second sodomy charge was overturned on a government appeal. In February 2015, the Federal Court – the highest in the land – upheld the government's appeal, and Anwar was sent to prison once again at the age of 67. Under the electoral rules, he was thus removed from front-line politics; he was released with a full royal pardon in 2018, and won a hastily-arranged by-election later the same year.

It seems clear that Malaysia is entering ever more uncertain waters. On the one hand, the country remains a working example of a multiethnic, multicultural state. On the other, it is also a collection of little powder kegs, any one of which could spark a

2015	**2015**	**2016**
1MDB financial scandal erupts, eventually landing Najib Tun Razak in jail	Golden jubilee of Singapore independence, months after the death of Lee Kuan Yew	Singapore wins first – and so far only – Olympic gold, in the men's 100m butterfly swim

conflagration at any time. Scarcely a year seems to go by without some new corruption scandal involving politicians or officials who eventually get off scot-free, and none has been as shocking as the **1MDB affair**, which erupted in 2015 with allegations that prime minister Najib had somehow received billions of ringgit siphoned from 1MDB, a state-owned investment company. The ramifications were wide-ranging, with international criminal investigations into potential money-laundering taking place from Switzerland to the Seychelles. In the US, Najib's stepson was found to have used 1MDB money to fund his film production company (somewhat hilariously, in a case of life not only imitating art but paying for art to imitate itself, the funds were used to make *The Wolf of Wall Street*), and in 2016 the Department of Justice launched an eventually successful effort to recover some US$1 billion in misappropriated 1MDB funds. Domestically, Malaysia's attorney general was investigating the matter when he was replaced; months later, that replacement gave Najib a clean bill of health, raising eyebrows. There was more scepticism when the head of Malaysian's Anti-Corruption Commission chose to step down early and was replaced with an official who had previously worked for the new attorney general.

Malaysia's official news agency also reported that Saudi donors provided the billions in Najib's bank accounts, an "explanation" that, even if true, raised grave questions as to why a politician came into receipt of massive backdoor donations from abroad. In 2018, Mahathir returned to power in a new Malay party, **Bersatu** (making him the first Malaysian prime minister not to represent the BN), and immediately reopened investigations into the scandal. Najib and eleven others were prevented from leaving the country, and US$270m of property was seized. In 2020, Najib was found guilty on seven charges, and sentenced to twelve years in jail, though the appeals process kept him free on bail until August 2022, when he was finally locked up, with a further 35 charges still yet to be faced in four potential trials.

2020 saw a political crisis, when Mahathir – by then the world's oldest leader, at 94 years of age – refused to hand over power to his old deputy Anwar. The subsequent assembling and crumbling of coalitions saw **Muhyiddin Yassin** (also of Bersatu) appointed prime minister in March 2020; these were, of course, testing times globally, and while Muhyiddin was praised for Malaysia's initial response to the **Covid crisis**, subsequent waves of the virus eventually led to his resignation in 2021, with **Ismail Sabri** returning the BN to power. He only lasted for fifteen months (Malaysia's shortest ever Prime Ministerial rule) before the BN were trounced in elections the following year by the Pakatan Harapan (PH) coalition, led by Anwar Ibrahim.

If Malaysia is sleepwalking towards crisis or stagnation, at least Malaysian democracy is enjoying a small renaissance. The press is less cowed now about reporting the policies of opposition politicians, and civil rights organizations are campaigning ever more vocally, as borne out by several massive **Bersih** (Malay for "clean") demonstrations in KL in recent years, calling for an end to corruption and electoral fraud. Thorny issues around race and religion (including the Sedition Act, which could in principle be used to imprison anyone questioning the country's ethnic or religious policies), long swept under the carpet in the name of economic progress, are being debated with some rancour. However, purposeful discussion could ultimately lead to the country taking a more progressive path.

2017	**2023**	**2024**	**2025**
Halimah Jacob becomes first female president of Singapore	Malaysian actress Michelle Yeoh becomes the first Asian woman to win the Oscar for Best Actress	Opening of Merdeka 118, the second-tallest structure in the world at 679m	Singapore hosts World Aquatics Championships

Religion

Islam is a significant force in Malaysia, given that virtually all Malays, who comprise just over half the population, are Muslim; in Singapore, where three-quarters of the population are Chinese, Buddhism is the main religion. There's a smaller, but no less significant, Hindu Indian presence in both countries, while the other chief belief system is animism, adhered to by many of the Indigenous peoples of Malaysia. While the colonial period drew Christian missionaries to the region, the British, in a bid to avoid unrest among the Malays, were restrained in their evangelical efforts. Christian missionaries had more success in Borneo than on the Peninsula; indeed, the main Indigenous group in Sabah, the Kadazan/Dusun, is Christian, as are many or most Kelabit and Iban in Sarawak. That said, Christianity is a significant minority religion in Peninsular Malaysia and Singapore, with a notable following among middle-class Chinese and Indians.

One striking feature of religion here is that it can be a **syncretic** blend of beliefs and influences. In a region where fusion is visible in everything from food to language, it's not hard to come across individuals who profess one faith, yet pray or make offerings to deities of another, in the warm-hearted belief that all religions contain some truth and that it therefore makes sense not to put all your spiritual eggs in one devotional basket.

Animism

Although many of Malaysia's Indigenous groups are now nominally Christian or Muslim, many of their old animist beliefs and rites still survive. In the animist worldview, everything in nature – mountains, trees, rocks and lakes – has a controlling soul or spirit (**semangat** in Malay) that has to be mollified. For the Orang Asli groups in the interior of the Peninsula, remaining animist beliefs often centre on healing and funeral ceremonies. A sick person, particularly a child, is believed to be invaded by a bad spirit, and drums are played and incantations performed to persuade the spirit to depart. The death of a member of the family is followed by a complex process of burial and reburial – a procedure that, it is hoped, ensures an easy passage for the person's spirit.

In Sarawak, **birds**, especially the **hornbill**, are of particular significance to the Iban and Kelabit peoples. Many Kelabit depend upon the arrival of migrating flocks to decide when to plant their rice crop, while Iban augury interprets sightings of the hornbill and other birds as good or bad omens. In some accounts of Iban beliefs, two bird spirits are involved in the creation of the Earth and sky, and the Iban themselves are descended from a bird spirit named Sengalang Burong.

Hinduism

Hinduism arrived in Malaysia long before Islam, brought by Indian traders more than a thousand years ago. While almost all of Malaysia's ancient Hindu past has been obliterated, elements live on in the popular arts like *wayang kulit* (shadow plays), the plots of which are drawn from the sacred *Ramayana*.

The central tenet of Hinduism is the belief that life is a series of rebirths and reincarnations that eventually lead to spiritual release. A whole variety of deities are worshipped, which on the surface makes Hinduism appear complex; however, a loose understanding of the *Vedas* – the religion's holy books – is enough for the characters and roles of the main gods to become apparent. The deities you'll come across most often are the three manifestations of the faith's supreme divine being: **Brahma** the creator, **Vishnu** the preserver and **Shiva** the destroyer.

Hinduism returned to the Peninsula in the late nineteenth century when immigrants from southern India arrived to work on the Malayan rubber and oil-palm plantations. The Hindu celebration of Rama's victory – the central theme of the *Ramayana* – in time became the national holiday of **Deepavali** (or Diwali; the festival of lights), while another Hindu festival, **Thaipusam**, when Lord Subramaniam and elephant-headed Ganesh, the sons of Shiva, are worshipped, is marked by some of the region's most prominent religious gatherings.

Step over the threshold of a **Hindu temple** in Malaysia or Singapore and you enter a kaleidoscope world of gods and fanciful creatures. The style is typically Dravidian (South Indian), as befits the largely Tamil population, with a soaring **gopura**, or entrance tower, teeming with sculptures and a central courtyard leading to an inner sanctum housing the presiding deity. In the temple precinct, you'll invariably witness incense being burned, the application of sandalwood paste to the forehead, and *puja* (ritualistic acts of worship).

Islam

Islam gained its first firm foothold in the Malay Peninsula with the conversion of Paramesvara, the ruler of **Melaka**, in the early fifteenth century. The commercial success of Melaka accelerated the spread of Islam; one after another the powerful Malay court rulers took to the religion, adopting the Arabic title "sultan", either because of sincere conversion or because they took a shrewd view of the advantages to be gained by embracing this international faith. On a cultural level, too, Islam had its attractions – its concepts of equality before Allah freed people from the Hindu caste system that had dominated parts of the region. Even after the Melaka Sultanate fell in 1511, the hold of Islam was strengthened by the migration of Muslim merchants to Brunei.

The first wave of Islamic missionaries were mostly **Sufis**, representing the mystical and generally more liberal wing of Islam. In the region Sufism absorbed some animist and Hindu beliefs, including the tradition of pluralist deity worship. However, Sufism's influence declined in the early nineteenth century when the puritanical **Wahhabi** sect of mainstream **Sunni** Islam captured Mecca. The return to the Koran's basic teachings became identified with a more militant approach, leading to jihads in Kedah, Kelantan and Terengganu against the Malay rulers' Siamese overlords and, subsequently, the British.

Islam in Malaysia and Singapore today is a mixture of Sunni and Sufi elements, and its adherents are still largely comprised of Malays, though a minority of the Indian community is Muslim, too. While Islam as practised locally is relatively liberal, the trend away from tacit secularism that has swept the Muslim world in the last two or three decades, has not left the two countries untouched. There's now a better understanding of Islam's tenets – and thus better compliance with them – among Muslims in both countries.

Of course, this drift has its social and political dimensions. In Malaysia, with its history of sometimes awkward race relations, Islam is something of a badge of identity for the Malays; it's significant that the Malaysian **constitution** practically regards being Malay as equivalent to being Muslim. Thus Malaysia has seen an increase in religious programming on TV and in state spending on often ostentatious new mosques, while even in consumerist Singapore, the Malay minority is becoming more actively engaged in religion. Malaysia's religious establishment has also become more vocal, making proclamations to discourage Muslims from practising yoga (because of its supposed

Hindu origins) and Muslim women from wearing short hair and trousers (because this would apparently encourage lesbianism). In 2017, there were also instances of Muslim-owned launderettes displaying signs barring non-Muslims from using the facilities; the government, seemingly afraid of confronting part of its support base, merely noted that it disapproved of segregation, and it took intervention from Malaysia's sultans – who normally avoid getting embroiled in politics – to force them to back down, at least for now.

Islam and the law

One striking way in which Islam influences day-to-day affairs is that in certain areas, Muslim and non-Muslim citizens are subject to different **laws**. In Malaysia, for example, while it would be acceptable for an unmarried couple to share a hotel room if neither person is Muslim, it would be illegal (an act known as **khalwat**) if both were Muslim; if only one of them were Muslim, only that person would be committing an illegal act. This legal divide is reflected in the judicial systems of both Malaysia and Singapore, in which **syariah** (sharia) courts interpreting Islamic law exist alongside courts and laws derived from the British legal system.

Both Malaysia and Singapore limit Islamic jurisprudence to matters concerning the family and certain types of behaviour deemed transgressions against Islam, such as *khalwat*, or for a Muslim to consume alcohol in public. In this regard, the *syariah* courts are in many ways subservient to the secular legal framework. This also means the harsher aspects of Islamic justice, such as stoning or the cutting off of a thief's hand, are not deemed permissible; an attempt in the 1990s by the state government of Kelantan, run by the Islamist opposition PAS party, to introduce them within the state was thwarted by Malaysia's federal government. The Islamic standard of proof in a case concerning rape – requiring the victim to be able to produce four witnesses – also does not apply, since rape cases are tried within the secular system.

However, the two juridical systems are experiencing a sort of territorial dispute in the important area of **religious conversion**. It's very difficult for Malaysian Muslims to convert out of Islam as the secular courts are unwilling to uphold their choice without the involvement of the *syariah* court, which might refuse permission or, worse, wish to punish them as apostates. In this Catch-22 situation, any Muslims who take up a new faith or no faith at all can never make their choice official, and for the most part simply keep mum. Controversy has also arisen when one person in a marriage converts to Islam and then wants to use Islamic law to divorce the spouse or change the registered religion of their children, for example. The roles of the two legal systems in these situations ought to be clarified as a matter of urgency, but there has been little progress.

Mosques

In Malaysia, every town, village and hamlet has its mosque, while the capital city of each state hosts a grandiose **Masjid Negeri** (state mosque). You'll rarely see

THE BOMOH

An important link between animism and the Islam of today is provided by the Malay **bomoh**, a kind of shaman. While *bomohs* keep a low profile in these times of greater Islamic orthodoxy – no *bomoh* operates out of an office, and there are no college courses to train *bomohs* or listings of practitioners in the telephone directory – the fact is that every Malay community can still summon a *bomoh* when it's felt one is needed to cure disease, bring rain during droughts, exorcize spirits from a newly cleared plot before building work starts, or rein in the behaviour of a wayward spouse. A central part of the *bomoh*'s trade is recitation, often of sections of the Koran, while – like his Orang Asli counterparts – he uses techniques such as burning herbs to cure or ease pain and disease.

contemporary mosques varying from the standard square building topped by onion domes and minarets, though the oldest mosques reveal unusual Sumatran or other Southeast Asian influences. Two additional standard features can be found inside the prayer hall, namely the **mihrab**, a niche indicating the direction of Mecca, towards which believers face during prayers (the green *kiblat* arrow on the ceiling of most Malaysian hotel rooms fulfils the same function), and the **mimbar** (pulpit), used by the imam.

One of the five **pillars of Islam** is that the faithful should pray five times a day – at dawn (called the *subuh* prayer in Malay), midday (*zuhur*, or *jumaat* on a Friday), mid-afternoon (*asar*), dusk (*maghrib*) and mid-evening (*isyak*). On **Friday**, the day of the communal *jumaat* prayer, Muslims converge on their nearest mosque around noon to hear the imam deliver a *khutbah* (sermon); all employers allow Muslim staff a three-hour break for the purpose.

Chinese beliefs

The three different strands in Chinese belief ostensibly point in very different directions. **Confucianism** is a philosophy based on piety, loyalty, humanitarianism and familial devotion, a set of principles that permeate every aspect of Chinese life; **Buddhism** is a religion primarily concerned with the attainment of a state of personal enlightenment, nirvana; and **Taoism** propounds unity with nature as its chief tenet.

The Chinese are seldom doctrinaire; someone who claims to be Buddhist, Taoist or Confucianist may be in practice be a mixture of all three. **Ancestor worship** is also common, as is devotion to folk deities such as **Tua Peh** (or **Pek**) **Kong**, sometimes described as the God of Prosperity.

Chinese temples

The rules of **feng shui** are rigorously applied to the construction of Chinese temples, so that each building has a layout and orientation rendering it free from evil influences. Visitors wishing to cross the threshold of a temple have to step over a kerb intended to trip up evil spirits, and walk through doors flanked by fearsome door gods; fronting the doors may be two stone lions, providing yet another defence.

Temples are normally constructed around a framework of huge, lacquered timber beams, adorned with intricately carved warriors, animals and flowers. More figures are moulded onto outer walls, which are dotted with octagonal, hexagonal or round grille-worked windows. Larger temples typically consist of a front entrance hall opening onto a walled-in courtyard, beyond which is the hall of worship, where joss sticks are burned below images of the deities. The most striking element of a Chinese temple is often its **roof** – a grand, multitiered affair with low, overhanging eaves, the ridges alive with dragons, phoenixes and folkloric characters in scenes often assembled using multicoloured pottery shards, an artistic technique known as *jiannian*. In the temple grounds you'll see sizeable ovens, stuffed constantly with paper money, prayer books and other offerings; and possibly a **pagoda** – the presence of which is, once again, a defence against evil spirits. Temples linked to individual clans may also have an **ancestral hall** displaying ranks of upright **ancestral tablets**, each representing a forebear of a clan member.

Peoples

Largely because of their pivotal position on maritime trade routes between the Middle East, India and China, the present-day countries of Malaysia, Singapore and Brunei have always been a cultural melting pot. During the first millennium AD, Malays arrived from Sumatra and Indians from India and Sri Lanka, while later the Chinese migrated from mainland China and Hainan Island. All these traders and settlers arrived to find that the region already held a gamut of Indigenous groups, thought to have migrated around 50,000 years ago from the Philippines, then connected by a land bridge to Borneo and Southeast Asia. The Indigenous groups who still live on the Peninsula are known as the Orang Asli, Malay for "the original people".

Original people they may have been, but their descendants now form a minority of the overall populations of the three countries. Over the last 150 years a massive influx of Chinese and Indian immigrants, escaping poverty, war and revolution, has swelled the population of **Malaysia**, which now stands at just under 35 million. Just over half are Malays, while the Chinese make up nearly a quarter of the population, the Indians seven percent, and the various Indigenous groups just over a tenth.

Brunei's population of around 465,000 is heavily dominated by Malays, with minorities of Chinese, Indians and indigenous peoples. In **Singapore**, only tiny numbers of Indigenes were left on the island when Raffles arrived. They have no modern-day presence in the state, where around three-quarters of the six million-strong population are of Chinese extraction, around 15 percent are Malay, and nearly 9 percent Indian.

The Malays

The **Malays** are believed to have originated from the meeting of Mainland Southeast Asian, Taiwanese and even Papuan groups over the last 5000 years. Also known as Orang Laut (sea people), they sustained an economy built around fishing, boatbuilding and, in some communities, piracy. The growth in power of the Malay sultanates from the fifteenth century onwards – coinciding with the arrival of Islam – established Malays as a force to be reckoned with in the Malay Peninsula and Borneo. They developed an aristocratic tradition, courtly rituals and a social hierarchy that have a continued influence today. The rulers of Malaysia's states still wield great influence, reflected in the fact that they elect one of their number to hold the post of Yang di-Pertuan Agong, a pre-eminent sultan who holds the title for a five-year term. Although a purely ceremonial position, the *agong* is seen as the ultimate guardian of Malay Muslim culture and, despite recent legislation to reduce his powers, is still considered to be above the law. The situation is even more pronounced in **Brunei**, to which many Muslim Malay traders fled after the fall of Melaka to the Portuguese in 1511. There, the sultan remains the supreme ruler (as his descendants have been, on and off, for over five hundred years).

Even though Malays have been Muslims since the fifteenth century, the region as a whole is not fundamentalist in character. Only in Brunei is alcohol banned across the board, for instance. Perhaps the most significant recent development affecting Malays in Malaysia has been the introduction of the **Bumiputra** policy (see box, page 538).

THE BABA-NYONYAS

The **Baba-Nyonyas** are a Chinese subgroup with deep roots in the Malay Peninsula and a distinctive hybrid culture. It's often glibly said that they are the product of Chinese/Malay intermarriage, though this ignores the practical difficulties of marrying into a Muslim family without converting to Islam. What's more likely is that male migrants, arriving from China from at least the sixteenth century onwards, married local women, some Malay, others from the region's various communities such as Orang Asli or ethnic Thais. Eventually their descendants became a community in their own right – the menfolk known as **Babas**, the women **Nyonyas** – although confusingly the terms **Straits Chinese** and **Peranakan** are also used for them as a whole (Peranakan can also refer to other mixed-race groups, such as the Chitties of Melaka).

The Baba-Nyonyas clung on to some aspects of Chinese culture while absorbing influences from the Peninsula, most notably in terms of their dress – Nyonyas wore beautiful Malay-style batik-print clothes – and food (see page 40), but also in their language: many spoke Chinese dialects, notably Hokkien, but they also had their own Malay dialect. With the arrival of the British, they mastered English too, and this was to prove the foundation for a golden era when many Baba-Nyonyas became immensely wealthy. They were the bridge between the Western world and the *sinkeh*, the newly arrived Chinese migrants, who were eager to succeed. Many *sinkeh* married Nyonyas and the resulting family businesses flourished; choice residential areas such as Singapore's Katong were packed with Peranakan mansions.

It wasn't to last. In the interwar years, the British loosened the immigration rules to allow migrants to bring their wives with them, and some members of an older generation of migrants were, by then, giving their children a Western education. The Baba-Nyonyas became far less useful to the new blood from China and were simply outnumbered by them. They were also viewed with disdain by the mainstream community as being not properly Chinese. The Baba-Nyonya identity has now been largely subsumed into a wider Chinese one, though in recent decades their culture has at least been showcased in museums and their culinary heritage, at least, shows no signs of going away.

The Chinese and Straits Chinese

Although **Chinese traders** began visiting the region in the seventh century, the first significant community established itself in Melaka in the fifteenth century. However, the ancestors of most of the Chinese now living in Malaysia – ethnic Hakka, and migrants from Teochew (Chaozhou) and Hokkien (Fujian) – emigrated from southeastern China during the nineteenth century to work in the burgeoning tin-mining industry and, later, rubber and oil plantations. A large number came as labourers, but they swiftly graduated to shopkeeping and business ventures, both in established towns like Melaka and fast-expanding centres like KL, Penang and Kuching. Chinatowns developed throughout the region, even in Malay strongholds like Kota Bharu and Kuala Terengganu, while **Chinese traditions**, religious festivities, theatre and music became an integral part of a wider multiracial culture. On the political level, the Malaysian Chinese are well represented in parliament and occupy around a quarter of current ministerial positions. By way of contrast, **Chinese Bruneians** are not automatically classed as citizens and suffer significant discrimination at the hands of the majority Malay population. **Singapore**'s nineteenth-century trade boom drew many Cantonese, Teochew, Hokkien and Hakka traders and labourers, who established a Chinatown on the south bank of the Singapore River. Today, the Chinese are the most economically successful racial group in Singapore.

One physical reminder of the Chinese presence in major cities is the presence of **kongsi** (literally "company") or **clan halls** (also called clan houses or associations). Each once functioned like a clan or regional club, providing help and protection for newly arrived migrants, who naturally tended to band together with others from the same part of China. At times they could also be a focus for community rivalry, as in the case of the Penang riots (see page 148). Many clan halls are excellent examples of traditional southern Chinese architecture, incorporating courtyards, shrines and sometimes living quarters.

The Indians

The second largest non-*bumiputra* group in Malaysia, the **Indians**, first arrived as traders more than two thousand years ago, although few settled; only in the early fifteenth century did a small community of Indians (from present-day Tamil Nadu and Sri Lanka) become based in Melaka. Like the majority of Chinese, however, the first large wave of Indians – Tamil labourers – arrived as indentured workers in the nineteenth century, to build the roads and rail lines and work on the European-run rubber estates. An embryonic entrepreneurial class from North India soon followed, and set up businesses in Penang and Singapore; mostly Muslim, these merchants and traders found it easier to assimilate themselves within the existing Malay community than did the Hindu Tamils.

Although Indians comprise under a tenth of the populations of Malaysia and Singapore, their impact is widely felt. The Hindu festival of Thaipusam is celebrated annually at KL's Batu Caves by upwards of a million people (with smaller but still significant celebrations in Singapore and Penang); the festival of Deepavali is a national holiday; and Indians dominate certain professional areas like medicine and law. And then, of course, there's the food – very few Malaysians these days could do without a daily dose of *roti canai*, so much so that this Indian snack has been virtually appropriated by Malay and Chinese cafés and hawkers.

The Orang Asli

Most of the **Orang Asli** – the Indigenous peoples of Peninsular Malaysia – belong to three distinct groups, within which various Indigenous groups are related by geography, language or physiological features. It's difficult to witness much of Orang Asli life as they largely live off the beaten track, though touristed communities at Taman Negara and the Cameron Highlands can be visited. To learn more about the disappearing Asli culture, the best stop is KL's Orang Asli Museum (see page 104).

Senoi

The largest group, the **Senoi** (the Asli word for "person"), number about sixty thousand. They live in the large, still predominantly forested interior, within the states of Perak, Pahang and Kelantan, and divide into two main Indigenous groups, the Semiar and the Temiar. These still adhere to a traditional lifestyle, following animist customs in marriage ceremonies and burial rites. On the whole they follow the practice of shifting cultivation (a regular rotation of jungle clearance and crop planting), although government resettlement drives have persuaded many to settle and farm just one area.

Semang

The two thousand or so **Semang** live in the northern areas of the Peninsula. They comprise six distinct, if small, Indigenous groups, related to each other in appearance – most are dark-skinned and curly-haired – and traditionally shared a nomadic, hunter-gatherer lifestyle. However, most Semang nowadays live in settled communities and work within the cash economy, either as labourers or selling jungle produce in markets. Perhaps the most frequently seen Semang Indigenous groups are the Batek, who live in and around Taman Negara.

Aboriginals

The third group, the so-called **Aboriginal Malays**, live in an area roughly south of the Kuala Lumpur–Kuantan road. Some Indigenous groups in this category, like the Jakun and the Semelais who live around the lakes of the southern interior, vigorously retain their animist religion and artistic traditions despite living in permanent villages near Malay communities, and working within the regular economy.

Others

One of Malaysia's other Orang Asli Indigenous groups, the Lanoh in Perak are sometimes regarded as Semang, their language is closer to that of the Temiar. Another group, the semi-nomadic Che Wong, of whom just a few hundred survive on the slopes of Gunung Benom in central Pahang, still depend on foraging to survive, and live in temporary huts made from bamboo and rattan. Two more groups, the Jah Hut of Pahang and the Mah Meri of Selangor, are particularly fine carvers, and it's possible to buy their sculptures at regional craft shops.

Indigenous Sarawak: the Dyak

In direct contrast to the Peninsula, Indigenous groups make up a larger chunk of the population in **Sarawak**, which stands at around three million. Although the Chinese comprise 18 percent of the state's population and the Malays and Indians around 20 percent together, the remainder are made up of various Indigenous **Dyak** groups – a word derived from the Malay for "upcountry". Certain general aspects of their culture – for instance, the importance of bronze drums and reburial ceremonies – might indicate that the Dyak arrived in the region from mainland Southeast Asia around 2000 years ago.

The largest Dyak groups are the Iban, Bidayuh, Melanau, Kayan, Kenyah, Kelabit and Penan Indigenous groups. They have very distinct cultures as well as a few commonalities. Many live in **longhouses** along the rivers or on hillsides in the mountainous interior, and maintain a proud cultural legacy that draws on animist religion, arts and crafts production and jungle skills.

The Iban

The **Iban** (see page 325) make up nearly thirty percent of Sarawak's population. Originating hundreds of miles south of present-day Sarawak, in the Kapuas Valley in Kalimantan, the Iban migrated north in the sixteenth century, and came into conflict over the next two hundred years with the Kayan and Kenyah Indigenous groups and, later, the British. Nowadays, Iban longhouse communities are found in the Batang Ai river system in the southwest and along Batang Rajang and tributaries. These communities are quite accessible, their inhabitants always hospitable and keen to demonstrate such aspects of their culture as traditional dance and textile weaving. In their time, the Iban were infamous head-hunters – some longhouses are still decorated with heads taken in battle long ago.

The Bidayuh

Unlike most Dyak groups, the **Bidayuh** traditionally lived away from the rivers, building their longhouse on the sides of hills. Culturally, the most southerly of Sarawak's Indigenous groups are similar to the Iban, although in temperament they are much milder and less gregarious, keeping themselves to themselves in their inaccessible homes on Sarawak's mountainous southern border with Kalimantan.

The Melanau and Kelabit

The **Melanau** are a coastal people, living north of Kuching in a region dominated by mangrove swamps. Many Melanau, however, now live in towns, preferring the kampung-style houses of the Malays to the elegant longhouses of the past. They are expert fishermen and cultivate sago as an alternative to rice. The **Kelabit** people live on the highland plateau separating north Sarawak from Kalimantan. Like the Iban, they live in longhouses and maintain a traditional lifestyle, but differ from some other groups in being Christian.

The Penan
The semi-nomadic **Penan** traditionally live in temporary lean-tos or small huts in the upper Rejang and Limbang areas of Sarawak. They rely, like some Orang Asli groups in the Peninsula, on hunting and gathering and collecting jungle produce for sale in local markets. In recent years, however, the state government has tried to resettle the Penan in small villages – a controversial policy not entirely unconnected with the advance of logging in traditional Penan land.

The Kenyah and Kayan
Most of the other groups in Sarawak fall into the all-embracing ethnic classification of **Orang Ulu** (people of the interior), who inhabit remote inland areas, further north than the Iban, along the upper Rajang, Balui and Linau rivers. The most numerous, the **Kayan** and the **Kenyah**, are closely related and in the past often teamed up to defend their lands from the invading Iban. But they also have much in common with their traditional enemy, since they are longhouse-dwellers, animists and shifting cultivators.

Indigenous Sabah
Sabah's population of around 3.5 million encompasses remarkable diversity, with forty-plus ethnic groups, some of which are interrelated; between them, they speak over eighty different languages and dialects. The **Kadazan/Dusun** and their various subgroups account for around a third of the population. Traditionally agriculturists (the word Dusun means "orchard", while the "Kadazan" part of the name was originally preferred by those from the Penampang area), they inhabit the western coastal plains and parts of the interior. Other Kadazan/Dusun branches include the Lotud of Tuaran and the Rungus of the Kudat Peninsula, whose longhouses – some characterized by walls that bulge outwards – are all that remain of the group's longhouse-building tradition. Although most Kadazan/Dusun are now Christians, remnants of their animist past are still evident, most obviously in the harvest festival, or **Kaamatan**, when their *bobohizans* (priestesses) perform rituals to honour the *bambaazon*, or rice spirit.

The mainly Muslim **Bajau** Indigenous group, who drifted over from the southern Philippines some two hundred years ago, has overtaken the Chinese as Sabah's second largest ethnic group, accounting for around a tenth of the population. Their penchant for piracy once earned them the sobriquet "sea gypsies", though nowadays they are either fisher-folk or agriculturalists noted for their horsemanship and buffalo rearing. The Bajau live in the northwest of Sabah, where they annually appear on horseback at Kota Belud's market (see page 389), as well as in Semporna and the islands offshore.

Sabah's third sizeable Indigenous group, the **Murut**, inhabit the area south of Keningau. Their name means "hill people", though some prefer to be known by their individual Indigenous names, such as Timugon, Tagal and Nabai. The Murut traditionally farm rice and cassava by a system of shifting cultivation. Their head-hunting days are over, but they retain other cultural traditions, such as constructing brightly adorned huts to house the graves and belongings of the dead.

Development and the environment

Malaysia is gradually becoming more environmentally friendly, largely as a result of well-organized and scientifically persuasive organizations within the country, rather than pressures from outside, but the pace of change is slow and huge problems remain. Logging and large-scale development projects, like dams, hog the spotlight, and remain a prime focus for NGOs, but just as pressing are the concerns over oil-palm cultivation and wetlands erosion, as well as the impact of environmental degradation on the lifestyles of Indigenous groups.

As a small, highly built-up island, **Singapore** has few wild areas left to spoil. Nevertheless, the country maintains an area of rainforest around its central reservoirs as well as other nature reserves, such the wetland area at Sungai Buloh. Singapore's very compactness dictates that it has to be vigilant on matters of pollution, and thus the island has strict laws on waste emissions and even an island, Semakau, created largely out of ash from incinerated refuse.

The tiny sultanate of **Brunei** has interfered least with its forest, but then, its enormous oil wealth and tiny population ensure it has little need to.

Logging and deforestation

The **sustainable exploitation** of forest products by the Indigenous population has always played a vital part in the domestic and export economy of the region – for almost two thousand years, ethnic Indigenous groups have bartered products like rattan, wild rubber and forest plants with foreign traders.

Although blamed for much of the deforestation in Sarawak and Sabah, the bulk of Indigenous agricultural activity occurs in secondary rather than primary (untouched) forest. Indeed, environmental groups believe that only around one hundred square kilometres of primary forest – a tiny proportion compared to the haul by commercial timber companies – is cleared by the Indigenous groups annually. **Logging**, despite having slowed, is still a cause of huge grievances among the Indigenous peoples of east Malaysia.

The Peninsula

Peninsular Malaysia's pre-independence economy was not as reliant on timber revenues as those of Sabah and Sarawak. Although one sixth of the region's 120,000 square kilometres of forest, predominantly in Johor, Perak and Negeri Sembilan states, had been cut down by 1957, most of the logging had been done gradually and on a small, localized scale. As in Sabah, it was the demand for rail sleepers during the 1920s' expansion of the Malayan train network that first attracted the commercial logging companies. Wide-scale clearing and conversion to rubber and oil-palm plantations in the more remote areas of Pahang, Perlis, Kedah and Terengganu intensified in the 1960s. By the end of the 1970s, more efficient extraction methods, coupled with a massive increase in foreign investment in the logging industry, had led to over forty percent of the Peninsula's remaining forests being either cleared for plantation purposes or partially logged.

Logging in west Malaysia has, however, slowed significantly in the last few decades, with environmental impact assessments being carried out before logging is allowed to proceed. One positive piece of legislation is the creation, more than a century ago, of Permanent Forest Reserves. Any logging in these areas must be carried out in a sustainable manner integrating checks and impact assessments.

Sabah

Commercial logging began in **Sabah** in the late nineteenth century, when the British Borneo Trading and Planting Company started to extract timber for use as railway sleepers in China. By World War II, the larger **British Borneo Timber Company** (BBTC) was primarily responsible for the extraction of five million cubic metres of rainforest timber, and Sandakan became one of the world's main timber ports. Areas were logged indiscriminately, and the Indigenous groups who lived there became employees of the rubber and tobacco plantations that replaced the forests. By 1970, nearly a third of Sabah's forests had been logged, accounting for over seventy percent of exports.

Since then, oil-palm cultivation has taken over much of the logged land, and at the same time Sabah's conservation policies have improved considerably. Half to sixty percent of the state remains under forest cover, and although some of this is previously logged areas, active reforestation programmes are under way. While logging continues, the emphasis is starting to shift towards **plantations** of fast-growing trees like acacias, meaning more forest can be left undisturbed. Cynics might say that Sabah is merely the best of a bad bunch in the context of the whole country, but there is a clearer commitment to sustainable forest use, wildlife protection and transparency here than anywhere else in Malaysia – as exemplified at **Deramakot**, the country's only reserve with international Forest Stewardship Council certification.

Sarawak

In many ways **Sarawak** seems to exemplify Malaysia's environmental policies at their worst. It's here that all the problems come into sharp focus – the forest is either being degraded by commercial logging or felled altogether for oil-palm cultivation, in the process ruining the ancestral lands of native peoples.

Having accelerated in northern Sarawak under Vyner Brooke during the 1930s, timber extraction became a major revenue earner for the state during its short postwar period as a Crown Colony and after independence as part of Malaysia. Accurate figures as to the current state of Sarawak's rainforest are notoriously hard to come by, though perhaps less than thirty percent of the primary forest cover remains, and even that can be so fragmented that it's practically useless from a wildlife conservation point of view.

In principle the Indigenous peoples have so-called **native customary rights** over their ancestral forest, and can use them in court to block the government granting logging or other concessions. However, the system is fraught with difficulty, partly because such rights are based on incomplete colonial-era data on agricultural settlement. What's more, in 2016 Malaysia's highest court ruled that existing Sarawak law did not actually recognize two important native customs establishing ties to the land, a situation that can only be corrected with new legislation. Even where Indigenous people can establish their rights, the demands of the cash economy may mean they are more interested in the jobs and amenities that the logging firms can bring.

Of course, logging, unlike clearing land for oil palm, does not mean the wholesale destruction of the forest: the logging companies are after hardwood trees, which they should try to remove as cleanly as possible. In practice, felling may involve collateral damage to other trees, and it's notable that only one timber concession in Sarawak has been certified under the Malaysian Timber Certification Scheme (MTCS) to indicate some compliance with responsible forest management practices.

Meanwhile the state continues to trumpet its target of gazetting 10,000 square kilometres (eight percent of Sarawak's land area) as national parks or wildlife reserves that are off-limits to the public, plus a further 60,000 square kilometres as permanent forest reserve. Impressive though these figures may sound, it's notable that many of the newer national parks scarcely function as such, since they are sited in inaccessible areas and have barely any facilities. This haphazard creation of parks might be thought to augment their effectiveness as conservation areas, but there is no such fringe benefit – policing to stop logging or poaching is minimal. It could be argued that the parks are,

> **OIL-PALM CULTIVATION IN MALAYSIA**
>
> Anyone who travels around Malaysia immediately notices the ubiquity of the **oil palm**. Native to West Africa, the plant is now widely cultivated on both plantations and smallholdings for its fruit, which yields **palm oil**, used for cooking, in food products and as a biofuel; Malaysia, together with Indonesia, account for at least eighty percent of world production of this valuable commodity. The industry has brought employment to many as well as improved infrastructure, with roads, cellular networks, schools and clinics springing up to serve plantation areas.
>
> Although some cultivation takes place on land long used for agriculture, **forest clearance** for plantations is a huge problem, not just because it threatens many animal species, including the orangutan. The practice also contributes significantly to global warming, notably via greenhouse gas emissions when fire is used to destroy trees, and can trigger conflict between plantation operators and local people who are forced off their land. Certification schemes exist to try to make palm oil production sustainable, although some critics view the very idea as an oxymoron and mere window-dressing.
>
> While there is some local awareness of oil palm's negative impact, Malaysian media coverage of the issue is largely uncritical; in 2017, European Parliament proposals to eventually ban the import of any palm oil linked with deforestation or human rights violations were reported with some indigation in Malaysia as a snub to the supposedly well-regulated industry.

in fact, a smokescreen for what's happening elsewhere in Sarawak – for example, the intensive logging of the Baram River basin in the north, in areas around the Kelabit Highlands and Mulu National Park. **Dam-building** is another major issue on the Sarawak environmental agenda. Some dams have already been completed, notably the one at Bakun (see page 336), and a couple more are set to be built, all to generate electricity for no obvious market. Overall, the picture in Sarawak does appear bleak, although there is genuine commitment among some government biodiversity managers to try to reform the state's policies.

Air pollution

The environmental issue that has most affected the inhabitants of Peninsular Malaysia and Singapore has been air pollution, specifically dust and smoke caused by sporadic forest fires – dubbed "the **haze**" by the local media. During severe, prolonged episodes in 1997/98, 2005 and 2015, things got so bad that respiratory illnesses spiked and schools were closed. Visibility in the Strait of Malacca, one of the world's busiest shipping routes, dropped dramatically.

At one time, the Malaysian government suggested that the agricultural methods of the Indigenous peoples – which involve the burning of excess vegetation at the end of growing cycles – were to blame. However, small longhouse communities could not have caused such extensive pollution, and it is now clear that Indonesian plantation companies burning large areas of forest to facilitate the planting of crops such as oil palm and acacia are the culprits. The Indonesian government does not appear to be able to rein in such practices, and the haze must be regarded as a recurrent threat that can plague a visit to Malaysia and Singapore with little warning.

The threat to traditional lifestyles

Although large-scale projects such as the Bakun Dam are the most prevalent threat to Indigenous peoples' way of life, **logging**, whether licensed or illicit, represents a constant challenge. The effect on wildlife has an obvious impact on communities' ability to hunt, but the failure to respect native customary rights has also led to the desecration of burial places and sections of rivers used for fishing – notably in the forests around Bintulu, Belaga and Limbang. In southwest Sarawak, the Iban have had some success in challenging logging, however: a historic court case in 2001, Rumah Nor v. Borneo Pulp and Paper, led to a ruling in favour of the longhouse community, after the community's map was accepted as court evidence for ownership of land. Emboldened by this ruling, several communities have filed petitions, but in many cases the courts have not revoked the state-awarded logging concessions.

The **Penan** have arguably been the worst hit by logging, as their traditionally semi-nomadic lifestyle makes it hard for their land rights to be defined and recognized. In addition, the Sarawak state government's avowed policy since the mid-1980s has been to bring the Penan into what it views as the development process (as applied to the more settled Dyak and Orang Ulu groups for many decades), urging them to move to permanent longhouses, work in the cash economy and send their children to school. Very often, the Penan receive no notice that their land has been earmarked for logging until extraction actually begins – examples in remote areas around Belaga have been documented by the environmental group **Sahabat Alam Malaysia** (SAM). Reports from one of the remaining semi-nomadic Penan communities situated in Sarawak's Ulu Baram area reveal that loggers continue to penetrate their last reserves illegally.

Wildlife

Set well inside the tropics and comprising everything from pristine ocean to coastal mangroves, lowland rainforest and mountain moorland, the range of habitats on the Malay Peninsula and Borneo is only matched by the diversity of its fauna – over 700 species of birds and more than 200 kinds of mammals. You don't have to be an ardent nature-spotter to appreciate this: even a brief visit to any of the region's national parks – or just the FRIM forestry reserve on Kuala Lumpur's outskirts – will put you face to face with clouds of butterflies, troops of monkeys, and an incessant background orchestra of insect noise.

Despite being separated by the South China Sea, the wildlife and plant communities of the Peninsula and east Malaysia are similar (the two were joined by a land bridge until after the last Ice Age), though the various regional wildlife reserves offer a range of experiences. On Peninsular Malaysia, **Taman Negara** provides full-on tropical jungle, a good place to see large mammals; **Fraser's Hill**, on the other hand, is better known for its birdlife. Sabah's **Kinabatangan River** and **Bako National Park** in Sarawak are good for estuarine and river forest creatures, while shallow lakes at Sarawak's **Loagan Bunut National Park** are home to many different bird species, as is Brunei's **Ulu Temburong National Park**.

Even though it's now predominantly urban, with little plant or animal life, **Singapore** still holds several remnants of its verdant tropical past, particularly at **Bukit Timah Nature Reserve**, the splendidly manicured Botanic Gardens, and the **Sungai Buloh Nature Wetland Reserve** in the far north of the island. Day-trippers to Pulau Ubin, just off Singapore and easily accessible by boat from the Changi Point ferry terminal, can also see the mangrove flats of **Chek Jawa**.

Poaching and habitation loss due to deforestation mean that the future of the region's wildlife is far from assured. Fortunately, many **not-for-profit organizations**, such as

FORESTS

Coastal mud flats are usually protected by **mangroves**, a diverse family of trees that thrive in brackish water and tend to support themselves on a platform of elevated roots that form an impenetrable barrier to exploration – and refuge for small creatures such as mudskippers, crabs and young fish.

Moving inland, the region's lowland forests are thick with **dipterocarps** (meaning "two-winged fruit"), a diverse group of trees often prized for timber. Other forest species include several palm trees (one of which, the spiky, vine-like rattan palm, is used to make cane furniture and the like); liana vines; massive fig trees (many of which support their huge trunks with buttress roots); 50m-tall *tualang*, Southeast Asia's tallest tree; and wild **fruit trees**, such as durian, mango, guava and rambutan. You'll seldom see flowers though (except fallen petals); so little light reaches the forest floor that trees and climbing plants only flower high up in the canopy. To get around this, a whole group of small plants have become epiphytes – using the trees as perches to get nearer the sunlight – including orchids and a wide range of small ferns, which sometimes cover the upper surface of larger branches.

Montane forest predominates above 1000m, comprising mainly oak and evergreen native conifers with a shrub layer of bamboo and dwarf palm. Above 1500m is **cloud forest**, where trees are often cloaked by swirling mist, and the stunted, damp boughs bear thick growths of mosses and ferns; at elevations of over 1700m, you'll find miniature montane forest of rhododendrons, the boughs heavily laden with dripping mosses, pitcher plants and colourful orchids.

> **HOW TO FIND WILDLIFE**
>
> Tropical wildlife is most active at dawn and dusk, though some larger mammals forage through the night. It's surprising how even large animals can be fairly invisible, especially in forest, where low light and random vegetation can break up their otherwise recognizable outlines. Here are some tips for finding creatures, without doing anything dangerous (such as turning over logs to look for snakes):
>
> **Listen** – aside from calls, many creatures make distinctive noises as they move, from the raucous crashing of active monkey troops, to staccato rustlings of mice and lizards in leaf litter.
>
> **Look** – many smaller creatures spend the day hidden under leaves and in hollows and crevices in tree trunks. At night, insects – and insect-eating animals – are attracted to lights; check ranger offices, chalets and huts around national park headquarters.
>
> **Signs** – footprints, scarred bark, mud wallows and flowers, fruit and torn twigs strewn along paths are all signs of animals, some of which might be feeding in the canopy above you.
>
> **Eyeshine** – if on a guided night trek or drive, use a torch held at or above eye level to reflect eyeshine, either from invertebrates such as crickets and spiders, or nocturnal mammals – anything from tapir to deer, mice and civets.

WWF Malaysia (http://wwfmalaysia.org), are campaigning to preserve the species and terrains most under threat.

Mammals

Big mammals are exciting to encounter in the wild, and several are unique to the region. Asian **elephants** are found both in Peninsular Malaysia and Borneo, though probably the best chance to see them is at Taman Negara, which is also good for **tapir** – a pony-sized relative of the rhino, with a black-and-white body and vestigial trunk.

Other mammals you might encounter include the **Sunda clouded leopard** – a rare cat species with a pattern of cloud-like markings on the sides of the body, spotted **leopard cat** (around the size of a large domestic cat), and nocturnal **civet**, tree-dwelling creatures that look like a cross between a cat and a weasel. Don't get your hopes up about seeing **tigers**, now thought to number under 150 in the Peninsula, or reclusive **sun bears**, marked with a white crescent across their chest – though you do occasionally see their deep claw grooves in tree bark.

Another possibility in undisturbed forest on the Peninsula are seladang, a Malaysian sub-species of **gaur**, a giant type of wild cattle with white leg patches, which look like socks. There are also several species of **deer**: the larger sambar; the muntjac or barking deer, the size of a roe deer; and the lesser and greater mouse deer.

Primates (monkeys and gibbons) are found throughout the Peninsula and Borneo. Most common are the long-tailed and pig-tailed **macaques**, which come to the ground to feed, the latter identified by its shorter tail, brown fur and pinkish-brown face. There are dusky and spectacled **langurs** too, elegant grey monkeys with white patterns that spend most of their time up in the trees – they're also known as leaf-monkeys, after their diet. The region's several gibbon species are entirely arboreal, with specially elongated forearms that allow them to swing athletically through the canopy – they tend to have very loud, wailing calls too, easily recognized. Big-nosed, pot-bellied proboscis monkeys – and Southeast Asia's sole ape, the **orangutan** – are found only in Borneo.

One of the most unusual smaller mammals to keep eyes peeled for is the **colugo**, a bizarre forest creature that looks like a cross between a fruit bat and a squirrel. It spends the day sleeping in tree hollows, and the night gliding through the forest looking for flowers and fruits.

Birds

One fairly common bird that epitomizes the entire Malay region – and is even a totem to some Dyak Indigenous groups– is the **hornbill** (see box, page 557). Its huge size, bold black-and-white markings, large curved beak and noisy, swooshing flight make it easily identifiable, even in thick jungle. Other forest birds include **trogons** (brightly coloured, mid-storey birds); green **fruit pigeons** – strongly coloured but strangely hard to see; **bulbuls**, vocal, fruit-eating birds that often flock to feed; **minivets**, slender birds with long, graduated tails and white, yellow or red bands in the wings; and round-winged **babblers**.

Plump and brilliantly coloured, **pitas** are notoriously shy and difficult to approach, though sometimes easily found thanks to their noisy progress through leaf litter on the forest floor. Other ground-dwelling birds to look for include the shy **Malaysian peacock pheasant**, with a blue-green crest and distinctive "eye spots" along its back and long tail; the similar **fireback**; and the 1.7m-long **great argus pheasant**.

The most common birds of prey are kites, buzzards and, along the coast, fish eagles, very large white and grey birds with a wedge-shaped tail. In forest, you might encounter the **crested serpent eagle** and the **changeable hawk eagle**, often spotted soaring over gaps in the forest canopy.

Other species confined to tropical forests are **trogons**, of which five species are present at Taman Negara, and several species of **hornbill** – large, broad-winged, long-tailed forest birds, some of which have huge, almost outlandish bills.

A feature of montane forest bird flocks is the **mixed feeding flock**, which may contain many different species. These pass rapidly through an area of forest searching for insects as they go, and different observers are likely to register entirely different species in the same flock. Look for **racket-tailed drongo**, a black bird with long tail streamers; the **speckled piculet**, a small spotted woodpecker; and the **blue nuthatch**, a small species – blue-black in colour with a white throat and pale eye ring – which runs up and down tree trunks. Several species of brightly coloured **laughing thrushes**, thrush-sized birds that spend time foraging on the ground or in the understorey, also occur in these flocks.

Reptiles

Small lizards – mostly skinks – are probably the commonest **reptiles** in the region; you'll often hear their frantic scuffling among forest-floor leaf litter. Nocturnal geckos

---

HORNBILLS

You should have little difficulty in identifying **hornbills**: they are large, black-and-white birds with disproportionately huge bills (often bent downwards), topped with an ornamental **casque** – a generally hollow structure attached to the upper mandible. The function of the casque is unknown; it may play a role in attracting a mate and courtship ceremonies. Ten of the world's 46 species of hornbill are found in Malaysia, many of them endangered or present only in small, isolated populations.

One of the smallest and most commonly seen species, the **pied hornbill**, can be identified by its white abdomen and tail, and white wingtips in flight. Reaching only 75cm in length, it may even be spotted in leafy suburban areas. Also widely seen, the **black hornbill** is only slightly larger and black, save for the white tips of the outer tail feathers (some individuals also show a white patch behind the eye).

Larger species include the **helmeted hornbill** and the **rhinoceros hornbill**, both over 120cm in length, mainly black, but with white tails and bellies. Although it's the symbol of Sarawak, the rhinoceros hornbill is rarely seen there (you may have better luck in Sabah); it has a bright orange rhino-horn-shaped casque, whereas the helmeted hornbill has a bright red head, neck and helmet-shaped casque. The call of the helmeted hornbill is notable for being a remarkable series of "took" notes that start slowly and accelerate to a cackling crescendo.

RAFFLESIAS

The *Rafflesia* is a strange plant that parasitizes tree roots, and whose presence can only be detected when its rubbery flowers, up to a metre across, burst into bloom. Its full name, *Rafflesia arnoldii*, recalls its discovery in Sumatra in 1818 by Sir Stamford Raffles (see page 530) and his physician, the naturalist Dr Joseph Arnold, who collected a 7kg specimen and sent a description of it to the Royal Society in London. The blooms, which are the world's largest and stink of rotting meat, are pollinated by carrion flies. Each flower's central "bowl" holds around 7 litres of nectar, while the petals, as Raffles recorded, "are of a brick-red with numerous pustular spots of a lighter colour. The whole substance of the flower is not less than half an inch thick, and of a firm fleshy consistence". The flower buds have been very much in demand by *bomohs* (Malay shamen) and their Chinese *sinseh* counterparts for use in medicine, particularly as an aid to accelerate the shrinking of a woman's womb after she has given birth. There's no specific flowering season, though in any one locality the plants seem to bloom at particular times of the year. As each flower lasts only a few days, however, there's a lot of luck involved in actually seeing one; national park rangers might be able to give likely times.

have sucker-like pads on their toes that enable them to run up walls (and even glass); they're often seen around lights, stalking any insects that settle nearby. On forest fringes, look for flying lizards, which at rest are small, bony, grey and unimpressive – until they unfold wings and glide between trees like paper darts. Fairly common, even in semi-rural parks, they're easily missed. Around water – and especially near popular picnic spots, where they can pick up scraps – you'll see heavily built **monitor lizards**, the largest of which can approach 2m.

Snakes – Malaysia and Borneo hold over 200 species, including poisonous cobras, kraits and pit vipers – are another common but seldom-seen creature; they tend to move off as soon as they detect your footfalls. The largest, the reticulated python, is capable of growing 8m long, though you're much more likely to see either harmless **whip snakes** (which eat insects and lizards) and green **tree snakes**.

Saltwater **crocodiles** – the world's largest, heaviest reptile – are now virtually extinct throughout Peninsular Malaysia, though numbers are increasing in Borneo. Scuba divers might encounter several species of marine **turtle**, all of whose populations are declining; certain beaches are also famous as turtle rookeries, where you might see adults coming ashore to lay eggs above the high tide line, or young turtles hatching, digging themselves out of the sand and heading for the sea en masse.

Books

Singapore and, to a lesser extent, Malaysia have healthy English-language publishing scenes, churning out books on local history, politics, society and culture, plus a modest amount of fiction.

In the reviews that follow, books marked ★ are especially recommended, while o/p signifies a title is out of print. As per Chinese custom, surnames are given first for Chinese authors who don't have Christian names; also, some Malay and Indian authors who do not have surnames are listed under their given name.

TRAVEL AND GENERAL INTEREST

★ *Encyclopedia of Malaysia*. A brilliantly produced series of tomes on different aspects of Malaysia, all beautifully illustrated and – not always the case with locally published material – competently edited. The volumes on the performing arts and architecture are particularly recommended. Available as individual volumes or as a set.

Isabella Bird *The Golden Chersonese*. Delightful epistolary romp through old Southeast Asia, penned by the intrepid Bird, whose adventures in the Malay states in 1879 ranged from strolls through Singapore's streets to elephant-back rides. A free download from various online libraries.

Robin Hanbury-Tenison *Finding Eden*. Forty years after leading the pioneering Royal Geographical Society expedition to the then newly established Mulu National Park, Hanbury-Tenison revisits the experience in this book, much of which dwells on the minutiae of the enterprise, as noted in his diaries. The book is at its best when recounting the discovery of the Garden of Eden and his close bond with the Penan people.

Tom Harrisson *Borneo Jungle* and *World Within*. The abrasive, eccentric polymath Tom Harrisson spent much of his professional life studying Sarawak's Dyak groups, especially the Kayan, Kenyah and Punan, whom he greatly admired. *Borneo Jungle* is a lively account of his first trip during the 1930s; *World Within* the story of how he parachuted into the highlands during World War II to organize Dyak resistance against the Japanese.

Sebastian Hope *Outcasts of the Islands*. Still available as an e-book, this is the 2001 account of the writer's extraordinary attempts to get to know Southeast Asia's itinerant sea peoples, notably Sabah's Bajau Laut at Semporna, at a time when many still lived at sea off Semporna and there were just two resorts at Mabul.

★ **Agnes Keith** *Land Below the Wind*. Bornean memories galore, in this charming account of expat life in prewar Sabah; Keith's true eye and assured voice produce a heartwarming picture of a way of life now long gone. Her naive sketches perfectly complement the childlike wonder of the prose.

Redmond O'Hanlon *Into The Heart of Borneo*. A hugely entertaining yarn recounting O'Hanlon's refreshingly amateurish romp through the jungle to a remote summit on the Sarawak/Kalimantan border, partnered by the English poet James Fenton.

HISTORY AND POLITICS

★ **Munshi Abdullah** *The Hikayat Abdullah*. Raffles' one-time clerk, Melaka-born Abdullah became diarist of some of the most formative years of Southeast Asian history; his firsthand account is crammed with illuminating vignettes and character portraits.

★ **Barbara Watson Andaya and Leonard Andaya** *The History of Malaysia*. Unlike more paternalistic histories penned by former colonists, this newly updated standard text on the region takes a more even-handed view of Malaysia, and finds time for cultural coverage, too.

Farish Noor *What Your Teacher Didn't Tell You*. An enjoyable series of lectures on subjects that remain awkward in Malaysia, from ethnicity to sexual attitudes.

Victoria Glendinning *Raffles and the Golden Opportunity*. An enjoyable, thorough biography of Singapore's founder Sir Stamford Raffles, though occasionally bogged down in the details of his upbringing and domestic life.

★ **Patrick Keith** *Ousted*. Most of the largely young population of Malaysia and Singapore know little of the events that saw Singapore leaving the federation in 1965. But, as this fine memoir by a former Malaysian government adviser demonstrates, many of the issues that led to the rift continue to shape both countries and their mutual ties today – Malaysia is still laden with ethnically based politics, while Singapore remains the fiefdom of the PAP.

★ **Sonny Liew** *The Art of Charlie Chan Hock Chye*. This internationally acclaimed graphic novel appears to celebrate an overlooked genius of Singapore comic art. In reality, Liew's "retrospective" on the fictional Mr Chan's satirical work and struggle for recognition is a savage indictment of the autocratic trajectory of postwar Singapore politics – a useful antidote to establishment accounts.

James Minchin *No Man Is An Island* (o/p). This well-researched, and at times critical, study of Lee Kuan Yew refuses to kowtow to Singapore's ex-prime minister and is hence unavailable in Singapore itself.

John Curtis Perry *Singapore: Unlikely Power*. Not quite as critical as it could be, but a highly readable history nonetheless, focusing mainly on development and economic influence rather than society and politics.

★ **C.M. Turnbull** *A History of Modern Singapore 1819–2005*. Mary Turnbull had barely completed a major update of this standard work when she died in 2008, and what a fine legacy: the final edition is lucid, thorough, nearly always spot-on in its analysis and utterly readable.

WORLD WAR II

★ **Russell Braddon** *The Naked Island* (o/p). Southeast Asia under the Japanese: Braddon's disturbing yet moving first-hand account of the POW camps of Malaya, Singapore and Siam salutes courage in the face of appalling conditions and treatment; worth scouring secondhand stores for.

★ **Spencer Chapman** *The Jungle is Neutral*. This riveting firsthand account of being lost, and surviving, in the Malay jungle during World War II reads like a breathless novel.

★ **Agnes Keith** *Three Came Home*. Pieced together from scraps of paper secreted in latrines and teddy bears, this is a remarkable story of survival in the face of Japanese attempts to eradicate the "proudery and arrogance" of the West in the World War II prison camps of Borneo.

Eric Lomax *The Railway Man*. Such is the power of Lomax's artless, redemptive and moving story of capture during the fall of Singapore, torture by the Japanese and reconciliation with his tormentor after fifty years, that many reviewers were moved to tears.

★ **Lucy Lum** *The Thorn of Lion City*. You might expect a memoir of a wartime childhood in Singapore to be dominated by the savagery of the Japanese, but that's nothing compared to the torment inflicted on the author at the hands of her manipulative and violent mother and grandmother. That it's all told with zero artifice only makes it more compelling.

CULTURE AND SOCIETY

James Harding and Ahmad Sarji *P. Ramlee: The Bright Star*. An uncritical but enjoyable biography of the Malay singer, actor and director sometimes likened to Malaysia's Harry Belafonte. More importantly, it's a window onto what seems like a different era – though little more than half a century ago – when Singapore was the centre of the Malay entertainment universe, and when Malay life was, frankly, more carefree than today.

Michael Heppell *Iban Art: Sexual Selection and Severed Heads* This excellent illustrated volume provides a deeper coverage of Iban art than the pretty pictures might lead you to assume, detailing the motifs and symbolism of traditional clothes, tattoos and carvings.

★ **Erik Jensen** *Where Hornbills Fly*. In the 1950s, before he became a British diplomat, the author arrived in Sarawak as a callow young man with idealistic notions of learning about the Iban. He soon wound up living in longhouses in the Lemanak area (near Batang Ai), helping the Iban make the change to a settled existence without imposing upon them as a "superior" foreigner. His memoir is so intricately and tenderly observed you can only wonder why he waited half a century to write up his experiences.

Lat *Kampung Boy* and *Town Boy*. Two comic-strip albums by the country's foremost cartoonist about growing up in Malaysia during the 1950s and 60s; gentle and fun, though without any sentimentality.

Charmaine Leung *17A Keong Saik Road*. This likeable autobiography recounts the author's childhood in a Singapore brothel. The nonlinear narrative spans many decades and can be confusing, but is ultimately rewarding for its insights into how ordinary people kept afloat as Chinatown (and Singapore at large) changed dramatically around them.

★ **Paul Malone** *The Peaceful People*. A moving, accessible study of the Penan people of Sarawak and of the enormous upheavals they have been through, transitioning from hunter-gatherers to a largely settled existence in just a few decades. Along the way Malone recounts their run-ins with authority and their ambivalent, unequal relationship with the logging industry eating into their ancestral lands.

Bernard Sellato *Innermost Borneo: Studies in Dayak Cultures*. Anthropologist Sellato spent much of the 1990s with the Indigenous Borneo groups of Kalimantan, who are related to the Sea Dyaks of Sarawak. This excellent ethnographic work contains ravishing images of a traditional, isolated world that will eventually be subsumed into greater Indonesia.

★ **Dina Zaman** *I Am Muslim*. A well-observed set of wry essays, with more candour than would have been appropriate in this guidebook, on Islam as practised in Malaysia; form without enough substance is, sadly, often the verdict. The section on sexual attitudes is particularly recommended.

FOOD AND COOKERY

Aziza Ali *Aziza's Creative Malay Cuisine; Sambal Days, Kampong Cuisine*. For years, Aziza Ali ran the only worthwhile high-end Malay restaurant in Singapore, and her *Creative Malay Cuisine* cookbook is packed with great recipes, though the emphasis is firmly on southern rather than east coast dishes. *Sambal Days* is quite different, a memoir of a middle-class Malay childhood that soon morphs into a reverie of special foods for just about every occasion.

★ **Betty Saw** *Rasa Malaysia: the complete Malaysian*

cookbook. A nicely illustrated cookbook that covers dozens of the standard dishes you'll find served at food courts and in homes around the country, including various Chinese and Nyonya recipes, though very little South Indian fare. It's all organized by state, which helps give a feel for regional cuisine, though annoyingly there's no index.

NATURAL HISTORY AND THE ENVIRONMENT

Chin Shui Hiung, Ravi Mandalam and Christopher Chin *East Kinabalu*. Gorgeous photos of montane plants and Mount Kinabalu's incredible vistas, taken on multi-day expeditions in little-visited areas which have since been altered by the 2015 earthquake.
G.W.H. Davison and Chew Yen Fook *A Photographic Guide to Birds of Borneo*; **M. Strange and A. Jeyarajasingam** *A Photographic Guide to Birds of Peninsular Malaysia and Singapore*; **Charles M. Francis** *A Photographic Guide to the Mammals of Southeast Asia*. Well keyed and user-friendly, these slender volumes carry oodles of glossy plates that make positive identifying a breeze.
Junaidi Payne *Wild Malaysia: The Wildlife and Landscapes of Peninsular Malaysia, Sarawak and Sabah*. Coffee-table book, recently reissued, capturing forest and beach vistas of the kind that linger in the mind long after you've left Malaysia.
★ **Alfred Russel Wallace** *The Malay Archipelago*. The immensely readable journal of Wallace's 1854–62 expedition to collect natural history specimens in Borneo and Indonesia, during which he independently formulated the theory of evolution by natural selection – prompting Charles Darwin to publish his landmark *On the Origin of Species*.
Lukas Straumann *Money Logging: On the Trail of the Asian Timber Mafia*. An unrelenting exposé of avarice and corruption at the heart of Sarawak's government and timber corporations, by the executive director of the Bruno Manser Fund, which campaigns on behalf of the state's Indigenous groups.

ART AND ARCHITECTURE

Julian Davison and Luca Invernizzi Tettoni *Black & White: The Singapore House*; **Peter and Waveney Jenkins** *The Planter's Bungalow*. Two tomes dealing with colonial "Anglo-Malay" residences, often strange hybrids of mock-Tudor and Southeast Asian elements, and sometimes raised off the ground on posts like a kampung house. Both volumes also examine the lives of those who occupied these houses, not always as wealthy as you might assume.
★ **Farish A. Noor and Eddin Khoo** *The Spirit of Wood: The Art of Malay Woodcarving*. Much weightier in tone than your average coffee-table book, this deals not only with the superb woodcarving produced on the east coast of the Peninsula and in southern Thailand, but also with the whole pre-Islamic consciousness that subtly imbues the woodcarver's art. Packed with great photos, too, of gorgeous timber mosques, incredibly detailed *kris* hilts and the like.
★ **Kang Ger-Wen** *Decoration & Symbolism in Chinese Architecture*. This beautifully photographed book focuses on temples and clan houses in Singapore, but will come in handy at any Chinese historic building in Malaysia, dissecting the meanings and stories hidden in roofing styles, vegetal motifs, altars and so on.
Peter Lee and Jennifer Chen *The Straits Chinese House*. A beautifully illustrated volume exploring Peranakan domestic artefacts and their now largely vanished traditions; an excellent memento of a visit to the Baba-Nyonya museums of Penang, Melaka and Singapore.
Anthony Ratos and H. Berber *Orang Asli and their Wood Art*. One of few accessible explorations of Orang Asli lifestyles and cultures, though note that only a third of this picture-heavy volume is devoted to their fantastical carvings; the rest of the photos are of Asli settlements and generic, if pretty, jungle scenes.
★ **Robert Winzeler** *The Architecture of Life and Death in Borneo*. Highly readable, illustrated study of the traditional architecture of Borneo, looking at the evolution of longhouses over the years and symbolism in building design.

FICTION

Eric Ambler *Passage of Arms*. Recently reissued, this 1959 thriller centres on a lowly Indian rubber-estate clerk who finds a valuable guerrilla arms cache during the Malayan Emergency. Hankering to launch his own bus company, he partners with some wily Chinese businessmen and a naive American in an attempt to peddle the booty. Things go awry, inevitably; the fun is in finding out who comes out on top.
★ **Anthony Burgess** *The Long Day Wanes*. Burgess taught at Kuala Kangsar's posh Malay College in the mid-1950s. His Malayan trilogy (*Time for a Tiger*, *The Enemy in the Blanket* and *Beds in the East*), currently available in one volume, provides a witty and acutely observed vision of the country, underscoring the various racial tensions and prejudices during the closing years of colonial rule.
Bernice Chauly *Once We Were There*. Probably the most explicit novel ever written about Malaysia (tellingly, it was published in Singapore), with plenty of sex and drugs as a bunch of Westernized activists in KL graduate from anti-establishment journalism to the messiness of married life and "proper" jobs. The one flaw is the lack of a satisfying resolution to a shocking incident midway through.

James Clavell *King Rat*. Set in Japanese-occupied Singapore, a gripping tale of survival in the notorious Changi Prison.

★ **Joseph Conrad** *Lord Jim*. Southeast Asia provides the backdrop to the story of Jim's desertion of an apparently sinking ship and subsequent efforts to redeem himself; modelled upon the sailor A.P. Williams, Jim's character also yields echoes of Rajah Brooke of Sarawak.

★ **J.G. Farrell** *The Singapore Grip*. Lengthy novel – Farrell's last – of World War II Singapore in which real and fictitious characters flit from tennis to dinner party as the countdown to the Japanese occupation begins.

Barbara Ismail *Shadow Play*. Lightweight whodunnits seem to be taking off in Malaysia and Singapore: the latter has its Inspector Singh franchise, and now there's Ismail's Kelantan-based Kain Songket Mysteries series. It kicks off with this decent enough novel about a Kota Bharu woman who, not content with selling brocade, turns out to be surprisingly good at solving murders – though not all the allusions to Kelantan's distinctive culture are convincing.

★ **W. Somerset Maugham** *Collected Short Stories Volume 4*. Peopled by hoary sailors, bored plantation-dwellers and colonials wearing mutton-chop whiskers and topees, this volume of Maugham's short stories resuscitates the Malaya of the 1900s; quintessential colonial literature graced by an easy style and a ready eye for a story.

Golda Mowe *Iban Dream*. The fabulous saga of a boy raised by apes who has to tackle a series of quests as a rite of passage. Just about every Indigenous group in Sarawak makes an appearance at some point in what isn't a bad read once you get used to the mystical-fable style. A sequel, *Iban Journey*, is also available.

Preeta Samarasan *Evening Is The Whole Day*. Set mostly in 1950s Ipoh, this debut novel ruthlessly dissects the lives of a dysfunctional upper-middle-class Indian family, with precious few laughs to be had in a tale of infidelity, class disparities and violence behind closed doors.

★ **Han Suyin** *And The Rain My Drink*. Han is best remembered for her autobiographical novel, which inspired the 1950s Hollywood hit *Love is a Many-Splendored Thing*, but the newly reissued *And The Rain My Drink*, published in 1956, deserves wider attention; there is no better novel of the upheavals of the Communist insurgency and the fag-end of British rule in Malaya, informed by Han's time living in 1950s Johor Bahru.

Tan Twan Eng *The Gift of Rain* and *The Garden of Evening Mists*. By a South Africa-based Malaysian, both these novels are deliberately paced and infused with the author's passion for Japanese culture. The first, set in Penang, focuses on the curious relationship between a Eurasian boy and his family's Japanese tenant as war breaks out, while the second follows a Chinese wartime internee during the subsequent Emergency, when she returns to the Cameron Highlands to confront her ghosts and an old Japanese acquaintance.

Language

Malay, officially referred to as Bahasa Melayu (literally "Malay language"), is the national language of Malaysia, Singapore and Brunei. Part of the Austronesian language family, it's an old tongue that became a regional lingua franca through its use in the ancient kingdom of Srivijaya and during the fifteenth-century Melaka Sultanate. Native speakers of the language are found not just in Peninsular Malaysia and northern Borneo but also in pockets of Indonesia, where a version of Malay has been adopted as the official language.

Malay is only one of many languages used in the three countries covered in this book. In Singapore, English, Mandarin and Tamil are also official tongues, with English pre-eminent as the language of government and business, while Hokkien is the most used regional Chinese dialect. In Malaysia itself, English retains an important position in business, law and government, Tamil is widely spoken among the Indian community, while Mandarin is much used by the Chinese, as are Chinese dialects such as Cantonese (especially in KL and Ipoh) and Hokkien (in Penang and on the east coast).

In practice, **English** is fairly widely understood except in rural areas and in the Malay-dominated east coast and the north of the Peninsula, where it really does pay to pick up a few words of Malay, especially since the basics are simple enough to learn. Besides, it's entertaining to get to grips with a tongue that, like English, is a ready absorber of loan words. The influence of English on modern Malay is apparent to most travellers, and with an awareness of Asian languages, it's not hard to discern the infusion of words from Sanskrit (stemming from the ancient impact of Hinduism on Southeast Asia), such as *jaya* ("success") and *negara* ("country"), as well as from Arabic, which has contributed words like *maaf* ("sorry") and many terms to do with Islam.

To pick up the language, it's best to buy a coursebook that focuses on **vernacular** Malay, as our vocabulary section does, rather than the formal language used in print and broadcasting. A good choice is *A Course in Conversational Malay* by Malcolm W. Mintz (SNP Publishing, Singapore).

Pronunciation

Malay was once written in Arabic script, but over the years this has been almost completely supplanted by a Romanized form. However, the Romanized **spellings** are prone to inconsistencies: for example, *baru*, "new", crops up in variant forms in place names like Johor Bahru and Kota Bharu, while new and old spellings of certain common words still coexist, for example *sungai/sungei, kampung/kampong*, and so forth.

Spelling quirks aside, Bahasa Malaysia is one of the more straightforward languages to pronounce, once you get your head round a few rules. One basic point to remember is that the consonants **k, p, t** have slightly less force in Malay than in English (to be precise, they aren't aspirated in Malay); if you emulate the sounds at the start of the Spanish words *cuatro, pero* and *toro*, you'd be in the right ball park. Other points of difference are listed below.

Syllable stress isn't complicated in Malay, though it can seem unnatural to English speakers. As a general rule, the stress lands on the **penultimate syllable** of a word (or, with words of two syllables, on the first syllable), hence SaRAwak, TerengGAnu. The chief exception concerns two-syllable words whose first syllable contains a short vowel (usually denoted by an "e"); in such cases, the stress sometimes falls on the second syllable – as in *beSAR* (big), *leKAS* (fast), and so forth; unfortunately, this isn't predictable.

MANGLISH AND SINGLISH

Manglish and **Singlish**, the distinctive forms of English widely spoken in Malaysia and Singapore respectively, can be as confusing to the uninitiated as Jamaican patois. They're really two sides of the same coin: in both, conventional English syntax gives way to a word order that's more akin to Malay or Chinese, and tenses and pronouns are discarded. Ask someone if they've ever been abroad, and you might be answered "I ever", while enquiring whether they've just been shopping might yield "Go, come back already". Responses are almost invariably distilled down to single-word replies, often repeated for stress. Request something in a shop and you'll hear "have, have", or "got, got". Other stock manglings of English include:

aidontch-main "I don't mind"
betayudon(lah) "You'd better not do that!"
debladigarmen A contraction of "the bloody government"
is it? (pronounced *eezeet?*) "Really?"
tingwat? "What do you think?"
watudu? "What can we do?", a rhetorical question
yusobadwan "You're such a bad one!" meaning "that's not very nice!"

Suffixes and **exclamations** drawn from Malay and Hokkien complete this patois, the most notable being the Malay intensifier "lah", which seems to finish off just about every other utterance. In Malaysia you may hear the Malay question marker "kah" at the ends of queries, while Chinese on both sides of the Causeway might apply the suffix "ah", as in "so cheap one ah", which translates as "is it really that cheap?" or "wow, that's cheap" depending on the intonation; "ah" on its own can also mean "yes", especially if accompanied by a nod of the head. If Manglish and Singlish have you baffled, you might try raising your eyes to the heavens and crying either "ayoh" (with a drop of tone on the second syllable) or "alamak", both expressions denoting exasperation or dismay.

While these linguistic quirks often amuse foreigners and locals alike, both countries are worried that an apparent decline in **English standards** could affect their ability to do business globally. During the colonial era, the minority who could speak English tended to have a decent facility for the language. Now all students learn some English in school (in Singapore, English is actually the official language of education), but often they emerge with a weak grasp of the language. In Malaysia, there is an ongoing debate over English, with Malay nationalists wanting to emphasize Malay and other communities wanting English to get more prominence in the school curriculum. For its part, Singapore, a country with a history of preachy state campaigns, has seen the creation of a government-backed Speak Good English movement (languagecouncils.sg/goodenglish).

VOWELS AND DIPHTHONGS

a somewhere in between the vowels of c**a**rp and c**u**p, but changes to a short indeterminate vowel if at the end of a word, as in banan**a**
aa like two "a" vowels separated by the merest pause; thus *maaf* (forgiveness) is rendered *ma + af*
ai as in f**i**ne (written "ei" in older spellings)
au as in h**ow**
e as in h**er**, though in many instances (not predictable) it is like the é of sauté, as in *kereta* (car), pronounced *keréta*; in yet others it denotes a short indeterminate vowel
i somewhere between the **i** of t**i**n and the **ee** of t**ee**n
o as in st**o**ne, though shorter and not as rounded as in English
u sometimes short as in p**u**ll, sometimes long (eg, if at the end of a word) as in p**oo**l
ua as in d**oer**

CONSONANTS

c as in **ch**ip (and written "ch" in older spellings), though slightly gentler than in English
d becomes **t** when at the end of a word
g hard, as in **g**irl
h can drop out when flanked by vowels; thus *tahu*, "know", is usually pronounced as though spelt *tau*
k drops out if at the end of the word or if followed by another consonant, becoming a glottal stop (a brief pause); thus *rakyat* (people) is pronounced *ra + yat*

kh as in the Scottish lo**ch**; found in loan words from Arabic
l unlike in English, l is not swallowed if it occurs at the end of a word
ng as in tang (the "g" is never hard – thus *telinga*, "ear", is *te-ling-a* and not *te-lin-ga*); can occur at the start of a word
ngg as in ta**ng**o
ny as in ca**ny**on; can occur at the start of a word
r is lightly trilled (though in some accents it can be rendered like the French r of Paris); drops out at the ends of words when preceded by a vowel
sy as in **sh**ut

Grammar

Word order in Malay is similar to that in English, though note that adjectives usually follow nouns. **Nouns** have no genders and don't require an article, while the **plural** form is constructed either by saying the word twice, if the number of objects is unspecified (thus "book" is *buku*, "books" *buku-buku*, sometimes written *buku2*), or by specifying the number of objects before the singular noun ("three books" is thus *tiga buku*). **Verbs** have no tenses either, the time of the action being indicated either by the context, or by the use of words such as *akan* (functioning like "will") and *sudah* ("already") for the future and past. The verb "to be" seldom appears explicitly, so, for example, *saya lapar* literally means "I [am] hungry". There are two words for **negation**: *bukan*, used before nouns (for example *saya bukan doktor*, "I'm not a doctor"), and *tak* (formally *tidak*), used before verbs and adjectives (as in *saya tak lapar*, "I'm not hungry"; *saya tak makan*, "I've not eaten"). Possessive constructions are achieved simply by putting the "owner" after the thing that's "owned"; thus *kampung saya*, literally "village [of] I", is "my village".

Malay words and phrases

One point to note regarding **pronouns** is that Malay lacks a convenient word for "you", all the options being either too formal or informal. In fact, the normal way to address someone is to use their name to their face, which can seem strange to English-speakers. If you don't know someone's name, then you can use *abang* (brother) or *kak* (sister) to address a person of roughly the same age as you, or *adik* to a child, or *pak cik* or *mak cik* to a much older man or woman respectively.

You'll often see the word Dato' (or Datuk) or Tun placed before the name of a government official or some other worthy. Both are honorific titles of distinction roughly equivalent to the British "Sir". Royalty are always addressed as Tuanku.

PERSONAL PRONOUNS

I/my saya
we (excludes the person kami being spoken to) or **kita** (includes the person being spoken to)
you (formal) or anda
  awak (informal)

he/she dia
they mereka
Mr Encik *or* Tuan
Mrs Puan
Miss Cik

GREETINGS AND OTHER BASICS

"Selamat" is the all-purpose greeting derived from Arabic, which communicates a general goodwill.
good morning selamat pagi
good afternoon selamat petang
good midday selamat tengah hari (used around noon)
good evening selamat malam
good night (literally selamat tidur "peaceful sleep")
goodbye (literally selamat tinggal "peaceful stay"; used by someone leaving)
safe journey selamat jalan

welcome selamat datang
bon appetit selamat makan
how are you? apa khabar?
fine baik *or* bagus
see you again jumpa lagi
please tolong
thank you terima kasih
you're welcome sama-sama
sorry/excuse me maaf
never mind, no matter tak apalah

yes ya (sometimes pronounced a bit like "year")
no tidak
this/that ini/itu
here sini
there (very nearby), situ
   (further away) sana
what is your name? siapa nama awak?
my name is… nama saya…
where are you from? dari mana?
I come from… saya dari…
…England …England
…America …Amerika
…Australia …Australia
…Canada …Kanada
…New Zealand …Zealandia Baru (*or just* "New Zeelan")
…Ireland …Irlandia
…Scotland …Skotlandia

husband suami
wife isteri
friend kawan
person orang
do you speak English? boleh cakap Bahasa inggeris?
I (don't) understand saya (tak) faham
that's fine/allowed boleh
can you help me? boleh tolong saya?
can I…? boleh saya…?
to have, there is/are ada
what? apa?
what is this/that? apa ini/itu?
when? bila?
where? di mana?
who? siapa?
why? mengapa? *or* kenapa?
how? bagaimana?
how much/many? berapa?

USEFUL ADJECTIVES

good bagus
a lot banyak
a little sikit *or* sedikit
cheap/expensive murah/mahal
hot/cold panas/sejuk
big/small besar/kecil

enough cukup
open/closed buka/tutup
hungry lapar
thirsty haus
tired letih
ill sakit

USEFUL VERBS

come/go datang/pergi
do buat
eat/drink makan/minum
enter, go in masuk
give/take beri/ambil
have, possess punya *or* ada
hear dengar
help tolong
know (something) tahu

know (someone) kenal
like suka
push/pull tolak/tarik
see tengok
sit duduk
sleep tidur
want mahu
wish to, intend to nak

GETTING AROUND AND DIRECTIONS

where is…? di mana…?
I want to go to… saya mahu pergi ke…
how do I get there? bagaimanakah saya boleh ke sana?
how far? berapa jauh?
how long will it take? berapa lama?
when will the bus leave? bila bas berangkat?
what time does the train arrive? jam berapa keretapi sampai?
go up, ride naik
get down, disembark turun
nearby/far away dekat/jauh
stop berhenti
wait tunggu
turn belok

left kiri
right kanan
straight on terus
in front di depan *or* di hadapan
behind di belakang
north utara
south selatan
east timur
west barat
street jalan
airport lapangan terbang
bus station stesen bas *or sometimes* hentian bas
train station stesen keretapi
jetty jeti *or* pangkalan
bicycle baisikal

boat bot *or* bot penambang (the latter is used of small passenger-carrying craft)
longboat perahu *or* bot panjang
car kereta
motorcycle motosikal
plane kapal terbang
taxi teksi
trishaw beca
ticket tiket
fare (adults/children) tambang (dewasa/kanak-kanak)
house rumah

post office pejabat pos
restaurant restoran
church gereja
mosque masjid
Chinese temple tokong
museum muzium
park, reserve taman
toilet (men/women) tandas (lelaki/perempuan)
entrance masuk
exit keluar

ACCOMMODATION

hotel hotel
guesthouse rumah tumpangan *or* rumah rehat
dorm asrama
room (double/single) bilik (untuk dua/satu)
bed (double/single) katil (kelamin/bujang)
fan kipas
air-conditioned berhawa dingin

bath, shower mandi
I need a room saya perlu satu bilik
I'm staying for... nights saya mahu tinggal... malam
please clean my room tolong bersih-kan bilik saya
can I store my luggage here? boleh titip barang?
I want to pay saya nak bayar

BANKING AND SHOPPING

how much is...? berapa harga...?
I want to buy... saya mahu beli...
can you reduce the price? boleh kurang?
I'll give you no more than... saya bayar tidak lebih dari...
I'm just looking saya hanya lihat-lihat
shop kedai

market pasar
night market pasar malam
supermarket pasaraya
bank bank
money wang *or* duit
moneychanger pengurup wang

NUMBERS

0 kosong
1 satu (sometimes shortened to the prefix "se-" when used with a noun)
2 dua
3 tiga
4 empat
5 lima
6 enam
7 tujuh
8 lapan
9 sembilan
10 sepuluh

11 sebelas
12 duabelas
20 duapuluh
21 duapuluh satu
100 seratus
121 seratus duapuluh satu
200 duaratus
1000 seribu
2000 duaribu
1 million sejuta
a half setengah

TIME AND DAYS OF THE WEEK

what time is it? pukul jam berapa?
time is... pukul...
three o'clock tiga
ten past four empat sepuluh
quarter past five lima suku
quarter to six ("five lima tiga suku
three-quarters")
six-thirty ("six half") enam setengah
7am tujuh pagi

8pm lapan malam
hour jam
minute minit
second detik
day hari
week minggu
month bulan
year tahun
today hari ini

tomorrow esok *or* besok
yesterday semalam *or on the east coast* kelmarin
now sekarang
later nanti
next... ...depan
last... ....yang lalu, ...lepas
not yet belum lagi
never tak pernah

Monday hari Isnin
Tuesday hari Selasa
Wednesday hari Rabu
Thursday hari Kamis
Friday hari Jumaat
Saturday hari Sabtu
Sunday hari Ahad *or* Minggu

Food and drink glossary

The list below concentrates on Malay terminology, though a few Chinese and Indian terms appear (unfortunately, transliteration of these varies widely), as well as definitions of some culinary words used in local English.

BASICS, INCLUDING COOKING METHODS

Deciphering menus and ordering is sometimes a matter of matching ingredients and cooking methods – for example, to get an approximation of chips or French fries, you'd ask for *kentang goreng*, literally "fried potatoes". If you don't want your food spicy, say *jangan taruh cili* ("don't add chilli") or *saya tak suka pedas* ("I don't like spicy [food]").

bakar baked
bubur porridge
garpu fork
goreng fried
istimewa special (as in "today's special")
kari curry
kedai kek bakery ("cake shop")
kedai kopis a diner ("coffee shop") concentrating on inexpensive rice spreads, noodles and other dishes, while serving some beverages
kering dried
kopitiam Hokkien Chinese term for a *kedai kopis*; commonly used in Singapore
kuah gravy
kukus steamed
layan diri self-service
lemak "fatty"; often denotes use of coconut milk
makanan/minuman food/drink
mangkuk bowl
manis sweet
masam sour
masin salty
medan selera food court
panggang grilled
pedas spicy
pinggan plate
pisau knife
rebus boiled
restoran restaurant
sedap tasty
sudu spoon
sup/sop soup
tumis stir-fried, sautéed
warung stall

MEAT (DAGING) AND POULTRY

ayam chicken
babi pork
burong puyuh quail
char siew Cantonese honey roast pork
daging lembu (**sapi** in Borneo) beef
itek duck
kambing mutton
lap cheong sweetish, fatty pork sausage (Cantonese)

FISH (IKAN) AND OTHER SEAFOOD

ambal bamboo clams, a Sarawak delicacy
fishball spherical fish dumpling, rubbery in texture, often added to noodles and soups
fishcake fish dumpling in slices, often added to noodles
ikan bawal pomfret
lian bilis anchovy
ikan keli catfish
ikan kembong mackerel
ikan kerapu grouper
ikan kurau threadfin
ikan merah red snapper
ikan pari skate
ikan siakap sea bass
ikan tongkol tuna
ikan yu or **jerung** shark
kepiting or **ketam** crab
kerang cockles
keropok lekor tubular fish dumplings (an east coast speciality)

sotong squid, cuttlefish
udang prawn

udang galah lobster

VEGETABLES (SAYUR)

bangkwang a radish-like root (also called *jicama*), used in Chinese *rojak* and in *popiah* fillings
bawang onion
bawang putih garlic
bayam spinach or spinach-like greens
bendi okra, ladies' fingers
bunga kobis cauliflower
bendawan mushroom
chye sim or choy sum brassica greens, similar to *pak choy*
cili chilli
halia ginger
jagung corn
kacang beans, pulses or nuts
kangkung convolvulus greens with narrow leaves and hollow stems; aka water spinach or morning glory
keladi yam

keledek sweet potato
kentang potatoes
kobis cabbage
lada chilli
lobak radish
lobak merah carrot
midin jungle fern, much served in Sarawak
pak choy or pek chye soft-leaved brassica greens with broad stalks
petai beans in large pods from a tree, often sold in bunches
pucuk paku fern tips, eaten as greens
rebung bamboo shoots
tauge beansprouts
terung aubergine
timun cucumber
ubi kayu tapioca

OTHER INGREDIENTS

asam tamarind; also used to indicate a dish flavoured with tamarind
belacan pungent fermented shrimp paste
daun pandan pandanus (screwpine) leaf, imparting a sweet bouquet to foods with which it's cooked; used not only in desserts but also in some rice dishes
garam salt
gula sugar
gula Melaka palm-sugar molasses, used to sweeten *cendol* and other desserts

kaya orange or green curd jam made with egg and coconut; delicious on toast
kicap soy sauce
kicap manis sweet dark soy sauce
mentega butter
minyak oil
tahu tofu (beancurd)
telur egg
tempeh fermented soybean cakes, nutty and slightly sour

NOODLES AND NOODLE DISHES

The three most common types of noodle are *mee* (or *mi*), yellow egg noodles made from wheat flour; *bee hoon* (or *bihun* or *mee hoon*), like vermicelli; and *kuay teow* (or *hor fun*), like tagliatelle.

char kuay teow Chinese fried *kuay teow*, often seasoned with *kicap manis*, and featuring any combination of prawns, Chinese sausage, fishcake, egg, vegetables and chilli
Foochow noodles steamed and served in soy and oyster sauce with spring onions and dried fish
Hokkien fried mee *mee* and *bee hoon* fried with pieces of pork, prawn and vegetables; a variant in KL has the noodles cooked in soy sauce with *tempeh*
kang puan (or kampua) mee a rich Sibu speciality – noodles cooked in lard
kolok mee *mee* served dryish, accompanied by *char siew* slices
laksa basically noodles in a curried soup featuring some seafood and flavoured with the *laksa*-leaf herb (*daun kesom*); variations include Nyonya *laksa* (featuring coconut milk), *asam laksa* (Penang-style, with tamarind) and *laksa Johor* (made with spaghetti)
laksam *kuay teow* rice noodles in a fish sauce made with coconut milk and served with *ulam* (salad); an east coast speciality
mee bandung *mee* served in thickish gravy flavoured with beef and prawn (both of which garnish the dish)
mee goreng Indian or Malay fried noodles; Indian versions are particularly spicy
mee hailam *mee* in an oyster-sauce-based gravy
mee kari noodles in a curried soup
mee pok Teochew dish using ribbon-like yellow noodles, served with fishballs and a chilli dressing
mee rebus boiled *mee*; varies regionally, but one of the best is that sold in Singapore, featuring *mee* in a sweetish sauce made with yellow bean paste, and garnished with boiled egg and tofu

mee siam *bee hoon* cooked in tangy-sweet soup flavoured with tamarind, and garnished with slices of hard-boiled egg and beancurd

mee suah like *bee hoon* but even more threadlike and soft; can be made crispy if fried

sar hor fun flat rice noodles served in a chicken-stock soup, to which prawns, fried shallots and beansprouts are added; a speciality in Ipoh

wan tan mee roast pork, noodles and vegetables, accompanied by pork dumplings

RICE (NASI) DISHES AND SPREADS

char siew fan common one-plate meal, featuring *char siew* and gravy on a bed of steamed rice

claypot rice Chinese dish of rice topped with meat (such as *lap cheong*), cooked in an earthenware pot over a fire to create a smoky taste

daun pisang Malay term for banana-leaf curry, a Southern Indian meal with chutneys and curries, served on a mound of rice, and presented on a banana leaf with poppadums

Hainanese chicken rice Singapore's unofficial national rice dish: steamed or boiled chicken slices served on rice cooked in chicken stock, and accompanied by chicken broth, and a chilli and ginger dip

lemang glutinous rice stuffed into lengths of bamboo

nasi ayam Malay version of Hainanese chicken rice

nasi berlauk simply "rice with dishes"

nasi biriyani saffron-flavoured rice cooked with chicken, beef or fish; a North Indian speciality

nasi campur standard term for a rice spread, served with an array of meat, fish and vegetable dishes to choose from

nasi dagang east coast speciality; a slightly glutinous rice steamed with coconut milk, and often brownish in appearance, usually served with fish curry

nasi goreng rice fried with diced meat and vegetables and sometimes a little spice

nasi kandar a spread of rice and curries originating with Indian Muslim caterers in Penang; the rice is often stored in a container made of wood, which is said to give it a distinctive flavour

nasi kerabu blue or green rice traditionally coloured with flower pigments, though these days food colourings may be used; found particularly in Kelantan, it's usually served with a fish curry

nasi kunyit rice given a bright yellow colour by turmeric

nasi lemak a Malay classic, rice cooked with a little coconut milk and served with *ikan bilis*, cucumber, fried peanuts, fried or hard-boiled egg slices and *sambal*

nasi Minang rice spread featuring dishes cooked in the style of the Minang Highlands of western Sumatra; similar to **nasi Padang**

nasi minyak rice cooked with *ghee*

nasi Padang rice spread with the dishes cooked in the style of Padang, Sumatra

nasi putih plain boiled rice

nasi ulam rice containing blanched herbs and greens

pulut glutinous rice

ROTI (BREAD) DISHES

The word *roti* refers both to griddle breads and to Western bread, depending on the context.

murtabak thick griddle bread, usually savoury stuffed with onion, egg and chicken or mutton

murtabak pisang a sweet version of *murtabak*, stuffed with banana.

roti bakar toast, usually served with butter and *kaya*

roti bom an especially greasy *roti canai*, containing a cheesy-tasting margarine

roti canai light, layered griddle bread served with a thin curry sauce

roti John simple Indian dish, a French loaf split and stuffed with an egg, onion and sweet chilli sauce mixture; versions containing meat are occasionally seen

roti kahwin toast spread with butter and *kaya*

roti prata Singapore name for *roti canai*

roti telur *roti canai* with an egg mixed into the dough

roti telur bawang *roti canai* with an egg and chopped onion mixed into the dough

OTHER SPECIALITIES

ayam goreng Malay-style fried chicken

ayam percik barbecued chicken with a creamy coconut sauce; a Kota Bharu speciality

bak kut teh literally "meat bone tea", a Chinese soup made by boiling up pork ribs with soy sauce, ginger, herbs and spices

chap chye a Nyonya stew of mixed vegetables, fungi and sometimes also glass noodles (aka *tang hoon*, a rather elastic vermicelli)

chee cheong fun Cantonese speciality, vaguely like ravioli, featuring minced shrimp rolled up in rice-flour sheets, steamed and dredged in a sweet-salty red sauce

chye tow kuay also known as "carrot cake", comprising a rice flour/white radish mixture formed into cubes and fried with egg and garlic; a savoury-sweet version with added *kicap manis* is also worth trying

congee watery rice gruel eaten with slices of meat or fish or omelette; sometimes listed on menus as "porridge"

dim sum Chinese meal of titbits – dumplings, pork ribs, etc – steamed or fried and served in bamboo baskets

dosai/dosa/thosai Southern Indian pancake, made from ground rice and lentils, and served with dhal (lentils); *masala dosai* features a potato stuffing, while *rava dosai* has grated carrot in the batter

fish-head curry the head of a red snapper (usually), cooked in a spicy curry sauce with tomatoes and okra

gado-gado Malay/Indonesian salad of lightly cooked vegetables, boiled egg, slices of rice cake and a crunchy peanut sauce

idli South Indian rice-and-lentil cakes, steamed

kari kepala ikan *see* fish-head curry

kongbian Chinese-style bagels, found only in Sibu

kuih pai tee Nyonya dish vaguely resembling fried spring rolls, except that the *pai tee* are shaped like cup cakes; filling is like that for *popiah*

lontong a pairing of a *sayur lodeh*-like curry with rice cakes similar to *ketupat*

oothapam rice-and-lentil pancakes; South Indian

otak-otak mashed fish mixed with coconut milk and chilli paste, then steamed in strips wrapped in banana leaf; a Nyonya dish

popiah spring rolls, consisting of a steamed dough wrapper filled with peanuts, egg, bean shoots, vegetables and a sweet sauce; sometimes known as *lumpia*

rendang dry, highly spiced coconut curry with beef, chicken or mutton

rojak the Chinese version is a salad of greens, beansprouts, pineapple and cucumber in a peanut and prawn-paste sauce; quite different is Indian *rojak*, a variety of fritters with sweet chilli dips

satar similar to *otak-otak* but made in triangular shapes; found on the east coast

satay marinated pieces of meat, skewered on small sticks and cooked over charcoal; served with peanut sauce, cucumber, raw onion and *ketupat* (rice cake)

sayur lodeh mixed vegetables stewed in a curry sauce containing coconut milk

sop ekor Malay oxtail soup

sop kambing spicy Malay mutton soup

sop tulang Malay beef-bone soup

steamboat Chinese fondue: raw meat, fish, veggies and other titbits dunked into a steaming broth until cooked

umai raw fish salad, mixed with shallots and lime, found in east Malaysia and Brunei

umbut kelapa masak lemak young coconut shoots, cooked in coconut milk

vadai South Indian fried lentil patty

yam basket Sarawak speciality: meat, vegetables and soya bean curd in a fried yam crust

yong tau foo bean curd, fishballs and assorted vegetables, poached and served with broth and sweet dipping sauces

SNACKS AND ACCOMPANIMENTS

acar pickle, often sweet and spicy

bak kwa Chinese-style sweet barbecued pork slices, eaten as a snack

budu fermented fish sauce

cempedak goreng *cempedak*, similar to jackfruit, fried in batter, allowing not just the flesh but also the floury stones to be eaten

curry puff also called *karipap* in Malay; a semicircular pastry parcel stuffed with curried meat and vegetables

kerabu not to be confused with *nasi kerabu*, this is a salad of grated unripe fruit, mixed with chilli, grated coconut, cucumber and other ingredients

keropok (goreng) deep-fried prawn or fish crackers, derived from a dough like that used to make *keropok lekor* (see page 568)

ketupat unseasoned rice cubes boiled in packets of woven coconut-leaf strips, served as an accompaniment to satay

pau or **pow** Chinese stuffed bun made with a sweetish dough and steamed; *char siew pau* contains Cantonese honey-roast pork, *kai pau* chicken and egg, while there are also *pau* with sweet fillings include bean paste, dried coconut or *kaya*

rasam sour-spicy South Indian soup flavoured with tamarind and tomato

sambal dip made with pounded or ground chilli; *sambal belacan* is augmented with a little *belacan* for extra depth of flavour

sambar watery South Indian curry served with *dosa*

tempoyak fermented durian paste, a Malay condiment

ulam Malay salad of raw vegetables and herbs

yew char kuay Chinese fried dough sticks, good dunked in coffee; not unlike Spanish *churros* in flavour and texture

DRINKS

When ordering beverages in a *kedai kopis*, there are various standard terms to bear in mind. *Kosong* ("zero") after the name of the drink means you want it black and unsugared; the suffix *-o* (pronounced "oh") means black with sugar, *susu* means with milk (invariably of the sweetened condensed variety), *ais* or *peng* means iced, *tarik* ("pulled") denotes the popular practice of frothing a drink by pouring it repeatedly from one mug to another and back, and *kurang manis* ("lacking sweetness") means to go easy on the sugar or condensed milk. A few places also allow you to order your drink *see* or *si*, meaning with unsweetened evaporated milk. It's quite possible to combine these terms, so in theory you could order *kopi susu tarik kurang manis peng*, which would be a frothy milky coffee, iced and not too sweet. Note that condensed milk is often assumed to be wanted even if you don't say *susu*.

air botol a bottled drink (usually refers to soft drinks)
air kelapa coconut water
air laici tinned lychee juice, very sweet, usually with a couple of lychees in the glass
air minum drinking water
air tebu sugar-cane juice
bandung or **air sirap bandung** a sweet drink, bright pink in colour, made with rose essence and a little milk
bir beer
chrysanthemum tea delicately fragrant tea made from chrysanthemum blossom, and served slightly sweet, either hot or cold
cincau or **chinchow** sweet drink, the colour of cola or stout, made with strips of jelly-like seaweed
jus juice (the word *jus* is usually followed by the name of the fruit in question)
kopi coffee; some *kedai kopis* offer it freshly brewed, others serve instant
kopi jantan coffee that's claimed to be a male tonic, often advertised with posters showing avuncular Malay men apparently endorsing the drink
kopi tongkat Ali similar to *kopi jantan* (*tongkat Ali* is a herb that Malays believe has aphrodisiac qualities for men)
lassi Indian sweet or salty yoghurt drink
susu milk
teh tea
teh bunga kekwa chrysanthemum
teh limau ais iced lemon tea
tuak rice wine (Borneo)

FRUIT (BUAH)

belimbing starfruit
betik papaya
cempedak similar to jackfruit
duku, duku langsat small round fruits containing bittersweet segments
durian famously stinky large fruit containing rows of seeds coated in sweet creamy flesh
durian belanda soursop
epal apple
jambu batu guava
kelapa coconut
laici lychee
limau lime or lemon
limau bali pomelo
mangga mango
manggis mangosteen
nanas pineapple
nangka jackfruit
nyiur alternative term for coconut
oren orange
pisang banana
rambutan hairy-skinned stone fruit with sweet white flesh
salak teardrop-shaped fruit with scaly brown skin and bitter flesh
tembikai watermelon

DESSERTS

agar-agar seaweed-derived jelly served in squares or diamonds, and often with coconut milk for richness
air batu campur ("ABC") another name for *ais kacang*
ais kacang ice flakes with red beans, cubes of jelly, sweetcorn, rose syrup and evaporated milk
bubur cha cha sweetened coconut milk with pieces of sweet potato, yam and tapioca
cendol coconut milk, palm sugar syrup and pea-flour noodles poured over shaved ice
cheng tng clear, sweet Chinese broth containing fungi and dried fruit
kuih or **kuih-muih** Malay/Nyonya sweetmeats, ranging from something like a Western cake to fudge-like morsels made of mung bean or rice flour
kuih lapis layer cake; either a simple rice-flour confection, or an elaborate wheat-flour sponge comprising numerous very thin layers and unusually rich in egg
pisang goreng bananas or plantains coated in a thin batter and fried

Glossary

adat customary or traditional law
air water
air panas hot springs
air terjun waterfall
ancestral hall building at clan temple housing ancestral tablets
ancestral tablet small upright object representing a departed forebear, venerated in Chinese ancestor worship
atap/attap palm thatch
Baba Straits-born Chinese (male)
bandar town
bandaraya city
bangunan building
banjaran mountain range
batang river system
batik wax and dye technique of cloth decoration
batu rock/stone
bejalai period in an Iban youth's life when he ventures out from the longhouse to experience life in the towns
belian a hardwood traditionally used to construct Sarawak longhouses
belukar secondary rainforest, essentially woodland that regrows in areas where primary forest has been disturbed or cut down
bomoh traditional spiritualist healer
bukit hill
bumbun hide
bumiputra person deemed Indigenous to Malaysia ("son of the soil")
bungalow in local English, any detached house
candi temple
Cantonese pertaining to the Guangdong province of southeast China
clan association social club and welfare organization, its members drawn from Chinese migrants from a particular city or area; its premises are called a clan hall/house
coolie colonial-era term for an unskilled labourer
daerah an administrative district
daulat divine force possessed by a ruler that commands unquestioning loyalty
Dayak/Dyak a largely obsolete umbrella term once used to denote the Indigenous peoples of Borneo
dipterocarp the predominant family of trees in the rainforest, comprising many types of exceptionally tall trees reaching up to the top of the forest canopy
ekspres express (used of boats and buses)
empangan dam
Foochow pertaining to Fuzhou, a city in Fujian province, southeast China
gasing spinning top
gawai annual festivals celebrated by Indigenous groups in Sarawak
gelanggang seni cultural centre
gereja church
godown warehouse
gopuram pyramidal tower decorated with deities and placed over the entrance to a Hindu temple
gua cave
gunung mountain
Hainanese pertaining to Hainan Island, southeast China
halal something permissible in Islam
hill station a settlement or resort at relatively high altitude usually founded in colonial times
Hokkien pertaining to the Fujian province of southeast China, the main dialect of which is more formally called **minnan**
huay guan/kuan another term for clan association
hutan forest
ikat woven fabric
istana palace
jalan road, street
jambatan bridge
kampung/kampong village
kelong a fishing platform extending out to sea from some beaches, acting to lure fish to nets at the far end
kemah campsite
kerangas sparse forest ("poor soil")
khalwat an offence under Islamic law, typically involving an unmarried Muslim couple being together in private
kongsi Chinese clan house/temple; has entered Malay as a word meaning "share"
kota fort
kris wavy-bladed Malay dagger
kuala river confluence or estuary
labu gourd; also used of the gourd-like ceramic bottles made as souvenirs in some parts of the Peninsula
lata waterfall
laut sea
lebuh avenue, street
lebuhraya highway/expressway
lorong lane
mak yong courtly dance-drama
makam grave or tomb
Malaya old name for the area now called Peninsular Malaysia
Mamak Indian Muslim; used particularly of restaurants run by Indian Muslims
mandi Asian method of showering by dousing with water from a tank using a small bucket or dipper

masjid mosque
Mat Salleh Malaysian slang for a white person
Melayu Malay
menara minaret or tower
merdeka freedom, in general; can specifically refer to Malaysian independence
Minangkabau matriarchal people from Sumatra
negara national
nipah a type of palm tree
Nyonya/Nonya Straits-born Chinese (female)
Orang Asli Peninsular Malaysia aborigines ("original people"); also Orang Ulu (upriver people) and Orang Laut (sea people)
padang field/square; usually the main town square
pangkalan jetty or port (literally "base")
pantai beach
parang machete
pasar market
pasar malam night market
pasir sand
pejabat Pos post office
pekan town
pelabuhan port/harbour
penghulu chieftain, leader
Peranakan Straits-born Chinese
perigi well
persekutuan federal
pintu arch/gate/door
pondok hut or shelter
pulau island
rajah prince
Ramadan Muslim fasting month
rebana drum
rotan rattan, and the rattan cane used to inflict corporal punishment
rumah persinggahan lodging house
rumah rehat older guesthouse (literally "resthouse"), now mainly privately run, though once state-owned
rumah tumpangan boarding house

samping songket worn by a man as a short sarong over loose trousers
saree traditional Indian woman's garment, worn in conjunction with a **choli** (short-sleeved blouse)
sarung/sarong cloth worn as a wrap around the lower body
sekolah school
semenanjung Peninsula
seni art or skill
shophouse a two-storey terraced building found mainly in town centres, and often featuring a facade that is recessed at street level, providing a shaded walkway that serves as a pavement
silat Malay art of self-defence
songket brocade
songkok Malay male headgear, a little like a flattish fez, made of black velvet over cardboard
sulap hut (East Malaysia, especially Sabah)
sultan ruler
sungai/sungei river
taman park
tamu market/fair
tanjung/tanjong cape, headland
tasik/tasek lake
telaga freshwater spring or well
teluk/telok bay or inlet
Teochew pertaining to Chaozhou, a city in Fujian province, southeast China
tokong Chinese temple
towkay Chinese merchant
tuai headman (Sarawak)
wasai waterfall or area with a pool (Brunei), Sabah
wau kite
wayang show, ranging from a film screening to Chinese opera
wayang kulit shadow-puppet play (literally "skin show", after the fact that the puppets are made of hide)
wisma building, especially a commercial one

ACRONYMS

BN Barisan Nasional or National Front – the coalition, dominated by UMNO, which has governed Malaysia since 1974
KTM Keretapi Tanah Melayu, the Malaysian national railway company
MAS Malaysia Airlines
MCA Malaysian Chinese Association, the Chinese wing of the governing BN
MCP Malayan Communist Party

MRT Singapore's Mass Rapid Transit system
PAP Singaporean People's Action Party
PAS Parti Islam SeMalaysia, the Pan-Malaysian Islamic Party
PKR Parti Keadilan Rakyat, the Malaysian opposition People's Justice Party (usually called simply Keadilan)
SIA Singapore Airlines
UMNO United Malays National Organization

Small print and index

575 About the author
577 Index
583 Map symbols

ABOUT THE AUTHOR
Martin Zatko has been in a near-constant state of motion since 2002. During some of his more productive moments, he has written or contributed to the Rough Guides to Korea, China, Japan, Taiwan, Vietnam, Myanmar, India, Fiji, Australia, Turkey, Morocco, Greece and Europe.

A ROUGH GUIDE TO ROUGH GUIDES
Published in 1982, the first Rough Guide – to Greece – was a student scheme that became a publishing phenomenon. Mark Ellingham, a recent graduate in English from Bristol University, had been travelling in Greece the previous summer and couldn't find the right guidebook. With a small group of friends he wrote his own guide, combining a contemporary, journalistic style with a thoroughly practical approach to travellers' needs.

The immediate success of the book spawned a series that rapidly covered dozens of destinations. And, in addition to impecunious backpackers, Rough Guides soon acquired a much broader readership that relished the guides' wit and inquisitiveness as much as their enthusiastic, critical approach and value-for-money ethos. These days, Rough Guides include recommendations from budget to luxury and cover more than 120 destinations around the globe, from Amsterdam to Zanzibar, all regularly updated by our team of roaming writers.

Browse all our latest guides, read inspirational features and book your trip at **roughguides.com**.

SMALL PRINT

Rough Guide credits
Editor: Siobhan Warwicker
Cartography: Carte
Picture Manager: Tom Smyth
Layout: Pradeep Thapliyal
Publishing Technology Manager: Rebeka Davies
Production Operations Manager: Katie Bennett
Head of Publishing: Sarah Clark

Publishing information
Eleventh Edition 2026

ISBN: 9781835294055

Distribution
UK, Ireland and Europe
Apa Publications (UK) Ltd; mail@roughguides.com
United States and Canada
Two Rivers; ips@ingramcontent.com
Australia and New Zealand
Woodslane; info@woodslane.com.au
Worldwide
Apa Publications (UK) Ltd; mail@roughguides.com

This book was produced using **Typefi** automated publishing software.

A catalogue record for this book is available from the British Library.

All rights reserved
© 2026 Apa Digital AG
License edition © Apa Publications Ltd UK

Special Sales, Content Licensing and CoPublishing
Rough Guides can be purchased in bulk quantities at discounted prices. We can create special editions, personalized jackets and corporate imprints tailored to your needs. mail@roughguides.com.

No part of this book may be reproduced, stored in a retrieval system, or transmitted in any form or by any means – electronic, mechanical, photocopying, recording, or otherwise – without prior written permission from Apa Publications.

roughguides.com

No part of this book may be used or reproduced in any manner for the purpose of training artificial intelligence technologies or systems.

EU Representative
LOGOS EUROPE, 9 rue Nicolas Poussin, 17000, LA ROCHELLE, France; Contact@logoseurope.eu; +33 (0) 667937378

Every effort has been made to ensure that this publication is accurate, free from safety risks, and provides accurate information. However, changes and errors are inevitable. The publisher is not responsible for any resulting loss, inconvenience, injury or safety concerns arising from the use of this book.

Printed by Omur in Turkey

Help us update
We've gone to a lot of effort to ensure that this edition of **The Rough Guide to Malaysia, Singapore and Brunei** is accurate and up-to-date. However, things change – places get "discovered", transport routes are altered, restaurants and hotels raise prices or lower standards, and businesses cease trading. If you feel we've got it wrong or left something out, we'd like to know, and if you can direct us to the web address, so much the better.

Please send your comments with the subject line **"Rough Guide Malaysia, Singapore and Brunei Update"** to mail@roughguides.com. We'll send a copy of the next edition (or any other Rough Guide if you prefer) for the very best emails.

Photo credits
(Key: T-top; C-centre; B-bottom; L-left; R-right)

Adobe Stock 4, 13T, 14, 15TL, 15TR, 15C, 15B, 17T, 17B, 18T, 18B, 19T, 19BL, 20B, 20T, 21T, 22TR, 22TL, 23B, 26, 58/59, 61, 108/109, 111, 176/177, 250/251, 367

Shutterstock 1, 5, 9, 10, 13B, 16B, 16T, 16C, 19BR, 21C, 21B, 22B, 23T, 24, 179, 204/205, 207, 253, 294/295, 297, 364/365, 424/425, 427, 446/447, 449, 524

Cover: Penang floating mosque at Tanjung Bungah, Malaysia **Shutterstock**

Index

A

accessible travel 52
accommodation 36
activities, outdoor 48
addresses 29
adventure caving 352
Air Batang (MY) 285
Air Hitam (MY). *See* Ayer Itam
Ai River (MY) 326
Air Terjun Jelawang (MY) 203
alcohol 42
Alor Setar (MY) 8, 162
altitude sickness 45
Animism 542
Annah Rais (MY) 322
Ayer Itam (MY) 156
Ayer Keroh (MY) 271

B

Bajau Laut people 413
Ba' Kelalan (MY) 361
bakeries 39
Bako National Park (MY) 49, 318
Bakun Dam (MY) 336
Balik Pulau (MY) 160
Bandar Seri Begawan (BN) 11, 431
   accommodation 438
   arrival and deparure 436
   Arts and Handicrafts Centre 435
   directory 440
   eating 439
   Gadong 436
   getting around 437
   information 437
   Istana Nurul Iman 435
   Jame 'Asr Hassanal Bolkiah 436
   Kampong Ayer 434
   Kampong Ayer Tourism and Culture Gallery 433
   Kota Batu 435
   Malay Technology Museum 435
   Maritime Museum 435
   Omar Ali Saifuddien Mosque 433
   Royal Regalia Building 434
   shopping 440
   Tamu Kianggeh 434
   tour operators 437
   waterfront 431
Bangar (BN) 442
banks 55, 56
Bario (MY) 358, 361
Batang Ai (MY) 324
Batang Ai National Park (MY) 326
Batang Rejang (MY) 332
Batu Bungan (MY) 353
Batu Caves (MY) 102
Batu Ferringhi (MY) 157
Batu Punggul (MY) 422
Bau caves (MY) 323
Bau (MY) 323
Bavanggazo (MY) 390
bears 406
Belaga (MY) 334, 338
Belait district (BN) 443
Besar Island (MY) 272, 291
Bidayuh people 296
bike rental 35
Bilit (MY) 409
Bintulu (MY) 336, 337, 338
birdlife and birdwatching 106, 407, 408, 557
Black Sand Beach (MY) 169
boat travel 33
body language 50
Bolkiah, Sultan Hassanal 426, 429
bomohs 544
books 559
Bornean Sun Bear Conservation Centre (Sepilok, MY) 406
Borneo 296, 532
Brinchang (MY) 134
British era 530
Brooke, Charles 301
Brooke, James 300, 303, 429
Brooke, Vyner 301
Brunei 11, 426, 529
Brunei river trips 436
Buddhism 5
Buddhist temples (MY) 213
Bugis people 529
Bujang Valley (MY) 162
Bukit Indah (MY) 189
Bukit Nenek Semukut (MY) 288
Bukit Piton reserve (MY) 412
Bukit Teresek (MY) 189
Bumbun Kumbang (MY) 191
bumiputra policy 538
Burgess, Anthony 124
buses 31
Butterworth (MY) 140

C

cafés 39
Cameron Highland Butterfly Garden (MY) 134
Cameron Highlands (MY) 8, 130
Cameron Highlands walking trails (MY) 136
Cameron Lavender Garden (MY) 135
camping 37, 49
card payments 55
car rental 35
car travel 34
caving 352
Cenang Beach (MY) 166
ceramic jars, Sarawak (MY) 308
Cherating (MY) 240
children, travelling with 57
Chinese beliefs 545
Chinese cave temples (MY) 115
Chukai (MY) 239
climate 11
clinics 45
clothing 50
coffee shops 39
costs 52
crime 53
Crocker Range Park (MY) 419
crocodiles 339
cuisines 39
culture 49
currencies 55
customs allowances 30

D

Dabong (MY) 202
Damai Beach (MY) 317
Damai (MY) 316
Danum Valley (MY) 412
Danum Valley reserves (MY) 412
dengue fever 44
Deramakot Forest Reserve (MY) 422
diving and snorkelling 170, 223, 227, 228, 238, 283, 288, 382, 387, 414
dolphins 317
dress 50
drinks 42
driving 34
drugs, illegal 31
Dungun (MY) 239
Dutch East India Company 528
duty-free allowances 30
duty-free goods 51
Duyong Island (MY) 231, 233

INDEX

E

earthquakes 398
Eastern & Oriental Express 28
economy 8, 539
electricity 53
elephants 185, 234
embassies and consulates 30
emergency numbers 53
employment opportunities 54
Endau Rompin National Park (MY) 292
entry requirements 29
environmental issues 130, 301, 551
etiquette 39, 49

F

fabrics 51
fact file 8
federation 537
ferries 33
festivals and events 12, 47
   Kaamatan (Sabah, MY) 379
   Penang (MY) festival calendar 154
   Rainforest Music Festival (Sarawak Cultural Village, MY) 318
   tamu besar (Kota Belud, MY) 390
   Thaipusam at the Batu Caves (MY) 101
firefly-spotting trips (MY) 104
fish massages 400
flights 27, 349
flights, domestic 34
food and drink 38, 39, 41, 42
food and drink glossary 568
Forest Research Institute of Malaysia (MY) 100
forests 555
Fraser's Hill (MY) 106
fruit 43

G

Gaharu Tea Valley (MY) 118
Gaya Island (MY) 381
Genting (MY) 288
George Town (MY) 8, 141
getting around 31
getting there 27
ghazal music 272
glossary 573. See also food and drink glossary
golf 106
Gomantong Caves (MY) 408
gong-making 390
Gopeng (MY) 118

Gua Charas (MY) 247
Gua Musang (MY) 200
Gunung Gading National Park (MY) 323
Gunung Mulu National Park (MY) 10, 350
Gunung Stong State Park (MY) 202

H

Halal food 42
health 43
Hinduism 542
history 4, 451
history timeline 525
homestays 38
hornbills 557
hospitals 45
hot springs 398

I

Iban longhouses (MY) 324
Iban people 296, 325
Iban tattoos 315
independence 536
insurance 53, 54
internet 54
Ipoh (MY) 113
Irrawaddy dolphin 317
Iskandar Malaysia (MY) 274
Islam 5, 429, 527, 543

J

Japanese occupation 533
Jelawang Jungle (MY) 202
Jerantut (MY) 181
Jerudong (BN) 441
Johor Bahru (MY) 274
Johor (MY) 529
Juara (MY) 289
Juara Turtle Project (MY) 289
Jungle Railway (MY) 193

K

Kampung Pulai (MY) 201
Kampung Tellian (MY) 336
Kampung Teluk Gedong (MY) 120
Kangar (MY) 174
Kapalai Island (MY) 415
Kapas Island (MY) 236
Kapit (MY) 332
Kawag reserve (MY) 412

Kayan art 335
Kayan people 335
Kedah (MY) 161
kedai kopis 39
Keith, Agnes 401
Kelabit Highlands (MY) 10, 356
Kelam Cave (MY) 174
Kellie's Castle (MY) 115
Kemah Keladong (MY) 190
Kemaman (MY) 239
Keningau (MY) 420
Kenong Rimba State Park (MY) 195
Kenyah people 335
Kenyir Elephant Conservation Village (MY) 234
kerata sapu (taxis) 34
Ketam Island (MY) 105
Kilim Geoforest Park (MY) 169
Kinabalu earthquake (MY) 398
Kinabalu, Mount (MY) 11, 393, 396, 397
Kinabalu Park (MY) 49, 392
Kinabatangan River (MY) 408
kitesurfing 241
Klias Peninsula (MY) 383
Konfrontasi 537
Kota Belud (MY) 389
Kota Bharu (MY) 10, 209
Kota Gelanggi Cave Complex (MY) 181
Kota Kinabalu (MY) 371
kris, the 231
Kuah (MY) 166
Kuala Besut (MY) 218
Kuala Gandah elephant sanctuary (MY) 185
Kuala Kangsar (MY) 122
Kuala Keniam (MY) 191, 192
Kuala Koh (MY) 201
Kuala Lipis (MY) 196
Kuala Lumpur (MY) 5, 60
   accommodation 86
   airports 82
   Aquaria KLCC 72
   architecture 64
   Badan Warisan 73
   Bangsar 81
   Banks and exchange 99
   Brickfields 80
   Bukit Bintang 73
   Bukit Nanas 73
   buses 83, 85
   Casino 99
   Central Market 69
   Chan See Shu Yuen 69
   Chinatown 65
   Chow Kit 70
   cinemas 97
   clubs 95

Colonial district 64
Court Hill Ganesh Temple 70
Cultural centres 99
directory 99
drinking 94
driving 83
eating 90
embassies and consulates 99
emergencies 100
entertainment 96
Golden Triangle 72
history 60
information 85
Islamic Arts Museum 79
Jalan Alor 91
Jalan Petaling 68
Jamek Mosque (Masjid Jamek) 65
Kampung Baru 71
Kompleks Kraf 73
Lake Gardens 76
left luggage 100
listings 85
Little India 70
live music venues 96
Masjid Negara 78
Menara KL 76
Merdeka 118 76
National Museum 78
National Textile Museum 65
nightlife 94
Old Kuala Lumpur train station 79
Petronas Towers 72
police 100
REXKL 69
Royal Malaysia Police Museum 78
Royal Selangor Club 64
shopping 97
sports and activities 99
Sri Kandaswamy Temple 80
Sri Maha Mariamman Temple 69
taxis 83, 85
Thean Hou Temple 80
Touch 'n Go cards 85
Tourism Malaysia 85
tours 86
trains 82, 84
train stations 82
transport 83
travel agents and tour operators 82
visa extensions 100
Kuala Penyu (MY) 384
Kuala Selangor (MY) 104
Kuala Tahan (MY) 178, 185, 188, 191, 192
Kuala Terengganu (MY) 10, 228
Kuantan (MY) 243
Kubah National Park (MY) 321
Kuching (MY) 10, 303
Kuching Wetland National Park (MY) 317

Kudat (MY) 390
Kudat Peninsula (MY) 389
Kukup (MY) 273
Kundasang War Memorial (MY) 399

L

Labi Road (BN) 444
Labuan Island (MY) 385
Labuan Town (MY) 385
Labuk Bay Proboscis Monkey Sanctuary (Labuk Bay, MY) 407
Lahad Datu (MY) 410
Lambir Hills National Park (MY) 345
Land Dyak people 296
Langkawi Cable Car (MY) 168
Langkawi (MY) 8, 166
Langkawi tours and activities (MY) 170
Lang Tengah Island (MY) 228
language 563, 564
Lankayan Island (MY) 407
Lata Berkoh (MY) 190
laundry 54
Lawas (MY) 348
leeches 45, 359
Legoland (MY) 276
Lemanak River (MY) 326
Lenggong Valley (MY) 129
LGBTQ+ travellers 54
living in Malaysia and Singapore 54
Loagan Bunut National Park (MY) 356
Lojing Highlands (MY) 135
longhouses 37, 326, 331
Lower Kinabatangan Wildlife Sanctuary (MY) 408

M

Mabul Island (MY) 415
Ma'Daerah Turtle Sanctuary (MY) 239
magazines 46
Mahmud, Taib 301
malaria 44
Malaysia 60
east coast 206
history 525
South 252
west coast 110
Maliau Basin 49
Maliau Basin Conservation Area (MY) 422
mammals 556

Mamutik Island (MY) 381
Manglish 564
Mantanani Islands (MY) 390
Manukan Island (MY) 381
maps 55
Alor Setar 163
Around Kota Bharu 214
Bako National Park 319
Bandar Seri Begawan 432
Bangsar Baru 81
Batu Ferringhi 158
Bintulu 337
Bras Basah Road to Rochor Road 462
Brickfields and KL Sentral 80
Brinchang 134
Brunei 428
Cameron Highlands 131
Cenang and Tengah beaches 168
Cherating 240
Chinatown and the Financial District 472
Colonial District 454
Colonial District and Chinatown 68
Day-trips and short trails 190
Downtown Singapore 453
George Town 143
George Town Colonial District 144
Geylang and Katong 490
Gua Musang 200
Gunung Mulu National Park 351
Ipoh 114
itineraries 24, 25
Jerantut 184
Johor Bahru 275
Juara 289
Kapas Island 236
Kelabit Highlands 357
Kenong Rimba State Park 196
Kinabalu Park HQ 395
Kota Bharu 210
Kota Kinabalu 372
Kuala Kangsar 123
Kuala Lipis 197
Kuala Lumpur 66
Kuala Lumpur and around 62
Kuala Lumpur transport system 84
Kuala Tahan 186
Kuala Terengganu 229
Kuantan 245
Kuching 304
Labuan 386
Langkawi 167
Little India and Arab Street 465
Little India and Chow Kit 71
Malaysia, Singapore and Brunei 6
Marang 235
Marina Bay 480
Melaka 259
Mersing 280
Miri 341

Mount Kinabalu 394
MRT System 502
Niah National Park 347
Orchard Road 484
Pangkor Island 119
Pekan 249
Penang Island 140
Perhentian Islands 220
Sabah 368
Salang 287
Sandakan 402
Sarawak 298
Semporna 413
Seremban 256
Sibu 328
Singapore 450
Taiping 125
Taman Negara 182
Tanah Rata 133
Tawau 417
Tekek and Air Batang 284
The east coast 208
The Golden Triangle 74
The interior 180
The Malaysian Rail Network 33
The south 254
The west coast 112
Tioman Island 282
Marang (MY) 235
Mari Mari Cultural Village (MY) 382
marine life 10
marine park (Labuan, MY) 388
marine turtles 242
Matang Mangrove Forest Reserve (MY) 128
Maxwell Hill (Bukit Larut) (MY) 128
media 46
Melaka (MY) 8, 258, 527
Melaka Wonderland (Ayer Keroh, MY) 271
Melanau people 296
Menumbok (MY) 384
Merang (MY) 226
Merapoh (MY) 199
Mersing (MY) 279
metalwork 51
Minangkabau people 257, 529
Miri (MY) 340
money 55
monkeys 317, 319, 384, 407, 431, 433
monsoons 166, 209
Monsopiad Heritage Village (MY) 382
mosque etiquette 50
Mount Alab (MY) 419
Mount Kinabalu (MY) 11, 45, 393, 396, 397

Mount Mulu (MY) 354
Mount Murud (MY) 362
Mount Raya (MY) 170
Mount Santubong (MY) 316
Mount Silam (MY) 411
Mount Stong (MY) 202
Mount Tahan (MY) 178, 193
Mount Trus Madi (MY) 49, 420
Muara (BN) 440
Muara district (BN) 440
Muar (MY) 272
Mukut (MY) 288
Mulu National Park 49
musical traditions 335

N

national parks 49
Bako (MY) 318
Batang Ai (MY) 326
Endau Rompin (MY) 292
Gunung Gading (MY) 323
Gunung Mulu (MY) 10, 350
Kubah (MY) 321
Lambir Hills (MY) 345
Loagan Bunut (MY) 356
Niah (MY) 346
Sarawak's national parks (MY) 320
Similajau (MY) 339
Taman Negara (MY) 8
Tanjung Datu (MY) 324
Negeri Sembilan (MY) 252
newspapers 46
Niah National Park (MY) 346
Nipah (MY) 288

O

oil 430, 444
opening hours 56
Orang Asli people 8, 181, 535
Orang Sungai people 408
Orang Ulu people 296, 335
orangutans 322, 326, 405, 412

P

Padang Kemunting Turtle Conservation and Information Centre (MY) 271
Pa' Lungan (MY) 360, 361, 362
Pangkor (MY) 119
Pangkor Treaty 531
Pantai Kok (MY) 168
Pantai Pasir Panjang (MY) 160
paragliding 399
parasailing 170

Pasir Bogak (MY) 120
Paya (MY) 287
Pekan (MY) 248
Penang International Airport (MY) 150
Penang (MY) 8, 139, 529
Penang National Park (MY) 158
Penan people 363
peoples 546
Perak (MY) 110
performing arts 213
Perhentian Besar (MY) 224
Perhentian Islands (MY) 10, 219, 221
Perhentian Kecil (MY) 221
Perlis (MY) 161
petroleum industry 340
Pewanis community (MY) 226
pharmacies 45
phones 56
place names 29
politics 534
Poring Hot Springs (MY) 398
Portuguese conquest 528
Princess Hill (MY) 201
proboscis monkeys. 407.
  See monkeys
public holidays 31, 56
Pulau Tiga Park (MY) 384
Putrajaya (MY) 101

R

rafflesias 8, 130, 420, 558
rafting 48
rail journeys (MY) 383
Rainforest Discovery Centre (Sepilok, MY) 406
Ranau (MY) 399
Rantau Abang (MY) 238
Rawa Island (MY) 291
Redang Island (MY) 227
Rejang River boats (MY) 332
Rejang river (MY) 332
religion 5, 542
reptiles 557
restaurants 39
road sign translations 35
roads, Malaysian 34
Rose Valley Garden (MY) 134
Royal Belum State Park (MY) 129

S

Sabah Agriculture Park (MY) 421
Sabah (MY) 10, 366
Sabah Tea Garden (MY) 400
safety 53

INDEX

Salang (MY) 286
Sama Jaya Nature Reserve (Kuching, MY) 308
Sandakan (MY) 400
sandflies 290
Santubong Peninsula (MY) 316
Sapi Island (MY) 381
Sapulut (MY) 422
Sarawak Cultural Village (MY) 316
Sarawak (MY) 10, 296, 384
Sayong (MY) 123
school holidays 56
Sea Dyak people 296
security 370
Semenggoh Wildlife Centre (MY) 322
Semporna (MY) 413
Sepilok (MY) 405
Sepilok Orangutan Rehabilitation Centre (Sepilok, MY) 405
Seremban (MY) 252
Seria (BN) 444
Seribuat Archipelago (MY) 290
service charges 52
Setiu Wetlands (MY) 225
Seven Wells Waterfall (Telaga Tujuh) (MY) 169
sharia law 430
shophouses 11
shopping 51
Sibu (MY) 10, 327, 336
Similajau National Park (MY) 339
Singapore 11, 448
  Abdul Gafoor Mosque 466
  access from Malaysia 274, 277
  accommodation 504, 506
  addresses and maps 500
  Adventure Cove Waterpark 497
  Albert Street 463
  Alexandra Arch 494
  Amoy Street 474
  Ann Siang Hill 474
  Arab Street (Kampong Glam) 467
  arrival and departure 499
  ArtScience Museum 481
  Asian Civilizations Museum 456
  Baba House 476
  Bali Lane 468
  Battery Road 478
  Battlebox 460
  Boat Quay 477
  Botanic Gardens 483
  Bras Basah Road 461
  Buddhas of the World Museum 471
  Buddha Tooth Relic Temple 470
  Buffalo Road 464
  Bugis Junction 463
  Bugis Village 463
  Bukit Pasoh conservation area 471
  Bukit Timah 487
  Bukit Timah Nature Reserve 487
  cable cars 496
  Cathay Gallery 483
  Cathedral of the Good Shepherd 458
  Cavenagh Bridge 457
  Central Catchment Nature Reserve 486
  Central Fire Station 458
  Changi 492
  Changi Museum 492
  Changi Point and the beach 492
  Chettiar Temple 461
  CHIJMES 458
  Chinatown 469
  Chinatown Heritage Centre 469
  Church of St Gregory the Illuminator 458
  Clarke Quay 461
  Clifford Pier 478
  Club Street 474
  Collyer Quay 478
  Colonial District 452
  cookery classes 509
  Cuff Road 466
  DBS Singapore Gallery 455
  Desker Road 466
  Dhoby Ghaut 482
  directory 523
  drinking 516
  driving 503
  eating 510
  Emerald Hill 483
  entertainment 519
  Esplanade – Theatres on the Bay 482
  Eu Tong Sen Street 474
  Financial District 477
  Former Ford Factory 487
  Fort Canning Park 460
  Fort Siloso 498
  Freemasons' Hall 458
  Fullerton Building 478
  Gardens by the Bay South 481
  getting around 501
  Geylang 490
  Goodwood Park Hotel 483
  Haji Lane 468
  Hajjah Fatimah mosque 469
  HarbourFront Centre 495
  Hastings Road 466
  Haw Par Villa 493
  history 451
  Hong Lim Park 477
  ice cream 510
  Imbiah Lookout 497
  Indian Heritage Centre 466
  information 504
  ION Orchard 483
  Istana, The 483
  Jurong 495
  Katong 490
  Kerbau Road 464
  Kranji War Cemetery and Memorial 489
  Kwan Im Temple 463
  Lau Pa Sat 479
  Little India 464
  Luge 497
  Madame Tussauds 497
  Maghain Aboth Synagogue 463
  Malabar Mosque 469
  Malay Heritage Centre 468
  Marina Bay 479
  Marina Bay Sands 479
  Marina Centre 482
  Megazip Adventure Park 498
  Mount Faber 494
  Museum of Ice Cream 486
  Muslim cemetery 469
  Mustafa Centre 466
  Nagore Durgha Shrine 475
  National Gallery 455
  National Orchid Garden 485
  New Bridge Road 474
  nightlife 516
  North Bridge Road 468
  Omni-Theatre 496
  Orchard Road 482
  Padang 454
  parliament buildings 455
  Pasir Panjang 493
  Peirce Reservoirs 486
  Peranakan Museum 459
  Peranakan shophouses 467
  Petain Road 466
  Raffles Hotel 461
  Raffles Place 478
  Raffles Terrace 460
  Red Dot Design Museum 481
  Reflections at Bukit Chandu 494
  Resorts World Sentosa 496
  restaurants 510
  River Valley Road 460
  Rochor Road 461
  Rowell Road 466
  Sacred Buddha Tooth Relic Stupa 471
  Sago Street 471
  Sakaya Muni Buddha Gaya Temple 467
  Sentosa Island 496
  Sentosa, transport to 499
  shopping 521
  Siloso Beach 498
  Singapore City Gallery 474
  Singapore Flyer 482
  Singapore River Experience 457
  Singapore Science Centre 495
  Singapore Zoo 488
  Skyhelix Sentosa 497

INDEX

SkyPark 480
Skypark Sentosa 498
Skyride 497
Smith Street 471
South Bridge Road 470
Southern Ridges 493
Spectra sound-and-light show 480
Sri Krishnan Temple 463
Sri Mariamman Temple 470
Sri Srinivasa Perumal Temple 467
Sri Veeramakaliamman Temple 466
St Andrew's Cathedral 457
Sultan Mosque 468
Sungei Buloh Wetland Reserve 489
Syed Alwi Road 466
Tanjong Pagar 476
tea tastings 478
Tekka Market 464
Telok Ayer Market 479
Telok Ayer Street 475
Thian Hock Keng Temple 475
tours 503
transport 501
TreeTop Walk 486
Tuas 495
Universal Studios Singapore 496
UOB Southeast Asia Gallery 455
Victoria Concert Hall 456
Victoria Theatre 456
VivoCity 495
War Memorial 458
Waterloo Street 463
watersports 498
Windsor Nature Park 486
Wings of Time 498
Ying Fo Fui Kun 476
Yueh Hai Ching Temple 477
Singapore River 457
Singlish 564
Sipadan Island (MY) 11, 415
Skytrex Adventure (MY) 169
snakes 160
snorkelling 170
souvenirs 51
sports 48
Sri Menanti (MY) 256
Stamford Raffles, Sir Thomas 451, 456
state parks 371. See also parks by name
study programmes 55
Sukau (MY) 409
Sulug Island (MY) 381
Sumangkap (MY) 390
sun bears 406
Sungai Lembing (MY) 247
Sungai Petani (MY) 161
Sunway Lagoon (MY) 101
surfing 241
Suri Island (MY) 215

T

Tabin Wildlife Reserve (MY) 412
Taiping (MY) 124
Taiping Zoo and Night Safari (MY) 126
Taman Mini Malaysia & ASEAN (Ayer Keroh, MY) 271
Taman Negara (MY) 8, 49, 178
Tambunan (MY) 420
Tambunan Rafflesia Information Centre (MY) 420
Tanah Rata (MY) 132
Tanjung Datu National Park (MY) 324
Tanjung Rhu (MY) 169
Taoism 5
Tasik Kenyir (MY) 234
tattoos 315
Tawau Hills Park (MY) 418
Tawau (MY) 416
taxes 52
taxis 34
taxis, long-distance 33
tea 400
tea plantations 130, 132
Tekek (MY) 284
television 46
Teluk Bahang Road (MY) 158
Teluk Ketapang (MY) 120
Teluk Nipah (MY) 120
Temburong district (BN) 442
temple etiquette 50
Tengah Beach (MY) 168
Tengah Island (MY) 291
Tenggol Island (MY) 239
Tenom (MY) 421
Terengganu, Southern (MY) 238
Thailand border crossings (MY) 175
ticket booking engines 31
Tiga (MY) 387
time zones 57
Tioman Island (MY) 10, 281, 283
Tip of Borneo (MY) 391
tipping 57
tourist information 57
tourist offices 55
tour operators 29
trains 32
transport 31
transport, urban 35
travel agents 29
travel essentials 52
trekking 48, 49, 359, 361, 363
Tropical Spice Garden (MY) 158
tubing 48
Tunku Abdul Rahman Park (MY) 380
Tun Mustapha Park (MY) 392
Tun Sakaran Marine Park (MY) 415
Turtle Conservation and Information Centre (Rantau Abang, MY) 238
Turtle Islands National Park (MY) 407
turtles 219, 228, 238, 239, 242, 271, 289, 324, 407
Turtle sanctuary (Cherating, MY) 241
Twin Otter planes 349

U

Ulu Baram (MY) 362
Ulu Muda Eco Park (MY) 165
Ulu Temburong National Park (BN) 11, 442
Umgawa Zipline Eco Adventures (MY) 169
Underwater World (MY) 166
UNESCO World Heritage sites 146

V

vegetarian food 42
via ferrata, Mount Kinabalu (MY) 397
visas 29

W

Wang Kelian (MY) 174
water, drinking 42
watersports 48, 121, 170
weather 11
whitewater rafting 48, 384
wi-fi 36, 54
wildlife 10, 10, 405, 408, 555. See also species by name, birdlife and birdwatching
windsurfing 241
women's status 50
women travellers 50
woodcarving 51
work programmes 55
World War II 369

Z

Zika virus 44
ziplining 169

Map symbols

The symbols below are used on maps throughout the book

	International boundary		Tourist office		Viewpoint
	Province boundary		Post office		Lighthouse
	Chapter division boundary		Hospital		Radio Tower
	Major road		Telephone		Campsite
	Minor road		Public gardens/fountain		Hut/hide
	Motorway		Golf course		Park HQ
	Pedestrian road		Arch		Mosque
	Steps		Castle/fort		Buddhist temple
	Unpaved road		Museum		Hindu/Sikh temple
	Funicular		Monument		Chinese temple
	Railway		Tower		Synagogue
	Footpath		Swimming pool		Snorkelling
	Ferry route		Gate/entrance		Church (regional map)
	River		Peak		Church (town map)
	Airport (international)		Rock		Market
	Airport (regional)		Bridge		Stadium
	Helipad		Hill		Building
	MRT station (Singapore)		Cave		Water village
	Transport stop		Ruin		Park
	Parking		Marshland		Beach
	Petrol station		Tree		Christian cemetery
	Point of interest		Waterfall		Muslim cemetery
	Internet access		Gorge		

Listings key

- Accommodation
- Eating
- Drinking/nightlife
- Shopping

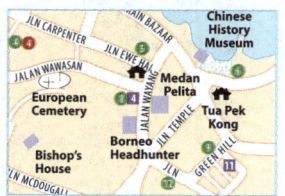